Class Library Reference

For the Microsoft® Foundation Class Library

Microsoft Visual C++™

**Development System for Windows™ and Windows NT™
Version 2.0**

Microsoft Corporation

PUBLISHED BY
Microsoft Press
A Division of Microsoft Corporation
One Microsoft Way
Redmond, Washington 98052-6399

Library of Congress Cataloging-in-Publication Data
Microsoft foundation class library reference / Microsoft Corporation.
     p.   cm.
   Includes index.
   ISBN 1-55615-801-7
   1. C (Computer program language)   2. C++ (Computer program
language) I. Microsoft Corporation.
QA76.76.C15M523   1994
005.26'2--dc20   94-26962
                                      CIP

Printed and bound in the United States of America.

1 2 3 4 5 6 7 8 9 MLML 9 8 7 6 5 4

Distributed to the book trade in Canada by Macmillan of Canada, a division of Canada Publishing Corporation.

A CIP catalogue record for this book is available from the British Library.

Microsoft Press books are available through booksellers and distributors worldwide. For further information about international editions, contact your local Microsoft Corporation office. Or contact Microsoft Press International directly at fax (206) 936-7329.

Document No. DB57158-0794

Contents

Introduction

The *Class Library Reference* covers the classes, global functions, global variables, and macros that make up the Microsoft® Foundation Class Library, version 3.0. Figure I.1 overleaf is a class hierarchy chart that details the class relationships in the class library.

The Class Library Overview lists the classes in helpful categories. Use these lists to help locate a class that contains the functionality you are interested in. *Programming with the Microsoft Foundation Class Library* explains how to use the class library to program for Microsoft Windows NT™ and other Win32 platforms. Practical examples and techniques are supplied in the tutorials in *Introducing Visual C++*.

The remainder of the *Class Library Reference* consists of an alphabetical listing of the classes and a "Macros and Globals" section that explains the global functions, global variables, and macros used with the class library.

The hierarchy chart and the subset charts included with each class are useful for locating base classes. The reference does not describe inherited member functions, inherited operators, and overridden virtual member functions. You must always refer to the base classes depicted in the hierarchy diagrams.

In the alphabetical listing section, each class description includes a member summary by category, followed by alphabetical listings of member functions, overloaded operators, and data members.

Public and protected class members are documented only when they are normally used in application programs or derived classes. Occasionally, private members are listed because they override a public or protected member in the base class. See the class header files for a complete listing of class members.

Some C-language structures defined by Windows are so widely applicable that their descriptions have been reproduced completely in a section following the alphabetical reference.

Please note that the "See Also" sections refer to Win32 API functions by prefacing them with the scope resolution operator (::), for example, **::EqualRect**. More information on these functions can be found in the *Programmer's Reference* for Win32.

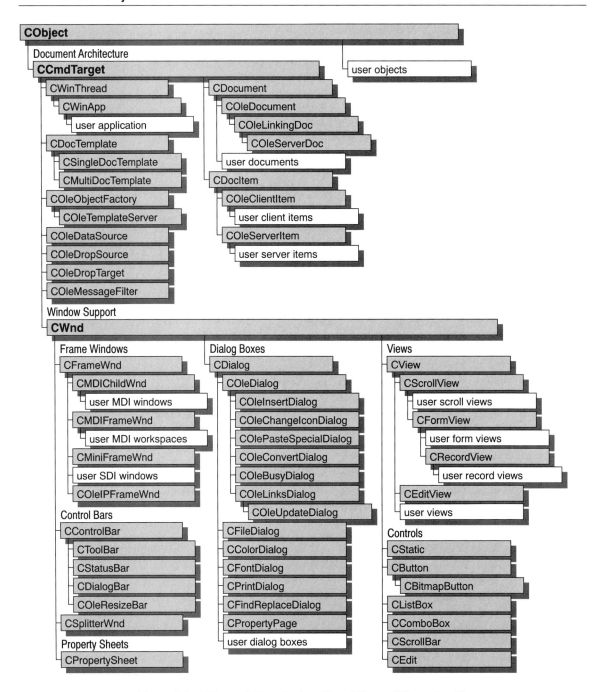

Figure I.1   Microsoft Foundation Class Library Hierarchy Chart

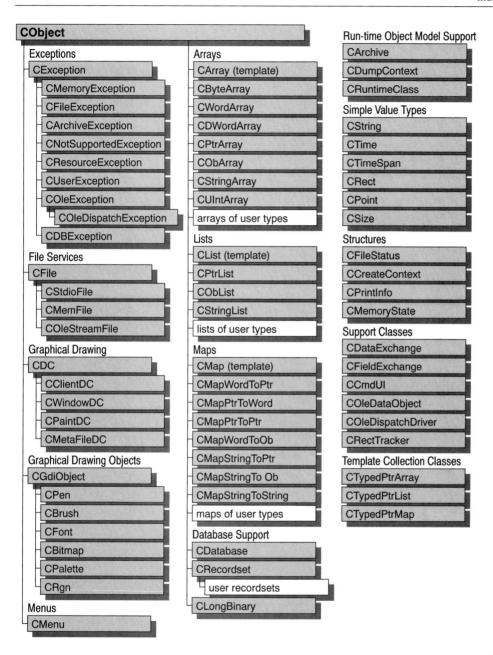

CObject

Exceptions
- CException
  - CMemoryException
  - CFileException
  - CArchiveException
  - CNotSupportedException
  - CResourceException
  - CUserException
  - COleException
    - COleDispatchException
  - CDBException

File Services
- CFile
  - CStdioFile
  - CMemFile
  - COleStreamFile

Graphical Drawing
- CDC
  - CClientDC
  - CWindowDC
  - CPaintDC
  - CMetaFileDC

Graphical Drawing Objects
- CGdiObject
  - CPen
  - CBrush
  - CFont
  - CBitmap
  - CPalette
  - CRgn

Menus
- CMenu

Arrays
- CArray (template)
  - CByteArray
  - CWordArray
  - CDWordArray
  - CPtrArray
  - CObArray
  - CStringArray
  - CUIntArray
  - arrays of user types

Lists
- CList (template)
  - CPtrList
  - CObList
  - CStringList
  - lists of user types

Maps
- CMap (template)
  - CMapWordToPtr
  - CMapPtrToWord
  - CMapPtrToPtr
  - CMapWordToOb
  - CMapStringToPtr
  - CMapStringTo Ob
  - CMapStringToString
  - maps of user types

Database Support
- CDatabase
- CRecordset
  - user recordsets
- CLongBinary

Run-time Object Model Support
- CArchive
- CDumpContext
- CRuntimeClass

Simple Value Types
- CString
- CTime
- CTimeSpan
- CRect
- CPoint
- CSize

Structures
- CFileStatus
- CCreateContext
- CPrintInfo
- CMemoryState

Support Classes
- CDataExchange
- CFieldExchange
- CCmdUI
- COleDataObject
- COleDispatchDriver
- CRectTracker

Template Collection Classes
- CTypedPtrArray
- CTypedPtrList
- CTypedPtrMap

Class Library Overview

This chapter categorizes and describes the classes in the Microsoft Foundation
Class Library (MFC) version 3.0. The classes in MFC, taken together, constitute an
"application framework"—the framework of an application written for the
Windows API. Your programming task is to fill in the code that is unique to your
application.

The library's classes are presented here in the following categories:

- Root Class
- Application Architecture Classes
  - Application Class
  - Command-Related Classes
  - Document/View Classes
  - Threading Base Class
- Visual Object Classes
  - Window Classes
  - View Classes
  - Dialog Classes
  - Property Sheet Classes
  - Control Classes
  - Menu Class
  - Device-Context Classes
  - Drawing Object Classes
- General-Purpose Classes
  - File Classes
  - Diagnostics
  - Exceptions
  - Collections
  - Template Collections
  - Miscellaneous Support Classes
- OLE 2 Classes
  - OLE Base Classes
  - OLE Visual Editing Container Classes
  - OLE Visual Editing Server Classes

- OLE Data Transfer Classes
- OLE Dialog Box Classes
- Miscellaneous OLE Classes
- Database Classes
- Macros and Globals

The section "General Class Design Philosophy" at the end of this chapter explains how the Microsoft Foundation Class Library was designed.

The framework is explained in detail in Chapters 1 though 7 of *Programming with the Microsoft Foundation Class Library*.

Some of the classes listed above are general-purpose classes that can be used with the framework. Chapter 7 of *Programming with the Microsoft Foundation Class Library* details these classes, which provide useful abstractions such as collections, exceptions, files, and strings.

Class Summary

The following is a brief summary of the classes in the Microsoft Foundation Class Library, divided by category to help you locate what you need. In some cases, a class is listed in more than one category. To see the inheritance of a class, use the class hierarchy charts on pages x and xi.

Root Class

Most of the classes in the Microsoft Foundation Class Library are derived from a single base class at the root of the class hierarchy. **CObject** provides a number of useful capabilities to all classes derived from it, with very low overhead. For more information about **CObject** and its capabilities, see the article "CObject Class" in *Programming with the Microsoft Foundation Class Library*.

CObject
The ultimate base class of most MFC classes. Supports serializing data and obtaining run-time information about a class.

Application Architecture Classes

Classes in this category contribute to the architecture of a framework application. They supply functionality common to most applications. You fill in the framework to add application-specific functionality. Typically, you do so by deriving new classes from the architecture classes, sometimes adding new members or overriding existing member functions.

The framework consists of class objects that cooperate at run time to function as an application for Windows. The principal objects are as follows:

- An application object derived from class **CWinApp**.
- One or more document objects derived from class **CDocument** and usually associated with a data file.
- One or more view objects derived from class **CView**, each attached to a document and associated with a window.

Window Application Class

Each application has one and only one application object; this object coordinates other objects in the running program and is derived from **CWinApp**.

CWinApp
  Encapsulates the code to initialize, run, and terminate the application.

Command-Related Classes

As the user interacts with the application by choosing menus or control-bar buttons with the mouse, the application sends messages from the affected user-interface object to an appropriate command-target object, which is of class **CCmdTarget**. Command-target classes derived from **CCmdTarget** include **CWinApp**, **CWnd**, **CDocTemplate**, **CDocument**, **CView**, and the classes derived from them. Class **CCmdUI** represents a command user-interface object, such as a menu or button, for updating the object's state.

CCmdTarget
  Serves as the base class for all classes of objects that can receive and respond to messages.

CCmdUI
  Provides a programmatic interface for updating user-interface objects such as menu items or control-bar buttons. The command-target object enables, disables, checks, and/or unchecks the user-interface object via this object.

Document/View Classes

Document objects, created by document template objects, manage the application's data. View objects, which represent the client area of a window, display a document's data and allow users to interact with it.

CDocTemplate
  The base class for document templates. A document template coordinates the creation of document, view, and frame window objects.

CSingleDocTemplate
  A template for documents in the single document interface (SDI). SDI applications have only one document open at a time.

CMultiDocTemplate
A template for documents in the multiple document interface (MDI). MDI applications can have multiple documents open at a time.

CDocument
The base class for application-specific documents. Derive your document class(es) from **CDocument**.

CView
The base class for application-specific views of a document's data. Views display data and accept user input to edit or select the data. Derive your view class(es) from **CView**. See the description of **CView** and its derived classes under "View Classes."

CPrintInfo
A structure containing information about a print or print preview job. Used by **CView**'s printing architecture.

CCreateContext
A structure passed by a document template to window-creation functions to coordinate the creation of document, view, and frame-window objects.

Threading Base Class

The Microsoft Foundation Class Library supports multiple threads of execution within an application. All applications must have at least one thread, called the "primary" thread. **CWinThread** encapsulates a portion of the operating system's threading capabilities.

CWinThread
The base class for all threads. Use directly, or derive a class from **CWinThread** if your thread performs user-interface functions. **CWinApp** is derived from **CWinThread**.

Visual Object Classes

Classes in this category represent visual user-interface objects: windows, dialog boxes, controls, and menus. Also included are associated objects employed in rendering the contents of a window: device contexts and drawing objects such as pens and brushes.

Window Classes

Class **CWnd** and its derived classes encapsulate an **HWND**, a handle to a Windows window. **CWnd** can be used by itself or as a base for deriving new classes. The derived classes supplied by the class library represent various kinds of windows.

CWnd
> The base class for all windows. Use the derived classes below, or derive your own classes directly from **CWnd**.

CFrameWnd
> The base class for an SDI application's main frame window.

CMDIFrameWnd
> The base class for an MDI application's main frame window.

CMDIChildWnd
> The base class for an MDI application's document frame windows.

CMiniFrameWnd
> A half-height frame window typically seen around floating toolbars.

View Classes

Class **CView** and its derived classes are child windows that represent the client area of a frame window and that show data and accept input for a document.

CView
> The base class for application-specific views of a document's data. Views display data and accept user input to edit or select the data. Derive your view classes from **CView** or use **CScrollView** for automatic scrolling.

CScrollView
> The base class for views with scrolling capabilities. Derive your view class from **CScrollView** for automatic scrolling.

CFormView
> A scroll view whose layout is defined in a dialog resource. Derive classes from **CFormView** to implement user interfaces quickly based on dialog resources.

CEditView
> A view with text-editing, searching, replacing, and scrolling capabilities. Use this class to provide a text-based user interface for a document.

Dialog Classes

Class **CDialog** and its derived classes encapsulate dialog-box functionality. Since a dialog box is a special kind of window, **CDialog** is derived from **CWnd**. Derive your dialog classes from **CDialog** or use one of the common dialog classes for standard dialog boxes, such as opening or saving a file, printing, selecting a font or color, or initiating a search-and-replace operation.

CDialog
> The base class for all dialog boxes—both modal and modeless.

CDataExchange
> Supplies initialization and validation information for dialog boxes.

CFileDialog
Provides a standard dialog box for opening or saving a file.

CPrintDialog
Provides a standard dialog box for printing a file.

CFontDialog
Provides a standard dialog box for selecting a font.

CColorDialog
Provides a standard dialog box for selecting a color.

CFindReplaceDialog
Provides a standard dialog box for a search-and-replace operation.

Property Sheet Classes

The property sheet classes allow your applications to use property sheets, also known as "tab dialogs." Property sheets are an efficient way to organize a large number of controls in a single dialog box.

CPropertySheet
Provides the frame for multiple property pages. Derive your property sheet class from **CPropertySheet** to implement your property sheets quickly.

CPropertyPage
Provides the individual pages within a property sheet. Derive a class from **CPropertyPage** for each page to be added to your property sheet.

Control Classes

Control classes encapsulate standard Windows controls such as buttons, list boxes, and combo boxes, as well as new controls, including buttons with bitmaps and control bars.

CStatic
A static-text control window. Static controls are used to label, box, or separate other controls in a dialog box or window.

CButton
A button control window. The class provides a programmatic interface for a pushbutton, check box, or radio button in a dialog box or window.

CEdit
An editable-text control window. Edit controls are used to accept textual input from the user.

CScrollBar
A scroll-bar control window. The class provides the functionality of a scroll bar, for use as a control in a dialog box or window, through which the user can specify a position within a range.

CListBox

A list-box control window. A list box displays a list of items that the user can view and select.

CComboBox

A combo-box control window. A combo box consists of an edit control plus a list box.

CControlBar

The base class for control bars such as toolbars and status bars. A window aligned to the top or bottom of a frame window that contains either **HWND**-based child controls or controls not based on an **HWND**, such as toolbar buttons.

CStatusBar

The base class for status-bar control windows.

CToolBar

Toolbar control windows that contain bitmap command buttons not based on an **HWND**.

CDialogBar

A modeless dialog box in the form of a control bar.

CBitmapButton

A button with a bitmap rather than a text caption.

CSplitterWnd

A window that the user can split into multiple panes.

Menu Class

Class **CMenu** provides an interface through which to access your application's menus. It is useful for manipulating menus dynamically at run time; for example, when adding or deleting menu items according to context.

CMenu

Encapsulates an **HMENU** handle to the application's menu bar and pop-up menus.

Device-Context Classes

Most of the following classes encapsulate a handle to a Windows device context. A device context is a Windows object that contains information about the drawing attributes of a device such as a display or a printer. All drawing calls are made through a device-context object. Additional classes derived from **CDC** encapsulate specialized device-context functionality, including support for Windows metafiles.

CDC

The base class for device contexts. Used directly for accessing the whole display and for accessing non-display contexts such as printers.

CPaintDC

A display context used in **OnPaint** member functions of windows and **OnDraw** member functions of views. Automatically calls **BeginPaint** on construction and **EndPaint** on destruction.

CClientDC

A display context for client areas of windows. Used, for example, to draw in an immediate response to mouse events.

CWindowDC

A display context for entire windows, including both the client and frame areas.

CMetaFileDC

A device context for Windows metafiles. A Windows metafile contains a sequence of graphics device interface (GDI) commands that can be replayed to create an image. Calls made to the member functions of a **CMetaFileDC** are recorded in a metafile.

Drawing Object Classes

The following classes encapsulate handle-based GDI objects. They allow you to manipulate common GDI drawing objects with C++ syntax.

CGdiObject

The base class for GDI drawing tools.

CBitmap

Encapsulates a GDI bitmap, providing an interface for manipulating bitmaps.

CBrush

Encapsulates a GDI brush that can be selected as the current brush in a device context.

CFont

Encapsulates a GDI font that can be selected as the current font in a device context.

CPalette

Encapsulates a GDI color palette for use as an interface between the application and a color output device such as a display.

CPen

Encapsulates a GDI pen that can be selected as the current pen in a device context.

CRgn

Encapsulates a GDI region for manipulating an elliptical or polygonal area within a window. Used in conjunction with the clipping member functions in class **CDC**.

General-Purpose Classes

Classes in this category provide a variety of general-purpose services such as file I/O, diagnostics, and exception handling. Also included are classes such as arrays and lists for storing aggregates of data.

File Classes

Use the following classes, particularly **CArchive** and **CFile**, if you write your own input/output processing. Normally you don't need to derive from these classes. If you use the application framework, the default implementations of the Open and Save commands on the File menu will handle file I/O (using class **CArchive**), as long as you supply details about how a document "serializes" its contents. For more information about the file classes and serialization, see the article "Files" and the article "Serialization (Object Persistence)" in *Programming with the Microsoft Foundation Class Library*.

CFile
Provides a programmatic interface to binary disk files.

CMemFile
Provides a programmatic interface to in-memory files.

CStdioFile
Provides a programmatic interface to buffered stream disk files, usually in text mode.

CArchive
Cooperates with a **CFile** object to implement persistent storage for objects through serialization (see **CObject::Serialize**).

Diagnostics

Use classes **CDumpContext** and **CMemoryState** during development to assist with debugging, as described in the article "Diagnostics" in *Programming with the Microsoft Foundation Class Library*. Use **CRuntimeClass** to determine the class of any object at run time, as described in the article "CObject Class: Accessing Run-Time Information" in *Programming with the Microsoft Foundation Class Library*. The framework uses **CRuntimeClass** to create objects of a particular class dynamically.

CDumpContext
Provides a destination for diagnostic dumps.

CMemoryState
Structure that provides snapshots of memory use. Also used to compare earlier and later memory snapshots.

CRuntimeClass
Structure used to determine the exact class of an object at run time.

Exceptions

The class library provides an exception-handling mechanism based on class **CException**. The application framework uses exceptions in its code; you can also use them in yours. For more information, see the article "Exceptions" in *Programming with the Microsoft Foundation Class Library*. You can derive your own exception types from **CException**.

CException
> The base class for exceptions.

CArchiveException
> An archive exception.

CFileException
> A file-oriented exception.

CMemoryException
> An out-of-memory exception.

CNotSupportedException
> An exception resulting from using an unsupported feature.

CResourceException
> An exception resulting from a failure to load a Windows resource.

CUserException
> An exception used to stop a user-initiated operation. Typically the user has been notified of the problem before this exception is thrown.

Collections

For handling aggregates of data, the class library provides a group of collection classes—arrays, lists, and "maps"—that can hold a variety of object and predefined types. The collections are dynamically sized. These classes can be used in any program, whether written for Windows or not. However, they are most useful for implementing the data structures that define your document classes in the application framework. You can readily derive specialized collection classes from these, or you can create them with a template tool supplied with the class library. For more information about these approaches, see the article "Collections" in *Programming with the Microsoft Foundation Class Library* and see "Template Collections" in this overview for a list of the template collection classes.

CByteArray
> Stores elements of type **BYTE** in an array.

CDWordArray
> Stores elements of type doubleword in an array.

CObArray
> Stores pointers to objects of class **CObject** or to objects of classes derived from **CObject** in an array.

CPtrArray
Stores pointers to **void** (generic pointers) in an array.

CStringArray
Stores **CString** objects in an array.

CWordArray
Stores elements of type **WORD** in an array.

CUIntArray
Stores elements of type **UINT** in an array.

CObList
Stores pointers to objects of class **CObject** or to objects of classes derived from **CObject** in a linked list.

CPtrList
Stores pointers to **void** (generic pointers) in a linked list.

CStringList
Stores **CString** objects in a linked list.

CMapPtrToPtr
Maps void pointers to void pointers. Uses void pointers as keys for finding other void pointers.

CMapPtrToWord
Maps void pointers to data of type **WORD**. Uses void pointers as keys for finding data of type **WORD**.

CMapStringToOb
Maps **CString** objects to **CObject** pointers. Uses **CString** objects as keys for finding **CObject** pointers.

CMapStringToPtr
Maps **CString** objects to void pointers. Uses **CString** objects as keys for finding void pointers.

CMapStringToString
Maps **CString** objects to **CString** objects. Uses **CString** objects as keys for finding other **CString** objects.

CMapWordToOb
Maps data of type **WORD** to **CObject** pointers. Uses data of type **WORD** to find **CObject** pointers.

CMapWordToPtr
Maps data of type **WORD** to void pointers. Uses data of type **WORD** to find void pointers.

Template Collections

These classes, like those listed under "Collections," can hold a variety of objects in arrays, lists, and "maps." These collection classes are templates whose parameters determine the types of the objects stored in the aggregates. The **CArray**, **CMap**, and **CList** classes use global helper functions that must usually be customized. For more information about these helper functions, see "Collection Class Helpers." The typed pointer classes are "wrappers" for other classes in the class library. By using these wrappers you enlist the compiler's type-checking to help you avoid errors. For more information on using these classes, see the article "Collections" in *Programming with the Microsoft Foundation Class Library*.

CArray
Stores elements in an array.

CMap
Maps keys to values.

CList
Stores elements in a linked list.

CTypedPtrList
Type-safe collection that stores pointers to objects in a linked list.

CTypedPtrArray
Type-safe collection that stores pointers to objects in an array.

CTypedPtrMap
Type-safe collection that maps keys to values; both keys and values are pointers.

Miscellaneous Support Classes

The following classes encapsulate drawing coordinates, character strings, and time and date information, allowing convenient use of C++ syntax. These objects are used widely as parameters to the member functions of Windows classes in the class library. Because **CPoint**, **CSize**, and **CRect** correspond to the **POINT**, **SIZE**, and **RECT** structures, respectively, in the Windows Software Development Kit (SDK), you can use objects of these C++ classes wherever you can use these C-language structures. The classes provide useful interfaces through their member functions. **CString** provides very flexible dynamic character strings. **CTime** and **CTimeSpan** represent time and date values. For more information about these classes, see the article "Date and Time" in *Programming with the Microsoft Foundation Class Library*.

CPoint
Holds coordinate (x, y) pairs.

CSize
Holds distance, relative positions, or paired values.

CRect
Holds rectangular areas.

CString
Holds character strings.

CTime
Holds absolute time and date values.

CTimeSpan

Holds relative time and date values.

CRectTracker

Displays and handles user interface for resizing and moving rectangular objects.

OLE 2 Classes

The OLE 2 classes work with the other application framework classes to provide easy access to the OLE 2 API, allowing users to create and edit documents containing data created by multiple applications. This allows a single document to contain text, graphics, spreadsheets, sound, or other types of data.

Six categories of classes support OLE 2: OLE base classes, OLE visual (in-place) editing container classes, OLE Visual Editing server classes, OLE data transfer classes, OLE dialog box classes, and miscellaneous OLE classes. To see the inheritance of a class, refer to the class hierarchy charts on pages x and xi.

OLE Base Classes

These classes serve as base classes for more specialized OLE classes in the other categories.

CDocItem

Abstract base class of **COleClientItem** and **OleServerItem**. Objects of classes derived from **CDocItem** represent parts of documents.

COleDispatchDriver

Used to call automation servers from your automation client. ClassWizard uses this class to create type-safe classes for automation servers that provide a type library.

COleDocument

Used for OLE compound document implementation as well as basic container support. Serves as a container for classes derived from **CDocItem**. This class can be used as the base class for container documents and is the base class for **COleServerDoc**.

OLE Visual Editing Container Classes

These two classes are used by container applications. Both **COleLinkingDoc** and **COleDocument** manage collections of **COleClientItem** objects.

COleLinkingDoc

A class derived from **COleDocument** which provides the infrastructure for linking. You should derive the document classes for your container applications from this class instead of from **COleDocument** if you want them to support links to embedded objects.

COleClientItem

A client item class that represents the client's side of the connection to an embedded or linked OLE item. You must derive your client items from this class.

OLE Visual Editing Server Classes

These classes are used by servers to handle various required tasks.

COleObjectFactory

Used to create items when requested from other OLE containers. This class serves as the base class for more specific types of factories, including **COleTemplateServer**.

COleTemplateServer

Used to create documents using the framework's document/view architecture. A **COleTemplateServer** object delegates most of its work to an associated **CDocTemplate** object.

COleServerDoc

Used as the base class for server application document classes. **COleServerDoc** objects provide the bulk of server support through interactions with **COleServerItem** objects. Visual editing capability is provided using the class library's document/view architecture.

COleServerItem

Used to represent the OLE interface to **COleServerDoc** objects. There is usually one **COleServerItem** object, which represents the embedded part of a document, and many **COleServerItem** objects, which represent links to portions of the document.

COleIPFrameWnd

Provides the frame window for a view when a server document is being edited in place.

COleResizeBar

Provides the standard user interface for in-place resizing. Objects of this class are always used in conjunction with **COleIPFrameWnd** objects.

OLE Data Transfer Classes

These classes are used in OLE data transfers. They allow data to be transferred between applications by using the Clipboard or through drag and drop.

COleDropSource

Controls the drag-and-drop operation from start to finish. This class determines when the drag operation starts and when it ends. It also displays cursor feedback during the drag-and-drop operation.

COleDropTarget

Represents the target of a drag-and-drop operation. A **COleDropTarget** object corresponds to a window on screen. It determines whether to accept any data dropped onto it and implements the actual drop operation.

COleDataSource

Used when an application provides data for a data transfer. **COleDataSource** could be viewed as an object-oriented clipboard object.

COleDataObject

Used as the client side to **COleDataSource**. **COleDataObject** objects provide access to the data contained in a **COleDataSource** object.

OLE Dialog Box Classes

These classes handle common OLE tasks by implementing a number of standard OLE dialog boxes.

COleDialog

Used by the framework to contain common implementations for all OLE dialog boxes. All dialog box classes in the user-interface category are derived from this base class. Cannot be used directly.

COleInsertDialog

Displays the Insert Object dialog box, the standard user interface for inserting new OLE linked or embedded items.

COleConvertDialog

Displays the Convert dialog box, the standard user interface for converting OLE items from one type to another.

COleChangeIconDialog

Displays the Change Icon dialog box, the standard user interface for changing the icon associated with an OLE embedded or linked item.

COlePasteSpecialDialog

Displays the Paste Special dialog box, the standard user interface for implementing the Edit Paste Special command.

COleLinksDialog

Displays the Edit Links dialog box, the standard user interface for modifying information about linked items.

COleUpdateDialog

Displays the Update dialog box, the standard user interface for updating all links in a document. The dialog box contains a progress indicator to indicate how close the update procedure is to completion.

COleBusyDialog

Displays the Server Busy and Server Not Responding dialog boxes, the standard user interface for handling calls to busy applications. Usually displayed automatically by the **COleMessageFilter** implementation.

Miscellaneous OLE Classes

These classes provide a number of different services, ranging from exceptions to file input and output.

COleException

An exception resulting from a failure in OLE processing. This class is used by both containers and servers.

COleDispatchException

An exception resulting from an error during OLE automation. OLE automation exceptions are thrown by automation servers and caught by automation clients.

CRectTracker

Used to allow moving, resizing, and reorientation of in-place items.

COleStreamFile

Uses the OLE 2 **IStream** interface to provide **CFile** access to compound files. This class (derived from **CFile**) enables MFC serialization to use OLE 2 structured storage.

COleMessageFilter

Used to manage concurrency with OLE Lightweight Remote Procedure Calls (LRPC).

Database Classes

These classes work with the other application framework classes to give easy access to a wide variety of databases for which Open Database Connectivity (ODBC) drivers are available.

CDatabase

Encapsulates a connection to a data source, through which you can operate on the data source.

CRecordset

Encapsulates a set of records selected from a data source. Recordsets enable scrolling from record to record, updating records (adding, editing, and deleting records), qualifying the selection with a filter, sorting the selection, and parameterizing the selection with information obtained or calculated at run time.

CRecordView

Provides a form view directly connected to a recordset object. The DDX mechanism exchanges data between the recordset and the controls of the record view. Like all form views, a record view is based on a dialog template resource. Record views also support moving from record to record in the recordset, updating records, and closing the associated recordset when the record view closes.

CFieldExchange

Supplies context information to support record field exchange (RFX), which exchanges data between the field data members and parameter data members of a recordset object and the corresponding table columns on the data source. Analogous to class **CDataExchange**, used similarly for dialog data exchange (DDX).

CLongBinary

Encapsulates a handle to storage for a binary large object (or BLOB), such as a bitmap. **CLongBinary** objects are used to manage large data objects stored in database tables.

CDBException

An exception resulting from failures in data access processing. This class serves the same purpose as other exception classes in the exception-handling mechanism of the class library.

Macros and Globals

The "Macros and Globals" section of this manual documents the elements of the Microsoft Foundation Class Library that are not defined as members of specific classes. These include macros and global functions and variables in the following general categories:

- Data types
- Run-time object model services
- Diagnostic services
- Exception processing
- **CString** formatting and message-box display
- Message maps
- Dialog data exchange and validation
- Application information and management
- Standard commands and window IDs

General Class Design Philosophy

Microsoft Windows was designed long before the C++ language became popular. Because thousands of applications use the C-language Windows application programming interface (API), that interface will be maintained for the foreseeable future. Any C++ Windows interface must therefore be built on top of the procedural C-language API. This guarantees that C++ applications will be able to coexist with C applications.

Design Goals

The Microsoft Foundation Class Library is truly an object-oriented interface to Windows that meets the following design goals:

- Effort of programming an application for Windows is significantly reduced
- Execution speed comparable to that of the C-language API
- Minimum code size overhead
- Ability to call any Windows C function directly
- Easier conversion of existing C applications to C++
- Ability to leverage from the existing base of C-language Windows programming experience
- Easier use of the Windows API with C++ than with C
- True Windows API for C++ that effectively uses C++ language features

The Application Framework

The core of the Microsoft Foundation Class Library is an encapsulation of a large portion of the Windows API in C++ form. Library classes represent windows, dialog boxes, device contexts, common GDI objects such as brushes and pens, controls, and other standard Windows items. These classes provide a convenient C++ member function interface to the structures in Windows that they encapsulate. For more information about these core classes, see "Windows of Your Own with CWnd" in Chapter 1 of *Programming with the Microsoft Foundation Class Library*.

But the Microsoft Foundation Class Library also supplies a layer of additional application functionality built on the C++ encapsulation of the Windows API. This layer is a working application framework for Windows that provides most of the common user interface expected of programs for Windows. Chapter 1 of *Programming with the Microsoft Foundation Class Library* explains the framework in detail, and *Introducing Visual C++* provides a tutorial that teaches application-framework programming.

Relationship to the C-Language API

The single characteristic that sets the Microsoft Foundation Class Library apart from other class libraries for Windows is the very close mapping to the Windows API written in the C language. Further, you can generally mix calls to the class library freely with direct calls to the Windows API. This direct access does not, however, imply that the classes are a complete replacement for that API. Developers must still occasionally make direct calls to some Windows functions— **GetSystemMetrics**, for example. A Windows function is wrapped by a class member function only when there is a clear advantage to doing so.

Because you sometimes need to make native Windows function calls, you should have access to the C-language Windows API documentation. This is included with Microsoft Visual C++ as Help. One useful book is *Programming Windows 3.1*, third edition, by Charles Petzold, from Microsoft Press. Many of that book's examples can be easily converted to the Microsoft Foundation classes. For examples and additional information about programming with the Microsoft Foundation Class Library, see *Inside Visual C++* by David J. Kruglinski from Microsoft Press. Both of these books are specific to programming for Windows version 3.1.

Note For an overview of how the Microsoft Foundation Class Library framework operates, see Chapter 1, "Using the Classes to Write Applications for Windows," in *Programming with the Microsoft Foundation Class Library*. The overview material is no longer located in the *Class Library Reference*.

class CArchive

The **CArchive** class allows you to save a complex network of objects in a permanent binary form (usually disk storage) that persists after those objects are deleted. Later you can load the objects from persistent storage, reconstituting them in memory. This process of making data persistent is called "serialization."

You can think of an archive object as a kind of binary stream. Like an input/output stream, an archive is associated with a file and permits the buffered writing and reading of data to and from storage. An input/output stream processes sequences of ASCII characters, but an archive processes binary object data in an efficient, nonredundant format.

You must create a **CFile** object before you can create a **CArchive** object. In addition, you must ensure that the archive's load/store status is compatible with the file's open mode. You are limited to one active archive per file.

When you construct a **CArchive** object, you attach it to an object of class **CFile** (or a derived class) that represents an open file. You also specify whether the archive will be used for loading or storing. A **CArchive** object can process not only primitive types but also objects of **CObject**-derived classes designed for serialization. A serializable class must have a **Serialize** member function, and it must use the **DECLARE_SERIAL** and **IMPLEMENT_SERIAL** macros, as described under class **CObject**.

The overloaded extraction (**>>**) and insertion (**<<**) operators are convenient archive programming interfaces that support both primitive types and **CObject**-derived classes.

#include <afx.h>

See Also   **CFile**, **CObject**

Data Members
m_pDocument	Points to the **CDocument** object being serialized.

Construction
CArchive	Creates a **CArchive** object.
Close	Flushes unwritten data and disconnects from the **CFile**.

Basic Input/Output

Flush	Flushes unwritten data from the archive buffer.
operator >>	Loads objects and primitive types from the archive.
operator <<	Stores objects and primitive types to the archive.
Read	Reads raw bytes.
Write	Writes raw bytes.

Status

GetFile	Gets the **CFile** object pointer for this archive.
GetObjectSchema	Called from the **Serialize** function to determine the version of the object that is being deserialized.
IsLoading	Determines whether the archive is loading.
IsStoring	Determines whether the archive is storing.

Object Input/Output

ReadObject	Calls an object's **Serialize** function for loading.
WriteObject	Calls an object's **Serialize** function for storing.

Member Functions

CArchive::CArchive

CArchive(CFile* *pFile*, **UINT** *nMode*, **int** *nBufSize* **= 512,**
    void* *lpBuf* **= NULL)**
    throw(CMemoryException, CArchiveException, CFileException);

Parameters   *pFile*   A pointer to the **CFile** object that is the ultimate source or destination of the persistent data.

nMode   A flag that specifies whether objects will be loaded from or stored to the archive. The *nMode* parameter must have one of the following values:

- **CArchive::load**   Loads data from the archive. Requires only **CFile** read permission.
- **CArchive::store**   Saves data to the archive. Requires **CFile** write permission.
- **CArchive::bNoFlushOnDelete**   Prevents the archive from automatically calling **Flush** when the archive destructor is called. If you set this flag, you are responsible for explicitly calling **Close** before the destructor is called. If you do not, your data will be corrupted.

nBufSize   An integer that specifies the size of the internal file buffer, in bytes. Note that the default buffer size is 512 bytes. If you routinely archive large objects, you will improve performance if you use a larger buffer size that is a multiple of the file buffer size.

lpBuf   An optional pointer to a user-supplied buffer of size *nBufSize*. If you do not specify this parameter, the archive allocates a buffer from the local heap and frees it when the object is destroyed. The archive does not free a user-supplied buffer.

Remarks   Constructs a **CArchive** object and specifies whether it will be used for loading or storing objects. You cannot change this specification after you have created the archive. You may not use **CFile** operations to alter the state of the file until you have closed the archive. Any such operation will damage the integrity of the archive. You may access the position of the file pointer at any time during serialization by obtaining the archive's file object from the **GetFile** member function and then using the **CFile::GetPosition** function. You should call **CArchive::Flush** before obtaining the position of the file pointer.

See Also   **CArchive::Close, CArchive::Flush, CFile::Close**

Example
```
extern char* pFileName;
CFile f;
char buf[512];
if( !f.Open( pFileName, CFile::modeCreate | CFile::modeWrite ) ) {
   #ifdef _DEBUG
      afxDump << "Unable to open file" << "\n";
      exit( 1 );
   #endif
}
CArchive ar( &f, CArchive::store, 512, buf );
```

CArchive::Close

void Close( )
    throw(CArchiveException, CFileException);

Remarks   Flushes any data remaining in the buffer, closes the archive, and disconnects the archive from the file. No further operations on the archive are permitted. After you close an archive, you can create another archive for the same file or you can close the file. The member function **Close** ensures that all data is transferred from the archive to the file, and it makes the archive unavailable. To complete the transfer from the file to the storage medium, you must first use **CFile::Close** and then destroy the **CFile** object.

See Also   **CArchive::Flush**

CArchive::Flush

> **void Flush( )**
>   **throw(CFileException);**

Remarks   Forces any data remaining in the archive buffer to be written to the file. The member function **Flush** ensures that all data is transferred from the archive to the file. You must call **CFile::Close** to complete the transfer from the file to the storage medium.

See Also   **CArchive::Close, CFile::Flush, CFile::Close**

CArchive::GetFile

> **CFile* GetFile( ) const;**

Return Value   A constant pointer to the **CFile** object in use.

Remarks   Gets the **CFile** object pointer for this archive. You must flush the archive before using **GetFile**.

Example
```
extern CArchive ar;
const CFile* fp = ar.GetFile();
```

CArchive::GetObjectSchema

> **UINT GetObjectSchema( );**

Return Value   During deserialization, the version of the object being read.

Remarks   Call this function from the **Serialize** function to determine the version of the object that is currently being deserialized. Calling this function is only valid when the **CArchive** object is being loaded (**CArchive::IsLoading** returns nonzero). It should be the first call in the **Serialize** function and called only once. A return value of (**UINT**)–1 indicates that the version number is unknown).

A **CObject**-derived class may use **VERSIONABLE_SCHEMA** combined (using bitwise **OR**) with the schema version itself (in the **IMPLEMENT_SERIAL** macro) to create a "versionable object," that is, an object whose **Serialize** member function can read multiple versions. The default framework functionality (without **VERSIONABLE_SCHEMA**) is to throw an exception when the version is mismatched.

See Also   **CObject::Serialize, CObject::IsSerializable, IMPLEMENT_SERIAL, DECLARE_SERIAL**

Example

```
DECLARE_SERIAL(CMyObject, CObject, VERSIONABLE_SCHEMA|1)
    // defines version as 1 and "versionable"

CMyObject::Serialize(CArchive& ar)
{
    switch (nVersion)
    {
        case -1:
            // read in current version
            // or report error
            break;
        case 0:
            // read in old version
            break;
        case 1;
            // read in latest version of this object
            break;
        default:
            //report unknown version
            break;
    }
}
```

CArchive::IsLoading

BOOL IsLoading( ) const;

Return Value   Nonzero if the archive is currently being used for loading; otherwise 0.

Remarks   Determines whether the archive is loading data. This member function is called by the **Serialize** functions of the archived classes.

See Also   **CArchive::IsStoring**

Example
```
int i;
extern CArchive ar;
if( ar.IsLoading() )
  ar >> i;
else
  ar << i;
```

CArchive::IsStoring

BOOL IsStoring( ) const;

Return Value   Nonzero if the archive is currently being used for storing; otherwise 0.

Remarks   Determines whether the archive is storing data. This member function is called by
the **Serialize** functions of the archived classes. If the **IsStoring** status of an archive
is nonzero, then its **IsLoading** status is 0, and vice versa.

See Also   **CArchive::IsLoading**

Example
```
int i;
extern CArchive ar;
if( ar.IsStoring() )
  ar << i;
else
  ar >> i;
```

CArchive::Read

UINT Read(void* *lpBuf*, **UINT** *nMax*)
   throw(CFileException);

Return Value An unsigned integer containing the number of bytes actually read. If the return
value is less than the number requested, the end of file has been reached. No
exception is thrown on the end-of-file condition.

Parameters   *lpBuf*   A pointer to a user-supplied buffer that is to receive the data read from the
archive.

nMax   An unsigned integer specifying the number of bytes to be read from the
archive.

Remarks   Reads a specified number of bytes from the archive. The archive does not interpret
the bytes. You can use the **Read** member function within your **Serialize** function
for reading ordinary structures that are contained in your objects.

Example
```
extern CArchive ar;
char pb[100];
UINT nr = ar.Read( pb, 100 );
```

CArchive::ReadObject

CObject* ReadObject(const CRuntimeClass* *pClass*)
   throw(CFileException, CArchiveException, CMemoryException);

Return Value A **CObject** pointer that must be safely cast to the correct derived class by using
CObject::IsKindOf.

Parameters   *pClass*   A constant pointer to the **CRuntimeClass** structure that corresponds to
the object you expect to read.

Remarks	Reads object data from the archive and constructs an object of the appropriate type. If the object contains pointers to other objects, those objects' constructors are called. This function is normally called by the **CArchive** extraction (**>>**) operator overloaded for a **CObject** pointer. **ReadObject**, in turn, calls the **Serialize** function of the archived class. If you supply a nonzero *pClass* parameter, which is obtained by the **RUNTIME_CLASS** macro, then the function verifies the run-time class of the archived object. This assumes you have used the **IMPLEMENT_SERIAL** macro in the implementation of the class.
See Also	**CArchive::WriteObject, CObject::IsKindOf**

CArchive::Write

void Write(const void* *lpBuf*, UINT *nMax*)
    throw(CFileException);

Parameters	*lpBuf* A pointer to a user-supplied buffer that contains the data to be written to the archive. *nMax* An integer that specifies the number of bytes to be written to the archive.
Remarks	Writes a specified number of bytes to the archive. The archive does not format the bytes. You can use the **Write** member function within your **Serialize** function to write ordinary structures that are contained in your objects.
See Also	**CArchive::Read**
| **Example** | ```
extern CArchive ar;
char pb[100];
ar.Write( pb, 100 );
``` |

CArchive::WriteObject

void WriteObject(const CObject* *pOb*)
    throw(CFileException, CArchiveException);

Parameters	*pOb* A constant pointer to the object being stored.
Remarks	Stores the specified **CObject** to the archive. If the object contains pointers to other objects, this function calls those objects' **Serialize** functions. This function is normally called by the **CArchive** insertion (**<<**) operator overloaded for **CObject**. **WriteObject**, in turn, calls the **Serialize** function of the archived class. You must use the **IMPLEMENT_SERIAL** macro to enable archiving. **WriteObject** writes the ASCII class name to the archive. This class name is validated later during the load process. A special encoding scheme prevents unnecessary duplication of the class name for multiple objects of the class. This scheme also prevents redundant storage of objects that are targets of more than one pointer. The exact object
```

encoding method (including the presence of the ASCII class name) is an implementation detail and could change in future versions of the library.

Note Finish creating, deleting, and updating all your objects before you begin to archive them. Your archive will be corrupted if you mix archiving with object modification.

See Also   **CArchive::ReadObject**

Operators

CArchive::operator <<

friend CArchive& operator <<(CArchive& *ar***, const CObject*** *pOb* **)**
   throw(CArchiveException, CFileException);

CArchive& operator <<(BYTE *by* **)**
   throw(CArchiveException, CFileException);

CArchive& operator <<(WORD *w* **)**
   throw(CArchiveException, CFileException);

CArchive& operator <<(LONG *l* **)**
   throw(CArchiveException, CFileException);

CArchive& operator <<(DWORD *dw* **)**
   throw(CArchiveException, CFileException);

CArchive& operator <<(float *f* **)**
   throw(CArchiveException, CFileException);

CArchive& operator <<(double *d* **)**
   throw(CArchiveException, CFileException);

Return Value   A **CArchive** reference that enables multiple extraction operators on a single line.

Remarks   Stores the indicated object or primitive type to the archive. If you used the **IMPLEMENT_SERIAL** macro in your class implementation, then the insertion operator overloaded for **CObject** calls the protected **WriteObject**. This function, in turn, calls the **Serialize** function of the class.

See Also   **CArchive::WriteObject, CObject::Serialize**

Example
```
long l;
int i;
extern CArchive ar;
if( ar.IsStoring() )
  ar << l << i;
```

CArchive::operator >>

friend CArchive& operator >>(CArchive& *ar*, **CObject *&** *pOb*)
    throw(CArchiveException, CFileException, CMemoryException);

friend CArchive& operator >>(CArchive& *ar*, **const CObject *&** *pOb*)
    throw(CArchiveException, CFileException, CMemoryException);

CArchive& operator >>(BYTE& *by*)
    throw(CArchiveException, CFileException);

CArchive& operator >>(WORD& *w*)
    throw(CArchiveException, CFileException);

CArchive& operator >>(LONG& *l*)
    throw(CArchiveException, CFileException);

CArchive& operator >>(DWORD& *dw*)
    throw(CArchiveException, CFileException);

CArchive& operator >>(float& *f*)
    throw(CArchiveException, CFileException);

CArchive& operator >>(double& *d*)
    throw(CArchiveException, CFileException);

Return Value   A **CArchive** reference that enables multiple insertion operators on a single line.

Remarks   Loads the indicated object or primitive type from the archive. If you used the **IMPLEMENT_SERIAL** macro in your class implementation, then the extraction operators overloaded for **CObject** call the protected **ReadObject** function (with a nonzero run-time class pointer). This function, in turn, calls the **Serialize** function of the class.

See Also   **CArchive::ReadObject, CObject::Serialize**

Example
```
int i;
extern CArchive ar;
if( ar.IsLoading() )
  ar >> i;
```

Data Members

CArchive::m_pDocument

Remarks

Set to **NULL** by default, this pointer to a **CDocument** can be set to anything the user of the **CArchive** instance wants. A common usage of this pointer is to convey additional information about the serialization process to all objects being serialized. This is achieved by initializing the pointer with the document (a **CDocument**-derived class) that is being serialized, in such a way that objects within the document can access the document if necessary. This pointer is also used by **COleClientItem** objects during serialization.

The framework sets **m_pDocument** to the document being serialized when a user issues a File Open or Save command. If you serialize an Object Linking and Embedding (OLE) container document for reasons other than File Open or Save, you must explicitly set **m_pDocument**. For example, you would do this when serializing a container document to the Clipboard.

See Also

CDocument, **COleClientItem**

class CArchiveException : public CException

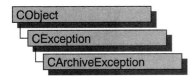

A **CArchiveException** object represents a serialization exception condition. The **CArchiveException** class includes a public data member that indicates the cause of the exception.

CArchiveException objects are constructed and thrown inside **CArchive** member functions. You can access these objects within the scope of a **CATCH** expression. The cause code is independent of the operating system. For more information about exception processing, see the article "Exceptions" in *Programming with the Microsoft Foundation Class Library*.

#include <afx.h>

See Also   **CArchive, AfxThrowArchiveException**

Data Members

m_cause	Indicates the exception cause.

Construction

CArchiveException	Constructs a **CArchiveException** object.

Member Functions

CArchiveException::CArchiveException

CArchiveException(int *cause* **= CArchiveException::none);**

Parameters   *cause*   An enumerated type variable that indicates the reason for the exception. For a list of the enumerators, see the **m_cause** data member.

Remarks   Constructs a **CArchiveException** object, storing the value of *cause* in the object. You can create a **CArchiveException** object on the heap and throw it yourself or let the global function **AfxThrowArchiveException** handle it for you.

Do not use this constructor directly; instead, call the global function **AfxThrowArchiveException**.

Data Members

CArchiveException::m_cause

Remarks   Specifies the cause of the exception. This data member is a public variable of type **int**. Its values are defined by a **CArchiveException** enumerated type. The enumerators and their meanings are as follows:

- **CArchiveException::none**   No error occurred.
- **CArchiveException::generic**   Unspecified error.
- **CArchiveException::readOnly**   Tried to write into an archive opened for loading.
- **CArchiveException::endOfFile**   Reached end of file while reading an object.
- **CArchiveException::writeOnly**   Tried to read from an archive opened for storing.
- **CArchiveException::badIndex**   Invalid file format.
- **CArchiveException::badClass**   Tried to read an object into an object of the wrong type.
- **CArchiveException::badSchema**   Tried to read an object with a different version of the class.

Note   These **CArchiveException** cause enumerators are distinct from the **CFileException** cause enumerators.

class CArray : public CObject

CObject

CArray

template< class *TYPE*, class *ARG_TYPE* >
class CArray : public CObject

Parameters   *TYPE*   Template parameter specifying the type of objects stored in the array.

ARG_TYPE   Template parameter specifying the argument type used to access objects stored in the array. Often a reference to *TYPE*.

Remarks   The **CArray** class supports arrays that are similar to C arrays, but can dynamically shrink and grow as necessary.

Array indexes always start at position 0. You can decide whether to fix the upper bound or allow the array to expand when you add elements past the current bound. Memory is allocated contiguously to the upper bound, even if some elements are null.

As with a C array, the access time for a **CArray** indexed element is constant and is independent of the array size.

Tip   Before using an array, use **SetSize** to establish its size and allocate memory for it. If you do not use SetSize, adding elements to your array causes it to be frequently reallocated and copied. Frequent reallocation and copying are inefficient and can fragment memory.

If you need a dump of individual elements in an array, you must set the depth of the **CDumpContext** object to 1 or greater.

Certain member functions of this class call global helper functions that must be customized for most uses of the **CArray** class. See Collection Class Helpers.

When elements are removed from a **CArray** object, the helper function **DestructElements** is called. When elements are added, the helper function **ConstructElements** is called.

Array class derivation is similar to list derivation.

#include <afxtempl.h>

See Also   **CObArray**, **DestructElements**, **ConstructElements**, Collection Class Helpers

Construction

CArray	Constructs an empty array.

Bounds

GetSize	Gets the number of elements in this array.
GetUpperBound	Returns the largest valid index.
SetSize	Sets the number of elements to be contained in this array.

Operations

FreeExtra	Frees all unused memory above the current upper bound.
RemoveAll	Removes all the elements from this array.

Element Access

GetAt	Returns the value at a given index.
SetAt	Sets the value for a given index; array not allowed to grow.
ElementAt	Returns a temporary reference to the element pointer within the array.

Growing the Array

SetAtGrow	Sets the value for a given index; grows the array if necessary.
Add	Adds an element to the end of the array; grows the array if necessary.

Insertion/Removal

InsertAt	Inserts an element (or all the elements in another array) at a specified index.
RemoveAt	Removes an element at a specific index.

Operators

operator [ ]	Sets or gets the element at the specified index.

Member Functions

CArray::Add

int Add(*ARG_TYPE newElement* **)**
throw(CMemoryException);

Return Value   The index of the added element.

Parameters	*ARG_TYPE* Template parameter specifying the type of arguments referencing elements in this array.
	newElement The element to be added to this array.
Remarks	Adds a new element to the end of an array, growing the array by 1. If **SetSize** has been used with an *nGrowBy* value greater than 1, then extra memory may be allocated. However, the upper bound will increase by only 1.
See Also	**CArray::SetAt**, **CArray::SetAtGrow**, **CArray::InsertAt**, **CArray::operator []**
Example	

```
CArray<CPoint,CPoint> ptArray;

CPoint pt(10,20);
ptArray.Add(pt);                // Element 0
ptArray.Add(CPoint(30,40));  // Element 1
```

CArray::CArray

CArray( );

Remarks	Constructs an empty array. The array grows one element at a time.
See Also	**CObArray::CObArray**

CArray::ElementAt

*TYPE***& ElementAt(int *nIndex*);**

Return Value	A reference to an array element.
Parameters	*TYPE* Template parameter specifying the type of elements in the array.
	nIndex An integer index that is greater than or equal to 0 and less than or equal to the value returned by **GetUpperBound**.
Remarks	Returns a temporary reference to the specified element within the array. It is used to implement the left-side assignment operator for arrays.
See Also	**CArray::operator []**

CArray::FreeExtra

void FreeExtra( );

Remarks	Frees any extra memory that was allocated while the array was grown. This function has no effect on the size or upper bound of the array.

CArray::GetAt

TYPE **GetAt(int** *nIndex* **) const;**

Return Value   The array element currently at this index. If no element is at the index, a new object as constructed by the **ConstructElements** helper function is returned.

Parameters   *TYPE*   Template parameter specifying the type of the array elements.

nIndex   An integer index that is greater than or equal to 0 and less than or equal to the value returned by **GetUpperBound**.

Remarks   Returns the array element at the specified index.

See Also   **CArray::SetAt, CArray::operator [], ConstructElements**

CArray::GetSize

int GetSize( ) const;

Remarks   Returns the size of the array. Since indexes are zero-based, the size is 1 greater than the largest index.

See Also   **CArray::GetUpperBound, CArray::SetSize**

CArray::GetUpperBound

int GetUpperBound( ) const;

Remarks   Returns the current upper bound of this array. Because array indexes are zero-based, this function returns a value 1 less than **GetSize**. The condition **GetUpperBound( ) = –1** indicates that the array contains no elements.

See Also   **CArray::GetSize, CArray::SetSize**

CArray::InsertAt

void InsertAt(int *nIndex*, *ARG_TYPE newElement*, **int** *nCount* **= 1)**
throw(CMemoryException);

void InsertAt(int *nStartIndex*, **CArray*** *pNewArray* **)**
throw(CMemoryException);

Parameters   *nIndex*   An integer index that may be greater than the value returned by **GetUpperBound**.

ARG_TYPE   Template parameter specifying the type of elements in this array.

newElement   The element to be placed in this array.

nCount   The number of times this element should be inserted (defaults to 1).

nStartIndex   An integer index that may be greater than the value returned by **GetUpperBound**.

pNewArray   Another array that contains elements to be added to this array.

Remarks   The first version of **InsertAt** inserts one element (or multiple copies of an element) at a specified index in an array. In the process, it shifts up (by incrementing the index) the existing element at this index, and it shifts up all the elements above it. The second version inserts all the elements from another **CArray** collection, starting at the *nStartIndex* position. The **SetAt** function, in contrast, replaces one specified array element and does not shift any elements.

See Also   **CArray::SetAt**, **CArray::RemoveAt**

Example

```
CArray<CPoint,CPoint> ptArray;

ptArray.Add(CPoint(10,20)); // Element 0
ptArray.Add(CPoint(30,40)); // Element 1 (will become element 2)
ptArray.InsertAt(1, CPoint(50,60)); // New element 1
```

CArray::RemoveAll

void RemoveAll( );

Remarks   Removes all the elements from this array. If the array is already empty, the function still works.

CArray::RemoveAt

void RemoveAt(int *nIndex*, int *nCount* = 1);

Parameters   *nIndex*   An integer index that is greater than or equal to 0 and less than or equal to the value returned by **GetUpperBound**.

nCount   The number of elements to remove.

Remarks   Removes one or more elements starting at a specified index in an array. In the process, it shifts down all the elements above the removed element(s). It decrements the upper bound of the array but does not free memory. If you try to remove more elements than are contained in the array above the removal point, then the Debug version of the library asserts.

See Also   **CArray::SetAt**, **CArray::SetAtGrow**, **CArray::InsertAt**

CArray::SetAt

void SetAt(int *nIndex***,** *ARG_TYPE newElement* **);**

Parameters   *nIndex*   An integer index that is greater than or equal to 0 and less than or equal to the value returned by **GetUpperBound**.

ARG_TYPE   Template parameter specifying the type of arguments used for referencing array elements.

newElement   The new element value to be stored at the specified position.

Remarks   Sets the array element at the specified index. **SetAt** will not cause the array to grow. Use **SetAtGrow** if you want the array to grow automatically.

You must ensure that your index value represents a valid position in the array. If it is out of bounds, then the Debug version of the library asserts.

See Also   **CArray::GetAt**, **CArray::SetAtGrow**, **CArray::ElementAt**, **CArray::operator []**

CArray::SetAtGrow

void SetAtGrow(int *nIndex***,** *ARG_TYPE newElement* **)**
throw(CMemoryException);

Parameters   *nIndex*   An integer index that is greater than or equal to 0.

ARG_TYPE   Template parameter specifying the type of elements in the array.

newElement   The element to be added to this array. A **NULL** value is allowed.

Remarks   Sets the array element at the specified index. The array grows automatically if necessary (that is, the upper bound is adjusted to accommodate the new element).

See Also   **CArray::GetAt**, **CArray::SetAt**, **CArray::ElementAt**, **CArray::operator []**

Example
```
CArray<CPoint,CPoint> ptArray;

ptArray.Add(CPoint(10,20)); // Element 0
ptArray.Add(CPoint(30,40)); // Element 1
                            // Element 2 deliberately skipped
ptArray.SetAtGrow(3, CPoint(50,60)); // Element 3
```

CArray::SetSize

void SetSize(int *nNewSize***, int** *nGrowBy* **= –1)**
throw(CMemoryException);

Parameters   *nNewSize*   The new array size (number of elements). Must be greater than or equal to 0.

nGrowBy   The minimum number of element slots to allocate if a size increase is necessary.

Remarks   Establishes the size of an empty or existing array; allocates memory if necessary. If the new size is smaller than the old size, then the array is truncated and all unused memory is released. Use this function to set the size of your array before you begin using the array. If you do not use **SetSize**, adding elements to your array causes it to be frequently reallocated and copied. Frequent reallocation and copying are inefficient and can fragment memory.

The *nGrowBy* parameter affects internal memory allocation while the array is growing. Its use never affects the array size as reported by **GetSize** and **GetUpperBound**. If the default value is used, MFC allocates memory in a way calculated to avoid memory fragmentation and optimize efficiency for most cases.

Operators

CArray::operator [ ]

*TYPE***& operator [ ](** **int** *nIndex* **);**

TYPE **operator [ ](** **int** *nIndex* **) const;**

Parameters   *TYPE*   Template parameter specifying the type of elements in this array.

nIndex   Index of the element to be accessed.

Remarks   These subscript operators are a convenient substitute for the **SetAt** and **GetAt** functions. The first operator, called for arrays that are not **const**, may be used on either the right (r-value) or the left (l-value) of an assignment statement. The second, called for **const** arrays, may be used only on the right. The Debug version of the library asserts if the subscript (either on the left or right side of an assignment statement) is out of bounds.

See Also   **CArray::GetAt**, **CArray::SetAt**

class CBitmap : public CGdiObject

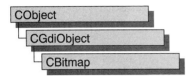

The **CBitmap** class encapsulates a Windows graphics device interface (GDI) bitmap and provides member functions to manipulate the bitmap. To use a **CBitmap** object, construct the object, install a bitmap handle in it with one of the initialization member functions, and then call the object's member functions.

#include <afxwin.h>

Construction

CBitmap	Constructs a **CBitmap** object.

Initialization

LoadBitmap	Initializes the object by loading a named bitmap resource from the application's executable file and attaching the bitmap to the object.
LoadOEMBitmap	Initializes the object by loading a predefined Windows bitmap and attaching the bitmap to the object.
CreateBitmap	Initializes the object with a device-dependent memory bitmap that has a specified width, height, and bit pattern.
CreateBitmapIndirect	Initializes the object with a bitmap with the width, height, and bit pattern (if one is specified) given in a **BITMAP** structure.
CreateCompatibleBitmap	Initializes the object with a bitmap so that it is compatible with a specified device.
CreateDiscardableBitmap	Initializes the object with a discardable bitmap that is compatible with a specified device.

Operations

FromHandle	Returns a pointer to a **CBitmap** object when given a handle to a Windows **HBITMAP** bitmap.
SetBitmapBits	Sets the bits of a bitmap to the specified bit values.
GetBitmapBits	Copies the bits of the specified bitmap into the specified buffer.
SetBitmapDimension	Assigns a width and height to a bitmap in 0.1-millimeter units.
GetBitmapDimension	Returns the width and height of the bitmap. The height and width are assumed to have been set previously by the **SetBitmapDimension** member function.

Member Functions

CBitmap::CBitmap

CBitmap( );

Remarks   Constructs a **CBitmap** object. The resulting object must be initialized with one of the initialization member functions.

See Also   **CBitmap::LoadBitmap**, **CBitmap::LoadOEMBitmap**, **CBitmap::CreateBitmap**, **CBitmap::CreateBitmapIndirect**, **CBitmap::CreateCompatibleBitmap**, **CBitmap::CreateDiscardableBitmap**

CBitmap::CreateBitmap

BOOL CreateBitmap(int *nWidth*, **int** *nHeight*, **UINT** *nPlanes*, **UINT** *nBitcount*, **const void*** *lpBits* **);**

Return Value   Nonzero if successful; otherwise 0.

Parameters   *nWidth*   Specifies the width (in pixels) of the bitmap.

nHeight   Specifies the height (in pixels) of the bitmap.

nPlanes   Specifies the number of color planes in the bitmap.

nBitcount   Specifies the number of color bits per display pixel.

lpBits   Points to a short-integer array that contains the initial bitmap bit values. If it is **NULL**, the new bitmap is left uninitialized.

For more information, see the description of the **bmBits** field in the **BITMAP** structure. In this manual, the **BITMAP** structure is described under the **CBitmap::CreateBitmapIndirect** member function.

Remarks

Initializes a device-dependent memory bitmap that has the specified width, height, and bit pattern. For a color bitmap, either the *nPlanes* or *nBitcount* parameter should be set to 1. If both of these parameters are set to 1, **CreateBitmap** creates a monochrome bitmap. Although a bitmap cannot be directly selected for a display device, it can be selected as the current bitmap for a "memory device context" by using **CDC::SelectObject** and copied to any compatible device context by using the **CDC::BitBlt** function.

When you finish with the **CBitmap** object created by the **CreateBitmap** function, first select the bitmap out of the device context, then delete the **CBitmap** object.

See Also

CDC::SelectObject, **CGdiObject::DeleteObject**, **CDC::BitBlt**, **::CreateBitmap**

CBitmap::CreateBitmapIndirect

BOOL CreateBitmapIndirect(LPBITMAP *lpBitmap* **);**

Return Value

Nonzero if successful; otherwise 0.

Parameters

lpBitmap   Points to a **BITMAP** structure that contains information about the bitmap.

Remarks

Initializes a bitmap that has the width, height, and bit pattern (if one is specified) given in the structure pointed to by *lpBitmap*. Although a bitmap cannot be directly selected for a display device, it can be selected as the current bitmap for a memory device context by using **CDC::SelectObject** and copied to any compatible device context by using the **CDC::BitBlt** or **CDC::StretchBlt** function. (The **CDC::PatBlt** function can copy the bitmap for the current brush directly to the display device context.)

If the **BITMAP** structure pointed to by the *lpBitmap* parameter has been filled in by using the **GetObject** function, the bits of the bitmap are not specified and the bitmap is uninitialized. To initialize the bitmap, an application can use a function such as **CDC::BitBlt** or **::SetDIBits** to copy the bits from the bitmap identified by the first parameter of **CGdiObject::GetObject** to the bitmap created by **CreateBitmapIndirect**.

When you finish with the **CBitmap** object created with **CreateBitmapIndirect** function, first select the bitmap out of the device context, then delete the **CBitmap** object.

See Also

CDC::SelectObject, **CDC::BitBlt**, **CGdiObject::DeleteObject**, **CGdiObject::GetObject**, **::CreateBitmapIndirect**

CBitmap::CreateCompatibleBitmap

BOOL CreateCompatibleBitmap(CDC* *pDC*, **int** *nWidth*, **int** *nHeight* **);**

Return Value   Nonzero if successful; otherwise 0.

Parameters   *pDC*   Specifies the device context.

nWidth   Specifies the width (in bits) of the bitmap.

nHeight   Specifies the height (in bits) of the bitmap.

Remarks   Initializes a bitmap that is compatible with the device specified by *pDC*. The bitmap has the same number of color planes or the same bits-per-pixel format as the specified device context. It can be selected as the current bitmap for any memory device that is compatible with the one specified by *pDC*. If *pDC* is a memory device context, the bitmap returned has the same format as the currently selected bitmap in that device context. A "memory device context" is a block of memory that represents a display surface. It can be used to prepare images in memory before copying them to the actual display surface of the compatible device. When a memory device context is created, GDI automatically selects a monochrome stock bitmap for it.

Since a color memory device context can have either color or monochrome bitmaps selected, the format of the bitmap returned by the **CreateCompatibleBitmap** function is not always the same; however, the format of a compatible bitmap for a nonmemory device context is always in the format of the device.

When you finish with the **CBitmap** object created with the **CreateCompatibleBitmap** function, first select the bitmap out of the device context, then delete the **CBitmap** object.

See Also   **::CreateCompatibleBitmap**, **CGdiObject::DeleteObject**

CBitmap::CreateDiscardableBitmap

BOOL CreateDiscardableBitmap(CDC* *pDC*, **int** *nWidth*, **int** *nHeight* **);**

Return Value   Nonzero if successful; otherwise 0.

Parameters   *pDC*   Specifies a device context.

nWidth   Specifies the width (in bits) of the bitmap.

nHeight   Specifies the height (in bits) of the bitmap.

Remarks   Initializes a discardable bitmap that is compatible with the device context identified by *pDC*. The bitmap has the same number of color planes or the same bits-per-pixel format as the specified device context. An application can select this bitmap as the current bitmap for a memory device that is compatible with the one specified by *pDC*. Windows can discard a bitmap created by this function only if an application has not selected it into a display context. If Windows discards the bitmap when it is not selected and the application later attempts to select it, the **CDC::SelectObject** function will return **NULL**.

When you finish with the **CBitmap** object created with the **CreateDiscardableBitmap** function, first select the bitmap out of the device context, then delete the **CBitmap** object.

See Also   **::CreateDiscardableBitmap**, **CGdiObject::DeleteObject**

CBitmap::FromHandle

static CBitmap* PASCAL FromHandle(HBITMAP *hBitmap* **);**

Return Value   A pointer to a **CBitmap** object if successful; otherwise **NULL**.

Parameters   *hBitmap*   Specifies a Windows GDI bitmap.

Remarks   Returns a pointer to a **CBitmap** object when given a handle to a Windows GDI bitmap. If a **CBitmap** object is not already attached to the handle, a temporary **CBitmap** object is created and attached. This temporary **CBitmap** object is valid only until the next time the application has idle time in its event loop, at which time all temporary graphic objects are deleted. Another way of saying this is that the temporary object is only valid during the processing of one window message.

CBitmap::GetBitmapBits

DWORD GetBitmapBits(DWORD *dwCount*, **LPVOID** *lpBits* **) const;**

Return Value   The actual number of bytes in the bitmap, or 0 if there is an error.

Parameters   *dwCount*   Specifies the number of bytes to be copied.

lpBits   Points to the buffer that is to receive the bitmap. The bitmap is an array of bytes. The bitmap byte array conforms to a structure where horizontal scan lines are multiples of 16 bits.

Remarks   Copies the bit pattern of the **CBitmap** object into the buffer that is pointed to by *lpBits*. The *dwCount* parameter specifies the number of bytes to be copied to the buffer. Use **GetObject** to determine the correct *dwCount* value for the given bitmap.

See Also   **CGdiObject::GetObject**, **::GetBitmapBits**

CBitmap::GetBitmapDimension

CSize GetBitmapDimension( ) const;

Return Value
The width and height of the bitmap, measured in 0.1-millimeter units. The height is in the **cy** member of the **CSize** object, and the width is in the **cx** member. If the bitmap width and height have not been set by using **SetBitmapDimension**, the return value is 0.

Remarks
Returns the width and height of the bitmap. The height and width are assumed to have been set previously by using the **SetBitmapDimension** member function.

See Also
CBitmap::SetBitmapDimension, ::GetBitmapDimension

CBitmap::LoadBitmap

BOOL LoadBitmap(LPCTSTR *lpszResourceName* **);**

BOOL LoadBitmap(UINT *nIDResource* **);**

Return Value
Nonzero if successful; otherwise 0.

Parameters
lpszResourceName   Points to a null-terminated string that contains the name of the bitmap resource.

nIDResource   Specifies the resource ID number of the bitmap resource.

Remarks
Loads the bitmap resource named by *lpszResourceName* or identified by the ID number in *nIDResource* from the application's executable file. The loaded bitmap is attached to the **CBitmap** object. If the bitmap identified by *lpszResourceName* does not exist or if there is insufficient memory to load the bitmap, the function returns 0. An application must call the **CGdiObject::DeleteObject** function to delete any bitmap loaded by the **LoadBitmap** function.

The following bitmaps were added to Windows versions 3.1 and later:

OBM_UPARRROWI
OBM_DNARROWI
OBM_RGARROWI
OBM_LFARROWI

These bitmaps are not found in device drivers for Windows versions 3.0 and earlier. For a complete list of bitmaps and a display of their appearance, see the *Programmer's Reference* in the Win32.

See Also
CBitmap::LoadOEMBitmap, ::LoadBitmap, CGdiObject::DeleteObject

CBitmap::LoadOEMBitmap

BOOL LoadOEMBitmap(UINT *nIDBitmap* **);**

Return Value   Nonzero if successful; otherwise 0.

Parameters   *nIDBitmap*   ID number of the predefined Windows bitmap. The possible values are listed below from WINDOWS.H:

OBM_BTNCORNERS	**OBM_OLD_RESTORE**
OBM_BTSIZE	**OBM_OLD_RGARROW**
OBM_CHECK	**OBM_OLD_UPARROW**
OBM_CHECKBOXES	**OBM_OLD_ZOOM**
OBM_CLOSE	**OBM_REDUCE**
OBM_COMBO	**OBM_REDUCED**
OBM_DNARROW	**OBM_RESTORE**
OBM_DNARROWD	**OBM_RESTORED**
OBM_DNARROWI	**OBM_RGARROW**
OBM_LFARROW	**OBM_RGARROWD**
OBM_LFARROWD	**OBM_RGARROWI**
OBM_LFARROWI	**OBM_SIZE**
OBM_MNARROW	**OBM_UPARROW**
OBM_OLD_CLOSE	**OBM_UPARROWD**
OBM_OLD_DNARROW	**OBM_UPARROWI**
OBM_OLD_LFARROW	**OBM_ZOOM**
OBM_OLD_REDUCE	**OBM_ZOOMD**

Remarks   Loads a predefined bitmap used by Windows. Bitmap names that begin with **OBM_OLD** represent bitmaps used by Windows versions prior to 3.0. Note that the constant **OEMRESOURCE** must be defined before including WINDOWS.H in order to use any of the **OBM_** constants.

See Also   **CBitmap::LoadBitmap**, **::LoadBitmap**

CBitmap::SetBitmapBits

DWORD SetBitmapBits(DWORD *dwCount*, **const void*** *lpBits* **);**

Return Value   The number of bytes used in setting the bitmap bits; 0 if the function fails.

Parameters   *dwCount*   Specifies the number of bytes pointed to by *lpBits*.

lpBits   Points to the **BYTE** array that contains the bit values to be copied to the **CBitmap** object.

Remarks   Sets the bits of a bitmap to the bit values given by *lpBits*.

See Also   **::SetBitmapBits**

CBitmap::SetBitmapDimension

CSize SetBitmapDimension(int *nWidth*, **int** *nHeight* **);**

Return Value   The previous bitmap dimensions. Height is in the **cy** member variable of the **CSize** object, and width is in the **cx** member variable.

Parameters   *nWidth*   Specifies the width of the bitmap (in 0.1-millimeter units).

nHeight   Specifies the height of the bitmap (in 0.1-millimeter units).

Remarks   Assigns a width and height to a bitmap in 0.1-millimeter units. The GDI does not use these values except to return them when an application calls the **GetBitmapDimension** member function.

See Also   **CBitmap::GetBitmapDimension**, **::SetBitmapDimension**

class CBitmapButton : public CButton

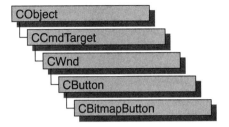

Use the **CBitmapButton** class to create pushbutton controls labeled with bitmapped images instead of text. **CBitmapButton** objects contain up to four bitmaps, which contain images for the different states a button can assume: up (or normal), down (or selected), focused, and disabled. Only the first bitmap is required; the others are optional.

Bitmap-button images include the border around the image as well as the image itself. The border typically plays a part in showing the state of the button. For example, the bitmap for the focused state usually is like the one for the up state but with a dashed rectangle inset from the border or a thick solid line at the border. The bitmap for the disabled state usually resembles the one for the up state but has lower contrast (like a dimmed or grayed menu selection).

These bitmaps can be of any size, but all are treated as if they were the same size as the bitmap for the up state.

Various applications demand different combinations of bitmap images:

Up	Down	Focused	Disabled	Application
×				Bitmap
×	×			Button without **WS_TABSTOP** style
×	×	×	×	Dialog button with all states
×	×	×		Dialog button with **WS_TABSTOP** style

When creating a bitmap-button control, set the **BS_OWNERDRAW** style to specify that the button is owner-drawn. This causes Windows to send the **WM_MEASUREITEM** and **WM_DRAWITEM** messages for the button; the framework handles these messages and manages the appearance of the button for you.

To create a bitmap-button control in a window's client area, follow these steps:

1. Create one to four bitmap images for the button.
2. Construct the **CBitmapButton** object.
3. Call the **Create** function to create the Windows button control and attach it to the **CBitmapButton** object.
4. Call the **LoadBitmaps** member function to load the bitmap resources after the bitmap button is constructed.

To include a bitmap-button control in a dialog box, follow these steps:

1. Create one to four bitmap images for the button.
2. Create a dialog template with an owner-draw button positioned where you want the bitmap button. The size of the button in the template does not matter.
3. Set the button's caption to a value such as "MYIMAGE" and define a symbol for the button such as IDC_MYIMAGE.
4. In your application's resource script, give each of the images created for the button an ID constructed by appending one of the letters "U," "D," "F," or "X" (for up, down, focused, and disabled) to the string used for the button caption in step 3. For the button caption "MYIMAGE," for example, the IDs would be "MYIMAGEU," "MYIMAGED," "MYIMAGEF," and "MYIMAGEX."
5. In your application's dialog class (derived from **CDialog**), add a **CBitmapButton** member object.
6. In the **CDialog** object's **OnInitDialog** routine, call the **CBitmapButton** object's **AutoLoad** function, using as parameters the button's control ID and the **CDialog** object's **this** pointer.

If you want to handle Windows notification messages, such as **BN_CLICKED**, sent by a bitmap-button control to its parent (usually a class derived from **CDialog**), add to the **CDialog**-derived object a message-map entry and message-handler member function for each message. The notifications sent by a **CBitmapButton** object are the same as those sent by a **CButton** object.

The class **CToolBar** takes a different approach to bitmap buttons. See **CToolBar** for more information.

#include <afxext.h>

See Also   **CButton**, **CBitmapButton::AutoLoad**, **CToolBar**

Construction

CBitmapButton	Constructs a **CBitmapButton** object.
LoadBitmaps	Initializes the object by loading one or more named bitmap resources from the application's resource file and attaching the bitmaps to the object.
AutoLoad	Associates a button in a dialog with an object of the **CBitmapButton** class, loads the bitmap(s) by name, and sizes the button to fit the bitmap.

Operations

SizeToContent	Sizes the button to accommodate the bitmap.

Member Functions

CBitmapButton::AutoLoad

BOOL AutoLoad(UINT *nID*, **CWnd*** *pParent* **);**

Return Value   Nonzero if successful; otherwise 0.

Parameters   *nID*   The button's control ID.

pParent   Pointer to the object that owns the button.

Remarks   Associates a button in a dialog box with an object of the **CBitmapButton** class, loads the bitmap(s) by name, and sizes the button to fit the bitmap.

Use the **AutoLoad** function to initialize an owner-draw button in a dialog box as a bitmap button. Instructions for using this function are in the remarks for the **CBitmapButton** class.

See Also   **CBitmapButton, CBitmapButton::LoadBitmaps, CBitmapButton::SizeToContent**

CBitmapButton::CBitmapButton

CBitmapButton( );

Remarks   Creates a **CBitmapButton** object.

See Also   **CBitmapButton::LoadBitmaps, CBitmapButton::AutoLoad, CBitmapButton::SizeToContent, CButton::Create**

CBitmapButton::LoadBitmaps

BOOL LoadBitmaps(LPCTSTR *lpszBitmapResource*, **LPCTSTR** *lpszBitmapResourceSel* = **NULL, LPCTSTR** *lpszBitmapResourceFocus* = **NULL, LPCTSTR** *lpszBitmapResourceDisabled* = **NULL**);

BOOL LoadBitmaps(UINT *nIDBitmapResource*, **UINT** *nIDBitmapResourceSel* = **0, UINT** *nIDBitmapResourceFocus* = **0, UINT** *nIDBitmapResourceDisabled* = **0**);

Return Value   Nonzero if successful; otherwise 0.

Parameters   *lpszBitmapResource*   Points to the null-terminated string that contains the name of the bitmap for a bitmap button's normal or "up" state. Required.

lpszBitmapResourceSel   Points to the null-terminated string that contains the name of the bitmap for a bitmap button's selected or "down" state. May be **NULL**.

lpszBitmapResourceFocus   Points to the null-terminated string that contains the name of the bitmap for a bitmap button's focused state. May be **NULL**.

lpszBitmapResourceDisabled   Points to the null-terminated string that contains the name of the bitmap for a bitmap button's disabled state. May be **NULL**.

nIDBitmapResource   Specifies the resource ID number of the bitmap resource for a bitmap button's normal or "up" state. Required.

nIDBitmapResourceSel   Specifies the resource ID number of the bitmap resource for a bitmap button's selected or "down" state. May be 0.

nIDBitmapResourceFocus   Specifies the resource ID number of the bitmap resource for a bitmap button's focused state. May be 0.

nIDBitmapResourceDisabled   Specifies the resource ID number of the bitmap resource for a bitmap button's disabled state. May be 0.

Remarks   Use this function when you want to load bitmap images identified by their resource names or ID numbers, or when you cannot use the **AutoLoad** function because, for example, you are creating a bitmap button that is not part of a dialog box.

See Also   **CBitmapButton, CBitmapButton::AutoLoad, CBitmapButton::SizeToContent, CButton::Create, CBitmap::LoadBitmap**

CBitmapButton::SizeToContent

void SizeToContent( );

Remarks   Call this function to resize a bitmap button to the size of the bitmap.

See Also   **CBitmapButton**, **CBitmapButton::LoadBitmaps**, **CBitmapButton::AutoLoad**

class CBrush : public CGdiObject

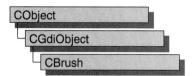

CObject
CGdiObject
CBrush

The **CBrush** class encapsulates a Windows graphics device interface (GDI) brush. To use a **CBrush** object, construct a **CBrush** object and pass it to any **CDC** member function that requires a brush. Brushes can be solid, hatched, or patterned.

#include <afxwin.h>

See Also   **CBitmap, CDC**

Construction

CBrush	Constructs a **CBrush** object.

Initialization

CreateSolidBrush	Initializes a brush with the specified solid color.
CreateHatchBrush	Initializes a brush with the specified hatched pattern and color.
CreateBrushIndirect	Initializes a brush with the style, color, and pattern specified in a **LOGBRUSH** structure.
CreatePatternBrush	Initializes a brush with a pattern specified by a bitmap.
CreateDIBPatternBrush	Initializes a brush with a pattern specified by a device-independent bitmap (DIB).

Operations

FromHandle	Returns a pointer to a **CBrush** object when given a handle to a Windows **HBRUSH** object.

Member Functions

CBrush::CBrush

CBrush( );

CBrush(COLORREF *crColor* **)**
  throw(CResourceException);

CBrush(int *nIndex*, **COLORREF** *crColor* **)**
  throw(CResourceException);

CBrush(CBitmap* *pBitmap* **)**
  throw(CResourceException);

Parameters   *crColor*   Specifies the foreground color of the brush as an RGB color. If the brush
        is hatched, this parameter specifies the color of the hatching.

nIndex   Specifies the hatch style of the brush. It can be any one of the following
        values:

- **HS_BDIAGONAL**   Downward hatch (left to right) at 45 degrees
- **HS_CROSS**   Horizontal and vertical crosshatch
- **HS_DIAGCROSS**   Crosshatch at 45 degrees
- **HS_FDIAGONAL**   Upward hatch (left to right) at 45 degrees
- **HS_HORIZONTAL**   Horizontal hatch
- **HS_VERTICAL**   Vertical hatch

pBitmap   Points to a **CBitmap** object that specifies a bitmap with which the brush
        paints.

Remarks   Has four overloaded constructors. The constructor with no arguments constructs an
        uninitialized **CBrush** object that must be initialized before it can be used. If you
        use the constructor with no arguments, you must initialize the resulting **CBrush**
        object with **CreateSolidBrush**, **CreateHatchBrush**, **CreateBrushIndirect**,
        CreatePatternBrush, or **CreateDIBPatternBrush**. If you use one of the
        constructors that takes arguments, then no further initialization is necessary. The
        constructors with arguments can throw an exception if errors are encountered, while
        the constructor with no arguments will always succeed.

The constructor with a single **COLORREF** parameter constructs a solid brush with
the specified color. The color specifies an RGB value and can be constructed with
the **RGB** macro in WINDOWS.H.

The constructor with two parameters constructs a hatch brush. The *nIndex* parameter specifies the index of a hatched pattern. The *crColor* parameter specifies the color.

The constructor with a **CBitmap** parameter constructs a patterned brush. The parameter identifies a bitmap. The bitmap is assumed to have been created by using **CBitmap::CreateBitmap**, **CBitmap::CreateBitmapIndirect**, **CBitmap::LoadBitmap**, or **CBitmap::CreateCompatibleBitmap**. The minimum size for a bitmap to be used in a fill pattern is 8 pixels by 8 pixels.

See Also   CBitmap::CreateBitmap, CBitmap::CreateBitmapIndirect, CBitmap::LoadBitmap, CBitmap::CreateCompatibleBitmap, CBrush::CreateSolidBrush, CBrush::CreateHatchBrush, CBrush::CreateBrushIndirect, CBrush::CreatePatternBrush, CBrush::CreateDIBPatternBrush, CGdiObject::CreateStockObject

CBrush::CreateBrushIndirect

BOOL CreateBrushIndirect(LPLOGBRUSH *lpLogBrush* **);**

Return Value   Nonzero if the function is successful; otherwise 0.

Parameters   *lpLogBrush*   Points to a **LOGBRUSH** structure that contains information about the brush.

The **LOGBRUSH** structure has the following form:

```
typedef struct tagLOGBRUSH {
    UINT      lbStyle;
    COLORREF  lbColor;
    int lbHatch;
} LOGBRUSH;
```

Remarks   Initializes a brush with a style, color, and pattern specified in a **LOGBRUSH** structure. The brush can subsequently be selected as the current brush for any device context. A brush created using a monochrome (1 plane, 1 bit per pixel) bitmap is drawn using the current text and background colors. Pixels represented by a bit set to 0 will be drawn with the current text color. Pixels represented by a bit set to 1 will be drawn with the current background color.

See Also   CBrush::CreateDIBPatternBrush, CBrush::CreatePatternBrush, CBrush::CreateSolidBrush, CBrush::CreateHatchBrush, CGdiObject::CreateStockObject, CGdiObject::DeleteObject, ::CreateBrushIndirect

CBrush::CreateDIBPatternBrush

BOOL CreateDIBPatternBrush(HGLOBAL *hPackedDIB*, **UINT** *nUsage* **);**

BOOL CreateDIBPatternBrush(const void* *lpPackedDIB*, **UINT** *nUsage* **);**

Return Value   Nonzero if successful; otherwise 0.

Parameters   *hPackedDIB*   Identifies a global-memory object containing a packed device-independent bitmap (DIB).

nUsage   Specifies whether the **bmiColors[]** fields of the **BITMAPINFO** data structure (a part of the "packed DIB") contain explicit RGB values or indices into the currently realized logical palette. The parameter must be one of the following values:

- **DIB_PAL_COLORS**   The color table consists of an array of 16-bit indexes.
- **DIB_RGB_COLORS**   The color table contains literal RGB values.

The following value is available only in the second version of this member function:

- **DIB_PAL_INDICES**   No color table is provided. The bitmap itself contains indices into the logical palette of the DC into which the brush is to be selected.

lpPackedDIB   Points to a packed DIB consisting of a **BITMAPINFO** structure immediately followed by an aray of bytes defining the pixels of the bitmap.

Remarks   Initializes a brush with the pattern specified by a device-independent bitmap (DIB). The brush can subsequently be selected for any device context that supports raster operations.

The two versions differ in the way you handle the DIB:

- In the first version, to obtain a handle to the DIB you call the Windows **::GlobalAlloc** function to allocate a block of global memory and then fill the memory with the packed DIB.
- In the second version, it is not necessary to call **::GlobalAlloc** to allocate memory for the packed DIB.

A packed DIB consists of a **BITMAPINFO** data structure immediately followed by the array of bytes that defines the pixels of the bitmap. Bitmaps used as fill patterns should be 8 pixels by 8 pixels. If the bitmap is larger, Windows creates a fill pattern using only the bits corresponding to the first 8 rows and 8 columns of pixels in the upper-left corner of the bitmap.

When an application selects a two-color DIB pattern brush into a monochrome device context, Windows ignores the colors specified in the DIB and instead displays the pattern brush using the current text and background colors of the device context. Pixels mapped to the first color (at offset 0 in the DIB color table) of the DIB are displayed using the text color. Pixels mapped to the second color (at offset 1 in the color table) are displayed using the background color.

See Also   **CBrush::CreatePatternBrush, CBrush::CreateBrushIndirect, CBrush::CreateSolidBrush, CBrush::CreateHatchBrush, CGdiObject::CreateStockObject, CDC::SelectObject, CGdiObject::DeleteObject, CDC::GetBrushOrg, CDC::SetBrushOrg, ::CreateDIBPatternBrush, ::CreateDIBPatternBrushPt, ::GlobalAlloc**

CBrush::CreateHatchBrush

BOOL CreateHatchBrush(int *nIndex***, COLORREF** *crColor* **);**

Return Value   Nonzero if successful; otherwise 0.

Parameters   *nIndex*   Specifies the hatch style of the brush. It can be any one of the following values:

- **HS_BDIAGONAL**   Downward hatch (left to right) at 45 degrees
- **HS_CROSS**   Horizontal and vertical crosshatch
- **HS_DIAGCROSS**   Crosshatch at 45 degrees
- **HS_FDIAGONAL**   Upward hatch (left to right) at 45 degrees
- **HS_HORIZONTAL**   Horizontal hatch
- **HS_VERTICAL**   Vertical hatch

crColor   Specifies the foreground color of the brush as an RGB color (the color of the hatches).

Remarks   Initializes a brush with the specified hatched pattern and color. The brush can subsequently be selected as the current brush for any device context.

See Also   **CBrush::CreateBrushIndirect, CBrush::CreateDIBPatternBrush, CBrush::CreatePatternBrush, CBrush::CreateSolidBrush, CGdiObject::CreateStockObject, ::CreateHatchBrush**

CBrush::CreatePatternBrush

BOOL CreatePatternBrush(CBitmap* *pBitmap* **);**

Return Value   Nonzero if successful; otherwise 0.

Parameters   *pBitmap*   Identifies a bitmap.

Remarks   Initializes a brush with a pattern specified by a bitmap. The brush can subsequently be selected for any device context that supports raster operations. The bitmap identified by *pBitmap* is typically initialized by using the **CBitmap::CreateBitmap, CBitmap::CreateBitmapIndirect, CBitmap::LoadBitmap,** or **CBitmap::CreateCompatibleBitmap** function.

Bitmaps used as fill patterns should be 8 pixels by 8 pixels. If the bitmap is larger, the Windows operating system will only use the bits corresponding to the first 8 rows and columns of pixels in the upper-left corner of the bitmap. A pattern brush can be deleted without affecting the associated bitmap. This means the bitmap can be used to create any number of pattern brushes. A brush created using a monochrome bitmap (1 color plane, 1 bit per pixel) is drawn using the current text and background colors. Pixels represented by a bit set to 0 are drawn with the current text color. Pixels represented by a bit set to 1 are drawn with the current background color.

See Also   **CBrush::CreateBrushIndirect, CBrush::CreateDIBPatternBrush, CBrush::CreateHatchBrush, CBrush::CreateSolidBrush, CGdiObject::CreateStockObject, CBitmap::CreateBitmap, CBitmap::CreateBitmapIndirect, CBitmap::CreateCompatibleBitmap, CBitmap::LoadBitmap, ::CreatePatternBrush**

CBrush::CreateSolidBrush

BOOL CreateSolidBrush(COLORREF *crColor* **);**

Return Value   Nonzero if successful; otherwise 0.

Parameters   *crColor*   Specifies the color of the brush. The color specifies an RGB value and can be constructed with the **RGB** macro in WINDOWS.H.

Remarks   Initializes a brush with a specified solid color. The brush can subsequently be selected as the current brush for any device context. When an application has finished using the brush created by **CreateSolidBrush**, it should select the brush out of the device context.

See Also   **CBrush::CreateBrushIndirect, CBrush::CreateDIBPatternBrush, CBrush::CreateHatchBrush, CBrush::CreatePatternBrush, ::CreateSolidBrush, CGdiObject::DeleteObject**

CBrush::FromHandle

static CBrush* PASCAL FromHandle(HBRUSH *hBrush* **);**

Return Value   A pointer to a **CBrush** object if successful; otherwise **NULL**.

Parameters   *hBrush*   **HANDLE** to a Windows GDI brush.

Remarks   Returns a pointer to a **CBrush** object when given a handle to a Windows
HBRUSH object. If a **CBrush** object is not already attached to the handle, a
temporary **CBrush** object is created and attached. This temporary **CBrush** object is
valid only until the next time the application has idle time in its event loop. At this
time, all temporary graphic objects are deleted. In other words, the temporary object
is valid only during the processing of one window message.

class CButton : public CWnd

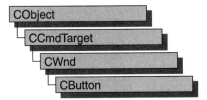

The **CButton** class provides the functionality of Windows button controls. A button control is a small, rectangular child window that can be clicked on and off. Buttons can be used alone or in groups and can either be labeled or appear without text. A button typically changes appearance when the user clicks it. Typical buttons are the check box, radio button, and pushbutton. A **CButton** object can become any of these, according to the button style specified at its initialization by the **Create** member function. For a list of button styles, see the section "Button Styles" on page 1246.

In addition, the **CBitmapButton** class derived from **CButton** supports creation of button controls labeled with bitmap images instead of text. A **CBitmapButton** can have separate bitmaps for a button's up, down, focused, and disabled states.

You can create a button control either from a dialog template or directly in your code. In both cases, first call the constructor **CButton** to construct the **CButton** object; then call the **Create** member function to create the Windows button control and attach it to the **CButton** object. Construction can be a one-step process in a class derived from **CButton**. Write a constructor for the derived class and call **Create** from within the constructor.

If you want to handle Windows notification messages sent by a button control to its parent (usually a class derived from **CDialog**), add a message-map entry and message-handler member function to the parent class for each message.

Each message-map entry takes the following form:

ON_ Notification(*id*, *memberFxn*)

where *id* specifies the child window ID of the control sending the notification and *memberFxn* is the name of the parent member function you have written to handle the notification.

The parent's function prototype is as follows:

afx_msg void memberFxn( ) **;**

Potential message-map entries are as follows:

Map Entry	Sent To Parent When...
ON_BN_CLICKED	The user clicks a button.
ON_BN_DOUBLECLICKED	The user double-clicks a button.

If you create a **CButton** object from a dialog resource, the **CButton** object is automatically destroyed when the user closes the dialog box.

If you create a **CButton** object within a window, you may need to destroy it. If you create the **CButton** object on the heap by using the **new** function, you must call **delete** on the object to destroy it when the user closes the Windows button control. If you create the **CButton** object on the stack, or it is embedded in the parent dialog object, it is destroyed automatically.

#include <afxwin.h>

See Also   CWnd, CComboBox, CEdit, CListBox, CScrollBar, CStatic, CBitmapButton, CDialog

Construction

CButton	Constructs a **CButton** object.

Initialization

Create	Creates the Windows button control and attaches it to the **CButton** object.

Operations

GetState	Retrieves the check state, highlight state, and focus state of a button control.
SetState	Sets the highlighting state of a button control.
GetCheck	Retrieves the check state of a button control.
SetCheck	Sets the check state of a button control.
GetButtonStyle	Retrieves information about the button control style.
SetButtonStyle	Changes the style of a button.

Overridables

DrawItem	Override to draw an owner-drawn **CButton** object.

Member Functions

CButton::CButton

CButton( );

Remarks   Constructs a **CButton** object.

See Also   **CButton::Create**

CButton::Create

BOOL Create(LPCTSTR *lpszCaption*, **DWORD** *dwStyle*, **const RECT&** *rect*, **CWnd*** *pParentWnd*, **UINT** *nID* **);**

Return Value   Nonzero if successful; otherwise 0.

Parameters   *lpszCaption*   Specifies the button control's text.

dwStyle   Specifies the button control's style. Apply any combination of button styles to the button.

rect   Specifies the button control's size and position. It can be either a **CRect** object or a **RECT** structure.

pParentWnd   Specifies the button control's parent window, usually a **CDialog**. It must not be **NULL**.

nID   Specifies the button control's ID.

Remarks   You construct a **CButton** object in two steps. First call the constructor, then call **Create**, which creates the Windows button control and attaches it to the **CButton** object.

If the **WS_VISIBLE** style is given, Windows sends the button control all the messages required to activate and show the button.

Apply the following window styles to a button control: For a list of window styles, see the section "Window Styles" on page 1253.

- **WS_CHILD**   Always
- **WS_VISIBLE**   Usually
- **WS_DISABLED**   Rarely
- **WS_GROUP**   To group controls
- **WS_TABSTOP**   To include the button in the tabbing order

See Also   **CButton::CButton**

CButton::DrawItem

virtual void DrawItem(LPDRAWITEMSTRUCT *lpDrawItemStruct* **);**

Parameters   *lpDrawItemStruct*   A long pointer to a **DRAWITEMSTRUCT** structure. The structure contains information about the item to be drawn and the type of drawing required.

Remarks   Called by the framework when a visual aspect of an owner-drawn button has changed. An owner-drawn button has the **BS_OWNERDRAW** style set. Override this member function to implement drawing for an owner-drawn **CButton** object. The application should restore all graphics device interface (GDI) objects selected for the display context supplied in *lpDrawItemStruct* before the member function terminates.

For a list of button styles, see the section "Button Styles" on page 1246.

See Also   **CButton::SetButtonStyle**, **WM_DRAWITEM**

CButton::GetButtonStyle

UINT GetButtonStyle( ) const;

Remarks   Retrieves the window style of **CButton**. It returns only the **BS_** style values, not any of the other window styles.

For a list of button styles, see the section "Button Styles" on page 1246.

See Also   **CButton::SetButtonStyle**, **::GetWindowLong**

CButton::GetCheck

int GetCheck( ) const;

Return Value   The return value from a button control created with the **BS_AUTOCHECKBOX**, **BS_AUTORADIOBUTTON**, **BS_AUTO3STATE**, **BS_CHECKBOX**, **BS_RADIOBUTTON**, or **BS_3STATE** style is one of the following values:

Value	Meaning
0	Button state is unchecked.
1	Button state is checked.
2	Button state is indeterminate (applies only if the button has the **BS_3STATE** or **BS_AUTO3STATE** style).

If the button has any other style, the return value is 0.

Remarks   Retrieves the check state of a radio button or check box.

See Also	CButton::GetState, CButton::SetState, CButton::SetCheck, BM_GETCHECK

CButton::GetState

UINT GetState( ) const;

Return Value	Specifies the current state of the button control. You can use the following masks against the return value to extract information about the state:

Mask	Meaning
0x0003	Specifies the check state (radio buttons and check boxes only). A 0 indicates the button is unchecked. A 1 indicates the button is checked. A radio button is checked when it contains a bullet (•). A check box is checked when it contains an **X**. A 2 indicates the check state is indeterminate (three-state check boxes only). The state of a three-state check box is indeterminate when it contains a halftone pattern.
0x0004	Specifies the highlight state. A nonzero value indicates that the button is highlighted. A button is highlighted when the user clicks and holds the left mouse button. The highlighting is removed when the user releases the mouse button.
0x0008	Specifies the focus state. A nonzero value indicates that the button has the focus.

See Also	CButton::GetCheck, CButton::SetCheck, CButton::SetState, BM_GETSTATE

CButton::SetButtonStyle

void SetButtonStyle(UINT *nStyle*, BOOL *bRedraw* = TRUE);

Parameters	*nStyle* Specifies the button style.
	bRedraw Specifies whether the button is to be redrawn. A nonzero value redraws the button. A 0 value does not redraw the button. The button is redrawn by default.

Remarks	Changes the style of a button. Use the **GetButtonStyle** member function to retrieve the button style. The low-order word of the complete button style is the button-specific style.
	For a list of possible button styles, see the section "Button Styles" on page 1246.

See Also	CButton::GetButtonStyle, BM_SETSTYLE

CButton::SetCheck

void SetCheck(int *nCheck* **);**

Parameters   *nCheck*   Specifies the check state. This parameter can be one of the following:

Value	Meaning
0	Set the button state to unchecked.
1	Set the button state to checked.
2	Set the button state to indeterminate. This value can be used only if the button has the **BS_3STATE** or **BS_AUTO3STATE** style.

Remarks   Sets or resets the check state of a radio button or check box. This member function has no effect on a pushbutton.

See Also   **CButton::GetCheck**, **CButton::GetState**, **CButton::SetState**, **BM_SETCHECK**

CButton::SetState

void SetState(BOOL *bHighlight* **);**

Parameters   *bHighlight*   Specifies whether the button is to be highlighted. A nonzero value highlights the button; a 0 value removes any highlighting.

Remarks   Sets the highlighting state of a button control. Highlighting affects the exterior of a button control. It has no effect on the check state of a radio button or check box. A button control is automatically highlighted when the user clicks and holds the left mouse button. The highlighting is removed when the user releases the mouse button.

See Also   **CButton::GetState**, **CButton::SetCheck**, **CButton::GetCheck**, **BM_SETSTATE**

class CByteArray : public CObject

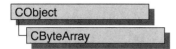

The **CByteArray** class supports dynamic arrays of bytes. The member functions of **CByteArray** are similar to the member functions of class **CObArray**. Because of this similarity, you can use the **CObArray** reference documentation for member function specifics. Wherever you see a **CObject** pointer as a function parameter or return value, substitute a **BYTE**.

```
CObject* CObArray::GetAt( int <nIndex> ) const;
```

for example, translates to

```
BYTE CByteArray::GetAt( int <nIndex> ) const;
```

Note   Before using an array, use **SetSize** to establish its size and allocate memory for it. If you do not use **SetSize**, adding elements to your array causes it to be frequently reallocated and copied. Frequent reallocation and copying are inefficient and can fragment memory.

If you need debug output from individual elements in the array, you must set the depth of the **CDumpContext** object to 1 or greater.

#include <afxcoll.h>

See Also   **CObArray**

Construction
CByteArray	Constructs an empty array for bytes.

Bounds
GetSize	Gets the number of elements in this array.
GetUpperBound	Returns the largest valid index.
SetSize	Sets the number of elements to be contained in this array.

Operations
FreeExtra	Frees all unused memory above the current upper bound.
RemoveAll	Removes all the elements from this array.

Element Access

GetAt	Returns the value at a given index.
SetAt	Sets the value for a given index; array not allowed to grow.
ElementAt	Returns a temporary reference to the byte within the array.

Growing the Array

SetAtGrow	Sets the value for a given index; grows the array if necessary.
Add	Adds an element to the end of the array; grows the array if necessary.

Insertion/Removal

InsertAt	Inserts an element (or all the elements in another array) at a specified index.
RemoveAt	Removes an element at a specific index.

Operators

operator []	Sets or gets the element at the specified index.

class CClientDC : public CDC

The **CClientDC** class is derived from **CDC** and takes care of calling the Windows functions **GetDC** at construction time and **ReleaseDC** at destruction time. This means that the device context associated with a **CClientDC** object is the client area of a window.

#include <afxwin.h>

See Also   **CDC**

Construction
CClientDC   Constructs a **CClientDC** object connected to the **CWnd**.

Data Members
m_hWnd   The **HWND** of the window for which this **CClientDC** is valid.

Member Functions

CClientDC::CClientDC

CClientDC(CWnd* *pWnd* **)**
    throw(CResourceException);

Parameters   *pWnd*   The window whose client area the device context object will access.

Remarks   Constructs a **CClientDC** object that accesses the client area of the **CWnd** pointed to by *pWnd*. The constructor calls the Windows function **GetDC**. An exception (of type **CResourceException**) is thrown if the Windows **GetDC** call fails. A device context may not be available if Windows has already allocated all of its available device contexts. Your application competes for the five common display contexts available at any given time under Windows.

Data Members

CClientDC::m_hWnd

Remarks   The **HWND** of the **CWnd** pointer used to construct the **CClientDC** object.
m_hWnd is a protected variable.

class CCmdTarget : public CObject

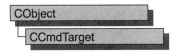

CCmdTarget is the base class for the Microsoft Foundation Class Library message-map architecture. A message map routes commands or messages to the member functions you write to handle them. (A command is a message from a menu item, command button, or accelerator key.)

Key framework classes derived from **CCmdTarget** include **CView**, **CWinApp**, **CDocument**, **CWnd**, and **CFrameWnd**. If you intend for a new class to handle messages, derive the class from one of these **CCmdTarget**-derived classes. You will rarely derive a class from **CCmdTarget** directly.

For an overview of command targets and **OnCmdMsg** routing, see Chapter 2, "Working with Messages and Commands" in *Programming with the Microsoft Foundation Class Library*.

CCmdTarget includes member functions that handle the display of an hourglass cursor. Display the hourglass cursor when you expect a command to take a noticeable time interval to execute.

Dispatch maps, similar to message maps, are used to expose Object Linking and Embedding (OLE) Automation **IDispatch** functionality. By exposing this interface, other applications (such as Visual Basic) can call into your application. For more information on OLE automation and **IDispatch** interfaces, see Chapter 5 of *Creating Programmable Applications*.

#include <afxwin.h>

See Also   **CCmdUI, CDocument, CDocTemplate, CWinApp, CWnd, CView, CFrameWnd, COleDispatchDriver**

Attributes

FromIDispatch	Returns a pointer to the **CCmdTarget** object associated with the **IDispatch** pointer.
GetIDispatch	Returns a pointer to the **IDispatch** object associated with the **CCmdTarget** object.
IsResultExpected	Returns **TRUE** if an automation function should return a value.

Operations

BeginWaitCursor	Displays the cursor as an hourglass cursor.
EnableAutomation	Allows OLE automation for the **CCmdTarget** object.
EndWaitCursor	Returns to the previous cursor.
RestoreWaitCursor	Restores the hourglass cursor.

Overridables

OnCmdMsg	Routes and dispatches command messages.
OnFinalRelease	Cleans up after last OLE reference is released.

Member Functions

CCmdTarget::BeginWaitCursor

void BeginWaitCursor( );

Remarks

Call this function to display the cursor as an hourglass when you expect a command to take a noticeable time interval to execute. The framework calls this function to show the user that it is busy, such as when a **CDocument** object loads or saves itself to a file.

The actions of **BeginWaitCursor** are not always effective outside of a single message handler as other actions, such as **OnSetCursor** handling, could change the cursor.

Call **EndWaitCursor** to restore the previous cursor.

See Also

CCmdTarget::EndWaitCursor, CCmdTarget::RestoreWaitCursor, CWinApp::DoWaitCursor

Example

```
// The following example illustrates the most common case
// of displaying the hourglass cursor during some lengthy
// processing of a command handler implemented in some
// CCmdTarget-derived class, such as a document or view.


void CMyView::OnSomeCommand()
{
   BeginWaitCursor(); // display the hourglass cursor

   // do some lengthy processing


   EndWaitCursor(); // remove the hourglass cursor
}
```

```
// The next example illustrates RestoreWaitCursor.
void CMyView::OnSomeCommand()
{
   BeginWaitCursor(); // display the hourglass cursor

   // do some lengthy processing


   // The dialog box will normally change the cursor to
   // the standard arrow cursor, and leave the cursor in
   // as the standard arrow cursor when the dialog box is
   // closed.
   CMyDialog dlg;
   dlg.DoModal();

   // It is necessary to call RestoreWaitCursor here in order
   // to change the cursor back to the hourglass cursor.
   RestoreWaitCursor();

   // do some more lengthy processing


   EndWaitCursor(); // remove the hourglass cursor
}


// In the above example, the dialog was clearly invoked between
// the pair of calls to BeginWaitCursor and EndWaitCursor.
// Sometimes it may not be clear whether the dialog is invoked
// in between a pair of calls to BeginWaitCursor and EndWaitCursor.
// It is permissable to call RestoreWaitCursor, even if
// BeginWaitCursor was not previously called.  This case is
// illustrated below, where CMyView::AnotherFunction does not
// need to know whether it was called in the context of an
// hourglass cursor.
void CMyView::AnotherFunction()
{
   // some processing ...

   CMyDialog dlg;
   dlg.DoModal();
   RestoreWaitCursor();

   // some more processing ...
}
```

```
// If the dialog is invoked from a member function of
// some non-CCmdTarget, then you can call CWinApp::DoWaitCursor
// with a 0 parameter value to restore the hourglass cursor.
void CMyObject::AnotherFunction()
{
   CMyDialog dlg;
   dlg.DoModal();
   AfxGetApp()->DoWaitCursor(0); // same as
CCmdTarget::RestoreWaitCursor
}
```

CCmdTarget::EnableAutomation

void EnableAutomation( );

Remarks Call this function to enable OLE automation for an object. This function is typically called from the constructor of your object and should only be called if a dispatch map has been declared for the class. For more information on automation see the articles "Automation Clients" and "Automation Servers" in *Programming with the Microsoft Foundation Class Library*.

See Also **DECLARE_DISPATCH_MAP, DECLARE_OLECREATE**

CCmdTarget::EndWaitCursor

void EndWaitCursor( );

Remarks Call this function after you have called the **BeginWaitCursor** member function to return from the hourglass cursor to the previous cursor. The framework also calls this member function after it has called the hourglass cursor.

See Also **CCmdTarget::BeginWaitCursor, CCmdTarget::RestoreWaitCursor, CWinApp::DoWaitCursor**

Example
```
// The following example illustrates the most common case
// of displaying the hourglass cursor during some lengthy
// processing of a command handler implemented in some
// CCmdTarget-derived class, such as a document or view.


void CMyView::OnSomeCommand()
{
   BeginWaitCursor(); // display the hourglass cursor

   // do some lengthy processing


   EndWaitCursor(); // remove the hourglass cursor
}
```

```
// The next example illustrates RestoreWaitCursor.
void CMyView::OnSomeCommand()
{
   BeginWaitCursor(); // display the hourglass cursor

   // do some lengthy processing


   // The dialog box will normally change the cursor to
   // the standard arrow cursor, and leave the cursor in
   // as the standard arrow cursor when the dialog box is
   // closed.
   CMyDialog dlg;
   dlg.DoModal();

   // It is necessary to call RestoreWaitCursor here in order
   // to change the cursor back to the hourglass cursor.
   RestoreWaitCursor();

   // do some more lengthy processing


   EndWaitCursor(); // remove the hourglass cursor
}


// In the above example, the dialog was clearly invoked between
// the pair of calls to BeginWaitCursor and EndWaitCursor.
// Sometimes it may not be clear whether the dialog is invoked
// in between a pair of calls to BeginWaitCursor and EndWaitCursor.
// It is permissable to call RestoreWaitCursor, even if
// BeginWaitCursor was not previously called.  This case is
// illustrated below, where CMyView::AnotherFunction does not
// need to know whether it was called in the context of an
// hourglass cursor.
void CMyView::AnotherFunction()
{
   // some processing ...

   CMyDialog dlg;
   dlg.DoModal();
   RestoreWaitCursor();

   // some more processing ...
}
```

```
// If the dialog is invoked from a member function of
// some non-CCmdTarget, then you can call CWinApp::DoWaitCursor
// with a 0 parameter value to restore the hourglass cursor.
void CMyObject::AnotherFunction()
{
   CMyDialog dlg;
   dlg.DoModal();
   AfxGetApp()->DoWaitCursor(0); // same as
CCmdTarget::RestoreWaitCursor
}
```

CCmdTarget::FromIDispatch

static CCmdTarget* FromIDispatch(LPDISPATCH *lpDispatch* **);**

Return Value   A pointer to the **CCmdTarget** object associated with *lpDispatch*. This function returns **NULL** if the **IDispatch** object is not recognized as a Microsoft Foundation Class **IDispatch** object.

Parameters   *lpDispatch*   A pointer to an **IDispatch** object.

Remarks   Call this function to map an **IDispatch** pointer, received from automation member functions of a class, into the **CCmdTarget** object that implements the interfaces of the **IDispatch** object.

The result of this function is the inverse of a call to the member function **GetIDispatch**.

See Also   **CCmdTarget::GetIDispatch**, **COleDispatchDriver**

CCmdTarget::GetIDispatch

LPDISPATCH GetIDispatch(BOOL *bAddRef* **);**

Return Value   The **IDispatch** pointer associated with the object.

Parameters   *bAddRef*   Specifies whether to increment the reference count for the object.

Remarks   Call this member function to retrieve the **IDispatch** pointer from an automation method that either returns an **IDispatch** pointer or takes an **IDispatch** pointer by reference.

For objects that call **EnableAutomation** in their constructors, making them automation enabled, this function returns a pointer to the Foundation Class implementation of **IDispatch** that is used by clients who communicate via the **IDispatch** interface. Calling this function automatically adds a reference to the pointer, so it is not necessary to make a call to **IUnknown::AddRef**.

See Also   **CCmdTarget::EnableAutomation**, **COleDispatchDriver**

CCmdTarget::IsResultExpected

BOOL IsResultExpected( );

Return Value   Non-zero if an automation function should return a value; otherwise 0.

Remarks   Use **IsResultExpected** to ascertain whether a client expects a return value from its call to an automation function. The OLE interface supplies information to MFC about whether the client is using or ignoring the result of a function call, and MFC in turn uses this information to determine the result of a call to **IsResultExpected**. If production of a return value is time- or resource-intensive, you can increase efficiency by calling this function before computing the return value.

This function returns 0 only once so that you will get valid return values from other automation functions if you call them from the automation function that the client has called.

IsResultExpected returns a non-zero value if called when an automation function call is not in progress.

See Also   **CCmdTarget::GetIDispatch**, **CCmdTarget::EnableAutomation**

CCmdTarget::OnCmdMsg

virtual BOOL OnCmdMsg(UINT *nID***, int** *nCode***, void*** *pExtra***,**
    AFX_CMDHANDLERINFO* *pHandlerInfo* **);**

Return Value   Nonzero if the message is handled; otherwise 0.

Parameters   *nID*   Contains the command ID.

nCode   Identifies the command notification code.

pExtra   Used according to the value of *nCode*.

pHandlerInfo   If not **NULL**, **OnCmdMsg** fills in the *pHandlerInfo* structure with the **pTarget** and **pmf** members of the **CMDHANDLERINFO** structure instead of dispatching the command. Typically, this parameter should be **NULL**.

Remarks   Called by the framework to route and dispatch command messages and to handle the update of command user-interface objects. This is the main implementation routine of the framework command architecture.

At run time, **OnCmdMsg** dispatches a command to other objects or handles the command itself by calling the root class **CCmdTarget::OnCmdMsg**, which does the actual message-map lookup. For a complete description of the default command routing, see *Programming with the Microsoft Foundation Class Library*.

On rare occasions, you may want to override this member function to extend the framework's standard command routing. Please refer to Technical Note 21 under MFC in Books Online for advanced details of the command-routing architecture.

See Also   **CCmdUI**

Example

```
// This example illustrates extending the framework's standard command
// route from the view to objects managed by the view. This example
// is from an object-oriented drawing application, similar to the
// DRAWCLI sample application, which draws and edits "shapes".

BOOL CMyView::OnCmdMsg(UINT nID, int nCode, void* pExtra,
    AFX_CMDHANDLERINFO* pHandlerInfo)
{
    // Extend the framework's command route from the view to
    // the application-specific CMyShape that is currently selected
    // in the view. m_pActiveShape is NULL if no shape object
    // is currently selected in the view.
    if ((m_pActiveShape != NULL)
        && m_pActiveShape->OnCmdMsg(nID, nCode, pExtra, pHandlerInfo))
        return TRUE;

    // If the object(s) in the extended command route don't handle
    // the command, then let the base class OnCmdMsg handle it.
    return CView::OnCmdMsg(nID, nCode, pExtra, pHandlerInfo);
}

// The command handler for ID_SHAPE_COLOR (menu command to change
// the color of the currently selected shape) was added to
// the message map of CMyShape (note, not CMyView) using ClassWizard.

// The menu item will be automatically enabled or disabled, depending
// on whether a CMyShape is currently selected in the view, that is,
// depending on whether CMyView::m_pActiveView is NULL. It is not
// necessary to implement an ON_UPDATE_COMMAND_UI handler to enable
// or disable the menu item.

BEGIN_MESSAGE_MAP(CMyShape, CCmdTarget)
    //{{AFX_MSG_MAP(CMyShape)
    ON_COMMAND(ID_SHAPE_COLOR, OnShapeColor)
    //}}AFX_MSG_MAP
END_MESSAGE_MAP()
```

CCmdTarget::OnFinalRelease

virtual void OnFinalRelease( );

Remarks   Called by the framework when the last OLE reference to or from the object is released. Override this function to provide special handling for this situation. The default implementation deletes the object.

See Also   **COleServerItem**

CCmdTarget::RestoreWaitCursor

void RestoreWaitCursor( );

Remarks   Call this function to restore the appropriate hourglass cursor after the system cursor has changed (for example, after a message box has opened and then closed while in the middle of a lengthy operation).

See Also   **CCmdTarget::EndWaitCursor, CCmdTarget::BeginWaitCursor, CWinApp::DoWaitCursor**

Example
```
// The following example illustrates the most common case
// of displaying the hourglass cursor during some lengthy
// processing of a command handler implemented in some
// CCmdTarget-derived class, such as a document or view.


void CMyView::OnSomeCommand()
{
   BeginWaitCursor(); // display the hourglass cursor

   // do some lengthy processing


   EndWaitCursor(); // remove the hourglass cursor
}
```

```
// The next example illustrates RestoreWaitCursor.
void CMyView::OnSomeCommand()
{
   BeginWaitCursor(); // display the hourglass cursor

   // do some lengthy processing


   // The dialog box will normally change the cursor to
   // the standard arrow cursor, and leave the cursor in
   // as the standard arrow cursor when the dialog box is
   // closed.
   CMyDialog dlg;
   dlg.DoModal();

   // It is necessary to call RestoreWaitCursor here in order
   // to change the cursor back to the hourglass cursor.
   RestoreWaitCursor();

   // do some more lengthy processing


   EndWaitCursor(); // remove the hourglass cursor
}


// In the above example, the dialog was clearly invoked between
// the pair of calls to BeginWaitCursor and EndWaitCursor.
// Sometimes it may not be clear whether the dialog is invoked
// in between a pair of calls to BeginWaitCursor and EndWaitCursor.
// It is permissable to call RestoreWaitCursor, even if
// BeginWaitCursor was not previously called.  This case is
// illustrated below, where CMyView::AnotherFunction does not
// need to know whether it was called in the context of an
// hourglass cursor.
void CMyView::AnotherFunction()
{
   // some processing ...

   CMyDialog dlg;
   dlg.DoModal();
   RestoreWaitCursor();

   // some more processing ...
}
```

```
// If the dialog is invoked from a member function of
// some non-CCmdTarget, then you can call CWinApp::DoWaitCursor
// with a 0 parameter value to restore the hourglass cursor.
void CMyObject::AnotherFunction()
{
   CMyDialog dlg;
   dlg.DoModal();
   AfxGetApp()->DoWaitCursor(0); // same as
CCmdTarget::RestoreWaitCursor
}
```

class CCmdUI

The **CCmdUI** class is used only within an **ON_UPDATE_COMMAND_UI** handler in a **CCmdTarget**-derived class.

When a user of your application pulls down a menu, each menu item needs to know whether it should be displayed as enabled or disabled (dimmed). The target of a menu command provides this information by implementing an **ON_UPDATE_COMMAND_UI** handler. Use ClassWizard to browse the command user-interface objects in your application and create a message-map entry and function prototype for each handler.

When the menu is pulled down, the framework searches for and calls each **ON_UPDATE_COMMAND_UI** handler, each handler calls **CCmdUI** member functions such as **Enable** and **Check**, and the framework then appropriately displays each menu item.

A menu item can be replaced with a control-bar button or other command user-interface object without changing the code within the **ON_UPDATE_COMMAND_UI** handler.

Table R.1 summarizes the effect **CCmdUI**'s member functions have on various command user-interface items.

Table R.1   Using CCmdUI Member Functions

User-Interface Item	Enable	SetCheck	SetRadio	SetText
Menu item	Enables or disables	Checks (×) or unchecks	Checks using dot (•)	Sets item text
Toolbar button	Enables or disables	Selects, unselects, or indeterminate	Same as **SetCheck**	(Not applicable)
Status-bar pane	Makes text visible or invisible	Sets pop-out or normal border	Same as **SetCheck**	Sets pane text
Normal button in **CDialogBar**	Enables or disables	Checks or unchecks check box	Same as **SetCheck**	Sets button text
Normal control in **CDialogBar**	Enables or disables	(Not applicable)	(Not applicable)	Sets window text

For more on the use of this class, see Chapter 10 in *Introducing Visual C++* and Chapter 2 in *Programming with the Microsoft Foundation Class Library*.

#include <afxwin.h>

See Also	CCmdTarget

Operations

Enable	Enables or disables the user-interface item for this command.
SetCheck	Sets the check state of the user-interface item for this command.
SetRadio	Like the **SetCheck** member function, but operates on radio groups.
SetText	Sets the text for the user-interface item for this command.
ContinueRouting	Tells the command-routing mechanism to continue routing the current message down the chain of handlers.

Member Functions

CCmdUI::ContinueRouting

void ContinueRouting( );

Remarks   Call this member function to tell the command-routing mechanism to continue routing the current message down the chain of handlers.

This is an advanced member function that should be used in conjunction with an **ON_COMMAND_EX** handler that returns **FALSE**. For more information, see Technical Note 21 under MFC in Books Online.

CCmdUI::Enable

virtual void Enable(BOOL *bOn* = TRUE);

Parameters   *bOn*   **TRUE** to enable the item, **FALSE** to disable it.

Remarks   Call this member function to enable or disable the user-interface item for this command.

See Also   CCmdUI::SetCheck

CCmdUI::SetCheck

virtual void SetCheck(int *nCheck* = 1);

Parameters   *nCheck*   Specifies the check state to set. If 0, unchecks; if 1, checks; and if 2, sets indeterminate.

Remarks   Call this member function to set the user-interface item for this command to the appropriate check state. This member function works for menu items and toolbar buttons. The indeterminate state applies only to toolbar buttons.

See Also   **CCmdUI::SetRadio**

CCmdUI::SetRadio

virtual void SetRadio(BOOL *bOn* = TRUE);

Parameters *bOn*   **TRUE** to enable the item; otherwise **FALSE**.

Remarks   Call this member function to set the user-interface item for this command to the appropriate check state. This member function operates like **SetCheck**, except that it operates on user-interface items acting as part of a radio group. Unchecking the other items in the group is not automatic unless the items themselves maintain the radio-group behavior.

See Also   **CCmdUI::SetCheck**

CCmdUI::SetText

virtual void SetText(LPCTSTR *lpszText*);

Parameters *lpszText*   A pointer to a text string.

Remarks   Call this member function to set the text of the user-interface item for this command.

See Also   **CCmdUI::Enable**

class CColorDialog : public CDialog

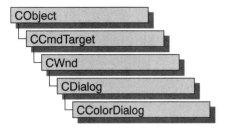

The **CColorDialog** class allows you to incorporate a color-selection dialog box into your application. A **CColorDialog** object is a dialog box with a list of colors that are defined for the display system. The user can select or create a particular color from the list, which is then reported back to the application when the dialog box exits.

To construct a **CColorDialog** object, use the provided constructor or derive a new class and use your own custom constructor.

Once the dialog box has been constructed, you can set or modify any values in the **m_cc** structure to initialize the values of the dialog box's controls. The **m_cc** structure is of type **CHOOSECOLOR**. For more information on this structure, see the Windows Software Development Kit (SDK) documentation.

After initializing the dialog box's controls, call the **DoModal** member function to display the dialog box and allow the user to select a color. **DoModal** returns the user's selection of either the dialog box's OK (**IDOK**) or Cancel (**IDCANCEL**) button.

If **DoModal** returns **IDOK**, you can use one of **CColorDialog**'s member functions to retrieve the information input by the user.

You can use the Windows **CommDlgExtendedError** function to determine whether an error occurred during initialization of the dialog box and to learn more about the error. For more information on this function, see the Windows SDK documentation.

CColorDialog relies on the COMMDLG.DLL file that ships with Windows versions 3.1 and later. For details about redistributing COMMDLG.DLL to Windows version 3.0 users, see the *Getting Started* manual for the Windows SDK.

To customize the dialog box, derive a class from **CColorDialog**, provide a custom dialog template, and add a message map to process the notification messages from the extended controls. Any unprocessed messages should be passed to the base class.

Customizing the hook function is not required.

Note On some installations the **CColorDialog** object will not display with a gray background if you have used the framework to make other **CDialog** objects gray.

#include <afxdlgs.h>

Data Members

m_cc	A structure used to customize the settings of the dialog box.

Construction

CColorDialog	Constructs a **CColorDialog** object.

Operations

DoModal	Displays a color dialog box and allows the user to make a selection.
GetColor	Returns a **COLORREF** structure containing the values of the selected color.
GetSavedCustomColors	Retrieves custom colors created by the user.
SetCurrentColor	Forces the current color selection to the specified color.

Overridables

OnColorOK	Override to validate the color entered into the dialog box.

Member Functions

CColorDialog::CColorDialog

CColorDialog(COLORREF *clrInit* = 0, DWORD *dwFlags* = 0, CWnd* *pParentWnd* = NULL);

Parameters   *clrInit*   The default color selection. If no value is specified, the default is RGB(0,0,0) (black).

dwFlags   A set of flags that customize the function and appearance of the dialog box. For more information, see the **CHOOSECOLOR** structure in the Windows SDK documentation.

pParentWnd   A pointer to the dialog box's parent or owner window.

Remarks   Constructs a **CColorDialog** object.

See Also   CDialog::DoModal

CColorDialog::DoModal

virtual int DoModal( );

Return Value   IDOK or IDCANCEL if the function is successful; otherwise 0. IDOK and
IDCANCEL are constants that indicate whether the user selected the OK or
Cancel button.

If IDCANCEL is returned, you can call the Windows CommDlgExtendedError
function to determine whether an error occurred.

Remarks   Call this function to display the Windows common color dialog box and allow the
user to select a color.

If you want to initialize the various color dialog-box options by setting members of
the m_cc structure, you should do this before calling DoModal but after the dialog-
box object is constructed.

After calling DoModal, you can call other member functions to retrieve the settings
or information input by the user into the dialog box.

See Also   CDialog::DoModal, CColorDialog::CColorDialog

CColorDialog::GetColor

COLORREF GetColor( ) const;

Return Value   A COLORREF value that contains the RGB information for the color selected in
the color dialog box.

Remarks   Call this function after calling DoModal to retrieve the information about the color
the user selected.

See Also   CColorDialog::SetCurrentColor

CColorDialog::GetSavedCustomColors

static COLORREF * GetSavedCustomColors( );

Return Value   A pointer to an array of 16 RGB color values that stores custom colors created by
the user.

Remarks   CColorDialog objects permit the user, in addition to choosing colors, to define up
to 16 custom colors. The GetSavedCustomColors member function provides
access to these colors. These colors can be retrieved after DoModal returns IDOK.

Each of the 16 RGB values in the returned array is initialized to RGB(255,255,255) (white). The custom colors chosen by the user are saved only between dialog box invocations within the application. If you wish to save these colors between invocations of the application, you must save them in some other manner, such as in an initialization (.INI) file.

See Also   CColorDialog::GetColor

CColorDialog::OnColorOK

Protected→
virtual BOOL OnColorOK( );
END Protected

Return Value   Nonzero if the dialog box should not be dismissed; otherwise 0 to accept the color that was entered.

Remarks   Override this function only if you want to provide custom validation of the color entered into the dialog box. This function allows you to reject a color entered by a user into a common color dialog box for any application-specific reason. Normally, you do not need to use this function because the framework provides default validation of colors and displays a message box if an invalid color is entered.

Use the **GetColor** member function to get the RGB value of the color.

If 0 is returned, the dialog box will remain displayed in order for the user to enter another filename.

CColorDialog::SetCurrentColor

void SetCurrentColor(COLORREF *clr*);

Parameters   *clr*   An RGB color value.

Remarks   Call this function after calling **DoModal** to force the current color selection to the color value specified in *clr*. This function is called from within a message handler or **OnColorOK**. The dialog box will automatically update the user's selection based on the value of the *clr* parameter.

See Also   CColorDialog::GetColor

Data Members

CColorDialog::m_cc

CHOOSECOLOR m_cc;

Remarks   A structure of type **CHOOSECOLOR**, whose members store the characteristics and values of the dialog box. After constructing a **CColorDialog** object, you can use **m_cc** to set various aspects of the dialog box before calling the **DoModal** member function.

class CComboBox : public CWnd

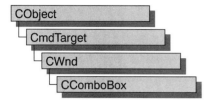

The **CComboBox** class provides the functionality of a Windows combo box.

A combo box consists of a list box combined with either a static control or edit control. The list-box portion of the control may be displayed at all times or may only drop down when the user selects the drop-down arrow next to the control.

The currently selected item (if any) in the list box is displayed in the static or edit control. In addition, if the combo box has an edit control, the user can type text in the edit control and the list box, if it is visible, will highlight the first selection that matches the typed entry.

The following table compares the three combo-box styles: For a list of combo-box styles, see the section "Combo-Box Styles" on page 1247.

Style	When Is List Box Visible?	Static or Edit Control?
Simple	Always	Edit
Drop-down	When dropped down	Edit
Drop-down list	When dropped down	Static

You can create a **CComboBox** object from either a dialog template or directly in your code. In both cases, first call the constructor **CComboBox** to construct the **CComboBox** object; then call the **Create** member function to create the control and attach it to the **CComboBox** object. If you want to handle Windows notification messages sent by a combo box to its parent (usually a class derived from **CDialog**), add a message-map entry and message-handler member function to the parent class for each message.

Each message-map entry takes the following form:

ON_ Notification(*id*, *memberFxn*)

where *id* specifies the child-window ID of the combo-box control sending the notification and *memberFxn* is the name of the parent member function you have written to handle the notification.

The parent's function prototype is as follows:

afx_msg void memberFxn( );

The order in which certain notifications will be sent cannot be predicted. In particular, a **CBN_SELCHANGE** notification may occur either before or after a **CBN_CLOSEUP** notification.

Potential message-map entries are the following:

- **ON_CBN_CLOSEUP**   (Windows 3.1 and later.) The list box of a combo box has closed. This notification message is not sent for a combo box that has the **CBS_SIMPLE** style.

- **ON_CBN_DBLCLK**   The user double-clicks a string in the list box of a combo box. This notification message is only sent for a combo box with the **CBS_SIMPLE** style. For a combo box with the **CBS_DROPDOWN** or **CBS_DROPDOWNLIST** style, a double-click cannot occur because a single click hides the list box.

- **ON_CBN_DROPDOWN**   The list box of a combo box is about to drop down (be made visible). This notification message can occur only for a combo box with the **CBS_DROPDOWN** or **CBS_DROPDOWNLIST** style.

- **ON_CBN_EDITCHANGE**   The user has taken an action that may have altered the text in the edit-control portion of a combo box. Unlike the **CBN_EDITUPDATE** message, this message is sent after Windows updates the screen. It is not sent if the combo box has the **CBS_DROPDOWNLIST** style.

- **ON_CBN_EDITUPDATE**   The edit-control portion of a combo box is about to display altered text. This notification message is sent after the control has formatted the text but before it displays the text. It is not sent if the combo box has the **CBS_DROPDOWNLIST** style.

- **ON_CBN_ERRSPACE**   The combo box cannot allocate enough memory to meet a specific request.

- **ON_CBN_SELENDCANCEL**   (Windows 3.1 and later.) Indicates the user's selection should be canceled. The user clicks an item and then clicks another window or control to hide the list box of a combo box. This notification message is sent before the **CBN_CLOSEUP** notification message to indicate that the user's selection should be ignored. The **CBN_SELENDCANCEL** or **CBN_SELENDOK** notification message is sent even if the **CBN_CLOSEUP** notification message is not sent (as in the case of a combo box with the **CBS_SIMPLE** style).

- **ON_CBN_SELENDOK**   The user selects an item and then either presses the ENTER key or clicks the DOWN ARROW key to hide the list box of a combo box. This notification message is sent before the **CBN_CLOSEUP** message to indicate that the user's selection should be considered valid. The **CBN_SELENDCANCEL** or **CBN_SELENDOK** notification message is sent even if the **CBN_CLOSEUP** notification message is not sent (as in the case of a combo box with the **CBS_SIMPLE** style).

- **ON_CBN_KILLFOCUS**   The combo box is losing the input focus.
- **ON_CBN_SELCHANGE**   The selection in the list box of a combo box is about to be changed as a result of the user either clicking in the list box or changing the selection by using the arrow keys. When processing this message, the text in the edit field of the combo box can only be retrieved via **GetLBText** or another similar function. **GetWindowText** cannot be used.
- **ON_CBN_SETFOCUS**   The combo box receives the input focus.

If you create a **CComboBox** object within a dialog box (through a dialog resource), the **CComboBox** object is automatically destroyed when the user closes the dialog box. If you embed a **CComboBox** object within another window object, you do not need to destroy it. If you create the **CComboBox** object on the stack, it is destroyed automatically. If you create the **CComboBox** object on the heap by using the **new** function, you must call **delete** on the object to destroy it when the Windows combo box is destroyed.

#include <afxwin.h>

See Also   **CWnd, CButton, CEdit, CListBox, CScrollBar, CStatic, CDialog**

Construction

CComboBox	Constructs a **CComboBox** object.

Initialization

Create	Creates the combo box and attaches it to the **CComboBox** object.

General Operations

GetCount	Retrieves the number of items in the list box of a combo box.
GetCurSel	Retrieves the index of the currently selected item, if any, in the list box of a combo box.
SetCurSel	Selects a string in the list box of a combo box.
GetEditSel	Gets the starting and ending character positions of the current selection in the edit control of a combo box.
SetEditSel	Selects characters in the edit control of a combo box.

SetItemData	Sets the 32-bit value associated with the specified item in a combo box.
SetItemDataPtr	Sets the 32-bit value associated with the specified item in a combo box to the specified pointer (**void***).
GetItemData	Retrieves the application-supplied 32-bit value associated with the specified combo-box item.
GetItemDataPtr	Retrieves the application-supplied 32-bit value associated with the specified combo-box item as a pointer (**void***).
Clear	Deletes (clears) the current selection (if any) in the edit control.
Copy	Copies the current selection (if any) onto the Clipboard in **CF_TEXT** format.
Cut	Deletes (cuts) the current selection, if any, in the edit control and copies the deleted text onto the Clipboard in **CF_TEXT** format.
Paste	Inserts the data from the Clipboard into the edit control at the current cursor position. Data is inserted only if the Clipboard contains data in **CF_TEXT** format.
LimitText	Limits the length of the text that the user may enter into the edit control of a combo box.
SetItemHeight	Sets the height of list items in a combo box or the height of the edit-control (or static-text) portion of a combo box.
GetItemHeight	Retrieves the height of list items in a combo box.
GetLBText	Gets a string from the list box of a combo box.
GetLBTextLen	Gets the length of a string in the list box of a combo box.
ShowDropDown	Shows or hides the list box of a combo box that has the **CBS_DROPDOWN** or **CBS_DROPDOWNLIST** style.
GetDroppedControlRect	Retrieves the screen coordinates of the visible (dropped-down) list box of a drop-down combo box.
GetDroppedState	Determines whether the list box of a drop-down combo box is visible (dropped down).
SetExtendedUI	Selects either the default user interface or the extended user interface for a combo box that has the **CBS_DROPDOWN** or **CBS_DROPDOWNLIST** style.

GetExtendedUI	Determines whether a combo box has the default user interface or the extended user interface.
GetLocale	Retrieves the locale identifier for a combo box.
SetLocale	Sets the locale identifier for a combo box.

String Operations

AddString	Adds a string to the end of the list in the list box of a combo box or at the sorted position for list boxes with the **CBS_SORT** style.
DeleteString	Deletes a string from the list box of a combo box.
InsertString	Inserts a string into the list box of a combo box.
ResetContent	Removes all items from the list box and edit control of a combo box.
Dir	Adds a list of filenames to the list box of a combo box.
FindString	Finds the first string that contains the specified prefix in the list box of a combo box.
FindStringExact	Finds the first list-box string (in a combo box) that matches the specified string.
SelectString	Searches for a string in the list box of a combo box and, if the string is found, selects the string in the list box and copies the string to the edit control.

Overridables

DrawItem	Called by the framework when a visual aspect of an owner-draw combo box changes.
MeasureItem	Called by the framework to determine combo box dimensions when an owner-draw combo box is created.
CompareItem	Called by the framework to determine the relative position of a new list item in a sorted owner-draw combo box.
DeleteItem	Called by the framework when a list item is deleted from an owner-draw combo box.

Member Functions

CComboBox::AddString

int AddString(LPCTSTR *lpszString* **);**

Return Value   If the return value is greater than or equal to 0, it is the zero-based index to the string in the list box. The return value is **CB_ERR** if an error occurs; the return value is **CB_ERRSPACE** if insufficient space is available to store the new string.

Parameters   *lpszString*   Points to the null-terminated string that is to be added.

Remarks   Adds a string to the list box of a combo box. If the list box was not created with the **CBS_SORT** style, the string is added to the end of the list. Otherwise, the string is inserted into the list, and the list is sorted. To insert a string into a specific location within the list, use the **InsertString** member function.

See Also   **CComboBox::InsertString, CComboBox::DeleteString, CB_ADDSTRING**

CComboBox::CComboBox

CComboBox( );

Remarks   Constructs a **CComboBox** object.

See Also   **CComboBox::Create**

CComboBox::Clear

void Clear( );

Remarks   Deletes (clears) the current selection, if any, in the edit control of the combo box. To delete the current selection and place the deleted contents onto the Clipboard, use the **Cut** member function.

See Also   **CComboBox::Copy, CComboBox::Cut, CComboBox::Paste, WM_CLEAR**

CComboBox::CompareItem

virtual int CompareItem(LPCOMPAREITEMSTRUCT *lpCompareItemStruct* **);**

Return Value   Indicates the relative position of the two items described in the **COMPAREITEMSTRUCT** structure. It may be any of the following values:

Value	Meaning
−1	Item 1 sorts before item 2.
0	Item 1 and item 2 sort the same.
1	Item 1 sorts after item 2.

See **CWnd::OnCompareItem** on page 1053 for a description of **COMPAREITEMSTRUCT**.

Parameters   *lpCompareItemStruct*   A long pointer to a **COMPAREITEMSTRUCT** structure.

Remarks   Called by the framework to determine the relative position of a new item in the list-box portion of a sorted owner-draw combo box. By default, this member function does nothing. If you create an owner-draw combo box with the **LBS_SORT** style, you must override this member function to assist the framework in sorting new items added to the list box.

See Also   **WM_COMPAREITEM, CComboBox::DrawItem, CComboBox::MeasureItem, CComboBox::DeleteItem**

CComboBox::Copy

void Copy( );

Remarks   Copies the current selection, if any, in the edit control of the combo box onto the Clipboard in **CF_TEXT** format.

See Also   **CComboBox::Clear, CComboBox::Cut, CComboBox::Paste, WM_COPY**

CComboBox::Create

BOOL Create(DWORD *dwStyle***, const RECT&** *rect***, CWnd*** *pParentWnd***, UINT** *nID* **);**

Return Value   Nonzero if successful; otherwise 0.

Parameters   *dwStyle*   Specifies the style of the combo box. Apply any combination of combo-box styles to the box.

rect   Points to the position and size of the combo box. Can be a **RECT** structure or a **CRect** object.

pParentWnd   Specifies the combo box's parent window (usually a **CDialog**). It must not be **NULL**.

nID   Specifies the combo box's control ID.

Remarks   You construct a **CComboBox** object in two steps. First call the constructor, then call **Create**, which creates the Windows combo box and attaches it to the **CComboBox** object. When **Create** executes, Windows sends the **WM_NCCREATE**, **WM_CREATE**, **WM_NCCALCSIZE**, and **WM_GETMINMAXINFO** messages to the combo box.

These messages are handled by default by the **OnNcCreate**, **OnCreate**, **OnNcCalcSize**, and **OnGetMinMaxInfo** member functions in the **CWnd** base class. To extend the default message handling, derive a class from **CComboBox**, add a message map to the new class, and override the preceding message-handler member functions. Override **OnCreate**, for example, to perform needed initialization for a new class.

Apply the following window styles to a combo-box control: For a list of window styles, see the section "Window Styles" on page 1253.

- **WS_CHILD**   Always
- **WS_VISIBLE**   Usually
- **WS_DISABLED**   Rarely
- **WS_VSCROLL**   To add vertical scrolling for the list box in the combo box
- **WS_HSCROLL**   To add horizontal scrolling for the list box in the combo box
- **WS_GROUP**   To group controls
- **WS_TABSTOP**   To include the combo box in the tabbing order

See Also   **CComboBox::CComboBox**

CComboBox::Cut

void Cut( );

Remarks   Deletes (cuts) the current selection, if any, in the combo-box edit control and copies the deleted text onto the Clipboard in **CF_TEXT** format.

To delete the current selection without placing the deleted text onto the Clipboard, call the **Clear** member function.

See Also   **CComboBox::Clear**, **CComboBox::Copy**, **CComboBox::Paste**, **WM_CUT**

CComboBox::DeleteItem

virtual void DeleteItem(LPDELETEITEMSTRUCT *lpDeleteItemStruct* **);**

Parameters   *lpDeleteItemStruct*   A long pointer to a Windows **DELETEITEMSTRUCT** structure that contains information about the deleted item.

See **CWnd::OnDeleteItem** on page 1056 for a description of this structure.

Remarks   Called by the framework when the user deletes an item from an owner-draw
CComboBox object or destroys the combo box. The default implementation of this
function does nothing. Override this function to redraw the combo box as needed.

See Also   **CComboBox::CompareItem, CComboBox::DrawItem,
CComboBox::MeasureItem, WM_DELETEITEM**

CComboBox::DeleteString

int DeleteString(UINT *nIndex* **);**

Return Value   If the return value is greater than or equal to 0, then it is a count of the strings
remaining in the list. The return value is **CB_ERR** if *nIndex* specifies an index
greater then the number of items in the list.

Parameters   *nIndex*   Specifies the index to the string that is to be deleted.

Remarks   Deletes a string in the list box of a combo box.

See Also   **CComboBox::InsertString, CComboBox::AddString, CB_DELETESTRING**

CComboBox::Dir

int Dir(UINT *attr*, **LPCTSTR** *lpszWildCard* **);**

Return Value   If the return value is greater than or equal to 0, it is the zero-based index of the last
filename added to the list. The return value is **CB_ERR** if an error occurs; the
return value is **CB_ERRSPACE** if insufficient space is available to store the new
strings.

Parameters   *attr*   Can be any combination of the **enum** values described in **CFile::GetStatus**
or any combination of the following values:

- **DDL_READWRITE**   File can be read from or written to.

- **DDL_READONLY**   File can be read from but not written to.

- **DDL_HIDDEN**   File is hidden and does not appear in a directory listing.

- **DDL_SYSTEM**   File is a system file.

- **DDL_DIRECTORY**   The name specified by *lpszWildCard* specifies a
  directory.

- **DDL_ARCHIVE**   File has been archived.

- **DDL_DRIVES**   Include all drives that match the name specified by
  lpszWildCard.

- **DDL_EXCLUSIVE**   Exclusive flag. If the exclusive flag is set, only files
  of the specified type are listed. Otherwise, files of the specified type are
  listed in addition to "normal" files.

lpszWildCard   Points to a file-specification string. The string can contain wildcards (for example, *.*).

Remarks   Adds a list of filenames and/or drives to the list box of a combo box.

See Also   **CWnd::DlgDirList, CB_DIR, CFile::GetStatus**

CComboBox::DrawItem

virtual void DrawItem(LPDRAWITEMSTRUCT *lpDrawItemStruct* **);**

Parameters   *lpDrawItemStruct*   A pointer to a **DRAWITEMSTRUCT** structure that contains information about the type of drawing required.

Remarks   Called by the framework when a visual aspect of an owner-draw combo box changes. The **itemAction** member of the **DRAWITEMSTRUCT** structure defines the drawing action that is to be performed.

See **CWnd::OnDrawItem** on page 1058 for a description of this structure.

By default, this member function does nothing. Override this member function to implement drawing for an owner-draw **CComboBox** object. Before this member function terminates, the application should restore all graphics device interface (GDI) objects selected for the display context supplied in *lpDrawItemStruct*.

See Also   **CComboBox::CompareItem, ::DrawItem, CComboBox::MeasureItem, CComboBox::DeleteItem**

CComboBox::FindString

int FindString(int *nStartAfter*, **LPCTSTR** *lpszString* **) const;**

Return Value   If the return value is greater than or equal to 0, it is the zero-based index of the matching item. It is **CB_ERR** if the search was unsuccessful.

Parameters   *nStartAfter*   Contains the zero-based index of the item before the first item to be searched. When the search reaches the bottom of the list box, it continues from the top of the list box back to the item specified by *nStartAfter*. If −1, the entire list box is searched from the beginning.

lpszString   Points to the null-terminated string that contains the prefix to search for. The search is case independent, so this string may contain any combination of uppercase and lowercase letters.

Remarks   Finds, but doesn't select, the first string that contains the specified prefix in the list box of a combo box.

See Also   **CComboBox::SelectString, CComboBox::SetCurSel, CB_FINDSTRING**

CComboBox::FindStringExact

int FindStringExact(int *nIndexStart*, **LPCTSTR** *lpszFind* **) const;**

Return Value   The zero-based index of the matching item, or **CB_ERR** if the search was unsuccessful.

Parameters   *nIndexStart*   Specifies the zero-based index of the item before the first item to be searched. When the search reaches the bottom of the list box, it continues from the top of the list box back to the item specified by *nIndexStart*. If *nIndexStart* is –1, the entire list box is searched from the beginning.

lpszFind   Points to the null-terminated string to search for. This string can contain a complete filename, including the extension. The search is not case sensitive, so this string can contain any combination of uppercase and lowercase letters.

Remarks   Call the **FindStringExact** member function to find the first list-box string (in a combo box) that matches the string specified in *lpszFind*.

If the combo box was created with an owner-draw style but without the **CBS_HASSTRINGS** style, **FindStringExact** attempts to match the doubleword value against the value of *lpszFind*.

See Also   **CComboBox::FindString, CB_FINDSTRINGEXACT**

CComboBox::GetCount

int GetCount( ) const;

Return Value   The number of items in the list box of a combo box. The returned count is one greater then the index value of the last item (the index is zero-based). It is **CB_ERR** if an error occurs.

See Also   **CB_GETCOUNT**

CComboBox::GetCurSel

int GetCurSel( ) const;

Return Value   The zero-based index of the currently selected item in the list box of a combo box, or **CB_ERR** if no item is selected.

See Also   **CComboBox::SetCurSel, CB_GETCURSEL**

CComboBox::GetDroppedControlRect

void GetDroppedControlRect(LPRECT *lprect* **) const;**

Parameters   *lprect*   Points to the **RECT** structure that is to receive the coordinates.

Remarks   Call the **GetDroppedControlRect** member function to retrieve the screen coordinates of the visible (dropped-down) list box of a drop-down combo box.

See Also   **CB_GETDROPPEDCONTROLRECT**

CComboBox::GetDroppedState

BOOL GetDroppedState( ) const;

Return Value   Nonzero if the listbox is visible; otherwise 0.

Remarks   Call the **GetDroppedState** member function to determine whether the list box of a drop-down combo box is visible (dropped down).

See Also   **CB_SHOWDROPDOWN, CB_GETDROPPEDSTATE**

CComboBox::GetEditSel

DWORD GetEditSel( ) const;

Return Value   A 32-bit value that contains the starting position in the low-order word and the position of the first nonselected character after the end of the selection in the high-order word. If this function is used on a combo box without an edit control, **CB_ERR** is returned.

Remarks   Gets the starting and ending character positions of the current selection in the edit control of a combo box.

See Also   **CComboBox::SetEditSel, CB_GETEDITSEL**

CComboBox::GetExtendedUI

BOOL GetExtendedUI( ) const;

Return Value   Nonzero if the combo box has the extended user interface; otherwise 0.

Remarks   Call the **GetExtendedUI** member function to determine whether a combo box has the default user interface or the extended user interface. The extended user interface can be identified in the following ways:

- Clicking the static control displays the list box only for combo boxes with the **CBS_DROPDOWNLIST** style.
- Pressing the DOWN ARROW key displays the list box (F4 is disabled).
- Scrolling in the static control is disabled when the item list is not visible (arrow keys are disabled).

See Also   **CComboBox::SetExtendedUI, CB_GETEXTENDEDUI**

CComboBox::GetItemData

DWORD GetItemData(int *nIndex*) const;

Return Value	The 32-bit value associated with the item, or **CB_ERR** if an error occurs.
Parameters	*nIndex* Contains the zero-based index of an item in the combo box's list box.
Remarks	Retrieves the application-supplied 32-bit value associated with the specified combo-box item. The 32-bit value can be set with the *dwItemData* parameter of a **SetItemData** member function call. Use the **GetItemDataPtr** member function if the 32-bit value to be retrieved is a pointer (**void***).
See Also	**CComboBox::SetItemData, CComboBox::GetItemDataPtr, CComboBox::SetItemDataPtr, CB_GETITEMDATA**

CComboBox::GetItemDataPtr

void* GetItemDataPtr(int *nIndex*) const;

Return Value	Retrieves a pointer, or –1 if an error occurs.
Parameters	*nIndex* Contains the zero-based index of an item in the combo box's list box.
Remarks	Retrieves the application-supplied 32-bit value associated with the specified combo-box item as a pointer (**void***).
See Also	**CComboBox::SetItemDataPtr, CComboBox::GetItemData, CComboBox::SetItemData, CB_GETITEMDATA**

CComboBox::GetItemHeight

int GetItemHeight(int *nIndex*) const;

Return Value	The height, in pixels, of the specified item in a combo box. The return value is **CB_ERR** if an error occurs.
Parameters	*nIndex* Specifies the component of the combo box whose height is to be retrieved. If the *nIndex* parameter is –1, the height of the edit-control (or static-text) portion of the combo box is retrieved. If the combo box has the **CBS_OWNERDRAWVARIABLE** style, *nIndex* specifies the zero-based index of the list item whose height is to be retrieved. Otherwise, *nIndex* should be set to 0.
Remarks	Call the **GetItemHeight** member function to retrieve the height of list items in a combo box.
See Also	**CComboBox::SetItemHeight, WM_MEASUREITEM, CB_GETITEMHEIGHT**

CComboBox::GetLBText

int GetLBText(int *nIndex*, LPTSTR *lpszText*) const;

void GetLBText(int *nIndex*, CString& *rString*) const;

Return Value   The length (in bytes) of the string, excluding the terminating null character. If *nIndex* does not specify a valid index, the return value is **CB_ERR**.

Parameters   *nIndex*   Contains the zero-based index of the list-box string to be copied.

lpszText   Points to a buffer that is to receive the string. The buffer must have sufficient space for the string and a terminating null character.

rString   A reference to a **CString**.

Remarks   Gets a string from the list box of a combo box. The second form of this member function fills a **CString** object with the item's text.

See Also   **CComboBox::GetLBTextLen, CB_GETLBTEXT**

CComboBox::GetLBTextLen

int GetLBTextLen(int *nIndex*) const;

Return Value   The length of the string in bytes, excluding the terminating null character. If *nIndex* does not specify a valid index, the return value is **CB_ERR**.

Parameters   *nIndex*   Contains the zero-based index of the list-box string.

Remarks   Gets the length of a string in the list box of a combo box.

See Also   **CComboBox::GetLBText, CB_GETLBTEXTLEN**

CComboBox::GetLocale

LCID GetLocale( ) const;

Return Value   The locale identifier (LCID) value for the strings in the combo-box.

Remarks   Retrieves the locale used by the combo-box. The locale is used, for example, to determine the sort order of the strings in a sorted combo-box.

See Also   **CComboBox::SetLocale, ::GetStringTypeW, ::GetSystemDefaultLCID, ::GetUserDefaultLCID**

CComboBox::InsertString

int InsertString(int *nIndex*, **LPCTSTR** *lpszString*);

Return Value

The zero-based index of the position at which the string was inserted. The return value is **CB_ERR** if an error occurs. The return value is **CB_ERRSPACE** if insufficient space is available to store the new string.

Parameters

nIndex   Contains the zero-based index to the position in the list box that will receive the string. If this parameter is –1, the string is added to the end of the list.

lpszString   Points to the null-terminated string that is to be inserted.

Remarks

Inserts a string into the list box of a combo box. Unlike the **AddString** member function, the **InsertString** member function does not cause a list with the **CBS_SORT** style to be sorted.

See Also

CComboBox::AddString, CComboBox::DeleteString, CComboBox::ResetContent, CB_INSERTSTRING

CComboBox::LimitText

BOOL LimitText(int *nMaxChars*);

Return Value

Nonzero if successful. If called for a combo box with the style **CBS_DROPDOWNLIST** or for a combo box without an edit control, the return value is **CB_ERR**.

Parameters

nMaxChars   Specifies the length (in bytes) of the text that the user can enter. If this parameter is 0, the text length is set to 65,535 bytes.

Remarks

Limits the length in bytes of the text that the user can enter into the edit control of a combo box.

If the combo box does not have the style **CBS_AUTOHSCROLL**, setting the text limit to be larger than the size of the edit control will have no effect.

LimitText only limits the text the user can enter. It has no effect on any text already in the edit control when the message is sent, nor does it affect the length of the text copied to the edit control when a string in the list box is selected.

See Also

CB_LIMITTEXT

CComboBox::MeasureItem

>**virtual void MeasureItem(LPMEASUREITEMSTRUCT**
>   *lpMeasureItemStruct* **);**

Parameters   *lpMeasureItemStruct*   A long pointer to a **MEASUREITEMSTRUCT** structure.

Remarks   Called by the framework when a combo box with an owner-draw style is created.

By default, this member function does nothing. Override this member function and fill in the **MEASUREITEM** structure to inform Windows of the dimensions of the list box in the combo box. If the combo box is created with the **CBS_OWNERDRAWVARIABLE** style, the framework calls this member function for each item in the list box. Otherwise, this member is called only once.

Using the **CBS_OWNERDRAWFIXED** style in an owner-draw combo box created with the **SubclassDlgItem** member function of **CWnd** involves further programming considerations. See the discussion in Technical Note 14 under MFC in Books Online.

See **CWnd::OnMeasureItem** on page 1073 for a description of the **MEASUREITEMSTRUCT** structure.

See Also   **CComboBox::CompareItem, CComboBox::DrawItem, ::MeasureItem, CComboBox::DeleteItem**

CComboBox::Paste

>**void Paste( );**

Remarks   Inserts the data from the Clipboard into the edit control of the combo box at the current cursor position. Data is inserted only if the Clipboard contains data in **CF_TEXT** format.

See Also   **CComboBox::Clear, CComboBox::Copy, CComboBox::Cut, WM_PASTE**

CComboBox::ResetContent

>**void ResetContent( );**

Remarks   Removes all items from the list box and edit control of a combo box.

See Also   **CB_RESETCONTENT**

CComboBox::SelectString

int SelectString(int *nStartAfter***, LPCTSTR** *lpszString* **);**

Return Value   The zero-based index of the selected item if the string was found. If the search was unsuccessful, the return value is **CB_ERR** and the current selection is not changed.

Parameters   *nStartAfter*   Contains the zero-based index of the item before the first item to be searched. When the search reaches the bottom of the list box, it continues from the top of the list box back to the item specified by *nStartAfter*. If –1, the entire list box is searched from the beginning.

   lpszString   Points to the null-terminated string that contains the prefix to search for. The search is case independent, so this string may contain any combination of uppercase and lowercase letters.

Remarks   Searches for a string in the list box of a combo box, and if the string is found, selects the string in the list box and copies it to the edit control.

   A string is selected only if its initial characters (from the starting point) match the characters in the prefix string.

   Note that the **SelectString** and **FindString** member functions both find a string, but the **SelectString** member function also selects the string.

See Also   **CComboBox::FindString, CB_SELECTSTRING**

CComboBox::SetCurSel

int SetCurSel(int *nSelect* **);**

Return Value   The zero-based index of the item selected if the message is successful. The return value is **CB_ERR** if *nSelect* is greater than the number of items in the list or if *nSelect* is set to –1, which clears the selection.

Parameters   *nSelect*   Specifies the zero-based index of the string to select. If –1, any current selection in the list box is removed and the edit control is cleared.

Remarks   Selects a string in the list box of a combo box. If necessary, the list box scrolls the string into view (if the list box is visible). The text in the edit control of the combo box is changed to reflect the new selection. Any previous selection in the list box is removed.

See Also   **CComboBox::GetCurSel, CB_SETCURSEL**

CComboBox::SetEditSel

BOOL SetEditSel(int *nStartChar***, int** *nEndChar* **);**

Return Value

Nonzero if the member function is successful; otherwise 0. It is **CB_ERR** if **CComboBox** has the **CBS_DROPDOWNLIST** style or does not have a list box.

Parameters

nStartChar   Specifies the starting position. If the starting position is set to –1, then any existing selection is removed.

nEndChar   Specifies the ending position. If the ending position is set to –1, then all text from the starting position to the last character in the edit control is selected.

Remarks

Selects characters in the edit control of a combo box. The positions are zero-based. To select the first character of the edit control, you specify a starting position of 0. The ending position is for the character just after the last character to select. For example, to select the first four characters of the edit control, you would use a starting position of 0 and an ending position of 4.

See Also

CComboBox::GetEditSel, **CB_SETEDITSEL**

CComboBox::SetExtendedUI

int SetExtendedUI(BOOL *bExtended* **= TRUE);**

Return Value

CB_OKAY if the operation is successful, or **CB_ERR** if an error occurs.

Parameters

bExtended   Specifies whether the combo box should use the extended user interface or the default user interface. A value of **TRUE** selects the extended user interface; a value of **FALSE** selects the standard user interface.

Remarks

Call the **SetExtendedUI** member function to select either the default user interface or the extended user interface for a combo box that has the **CBS_DROPDOWN** or **CBS_DROPDOWNLIST** style.

The extended user interface can be identified in the following ways:

- Clicking the static control displays the list box only for combo boxes with the **CBS_DROPDOWNLIST** style.
- Pressing the DOWN ARROW key displays the list box (F4 is disabled).
- Scrolling in the static control is disabled when the item list is not visible (the arrow keys are disabled).

See Also

CComboBox::GetExtendedUI, **CB_SETEXTENDEDUI**

CComboBox::SetItemData

int **SetItemData**(int *nIndex*, DWORD *dwItemData*);

Return Value   **CB_ERR** if an error occurs.

Parameters   *nIndex*   Contains a zero-based index to the item to set.

                      dwItemData   Contains the new value to associate with the item.

Remarks   Sets the 32-bit value associated with the specified item in a combo box. Use the **SetItemDataPtr** member function if the 32-bit item is to be a pointer.

See Also   **CComboBox::GetItemData, CComboBox::GetItemDataPtr, CComboBox::SetItemDataPtr, CB_SETITEMDATA, CComboBox::AddString, CComboBox::InsertString**

CComboBox::SetItemDataPtr

int **SetItemDataPtr**(int *nIndex*, void* *pData*);

Return Value   **CB_ERR** if an error occurs.

Parameters   *nIndex*   Contains a zero-based index to the item.

                      pData   Contains the pointer to associate with the item.

Remarks   Sets the 32-bit value associated with the specified item in a combo box to be the specified pointer (**void***).

See Also   **CComboBox::GetItemData, CComboBox::GetItemDataPtr, CComboBox::SetItemData, CB_SETITEMDATA, CComboBox::AddString, CComboBox::InsertString**

CComboBox::SetItemHeight

int **SetItemHeight**(int *nIndex*, UINT *cyItemHeight*);

Return Value   **CB_ERR** if the index or height is invalid; otherwise 0.

Parameters   *nIndex*   Specifies whether the height of list items or the height of the edit-control (or static-text) portion of the combo box is set.

                    If the combo box has the **CBS_OWNERDRAWVARIABLE** style, *nIndex* specifies the zero-based index of the list item whose height is to be set; otherwise, *nIndex* must be 0 and the height of all list items will be set.

                    If *nIndex* is –1, the height of the edit-control or static-text portion of the combo box is to be set.

     cyItemHeight   Specifies the height, in pixels, of the combo-box component identified by *nIndex*.

Remarks   Call the **SetItemHeight** member function to set the height of list items in a combo box or the height of the edit-control (or static-text) portion of a combo box.

The height of the edit-control (or static-text) portion of the combo box is set independently of the height of the list items. An application must ensure that the height of the edit-control (or static-text) portion is not smaller than the height of a particular list-box item.

See Also   **CComboBox::GetItemHeight**, **WM_MEASUREITEM**, **CB_SETITEMHEIGHT**

CComboBox::SetLocale

    LCID SetLocale(LCID *nNewLocale* **);**

Return Value   The previous locale identifier (LCID) value for this combo-box.

Parameters   *nNewLocale*   The new locale identifier (LCID) value to set for the combo-box.

Remarks   Sets the locale identifier for this combo-box. If **SetLocale** is not called, the default locale is obtained from the system. This system default locale can be modified by using Control Panel's International application.

See Also   **CComboBox::GetLocale**

CComboBox::ShowDropDown

    void ShowDropDown(BOOL *bShowIt* **= TRUE);**

Parameters   *bShowIt*   Specifies whether the drop-down list box is to be shown or hidden. A value of **TRUE** shows the list box. A value of **FALSE** hides the list box.

Remarks   Shows or hides the list box of a combo box that has the **CBS_DROPDOWN** or **CBS_DROPDOWNLIST** style. By default, a combo box of this style will show the list box.

This member function has no effect on a combo box created with the **CBS_SIMPLE** style.

See Also   **CB_SHOWDROPDOWN**

class CControlBar : public CWnd

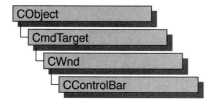

CObject
CmdTarget
CWnd
CControlBar

CControlBar is the base class for the control-bar classes **CStatusBar**, **CToolBar**, and **CDialogBar**. A control bar is a window that is usually aligned to the top or bottom of a frame window. It may contain child items that are either **HWND**-based controls, which are Windows windows that generate and respond to Windows messages, or non-**HWND**-based items, which are not windows and are managed by application code or framework code. List boxes and edit controls are examples of **HWND**-based controls; status-bar panes and bitmap buttons are examples of non-**HWND**-based controls.

Control-bar windows are usually child windows of a parent frame window and are usually "siblings" to the client view or MDI client of the frame window. A **CControlBar** object uses information about the parent window's client rectangle to position itself. It then informs the parent window as to how much space remains unallocated in the parent window's client area.

#include <afxext.h>

See Also   **CStatusBar**, **CToolBar**, **CDialogBar**

Data Members

m_bAutoDelete	If nonzero, the **CControlBar** object is deleted when the Windows control bar is destroyed.

Attributes

GetBarStyle	Retrieves the control bar style settings.
SetBarStyle	Modifies the control bar style settings.
GetCount	Returns the number of non-**HWND** elements in the control bar.

Operations

EnableDocking	Allows a toolbar to be docked or floating.

Member Functions

CControlBar::EnableDocking

void EnableDocking(DWORD *dwStyle* **);**

Parameters   *dwStyle*   Specifies the sides of its parent window to which the control bar can be docked and whether the control bar supports tool tips. Can be one or more of the following:

- **CBRS_ALIGN_TOP**   Allows docking at the top of the client area.
- **CBRS_ALIGN_BOTTOM**   Allows docking at the bottom of the client area.
- **CBRS_ALIGN_LEFT**   Allows docking on the left side of the client area.
- **CBRS_ALIGN_RIGHT**   Allows docking on the right side of the client area.
- **CBRS_ALIGN_ANY**   Allows docking on any side of the client area.

Remarks   Call this function to enable a control bar to be docked. The sides specified must match one of the sides enabled for docking in the destination frame window, or the control bar cannot be docked to that frame window.

See Also   **CFrameWnd::EnableDocking, CFrameWnd::DockControlBar, CFrameWnd::FloatControlBar**

CControlBar::GetCount

int GetCount( );

Return Value   The number of non-**HWND** items on the **CControlBar** object. This function returns 0 for a **CDialogBar** object.

Remarks   Returns the number of non-**HWND** items on the **CControlBar** object. The type of the item depends on the derived object: panes for **CStatusBar** objects, and buttons and separators for **CToolBar** objects.

See Also   **CToolBar::SetButtons, CStatusBar::SetIndicators**

CControlBar::GetBarStyle

DWORD GetBarStyle( );

Return Value   The current **CBRS_** (control bar styles) settings for the control bar. See **CControlBar::SetBarStyle** for the complete list of available styles.

Remarks   Call this function to determine which **CBRS_** (control bar styles) settings are currently set for the control bar. Does not handle **WS_** (window style) styles.

CControlBar::SetBarStyle

void SetBarStyle(DWORD *dwStyle* **);**

Parameters   *dwStyle*   The desired styles for the control bar. Can be one or more of the following:

- **CBRS_ALIGN_TOP**   Allows the control bar to be docked to the top of the client area of a frame window.

- **CBRS_ALIGN_BOTTOM**   Allows the control bar to be docked to the bottom of the client area of a frame window.

- **CBRS_ALIGN_LEFT**   Allows the control bar to be docked to the left side of the client area of a frame window.

- **CBRS_ALIGN_RIGHT**   Allows the control bar to be docked to the right side of the client area of a frame window.

- **CBRS_ALIGN_ANY**   Allows the control bar to be docked to any side of the client area of a frame window.

- **CBRS_BORDER_TOP**   Causes a border to be drawn on the top edge of the control bar when it would be visible.

- **CBRS_BORDER_BOTTOM**   Causes a border to be drawn on the top edge of the control bar when it would be visible.

- **CBRS_BORDER_LEFT**   Causes a border to be drawn on the left edge of the control bar when it would be visible.

- **CBRS_BORDER_RIGHT**   Causes a border to be drawn on the right edge of the control bar when it would be visible.

- **CBRS_TOOLTIPS**   Causes tool tips to be displayed for the control bar.

- **CBRS_FLYBY**   Causes message text to be updated at the same time as tool tips.

- **CBRS_FLOAT_MULTI**   Allows multiple control bars to be floated in a single mini-frame window.

Remarks   Call this function to set the desired **CBRS_** styles for the control bar. Does not affect the **WS_** (window style) settings.

See Also   **CControlBar::GetBarStyle**

Data Members

CControlBar::m_bAutoDelete

Remarks

m_bAutoDelete is a public variable of type **BOOL**. If it is nonzero when the Windows control-bar object is destroyed, the **CControlBar** object is deleted.

A control-bar object is usually embedded in a frame-window object. In this case, **m_bAutoDelete** is 0 because the embedded control-bar object is destroyed when the frame window is destroyed.

Set this variable to a nonzero value if you allocate a **CControlBar** object on the heap and you do not plan to call **delete**.

See Also   **CWnd::DestroyWindow**

structure CCreateContext

The framework uses the **CCreateContext** structure when it creates the frame windows and views associated with a document. When creating a window, the values in this structure provide information used to connect the components that make up a document and the view of its data. You will only need to use **CCreateContext** if you are overriding parts of the creation process.

A **CCreateContext** structure contains pointers to the document, the frame window, the view, and the document template. It also contains a pointer to a **CRuntimeClass** that identifies the type of view to create. The run-time class information and the current document pointer are used to create a new view dynamically. The following table suggests how and when each **CCreateContext** member might be used:

Member	What It Is For
m_pNewViewClass	**CRuntimeClass** of the new view to create.
m_pCurrentDoc	The existing document to be associated with the new view.
m_pNewDocTemplate	The document template associated with the creation of a new MDI frame window.
m_pLastView	The original view upon which additional views are modeled, as in the creation of a splitter window's views or the creation of a second view on a document.
m_pCurrentFrame	The frame window upon which additional frame windows are modeled, as in the creation of a second frame window on a document.

When a document template creates a document and its associated components, it validates the information stored in the **CCreateContext** structure. For example, a view should not be created for a nonexistent document.

Note All of the pointers in **CCreateContext** are optional and may be **NULL** if unspecified or unknown.

CCreateContext is used by the member functions listed under "See Also." Consult the descriptions of these functions for specific information if you plan to override them.

Here are a few general guidelines:

- When passed as an argument for window creation, as in **CWnd::Create**, **CFrameWnd::Create**, and **CFrameWnd::LoadFrame**, the create context specifies what the new window should be connected to. For most windows, the entire structure is optional and a **NULL** pointer may be passed.

- For overridable member functions, such as **CFrameWnd::OnCreateClient**, the **CCreateContext** argument is optional.

- For member functions involved in view creation, you must provide enough information to create the view. For example, for the first view in a splitter window, you must supply the view class information and the current document.

In general, if you use the framework defaults, you can ignore **CCreateContext**. If you attempt more advanced modifications, the Microsoft Foundation Class Library source code or the sample programs, such as VIEWEX, will guide you. If you do forget a required parameter, a framework assertion will tell you what you forgot.

#include <afxext.h>

See Also   **CFrameWnd::Create, CFrameWnd::LoadFrame, CFrameWnd::OnCreateClient, CSplitterWnd::Create, CSplitterWnd::CreateView, CWnd::Create**

class CDatabase : public CObject

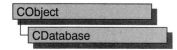

A **CDatabase** object represents a connection to a data source, through which you can operate on the data source. A data source is a specific instance of data hosted by some database management system (DBMS). Examples include Microsoft SQL Server, Microsoft Access, Borland dBASE, and xBASE. You can have one or more **CDatabase** objects active at a time in your application.

To use **CDatabase**, construct a **CDatabase** object and call its **Open** member function. This opens a connection. When you then construct **CRecordset** objects for operating on the connected data source, pass the recordset constructor a pointer to your **CDatabase** object. When you finish using the connection, call the **Close** member function and destroy the **CDatabase** object. **Close** closes any recordsets you have not closed previously.

For more information about **CDatabase**, see the article "Data Source" in *Programming with the Microsoft Foundation Class Library*.

#include <afxdb.h>

See Also   **CRecordset**

Data Members
m_hdbc	Open Database Connectivity (ODBC) connection handle to a data source. Type **HDBC**.

Construction
CDatabase	Constructs a **CDatabase** object. You must initialize the object by calling **Open**.
Open	Establishes a connection to a data source (through an ODBC driver).
Close	Closes the data source connection.

Database Attributes

GetConnect	Returns the ODBC connect string used to connect the **CDatabase** object to a data source.
IsOpen	Returns nonzero if the **CDatabase** object is currently connected to a data source.
GetDatabaseName	Returns the name of the database currently in use.
CanUpdate	Returns nonzero if the **CDatabase** object is updatable (not read-only).
CanTransact	Returns nonzero if the data source supports transactions.
InWaitForDataSource	Returns nonzero if the **CDatabase** object is currently waiting for the server to respond.
SetLoginTimeout	Sets the number of seconds after which a data source connection attempt will time out.
SetQueryTimeout	Sets the number of seconds after which database query operations will time out. Affects all subsequent **Open**, **AddNew**, **Edit**, and **Delete** calls.
SetSynchronousMode	Enables or disables synchronous processing for all recordsets and SQL statements associated with the **CDatabase** object. Asynchronous processing is the default.

Database Operations

BeginTrans	Starts a "transaction"—a series of reversible calls to the **AddNew**, **Edit**, **Delete**, and **Update** member functions of class **CRecordset**—on the connected data source. The data source must support transactions for **BeginTrans** to have any effect.
CommitTrans	Completes a transaction begun by **BeginTrans**. Commands in the transaction that alter the data source are carried out.
Rollback	Reverses changes made during the current transaction. The data source returns to its previous state, as defined at the **BeginTrans** call, unaltered.
Cancel	Cancels an asynchronous operation.
ExecuteSQL	Executes an SQL statement. Any result sets or errors are ignored.

Database Overridables

OnSetOptions	Called by the framework to set standard connection options. The default implementation sets the query timeout value and the processing mode (asynchronous or synchronous). You can establish these options ahead of time by calling **SetQueryTimeout** and **SetSynchronousMode**.
OnWaitForDataSource	Called by the framework to yield processing time to other applications during a lengthy operation.

Member Functions

CDatabase::BeginTrans

BOOL BeginTrans( );

Return Value   Nonzero if the call was successful and changes are committed only manually; otherwise 0.

Remarks   Call this member function to begin a transaction with the connected data source. A transaction consists of one or more calls to the **AddNew**, **Edit**, **Delete**, and **Update** **CDatabase** object. Before beginning a transaction, the **CDatabase** object must already have been connected to the data source by calling its **Open** member function. To end the transaction, call **CommitTrans** to accept all changes to the data source (and carry them out) or call **Rollback** to abort the entire transaction. Call **BeginTrans** after you open any recordsets involved in the transaction and as close to the actual update operations as possible.

Warning If you call BeginTrans before opening recordsets, you may have problems when you call Rollback. Your recordsets will be unsafe because the ODBC "cursors" the database classes use to implement your recordsets did not exist when you called BeginTrans.

BeginTrans may also lock data records on the server, depending on the requested concurrency and the capabilities of the data source. For information about locking data, see the article "Recordset: Locking Records."

User-defined transactions are explained in the article "Transaction" in *Programming with the Microsoft Foundation Class Library*.

BeginTrans establishes the state to which the sequence of transactions can be rolled back (reversed). To establish a new state for rollbacks, commit any current transaction, then call **BeginTrans** again.

> **Warning** Calling **BeginTrans** again without calling **CommitTrans** or **Rollback** is an error.

Your data source may or may not sufficiently support transactions for the database classes to use them. To determine the transaction behavior of your driver, call **CanTransact**. If the data source does not sufficiently support transactions, **CDatabase** ignores transaction calls. For more information about transactions and how to tell whether they are supported, see the article "Transaction" in *Programming with the Microsoft Foundation Class Library*.

See Also   **CDatabase::CommitTrans**, **CDatabase::Rollback**, **CRecordset::CanTransact**

Example   See the article "Transaction: Performing a Transaction in a Recordset" in *Programming with the Microsoft Foundation Class Library*.

CDatabase::Cancel

void Cancel( );

Remarks   Call this member function to cancel an asynchronous operation in progress. This requests that the data source abort the current operation. The **OnWaitForDataSource** member function will continue to call the ODBC function until it no longer returns **SQL_STILL_EXECUTING**.

See Also   **CDatabase::SetSynchronousMode**, **CDatabase::InWaitForDataSource**, **CDatabase::OnWaitForDataSource**

CDatabase::CanTransact

BOOL CanTransact( ) const;

Return Value   Nonzero if recordsets using this **CDatabase** object allow transactions; otherwise 0.

Remarks   Call this member function to determine whether the database allows transactions. For information about transactions, see the article "Transaction" in *Programming with the Microsoft Foundation Class Library*.

See Also   **CDatabase::BeginTrans**, **CDatabase::CommitTrans**, **CDatabase::Rollback**

CDatabase::CanUpdate

BOOL CanUpdate( ) const;

Return Value   Nonzero if the **CDatabase** object allows updates; otherwise 0, indicating either that you passed **TRUE** in *bReadOnly* when you opened the **CDatabase** object or that the data source itself is read-only. The data source is read-only if a call to the

ODBC API function **::SQLGetInfo** for **SQL_DATASOURCE_READ_ONLY** returns "y".

Remarks   Call this member function to determine whether the **CDatabase** object allows updates. Not all drivers support updates.

CDatabase::CDatabase

CDatabase( );

Remarks   Constructs a **CDatabase** object. After constructing the object, you must call its **Open** member function to establish a connection to a specified data source.

You may find it convenient to embed the **CDatabase** object in your document class.

See Also   **CDatabase::Open**

Example   This example illustrates using **CDatabase** in a **CDocument**-derived class.

```
class CMyDocument : public CDocument
{
public:
    // Declare a CDatabase embedded in the document
    CDatabase m_dbCust;
    // ...
};
// ...
// Initialize when needed
CDatabase* CMyDocument::GetDatabase( )
{
    // Connect the object to a data source
    if( !m_dbCust.IsOpen( ) && !m_dbCust.Open( NULL ) )
        return NULL;
    return &m_dbCust;
}
```

CDatabase::Close

virtual void Close( );

Remarks   Call this member function if you want to disconnect from a data source. You must close any recordsets associated with the **CDatabase** object before you call this member function. Because **Close** does not destroy the **CDatabase** object, you can reuse the object by opening a new connection to the same data source or a different data source.

All pending **AddNew** or **Edit** statements of recordsets using the database are canceled, and all pending transactions are rolled back. Any recordsets dependent on the **CDatabase** object are left in an undefined state.

See Also   **CDatabase::Open**

Example
```
// Close the current connection
m_dbCust.Close( );
// Perhaps connect the object to a different data source
m_dbCust.Open("DSN=MYDATASOURCE",
                          FALSE, FALSE,  "ODBC;UID=JOES");
// ...
```

CDatabase::CommitTrans

BOOL CommitTrans( );

Return Value   Nonzero if the updates were successfully committed; otherwise 0. If **Commit** fails, the state of the data source is undefined. You must check the data to determine its state.

Remarks   Call this member function upon completing transactions. A transaction consists of a series of calls to the **AddNew**, **Edit**, **Delete**, and **Update** member functions of a **CRecordset** object that began with a call to **BeginTrans**. **CommitTrans** commits the transaction. By default, updates are committed immediately; calling **BeginTrans** causes commitment of updates to be delayed until **CommitTrans** is called.

Until you call **CommitTrans** to end a transaction, you can call the **Rollback** member function to abort the transaction and leave the data source in its original state. To begin a new transaction, call **BeginTrans** again.

For more information about transactions, see the article "Transaction" in *Programming with the Microsoft Foundation Class Library*.

See Also   **CDatabase::BeginTrans**, **CDatabase::Rollback**

Example   See the article "Transaction: Performing a Transaction in a Recordset" in *Programming with the Microsoft Foundation Class Library*.

CDatabase::ExecuteSQL

void ExecuteSQL(LPCSTR *lpszSQL* **);**
    throw(CDBException);

Parameters   *lpszSQL*   Pointer to a null-terminated string containing a valid SQL command to execute. You may pass a **CString**.

Remarks   Call this member function when you need to execute an SQL command directly. Create the command as a null-terminated string. **ExecuteSQL** does not return data records. If you want to operate on records, use a recordset object instead.

Most of your commands for a data source are issued through recordset objects, which support commands for selecting data, inserting new records, deleting records, and editing records. However, not all ODBC functionality is directly supported by the database classes, so you may at times need to make a direct SQL call with **ExecuteSQL**.

See Also   **CDatabase::SetSynchronousMode**, **CDatabase::SetLoginTimeout**, **CRecordset**

Example
```
CString strCmd = "UPDATE Taxes SET Federal = 36%";
if( !m_dbCust.ExecuteSQL( strCmd ) )
    // ...
```

CDatabase::GetConnect

const CString& GetConnect( ) const;

Return Value   A **const** reference to a **CString** containing the connect string if **Open** has been called; otherwise, an empty string.

Remarks   Call this member function to retrieve the connect string used during the call to **Connect** that connected the **CDatabase** object to a data source.

See **Open** for a description of how the connect string is created.

See Also   **CDatabase::Open**

CDatabase::GetDatabaseName

CString GetDatabaseName( ) const;

Return Value   A **CString** containing the database name if successful; otherwise, an empty **CString**.

Remarks   Call this member function to retrieve the name of the currently connected database (provided that the data source defines a named object called "database"). This is not the same as the data source name (DSN) specified in the **Open** call. What **GetDatabaseName** returns depends on ODBC. In general, a database is a collection of tables. If this entity has a name, **GetDatabaseName** returns it.

You might, for example, want to display this name in a heading. If an error occurs while retrieving the name from ODBC, **GetDatabaseName** returns an empty **CString**.

See Also   **CDatabase::Open**, **CDatabase::GetConnect**

CDatabase::InWaitForDataSource

static BOOL PASCAL InWaitForDataSource( );

Return Value   Nonzero if the application is still waiting for a server to complete an operation; otherwise 0.

Remarks   Call this function from your main window's **OnCommand** or **OnCmdMsg** member function to disable user commands until a data source responds.

CDatabase::IsOpen

BOOL IsOpen( ) const;

Return Value   Nonzero if the **CDatabase** object is currently connected; otherwise 0.

Remarks   Call this member function to determine whether the **CDatabase** object is currently connected to a data source.

See Also   **CDatabase::Open**

CDatabase::OnSetOptions

virtual void OnSetOptions(HSTMT *hstmt* **);**

Parameters   *hstmt*   The ODBC statement handle for which options are being set.

Remarks   The framework calls this member function when directly executing an SQL statement with the **ExecuteSQL** member function. **CRecordset::OnSetOptions** also calls this member function. **OnSetOptions** sets options for synchronous or asynchronous processing and the login timeout value. If there have been previous calls to the **SetQueryTimeout** and **SetSynchronousMode** member functions, **OnSetOptions** reflects the current values; otherwise, it sets default values.

You do not need to override **OnSetOptions** to change the timeout and synchronous mode options. Instead, to customize the query timeout value, call **SetQueryTimeout** before creating a recordset; **OnSetOptions** will use the new value. To change the default processing mode from asynchronous to synchronous, call **SetSynchronousMode** before creating a recordset; **OnSetOptions** sets the mode to asynchronous unless you have changed it to synchronous. The values set apply to subsequent operations on all recordsets or direct SQL calls.

Override **OnSetOptions** if you want to set additional options. Your override should call the base class **OnSetOptions** either before or after you call the ODBC API function **::SQLSetStmtOption**. Follow the method illustrated in the framework's default implementation of **OnSetOptions**.

See Also   **CDatabase::ExecuteSQL, CDatabase::SetQueryTimeout, CDatabase::SetSynchronousMode, CRecordset::OnSetOptions**

CDatabase::OnWaitForDataSource

virtual void OnWaitForDataSource(BOOL *bStillExecuting* **);**

Parameters   *bStillExecuting*   **TRUE** if this is the first time the function is called before an
asynchronous operation. Data access operations are asynchronous by default.

Remarks   The framework calls this member function to yield processing time to other
applications. You can also override it to give the user a chance to cancel a long
operation.

Override **OnWaitForDataSource** if you want to fine-tune the behavior of the
default version. For example, you may also want to detect the ESC key in your
override and, if you detect it, call the **Cancel** member function to break out of the
wait loop.

CDatabase::Open

virtual BOOL Open(LPCSTR *lpszDSN*, **BOOL** *bExclusive* = **FALSE, BOOL**
bReadOnly = **FALSE, LPCSTR** *lpszConnect* = "ODBC;", **BOOL**
bUseCursorLib = **TRUE**);
throw(CDBException, CMemoryException);

Return Value   Nonzero if the connection is successfully made; otherwise 0 if the user chooses
Cancel when presented a dialog box asking for more connection information. In all
other cases, the framework throws an exception.

Parameters   *lpszDSN*   Specifies a data source name—a name registered with ODBC through
the ODBC Administrator program. If a DSN value is specified in *lpszConnect*
(in the form "DSN=<data-source>"), it need not be specified again in lpszDSN.
In this case, *lpszDSN* can be **NULL**. Otherwise, you can pass **NULL** if you
want to present the user with a Data Source dialog box in which the user can
select a data source. If a data source name is passed in both *lpszDSN* and
lpszConnect, the version in *lpszDSN* is ignored. For further information, see
Remarks.

bExclusive   Not supported in this version of the class library. Currently, an
assertion fails if this parameter is **TRUE**. The data source is always opened as
shared (not exclusive).

bReadOnly   **TRUE** if you intend the connection to be read-only and to prohibit
updates to the data source. All dependent recordsets inherit this attribute.

lpszConnect   Specifies a connect string. The connect string concatenates
information, possibly including a data source name, a user ID valid on the data
source, a user authentication string (password, if the data source requires one),
and other information. The whole connect string must be prefixed by the string

"ODBC;" (uppercase or lowercase). The "ODBC;" string is used to indicate that the connection is to an ODBC data source; this is for upward compatibility when future versions of the class library might support non-ODBC data sources. If you do not supply *lpszConnect*, its value defaults to "ODBC;". For further information, see Remarks.

bUseCursorLib   **TRUE** if you want the ODBC Cursor Library DLL to be loaded. The Cursor Library masks some functionality of the underlying ODBC driver, effectively preventing the use of dynasets (if the driver supports them). The only cursors supported if the Cursor Library is loaded are static snapshots and "forwardOnly" cursors. The default value is **TRUE**.

Remarks

You must call this member function to initialize a newly-constructed **CDatabase** object. You cannot use the database object to construct recordset objects until it is initialized.

If the parameters in your **Open** call do not contain enough information to make the connection, the ODBC driver opens a dialog box to obtain the necessary information from the user. When you call **Open**, your connect string, *lpszConnect*, is stored privately in the **CDatabase** object and is available by calling the **GetConnect** member function.

If you wish, you can open your own dialog box before you call **Open** to get information from the user, such as a password, then add that information to the connect string you pass to **Open**. Or you might want to save the connect string you pass (perhaps in an INI file) so you can reuse it the next time your application calls **Open** on a **CDatabase** object.

You can also use the connect string for multiple levels of login authorization (each for a different **CDatabase** object) or to convey other data source-specific information. For more information about connect strings, see Chapter 5 in the *Programmer's Reference* for the Open Database Connectivity Software Development Kit.

It is possible for a connection attempt to time out if, for example, the DBMS host is unavailable. If the connection attempt fails, **Open** throws a **CDBException**.

See Also   **CDatabase::CDatabase, CDatabase::Close, CDBException, CRecordset::Open**

Example

```
// Embed the CDatabase object in your document class
CDatabase m_dbCust( );
// ...
// Connect the object to a data source (no password)
// Instead of hard-coded values, you might use user-supplied values
m_dbCust.Open( "MYDATASOURCE", FALSE, FALSE,
                              "ODBC;UID=JOES" );
// Or query the user for all connection information
```

```
m_dbCust.Open( NULL );
```

CDatabase::Rollback

BOOL Rollback( );

Return Value   Nonzero if the transaction was successfully reversed; otherwise 0. If a **Rollback** call fails, the data source and transaction states are undefined. If **Rollback** returns 0, you must check the data source to determine its state.

Remarks   Call this member function to reverse the changes made during a transaction. All **CRecordset AddNew**, **Edit**, **Delete**, and **Update** calls executed since the last **BeginTrans** are rolled back to the state that existed at the time of that call.

After a call to **Rollback**, the transaction is over, and you must call **BeginTrans** again for another transaction. The record that was current before you called **BeginTrans** becomes the current record again after **Rollback**.

After a rollback, the record that was current before the rollback remains current. For details about the state of the recordset and the data source after a rollback, see the article "Transaction" in *Programming with the Microsoft Foundation Class Library*.

See Also   **CDatabase::BeginTrans, CDatabase::CommitTrans**

Example   See "Transaction: Performing a Transaction in a Recordset" in *Programming with the Microsoft Foundation Class Library*.

CDatabase::SetSynchronousMode

void SetSynchronousMode(BOOL *bSynchronous* **);**

Parameters   *bSynchronous*   **TRUE** to enable synchronous processing; **FALSE** to disable.

Remarks   Call this member function to enable or disable synchronous processing of database transactions. This state applies to all subsequently opened recordsets or direct SQL calls on the **CDatabase** connection.

By default, functions are processed asynchronously. The driver returns control to an application before a function call completes; the application can continue non-database processing while the driver completes the function in progress.

Not all data sources support the ability to specify asynchronous processing.

See Also   **CDatabase::OnSetOptions, CDatabase::InWaitForDataSource**

CDatabase::SetLoginTimeout

void SetLoginTimeout(DWORD *dwSeconds* **);**

Parameters   *dwSeconds*   The number of seconds to allow before a connection attempt times out.

Remarks   Call this member function—before you call **Open**—to override the default number of seconds allowed before an attempted data source connection times out. A connection attempt might time out if, for example, the DBMS is not available. Call **SetLoginTimeout** after you construct the uninitialized **CDatabase** object but before you call **Open**.

The default value for login timeouts is 15 seconds. Not all data sources support the ability to specify a login timeout value. If the data source does not support timeout, you get trace output but not an exception. A value of 0 means "infinite."

See Also   **CDatabase::OnSetOptions, CDatabase::SetQueryTimeout**

CDatabase::SetQueryTimeout

void SetQueryTimeout(DWORD *dwSeconds* **);**

Parameters   *dwSeconds*   The number of seconds to allow before a query attempt times out.

Remarks   Call this member function to override the default number of seconds to allow before subsequent operations on the connected data source time out. An operation might time out due to network access problems, excessive query processing time, and so on. Call **SetQueryTimeout** prior to opening your recordset or prior to calling the recordset's **AddNew**, **Update** or **Delete** member functions if you want to change the query timeout value. The setting affects all subsequent **Open**, **AddNew**, **Update**, and **Delete** calls to any recordsets associated with this **CDatabase** object. Changing the query timeout value for a recordset after opening does not change the value for the recordset. For example, subsequent **Move** operations do not use the new value.

The default value for query timeouts is 15 seconds. Not all data sources support the ability to set a query timeout value. If you set a query timeout value of 0, no timeout occurs; the communication with the data source may hang. This behavior may be useful during development. If the data source does not support timeout, you get trace output but not an exception.

See Also   **CDatabase::SetLoginTimeout**

Data Members

CDatabase::m_hdbc

Remarks   Contains a public handle to an ODBC data source connection—a "connection handle." Normally, you will have no need to access this member variable directly. Instead, the framework allocates the handle when you call **Open**. The framework deallocates the handle when you call the **delete** operator on the **CDatabase** object. Note that the **Close** member function does not deallocate the handle.

Under some circumstances, however, you may need to use the handle directly. For example, if you need to call ODBC API functions directly rather than through class **CDatabase**, you may need a connection handle to pass as a parameter. See the code example below.

See Also   **CDatabase::Open**, **CDatabase::Close**

Example
```
// Using m_hdbc for a direct ODBC API call
// m_db is the CDatabase object; m_hdbc is its HDBC member variable
nRetcode = ::SQLGetInfo(m_db.m_hdbc, SQL_ODBC_SQL_CONFORMANCE,
                        &nValue, sizeof(nValue), &cbValue);
```

class CDataExchange

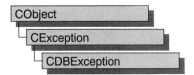

The **CDataExchange** class supports the dialog data exchange (DDX) and dialog data validation (DDV) routines used by the Microsoft Foundation classes. Use this class if you are writing data exchange routines for custom data types or controls, or if you are writing your own data validation routines. For more information on writing your own DDX and DDV routines, see Technical Note 26 under MFC in Books Online. For an overview of DDX and DDV, see Chapter 4, "Working with Dialog Boxes, Controls, and Control Bars," in *Programming with the Microsoft Foundation Class Library*.

A **CDataExchange** object provides the context information needed for DDX and DDV to take place. The flag **m_bSaveAndValidate** is **FALSE** when DDX is used to fill the initial values of dialog controls from data members. The flag **m_bSaveAndValidate** is **TRUE** when DDX is used to set the current values of dialog controls into data members and when DDV is used to validate the data values. If the DDV validation fails, the DDV procedure will display a message box explaining the input error. The DDV procedure will then call **Fail** to reset the focus to the offending control and throw an exception to stop the validation process.

#include <afxwin.h>

See Also   **CWnd::DoDataExchange**, **CWnd::UpdateData**

Data Members

m_bSaveAndValidate	Flag for the direction of DDX and DDV.
m_pDlgWnd	The dialog box or window where the data exchange takes place.

Operations

PrepareCtrl	Prepares the specified control for data exchange or validation. Use for nonedit controls.
PrepareEditCtrl	Prepares the specified edit control for data exchange or validation.
Fail	Called when validation fails. Resets focus to the previous control and throws an exception.

class CDBException : public CException

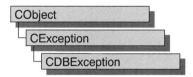

CObject
CException
CDBException

A **CDBException** object represents an exception condition arising from the database classes. The class includes two public data members you can use to determine the cause of the exception or to display a text message describing the exception. **CDBException** objects are constructed and thrown by member functions of the database classes.

Exceptions are cases of abnormal execution involving conditions outside the program's control, such as data source or network I/O errors. Errors that you might expect to see in the normal course of executing your program are usually not considered exceptions.

You can access these objects within the scope of a **CATCH** expression. You can also throw **CDBException** objects from your own code with the **AfxThrowDBException** global function.

For more information about exception handling in general, or about **CDBException** objects, see the article "Exceptions" in *Programming with the Microsoft Foundation Class Library*.

#include <afxdb.h>

See Also   **CDatabase, CRecordset, CFieldExchange, AfxThrowDBException, CRecordset::Update, CRecordset::Delete, CException**

Data Members

m_nRetCode	Contains an Open Database Connectivity (ODBC) return code, of type **RETCODE**.
m_strError	Contains a string that describes the error in alphanumeric terms.
m_strStateNativeOrigin	Contains a string describing the error in terms of the error codes returned by ODBC.

Data Members

CDBException::m_nRetCode

Remarks   Contains an ODBC error code of type **RETCODE** returned by an ODBC application programming interface (API) function. This type includes SQL-prefixed codes defined by ODBC and AFX_SQL-prefixed codes defined by the database classes. For a **CDBException**, this member will contain one of the following values:

- **AFX_SQL_ERROR_API_CONFORMANCE**   The driver for a **CDatabase::Open** call does not conform to required ODBC API Conformance level 1 (**SQL_OAC_LEVEL1**).

- **AFX_SQL_ERROR_CONNECT_FAIL**   Connection to the data source failed. You passed a **NULL CDatabase** pointer to your recordset constructor and the subsequent attempt to create a connection based on **GetDefaultConnect** failed.

- **AFX_SQL_ERROR_DATA_TRUNCATED**   You requested more data than you have provided storage for. For information on increasing the provided data storage for **CString** or **CByteArray** data types, see the *nMaxLength* argument for **RFX_Text** and **RFX_Binary** under "Macros and Globals."

- **AFX_SQL_ERROR_DYNASET_NOT_SUPPORTED**   A call to **CRecordset::Open** requesting a dynaset failed. Dynasets are not supported by the driver.

- **AFX_SQL_ERROR_EMPTY_COLUMN_LIST**   You attempted to open a table (or what you gave could not be identified as a procedure call or **SELECT** statement) but there are no columns identified in record field exchange (RFX) function calls in your **DoFieldExchange** override.

- **AFX_SQL_ERROR_FIELD_SCHEMA_MISMATCH**   The type of an RFX function in your **DoFieldExchange** override is not compatible with the column data type in the recordset.

- **AFX_SQL_ERROR_ILLEGAL_MODE**   You called **CRecordset::Update** without previously calling **CRecordset::AddNew** or **CRecordset::Edit**.

- **AFX_SQL_ERROR_LOCK_MODE_NOT_SUPPORTED**   Your request to lock records for update could not be fulfilled because your ODBC driver does not support locking.

- **AFX_SQL_ERROR_MULTIPLE_ROWS_AFFECTED**   You called **CRecordset::Update** or **Delete** for a table with no unique key and changed multiple records.

- **AFX_SQL_ERROR_NO_CURRENT_RECORD**   You attempted to edit or delete a previously deleted record. You must scroll to a new current record after a deletion.

- **AFX_SQL_ERROR_NO_POSITIONED_UPDATES**   Your request for a dynaset could not be fulfilled because your ODBC driver does not support positioned updates.

- **AFX_SQL_ERROR_NO_ROWS_AFFECTED**   You called **CRecordset::Update** or **Delete**, but when the operation began the record could no longer be found.

- **AFX_SQL_ERROR_ODBC_LOAD_FAILED**   An attempt to load the ODBC.DLL failed; Windows could not find or could not load this DLL. This error is fatal.

- **AFX_SQL_ERROR_ODBC_V2_REQUIRED**   Your request for a dynaset could not be fulfilled because a Level 2-compliant ODBC driver is required.

- **AFX_SQL_ERROR_RECORDSET_FORWARD_ONLY**   An attempt to scroll did not succeed because the data source does not support backward scrolling.

- **AFX_SQL_ERROR_SNAPSHOT_NOT_SUPPORTED**   A call to **CRecordset::Open** requesting a snapshot failed. Snapshots are not supported by the driver. (This should only occur when the ODBC cursor library— ODBCCURS.DLL—is not present.)

- **AFX_SQL_ERROR_SQL_CONFORMANCE**   The driver for a **CDatabase::Open** call does not conform to the required ODBC SQL Conformance level of "Minimum" (**SQL_OSC_MINIMUM**).

- **AFX_SQL_ERROR_SQL_NO_TOTAL**   The ODBC driver was unable to specify the total size of a **CLongBinary** data value. The operation probably failed because a global memory block could not be preallocated.

- **AFX_SQL_ERROR_RECORDSET_READONLY**   You attempted to update a read-only recordset, or the data source is read-only. No update operations can be performed with the recordset or the **CDatabase** object it is associated with.

- **SQL_ERROR**   Function failed. The error message returned by **::SQLError** is stored in the **m_strError** data member.

- **SQL_INVALID_HANDLE**   Function failed due to an invalid environment handle, connection handle, or statement handle. This indicates a programming error. No additional information is available from **::SQLError**.

The SQL-prefixed codes are defined by ODBC. The AFX-prefixed codes are defined in AFXDB.H, found in \MSVC20\MFC\INCLUDE.

See Also   **CDatabase**, **CLongBinary**, **CRecordset**

CDBException::m_strError

Remarks

Contains a string describing the error that caused the exception. The string describes the error in alphanumeric terms. For more detailed information and an example, see **m_strStateNativeOrigin**.

See Also

CDBException::m_strStateNativeOrigin

CDBException::m_strStateNativeOrigin

Remarks

Contains a string describing the error that caused the exception. The string is of the form "State:%s,Native:%ld,Origin:%s", where the format codes, in order, are replaced by values that describe:

- The **SQLSTATE**, a null-terminated string containing a five-character error code returned in the *szSqlState* parameter of the **::SQLError** function. **SQLSTATE** values are listed in Appendix A, "ODBC Error Codes," in the ODBC SDK *Programmer's Reference*. Example: "S0022".

- The native error code, specific to the data source, returned in the *pfNativeError* parameter of the **::SQLError** function. Example: 207.

- The error message text returned in the *szErrorMsg* parameter of the **::SQLError** function. This message consists of several bracketed names. As an error is passed from its source to the user, each ODBC component (data source, driver, Driver Manager) appends its own name. This information helps to pinpoint the origin of the error. Example: [Microsoft][ODBC SQL Server Driver][SQL Server]

The framework interprets the error string and puts its components into **m_strStateNativeOrigin**; if **m_strStateNativeOrigin** contains information for more than one error, the errors are separated by newlines. The framework puts the alphanumeric error text into **m_strError**.

For additional information about the codes used to make up this string, see the **SQLError** function in the ODBC SDK *Programmer's Reference*.

See Also

CDBException::m_strError

Example

From ODBC: "State:S0022,Native:207,Origin:[Microsoft][ODBC SQL Server Driver][SQL Server] Invalid column name 'ColName'"

In **m_strStateNativeOrigin**: "State:S0022,Native:207,Origin:[Microsoft][ODBC SQL Server Driver][SQL Server]"

In **m_strError**: "Invalid column name 'ColName'"

class CDC : public CObject

The **CDC** class defines a class of device-context objects. The **CDC** object provides member functions for working with a device context, such as a display or printer, as well as members for working with a display context associated with the client area of a window.

Do all drawing through the member functions of a **CDC** object. The class provides member functions for device-context operations, working with drawing tools, type-safe graphics device interface (GDI) object selection, and working with colors and palettes. It also provides member functions for getting and setting drawing attributes, mapping, working with the viewport, working with the window extent, converting coordinates, working with regions, clipping, drawing lines, and drawing simple shapes, ellipses, and polygons. Member functions are also provided for drawing text, working with fonts, using printer escapes, scrolling, and playing metafiles.

To use a **CDC** object, construct it, and then call its member functions, which parallel Windows functions that use device contexts or display contexts.

For specific uses, the Microsoft Foundation Class Library provides several classes derived from **CDC**. **CPaintDC** encapsulates calls to **BeginPaint** and **EndPaint**. **CClientDC** manages a display context associated with a window's client area. **CWindowDC** manages a display context associated with an entire window, including its frame and controls. **CMetaFileDC** associates a device context with a metafile.

CDC contains two device contexts, **m_hDC** and **m_hAttribDC**, which, on creation of a **CDC** object, refer to the same device. **CDC** directs all output GDI calls to **m_hDC** and most attribute GDI calls to **m_hAttribDC**. (An example of an attribute call is **GetTextColor**, while **SetTextColor** is an output call.)

For example, the framework uses these two device contexts to implement a **CMetaFileDC** object that will send output to a metafile while reading attributes from a physical device. Print preview is implemented in the framework in a similar fashion. You can also use the two device contexts in a similar way in your application-specific code.

There are times when you may need text-metric information from both the **m_hDC** and **m_hAttribDC** device contexts. The following pairs of functions provide this capability:

Uses **m_hAttribDC**	Uses **m_hDC**
GetTextExtent	**GetOutputTextExtent**
GetTabbedTextExtent	**GetOutputTabbedTextExtent**
GetTextMetrics	**GetOutputTextMetrics**
GetCharWidth	**GetOutputCharWidth**

#include <afxwin.h>

See Also   **CPaintDC**, **CWindowDC**, **CClientDC**, **CMetaFileDC**

Data Members

m_hDC	The output-device context used by this **CDC** object.
m_hAttribDC	The attribute-device context used by this **CDC** object.

Construction

CDC	Constructs a **CDC** object.

Initialization

CreateDC	Creates a device context for a specific device.
CreateIC	Creates an information context for a specific device. This provides a fast way to get information about the device without creating a device context.
CreateCompatibleDC	Creates a memory-device context that is compatible with another device context. You can use it to prepare images in memory.
DeleteDC	Deletes the Windows device context associated with this **CDC** object.
FromHandle	Returns a pointer to a **CDC** object when given a handle to a device context. If a **CDC** object is not attached to the handle, a temporary **CDC** object is created and attached.
DeleteTempMap	Called by the **CWinApp** idle-time handler to delete any temporary **CDC** object created by **FromHandle**. Also detaches the device context.

Attach	Attaches a Windows device context to this **CDC** object.
Detach	Detaches the Windows device context from this **CDC** object.
SetAttribDC	Sets **m_hAttribDC**, the attribute device context.
SetOutputDC	Sets **m_hDC**, the output device context.
ReleaseAttribDC	Releases **m_hAttribDC**, the attribute device context.
ReleaseOutputDC	Releases **m_hDC**, the output device context.
GetCurrentBitmap	Returns a pointer to the currently selected **CBitmap** object.
GetCurrentBrush	Returns a pointer to the currently selected **CBrush** object.
GetCurrentFont	Returns a pointer to the currently selected **CFont** object.
GetCurrentPalette	Returns a pointer to the currently selected **CPalette** object.
GetCurrentPen	Returns a pointer to the currently selected **CPen** object.
GetWindow	Returns the window associated with the display device context.

Device-Context Functions

GetSafeHdc	Returns **m_hDC**, the output device context.
SaveDC	Saves the current state of the device context.
RestoreDC	Restores the device context to a previous state saved with **SaveDC**.
ResetDC	Updates the **m_hAttribDC** device context.
GetDeviceCaps	Retrieves a specified kind of device-specific information about a given display device's capabilities.
IsPrinting	Determines whether the device context is being used for printing.

Drawing-Tool Functions

GetBrushOrg	Retrieves the origin of the current brush.
SetBrushOrg	Specifies the origin for the next brush selected into a device context.
EnumObjects	Enumerates the pens and brushes available in a device context.

Type-Safe Selection Helpers

SelectObject	Selects a GDI drawing object such as a pen.
SelectStockObject	Selects one of the predefined stock pens, brushes, or fonts provided by Windows.

Color and Color Palette Functions

GetNearestColor	Retrieves the closest logical color to a specified logical color that the given device can represent.
SelectPalette	Selects the logical palette.
RealizePalette	Maps palette entries in the current logical palette to the system palette.
UpdateColors	Updates the client area of the device context by matching the current colors in the client area to the system palette on a pixel-by-pixel basis.

Drawing-Attribute Functions

GetBkColor	Retrieves the current background color.
SetBkColor	Sets the current background color.
GetBkMode	Retrieves the background mode.
SetBkMode	Sets the background mode.
GetPolyFillMode	Retrieves the current polygon-filling mode.
SetPolyFillMode	Sets the polygon-filling mode.
GetROP2	Retrieves the current drawing mode.
SetROP2	Sets the current drawing mode.
GetStretchBltMode	Retrieves the current bitmap-stretching mode.
SetStretchBltMode	Sets the bitmap-stretching mode.

GetTextColor	Retrieves the current text color.
SetTextColor	Sets the text color.
GetColorAdjustment	Retrieves the color adjustment values for the device context.
SetColorAdjustment	Sets the color adjustment values for the device context using the specified values.

Mapping Functions

GetMapMode	Retrieves the current mapping mode.
SetMapMode	Sets the current mapping mode.
GetViewportOrg	Retrieves the x- and y-coordinates of the viewport origin.
SetViewportOrg	Sets the viewport origin.
OffsetViewportOrg	Modifies the viewport origin relative to the coordinates of the current viewport origin.
GetViewportExt	Retrieves the x- and y-extents of the viewport.
SetViewportExt	Sets the x- and y-extents of the viewport.
ScaleViewportExt	Modifies the viewport extent relative to the current values.
GetWindowOrg	Retrieves the x- and y-coordinates of the origin of the associated window.
SetWindowOrg	Sets the window origin of the device context.
OffsetWindowOrg	Modifies the window origin relative to the coordinates of the current window origin.
GetWindowExt	Retrieves the x- and y-extents of the associated window.
SetWindowExt	Sets the x- and y-extents of the associated window.
ScaleWindowExt	Modifies the window extents relative to the current values.

Coordinate Functions

DPtoHIMETRIC	Converts device units into **HIMETRIC** units.
DPtoLP	Converts device units into logical units.
HIMETRICtoDP	Converts **HIMETRIC** units into device units.
HIMETRICtoLP	Converts **HIMETRIC** units into logical units.
LPtoDP	Converts logical units into device units.
LPtoHIMETRIC	Converts logical units into **HIMETRIC** units.

Region Functions

FillRgn	Fills a specific region with the specified brush.
FrameRgn	Draws a border around a specific region using a brush.
InvertRgn	Inverts the colors in a region.
PaintRgn	Fills a region with the selected brush.

Clipping Functions

SetBoundsRect	Controls the accumulation of bounding-rectangle information for the specified device context.
GetBoundsRect	Returns the current accumulated bounding rectangle for the specified device context.
GetClipBox	Retrieves the dimensions of the tightest bounding rectangle around the current clipping boundary.
SelectClipRgn	Combines the given region with the current clipping region by using the specified mode.
ExcludeClipRect	Creates a new clipping region that consists of the existing clipping region minus the specified rectangle.
ExcludeUpdateRgn	Prevents drawing within invalid areas of a window by excluding an updated region in the window from a clipping region.
IntersectClipRect	Creates a new clipping region by forming the intersection of the current region and a rectangle.
OffsetClipRgn	Moves the clipping region of the given device.
PtVisible	Specifies whether the given point is within the clipping region.
RectVisible	Determines whether any part of the given rectangle lies within the clipping region.

Line-Output Functions

GetCurrentPosition	Retrieves the current position of the pen (in logical coordinates).
MoveTo	Moves the current position.
LineTo	Draws a line from the current position up to, but not including, a point.
Arc	Draws an elliptical arc.
ArcTo	Draws an elliptical arc. This function is similar to **Arc**, except that the current position is updated.
AngleArc	Draws a line segment and an arc, and moves the current position to the ending point of the arc.
GetArcDirection	Returns the current arc direction for the device context.
SetArcDirection	Sets the drawing direction to be used for arc and rectangle functions.
PolyDraw	Draws a set of line segments and Bézier splines. This function updates the current position.
Polyline	Draws a set of line segments connecting the specified points.
PolyPolyline	Draws multiple series of connected line segments. The current position is neither used nor updated by this function.
PolylineTo	Draws one or more straignt lines and moves the current position to the ending point of the last line.
PolyBezier	Draws one or more Bézier splines. The current position is neither used nor updated.
PolyBezierTo	Draws one or more Bézier splines, and moves the current position to the ending point of the last Bézier spline.

Simple Drawing Functions

FillRect	Fills a given rectangle by using a specific brush.
FrameRect	Draws a border around a rectangle.
InvertRect	Inverts the contents of a rectangle.
DrawIcon	Draws an icon.

Ellipse and Polygon Functions

Chord	Draws a chord (a closed figure bounded by the intersection of an ellipse and a line segment).
DrawFocusRect	Draws a rectangle in the style used to indicate focus.
Ellipse	Draws an ellipse.
Pie	Draws a pie-shaped wedge.
Polygon	Draws a polygon consisting of two or more points (vertices) connected by lines.
PolyPolygon	Creates two or more polygons that are filled using the current polygon-filling mode. The polygons may be disjoint or they may overlap.
Polyline	Draws a polygon consisting of a set of line segments connecting specified points.
Rectangle	Draws a rectangle using the current pen and fills it using the current brush.
RoundRect	Draws a rectangle with rounded corners using the current pen and filled using the current brush.

Bitmap Functions

PatBlt	Creates a bit pattern.
BitBlt	Copies a bitmap from a specified device context.
StretchBlt	Moves a bitmap from a source rectangle and device into a destination rectangle, stretching or compressing the bitmap if necessary to fit the dimensions of the destination rectangle.
GetPixel	Retrieves the RGB color value of the pixel at the specified point.
SetPixel	Sets the pixel at the specified point to the closest approximation of the specified color.
SetPixelV	Sets the pixel at the specified coordinates to the closest approximation of the specified color. **SetPixelV** is faster than **SetPixel** because it does not need to return the color value of the point actually painted.

FloodFill	Fills an area with the current brush.
ExtFloodFill	Fills an area with the current brush. Provides more flexibility than the **FloodFill** member function.
MaskBlt	Combines the color data for the source and destination bitmaps using the given mask and raster operation.
PlgBlt	Performs a bit-block transfer of the bits of color data from the specified rectangle in the source device context to the specified parallelogram in the given device context.

Text Functions

TextOut	Writes a character string at a specified location using the currently selected font.
ExtTextOut	Writes a character string within a rectangular region using the currently selected font.
TabbedTextOut	Writes a character string at a specified location, expanding tabs to the values specified in an array of tab-stop positions.
DrawText	Draws formatted text in the specified rectangle.
GetTextExtent	Computes the width and height of a line of text on the attribute device context using the current font to determine the dimensions.
GetOutputTextExtent	Computes the width and height of a line of text on the output device context using the current font to determine the dimensions.
GetTabbedTextExtent	Computes the width and height of a character string on the attribute device context.
GetOutputTabbedTextExtent	Computes the width and height of a character string on the output device context.

GrayString	Draws dimmed (grayed) text at the given location.
GetTextAlign	Retrieves the text-alignment flags.
SetTextAlign	Sets the text-alignment flags.
GetTextFace	Copies the typeface name of the current font into a buffer as a null-terminated string.
GetTextMetrics	Retrieves the metrics for the current font from the attribute device context.
GetOutputTextMetrics	Retrieves the metrics for the current font from the output device context.
SetTextJustification	Adds space to the break characters in a string.
GetTextCharacterExtra	Retrieves the current setting for the amount of intercharacter spacing.
SetTextCharacterExtra	Sets the amount of intercharacter spacing.

Font Functions

GetFontData	Retrieves font metric information from a scalable font file. The information to retrieve is identified by specifying an offset into the font file and the length of the information to return.
GetKerningPairs	Retrieves the character kerning pairs for the font that is currently selected in the specified device context.
GetOutlineTextMetrics	Retrieves font metric information for TrueType fonts.
GetGlyphOutline	Retrieves the outline curve or bitmap for an outline character in the current font.
GetCharABCWidths	Retrieves the widths, in logical units, of consecutive characters in a given range from the current font.
GetCharWidth	Retrieves the fractional widths of consecutive characters in a given range from the current font.
GetOutputCharWidth	Retrieves the widths of individual characters in a consecutive group of characters from the current font using the output device context.
SetMapperFlags	Alters the algorithm that the font mapper uses when it maps logical fonts to physical fonts.
GetAspectRatioFilter	Retrieves the setting for the current aspect-ratio filter.

Printer Escape Functions

QueryAbort Calls the **AbortProc** callback function for a printing application and queries whether the printing should be terminated.

Escape Allows applications to access facilities that are not directly available from a particular device through GDI. Also allows access to Windows escape functions. Escape calls made by an application are translated and sent to the device driver.

DrawEscape Accesses drawing capabilities of a video display that are not directly available through the graphics device interface (GDI).

StartDoc Informs the device driver that a new print job is starting.

StartPage Informs the device driver that a new page is starting.

EndPage Informs the device driver that a page is ending.

SetAbortProc Sets a programmer-supplied callback function that Windows calls if a print job must be aborted.

AbortDoc Terminates the current print job, erasing everything the application has written to the device since the last call of the **StartDoc** member function.

EndDoc Ends a print job started by the **StartDoc** member function.

Scrolling Functions

ScrollDC Scrolls a rectangle of bits horizontally and vertically.

Metafile Functions

PlayMetaFile Plays the contents of the specified metafile on the given device. The enhanced version of **PlayMetaFile** displays the picture stored in the given enhanced-format metafile. The metafile can be played any number of times.

AddMetaFileComment Copies the comment from a buffer into a specified enhanced-format metafile.

Path Functions

AbortPath	Closes and discards any paths in the device context.
BeginPath	Opens a path bracket in the device context.
CloseFigure	Closes an open figure in a path.
EndPath	Closes a path bracket and selects the path defined by the bracket into the device context.
FillPath	Closes any open figures in the current path and fills the path's interior by using the current brush and polygon-filling mode.
FlattenPath	Transforms any curves in the path selected into the current device context, and turns each curve into a sequence of lines.
GetMiterLimit	Returns the miter limit for the device context.
GetPath	Retrieves the coordinates defining the endpoints of lines and the control points of curves found in the path that is selected into the device context.
SelectClipPath	Selects the current path as a clipping region for the device context, combining the new region with any existing clipping region by using the specified mode.
SetMiterLimit	Sets the limit for the length of miter joins for the device context.
StrokeandFillPath	Closes any open figures in a path, strikes the outline of the path by using the current pen, and fills its interior by using the current brush.
StrokePath	Renders the specified path by using the current pen.
WidenPath	Redefines the current path as the area that would be painted if the path were stroked using the pen currently selected into the device context.

Member Functions

CDC::AbortDoc

int AbortDoc( );

Return Value   A value greater than or equal to 0 if successful, or a negative value if an error has occurred. The following list shows common error values and their meanings:

- **SP_ERROR**   General error.
- **SP_OUTOFDISK**   Not enough disk space is currently available for spooling, and no more space will become available.
- **SP_OUTOFMEMORY**   Not enough memory is available for spooling.
- **SP_USERABORT**   User terminated the job through the Print Manager.

Remarks   Terminates the current print job and erases everything the application has written to the device since the last call to the **StartDoc** member function. This member function replaces the **ABORTDOC** printer escape.

AbortDoc should be used to terminate the following:

- Printing operations that do not specify an abort function using **SetAbortProc**.
- Printing operations that have not yet reached their first **NEWFRAME** or **NEXTBAND** escape call.

If an application encounters a printing error or a canceled print operation, it must not attempt to terminate the operation by using either the **EndDoc** or **AbortDoc** member functions of class **CDC**. GDI automatically terminates the operation before returning the error value.

If the application displays a dialog box to allow the user to cancel the print operation, it must call **AbortDoc** before destroying the dialog box.

If Print Manager was used to start the print job, calling **AbortDoc** erases the entire spool job—the printer receives nothing. If Print Manager was not used to start the print job, the data may have been sent to the printer before **AbortDoc** was called. In this case, the printer driver would have reset the printer (when possible) and closed the print job.

When running under Windows version 3.0, this member function sends an **ABORTDOC** printer escape.

See Also   **CDC::StartDoc**, **CDC::EndDoc**, **CDC::SetAbortProc**

CDC::AbortPath

BOOL AbortPath( )

Return Value   Nonzero if the function is successful; otherwise 0.

Remarks   Closes and discards any paths in the device context. If there is an open path bracket in the device context, the path bracket is closed and the path is discarded. If there is a closed path in the device context, the path is discarded.

See Also   **CDC::BeginPath**, **CDC::EndPath**

CDC::AddMetaFileComment

BOOL AddMetaFileComment(UINT *nDataSize*, **const BYTE***
pCommentData **);**

Return Value   Nonzero if the function is successful; otherwise 0.

Parameters   *nDataSize*   Specifies the length of the comment buffer, in bytes.

pCommentData   Points to the buffer that contains the comment.

Remarks   Copies the comment from a buffer into a specified enhanced-format metafile. A comment may include any private information—for example, the source of the picture and the date it was created. A comment should begin with an application signature, followed by the data. Comments should not contain position-specific data. Position-specific data specifies the location of a record, and it should not be included because one metafile may be embedded within another metafile. This function can only be used with enhanced metafiles.

See Also   **CMetaFileDC::CreateEnhanced**, **::GdiComment**

CDC::AngleArc

BOOL AngleArc(int *x*, **int** *y*, **int** *nRadius*, **float** *fStartAngle*,
float *fSweepAngle* **);**

Return Value   Nonzero if successful; otherwise 0.

Parameters   *x*   Specifies the logical x-coordinate of the center of the circle.

y   Specifies the logical y-coordinate of the center of the circle.

nRadius   Specifies the radius of the circle in logical units. This value must be positive.

fStartAngle   Specifies the starting angle in degrees relative to the x-axis.

fSweepAngle   Specifies the sweep angle in degrees relative to the starting angle.

Remarks   Draws a line segment and an arc. The line segment is drawn from the current position to the beginning of the arc. The arc is drawn along the perimeter of a circle with the given radius and center. The length of the arc is defined by the given start and sweep angles.

AngleArc moves the current position to the ending point of the arc. The arc drawn by this function may appear to be elliptical, depending on the current transformation and mapping mode. Before drawing the arc, this function draws the line segment from the current position to the beginning of the arc. The arc is drawn by constructing an imaginary circle with the specified radius around the specified center point. The starting point of the arc is determined by measuring counterclockwise from the x-axis of the circle by the number of degrees in the start angle. The ending point is similarly located by measuring counterclockwise from the starting point by the number of degrees in the sweep angle.

If the sweep angle is greater than 360 degrees the arc is swept multiple times. This function draws lines by using the current pen. The figure is not filled.

See Also   **CDC::Arc**, **CDC::ArcTo**, **CDC::MoveTo**, **::AngleArc**

CDC::Arc

BOOL Arc(int *x1*, **int** *y1*, **int** *x2*, **int** *y2*, **int** *x3*, **int** *y3*, **int** *x4*, **int** *y4* **);**

BOOL Arc(LPCRECT *lpRect*, **POINT** *ptStart*, **POINT** *ptEnd* **);**

Return Value   Nonzero if the function is successful; otherwise 0.

Parameters   *x1*   Specifies the x-coordinate of the upper-left corner of the bounding rectangle (in logical units).

y1   Specifies the y-coordinate of the upper-left corner of the bounding rectangle (in logical units).

x2   Specifies the x-coordinate of the lower-right corner of the bounding rectangle (in logical units).

y2   Specifies the y-coordinate of the lower-right corner of the bounding rectangle (in logical units).

x3   Specifies the x-coordinate of the point that defines the arc's starting point (in logical units). This point does not have to lie exactly on the arc.

y3   Specifies the y-coordinate of the point that defines the arc's starting point (in logical units). This point does not have to lie exactly on the arc.

x4   Specifies the x-coordinate of the point that defines the arc's endpoint (in logical units). This point does not have to lie exactly on the arc.

y4   Specifies the y-coordinate of the point that defines the arc's endpoint (in logical units). This point does not have to lie exactly on the arc.

lpRect   Specifies the bounding rectangle (in logical units). You can pass either an **LPRECT** or a **CRect** object for this parameter.

ptStart   Specifies the x- and y-coordinates of the point that defines the arc's starting point (in logical units). This point does not have to lie exactly on the arc. You can pass either a **POINT** structure or a **CPoint** object for this parameter.

ptEnd   Specifies the x- and y-coordinates of the point that defines the arc's ending point (in logical units). This point does not have to lie exactly on the arc. You can pass either a **POINT** structure or a **CPoint** object for this parameter.

Remarks   Draws an elliptical arc. The arc drawn by using the function is a segment of the ellipse defined by the specified bounding rectangle. The actual starting point of the arc is the point at which a ray drawn from the center of the bounding rectangle through the specified starting point intersects the ellipse. The actual ending point of the arc is the point at which a ray drawn from the center of the bounding rectangle through the specified ending point intersects the ellipse. The arc is drawn in a counterclockwise direction. Since an arc is not a closed figure, it is not filled. Both the width and height of the rectangle must be greater than 2 units and less than 32,767 units.

See Also   **CDC::Chord, ::Arc, POINT, RECT**

CDC::ArcTo

BOOL ArcTo(int *x1***, int** *y1***, int** *x2***, int** *y2***, int** *x3***, int** *y3***, int** *x4***, int** *y4* **);**

BOOL ArcTo(LPCRECT *lpRect***, POINT** *ptStart***, POINT** *ptEnd* **);**

Return Value   Nonzero if the function is successful; otherwise 0.

Parameters   *x1*   Specifies the x-coordinate of the upper-left corner of the bounding rectangle (in logical units).

y1   Specifies the y-coordinate of the upper-left corner of the bounding rectangle (in logical units).

x2   Specifies the x-coordinate of the lower-right corner of the bounding rectangle (in logical units).

y2   Specifies the y-coordinate of the lower-right corner of the bounding rectangle (in logical units).

x3   Specifies the x-coordinate of the point that defines the arc's starting point (in logical units). This point does not have to lie exactly on the arc.

y3   Specifies the y-coordinate of the point that defines the arc's starting point (in logical units). This point does not have to lie exactly on the arc.

x4   Specifies the x-coordinate of the point that defines the arc's endpoint (in logical units). This point does not have to lie exactly on the arc.

y4   Specifies the y-coordinate of the point that defines the arc's endpoint (in logical units). This point does not have to lie exactly on the arc.

lpRect   Specifies the bounding rectangle (in logical units). You can pass either a pointer to a **RECT** data structure or a **CRect** object for this parameter.

ptStart   Specifies the x- and y-coordinates of the point that defines the arc's starting point (in logical units). This point does not have to lie exactly on the arc. You can pass either a **POINT** data structure or a **CPoint** object for this parameter.

ptEnd   Specifies the x- and y-coordinates of the point that defines the arc's ending point (in logical units). This point does not have to lie exactly on the arc. You can pass either a **POINT** data structure or a **CPoint** object for this parameter.

Remarks   Draws an elliptical arc. This function is similar to **CDC::Arc**, except that the current position is updated. The points ($x1,y1$) and ($x2,y2$) specify the bounding rectangle. An ellipse formed by the given bounding rectangle defines the curve of the arc. The arc extends counterclockwise (the default arc direction) from the point where it intersects the radial line from the center of the bounding rectangle to ($x3,y3$). The arc ends where it intersects the radial line from the center of the bounding rectangle to ($x4,y4$). If the starting point and ending point are the same, a complete ellipse is drawn.

A line is drawn from the current position to the starting point of the arc. If no error occurs, the current position is set to the ending point of the arc. The arc is drawn using the current pen; it is not filled.

See Also   **CDC::AngleArc, CDC::Arc, CDC::SetArcDirection, ::ArcTo**

CDC::Attach

BOOL Attach(HDC *hDC*);

Return Value   Nonzero if the function is successful; otherwise 0.

Parameters   *hDC*   A Windows device context.

Remarks   Use this member function to attach an *hDC* to the **CDC** object. The *hDC* is stored in both **m_hDC**, the output device context, and in **m_hAttribDC**, the attribute device context.

See Also   **CDC::Detach, CDC::m_hDC, CDC::m_hAttribDC**

CDC::BeginPath

BOOL BeginPath( );

Return Value   Nonzero if the function is successful; otherwise 0.

Remarks   Opens a path bracket in the device context. After a path bracket is open, an application can begin calling GDI drawing functions to define the points that lie in the path. An application can close an open path bracket by calling the **EndPath** member function. When an application calls **BeginPath**, any previous paths are discarded.

The following drawing functions define points in a path:

AngleArc	**PolyBezierTo**
Arc	**PolyDraw**
ArcTo	**Polygon**
Chord	**Polyline**
CloseFigure	**PolylineTo**
Ellipse	**PolyPolygon**
ExtTextOut	**PolyPolyline**
LineTo	**Rectangle**
MoveToEx	**RoundRec**
Pie	**TextOut**
PolyBezier	

See Also   **CDC::EndPath, CDC::FillPath, CRgn::CreateFromPath, CDC::SelectClipPath, CDC::StrokeAndFillPath, CDC::StrokePath, CDC::WidenPath, ::BeginPath**

CDC::BitBlt

BOOL BitBlt(int *x***, int** *y***, int** *nWidth***, int** *nHeight***, CDC*** *pSrcDC***, int** *xSrc***, int** *ySrc***, DWORD** *dwRop* **);**

Return Value   Nonzero if the function is successful; otherwise 0.

Parameters   *x*   Specifies the logical x-coordinate of the upper-left corner of the destination rectangle.

y   Specifies the logical y-coordinate of the upper-left corner of the destination rectangle.

nWidth   Specifies the width (in logical units) of the destination rectangle and source bitmap.

nHeight   Specifies the height (in logical units) of the destination rectangle and source bitmap.

pSrcDC   Pointer to a **CDC** object that identifies the device context from which the bitmap will be copied. It must be **NULL** if *dwRop* specifies a raster operation that does not include a source.

xSrc   Specifies the logical x-coordinate of the upper-left corner of the source bitmap.

ySrc   Specifies the logical y-coordinate of the upper-left corner of the source bitmap.

dwRop   Specifies the raster operation to be performed. Raster-operation codes define how the GDI combines colors in output operations that involve a current brush, a possible source bitmap, and a destination bitmap. The following lists raster-operation codes for *dwRop* and their descriptions:

- **BLACKNESS**   Turns all output black.
- **DSTINVERT**   Inverts the destination bitmap.
- **MERGECOPY**   Combines the pattern and the source bitmap using the Boolean AND operator.
- **MERGEPAINT**   Combines the inverted source bitmap with the destination bitmap using the Boolean OR operator.
- **NOTSRCCOPY**   Copies the inverted source bitmap to the destination.
- **NOTSRCERASE**   Inverts the result of combining the destination and source bitmaps using the Boolean OR operator.
- **PATCOPY**   Copies the pattern to the destination bitmap.
- **PATINVERT**   Combines the destination bitmap with the pattern using the Boolean XOR operator.
- **PATPAINT**   Combines the inverted source bitmap with the pattern using the Boolean OR operator. Combines the result of this operation with the destination bitmap using the Boolean OR operator.
- **SRCAND**   Combines pixels of the destination and source bitmaps using the Boolean AND operator.
- **SRCCOPY**   Copies the source bitmap to the destination bitmap.

- **SRCERASE**   Inverts the desination bitmap and combines the result with the source bitmap using the Boolean AND operator.

- **SRCINVERT**   Combines pixels of the destination and source bitmaps using the Boolean XOR operator.

- **SRCPAINT**   Combines pixels of the destination and source bitmaps using the Boolean OR operator.

- **WHITENESS**   Turns all output white.

For a complete list of raster-operation codes, see the Windows Software Development Kit (SDK) documentation.

Remarks

Copies a bitmap from the source device context to this current device context. The application can align the windows or client areas on byte boundaries to ensure that the **BitBlt** operations occur on byte-aligned rectangles. (Set the **CS_BYTEALIGNWINDOW** or **CS_BYTEALIGNCLIENT** flags when you register the window classes.) **BitBlt** operations on byte-aligned rectangles are considerably faster than **BitBlt** operations on rectangles that are not byte aligned. If you want to specify class styles such as byte-alignment for your own device context, you will have to register a window class rather than relying on the Microsoft Foundation classes to do it for you. Use the global function **AfxRegisterWndClass**.

GDI transforms *nWidth* and *nHeight*, once by using the destination device context, and once by using the source device context. If the resulting extents do not match, GDI uses the Windows **StretchBlt** function to compress or stretch the source bitmap as necessary.

If destination, source, and pattern bitmaps do not have the same color format, the **BitBlt** function converts the source and pattern bitmaps to match the destination. The foreground and background colors of the destination bitmap are used in the conversion. When the **BitBlt** function converts a monochrome bitmap to color, it sets white bits (1) to the background color and black bits (0) to the foreground color. The foreground and background colors of the destination device context are used. To convert color to monochrome, **BitBlt** sets pixels that match the background color to white and sets all other pixels to black. **BitBlt** uses the foreground and background colors of the color device context to convert from color to monochrome.

Note that not all device contexts support **BitBlt**. To check whether a given device context does support **BitBlt**, use the **GetDeviceCaps** member function and specify the **RASTERCAPS** index.

See Also

CDC::GetDeviceCaps, CDC::PatBlt, CDC::SetTextColor, CDC::StretchBlt, ::StretchDIBits, ::BitBlt

CDC::CDC

CDC( );

Remarks Constructs a **CDC** object.

See Also **CDC::CreateDC**, **CDC::CreateIC**, **CDC::CreateCompatibleDC**

CDC::Chord

BOOL Chord(int *x1*, **int** *y1*, **int** *x2*, **int** *y2*, **int** *x3*, **int** *y3*, **int** *x4*, **int** *y4* **);**

BOOL Chord(LPCRECT *lpRect*, **POINT** *ptStart*, **POINT** *ptEnd* **);**

Return Value Nonzero if the function is successful; otherwise 0.

Parameters *x1* Specifies the x-coordinate of the upper-left corner of the chord's bounding rectangle (in logical units).

y1 Specifies the y-coordinate of the upper-left corner of the chord's bounding rectangle (in logical units).

x2 Specifies the x-coordinate of the lower-right corner of the chord's bounding rectangle (in logical units).

y2 Specifies the y-coordinate of the lower-right corner of the chord's bounding rectangle (in logical units).

x3 Specifies the x-coordinate of the point that defines the chord's starting point (in logical units).

y3 Specifies the y-coordinate of the point that defines the chord's starting point (in logical units).

x4 Specifies the x-coordinate of the point that defines the chord's endpoint (in logical units).

y4 Specifies the y-coordinate of the point that defines the chord's endpoint (in logical units).

lpRect Specifies the bounding rectangle (in logical units). You can pass either a **LPRECT** or a **CRect** object for this parameter.

ptStart Specifies the x- and y-coordinates of the point that defines the chord's starting point (in logical units). This point does not have to lie exactly on the chord. You can pass either a **POINT** structure or a **CPoint** object for this parameter.

ptEnd   Specifies the x- and y-coordinates of the point that defines the chord's ending point (in logical units). This point does not have to lie exactly on the chord. You can pass either a **POINT** structure or a **CPoint** object for this parameter.

Remarks   Draws a chord (a closed figure bounded by the intersection of an ellipse and a line segment). The (*x1*, *y1*) and (*x2*, *y2*) parameters specify the upper-left and lower-right corners, respectively, of a rectangle bounding the ellipse that is part of the chord. The (*x3*, *y3*) and (*x4*, *y4*) parameters specify the endpoints of a line that intersects the ellipse. The chord is drawn by using the selected pen and filled by using the selected brush. The figure drawn by the **Chord** function extends up to, but does not include the right and bottom coordinates. This means that the height of the figure is *y2* − *y1* and the width of the figure is *x2* − *x1*.

See Also   **CDC::Arc**, **::Chord**, **POINT**

CDC::CloseFigure

BOOL CloseFigure( );

Return Value   Nonzero if the function is successful; otherwise 0.

Remarks   Closes an open figure in a path. The function closes the figure by drawing a line from the current position to the first point of the figure (usually, the point specified by the most recent call to the **MoveTo** member function) and connects the lines by using the line join style. If a figure is closed by using the **LineTo** member function instead of **CloseFigure**, end caps are used to create the corner instead of a join. **CloseFigure** should only be called if there is an open path bracket in the device context.

A figure in a path is open unless it is explicitly closed by using this function. (A figure can be open even if the current point and the starting point of the figure are the same.) Any line or curve added to the path after **CloseFigure** starts a new figure.

See Also   **CDC::BeginPath**, **CDC::EndPath**, **CDC::MoveTo**, **::CloseFigure**

CDC::CreateCompatibleDC

virtual BOOL CreateCompatibleDC(CDC* *pDC*);

Return Value   Nonzero if the function is successful; otherwise 0.

Parameters   *pDC*   A pointer to a device context. If *pDC* is **NULL**, the function creates a memory device context that is compatible with the system display.

Remarks Creates a memory device context that is compatible with the device specified by *pDC*. A memory device context is a block of memory that represents a display surface. It can be used to prepare images in memory before copying them to the actual device surface of the compatible device.

When a memory device context is created, GDI automatically selects a 1-by-1 monochrome stock bitmap for it. GDI output functions can be used with a memory device context only if a bitmap has been created and selected into that context.

This function can only be used to create compatible device contexts for devices that support raster operations. See the **CDC::BitBlt** member function for information regarding bit-block transfers between device contexts. To determine whether a device context supports raster operations, see the **RC_BITBLT** raster capability in the member function **CDC::GetDeviceCaps**.

See Also **CDC::CDC**, **CDC::GetDeviceCaps**, **::CreateCompatibleDC**, **CDC::BitBlt**, **CDC::CreateDC**, **CDC::CreateIC**, **CDC::DeleteDC**

CDC::CreateDC

virtual BOOL CreateDC(LPCTSTR *lpszDriverName*, **LPCTSTR** *lpszDeviceName*, **LPCTSTR** *lpszOutput*, **const void*** *lpInitData* **);**

Return Value Nonzero if the function is successful; otherwise 0.

Parameters *lpszDriverName* Points to a null-terminated string that specifies the filename (without extension) of the device driver (for example, "EPSON"). You can also pass a **CString** object for this parameter.

lpszDeviceName Points to a null-terminated string that specifies the name of the specific device to be supported (for example, "EPSON FX-80"). The *lpszDeviceName* parameter is used if the module supports more than one device. You can also pass a **CString** object for this parameter.

lpszOutput Points to a null-terminated string that specifies the file or device name for the physical output medium (file or output port). You can also pass a **CString** object for this parameter.

lpInitData Points to a **DEVMODE** structure containing device-specific initialization data for the device driver. The Windows **ExtDeviceMode** function retrieves this structure filled in for a given device. The *lpInitData* parameter must be **NULL** if the device driver is to use the default initialization (if any) specified by the user through the Control Panel.

Remarks Creates a device context for the specified device. The PRINT.H header file is required if the **DEVMODE** structure is used.

Device names follow these conventions: an ending colon (:) is recommended, but optional. Windows strips the terminating colon so that a device name ending with a colon is mapped to the same port as the same name without a colon. The driver and port names must not contain leading or trailing spaces. GDI output functions cannot be used with information contexts.

See Also   **::ExtDeviceMode**, **::CreateDC**, **CDC::DeleteDC**, **CDC::CreateIC**

CDC::CreateIC

virtual BOOL CreateIC(LPCTSTR *lpszDriverName*, **LPCTSTR** *lpszDeviceName*, **LPCTSTR** *lpszOutput*, **const void*** *lpInitData* **);**

Return Value   Nonzero if successful; otherwise 0.

Parameters   *lpszDriverName*   Points to a null-terminated string that specifies the filename (without extension) of the device driver (for example, "EPSON"). You can pass a **CString** object for this parameter.

lpszDeviceName   Points to a null-terminated string that specifies the name of the specific device to be supported (for example, "EPSON FX-80"). The *lpszDeviceName* parameter is used if the module supports more than one device. You can pass a **CString** object for this parameter.

lpszOutput   Points to a null-terminated string that specifies the file or device name for the physical output medium (file or port). You can pass a **CString** object for this parameter.

lpInitData   Points to device-specific initialization data for the device driver. The *lpInitData* parameter must be **NULL** if the device driver is to use the default initialization (if any) specified by the user through the Control Panel. See **CreateDC** for the data format for device-specific initialization.

Remarks   Creates an information context for the specified device. The information context provides a fast way to get information about the device without creating a device context.

Device names follow these conventions: an ending colon (:) is recommended, but optional. Windows strips the terminating colon so that a device name ending with a colon is mapped to the same port as the same name without a colon. The driver and port names must not contain leading or trailing spaces. GDI output functions cannot be used with information contexts.

See Also   **CDC::CreateDC**, **::CreateIC**, **CDC::DeleteDC**

CDC::DeleteDC

virtual BOOL DeleteDC( );

Return Value   Nonzero if the function completed successfully; otherwise 0.

Remarks   In general, do not call this function; the destructor will do it for you. The **DeleteDC** member function deletes the Windows device contexts that are associated with **m_hDC** in the current **CDC** object. If this **CDC** object is the last active device context for a given device, the device is notified and all storage and system resources used by the device are released. An application should not call **DeleteDC** if objects have been selected into the device context. Objects must first be selected out of the device context before it it is deleted. An application must not delete a device context whose handle was obtained by calling **CWnd::GetDC**. Instead, it must call **CWnd::ReleaseDC** to free the device context. The **CClientDC** and **CWindowDC** classes are provided to wrap this functionality. The **DeleteDC** function is generally used to delete device contexts created with **CreateDC**, **CreateIC**, or **CreateCompatibleDC**.

See Also   **CDC::CDC, ::DeleteDC, CDC::CreateDC, CDC::CreateIC, CDC::CreateCompatibleDC, CWnd::GetDC, CWnd::ReleaseDC**

CDC::DeleteTempMap

static void PASCAL DeleteTempMap( );

Remarks   Called automatically by the **CWinApp** idle-time handler, **DeleteTempMap** deletes any temporary **CDC** objects created by **FromHandle**, but does not destroy the device context handles (**HDCs**) temporarily associated with the **CDC** objects.

See Also   **CDC::Detach, CDC::FromHandle, CWinApp::OnIdle**

CDC::Detach

HDC Detach( );

Return Value   A Windows device context.

Remarks   Call this function to detach **m_hDC** (the output device context) from the **CDC** object and set both **m_hDC** and **m_hAttribDC** to **NULL**.

See Also   **CDC::Attach, CDC::m_hDC, CDC::m_hAttribDC**

CDC::DPtoHIMETRIC

void DPtoHIMETRIC(LPSIZE *lpSize* **) const;**

Parameters   *lpSize*   Points to a **SIZE** structure or **CSize** object.

Remarks   Use this function when you give **HIMETRIC** sizes to OLE, converting pixels to **HIMETRIC**.

If the mapping mode of the device context object is **MM_LOENGLISH**, **MM_HIENGLISH**, **MM_LOMETRIC** or **MM_HIMETRIC**, then the conversion is based on the number of pixels in the physical inch. If the mapping mode is one of the other non-constrained modes (e.g., **MM_TEXT**), then the conversion is based on the number of pixels in the logical inch.

See Also   **CDC::DPtoLP, CDC::LPtoDP, CDC::HIMETRICtoLP, CDC::HIMETRICtoDP, CDC::LPtoHIMETRIC**

CDC::DPtoLP

void DPtoLP(LPPOINT *lpPoints*, **int** *nCount* = **1**) **const;**

void DPtoLP(LPRECT *lpRect*) **const;**

void DPtoLP(LPSIZE *lpSize*) **const;**

Parameters *lpPoints* Points to an array of **POINT** structures or **CPoint** objects.

nCount The number of points in the array.

lpRect Points to a **RECT** structure or **CRect** object. This parameter is used for the simple case of converting one rectangle from device points to logical points.

lpSize Points to a **SIZE** structure or **CSize** object.

Remarks   Converts device units into logical units. The function maps the coordinates of each point, or dimension of a size, from the device coordinate system into GDI's logical coordinate system. The conversion depends on the current mapping mode and the settings of the origins and extents for the device's window and viewport.

See Also   **CDC::LPtoDP, CDC::HIMETRICtoDP, ::DPtoLP, POINT, RECT, CDC::GetWindowExt, CDC::GetWindowOrg**

CDC::DrawEscape

int DrawEscape(int *nEscape*, **int** *nInputSize*, **LPCSTR** *lpszInputData*);

Return Value Specifies the outcome of the function. Greater than zero if successful, except for the **QUERYESCSUPPORT** draw escape, which checks for implementation only; or zero if the escape is not implemented; or less than zero if an error occurred.

Parameters *nEscape* Specifies the escape function to be performed.

nInputSize Specifies the number of bytes of data pointed to by the *lpszInputData* parameter.

lpszInputData   Points to the input structure required for the specified escape.

Remarks   Accesses drawing capabilities of a video display that are not directly available through the graphics device interface (GDI). When an application calls **DrawEscape**, the data identified by *nInputSize* and *lpszInputData* is passed directly to the specified display driver.

See Also   **CDC::Escape**, **::DrawEscape**

CDC::DrawFocusRect

void DrawFocusRect(LPCRECT *lpRect* **);**

Parameters   *lpRect*   Points to a **RECT** structure or a **CRect** object that specifies the logical coordinates of the rectangle to be drawn.

Remarks   Draws a rectangle in the style used to indicate that the rectangle has the focus. Since this is a Boolean XOR function, calling this function a second time with the same rectangle removes the rectangle from the display. The rectangle drawn by this function cannot be scrolled. To scroll an area containing a rectangle drawn by this function, first call **DrawFocusRect** to remove the rectangle from the display, then scroll the area, and then call **DrawFocusRect** again to draw the rectangle in the new position.

See Also   **CDC::FrameRect**, **::DrawFocusRect**, **RECT**

CDC::DrawIcon

BOOL DrawIcon(int *x*, **int** *y*, **HICON** *hIcon* **);**

BOOL DrawIcon(POINT *point*, **HICON** *hIcon* **);**

Return Value   Nonzero if the function completed successfully; otherwise 0.

Parameters   *x*   Specifies the logical x-coordinate of the upper-left corner of the icon.

y   Specifies the logical y-coordinate of the upper-left corner of the icon.

hIcon   Identifies the handle of the icon to be drawn.

point   Specifies the logical x- and y-coordinates of the upper-left corner of the icon. You can pass a **POINT** structure or a **CPoint** object for this parameter.

Remarks   Draws an icon on the device represented by the current **CDC** object. The function places the icon's upper-left corner at the location specified by *x* and *y*. The location is subject to the current mapping mode of the device context. The icon resource must have been previously loaded by using the functions **CWinApp::LoadIcon**, **CWinApp::LoadStandardIcon**, or **CWinApp::LoadOEMIcon**. The **MM_TEXT** mapping mode must be selected prior to using this function.

See Also   CWinApp::LoadIcon, CWinApp::LoadStandardIcon,
CWinApp::LoadOEMIcon, CDC::GetMapMode, CDC::SetMapMode,
::DrawIcon, POINT

CDC::DrawText

virtual int DrawText(LPCTSTR *lpszString*, **int** *nCount*, **LPRECT** *lpRect*,
UINT *nFormat* **);**

Return Value   The height of the text if the function is successful.

Parameters   *lpszString*   Points to the string to be drawn. If *nCount* is –1, the string must be
null-terminated.

nCount   Specifies the number of bytes in the string. If *nCount* is –1, then
lpszString is assumed to be a long pointer to a null-terminated string and
DrawText computes the character count automatically.

lpRect   Points to a **RECT** structure or **CRect** object that contains the rectangle (in
logical coordinates) in which the text is to be formatted.

nFormat   Specifies the method of formatting the text. It can be any combination of
the following values (combine using the bitwise OR operator):

- **DT_BOTTOM**   Specifies bottom-justified text. This value must be
combined with **DT_SINGLELINE**.

- **DT_CALCRECT**   Determines the width and height of the rectangle. If
there are multiple lines of text, **DrawText** will use the width of the rectangle
pointed to by *lpRect* and extend the base of the rectangle to bound the last
line of text. If there is only one line of text, **DrawText** will modify the right
side of the rectangle so that it bounds the last character in the line. In either
case, **DrawText** returns the height of the formatted text but does not draw
the text.

- **DT_CENTER**   Centers text horizontally.

- **DT_EXPANDTABS**   Expands tab characters. The default number of
characters per tab is eight.

- **DT_EXTERNALLEADING**   Includes the font's external leading in the
line height. Normally, external leading is not included in the height of a line
of text.

- **DT_LEFT**   Aligns text flush-left.

- **DT_NOCLIP**   Draws without clipping. **DrawText** is somewhat faster
when **DT_NOCLIP** is used.

- **DT_NOPREFIX**   Turns off processing of prefix characters. Normally,
DrawText interprets the ampersand (**&**) mnemonic-prefix character as a
directive to underscore the character that follows, and the two-ampersand

(**&&**) mnemonic-prefix characters as a directive to print a single ampersand. By specifying **DT_NOPREFIX** this processing is turned off.

- **DT_RIGHT**   Aligns text flush-right.

- **DT_SINGLELINE**   Specifies single line only. Carriage returns and linefeeds do not break the line.

- **DT_TABSTOP**   Sets tab stops. The high-order byte of *nFormat* is the number of characters for each tab. The default number of characters per tab is eight.

- **DT_TOP**   Specifies top-justified text (single line only).

- **DT_VCENTER**   Specifies vertically centered text (single line only).

- **DT_WORDBREAK**   Specifies word-breaking. Lines are automatically broken between words if a word would extend past the edge of the rectangle specified by *lpRect*. A carriage return–linefeed sequence will also break the line.

Note that the values **DT_CALCRECT**, **DT_EXTERNALLEADING**, **DT_INTERNAL**, **DT_NOCLIP**, and **DT_NOPREFIX** cannot be used with the **DT_TABSTOP** value.

Remarks   Draws formatted text in the rectangle specified by *lpRect*. It formats text by expanding tabs into appropriate spaces, aligning text to the left, right, or center of the given rectangle, and breaking text into lines that fit within the given rectangle. The type of formatting is specified by *nFormat*. This member function uses the device context's selected font, text color, and background color to draw the text. Unless the **DT_NOCLIP** format is used, **DrawText** clips the text so that the text does not appear outside the given rectangle. All formatting is assumed to have multiple lines unless the **DT_SINGLELINE** format is given. If the selected font is too large for the specified rectangle, the **DrawText** member function does not attempt to substitute a smaller font.

If the **DT_CALCRECT** flag is specified, the rectangle specified by *lpRect* will be updated to reflect the width and height needed to draw the text.

If the **TA_UPDATECP** text-alignment flag has been set (see **CDC::SetTextAlign**), **DrawText** will display text starting at the current position, rather than at the left of the given rectangle. **DrawText** will not wrap text when the **TA_UPDATECP** flag has been set (that is, the **DT_WORDBREAK** flag will have no effect).

The text color may be set by **CDC::SetTextColor**.

See Also   CDC::SetTextColor, CDC::ExtTextOut, CDC::TabbedTextOut, CDC::TextOut, ::DrawText, RECT, CDC::SetTextAlign

CDC::Ellipse

BOOL Ellipse(int *x1***, int** *y1***, int** *x2***, int** *y2* **);**

BOOL Ellipse(LPCRECT *lpRect* **);**

Return Value   Nonzero if the function is successful; otherwise 0.

Parameters   *x1*   Specifies the logical x-coordinate of the upper-left corner of the ellipse's bounding rectangle.

y1   Specifies the logical y-coordinate of the upper-left corner of the ellipse's bounding rectangle.

x2   Specifies the logical x-coordinate of the lower-right corner of the ellipse's bounding rectangle.

y2   Specifies the logical y-coordinate of the lower-right corner of the ellipse's bounding rectangle.

lpRect   Specifies the ellipse's bounding rectangle. You can also pass a **CRect** object for this parameter.

Remarks   Draws an ellipse. The center of the ellipse is the center of the bounding rectangle specified by *x1*, *y1*, *x2*, and *y2*, or *lpRect*. The ellipse is drawn with the current pen and its interior is filled with the current brush. The figure drawn by this function extends up to but does not include the right and bottom coordinates. This means that the height of the figure is $y2 - y1$ and the width of the figure is $x2 - x1$. If either the width or the height of the bounding rectangle is 0, no ellipse is drawn.

See Also   **CDC::Arc**, **CDC::Chord**, **::Ellipse**

CDC::EndDoc

int EndDoc( );

Return Value   Greater than or equal to 0 if the function is successful, or a negative value if an error occurred. The following list shows common error values:

- **SP_ERROR**   General error.
- **SP_OUTOFDISK**   Not enough disk space is currently available for spooling, and no more space will become available.
- **SP_OUTOFMEMORY**   Not enough memory is available for spooling.
- **SP_USERABORT**   User ended the job through the Print Manager.

Remarks   Ends a print job started by a call to the **StartDoc** member function. This member function replaces the **ENDDOC** printer escape, and should be called immediately after finishing a successful print job. If an application encounters a printing error or a canceled print operation, it must not attempt to terminate the operation by using either **EndDoc** or **AbortDoc**. GDI automatically terminates the operation before returning the error value.

This function should not be used inside metafiles.

When used with Windows version 3.0, this member function sends the **ENDDOC** escape.

See Also   **CDC::AbortDoc, CDC::Escape, CDC::StartDoc**

CDC::EndPage

int EndPage( );

Return Value   Greater than or equal to 0 if successful; otherwise it is an error value, which can be one of the following:

- **SP_ERROR**   General error.
- **SP_APPABORT**   Job was ended because the application's abort function returned 0.
- **SP_USERABORT**   User ended the job through Print Manager.
- **SP_OUTOFDISK**   Not enough disk space is currently available for spooling, and no more space will become available.
- **SP_OUTOFMEMORY**   Not enough memory is available for spooling.

Remarks   Informs the device that the application has finished writing to a page. This member function is typically used to direct the device driver to advance to a new page. This member function replaces the **NEWFRAME** printer escape. Unlike **NEWFRAME**, this function is always called after printing a page.

When used with Windows version 3.0, this member function sends the **NEWFRAME** escape.

See Also   **CDC::StartPage, CDC::StartDoc, CDC::Escape**

CDC::EndPath

BOOL EndPath( );

Return Value   Nonzero if the function is successful; otherwise 0.

Remarks   Closes a path bracket and selects the path defined by the bracket into the device context.

See Also   **CDC::BeginPath**

CDC::EnumObjects

int EnumObjects(int *nObjectType***, int (CALLBACK EXPORT*** *lpfn* **)(**
LPVOID, LPARAM), LPARAM *lpData* **);**

Return Value   Specifies the last value returned by the callback function. Its meaning is user-defined. For more information about the callback function, see the section "Callback Function for CDC::EnumObjects" on page 1256.

Parameters   *nObjectType*   Specifies the object type. It can have the values **OBJ_BRUSH** or **OBJ_PEN**.

lpfn   Is the procedure-instance address of the application-supplied callback function. See the "Remarks" section below.

lpData   Points to the application-supplied data. The data is passed to the callback function along with the object information.

Remarks   Enumerates the pens and brushes available in a device context. For each object of a given type, the callback function that you pass is called with the information for that object. The system calls the callback function until there are no more objects or the callback function returns 0.

Note that new features of Microsoft Visual C++ let you use an ordinary function as the function passed to **EnumObjects**. The address passed to **EnumObjects** is a pointer to a function exported with **EXPORT** and with the Pascal calling convention. In protect-mode applications, you do not have to create this function with the Windows **MakeProcInstance** function or free the function after use with the **FreeProcInstance** Windows function. You also do not have to export the function name in an **EXPORTS** statement in your application's module-definition file. You can instead use the **EXPORT** function modifier, as in

int CALLBACK EXPORT AFunction(**LPSTR, LPSTR**);

to cause the compiler to emit the proper export record for export by name without aliasing. This works for most needs. For some special cases, such as exporting a function by ordinal or aliasing the export, you still need to use an **EXPORTS** statement in a module-definition file.

For compiling Microsoft Foundation programs, you will normally use the /GA and /GEs compiler options. The /Gw compiler option is not used with the Microsoft Foundation classes. (If you do use the Windows function **MakeProcInstance**, you will need to explicitly cast the returned function pointer from **FARPROC** to the type needed in this API.) Callback registration interfaces are now type-safe (you must pass in a function pointer that points to the right kind of function for the specific callback).

Also note that all callback functions must trap Microsoft Foundation exceptions before returning to Windows, since exceptions cannot be thrown across callback boundaries. For more information about exceptions, see the article "Exceptions" in *Programming with the Microsoft Foundation Class Library*.

See Also   **::EnumObjects**

CDC::Escape

virtual int Escape(int *nEscape*, **int** *nCount*, **LPCSTR** *lpszInData*, **LPVOID** *lpOutData* **);**

int ExtEscape(int *nEscape*, **int** *nInputSize*, **LPCSTR** *lpszInputData*, **int** *nOutputSize*, **LPSTR** *lpszOutputData* **);**

Return Value   Positive if the function is successful, except for the **QUERYESCSUPPORT** escape, which only checks for implementation. Zero is returned if the escape is not implemented, and a negative value is returned if an error occurred. The following are common error values:

- **SP_ERROR**   General error.
- **SP_OUTOFDISK**   Not enough disk space is currently available for spooling, and no more space will become available.
- **SP_OUTOFMEMORY**   Not enough memory is available for spooling.
- **SP_USERABORT**   User ended the job through the Print Manager.

Parameters   *nEscape*   Specifies the escape function to be performed.

For a complete list of escape functions, see the information on printer escapes in the Windows Software Development Kit documentation.

nCount   Specifies the number of bytes of data pointed to by *lpszInData*.

lpszInData   Points to the input data structure required for this escape.

lpOutData   Points to the structure that is to receive output from this escape. The *lpOutData* parameter is **NULL** if no data is returned.

nInputSize   Specifies the number of bytes of data pointed to by the *lpszInputData* parameter.

lpszInputData   Points to the input structure required for the specified escape.

nOutputSize   Specifies the number of bytes of data pointed to by the *lpszOutputData* parameter.

lpszOutputData   Points to the structure that receives output from this escape. This parameter should be **NULL** if no data is returned.

Remarks   Allows applications to access facilities of a particular device that are not directly available through GDI. Use the first version of **Escape** to pass a driver-defined escape value to a device. Use the second version of **Escape** to pass one of the escape values defined by Windows to a device. Escape calls made by an application are translated and sent to the device driver. The *nEscape* parameter specifies the escape function to be performed. For possible values, see the information on printer escapes in the Windows SDK documentation. See Also

CDC::StartDoc, **CDC::StartPage**, **CDC::EndPage**, **CDC::SetAbortProc**, **CDC::AbortDoc**, **CDC::EndDoc**, **CDC::GetDeviceCaps**, **::ExtEscape**, **::Escape**

CDC::ExcludeClipRect

virtual int ExcludeClipRect(int *x1*, **int** *y1*, **int** *x2*, **int** *y2* **);**

virtual int ExcludeClipRect(LPCRECT *lpRect* **);**

Return Value   Specifies the new clipping region's type. It can be any of the following values:

- **COMPLEXREGION**   The region has overlapping borders.
- **ERROR**   No region was created.
- **NULLREGION**   The region is empty.
- **SIMPLEREGION**   The region has no overlapping borders.

Parameters   *x1*   Specifies the logical x-coordinate of the upper-left corner of the rectangle.

y1   Specifies the logical y-coordinate of the upper-left corner of the rectangle.

x2   Specifies the logical x-coordinate of the lower-right corner of the rectangle.

y2   Specifies the logical y-coordinate of the lower-right corner of the rectangle.

lpRect   Specifies the rectangle. Can also be a **CRect** object.

Remarks   Creates a new clipping region that consists of the existing clipping region minus the specified rectangle. The width of the rectangle, specified by the absolute value of $x2 - x1$, must not exceed 32,767 units. This limit applies to the height of the rectangle as well.

See Also   **CDC::ExcludeUpdateRgn**, **::ExcludeClipRect**

CDC::ExcludeUpdateRgn

int ExcludeUpdateRgn(CWnd* *pWnd* **);**

Return Value   The type of excluded region. It can be any one of the following values:

- **COMPLEXREGION**   The region has overlapping borders.
- **ERROR**   No region was created.
- **NULLREGION**   The region is empty.
- **SIMPLEREGION**   The region has no overlapping borders.

Parameters   *pWnd*   Points to the window object whose window is being updated.

Remarks   Prevents drawing within invalid areas of a window by excluding an updated region in the window from the clipping region associated with the **CDC** object.

See Also   **CDC::ExcludeClipRect**, **::ExcludeUpdateRgn**

CDC::ExtFloodFill

BOOL ExtFloodFill(int *x*, **int** *y*, **COLORREF** *crColor*, **UINT** *nFillType* **);**

Return Value   Nonzero if the function is successful; otherwise 0 if the filling could not be completed, if the given point has the boundary color specified by *crColor* (if **FLOODFILLBORDER** was requested), if the given point does not have the color specified by *crColor* (if **FLOODFILLSURFACE** was requested), or if the point is outside the clipping region.

Parameters   *x*   Specifies the logical x-coordinate of the point where filling begins.

y   Specifies the logical y-coordinate of the point where filling begins.

crColor   Specifies the color of the boundary or of the area to be filled. The interpretation of *crColor* depends on the value of *nFillType*.

nFillType   Specifies the type of flood fill to be performed. It must be either of the following values:

- **FLOODFILLBORDER**   The fill area is bounded by the color specified by *crColor*. This style is identical to the filling performed by **FloodFill**.
- **FLOODFILLSURFACE**   The fill area is defined by the color specified by *crColor*. Filling continues outward in all directions as long as the color is encountered. This style is useful for filling areas with multicolored boundaries.

Remarks   Fills an area of the display surface with the current brush. This member function offers more flexibility than **FloodFill** because you can specify a fill type in *nFillType*.

If *nFillType* is set to **FLOODFILLBORDER**, the area is assumed to be completely bounded by the color specified by *crColor*. The function begins at the point specified by *x* and *y* and fills in all directions to the color boundary.

If *nFillType* is set to **FLOODFILLSURFACE**, the function begins at the point specified by *x* and *y* and continues in all directions, filling all adjacent areas containing the color specified by *crColor*.

Only memory-device contexts and devices that support raster-display technology support **ExtFloodFill**. For more information, see the **GetDeviceCaps** member function.

See Also   **CDC::FloodFill**, **CDC::GetDeviceCaps**, **::ExtFloodFill**

CDC::ExtTextOut

virtual BOOL ExtTextOut(int *x*, **int** *y*, **UINT** *nOptions*, **LPCRECT** *lpRect*, **LPCTSTR** *lpszString*, **UINT** *nCount*, **LPINT** *lpDxWidths* **);**

Return Value   Nonzero if the function is successful; otherwise 0.

Parameters   *x*   Specifies the logical x-coordinate of the character cell for the first character in the specified string.

y   Specifies the logical y-coordinate of the character cell for the first character in the specified string.

nOptions   Specifies the rectangle type. This parameter can be one, both, or neither of the following values:

- **ETO_CLIPPED**   Specifies that text is clipped to the rectangle.
- **ETO_OPAQUE**   Specifies that the current background color fills the rectangle. (You can set and query the current background color with the **SetBkColor** and **GetBkColor** member functions).

lpRect   Points to a **RECT** structure that determines the dimensions of the rectangle. This parameter can be **NULL**. You can also pass a **CRect** object for this parameter.

lpszString   Points to the specified character string. You can also pass a **CString** object for this parameter.

nCount   Specifies the number of characters in the string.

lpDxWidths   Points to an array of values that indicate the distance between origins of adjacent character cells. For instance, *lpDxWidths*[*i*] logical units will separate the origins of character cell *i* and character cell *i* + 1. If *lpDxWidths* is **NULL**, **ExtTextOut** uses the default spacing between characters.

Remarks   Writes a character string within a rectangular region using the currently selected font. The rectangular region can be opaque (filled with the current background color) and it can be a clipping region.

If *nOptions* is 0 and *lpRect* is **NULL**, the function writes text to the device context without using a rectangular region. By default, the current position is not used or updated by the function. If an application needs to update the current position when it calls **ExtTextOut**, the application can call the **CDC** member function **SetTextAlign** with *nFlags* set to **TA_UPDATECP**. When this flag is set, Windows ignores *x* and *y* on subsequent calls to **ExtTextOut** and uses the current position instead. When an application uses **TA_UPDATECP** to update the current position, **ExtTextOut** sets the current position either to the end of the previous line of text or to the position specified by the last element of the array pointed to by *lpDxWidths*, whichever is greater.

See Also   **CDC::SetTextAlign**, **CDC::TabbedTextOut**, **CDC::TextOut**, **CDC::GetBkColor**, **CDC::SetBkColor**, **CDC::SetTextColor**, **::ExtTextOut**, **RECT**

CDC::FillPath

BOOL FillPath( );

Return Value   Nonzero if the function is successful; otherwise 0.

Remarks   Closes any open figures in the current path and fills the path's interior by using the current brush and polygon-filling mode. After its interior is filled, the path is discarded from the device context.

See Also   **CDC::BeginPath**, **CDC::SetPolyFillMode**, **CDC::StrokeAndFillPath**, **CDC::StrokePath**, **::FillPath**

CDC::FillRect

void FillRect(LPCRECT *lpRect*, CBrush* *pBrush*);

Parameters   *lpRect*   Points to a **RECT** structure that contains the logical coordinates of the rectangle to be filled. You can also pass a **CRect** object for this parameter.

pBrush   Identifies the brush used to fill the rectangle.

Remarks   Fills a given rectangle using the specified brush. The function fills the complete rectangle, including the left and top borders, but it does not fill the right and bottom borders.

The brush needs to either be created using the **CBrush** member functions **CreateHatchBrush**, **CreatePatternBrush**, and **CreateSolidBrush**, or retrieved by the **GetStockObject** Windows function. When filling the specified rectangle, **FillRect** does not include the rectangle's right and bottom sides. GDI fills a rectangle up to, but does not include, the right column and bottom row, regardless of the current mapping mode. **FillRect** compares the values of the **top**, **bottom**,

left, and **right** members of the specified rectangle. If **bottom** is less than or equal to **top**, or if **right** is less than or equal to **left**, the rectangle is not drawn.

See Also   **CBrush::CreateHatchBrush**, **CBrush::CreatePatternBrush**, **CBrush::CreateSolidBrush**, **::FillRect**, **::GetStockObject**, **RECT**, **CBrush**

CDC::FillRgn

BOOL FillRgn(CRgn* *pRgn*, **CBrush*** *pBrush* **);**

Return Value   Nonzero if the function is successful; otherwise 0.

Parameters   *pRgn*   A pointer to the region to be filled. The coordinates for the given region are specified in device units.

pBrush   Identifies the brush to be used to fill the region.

Remarks   Fills the region specified by *pRgn* with the brush specified by *pBrush*.

The brush must either be created using the **CBrush** member functions **CreateHatchBrush**, **CreatePatternBrush**, **CreateSolidBrush**, or be retrieved by **GetStockObject**.

See Also   **CDC::PaintRgn**, **CDC::FillRect**, **CBrush**, **CRgn**, **::FillRgn**

CDC::FlattenPath

BOOL FlattenPath( );

Return Value   Nonzero if the function is successful; otherwise 0.

Remarks   Transforms any curves in the path selected into the current device context, and turns each curve into a sequence of lines.

See Also   **CDC::WidenPath**

CDC::FloodFill

BOOL FloodFill(int *x*, **int** *y*, **COLORREF** *crColor* **);**

Return Value   Nonzero if the function is successful; otherwise 0 is returned if the filling could not be completed, the given point has the boundary color specified by *crColor*, or the point is outside the clipping region.

Parameters   *x*   Specifies the logical x-coordinate of the point where filling begins.

y   Specifies the logical y-coordinate of the point where filling begins.

crColor   Specifies the color of the boundary.

Remarks   Fills an area of the display surface with the current brush. The area is assumed to be bounded as specified by *crColor*. The **FloodFill** function begins at the point specified by *x* and *y* and continues in all directions to the color boundary. Only memory-device contexts and devices that support raster-display technology support the **FloodFill** member function. For information about **RC_BITBLT** capability, see the **GetDeviceCaps** member function. The **ExtFloodFill** function provides similar capability but greater flexibility.

See Also   **CDC::ExtFloodFill, CDC::GetDeviceCaps, ::FloodFill**

CDC::FrameRect

void FrameRect(LPCRECT *lpRect*, **CBrush*** *pBrush* **);**

Parameters   *lpRect*   Points to a **RECT** structure or **CRect** object that contains the logical coordinates of the upper-left and lower-right corners of the rectangle. You can also pass a **CRect** object for this parameter.

pBrush   Identifies the brush to be used for framing the rectangle.

Remarks   Draws a border around the rectangle specified by *lpRect*. The function uses the given brush to draw the border. The width and height of the border is always 1 logical unit. If the rectangle's **bottom** coordinate is less than or equal to **top**, or if **right** is less than or equal to **left**, the rectangle is not drawn. The border drawn by **FrameRect** is in the same position as a border drawn by the **Rectangle** member function using the same coordinates (if **Rectangle** uses a pen that is 1 logical unit wide). The interior of the rectangle is not filled by **FrameRect**.

See Also   **CBrush, CDC::Rectangle, CDC::FrameRgn, ::FrameRect, RECT**

CDC::FrameRgn

BOOL FrameRgn(CRgn* *pRgn*, **CBrush*** *pBrush*, **int** *nWidth*, **int** *nHeight* **);**

Return Value   Nonzero if the function is successful; otherwise 0.

Parameters   *pRgn*   Points to the **CRgn** object that identifies the region to be enclosed in a border. The coordinates for the given region are specified in device units.

pBrush   Points to the **CBrush** object that identifies the brush to be used to draw the border.

nWidth   Specifies the width of the border in vertical brush strokes in device units (or logical units if running with Windows versions 3.0 and earlier).

nHeight   Specifies the height of the border in horizontal brush strokes in device units (or logical units if running with Windows versions 3.0 and earlier).

Remarks   Draws a border around the region specified by *pRgn* using the brush specified by *pBrush*.

See Also   **CDC::Rectangle, CDC::FrameRect, CBrush, CRgn, ::FrameRgn**

CDC::FromHandle

static CDC* PASCAL FromHandle(HDC *hDC* **);**

Return Value The pointer may be temporary and should not be stored beyond immediate use.

Parameters   *hDC*   Contains a handle to a Windows device context.

Remarks   Returns a pointer to a **CDC** object when given a handle to a device context. If a **CDC** object is not attached to the handle, a temporary **CDC** object is created and attached.

See Also   **CDC::DeleteTempMap**

CDC::GetArcDirection

int GetArcDirection( ) const;

Return Value Specifies the current arc direction, if successful. Following are the valid return values:

- **AD_COUNTERCLOCKWISE**   Arcs and rectangles drawn counterclockwise.
- **AD_CLOCKWISE**   Arcs and rectangles drawn clockwise.

If an error occurs, the return value is zero.

Remarks   Returns the current arc direction for the device context. Arc and rectangle functions use the arc direction.

See Also   **CDC::SetArcDirection, ::GetArcDirection**

CDC::GetAspectRatioFilter

CSize GetAspectRatioFilter( ) const;

Return Value A **CSize** object representing the aspect ratio used by the current aspect ratio filter.

Remarks   Retrieves the setting for the current aspect-ratio filter. The aspect ratio is the ratio formed by a device's pixel width and height. Information about a device's aspect ratio is used in the creation, selection, and display of fonts. Windows provides a special filter, the aspect-ratio filter, to select fonts designed for a particular aspect ratio from all of the available fonts. The filter uses the aspect ratio specified by the **SetMapperFlags** member function.

See Also   CDC::SetMapperFlags, ::GetAspectRatioFilter, CSize

CDC::GetBkColor

COLORREF GetBkColor( ) const;

Return Value   An RGB color value.

Remarks   Returns the current background color. If the background mode is **OPAQUE**, the system uses the background color to fill the gaps in styled lines, the gaps between hatched lines in brushes, and the background in character cells. The system also uses the background color when converting bitmaps between color and monochrome device contexts.

See Also   CDC::GetBkMode, CDC::SetBkColor, CDC::SetBkMode, ::GetBkColor

CDC::GetBkMode

int GetBkMode( ) const;

Return Value   The current background mode, which can be **OPAQUE**, **TRANSPARENT**, or **TRANSPARENT1**.

Remarks   Returns the background mode. The background mode defines whether the system removes existing background colors on the drawing surface before drawing text, hatched brushes, or any pen style that is not a solid line.

See Also   CDC::GetBkColor, CDC::SetBkColor, CDC::SetBkMode, ::GetBkMode

CDC::GetBoundsRect

UINT GetBoundsRect(LPRECT *lpRectBounds*, **UINT** *flags* **);**

Return Value   Specifies the current state of the bounding rectangle if the function is successful. It can be a combination of the following values:

- **DCB_ACCUMULATE**   Bounding rectangle accumulation is occurring.
- **DCB_RESET**   Bounding rectangle is empty.
- **DCB_SET**   Bounding rectangle is not empty.
- **DCB_ENABLE**   Bounding accumulation is on.
- **DCB_DISABLE**   Bounding accumulation is off.

Parameters

lpRectBounds   Points to a buffer that will receive the current bounding rectangle. The rectangle is returned in logical coordinates.

flags   Specifies whether the bounding rectangle is to be cleared after it is returned. This parameter can be either of the following values:

- **DCB_RESET**   Forces the bounding rectangle to be cleared after it is returned.
- **DCB_WINDOWMGR**   Queries the Windows bounding rectangle instead of the application's.

Remarks

Returns the current accumulated bounding rectangle for the specified device context.

See Also

CDC::SetBoundsRect, **::GetBoundsRect**

CDC::GetBrushOrg

CPoint GetBrushOrg( ) const;

Return Value

The current origin of the brush (in device units) as a **CPoint** object.

Remarks

Retrieves the origin (in device units) of the brush currently selected for the device context. The initial brush origin is at (0,0) of the client area. The return value specifies this point in device units relative to the origin of the desktop window.

See Also

CDC::SetBrushOrg, **::GetBrushOrg**, **CPoint**

CDC::GetCharABCWidths

BOOL GetCharABCWidths(UINT *nFirstChar*, **UINT** *nLastChar*, **LPABC** *lpabc*) **const;**

BOOL GetCharABCWidths(UINT *nFirstChar*, **UINT** *nLastChar*, **LPABCFLOAT** *lpABCF*) **const;**

Return Value

Nonzero if the function is successful; otherwise 0.

Parameters

nFirstChar   Specifies the first character in the range of characters from the current font for which character widths are returned.

nLastChar   Specifies the last character in the range of characters from the current font for which character widths are returned.

lpabc   Points to an array of **ABC** structures that receive the character widths when the function returns. This array must contain at least as many **ABC** structures as there are characters in the range specified by the *nFirstChar* and *nLastChar* parameters.

lpABCF   Points to an application-supplied buffer with an array of **ABCFLOAT** structures to receive the character widths when the function returns. The widths returned by this function are in the IEEE floating-point format.

Remarks   Retrieves the widths of consecutive characters in a specified range from the current TrueType font. The widths are returned in logical units. This function succeeds only with TrueType fonts.

The TrueType rasterizer provides "ABC" character spacing after a specific point size has been selected. "A" spacing is the distance that is added to the current position before placing the glyph. "B" spacing is the width of the black part of the glyph. "C" spacing is added to the current position to account for the white space to the right of the glyph. The total advanced width is given by A + B + C.

When the **GetCharABCWidths** member function retrieves negative "A" or "C" widths for a character, that character includes underhangs or overhangs.

To convert the ABC widths to font design units, an application should create a font whose height (as specified in the **lfHeight** member of the **LOGFONT** structure) is equal to the value stored in the **ntmSizeEM** member of the **NEWTEXTMETRIC** structure. (The value of the **ntmSizeEM** member can be retrieved by calling the **EnumFontFamilies** Windows function.)

The ABC widths of the default character are used for characters that are outside the range of the currently selected font. To retrieve the widths of characters in non-TrueType fonts, applications should use the **GetCharWidth** member function.

See Also   **::EnumFontFamilies, CDC::GetCharWidth, ::GetCharABCWidths, ::GetCharABCWidthsFloat, ::GetCharWidthFloat, ::EnumFontFamilies, ::GetCharABCWidths**

CDC::GetCharWidth

BOOL GetCharWidth(UINT *nFirstChar*, **UINT** *nLastChar*, **LPINT** *lpBuffer* **) const;**

BOOL GetCharWidth(UINT *nFirstChar*, **UINT** *nLastChar*, **float*** *lpFloatBuffer* **) const;**

Return Value   Nonzero if the function is successful; otherwise 0.

Parameters   *nFirstChar*   Specifies the first character in a consecutive group of characters in the current font.

nLastChar   Specifies the last character in a consecutive group of characters in the current font.

lpBuffer   Points to a buffer that will receive the width values for a consecutive group of characters in the current font.

lpFloatBuffer   Points to a buffer to receive the character widths. The returned widths are in the 32-bit IEEE floating-point format. (The widths are measured along the base line of the characters.)

Remarks   Retrieves the widths of individual characters in a consecutive group of characters from the current font, using **m_hAttribDC**, the input device context. For example, if *nFirstChar* identifies the letter 'a' and *nLastChar* identifies the letter 'z', the function retrieves the widths of all lowercase characters. The function stores the values in the buffer pointed to by *lpBuffer*. This buffer must be large enough to hold all of the widths. That is, there must be at least 26 entries in the example given. If a character in the consecutive group of characters does not exist in a particular font, it will be assigned the width value of the default character.

See Also   **CDC::GetOutputCharWidth, CDC::m_hAttribDC, CDC::m_hDC, CDC::GetCharABCWidths, ::GetCharWidth, ::GetCharABCWidths, ::GetCharABCWidthsFloat, ::GetCharWidthFloat**

CDC::GetClipBox

virtual int GetClipBox(LPRECT *lpRect* **) const;**

Return Value   The clipping region's type. It can be any of the following values:

- **COMPLEXREGION**   Clipping region has overlapping borders.
- **ERROR**   Device context is not valid.
- **NULLREGION**   Clipping region is empty.
- **SIMPLEREGION**   Clipping region has no overlapping borders.

Parameters   *lpRect*   Points to the **RECT** structure or **CRect** object that is to receive the rectangle dimensions.

Remarks   Retrieves the dimensions of the tightest bounding rectangle around the current clipping boundary. The dimensions are copied to the buffer pointed to by *lpRect*.

See Also   **CDC::SelectClipRgn, ::GetClipBox, RECT**

CDC::GetColorAdjustment

BOOL GetColorAdjustment(LPCOLORADJUSTMENT *lpColorAdjust*) const;

Return Value   Nonzero if the function is successful; otherwise 0.

Parameters   *lpColorAdjust*   Points to a **COLORADJUSTMENT** data structure to receive the color adjustment values.

Remarks   Retrieves the color adjustment values for the device context.

See Also   CDC::SetColorAdjustment

CDC::GetCurrentBitmap

CBitmap* GetCurrentBitmap( ) const;

Return Value   Pointer to a **CBitmap** object, if successful; otherwise **NULL**.

Remarks   Returns a pointer to the currently selected **CBitmap** object. This member function may return temporary objects.

See Also   CDC::SelectObject, ::GetCurrentObject

CDC::GetCurrentBrush

CBrush* GetCurrentBrush( ) const;

Return Value   Pointer to a **CBrush** object, if successful; otherwise **NULL**.

Remarks   Returns a pointer to the currently selected **CBrush** object. This member function may return temporary objects.

See Also   CDC::SelectObject, ::GetCurrentObject

CDC::GetCurrentFont

CFont* GetCurrentFont( ) const;

Return Value   Pointer to a **CFont** object, if successful; otherwise **NULL**.

Remarks   Returns a pointer to the currently selected **CFont** object. This member function may return temporary objects.

See Also   CDC::SelectObject, ::GetCurrentObject

CDC::GetCurrentPalette

CPalette* GetCurrentPalette( ) const;

Return Value   Pointer to a **CPalette** object, if successful; otherwise **NULL**.

Remarks   Returns a pointer to the currently selected **CPalette** object. This member function may return temporary objects.

See Also   **CDC::SelectObject**, **::GetCurrentObject**

CDC::GetCurrentPen

CPen* GetCurrentPen( ) const;

Return Value   Pointer to a **CPen** object, if successful; otherwise **NULL**.

Remarks   Returns a pointer to the currently selected **CPen** object. This member function may return temporary objects.

See Also   **CDC::SelectObject**, **::GetCurrentObject**

CDC::GetCurrentPosition

CPoint GetCurrentPosition( ) const;

Return Value   The current position as a **CPoint** object.

Remarks   Retrieves the current position (in logical coordinates). The current position can be set with the **MoveTo** member function.

See Also   **CDC::MoveTo**, **CPoint**, **::GetCurrentPosition**

CDC::GetDeviceCaps

int GetDeviceCaps(int *nIndex*) const;

Return Value   The value of the requested capability if the function is successful.

Parameters   *nIndex*   Specifies the type of information to return. It can be any one of the following values:

- **DRIVERVERSION**   Version number; for example, 0x100 for 1.0.
- **TECHNOLOGY**   Device technology. It can be any one of the following:

Value	Meaning
DT_PLOTTER	Vector plotter
DT_RASDISPLAY	Raster display
DT_RASPRINTER	Raster printer
DT_RASCAMERA	Raster camera
DT_CHARSTREAM	Character stream
DT_METAFILE	Metafile
DT_DISPFILE	Display file

- **HORZSIZE**   Width of the physical display (in millimeters).
- **VERTSIZE**   Height of the physical display (in millimeters).
- **HORZRES**   Width of the display (in pixels).
- **VERTRES**   Height of the display (in raster lines).
- **LOGPIXELSX**   Number of pixels per logical inch along the display width.
- **LOGPIXELSY**   Number of pixels per logical inch along the display height.
- **BITSPIXEL**   Number of adjacent color bits for each pixel.
- **PLANES**   Number of color planes.
- **NUMBRUSHES**   Number of device-specific brushes.
- **NUMPENS**   Number of device-specific pens.
- **NUMFONTS**   Number of device-specific fonts.
- **NUMCOLORS**   Number of entries in the device's color table.
- **ASPECTX**   Relative width of a device pixel as used for line drawing.
- **ASPECTY**   Relative height of a device pixel as used for line drawing.
- **ASPECTXY**   Diagonal width of the device pixel as used for line drawing.
- **PDEVICESIZE**   Size of the **PDEVICE** internal data structure.
- **CLIPCAPS**   Clipping capabilities of the device. It can be one of the following:

Value	Meaning
CP_NONE	Output is not clipped.
CP_RECTANGLE	Output is clipped to rectangles.
CP_REGION	Output is clipped to regions.

- **SIZEPALETTE**   Number of entries in the system palette. This index is valid only if the device driver sets the **RC_PALETTE** bit in the **RASTERCAPS** index. It is available only if the driver is written for Windows version 3.0 or later.

- **NUMRESERVED**   Number of reserved entries in the system palette. This index is valid only if the device driver sets the **RC_PALETTE** bit in the **RASTERCAPS** index and is available only if the driver is written for Windows version 3.0 or later.

- **COLORRES**   Actual color resolution of the device in bits per pixel. This index is valid only if the device driver sets the **RC_PALETTE** bit in the **RASTERCAPS** index and is available only if the driver is written for Windows version 3.0 or later.

- **RASTERCAPS**   Value that indicates the raster capabilities of the device. It can be a combination of the following:

Value	Meaning
RC_BANDING	Requires banding support.
RC_BIGFONT	Supports fonts larger than 64K.
RC_BITBLT	Capable of transferring bitmaps.
RC_BITMAP64	Supports bitmaps larger than 64K.
RC_DEVBITS	Supports device bitmaps.
RC_DI_BITMAP	Capable of supporting the **SetDIBits** and **GetDIBits** Windows functions.
RC_DIBTODEV	Capable of supporting the **SetDIBitsToDevice** Windows function.
RC_FLOODFILL	Capable of performing flood fills.
RC_GDI20_OUTPUT	Capable of supporting Windows version 2.0 features.
RC_GDI20_STATE	Includes a state block in the device context.
RC_NONE	Supports no raster operations.
RC_OP_DX_OUTPUT	Supports dev opaque and DX array.
RC_PALETTE	Specifies a palette-based device.
RC_SAVEBITMAP	Capable of saving bitmaps locally.
RC_SCALING	Capable of scaling.
RC_STRETCHBLT	Capable of performing the **StretchBlt** member function.
RC_STRETCHDIB	Capable of performing the **StretchDIBits** Windows function.

- **CURVECAPS**   The curve capabilities of the device. It can be a combination of the following:

Value	Meaning
CC_NONE	Supports curves.
CC_CIRCLES	Supports circles.
CC_PIE	Supports pie wedges.
CC_CHORD	Supports chords.
CC_ELLIPSES	Supports ellipses.
CC_WIDE	Supports wide borders.
CC_STYLED	Supports styled borders.
CC_WIDESTYLED	Supports wide, styled borders.
CC_INTERIORS	Supports interiors.
CC_ROUNDRECT	Supports rectangles with rounded corners.

- **LINECAPS**   Line capabilities the device supports. It can be a combination of the following:

Value	Meaning
LC_NONE	Supports no lines.
LC_POLYLINE	Supports polylines.
LC_MARKER	Supports markers.
LC_POLYMARKER	Supports polymarkers.
LC_WIDE	Supports wide lines.
LC_STYLED	Supports styled lines.
LC_WIDESTYLED	Supports wide, styled lines.
LC_INTERIORS	Supports interiors.

- **POLYGONALCAPS**   Polygonal capabilities the device supports. It can be a combination of the following:

Value	Meaning
PC_NONE	Supports no polygons.
PC_POLYGON	Supports alternate fill polygons.
PC_RECTANGLE	Supports rectangles.
PC_WINDPOLYGON	Supports winding number fill polygons.
PC_SCANLINE	Supports scan lines.
PC_WIDE	Supports wide borders.
PC_STYLED	Supports styled borders.
PC_WIDESTYLED	Supports wide, styled borders.
PC_INTERIORS	Supports interiors.

- **TEXTCAPS** Text capabilities the device supports. It can be a combination of the following:

Value	Meaning
TC_OP_CHARACTER	Supports character output precision, which indicates the device can place device fonts at any pixel location. This is required for any device with device fonts.
TC_OP_STROKE	Supports stroke output precision, which indicates the device can omit any stroke of a device font.
TC_CP_STROKE	Supports stroke clip precision, which indicates the device can clip device fonts to a pixel boundary.
TC_CR_90	Supports 90-degree character rotation, which indicates the device can rotate characters only 90 degrees at a time.
TC_CR_ANY	Supports character rotation at any degree, which indicates the device can rotate device fonts through any angle.
TC_SF_X_YINDEP	Supports scaling independent of x and y directions, which indicates the device can scale device fonts separately in x and y directions.
TC_SA_DOUBLE	Supports doubled characters for scaling, which indicates the device can double the size of device fonts.
TC_SA_INTEGER	Supports integer multiples for scaling, which indicates the device can scale the size of device fonts in any integer multiple.
TC_SA_CONTIN	Supports any multiples for exact scaling, which indicates the device can scale device fonts by any amount but still preserve the x and y ratios.
TC_EA_DOUBLE	Supports double-weight characters, which indicates the device can make device fonts bold. If this bit is not set for printer drivers, GDI attempts to create bold device fonts by printing them twice.
TC_IA_ABLE	Supports italics, which indicates the device can make device fonts italic. If this bit is not set, GDI assumes italics are not available.
TC_UA_ABLE	Supports underlining, which indicates the device can underline device fonts. If this bit is not set, GDI creates underlines for device fonts.
TC_SO_ABLE	Supports strikeouts, which indicates the device can strikeout device fonts. If this bit is not set, GDI creates strikeouts for device fonts.

TC_RA_ABLE	Supports raster fonts, which indicates that GDI should enumerate any raster or TrueType fonts available for this device in response to a call to the **EnumFonts** or **EnumFontFamilies** Windows functions. If this bit is not set, GDI-supplied raster or TrueType fonts are not enumerated when these functions are called.
TC_VA_ABLE	Supports vector fonts, which indicates that GDI should enumerate any vector fonts available for this device in response to a call to the **EnumFonts** or **EnumFontFamilies** Windows functions. This is significant for vector devices only (that is, for plotters). Display drivers (which must be able to use raster fonts) and raster printer drivers always enumerate vector fonts, because GDI rasterizes vector fonts before sending them to the driver.
TC_RESERVED	Reserved; must be 0.

Remarks   Retrieves a wide range of device-specific information about the display device.

See Also   **::GetDeviceCaps**

CDC::GetFontData

DWORD GetFontData(DWORD *dwTable*, DWORD *dwOffset*, LPVOID *lpData*, DWORD *cbData*) const;

Return Value   Specifies the number of bytes returned in the buffer pointed to by *lpData* if the function is successful; otherwise −1.

Parameters   *dwTable*   Specifies the name of the metric table to be returned. This parameter can be one of the metric tables documented in the TrueType Font Files specification published by Microsoft Corporation. If this parameter is 0, the information is retrieved starting at the beginning of the font file.

dwOffset   Specifies the offset from the beginning of the table at which to begin retrieving information. If this parameter is 0, the information is retrieved starting at the beginning of the table specified by the *dwTable* parameter. If this value is greater than or equal to the size of the table, **GetFontData** returns 0.

lpData   Points to a buffer that will receive the font information. If this value is **NULL**, the function returns the size of the buffer required for the font data specified in the *dwTable* parameter.

cbData   Specifies the length, in bytes, of the information to be retrieved. If this parameter is 0, **GetFontData** returns the size of the data specified in the *dwTable* parameter.

Remarks   Retrieves font-metric information from a scalable font file. The information to retrieve is identified by specifying an offset into the font file and the length of the information to return. An application can sometimes use the **GetFontData** member function to save a TrueType font with a document. To do this, the application determines whether the font can be embedded and then retrieves the entire font file, specifying 0 for the *dwTable*, *dwOffset*, and *cbData* parameters.

Applications can determine whether a font can be embedded by checking the **otmfsType** member of the **OUTLINETEXTMETRIC** structure. If bit 1 of **otmfsType** is set, embedding is not permitted for the font. If bit 1 is clear, the font can be embedded. If bit 2 is set, the embedding is read only. If an application attempts to use this function to retrieve information for a non-TrueType font, the **GetFontData** member function returns –1.

See Also   **CDC::GetOutlineTextMetrics**, **::GetFontData**, **OUTLINETEXTMETRIC**

CDC::GetGlyphOutline

DWORD GetGlyphOutline(UINT *nChar*, **UINT** *nFormat*,
    LPGLYPHMETRICS *lpgm*, **DWORD** *cbBuffer*, **LPVOID** *lpBuffer*, **const
    MAT2 FAR*** *lpmat2* **) const;**

Return Value   The size, in bytes, of the buffer required for the retrieved information if *cbBuffer* is 0 or *lpBuffer* is **NULL**. Otherwise, it is a positive value if the function is successful, or –1 if there is an error.

Parameters   *nChar*   Specifies the character for which information is to be returned.

nFormat   Specifies the format in which the function is to return information. It can be one of the following values, or 0:

Value	Meaning
GGO_BITMAP	Returns the glyph bitmap. When the function returns, the buffer pointed to by *lpBuffer* contains a 1-bit-per-pixel bitmap whose rows start on doubleword boundaries.
GGO_NATIVE	Returns the curve data points in the rasterizer's native format, using device units. When this value is specified, any transformation specified in *lpmat2* is ignored.

When the value of *nFormat* is 0, the function fills in a **GLYPHMETRICS** structure but does not return glyph-outline data.

lpgm   Points to a **GLYPHMETRICS** structure that describes the placement of the glyph in the character cell.

cbBuffer   Specifies the size of the buffer into which the function copies information about the outline character. If this value is 0 and the *nFormat* parameter is either the **GGO_BITMAP** or **GGO_NATIVE** values, the function returns the required size of the buffer.

lpBuffer   Points to a buffer into which the function copies information about the outline character. If *nFormat* specifies the **GGO_NATIVE** value, the information is copied in the form of **TTPOLYGONHEADER** and **TTPOLYCURVE** structures. If this value is **NULL** and *nFormat* is either the **GGO_BITMAP** or **GGO_NATIVE** value, the function returns the required size of the buffer.

lpmat2   Points to a **MAT2** structure that contains a transformation matrix for the character. This parameter cannot be **NULL**, even when the **GGO_NATIVE** value is specified for *nFormat*.

Remarks   Retrieves the outline curve or bitmap for an outline character in the current font. An application can rotate characters retrieved in bitmap format by specifying a 2-by-2 transformation matrix in the structure pointed to by *lpmat2*.

A glyph outline is returned as a series of contours. Each contour is defined by a **TTPOLYGONHEADER** structure followed by as many **TTPOLYCURVE** structures as are required to describe it. All points are returned as **POINTFX** structures and represent absolute positions, not relative moves. The starting point given by the **pfxStart** member of the **TTPOLYGONHEADER** structure is the point at which the outline for a contour begins. The **TTPOLYCURVE** structures that follow can be either polyline records or spline records. Polyline records are a series of points; lines drawn between the points describe the outline of the character. Spline records represent the quadratic curves used by TrueType (that is, quadratic b-splines).

See Also   **CDC::GetOutlineTextMetrics**, **::GetGlyphOutline**, **GLYPHMETRICS**, **TTPOLYGONHEADER**, **TTPOLYCURVE**

CDC::GetKerningPairs

int GetKerningPairs(int *nPairs***, LPKERNINGPAIR** *lpkrnpair* **) const;**

Return Value   Specifies the number of kerning pairs retrieved or the total number of kerning pairs in the font, if the function is successful. Zero is returned if the function fails or there are no kerning pairs for the font.

Parameters   *nPairs*   Specifies the number of **KERNINGPAIR** structures pointed to by *lpkrnpair*. The function will not copy more kerning pairs than specified by *nPairs*.

lpkrnpair   Points to an array of **KERNINGPAIR** structures that receive the kerning pairs when the function returns. This array must contain at least as many structures as specified by *nPairs*. If this parameter is **NULL**, the function returns the total number of kerning pairs for the font.

Remarks   Retrieves the character kerning pairs for the font that is currently selected in the specified device context.

See Also   **::GetKerningPairs**, **KERNINGPAIR**

CDC::GetMapMode

int GetMapMode( ) const;

Return Value   The mapping mode.

Remarks   Retrieves the current mapping mode. See the **SetMapMode** member function for a description of the mapping modes.

See Also   **CDC::SetMapMode**, **::GetMapMode**

CDC::GetMiterLimit

float GetMiterLimit( ) const;

Return Value   Nonzero if the function is successful; otherwise 0.

Remarks   Returns the miter limit for the device context. The miter limit is used when drawing geometric lines that have miter joins.

See Also   **CDC::SetMiterLimit**, **::GetMiterLimit**

CDC::GetNearestColor

COLORREF GetNearestColor(COLORREF *crColor*) const;

Return Value   An RGB (red, green, blue) color value that defines the solid color closest to the *crColor* value that the device can represent.

Parameters   *crColor*   Specifies the color to be matched.

Remarks   Returns the solid color that best matches a specified logical color. The given device must be able to represent this color.

See Also   **::GetNearestColor**, **CPalette::GetNearestPaletteIndex**

CDC::GetOutlineTextMetrics

Protected→
UINT GetOutlineTextMetrics(UINT *cbData*, LPOUTLINETEXTMETRIC *lpotm*) const;
END Protected

Return Value   Nonzero if the function is successful; otherwise 0.

Parameters   *cbData*   Specifies the size, in bytes, of the buffer to which information is returned.

lpotm   Points to an **OUTLINETEXTMETRIC** structure. If this parameter is **NULL**, the function returns the size of the buffer required for the retrieved metric information.

Remarks   Retrieves metric information for TrueType fonts. The **OUTLINETEXTMETRIC** structure contains most of the font metric information provided with the TrueType format, including a **TEXTMETRIC** structure. The last four members of the **OUTLINETEXTMETRIC** structure are pointers to strings. Applications should allocate space for these strings in addition to the space required for the other members. Because there is no system-imposed limit to the size of the strings, the simplest method for allocating memory is to retrieve the required size by specifying **NULL** for *lpotm* in the first call to the **GetOutlineTextMetrics** function.

See Also   **::GetTextMetrics**, **::GetOutlineTextMetrics**, **CDC::GetTextMetrics**

CDC::GetOutputCharWidth

BOOL GetOutputCharWidth(UINT *nFirstChar*, **UINT** *nLastChar*, **LPINT** *lpBuffer* **) const;**

Return Value   Nonzero if the function is successful; otherwise 0.

Parameters   *nFirstChar*   Specifies the first character in a consecutive group of characters in the current font.

nLastChar   Specifies the last character in a consecutive group of characters in the current font.

lpBuffer   Points to a buffer that will receive the width values for a consecutive group of characters in the current font.

Remarks   Uses the output device context, **m_hDC**, and retrieves the widths of individual characters in a consecutive group of characters from the current font. For example, if *nFirstChar* identifies the letter 'a' and *nLastChar* identifies the letter 'z', the function retrieves the widths of all lowercase characters. The function stores the values in the buffer pointed to by *lpBuffer*. This buffer must be large enough to hold all of the widths; that is, there must be at least 26 entries in the example given. If a character in the consecutive group of characters does not exist in a particular font, it will be assigned the width value of the default character.

See Also   **CDC::GetCharWidth**, **CDC::m_hAttribDC**, **CDC::m_hDC**, **::GetCharWidth**

CDC::GetOutputTabbedTextExtent

CSize GetOutputTabbedTextExtent(LPCTSTR *lpszString***, int** *nCount***, int** *nTabPositions***, LPINT** *lpnTabStopPositions* **) const;**

Return Value   The dimensions of the string (in logical units).

Parameters   *lpszString*   Points to a character string. You can also pass a **CString** object for this parameter.

nCount   Specifies the number of characters in the string.

nTabPositions   Specifies the number of tab-stop positions in the array pointed to by *lpnTabStopPositions*.

lpnTabStopPositions   Points to an array of integers containing the tab-stop positions in logical units. The tab stops must be sorted in increasing order; the smallest x-value should be the first item in the array. Back tabs are not allowed.

Remarks   Computes the width and height of a character string using **m_hDC**, the output device context. If the string contains one or more tab characters, the width of the string is based upon the tab stops specified by *lpnTabStopPositions*. The function uses the currently selected font to compute the dimensions of the string. The current clipping region does not offset the width and height returned by the **GetOutputTabbedTextExtent** function.

Since some devices do not place characters in regular cell arrays (that is, they kern the characters), the sum of the extents of the characters in a string may not be equal to the extent of the string.

If *nTabPositions* is 0 and *lpnTabStopPositions* is **NULL**, tabs are expanded to eight average character widths. If *nTabPositions* is 1, the tab stops will be separated by the distance specified by the first value in the array to which *lpnTabStopPositions* points. If *lpnTabStopPositions* points to more than a single value, a tab stop is set for each value in the array, up to the number specified by *nTabPositions*.

See Also   **CDC::GetTextExtent, CDC::m_hAttribDC, CDC::m_hDC, CDC::GetTabbedTextExtent, CDC::GetOutputTextExtent, CDC::TabbedTextOut, ::GetTabbedTextExtent, CSize**

CDC::GetOutputTextExtent

CSize GetOutputTextExtent(LPCTSTR *lpszString***, int** *nCount* **) const;**

Return Value   The dimensions of the string (in logical units) returned in a **CSize** object.

| Parameters | *lpszString*   Points to a string of characters. You can also pass a **CString** object for this parameter. |

Parameters

lpszString   Points to a string of characters. You can also pass a **CString** object for this parameter.

nCount   Specifies the number of characters in the string.

Remarks

This member function uses the output device context, **m_hDC**, and computes the width and height of a line of text, using the current font. The current clipping region does not affect the width and height returned by **GetOutputTextExtent**.

Since some devices do not place characters in regular cell arrays (that is, they carry out kerning), the sum of the extents of the characters in a string may not be equal to the extent of the string.

See Also

CDC::GetTabbedTextExtent, **CDC::m_hAttribDC**, **CDC::m_hDC**, **CDC::GetTextExtent**, **::GetTextExtent**, **CDC::SetTextJustification**, **CSize**

CDC::GetOutputTextMetrics

BOOL GetOutputTextMetrics(LPTEXTMETRIC *lpMetrics* **) const;**

Return Value

Nonzero if the function is successful; otherwise 0.

Parameters

lpMetrics   Points to the **TEXTMETRIC** structure that receives the metrics.

Remarks

Retrieves the metrics for the current font using **m_hDC**, the output device context.

See Also

CDC::GetTextAlign, **CDC::m_hAttribDC**, **CDC::m_hDC**, **CDC::GetTextMetrics**, **CDC::GetTextExtent**, **CDC::GetTextFace**, **CDC::SetTextJustification**, **::GetTextMetrics**

CDC::GetPath

int GetPath(LPPOINT *lpPoints*, **LPBYTE** *lpTypes*, **int** *nCount* **) const;**

Return Value

If the *nCount* parameter is nonzero, the number of points enumerated. If *nCount* is 0, the total number of points in the path (and **GetPath** writes nothing to the buffers). If *nCount* is nonzero and is less than the number of points in the path, the return value is -1.

Parameters

lpPoints   Points to an array of **POINT** data structures or **CPoint** objects where the line endpoints and curve control points are placed.

lpTypes   Points to an array of bytes where the vertex types are placed. Values are one of the following:

- **PT_MOVETO**   Specifies that the corresponding point in *lpPoints* starts a disjoint figure.
- **PT_LINETO**   Specifies that the previous point and the corresponding point in *lpPoints* are the endpoints of a line.

- **PT_BEZIERTO**   Specifies that the corresponding point in *lpPoints* is a control point or ending point for a Bézier curve.

PT_BEZIERTO types always occur in sets of three. The point in the path immediately preceding them defines the starting point for the Bézier curve. The first two **PT_BEZIERTO** points are the control points, and the third **PT_BEZIERTO** point is the end point (if hard-coded).

A **PT_LINETO** or **PT_BEZIERTO** type may be combined with the following flag (by using the bitwise operator **OR**) to indicate that the corresponding point is the last point in a figure and that the figure should be closed:

- **PT_CLOSEFIGURE**   Specifies that the figure is automatically closed after the corresponding line or curve is drawn. The figure is closed by drawing a line from the line or curve endpoint to the point corresponding to the last **PT_MOVETO**.

nCount   Specifies the total number of **POINT** data structures that may be placed in the *lpPoints* array. This value must be the same as the number of bytes that may be placed in the *lpTypes* array.

Remarks   Retrieves the coordinates defining the endpoints of lines and the control points of curves found in the path that is selected into the device context. The device context must contain a closed path. The points of the path are returned in logical coordinates. Points are stored in the path in device coordinates, so **GetPath** changes the points from device coordinates to logical coordinates by using the inverse of the current transformation. The **FlattenPath** member function may be called before **GetPath**, to convert all curves in the path into line segments.

See Also   **CDC::FlattenPath, CDC::PolyDraw, CDC::WidenPath**

CDC::GetPixel

COLORREF GetPixel(int *x*, int *y*) const;

COLORREF GetPixel(POINT *point*) const;

Return Value   For either version of the function, an RGB color value for the color of the given point. It is –1 if the coordinates do not specify a point in the clipping region.

Parameters   *x*   Specifies the logical x-coordinate of the point to be examined.

y   Specifies the logical y-coordinate of the point to be examined.

point   Specifies the logical x- and y-coordinates of the point to be examined.

Remarks   Retrieves the RGB color value of the pixel at the point specified by *x* and *y*. The point must be in the clipping region. If the point is not in the clipping region, the function has no effect and returns –1. Not all devices support the **GetPixel** function.

For more information, see the **RC_BITBLT** raster capability under the **GetDeviceCaps** member function.

The **GetPixel** member function has two forms. The first takes two coordinate values; the second takes either a **POINT** structure or a **CPoint** object.

See Also   **CDC::GetDeviceCaps, CDC::SetPixel, ::GetPixel, POINT, CPoint**

CDC::GetPolyFillMode

int GetPolyFillMode( ) const;

Return Value   The current polygon-filled mode, **ALTERNATE** or **WINDING**, if the function is successful.

Remarks   Retrieves the current polygon-filling mode. See the **SetPolyFillMode** member function for a description of the polygon-filling modes.

See Also   **CDC::SetPolyFillMode, ::GetPolyFillMode**

CDC::GetROP2

int GetROP2( ) const;

Return Value   The drawing mode. For a list of the drawing mode values, see the **SetROP2** member function.

Remarks   Retrieves the current drawing mode. The drawing mode specifies how the colors of the pen and the interior of filled objects are combined with the color already on the display surface.

See Also   **CDC::GetDeviceCaps, CDC::SetROP2, ::GetROP2**

CDC::GetSafeHdc

HDC GetSafeHdc( ) const;

Return Value   A device context handle.

Remarks   Call this member function to get **m_hDC**, the output device context. This member function also works with null pointers.

CDC::GetStretchBltMode

int GetStretchBltMode( ) const;

Return Value   The return value specifies the current bitmap-stretching mode— **STRETCH_ANDSCANS, STRETCH_DELETESCANS**, or **STRETCH_ORSCANS**—if the function is successful.

Remarks   Retrieves the current bitmap-stretching mode. The bitmap-stretching mode defines how information is removed from bitmaps that are stretched or compressed by the **StretchBlt** member function. The **STRETCH_ANDSCANS** and **STRETCH_ORSCANS** modes are typically used to preserve foreground pixels in monochrome bitmaps. The **STRETCH_DELETESCANS** mode is typically used to preserve color in color bitmaps.

See Also   **CDC::StretchBlt**, **CDC::SetStretchBltMode**, **::GetStretchBltMode**

CDC::GetTabbedTextExtent

CSize GetTabbedTextExtent(LPCTSTR *lpszString*, **int** *nCount*, **int** *nTabPositions*, **LPINT** *lpnTabStopPositions*) **const;**

Return Value   The dimensions of the string (in logical units).

Parameters   *lpszString*   Points to a character string. You can also pass a **CString** object for this parameter.

nCount   Specifies the number of characters in the string.

nTabPositions   Specifies the number of tab-stop positions in the array pointed to by *lpnTabStopPositions*.

lpnTabStopPositions   Points to an array of integers containing the tab-stop positions in logical units. The tab stops must be sorted in increasing order; the smallest x-value should be the first item in the array. Back tabs are not allowed.

Remarks   Computes the width and height of a character string using **m_hAttribDC**, the attribute device context. If the string contains one or more tab characters, the width of the string is based upon the tab stops specified by *lpnTabStopPositions*. The function uses the currently selected font to compute the dimensions of the string. The current clipping region does not offset the width and height returned by the **GetTabbedTextExtent** function.

Since some devices do not place characters in regular cell arrays (that is, they kern the characters), the sum of the extents of the characters in a string may not be equal to the extent of the string.

If *nTabPositions* is 0 and *lpnTabStopPositions* is **NULL**, tabs are expanded to eight times the average character width. If *nTabPositions* is 1, the tab stops will be separated by the distance specified by the first value in the array to which *lpnTabStopPositions* points. If *lpnTabStopPositions* points to more than a single value, a tab stop is set for each value in the array, up to the number specified by *nTabPositions*.

See Also   CDC::GetTextExtent, CDC::GetOutputTabbedTextExtent,
CDC::GetOutputTextExtent, CDC::TabbedTextOut,
::GetTabbedTextExtent, CSize

CDC::GetTextAlign

UINT GetTextAlign( ) const;

Return Value   The status of the text-alignment flags. The return value is one or more of the following values:

- **TA_BASELINE**   Specifies alignment of the x-axis and the baseline of the chosen font within the bounding rectangle.
- **TA_BOTTOM**   Specifies alignment of the x-axis and the bottom of the bounding rectangle.
- **TA_CENTER**   Specifies alignment of the y-axis and the center of the bounding rectangle.
- **TA_LEFT**   Specifies alignment of the y-axis and the left side of the bounding rectangle.
- **TA_NOUPDATECP**   Specifies that the current position is not updated.
- **TA_RIGHT**   Specifies alignment of the y-axis and the right side of the bounding rectangle.
- **TA_TOP**   Specifies alignment of the x-axis and the top of the bounding rectangle.
- **TA_UPDATECP**   Specifies that the current position is updated.

Remarks   Retrieves the status of the text-alignment flags for the device context. The text-alignment flags determine how the **TextOut** and **ExtTextOut** member functions align a string of text in relation to the string's starting point. The text-alignment flags are not necessarily single-bit flags and may be equal to 0. To test whether a flag is set, an application should follow these steps:

1. Apply the bitwise OR operator to the flag and its related flags, grouped as follows:
   - **TA_LEFT, TA_CENTER**, and **TA_RIGHT**
   - **TA_BASELINE, TA_BOTTOM**, and **TA_TOP**
   - **TA_NOUPDATECP** and **TA_UPDATECP**

2. Apply the bitwise-AND operator to the result and the return value of **GetTextAlign**.

3. Test for the equality of this result and the flag.

See Also   CDC::ExtTextOut, CDC::SetTextAlign, CDC::TextOut, ::GetTextAlign

CDC::GetTextCharacterExtra

int GetTextCharacterExtra( ) const;

Return Value The amount of the intercharacter spacing.

Remarks Retrieves the current setting for the amount of intercharacter spacing. GDI adds this spacing to each character, including break characters, when it writes a line of text to the device context. The default value for the amount of intercharacter spacing is 0.

See Also **CDC::SetTextCharacterExtra, ::GetTextCharacterExtra**

CDC::GetTextColor

COLORREF GetTextColor( ) const;

Return Value The current text color as an RGB color value.

Remarks Retrieves the current text color. The text color is the foreground color of characters drawn by using the GDI text-output member functions **TextOut**, **ExtTextOut**, and **TabbedTextOut**.

See Also **CDC::GetBkColor, CDC::GetBkMode, CDC::SetBkMode, CDC::SetTextColor, ::GetTextColor**

CDC::GetTextExtent

CSize GetTextExtent(LPCTSTR *lpszString*, **int** *nCount* **) const;**

Return Value The dimensions of the string (in logical units) in a **CSize** object.

Parameters *lpszString*   Points to a string of characters. You can also pass a **CString** object for this parameter.

nCount   Specifies the number of characters in the string.

Remarks Computes the width and height of a line of text using the current font to determine the dimensions. The information is retrieved from **m_hAttribDC**, the attribute device context. The current clipping region does not affect the width and height returned by **GetTextExtent**.

Since some devices do not place characters in regular cell arrays (that is, they carry out kerning), the sum of the extents of the characters in a string may not be equal to the extent of the string.

See Also **CDC::GetTabbedTextExtent, CDC::m_hAttribDC, CDC::m_hDC, CDC::GetOutputTextExtent, ::GetTextExtent, CDC::SetTextJustification, CSize**

CDC::GetTextFace

int GetTextFace(int *nCount*, LPTSTR *lpszFacename*) **const;**

Return Value
The number of bytes copied to the buffer, not including the terminating null character. It is 0 if an error occurs.

Parameters
nCount   Specifies the size of the buffer (in bytes). If the typeface name is longer than the number of bytes specified by this parameter, the name is truncated.

lpszFacename   Points to the buffer for the typeface name.

Remarks
Copies the typeface name of the current font into a buffer. The typeface name is copied as a null-terminated string.

See Also
CDC::GetTextMetrics, CDC::SetTextAlign, CDC::TextOut, ::GetTextFace

CDC::GetTextMetrics

BOOL GetTextMetrics(LPTEXTMETRIC *lpMetrics*) **const;**

Return Value
Nonzero if the function is successful; otherwise 0.

Parameters
lpMetrics   Points to the **TEXTMETRIC** structure that receives the metrics.

Remarks
Retrieves the metrics for the current font using the attribute device context.

See Also
CDC::GetTextAlign, CDC::m_hAttribDC, CDC::m_hDC, CDC::GetOutputTextMetrics, CDC::GetTextExtent, CDC::GetTextFace, CDC::SetTextJustification, ::GetTextMetrics

CDC::GetViewportExt

CSize GetViewportExt( ) **const;**

Return Value
The x- and y-extents (in device units) as a **CSize** object.

Remarks
Retrieves the x- and y-extents of the device context's viewport.

See Also
CDC::SetViewportExt, CSize, ::GetViewportExt, CDC::SetWindowExt

CDC::GetViewportOrg

CPoint GetViewportOrg( ) **const;**

Return Value
The origin of the viewport (in device coordinates) as a **CPoint** object.

Remarks
Retrieves the x- and y-coordinates of the origin of the viewport associated with the device context.

See Also	CDC::GetWindowOrg, CPoint, ::GetViewportOrg, CDC::SetViewportOrg

CDC::GetWindow

CWnd* GetWindow( ) const;

Return Value   Pointer to a **CWnd** object if successful; otherwise **NULL**.

Remarks   Returns the window associated with the display device context. This is an advanced function. For example, this member function may not return the view window when printing or in print preview. It always returns the window associated with output. Output functions that use the given DC draw into this window.

See Also   **CWnd::GetDC**, **CWnd::GetWindowDC**, **::GetWindow**

CDC::GetWindowExt

CSize GetWindowExt( ) const;

Return Value   The x- and y-extents (in logical units) as a **CSize** object.

Remarks   Retrieves the x- and y-extents of the window associated with the device context.

See Also   **CDC::SetWindowExt**, **CSize**, **::GetWindowExt**, **CDC::GetViewportExt**

CDC::GetWindowOrg

CPoint GetWindowOrg( ) const;

Return Value   The origin of the window (in logical coordinates) as a **CPoint** object.

Remarks   Retrieves the x- and y-coordinates of the origin of the window associated with the device context.

See Also   **CDC::GetViewportOrg**, **CDC::SetWindowOrg**, **CPoint**, **::GetWindowOrg**

CDC::GrayString

virtual BOOL GrayString(CBrush* *pBrush***, BOOL (CALLBACK EXPORT*** *lpfnOutput* **)(HDC, LPARAM, int), LPARAM** *lpData***, int** *nCount***, int** *x***, int** *y***, int** *nWidth***, int** *nHeight* **);**

Return Value   Nonzero if the string is drawn, or 0 if either the **TextOut** function or the application-supplied output function returned 0, or if there was insufficient memory to create a memory bitmap for dimming.

Parameters   *pBrush*   Identifies the brush to be used for dimming (graying).

lpfnOutput   Specifies the procedure-instance address of the application-supplied callback function that will draw the string. For more information, see the description of the Windows **OutputFunc** callback function in the section "Callback Function for CDC::Gray String" on page ???. If this parameter is **NULL,** the system uses the Windows **TextOut** function to draw the string, and *lpData* is assumed to be a long pointer to the character string to be output.

lpData   Specifies a far pointer to data to be passed to the output function. If *lpfnOutput* is **NULL,** *lpData* must be a long pointer to the string to be output.

nCount   Specifies the number of characters to be output. If this parameter is 0, **GrayString** calculates the length of the string (assuming that *lpData* is a pointer to the string). If *nCount* is –1 and the function pointed to by *lpfnOutput* returns 0, the image is shown but not dimmed.

x   Specifies the logical x-coordinate of the starting position of the rectangle that encloses the string.

y   Specifies the logical y-coordinate of the starting position of the rectangle that encloses the string.

nWidth   Specifies the width (in logical units) of the rectangle that encloses the string. If *nWidth* is 0, **GrayString** calculates the width of the area, assuming *lpData* is a pointer to the string.

nHeight   Specifies the height (in logical units) of the rectangle that encloses the string. If *nHeight* is 0, **GrayString** calculates the height of the area, assuming *lpData* is a pointer to the string.

Remarks   Draws dimmed (gray) text at the given location by writing the text in a memory bitmap, dimming the bitmap, and then copying the bitmap to the display. The function dims the text regardless of the selected brush and background. The **GrayString** member function uses the currently selected font. The **MM_TEXT** mapping mode must be selected before using this function.

An application can draw dimmed (grayed) strings on devices that support a solid gray color without calling the **GrayString** member function. The system color **COLOR_GRAYTEXT** is the solid-gray system color used to draw disabled text. The application can call the **GetSysColor** Windows function to retrieve the color value of **COLOR_GRAYTEXT**. If the color is other than 0 (black), the application can call the **SetTextColor** member function to set the text color to the color value and then draw the string directly. If the retrieved color is black, the application must call **GrayString** to dim (gray) the text.

If *lpfnOutput* is **NULL,** GDI uses the Windows **TextOut** function, and *lpData* is assumed to be a far pointer to the character to be output. If the characters to be output cannot be handled by the **TextOut** member function (for example, the string is stored as a bitmap), the application must supply its own output function. Also note that all callback functions must trap Microsoft Foundation exceptions before returning to Windows, since exceptions cannot be thrown across callback boundaries. For more information about exceptions, see the article "Exceptions" in *Programming with the Microsoft Foundation Class Library*. The callback function passed to **GrayString** must use the Pascal calling convention, must be exported with **__export**, and must be declared **FAR**.

When the framework is in preview mode, a call to the **GrayString** member function is translated to a **TextOut** call, and the callback function is not called.

See Also   **::GetSysColor, CDC::SetTextColor, CDC::TextOut, ::GrayString**

CDC::HIMETRICtoDP

void HIMETRICtoDP(LPSIZE *lpSize* **) const;**

Parameters   *lpSize*   Points to a **SIZE** structure or **CSize** object.

Remarks   Use this function when you convert **HIMETRIC** sizes from OLE to pixels.

If the mapping mode of the device context object is **MM_LOENGLISH**, **MM_HIENGLISH, MM_LOMETRIC** or **MM_HIMETRIC**, then the conversion is based on the number of pixels in the physical inch. If the mapping mode is one of the other non-constrained modes (e.g., **MM_TEXT**), then the conversion is based on the number of pixels in the logical inch.

See Also   **CDC::LPtoDP, CDC::HIMETRICtoLP**

CDC::HIMETRICtoLP

void HIMETRICtoLP(LPSIZE *lpSize* **) const;**

Parameters   *lpSize*   Points to a **SIZE** structure or **CSize** object.

Remarks   Call this function to convert **HIMETRIC** units into logical units. Use this function when you get **HIMETRIC** sizes from OLE and wish to convert them to your application's natural mapping mode.

The conversion is accomplished by first converting the **HIMETRIC** units into pixels and then converting these units into logical units using the device context's current mapping units. Note that the extents of the device's window and viewport will affect the result.

See Also   **CDC::HIMETRICtoDP, CDC::DPtoLP**

CDC::IntersectClipRect

virtual int IntersectClipRect(int *x1*, int *y1*, int *x2*, int *y2*);

virtual int IntersectClipRect(LPCRECT *lpRect*);

Return Value The new clipping region's type. It can be any one of the following values:

- **COMPLEXREGION** New clipping region has overlapping borders.
- **ERROR** Device context is not valid.
- **NULLREGION** New clipping region is empty.
- **SIMPLEREGION** New clipping region has no overlapping borders.

Parameters *x1* Specifies the logical x-coordinate of the upper-left corner of the rectangle.

y1 Specifies the logical y-coordinate of the upper-left corner of the rectangle.

x2 Specifies the logical x-coordinate of the lower-right corner of the rectangle.

y2 Specifies the logical y-coordinate of the lower-right corner of the rectangle.

lpRect Specifies the rectangle. You can pass either a **CRect** object or a pointer to a **RECT** structure for this parameter.

Remarks Creates a new clipping region by forming the intersection of the current region and the rectangle specified by *x1*, *y1*, *x2*, and *y2*. GDI clips all subsequent output to fit within the new boundary. The width and height must not exceed 32,767.

See Also **::IntersectClipRect, CRect, RECT**

CDC::InvertRect

void InvertRect(LPCRECT *lpRect*);

Parameters *lpRect* Points to a **RECT** that contains the logical coordinates of the rectangle to be inverted. You can also pass a **CRect** object for this parameter.

Remarks Inverts the contents of the given rectangle. Inversion is a logical NOT operation and flips the bits of each pixel. On monochrome displays, the function makes white pixels black and black pixels white. On color displays, the inversion depends on how colors are generated for the display. Calling **InvertRect** twice with the same rectangle restores the display to its previous colors. If the rectangle is empty, nothing is drawn.

See Also **CDC::FillRect, ::InvertRect, CRect, RECT struct**

CDC::InvertRgn

BOOL InvertRgn(CRgn* *pRgn*);

Return Value   Nonzero if the function is successful; otherwise 0.

Parameters   *pRgn*   Identifies the region to be inverted. The coordinates for the region are specified in device units.

Remarks   Inverts the colors in the region specified by *pRgn*. On monochrome displays, the function makes white pixels black and black pixels white. On color displays, the inversion depends on how the colors are generated for the display.

See Also   **CDC::FillRgn, CDC::PaintRgn, CRgn, ::InvertRgn**

CDC::IsPrinting

BOOL IsPrinting( ) const;

Return Value   Nonzero if the **CDC** object is currently printing; otherwise 0.

CDC::LineTo

BOOL LineTo(int *x*, int *y*);

BOOL LineTo(POINT *point*);

Return Value   Nonzero if the line is drawn; otherwise 0.

Parameters   *x*   Specifies the logical x-coordinate of the endpoint for the line.

y   Specifies the logical y-coordinate of the endpoint for the line.

point   Specifies the endpoint for the line. You can pass either a **POINT** structure or a **CPoint** object for this parameter.

Remarks   Draws a line from the current position up to, but not including, the point specified by *x* and *y* (or *point*). The line is drawn with the selected pen. The current position is set to *x,y* or to *point*.

See Also   **CDC::MoveTo, CDC::GetCurrentPosition, ::LineTo, CPoint, POINT**

CDC::LPtoDP

> void **LPtoDP**(**LPPOINT** *lpPoints*, **int** *nCount* = **1**) **const**;
>
> void **LPtoDP**(**LPRECT** *lpRect*) **const**;
>
> void **LPtoDP**(**LPSIZE** *lpSize*) **const**;

Parameters   *lpPoints*   Points to an array of points. Each point in the array is a **POINT** structure or a **CPoint** object.

nCount   The number of points in the array.

lpRect   Points to a **RECT** structure or a **CRect** object. This parameter is used for the common case of mapping a rectangle from logical to device units.

lpSize   Points to a **SIZE** structure or a **CSize** object.

Remarks   Converts logical units into device units. The function maps the coordinates of each point, or dimensions of a size, from GDI's logical coordinate system into a device coordinate system. The conversion depends on the current mapping mode and the settings of the origins and extents of the device's window and viewport.

The x- and y-coordinates of points are 2-byte signed integers in the range –32,768 through 32,767. In cases where the mapping mode would result in values larger than these limits, the system sets the values to –32,768 and 32,767, respectively.

See Also   **CDC::DPtoLP**, **CDC::HIMETRICtoLP**, **::LPtoDP**, **CDC::GetWindowOrg**, **CDC::GetWindowExt**

CDC::LPtoHIMETRIC

> void **LPToHIMETRIC**(**LPSIZE** *lpSize*) **const**;

Parameters   *lpSize*   Points to a **SIZE** structure or a **CSize** object.

Remarks   Call this function to convert logical units into **HIMETRIC** units. Use this function when you give **HIMETRIC** sizes to OLE, converting from your application's natural mapping mode. Note that the extents of the device's window and viewport will affect the result.

The conversion is accomplished by first converting the logical units into pixels using the device context's current mapping units and then converting these units into **HIMETRIC** units.

See Also   **CDC::HIMETRICtoLP**, **CDC::LPtoDP**, **CDC::DPtoHIMETRIC**

CDC::MaskBlt

BOOL MaskBlt(int *x*, **int** *y*, **int** *nWidth*, **int** *nHeight*, **CDC*** *pSrcDC*, **int** *xSrc*, **int** *ySrc*, **CBitmap&** *maskBitmap*, **int** *xMask*, **int** *yMask*, **DWORD** *dwRop* **);**

Return Value   Nonzero if the function is successful; otherwise 0.

Parameters

x   Specifies the logical x-coordinate of the upper-left corner of the destination rectangle.

y   Specifies the logical y-coordinate of the upper-left corner of the destination rectangle.

nWidth   Specifies the width, in logical units, of the destination rectangle and source bitmap.

nHeight   Specifies the height, in logical units, of the destination rectangle and source bitmap.

pSrcDC   Identifies the device context from which the bitmap is to be copied. It must be zero if the *dwRop* parameter specifies a raster operation that does not include a source.

xSrc   Specifies the logical x-coordinate of the upper-left corner of the source bitmap.

ySrc   Specifies the logical y-coordinate of the upper-left corner of the source bitmap.

maskBitmap   Identifies the monochrome mask bitmap combined with the color bitmap in the source device context.

xMask   Specifies the horizontal pixel offset for the mask bitmap specified by the *maskBitmap* parameter.

yMask   Specifies the vertical pixel offset for the mask bitmap specified by the *maskBitmap* parameter.

dwRop   Specifies both foreground and background ternary raster operation codes, which the function uses to control the combination of source and destination data. The background raster operation code is stored in the high byte of the high word of this value; the foreground raster operation code is stored in the low byte of the high word of this value; the low word of this value is ignored, and should be zero. The macro **MAKEROP4** creates such combinations of foreground and background raster operation codes. See the Remarks section below for a discussion of foreground and background in the context of this function. See the **BitBlt** member function for a list of common raster operation codes.

Remarks   Combines the color data for the source and destination bitmaps using the given mask and raster operation. A value of 1 in the mask specified by *maskBitmap* indicates that the foreground raster operation code specified by *dwRop* should be applied at that location. A value of 0 in the mask indicates that the background raster operation code specified by *dwRop* should be applied at that location. If the raster operations require a source, the mask rectangle must cover the source rectangle. If it does not, the function will fail. If the raster operations do not require a source, the mask rectangle must cover the destination rectangle. If it does not, the function will fail.

If a rotation or shear transformation is in effect for the source device context when this function is called, an error occurs. However, other types of transformations are allowed.

If the color formats of the source, pattern, and destination bitmaps differ, this function converts the pattern or source format, or both, to match the destination format. If the mask bitmap is not a monochrome bitmap, an error occurs. When an enhanced metafile is being recorded, an error occurs (and the function returns 0) if the source device context identifies an enhanced-metafile device context. Not all devices support **MaskBlt**. An application should call **GetDeviceCaps** to determine whether a device supports this function. If no mask bitmap is supplied, this function behaves exactly like **BitBlt**, using the foreground raster operation code. The pixel offsets in the mask bitmap map to the point (0,0) in the source device context's bitmap. This is useful for cases in which a mask bitmap contains a set of masks; an application can easily apply any one of them to a mask-blitting task by adjusting the pixel offsets and rectangle sizes sent to **MaskBlt**.

See Also   **CDC::BitBlt, CDC::GetDeviceCaps, CDC::PlgBlt, CDC::StretchBlt, ::MaskBlt**

CDC::MoveTo

CPoint MoveTo(int *x*, int *y*);

CPoint MoveTo(POINT *point*);

Return Value   The x- and y-coordinates of the previous position as a **CPoint** object.

Parameters   *x*   Specifies the logical x-coordinate of the new position.

y   Specifies the logical y-coordinate of the new position.

point   Specifies the new position. You can pass either a **POINT** structure or a **CPoint** object for this parameter.

Remarks   Moves the current position to the point specified by *x* and *y* (or by *point*).

See Also   **CDC::GetCurrentPosition, CDC::LineTo, ::MoveTo, CPoint, POINT**

CDC::OffsetClipRgn

virtual int OffsetClipRgn(int *x***, int** *y* **);**

virtual int OffsetClipRgn(SIZE *size* **);**

Return Value   The new region's type. It can be any one of the following values:

- **COMPLEXREGION**   Clipping region has overlapping borders.
- **ERROR**   Device context is not valid.
- **NULLREGION**   Clipping region is empty.
- **SIMPLEREGION**   Clipping region has no overlapping borders.

Parameters   *x*   Specifies the number of logical units to move left or right.

y   Specifies the number of logical units to move up or down.

size   Specifies the amount to offset.

Remarks   Moves the clipping region of the device context by the specified offsets. The function moves the region *x* units along the x-axis and *y* units along the y-axis.

See Also   **CDC::SelectClipRgn**, **::OffsetClipRgn**

CDC::OffsetViewportOrg

virtual CPoint OffsetViewportOrg(int *nWidth***, int** *nHeight* **);**

Return Value   The previous viewport origin (in device coordinates) as a **CPoint** object.

Parameters   *nWidth*   Specifies the number of device units to add to the current origin's x-coordinate.

nHeight   Specifies the number of device units to add to the current origin's y-coordinate.

Remarks   Modifies the coordinates of the viewport origin relative to the coordinates of the current viewport origin.

See Also   **CDC::GetViewportOrg**, **CDC::OffsetWindowOrg**, **CDC::SetViewportOrg**, **::OffsetViewportOrg**, **CPoint**

CDC::OffsetWindowOrg

CPoint OffsetWindowOrg(int *nWidth***, int** *nHeight* **);**

Return Value   The previous window origin (in logical coordinates) as a **CPoint** object.

Parameters	*nWidth* Specifies the number of logical units to add to the current origin's x-coordinate.

nHeight Specifies the number of logical units to add to the current origin's y-coordinate.

Remarks Modifies the coordinates of the window origin relative to the coordinates of the current window origin.

See Also **CDC::GetWindowOrg, CDC::OffsetViewportOrg, CDC::SetWindowOrg, ::OffsetWindowOrg, CPoint**

CDC::PaintRgn

BOOL PaintRgn(CRgn* *pRgn* **);**

Return Value Nonzero if the function is successful; otherwise 0.

Parameters *pRgn* Identifies the region to be filled. The coordinates for the given region are specified in device units.

Remarks Fills the region specified by *pRgn* using the current brush.

See Also **CBrush, CDC::SelectObject, CDC::FillRgn, ::PaintRgn, CRgn**

CDC::PatBlt

BOOL PatBlt(int *x***, int** *y***, int** *nWidth***, int** *nHeight***, DWORD** *dwRop* **);**

Return Value Nonzero if the function is successful; otherwise 0.

Parameters *x* Specifies the logical x-coordinate of the upper-left corner of the rectangle that is to receive the pattern.

y Specifies the logical y-coordinate of the upper-left corner of the rectangle that is to receive the pattern.

nWidth Specifies the width (in logical units) of the rectangle that is to receive the pattern.

nHeight Specifies the height (in logical units) of the rectangle that is to receive the pattern.

dwRop Specifies the raster-operation code. Raster-operation codes (ROPs) define how GDI combines colors in output operations that involve a current brush, a possible source bitmap, and a destination bitmap. This parameter can be one of the following values:

- **PATCOPY**   Copies pattern to destination bitmap.
- **PATINVERT**   Combines destination bitmap with pattern using the Boolean XOR operator.
- **DSTINVERT**   Inverts the destination bitmap.
- **BLACKNESS**   Turns all output black.
- **WHITENESS**   Turns all output white.
- **PATPAINT**   Paints the destination bitmap.

Remarks

Creates a bit pattern on the device. The pattern is a combination of the selected brush and the pattern already on the device. The raster-operation code specified by *dwRop* defines how the patterns are to be combined. The raster operations listed for this function are a limited subset of the full 256 ternary raster-operation codes; in particular, a raster-operation code that refers to a source cannot be used.

Not all device contexts support the **PatBlt** function. To determine whether a device context supports **PatBlt**, call the **GetDeviceCaps** member function with the **RASTERCAPS** index and check the return value for the **RC_BITBLT** flag.

See Also

CDC::GetDeviceCaps, **::PatBlt**

CDC::Pie

BOOL Pie(int *x1*, **int** *y1*, **int** *x2*, **int** *y2*, **int** *x3*, **int** *y3*, **int** *x4*, **int** *y4* **);**

BOOL Pie(LPCRECT *lpRect*, **POINT** *ptStart*, **POINT** *ptEnd* **);**

Return Value

Nonzero if the function is successful; otherwise 0.

Parameters

x1   Specifies the x-coordinate of the upper-left corner of the bounding rectangle (in logical units).

y1   Specifies the y-coordinate of the upper-left corner of the bounding rectangle (in logical units).

x2   Specifies the x-coordinate of the lower-right corner of the bounding rectangle (in logical units).

y2   Specifies the y-coordinate of the lower-right corner of the bounding rectangle (in logical units).

x3   Specifies the x-coordinate of the arc's starting point (in logical units). This point does not have to lie exactly on the arc.

y3   Specifies the y-coordinate of the arc's starting point (in logical units). This point does not have to lie exactly on the arc.

x4   Specifies the x-coordinate of the arc's endpoint (in logical units). This point does not have to lie exactly on the arc.

y4   Specifies the y-coordinate of the arc's endpoint (in logical units). This point does not have to lie exactly on the arc.

lpRect   Specifies the bounding rectangle. You can pass either a **CRect** object or a pointer to a **RECT** structure for this parameter.

ptStart   Specifies the starting point of the arc. This point does not have to lie exactly on the arc. You can pass either a **POINT** structure or a **CPoint** object for this parameter.

ptEnd   Specifies the endpoint of the arc. This point does not have to lie exactly on the arc. You can pass either a **POINT** structure or a **CPoint** object for this parameter.

Remarks   Draws a pie-shaped wedge by drawing an elliptical arc whose center and two endpoints are joined by lines. The center of the arc is the center of the bounding rectangle specified by *x1*, *y1*, *x2*, and *y2* (or by *lpRect*). The starting and ending points of the arc are specified by *x3*, *y3*, *x4*, and *y4* (or by *ptStart* and *ptEnd*). The arc is drawn with the selected pen, moving in a counterclockwise direction. Two additional lines are drawn from each endpoint to the arc's center. The pie-shaped area is filled with the current brush. If *x3* equals *x4* and *y3* equals *y4*, the result is an ellipse with a single line from the center of the ellipse to the point (*x3*, *y3*) or (*x4*, *y4*). The figure drawn by this function extends up to but does not include the right and bottom coordinates. This means that the height of the figure is *y2* − *y1* and the width of the figure is *x2* − *x1*. Both the width and the height of the bounding rectangle must be greater than 2 units and less than 32,767 units.

See Also   **CDC::Chord**, **::Pie**, **RECT**, **POINT**, **CRect**, **CPoint**

CDC::PlayMetaFile

BOOL PlayMetaFile(HMETAFILE *hMF* **);**

BOOL PlayMetaFile(HENHMETAFILE *hEnhMetaFile*,
    LPCRECT *lpBounds* **);**

Return Value   Nonzero if the function is successful; otherwise 0.

Parameters   *hMF*   Identifies the metafile to be played.

hEnhMetaFile   Identifies the enhanced metafile.

lpBounds   Points to a **RECT** structure or a **CRect** object that contains the coordinates of the bounding rectangle used to display the picture. The coordinates are specified in logical units.

Remarks

Plays the contents of the specified metafile on the device context. The metafile can be played any number of times.

The second version of **PlayMetaFile** displays the picture stored in the given enhanced-format metafile. When an application calls the second version of **PlayMetaFile**, Windows uses the picture frame in the enhanced-metafile header to map the picture onto the rectangle pointed to by the *lpBounds* parameter. (This picture may be sheared or rotated by setting the world transform in the output device before calling **PlayMetaFile**.) Points along the edges of the rectangle are included in the picture. An enhanced-metafile picture can be clipped by defining the clipping region in the output device before playing the enhanced metafile.

If an enhanced metafile contains an optional palette, an application can achieve consistent colors by setting up a color palette on the output device before calling the second version of **PlayMetaFile**. To retrieve the optional palette, use the **::GetEnhMetaFilePaletteEntries** function. An enhanced metafile can be embedded in a newly created enhanced metafile by calling the second version of **PlayMetaFile** and playing the source enhanced metafile into the device context for the new enhanced metafile.

The states of the output device context are preserved by this function. Any object created but not deleted in the enhanced metafile is deleted by this function. To stop this function, an application can call the **::CancelDC** function from another thread to terminate the operation. In this case, the function returns zero.

See Also

::CancelDC, **::GetEnhMetaFileHeader**, **::GetEnhMetaFilePaletteEntries**, **::SetWorldTransform**, **::PlayMetaFile**, **::PlayEnhMetaFile**, **::PlayMetaFile**

CDC::PlgBlt

BOOL PlgBlt(POINT *lpPoint*, **CDC*** *pSrcDC*, **int** *xSrc*, **int** *ySrc*, **int** *nWidth*, **int** *nHeight*, **CBitmap&** *maskBitmap*, **int** *xMask*, **int** *yMask* **);**

Return Value

Nonzero if the function is successful; otherwise 0.

Parameters

lpPoint   Points to an array of three points in logical space that identifies three corners of the destination parallelogram. The upper-left corner of the source rectangle is mapped to the first point in this array, the upper-right corner to the second point in this array, and the lower-left corner to the third point. The lower-right corner of the source rectangle is mapped to the implicit fourth point in the parallelogram.

pSrcDC   Identifies the source device context.

xSrc   Specifies the x-coordinate, in logical units, of the upper-left corner of the source rectangle.

ySrc   Specifies the y-coordinate, in logical units, of the upper-left corner of the source rectangle.

nWidth   Specifies the width, in logical units, of the source rectangle.

nHeight   Specifies the height, in logical units, of the source rectangle.

maskBitmap   Identifies an optional monochrome bitmap that is used to mask the colors of the source rectangle.

xMask   Specifies the x-coordinate of the upper-left corner of the the monochrome bitmap.

yMask   Specifies the y-coordinate of the upper-left corner of the the monochrome bitmap.

Remarks   Performs a bit-block transfer of the bits of color data from the specified rectangle in the source device context to the specified parallelogram in the given device context. If the given bitmask handle identifies a valid monochrome bitmap, the function uses this bitmap to mask the bits of color data from the source rectangle.

The fourth vertex of the parallelogram (D) is defined by treating the first three points (A, B, and C) as vectors and computing D = B + C - A.

If the bitmask exists, a value of 1 in the mask indicates that the source pixel color should be copied to the destination. A value of 0 in the mask indicates that the destination pixel color is not to be changed.

If the mask rectangle is smaller than the source and destination rectangles, the function replicates the mask pattern.

Scaling, translation, and reflection transformations are allowed in the source device context; however, rotation and shear transformations are not. If the mask bitmap is not a monochrome bitmap, an error occurs. The stretching mode for the destination device context is used to determine how to stretch or compress the pixels, if that is necessary. When an enhanced metafile is being recorded, an error occurs if the source device context identifies an enhanced-metafile device context.

The destination coordinates are transformed according to the destination device context; the source coordinates are transformed according to the source device context. If the source transformation has a rotation or shear, an error is returned. If the destination and source rectangles do not have the same color format, **PlgBlt** converts the source rectangle to match the destination rectangle. Not all devices support **PlgBlt**. For more information, see the description of the **RC_BITBLT** raster capability in the **CDC::GetDeviceCaps** member function.

If the source and destination device contexts represent incompatible devices, **PlgBlt** returns an error.

See Also   **CDC::BitBlt**, **CDC::GetDeviceCaps**, **CDC::MaskBlt**, **CDC::StretchBlt**, **::SetStretchBltMode**, **::PlgBlt**

CDC::PolyBezier

BOOL PolyBezier(const POINT* *lpPoints***, int** *nCount* **);**

Return Value   Nonzero if the function is successful; otherwise 0.

Parameters   *lpPoints*   Points to an array of **POINT** data structures that contain the endpoints and control points of the spline(s).

nCount   Specifies the number of points in the *lpPoints* array. This value must be one more than three times the number of splines to be drawn, because each Bézier spline requires two control points and an endpoint, and the initial spline requires an additional starting point.

Remarks   Draws one or more Bézier splines. This function draws cubic Bézier splines by using the endpoints and control points specified by the *lpPoints* parameter. The first spline is drawn from the first point to the fourth point by using the second and third points as control points. Each subsequent spline in the sequence needs exactly three more points: the end point of the previous spline is used as the starting point, the next two points in the sequence are control points, and the third is the end point.

The current position is neither used nor updated by the **PolyBezier** function. The figure is not filled. This function draws lines by using the current pen.

See Also   **CDC::PolyBezierTo**, **::PolyBezier**

CDC::PolyBezierTo

BOOL PolyBezierTo(const POINT* *lpPoints***, int** *nCount* **);**

Return Value   Nonzero if the function is successful; otherwise 0.

Parameters   *lpPoints*   Points to an array of **POINT** data structures that contains the endpoints and control points.

nCount   Specifies the number of points in the *lpPoints* array. This value must be three times the number of splines to be drawn, because each Bézier spline requires two control points and an end point.

Remarks   Draws one or more Bézier splines. This function draws cubic Bézier splines by using the control points specified by the *lpPoints* parameter. The first spline is drawn from the current position to the third point by using the first two points as control points. For each subsequent spline, the function needs exactly three more points, and uses the end point of the previous spline as the starting point for the next. **PolyBezierTo** moves the current position to the end point of the last Bézier spline. The figure is not filled. This function draws lines by using the current pen.

See Also   **CDC::MoveTo**, **CDC::PolyBezier**, **::PolyBezierTo**

CDC::PolyDraw

BOOL PolyDraw(const POINT* *lpPoints*, **const BYTE*** *lpTypes*, **int** *nCount* **);**

Return Value   Nonzero if the function is successful; otherwise 0.

Parameters   *lpPoints*   Points to an array of **POINT** data structures that contains the endpoints for each line segment and the endpoints and control points for each Bézier spline.

lpTypes   Points to an array that specifies how each point in the *lpPoints* array is used. Values can be one of the following:

- **PT_MOVETO**   Specifies that this point starts a disjoint figure. This point becomes the new current position.
- **PT_LINETO**   Specifies that a line is to be drawn from the current position to this point, which then becomes the new current position.
- **PT_BEZIERTO**   Specifies that this point is a control point or ending point for a Bézier spline.

PT_BEZIERTO types always occur in sets of three. The current position defines the starting point for the Bézier spline. The first two **PT_BEZIERTO** points are the control points, and the third **PT_BEZIERTO** point is the ending point. The ending point becomes the new current position. If there are not three consecutive **PT_BEZIERTO** points, an error results.

A **PT_LINETO** or **PT_BEZIERTO** type can be combined with the following constant by using the bitwise operator OR to indicate that the corresponding point is the last point in a figure and the figure is closed:

- **PT_CLOSEFIGURE**   Specifies that the figure is automatically closed after the **PT_LINETO** or **PT_BEZIERTO** type for this point is done. A line is drawn from this point to the most recent **PT_MOVETO** or **MoveTo** point.

    This flag is combined with the **PT_LINETO** type for a line, or with the **PT_BEZIERTO** type of ending point for a Bézier spline, by using the bitwise **OR** operator. The current position is set to the ending point of the closing line.

nCount   Specifies the total number of points in the *lpPoints* array, the same as the number of bytes in the *lpTypes* array.

Remarks   Draws a set of line segments and Bézier splines. This function can be used to draw disjoint figures in place of consecutive calls to **CDC::MoveTo**, **CDC::LineTo**, and **CDC::PolyBezierTo** member functions. The lines and splines are drawn using the current pen, and figures are not filled. If there is an active path started by calling the **CDC::BeginPath** member function, **PolyDraw** adds to the path. The points contained in the *lpPoints* array and in *lpTypes* indicate whether each point is part of a **CDC::MoveTo**, a **CDC::LineTo**, or a **CDC::BezierTo** operation. It is also possible to close figures. This function updates the current position.

See Also   **CDC::BeginPath**, **CDC::EndPath**, **CDC::LineTo**, **CDC::MoveTo**, **CDC::PolyBezierTo**, **CDC::PolyLine**, **::PolyDraw**

CDC::Polygon

BOOL Polygon(LPPOINT *lpPoints*, **int** *nCount* **);**

Return Value   Nonzero if the function is successful; otherwise 0.

Parameters   *lpPoints*   Points to an array of points that specifies the vertices of the polygon. Each point in the array is a **POINT** structure or a **CPoint** object.

nCount   Specifies the number of vertices in the array.

Remarks   Draws a polygon consisting of two or more points (vertices) connected by lines, using the current pen. The system closes the polygon automatically, if necessary, by drawing a line from the last vertex to the first. The current polygon-filling mode can be retrieved or set by using the **GetPolyFillMode** and **SetPolyFillMode** member functions.

See Also   **CDC::GetPolyFillMode**, **CDC::Polyline**, **CDC::PolyPolygon**, **CDC::SetPolyFillMode**, **CPoint**

In the Win32 *Programmer's Reference*: **::Polygon**

CDC::Polyline

BOOL Polyline(LPPOINT *lpPoints*, **int** *nCount* **);**

Return Value   Nonzero if the function is successful; otherwise 0.

Parameters   *lpPoints*   Points to an array of **POINT** structures or **CPoint** objects to be connected.

nCount   Specifies the number of points in the array. This value must be at least 2.

Remarks   Draws a set of line segments connecting the points specified by *lpPoints*. The lines are drawn from the first point through subsequent points using the current pen. Unlike the **LineTo** member function, the **Polyline** function neither uses nor updates the current position.

See Also   **CDC::LineTo**, **CDC::Polygon**, **POINT**, **CPoint**

In the Win32 *Programmer's Reference*: **::PolyLine**

CDC::PolylineTo

BOOL PolylineTo(const POINT* *lpPoints*, **int** *nCount* **);**

Return Value   Nonzero if the function is successful; otherwise 0.

Parameters   *lpPoints*   Points to an array of **POINT** data structures that contains the vertices of the line.

nCount   Specifies the number of points in the array

Remarks   Draws one or more straight lines. A line is drawn from the current position to the first point specified by the *lpPoints* parameter by using the current pen. For each additional line, the function draws from the ending point of the previous line to the next point specified by *lpPoints*. **PolylineTo** moves the current position to the ending point of the last line. If the line segments drawn by this function form a closed figure, the figure is not filled.

See Also   **CDC::LineTo**, **CDC::Polyline**, **CDC::MoveTo**, **::PolylineTo**

CDC::PolyPolygon

BOOL PolyPolygon(LPPOINT *lpPoints*, **LPINT** *lpPolyCounts*, **int** *nCount* **);**

Return Value   Nonzero if the function is successful; otherwise 0.

Parameters   *lpPoints*   Points to an array of **POINT** structures or **CPoint** objects that define the vertices of the polygons.

lpPolyCounts   Points to an array of integers, each of which specifies the number of points in one of the polygons in the *lpPoints* array.

nCount   The number of entries in the *lpPolyCounts* array. This number specifies the number of polygons to be drawn. This value must be at least 2.

Remarks   Creates two or more polygons that are filled using the current polygon-filling mode. The polygons may be disjoint or overlapping. Each polygon specified in a call to the **PolyPolygon** function must be closed. Unlike polygons created by the **Polygon** member function, the polygons created by **PolyPolygon** are not closed automatically.

The function creates two or more polygons. To create a single polygon, an application should use the **Polygon** member function. The current polygon-filling mode can be retrieved or set by using the **GetPolyFillMode** and **SetPolyFillMode** member functions.

See Also   **CDC::GetPolyFillMode**, **CDC::Polygon**, **CDC::Polyline**,
CDC::SetPolyFillMode, **::PolyPolygon**, **POINT**, **CPoint**

CDC::PolyPolyline

BOOL PolyPolyline(const POINT* *lpPoints***, const DWORD*** *lpPolyPoints***,**
int *nCount* **);**

Return Value   Nonzero if the function is successful; otherwise 0.

Parameters   *lpPoints*   Points to an array of structures that contains the vertices of the polylines. The polylines are specified consecutively.

lpPolyPoints   Points to an array of variables specifying the number of points in the *lpPoints* array for the corresponding polygon. Each entry must be greater than or equal to two.

nCount   Specifies the total number of counts in the *lpPolyPoints* array.

Remarks   Draws multiple series of connected line segments. The line segments are drawn by using the current pen. The figures formed by the segments are not filled. The current position is neither used nor updated by this function.

See Also   **CDC::Polyline**, **CDC::PolylineTo**, **::PolyPolyline**

CDC::PtVisible

virtual BOOL PtVisible(int *x***, int** *y* **) const;**

virtual BOOL PtVisible(POINT *point* **) const;**

Return Value   Nonzero if the specified point is within the clipping region; otherwise 0.

Parameters   *x*   Specifies the logical x-coordinate of the point.

y   Specifies the logical y-coordinate of the point.

point   Specifies the point to check in logical coordinates. You can pass either a **POINT** structure or a **CPoint** object for this parameter.

Remarks   Determines whether the given point is within the clipping region of the device context.

See Also   **CDC::RectVisible**, **CDC::SelectClipRgn**, **CPoint**, **::PtVisible**, **POINT**

CDC::QueryAbort

BOOL QueryAbort( ) const;

Return Value   The return value is nonzero if printing should continue or if there is no abort procedure. It is 0 if the print job should be terminated. The return value is supplied by the abort function.

Remarks   Calls the abort function installed by the **SetAbortProc** member function for a printing application and queries whether the printing should be terminated.

See Also   **CDC::SetAbortProc**

CDC::RealizePalette

UINT RealizePalette( );

Return Value   Indicates how many entries in the logical palette were mapped to different entries in the system palette. This represents the number of entries that this function remapped to accommodate changes in the system palette since the logical palette was last realized.

Remarks   Maps entries from the current logical palette to the system palette. A logical color palette acts as a buffer between color-intensive applications and the system, allowing an application to use as many colors as needed without interfering with its own displayed colors or with colors displayed by other windows. When a window has the input focus and calls **RealizePalette**, Windows ensures that the window will display all the requested colors, up to the maximum number simultaneously available on the screen. Windows also displays colors not found in the window's palette by matching them to available colors. In addition, Windows matches the colors requested by inactive windows that call the function as closely as possible to the available colors. This significantly reduces undesirable changes in the colors displayed in inactive windows.

See Also   **CDC::SelectPalette, CPalette, ::RealizePalette**

CDC::Rectangle

BOOL Rectangle(int *x1*, int *y1*, int *x2*, int *y2*);

BOOL Rectangle(LPCRECT *lpRect*);

Return Value   Nonzero if the function is successful; otherwise 0.

Parameters   *x1*   Specifies the x-coordinate of the upper-left corner of the rectangle (in logical units).

y1   Specifies the y-coordinate of the upper-left corner of the rectangle (in logical units).

x2   Specifies the x-coordinate of the lower-right corner of the rectangle (in logical units).

y2   Specifies the y-coordinate of the lower-right corner of the rectangle (in logical units).

lpRect   Specifies the rectangle in logical units. You can pass either a **CRect** object or a pointer to a **RECT** structure for this parameter.

Remarks   Draws a rectangle using the current pen. The interior of the rectangle is filled using the current brush. The rectangle extends up to, but does not include, the right and bottom coordinates. This means that the height of the rectangle is $y2 - y1$ and the width of the rectangle is $x2 - x1$. Both the width and the height of a rectangle must be greater than 2 units and less than 32,767 units.

See Also   **::Rectangle**, **CDC::PolyLine**, **CDC::RoundRect**, **RECT**, **CRect**

CDC::RectVisible

virtual BOOL RectVisible(LPCRECT *lpRect* **) const;**

Return Value   Nonzero if any portion of the given rectangle lies within the clipping region; otherwise 0.

Parameters   *lpRect*   Points to a **RECT** structure or a **CRect** object that contains the logical coordinates of the specified rectangle.

Remarks   Determines whether any part of the given rectangle lies within the clipping region of the display context.

See Also   **CDC::PtVisible**, **CDC::SelectClipRgn**, **CRect**, **::RectVisible**, **RECT**

CDC::ReleaseAttribDC

virtual void ReleaseAttribDC( );

Remarks   Call this member function to set **m_hAttribDC** to **NULL**. This does not cause a **Detach** to occur. Only the output device context is attached to the **CDC** object, and only it can be detached.

See Also   **CDC::SetOutputDC**, **CDC::SetAttribDC**, **CDC::ReleaseOutputDC**, **CDC::m_hAttribDC**

CDC::ReleaseOutputDC

virtual void ReleaseOutputDC( );

Remarks   Call this member function to set the **m_hDC** member to **NULL**. This member function cannot be called when the output device context is attached to the **CDC** object. Use the **Detach** member function to detach the output device context.

See Also   **CDC::SetAttribDC, CDC::SetOutputDC, CDC::ReleaseAttribDC, CDC::m_hDC**

CDC::ResetDC

BOOL ResetDC(const DEVMODE* *lpDevMode* **);**

Return Value   Nonzero if the function is successful; otherwise 0.

Parameters   *lpDevMode*   A pointer to a Windows **DEVMODE** structure.

Remarks   Call this member function to update the device context wrapped by the **CDC** object. The device context is updated from the information specified in the Windows **DEVMODE** structure. This member function only resets the attribute device context.

An application will typically use the **ResetDC** member function when a window handles a **WM_DEVMODECHANGE** message. You can also use this member function to change the paper orientation or paper bins while printing a document.

You cannot use this member function to change the driver name, device name, or output port. When the user changes the port connection or device name, you must delete the original device context and create a new device context with the new information.

Before you call this member function, you must ensure that all objects (other than stock objects) that had been selected into the device context have been selected out.

See Also   **CDC::m_hAttribDC, ::ResetDC, WM_DEVMODECHANGE, DEVMODE**

CDC::RestoreDC

virtual BOOL RestoreDC(int *nSavedDC* **);**

Return Value   Nonzero if the specified context was restored; otherwise 0.

Parameters   *nSavedDC*   Specifies the device context to be restored. It can be a value returned by a previous **SaveDC** function call. If *nSavedDC* is –1, the most recently saved device context is restored.

Remarks   Restores the device context to the previous state identified by *nSavedDC*.
RestoreDC restores the device context by popping state information off a stack
created by earlier calls to the **SaveDC** member function. The stack can contain the
state information for several device contexts. If the context specified by *nSavedDC*
is not at the top of the stack, **RestoreDC** deletes all state information between the
device context specified by *nSavedDC* and the top of the stack. The deleted
information is lost.

See Also   **CDC::SaveDC**, **::RestoreDC**

CDC::RoundRect

BOOL RoundRect(LPCRECT *lpRect*, **POINT** *point* **);**

Return Value   Nonzero if the function is successful; otherwise 0.

Parameters   *x1*   Specifies the x-coordinate of the upper-left corner of the rectangle (in logical
units).

y1   Specifies the y-coordinate of the upper-left corner of the rectangle (in logical
units).

x2   Specifies the x-coordinate of the lower-right corner of the rectangle (in logical
units).

y2   Specifies the y-coordinate of the lower-right corner of the rectangle (in logical
units).

x3   Specifies the width of the ellipse used to draw the rounded corners (in logical
units).

y3   Specifies the height of the ellipse used to draw the rounded corners (in logical
units).

lpRect   Specifies the bounding rectangle in logical units. You can pass either a
CRect object or a pointer to a **RECT** structure for this parameter.

point   The x-coordinate of *point* specifies the width of the ellipse to draw the
rounded corners (in logical units). The y-coordinate of *point* specifies the height
of the ellipse to draw the rounded corners (in logical units). You can pass either
a **POINT** structure or a **CPoint** object for this parameter.

Remarks   Draws a rectangle with rounded corners using the current pen. The interior of the
rectangle is filled using the current brush. The figure this function draws extends up
to but does not include the right and bottom coordinates. This means that the height
of the figure is *y2 – y1* and the width of the figure is *x2 – x1*. Both the height and
the width of the bounding rectangle must be greater than 2 units and less than
32,767 units.

See Also   CDC::**Rectangle**, ::**RoundRect**, **CRect**, **RECT**, **POINT**, **CPoint**

CDC::SaveDC

virtual int SaveDC( );

Return Value   An integer identifying the saved device context. It is 0 if an error occurs. This
                     return value can be used to restore the device context by calling **RestoreDC**.

Remarks   Saves the current state of the device context by copying state information (such as
                     clipping region, selected objects, and mapping mode) to a context stack maintained
                     by Windows. The saved device context can later be restored by using **RestoreDC**.

                     SaveDC can be used any number of times to save any number of device-context
                     states.

See Also   CDC::**RestoreDC**, ::**SaveDC**

CDC::ScaleViewportExt

virtual CSize ScaleViewportExt(int *xNum*, **int** *xDenom*, **int** *yNum*, **int**
     yDenom **);**

Return Value   The previous viewport extents (in device units) as a **CSize** object.

Parameters   *xNum*   Specifies the amount by which to multiply the current x-extent.

                     xDenom   Specifies the amount by which to divide the result of multiplying the
                          current x-extent by the value of the *xNum* parameter.

                     yNum   Specifies the amount by which to multiply the current y-extent.

                     yDenom   Specifies the amount by which to divide the result of multiplying the
                          current y-extent by the value of the *yNum* parameter.

Remarks   Modifies the viewport extents relative to the current values. The formulas are
                     written as follows:

```
xNewVE = ( xOldVE * xNum ) / xDenom
yNewVE = ( yOldVE * yNum ) / yDenom
```

                     The new viewport extents are calculated by multiplying the current extents by the
                     given numerator and then dividing by the given denominator.

See Also   CDC::**GetViewportExt**, ::**ScaleViewportExt**, **CSize**

CDC::ScaleWindowExt

virtual CSize ScaleWindowExt(int *xNum***, int** *xDenom***, int** *yNum***, int** *yDenom* **);**

Return Value

The previous window extents (in logical units) as a **CSize** object.

Parameters

xNum   Specifies the amount by which to multiply the current x-extent.

xDenom   Specifies the amount by which to divide the result of multiplying the current x-extent by the value of the *xNum* parameter.

yNum   Specifies the amount by which to multiply the current y-extent.

yDenom   Specifies the amount by which to divide the result of multiplying the current y-extent by the value of the *yNum* parameter.

Remarks

Modifies the window extents relative to the current values. The formulas are written as follows:

```
xNewWE = ( xOldWE * xNum ) / xDenom
yNewWE = ( yOldWE * yNum ) / yDenom
```

The new window extents are calculated by multiplying the current extents by the given numerator and then dividing by the given denominator.

See Also

CDC::GetWindowExt, **::ScaleWindowExt**, **CSize**

CDC::ScrollDC

BOOL ScrollDC(int *dx***, int** *dy***, LPCRECT** *lpRectScroll***, LPCRECT** *lpRectClip***, CRgn*** *pRgnUpdate***, LPRECT** *lpRectUpdate* **);**

Return Value

Nonzero if scrolling is executed; otherwise 0.

Parameters

dx   Specifies the number of horizontal scroll units.

dy   Specifies the number of vertical scroll units.

lpRectScroll   Points to the **RECT** structure or **CRect** object that contains the coordinates of the scrolling rectangle.

lpRectClip   Points to the **RECT** structure or **CRect** object that contains the coordinates of the clipping rectangle. When this rectangle is smaller than the original one pointed to by *lpRectScroll*, scrolling occurs only in the smaller rectangle.

pRgnUpdate   Identifies the region uncovered by the scrolling process. The **ScrollDC** function defines this region; it is not necessarily a rectangle.

lpRectUpdate   Points to the **RECT** structure or **CRect** object that receives the coordinates of the rectangle that bounds the scrolling update region. This is the largest rectangular area that requires repainting. The values in the structure or object when the function returns are in client coordinates, regardless of the mapping mode for the given device context.

Remarks   Scrolls a rectangle of bits horizontally and vertically. If *lpRectUpdate* is **NULL**, Windows does not compute the update rectangle. If both *pRgnUpdate* and *lpRectUpdate* are **NULL**, Windows does not compute the update region. If *pRgnUpdate* is not **NULL**, Windows assumes that it contains a valid pointer to the region uncovered by the scrolling process (defined by the **ScrollDC** member function). The update region returned in *lpRectUpdate* can be passed to **CWnd::InvalidateRgn** if required.

An application should use the **ScrollWindow** member function of class **CWnd** when it is necessary to scroll the entire client area of a window. Otherwise it should use **ScrollDC**.

See Also   **CWnd::InvalidateRgn**, **CWnd::ScrollWindow**, **::ScrollDC**, **CRgn**, **RECT**, **CRect**

CDC::SelectClipPath

BOOL SelectClipPath(int *nMode* **);**

Return Value   Nonzero if the function is successful; otherwise 0.

Parameters   *nMode*   Specifies the way to use the path. The following values are allowed:

- **RGN_AND**   The new clipping region includes the intersection (overlapping areas) of the current clipping region and the current path.
- **RGN_COPY**   The new clipping region is the current path.
- **RGN_DIFF**   The new clipping region includes the areas of the current clipping region, and those of the current path are excluded.
- **RGN_OR**   The new clipping region includes the union (combined areas) of the current clipping region and the current path.
- **RGN_XOR**   The new clipping region includes the union of the current clipping region and the current path, but without the overlapping areas.

Remarks   Selects the current path as a clipping region for the device context, combining the new region with any existing clipping region by using the specified mode. The device context identified must contain a closed path.

See Also   **CDC::BeginPath**, **CDC::EndPath**

CDC::SelectClipRgn

virtual int SelectClipRgn(CRgn* *pRgn* **);**

int SelectClipRgn(CRgn* *pRgn*, **int** *nMode* **);**

Return Value   The region's type. It can be any of the following values:

- **COMPLEXREGION**   New clipping region has overlapping borders.
- **ERROR**   Device context or region is not valid.
- **NULLREGION**   New clipping region is empty.
- **SIMPLEREGION**   New clipping region has no overlapping borders.

Parameters   *pRgn*   Identifies the region to be selected.

- For the first version of this function, if this value is **NULL**, the entire client area is selected and output is still clipped to the window.
- For the second version of this function, this handle can be **NULL** only when the **RGN_COPY** mode is specified.

nMode   Specifies the operation to be performed. It must be one of the following values:

- **RGN_AND**   The new clipping region combines the overlapping areas of the current clipping region and the region identified by *pRgn*.
- **RGN_COPY**   The new clipping region is a copy of the region identified by *pRgn*. This is functionality is identical to the first version of **SelectClipRgn**. If the region identified by *pRgn* is **NULL**, the new clipping region becomes the default clipping region (a null region).
- **RGN_DIFF**   The new clipping region combines the areas of the current clipping region with those areas excluded from the region identified by *pRgn*.
- **RGN_OR**   The new clipping region combines the current clipping region and the region identified by *pRgn*.
- **RGN_XOR**   The new clipping region combines the current clipping region and the region identified by *pRgn* but excludes any overlapping areas.

Remarks   Selects the given region as the current clipping region for the device context. Only a copy of the selected region is used. The region itself can be selected for any number of other device contexts, or it can be deleted.

The function assumes that the coordinates for the given region are specified in device units. Some printer devices support text output at a higher resolution than graphics output in order to retain the precision needed to express text metrics. These devices report device units at the higher resolution, that is, in text units. These devices then scale coordinates for graphics so that several reported device units map to only 1 graphic unit. You should always call the **SelectClipRgn** function using text units.

Applications that must take the scaling of graphics objects in the GDI can use the **GETSCALINGFACTOR** printer escape to determine the scaling factor. This scaling factor affects clipping. If a region is used to clip graphics, GDI divides the coordinates by the scaling factor. If the region is used to clip text, GDI makes no scaling adjustment. A scaling factor of 1 causes the coordinates to be divided by 2; a scaling factor of 2 causes the coordinates to be divided by 4; and so on.

See Also   **CDC::GetClipBox**, **CDC::Escape**, **CRgn**, ExtSelectClipRgn , **::SelectClipRgn**

CDC::SelectObject

CPen* SelectObject(CPen* *pPen* **);**

CBrush* SelectObject(CBrush* *pBrush* **);**

virtual CFont* SelectObject(CFont* *pFont* **);**

CBitmap* SelectObject(CBitmap* *pBitmap* **);**

int SelectObject(CRgn* *pRgn* **);**

Return Value   A pointer to the object being replaced. This is a pointer to an object of one of the classes derived from **CGdiObject**, such as **CPen**, depending on which version of the function is used. The return value is **NULL** if there is an error. This function may return a pointer to a temporary object. This temporary object is only valid during the processing of one Windows message. For more information, see **CGdiObject::FromHandle**.

The version of the member function that takes a region parameter performs the same task as the **SelectClipRgn** member function. Its return value can be any of the following:

- **COMPLEXREGION**   New clipping region has overlapping borders.
- **ERROR**   Device context or region is not valid.
- **NULLREGION**   New clipping region is empty.
- **SIMPLEREGION**   New clipping region has no overlapping borders.

Parameters   *pPen*   A pointer to a **CPen** object to be selected.

pBrush   A pointer to a **CBrush** object to be selected.

pFont   A pointer to a **CFont** object to be selected.

pBitmap   A pointer to a **CBitmap** object to be selected.

pRgn   A pointer to a **CRgn** object to be selected.

Remarks   Selects an object into the device context. Class **CDC** provides five versions specialized for particular kinds of GDI objects, including pens, brushes, fonts, bitmaps, and regions. The newly selected object replaces the previous object of the same type. For example, if *pObject* of the general version of **SelectObject** points to a **CPen** object, the function replaces the current pen with the pen specified by *pObject*.

An application can select a bitmap into memory device contexts only and into only one memory device context at a time. The format of the bitmap must either be monochrome or compatible with the device context; if it is not, **SelectObject** returns an error.

For Windows 3.1 and later, the **SelectObject** function returns the same value whether it is used in a metafile or not. Under previous versions of Windows, **SelectObject** returned a nonzero value for success and 0 for failure when it was used in a metafile.

See Also   **CGdiObject::DeleteObject, CGdiObject::FromHandle, CDC::SelectClipRgn, CDC::SelectPalette, ::SelectObject**

CDC::SelectPalette

CPalette* SelectPalette(CPalette* *pPalette*, **BOOL** *bForceBackground* **);**

Return Value   A pointer to a **CPalette** object identifying the logical palette replaced by the palette specified by *pPalette*. It is **NULL** if there is an error.

Parameters   *pPalette*   Identifies the logical palette to be selected. This palette must already have been created with the **CPalette** member function **CreatePalette**.

bForceBackground   Specifies whether the logical palette is forced to be a background palette. If *bForceBackground* is nonzero, the selected palette is always a background palette, regardless of whether the window has the input focus. If *bForceBackground* is 0 and the device context is attached to a window, the logical palette is a foreground palette when the window has the input focus.

Remarks   Selects the logical palette that is specified by *pPalette* as the selected palette object of the device context. The new palette becomes the palette object used by GDI to control colors displayed in the device context and replaces the previous palette. An application can select a logical palette into more than one device context. However, changes to a logical palette will affect all device contexts for which it is selected. If an application selects a palette into more than one device context, the device contexts must all belong to the same physical device.

See Also   **CDC::RealizePalette**, **CPalette**, **::SelectPalette**

CDC::SelectStockObject

virtual CGdiObject* SelectStockObject(int *nIndex* **);**

Return Value   A pointer to the **CGdiObject** object that was replaced if the function is successful. The actual object pointed to is a **CPen**, **CBrush**, or **CFont** object. If the call is unsuccessful, the return value is **NULL**.

Parameters   *nIndex*   Specifies the kind of stock object desired. It can be one of the following values:

- **BLACK_BRUSH**   Black brush.
- **DKGRAY_BRUSH**   Dark gray brush.
- **GRAY_BRUSH**   Gray brush.
- **HOLLOW_BRUSH**   Hollow brush.
- **LTGRAY_BRUSH**   Light gray brush.
- **NULL_BRUSH**   Null brush.
- **WHITE_BRUSH**   White brush.
- **BLACK_PEN**   Black pen.
- **NULL_PEN**   Null pen.
- **WHITE_PEN**   White pen.
- **ANSI_FIXED_FONT**   ANSI fixed system font.
- **ANSI_VAR_FONT**   ANSI variable system font.
- **DEVICE_DEFAULT_FONT**   Device-dependent font.
- **OEM_FIXED_FONT**   OEM-dependent fixed font.
- **SYSTEM_FONT**   The system font. By default, Windows uses the system font to draw menus, dialog-box controls, and other text. In Windows versions 3.0 and later, the system font is proportional width; earlier versions of Windows use a fixed-width system font.
- **SYSTEM_FIXED_FONT**   The fixed-width system font used in Windows prior to version 3.0. This object is available for compatibility with earlier versions of Windows.
- **DEFAULT_PALETTE**   Default color palette. This palette consists of the 20 static colors in the system palette.

Remarks   Selects a **CGdiObject** object that corresponds to one of the predefined stock pens, brushes, or fonts.

See Also   **CGdiObject::GetObject**

CDC::SetAbortProc

int SetAbortProc(BOOL (CALLBACK EXPORT* *lpfn* **)(HDC, int));**

Return Value

Specifies the outcome of the **SetAbortProc** function. Some of the following values are more probable than others, but all are possible.

- **SP_ERROR**   General error.
- **SP_OUTOFDISK**   Not enough disk space is currently available for spooling, and no more space will become available.
- **SP_OUTOFMEMORY**   Not enough memory is available for spooling.
- **SP_USERABORT**   User ended the job through the Print Manager.

Parameters

lpfn   A pointer to the abort function to install as the abort procedure. For more about the callback function, see the section "Callback Function for CDC::SetAbortProc" on page 1257.

Remarks

Installs the abort procedure for the print job. If an application is to allow the print job to be canceled during spooling, it must set the abort function before the print job is started with the **StartDoc** member function. The Print Manager calls the abort function during spooling to allow the application to cancel the print job or to process out-of-disk-space conditions. If no abort function is set, the print job will fail if there is not enough disk space for spooling.

Note that the features of Microsoft Visual C++ simplify the creation of the callback function passed to **SetAbortProc**. The address passed to the **EnumObjects** member function is a pointer to a function exported with **__export** and with the Pascal calling convention. In protect-mode applications, you do not have to create this function with the Windows **MakeProcInstance** function or free the function after use with the Windows function **FreeProcInstance**

You also do not have to export the function name in an **EXPORTS** statement in your application's module-definition file. You can instead use the **EXPORT** function modifier, as in

BOOL CALLBACK EXPORT AFunction(**HDC, int**);

to cause the compiler to emit the proper export record for export by name without aliasing. This works for most needs. For some special cases, such as exporting a function by ordinal or aliasing the export, you still need to use an **EXPORTS** statement in a module-definition file.

For compiling Microsoft Foundation programs, you'll normally use the /GA and /GEs compiler options. The /Gw compiler option is not used with the Microsoft Foundation classes. (If you do use the Windows function **MakeProcInstance**, you will need to explicitly cast the returned function pointer from **FARPROC** to the type needed by this member function.) Callback registration interfaces are now type-safe (you must pass in a function pointer that points to the right kind of function for the specific callback).

Also note that all callback functions must trap Microsoft Foundation exceptions before returning to Windows, since exceptions cannot be thrown across callback boundaries. For more information about exceptions, see the article "Exceptions" in *Programming with the Microsoft Foundation Class Library*.

CDC::SetArcDirection

int SetArcDirection(int *nArcDirection* **);**

Return Value   Specifies the old arc direction, if successful; otherwise 0.

Parameters   *nArcDirection*   Specifies the new arc direction. This parameter can be either of the following values:

- **AD_COUNTERCLOCKWISE**   Figures drawn counterclockwise.
- **AD_CLOCKWISE**   Figures drawn clockwise.

Remarks   Sets the drawing direction to be used for arc and rectangle functions. The default direction is counterclockwise. The **SetArcDirection** function specifies the direction in which the following functions draw:

Arc	**Pie**
ArcTo	**Rectangle**
Chord	**RoundRect**
Ellipse	

See Also   **CDC::GetArcDirection**, **::SetArcDirection**

CDC::SetAttribDC

virtual void SetAttribDC(HDC *hDC* **);**

Parameters   *hDC*   A Windows device context.

Remarks   Call this function to set the attribute device context, **m_hAttribDC**. This member function does not attach the device context to the **CDC** object. Only the output device context is attached to a **CDC** object.

See Also   **CDC::SetOutputDC**, **CDC::ReleaseAttribDC**, **CDC::ReleaseOutputDC**

CDC::SetBkColor

virtual COLORREF SetBkColor(COLORREF *crColor* **);**

Return Value

The previous background color as an RGB color value. If an error occurs, the return value is 0x80000000.

Parameters

crColor   Specifies the new background color.

Remarks

Sets the current background color to the specified color. If the background mode is **OPAQUE**, the system uses the background color to fill the gaps in styled lines, the gaps between hatched lines in brushes, and the background in character cells. The system also uses the background color when converting bitmaps between color and monochrome device contexts. If the device cannot display the specified color, the system sets the background color to the nearest physical color.

See Also

CDC::BitBlt, **CDC::GetBkColor**, **CDC::GetBkMode**, **CDC::SetBkMode**, **CDC::StretchBlt**, **::SetBkColor**

CDC::SetBkMode

int SetBkMode(int *nBkMode* **);**

Return Value

The previous background mode.

Parameters

nBkMode   Specifies the mode to be set. This parameter can be either of the following values:

- **OPAQUE**   Background is filled with the current background color before the text, hatched brush, or pen is drawn. This is the default background mode.

- **TRANSPARENT**   Background is not changed before drawing.

Remarks

Sets the background mode. The background mode defines whether the system removes existing background colors on the drawing surface before drawing text, hatched brushes, or any pen style that is not a solid line.

See Also

CDC::GetBkColor, **CDC::GetBkMode**, **CDC::SetBkColor**, **::SetBkMode**

CDC::SetBoundsRect

UINT SetBoundsRect(LPCRECT *lpRectBounds***, UINT** *flags* **);**

Return Value

The current state of the bounding rectangle, if the function is successful. Like *flags*, the return value can be a combination of **DCB_** values:

- **DCB_ACCUMULATE**   The bounding rectangle is not empty. This value will always be set.
- **DCB_DISABLE**   Bounds accumulation is off.
- **DCB_ENABLE**   Bounds accumulation is on.

Parameters

lpRectBounds   Points to a **RECT** structure or **CRect** object that is used to set the bounding rectangle. Rectangle dimensions are given in logical coordinates. This parameter can be **NULL**.

flags   Specifies how the new rectangle will be combined with the accumulated rectangle. This parameter can be a combination of the following values:

- **DCB_ACCUMULATE**   Add the rectangle specified by *lpRectBounds* to the bounding rectangle (using a rectangle-union operation).
- **DCB_DISABLE**   Turn off bounds accumulation.
- **DCB_ENABLE**   Turn on bounds accumulation. (The default setting for bounds accumulation is disabled.)

Remarks

Controls the accumulation of bounding-rectangle information for the specified device context. Windows can maintain a bounding rectangle for all drawing operations. This rectangle can be queried and reset by the application. The drawing bounds are useful for invalidating bitmap caches.

See Also

CDC::GetBoundsRect, **::SetBoundsRect**, **RECT**, **CRect**

CDC::SetBrushOrg

CPoint SetBrushOrg(int *x*, int *y*);

CPoint SetBrushOrg(POINT *point*);

Return Value

The previous origin of the brush in device units.

Parameters

x   Specifies the x-coordinate (in device units) of the new origin. This value must be in the range 0–7.

y   Specifies the y-coordinate (in device units) of the new origin. This value must be in the range 0–7.

point   Specifies the x- and y-coordinates of the new origin. Each value must be in the range 0–7. You can pass either a **POINT** structure or a **CPoint** object for this parameter.

Remarks

Specifies the origin that GDI will assign to the next brush that the application selects into the device context. The default coordinates for the brush origin are (0, 0). To alter the origin of a brush, call the **UnrealizeObject** function for the

CBrush object, call **SetBrushOrg**, and then call the **SelectObject** member function to select the brush into the device context. Do not use **SetBrushOrg** with stock **CBrush** objects.

See Also   **CBrush**, **CDC::GetBrushOrg**, **CDC::SelectObject**, **CGdiObject::UnrealizeObject**, **::SetBrushOrg**, **POINT**, **CPoint**

CDC::SetColorAdjustment

BOOL SetColorAdjustment(const COLORADJUSTMENT* *lpColorAdjust* **);**

Return Value   Nonzero if successful; otherwise 0.

Parameters   *lpColorAdjust*   Points to a **COLORADJUSTMENT** data structure containing the color adjustment values.

Remarks   Sets the color adjustment values for the device context using the specified values. The color adjustment values are used to adjust the input color of the source bitmap for calls to the **CDC::StretchBlt** member function when **HALFTONE** mode is set.

See Also   **CDC::SetStretchBltMode**, **CDC::StretchBlt**, **::StretchDIBits**

CDC::SetMapMode

virtual int SetMapMode(int *nMapMode* **);**

Return Value   The previous mapping mode.

Parameters   *nMapMode*   Specifies the new mapping mode. It can be any one of the following values:

- **MM_ANISOTROPIC**   Logical units are converted to arbitrary units with arbitrarily scaled axes. Setting the mapping mode to **MM_ANISOTROPIC** does not change the current window or viewport settings. To change the units, orientation, and scaling, call the **SetWindowExt** and **SetViewportExt** member functions.

- **MM_HIENGLISH**   Each logical unit is converted to 0.001 inch. Positive x is to the right; positive y is up.

- **MM_HIMETRIC**   Each logical unit is converted to 0.01 millimeter. Positive x is to the right; positive y is up.

- **MM_ISOTROPIC**   Logical units are converted to arbitrary units with equally scaled axes; that is, 1 unit along the x-axis is equal to 1 unit along the y-axis. Use the **SetWindowExt** and **SetViewportExt** member functions to specify the desired units and the orientation of the axes. GDI makes adjustments as necessary to ensure that the x and y units remain the same size.

- **MM_LOENGLISH**   Each logical unit is converted to 0.01 inch. Positive x is to the right; positive y is up.

- **MM_LOMETRIC**   Each logical unit is converted to 0.1 millimeter. Positive x is to the right; positive y is up.

- **MM_TEXT**   Each logical unit is converted to 1 device pixel. Positive x is to the right; positive y is down.

- **MM_TWIPS**   Each logical unit is converted to 1/20 of a point. (Because a point is 1/72 inch, a twip is 1/1440 inch.) Positive x is to the right; positive y is up.

Remarks   Sets the mapping mode. The mapping mode defines the unit of measure used to convert logical units to device units; it also defines the orientation of the device's x- and y-axes. GDI uses the mapping mode to convert logical coordinates into the appropriate device coordinates. The **MM_TEXT** mode allows applications to work in device pixels, where 1 unit is equal to 1 pixel. The physical size of a pixel varies from device to device. The **MM_HIENGLISH**, **MM_HIMETRIC**, **MM_LOENGLISH**, **MM_LOMETRIC**, and **MM_TWIPS** modes are useful for applications that must draw in physically meaningful units (such as inches or millimeters). The **MM_ISOTROPIC** mode ensures a 1:1 aspect ratio, which is useful when it is important to preserve the exact shape of an image. The **MM_ANISOTROPIC** mode allows the x- and y-coordinates to be adjusted independently.

See Also   **CDC::SetViewportExt**, **CDC::SetWindowExt**, **::SetMapMode**

CDC::SetMapperFlags

DWORD SetMapperFlags(DWORD *dwFlag* **);**

Return Value   The previous value of the font-mapper flag.

Parameters   *dwFlag*   Specifies whether the font mapper attempts to match a font's aspect height and width to the device. When this value is **ASPECT_FILTERING**, the mapper selects only fonts whose x-aspect and y-aspect exactly match those of the specified device.

Remarks   Changes the method used by the font mapper when it converts a logical font to a physical font. An application can use **SetMapperFlags** to cause the font mapper to attempt to choose only a physical font that exactly matches the aspect ratio of the specified device. An application that uses only raster fonts can use the **SetMapperFlags** function to ensure that the font selected by the font mapper is attractive and readable on the specified device. Applications that use scalable (TrueType) fonts typically do not use **SetMapperFlags**. If no physical font has an aspect ratio that matches the specification in the logical font, GDI chooses a new aspect ratio and selects a font that matches this new aspect ratio.

See Also   **::SetMapperFlags**

CDC::SetMiterLimit

BOOL SetMiterLimit(float *fMiterLimit* **);**

Return Value   Nonzero if the function is successful; otherwise 0.

Parameters   *fMiterLimit*   Specifies the new miter limit for the device context.

Remarks   Sets the limit for the length of miter joins for the device context. The miter length is defined as the distance from the intersection of the line walls on the inside of the join to the intersection of the line walls on the outside of the join. The miter limit is the maximum allowed ratio of the miter length to the line width. The default miter limit is 10.0.

See Also   **CDC::GetMiterLimit**, **::SetMiterLimit**

CDC::SetOutputDC

virtual void SetOutputDC(HDC *hDC* **);**

Parameters   *hDC*   A Windows device context.

Remarks   Call this member function to set the output device context, **m_hDC**. This member function can only be called when a device context has not been attached to the **CDC** object. This member function sets **m_hDC** but does not attach the device context to the **CDC** object.

See Also   **CDC::SetAttribDC**, **CDC::ReleaseAttribDC**, **CDC::ReleaseOutputDC**, **CDC::m_hDC**

CDC::SetPixel

COLORREF SetPixel(int *x*, **int** *y*, **COLORREF** *crColor* **);**

COLORREF SetPixel(POINT *point*, **COLORREF** *crColor* **);**

Return Value   An RGB value for the color that the point is actually painted. This value can be different from that specified by *crColor* if an approximation of that color is used. If the function fails (if the point is outside the clipping region), the return value is −1.

Parameters   *x*   Specifies the logical x-coordinate of the point to be set.

y   Specifies the logical y-coordinate of the point to be set.

crColor   Specifies the color used to paint the point.

point   Specifies the logical x- and y-coordinates of the point to be set. You can pass either a **POINT** structure or a **CPoint** object for this parameter.

Remarks   Sets the pixel at the point specified to the closest approximation of the color specified by *crColor*. The point must be in the clipping region. If the point is not in the clipping region, the function does nothing. Not all devices support the **SetPixel** function. To determine whether a device supports **SetPixel**, call the **GetDeviceCaps** member function with the **RASTERCAPS** index and check the return value for the **RC_BITBLT** flag.

See Also   **CDC::GetDeviceCaps**, **CDC::GetPixel**, **::SetPixel**, **POINT**, **CPoint**

CDC::SetPixelV

BOOL SetPixelV(int *x*, **int** *y*, **COLORREF** *crColor*);

BOOL SetPixelV(POINT *point*, **COLORREF** *crColor*);

Return Value   Nonzero if the function is successful; otherwise 0.

Parameters   *x*   Specifies the x-coordinate, in logical units, of the point to be set.

y   Specifies the y-coordinate, in logical units, of the point to be set.

crColor   Specifies the color to be used to paint the point.

point   Specifies the logical x- and y-coordinates of the point to be set. You can pass either a **POINT** data structure or a **CPoint** object for this parameter.

Remarks   Sets the pixel at the specified coordinates to the closest approximation of the specified color. The point must be in both the clipping region and the visible part of the device surface. Not all devices support the member function. For more information, see the **RC_BITBLT** capability in the **CDC::GetDeviceCaps** member function. **SetPixelV** is faster than **SetPixel** because it does not need to return the color value of the point actually painted.

See Also   **CDC::GetDeviceCaps**, **CDC::SetPixel**, **::SetPixelV**

CDC::SetPolyFillMode

int SetPolyFillMode(int *nPolyFillMode*);

Return Value   The previous filling mode, if successful; otherwise 0.

Parameters   *nPolyFillMode*   Specifies the new filling mode. This value may be either **ALTERNATE** or **WINDING**. The default mode set in Windows is **ALTERNATE**.

Remarks   Sets the polygon-filling mode. When the polygon-filling mode is **ALTERNATE**, the system fills the area between odd-numbered and even-numbered polygon sides on each scan line. That is, the system fills the area between the first and second side, between the third and fourth side, and so on. This mode is the default. When the polygon-filling mode is **WINDING**, the system uses the direction in which a figure was drawn to determine whether to fill an area. Each line segment in a polygon is drawn in either a clockwise or a counterclockwise direction. Whenever an imaginary line drawn from an enclosed area to the outside of a figure passes through a clockwise line segment, a count is incremented. When the line passes through a counterclockwise line segment, the count is decremented. The area is filled if the count is nonzero when the line reaches the outside of the figure.

See Also   **CDC::GetPolyFillMode**, **CDC::PolyPolygon**, **::SetPolyFillMode**

CDC::SetROP2

int SetROP2(int *nDrawMode* **);**

Return Value   The previous drawing mode. It can be any of the values given in the Windows SDK documentation.

Parameters   *nDrawMode*   Specifies the new drawing mode. It can be any of the following values:

- **R2_BLACK**   Pixel is always black.
- **R2_WHITE**   Pixel is always white.
- **R2_NOP**   Pixel remains unchanged.
- **R2_NOT**   Pixel is the inverse of the screen color.
- **R2_COPYPEN**   Pixel is the pen color.
- **R2_NOTCOPYPEN**   Pixel is the inverse of the pen color.
- **R2_MERGEPENNOT**   Pixel is a combination of the pen color and the inverse of the screen color (final pixel = (NOT screen pixel) OR pen).
- **R2_MASKPENNOT**   Pixel is a combination of the colors common to both the pen and the inverse of the screen (final pixel = (NOT screen pixel) AND pen).
- **R2_MERGENOTPEN**   Pixel is a combination of the screen color and the inverse of the pen color (final pixel = (NOT pen) OR screen pixel).
- **R2_MASKNOTPEN**   Pixel is a combination of the colors common to both the screen and the inverse of the pen (final pixel = (NOT pen) AND screen pixel).

- **R2_MERGEPEN**   Pixel is a combination of the pen color and the screen color (final pixel = pen OR screen pixel).

- **R2_NOTMERGEPEN**   Pixel is the inverse of the **R2_MERGEPEN** color (final pixel = NOT(pen OR screen pixel)).

- **R2_MASKPEN**   Pixel is a combination of the colors common to both the pen and the screen (final pixel = pen AND screen pixel).

- **R2_NOTMASKPEN**   Pixel is the inverse of the **R2_MASKPEN** color (final pixel = NOT(pen AND screen pixel)).

- **R2_XORPEN**   Pixel is a combination of the colors that are in the pen or in the screen, but not in both (final pixel = pen XOR screen pixel).

- **R2_NOTXORPEN**   Pixel is the inverse of the **R2_XORPEN** color (final pixel = NOT(pen XOR screen pixel)).

Remarks   Sets the current drawing mode. The drawing mode specifies how the colors of the pen and the interior of filled objects are combined with the color already on the display surface. The drawing mode is for raster devices only; it does not apply to vector devices. Drawing modes are binary raster-operation codes representing all possible Boolean combinations of two variables, using the binary operators AND, OR, and XOR (exclusive OR), and the unary operation NOT.

See Also   **CDC::GetDeviceCaps, CDC::GetROP2, ::SetROP2**

CDC::SetStretchBltMode

int SetStretchBltMode(int *nStretchMode* **);**

Return Value   The previous stretching mode. It can be **STRETCH_ANDSCANS**, **STRETCH_DELETESCANS**, or **STRETCH_ORSCRANS**.

Parameters   *nStretchMode*   Specifies the new bitmap-stretching mode. It can be any of the following values:

- **STRETCH_ANDSCANS**   Uses the AND operator to combine eliminated lines with the remaining lines. This mode preserves black pixels at the expense of colored or white pixels.

- **STRETCH_DELETESCANS**   Deletes the eliminated lines. Information in the eliminated lines is not preserved.

- **STRETCH_ORSCANS**   Uses the OR operator to combine eliminated lines with the remaining lines. This mode preserves colored or white pixels at the expense of black pixels.

Remarks   Sets the bitmap-stretching mode for the **StretchBlt** member function. The bitmap-stretching mode defines how information is removed from bitmaps that are compressed by using the function. The default mode is **STRETCH_ANDSCANS**.

The **STRETCH_ANDSCANS** and **STRETCH_ORSCANS** modes are typically used to preserve foreground pixels in monochrome bitmaps. The **STRETCH_DELETESCANS** mode is typically used to preserve color in color bitmaps.

See Also   **CDC::GetStretchBltMode**, **CDC::StretchBlt**, **::SetStretchBltMode**

CDC::SetTextAlign

UINT SetTextAlign(UINT *nFlags* **);**

Return Value   The previous text-alignment setting, if successful. The low-order byte contains the horizontal setting and the high-order byte contains the vertical setting; otherwise 0.

Parameters   *nFlags*   Specifies text-alignment flags. The flags specify the relationship between a point and a rectangle that bounds the text. The point can be either the current position or coordinates specified by a text-output function. The rectangle that bounds the text is defined by the adjacent character cells in the text string. The *nFlags* parameter can be one or more flags from the following three categories. Choose only one flag from each category. The first category affects text alignment in the x-direction:

- **TA_CENTER**   Aligns the point with the horizontal center of the bounding rectangle.
- **TA_LEFT**   Aligns the point with the left side of the bounding rectangle. This is the default setting.
- **TA_RIGHT**   Aligns the point with the right side of the bounding rectangle.

The second category affects text alignment in the y-direction:

- **TA_BASELINE**   Aligns the point with the baseline of the chosen font.
- **TA_BOTTOM**   Aligns the point with the bottom of the bounding rectangle.
- **TA_TOP**   Aligns the point with the top of the bounding rectangle. This is the default setting.

The third category determines whether the current position is updated when text is written:

- **TA_NOUPDATECP**   Does not update the current position after each call to a text-output function. This is the default setting.
- **TA_UPDATECP**   Updates the current x-position after each call to a text-output function. The new position is at the right side of the bounding rectangle for the text. When this flag is set, the coordinates specified in calls to the **TextOut** member function are ignored.

Remarks   Sets the text-alignment flags. The **TextOut** and **ExtTextOut** member functions use these flags when positioning a string of text on a display or device. The flags specify the relationship between a specific point and a rectangle that bounds the text. The coordinates of this point are passed as parameters to the **TextOut** member function. The rectangle that bounds the text is formed by the adjacent character cells in the text string.

See Also   **CDC::ExtTextOut, CDC::GetTextAlign, CDC::TabbedTextOut, CDC::TextOut, ::SetTextAlign**

CDC::SetTextCharacterExtra

int SetTextCharacterExtra(int *nCharExtra* **);**

Return Value   The amount of the previous intercharacter spacing.

Parameters   *nCharExtra*   Specifies the amount of extra space (in logical units) to be added to each character. If the current mapping mode is not **MM_TEXT**, *nCharExtra* is transformed and rounded to the nearest pixel.

Remarks   Sets the amount of intercharacter spacing. GDI adds this spacing to each character, including break characters, when it writes a line of text to the device context. The default value for the amount of intercharacter spacing is 0.

See Also   **CDC::GetTextCharacterExtra, ::SetTextCharacterExtra**

CDC::SetTextColor

virtual COLORREF SetTextColor(COLORREF *crColor* **);**

Return Value   An RGB value for the previous text color.

Parameters   *crColor*   Specifies the color of the text as an RGB color value.

Remarks   Sets the text color to the specified color. The system will use this text color when writing text to this device context and also when converting bitmaps between color and monochrome device contexts. If the device cannot represent the specified color, the system sets the text color to the nearest physical color. The background color for a character is specified by the **SetBkColor** and **SetBkMode** member functions.

See Also   **CDC::GetTextColor, CDC::BitBlt, CDC::SetBkColor, CDC::SetBkMode, ::SetTextColor**

CDC::SetTextJustification

int SetTextJustification(int *nBreakExtra***, int** *nBreakCount* **);**

Return Value   One if the function is successful; otherwise 0.

Parameters   *nBreakExtra*   Specifies the total extra space to be added to the line of text (in logical units). If the current mapping mode is not **MM_TEXT**, the value given by this parameter is converted to the current mapping mode and rounded to the nearest device unit.

nBreakCount   Specifies the number of break characters in the line.

Remarks   Adds space to the break characters in a string. An application can use the **GetTextMetrics** member functions to retrieve a font's break character. After the **SetTextJustification** member function is called, a call to a text-output function (such as **TextOut**) distributes the specified extra space evenly among the specified number of break characters. The break character is usually the space character (ASCII 32), but may be defined by a font as some other character.

The member function **GetTextExtent** is typically used with **SetTextJustification**. **GetTextExtent** computes the width of a given line before alignment. An application can determine how much space to specify in the *nBreakExtra* parameter by subtracting the value returned by **GetTextExtent** from the width of the string after alignment.

The **SetTextJustification** function can be used to align a line that contains multiple runs in different fonts. In this case, the line must be created piecemeal by aligning and writing each run separately. Because rounding errors can occur during alignment, the system keeps a running error term that defines the current error. When aligning a line that contains multiple runs, **GetTextExtent** automatically uses this error term when it computes the extent of the next run. This allows the text-output function to blend the error into the new run. After each line has been aligned, this error term must be cleared to prevent it from being incorporated into the next line. The term can be cleared by calling **SetTextJustification** with *nBreakExtra* set to 0.

See Also   **CDC::GetMapMode**, **CDC::GetTextExtent**, **CDC::GetTextMetrics**, **CDC::SetMapMode**, **CDC::TextOut**, **::SetTextJustification**

CDC::SetViewportExt

virtual CSize SetViewportExt(int *cx*, **int** *cy* **);**

virtual CSize SetViewportExt(SIZE *size* **);**

Return Value   The previous extents of the viewport as a **CSize** object. When an error occurs, the x- and y-coordinates of the returned **CSize** object are both set to 0.

Parameters   *cx*   Specifies the x-extent of the viewport (in device units).

cy   Specifies the y-extent of the viewport (in device units).

size   Specifies the x- and y-extents of the viewport (in device units).

Remarks   Sets the x- and y-extents of the viewport of the device context. The viewport, along with the device-context window, defines how GDI maps points in the logical coordinate system to points in the coordinate system of the actual device. In other words, they define how GDI converts logical coordinates into device coordinates. When the following mapping modes are set, calls to **SetWindowExt** and **SetViewportExt** are ignored:

MM_HIENGLISH	**MM_LOMETRIC**
MM_HIMETRIC	**MM_TEXT**
MM_LOENGLISH	**MM_TWIPS**

When **MM_ISOTROPIC** mode is set, an application must call the **SetWindowExt** member function before it calls **SetViewportExt**.

See Also   **CDC::SetWindowExt, ::SetViewportExt, CSize, CDC::GetViewportExt**

CDC::SetViewportOrg

virtual CPoint SetViewportOrg(int *x*, int *y*);

virtual CPoint SetViewportOrg(POINT *point*);

Return Value   The previous origin of the viewport (in device coordinates) as a **CPoint** object.

Parameters   *x*   Specifies the x-coordinate (in device units) of the origin of the viewport. The value must be within the range of the device coordinate system.

y   Specifies the y-coordinate (in device units) of the origin of the viewport. The value must be within the range of the device coordinate system.

point   Specifies the origin of the viewport. The values must be within the range of the device coordinate system. You can pass either a **POINT** structure or a **CPoint** object for this parameter.

Remarks   Sets the viewport origin of the device context. The viewport, along with the device-context window, defines how GDI maps points in the logical coordinate system to points in the coordinate system of the actual device. In other words, they define how GDI converts logical coordinates into device coordinates. The viewport origin marks the point in the device coordinate system to which GDI maps the window origin, a point in the logical coordinate system specified by the **SetWindowOrg** member function. GDI maps all other points by following the same process required to map the window origin to the viewport origin. For example, all points in a circle around the point at the window origin will be in a circle around the point at the viewport origin. Similarly, all points in a line that passes through the window origin will be in a line that passes through the viewport origin.

See Also   **CDC::SetWindowOrg**, **::SetViewportOrg**, **CPoint**, **POINT**, **CDC::GetViewportOrg**

CDC::SetWindowExt

virtual CSize SetWindowExt(int *cx,* **int** *cy* **);**

virtual CSize SetWindowExt(SIZE *size* **);**

Return Value   The previous extents of the window (in logical units) as a **CSize** object. If an error occurs, the x- and y-coordinates of the returned **CSize** object are both set to 0.

Parameters   *cx*   Specifies the x-extent (in logical units) of the window.

cy   Specifies the y-extent (in logical units) of the window.

size   Specifies the x- and y-extents (in logical units) of the window.

Remarks   Sets the x- and y-extents of the window associated with the device context. The window, along with the device-context viewport, defines how GDI maps points in the logical coordinate system to points in the device coordinate system. When the following mapping modes are set, calls to **SetWindowExt** and **SetViewportExt** functions are ignored:

- **MM_HIENGLISH**
- **MM_HIMETRIC**
- **MM_LOENGLISH**
- **MM_LOMETRIC**
- **MM_TEXT**
- **MM_TWIPS**

When **MM_ISOTROPIC** mode is set, an application must call the **SetWindowExt** member function before calling **SetViewportExt**.

See Also   **CDC::GetWindowExt**, **CDC::SetViewportExt**, **::SetWindowExt**, **CSize**

CDC::SetWindowOrg

CPoint SetWindowOrg(int *x,* **int** *y* **);**

CPoint SetWindowOrg(POINT *point* **);**

Return Value   The previous origin of the window as a **CPoint** object.

Parameters   *x*   Specifies the logical x-coordinate of the new origin of the window.

y   Specifies the logical y-coordinate of the new origin of the window.

point   Specifies the logical coordinates of the new origin of the window. You can pass either a **POINT** structure or a **CPoint** object for this parameter.

Remarks   Sets the window origin of the device context. The window, along with the device-context viewport, defines how GDI maps points in the logical coordinate system to points in the device coordinate system. The window origin marks the point in the logical coordinate system from which GDI maps the viewport origin, a point in the device coordinate system specified by the **SetWindowOrg** function. GDI maps all other points by following the same process required to map the window origin to the viewport origin. For example, all points in a circle around the point at the window origin will be in a circle around the point at the viewport origin. Similarly, all points in a line that passes through the window origin will be in a line that passes through the viewport origin.

See Also   **::SetWindowOrg, ::SetViewportOrg, CPoint, POINT, CDC::GetWindowOrg**

CDC::StartDoc

int StartDoc(LPDOCINFO *lpDocInfo* **);**

Return Value   The value −1 if there is an error such as insufficient memory or an invalid port specification occurs; otherwise a positive value.

Parameters   *lpDocInfo*   Points to a **DOCINFO** structure containing the name of the document file and the name of the output file.

Remarks   Informs the device driver that a new print job is starting and that all subsequent **StartPage** and **EndPage** calls should be spooled under the same job until an **EndDoc** call occurs. This ensures that documents longer than one page will not be interspersed with other jobs.

For Windows versions 3.1 and later, this function replaces the **STARTDOC** printer escape. Using this function ensures that documents containing more than one page are not interspersed with other print jobs.

When running under Windows version 3.0, this member functions sends a **STARTDOC** printer escape.

StartDoc should not be used inside metafiles.

See Also   **CDC::Escape, CDC::EndDoc, CDC::AbortDoc**

CDC::StartPage

int StartPage( );

Remarks   Call this member function to prepare the printer driver to receive data. **StartPage** supersedes the **NEWFRAME** and **BANDINFO** escapes. For an overview of the sequence of printing calls, see the **StartDoc** member function.

The system disables the **ResetDC** member function between calls to **StartPage** and **EndPage**.

When running under Windows version 3.0, this member function does nothing.

See Also   **CDC::Escape, CDC::EndPage**

CDC::StretchBlt

BOOL StretchBlt(int *x*, **int** *y*, **int** *nWidth*, **int** *nHeight*, **CDC*** *pSrcDC*, **int** *xSrc*, **int** *ySrc*, **int** *nSrcWidth*, **int** *nSrcHeight*, **DWORD** *dwRop*);

Return Value   Nonzero if the bitmap is drawn; otherwise 0.

Parameters   *x*   Specifies the x-coordinate (in logical units) of the upper-left corner of the destination rectangle.

y   Specifies the y-coordinate (in logical units) of the upper-left corner of the destination rectangle.

nWidth   Specifies the width (in logical units) of the destination rectangle.

nHeight   Specifies the height (in logical units) of the destination rectangle.

pSrcDC   Specifies the source device context.

xSrc   Specifies the x-coordinate (in logical units) of the upper-left corner of the source rectangle.

ySrc   Specifies the x-coordinate (in logical units) of the upper-left corner of the source rectangle.

nSrcWidth   Specifies the width (in logical units) of the source rectangle.

nSrcHeight   Specifies the height (in logical units) of the source rectangle.

dwRop   Specifies the raster operation to be performed. Raster operation codes define how GDI combines colors in output operations that involve a current brush, a possible source bitmap, and a destination bitmap. This parameter may be one of the following values:

- **BLACKNESS**   Turns all output black.
- **DSTINVERT**   Inverts the destination bitmap.
- **MERGECOPY**   Combines the pattern and the source bitmap using the Boolean AND operator.
- **MERGEPAINT**   Combines the inverted source bitmap with the destination bitmap using the Boolean OR operator.
- **NOTSRCCOPY**   Copies the inverted source bitmap to the destination.

- **NOTSRCERASE**   Inverts the result of combining the destination and source bitmaps using the Boolean OR operator.

- **PATCOPY**   Copies the pattern to the destination bitmap.

- **PATINVERT**   Combines the destination bitmap with the pattern using the Boolean XOR operator.

- **PATPAINT**   Combines the inverted source bitmap with the pattern using the Boolean OR operator. Combines the result of this operation with the destination bitmap using the Boolean OR operator.

- **SRCAND**   Combines pixels of the destination and source bitmaps using the Boolean AND operator.

- **SRCCOPY**   Copies the source bitmap to the destination bitmap.

- **SRCERASE**   Inverts the destination bitmap and combines the result with the source bitmap using the Boolean AND operator.

- **SRCINVERT**   Combines pixels of the destination and source bitmaps using the Boolean XOR operator.

- **SRCPAINT**   Combines pixels of the destination and source bitmaps using the Boolean OR operator.

- **WHITENESS**   Turns all output white.

Remarks

Copies a bitmap from a source rectangle into a destination rectangle, stretching or compressing the bitmap if necessary to fit the dimensions of the destination rectangle. The function uses the stretching mode of the destination device context (set by **SetStretchBltMode**) to determine how to stretch or compress the bitmap.

The **StretchBlt** function moves the bitmap from the source device given by *pSrcDC* to the destination device represented by the device-context object whose member function is being called. The *xSrc*, *ySrc*, *nSrcWidth*, and *nSrcHeight* parameters define the upper-left corner and dimensions of the source rectangle. The *x*, *y*, *nWidth*, and *nHeight* parameters give the upper-left corner and dimensions of the destination rectangle. The raster operation specified by *dwRop* defines how the source bitmap and the bits already on the destination device are combined.

The **StretchBlt** function creates a mirror image of a bitmap if the signs of the *nSrcWidth* and *nWidth* or *nSrcHeight* and *nHeight* parameters differ. If *nSrcWidth* and *nWidth* have different signs, the function creates a mirror image of the bitmap along the x-axis. If *nSrcHeight* and *nHeight* have different signs, the function creates a mirror image of the bitmap along the y-axis.

The **StretchBlt** function stretches or compresses the source bitmap in memory and then copies the result to the destination. If a pattern is to be merged with the result, it is not merged until the stretched source bitmap is copied to the destination. If a brush is used, it is the selected brush in the destination device context. The destination coordinates are transformed according to the destination device context; the source coordinates are transformed according to the source device context.

If the destination, source, and pattern bitmaps do not have the same color format, **StretchBlt** converts the source and pattern bitmaps to match the destination bitmaps. The foreground and background colors of the destination device context are used in the conversion. If **StretchBlt** must convert a monochrome bitmap to color, it sets white bits (1) to the background color and black bits (0) to the foreground color. To convert color to monochrome, it sets pixels that match the background color to white (1) and sets all other pixels to black (0). The foreground and background colors of the device context with color are used.

Not all devices support the **StretchBlt** function. To determine whether a device supports **StretchBlt**, call the **GetDeviceCaps** member function with the **RASTERCAPS** index and check the return value for the **RC_STRETCHBLT** flag.

See Also   **CDC::BitBlt, CDC::GetDeviceCaps, CDC::SetStretchBltMode, ::StretchBlt**

CDC::StrokeAndFillPath

BOOL StrokeAndFillPath( );

Return Value   Nonzero if the function is successful; otherwise 0.

Remarks   Closes any open figures in a path, strokes the outline of the path by using the current pen, and fills its interior by using the current brush. The device context must contain a closed path. The **StrokeAndFillPath** member function has the same effect as closing all the open figures in the path, and stroking and filling the path separately, except that the filled region will not overlap the stroked region even if the pen is wide.

See Also   **CDC::BeginPath, CDC::FillPath, CDC::SetPolyFillMode, CDC::StrokePath, ::StrokeAndFillPath**

CDC::StrokePath

BOOL StrokePath( );

Return Value   Nonzero if the function is successful; otherwise 0.

Remarks   Renders the specified path by using the current pen. The device context must contain a closed path.

See Also   **CDC::BeginPath, CDC::EndPath, ::StrokePath**

CDC::TabbedTextOut

virtual CSize TabbedTextOut(int *x*, **int** *y*, **LPCTSTR** *lpszString*, **int** *nCount*,
int *nTabPositions*, **LPINT** *lpnTabStopPositions*, **int** *nTabOrigin* **);**

Return Value   The dimensions of the string (in logical units) as a **CSize** object.

Parameters   *x*   Specifies the logical x-coordinate of the starting point of the string.

y   Specifies the logical y-coordinate of the starting point of the string.

lpszString   Points to the character string to draw. You can pass either a pointer to an array of characters or a **CString** object for this parameter.

nCount   Specifies the number of characters in the string.

nTabPositions   Specifies the number of values in the array of tab-stop positions.

lpnTabStopPositions   Points to an array containing the tab-stop positions (in logical units). The tab stops must be sorted in increasing order; the smallest x-value should be the first item in the array.

nTabOrigin   Specifies the x-coordinate of the starting position from which tabs are expanded (in logical units).

Remarks   Writes a character string at the specified location, expanding tabs to the values specified in the array of tab-stop positions. Text is written in the currently selected font. If *nTabPositions* is 0 and *lpnTabStopPositions* is **NULL**, tabs are expanded to eight times the average character width. If *nTabPositions* is 1, the tab stops are separated by the distance specified by the first value in the *lpnTabStopPositions* array. If the *lpnTabStopPositions* array contains more than one value, a tab stop is set for each value in the array, up to the number specified by *nTabPositions*.

The *nTabOrigin* parameter allows an application to call the **TabbedTextOut** function several times for a single line. If the application calls the function more than once with the *nTabOrigin* set to the same value each time, the function expands all tabs relative to the position specified by *nTabOrigin*.

By default, the current position is not used or updated by the function. If an application needs to update the current position when it calls the function, the application can call the **SetTextAlign** member function with *nFlags* set to **TA_UPDATECP**. When this flag is set, Windows ignores the *x* and *y* parameters on subsequent calls to **TabbedTextOut**, using the current position instead.

See Also   **CDC::GetTabbedTextExtent, CDC::SetTextAlign, CDC::TextOut, CDC::SetTextColor, ::TabbedTextOut, CSize**

CDC::TextOut

virtual BOOL TextOut(int *x*, **int** *y*, **LPCTSTR** *lpszString*, **int** *nCount* **);**

virtual BOOL TextOut(int *x*, **int** *y*, **const CString&** *str* **);**

Return Value   Nonzero if the function is successful; otherwise 0.

Parameters   *x*   Specifies the logical x-coordinate of the starting point of the text.

y   Specifies the logical y-coordinate of the starting point of the text.

lpszString   Points to the character string to be drawn.

nCount   Specifies the number of bytes in the string.

str   A **CString** object that contains the characters to be drawn.

Remarks   Writes a character string at the specified location using the currently selected font. Character origins are at the upper-left corner of the character cell. By default, the current position is not used or updated by the function. If an application needs to update the current position when it calls **TextOut**, the application can call the **SetTextAlign** member function with *nFlags* set to **TA_UPDATECP**. When this flag is set, Windows ignores the *x* and *y* parameters on subsequent calls to **TextOut**, using the current position instead.

See Also   **CDC::ExtTextOut, CDC::GetTextExtent, CDC::SetTextAlign, CDC::SetTextColor, CDC::TabbedTextOut, ::TextOut**

CDC::UpdateColors

void UpdateColors( );

Remarks   Updates the client area of the device context by matching the current colors in the client area to the system palette on a pixel-by-pixel basis. An inactive window with a realized logical palette may call **UpdateColors** as an alternative to redrawing its client area when the system palette changes. For more information on using color palettes, see the Windows SDK documentation. The **UpdateColors** member function typically updates a client area faster than redrawing the area. However, because the function performs the color translation based on the color of each pixel before the system palette changed, each call to this function results in the loss of some color accuracy.

See Also   **CDC::RealizePalette, CPalette, ::UpdateColors**

CDC::WidenPath

BOOL WidenPath( );

Return Value Nonzero if the function is successful; otherwise 0.

Remarks Redefines the current path as the area that would be painted if the path were stroked using the pen currently selected into the device context. This function is successful only if the current pen is a geometric pen created by the second version of **CreatePen** member function, or if the pen is created with the first version of **CreatePen** and has a width, in device units, of greater than 1. The device context must contain a closed path. Any Bézier curves in the path are converted to sequences of straight lines approximating the widened curves. As such, no Bézier curves remain in the path after **WidenPath** is called.

See Also **CDC::BeginPath, CDC::EndPath, CDC::SetMiterLimit, ::WidenPath**

Data Members

CDC::m_hAttribDC

Remarks The attribute device context for this **CDC** object. By default, this device context is equal to **m_hDC**. In general, **CDC** GDI calls that request information from the device context are directed to **m_hAttribDC**. See the **CDC** class description for more on the use of these two device contexts.

See Also **CDC::m_hDC, CDC::SetAttribDC, CDC::ReleaseAttribDC**

CDC::m_hDC

Remarks The output device context for this **CDC** object. By default, **m_hDC** is equal to **m_hAttribDC**, the other device context wrapped by **CDC**. In general, **CDC** GDI calls that create output go to the **m_hDC** device context. You can initialize **m_hDC** and **m_hAttribDC** to point to different devices. See the **CDC** class description for more on the use of these two device contexts.

See Also **CDC::m_hAttribDC, CDC::SetOutputDC, CDC::ReleaseOutputDC**

class CDialog : public CWnd

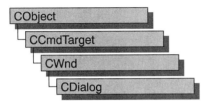

The **CDialog** class is the base class used for displaying dialog boxes on the screen. Dialog boxes are of two types: modal and modeless. A modal dialog box must be closed by the user before the application continues. A modeless dialog box allows the user to display the dialog box and return to another task without canceling or removing the dialog box.

A **CDialog** object is a combination of a dialog template and a **CDialog**-derived class. Use the dialog editor to create the dialog template and store it in a resource, then use ClassWizard to create a class derived from **CDialog**.

A dialog box, like any other window, receives messages from Windows. In a dialog box, you are particularly interested in handling notification messages from the dialog box's controls since that is how the user interacts with your dialog box. ClassWizard browses through the potential messages generated by each control in your dialog box, and you can select which messages you wish to handle. ClassWizard then adds the appropriate message-map entries and message-handler member functions to the new class for you. You only need to write application-specific code in the handler member functions.

If you prefer, you can always write message-map entries and member functions yourself instead of using ClassWizard.

In all but the most trivial dialog box, you add member variables to your derived dialog class to store data entered in the dialog box's controls by the user or to display data for the user. ClassWizard browses through those controls in your dialog box that can be mapped to data and prompts you to create a member variable for each control. At the same time, you choose a variable type and permissible range of values for each variable. ClassWizard adds the member variables to your derived dialog class.

ClassWizard then writes a data map to automatically handle the exchange of data between the member variables and the dialog box's controls. The data map provides functions that initialize the controls in the dialog box with the proper values, retrieve the data, and validate the data.

To create a modal dialog box, construct an object on the stack using the constructor for your derived dialog class and then call **DoModal** to create the dialog window and its controls. If you wish to create a modeless dialog, call **Create** in the constructor of your dialog class.

You can also create a template in memory by using a **DialogBoxResource** data structure as described in the Windows Software Development Kit documentation. After you construct a **CDialog** object, call **CreateIndirect** to create a modeless dialog box, or call **InitModalIndirect** and **DoModal** to create a modal dialog box.

ClassWizard writes the exchange and validation data map in an override of **CWnd::DoDataExchange** that ClassWizard adds to your new dialog class. See the **DoDataExchange** member function in **CWnd** for more on the exchange and validation functionality.

Both the programmer and the framework call **DoDataExchange** indirectly through a call to **CWnd::UpdateData**.

The framework calls **UpdateData** when the user clicks the OK button to close a modal dialog box. (The data is not retrieved if the Cancel button is clicked.) The default implementation of **OnInitDialog** also calls **UpdateData** to set the initial values of the controls. You typically override **OnInitDialog** to further initialize controls. **OnInitDialog** is called after all the dialog controls are created and just before the dialog box is displayed.

You can call **CWnd::UpdateData** at any time during the execution of a modal or modeless dialog box.

If you develop a dialog box by hand, you add the necessary member variables to the derived dialog-box class yourself, and you add member functions to set or get these values.

For more on ClassWizard, see the *Visual C++ User's Guide*, Chapter 12, and Chapter 12 of *Introducing Visual C++*.

Call **CWinApp::SetDialogBkColor** to set the background color for dialog boxes in your application.

A modal dialog box closes automatically when the user presses the OK or Cancel buttons or when your code calls the **EndDialog** member function.

When you implement a modeless dialog box, always override the **OnCancel** member function and call **DestroyWindow** from within it. Don't call the base class **CDialog::OnCancel**, because it calls **EndDialog**, which will make the dialog box invisible but will not destroy it. You should also override **PostNcDestroy** for modeless dialog boxes in order to delete **this**, since modeless dialog boxes are usually allocated with **new**. Modal dialog boxes are usually constructed on the frame and do not need **PostNcDestroy** cleanup.

#include <afxwin.h>

Construction

CDialog	Constructs a **CDialog** object.

Initialization

Create	Initializes the **CDialog** object. Creates a modeless dialog box and attaches it to the **CDialog** object.
CreateIndirect	Creates a modeless dialog box from a dialog-box template in memory (not resource-based).
InitModalIndirect	Creates a modal dialog box from a dialog-box template in memory (not resource-based). The parameters are stored until the function **DoModal** is called.

Operations

DoModal	Calls a modal dialog box and returns when done.
MapDialogRect	Converts the dialog-box units of a rectangle to screen units.
IsDialogMessage	Determines whether the given message is intended for the modeless dialog box and, if so, processes it.
NextDlgCtrl	Moves the focus to the next dialog-box control in the dialog box.
PrevDlgCtrl	Moves the focus to the previous dialog-box control in the dialog box.
GotoDlgCtrl	Moves the focus to a specified dialog-box control in the dialog box.
SetDefID	Changes the default pushbutton control for a dialog box to a specified pushbutton.
GetDefID	Gets the ID of the default pushbutton control for a dialog box.
SetHelpID	Sets a context-sensitive help ID for the dialog box.
EndDialog	Closes a modal dialog box.

Overridables

OnInitDialog	Override to augment dialog-box initialization.
OnSetFont	Override to specify the font that a dialog-box control is to use when it draws text.
OnOK	Override to perform the OK button action in a modal dialog box. The default closes the dialog box and **DoModal** returns **IDOK**.
OnCancel	Override to perform the Cancel button or ESC key action. The default closes the dialog box and **DoModal** returns **IDCANCEL**.

Member Functions

CDialog::CDialog

CDialog(LPCTSTR *lpszTemplateName,* **CWnd*** *pParentWnd* **= NULL);**

CDialog(UINT *nIDTemplate,* **CWnd*** *pParentWnd* **= NULL);**

Protected→
CDialog( );
END Protected

Parameters   *lpszTemplateName*   Contains a null-terminated string that is the name of a dialog-box template resource.

nIDTemplate   Contains the ID number of a dialog-box template resource.

pParentWnd   Points to the parent or owner window object (of type **CWnd**) to which the dialog object belongs. If it is **NULL**, the dialog object's parent window is set to the main application window.

Remarks   To construct a resource-based modal dialog box, call either public form of the constructor. One form of the constructor provides access to the dialog resource by template name. The other constructor provides access by template ID number, usually with an **IDD_** prefix (for example, IDD_DIALOG1).

To construct a modal dialog box from a template in memory, first invoke the parameterless, protected constructor and then call **InitModalIndirect**.

After you construct a modal dialog box with one of the above methods, call **DoModal**.

To construct a modeless dialog box, use the protected form of the **CDialog** constructor. The constructor is protected because you must derive your own dialog-box class to implement a modeless dialog box. Construction of a modeless dialog box is a two-step process. First call the constructor; then call the **Create** member function to create a resource-based dialog box, or call **CreateIndirect** to create the dialog box from a template in memory.

See Also   **CDialog::Create, CWnd::DestroyWindow, CDialog::InitModalIndirect, CDialog::DoModal, ::CreateDialog**

CDialog::Create

BOOL Create(LPCTSTR *lpszTemplateName***, CWnd*** *pParentWnd* **= NULL);**

BOOL Create(UINT *nIDTemplate***, CWnd*** *pParentWnd* **= NULL);**

Return Value   Both forms return nonzero if dialog-box creation and initialization were successful; otherwise 0.

Parameters   *lpszTemplateName*   Contains a null-terminated string that is the name of a dialog-box template resource.

pParentWnd   Points to the parent window object (of type **CWnd**) to which the dialog object belongs. If it is **NULL**, the dialog object's parent window is set to the main application window.

nIDTemplate   Contains the ID number of a dialog-box template resource.

Remarks   Call **Create** to create a modeless dialog box using a dialog-box template from a resource. You can put the call to **Create** inside the constructor or call it after the constructor is invoked.

Two forms of the **Create** member function are provided for access to the dialog-box template resource by either template name or template ID number (for example, IDD_DIALOG1).

For either form, pass a pointer to the parent window object. If *pParentWnd* is **NULL**, the dialog box will be created with its parent or owner window set to the main application window.

The **Create** member function returns immediately after it creates the dialog box.

Use the **WS_VISIBLE** style in the dialog-box template if the dialog box should appear when the parent window is created. Otherwise, you must call **ShowWindow**. For further dialog-box styles and their application, see the Windows Software Development Kit (SDK) and the *Class Library Reference*.

Use the **CWnd::DestroyWindow** function to destroy a dialog box created by the **Create** function.

See Also   **CDialog::CDialog, CWnd::DestroyWindow, CDialog::InitModalIndirect, CDialog::DoModal, ::CreateDialog**

CDialog::CreateIndirect

BOOL CreateIndirect(const void* *lpDialogTemplate***, CWnd*** *pParentWnd* **= NULL);**

Return Value   Nonzero if the dialog box was created and initialized successfully; otherwise 0.

Parameters   *lpDialogTemplate*   Points to memory that contains a dialog-box template used to create the dialog box. This template is in the form of a **DialogBoxHeader** structure and control information. For more information on this structure, see the Windows SDK.

pParentWnd   Points to the dialog object's parent window object (of type **CWnd**). If it is **NULL**, the dialog object's parent window is set to the main application window.

Remarks   Call this member function to create a modeless dialog box from a dialog-box template in memory.

The **CreateIndirect** member function returns immediately after it creates the dialog box.

Use the **WS_VISIBLE** style in the dialog-box template if the dialog box should appear when the parent window is created. Otherwise, you must call **ShowWindow** to cause it to appear. For more information on how you can specify other dialog-box styles in the template, see the Windows SDK and the *Visual C++ User's Guide*.

Use the **CWnd::DestroyWindow** function to destroy a dialog box created by the **CreateIndirect** function.

See Also   **CDialog::CDialog**, **CWnd::DestroyWindow**, **CDialog::Create**, **::CreateDialogIndirect**

CDialog::DoModal

virtual int DoModal( );

Return Value   An **int** value that specifies the value of the *nResult* parameter that was passed to the **CDialog::EndDialog** member function, which is used to close the dialog box. The return value is –1 if the function could not create the dialog box, or **IDABORT** if some other error occurred.

Remarks   Call this member function to invoke the modal dialog box and return the dialog-box result when done. This member function handles all interaction with the user while the dialog box is active. This is what makes the dialog box modal; that is, the user cannot interact with other windows until the dialog box is closed.

If the user clicks one of the pushbuttons in the dialog box, such as OK or Cancel, a message-handler member function, such as **OnOK** or **OnCancel**, is called to attempt to close the dialog box. The default **OnOK** member function will validate and update the dialog-box data and close the dialog box with result **IDOK**, and the default **OnCancel** member function will close the dialog box with result **IDCANCEL** without validating or updating the dialog-box data. You can override these message-handler functions to alter their behavior.

See Also   **::DialogBox**

CDialog::EndDialog

void EndDialog(int *nResult* **);**

Parameters   *nResult*   Contains the value to be returned from the dialog box to the caller of **DoModal**.

Remarks   Call this member function to terminate a modal dialog box. This member function returns *nResult* as the return value of **DoModal**. You must use the **EndDialog** function to complete processing whenever a modal dialog box is created.

You can call **EndDialog** at any time, even in **OnInitDialog**, in which case you should close the dialog box before it is shown or before the input focus is set.

EndDialog does not close the dialog box immediately. Instead, it sets a flag that directs the dialog box to close as soon as the current message handler returns.

See Also   **CDialog::DoModal**, **CDialog::OnOK**, **CDialog::OnCancel**

CDialog::GetDefID

DWORD GetDefID( ) const;

Return Value   A 32-bit value (**DWORD**). If the default pushbutton has an ID value, the high-order word contains **DC_HASDEFID** and the low-order word contains the ID value. If the default pushbutton does not have an ID value, the return value is 0.

Remarks   Call the **GetDefID** member function to get the ID of the default pushbutton control for a dialog box. This is usually an OK button.

See Also   **CDialog::SetDefID**, **DM_GETDEFID**

CDialog::GotoDlgCtrl

void GotoDlgCtrl(CWnd* *pWndCtrl* **);**

Parameters   *pWndCtrl*   Identifies the window (control) that is to receive the focus.

Remarks   Moves the focus to the specified control in the dialog box.

To get a pointer to the control (child window) to pass as *pWndCtrl*, call the **CWnd::GetDlgItem** member function, which returns a pointer to a **CWnd** object.

See Also   **CWnd::GetDlgItem**, **CDialog::PrevDlgCtrl**, **CDialog::NextDlgCtrl**

CDialog::InitModalIndirect

BOOL InitModalIndirect(HGLOBAL *hDialogTemplate* **);**

Return Value   Nonzero if the dialog object was created and initialized successfully; otherwise 0.

Parameters   *hDialogTemplate*   Contains a handle to global memory containing a dialog-box template. This template is in the form of a **DialogBoxHeader** structure and data for each control in the dialog box. For more information on this structure, see the Windows SDK.

Remarks   Call this member function to initialize a modal dialog object using a dialog-box template that you construct in memory.

To create a modal dialog box indirectly, first allocate a global block of memory and fill it with the dialog box template. Then call the empty **CDialog** constructor to construct the dialog-box object. Next, call **InitModalIndirect** to store your handle to the in-memory dialog-box template. The Windows dialog box is created and displayed later, when the **DoModal** member function is called.

See Also   **::DialogBoxIndirect**, **CDialog::DoModal**, **CWnd::DestroyWindow**, **CDialog::CDialog**

CDialog::IsDialogMessage

BOOL IsDialogMessage(LPMSG *lpMsg* **);**

Return Value   Specifies whether the member function has processed the given message. It is nonzero if the message has been processed; otherwise 0. If the return is 0, call the **PreTranslateMessage** member function of the base class to process the message. In an override of the **CDialog::PreTranslateMessage** member function the code looks like this :

```
BOOL CMyDlg::PreTranslateMessage( msg )
{
    if( IsDialogMessage( msg ) )
        return TRUE;
    else
        return CDialog::PreTranslateMessage( msg );
}
```

Parameters   *lpMsg*   Points to an **MSG** structure that contains the message to be checked.

Remarks   Call this member function to determine whether the given message is intended for a modeless dialog box; if it is, this function processes the message. When the **IsDialogMessage** function processes a message, it checks for keyboard messages and converts them to selection commands for the corresponding dialog box. For example, the TAB key selects the next control or group of controls, and the DOWN ARROW key selects the next control in a group.

You must not pass a message processed by **IsDialogMessage** to the **TranslateMessage** or **DispatchMessage** Windows functions, because it has already been processed.

See Also   **::DispatchMessage**, **::TranslateMessage**, **::GetMessage**, **CWnd::PreTranslateMessage**, **::IsDialogMessage**

CDialog::MapDialogRect

void **MapDialogRect**(**LPRECT** *lpRect*) **const;**

Parameters   *lpRect*   Points to a **RECT** structure or **CRect** object that contains the dialog-box coordinates to be converted.

Remarks   Call to convert the dialog-box units of a rectangle to screen units. Dialog-box units are stated in terms of the current dialog-box base unit derived from the average width and height of characters in the font used for dialog-box text. One horizontal unit is one-fourth of the dialog-box base-width unit, and one vertical unit is one-eighth of the dialog-box base height unit.

The **GetDialogBaseUnits** Windows function returns size information for the system font, but you can specify a different font for each dialog box if you use the **DS_SETFONT** style in the resource-definition file. The **MapDialogRect** Windows function uses the appropriate font for this dialog box.

The **MapDialogRect** member function replaces the dialog-box units in *lpRect* with screen units (pixels) so that the rectangle can be used to create a dialog box or position a control within a box.

See Also   **::GetDialogBaseUnits**, **::MapDialogRect**, **WM_SETFONT**

CDialog::NextDlgCtrl

void **NextDlgCtrl**( ) **const;**

Remarks   Moves the focus to the next control in the dialog box. If the focus is at the last control in the dialog box, it moves to the first control.

See Also   **CDialog::PrevDlgCtrl**, **CDialog::GotoDlgCtrl**

CDialog::OnCancel

Protected→
virtual void OnCancel( );
END Protected

Remarks

The framework calls this member function when the user clicks the Cancel button or presses the ESC key in a modal or modeless dialog box.

Override this member function to perform Cancel button action. The default simply terminates a modal dialog box by calling **EndDialog** and causing **DoModal** to return **IDCANCEL**.

If you implement the Cancel button in a modeless dialog box, you must override the **OnCancel** member function and call **DestroyWindow** from within it. Don't call the base-class member function, because it calls **EndDialog**, which will make the dialog box invisible but not destroy it.

See Also

CDialog::OnOK, **CDialog::EndDialog**

CDialog::OnInitDialog

virtual BOOL OnInitDialog( );

Return Value

Specifies whether the application has set the input focus to one of the controls in the dialog box. If **OnInitDialog** returns nonzero, Windows sets the input focus to the first control in the dialog box. The application can return 0 only if it has explicitly set the input focus to one of the controls in the dialog box.

Remarks

This member function is called in response to the **WM_INITDIALOG** message. This message is sent to the dialog box during the **Create**, **CreateIndirect**, or **DoModal** calls, which occur immediately before the dialog box is displayed.

Override this member function if you need to perform special processing when the dialog box is initialized. In the overridden version, first call the base class **OnInitDialog** but disregard its return value. You will normally return **TRUE** from your overridden member function.

Windows calls the **OnInitDialog** function via the standard global dialog-box procedure common to all Microsoft Foundation Class Library dialog boxes, rather than through your message map, so you do not need a message-map entry for this member function.

See Also

CDialog::Create, **CDialog::CreateIndirect**, **WM_INITDIALOG**

CDialog::OnOK

Protected→
virtual void OnOK( );
END Protected

Remarks   Called when the user clicks the OK button (the button with an ID of **IDOK**).

Override this member function to perform the OK button action. If the dialog box includes automatic data validation and exchange, the default implementation of this member function validates the dialog-box data and updates the appropriate variables in your application.

If you implement the OK button in a modeless dialog box, you must override the **OnOK** member function and call **DestroyWindow** from within it. Don't call the base-class member function, because it calls **EndDialog**, which makes the dialog box invisible but does not destroy it.

See Also   **CDialog::OnCancel**, **CDialog::EndDialog**

CDialog::OnSetFont

virtual void OnSetFont(CFont* *pFont* **);**

Parameters   *pFont*   Specifies a pointer to the font. Used as the default font for all controls in this dialog box.

Remarks   Specifies the font a dialog-box control will use when drawing text. The dialog-box control will use the specified font as the default for all dialog-box controls. The dialog editor typically sets the dialog-box font as part of the dialog-box template resource.

See Also   **WM_SETFONT**, **CWnd::SetFont**

CDialog::PrevDlgCtrl

void PrevDlgCtrl( ) const;

Remarks   Sets the focus to the previous control in the dialog box. If the focus is at the first control in the dialog box, it moves to the last control in the box.

See Also   **CDialog::NextDlgCtrl**, **CDialog::GotoDlgCtrl**

CDialog::SetDefID

void SetDefID(UINT *nID* **);**

Parameters   *nID*   Specifies the ID of the pushbutton control that will become the default.

Remarks	Changes the default pushbutton control for a dialog box.
See Also	**CDialog::GetDefID**

CDialog::SetHelpID

void SetHelpID(UINT *nIDR*);

Parameters   *nIDR*   Specifies the context-sensitive help ID.

Remarks   Sets a context-sensitive help ID for the dialog box.

class CDialogBar : public CControlBar

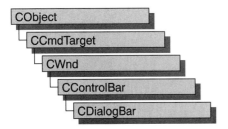

The **CDialogBar** class provides the functionality of a Windows modeless dialog box in a control bar. A dialog bar resembles a dialog box in that it contains standard Windows controls that the user can tab between. Another similarity is that you create a dialog template to represent the dialog bar.

Creating and using a dialog bar is similar to creating and using a **CFormView** object. First, use the dialog editor to define a dialog template with the style **WS_CHILD** and no other style (see *Visual C++ User's Guide*, Chapter 5, "Using the Dialog Editor"). The template must not have the style **WS_VISIBLE**. In your application code, call the constructor to construct the **CDialogBar** object, then call **Create** to create the dialog-bar window and attach it to the **CDialogBar** object.

#include <afxext.h>

See Also   **CControlBar**, **CFormView**

Construction

CDialogBar	Constructs a **CDialogBar** object.
Create	Creates a Windows dialog bar and attaches it to the **CDialogBar** object.

Member Functions

CDialogBar::CDialogBar

CDialogBar( );

Remarks   Constructs a **CDialogBar** object.

See Also   **CControlBar**

CDialogBar::Create

BOOL Create(CWnd* *pParentWnd*, **LPCTSTR** *lpszTemplateName*, **UINT** *nStyle*, **UINT** *nID*);

BOOL Create(CWnd* *pParentWnd*, **UINT** *nIDTemplate*, **UINT** *nStyle*, **UINT** *nID*);

Return Value   Nonzero if successful; otherwise 0.

Parameters   *pParentWnd*   A pointer to the parent **CWnd** object.

lpszTemplateName   A pointer to the name of the **CDialogBar** object's dialog-box resource template.

nStyle   The alignment style of the dialog bar. The following styles are supported:

- **CBRS_TOP**   Control bar is at the top of the frame window.
- **CBRS_BOTTOM**   Control bar is at the bottom of the frame window.
- **CBRS_NOALIGN**   Control bar is not repositioned when the parent is resized.
- **CBRS_LEFT**   Control bar is at the left of the frame window.
- **CBRS_RIGHT**   Control bar is at the right of the frame window.

nID   The control ID of the dialog bar.

nIDTemplate   The resource ID of the **CDialogBar** object's dialog-box template.

Remarks   Loads the dialog-box resource template specified by *lpszTemplateName* or *nIDTemplate*, creates the dialog-bar window, sets its style, and associates it with the **CDialogBar** object.

If you specify the **CBRS_TOP** or **CBRS_BOTTOM** alignment style, the dialog bar's width is that of the frame window and its height is that of the resource specified by *nIDTemplate*. If you specify the **CBRS_LEFT** or **CBRS_RIGHT** alignment style, the dialog bar's height is that of the frame window and its width is that of the resource specified by *nIDTemplate*.

See Also   **CDialogBar::CDialogBar**

class CDocItem : public CObject

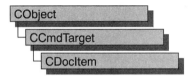

CDocItem is the base class for document items, which are components of a document's data. CDocItem objects are used to represent Object Linking and Embedding (OLE) items in both client and server documents.

#include <afxole.h>

See Also   COleDocument, COleServerItem, COleClientItem

Operations

GetDocument	Returns the document that contains the item.

Overridables

IsBlank	Determines whether the item contains any information.

Member Functions

CDocItem::IsBlank

virtual BOOL IsBlank( ) const;

Return Value   Nonzero if the item contains no information; otherwise 0.

Remarks   Called by the framework when default serialization occurs.

By default, **CDocItem** objects are not blank. **COleClientItem** objects are sometimes blank because they derive directly from **CDocItem**. However, **COleServerItem** objects are always blank. By default, OLE applications containing **COleClientItem** objects that have no x or y extent are serialized. This is done by returning **TRUE** from an override of **COleClientItem::IsBlank** when the item has no x or y extent.

Override this function if you want to implement other actions during serialization.

See Also   CObject::Serialize

CDocItem::GetDocument

CDocument* GetDocument( ) const;

Return Value

A pointer to the document that contains the item; **NULL**, if the item is not part of a document.

Remarks

Call this function to get the document that contains the item.

This function is overridden in the derived classes **COleClientItem** and **COleServerItem**, returning a pointer to either a **COleDocument** or a **COleServerDoc** object.

See Also

COleDocument, COleServerDoc, COleClientItem

class CDocTemplate : public CCmdTarget

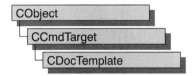

CDocTemplate is an abstract base class that defines the basic functionality for document templates. You usually create one or more document templates in the implementation of your application's **InitInstance** function. A document template defines the relationships among three types of classes:

- A document class, which you derive from **CDocument**.
- A view class, which displays data from the document class listed above. You can derive this class from **CView**, **CScrollView**, **CFormView**, or **CEditView**. (You can also use **CEditView** directly.)
- A frame window class, which contains the view. For a single document interface (SDI) application, you derive this class from **CFrameWnd**. For a multiple document interface (MDI) application, you derive this class from **CMDIChildWnd**. If you don't need to customize the behavior of the frame window, you can use **CFrameWnd** or **CMDIChildWnd** directly without deriving your own class.

Your application has one document template for each type of document that it supports. For example, if your application supports both spreadsheets and text documents, the application has two document template objects. Each document template is responsible for creating and managing all the documents of its type.

The document template stores pointers to the **CRuntimeClass** objects for the document, view, and frame window classes. These **CRuntimeClass** objects are specified when constructing a document template.

The document template contains the ID of the resources used with the document type (such as menu, icon, or accelerator table resources). The document template also has strings containing additional information about its document type. These include the name of the document type (for example, "Worksheet") and the file extension (for example, ".xls"). Optionally, it can contain other strings used by the application's user interface, the Windows File Manager, and Object Linking and Embedding (OLE) support.

If your application is an OLE container and/or server, the document template also defines the ID of the menu used during in-place activation. If your application is an OLE server, the document template defines the ID of the toolbar and menu used during in-place activation. You specify these additional OLE resources by calling **SetContainerInfo** and **SetServerInfo**.

Because **CDocTemplate** is an abstract class, you cannot use the class directly. A typical application uses one of the two **CDocTemplate**-derived classes provided by the Microsoft Foundation Class Library: **CSingleDocTemplate**, which implements SDI, and **CMultiDocTemplate**, which implements MDI. See those classes for more information on using document templates.

If your application requires a user-interface paradigm that is fundamentally different from SDI or MDI, you can derive your own class from **CDocTemplate**.

include# <afxwin.h>

See Also   **CSingleDocTemplate**, **CMultiDocTemplate**, **CDocument**, **CView**, **CScrollView**, **CEditView**, **CFormView**, **CFrameWnd**, **CMDIChildWnd**

Attributes

SetContainerInfo	Determines the resources for OLE containers when editing an in-place OLE item.
SetServerInfo	Determines the resources and classes when the server document is embedded or edited in-place.

Operations

CreateNewFrame	Creates a new frame window containing a document and view.
GetDocString	Retrieves a string describing the document type.
InitialUpdateFrame	Initializes the frame window, and optionally makes it visible.

Member Functions

CDocTemplate::CreateNewFrame

CFrameWnd* CDocTemplate::CreateNewFrame(CDocument* *pDoc*, **CFrameWnd*** *pOther* **);**

Return Value   The newly created frame window, or **NULL** if an error occurs.

Parameters   *pDoc*   The document to which the new frame window should refer. Can be **NULL**.

pOther   The frame window on which the new frame window is to be based. Can be **NULL**.

Remarks   **CreateNewFrame** uses the **CRuntimeClass** objects passed to the constructor to
create a new frame window with a view and document attached. If the *pDoc*
parameter is **NULL**, a new document will be created if the appropriate runtime
class is available; otherwise the new view will be associated with the existing
document specified by *pDoc*. The *pOther* parameter is used to implement the
Window New command. It provides a frame window on which to model the new
frame window. The new frame window is usually created invisible. Call this
function to create frame windows outside the standard framework implementation
of File New and File Open.

See Also   **CCreateContext**, **CFrameWnd::LoadFrame**,
CDocTemplate::InitialUpdateFrame

CDocTemplate::GetDocString

virtual BOOL GetDocString(CString& *rString*, **enum DocStringIndex** *index* **)**
const;

Return Value   Nonzero if the specified substring was found; otherwise 0.

Parameters   *rString*   A reference to a **CString** object that will contain the string when the
function returns.

index   An index of the substring being retrieved from the string that describes the
document type. This parameter can have one of the following values:

- **CDocTemplate::windowTitle**   Name that appears in the application
window's title bar (for example, "Microsoft Excel"). Present only in the
document template for SDI applications.

- **CDocTemplate::docName**   Root for the default document name (for
example, "Sheet"). This root, plus a number, is used for the default name of
a new document of this type whenever the user chooses the New command
from the File menu (for example, "Sheet1" or "Sheet2"). If not specified,
"Untitled" is used as the default.

- **CDocTemplate::fileNewName**   Name of this document type. If the
application supports more than one type of document, this string is displayed
in the File New dialog box (for example, "Worksheet"). If not specified, the
document type is inaccessible using the File New command.

- **CDocTemplate::filterName**   Description of the document type and a
wildcard filter matching documents of this type. This string is displayed in
the List Files Of Type drop-down list in the File Open dialog box (for
example, "Worksheets (*.xls)"). If not specified, the document type is
inaccessible using the File Open command.

- **CDocTemplate::filterExt**   Extension for documents of this type (for example, ".xls"). If not specified, the document type is inaccessible using the File Open command.

- **CDocTemplate::regFileTypeId**   Identifier for the document type to be stored in the registration database maintained by Windows. This string is for internal use only (for example, "ExcelWorksheet"). If not specified, the document type cannot be registered with the Windows File Manager.

- **CDocTemplate::regFileTypeName**   Name of the document type to be stored in the registration database. This string may be displayed in dialog boxes of applications that access the registration database (for example, "Microsoft Excel Worksheet").

Remarks

Call this function to retrieve a specific substring describing the document type. The string containing these substrings is stored in the document template and is derived from a string in the resource file for the application. The framework calls this function to get the strings it needs for the application's user interface. If you have specified a filename extension for your application's documents, the framework also calls this function when adding an entry to the Windows registration database; this allows documents to be opened from the Windows File Manager.

Call this function only if you are deriving your own class from **CDocTemplate**.

See Also

CMultiDocTemplate::CMultiDocTemplate,
CSingleDocTemplate::CSingleDocTemplate,
CWinApp::RegisterShellFileTypes

CDocTemplate::InitialUpdateFrame

void CDocTemplate::Initial UpdateFrame(CFrameWnd* *pFrame*,
CFrameWnd* *pDoc*, BOOL *bMakeVisible*);

Parameters

pFrame   The frame window that needs the initial update.

pDoc   The document to which the frame is associated. Can be **NULL**.

bMakeVisible   Indicates whether the frame should become visible and active.

Remarks

Call **IntitialUpdateFrame** after creating a new frame with **CreateNewFrame**. This causes the views in that frame window to receive their **OnInitialUpdate** calls. Also, if there was not previously an active view, the primary view of the frame window is made active. The primary view is a view with a child ID of AFX_IDW_PANE_FIRST. Finally, the frame window is made visible if *bMakeVisible* is nonzero. If *bMakeVisible* is zero, the current focus and visible state of the frame window will remain unchanged. It is not necessary to call this function when using the framework's implementation of File New and File Open.

See Also   CView::OnInititalUpdate, CFrameWnd::SetActiveView,
CDocTemplate::CreateNewFrame

CDocTemplate::SetContainerInfo

void SetContainerInfo(UINT *nIDOleInPlaceContainer* **);**

Parameters   *nIDOleInPlaceContainer*   The ID of the resources used when an embedded object
is activated.

Remarks   Call this function to set the resources to be used when an OLE 2 object is in-place
activated. These resources may include menus and accelerator tables. This function
is usually called in the **InitInstance** of your application.

The menu associated with *nIDOleInPlaceContainer* contains separators that allow
the menu of the activated in-place item to merge with the menu of the container
application. For more information about merging server and container menus, see
the article "Menus and Resources" in *Programming with the Microsoft Foundation
Class Library*.

See Also   CDocTemplate::SetServerInfo, CWinApp::InitInstance,
CMultiDocTemplate::CMultiDocTemplate

CDocTemplate::SetServerInfo

void SetServerInfo(UINT *nIDOleEmbedding*, **UINT** *nIDOleInPlaceServer* = 0,
CRuntimeClass* *pOleFrameClass* = **NULL, CRuntimeClass***
pOleViewClass = **NULL);**

Parameters   *nIDOleEmbedding*   The ID of the resources used when an embedded object is
opened in a separate window.

nIDOleInPlaceServer   The ID of the resources used when an embedded object is
activated in-place.

pOleFrameClass   Pointer to a **CRuntimeClass** structure containing class
information for the frame window object created when in-place activation
occurs.

pOleViewClass   Pointer to a **CRuntimeClass** structure containing class
information for the view object created when in-place activation occurs.

Remarks   Call this member function to identify resources that will be used by the server
application when the user requests activation of an embedded object. These
resources consist of menus and accelerator tables. This function is usually called in
the **InitInstance** of your application.

The menu associated with *nIDOleInPlaceServer* contains separators that allow the server menu to merge with the menu of the container. For more information about merging server and container menus, see the article "Menus and Resources" in *Programming with the Microsoft Foundation Class Library*.

See Also   **CMultiDocTemplate::CMultiDocTemplate**,
CDocTemplate::SetContainerInfo, **CWinApp::InitInstance**

class CDocument : public CCmdTarget

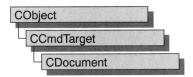

The **CDocument** class provides the basic functionality for user-defined document classes. A document represents the unit of data that the user typically opens with the File Open command and saves with the File Save command.

CDocument supports standard operations such as creating a document, loading it, and saving it. The framework manipulates documents using the interface defined by **CDocument**.

An application can support more than one type of document; for example, an application might support both spreadsheets and text documents. Each type of document has an associated document template; the document template specifies what resources (for example, menu, icon, or accelerator table) are used for that type of document. Each document contains a pointer to its associated **CDocTemplate** object.

Users interact with a document through the **CView** object(s) associated with it. A view renders an image of the document in a frame window and interprets user input as operations on the document. A document can have multiple views associated with it. When the user opens a window on a document, the framework creates a view and attaches it to the document. The document template specifies what type of view and frame window are used to display each type of document.

Documents are part of the framework's standard command routing and consequently receive commands from standard user-interface components (such as the File Save menu item). A document receives commands forwarded by the active view. If the document doesn't handle a given command, it forwards the command to the document template that manages it.

When a document's data is modified, each of its views must reflect those modifications. **CDocument** provides the **UpdateAllViews** member function for you to notify the views of such changes, so the views can repaint themselves as necessary. The framework also prompts the user to save a modified file before closing it.

To implement documents in a typical application, you must do the following:

- Derive a class from **CDocument** for each type of document.
- Add member variables to store each document's data.

- Implement member functions for reading and modifying the document's data. The document's views are the most important users of these member functions.

- Override the **Serialize** member function in your document class to write and read the document's data to and from disk.

#include <afxwin.h>

See Also   **CCmdTarget**, **CView**, **CDocTemplate**

Construction

CDocument	Constructs a **CDocument** object.

Operations

AddView	Attaches a view to the document.
GetDocTemplate	Returns a pointer to the document template that describes the type of the document.
GetFirstViewPosition	Returns the position of the first in the list of views; used to begin iteration.
GetNextView	Iterates through the list of views associated with the document.
GetPathName	Returns the path of the document's data file.
GetTitle	Returns the document's title.
IsModified	Indicates whether the document has been modified since it was last saved.
RemoveView	Detaches a view from the document.
SetModifiedFlag	Sets a flag indicating that you have modified the document since it was last saved.
SetPathName	Sets the path of the data file used by the document.
SetTitle	Sets the document's title.
UpdateAllViews	Notifies all views that document has been modified.

Overridables

CanCloseFrame	Advanced overridable; called before closing a frame window viewing this document.
DeleteContents	Called to perform cleanup of the document.
OnChangedViewList	Called after a view is added to or removed from the document.

OnCloseDocument	Called to close the document.
OnNewDocument	Called to create a new document.
OnOpenDocument	Called to open an existing document.
OnSaveDocument	Called to save the document to disk.
ReportSaveLoadException	Advanced overridable; called when an open or save operation cannot be completed because of an exception.
SaveModified	Advanced overridable; called to ask the user whether the document should be saved.

Member Functions

CDocument::AddView

void AddView(CView* *pView* **);**

Parameters

pView   Points to the view being added.

Remarks

Call this function to attach a view to the document. This function adds the specified view to the list of views associated with the document; the function also sets the view's document pointer to this document. The framework calls this function when attaching a newly created view object to a document; this occurs in response to a File New, File Open, or New Window command or when a splitter window is split.

Call this function only if you are manually creating and attaching a view. Typically you will let the framework connect documents and views by defining a **CDocTemplate** object to associate a document class, view class, and frame window class.

See Also

CDocTemplate, CDocument::GetFirstViewPosition, CDocument::GetNextView, CDocument::RemoveView, CView::GetDocument

Example

```
// The following example toggles two views in an SDI (single document
// interface) frame window.  A design decision must be made as to
// whether to leave the inactive view connected to the document,
// such that the inactive view continues to receive OnUpdate
// notifications from the document.  It is usually desirable to
// keep the inactive view continuously in sync with the document, even
// though it is inactive.  However, doing so incurs a performance cost,
// as well as the programming cost of implementing OnUpdate hints.
// It may be less expensive, in terms of performance and/or programming,
// to re-sync the inactive view with the document only with it is
// reactivated.  This example illustrates this latter approach, by
// reconnecting the newly active view and disconnecting the newly
// inactive view, via calls to CDocument::AddView and RemoveView.
```

```
BOOL CMainFrame::OnViewChange(UINT nCmdID)
{
   CView* pViewAdd;
   CView* pViewRemove;
   CDocument* pDoc = GetActiveDocument();
   if (nCmdID == ID_VIEW_VIEW2)
   {
      if (m_pView2 == NULL)
      {
         m_pView1 = GetActiveView();
         m_pView2 = new CMyView2;
         m_pView2->Create(NULL, NULL, AFX_WS_DEFAULT_VIEW,
            rectDefault, this, AFX_IDW_PANE_FIRST + 1, NULL);
      }
      pViewAdd = m_pView2;
      pViewRemove = m_pView1;
   }
   else
   {
      pViewAdd = m_pView1;
      pViewRemove = m_pView2;
   }

   // Set the child i.d. of the active view to AFX_IDW_PANE_FIRST,
   // so that CFrameWnd::RecalcLayout will allocate to this
   // "first pane" that portion of   the frame window's client area
   // not allocated to control   bars.  Set the child i.d. of the
   // other view to anything other than AFX_IDW_PANE_FIRST; this
   // examples switches the child id's of the two views.

   int nSwitchChildID = pViewAdd->GetDlgCtrlID();
   pViewAdd->SetDlgCtrlID(AFX_IDW_PANE_FIRST);
   pViewRemove->SetDlgCtrlID(nSwitchID);
     // Show the newly active view and hide the inactive view.
   pViewAdd->ShowWindow(SW_SHOW);
   pViewRemove->ShowWindow(SW_HIDE);

   // Connect the newly active view to the document, and
   // disconnect the inactive view.
   pDoc->AddView(pViewAdd);
   pDoc->RemoveView(pViewRemove);

   // Inform the frame window which view is now active;
   // and reallocate the frame window's client area to the
   // new view. Implement logic to resync the view to the
   // document in an override of CView::OnActivateView,
   // which is called from CFrameWnd::SetActiveView.
   SetActiveView(pViewAdd);
   RecalcLayout();
```

```
        return TRUE;
    }
```

CDocument::CanCloseFrame

virtual BOOL CanCloseFrame(CFrameWnd* *pFrame* **);**

Return Value   Nonzero if it is safe to close the frame window; otherwise 0.

Parameters   *pFrame*   Points to the frame window of a view attached to the document.

Remarks   Called by the framework before a frame window displaying the document is closed.
The default implementation checks if there are other frame windows displaying the
document. If the specified frame window is the last one that displays the document,
the function prompts the user to save the document if it has been modified. Override
this function if you want to perform special processing when a frame window is
closed. This is an advanced overridable.

See Also   **CDocument::SaveModified**

CDocument::CDocument

CDocument( );

Remarks   Constructs a **CDocument** object. The framework handles document creation for
you. Override the **OnNewDocument** member function to perform initialization on
a per-document basis; this is particularly important in single document interface
(SDI) applications.

See Also   **CDocument::OnNewDocument, CDocument::OnOpenDocument**

CDocument::DeleteContents

virtual void DeleteContents( );

Remarks   Called by the framework to delete the document's data without destroying the
document object itself. It is called just before the document is to be destroyed. It is
also called to ensure that a document is empty before it is reused. This is
particularly important for an SDI application, which uses only one document object;
the document object is reused whenever the user creates or opens another document.
Call this function to implement an "Edit Clear All" or similar command that deletes
all of the document's data. The default implementation of this function does
nothing. Override this function to delete the data in your document.

See Also   **CDocument::OnCloseDocument, CDocument::OnNewDocument,
CDocument::OnOpenDocument**

Example

```
// This example is the handler for an Edit Clear All command.

void CMyDoc::OnEditClearAll()
{
   DeleteContents();
   UpdateAllViews(NULL);
}


void CMyDoc::DeleteContents()
{
   // Re-initialize document data here.


}
```

CDocument::GetDocTemplate

CDocTemplate* GetDocTemplate( ) const;

Return Value   A pointer to the document template for this document type, or **NULL** if the document is not managed by a document template.

Remarks   Call this function to get a pointer to the document template for this document type.

See Also   **CDocTemplate**

Example

```
// This example accesses the doc template object to construct
// a default document name such as SHEET.XLS, where "sheet"
// is the base document name and ".xls" is the file extension
// for the document type.
CString strDefaultDocName, strBaseName, strExt;
CDocTemplate* pDocTemplate = GetDocTemplate();
if (!pDocTemplate->GetDocString(strBaseName, CDocTemplate::docName)
   || !pDocTemplate->GetDocString(strExt, CDocTemplate::filterExt))
{
   AfxThrowUserException(); // These doc template strings will
      // be available if you created the application using AppWizard
      // and specified the file extension as an option for
      // the document class produced by AppWizard.
}
strDefaultDocName = strBaseName + strExt;
```

CDocument::GetFirstViewPosition

virtual POSITION GetFirstViewPosition( ) const;

Return Value A **POSITION** value that can be used for iteration with the **GetNextView** member function.

Remarks Call this function to get the position of the first view in the list of views associated with the document.

See Also **CDocument::GetNextView**

Example To get the first view in the list of views:

```
POSITION pos = GetFirstViewPosition();
CView* pFirstView = GetNextView( pos );
// This example uses CDocument::GetFirstViewPosition
// and GetNextView to repaint each view.
void CMyDoc::OnRepaintAllViews()
{
   POSITION pos = GetFirstViewPosition();
   while (pos != NULL)
   {
      CView* pView = GetNextView(pos);
      pView->UpdateWindow();
   }
}

// An easier way to accomplish the same result is to call
// UpdateAllViews(NULL);
```

CDocument::GetNextView

virtual CView* GetNextView(POSITION& *rPosition*) const;

Return Value A pointer to the view identified by *rPosition*.

Parameters *rPosition*   A reference to a **POSITION** value returned by a previous call to the **GetNextView** or **GetFirstViewPosition** member functions. This value must not be **NULL**.

Remarks Call this function to iterate through all of the document's views. The function returns the view identified by *rPosition* and then sets *rPosition* to the **POSITION** value of the next view in the list. If the retrieved view is the last in the list, then *rPosition* is set to **NULL**.

See Also **CDocument::AddView, CDocument::GetFirstViewPosition, CDocument::RemoveView, CDocument::UpdateAllViews**

Example

```
// This example uses CDocument::GetFirstViewPosition
// and GetNextView to repaint each view.
void CMyDoc::OnRepaintAllViews()
{
    POSITION pos = GetFirstViewPosition();
    while (pos != NULL)
    {
        CView* pView = GetNextView(pos);
        pView->UpdateWindow();
    }
}

// An easier way to accomplish the same result is to call
// UpdateAllViews(NULL);
```

CDocument::GetPathName

const CString& GetPathName( ) const;

Return Value The document's fully qualified path. This string is empty if the document has not been saved or does not have a disk file associated with it.

Remarks Call this function to get the fully qualified path of the document's disk file.

See Also **CDocument::SetPathName**

CDocument::GetTitle

const CString& GetTitle( ) const;

Return Value The document's title.

Remarks Call this function to get the document's title, which is usually derived from the document's filename.

See Also **CDocument::SetTitle**

CDocument::IsModified

BOOL IsModified( );

Return Value Nonzero if the document has been modified since it was last saved; otherwise 0.

Remarks Call this function to determine whether the document has been modified since it was last saved.

See Also **CDocument::SetModifiedFlag**, **CDocument::SaveModified**

CDocument::OnChangedViewList

virtual void OnChangedViewList( );

Remarks   Called by the framework after a view is added to or removed from the document. The default implementation of this function checks whether the last view is being removed and, if so, deletes the document. Override this function if you want to perform special processing when the framework adds or removes a view. For example, if you want a document to remain open even when there are no views attached to it, override this function.

See Also   **CDocument::AddView**, **CDocument::RemoveView**

CDocument::OnCloseDocument

virtual void OnCloseDocument( );

Remarks   Called by the framework when the document is closed, typically as part of the File Close command. The default implementation of this function calls the **DeleteContents** member function to delete the document's data and then closes the frame windows for all the views attached to the document.

Override this function if you want to perform special cleanup processing when the framework closes a document. For example, if the document represents a record in a database, you may want to override this function to close the database. You should call the base class version of this function from your override.

See Also   **CDocument::DeleteContents**, **CDocument::OnNewDocument**, **CDocument::OnOpenDocument**

CDocument::OnNewDocument

virtual BOOL OnNewDocument( );

Return Value   Nonzero if the document was successfully initialized; otherwise 0.

Remarks   Called by the framework as part of the File New command. The default implementation of this function calls the **DeleteContents** member function to ensure that the document is empty and then marks the new document as clean. Override this function to initialize the data structure for a new document. You should call the base class version of this function from your override.

If the user chooses the File New command in an SDI application, the framework uses this function to reinitialize the existing document object, rather than creating a new one. If the user chooses File New in a multiple document interface (MDI) application, the framework creates a new document object each time and then calls this function to initialize it. You must place your initialization code in this function

instead of in the constructor for the File New command to be effective in SDI
applications.

See Also   **CDocument::CDocument, CDocument::DeleteContents,
CDocument::OnCloseDocument, CDocument::OnOpenDocument,
CDocument::OnSaveDocument**

Example
```
// The follow examples illustrate alternative methods of
// initializing a document object.

// Method 1: In an MDI application, the simplest place to do
// initialization is in the document constructor.  The framework
// always creates a new document object for File New or File Open.


CMyDoc::CMyDoc()
{
   // Do initialization of MDI document here.
   // ...
}


// Method 2: In an SDI or MDI application, do all initialization
// in an override of OnNewDocument, if you are certain that
// the initialization is effectively saved upon File Save
// and fully restored upon File Open, via serialization.


BOOL CMyDoc::OnNewDocument()
{
   if (!CDocument::OnNewDocument())
      return FALSE;

   // Do initialization of new document here.

   return TRUE;
}


// Method 3: If the initialization of your document is not
// effectively saved and restored by serialization (during File Save
// and File Open), then implement the initialization in single
// function (named InitMyDocument in this example).  Call the
// shared initialization function from overrides of both
// OnNewDocument and OnOpenDocument.
```

```
BOOL CMyDoc::OnNewDocument()
{
   if (!CDocument::OnNewDocument())
      return FALSE;

   InitMyDocument(); // call your shared initialization function

   // If your new document object requires additional initialization
   // not necessary when the document is deserialized via File Open,
   // then perform that additional initialization here.

   return TRUE;
}

BOOL CMyDoc::OnOpenDocument(LPCTSTR lpszPathName)
{
   if (!CDocument::OnOpenDocument(lpszPathName))
      return FALSE;

   InitMyDocument();

   return TRUE;
}
```

CDocument::OnOpenDocument

virtual BOOL OnOpenDocument(LPCTSTR *lpszPathName* **);**

Return Value   Nonzero if the document was successfully loaded; otherwise 0.

Parameters   *lpszPathName*   Points to the path of the document to be opened.

Remarks   Called by the framework as part of the File Open command. The default implementation of this function opens the specified file, calls the **DeleteContents** member function to ensure that the document is empty, calls **Serialize** to read the file's contents, and then marks the document as clean. Override this function if you want to use something other than the archive mechanism or the file mechanism. For example, you might write an application where documents represent records in a database rather than separate files.

If the user chooses the File Open command in an SDI application, the framework uses this function to reinitialize the existing document object, rather than creating a new one. If the user chooses File Open in an MDI application, the framework constructs a new document object each time and then calls this function to initialize it. You must place your initialization code in this function instead of in the constructor for the File Open command to be effective in SDI applications.

See Also   **CDocument::DeleteContents, CDocument::OnCloseDocument,**
CDocument::OnNewDocument, CDocument::OnSaveDocument,
CDocument::ReportSaveLoadException, CObject::Serialize

Example

```
// The follow examples illustrate alternative methods of
// initializing a document object.

// Method 1: In an MDI application, the simplest place to do
// initialization is in the document constructor.  The framework
// always creates a new document object for File New or File Open.


CMyDoc::CMyDoc()
{
   // Do initialization of MDI document here.
   // ...
}


// Method 2: In an SDI or MDI application, do all initialization
// in an override of OnNewDocument, if you are certain that
// the initialization is effectively saved upon File Save
// and fully restored upon File Open, via serialization.


BOOL CMyDoc::OnNewDocument()
{
   if (!CDocument::OnNewDocument())
      return FALSE;

   // Do initialization of new document here.

   return TRUE;
}


// Method 3: If the initialization of your document is not
// effectively saved and restored by serialization (during File Save
// and File Open), then implement the initialization in single
// function (named InitMyDocument in this example).  Call the
// shared initialization function from overrides of both
// OnNewDocument and OnOpenDocument.

BOOL CMyDoc::OnNewDocument()
{
   if (!CDocument::OnNewDocument())
      return FALSE;

   InitMyDocument(); // call your shared initialization function
```

```
                    // If your new document object requires additional initialization
                    // not necessary when the document is deserialized via File Open,
                    // then perform that additional initialization here.

                    return TRUE;
                }

                BOOL CMyDoc::OnOpenDocument(LPCTSTR lpszPathName)
                {
                    if (!CDocument::OnOpenDocument(lpszPathName))
                        return FALSE;

                    InitMyDocument();

                    return TRUE;
                }
```

CDocument::OnSaveDocument

virtual BOOL OnSaveDocument(LPCTSTR *lpszPathName* **);**

Return Value Nonzero if the document was successfully saved; otherwise 0.

Parameters *lpszPathName*   Points to the fully qualified path to which the file should be saved.

Remarks Called by the framework as part of the File Save or File Save As command. The default implementation of this function opens the specified file, calls **Serialize** to write the document's data to the file, and then marks the document as clean. Override this function if you want to perform special processing when the framework saves a document. For example, you might write an application where documents represent records in a database rather than separate files.

See Also **CDocument::OnCloseDocument**, **CDocument::OnNewDocument**, **CDocument::OnOpenDocument**, **CDocument::ReportSaveLoadException**, **CObject::Serialize**

CDocument::RemoveView

void RemoveView(CView* *pView* **);**

Parameters *pView*   Points to the view being removed.

Remarks Call this function to detach a view from a document. This function removes the specified view from the list of views associated with the document; it also sets the view's document pointer to **NULL**. This function is called by the framework when a frame window is closed or a pane of a splitter window is closed.

Call this function only if you are manually detaching a view. Typically you will let the framework detach documents and views by defining a **CDocTemplate** object to associate a document class, view class, and frame window class.

See Also   **CDocument::AddView**, **CDocument::GetFirstViewPosition**,
CDocument::GetNextView

Example
```
// The following example toggles two views in an SDI (single document
// interface) frame window.  A design decision must be made as to
// whether to leave the inactive view connected to the document,
// such that the inactive view continues to receive OnUpdate
// notifications from the document.  It is usually desirable to
// keep the inactive view continuously in sync with the document, even
// though it is inactive.  However, doing so incurs a performance cost,
// as well as the programming cost of implementing OnUpdate hints.
// It may be less expensive, in terms of performance and/or programming,
// to re-sync the inactive view with the document only with it is
// reactivated.  This example illustrates this latter approach, by
// reconnecting the newly active view and disconnecting the newly
// inactive view, via calls to CDocument::AddView and RemoveView.

BOOL CMainFrame::OnViewChange(UINT nCmdID)
{
   CView* pViewAdd;
   CView* pViewRemove;
   CDocument* pDoc = GetActiveDocument();
   if (nCmdID == ID_VIEW_VIEW2)
   {
      if (m_pView2 == NULL)
      {
         m_pView1 = GetActiveView();
         m_pView2 = new CMyView2;
         m_pView2->Create(NULL, NULL, AFX_WS_DEFAULT_VIEW,
            rectDefault, this, AFX_IDW_PANE_FIRST + 1, NULL);
      }
      pViewAdd = m_pView2;
      pViewRemove = m_pView1;
   }
   else
   {
      pViewAdd = m_pView1;
      pViewRemove = m_pView2;
   }

   // Set the child i.d. of the active view to AFX_IDW_PANE_FIRST,
   // so that CFrameWnd::RecalcLayout will allocate to this
   // "first pane" that portion of   the frame window's client area
   // not allocated to control   bars.  Set the child i.d. of the
   // other view to anything other than AFX_IDW_PANE_FIRST; this
   // examples switches the child id's of the two views.
```

```
            int nSwitchChildID = pViewAdd->GetDlgCtrlID();
            pViewAdd->SetDlgCtrlID(AFX_IDW_PANE_FIRST);
            pViewRemove->SetDlgCtrlID(nSwitchID);
              // Show the newly active view and hide the inactive view.
            pViewAdd->ShowWindow(SW_SHOW);
            pViewRemove->ShowWindow(SW_HIDE);

            // Connect the newly active view to the document, and
            // disconnect the inactive view.
            pDoc->AddView(pViewAdd);
            pDoc->RemoveView(pViewRemove);

            // Inform the frame window which view is now active;
            // and reallocate the frame window's client area to the
            // new view. Implement logic to resync the view to the
            // document in an override of CView::OnActivateView,
            // which is called from CFrameWnd::SetActiveView.
            SetActiveView(pViewAdd);
            RecalcLayout();

            return TRUE;
        }
```

CDocument::ReportSaveLoadException

virtual void ReportSaveLoadException(LPCTSTR *lpszPathName*,
CException* *e*, **BOOL** *bSaving*, **UINT** *nIDPDefault* **);**

Parameters   *lpszPathName*   Points to name of document that was being saved or loaded.

e   Points to the exception that was thrown. May be **NULL**.

bSaving   Flag indicating what operation was in progress; nonzero if the document
was being saved, 0 if the document was being loaded.

nIDPDefault   Identifier of the error message to be displayed if the function does
not specify a more specific one.

Remarks   Called if an exception is thrown (typically a **CFileException** or
CArchiveException) while saving or loading the document. The default
implementation examines the exception object and looks for an error message that
specifically describes the cause. If a specific message is not found or if *e* is **NULL**,
the general message specified by the *nIDPDefault* parameter is used. The function
then displays a message box containing the error message. Override this function if
you want to provide additional, customized failure messages. This is an advanced
overridable.

See Also   **CDocument::OnOpenDocument, CDocument::OnSaveDocument,
CFileException, CArchiveException**

CDocument::SaveModified

> **virtual BOOL SaveModified( );**

Return Value   Nonzero if it is safe to continue and close the document; 0 if the document should
not be closed.

Remarks   Called by the framework before a modified document is to be closed. The default
implementation of this function displays a message box asking the user whether to
save the changes to the document, if any have been made. Override this function if
your program requires a different prompting procedure. This is an advanced
overridable.

See Also   **CDocument::CanCloseFrame, CDocument::IsModified,
CDocument::OnNewDocument, CDocument::OnOpenDocument,
CDocument::OnSaveDocument**

CDocument::SetModifiedFlag

> **void SetModifiedFlag(BOOL *bModified* = TRUE);**

Parameters   *bModified*   Flag indicating whether the document has been modified.

Remarks   Call this function after you have made any modifications to the document. By
calling this function consistently, you ensure that the framework prompts the user to
save changes before closing a document. Typically you should use the default value
of **TRUE** for the *bModified* parameter. To mark a document as clean (unmodified),
call this function with a value of **FALSE**.

See Also   **CDocument::IsModified, CDocument::SaveModified**

CDocument::SetPathName

> **virtual void SetPathName(LPCTSTR *lpszPathName*, BOOL *bAddToMRU* =
TRUE);**

Parameters   *lpszPathName*   Points to the string to be used as the path for the document.

bAddToMRU   Determines whether the filename is added to the most recently used
(MRU) file list. If **TRUE,** the filename is added; if **FALSE**, it is not added.

Remarks   Call this function to specify the fully qualified path of the document's disk file.
Depending on the value of *bAddToMRU* the path is added, or not added, to the
MRU list maintained by the application. Note that some documents are not
associated with a disk file. Call this function only if you are overriding the default
implementation for opening and saving files used by the framework.

See Also   **CDocument::GetPathName**, **CWinApp::AddToRecentFileList**

CDocument::SetTitle

virtual void SetTitle(LPCTSTR *lpszTitle* **);**

Parameters   *lpszTitle*   Points to the string to be used as the document's title.

Remarks   Call this function to specify the document's title (the string displayed in the title bar of a frame window). Calling this function updates the titles of all frame windows that display the document.

See Also   **CDocument::GetTitle**

CDocument::UpdateAllViews

void UpdateAllViews(CView* *pSender*, **LPARAM** *lHint* **= 0L, CObject*** *pHint* **= NULL);**

Parameters   *pSender*   Points to the view that modified the document, or **NULL** if all views are to be updated.

lHint   Contains information about the modification.

pHint   Points to an object storing information about the modification.

Remarks   Call this function after the document has been modified. You should call this function after you call the **SetModifiedFlag** member function. This function informs each view attached to the document, except for the view specified by *pSender*, that the document has been modified. You typically call this function from your view class after the user has changed the document through a view.

This function calls the **OnUpdate** member function for each of the document's views except the sending view, passing *pHint* and *lHint*. Use these parameters to pass information to the views about the modifications made to the document. You can encode information using *lHint* and/or you can define a **CObject**-derived class to store information about the modifications and pass an object of that class using *pHint*. Override the **OnUpdate** member function in your **CView**-derived class to optimize the updating of the view's display based on the information passed.

See Also   **CDocument::SetModifiedFlag, CDocument::GetFirstViewPosition, CDocument::GetNextView, CView::OnUpdate**

class CDumpContext

The **CDumpContext** class supports stream-oriented diagnostic output in the form of human-readable text. You can use **afxDump**, a predeclared **CDumpContext** object, for most of your dumping. The **afxDump** object is available only in the Debug version of the Microsoft Foundation Class Library. Several of the memory diagnostic functions use **afxDump** for their output.

Under the Windows environment, the output from the predefined **afxDump** object, conceptually similar to the cerr stream, is routed to the debugger via the Windows function **OutputDebugString**.

The **CDumpContext** class has an overloaded insertion (**<<**) operator for **CObject** pointers that dumps the object's data. If you need a custom dump format for a derived object, override **CObject::Dump**. Most Microsoft Foundation classes implement an overridden **Dump** member function.

Classes that are not derived from **CObject**, such as **CString**, **CTime**, and **CTimeSpan**, have their own overloaded **CDumpContext** insertion operators, as do often-used structures such as **CFileStatus**, **CPoint**, and **CRect**.

If you use the **IMPLEMENT_DYNAMIC** or **IMPLEMENT_SERIAL** macros in the implementation of your class, then **CObject::Dump** will print the name of your **CObject**-derived class. Otherwise, it will print CObject.

The **CDumpContext** class is available with both the Debug and Release versions of the library, but the **Dump** member function is defined only in the Debug version. Use **#ifdef _DEBUG** / **#endif** statements to bracket your diagnostic code, including your custom **Dump** member functions.

Before you create your own **CDumpContext** object, you must create a **CFile** object that serves as the dump destination.

#define _DEBUG

#include <afx.h>

See Also   **CFile**, **CObject**

Construction

CDumpContext	Constructs a **CDumpContext** object.

Basic Input/Output

Flush	Flushes any data in the dump context buffer.
operator <<	Inserts variables and objects into the dump context.
HexDump	Dumps bytes in hexadecimal format.

Status

GetDepth	Gets an integer corresponding to the depth of the dump.
SetDepth	Sets the depth of the dump.

Member Functions

CDumpContext::CDumpContext

CDumpContext(CFile* *pFile*)
    throw(CMemoryException, CFileException);

Parameters   *pFile*   A pointer to the **CFile** object that is the dump destination.

Remarks   Constructs an object of class **CDumpContext**. The **afxDump** object is constructed automatically.

Do not write to the underlying **CFile** while the dump context is active; otherwise, you will interfere with the dump. Under the Windows environment, the output is routed to the debugger via the Windows function **OutputDebugString**.

Example
```
CFile f;
if( !f.Open( "dump.txt", CFile::modeCreate | CFile::modeWrite ) ) {
   afxDump << "Unable to open file" << "\n";
   exit( 1 );
}
CDumpContext dc( &f );
```

CDumpContext::Flush

void Flush( )
    throw(CFileException);

Remarks   Forces any data remaining in buffers to be written to the file attached to the dump context.

Example   `afxDump.Flush();`

CDumpContext::GetDepth

int GetDepth( ) const;

Return Value   The depth of the dump as set by **SetDepth**.

Remarks   Determines whether a deep or shallow dump is in process.

See Also   **CDumpContext::SetDepth**

Example   See the example for **SetDepth.**

CDumpContext::HexDump

void HexDump(LPCTSTR *lpszLine*, **BYTE*** *pby*, **int** *nBytes*, **int** *nWidth* **)**
throw(CFileException);

Parameters   *lpszLine*   A string to output at the start of a new line.

pby   A pointer to a buffer containing the bytes to dump.

nBytes   The number of bytes to dump.

nWidth   Maximum number of bytes dumped per line (not the width of the output line).

Remarks   Dumps an array of bytes formatted as hexadecimal numbers.

Example
```
char test[] = "This is a test of CDumpContext::HexDump\n";
afxDump.HexDump( ".", (BYTE*) test, sizeof test, 20 );
```

The output from this program is:

```
. 54 68 69 73 20 69 73 20 61 20 74 65 73 74 20 6F 66 20 43 44
. 75 6D 70 43 6F 6E 74 65 78 74 3A 3A 48 65 78 44 75 6D 70 0A
. 00
```

CDumpContext::SetDepth

void SetDepth(int *nNewDepth* **);**

Parameters   *nNewDepth*   The new depth value.

Remarks   Sets the depth for the dump. If you are dumping a primitive type or simple **CObject** that contains no pointers to other objects, then a value of 0 is sufficient. A value greater than 0 specifies a deep dump where all objects are dumped recursively. For example, a deep dump of a collection will dump all elements of the collection. You may use other specific depth values in your derived classes.

> **Note** Circular references are not detected in deep dumps and can result in infinite loops.

See Also   **CObject::Dump**

Example
```
afxDump.SetDepth( 1 );  // Specifies deep dump
ASSERT( afxDump.GetDepth() == 1 );
```

Operators

CDumpContext::operator <<

CDumpContext& operator <<(const CObject* *pOb* **)**
   throw(CFileException);

CDumpContext& operator <<(const CObject& *ob* **)**
   throw(CFileException);

CDumpContext& operator <<(LPCTSTR *lpsz* **)**
   throw(CFileException);

CDumpContext& operator <<(const void* *lp* **)**
   throw(CFileException);

CDumpContext& operator <<(BYTE *by* **)**
   throw(CFileException);

CDumpContext& operator <<(WORD *w* **)**
   throw(CFileException);

CDumpContext& operator <<(DWORD *dw* **)**
   throw(CFileException);

CDumpContext& operator <<(int *n* **)**
   throw(CFileException);

CDumpContext& operator <<(double *d* **)**
   throw(CFileException);

CDumpContext& operator <<(float *f* **)**
   throw(CFileException);

CDumpContext& operator <<(LONG *l* **)**
   throw(CFileException);

CDumpContext& operator <<(UINT *u* **)**
   throw(CFileException);

CDumpContext& operator <<(LPCWSTR *lpsz* **)**
   throw(CFileException);

CDumpContext& operator <<(LPCSTR *lpsz* **)**
   throw(CFileException);

Return Value

A **CDumpContext** reference. Using the return value, you can write multiple insertions on a single line of source code.

Remarks

Outputs the specified data to the dump context. The insertion operator is overloaded for **CObject** pointers as well as for most primitive types. A pointer to character results in a dump of string contents; a pointer to **void** results in a hexadecimal dump of the address only.

If you use the **IMPLEMENT_DYNAMIC** or **IMPLEMENT_SERIAL** macros in the implementation of your class, then the insertion operator, through **CObject::Dump**, will print the name of your **CObject**-derived class. Otherwise, it will print CObject. If you override the **Dump** function of the class, then you can provide a more meaningful output of the object's contents instead of a hexadecimal dump.

Example

```
extern CObList li;
CString s = "test";
int i = 7;
long lo = 1000000000L;
afxDump << "list=" << &li << "string="
        << s << "int=" << i << "long=" << lo << "\n";
```

class CDWordArray : public CObject

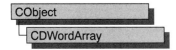

The **CDWordArray** class supports arrays of 32-bit doublewords. The member functions of **CDWordArray** are similar to the member functions of class **CObArray**. Because of this similarity, you can use the **CObArray** reference documentation for member function specifics. Wherever you see a **CObject** pointer as a function parameter or return value, substitute a **DWORD**.

```
CObject* CObArray::GetAt( int <nIndex> ) const;
```

for example, translates to

```
DWORD CDWordArray::GetAt( int <nIndex> ) const;
```

Note Before using an array, use **SetSize** to establish its size and allocate memory for it. If you do not use **SetSize**, adding elements to your array causes it to be frequently reallocated and copied. Frequent reallocation and copying are inefficient and can fragment memory.

If you need debug output from individual elements in the array, you must set the depth of the **CDumpContext** object to 1 or greater.

#include <afxcoll.h>

See Also   **CObArray**

Construction
CDWordArray	Constructs an empty array for doublewords.

Bounds
GetSize	Gets the number of elements in this array.
GetUpperBound	Returns the largest valid index.
SetSize	Sets the number of elements to be contained in this array.

Operations
FreeExtra	Frees all unused memory above the current upper bound.
RemoveAll	Removes all the elements from this array.

Element Access

GetAt	Returns the value at a given index.
SetAt	Sets the value for a given index; array not allowed to grow.
ElementAt	Returns a temporary reference to the doubleword within the array.

Growing the Array

SetAtGrow	Sets the value for a given index; grows the array if necessary.
Add	Adds an element to the end of the array; grows the array if necessary.

Insertion/Removal

InsertAt	Inserts an element (or all the elements in another array) at a specified index.
RemoveAt	Removes an element at a specific index.

Operators

operator [ ]	Sets or gets the element at the specified index.

class CEdit : public CWnd

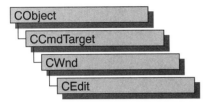

The **CEdit** class provides the functionality of a Windows edit control. An edit control is a rectangular child window in which the user can enter text.

You can create an edit control either from a dialog template or directly in your code. In both cases, first call the constructor **CEdit** to construct the **CEdit** object, then call the **Create** member function to create the Windows edit control and attach it to the **CEdit** object. Construction can be a one-step process in a class derived from **CEdit**. Write a constructor for the derived class and call **Create** from within the constructor.

CEdit inherits significant functionality from **CWnd**. To set and retrieve text from a **CEdit** object, use the **CWnd** member functions **SetWindowText** and **GetWindowText**, which set or get the entire contents of an edit control, even if it is a multiline control. Also, if an edit control is multiline, get and set part of the control's text by calling the **CWnd** member functions **GetLine**, **SetSel**, **GetSel**, and **ReplaceSel**.

If you want to handle Windows notification messages sent by an edit control to its parent (usually a class derived from **CDialog**), add a message-map entry and message-handler member function to the parent class for each message.

Each message-map entry takes the following form:

ON_ Notification(*id, memberFxn*)

where *id* specifies the child window ID of the edit control sending the notification, and *memberFxn* is the name of the parent member function you have written to handle the notification.

The parent's function prototype is as follows:

afx_msg void memberFxn( ) ;

Following is a list of potential message-map entries and a description of the cases in which they would be sent to the parent:

- **ON_EN_CHANGE**   The user has taken an action that may have altered text in an edit control. Unlike the **EN_UPDATE** notification message, this notification message is sent after Windows updates the display.

- **ON_EN_ERRSPACE**   The edit control cannot allocate enough memory to meet a specific request.

- **ON_EN_HSCROLL**   The user clicks an edit control's horizontal scroll bar. The parent window is notified before the screen is updated.

- **ON_EN_KILLFOCUS**   The edit control loses the input focus.

- **ON_EN_MAXTEXT**   The current insertion has exceeded the specified number of characters for the edit control and has been truncated. Also sent when an edit control does not have the **ES_AUTOHSCROLL** style and the number of characters to be inserted would exceed the width of the edit control. Also sent when an edit control does not have the **ES_AUTOVSCROLL** style and the total number of lines resulting from a text insertion would exceed the height of the edit control.

- **ON_EN_SETFOCUS**   Sent when an edit control receives the input focus.

- **ON_EN_UPDATE**   The edit control is about to display altered text. Sent after the control has formatted the text but before it screens the text so that the window size can be altered, if necessary.

- **ON_EN_VSCROLL**   The user clicks an edit control's vertical scroll bar. The parent window is notified before the screen is updated.

If you create a **CEdit** object within a dialog box, the **CEdit** object is automatically destroyed when the user closes the dialog box.

If you create a **CEdit** object from a dialog resource using the dialog editor, the **CEdit** object is automatically destroyed when the user closes the dialog box. If you create a **CEdit** object within a window, you may also need to destroy it. If you create the **CEdit** object on the stack, it is destroyed automatically. If you create the **CEdit** object on the heap by using the **new** function, you must call **delete** on the object to destroy it when the user terminates the Windows edit control. If you allocate any memory in the **CEdit** object, override the **CEdit** destructor to dispose of the allocations.

#include <afxwin.h>

See Also   **CWnd, CButton, CComboBox, CListBox, CScrollBar, CStatic, CDialog**

Construction

CEdit   Constructs a **CEdit** control object.

Initialization

Create	Creates the Windows edit control and attaches it to the **CEdit** object.

Multiple-Line Operations

GetLineCount	Retrieves the number of lines in a multiple-line edit control.
GetHandle	Retrieves a handle to the memory currently allocated for a multiple-line edit control.
SetHandle	Sets the handle to the local memory that will be used by a multiple-line edit control.
FmtLines	Sets the inclusion of soft line-break characters on or off within a multiple-line edit control.
LineIndex	Retrieves the character index of a line within a multiple-line edit control.
SetRect	Sets the formatting rectangle of a multiple-line edit control and updates the control.
SetRectNP	Sets the formatting rectangle of a multiple-line edit control without redrawing the control window.
SetTabStops	Sets the tab stops in a multiple-line edit control.

General Operations

CanUndo	Determines whether an edit-control operation can be undone.
GetModify	Determines whether the contents of an edit control have been modified.
SetModify	Sets or clears the modification flag for an edit control.
SetReadOnly	Sets the read-only state of an edit control.
GetPasswordChar	Retrieves the password character displayed in an edit control when the user enters text.
GetRect	Gets the formatting rectangle of an edit control.
GetSel	Gets the starting and ending character positions of the current selection in an edit control.
GetLine	Retrieves a line of text from an edit control.
GetFirstVisibleLine	Determines the topmost visible line in an edit control.

EmptyUndoBuffer	Resets (clears) the undo flag of an edit control.
LimitText	Limits the length of the text that the user may enter into an edit control.
LineFromChar	Retrieves the line number of the line that contains the specified character index.
LineLength	Retrieves the length of a line in an edit control.
LineScroll	Scrolls the text of a multiple-line edit control.
ReplaceSel	Replaces the current selection in an edit control with the specified text.
SetPasswordChar	Sets or removes a password character displayed in an edit control when the user enters text.
SetSel	Selects a range of characters in an edit control.
Undo	Reverses the last edit-control operation.
Clear	Deletes (clears) the current selection (if any) in the edit control.
Copy	Copies the current selection (if any) in the edit control to the Clipboard in **CF_TEXT** format.
Cut	Deletes (cuts) the current selection (if any) in the edit control and copies the deleted text to the Clipboard in **CF_TEXT** format.
Paste	Inserts the data from the Clipboard into the edit control at the current cursor position. Data is inserted only if the Clipboard contains data in **CF_TEXT** format.

Member Functions

CEdit::CanUndo

BOOL CanUndo( ) const;

Return Value   Nonzero if the last edit operation can be undone by a call to the **Undo** member function; 0 if it cannot be undone.

See Also   **CEdit::Undo, EM_CANUNDO**

CEdit::CEdit

CEdit( );

Remarks   Constructs a **CEdit** object.

See Also   **CEdit::Create**

CEdit::Clear

void Clear( );

Remarks   Deletes (clears) the current selection (if any) in the edit control. The deletion performed by **Clear** can be undone by calling the **Undo** member function.

To delete the current selection and place the deleted contents into the Clipboard, call the **Cut** member function.

See Also   **CEdit::CanUndo**, **CEdit::Undo**, **CEdit::Copy**, **CEdit::Cut**, **CEdit::Paste**, **WM_CLEAR**

CEdit::Copy

void Copy( );

Remarks   Copies the current selection (if any) in the edit control to the Clipboard in **CF_TEXT** format.

See Also   **CEdit::Clear**, **CEdit::Cut**, **CEdit::Paste**, **WM_COPY**

CEdit::Create

BOOL Create(DWORD *dwStyle*, **const RECT&** *rect*, **CWnd*** *pParentWnd*, **UINT** *nID* **);**

Return Value   **Create** returns nonzero if initialization is successful; 0 if unsuccessful.

Parameters   *dwStyle*   Specifies the edit control's style. Apply any combination of edit styles to the control. For a list of edit styles, see the section "Edit Styles" on page 1248.

rect   Specifies the edit control's size and position. Can be a **CRect** object or **RECT** structure.

pParentWnd   Specifies the edit control's parent window (usually a **CDialog**). It must not be **NULL**.

nID   Specifies the edit control's ID.

Remarks   You construct a **CEdit** object in two steps. First, call the **CEdit** constructor, then call **Create**, which creates the Windows edit control and attaches it to the **CEdit** object. When **Create** executes, Windows sends the **WM_NCCREATE**, **WM_NCCALCSIZE**, **WM_CREATE**, and **WM_GETMINMAXINFO** messages to the edit control. These messages are handled by default by the **OnNcCreate**, **OnNcCalcSize**, **OnCreate**, and **OnGetMinMaxInfo** member functions in the **CWnd** base class. To extend the default message handling, derive a class from **CEdit**, add a message map to the new class, and override the above message-handler member functions. Override **OnCreate**, for example, to perform needed initialization for the new class.

Apply the following window styles to an edit control: For a list of window styles, see the section "Window Styles" on page 1253.

- **WS_CHILD**   Always
- **WS_VISIBLE**   Usually
- **WS_DISABLED**   Rarely
- **WS_GROUP**   To group controls
- **WS_TABSTOP**   To include edit control in the tabbing order

See Also   **CEdit::CEdit**

CEdit::Cut

void Cut( );

Remarks   Deletes (cuts) the current selection (if any) in the edit control and copies the deleted text to the Clipboard in **CF_TEXT** format. The deletion performed by **Cut** can be undone by calling the **Undo** member function. To delete the current selection without placing the deleted text into the Clipboard, call the **Clear** member function.

See Also   **CEdit::Undo, CEdit::Clear, CEdit::Copy, CEdit::Paste, WM_CUT**

CEdit::EmptyUndoBuffer

void EmptyUndoBuffer( );

Remarks   Resets (clears) the undo flag of an edit control. The edit control will now be unable to undo the last operation. The undo flag is set whenever an operation within the edit control can be undone. The undo flag is automatically cleared whenever the **SetWindowText** or **SetHandle** member function is called.

See Also   **CEdit::CanUndo, CEdit::SetHandle, CEdit::Undo, CWnd::SetWindowText, EM_EMPTYUNDOBUFFER**

CEdit::FmtLines

BOOL FmtLines(BOOL *bAddEOL* **);**

Return Value   Nonzero if any formatting occurs; otherwise 0.

Parameters   *bAddEOL*   Specifies whether soft line-break characters are to be inserted. A value of **TRUE** inserts the characters; a value of **FALSE** removes them.

Remarks   Sets the inclusion of soft line-break characters on or off within a multiple-line edit control. A soft line break consists of two carriage returns and a linefeed inserted at the end of a line that is broken because of word wrapping. A hard line break consists of one carriage return and a linefeed. Lines that end with a hard line break are not affected by **FmtLines**. Windows will only respond if the **CEdit** object is a multiple-line edit control. **FmtLines** only affects the buffer returned by **GetHandle** and the text returned by **WM_GETTEXT** It has no impact on the display of the text within the edit control.

See Also   **CEdit::GetHandle**, **CWnd::GetWindowText**, **EM_FMTLINES**

CEdit::GetFirstVisibleLine

int GetFirstVisibleLine( ) const;

Return Value   The zero-based index of the topmost visible line. For single-line edit controls, the return value is 0.

Remarks   An application calls **GetFirstVisibleLine** to determine the topmost visible line in an edit control.

See Also   **EM_GETFIRSTVISIBLELINE**

CEdit::GetHandle

HLOCAL GetHandle( ) const;

Return Value   A local memory handle that identifies the buffer holding the contents of the edit control. If an error occurs, such as sending the message to a single-line edit control, the return value is 0.

Remarks   Retrieves a handle to the memory currently allocated for a multiple-line edit control. The handle is a local memory handle and may be used by any of the **Local** Windows memory functions that take a local memory handle as a parameter. **GetHandle** is processed only by multiple-line edit controls. Call **GetHandle** for a multiple-line edit control in a dialog box only if the dialog box was created with the **DS_LOCALEDIT** style flag set. If the **DS_LOCALEDIT** style is not set, you will still get a nonzero return value, but you will not be able to use the returned value.

See Also   **CEdit::SetHandle**, **EM_GETHANDLE**

CEdit::GetLine

int GetLine(int *nIndex*, **LPTSTR** *lpszBuffer* **) const;**

int GetLine(int *nIndex*, **LPTSTR** *lpszBuffer*, **int** *nMaxLength* **) const;**

Return Value   The number of bytes actually copied. The return value is 0 if the line number specified by *nIndex* is greater then the number of lines in the edit control.

Parameters   *nIndex*   Specifies the line number to retrieve from a multiple-line edit control. Line numbers are zero-based; a value of 0 specifies the first line. This parameter is ignored by a single-line edit control.

lpszBuffer   Points to the buffer that receives a copy of the line. The first word of the buffer must specify the maximum number of bytes that can be copied to the buffer.

nMaxLength   Specifies the maximum number of bytes that can be copied to the buffer. **GetLine** places this value in the first word of *lpszBuffer* before making the call to Windows.

Remarks   Retrieves a line of text from an edit control and places it in *lpszBuffer*. This call is not processed for a single-line edit control. The copied line does not contain a null-termination character.

See Also   **CEdit::LineLength**, **CWnd::GetWindowText**, **EM_GETLINE**

CEdit::GetLineCount

int GetLineCount( ) const;

Return Value   An integer containing the number of lines in the multiple-line edit control. If no text has been entered into the edit control, the return value is 1.

Remarks   Retrieves the number of lines in a multiple-line edit control. **GetLineCount** is only processed by multiple-line edit controls.

See Also   **EM_GETLINECOUNT**

CEdit::GetModify

BOOL GetModify( ) const;

Return Value   Nonzero if the edit-control contents have been modified; 0 if they have remained unchanged.

Remarks   Determines whether the contents of an edit control have been modified. Windows maintains an internal flag indicating whether the contents of the edit control have been changed. This flag is cleared when the edit control is first created and may also be cleared by calling the **SetModify** member function.

See Also   **CEdit::SetModify**, **EM_GETMODIFY**

CEdit::GetPasswordChar

TCHAR GetPasswordChar( ) const;

Return Value   Specifies the character to be displayed in place of the character typed by the user. The return value is **NULL** if no password character exists.

Remarks   An application calls the **GetPasswordChar** member function to retrieve the password character displayed in an edit control when the user enters text. If the edit control is created with the **ES_PASSWORD** style, the default password character is set to an asterisk (*).

See Also   **EM_GETPASSWORDCHAR, CEdit::SetPasswordChar**

CEdit::GetRect

void GetRect(LPRECT *lpRect* **) const;**

Parameters   *lpRect*   Points to the **RECT** structure that receives the formatting rectangle.

Remarks   Gets the formatting rectangle of an edit control. The formatting rectangle is the limiting rectangle of the text, which is independent of the size of the edit-control window. The formatting rectangle of a multiple-line edit control can be modified by the **SetRect** and **SetRectNP** member functions.

See Also   **CEdit::SetRect, CEdit::SetRectNP, EM_GETRECT**

CEdit::GetSel

DWORD GetSel( ) const;

void GetSel(int& *nStartChar***, int&** *nEndChar* **) const;**

Return Value   The version that returns a **DWORD** returns a value that contains the starting position in the low-order word and the position of the first nonselected character after the end of the selection in the high-order word.

Parameters   *nStartChar*   Reference to an integer that will receive the position of the first character in the current selection.

nEndChar   Reference to an integer that will receive the position of the first nonselected character past the end of the current selection.

Remarks   Gets the starting and ending character positions of the current selection (if any) in an edit control, using either the return value or the parameters.

See Also   **CEdit::SetSel, EM_GETSEL**

CEdit::LimitText

void LimitText(int *nChars* = 0);

Parameters   *nChars*   Specifies the length (in bytes) of the text that the user can enter. If this parameter is 0, the text length is set to **UINT_MAX** bytes. This is the default behavior.

Remarks   Limits the length of the text that the user may enter into an edit control. **LimitText** limits only the text the user can enter. It has no effect on any text already in the edit control when the message is sent, nor does it affect the length of the text copied to the edit control by the **SetWindowText** member function in **CWnd**. If an application uses the **SetWindowText** function to place more text into an edit control than is specified in the call to **LimitText**, the user can edit the entire contents of the edit control.

See Also   **CWnd::SetWindowText**, **EM_LIMITTEXT**

CEdit::LineFromChar

int **LineFromChar**(int *nIndex* = –1) const;

Return Value   The zero-based line number of the line containing the character index specified by *nIndex*. If *nIndex* is –1, the number of the line that contains the first character of the selection is returned. If there is no selection, the current line number is returned.

Parameters   *nIndex*   Contains the zero-based index value for the desired character in the text of the edit control, or contains –1. If *nIndex* is –1, it specifies the current line, that is, the line that contains the caret.

Remarks   Retrieves the line number of the line that contains the specified character index. A character index is the number of characters from the beginning of the edit control. This member function is only used by multiple-line edit controls.

See Also   **CEdit::LineIndex**, **EM_LINEFROMCHAR**

CEdit::LineIndex

int **LineIndex**(int *nLine* = –1) const;

Return Value   The character index of the line specified in *nLine* or –1 if the specified line number is greater then the number of lines in the edit control.

Parameters   *nLine*   Contains the index value for the desired line in the text of the edit control, or contains –1. If *nLine* is –1, it specifies the current line, that is, the line that contains the caret.

Remarks	Retrieves the character index of a line within a multiple-line edit control. The character index is the number of characters from the beginning of the edit control to the specified line. This member function is only processed by multiple-line edit controls.
See Also	**CEdit::LineFromChar**, **EM_LINEINDEX**

CEdit::LineLength

int **LineLength**(int *nLine* = –1) **const;**

Return Value	When **LineLength** is called for a multiple-line edit control, the return value is the length (in bytes) of the line specified by *nLine*. When **LineLength** is called for a single-line edit control, the return value is the length (in bytes) of the text in the edit control.
Parameters	*nLine* Specifies the character index of a character in the line whose length is to be retrieved. If this parameter is –1, the length of the current line (the line that contains the caret) is returned, not including the length of any selected text within the line. When **LineLength** is called for a single-line edit control, this parameter is ignored.
Remarks	Retrieves the length of a line in an edit control. Use the **LineIndex** member function to retrieve a character index for a given line number within a multiple-line edit control.
See Also	**CEdit::LineIndex**, **EM_LINELENGTH**

CEdit::LineScroll

void **LineScroll**(int *nLines*, int *nChars* = 0);

Parameters	*nLines* Specifies the number of lines to scroll vertically.
	nChars Specifies the number of character positions to scroll horizontally. This value is ignored if the edit control has either the **ES_RIGHT** or **ES_CENTER** style.
Remarks	Scrolls the text of a multiple-line edit control. This member function is processed only by multiple-line edit controls. The edit control does not scroll vertically past the last line of text in the edit control. If the current line plus the number of lines specified by *nLines* exceeds the total number of lines in the edit control, the value is adjusted so that the last line of the edit control is scrolled to the top of the edit-control window. **LineScroll** can be used to scroll horizontally past the last character of any line.
See Also	**EM_LINESCROLL**

CEdit::Paste

void Paste( );

Remarks   Inserts the data from the Clipboard into the edit control at the current cursor position. Data is inserted only if the Clipboard contains data in **CF_TEXT** format.

See Also   **CEdit::Clear, CEdit::Copy, CEdit::Cut, WM_PASTE**

CEdit::ReplaceSel

void ReplaceSel(LPCTSTR *lpszNewText* **);**

Parameters   *lpszNewText*   Points to a null-terminated string containing the replacement text.

Remarks   Replaces the current selection in an edit control with the text specified by *lpszNewText*. Replaces only a portion of the text in an edit control. If you want to replace all of the text, use the **CWnd::SetWindowText** member function. If there is no current selection, the replacement text is inserted at the current cursor location.

See Also   **CWnd::SetWindowText, EM_REPLACESEL**

CEdit::SetHandle

void SetHandle(HLOCAL *hBuffer* **);**

Parameters   *hBuffer*   Contains a handle to the local memory. This handle must have been created by a previous call to the **LocalAlloc** Windows function using the **LMEM_MOVEABLE** flag. The memory is assumed to contain a null-terminated string. If this is not the case, the first byte of the allocated memory should be set to 0.

Remarks   Sets the handle to the local memory that will be used by a multiple-line edit control. The edit control will then use this buffer to store the currently displayed text instead of allocating its own buffer. This member function is processed only by multiple-line edit controls. Before an application sets a new memory handle, it should use the **GetHandle** member function to get the handle to the current memory buffer and free that memory using the **LocalFree** Windows function. **SetHandle** clears the undo buffer (the **CanUndo** member function then returns 0) and the internal modification flag (the **GetModify** member function then returns 0). The edit-control window is redrawn. You can use this member function in a multiple-line edit control in a dialog box only if you have created the dialog box with the **DS_LOCALEDIT** style flag set.

See Also   **CEdit::CanUndo, CEdit::GetHandle, CEdit::GetModify, ::LocalAlloc, ::LocalFree, EM_SETHANDLE**

CEdit::SetModify

void SetModify(BOOL *bModified* **= TRUE);**

Parameters   *bModified*   A value of **TRUE** indicates that the text has been modified, and a value of **FALSE** indicates it is unmodified. By default, the modified flag is set.

Remarks   Sets or clears the modified flag for an edit control. The modified flag indicates whether or not the text within the edit control has been modified. It is automatically set whenever the user changes the text. Its value may be retrieved with the **GetModify** member function.

See Also   **CEdit::GetModify**, **EM_SETMODIFY**

CEdit::SetPasswordChar

void SetPasswordChar(TCHAR *ch* **);**

Parameters   *ch*   Specifies the character to be displayed in place of the character typed by the user. If *ch* is 0, the actual characters typed by the user are displayed.

Remarks   Sets or removes a password character displayed in an edit control when the user types text. When a password character is set, that character is displayed for each character the user types. This member function has no effect on a multiple-line edit control. When the **SetPasswordChar** member function is called, **CEdit** will redraw all visible characters using the character specified by *ch*. If the edit control is created with the **ES_PASSWORD** style, the default password character is set to an asterisk (*). This style is removed if **SetPasswordChar** is called with *ch* set to 0.

See Also   **CEdit::GetPasswordChar**, **EM_SETPASSWORDCHAR**

CEdit::SetReadOnly

BOOL SetReadOnly(BOOL *bReadOnly* **= TRUE);**

Return Value   Nonzero if the operation is successful, or 0 if an error occurs.

Parameters   *bReadOnly*   Specifies whether to set or remove the read-only state of the edit control. A value of **TRUE** sets the state to read-only; a value of **FALSE** sets the state to read/write.

Remarks   An application calls the **SetReadOnly** member function to set the read-only state of an edit control. The current setting can be found by testing the **ES_READONLY** flag in the return value of **CWnd::GetStyle**.

See Also   **EM_SETREADONLY**, **CWnd::GetStyle**

CEdit::SetRect

void SetRect(LPCRECT *lpRect* **);**

Parameters   *lpRect*   Points to the **RECT** structure or **CRect** object that specifies the new dimensions of the formatting rectangle.

Remarks   Sets the dimensions of a rectangle using the specified coordinates. This member is processed only by multiple-line edit controls. Use **SetRect** to set the formatting rectangle of a multiple-line edit control. The formatting rectangle is the limiting rectangle of the text, which is independent of the size of the edit-control window. When the edit control is first created, the formatting rectangle is the same as the client area of the edit-control window. By using the **SetRect** member function, an application can make the formatting rectangle larger or smaller than the edit-control window. If the edit control has no scroll bar, text will be clipped, not wrapped, if the formatting rectangle is made larger than the window. If the edit control contains a border, the formatting rectangle is reduced by the size of the border. If you adjust the rectangle returned by the **GetRect** member function, you must remove the size of the border before you pass the rectangle to **SetRect**. When **SetRect** is called, the edit control's text is also reformatted and redisplayed.

See Also   **CRect::CRect, CRect::CopyRect, CRect::operator =,
CRect::SetRectEmpty, CEdit::GetRect, CEdit::SetRectNP, EM_SETRECT**

CEdit::SetRectNP

void SetRectNP(LPCRECT *lpRect* **);**

Parameters   *lpRect*   Points to a **RECT** structure or **CRect** object that specifies the new dimensions of the rectangle.

Remarks   Sets the formatting rectangle of a multiple-line edit control. The formatting rectangle is the limiting rectangle of the text, which is independent of the size of the edit-control window. **SetRectNP** is identical to the **SetRect** member function except that the edit-control window is not redrawn. When the edit control is first created, the formatting rectangle is the same as the client area of the edit-control window. By calling the **SetRectNP** member function, an application can make the formatting rectangle larger or smaller than the edit-control window. If the edit control has no scroll bar, text will be clipped, not wrapped, if the formatting rectangle is made larger than the window. This member is processed only by multiple-line edit controls.

See Also   **CRect::CRect, CRect::CopyRect, CRect::operator =,
CRect::SetRectEmpty, CEdit::GetRect, CEdit::SetRect, EM_SETRECTNP**

CEdit::SetSel

void SetSel(DWORD *dwSelection*, BOOL *bNoScroll* = FALSE);

void SetSel(int *nStartChar*, int *nEndChar*, BOOL *bNoScroll* = FALSE);

Parameters   *dwSelection*   Specifies the starting position in the low-order word and the ending position in the high-order word. If the low-order word is 0 and the high-order word is –1, all the text in the edit control is selected. If the low-order word is –1, any current selection is removed.

bNoScroll   Indicates whether the caret should be scrolled into view. If **FALSE**, the caret is scrolled into view. If **TRUE**, the caret is not scrolled into view.

nStartChar   Specifies the starting position. If *nStartChar* is 0 and *nEndChar* is –1, all the text in the edit control is selected. If *nStartChar* is –1, any current selection is removed.

nEndChar   Specifies the ending position.

Remarks   Selects a range of characters in an edit control.

See Also   **CEdit::GetSel**, **CEdit::ReplaceSel**, **EM_SETSEL**

CEdit::SetTabStops

void SetTabStops( );

BOOL SetTabStops(const int& *cxEachStop*);

BOOL SetTabStops(int *nTabStops*, LPINT *rgTabStops*);

Return Value   Nonzero if the tabs were set; otherwise 0.

Parameters   *cxEachStop*   Specifies that tab stops are to be set at every *cxEachStop* dialog units.

nTabStops   Specifies the number of tab stops contained in *rgTabStops*. This number must be greater than 1.

rgTabStops   Points to an array of unsigned integers specifying the tab stops in dialog units. A dialog unit is a horizontal or vertical distance. One horizontal dialog unit is equal to one-fourth of the current dialog base width unit, and 1 vertical dialog unit is equal to one-eighth of the current dialog base height unit. The dialog base units are computed based on the height and width of the current system font. The **GetDialogBaseUnits** Windows function returns the current dialog base units in pixels.

Remarks   Sets the tab stops in a multiple-line edit control. When text is copied to a multiple-line edit control, any tab character in the text will cause space to be generated up to the next tab stop.

To set tab stops to the default size of 32 dialog units, call the parameterless version of this member function. To set tab stops to a size other than 32, call the version with the *cxEachStop* parameter. To set tab stops to an array of sizes, use the version with two parameters. This member function is only processed by multiple-line edit controls. **SetTabStops** does not automatically redraw the edit window. If you change the tab stops for text already in the edit control, call **CWnd::InvalidateRect** to redraw the edit window.

See Also   **::GetDialogBaseUnits**, **CWnd::InvalidateRect**, **EM_SETTABSTOPS**

CEdit::Undo

BOOL Undo( );

Return Value   For a single-line edit control, the return value is always nonzero. For a multiple-line edit control, the return value is nonzero if the undo operation is successful, or 0 if the undo operation fails.

Remarks   Use to undo the last edit-control operation. An undo operation can also be undone. For example, you can restore deleted text with the first call to **Undo**. As long as there is no intervening edit operation, you can remove the text again with a second call to **Undo**.

See Also   **CEdit::CanUndo**, **EM_UNDO**

class CEditView : public CView

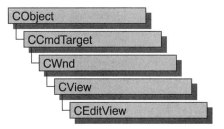

Like the **CEdit** class, the **CEditView** class provides the functionality of a Windows edit control. The **CEditView** class provides the following additional functions:

- Printing
- Find and replace
- Cut, copy, paste, clear, and undo

Because class **CEditView** is derived from class **CView**, objects of class **CEditView** can be used with documents and document templates.

Each **CEditView** control's text is kept in its own global memory object. Your application can have any number of **CEditView** controls.

Create objects of type **CEditView** if you want an edit control with the added functionality listed above. Derive your own classes from **CEditView** to add or modify the basic functionality, or to declare classes that can be added to a document template.

The default implementation of class **CEditView** handles the following commands: **ID_EDIT_CUT, ID_EDIT_COPY, ID_EDIT_PASTE, ID_EDIT_CLEAR, ID_EDIT_UNDO, ID_EDIT_SELECT_ALL, ID_EDIT_FIND, ID_EDIT_REPLACE, ID_EDIT_REPEAT**, and **ID_FILE_PRINT**.

Objects of type **CEditView** (or of types derived from **CEditView**) have the following limitations:

- **CEditView** does not implement true WYSIWYG (what you see is what you get) editing. Where there is a choice between readability on the screen and matching printed output, **CEditView** opts for screen readability.

- **CEditView** can display text in only a single font. No special character formatting is supported.

- The amount of text a **CEditView** can contain is limited. The limits are the same as for the **CEdit** control.

#include <afxext.h>

See Also   **CEdit**, **CDocument**, **CDocTemplate**, **CView**

Data Members
dwStyleDefault   Default style for objects of type **CEditView.**

Construction
CEditView   Constructs an object of type **CEditView**.

Attributes
GetEditCtrl   Provides access to the **CEdit** portion of a **CEditView** object (the Windows edit control).

GetPrinterFont   Retrieves the current printer font.

GetSelectedText   Retrieves the current text selection.

SetPrinterFont   Sets a new printer font.

SetTabStops   Sets tab stops for both screen display and printing.

Operations
FindText   Searches for a string within the text.

PrintInsideRect   Renders text inside a given rectangle.

SerializeRaw   Serializes a **CEditView** object to disk as raw text.

Overridables
OnFindNext   Finds next occurrence of a text string.

OnReplaceAll   Replaces all occurrences of a given string with a new string.

OnReplaceSel   Replaces current selection.

OnTextNotFound   Called when a find operation fails to match any further text.

Member Functions

CEditView::CEditView

CEditView( );

Remarks   Constructs an object of type **CEditView**. After constructing the object, you must call the **Create** function before the edit control is used. If you derive a class from

CEditView and add it to the template using **CWinApp::AddDocTemplate**, the framework calls both this constructor and the **Create** function.

See Also   **CWnd::Create**, **CWinApp::AddDocTemplate**

CEditView::FindText

BOOL FindText(LPCTSTR *lpszFind***, BOOL** *bNext* **= TRUE, BOOL** *bCase* **= TRUE);**

Return Value   Nonzero if the search text is found; otherwise 0.

Parameters   *lpszFind*   The text to be found.

bNext   Specifies the direction of the search. If **TRUE**, the search direction is toward the end of the buffer. If **FALSE**, the search direction is toward the beginning of the buffer.

bCase   Specifies whether the search is case sensitive. If **TRUE**, the search is case sensitive. If **FALSE**, the search is not case sensitive.

Remarks   Call the **FindText** function to search the **CEditView** object's text buffer. This function searches the text in the buffer for the text specified by *lpszFind*, starting at the current selection, in the direction specified by *bNext*, and with case sensitivity specified by *bCase*. If the text is found, it sets the selection to the found text and returns a nonzero value. If the text is not found, the function returns 0.

You normally do not need to call the **FindText** function unless you override **OnFindNext**, which calls **FindText**.

See Also   **CEditView::OnFindNext**, **CEditView::OnReplaceAll**, **CEditView::OnReplaceSel**, **CEditView::OnTextNotFound**

CEditView::GetEditCtrl

CEdit& GetEditCtrl( ) const;

Return Value   A reference to a **CEdit** object.

Remarks   Call **GetEditCtrl** to get a reference to the edit control used by the edit view. This control is of type **CEdit**, so you can manipulate the Windows edit control directly using the **CEdit** member functions.

> **Warning** Using the **CEdit** object can change the state of the underlying Windows edit control. For example, you should not change the tab settings using the **CEdit::SetTabStops** function because **CEditView** caches these settings for use both in the edit control and in printing. Instead, use **CEditView::SetTabStops**.

See Also   **CEdit, CEditView::SetTabStops**

CEditView::GetPrinterFont

CFont* GetPrinterFont( ) const;

Return Value   A pointer to a **CFont** object that specifies the current printer font; **NULL** if the printer font has not been set. The pointer may be temporary and should not be stored for later use.

Remarks   Call **GetPrinterFont** to get a pointer to a **CFont** object that describes the current printer font. If the printer font has not been set, the default printing behavior of the **CEditView** class is to print using the same font used for display.

Use this function to determine the current printer font. If it is not the desired printer font, use **CEditView::SetPrinterFont** to change it.

See Also   **CEditView::SetPrinterFont**

CEditView::GetSelectedText

void GetSelectedText(CString& *strResult* **) const;**

Parameters   *strResult*   A reference to the **CString** object that is to receive the selected text.

Remarks   Call **GetSelectedText** to copy the selected text into a **CString** object, up to the end of the selection or the character preceding the first carriage-return character in the selection.

See Also   **CEditView::OnReplaceSel**

CEditView::OnFindNext

Protected→
virtual void OnFindNext(LPCTSTR *lpszFind*, **BOOL** *bNext*, **BOOL** *bCase* **);**
END Protected

Parameters   *lpszFind*   The text to be found.

bNext   Specifies the direction of the search. If **TRUE**, the search direction is toward the end of the buffer. If **FALSE**, the search direction is toward the beginning of the buffer.

bCase   Specifies whether the search is case sensitive. If **TRUE**, the search is case sensitive. If **FALSE**, the search is not case sensitive.

Remarks   Searches the text in the buffer for the text specified by *lpszFind*, in the direction specified by *bNext*, with case sensitivity specified by *bCase*. The search starts at the beginning of the current selection and is accomplished through a call to **FindText**. In the default implementation, **OnFindNext** calls **OnTextNotFound** if the text is not found.

Override **OnFindNext** to change the way a **CEditView**-derived object searches text. **CEditView** calls **OnFindNext** when the user chooses the Find Next button in the standard Find dialog box.

See Also   **CEditView::OnTextNotFound**, **CEditView::FindText**, **CEditView::OnReplaceAll**, **CEditView::OnReplaceSel**

CEditView::OnReplaceAll

Protected→
virtual void OnReplaceAll(LPCTSTR *lpszFind*, **LPCTSTR** *lpszReplace*, **BOOL** *bCase* **);**
END Protected

Parameters   *lpszFind*   The text to be found.

lpszReplace   The text to replace the search text.

bCase   Specifies whether search is case sensitive. If **TRUE**, the search is case sensitive. If **FALSE**, the search is not case sensitive.

Remarks   **CEditView** calls **OnReplaceAll** when the user selects the Replace All button in the standard Replace dialog box. **OnReplaceAll** searches the text in the buffer for the text specified by *lpszFind*, with case sensitivity specified by *bCase*. The search starts at the beginning of the current selection. Each time the search text is found, this function replaces that occurrence of the text with the text specified by *lpszReplace*. The search is accomplished through a call to **FindText**. In the default implementation, **OnTextNotFound** is called if the text is not found.

If the current selection does not match *lpszFind*, the selection is updated to the first occurrence of the text specified by *lpszFind* and a replace is not performed. This allows the user to confirm that this is what they want to do when the selection does not match the text to be replaced.

Override **OnReplaceAll** to change the way a **CEditView**-derived object replaces text.

See Also **CEditView::OnFindNext**, **CEditView::OnTextNotFound**, **CEditView::FindText**, **CEditView::OnReplaceSel**

CEditView::OnReplaceSel

Protected→
virtual void OnReplaceSel(LPCTSTR *lpszFind*, **BOOL** *bNext*, **BOOL** *bCase*, **LPCTSTR** *lpszReplace* **);**
END Protected

Parameters *lpszFind*   The text to be found.

bNext   Specifies the direction of the search. If **TRUE**, the search direction is toward the end of the buffer. If **FALSE**, the search direction is toward the beginning of the buffer.

bCase   Specifies whether the search is case sensitive. If **TRUE**, the search is case sensitive. If **FALSE**, the search is not case sensitive.

lpszReplace   The text to replace the found text.

Remarks **CEditView** calls **OnReplaceSel** when the user selects the Replace button in the standard Replace dialog box. After replacing the selection, this function searches the text in the buffer for the next occurrence of the text specified by *lpszFind*, in the direction specified by *bNext*, with case sensitivity specified by *bCase*. The search is accomplished through a call to **FindText**. If the text is not found, **OnTextNotFound** is called.

Override **OnReplaceSel** to change the way a **CEditView**-derived object replaces the selected text.

See Also **CEditView::OnFindNext**, **CEditView::OnTextNotFound**, **CEditView::FindText**, **CEditView::OnReplaceAll**

CEditView::OnTextNotFound

Protected→
virtual void OnTextNotFound(LPCTSTR *lpszFind* **);**
END Protected

Parameters *lpszFind*   The text to be found.

Remarks Override this function to change the default implementation, which calls the Windows function **MessageBeep**.

See Also   **CEditView::FindText, CEditView::OnFindNext, CEditView::OnReplaceAll,
CEditView::OnReplaceSel**

CEditView::PrintInsideRect

UINT PrintInsideRect(CDC **pDC***, RECT&** *rectLayout***, UINT** *nIndexStart***,
UINT** *nIndexStop* **);**

Return Value   The index of the next character to be printed (i.e., the character following the last character rendered).

Parameters   *pDC*   Pointer to the printer device context.

rectLayout   Reference to a **CRect** object or **RECT** structure specifying the rectangle in which the text is to be rendered.

nIndexStart   Index within the buffer of the first character to be rendered.

nIndexStop   Index within the buffer of the character following the last character to be rendered.

Remarks   Call **PrintInsideRect** to print text in the rectangle specified by *rectLayout*.

If the **CEditView** control does not have the style **ES_AUTOHSCROLL**, text is wrapped within the rendering rectangle. If the control does have the style **ES_AUTOHSCROLL**, the text is clipped at the right edge of the rectangle.

The **rect.bottom** element of the *rectLayout* object is changed so that the rectangle's dimensions define the part of the original rectangle that is occupied by the text.

See Also   **CEditView::SetPrinterFont, CEditView::GetPrinterFont**

CEditView::SerializeRaw

void SerializeRaw(CArchive& *ar* **);**

Parameters   *ar*   Reference to the **CArchive** object that stores the serialized text.

Remarks   Call **SerializeRaw** to have a **CArchive** object read or write the text in the **CEditView** object to a text file. **SerializeRaw** differs from **CEditView**'s internal implementation of **Serialize** in that it reads and writes only the text, without preceding object-description data.

See Also   **CArchive, CObject::Serialize**

CEditView::SetPrinterFont

void SetPrinterFont(CFont* *pFont* **);**

Parameters   *pFont*   A pointer to an object of type **CFont**. If **NULL**, the font used for printing is based on the display font.

Remarks   Call **SetPrinterFont** to set the printer font to the font specified by *pFont*.

If you want your view to always use a particular font for printing, include a call to **SetPrinterFont** in your class's **OnPreparePrinting** function. This virtual function is called before printing occurs, so the font change takes place before the view's contents are printed.

See Also   **CWnd::SetFont**, **CFont**, **CView::OnPreparePrinting**

CEditView::SetTabStops

void SetTabStops(int *nTabStops* **);**

Parameters   *nTabStops*   Width of each tab stop, in dialog units.

Remarks   Call this function to set the tab stops used for display and printing. Only a single tab-stop width is supported. (**CEdit** objects support multiple tab widths.) Widths are in dialog units, which equal one-fourth of the average character width (based on uppercase and lowercase alphabetic characters only) of the font used at the time of printing or displaying. You should not use **CEdit::SetTabStops** because **CEditView** must cache the tab-stop value.

This function modifies only the tabs of the object for which it is called. To change the tab stops for each **CEditView** object in your application, call each object's **SetTabStops** function. **dwStyleDefault** is a public member variable of type **DWORD**.

See Also   **CWnd::SetFont**, **CEditView::SetPrinterFont**

Data Members

CEditView::dwStyleDefault

Remarks   Pass this static member as the *dwStyle* parameter of the **Create** function to obtain the default style for the **CEditView** object. **dwStyleDefault** is a public member of type **DWORD**.

class CException : public CObject

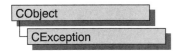

CException is the base class for all exceptions in the Microsoft Foundation Class Library. The derived classes and their descriptions are listed below:

CMemoryException	Out-of-memory exception
CNotSupportedException	Request for an unsupported operation
CArchiveException	Archive-specific exceptions
CFileException	File-specific exceptions
CResourceException	Windows resource not found or not createable

These exceptions are intended to be used with the **THROW**, **THROW_LAST**, **TRY**, **CATCH**, **AND_CATCH**, and **END_CATCH** macros. For more information on exceptions, see the article "Exceptions" in *Programming with the Microsoft Foundation Class Library*.

Use the derived classes to catch specific exceptions. Use **CException** if you need to catch all types of exceptions (and then use **CObject::IsKindOf** to differentiate among **CException**-derived classes). All derived **CException** classes use the **IMPLEMENT_DYNAMIC** macro. **CException** objects are deleted automatically. Do not delete them yourself.

Because **CException** is an abstract base class, you cannot create **CException** objects; you must create objects of derived classes. If you need to create your own **CException** type, use one of the derived classes listed above as a model.

#include <afx.h>

See Also   **Exception Processing**

class CFieldExchange

The **CFieldExchange** class supports the record field exchange (RFX) routines used by the database classes. Use this class if you are writing data exchange routines for custom data types; otherwise, you will not directly use this class. RFX exchanges data between the field data members of your recordset object and the corresponding fields of the current record on the data source. RFX manages the exchange in both directions, from the data source and to the data source.

A **CFieldExchange** object provides the context information needed for record field exchange to take place. **CFieldExchange** objects support a number of operations, including binding parameters and field data members and setting various flags on the fields of the current record. RFX operations are performed on recordset-class data members of types defined by the **enum FieldType** in **CFieldExchange**. Possible **FieldType** values are:

- **CFieldExchange::outputColumn** for field data members.
- **CFieldExchange::param** for parameter data members.

Most of the member functions and data members listed below are provided for writing your own custom RFX routines. You will use **SetFieldType** frequently. For more information about RFX and the use of **CFieldExchange** objects, see the article "Record Field Exchange" in *Programming with the Microsoft Foundation Class Library*. For details about the RFX global functions, see "Macros and Globals" in this manual.

#include <afxdb.h>

See Also   **CRecordset**

Operations

IsFieldType	Returns nonzero if the current operation is appropriate for the type of field being updated.
SetFieldType	Specifies the type of recordset data member—column or parameter—represented by all following calls to RFX functions until the next call to **SetFieldType**.

Member Functions

CFieldExchange::IsFieldType

BOOL IsFieldType(UINT* *pnField* **);**

Return Value   Nonzero if the current operation can be performed on the current field type.

Parameters   *pnField*   The sequential number of the field data member is returned in this parameter. This number corresponds to the field's order in the **DoFieldExchange** function.

Remarks   If you write your own RFX function, call **IsFieldType** at the beginning of your function to determine whether the current operation can be performed on a particular field data member type (a **CFieldExchange::outputColumn** or a **CFieldExchange::param**). Follow the model of the existing RFX functions.

CFieldExchange::SetFieldType

void SetFieldType(UINT *nFieldType* **);**

Parameters   *nFieldType*   A value of the **enum FieldType**, declared in **CFieldExchange**, which can be either of the following:

- **CFieldExchange::outputColumn**
- **CFieldExchange::param**

Remarks   ClassWizard places a call to **SetFieldType** in the field map section of your recordset class's **DoFieldExchange** override. The call precedes calls to RFX functions, one for each field data member of your class, and identifies the field type as **CFieldExchange::outputColumn**.

If you parameterize your recordset class, you must add RFX calls for all parameter data members (outside the field map) and precede these calls with a call to **SetFieldType**. Pass the value **CFieldExchange::param**.

In general, each group of RFX function calls associated with field data members or parameter data members must be preceded by a call to **SetFieldType**. The *nFieldType* parameter of each **SetFieldType** call identifies the type of the data members represented by the RFX function calls that follow the **SetFieldType** call.

See Also   **CRecordset::DoFieldExchange**

RFX global functions
listed under "Macros and Globals"

Example   This example shows several calls to RFX functions with accompanying calls to **SetFieldType**. ClassWizard normally writes the first call to **SetFieldType**, and its associated RFX calls. You must write the second, and its RFX call. Note that **SetFieldType** is called through the *pFX* pointer to a **CFieldExchange** object.

```
void CSections::DoFieldExchange(CFieldExchange* pFX)
{
    //{{AFX_FIELD_MAP(CSections)
    pFX->SetFieldType(pFX, CFieldExchange::outputColumn);
    RFX_Text(pFX, 1, "CourseID", m_strCourseID);
    RFX_Text(pFX, 2, "InstructorID", m_strInstructorID);
    RFX_Text(pFX, 3, "RoomNo", m_strRoomNo);
    RFX_Text(pFX, 4, "Schedule", m_strSchedule);
    RFX_Text(pFX, 5, "SectionNo", m_strSectionNo);
    //}}AFX_FIELD_MAP
    pFX->SetFieldType(pFX, CFieldExchange::param);
    RFX_Text(pFX, "Name," m_strNameParam);
}
```

class CFile : public CObject

CObject

CFile

CFile is the base class for Microsoft Foundation file classes. It directly provides unbuffered, binary disk input/output services, and it indirectly supports text files and memory files through its derived classes. CFile works in conjunction with the CArchive class to support serialization of Microsoft Foundation objects. The hierarchical relationship between this class and its derived classes allows your program to operate on all file objects through the polymorphic CFile interface. A memory file, for example, behaves like a disk file. Use CFile and its derived classes for general-purpose disk I/O. Use ofstream or other Microsoft iostream classes for formatted text sent to a disk file. Normally, a disk file is opened automatically on CFile construction and closed on destruction. Static member functions permit you to interrogate a file's status without opening the file.

#include <afx.h>

See Also   CStdioFile, CMemFile

Data Members
m_hFile	Usually contains the operating-system file handle.

Construction
CFile	Constructs a CFile object from a path or file handle.
Abort	Closes a file ignoring all warnings and errors.
Duplicate	Constructs a duplicate object based on this file.
Open	Safely opens a file with an error-testing option.
Close	Closes a file and deletes the object.

Input/Output
Read	Reads (unbuffered) data from a file at the current file position.
ReadHuge	Can read more than 64K of (unbuffered) data from a file at the current file position.
Write	Writes (unbuffered) data in a file to the current file position.
WriteHuge	Can write more than 64K of (unbuffered) data in a file to the current file position.
Flush	Flushes any data yet to be written.

Position

Seek Positions the current file pointer.

SeekToBegin Positions the current file pointer at the beginning of the file.

SeekToEnd Positions the current file pointer at the end of the file.

GetLength Obtains the length of the file.

SetLength Changes the length of the file.

Locking

LockRange Locks a range of bytes in a file.

UnlockRange Unlocks a range of bytes in a file.

Status

GetPosition Gets the current file pointer.

GetStatus Obtains the status of this open file.

Static

Rename Renames the specified file (static function).

Remove Deletes the specified file (static function).

GetStatus Obtains the status of the specified file (static, virtual function).

SetStatus Sets the status of the specified file (static, virtual function).

Member Functions

CFile::Abort

virtual void Abort( );

Remarks Closes the file associated with this object and makes the file unavailable for reading or writing. If you have not closed the file before destroying the object, the destructor closes it for you.

When handling exceptions, **CFile::Abort** differs from **CFile::Close** in two important ways. First, the **Abort** function will not throw an exception on failures because failures are ignored by **Abort**. Second, **Abort** will not **ASSERT** if the file has not been opened or was closed previously.

If you used **new** to allocate the **CFile** object on the heap, then you must delete it after closing the file. **Abort** sets **m_hFile** to **CFile::hFileNull**.

See Also **CFile::Close**, **CFile::Open**

Example

```
CStdioFile fileTest;
char* pFileName = "test.dat";
TRY
{
    // do stuff that may throw exceptions
    fileTest.Open( pFileName, CFile::modeWrite );
}
CATCH_ALL( e )
{
    fileTest.Abort();    // close file safely and quietly
    THROW_LAST();
}
END_CATCH_ALL
```

CFile::CFile

CFile( );

CFile(int *hFile* **);**

CFile(LPCTSTR *lpszFileName*, **UINT** *nOpenFlags* **)**
   throw(CFileException);

Parameters

hFile   The handle of a file that is already open.

lpszFileName   A string that is the path to the desired file. The path may be relative or absolute.

nOpenFlags   Sharing and access mode. Specifies the action to take when opening the file. You can combine options listed below by using the bitwise OR (|) operator. One access permission and one share option are required; the **modeCreate** and **modeNoInherit** modes are optional. The values are as follows:

- **CFile::modeCreate**   Directs the constructor to create a new file. If the file exists already, it is truncated to 0 length.

- **CFile::modeRead**   Opens the file for reading only.

- **CFile::modeReadWrite**   Opens the file for reading and writing.

- **CFile::modeWrite**   Opens the file for writing only.

- **CFile::modeNoInherit**   Prevents the file from being inherited by child processes.

- **CFile::shareDenyNone**   Opens the file without denying other processes read or write access to the file. **Create** fails if the file has been opened in compatibility mode by any other process.

- **CFile::shareDenyRead**   Opens the file and denies other processes read access to the file. **Create** fails if the file has been opened in compatibility mode or for read access by any other process.

- **CFile::shareDenyWrite**   Opens the file and denies other processes write access to the file. **Create** fails if the file has been opened in compatibility mode or for write access by any other process.

- **CFile::shareExclusive**   Opens the file with exclusive mode, denying other processes both read and write access to the file. Construction fails if the file has been opened in any other mode for read or write access, even by the current process.

- **CFile::shareCompat**   Opens the file with compatibility mode, allowing any process on a given machine to open the file any number of times. Construction fails if the file has been opened with any of the other sharing modes.

- **CFile::typeText**   Sets text mode with special processing for carriage return–linefeed pairs (used in derived classes only).

- **CFile::typeBinary**   Sets binary mode (used in derived classes only).

Remarks

The default constructor does not open a file but rather sets **m_hFile** to **CFile::hFileNull**. Because this constructor does not throw an exception, it does not make sense to use **TRY/CATCH** logic. Use the **Open** member function, then test directly for exception conditions. For a discussion of exception-processing strategy, see the article "Exceptions" in *Programming with the Microsoft Foundation Class Library*.

The constructor with one argument creates a **CFile** object that corresponds to an existing operating-system file identified by *hFile*. No check is made on the access mode or file type. When the **CFile** object is destroyed the operating-system file will not be closed. You must close the file yourself.

The constructor with two arguments creates a **CFile** object and opens the corresponding operating-system file with the given path. This constructor combines the functions of the first constructor and the **Open** member function. It throws an exception if there is an error while opening the file. Generally, this means that the error is unrecoverable and that the user should be alerted.

Example

```
char* pFileName = "test.dat";
TRY
{
    CFile f( pFileName, CFile::modeCreate | CFile::modeWrite );
}
CATCH( CFileException, e )
{
    #ifdef _DEBUG
        afxDump << "File could not be opened " << e->m_cause << "\n";
    #endif
}
END_CATCH
```

CFile::Close

virtual void Close( )
    throw(CFileException);

Remarks

Closes the file associated with this object and makes the file unavailable for reading or writing. If you have not closed the file before destroying the object, the destructor closes it for you. If you used **new** to allocate the **CFile** object on the heap, then you must delete it after closing the file. **Close** sets **m_hFile** to **CFile::hFileNull**.

See Also

CFile::Open

CFile::Duplicate

virtual CFile* Duplicate( ) const
    throw(CFileException);

Return Value

A pointer to a duplicate **CFile** object.

Remarks

Constructs a duplicate **CFile** object for a given file. This is equivalent to the C run-time function **_dup**.

CFile::Flush

virtual void Flush( )
    throw(CFileException);

Remarks

Forces any data remaining in the file buffer to be written to the file. The use of **Flush** does not guarantee flushing of **CArchive** buffers. If you are using an archive, call **CArchive::Flush** first.

CFile::GetLength

virtual DWORD GetLength( ) const
throw(CFileException);

Return Value   The length of the file.

Remarks   Obtains the current logical length of the file in bytes, not the amount physically allocated.

See Also   **CFile::SetLength**

CFile::GetPosition

virtual DWORD GetPosition( ) const
throw(CFileException);

Return Value   The file pointer as a 32-bit doubleword.

Remarks   Obtains the current value of the file pointer, which can be used in subsequent calls to **Seek**.

Example
```
extern CFile cfile;
DWORD dwPosition = cfile.GetPosition();
```

CFile::GetStatus

BOOL GetStatus(CFileStatus& *rStatus* **) const;**

static BOOL PASCAL GetStatus(LPCTSTR *lpszFileName*, **CFileStatus&**
rStatus **);**

Return Value   Nonzero if no error, in which case *rStatus* is valid; otherwise 0. A value of 0 indicates that the file does not exist.

Parameters   *rStatus*   A reference to a user-supplied **CFileStatus** structure that will receive the status information. The **CFileStatus** structure has the following fields:

- **CTime m_ctime**   The date and time the file was created
- **CTime m_mtime**   The date and time the file was last modified
- **CTime m_atime**   The date and time the file was last accessed for reading
- **LONG m_size**   The logical size of the file in bytes, as reported by the DIR command
- **BYTE m_attribute**   The attribute byte of the file
- **char m_szFullName[_MAX_PATH]**   The absolute filename in the Windows character set.

lpszFileName   A string in the Windows character set that is the path to the desired file. The path may be relative or absolute, but may not contain a network name.

Remarks

The virtual version of **GetStatus** retrieves the status of the open file associated with this **CFile** object. It does not insert a value into the **m_szFullName** structure member.

The static version gets the status of the named file and copies the filename to **m_szFullName**. This function obtains the file status from the directory entry without actually opening the file. It is useful for testing the existence and access rights of a file.

The **m_attribute** is the file attribute. The Microsoft Foundation classes provide an **enum** type attribute so that you can specify attributes symbolically:

```
enum Attribute {
    normal    =    0x00,
    readOnly  =    0x01,
    hidden    =    0x02,
    system    =    0x04,
    volume    =    0x08,
    directory =    0x10,
    archive   =    0x20
    };
```

See Also   **CFile::SetStatus**, **CTime**

Example
```
CFileStatus status;
extern CFile cfile;
if( cfile.GetStatus( status ) )     // virtual member function
    {
        #ifdef _DEBUG
          afxDump << "File size = " << status.m_size << "\n";
        #endif
    }
char* pFileName = "test.dat";
if( CFile::GetStatus( pFileName, status ) )   // static function
    {
        #ifdef _DEBUG
          afxDump << "Full file name = " << status.m_szFullName << "\n";
        #endif
    }
```

CFile::LockRange

virtual void LockRange(DWORD *dwPos*, **DWORD** *dwCount* **)**
 throw(CFileException);

Parameters   *dwPos*   The byte offset of the start of the byte range to lock.

dwCount   The number of bytes in the range to lock.

Remarks

Locks a range of bytes in an open file, throwing an exception if the file is already locked. Locking bytes in a file prevents access to those bytes by other processes. You can lock more than one region of a file, but no overlapping regions are allowed.

When you unlock the region, using the **UnlockRange** member function, the byte range must correspond exactly to the region that was previously locked. The **LockRange** function does not merge adjacent regions; if two locked regions are adjacent, you must unlock each region separately.

Note   This function is not available for the **CMemFile**-derived class.

See Also   **CFile::UnlockRange**

Example
```
extern DWORD dwPos;
extern DWORD dwCount;
extern CFile cfile;
cfile.LockRange( dwPos, dwCount );
```

CFile::Open

virtual BOOL Open(LPCTSTR *lpszFileName*, **UINT** *nOpenFlags*,
    CFileException* *pError* = **NULL);**

Return Value   Nonzero if the open was successful; otherwise 0. The *pError* parameter is meaningful only if 0 is returned.

Parameters   *lpszFileName*   A string that is the path to the desired file. The path may be relative or absolute but may not contain a network name.

nOpenFlags   A **UINT** that defines the file's sharing and access mode. It specifies the action to take when opening the file. You can combine options by using the bitwise OR (|) operator. One access permission and one share option are required; the **modeCreate** and **modeNoInherit** modes are optional. See the **CFile** constructor for a list of mode options.

pError   A pointer to an existing file-exception object that indicates the completion status of the open operation.

Remarks   **Open** is designed for use with the default **CFile** constructor. The two functions form a "safe" method for opening a file where a failure is a normal, expected condition. The constructor is guaranteed to succeed, and **Open** returns a pointer to an exception object, bypassing the **THROW/TRY/CATCH** mechanism.

See Also   **CFile::CFile**, **CFile::Close**

Example
```
CFile f;
CFileException e;
char* pFileName = "test.dat";
if( !f.Open( pFileName, CFile::modeCreate | CFile::modeWrite, &e ) )
    {
        #ifdef _DEBUG
            afxDump << "File could not be opened " << e.m_cause << "\n";
        #endif
    }
```

CFile::Read

virtual UINT Read(void* *lpBuf*, **UINT** *nCount* **)**
   throw(CFileException);

Return Value   The number of bytes transferred to the buffer. Note that for all **CFile** classes, the return value may be less than *nCount* if the end of file was reached.

Parameters   *lpBuf*   Pointer to the user-supplied buffer that is to receive the data read from the file.

   nCount   The maximum number of bytes to be read from the file. For text-mode files, carriage return–linefeed pairs are counted as single characters.

Remarks   Reads data into a buffer from the file associated with the **CFile** object.

See Also   **CFile::Write**

Example
```
extern CFile cfile;
char pbuf[100];
UINT nBytesRead = cfile.Read( pbuf, 100 );
```

CFile::ReadHuge

virtual UINT ReadHuge(void* *lpBuf*, **DWORD** *dwCount* **)**
   throw(CFileException);

Return Value   The number of bytes transferred to the buffer. Note that for all **CFile** objects, the return value can be less than *dwCount* if the end of file was reached.

Parameters   *lpBuf*   Pointer to the user-supplied buffer that is to receive the data read from the file.

   dwCount   The maximum number of bytes to be read from the file. For text-mode files, carriage return–linefeed pairs are counted as single characters.

Remarks   Reads data into a buffer from the file associated with the **CFile** object.

This function differs from **Read** in that more than 64K–1 bytes of data can be read by **ReadHuge**. This function can be used by any object derived from **CFile**.

See Also   **CFile::Write, CFile::WriteHuge, CFile::Read**

CFile::Remove

static void PASCAL Remove(LPCTSTR *lpszFileName* **)**
    throw(CFileException);

Parameters   *lpszFileName*   A string that is the path to the desired file. The path may be relative or absolute but may not contain a network name.

Remarks   This static function deletes the file specified by the path. It will not remove a directory. The **Remove** member function throws an exception if the connected file is open or if the file cannot be removed. This is equivalent to the DEL command.

Example

```
char* pFileName = "test.dat";
TRY
{
    CFile::Remove( pFileName );
}
CATCH( CFileException, e )
{
    #ifdef _DEBUG
        afxDump << "File " << pFileName << " cannot be removed\n";
    #endif
}
END_CATCH
```

CFile::Rename

static void PASCAL Rename(LPCTSTR *lpszOldName***,**
    LPCTSTR *lpszNewName* **)**
    throw(CFileException);

Parameters   *lpszOldName*   The old path.

    lpszNewName   The new path.

Remarks   This static function renames the specified file. Directories cannot be renamed. This is equivalent to the REN command.

Example

```
extern char* pOldName;
extern char* pNewName;
TRY
{
    CFile::Rename( pOldName, pNewName );
}
```

```
CATCH( CFileException, e )
{
    #ifdef _DEBUG
        afxDump << "File " << pOldName << " not found, cause = "
            << e->m_cause << "\n";
    #endif
}
END_CATCH
```

CFile::Seek

virtual LONG Seek(LONG *lOff*, **UINT** *nFrom* **)**
  throw(CFileException);

Return Value   If the requested position is legal, **Seek** returns the new byte offset from the beginning of the file. Otherwise, the return value is undefined and a **CFileException** object is thrown.

Parameters   *lOff*   Number of bytes to move the pointer.

nFrom   Pointer movement mode. Must be one of the following values:

- **CFile::begin**   Move the file pointer *lOff* bytes forward from the beginning of the file.
- **CFile::current**   Move the file pointer *lOff* bytes from the current position in the file.
- **CFile::end**   Move the file pointer backward *lOff* bytes from the end of the file.

Remarks   Repositions the pointer in a previously opened file. The **Seek** function permits random access to a file's contents by moving the pointer a specified amount, absolutely or relatively. No data is actually read during the seek. When a file is opened, the file pointer is positioned at offset 0, the beginning of the file.

Example
```
extern CFile cfile;
LONG lOffset = 1000, lActual;
lActual = cfile.Seek( lOffset, CFile::begin );
```

CFile::SeekToBegin

void SeekToBegin( )
  throw(CFileException);

Remarks   Sets the value of the file pointer to the beginning of the file. SeekToBegin() is equivalent to Seek(0L, CFile::begin).

Example
```
extern CFile cfile;
cfile.SeekToBegin();
```

CFile::SeekToEnd

DWORD SeekToEnd( )
   throw(CFileException);

Return Value

The length of the file in bytes.

Remarks

Sets the value of the file pointer to the logical end of the file. `SeekToEnd()` is equivalent to `CFile::Seek( 0L, CFile::end )`.

See Also

CFile::GetLength, CFile::Seek, CFile::SeekToBegin

Example
```
extern CFile cfile;
DWORD dwActual = cfile.SeekToEnd();
```

CFile::SetLength

virtual void SetLength(const DWORD *dwNewLen* **)**
   throw(CFileException);

Parameters

dwNewLen   Desired length of the file in bytes. This value may be larger or smaller than the current length of the file. The file will be extended or truncated as appropriate.

Remarks

Changes the length of the file.

Note   With **CMemFile**, this function could throw a **CMemoryException** object.

Example
```
extern CFile cfile;
DWORD dwNewLength = 10000;
cfile.SetLength( dwNewLength );
```

CFile::SetStatus

static void SetStatus(LPCTSTR *lpszFileName*, **const CFileStatus&** *status* **)**
   throw(CFileException);

Parameters

lpszFileName   A string that is the path to the desired file. The path may be relative or absolute but may not contain a network name.

status   The buffer containing the new status information. Call the **GetStatus** member function to prefill the **CFileStatus** structure with current values, then make changes as required. If a value is 0, then the corresponding status item is not updated. See the **GetStatus** member function for a description of the **CFileStatus** structure.

Remarks   Sets the status of the file associated with this file location. To set the time, modify the **m_mtime** field of *status*. Please note that when you make a call to **SetStatus** in an attempt to change only the attributes of the file, and the m_mtime member of the file status structure is non-zero, the attributes may also be affected (changing the time stamp may have side effects on the attributes). If you wish to only change the attributes of the file, first set the **m_mtime** member of the file status structure to zero and then make a call to **SetStatus**.

See Also   **CFile::GetStatus**

Example
```
char* pFileName = "test.dat";
extern BYTE newAttribute;
CFileStatus status;
CFile::GetStatus( pFileName, status );
status.m_attribute = newAttribute;
CFile::SetStatus( pFileName, status );
```

CFile::UnlockRange

virtual void UnlockRange(DWORD *dwPos***, DWORD** *dwCount* **)**
    throw(CFileException);

Parameters   *dwPos*   The byte offset of the start of the byte range to unlock.

dwCount   The number of bytes in the range to unlock.

Remarks   Unlocks a range of bytes in an open file. See the description of the **LockRange** member function for details.

Note   This function is not available for the **CMemFile**-derived class.

See Also   **CFile::LockRange**

Example
```
extern DWORD dwPos;
extern DWORD dwCount;
extern CFile cfile;
cfile.UnlockRange( dwPos, dwCount );
```

CFile::Write

virtual void Write(const void* *lpBuf*, UINT *nCount*)
   throw(CFileException);

Parameters   *lpBuf*   A pointer to the user-supplied buffer that contains the data to be written to the file.

nCount   The number of bytes to be transferred from the buffer. For text-mode files, carriage return–linefeed pairs are counted as single characters.

Remarks   Writes data from a buffer to the file associated with the **CFile** object. **Write** throws an exception in response to several conditions including the disk-full condition.

See Also   **CFile::Read**, **CStdioFile::WriteString**

Example
```
extern CFile cfile;
char pbuf[100];
cfile.Write( pbuf, 100 );
```

CFile::WriteHuge

virtual void WriteHuge(const void* *lpBuf*, DWORD *dwCount*)
   throw(CFileException);

Parameters   *lpBuf*   A pointer to the user-supplied buffer that contains the data to be written to the file.

dwCount   The number of bytes to be transferred from the buffer. For text-mode files, carriage return–linefeed pairs are counted as single characters.

Remarks   Writes data from a buffer to the file associated with the **CFile** object. **WriteHuge** throws an exception in response to several conditions, including the disk-full condition.

This function differs from **Write** in that more than 64K–1 bytes of data can be written by **WriteHuge**. This function can be used by any object derived from **CFile**.

Note   **WriteHuge** is provided only for backward compatiblity. **WriteHuge** and **Write** have the same semantics under Win32.

See Also   **CFile::Read**, **CFile::ReadHuge**, **CFile::Write**, **CStdioFile::WriteString**

Data Members

CFile::m_hFile

Remarks   Contains the operating-system file handle for an open file. **m_hFile** is a public variable of type **UINT**. It contains **CFile::hFileNull** (an operating-system-independent empty file indicator) if the handle has not been assigned.

Use of **m_hFile** is not recommended because the member's meaning depends on the derived class. **m_hFile** is made a public member for convenience in supporting nonpolymorphic use of the class.

class CFileDialog : public CDialog

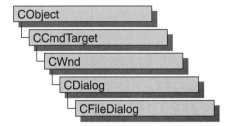

The **CFileDialog** class encapsulates the Windows common file dialog box. Common file dialog boxes provide an easy way to implement File Open and File Save As dialog boxes (as well as other file-selection dialog boxes) in a manner consistent with Windows standards.

You can use **CFileDialog** "as is" with the constructor provided, or you can derive your own dialog class from **CFileDialog** and write a constructor to suit your needs. In either case, these dialog boxes will behave like standard Microsoft Foundation class dialog boxes because they are derived from the **CDialog** class.

To use a **CFileDialog** object, first create the object using the **CFileDialog** constructor. After the dialog box has been constructed, you can set or modify any values in the **m_ofn** structure to initialize the values or states of the dialog box's controls. The **m_ofn** structure is of type **OPENFILENAME**. For more information on this structure, see the Windows Software Development Kit (SDK) documentation.

After initializing the dialog box's controls, call the **DoModal** member function to display the dialog box and allow the user to enter the path and file. **DoModal** returns whether the user selected the OK (**IDOK**) or the Cancel (**IDCANCEL**) button.

If **DoModal** returns **IDOK**, you can use one of **CFileDialog**'s public member functions to retrieve the information input by the user.

CFileDialog includes several protected members that enable you to do custom handling of share violations, filename validation, and list-box change notification. These protected members are callback functions that most applications do not need to use, since default handling is done automatically. Message-map entries for these functions are not necessary because they are standard virtual functions.

You can use the Windows **CommDlgExtendedError** function to determine whether an error occurred during initialization of the dialog box and to learn more about the error.

The destruction of **CFileDialog** objects is handled automatically. It is not necessary to call **CDialog::EndDialog**.

To allow the user to select multiple files, set the **OFN.ALLOW_MULTISELECT** flag before calling **DoModal**. You need to supply your own filename buffer to accommodate the returned list of multiple filenames. Do this by replacing **m_ofn.lpstrFile** with a pointer to a buffer you have allocated, after constructing the **CFileDialog**, but before calling **DoModal**.

CFileDialog relies on the COMMDLG.DLL file that ships with Windows versions 3.1 and later. For details about redistributing COMMDLG.DLL to Windows version 3.0 users, see the *Getting Started* manual in the Windows SDK.

If you derive a new class from **CFileDialog**, you can use a message map to handle any messages. To extend the default message handling, derive a class from **CWnd**, add a message map to the new class, and provide member functions for the new messages. You do not need to provide a hook function to customize the dialog box.

To customize the dialog box, derive a class from **CFileDialog**, provide a custom dialog template, and add a message map to process the notification messages from the extended controls. Any unprocessed messages should be passed to the base class.

Customizing the hook function is not required.

#include <afxdlgs.h>

Data Members

m_ofn	The Windows **OPENFILENAME** structure. Provides access to basic file dialog box parameters.

Construction

CFileDialog	Constructs a **CFileDialog** object.

Overridables

DoModal	Displays the dialog box and allows the user to make a selection.
GetPathName	Returns the full path of the selected file.
GetFileName	Returns the filename of the selected file.
GetFileExt	Returns the file extension of the selected file.
GetFileTitle	Returns the title of the selected file.
GetReadOnlyPref	Returns the read-only status of the selected file.

Operations

OnShareViolation	Called when a share violation occurs.
OnFileNameOK	Called to validate the filename entered in the dialog box.
OnLBSelChangedNotify	Called when the list box selection changes.

Member Functions

CFileDialog::CFileDialog

CFileDialog(BOOL *bOpenFileDialog*, **LPCTSTR** *lpszDefExt* = **NULL,**
   LPCTSTR *lpszFileName* = **NULL, DWORD** *dwFlags* =
   OFN_HIDEREADONLY | OFN_OVERWRITEPROMPT, LPCTSTR
   lpszFilter = **NULL, CWnd*** *pParentWnd* = **NULL);**

Parameters   *bOpenFileDialog*   Set to **TRUE** to construct a File Open dialog box or **FALSE** to construct a File Save As dialog box.

lpszDefExt   The default filename extension. If the user does not include an extension in the Filename edit box, the extension specified by *lpszDefExt* is automatically appended to the filename. If this parameter is **NULL**, no file extension is appended.

lpszFileName   The initial filename that appears in the filename edit box. If **NULL**, no filename initially appears.

dwFlags   A combination of one or more flags that allow you to customize the dialog box. For a description of these flags, see the **OPENFILENAME** structure description in the Windows SDK documentation. If you modify the **m_ofn.Flags** structure member, use a bitwise OR operator in your changes to keep the default behavior intact.

lpszFilter   A series of string pairs that specify filters you can apply to the file. If you specify file filters, only selected files will appear in the Files list box. See the Remarks section below for more information on how to work with file filters.

pParentWnd   A pointer to the file dialog-box object's parent or owner window.

Remarks   Call this function to construct a standard Windows file dialog box-object. Either a File Open or File Save As dialog box is constructed, depending on the value of *bOpenFileDialog*.

The *lpszFilter* parameter is used to determine the type of filename a file must have to be displayed in the file list box. The first string in the string pair describes the filter; the second string indicates the file extension to use. Multiple extensions may be specified using ';' as the delimiter. The string ends with two '|' characters, followed by a **NULL** character. You can also use a **CString** object for this parameter.

For example, Microsoft Excel permits users to open files with extensions .XLC (chart) or .XLS (worksheet), among others. The filter for Excel could be written as:

```
static char BASED_CODE szFilter[] = "Chart Files (*.xlc) | *.xlc |
Worksheet Files (*.xls) | *.xls | Data Files (*.xlc;*.xls) | *.xlc;
*.xls | All Files (*.*) | *.* ||"
```

See Also   **CFileDialog::DoModal**, **::GetOpenFileName**, **::GetSaveFileName**

CFileDialog::DoModal

virtual int DoModal( );

Return Value   **IDOK** or **IDCANCEL** if the function is successful; otherwise 0. **IDOK** and **IDCANCEL** are constants that indicate whether the user selected the OK or Cancel button.

If **IDCANCEL** is returned, you can call the Windows **CommDlgExtendedError** function to determine whether an error occurred.

Remarks   Call this function to display the Windows common file dialog box and allow the user to browse files and directories and enter a filename.

If you want to initialize the various file dialog-box options by setting members of the **m_ofn** structure, you should do this before calling **DoModal**, but after the dialog object is constructed.

When the user clicks the dialog box's OK or CANCEL buttons, or selects the CLOSE option from the dialog box's control menu, control is returned to your application. You can then call other member functions to retrieve the settings or information the user inputs into the dialog box.

DoModal is a virtual function overridden from class **CDialog**.

See Also   **CDialog::DoModal**, **CFileDialog::CFileDialog**

CFileDialog::GetFileExt

CString GetFileExt( ) const;

Return Value   The extension of the filename.

Remarks   Call this function to retrieve the extension of the filename entered into the dialog box. For example, if the name of the file entered is DATA.TXT, **GetFileExt** returns "TXT".

If **m_ofn.Flags** has the **OFN_ALLOWMULTISELECT** flag set, then this member function only applies to the first name.

See Also   **CFileDialog::GetPathName**, **CFileDialog::GetFileName**, **CFileDialog::GetFileTitle**

CFileDialog::GetFileName

CString GetFileName( ) const;

Return Value   The name of the file.

Remarks   Call this function to retrieve the name of the file entered in the dialog box. The name of the file includes only its prefix, without the path or the extension. For example, **GetFileName** will return "TEXT" for the file C:\FILES\TEXT.DAT.

If **m_ofn.Flags** has the **OFN_ALLOWMULTISELECT** flag set, then this member function only applies to the first name.

See Also   **CFileDialog::GetPathName**, **CFileDialog::GetFileExt**, **CFileDialog::GetFileTitle**

CFileDialog::GetFileTitle

CString GetFileTitle( ) const;

Return Value   The title of the file.

Remarks   Call this function to retrieve the title of the filename entered in the dialog box. The title of the filename includes both the name and the extension. For example, **GetFileTitle** will return "TEXT.DAT" for the file C:\FILES\TEXT.DAT.

If **m_ofn.Flags** has the **OFN_ALLOWMULTISELECT** flag set, then this member function only applies to the first name.

See Also   **CFileDialog::GetPathName**, **CFileDialog::GetFileName**, **CFileDialog::GetFileExt**, **::GetFileTitle**

CFileDialog::GetPathName

CString GetPathName( ) const;

Return Value   The full path of the file.

Remarks   Call this function to retrieve the full path of the file entered in the dialog box. The path of the filename includes the file's title plus the entire directory path. For example, **GetPathName** will return "C:\FILES\TEXT.DAT" for the file C:\FILES\TEXT.DAT.

If **m_ofn.Flags** has the **OFN_ALLOWMULTISELECT** flag set, then this member function only applies to the first name.

See Also   **CFileDialog::GetFileName**, **CFileDialog::GetFileExt**, **CFileDialog::GetFileTitle**

CFileDialog::GetReadOnlyPref

BOOL GetReadOnlyPref( ) const;

Return Value   Non-zero if the Read Only check box in the dialog box is selected; otherwise 0.

Remarks   Call this function to determine whether the Read Only check box has been selected in the Windows standard File Open and File Save As dialog boxes. The Read Only check box can be hidden by setting the **OFN_HIDEREADONLY** style in the **CFileDialog** constructor.

See Also   **CFileDialog::CFileDialog**, **CFileDialog::GetPathName**, **CFileDialog::GetFileExt**

CFileDialog::OnFileNameOK

Protected→
virtual BOOL OnFileNameOK( );
END **Protected**

Return Value   Nonzero if the filename is a valid filename; otherwise 0.

Remarks   Override this function only if you want to provide custom validation of filenames that are entered into a common file dialog box. This function allows you to reject a filename for any application-specific reason. Normally, you do not need to use this function because the framework provides default validation of filenames and displays a message box if an invalid filename is entered.

If a nonzero value is returned, the dialog box will remain displayed for the user to enter another filename.

See Also   **OPENFILENAME**

CFileDialog::OnLBSelChangedNotify

Protected→
virtual void OnLBSelChangedNotify(UINT *nIDBox***, UINT** *iCurSel***, UINT**
*nCode***);**
END Protected

Parameters
nIDBox The ID of the list box or combo box in which the selection occurred.

iCurSel The index of the current selection.

nCode The control notification code.

This parameter must have one of the following values:

- **CD_LBSELCHANGE** Specifies *iCurSel* is the selected item in a single-selection list box.
- **CD_LBSELSUB** Specifies that *iCurSel* is no longer selected in a multiselection list box.
- **CD_LBSELADD** Specifies that *iCurSel* is selected in a multiselection list box.
- **CD_LBSELNOITEMS** Specifies that no selection exists in a multiselection list box.

For more information, see "Filename Dialog Boxes" in the Windows SDK Help.

Remarks
This function is called whenever the current selection in a list box is about to change. Override this function to provide custom handling of selection changes in the list box. For example, you can use this function to display the access rights or date-last-modified of each file the user selects.

CFileDialog::OnShareViolation

Protected→
virtual UINT OnShareViolation(LPCTSTR *lpszPathName* **);**
END Protected

Return Value
One of the following values:

- **OFN_SHAREFALLTHROUGH** The filename is returned from the dialog box.
- **OFN_SHARENOWARN** No further action needs to be taken.
- **OFN_SHAREWARN** The user receives the standard warning message for this error.

Parameters
lpszPathName The path of the file on which the share violation occurred.

Remarks   Override this function to provide custom handling of share violations. Normally, you do not need to use this function because the framework provides default checking of share violations and displays a message box if a share violation occurs.

If you want to disable share violation checking, use the bitwise OR operator to combine the flag **OFN_SHAREAWARE** with **m_ofn.Flags**.

See Also   **CFileDialog::OnFileNameOK**

Data Members

CFileDialog::m_ofn

Remarks   **m_ofn** is a structure of type **OPENFILENAME**. Use this structure to initialize the appearance of a File Open or File Save As dialog box after it is constructed but before it is displayed with the **DoModal** member function. For example, you can set the **lpszTitle** member of **m_ofn** to the caption you want the dialog box to have.

For more information on this structure, including a listing of its members, see **OPENFILENAME** in the Windows SDK documentation.

class CFileException : public CException

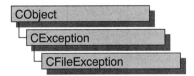

A **CFileException** object represents a file-related exception condition. The **CFileException** class includes public data members that hold the portable cause code and the operating-system-specific error number. The class also provides static member functions for throwing file exceptions and for returning cause codes for both operating-system errors and C run-time errors. **CFileException** objects are constructed and thrown in **CFile** member functions and in member functions of derived classes. You can access these objects within the scope of a **CATCH** expression. For portability, use only the cause code to get the reason for an exception. For more information about exceptions, see the article "Exceptions" in *Programming with the Microsoft Foundation Class Library*.

#include <afx.h>

See Also   **CFile**

Data Members

m_cause	Contains portable code corresponding to the exception cause.
m_lOsError	Contains the related operating-system error number.

Construction

CFileException	Constructs a **CFileException** object.

Code Conversion

OsErrorToException	Returns a cause code corresponding to an operating system error code.
ErrnoToException	Returns cause code corresponding to a run-time error number.

Helper Functions

ThrowOsError	Throws a file exception based on an operating-system error number.
ThrowErrno	Throws a file exception based on a run-time error number.

Member Functions

CFileException::CFileException

CFileException(int *cause* = CFileException::none, LONG *lOsError* = –1);

Parameters   *cause*   An enumerated type variable that indicates the reason for the exception. See **CFileException::m_cause** for a list of the possible values.

lOsError   An operating-system-specific reason for the exception, if available. The *lOsError* parameter provides more information than *cause* does.

Remarks   Constructs a **CFileException** object that stores the cause code and the operating-system code in the object. Do not use this constructor directly, but rather call the global function **AfxThrowFileException**.

Note   The variable *lOsError* applies only to **CFile** and **CStdioFile** objects. The **CMemFile** class does not handle this error code.

See Also   **AfxThrowFileException**

CFileException::ErrnoToException

static int PASCAL ErrnoToException(int *nErrno*);

Return Value   Enumerated value that corresponds to a given run-time library error value.

Parameters   *nErrno*   An integer error code as defined in the run-time include file ERRNO.H.

Remarks   Converts a given run-time library error value to a **CFileException** enumerated error value. See **CFileException::m_cause** for a list of the possible enumerated values.

See Also   **CFileException::OsErrorToException**

Example
```
#include <errno.h>
ASSERT( CFileException::ErrnoToException( EACCES ) ==
                    CFileException::accessDenied );
```

CFileException::OsErrorToException

static int PASCAL OsErrorToException(LONG *lOsError*);

Return Value   Enumerated value that corresponds to a given operating-system error value.

Parameters   *lOsError*   An operating-system-specific error code.

Remarks   Returns an enumerator that corresponds to a given *lOsError* value. If the error code is unknown, then the function returns **CFileException::generic**.

See Also   **CFileException::ErrnoToException**

Example
```
ASSERT( CFileException::OsErrorToException( 5 ) ==
                    CFileException::accessDenied );
```

CFileException::ThrowErrno

static void PASCAL ThrowErrno(int *nErrno*);

Parameters   *nErrno*   An integer error code as defined in the run-time include file ERRNO.H.

Remarks   Constructs a **CFileException** object corresponding to a given *nErrno* value, then throws the exception.

See Also   **CFileException::ThrowOsError**

Example
```
#include <errno.h>
CFileException::ThrowErrno( EACCES );  // "access denied"
```

CFileException::ThrowOsError

static void PASCAL ThrowOsError(LONG *lOsError*);

Parameters   *lOsError*   An operating-system-specific error code.

Remarks   Throws a **CFileException** corresponding to a given *lOsError* value. If the error code is unknown, then the function throws an exception coded as **CFileException::generic**.

See Also   **CFileException::ThrowErrno**

Example
```
FileException::ThrowOsError( 5 );  // "access denied"
```

Data Members

CFileException::m_cause

Remarks   Contains values defined by a **CFileException** enumerated type. This data member is a public variable of type **int**. The enumerators and their meanings are as follows:

- **CFileException::none**   No error occurred.
- **CFileException::generic**   An unspecified error occurred.
- **CFileException::fileNotFound**   The file could not be located.

- **CFileException::badPath**   All or part of the path is invalid.
- **CFileException::tooManyOpenFiles**   The permitted number of open files was exceeded.
- **CFileException::accessDenied**   The file could not be accessed.
- **CFileException::invalidFile**   There was an attempt to use an invalid file handle.
- **CFileException::removeCurrentDir**   The current working directory cannot be removed.
- **CFileException::directoryFull**   There are no more directory entries.
- **CFileException::badSeek**   There was an error trying to set the file pointer.
- **CFileException::hardIO**   There was a hardware error.
- **CFileException::sharingViolation**   SHARE.EXE was not loaded, or a shared region was locked.
- **CFileException::lockViolation**   There was an attempt to lock a region that was already locked.
- **CFileException::diskFull**   The disk is full.
- **CFileException::endOfFile**   The end of file was reached.

Note These **CFileException** cause enumerators are distinct from the **CArchiveException** cause enumerators.

Example

```
extern char* pFileName;
TRY
{
    CFile f( pFileName, CFile::modeCreate | CFile::modeWrite );
}
CATCH( CFileException, e)
{
    if( e->m_cause == CFileException::fileNotFound )
        printf( "ERROR: File not found\n");
}
```

CFileException::m_IOsError

Remarks

Contains the operating-system error code for this exception. See your operating-system technical manual for a listing of error codes. This data member is a public variable of type **LONG**.

class CFindReplaceDialog : public CDialog

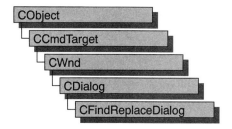

The **CFindReplaceDialog** class allows you to implement standard string Find/Replace dialog boxes in your application. Unlike the other Windows common dialog boxes, **CFindReplaceDialog** objects are modeless, allowing users to interact with other windows while they are on screen. There are two kinds of **CFindReplaceDialog** objects: Find dialog boxes and Find/Replace dialog boxes. Although the dialog boxes allow the user to input search and search/replace strings, they do not perform any of the searching or replacing functions. You must add these to the application.

To construct a **CFindReplaceDialog** object, use the provided constructor (which has no arguments). Since this is a modeless dialog box, allocate the object on the heap using the **new** operator, rather than on the stack.

Once a **CFindReplaceDialog** object has been constructed, you must call the **Create** member function to create and display the dialog box.

Use the **m_fr** structure to initialize the dialog box before calling **Create**. The **m_fr** structure is of type **FINDREPLACE**. For more information on this structure, see the Windows Software Development Kit (SDK) documentation.

In order for the parent window to be notified of find/replace requests, you must use the Windows **RegisterMessage** function and use the **ON_REGISTERED_MESSAGE** message-map macro in your frame window that handles this registered message. You can call any of the member functions listed in the following "Operations" section from the frame window's callback function.

You can determine whether the user has decided to terminate the dialog box with the **IsTerminating** member function.

CFindReplaceDialog relies on the COMMDLG.DLL file that ships with Windows versions 3.1 and later. For details about redistributing COMMDLG.DLL to Windows version 3.0 users, see the *Getting Started* manual in the Windows SDK.

To customize the dialog box, derive a class from **CFindReplaceDialog**, provide a custom dialog template, and add a message map to process the notification messages from the extended controls. Any unprocessed messages should be passed to the base class.

Customizing the hook function is not required.

#include <afxdlgs.h>

Data Members

m_fr	A structure used to customize a **CFindReplaceDialog** object.

Construction

CFindReplaceDialog	Call this function to construct a **CFindReplaceDialog** object.
Create	Creates and displays a **CFindReplaceDialog** dialog box.

Operations

FindNext	Call this function to determine whether the user wants to find the next occurrence of the find string.
GetNotifier	Call this function to retrieve the **FINDREPLACE** structure in your registered message handler.
GetFindString	Call this function to retrieve the current find string.
GetReplaceString	Call this function to retrieve the current replace string.
IsTerminating	Call this function to determine whether the dialog box is terminating.
MatchCase	Call this function to determine whether the user wants to match the case of the find string exactly.
MatchWholeWord	Call this function to determine whether the user wants to match entire words only.
ReplaceAll	Call this function to determine whether the user wants all occurrences of the string to be replaced.
ReplaceCurrent	Call this function to determine whether the user wants the current word to be replaced.
SearchDown	Call this function to determine whether the user wants the search to proceed in a downward direction.

Member Functions

CFindReplaceDialog::CFindReplaceDialog

CFindReplaceDialog( );

Remarks   Constructs a **CFindReplaceDialog** object. **CFindReplaceDialog** objects are constructed on the heap with the **new** operator. See the class description above for more information on the construction of **CFindReplaceDialog** objects. Use the **Create** member function to display the dialog box.

See Also   CFindReplaceDialog::Create

CFindReplaceDialog::Create

BOOL Create(BOOL *bFindDialogOnly*, **LPCTSTR** *lpszFindWhat*, **LPCTSTR** *lpszReplaceWith* = **NULL**, **DWORD** *dwFlags* = **FR_DOWN**, **CWnd*** *pParentWnd* = **NULL);**

Return Value   Nonzero if the dialog box object was successfully created; otherwise 0.

Parameters   *bFindDialogOnly*   Set this parameter to **TRUE** to display the standard Windows Find dialog box. Set it to **FALSE** to display the Windows Find/Replace dialog box.

lpszFindWhat   Specifies the string for which to search.

lpszReplaceWith   Specifies the default string with which to replace found strings.

dwFlags   One or more flags you can use to customize the settings of the dialog box, combined using the bitwise OR operator. The default value is **FR_DOWN**, which specifies that the search is to proceed in a downward direction. See the **FINDREPLACE** structure in the Windows SDK for more information on these flags.

pParentWnd   A pointer to the dialog box's parent or owner window. This is the window that will receive the special message indicating that a find/replace action is requested. If **NULL**, the application's main window is used.

Remarks   Creates and displays either a Find or Find/Replace dialog box object, depending on the value of *bFindDialogOnly*.

In order for the parent window to be notified of find/replace requests, you must use the Windows **RegisterMessage** function whose return value is a message number unique to the application's instance. Your frame window should have a message map entry that declares the callback function (**OnFindReplace** in the example that follows) that handles this registered message. The following code fragment is an example of how to do this for a frame window class named `CMyFrameWnd`:

```
class CMyFrameWnd : public CFrameWnd
{
protected:
    afx_msg LONG LRESULT OnFindReplace(WPARAM wParam, LPARAM
lParam);

    DECLARE_MESSAGE_MAP()
};
static UINT WM_FINREPLACE = ::RegisterMessage(FINDMSGSTRING);

BEGIN_MESSAGE_MAP( CMyFrameWnd, CFrameWnd )
    //Normal message map entries here.
    ON_REGISTERED_MESSAGE( WM_FINDREPLACE, OnFindReplace )
END_MESSAGE_MAP
```

Within your **OnFindReplace** function, you interpret the intentions of the user and create the code for the find/replace operations.

See Also	**CFindReplaceDialog::CFindReplaceDialog**

CFindReplaceDialog::FindNext

BOOL FindNext( ) const;

Return Value	Nonzero if the user wants to find the next occurrence of the search string; otherwise 0.
Remarks	Call this function from your callback function to determine whether the user wants to find the next occurrence of the search string.
See Also	**CFindReplaceDialog::GetFindString, CFindReplaceDialog::SearchDown**

CFindReplaceDialog::GetFindString

CString GetFindString( ) const;

Return Value	The default string to find.
Remarks	Call this function from your callback function to retrieve the default string to find.
See Also	**CFindReplaceDialog::FindNext, CFindReplaceDialog::GetReplaceString**

CFindReplaceDialog::GetNotifier

static CFindReplaceDialog* PASCAL GetNotifier(LPARAM *lParam*);

Return Value	A pointer to the current dialog box.

Parameters   *lParam*   The **lparam** value passed to the frame window's **OnFindReplace** member function.

Remarks   Call this function to retrieve a pointer to the current Find Replace dialog box. It should be used within your callback function to access the current dialog box, call its member functions, and access the **m_fr** structure.

CFindReplaceDialog::GetReplaceString

CString GetReplaceString( ) const;

Return Value   The default string with which to replace found strings.

See Also   **CFindReplaceDialog::GetFindString**

CFindReplaceDialog::IsTerminating

BOOL IsTerminating( ) const;

Return Value   Nonzero if the user has decided to terminate the dialog box; otherwise 0.

Remarks   Call this function within your callback function to determine whether the user has decided to terminate the dialog box. If this function returns nonzero, you should call the **DestroyWindow** member function of the current dialog box and set any dialog box pointer variable to **NULL**. Optionally, you can also store the find/replace text last entered and use it to initialize the next find/replace dialog box.

CFindReplaceDialog::MatchCase

BOOL MatchCase( ) const;

Return Value   Nonzero if the user wants to find occurrences of the search string that exactly match the case of the search string; otherwise 0.

See Also   **CFindReplaceDialog::MatchWholeWord**

CFindReplaceDialog::MatchWholeWord

BOOL MatchWholeWord( ) const;

Return Value   Nonzero if the user wants to match only the entire words of the search string; otherwise 0.

See Also   **CFindReplaceDialog::MatchCase**

CFindReplaceDialog::ReplaceAll

BOOL ReplaceAll( ) const;

Return Value   Nonzero if the user has requested that all strings matching the replace string be replaced; otherwise 0.

See Also   **CFindReplaceDialog::ReplaceCurrent**

CFindReplaceDialog::ReplaceCurrent

BOOL ReplaceCurrent( ) const;

Return Value   Nonzero if the user has requested that the currently selected string be replaced with the replace string; otherwise 0.

See Also   **CFindReplaceDialog::ReplaceAll**

CFindReplaceDialog::SearchDown

BOOL SearchDown( ) const;

Return Value   Nonzero if the user wants the search to proceed in a downward direction; 0 if the user wants the search to proceed in an upward direction.

Data Members

CFindReplaceDialog::m_fr

Remarks   **m_fr** is a structure of type **FINDREPLACE**. Its members store the characteristics of the dialog-box object. After constructing a **CFindReplaceDialog** object, you can use **m_fr** to initialize various values in the dialog box. You must initialize the dialog box's values before calling the **Create** member function. For more information on this structure, see the **FINDREPLACE** structure in the Windows SDK documentation.

class CFont : public CGdiObject

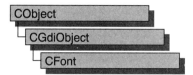

The **CFont** class encapsulates a Windows graphics device interface (GDI) font and provides member functions for manipulating the font. To use a **CFont** object, construct a **CFont** object and attach a Windows font to it with **CreateFont** or **CreateFontIndirect**, and then use the object's member functions to manipulate the font.

#include <afxwin.h>

Construction

CFont	Constructs a **CFont** object.

Initialization

CreateFontIndirect	Initializes a **CFont** object with the characteristics given in a **LOGFONT** structure.
CreateFont	Initializes a **CFont** with the specified characteristics.

Operations

FromHandle	Returns a pointer to a **CFont** object when given a Windows **HFONT**.

Member Functions

CFont::CFont

CFont( );

Remarks   Constructs a **CFont** object. The resulting object must be initialized with **CreateFont** or **CreateFontIndirect** before it can be used.

See Also   **CFont::CreateFontIndirect, CFont::CreateFont, ::EnumFonts**

CFont::CreateFont

BOOL CreateFont(int *nHeight*, **int** *nWidth*, **int** *nEscapement*,
int *nOrientation*, **int** *nWeight*, **BYTE** *bItalic*, **BYTE** *bUnderline*,
BYTE *cStrikeOut*, **BYTE** *nCharSet*, **BYTE** *nOutPrecision*,
BYTE *nClipPrecision*, **BYTE** *nQuality*, **BYTE** *nPitchAndFamily*,
LPCTSTR *lpszFacename* **);**

Return Value   Nonzero if successful; otherwise 0.

Parameters   *nHeight*   Specifies the desired height (in logical units) of the font. The font height can be specified in the following ways:

- Greater than 0, in which case the height is transformed into device units and matched against the cell height of the available fonts.

- Equal to 0, in which case a reasonable default size is used.

- Less than 0, in which case the height is transformed into device units and the absolute value is matched against the character height of the available fonts.

The absolute value of *nHeight* must not exceed 16,384 device units after it is converted. For all height comparisons, the font mapper looks for the largest font that does not exceed the requested size or the smallest font if all the fonts exceed the requested size.

nWidth   Specifies the average width (in logical units) of characters in the font. If *nWidth* is 0, the aspect ratio of the device will be matched against the digitization aspect ratio of the available fonts to find the closest match, which is determined by the absolute value of the difference.

nEscapement   Specifies the angle (in 0.1-degree units) between the escapement vector and the x-axis of the display surface. The escapement vector is the line through the origins of the first and last characters on a line. The angle is measured counterclockwise from the x-axis.

nOrientation   Specifies the angle (in 0.1-degree units) between the baseline of a character and the x-axis. The angle is measured counterclockwise from the x-axis for coordinate systems in which the y-direction is down and clockwise from the x-axis for coordinate systems in which the y-direction is up.

nWeight   Specifies the font weight (in inked pixels per 1000). Although *nWeight* can be any integer value from 0 to 1000, the common constants and values are as follows:

Constant	Value
FW_DONTCARE	0
FW_THIN	100
FW_EXTRALIGHT	200
FW_ULTRALIGHT	200
FW_LIGHT	300
FW_NORMAL	400
FW_REGULAR	400
FW_MEDIUM	500
FW_SEMIBOLD	600
FW_DEMIBOLD	600
FW_BOLD	700
FW_EXTRABOLD	800
FW_ULTRABOLD	800
FW_BLACK	900
FW_HEAVY	900

These values are approximate; the actual appearance depends on the typeface. Some fonts have only **FW_NORMAL**, **FW_REGULAR**, and **FW_BOLD** weights. If **FW_DONTCARE** is specified, a default weight is used.

bItalic   Specifies whether the font is italic.

bUnderline   Specifies whether the font is underlined.

cStrikeOut   Specifies whether characters in the font are struck out. Specifies a strikeout font if set to a nonzero value.

nCharSet   Specifies the font's character set. The following constants and values are predefined:

Constant	Value
ANSI_CHARSET	0
DEFAULT_CHARSET	1
SYMBOL_CHARSET	2
SHIFTJIS_CHARSET	128
OEM_CHARSET	255

The OEM character set is system-dependent.

Fonts with other character sets may exist in the system. An application that uses a font with an unknown character set must not attempt to translate or interpret strings that are to be rendered with that font. Instead, the strings should be passed directly to the output device driver.

The font mapper does not use the **DEFAULT_CHARSET** value. An application can use this value to allow the name and size of a font to fully describe the logical font. If a font with the specified name does not exist, a font from any character set can be substituted for the specified font. To avoid unexpected results, applications should use the **DEFAULT_CHARSET** value sparingly.

nOutPrecision   Specifies the desired output precision. The output precision defines how closely the output must match the requested font's height, width, character orientation, escapement, and pitch. It can be any one of the following values:

OUT_CHARACTER_PRECIS	**OUT_STRING_PRECIS**
OUT_DEFAULT_PRECIS	**OUT_STROKE_PRECIS**
OUT_DEVICE_PRECIS	**OUT_TT_PRECIS**
OUT_RASTER_PRECIS	

Applications can use the **OUT_DEVICE_PRECIS**, **OUT_RASTER_PRECIS**, and **OUT_TT_PRECIS** values to control how the font mapper chooses a font when the system contains more than one font with a given name. For example, if a system contains a font named Symbol in raster and TrueType form, specifying **OUT_TT_PRECIS** forces the font mapper to choose the TrueType version. (Specifying **OUT_TT_PRECIS** forces the font mapper to choose a TrueType font whenever the specified font name matches a device or raster font, even when there is no TrueType font of the same name.)

nClipPrecision   Specifies the desired clipping precision. The clipping precision defines how to clip characters that are partially outside the clipping region. It can be any one of the following values:

CLIP_CHARACTER_PRECIS	**CLIP_MASK**
CLIP_DEFAULT_PRECIS	**CLIP_STROKE_PRECIS**
CLIP_ENCAPSULATE	**CLIP_TT_ALWAYS**
CLIP_LH_ANGLES	

To use an embedded read-only font, an application must specify **CLIP_ENCAPSULATE**.

To achieve consistent rotation of device, TrueType, and vector fonts, an application can use the OR operator to combine the **CLIP_LH_ANGLES** value with any of the other *nClipPrecision* values. If the **CLIP_LH_ANGLES** bit is set, the rotation for all fonts depends on whether the orientation of the coordinate system is left-handed or right-handed. (For more information about the orientation of coordinate systems, see the description of the *nOrientation* parameter.) If **CLIP_LH_ANGLES** is not set, device fonts always rotate counterclockwise, but the rotation of other fonts is dependent on the orientation of the coordinate system.

nQuality   Specifies the font's output quality, which defines how carefully the GDI must attempt to match the logical-font attributes to those of an actual physical font. It can be one of the following values:

- **DEFAULT_QUALITY**   Appearance of the font does not matter.
- **DRAFT_QUALITY**   Appearance of the font is less important than when **PROOF_QUALITY** is used. For GDI raster fonts, scaling is enabled. Bold, italic, underline, and strikeout fonts are synthesized if necessary.
- **PROOF_QUALITY**   Character quality of the font is more important than exact matching of the logical-font attributes. For GDI raster fonts, scaling is disabled and the font closest in size is chosen. Bold, italic, underline, and strikeout fonts are synthesized if necessary.

nPitchAndFamily   Specifies the pitch and family of the font. The two low-order bits specify the pitch of the font and can be any one of the following values:

DEFAULT_PITCH   **VARIABLE_PITCH**
FIXED_PITCH

Applications can add **TMPF_TRUETYPE** to the *nPitchAndFamily* parameter to choose a TrueType font. The four high-order bits of the parameter specify the font family and can be any one of the following values:

- **FF_DECORATIVE**   Novelty fonts: Old English, for example.
- **FF_DONTCARE**   Don't care or don't know.
- **FF_MODERN**   Fonts with constant stroke width (fixed-pitch), with or without serifs. Fixed-pitch fonts are usually modern faces. Pica, Elite, and Courier New are examples.
- **FF_ROMAN**   Fonts with variable stroke width (proportionally spaced) and with serifs. Times New Roman and Century Schoolbook are examples.
- **FF_SCRIPT**   Fonts designed to look like handwriting. Script and Cursive are examples.
- **FF_SWISS**   Fonts with variable stroke width (proportionally spaced) and without serifs. MS Sans Serif is an example.

An application can specify a value for *nPitchAndFamily* by using the Boolean OR operator to join a pitch constant with a family constant.

Font families describe the look of a font in a general way. They are intended for specifying fonts when the exact typeface desired is not available.

lpszFacename   A **CString** or pointer to a null-terminated string that specifies the typeface name of the font. The length of this string must not exceed 30 characters. The Windows **EnumFontFamilies** function can be used to enumerate all currently available fonts. If *lpszFacename* is **NULL**, the GDI uses a device-independent typeface.

Remarks   Initializes a **CFont** object with the specified characteristics. The font can subsequently be selected as the font for any device context. The **CreateFont** function does not create a new Windows GDI font. It merely selects the closest match from the fonts available in the GDI's pool of physical fonts. Applications can use the default settings for most of these parameters when creating a logical font. The parameters that should always be given specific values are *nHeight* and *lpszFacename*. If *nHeight* and *lpszFacename* are not set by the application, the logical font that is created is device-dependent.

When you finish with the **CFont** object created by the **CreateFont** function, first select the font out of the device context, then delete the **CFont** object.

See Also   **CFont::CreateFontIndirect**, **::CreateFont**, **::EnumFontFamilies**, **::EnumFonts**

CFont::CreateFontIndirect

BOOL CreateFontIndirect(const LOGFONT* *lpLogFont* **);**

Return Value   Nonzero if successful; otherwise 0.

Parameters   *lpLogFont*   Points to a **LOGFONT** structure that defines the characteristics of the logical font.

Remarks   Initializes a **CFont** object with the characteristics given in a **LOGFONT** structure pointed to by *lpLogFont*. The font can subsequently be selected as the current font for any device. This font has the characteristics specified in the **LOGFONT** structure. When the font is selected by using the **CDC::SelectObject** member function, the GDI's font mapper attempts to match the logical font with an existing physical font. If it fails to find an exact match for the logical font, it provides an alternative whose characteristics match as many of the requested characteristics as possible.

When you finish with the **CFont** object created by the **CreateFontIndirect** function, first select the font out of the device context, then delete the **CFont** object.

See Also   **CFont::CreateFont**, **CDC::SelectObject**, **CGdiObject::DeleteObject**, **::CreateFontIndirect**

CFont::FromHandle

static CFont* PASCAL FromHandle(HFONT *hFont* **);**

Return Value   A pointer to a **CFont** object if successful; otherwise **NULL**.

Parameters   *hFont*   An **HFONT** handle to a Windows font.

Remarks   Returns a pointer to a **CFont** object when given an **HFONT** handle to a Windows GDI font object. If a **CFont** object is not already attached to the handle, a temporary **CFont** object is created and attached. This temporary **CFont** object is valid only until the next time the application has idle time in its event loop, at which time all temporary graphic objects are deleted. Another way of saying this is that the temporary object is valid only during the processing of one window message.

class CFontDialog : public CDialog

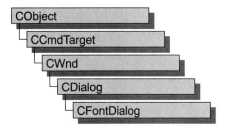

The **CFontDialog** class allows you to incorporate a font-selection dialog box into your application. A **CFontDialog** object is a dialog box with a list of fonts that are currently installed in the system. The user can select a particular font from the list, and this selection is then reported back to the application.

To construct a **CFontDialog** object, use the provided constructor or derive a new subclass and use your own custom constructor.

Once a **CFontDialog** object has been constructed, you can use the **m_cf** structure to initialize the values or states of controls in the dialog box. The **m_cf** structure is of type **CHOOSEFONT**. For more information on this structure, see the Windows Software Development Kit (SDK) documentation.

After initializing the dialog object's controls, call the **DoModal** member function to display the dialog box and allow the user to select a font. **DoModal** returns whether the user selected the OK (**IDOK**) or Cancel (**IDCANCEL**) button.

If **DoModal** returns **IDOK**, you can use one of **CFontDialog**'s member functions to retrieve the information input by the user.

You can use the Windows **CommDlgExtendedError** function to determine whether an error occurred during initialization of the dialog box to and learn more about the error. For more information on this function, see the Windows SDK documentation.

CFontDialog relies on the COMMDLG.DLL file that ships with Windows versions 3.1 and later. For details about redistributing COMMDLG.DLL to Windows version 3.0 users, see the *Getting Started* manual for the Windows SDK.

To customize the dialog box, derive a class from **CFontDialog**, provide a custom dialog template, and add a message-map to process the notification messages from the extended controls. Any unprocessed messages should be passed to the base class.

Customizing the hook function is not required.

#include <afxdlgs.h>

Data Members

m_cf   A structure used to customize a **CFontDialog** object.

Construction

CFontDialog   Constructs a **CFontDialog** object.

Operations

DoModal	Displays the dialog and allows the user to make a selection.
GetCurrentFont	Retrieves the name of the currently selected font.
GetFaceName	Returns the face name of the selected font.
GetStyleName	Returns the style name of the selected font.
GetSize	Returns the point size of the selected font.
GetColor	Returns the color of the selected font.
GetWeight	Returns the weight of the selected font.
IsStrikeOut	Determines whether the font is displayed with strikeout.
IsUnderline	Determines whether the font is underlined.
IsBold	Determines whether the font is bold.
IsItalic	Determines whether the font is italic.

Member Functions

CFontDialog::CFontDialog

CFontDialog(LPLOGFONT *lplfInitial* **= NULL,**
    DWORD *dwFlags* **= CF_EFFECTS | CF_SCREENFONTS,**
    CDC* *pdcPrinter* **= NULL,**
    CWnd* *pParentWnd* **= NULL);**

Parameters   *lplfInitial*   A pointer to a **LOGFONT** data structure that allows you to set some of the font's characteristics. The **LOGFONT** type is defined in WINDOWS.H as follows:

```
typedef struct tagLOGFONT
  {
    int      lfHeight;
    int      lfWidth;
    int      lfEscapement;
    int      lfOrientation;
    int      lfWeight;
    BYTE     lfItalic;
    BYTE     lfUnderline;
    BYTE     lfStrikeOut;
    BYTE     lfCharSet;
    BYTE     lfOutPrecision;
    BYTE     lfClipPrecision;
    BYTE     lfQuality;
    BYTE     lfPitchAndFamily;
    BYTE     lfFaceName[LF_FACESIZE];
  } LOGFONT;
```

For more information on the **LOGFONT** structure, see the Windows SDK documentation.

dwFlags   Specifies one or more choose-font flags. One or more preset values can be combined using the bitwise OR operator. If you modify the **m_ofn.Flags** structure member, be sure to use a bitwise OR operator in your changes to keep the default behavior intact. For details on each of these flags, see the description of the **CHOOSEFONT** structure in the Windows SDK documentation.

pdcPrinter   A pointer to a printer-device context. If supplied, this parameter points to a printer-device context for the printer on which the fonts are to be selected.

pParentWnd   A pointer to the font dialog box's parent or owner window.

Remarks   Constructs a **CFontDialog** object.

See Also   **CFontDialog::DoModal**

CFontDialog::DoModal

virtual int DoModal( );

Return Value   **IDOK** or **IDCANCEL** if the function is successful; otherwise 0. **IDOK** and **IDCANCEL** are constants that indicate whether the user selected the OK or Cancel button.

If **IDCANCEL** is returned, you can call the Windows **CommDlgExtendedError** function to determine whether an error occurred.

Remarks   Call this function to display the Windows common font dialog box and allow the user to choose a font.

If you want to initialize the various font dialog controls by setting members of the **m_cf** structure, you should do this before calling **DoModal**, but after the dialog object is constructed.

If **DoModal** returns **IDOK**, you can call other member functions to retrieve the settings or information input by the user into the dialog box.

See Also **CDialog::DoModal**, **CFontDialog::CFontDialog**

CFontDialog::GetColor

COLORREF GetColor( ) const;

Return Value The color of the selected font.

See Also **CFontDialog::GetCurrentFont**

CFontDialog::GetCurrentFont

void GetCurrentFont(LPLOGFONT *lplf* **);**

Parameters *lplf* A pointer to a **LOGFONT** structure.

Remarks Assigns the characteristics of the currently selected font to the members of a **LOGFONT** structure. For more information on the **LOGFONT** structure, see the Windows SDK documentation. Other **CFontDialog** member functions are provided to access individual characteristics of the current font.

See Also **CFontDialog::GetFaceName**, **CFontDialog::GetStyleName**

CFontDialog::GetFaceName

CString GetFaceName( ) const;

Return Value The face name of the font selected in the **CFontDialog** dialog box.

See Also **CFontDialog::GetCurrentFont**, **CFontDialog::GetStyleName**

CFontDialog::GetSize

int GetSize( ) const;

Return Value The font's point size.

See Also **CFontDialog::GetWeight**, **CFontDialog::GetCurrentFont**

CFontDialog::GetStyleName

CString GetStyleName( ) const;

Return Value   The style name of the font.

See Also   **CFontDialog::GetFaceName, CFontDialog::GetCurrentFont**

CFontDialog::GetWeight

int GetWeight( ) const;

Return Value   The weight of the selected font.

See Also   **CFontDialog::GetCurrentFont, CFontDialog::IsBold**

CFontDialog::IsBold

BOOL IsBold( ) const;

Return Value   Nonzero if the selected font has the Bold characteristic enabled; otherwise 0.

See Also   **CFontDialog::GetCurrentFont**

CFontDialog::IsItalic

BOOL IsItalic( ) const;

Return Value   Nonzero if the selected font has the Italic characteristic enabled; otherwise 0.

See Also   **CFontDialog::GetCurrentFont**

CFontDialog::IsStrikeOut

BOOL IsStrikeOut( ) const;

Return Value   Nonzero if the selected font has the Strikeout characteristic enabled; otherwise 0.

See Also   **CFontDialog::GetCurrentFont**

CFontDialog::IsUnderline

BOOL IsUnderline( ) const;

Return Value   Nonzero if the selected font has the Underline characteristic enabled; otherwise 0.

See Also   **CFontDialog::GetCurrentFont**

Data Members

CFontDialog::m_cf

Remarks   A structure whose members store the characteristics of the dialog object. After constructing a **CFontDialog** object, you can use **m_cf** to initialize various values in the dialog box. You must initialize the dialog box's values before calling the **Create** member function. For more information on this structure, see **CHOOSEFONT** in the Windows SDK documentation.

class CFormView : public CScrollView

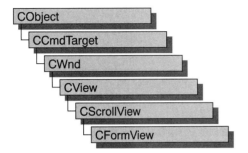

The **CFormView** class is the base class used for views containing controls. These controls are laid out based on a dialog-template resource. Use **CFormView** if you want form-based documents in your application. These views support scrolling, as needed, using the **CScrollView** functionality.

Creating a view based on **CFormView** is similar to creating a dialog box. For information on using AppWizard and ClassWizard with **CFormView**, see Technical Note 36 under MFC in Books Online.

To use **CFormView**, take the following steps:

1. Design a dialog template.

   Use the Visual C++ dialog editor to design the dialog box. Then, in the Styles property page, set the following properties:

   - In the Style box, select Child (**WS_CHILD** on).
   - In the Border box, select None (**WS_BORDER** off).
   - Clear the Visible check box (**WS_VISIBLE** off).
   - Clear the Titlebar check box (**WS_CAPTION** off).

   These steps are necessary because a form view is not a true dialog box. For more information about creating a dialog-box resource, see Chapter 5 in the *Visual C++ User's Guide*.

2. Create a view class.

   With your dialog template open, run ClassWizard and choose **CFormView** as the class type when you are filling in the Add Class dialog box. ClassWizard creates a **CFormView**-derived class and connects it to the dialog template you just designed. This connection is established in the constructor for your class; ClassWizard generates a call to the base-class constructor, **CFormView::CFormView**, and passes the resource ID of your dialog template. For example:

```
CMyFormView::CMyFormView()
    : CFormView( CMyFormView::IDD )
{
    //{{AFX_DATA_INIT( CMyFormView )
        // NOTE: the ClassWizard will add member initialization here
    //}}AFX_DATA_INIT

    // Other construction code, such as data initialization
}
```

Note If you choose not to use ClassWizard, you must define the appropriate ID you supply to the CFormView constructor (that is, `CMyFormView::IDD` is not predefined). ClassWizard declares `IDD` as an enum value in the class it creates for you.

If you want to define member variables in your view class that correspond to the controls in your form view, use the Edit Variables button in the ClassWizard dialog box. This allows you to use the dialog data exchange (DDX) mechanism. If you want to define message handlers for control-notification messages, use the Add Function button in the ClassWizard dialog box. For more information on using ClassWizard, see Chapter 12 in the *Visual C++ User's Guide*.

3. Override the **OnUpdate** member function.

   The **OnUpdate** member function is defined by **CView** and is called to update the form view's appearance. Override this function to update the member variables in your view class with the appropriate values from the current document. Then, if you are using DDX, use the **UpdateData** member function (defined by **CWnd**) with an argument of **FALSE** to update the controls in your form view.

   The **OnInitialUpdate** member function (also defined by **CView**) is called to perform one-time initialization of the view. **CFormView** overrides this function to use DDX to set the initial values of the controls you have mapped using ClassWizard. Override **OnInitialUpdate** if you want to perform custom initialization.

4. Implement a member function to move data from your view to your document.

   This member function is typically a message handler for a control-notification message or for a menu command. If you are using DDX, call the **UpdateData** member function to update the member variables in your view class. Then move their values to the document associated with the form view.

5. Override the **OnPrint** member function (optional).

   The **OnPrint** member function is defined by **CView** and prints the view. By default, printing and print preview are not supported by the **CFormView** class. To add printing support, override the **OnPrint** function in your derived class.

See the VIEWEX sample for more information about how to add printing capabilities to a view derived from **CFormView**.

6. Associate your view class with a document class and a frame-window class using a document template.

Unlike ordinary views, form views do not require you to override the **OnDraw** member function defined by **CView**. This is because controls are able to paint themselves. Only if you want to customize the display of your form view (for example, to provide a background for your view) should you override **OnDraw**. If you do so, be careful that your updating does not conflict with the updating done by the controls.

If the view becomes smaller than the dialog template, scroll bars appear automatically. Views derived from **CFormView** support only the **MM_TEXT** mapping mode.

If you are not using DDX, use the **CWnd** dialog functions to move data between the member variables in your view class and the controls in your form view.

For more information about DDX, see Chapter 12 of the *Visual C++ User's Guide*.

#include <afxext.h>

See Also   CDialog, CScrollView, CView::OnUpdate, CView::OnInitialUpdate, CView::OnPrint, CWnd::UpdateData, CScrollView::ResizeParentToFit

Construction
CFormView   Constructs a **CFormView** object.

Member Functions

CFormView::CFormView

Protected →
CFormView(LPCTSTR *lpszTemplateName* **);**

CFormView(UINT *nIDTemplate* **);**
END Protected

Parameters   *lpszTemplateName*   Contains a null-terminated string that is the name of a dialog-template resource.

nIDTemplate   Contains the ID number of a dialog-template resource.

Remarks

When you create an object of a type derived from **CFormView**, invoke one of the constructors to create the view object and identify the dialog resource on which the view is based. You can identify the resource either by name (pass a string as the argument to the constructor) or by its ID (pass an unsigned integer as the argument).

The form-view window and child controls are not created until **CWnd::Create** is called. **CWnd::Create** is called by the framework as part of the document and view creation process, which is driven by the document template.

Note Your derived class *must* supply its own constructor. In the constructor, invoke the constructor, **CFormView::CFormView**, with the resource name or ID as an argument as shown in the preceding class overview.

See Also   **CWnd::Create**

class CFrameWnd : public CWnd

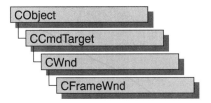

The **CFrameWnd** class provides the functionality of a Windows single document interface (SDI) overlapped or pop-up frame window, along with members for managing the window. To create a useful frame window for your application, derive a class from **CFrameWnd**. Add member variables to the derived class to store data specific to your application. Implement message-handler member functions and a message map in the derived class to specify what happens when messages are directed to the window. There are three ways to construct a frame window:

- Directly construct it using **Create**.
- Directly construct it using **LoadFrame**.
- Indirectly construct it using a document template.

Before you call either **Create** or **LoadFrame**, you must construct the frame-window object on the heap using the C++ **new** operator. Before calling **Create**, you may also register a window class with the **AfxRegisterWndClass** global function to set the icon and class styles for the frame.

Use the **Create** member function to pass the frame's creation parameters as immediate arguments.

LoadFrame requires fewer arguments than **Create**, and instead retrieves most of its default values from resources, including the frame's caption, icon, accelerator table, and menu. To be accessible by **LoadFrame**, all these resources must have the same resource ID (for example, **IDR_MAINFRAME**).

When a **CFrameWnd** object contains views and documents, they are created indirectly by the framework instead of directly by the programmer. The **CDocTemplate** object orchestrates the creation of the frame, the creation of the containing views, and the connection of the views to the appropriate document. The parameters of the **CDocTemplate** constructor specify the **CRuntimeClass** of the three classes involved (document, frame, and view). A **CRuntimeClass** object is used by the framework to dynamically create new frames when specified by the user (for example, by using the File New command or the multiple document interface [MDI] Window New command).

A frame-window class derived from **CFrameWnd** must be declared with **DECLARE_DYNCREATE** in order for the above **RUNTIME_CLASS** mechanism to work correctly.

A **CFrameWnd** contains default implementations to perform the following functions of a main window in a typical application for Windows:

- A **CFrameWnd** frame window keeps track of a currently active view that is independent of the Windows active window or the current input focus. When the frame is reactivated, the active view is notified by calling **CView::OnActivateView**.

- Command messages and many common frame-notification messages, including those handled by the **OnSetFocus**, **OnHScroll**, and **OnVScroll** functions of **CWnd**, are delegated by a **CFrameWnd** frame window to the currently active view.

- The currently active view (or currently active MDI child frame window in the case of an MDI frame) can determine the caption of the frame window. This feature can be disabled by turning off the **FWS_ADDTOTITLE** style bit of the frame window.

- A **CFrameWnd** frame window manages the positioning of the control bars, views, and other child windows inside the frame window's client area. A frame window also does idle-time updating of toolbar and other control-bar buttons. A **CFrameWnd** frame window also has default implementations of commands for toggling on and off the toolbar and status bar.

- A **CFrameWnd** frame window manages the main menu bar. When a pop-up menu is displayed, the frame window uses the **UPDATE_COMMAND_UI** mechanism to determine which menu items should be enabled, disabled, or checked. When the user selects a menu item, the frame window updates the status bar with the message string for that command.

- A **CFrameWnd** frame window has an optional accelerator table that automatically translates keyboard accelerators.

- A **CFrameWnd** frame window has an optional help ID set with **LoadFrame** that is used for context-sensitive help. A frame window is the main orchestrator of semimodal states such as context-sensitive help (SHIFT+F1) and print-preview modes.

- A **CFrameWnd** frame window will open a file dragged from the File Manager and dropped on the frame window. If a file extension is registered and associated with the application, the frame window responds to the dynamic data exchange (DDE) open request that occurs when the user opens a data file in the File Manager or when the **ShellExecute** Windows function is called.

- If the frame window is the main application window (that is, **CWinThread::m_pMainWnd**), when the user closes the application, the frame window prompts the user to save any modified documents (for **OnClose** and **OnQueryEndSession**).

- If the frame window is the main application window, the frame window is the context for running WinHelp. Closing the frame window will shut down WINHELP.EXE if it was launched for help for this application.

Do not use the C++ **delete** operator to destroy a frame window. Use **CWnd::DestroyWindow** instead. The **CFrameWnd** implementation of **PostNcDestroy** will delete the C++ object when the window is destroyed. When the user closes the frame window, the default **OnClose** handler will call **DestroyWindow**.

#include <afxwin.h>

See Also   **CWnd, CMDIFrameWnd, CMDIChildWnd**

Data Members

m_bAutoMenuEnable	Controls automatic enable and disable functionality for menu items.
rectDefault	Pass this static **CRect** as a parameter when creating a **CFrameWnd** object to allow Windows to choose the window's initial size and position.

Construction

CFrameWnd	Constructs a **CFrameWnd** object.

Initialization

Create	Call to create and initialize the Windows frame window associated with the **CFrameWnd** object.
LoadFrame	Call to dynamically create a frame window from resource information.
LoadAccelTable	Call to load an accelerator table.
LoadBarState	Call to restore control bar settings.
SaveBarState	Call to save control bar settings.

Operations

ActivateFrame	Makes the frame visible and available to the user.
GetActiveFrame	Returns the active **CFrameWnd** object.
SetActiveView	Sets the active **CView** object.
GetActiveView	Returns the active **CView** object.
GetActiveDocument	Returns the active **CDocument** object.
GetMessageString	Retrieves message corresponding to a command ID.

SetMessageText	Sets the text of a standard status bar.
EnableDocking	Allows a control bar to be docked.
DockControlBar	Docks a control bar.
FloatControlBar	Floats a control bar.
RecalcLayout	Repositions the control bars of the **CFrameWnd** object.

Overridables

| OnCreateClient | Creates a client window for the frame. |
| OnSetPreviewMode | Sets the application's main frame window into and out of print-preview mode. |

Command Handlers

| OnContextHelp | Handles SHIFT+F1 Help for in-place items. |

Member Functions

CFrameWnd::ActivateFrame

virtual void ActivateFrame(int *nCmdShow* **= –1);**

Parameters

nCmdShow   Specifies the parameter to pass to **CWnd::ShowWindow**. By default, the frame is shown and correctly restored.

Remarks

Call this member function to activate and restore the frame window so that it is visible and available to the user. This member function is usually called after a non-user interface event such as a DDE, Object Linking and Embedding (OLE), or other event that may show the frame window or its contents to the user.

The default implementation activates the frame and brings it to the top of the Z-order and, if necessary, carries out the same steps for the application's main frame window.

Override this member function to change how a frame is activated. For example, you can force MDI child windows to be maximized. Add the appropriate functionality, then call the base class version with an explicit *nCmdShow*.

CFrameWnd::CFrameWnd

CFrameWnd( );

Remarks

Constructs a **CFrameWnd** object, but does not create the visible frame window. Call **Create** to create the visible window.

See Also

CFrameWnd::Create, **CFrameWnd::LoadFrame**

CFrameWnd::Create

BOOL Create(LPCTSTR *lpszClassName*, LPCTSTR *lpszWindowName*,
DWORD *dwStyle* = WS_OVERLAPPEDWINDOW,
const RECT& *rect* = rectDefault, CWnd* *pParentWnd* = NULL,
LPCTSTR *lpszMenuName* = NULL, DWORD *dwExStyle* = 0,
CCreateContext* *pContext* = NULL);

Return Value   Nonzero if initialization is successful; otherwise 0.

Parameters   *lpszClassName*   Points to a null-terminated character string that names the
Windows class. The class name can be any name registered with the
AfxRegisterWndClass global function or the **RegisterClass** Windows
function. If **NULL**, uses the predefined default **CFrameWnd** attributes.

lpszWindowName   Points to a null-terminated character string that represents the
window name. Used as text for the title bar.

dwStyle   Specifies the window style attributes. Include the **FWS_ADDTOTITLE**
style if you want the title bar to automatically display the name of the document
represented in the window.

rect   Specifies the size and position of the window. The **rectDefault** value allows
Windows to specify the size and position of the new window.

pParentWnd   Specifies the parent window of this frame window. This parameter
should be **NULL** for top-level frame windows.

lpszMenuName   Identifies the name of the menu resource to be used with the
window. Use **MAKEINTRESOURCE** if the menu has an integer ID instead of
a string. This parameter can be **NULL**.

dwExStyle   Specifies the window extended style attributes. For a list of extended
window styles, see the section "Extended Window Styles" on page 1254.

pContext   Specifies a pointer to a **CCreateContext** structure. This parameter can
be **NULL**.

Remarks   Construct a **CFrameWnd** object in two steps. First invoke the constructor, which
constructs the **CFrameWnd** object, then call **Create**, which creates the Windows
frame window and attaches it to the **CFrameWnd** object. **Create** initializes the
window's class name and window name and registers default values for its style,
parent, and associated menu.

Use **LoadFrame** rather than **Create** to load the frame window from a resource
instead of specifying its arguments.

See Also   **CFrameWnd::CFrameWnd, CFrameWnd::LoadFrame, CCreateContext, CWnd::Create, CWnd::PreCreateWindow**

CFrameWnd::DockControlBar

void DockControlBar(CControlBar * *pBar***, UINT** *nDockBarID* **= 0, LPCRECT** *lpRect* **= NULL);**

Parameters   *pBar*   Points to the control bar to be docked.

nDockBarID   Determines which sides of the frame window to consider for docking. It can be 0, or one or more of the following:

- **AFX_IDW_DOCKBAR_TOP**   Dock to the top side of the frame window.
- **AFX_IDW_DOCKBAR_BOTTOM**   Dock to the bottom side of the frame window.
- **AFX_IDW_DOCKBAR_LEFT**   Dock to the left side of the frame window.
- **AFX_IDW_DOCKBAR_RIGHT**   Dock to the right side of the frame window.

If 0, the control bar can be docked to any side enabled for docking in the destination frame window.

lpRect   Determines, in screen coordinates, where control bar will be docked in the non-client area of the destination frame window.

Remarks   Causes a control bar to be docked to the frame window. The control bar will be docked to one of the sides of the frame window specified in the calls to both **CControlBar::EnableDocking** and **CFrameWnd::EnableDocking**. The side chosen is determined by *nDockBarID*.

See Also   **CFrameWnd::FloatControlBar**

CFrameWnd::EnableDocking

void EnableDocking(DWORD *dwDockStyle* **);**

Parameters   *dwDockStyle*   Specifies which sides of the frame window can serve as docking sites for control bars. It can be one or more of the following:

- **CBRS_ALIGN_TOP**   Allows docking at the top of the client area.
- **CBRS_ALIGN_BOTTOM**   Allows docking at the bottom of the client area.
- **CBRS_ALIGN_LEFT**   Allows docking on the left side of the client area.

- **CBRS_ALIGN_RIGHT**   Allows docking on the right side of the client area.
- **CBRS_ALIGN_ANY**   Allows docking on any side of the client area.
- **CBRS_FLOAT_MULTI**   Allows multiple floating control bars in one mini-frame window.

Remarks   Call this function to enable dockable control bars in a frame window. By default, control bars will be docked to a side of the frame window in the following order: top, bottom, left, right.

See Also   **CControlBar::EnableDocking**, **CFrameWnd::DockControlBar**, **CFrameWnd::FloatControlBar**

CFrameWnd::FloatControlBar

CFrameWnd* FloatControlBar(CControlBar * *pBar***, CPoint** *point***, DWORD** *dwStyle* **= CBRS_ALIGN_TOP);**

Return Value   Pointer to the current frame window.

Parameters   *pBar*   Points to the control bar to be floated.

point   The location, in screen coordinates, where the top left corner of the control bar will be placed.

dwStyle   Specifies whether to align the control bar horizontally or vertically within its new frame window. It can be any one of the following:

- **CBRS_ALIGN_TOP**   Orients the control bar vertically.
- **CBRS_ALIGN_BOTTOM**   Orients the control bar vertically.
- **CBRS_ALIGN_LEFT**   Orients the control bar horizontally.
- **CBRS_ALIGN_RIGHT**   Orients the control bar horizontally.

If styles are passed specifying both horizontal and vertical orientation, the toolbar will be oriented horizontally.

Remarks   Call this function to cause a control bar to not be docked to the frame window. Typically, this is done at application startup when the program is restoring settings from the previous execution.

This function is called by the framework when the user causes a drop operation by releasing the left mouse button while dragging the control bar over a location that is not available for docking.

See Also   **CFrameWnd::DockControlBar**

CFrameWnd::GetActiveDocument

virtual CDocument* GetActiveDocument( );

Return Value

A pointer to the current **CDocument**. If there is no current document, returns **NULL**.

Remarks

Call this member function to obtain a pointer to the current **CDocument** attached to the current active view.

See Also

CFrameWnd::GetActiveView

CFrameWnd::GetActiveFrame

virtual CFrameWnd* GetActiveFrame( );

Return Value

A pointer to the active MDI child window. If the application is an SDI application, or the MDI frame window has no active document, the implicit **this** pointer will be returned.

Remarks

Call this member function to obtain a pointer to the active multiple document interface (MDI) child window of an MDI frame window.

If there is no active MDI child or the application is a single document interface (SDI), the implicit **this** pointer is returned.

See Also

CFrameWnd::GetActiveView, CFrameWnd::GetActiveDocument, CMDIFrameWnd

CFrameWnd::GetActiveView

CView* GetActiveView( ) const;

Return Value

A pointer to the current **CView**. If there is no current view, returns **NULL**.

Remarks

Call this member function to obtain a pointer to the active view.

See Also

CFrameWnd::SetActiveView, CFrameWnd::GetActiveDocument

CFrameWnd::GetMessageString

virtual void GetMessageString(UINT *nID*, **CString&** *rMessage* **) const;**

Parameters

nID   Resource ID of the desired message.

rMessage   **CString** object into which to place message.

Remarks   Override this function to provide custom strings for command IDs. The default implementation simply loads the string specified by *nID* from the resource file. This function is called by the framework when the message string in the status bar needs updating.

See Also   **CFrameWnd::SetMessageText**

CFrameWnd::LoadAccelTable

BOOL LoadAccelTable(LPCTSTR *lpszResourceName* **);**

Return Value   Nonzero if the accelerator table was successfully loaded; otherwise 0.

Parameters   *lpszResourceName*   Identifies the name of the accelerator resource. Use **MAKEINTRESOURCE** if the resource is identified with an integer ID.

Remarks   Call to load the specified accelerator table. Only one table may be loaded at a time. Accelerator tables loaded from resources are freed automatically when the application terminates.

        If you call **LoadFrame** to create the frame window, the framework loads an accelerator table along with the menu and icon resources, and a subsequent call to this member function is then unnecessary.

See Also   **CFrameWnd::LoadFrame, ::LoadAccelerators**

CFrameWnd::LoadBarState

void LoadBarState(LPCTSTR *lpszProfileName* **);**

Parameters   *lpszProfileName*   Name of the initialization file where state information is stored.

Remarks   Call this function to restore the settings of each control bar owned by the frame window. This information is written to the initialization file using **SaveBarState**. Information restored includes visibility, horizontal/vertical orientation, docking state, and control bar position.

See Also   **CFrameWnd::SaveBarState**

CFrameWnd::LoadFrame

virtual BOOL LoadFrame(UINT *nIDResource*, **DWORD** *dwDefaultStyle* = **WS_OVERLAPPEDWINDOW | FWS_ADDTOTITLE,** **CWnd*** *pParentWnd* = **NULL, CCreateContext*** *pContext* = **NULL);**

Parameters   *nIDResource*   The ID of shared resources associated with the frame window.

dwDefaultStyle   The frame's style. Include the **FWS_ADDTOTITLE** style if you want the title bar to automatically display the name of the document represented in the window. For a list of window styles, see the section "Window Styles" on page 1253.

pParentWnd   A pointer to the frame's parent.

pContext   A pointer to a **CCreateContext** structure. This parameter can be **NULL**.

Remarks   Construct a **CFrameWnd** object in two steps. First invoke the constructor, which constructs the **CFrameWnd** object, then call **LoadFrame**, which loads the Windows frame window and associated resources and attaches the frame window to the **CFrameWnd** object. The *nIDResource* parameter specifies the menu, the accelerator table, the icon, and the string resource of the title for the frame window.

Use the **Create** member function rather than **LoadFrame** when you want to specify all of the frame window's creation parameters.

The framework calls **LoadFrame** when it creates a frame window using a document template object.

The framework uses the *pContext* argument to specify the objects to be connected to the frame window, including any contained view objects. You can set the *pContext* argument to **NULL** when you call **LoadFrame**.

See Also   **CDocTemplate**, **CFrameWnd::Create**, **CFrameWnd::CFrameWnd**, **CWnd::PreCreateWindow**

CFrameWnd::OnContextHelp

afx_msg void OnContextHelp( );

Remarks   To enable context-sensitive help, you must add an

```
ON_COMMAND( ID_CONTEXT_HELP, OnContextHelp )
```

statement to your **CFrameWnd** class message map and also add an accelerator-table entry, typically SHIFT+F1, to enable this member function.

If your application is an OLE Container, **OnContextHelp** puts all in-place items contained within the frame window object into Help mode. The cursor changes to an arrow and a question mark, and the user can then move the mouse pointer and press the left mouse button to select a dialog box, window, menu, or command button. This member function calls the Windows function **WinHelp** with the Help context of the object under the cursor.

See Also   **CWinApp::OnHelp**, **CWinApp::WinHelp**

CFrameWnd::OnCreateClient

Protected→

virtual BOOL OnCreateClient(LPCREATESTRUCT *lpcs***,
CCreateContext*** *pContext* **);**

END Protected

Parameters   *lpcs*   A pointer to a Windows **CREATESTRUCT** structure.

pContext   A pointer to a **CCreateContext** structure.

Remarks   Called by the framework during the execution of **OnCreate**. Never call this
function.

The default implementation of this function creates a **CView** object from the
information provided in *pContext*, if possible.

Override this function to override values passed in the **CCreateContext** object or
to change the way controls in the main client area of the frame window are created.
The **CCreateContext** members you can override are described in the
CCreateContext class.

Note Do not replace values passed in the **CREATESTRUCT** structure. They are
for informational use only. If you want to override the initial window rectangle, for
example, override the **CWnd** member function **PreCreateWindow**.

CFrameWnd::OnSetPreviewMode

virtual void OnSetPreviewMode(BOOL *bPreview***, CPrintPreviewState***
pModeStuff **);**

Parameters   *bPreview*   Specifies whether or not to place the application in print-preview mode.
Set to **TRUE** to place in print preview, **FALSE** to restore to cancel preview
mode.

pModeStuff   A pointer to a **CPrintPreviewState** structure.

Remarks   Call this member function to set the application's main frame window into and out
of print-preview mode.

The default implementation disables all standard toolbars and hides the main menu
and the main client window. This turns MDI frame windows into temporary SDI
frame windows.

Override this member function to customize the hiding and showing of control bars
and other frame window parts during print preview. Call the base class
implementation from within the overridden version.

CFrameWnd::RecalcLayout

virtual void RecalcLayout(BOOL *bNotify* = **TRUE**);

Parameters

bNotify   Determines whether the active in-place item for the frame window receives notification of the layout change. If **TRUE**, the item is notified; otherwise **FALSE**.

Remarks

Called by the framework when the standard control bars are toggled on or off or when the frame window is resized. The default implementation of this member function calls the **CWnd** member function **RepositionBars** to reposition all the control bars in the frame as well as in the main client window (usually a **CView** or **MDICLIENT**).

Override this member function to control the appearance and behavior of control bars after the layout of the frame window has changed. For example, call it when you turn control bars on or off or add another control bar.

See Also

CWnd::RepositionBars

CFrameWnd::SaveBarState

void SaveBarState(LPCTSTR *lpszProfileName*) **const;**

Parameters

lpszProfileName   Name of the initialization file where state information is to be stored.

Remarks

Call this function to store information about each control bar owned by the frame window. This information can be read from the initialization file using **LoadBarState**. Information stored includes visibility, horizontal/vertical orientation, docking state, and control bar position.

See Also

CFrameWnd::LoadBarState

CFrameWnd::SetActiveView

void SetActiveView(CView* *pViewNew*, **BOOL** *bNotify* = **TRUE**);

Parameters

pViewNew   Specifies a pointer to a **CView** object, or **NULL** for no active view.

bNotify   Specifies whether the view is to be notified of activation. If **TRUE**, **OnActivateView** is called for the new view; if **FALSE**, it is not.

Remarks

Call this member function to set the active view. The framework will call this function automatically as the user changes the focus to a view within the frame window. You may explicitly call **SetActiveView** to change the focus to the specified view.

See Also   CFrameWnd::GetActiveView, CView::OnActivateView,
             CFrameWnd::GetActiveDocument

CFrameWnd::SetMessageText

void SetMessageText(LPCTSTR *lpszText*);

void SetMessageText(UINT *nID*);

Parameters   *lpszText*   Points to the string to be placed on the status bar.

             nID   String resource ID of the string to be placed on the status bar.

Remarks   Call this function to place a string in the status bar pane that has an ID of 0. This is
             typically the leftmost, and longest, pane of the status bar.

See Also   CStatusBar

Data Members

CFrameWnd::m_bAutoMenuEnable

Remarks   When this data member is enabled (which is the default), menu items that do not
             have ON_UPDATE_COMMAND_UI or ON_COMMAND handlers will be
             automatically disabled when the user pulls down a menu. Menu items that have an
             ON_COMMAND handler but no ON_UPDATE_COMMAND_UI handler will
             be automatically enabled. When this data member is set, menu items are
             automatically enabled in the same way that toolbar buttons are enabled.

             This data member simplifies the implementation of optional commands based on the
             current selection and reduces the need for an application to write
             ON_UPDATE_COMMAND_UI handlers for enabling and disabling menu items.

See Also   CCmdUI, CCmdTarget

CFrameWnd::rectDefault

Remarks   Pass this static CRect as a parameter when creating a window to allow Windows to
             choose the window's initial size and position.

class CGdiObject : public CObject

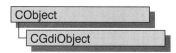

The **CGdiObject** class provides a base class for various kinds of Windows graphics device interface (GDI) objects such as bitmaps, regions, brushes, pens, palettes, and fonts. You never create a **CGdiObject** directly. Rather, you create an object from one of its derived classes, such as **CPen** or **CBrush**.

#include <afxwin.h>

See Also   **CBitmap**, **CBrush**, **CFont**, **CPalette**, **CPen**, **CRgn**

Data Members
m_hObject   A **HANDLE** containing the **HBITMAP**, **HPALETTE**, **HRGN**, **HBRUSH**, **HPEN**, or **HFONT** attached to this object.

Construction
CGdiObject   Constructs a **CGdiObject** object.

Operations
GetSafeHandle   Returns **m_hObject** unless **this** is NULL, in which case **NULL** is returned.

FromHandle   Returns a pointer to a **CGdiObject** object given a handle to a Windows GDI object.

Attach   Attaches a Windows GDI object to a **CGdiObject** object.

Detach   Detaches a Windows GDI object from a **CGdiObject** object and returns a handle to the Windows GDI object.

DeleteObject   Deletes the Windows GDI object attached to the **CGdiObject** object from memory by freeing all system storage associated with the object.

DeleteTempMap   Deletes any temporary **CGdiObject** objects created by **FromHandle**.

GetObject	Fills a buffer with data that describes the Windows GDI object attached to the **CGdiObject** object.
CreateStockObject	Retrieves a handle to one of the Windows predefined stock pens, brushes, or fonts.
UnrealizeObject	Resets the origin of a brush or resets a logical palette.
GetObjectType	Retrieves the type of the GDI object.

Member Functions

CGdiObject::Attach

BOOL Attach(HGDIOBJ *hObject* **);**

Return Value   Nonzero if attachment is successful; otherwise 0.

Parameters   *hObject*   A **HANDLE** to a Windows GDI object (for example, **HPEN** or **HBRUSH**).

Remarks   Attaches a Windows GDI object to a **CGdiObject** object.

See Also   **CGdiObject::Detach**

CGdiObject::CGdiObject

CGdiObject( );

Remarks   Constructs a **CGdiObject** object. You never create a **CGdiObject** directly. Rather, you create an object from one of its derived classes, such as **CPen** or **CBrush**.

See Also   **CPen, CBrush, CFont, CBitmap, CRgn, CPalette**

CGdiObject::CreateStockObject

BOOL CreateStockObject(int *nIndex* **);**

Return Value   Nonzero if the function is successful; otherwise 0.

Parameters   *nIndex*   A constant specifying the type of stock object desired. It can be one of the following values:

- **BLACK_BRUSH**   Black brush.
- **DKGRAY_BRUSH**   Dark gray brush.
- **GRAY_BRUSH**   Gray brush.
- **HOLLOW_BRUSH**   Hollow brush.

- **LTGRAY_BRUSH**   Light gray brush.
- **NULL_BRUSH**   Null brush.
- **WHITE_BRUSH**   White brush.
- **BLACK_PEN**   Black pen.
- **NULL_PEN**   Null pen.
- **WHITE_PEN**   White pen.
- **ANSI_FIXED_FONT**   ANSI fixed system font.
- **ANSI_VAR_FONT**   ANSI variable system font.
- **DEVICE_DEFAULT_FONT**   Device-dependent font.
- **OEM_FIXED_FONT**   OEM-dependent fixed font.
- **SYSTEM_FONT**   The system font. By default, Windows uses the system font to draw menus, dialog-box controls, and other text. In Windows versions 3.0 and later, the system font is proportional width; earlier versions of Windows use a fixed-width system font.
- **SYSTEM_FIXED_FONT**   The fixed-width system font used in Windows prior to version 3.0. This object is available for compatibility with earlier versions of Windows.
- **DEFAULT_PALETTE**   Default color palette. This palette consists of the 20 static colors in the system palette.

Remarks

Retrieves a handle to one of the predefined stock Windows GDI pens, brushes, or fonts, and attaches the GDI object to the **CGdiObject** object. Call this function with one of the derived classes that corresponds to the Windows GDI object type, such as **CPen** for a stock pen.

See Also

CPen::CPen, CBrush::CBrush, CFont::CFont, CPalette::CPalette

CGdiObject::DeleteObject

BOOL DeleteObject( );

Return Value

Nonzero if the GDI object was successfully deleted; otherwise 0.

Remarks

Deletes the attached Windows GDI object from memory by freeing all system storage associated with the Windows GDI object. The storage associated with the **CGdiObject** object is not affected by this call. An application should not call **DeleteObject** on a **CGdiObject** object that is currently selected into a device context. When a pattern brush is deleted, the bitmap associated with the brush is not deleted. The bitmap must be deleted independently.

See Also

CGdiObject::Detach

CGdiObject::DeleteTempMap

static void PASCAL DeleteTempMap( );

Remarks   Called automatically by the **CWinApp** idle-time handler, **DeleteTempMap** deletes any temporary **CGdiObject** objects created by **FromHandle**. **DeleteTempMap** detaches the Windows GDI object attached to a temporary **CGdiObject** object before deleting the **CGdiObject** object.

See Also   **CGdiObject::Detach**, **CGdiObject::FromHandle**

CGdiObject::Detach

HGDIOBJ Detach( );

Return Value   A **HANDLE** to the Windows GDI object detached; otherwise **NULL** if no GDI object is attached.

Remarks   Detaches a Windows GDI object from a **CGdiObject** object and returns a handle to the Windows GDI object.

See Also   **CGdiObject::Attach**

CGdiObject::FromHandle

static CGdiObject* PASCAL FromHandle(HGDIOBJ *hObject* **);**

Return Value   A pointer to a **CGdiObject** that may be temporary or permanent.

Parameters   *hObject*   A **HANDLE** to a Windows GDI object.

Remarks   Returns a pointer to a **CGdiObject** object given a handle to a Windows GDI object. If a **CGdiObject** object is not already attached to the Windows GDI object, a temporary **CGdiObject** object is created and attached. This temporary **CGdiObject** object is only valid until the next time the application has idle time in its event loop, at which time all temporary graphic objects are deleted. Another way of saying this is that the temporary object is only valid during the processing of one window message.

See Also   **CGdiObject::DeleteTempMap**

CGdiObject::GetObject

int GetObject(int *nCount,* **LPVOID** *lpObject* **) const;**

Return Value   The number of bytes retrieved; otherwise 0 if an error occurs.

Parameters   *nCount*   Specifies the number of bytes to copy into the *lpObject* buffer.

lpObject   Points to a user-supplied buffer that is to receive the information.

Remarks   Fills a buffer with data that defines a specified object. The function retrieves a data structure whose type depends on the type of graphic object, as shown by the following list:

Object	Buffer type
CPen	LOGPEN
CBrush	LOGBRUSH
CFont	LOGFONT
CBitmap	BITMAP
CPalette	int
CRgn	Not supported

If the object is a **CBitmap** object, **GetObject** returns only the width, height, and color format information of the bitmap. The actual bits can be retrieved by using **CBitmap::GetBitmapBits**. If the object is a **CPalette** object, **GetObject** retrieves an integer that specifies the number of entries in the palette. The function does not retrieve the **LOGPALETTE**structure that defines the palette. An application can get information on palette entries by calling **CPalette::GetPaletteEntries**.

See Also   **CBitmap::GetBitmapBits**, **CPalette::GetPaletteEntries**

CGdiObject::GetObjectType

UINT GetObjectType( ) const;

Return Value   The type of the object, if successful; otherwise 0. The value can be one of the following:

- **OBJ_BITMAP**   Bitmap
- **OBJ_BRUSH**   Brush
- **OBJ_FONT**   Font
- **OBJ_PAL**   Palette
- **OBJ_PEN**   Pen
- **OBJ_EXTPEN**   Extended pen
- **OBJ_REGION**   Region
- **OBJ_DC**   Device context
- **OBJ_MEMDC**   Memory device context
- **OBJ_METAFILE**   Metafile

- **OBJ_METADC**   Metafile device context
- **OBJ_ENHMETAFILE**   Enhanced metafile
- **OBJ_ENHMETADC**   Enhanced-metafile device context

Remarks   Retrieves the type of the GDI object.

See Also   **CGdiObject::GetObject**, **CDC::SelectObject**

CGdiObject::GetSafeHandle

HGDIOBJ GetSafeHandle( ) const;

Return Value   A **HANDLE** to the attached Windows GDI object; otherwise **NULL** if no object is
attached.

Remarks   Returns **m_hObject** unless **this** is **NULL**, in which case **NULL** is returned. This is
part of the general handle interface paradigm and is useful when **NULL** is a valid
or special value for a handle.

CGdiObject::UnrealizeObject

BOOL UnrealizeObject( );

Return Value   Nonzero if successful; otherwise 0.

Remarks   Resets the origin of a brush or resets a logical palette. While **UnrealizeObject** is a
member function of the **CGdiObject** class, it should be invoked only on **CBrush** or
CPalette objects. For **CBrush** objects, **UnrealizeObject** directs the system to
reset the origin of the given brush the next time it is selected into a device context.
If the object is a **CPalette** object, **UnrealizeObject** directs the system to realize the
palette as though it had not previously been realized. The next time the application
calls the **CDC::RealizePalette** function for the specified palette, the system
completely remaps the logical palette to the system palette. The **UnrealizeObject**
function should not be used with stock objects. The **UnrealizeObject** function must
be called whenever a new brush origin is set (by means of the **CDC::SetBrushOrg**
function). The **UnrealizeObject** function must not be called for the currently
selected brush or currently selected palette of any display context.

See Also   **CDC::RealizePalette**, **CDC::SetBrushOrg**

Data Members

CGdiObject::m_hObject

Remarks   A **HANDLE** containing the **HBITMAP**, **HRGN**, **HBRUSH**, **HPEN**,
HPALETTE, or **HFONT** attached to this object.

class CList : public CObject

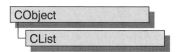

template< class *TYPE*, class *ARG_TYPE* >
  class CList : public CObject

Parameters   *TYPE*   Type of object stored in the list.

ARG_TYPE   Type used to reference objects stored in the list. May be a reference.

Remarks   The **CList** class supports ordered lists of nonunique objects accessible sequentially or by value. **CList** lists behave like doubly-linked lists.

A variable of type **POSITION** is a key for the list. You can use a **POSITION** variable as an iterator to traverse a list sequentially and as a bookmark to hold a place. A position is not the same as an index, however.

Element insertion is very fast at the list head, at the tail, and at a known **POSITION**. A sequential search is necessary to look up an element by value or index. This search can be slow if the list is long.

If you need a dump of individual elements in the list, you must set the depth of the dump context to 1 or greater.

Certain member functions of this class call global helper functions that must be customized for most uses of the **CList** class. See Collection Class Helpers.

#include <afxtempl.h>

See Also   **CMap**, **CArray**, Collection Class Helpers

Head/Tail Access

GetHead	Returns the head element of the list (cannot be empty).
GetTail	Returns the tail element of the list (cannot be empty).

Operations

RemoveHead	Removes the element from the head of the list.
RemoveTail	Removes the element from the tail of the list.
AddHead	Adds an element (or all the elements in another list) to the head of the list (makes a new head).

| AddTail | Adds an element (or all the elements in another list) to the tail of the list (makes a new tail). |
| RemoveAll | Removes all the elements from this list. |

Iteration

GetHeadPosition	Returns the position of the head element of the list.
GetTailPosition	Returns the position of the tail element of the list.
GetNext	Gets the next element for iterating.
GetPrev	Gets the previous element for iterating.

Retrieval/Modification

GetAt	Gets the element at a given position.
SetAt	Sets the element at a given position.
RemoveAt	Removes an element from this list, specified by position.

Insertion

| InsertBefore | Inserts a new element before a given position. |
| InsertAfter | Inserts a new element after a given position. |

Searching

| Find | Gets the position of an element specified by pointer value. |
| FindIndex | Gets the position of an element specified by a zero-based index. |

Status

| GetCount | Returns the number of elements in this list. |
| IsEmpty | Tests for the empty list condition (no elements). |

Member Functions

CList::AddHead

POSITION AddHead(*ARG_TYPE newElement* **);**

void AddHead(CList* *pNewList* **);**

Return Value   The first version returns the **POSITION** value of the newly inserted element.

Parameters   *ARG_TYPE*   Template parameter specifying the type of the list element (may be a reference).

newElement   The new element.

pNewList   A pointer to another **CList** list. The elements in *pNewList* will be added to this list.

Remarks   Adds a new element or list of elements to the head of this list. The list may be empty before the operation.

See Also   **CList::GetHead**, **CList::RemoveHead**

CList::AddTail

POSITION AddTail(*ARG_TYPE newElement* **);**

void AddTail(CList* *pNewList* **);**

Return Value   The first version returns the **POSITION** value of the newly inserted element.

Parameters   *ARG_TYPE*   Template parameter specifying the type of the list element (may be a reference).

newElement   The element to be added to this list.

pNewList   A pointer to another **CList** list. The elements in *pNewList* will be added to this list.

Remarks   Adds a new element or list of elements to the tail of this list. The list may be empty before the operation.

See Also   **CObList::GetTail**, **CObList::RemoveTail**

CList::Find

POSITION Find(*ARG_TYPE searchValue*, **POSITION** *startAfter* = **NULL)**
   const;

Return Value   A **POSITION** value that can be used for iteration or object pointer retrieval;
NULL if the object is not found.

Parameters   *ARG_TYPE*   Template parameter specifying the type of the list element (may be a
reference).

searchValue   The value to be found in the list.

startAfter   The start position for the search.

Remarks   Searches the list sequentially to find the first element matching the specified
searchValue. Note that the pointer values are compared, not the contents of the
objects.

See Also   **CList::GetNext**, **CList::GetPrev**

CList::FindIndex

POSITION FindIndex(**int** *nIndex* **) const;**

Return Value   A **POSITION** value that can be used for iteration or object pointer retrieval;
NULL if *nIndex* is negative or too large.

Parameters   *nIndex*   The zero-based index of the list element to be found.

Remarks   Uses the value of *nIndex* as an index into the list. It starts a sequential scan from
the head of the list, stopping on the *n*th element.

See Also   **CObList::Find**, **CObList::GetNext**, **CObList::GetPrev**

CList::GetAt

TYPE& **GetAt(** **POSITION** *position* **);**

TYPE **GetAt(** **POSITION** *position* **) const;**

Return Value   See the return value description for **GetHead**.

Parameters   *TYPE*   Template parameter specifying the type of object in the list.

position   A **POSITION** value returned by a previous **GetHeadPosition** or **Find**
member function call.

Remarks   A variable of type **POSITION** is a key for the list. It is not the same as an index, and you cannot operate on a **POSITION** value yourself. **GetAt** returns the element (or a reference to the element) associated with a given position.

You must ensure that your **POSITION** value represents a valid position in the list. If it is invalid, then the Debug version of the Microsoft Foundation Class Library asserts.

See Also   **CList::Find**, **CList::SetAt**, **CList::GetNext**, **CList::GetPrev**, **CList::GetHead**

CList::GetCount

int GetCount() const;

Return Value   An integer value containing the element count.

Remarks   Gets the number of elements in this list.

See Also   **CList::IsEmpty**

CList::GetHead

TYPE& **GetHead( );**

TYPE **GetHead( ) const;**

Return Value   If the list is **const**, **GetHead** returns a copy of the element at the head of the list. This allows the function to be used only on the right side of an assignment statement and protects the list from modification.

If the list is not **const**, **GetHead** returns a reference to an element of the list. This allows the function to be used on either side of an assignment statement and thus allows the list entries to be modified.

Parameters   *TYPE*   Template parameter specifying the type of object in the list.

Remarks   Gets the head element (or a reference to the head element) of this list.

You must ensure that the list is not empty before calling **GetHead**. If the list is empty, then the Debug version of the Microsoft Foundation Class Library asserts. Use **IsEmpty** to verify that the list contains elements.

See Also   **CList::GetTail**, **CList::GetTailPosition**, **CList::AddHead**, **CList::RemoveHead**

CList::GetHeadPosition

POSITION GetHeadPosition( ) const;

Return Value   A **POSITION** value that can be used for iteration or object pointer retrieval; **NULL** if the list is empty.

Remarks   Gets the position of the head element of this list.

See Also   **CList::GetTailPosition**

CList::GetNext

TYPE& **GetNext(POSITION&** *rPosition* **);**

TYPE **GetNext(POSITION&** *rPosition* **) const;**

Return Value   If the list is **const**, **GetNext** returns a copy of the element at the head of the list. This allows the function to be used only on the right side of an assignment statement and protects the list from modification.

If the list is not **const**, **GetNext** returns a reference to an element of the list. This allows the function to be used on either side of an assignment statement and thus allows the list entries to be modified.

Parameters   *TYPE*   Template parameter specifying the type of the elements in the list.

rPosition   A reference to a **POSITION** value returned by a previous **GetNext**, **GetHeadPosition**, or other member function call.

Remarks   Gets the list element identified by *rPosition*, then sets *rPosition* to the **POSITION** value of the next entry in the list. You can use **GetNext** in a forward iteration loop if you establish the initial position with a call to **GetHeadPosition** or **Find**.

You must ensure that your **POSITION** value represents a valid position in the list. If it is invalid, then the Debug version of the Microsoft Foundation Class Library asserts.

If the retrieved element is the last in the list, then the new value of *rPosition* is set to **NULL**.

See Also   **CList::Find, CList::GetHeadPosition, CList::GetTailPosition, CList::GetPrev, CList::GetHead**

CList::GetPrev

TYPE& **GetPrev(POSITION&** *rPosition* **);**

TYPE **GetPrev(POSITION&** *rPosition* **) const;**

Return Value   If the list is **const**, **GetPrev** returns a copy of the element at the head of the list. This allows the function to be used only on the right side of an assignment statement and protects the list from modification.

If the list is not **const**, **GetPrev** returns a reference to an element of the list. This allows the function to be used on either side of an assignment statement and thus allows the list entries to be modified.

Parameters   *TYPE*   Template parameter specifying the type of the elements in the list.

rPosition   A reference to a **POSITION** value returned by a previous **GetPrev** or other member function call.

Remarks   Gets the list element identified by *rPosition*, then sets *rPosition* to the **POSITION** value of the previous entry in the list. You can use **GetPrev** in a reverse iteration loop if you establish the initial position with a call to **GetTailPosition** or **Find**.

You must ensure that your **POSITION** value represents a valid position in the list. If it is invalid, then the Debug version of the Microsoft Foundation Class Library asserts.

If the retrieved element is the first in the list, then the new value of *rPosition* is set to **NULL**.

See Also   **CList::Find, CList::GetTailPosition, CList::GetHeadPosition, CList::GetNext, CList::GetHead**

CList::GetTail

TYPE& **GetTail( );**

TYPE **GetTail() const;**

Return Value   See the return value description for **GetHead**.

Parameters   *TYPE*   Template parameter specifying the type of elements in the list.

Remarks   Gets the **CObject** pointer that represents the tail element of this list.

You must ensure that the list is not empty before calling **GetTail**. If the list is empty, then the Debug version of the Microsoft Foundation Class Library asserts. Use **IsEmpty** to verify that the list contains elements.

See Also   **CList::AddTail, CList::AddHead, CList::RemoveHead, CList::GetHead**

CList::GetTailPosition

POSITION GetTailPosition( ) const;

Return Value   A **POSITION** value that can be used for iteration or object pointer retrieval; **NULL** if the list is empty.

Remarks   Gets the position of the tail element of this list; **NULL** if the list is empty.

See Also   **CList::GetHeadPosition**, **CList::GetTail**

CList::InsertAfter

POSITION InsertAfter(POSITION *position*, *ARG_TYPE newElement* **);**

Return Value   A **POSITION** value that can be used for iteration or list element retrieval.

Parameters   *position*   A **POSITION** value returned by a previous **GetNext**, **GetPrev**, or **Find** member function call.

     ARG_TYPE   Template parameter specifying the type of the list element.

     newElement   The element to be added to this list.

Remarks   Adds an element to this list after the element at the specified position.

See Also   **CList::Find**, **CList::InsertBefore**

CList::InsertBefore

POSITION InsertBefore(POSITION *position***,** *ARG_TYPE newElement* **);**

Return Value   A **POSITION** value that can be used for iteration or list element retrieval; **NULL** if the list is empty.

Parameters   *position*   A **POSITION** value returned by a previous **GetNext**, **GetPrev**, or **Find** member function call.

     ARG_TYPE   Template parameter specifying the type of the list element (may be a reference).

     newElement   The element to be added to this list.

Remarks   Adds an element to this list before the element at the specified position.

See Also   **CList::Find**, **CList::InsertAfter**

CList::IsEmpty

BOOL IsEmpty( ) const;

Return Value   Nonzero if this list is empty; otherwise 0.

Remarks   Indicates whether this list contains no elements.

See Also   **CList::GetCount**

CList::RemoveAll

void RemoveAll( )

Remarks   Removes all the elements from this list and frees the associated memory. No error is generated if the list is already empty.

See Also   **CList::RemoveAt**

CList::RemoveAt

void RemoveAt(POSITION *position* **);**

Parameters   *position*   The position of the element to be removed from the list.

Remarks   Removes the specified element from this list.

You must ensure that your **POSITION** value represents a valid position in the list. If it is invalid, then the Debug version of the Microsoft Foundation Class Library asserts.

See Also   **CList::RemoveAll**

CList::RemoveHead

TYPE **RemoveHead( );**

Return Value   The element previously at the head of the list.

Parameters   *TYPE*   Template parameter specifying the type of elements in the list.

Remarks   Removes the element from the head of the list and returns a pointer to it.

You must ensure that the list is not empty before calling **RemoveHead**. If the list is empty, then the Debug version of the Microsoft Foundation Class Library asserts. Use **IsEmpty** to verify that the list contains elements.

See Also   **CList::GetHead**, **CList::AddHead**

CList::RemoveTail

TYPE **RemoveTail( );**

Return Value   The element that was at the tail of the list.

Parameters   *TYPE*   Template parameter specifying the type of elements in the list.

Remarks   Removes the element from the tail of the list and returns a pointer to it.

You must ensure that the list is not empty before calling **RemoveTail**. If the list is empty, then the Debug version of the Microsoft Foundation Class Library asserts. Use **IsEmpty** to verify that the list contains elements.

See Also   **CList::GetTail**, **CList::AddTail**

CList::SetAt

void SetAt(POSITION *pos*, *ARG_TYPE newElement* **);**

Parameters   *pos*   The **POSITION** of the element to be set.

ARG_TYPE   Template parameter specifying the type of the list element (may be a reference).

newElement   The element to be added to the list.

Remarks   A variable of type **POSITION** is a key for the list. It is not the same as an index, and you cannot operate on a **POSITION** value yourself. **SetAt** writes the element to the specified position in the list.

You must ensure that your **POSITION** value represents a valid position in the list. If it is invalid, then the Debug version of the Microsoft Foundation Class Library asserts.

See Also   **CList::Find**, **CList::GetAt**, **CList::GetNext**, **CList::GetPrev**

class CListBox : public CWnd

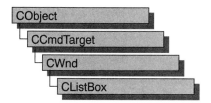

The **CListBox** class provides the functionality of a Windows list box. A list box displays a list of items, such as filenames, that the user can view and select. In a single-selection list box, the user can select only one item. In a multiple-selection list box, a range of items can be selected. When the user selects an item, it is highlighted and the list box sends a notification message to the parent window. You can create a list box either from a dialog template or directly in your code. In both cases, call the constructor **CListBox** to construct the **CListBox** object, then call the **Create** member function to create the Windows list-box control and attach it to the **CListBox** object. Construction can be a one-step process in a class derived from **CListBox**. Write a constructor for the derived class and call **Create** from within the constructor. If you want to handle Windows notification messages sent by a list box to its parent (usually a class derived from **CDialog**), add a message-map entry and message-handler member function to the parent class for each message.

Each message-map entry takes the following form:

ON_Notification(*id,* *memberFxn*)

Where *id* specifies the child window ID of the list-box control sending the notification and *memberFxn* is the name of the parent member function you have written to handle the notification.

The parent's function prototype is as follows:

afx_msg void memberFxn( );

Following is a list of potential message-map entries and a description of the cases in which they would be sent to the parent:

- **ON_LBN_DBLCLK**   The user double-clicks a string in a list box. Only a list box that has the **LBS_NOTIFY** style will send this notification message. For a list of list-box styles, see the section "List-Box Styles" on page 1249.
- **ON_LBN_ERRSPACE**   The list box cannot allocate enough memory to meet the request.
- **ON_LBN_KILLFOCUS**   The list box is losing the input focus.

- **ON_LBN_SELCANCEL**   The current list-box selection is canceled. This message is only sent when a list box has the **LBS_NOTIFY** style.
- **ON_LBN_SELCHANGE**   The selection in the list box is about to change. This notification is not sent if the selection is changed by the **CListBox::SetCurSel** member function. This notification applies only to a list box that has the **LBS_NOTIFY** style. The **LBN_SELCHANGE** notification message is sent for a multiple-selection list box whenever the user presses an arrow key, even if the selection does not change.
- **ON_LBN_SETFOCUS**   The list box is receiving the input focus.

If you create a **CListBox** object within a dialog box (through a dialog resource), the **CListBox** object is automatically destroyed when the user closes the dialog box. If you create a **CListBox** object within a window, you may need to destroy the **CListBox** object. If you create the **CListBox** object on the stack, it is destroyed automatically. If you create the **CListBox** object on the heap by using the **new** function, you must call **delete** on the object to destroy it when the user terminates the Windows list box. If you allocate any memory in the **CListBox** object, override the **CListBox** destructor to dispose of the allocations.

#include <afxwin.h>

See Also   **CWnd**, **CButton**, **CComboBox**, **CEdit**, **CScrollBar**, **CStatic**, **CDialog**

Construction

CListBox	Constructs a **CListBox** object.

Initialization

Create	Creates the Windows list box and attaches it to the **CListBox** object.

General Operations

GetCount	Returns the number of strings in a list box.
GetHorizontalExtent	Returns the width in pixels that a list box can be scrolled horizontally.
SetHorizontalExtent	Sets the width in pixels that a list box can be scrolled horizontally.
GetTopIndex	Returns the index of the first visible string in a list box.
SetTopIndex	Sets the zero-based index of the first visible string in a list box.

GetItemData	Returns the 32-bit value associated with the list-box item.
GetItemDataPtr	Returns a pointer to a list-box item.
SetItemData	Sets the 32-bit value associated with the list-box item.
SetItemDataPtr	Sets a pointer to the list-box item.
GetItemRect	Returns the bounding rectangle of the list-box item as it is currently displayed.
SetItemHeight	Sets the height of items in a list box.
GetItemHeight	Determines the height of items in a list box.
GetSel	Returns the selection state of a list-box item.
GetText	Copies a list-box item into a buffer.
GetTextLen	Returns the length in bytes of a list-box item.
SetColumnWidth	Sets the column width of a multicolumn list box.
SetTabStops	Sets the tab-stop positions in a list box.
GetLocale	Retrieves the locale identifier for a list box.
SetLocale	Sets the locale identifier for a list box.

Single-Selection Operations

| GetCurSel | Returns the zero-based index of the currently selected string in a list box. |
| SetCurSel | Selects a list-box string. |

Multiple-Selection Operations

SetSel	Selects or deselects a list-box item in a multiple-selection list box.
GetCaretIndex	Determines the index of the item that has the focus rectangle in a multiple-selection list box.
SetCaretIndex	Sets the focus rectangle to the item at the specified index in a multiple-selection list box.
GetSelCount	Returns the number of strings currently selected in a multiple-selection list box.
GetSelItems	Returns the indices of the strings currently selected in a list box.

SelItemRange	Selects or deselects a range of strings in a multiple-selection list box.
SetAnchorIndex	Sets the anchor in a multiple-selection list box to begin an extended selection.
GetAnchorIndex	Retrieves the zero-based index of the current anchor item list box.

String Operations

AddString	Adds a string to a list box.
DeleteString	Deletes a string from a list box.
InsertString	Inserts a string at a specific location in a list box.
ResetContent	Clears all the entries from a list box.
Dir	Adds filenames from the current directory to a list box.
FindString	Searches for a string in a list box.
FindStringExact	Finds the first list-box string that matches a specified string.
SelectString	Searches for and selects a string in a single-selection list box.

Overridables

DrawItem	Called by the framework when a visual aspect of an owner-draw list box changes.
MeasureItem	Called by the framework when an owner-draw list box is created to determine list-box dimensions.
CompareItem	Called by the framework to determine the position of a new item in a sorted owner-draw list box.
DeleteItem	Called by the framework when the user deletes an item from an owner-draw list box.

Member Functions

CListBox::AddString

int AddString(LPCTSTR *lpszItem* **);**

Return Value   The zero-based index to the string in the list box. The return value is **LB_ERR** if an error occurs; the return value is **LB_ERRSPACE** if insufficient space is available to store the new string.

Parameters   *lpszItem*   Points to the null-terminated string that is to be added.

Remarks   Call this member function to add a string to a list box. If the list box was not created with the **LBS_SORT** style, the string is added to the end of the list. Otherwise, the string is inserted into the list, and the list is sorted. If the list box was created with the **LBS_SORT** style but not the **LBS_HASSTRINGS** style, the framework sorts the list by one or more calls to the **CompareItem** member function. For a list of list-box styles, see the section "List-Box Styles" on page 1249.

Use **InsertString** to insert a string into a specific location within the list box.

See Also   **CListBox::InsertString**, **CListBox::CompareItem**, **LB_ADDSTRING**

CListBox::CListBox

CListBox( );

Remarks   You construct a **CListBox** object in two steps. First call the constructor **CListBox**, then call **Create**, which initializes the Windows list box and attaches it to the **CListBox**.

See Also   **CListBox::Create**

CListBox::CompareItem

virtual int CompareItem(LPCOMPAREITEMSTRUCT
   lpCompareItemStruct **);**

Return Value   Indicates the relative position of the two items described in the **COMPAREITEMSTRUCT** structure. It may be any of the following values:

Value	Meaning
–1	Item 1 sorts before item 2.
0	Item 1 and item 2 sort the same.
1	Item 1 sorts after item 2.

See **CWnd::OnCompareItem** on page 1053 for a description of the **COMPAREITEMSTRUCT** structure.

Parameters   *lpCompareItemStruct*   A long pointer to a **COMPAREITEMSTRUCT** structure.

Remarks   Called by the framework to determine the relative position of a new item in a sorted owner-draw list box. By default, this member function does nothing. If you create an owner-draw list box with the **LBS_SORT** style, you must override this member function to assist the framework in sorting new items added to the list box.

See Also   **WM_COMPAREITEM**, **CWnd::OnCompareItem**, **CListBox::DrawItem**, **CListBox::MeasureItem**, **CListBox::DeleteItem**

CListBox::Create

BOOL Create(DWORD *dwStyle*, const RECT& *rect*, CWnd* *pParentWnd*, UINT *nID*);

Return Value   Nonzero if successful; otherwise 0.

Parameters   *dwStyle*   Specifies the style of the list box. Apply any combination of list-box styles to the box. For a list of list-box styles, see the section "List-Box Styles" on page 1249.

rect   Specifies the list-box size and position. Can be either a **CRect** object or a **RECT** structure.

pParentWnd   Specifies the list box's parent window (usually a **CDialog** object). It must not be **NULL**.

nID   Specifies the list box's control ID.

Remarks   You construct a **CListBox** object in two steps. First call the constructor, then call **Create**, which initializes the Windows list box and attaches it to the **CListBox** object. When **Create** executes, Windows sends the **WM_NCCREATE**, **WM_CREATE**, **WM_NCCALCSIZE**, and **WM_GETMINMAXINFO** messages to the list-box control. These messages are handled by default by the **OnNcCreate**, **OnCreate**, **OnNcCalcSize**, and **OnGetMinMaxInfo** member functions in the **CWnd** base class. To extend the default message handling, derive a class from **CListBox**, add a message map to the new class, and override the preceding message-handler member functions. Override **OnCreate**, for example, to perform needed initialization for a new class.

Apply the following window styles to a list-box control: For a list of window styles, see the section "Window Styles" on page 1253.

- **WS_CHILD**   Always
- **WS_VISIBLE**   Usually
- **WS_DISABLED**   Rarely
- **WS_VSCROLL**   To add a vertical scroll bar
- **WS_HSCROLL**   To add a horizontal scroll bar
- **WS_GROUP**   To group controls
- **WS_TABSTOP**   To allow tabbing to this control

See Also   **CListBox::CListBox**

CListBox::DeleteItem

virtual void DeleteItem(LPDELETEITEMSTRUCT *lpDeleteItemStruct* **);**

Parameters   *lpDeleteItemStruct*   A long pointer to a Windows **DELETEITEMSTRUCT**
structure that contains information about the deleted item.

Remarks   Called by the framework when the user deletes an item from an owner-draw
CListBox object or destroys the list box. The default implementation of this
function does nothing. Override this function to redraw an owner-draw list box as
needed.

See **CWnd::OnDeleteItem** on page 1056 for a description of the
DELETEITEMSTRUCT structure.

See Also   **CListBox::CompareItem**, **CWnd::OnDeleteItem**, **CListBox::DrawItem**,
CListBox::MeasureItem, **::DeleteItem**

CListBox::DeleteString

int DeleteString(UINT *nIndex* **);**

Return Value   A count of the strings remaining in the list. The return value is **LB_ERR** if *nIndex*
specifies an index greater then the number of items in the list.

Parameters   *nIndex*   Specifies the zero-based index of the string to be deleted.

Remarks   Deletes an item in a list box.

See Also   **LB_DELETESTRING**, **CListBox::AddString**, **CListBox::InsertString**

CListBox::Dir

int Dir(UINT *attr*, **LPCTSTR** *lpszWildCard* **);**

Return Value

The zero-based index of the last filename added to the list. The return value is **LB_ERR** if an error occurs; the return value is **LB_ERRSPACE** if insufficient space is available to store the new strings.

Parameters

attr   Can be any combination of the **enum** values described in **CFile::GetStatus**, or any combination of the following values:

Value	Meaning
0x0000	File can be read from or written to.
0x0001	File can be read from but not written to.
0x0002	File is hidden and does not appear in a directory listing.
0x0004	File is a system file.
0x0010	The name specified by *lpszWildCard* specifies a directory.
0x0020	File has been archived.
0x4000	Include all drives that match the name specified by *lpszWildCard*.
0x8000	Exclusive flag. If the exclusive flag is set, only files of the specified type are listed. Otherwise, files of the specified type are listed in addition to "normal" files.

lpszWildCard   Points to a file-specification string. The string can contain wildcards (for example, *.*).

Remarks

Adds a list of filenames and/or drives to a list box.

See Also

CWnd::DlgDirList, **LB_DIR**, **CFile::GetStatus**

CListBox::DrawItem

virtual void DrawItem(LPDRAWITEMSTRUCT *lpDrawItemStruct* **);**

Parameters

lpDrawItemStruct   A long pointer to a **DRAWITEMSTRUCT** structure that contains information about the type of drawing required.

Remarks

Called by the framework when a visual aspect of an owner-draw list box changes. The member of the **DRAWITEMSTRUCT** structure defines the drawing action that is to be performed.

By default, this member function does nothing. Override this member function to implement drawing for an owner-draw **CListBox** object. The application should restore all graphics device interface (GDI) objects selected for the display context supplied in *lpDrawItemStruct* before this member function terminates.

See **CWnd::OnDrawItem** on page 1058 for a description of the **DRAWITEMSTRUCT** structure.

See Also   **CListBox::CompareItem, CWnd::OnDrawItem, ::DrawItem, CListBox::MeasureItem, CListBox::DeleteItem**

CListBox::FindString

int FindString(int *nStartAfter*, **LPCTSTR** *lpszItem*) **const;**

Return Value   The zero-based index of the matching item, or **LB_ERR** if the search was unsuccessful.

Parameters   *nStartAfter*   Contains the zero-based index of the item before the first item to be searched. When the search reaches the bottom of the list box, it continues from the top of the list box back to the item specified by *nStartAfter*. If *nStartAfter* is –1, the entire list box is searched from the beginning.

lpszItem   Points to the null-terminated string that contains the prefix to search for. The search is case independent, so this string may contain any combination of uppercase and lowercase letters.

Remarks   Finds the first string in a list box that contains the specified prefix without changing the list-box selection. Use the **SelectString** member function to both find and select a string.

See Also   **CListBox::SelectString, CListBox::AddString, CListBox::InsertString, LB_FINDSTRING**

CListBox::FindStringExact

int FindStringExact(int *nIndexStart*, **LPCTSTR** *lpszFind*) **const;**

Return Value   The index of the matching item, or **LB_ERR** if the search was unsuccessful.

Parameters   *nIndexStart*   Specifies the zero-based index of the item before the first item to be searched. When the search reaches the bottom of the list box, it continues from the top of the list box back to the item specified by *nIndexStart*. If *nIndexStart* is –1, the entire list box is searched from the beginning.

lpszFind   Points to the null-terminated string to search for. This string can contain a complete filename, including the extension. The search is not case sensitive, so the string can contain any combination of uppercase and lowercase letters.

Remarks   An application calls the **FindStringExact** member function to find the first list-box string that matches the string specified in *lpszFind*. If the list box was created with an owner-draw style but without the **LBS_HASSTRINGS** style, the

FindStringExact member function attempts to match the doubleword value against the value of *lpszFind*.

See Also   **CListBox::FindString, LB_FINDSTRING, LB_FINDSTRINGEXACT**

CListBox::GetAnchorIndex

int GetAnchorIndex( ) const;

Return Value   The index of the current anchor item, if successful; otherwise LB_ERR.

Class   **CListBox**

Remarks   Retrieves the zero-based index of the current anchor item in the list box. In a multiple-selection list box, the anchor item is the first or last item in a block of contiguous selected items.

See Also   **CListBox::SetAnchorIndex**

CListBox::GetCaretIndex

int GetCaretIndex( ) const;

Return Value   The zero-based index of the item that has the focus rectangle in a list box. If the list box is a single-selection list box, the return value is the index of the item that is selected, if any.

Remarks   An application calls the **GetCaretIndex** member function to determine the index of the item that has the focus rectangle in a multiple-selection list box. The item may or may not be selected.

See Also   **CListBox::SetCaretIndex, LB_GETCARETINDEX**

CListBox::GetCount

int GetCount( ) const;

Return Value   The number of items in the list box, or **LB_ERR** if an error occurs.

Remarks   Retrieves the number of items in a list box. The returned count is one greater than the index value of the last item (the index is zero-based).

See Also   **LB_GETCOUNT**

CListBox::GetCurSel

int GetCurSel( ) const;

Return Value   The zero-based index of the currently selected item. It is **LB_ERR** if no item is currently selected or if the list box is a multiple-selection list box.

Remarks   Retrieves the zero-based index of the currently selected item, if any, in a single-selection list box. **GetCurSel** should not be called for a multiple-selection list box.

See Also   **LB_GETCURSEL, CListBox::SetCurSel**

CListBox::GetHorizontalExtent

int GetHorizontalExtent( ) const;

Return Value   The scrollable width of the list box, in pixels.

Remarks   Retrieves from a list box the width in pixels by which the list box can be scrolled horizontally if the list box has horizontal scroll bars. To respond to **GetHorizontalExtent**, the list box must have been defined with the **WS_HSCROLL** style. For a list of window styles, see the section "Window Styles" on page 1253.

See Also   **CListBox::SetHorizontalExtent, LB_GETHORIZONTALEXTENT**

CListBox::GetItemData

DWORD GetItemData(int *nIndex*) const;

Return Value   The 32-bit value associated with the item, or **LB_ERR** if an error occurs.

Parameters   *nIndex*   Specifies the zero-based index of the item in the list box.

Remarks   Retrieves the application-supplied doubleword value associated with the specified list-box item. The doubleword value was the *dwItemData* parameter of a **SetItemData** call.

See Also   **CListBox::AddString, CListBox::GetItemDataPtr, CListBox::SetItemDataPtr, CListBox::InsertString, CListBox::SetItemData, LB_GETITEMDATA**

CListBox::GetItemDataPtr

void* GetItemDataPtr(int *nIndex*) const;

Return Value   Retrieves a pointer, or –1 if an error occurs.

Parameters   *nIndex*   Specifies the zero-based index of the item in the list box.

Remarks   Retrieves the application-supplied 32-bit value associated with the specified list-box item as a pointer (**void***).

See Also   **CListBox::AddString, CListBox::GetItemData, CListBox::InsertString, CListBox::SetItemData, LB_GETITEMDATA**

CListBox::GetItemHeight

int GetItemHeight(int *nIndex*) const;

Return Value   The height, in pixels, of the items in the list box. If the list box has the **LBS_OWNERDRAWVARIABLE** style, the return value is the height of the item specified by *nIndex*. If an error occurs, the return value is **LB_ERR**.

Parameters   *nIndex*   Specifies the zero-based index of the item in the list box. This parameter is used only if the list box has the **LBS_OWNERDRAWVARIABLE** style; otherwise, it should be set to 0.

Remarks   An application calls the **GetItemHeight** member function to determine the height of items in a list box.

See Also   **LB_GETITEMHEIGHT, CListBox::SetItemHeight**

CListBox::GetItemRect

int GetItemRect(int *nIndex*, LPRECT *lpRect*) const;

Return Value   **LB_ERR** if an error occurs.

Parameters   *nIndex*   Specifies the zero-based index of the item.

lpRect   Specifies a long pointer to a **RECT** data structure that receives the list-box client coordinates of the item.

Remarks   Retrieves the dimensions of the rectangle that bounds a list-box item as it is currently displayed in the list-box window.

See Also   **LB_GETITEMRECT**

CListBox::GetLocale

LCID GetLocale( ) const;

Return Value   The locale identifier (LCID) value for the strings in the list-box.

Remarks   Retrieves the locale used by the list-box. The locale is used, for example, to determine the sort order of the strings in a sorted list-box.

See Also	**CListBox::SetLocale**, **::GetStringTypeW**, **::GetSystemDefaultLCID**, **::GetUserDefaultLCID**

CListBox::GetSel

int GetSel(int *nIndex*) const;

Return Value	A positive number if the specified item is selected; otherwise, it is 0. The return value is **LB_ERR** if an error occurs.
Parameters	*nIndex* Specifies the zero-based index of the item.
Remarks	Retrieves the selection state of an item. This member function works with both single- and multiple-selection list boxes.
See Also	**LB_GETSEL**, **CListBox::SetSel**

CListBox::GetSelCount

int GetSelCount( ) const;

Return Value	The count of selected items in a list box. If the list box is a single-selection list box, the return value is **LB_ERR**.
Remarks	Retrieves the total number of selected items in a multiple-selection list box.
See Also	**CListBox::SetSel**, **LB_GETSELCOUNT**

CListBox::GetSelItems

int GetSelItems(int *nMaxItems*, LPINT *rgIndex*) const;

Return Value	The actual number of items placed in the buffer. If the list box is a single-selection list box, the return value is **LB_ERR**.
Parameters	*nMaxItems* Specifies the maximum number of selected items whose item numbers are to be placed in the buffer.
	rgIndex Specifies a long pointer to a buffer large enough for the number of integers specified by *nMaxItems*.
Remarks	Fills a buffer with an array of integers that specifies the item numbers of selected items in a multiple-selection list box.
See Also	**LB_GETSELITEMS**

CListBox::GetText

int GetText(int *nIndex*, **LPTSTR** *lpszBuffer* **) const;**

void GetText(int *nIndex*, **CString&** *rString* **) const;**

Return Value   The length (in bytes) of the string, excluding the terminating null character. If *nIndex* does not specify a valid index, the return value is **LB_ERR**.

Parameters   *nIndex*   Specifies the zero-based index of the string to be retrieved.

lpszBuffer   Points to the buffer that receives the string. The buffer must have sufficient space for the string and a terminating null character. The size of the string can be determined ahead of time by calling the **GetTextLen** member function.

rString   A reference to a **CString** object.

Remarks   Gets a string from a list box. The second form of this member function fills a **CString** object with the string text.

See Also   **CListBox::GetTextLen**, **LB_GETTEXT**

CListBox::GetTextLen

int GetTextLen(int *nIndex* **) const;**

Return Value   The length of the string in bytes, excluding the terminating null character. If *nIndex* does not specify a valid index, the return value is **LB_ERR**.

Parameters   *nIndex*   Specifies the zero-based index of the string.

Remarks   Gets the length of a string in a list-box item.

See Also   **CListBox::GetText**, **LB_GETTEXTLEN**

CListBox::GetTopIndex

int GetTopIndex( ) const;

Return Value   The zero-based index of the first visible item in a list box.

Remarks   Retrieves the zero-based index of the first visible item in a list box. Initially, item 0 is at the top of the list box, but if the list box is scrolled, another item may be at the top.

See Also   **CListBox::SetTopIndex**, **LB_GETTOPINDEX**

CListBox::InsertString

int InsertString(int *nIndex***, LPCTSTR** *lpszItem* **);**

Return Value   The zero-based index of the position at which the string was inserted. The return value is **LB_ERR** if an error occurs; the return value is **LB_ERRSPACE** if insufficient space is available to store the new string.

Parameters   *nIndex*   Specifies the zero-based index of the position to insert the string. If this parameter is −1, the string is added to the end of the list.

lpszItem   Points to the null-terminated string that is to be inserted.

Remarks   Inserts a string into the list box. Unlike the **AddString** member function, **InsertString** does not cause a list with the **LBS_SORT** style to be sorted.

See Also   **CListBox::AddString, LB_INSERTSTRING**

CListBox::MeasureItem

virtual void MeasureItem(LPMEASUREITEMSTRUCT *lpMeasureItemStruct* **);**

Parameters   *lpMeasureItemStruct*   A long pointer to a **MEASUREITEMSTRUCT** structure.

Remarks   Called by the framework when a list box with an owner-draw style is created.

By default, this member function does nothing. Override this member function and fill in the **MEASUREITEMSTRUCT** structure to inform Windows of the list-box dimensions. If the list box is created with the **LBS_OWNERDRAWVARIABLE** style, the framework calls this member function for each item in the list box. Otherwise, this member is called only once.

For further information about using the **OWNERDRAWFIXED** style in an owner-draw list box created with the **SubclassDlgItem** member function of **CWnd**, see the discussion in Technical Note 14 under MFC in Books Online.

See **CWnd::OnMeasureItem** on page 1073 for a description of the **MEASUREITEMSTRUCT** structure**.**

See Also   **CListBox::CompareItem, CWnd::OnMeasureItem, CListBox::DrawItem, ::MeasureItem, CListBox::DeleteItem**

CListBox::ResetContent

void ResetContent( );

Remarks   Removes all items from a list box.

See Also   **LB_RESETCONTENT**

CListBox::SelectString

int **SelectString**(int *nStartAfter*, **LPCTSTR** *lpszItem*);

Return Value   The index of the selected item if the search was successful. If the search was unsuccessful, the return value is **LB_ERR** and the current selection is not changed.

Parameters   *nStartAfter*   Contains the zero-based index of the item before the first item to be searched. When the search reaches the bottom of the list box, it continues from the top of the list box back to the item specified by *nStartAfter*. If *nStartAfter* is –1, the entire list box is searched from the beginning.

lpszItem   Points to the null-terminated string that contains the prefix to search for. The search is case independent, so this string may contain any combination of uppercase and lowercase letters.

Remarks   Searches for a list-box item that matches the specified string, and if a matching item is found, it selects the item. The list box is scrolled, if necessary, to bring the selected item into view. This member function cannot be used with a list box that has the **LBS_MULTIPLESEL** style. For a list of list-box styles, see the section "List-Box Styles" on page 1249. An item is selected only if its initial characters (from the starting point) match the characters in the string specified by *lpszItem*. Use the **FindString** member function to find a string without selecting the item.

See Also   **CListBox::FindString, LB_SELECTSTRING**

CListBox::SelItemRange

int **SelItemRange**(**BOOL** *bSelect*, int *nFirstItem*, int *nLastItem*);

Return Value   **LB_ERR** if an error occurs.

Parameters   *bSelect*   Specifies how to set the selection. If *bSelect* is **TRUE**, the string is selected and highlighted; if **FALSE**, the highlight is removed and the string is no longer selected.

nFirstItem   Specifies the zero-based index of the first item to set.

nLastItem   Specifies the zero-based index of the last item to set.

Remarks   Selects one or more consecutive items in a multiple-selection list box. Use this member function only with multiple-selection list boxes.

See Also   **LB_SELITEMRANGE, CListBox::GetSelItems**

CListBox::SetAnchorIndex

void SetAnchorIndex(int *nIndex*);

Return Value   Zero.

Parameters   *nIndex*   Specifies the zero-based index of the list-box item that will be the anchor.

Remarks   Sets the anchor in a multiple-selection list box to begin an extended selection. In a multiple-selection list box, the anchor item is the first or last item in a block of contiguous selected items.

See Also   **CListBox::GetAnchorIndex**

CListBox::SetCaretIndex

int SetCaretIndex(int *nIndex*, BOOL *bScroll* = TRUE);

Return Value   **LB_ERR** if an error occurs.

Parameters   *nIndex*   Specifies the zero-based index of the item to receive the focus rectangle in the list box.

bScroll   If this value is 0, the item is scrolled until it is fully visible. If this value is not 0, the item is scrolled until it is at least partially visible.

Remarks   An application calls the **SetCaretIndex** member function to set the focus rectangle to the item at the specified index in a multiple-selection list box. If the item is not visible, it is scrolled into view.

See Also   **CListBox::GetCaretIndex, LB_SETCARETINDEX**

CListBox::SetColumnWidth

void SetColumnWidth(int *cxWidth*);

Parameters   *cxWidth*   Specifies the width in pixels of all columns.

Remarks   Sets the width in pixels of all columns in a multicolumn list box (created with the **LBS_MULTICOLUMN** style). For more information on list-box styles, see the section "List-Box Styles" on page 1249.

See Also   **LB_SETCOLUMNWIDTH**

CListBox::SetCurSel

int SetCurSel(int *nSelect*);

Return Value   **LB_ERR** if an error occurs.

Parameters	*nSelect* Specifies the zero-based index of the string to be selected. If *nSelect* is −1, the list box is set to have no selection.
Remarks	Selects a string and scrolls it into view, if necessary. When the new string is selected, the list box removes the highlight from the previously selected string. Use this member function only with single-selection list boxes. It cannot be used to set or remove a selection in a multiple-selection list box.
See Also	**LB_SETCURSEL**, **CListBox::GetCurSel**

CListBox::SetHorizontalExtent

void SetHorizontalExtent(int *cxExtent*);

Parameters	*cxExtent* Specifies the number of pixels by which the list box can be scrolled horizontally.
Remarks	Sets the width, in pixels, by which a list box can be scrolled horizontally. If the size of the list box is smaller than this value, the horizontal scroll bar will horizontally scroll items in the list box. If the list box is as large or larger than this value, the horizontal scroll bar is hidden. To respond to a call to **SetHorizontalExtent**, the list box must have been defined with the **WS_HSCROLL** style. For a list of list-box styles, see the section "List-Box Styles" on page 1249. This member function is not useful for multicolumn list boxes. For multicolumn list boxes, call the **SetColumnWidth** member function.
See Also	**CListBox::GetHorizontalExtent**, **LB_SETHORIZONTALEXTENT**

CListBox::SetItemData

int SetItemData(int *nIndex*, DWORD *dwItemData*);

Return Value	**LB_ERR** if an error occurs.
Parameters	*nIndex* Specifies the zero-based index of the item.
	dwItemData Specifies the value to be associated with the item.
Remarks	Sets a 32-bit value associated with the specified item in a list box.
See Also	**CListBox::SetItemDataPtr**, **CListBox::GetItemData**, **LB_SETITEMDATA**

CListBox::SetItemDataPtr

int SetItemDataPtr(int *nIndex*, void* *pData*);

Return Value	**LB_ERR** if an error occurs.

Parameters	*nIndex* Specifies the zero-based index of the item.
	pData Specifies the pointer to be associated with the item.
Remarks	Sets the 32-bit value associated with the specified item in a combo box to be the specified pointer (**void***).
See Also	**CListBox::SetItemData, CListBox::GetItemData, CListBox::GetItemDataPtr, LB_SETITEMDATA**

CListBox::SetItemHeight

int SetItemHeight(int *nIndex***, UINT** *cyItemHeight* **);**

Return Value	**LB_ERR** if the index or height is invalid.
Parameters	*nIndex* Specifies the zero-based index of the item in the list box. This parameter is used only if the list box has the **LBS_OWNERDRAWVARIABLE** style; otherwise, it should be set to 0.
	cyItemHeight Specifies the height, in pixels, of the item.
Remarks	An application calls the **SetItemHeight** member function to set the height of items in a list box. If the list box has the **LBS_OWNERDRAWVARIABLE** style, this function sets the height of the item specified by *nIndex*. Otherwise, this function sets the height of all items in the list box.
See Also	**CListBox::GetItemHeight, LB_SETITEMHEIGHT**

CListBox::SetLocale

LCID SetLocale(LCID *nNewLocale* **);**

Return Value	The previous locale identifier (LCID) value for this list-box.
Parameters	*nNewLocale* The new locale identifier (LCID) value to set for the list-box.
Remarks	Sets the locale identifier for this list-box. If **SetLocale** is not called, the default locale is obtained from the system. This system default locale can be modified by using Control Panel's International application.
See Also	**CListBox::GetLocale**

CListBox::SetSel

int SetSel(int *nIndex***, BOOL** *bSelect* **= TRUE);**

Return Value	**LB_ERR** if an error occurs.

Parameters *nIndex*   Contains the zero-based index of the string to be set. If –1, the selection is added to or removed from all strings, depending on the value of *bSelect*.

bSelect   Specifies how to set the selection. If *bSelect* is **TRUE**, the string is selected and highlighted; if **FALSE**, the highlight is removed and the string is no longer selected. The specified string is selected and highlighted by default.

Remarks Selects a string in a multiple-selection list box. Use this member function only with multiple-selection list boxes.

See Also **CListBox::GetSel**, **LB_SETSEL**

CListBox::SetTabStops

void SetTabStops( );

BOOL SetTabStops(const int& *cxEachStop* **);**

BOOL SetTabStops(int *nTabStops*, **LPINT** *rgTabStops* **);**

Return Value Nonzero if all the tabs were set; otherwise 0.

Parameters *cxEachStop*   Tab stops are set at every *cxEachStop* dialog units. See *rgTabStops* for a description of a dialog unit.

nTabStops   Specifies the number of tab stops to have in the list box.

rgTabStops   Points to the first member of an array of integers containing the tab-stop positions in dialog units. A dialog unit is a horizontal or vertical distance. One horizontal dialog unit is equal to one-fourth of the current dialog base width unit, and one vertical dialog unit is equal to one-eighth of the current dialog base height unit. The dialog base units are computed based on the height and width of the current system font. The **GetDialogBaseUnits** Windows function returns the current dialog base units in pixels. The tab stops must be sorted in increasing order; back tabs are not allowed.

Remarks Sets the tab-stop positions in a list box.

To set tab stops to the default size of 2 dialog units, call the parameterless version of this member function. To set tab stops to a size other than 2, call the version with the *cxEachStop* argument.

To set tab stops to an array of sizes, use the version with the *rgTabStops* and *nTabStops* arguments. A tab stop will be set for each value in *rgTabStops*, up to the number specified by *nTabStops*. To respond to a call to the **SetTabStops** member function, the list box must have been created with the **LBS_USETABSTOPS** style.

See Also **LB_SETTABSTOPS**, **::GetDialogBaseUnits**

CListBox::SetTopIndex

int SetTopIndex(int *nIndex*);

Return Value   **LB_ERR** if an error occurs.

Parameters   *nIndex*   Specifies the zero-based index of the list-box item.

Remarks   Ensures that a particular list-box item is visible. The system scrolls the list box until either the list-box item appears at the top of the list box or the maximum scroll range has been reached.

See Also   **CListBox::GetTopIndex, LB_SETTOPINDEX**

class CLongBinary : public CObject

Class **CLongBinary** simplifies working with very large binary data objects (often called BLOBs, or "binary large objects") in a database. For example, a record field in an SQL table might contain a bitmap representing a picture. A **CLongBinary** object stores such an object and keeps track of its size.

To use a **CLongBinary** object, declare a field data member of type **CLongBinary** in your recordset class. This member will be an embedded member of the recordset class and will be constructed when the recordset is constructed. After the **CLongBinary** object is constructed, the record field exchange (RFX) mechanism loads the data object from a field in the current record on the data source and stores it back to the record when the record is updated. RFX queries the data source for the size of the binary large object, allocates storage for it (via the **CLongBinary** object's **m_hData** data member), and stores an **HGLOBAL** handle to the data in **m_hData**. RFX also stores the actual size of the data object in the **m_dwDataLength** data member. Work with the data in the object through **m_hData**, using the same techniques you would normally use to manipulate the data stored in a Windows **HGLOBAL** handle.

When you destroy your recordset, the embedded **CLongBinary** object is also destroyed, and its destructor deallocates the **HGLOBAL** data handle.

For more information about large objects and the use of **CLongBinary**, see the articles "Recordset" and "Recordset: Working with Large Data Items" in *Programming with the Microsoft Foundation Class Library*.

#include <afxdb.h>

See Also   **CRecordset**

Data Members

m_dwDataLength	Contains the actual size in bytes of the data object whose handle is stored in **m_hData**.
m_hData	Contains a Windows **HGLOBAL** handle to the actual image object.

Construction

CLongBinary	Constructs a **CLongBinary** object.

Member Functions

CLongBinary::CLongBinary

CLongBinary( );

Remarks   Constructs a **CLongBinary** object.

Data Members

CLongBinary::m_dwDataLength

Remarks   Stores the actual size in bytes of the data stored in the **HGLOBAL** handle in **m_hData**. This size may be smaller than the size of the memory block allocated for the data. Call **::GlobalSize** to get the allocated size.

CLongBinary::m_hData

Remarks   Stores a Windows **HGLOBAL** handle to the actual binary large object data.

class CMap : public CObject

> template< class *KEY*, class *ARG_KEY*, class *VALUE*, class *ARG_VALUE* >
> class CMap : public CObject

Parameters

KEY   Class of the object used as the key to the map.

ARG_KEY   Data type used for *KEY* arguments; usually a reference to *KEY*.

VALUE   Class of the object stored in the map.

ARG_VALUE   Data type used for *VALUE* arguments; usually a reference to *VALUE*.

Remarks

CMap is a dictionary collection class that maps unique keys to values. Once you have inserted a key-value pair (element) into the map, you can efficiently retrieve or delete the pair using the key to access it. You can also iterate over all the elements in the map.

A variable of type **POSITION** is used for alternate access to entries. You can use a **POSITION** to "remember" an entry and to iterate through the map. You might think that this iteration is sequential by key value; it is not. The sequence of retrieved elements is indeterminate.

Certain member functions of this class call global helper functions that must be customized for most uses of the **CMap** class. See Collection Class Helpers.

CMap incorporates the **IMPLEMENT_SERIAL** macro to support serialization and dumping of its elements. Each element is serialized in turn if a map is stored to an archive, either with the overloaded insertion (**<<**) operator or with the **Serialize** member function. If you need a diagnostic dump of the individual elements in the map (the keys and the values), you must set the depth of the dump context to 1 or greater.

When a **CMap** object is deleted, or when its elements are removed, the keys and values both are removed.

Map class derivation is similar to list derivation. See the article "Collections" in *Programming with the Microsoft Foundation Class Library* for an illustration of the derivation of a special-purpose list class.

#include <afxtempl.h>

See Also   Collections, Collection Class Helpers

Construction

CMap	Constructs a collection that maps keys to values.

Operations

Lookup	Looks up the value mapped to a given key.
SetAt	Inserts an element into the map; replaces an existing element if a matching key is found.
operator []	Inserts an element into the map—operator substitution for **SetAt**.
RemoveKey	Removes an element specified by a key.
RemoveAll	Removes all the elements from this map.
GetStartPosition	Returns the position of the first element.
GetNextAssoc	Gets the next element for iterating.
GetHashTableSize	Returns the size (number of elements) of the hash table.
InitHashTable	Initializes the hash table and specifies its size.

Status

GetCount	Returns the number of elements in this map.
IsEmpty	Tests for the empty-map condition (no elements).

Member Functions

CMap::CMap

CMap(int *nBlockSize* **= 10);**

Parameters   *nBlockSize*   Specifies the memory-allocation granularity for extending the map.

Remarks   Constructs an empty map. As the map grows, memory is allocated in units of *nBlockSize* entries.

CMap::GetCount

int GetCount( ) const;

Return Value   The number of elements in this map.

See Also   **CMap::IsEmpty**

CMap::GetHashTableSize

UINT GetHashTableSize( ) const;

Return Value   The number of elements in the hash table.

See Also   **CMap::InitHashTable**

CMap::GetNextAssoc

void GetNextAssoc(POSITION& *rNextPosition*, *KEY*& *rKey*,
    VALUE& *rValue* **) const;**

Parameters   *rNextPosition*   Specifies a reference to a **POSITION** value returned by a previous **GetNextAssoc** or **GetStartPosition** call.

    KEY   Template parameter specifying the type of the map's key.

    rKey   Specifies the returned key of the retrieved element (a string).

    VALUE   Template parameter specifying the type of the map's value.

    rValue   Specifies the returned value of the retrieved element (a **CObject** pointer).

Remarks   Retrieves the map element at *rNextPosition*, then updates *rNextPosition* to refer to the next element in the map. This function is most useful for iterating through all the elements in the map. Note that the position sequence is not necessarily the same as the key value sequence. If the retrieved element is the last in the map, then the new value of *rNextPosition* is set to **NULL**.

See Also   **CMap::GetStartPosition**

CMap::GetStartPosition

POSITION GetStartPosition( ) const;

Return Value   A **POSITION** value that indicates a starting position for iterating the map; or **NULL** if the map is empty.

Remarks   Starts a map iteration by returning a **POSITION** value that can be passed to a **GetNextAssoc** call. The iteration sequence is not predictable; therefore, the "first element in the map" has no special significance.

CMap::InitHashTable

void InitHashTable(UINT *hashSize* **);**

Parameters   *hashSize*   Number of entries in the hash table.

Remarks   Initializes the hash table. For best performance, the hash table size should be a prime number. To minimize collisions the size should be roughly 20 percent larger than the largest anticipated data set.

See Also   **CMap::GetHashTableSize**

CMap::IsEmpty

BOOL IsEmpty( ) const;

Return Value   Nonzero if this map contains no elements; otherwise 0.

See Also   **CMap::GetCount**

Example   See the example for **RemoveAll**.

CMap::Lookup

BOOL Lookup(*ARG_KEY key***,** *VALUE& rValue* **) const;**

Return Value   Nonzero if the element was found; otherwise 0.

Parameters   *ARG_KEY*   Template parameter specifying the type of the *key* value.

key   Specifies the string key that identifies the element to be looked up.

VALUE   Specifies the type of the value to be looked up.

rValue   Receives the looked-up value.

Remarks   **Lookup** uses a hashing algorithm to quickly find the map element with a key that exactly matches the given key.

See Also   **CMap::operator [ ]**

CMap::RemoveAll

void RemoveAll( );

Remarks   Removes all the values from this map by calling the global helper function **DestructElements**. The function works correctly if the map is already empty.

See Also   **CMap::RemoveKey**, **DestructElements**

CMap::RemoveKey

BOOL RemoveKey(*ARG_KEY key*);

Return Value   Nonzero if the entry was found and successfully removed; otherwise 0.

Parameters   *ARG_KEY*   Template parameter specifying the type of the key.

key   Key for the element to be removed.

Remarks   Looks up the map entry corresponding to the supplied key; then, if the key is found, removes the entry.

The **DestructElements** helper function is used to remove the entry.

See Also   **CMap::RemoveAll**

CMap::SetAt

void SetAt(*ARG_KEY key*, *ARG_VALUE newValue*);

Parameters   *ARG_KEY*   Template parameter specifying the type of the *key* parameter.

key   Specifies the string that is the key of the new element.

ARG_VALUE   Template parameter specifying the type of the *newValue* parameter.

newValue   Specifies the value of the new element.

Remarks   The primary means to insert an element in a map. First, the key is looked up. If the key is found, then the corresponding value is changed; otherwise a new key-value pair is created.

See Also   **CMap::Lookup, CMap::operator [ ]**

Operators

CMap::operator [ ]

VALUE& **operator[](*ARG_KEY key*);**

Parameters   *VALUE*   Template parameter specifying the type of the map value.

ARG_KEY   Template parameter specifying the type of the key value.

key   The key used to retrieve the value from the map.

Remarks   This operator is a convenient substitute for the **SetAt** member function. Thus it can be used only on the left side of an assignment statement (an l-value). If there is no map element with the specified key, then a new element is created. There is no "right side" (r-value) equivalent to this operator because there is a possibility that a key may not be found in the map. Use the **Lookup** member function for element retrieval.

See Also   **CMap::SetAt**, **CMap::Lookup**

class CMapPtrToPtr : public CObject

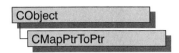

The **CMapPtrToPtr** class supports maps of void pointers keyed by void pointers. The member functions of **CMapPtrToPtr** are similar to the member functions of class **CMapStringToOb**. Because of this similarity, you can use the **CMapStringToOb** reference documentation for member function specifics. Wherever you see a **CObject** pointer as a function parameter or return value, substitute a pointer to **void**. Wherever you see a **CString** or a **const** pointer to **char** as a function parameter or return value, substitute a pointer to **void**.

```
BOOL CMapStringToOb::Lookup( const char* <key>,
                                 CObject*& <rValue> ) const;
```

for example, translates to

```
BOOL CMapPtrToPtr::Lookup( void* <key>, void*& <rValue> ) const;
```

CMapPtrToPtr incorporates the **IMPLEMENT_DYNAMIC** macro to support run-time type access and dumping to a **CDumpContext** object. If you need a dump of individual map elements (pointer values), you must set the depth of the dump context to 1 or greater. Pointer-to-pointer maps may not be serialized. When a **CMapPtrToPtr** object is deleted, or when its elements are removed, only the pointers are removed, not the entities they reference.

#include <afxcoll.h>

See Also   **CMapStringToOb**

Construction

CMapPtrToPtr   Constructs a collection that maps void pointers to void pointers.

Operations

Lookup   Looks up a void pointer based on the void pointer key. The pointer value, not the entity it points to, is used for the key comparison.

SetAt   Inserts an element into the map; replaces an existing element if a matching key is found.

operator [ ]   Inserts an element into the map—operator substitution for **SetAt**.

RemoveKey   Removes an element specified by a key.

RemoveAll   Removes all the elements from this map.

GetStartPosition   Returns the position of the first element.

GetNextAssoc   Gets the next element for iterating.

Status

GetCount   Returns the number of elements in this map.

IsEmpty   Tests for the empty-map condition (no elements).

class CMapPtrToWord : public CObject

The **CMapPtrToWord** class supports maps of 16-bit words keyed by void pointers. The member functions of **CMapPtrToWord** are similar to the member functions of class **CMapStringToOb**. Because of this similarity, you can use the **CMapStringToOb** reference documentation for member function specifics. Wherever you see a **CObject** pointer as a function parameter or return value, substitute **WORD**. Wherever you see a **CString** or a **const** pointer to **char** as a function parameter or return value, substitute a pointer to **void**.

```
BOOL CMapStringToOb::Lookup( const char* <key>,
                             CObject*& <rValue> ) const;
```

for example, translates to

```
BOOL CMapPtrToWord::Lookup( const void* <key>, WORD& <rValue> ) const;
```

CMapWordToPtr incorporates the **IMPLEMENT_DYNAMIC** macro to support run-time type access and dumping to a **CDumpContext** object. If you need a dump of individual map elements, you must set the depth of the dump context to 1 or greater. Pointer-to-word maps may not be serialized. When a **CMapPtrToWord** object is deleted, or when its elements are removed, the pointers and the words are removed. The entities referenced by the key pointers are not removed.

#include <afxcoll.h>

See Also   **CMapStringToOb**

Construction
CMapPtrToWord   Constructs a collection that maps void pointers to 16-bit words.

Operations

Lookup	Returns a **WORD** using a void pointer as a key. The pointer value, not the entity it points to, is used for the key comparison.
SetAt	Inserts an element into the map; replaces an existing element if a matching key is found.
operator [ ]	Inserts an element into the map—operator substitution for **SetAt**.
RemoveKey	Removes an element specified by a key.
RemoveAll	Removes all the elements from this map.
GetStartPosition	Returns the position of the first element.
GetNextAssoc	Gets the next element for iterating.

Status

GetCount	Returns the number of elements in this map.
IsEmpty	Tests for the empty-map condition (no elements).

class CMapStringToOb : public CObject

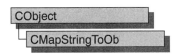

CMapStringToOb is a dictionary collection class that maps unique **CString** objects to **CObject** pointers. Once you have inserted a **CString-CObject*** pair (element) into the map, you can efficiently retrieve or delete the pair using a string or a **CString** value as a key. You can also iterate over all the elements in the map.

A variable of type **POSITION** is used for alternate entry access in all map variations. You can use a **POSITION** to "remember" an entry and to iterate through the map. You might think that this iteration is sequential by key value; it is not. The sequence of retrieved elements is indeterminate.

CMapStringToOb incorporates the **IMPLEMENT_SERIAL** macro to support serialization and dumping of its elements. Each element is serialized in turn if a map is stored to an archive, either with the overloaded insertion (**<<**) operator or with the **Serialize** member function. If you need a diagnostic dump of the individual elements in the map (the **CString** value and the **CObject** contents), you must set the depth of the dump context to 1 or greater.

When a **CMapStringToOb** object is deleted, or when its elements are removed, the **CString** objects and the **CObject** pointers are removed. The objects referenced by the **CObject** pointers are not destroyed.

Map class derivation is similar to list derivation. See the article "Collections" in *Programming with the Microsoft Foundation Class Library* for an illustration of the derivation of a special-purpose list class.

#include <afxcoll.h>

See Also **CMapPtrToPtr, CMapPtrToWord, CMapStringToPtr, CMapStringToString, CMapWordToOb, CMapWordToPtr**

Construction
CMapStringToOb   Constructs a collection that maps **CString** values to **CObject** pointers.

Operations

Lookup	Returns a **CObject** pointer based on a **CString** value.
SetAt	Inserts an element into the map; replaces an existing element if a matching key is found.
operator [ ]	Inserts an element into the map—operator substitution for **SetAt**.
RemoveKey	Removes an element specified by a key.
RemoveAll	Removes all the elements from this map.
GetStartPosition	Returns the position of the first element.
GetNextAssoc	Gets the next element for iterating.

Status

GetCount	Returns the number of elements in this map.
IsEmpty	Tests for the empty-map condition (no elements).

Member Functions

CMapStringToOb::CMapStringToOb

CMapStringToOb(int *nBlockSize* **= 10);**

Parameters *nBlockSize* Specifies the memory-allocation granularity for extending the map.

Remarks Constructs an empty **CString**-to-**CObject*** map. As the map grows, memory is allocated in units of *nBlockSize* entries.

Example See **CObList::CObList** for a listing of the CAge class used in all collection examples.

```
CMapStringToOb map(20);  // Map on the stack with blocksize of 20

CMapStringToOb* pm = new CMapStringToOb;  // Map on the heap
                                          // with default blocksize
```

CMapStringToOb::GetCount

int GetCount( ) const;

Return Value The number of elements in this map.

See Also **CMapStringToOb::IsEmpty**

Example
```
CMapStringToOb map;

map.SetAt( "Bart", new CAge( 13 ) );
map.SetAt( "Homer", new CAge( 36 ) );
ASSERT( map.GetCount() == 2 );
```

CMapStringToOb::GetNextAssoc

void GetNextAssoc(POSITION& *rNextPosition*, **CString&** *rKey*,
CObject*& *rValue*) **const;**

Parameters   *rNextPosition*   Specifies a reference to a **POSITION** value returned by a previous **GetNextAssoc** or **GetStartPosition** call.

rKey   Specifies the returned key of the retrieved element (a string).

rValue   Specifies the returned value of the retrieved element (a **CObject** pointer).

Remarks   Retrieves the map element at *rNextPosition*, then updates *rNextPosition* to refer to the next element in the map. This function is most useful for iterating through all the elements in the map. Note that the position sequence is not necessarily the same as the key value sequence. If the retrieved element is the last in the map, then the new value of *rNextPosition* is set to **NULL**.

See Also   **CMapStringToOb::GetStartPosition**

Example
```
CMapStringToOb map;
POSITION pos;
CString key;
CAge* pa;

map.SetAt( "Bart", new CAge( 13 ) );
map.SetAt( "Lisa", new CAge( 11 ) );
map.SetAt( "Homer", new CAge( 36 ) );
map.SetAt( "Marge", new CAge( 35 ) );
// Iterate through the entire map, dumping both name and age.
for( pos = map.GetStartPosition(); pos != NULL; )
{
map.GetNextAssoc( pos, key, pa );
#ifdef _DEBUG
    afxDump << key << " : " << pa << "\n";
#endif
}
```

The results from this program are as follows:

```
Lisa : a CAge at $4724 11
Marge : a CAge at $47A8 35
Homer : a CAge at $4766 36
Bart : a CAge at $45D4 13
```

CMapStringToOb::GetStartPosition

POSITION GetStartPosition( ) const;

Return Value   A **POSITION** value that indicates a starting position for iterating the map; or **NULL** if the map is empty.

Remarks   Starts a map iteration by returning a **POSITION** value that can be passed to a **GetNextAssoc** call. The iteration sequence is not predictable; therefore, the "first element in the map" has no special significance.

CMapStringToOb::IsEmpty

BOOL IsEmpty( ) const;

Return Value   Nonzero if this map contains no elements; otherwise 0.

See Also   **CMapStringToOb::GetCount**

Example   See the example for **RemoveAll**.

CMapStringToOb::Lookup

BOOL Lookup(LPCTSTR *key*, **CObject*&** *rValue* **) const;**

Return Value   Nonzero if the element was found; otherwise 0.

Parameters   *key*   Specifies the string key that identifies the element to be looked up.

rValue   Specifies the returned value from the looked-up element.

Remarks   **Lookup** uses a hashing algorithm to quickly find the map element with a key that matches exactly (**CString** value).

See Also   **CMapStringToOb::operator [ ]**

Example

```
CMapStringToOb map;
CAge* pa;

map.SetAt( "Bart", new CAge( 13 ) );
map.SetAt( "Lisa", new CAge( 11 ) );
map.SetAt( "Homer", new CAge( 36 ) );
map.SetAt( "Marge", new CAge( 35 ) );
ASSERT( map.Lookup( "Lisa", ( CObject*& ) pa ) ); // Is "Lisa" in the
map?
ASSERT( *pa ==  CAge( 11 ) ); // Is she 11?
```

CMapStringToOb::RemoveAll

void RemoveAll( );

Remarks

Removes all the elements from this map and destroys the **CString** key objects. The **CObject** objects referenced by each key are not destroyed. The **RemoveAll** function can cause memory leaks if you do not ensure that the referenced **CObject** objects are destroyed. The function works correctly if the map is already empty.

See Also

CMapStringToOb::RemoveKey

Example

```
{
    CMapStringToOb map;

    CAge age1( 13 ); // Two objects on the stack
    CAge age2( 36 );
    map.SetAt( "Bart", &age1 );
    map.SetAt( "Homer", &age2 );
    ASSERT( map.GetCount() == 2 );
    map.RemoveAll(); // CObject pointers removed; objects not removed.
    ASSERT( map.GetCount() == 0 );
    ASSERT( map.IsEmpty() );
} // The two CAge objects are deleted when they go out of scope.
```

CMapStringToOb::RemoveKey

BOOL RemoveKey(LPCTSTR *key*);

Return Value

Nonzero if the entry was found and successfully removed; otherwise 0.

Parameters

key   Specifies the string used for map lookup.

Remarks

Looks up the map entry corresponding to the supplied key; then, if the key is found, removes the entry. This can cause memory leaks if the **CObject** object is not deleted elsewhere.

See Also

CMapStringToOb::RemoveAll

Example
```
CMapStringToOb map;

map.SetAt( "Bart", new CAge( 13 ) );
map.SetAt( "Lisa", new CAge( 11 ) );
map.SetAt( "Homer", new CAge( 36 ) );
map.SetAt( "Marge", new CAge( 35 ) );
map.RemoveKey( "Lisa" ); // Memory leak: CAge object not
                         //                deleted.
#ifdef _DEBUG
    afxDump.SetDepth( 1 );
    afxDump << "RemoveKey example: " << &map << "\n";
#endif
```

The results from this program are as follows:

```
RemoveKey example: A CMapStringToOb with 3 elements
    [Marge] = a CAge at $49A0 35
    [Homer] = a CAge at $495E 36
    [Bart] = a CAge at $4634 13
```

CMapStringToOb::SetAt

void SetAt(LPCTSTR *key*, **CObject*** *newValue* **)**
 throw(CMemoryException);

Parameters   *key*   Specifies the string that is the key of the new element.

 newValue   Specifies the **CObject** pointer that is the value of the new element.

Remarks   The primary means to insert an element in a map. First, the key is looked up. If the key is found, then the corresponding value is changed; otherwise a new key-value element is created.

See Also   **CMapStringToOb::Lookup, CMapStringToOb::operator [ ]**

Example
```
CMapStringToOb map;
CAge* pa;

map.SetAt( "Bart", new CAge( 13 ) );
map.SetAt( "Lisa", new CAge( 11 ) ); // Map contains 2
                                     //      elements.
#ifdef _DEBUG
    afxDump.SetDepth( 1 );
    afxDump << "before Lisa's birthday: " << &map << "\n";
#endif
    if( map.Lookup( "Lisa", pa ) )
    { // CAge 12 pointer replaces CAge 11 pointer.
        map.SetAt( "Lisa", new CAge( 12 ) );
        delete pa;   // Must delete CAge 11 to avoid memory leak.
    }
```

```
#ifdef _DEBUG
    afxDump << "after Lisa's birthday: " << &map << "\n";
#endif
```

The results from this program are as follows:

```
before Lisa's birthday: A CMapStringToOb with 2 elements
    [Lisa] = a CAge at $493C 11
    [Bart] = a CAge at $4654 13
after Lisa's birthday: A CMapStringToOb with 2 elements
    [Lisa] = a CAge at $49C0 12
    [Bart] = a CAge at $4654 13
```

Operators

CMapStringToOb::operator [ ]

CObject*& operator [ ](LPCTSTR *key* **);**

Return Value   A reference to a pointer to a **CObject** object; or **NULL** if the map is empty or *key* is out of range.

Remarks   This operator is a convenient substitute for the **SetAt** member function. Thus it can be used only on the left side of an assignment statement (an l-value). If there is no map element with the specified key, then a new element is created. There is no "right side" (r-value) equivalent to this operator because there is a possibility that a key may not be found in the map. Use the **Lookup** member function for element retrieval.

See Also   **CMapStringToOb::SetAt, CMapStringToOb::Lookup**

Example
```
    CMapStringToOb map;

    map["Bart"] = new CAge( 13 );
    map["Lisa"] = new CAge( 11 );
#ifdef _DEBUG
    afxDump.SetDepth( 1 );
    afxDump << "Operator [] example: " << &map << "\n";
#endif
```

The results from this program are as follows:

```
Operator [] example: A CMapStringToOb with 2 elements
    [Lisa] = a CAge at $4A02 11
    [Bart] = a CAge at $497E 13
```

class CMapStringToPtr : public CObject

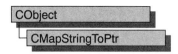

CObject

CMapStringToPtr

The **CMapStringToPtr** class supports maps of void pointers keyed by **CString** objects. The member functions of **CMapStringToPtr** are similar to the member functions of class **CMapStringToOb**. Because of this similarity, you can use the **CMapStringToOb** reference documentation for member function specifics. Wherever you see a **CObject** pointer as a function parameter or return value, substitute a pointer to **void**.

```
BOOL CMapStringToOb::Lookup( const char* <key>,
                            CObject*& <rValue> ) const;
```

for example, translates to

```
BOOL CMapStringToPtr::Lookup( LPCTSTR <key>, void*& <rValue> )
                        const;
```

CMapStringToPtr incorporates the **IMPLEMENT_DYNAMIC** macro to support run-time type access and dumping to a **CDumpContext** object. If you need a dump of individual map elements, you must set the depth of the dump context to 1 or greater. String-to-pointer maps may not be serialized. When a **CMapStringToPtr** object is deleted, or when its elements are removed, the **CString** key objects and the words are removed.

#include <afxcoll.h>

See Also   **CMapStringToOb**

Construction

CMapStringToPtr   Constructs a collection that maps **CString** objects to void pointers.

Operations

Lookup	Returns a void pointer based on a **CString** value.
SetAt	Inserts an element into the map; replaces an existing element if a matching key is found.
operator [ ]	Inserts an element into the map—operator substitution for **SetAt**.
RemoveKey	Removes an element specified by a key.
RemoveAll	Removes all the elements from this map.
GetStartPosition	Returns the position of the first element.
GetNextAssoc	Gets the next element for iterating.

Status

GetCount	Returns the number of elements in this map.
IsEmpty	Tests for the empty-map condition (no elements).

class CMapStringToString : public CObject

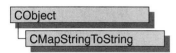

The **CMapStringToString** class supports maps of **CString** objects keyed by **CString** objects.

The member functions of **CMapStringToString** are similar to the member functions of class **CMapStringToOb**. Because of this similarity, you can use the **CMapStringToOb** reference documentation for member function specifics. Wherever you see a **CObject** pointer as a return value or "output" function parameter, substitute a pointer to **char**. Wherever you see a **CObject** pointer as an "input" function parameter, substitute a pointer to **char**.

```
BOOL CMapStringToOb::Lookup( const char* <key>,
                             CObject*& <rValue> ) const;
```

for example, translates to

```
BOOL CMapStringToString::Lookup( LPCTSTR <key>,
                                 CString& <rValue> ) const;
```

CMapStringToString incorporates the **IMPLEMENT_SERIAL** macro to support serialization and dumping of its elements. Each element is serialized in turn if a map is stored to an archive, either with the overloaded insertion (**<<**) operator or with the **Serialize** member function. If you need a dump of individual **CString**-**CString** elements, you must set the depth of the dump context to 1 or greater. When a **CMapStringToString** object is deleted, or when its elements are removed, the **CString** objects are removed as appropriate.

#include <afxcoll.h>

See Also   **CMapStringToOb**

Construction

CMapStringToString	Constructs a collection that maps **CString** objects to **CString** objects.

Operations

Lookup	Returns a **CString** using a **CString** value as a key.
SetAt	Inserts an element into the map; replaces an existing element if a matching key is found.
operator [ ]	Inserts an element into the map—operator substitution for **SetAt**.
RemoveKey	Removes an element specified by a key.
RemoveAll	Removes all the elements from this map.
GetStartPosition	Returns the position of the first element.
GetNextAssoc	Gets the next element for iterating.

Status

GetCount	Returns the number of elements in this map.
IsEmpty	Tests for the empty-map condition (no elements).

class CMapWordToOb : public CObject

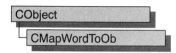

The **CMapWordToOb** class supports maps of **CObject** pointers keyed by 16-bit words. The member functions of **CMapWordToOb** are similar to the member functions of class **CMapStringToOb**. Because of this similarity, you can use the **CMapStringToOb** reference documentation for member function specifics. Wherever you see a **CString** or a **const** pointer to **char** as a function parameter or return value, substitute **WORD**.

```
BOOL CMapStringToOb::Lookup( const char* <key>,
                             CObject*& <rValue> ) const;
```

for example, translates to

```
BOOL CMapWordToOb::Lookup( WORD <key>, CObject*& <rValue> ) const;
```

CMapWordToOb incorporates the **IMPLEMENT_SERIAL** macro to support serialization and dumping of its elements. Each element is serialized in turn if a map is stored to an archive, either with the overloaded insertion (**<<**) operator or with the **Serialize** member function. If you need a dump of individual **WORD-CObject** elements, you must set the depth of the dump context to 1 or greater. When a **CMapWordToOb** object is deleted, or when its elements are removed, the **CObject** objects are deleted as appropriate.

#include <afxcoll.h>

See Also   **CMapStringToOb**

Construction
CMapWordToOb   Constructs a collection that maps words to **CObject** pointers.

Operations

Lookup	Returns a **CObject** pointer using a word value as a key.
SetAt	Inserts an element into the map; replaces an existing element if a matching key is found.
operator [ ]	Inserts an element into the map—operator substitution for **SetAt**.
RemoveKey	Removes an element specified by a key.
RemoveAll	Removes all the elements from this map.
GetStartPosition	Returns the position of the first element.
GetNextAssoc	Gets the next element for iterating.

Status

GetCount	Returns the number of elements in this map.
IsEmpty	Tests for the empty-map condition (no elements).

class CMapWordToPtr : public CObject

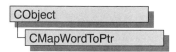

The **CMapWordToPtr** class supports maps of void pointers keyed by 16-bit words. The member functions of **CMapWordToPtr** are similar to the member functions of class **CMapStringToOb**. Because of this similarity, you can use the **CMapStringToOb** reference documentation for member function specifics. Wherever you see a **CObject** pointer as a function parameter or return value, substitute a pointer to **void**. Wherever you see a **CString** or a **const** pointer to **char** as a function parameter or return value, substitute **WORD**.

```
BOOL CMapStringToOb::Lookup( const char* <key>,
                                CObject*& <rValue> ) const;
```

for example, translates to

```
BOOL CMapWordToPtr::Lookup( WORD <key>, void*& <rValue> ) const;
```

CMapWordToPtr incorporates the **IMPLEMENT_DYNAMIC** macro to support run-time type access and dumping to a **CDumpContext** object. If you need a dump of individual map elements, you must set the depth of the dump context to 1 or greater. Word-to-pointer maps may not be serialized. When a **CMapWordToPtr** object is deleted, or when its elements are removed, the words and the pointers are removed. The entities referenced by the pointers are not removed.

#include <afxcoll.h>

See Also   **CMapStringToOb**

Construction

CMapWordToPtr   Constructs a collection that maps words to void pointers.

Operations

Lookup	Returns a void pointer using a word value as a key.
SetAt	Inserts an element into the map; replaces an existing element if a matching key is found.
operator []	Inserts an element into the map—operator substitution for **SetAt**.
RemoveKey	Removes an element specified by a key.
RemoveAll	Removes all the elements from this map.
GetStartPosition	Returns the position of the first element.
GetNextAssoc	Gets the next element for iterating.

Status

GetCount	Returns the number of elements in this map.
IsEmpty	Tests for the empty-map condition (no elements).

class CMDIChildWnd : public CFrameWnd

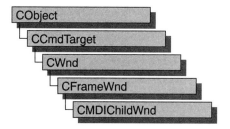

The **CMDIChildWnd** class provides the functionality of a Windows multiple document interface (MDI) child window, along with members for managing the window. An MDI child window looks much like a typical frame window, except that the MDI child window appears inside an MDI frame window rather than on the desktop. An MDI child window does not have a menu bar of its own, but instead shares the menu of the MDI frame window. The framework automatically changes the MDI frame menu to represent the currently active MDI child window.

To create a useful MDI child window for your application, derive a class from **CMDIChildWnd**. Add member variables to the derived class to store data specific to your application. Implement message-handler member functions and a message map in the derived class to specify what happens when messages are directed to the window. There are three ways to construct an MDI child window:

- Directly construct it using **Create**.
- Directly construct it using **LoadFrame**.
- Indirectly construct it through a document template.

Before you call **Create** or **LoadFrame**, you must construct the frame-window object on the heap using the C++ **new** operator. Before calling **Create** you may also register a window class with the **AfxRegisterWndClass** global function to set the icon and class styles for the frame.

Use the **Create** member function to pass the frame's creation parameters as immediate arguments.

LoadFrame requires fewer arguments than **Create**, and instead retrieves most of its default values from resources, including the frame's caption, icon, accelerator table, and menu. To be accessible by **LoadFrame**, all these resources must have the same resource ID (for example, **IDR_MAINFRAME**).

When a **CMDIChildWnd** object contains views and documents, they are created indirectly by the framework instead of directly by the programmer. The **CDocTemplate** object orchestrates the creation of the frame, the creation of the containing views, and the connection of the views to the appropriate document. The parameters of the **CDocTemplate** constructor specify the **CRuntimeClass** of the three classes involved (document, frame, and view). A **CRuntimeClass** object is used by the framework to dynamically create new frames when specified by the user (for example, by using the File New command or the MDI Window New command).

A frame-window class derived from **CMDIChildWnd** must be declared with **DECLARE_DYNCREATE** in order for the above **RUNTIME_CLASS** mechanism to work correctly.

The **CMDIChildWnd** class inherits much of its default implementation from **CFrameWnd**. For a detailed list of these features, please refer to the **CFrameWnd** class description. The **CMDIChildWnd** class has the following additional features:

- In conjunction with the **CMultiDocTemplate** class, multiple **CMDIChildWnd** objects from the same document template share the same menu, saving Windows system resources.

- The currently active MDI child window menu entirely replaces the MDI frame window's menu, and the caption of the currently active MDI child window is added to the MDI frame window's caption. For further examples of MDI child window functions that are implemented in conjunction with an MDI frame window, see the **CMDIFrameWnd** class description.

Do not use the C++ **delete** operator to destroy a frame window. Use **CWnd::DestroyWindow** instead. The **CFrameWnd** implementation of **PostNcDestroy** will delete the C++ object when the window is destroyed. When the user closes the frame window, the default **OnClose** handler will call **DestroyWindow**.

#include <afxwin.h>

See Also   CWnd, CFrameWnd, CMDIFrameWnd

Construction
CMDIChildWnd   Constructs a **CMDIChildWnd** object.

Initialization
Create   Creates the Windows MDI child window associated with the **CMDIChildWnd** object.

Operations

MDIDestroy	Destroys this MDI child window.
MDIActivate	Activates this MDI child window.
MDIMaximize	Maximizes this MDI child window.
MDIRestore	Restores this MDI child window from maximized or minimized size.
GetMDIFrame	Returns the parent MDI frame of the MDI client window.

Member Functions

CMDIChildWnd::CMDIChildWnd

CMDIChildWnd( );

Remarks   Call to construct a **CMDIChildWnd** object. Call **Create** to create the visible window.

See Also   **CMDIChildWnd::Create**

CMDIChildWnd::Create

BOOL Create(LPCTSTR *lpszClassName***, LPCTSTR** *lpszWindowName***, DWORD** *dwStyle* **= WS_CHILD | WS_VISIBLE | WS_OVERLAPPEDWINDOW, const RECT&** *rect* **= rectDefault, CMDIFrameWnd*** *pParentWnd* **= NULL, CCreateContext*** *pContext* **= NULL);**

Return Value   Nonzero if successful; otherwise 0.

Parameters   *lpszClassName*   Points to a null-terminated character string that names the Windows class (a **WNDCLASS** structure). The class name can be any name registered with the **AfxRegisterWndClass** global function. Should be **NULL** for a standard **CMDIChildWnd**.

lpszWindowName   Points to a null-terminated character string that represents the window name. Used as text for the title bar.

dwStyle   Specifies the window style attributes. The **WS_CHILD** style is required. For a list of window styles, see the section "Window Styles" on page 1253.

rect   Contains the size and position of the window. The **rectDefault** value allows Windows to specify the size and position of the new **CMDIChildWnd**.

pParentWnd   Specifies the window's parent. If **NULL**, the main application window is used.

pContext   Specifies a **CCreateContext** structure. This parameter can be **NULL**.

Remarks   Call this member function to create a Windows MDI child window and attach it to the **CMDIChildWnd** object. The currently active MDI child frame window can determine the caption of the parent frame window. This feature is disabled by turning off the **FWS_ADDTOTITLE** style bit of the child frame window.

The framework calls this member function in response to a user command to create a child window, and the framework uses the *pContext* parameter to properly connect the child window to the application. When you call **Create**, *pContext* may be **NULL**.

See Also   **CMDIChildWnd::CMDIChildWnd, CWnd::PreCreateWindow**

CMDIChildWnd::GetMDIFrame

CMDIFrameWnd* GetMDIFrame( );

Return Value   A pointer to the MDI parent frame window.

Remarks   Call this function to return the MDI parent frame. The frame returned is two parents removed from the **CMDIChildWnd** and is the parent of the window of type **MDICLIENT** that manages the **CMDIChildWnd** object. Call the **GetParent** member function to return the **CMDIChildWnd** object's immediate **MDICLIENT** parent as a temporary **CWnd** pointer.

See Also   **CWnd::GetParent**

CMDIChildWnd::MDIActivate

void MDIActivate( );

Remarks   Call this member function to activate an MDI child window independently of the MDI frame window. When the frame becomes active, the child window that was last activated will be activated as well.

See Also   **CMDIFrameWnd::MDIGetActive, CWnd::OnNcActivate, CMDIFrameWnd::MDINext, WM_MDIACTIVATE**

CMDIChildWnd::MDIDestroy

void MDIDestroy( );

Remarks

Call this member function to destroy an MDI child window. The member function removes the title of the child window from the frame window and deactivates the child window.

See Also

WM_MDIDESTROY, CMDIChildWnd::Create

CMDIChildWnd::MDIMaximize

void MDIMaximize( );

Remarks

Call this member function to maximize an MDI child window. When a child window is maximized, Windows resizes it to make its client area fill the client area of the frame window. Windows places the child window's Control menu in the frame's menu bar so that the user can restore or close the child window and adds the title of the child window to the frame-window title.

See Also

WM_MDIMAXIMIZE, CMDIChildWnd::MDIRestore

CMDIChildWnd::MDIRestore

void MDIRestore( );

Remarks

Call this member function to restore an MDI child window from maximized or minimized size.

See Also

CMDIChildWnd::MDIMaximize, WM_MDIRESTORE

class CMDIFrameWnd : public CFrameWnd

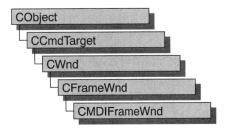

The **CMDIFrameWnd** class provides the functionality of a Windows multiple document interface (MDI) frame window, along with members for managing the window. To create a useful MDI frame window for your application, derive a class from **CMDIFrameWnd**. Add member variables to the derived class to store data specific to your application. Implement message-handler member functions and a message map in the derived class to specify what happens when messages are directed to the window.

You can construct an MDI frame window by calling the **Create** or **LoadFrame** member functions of **CFrameWnd**.

Before you call **Create** or **LoadFrame**, you must construct the frame window object on the heap using the C++ **new** operator. Before calling **Create** you may also register a window class with the **AfxRegisterWndClass** global function to set the icon and class styles for the frame.

Use the **Create** member function to pass the frame's creation parameters as immediate arguments.

LoadFrame requires fewer arguments than **Create**, and instead retrieves most of its default values from resources, including the frame's caption, icon, accelerator table, and menu. To be accessed by **LoadFrame**, all these resources must have the same resource ID (for example, **IDR_MAINFRAME**).

Though **MDIFrameWnd** is derived from **CFrameWnd**, a frame window class derived from **CMDIFrameWnd** need not be declared with **DECLARE_DYNCREATE**.

The **CMDIFrameWnd** class inherits much of its default implementation from **CFrameWnd**. For a detailed list of these features, refer to the **CFrameWnd** class description. The **CMDIFrameWnd** class has the following additional features:

- An MDI frame window manages the **MDICLIENT** window, repositioning it in conjunction with control bars. The MDI client window is the direct parent of MDI child frame windows. The **WS_HSCROLL** and **WS_VSCROLL** window styles specified on a **CMDIFrameWnd** apply to the MDI client window rather than the main frame window so the user can scroll the MDI client area (as in the Windows Program Manager, for example).

- An MDI frame window owns a default menu that is used as the menu bar when there is no active MDI child window. When there is an active MDI child, the MDI frame window's menu bar is automatically replaced by the MDI child window menu.

- An MDI frame window works in conjunction with the current MDI child window, if there is one. For instance, command messages are delegated to the currently active MDI child before the MDI frame window.

- An MDI frame window has default handlers for the following standard Window menu commands:

ID_WINDOW_TILE_VERT

ID_WINDOW_TILE_HORZ

ID_WINDOW_CASCADE

ID_WINDOW_ARRANGE

An MDI frame window also has an implementation of **ID_WINDOW_NEW**, which creates a new frame and view on the current document. An application can override these default command implementations to customize MDI window handling.

Do not use the C++ **delete** operator to destroy a frame window. Use **CWnd::DestroyWindow** instead. The **CFrameWnd** implementation of **PostNcDestroy** will delete the C++ object when the window is destroyed. When the user closes the frame window, the default **OnClose** handler will call **DestroyWindow**.

#include <afxwin.h>

See Also　　CWnd, CFrameWnd, CMDIChildWnd

Construction
| CMDIFrameWnd | Constructs a **CMDIFrameWnd**. |

Operations
MDIActivate	Activates a different MDI child window.
MDIGetActive	Retrieves the currently active MDI child window, along with a flag indicating whether or not the child is maximized.
MDIIconArrange	Arranges all minimized document child windows.
MDIMaximize	Maximizes an MDI child window.

MDINext	Activates the child window immediately behind the currently active child window and places the currently active child window behind all other child windows.
MDIRestore	Restores an MDI child window from maximized or minimized size.
MDISetMenu	Replaces the menu of an MDI frame window, the Window pop-up menu, or both.
MDITile	Arranges all child windows in a tiled format.
MDICascade	Arranges all child windows in a cascaded format.

Overridables

CreateClient	Creates a Windows **MDICLIENT** window for this **CMDIFrameWnd**. Called by the **OnCreate** member function of **CWnd**.
GetWindowMenuPopup	Returns the Window pop-up menu.

Member Functions

CMDIFrameWnd::CMDIFrameWnd

CMDIFrameWnd( );

Remarks   Call this member function to construct a **CMDIFrameWnd** object. Call the **Create** or **LoadFrame** member functions to create the visible MDI frame window.

See Also   **CFrameWnd::Create**, **CFrameWnd::LoadFrame**

CMDIFrameWnd::CreateClient

virtual BOOL CreateClient(LPCREATESTRUCT *lpCreateStruct*, **CMenu*** *pWindowMenu* **);**

Return Value   Nonzero if successful; otherwise 0.

Parameters   *lpCreateStruct*   A long pointer to a **CREATESTRUCT** structure.

                pWindowMenu   A pointer to the Window pop-up menu.

Remarks   Creates the MDI client window that manages the **CMDIChildWnd** objects.

           This member function should be called if you override the **OnCreate** member function directly.

See Also   **CMDIFrameWnd::CMDIFrameWnd**

CMDIFrameWnd::GetWindowMenuPopup

virtual HMENU GetWindowMenuPopup(HMENU *hMenuBar* **);**

Return Value   The Window pop-up menu if one exists; otherwise **NULL**.

Parameters   *hMenuBar*   The current menu bar.

Remarks   Call this member function to obtain a handle to the current pop-up menu named "Window" (the pop-up menu with menu items for MDI window management).

The default implementation looks for a pop-up menu containing standard Window menu commands such as **ID_WINDOW_NEW** and **ID_WINDOW_TILE_HORZ**.

Override this member function if you have a Window menu that does not use the standard menu command IDs.

See Also   **CMDIFrameWnd::MDIGetActive**

CMDIFrameWnd::MDIActivate

void MDIActivate(CWnd* *pWndActivate* **);**

Parameters   *pWndActivate*   Points to the MDI child window to be activated.

Remarks   Call this member function to activate a different MDI child window. This member function sends the **WM_MDIACTIVATE** message to both the child window being activated and the child window being deactivated. This is the same message that is sent if the user changes the focus to an MDI child window by using the mouse or keyboard.

Note   An MDI child window is activated independently of the MDI frame window. When the frame becomes active, the child window that was last activated is sent a **WM_NCACTIVATE** message to draw an active window frame and caption bar, but it does not receive another **WM_MDIACTIVATE** message.

See Also   **CMDIFrameWnd::MDIGetActive, CMDIFrameWnd::MDINext,
WM_ACTIVATE, WM_NCACTIVATE**

CMDIFrameWnd::MDICascade

void MDICascade( );

void MDICascade(int *nType* **);**

Parameters   *nType*   Specifies a cascade flag. Only the following flag may be specified: **MDITILE_SKIPDISABLED**, which prevents disabled MDI child windows from being cascaded.

Remarks   Call this member function to arrange all the MDI child windows in a cascade format.

The first version of **MDICascade**, with no parameters, cascades all MDI child windows, including disabled ones. The second version optionally does not cascade disabled MDI child windows if you specify **MDITILE_SKIPDISABLED** for the *nType* parameter.

See Also   **CMDIFrameWnd::MDIIconArrange**, **CMDIFrameWnd::MDITile**, **WM_MDICASCADE**

CMDIFrameWnd::MDIGetActive

CMDIChildWnd* MDIGetActive(BOOL* *pbMaximized* **= NULL) const;**

Return Value   A pointer to the active MDI child window.

Parameters   *pbMaximized*   A pointer to a **BOOL** return value. Set to **TRUE** on return if the window is maximized; otherwise **FALSE**.

Remarks   Retrieves the current active MDI child window, along with a flag indicating whether the child window is maximized.

See Also   **CMDIFrameWnd::MDIActivate**, **WM_MDIGETACTIVE**

CMDIFrameWnd::MDIIconArrange

void MDIIconArrange( );

Remarks   Arranges all minimized document child windows. It does not affect child windows that are not minimized.

See Also   **CMDIFrameWnd::MDICascade**, **CMDIFrameWnd::MDITile**, **WM_MDIICONARRANGE**

CMDIFrameWnd::MDIMaximize

void MDIMaximize(CWnd* *pWnd* **);**

Parameters   *pWnd*   Points to the window to maximize.

Remarks   Call this member function to maximize the specified MDI child window. When a child window is maximized, Windows resizes it to make its client area fill the client window. Windows places the child window's Control menu in the frame's menu bar so the user can restore or close the child window. It also adds the title of the child window to the frame-window title. If another MDI child window is activated when the currently active MDI child window is maximized, Windows restores the currently active child and maximizes the newly activated child window.

See Also   **WM_MDIMAXIMIZE, CMDIFrameWnd::MDIRestore**

CMDIFrameWnd::MDINext

void MDINext( );

Remarks   Activates the child window immediately behind the currently active child window and places the currently active child window behind all other child windows. If the currently active MDI child window is maximized, the member function restores the currently active child and maximizes the newly activated child.

See Also   **CMDIFrameWnd::MDIActivate, CMDIFrameWnd::MDIGetActive, WM_MDINEXT**

CMDIFrameWnd::MDIRestore

void MDIRestore(CWnd* *pWnd*);

Parameters   *pWnd*   Points to the window to restore.

Remarks   Restores an MDI child window from maximized or minimized size.

See Also   **CMDIFrameWnd::MDIMaximize, WM_MDIRESTORE**

CMDIFrameWnd::MDISetMenu

CMenu* MDISetMenu(CMenu* *pFrameMenu*, CMenu* *pWindowMenu*);

Return Value   A pointer to the frame-window menu replaced by this message. The pointer may be temporary and should not be stored for later use.

Parameters   *pFrameMenu*   Specifies the menu of the new frame-window menu. If **NULL**, the menu is not changed.

pWindowMenu   Specifies the menu of the new Window pop-up menu. If **NULL**, the menu is not changed.

Remarks   Call this member function to replace the menu of an MDI frame window, the Window pop-up menu, or both. After calling **MDISetMenu**, an application must call the **DrawMenuBar** member function of **CWnd** to update the menu bar. If this call replaces the Window pop-up menu, MDI child-window menu items are removed from the previous Window menu and added to the new Window pop-up menu. If an MDI child window is maximized and this call replaces the MDI frame-window menu, the Control menu and restore controls are removed from the previous frame-window menu and added to the new menu.

Do not call this member function if you use the framework to manage your MDI child windows.

See Also   **CWnd::DrawMenuBar**, **WM_MDISETMENU**

CMDIFrameWnd::MDITile

void MDITile( );

void MDITile(int *nType* **);**

Parameters   *nType*   Specifies a tiling flag. This parameter can be any one of the following flags:

- **MDITILE_HORIZONTAL**   Tiles MDI child windows so that one window appears above another.
- **MDITILE_SKIPDISABLED**   Prevents disabled MDI child windows from being tiled.
- **MDITILE_VERTICAL**   Tiles MDI child windows so that one window appears beside another.

Remarks   Call this member function to arrange all child windows in a tiled format.

The first version of **MDITile**, without parameters, tiles the windows vertically under Windows versions 3.1 and later, and arbitrarily under Windows version 3.0. The second version tiles windows vertically or horizontally, depending on the value of the *nType* parameter.

See Also   **CMDIFrameWnd::MDICascade**, **CMDIFrameWnd::MDIIconArrange**, **WM_MDITILE**

class CMemFile : public CFile

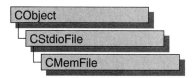

CObject
CStdioFile
CMemFile

CMemFile is the **CFile**-derived class that supports in-memory files. These in-memory files behave like binary disk files except that bytes are stored in RAM. An in-memory file is a useful means of transferring raw bytes or serialized objects between independent processes. Contiguous memory is automatically allocated in specified increments, and it is deleted when the object is destroyed. You can access this memory through a pointer supplied by a member function.

The **Duplicate**, **LockRange**, and **UnlockRange** functions are not implemented for **CMemFile**. If you call these functions on a **CMemFile** object, you will get a **CNotSupportedException**. The data member **CFile::m_hFile** is not used and has no meaning.

#include <afx.h>

Construction

CMemFile   Constructs a memory file using internally allocated memory.

Member Functions

CMemFile::CMemFile

CMemFile(UINT *nGrowBytes* **= 1024)**
        throw (CFileException, CMemoryException);

Parameters   *nGrowBytes*   The memory-allocation increment in bytes.

Remarks   Allocates memory and opens an empty memory file.

Example   `CMemFile f; // Ready to use - no Open necessary.`

class CMemoryException : public CException

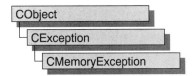

A **CMemoryException** object represents an out-of-memory exception condition. No further qualification is necessary or possible. Memory exceptions are thrown automatically by **new**. If you write your own memory functions, using **malloc**, for example, then you are responsible for throwing memory exceptions.

#include <afx.h>

Construction
CMemoryException   Constructs a **CMemoryException** object.

Member Functions

CMemoryException::CMemoryException

CMemoryException( );

Remarks   Constructs a **CMemoryException** object. Do not use this constructor directly, but rather call the global function **AfxThrowMemoryException**. This global function can succeed in an out-of-memory situation because it constructs the exception object in previously allocated memory. For more information about exception processing, see the article "Exceptions" in *Programming with the Microsoft Foundation Class Library*.

See Also   **AfxThrowMemoryException, Exception Processing**

structure CMemoryState

CMemoryState provides a convenient way to detect memory leaks in your program. A "memory leak" occurs when memory for an object is allocated on the heap but not deallocated when it is no longer required. Such memory leaks can eventually lead to out-of-memory errors. There are several ways to allocate and deallocate memory in your program:

- Using the **malloc/free** family of functions from the run-time library.
- Using the Windows API memory management functions, **LocalAlloc/LocalFree** and **GlobalAlloc/GlobalFree**.
- Using the C++ **new** and **delete** operators.

The **CMemoryState** diagnostics only help detect memory leaks caused when memory allocated using the **new** operator is not deallocated using **delete**. The other two groups of memory-management functions are for non-C++ programs, and mixing them with **new** and **delete** in the same program is not recommended. An additional macro, **DEBUG_NEW**, is provided to replace the **new** operator when you need file and line-number tracking of memory allocations. **DEBUG_NEW** is used whenever you would normally use the **new** operator.

As with other diagnostics, the **CMemoryState** diagnostics are only available in debug versions of your program. A debug version must have the **_DEBUG** constant defined.

If you suspect your program has a memory leak, you can use the **Checkpoint**, **Difference**, and **DumpStatistics** functions to discover the difference between the memory state (objects allocated) at two different points in program execution. This information can be useful in determining whether a function is cleaning up all the objects it allocates.

If simply knowing where the imbalance in allocation and deallocation occurs does not provide enough information, you can use the **DumpAllObjectsSince** function to dump all objects allocated since the a previous call to **Checkpoint**. This dump shows the order of allocation, the source file and line where the object was allocated (if you are using **DEBUG_NEW** for allocation), and the derivation of the object, its address, and its size. **DumpAllObjectsSince** also calls each object's **Dump** function to provide information about its current state.

For more information about how to use **CMemoryState** and other diagnostics, see the article "Diagnostics: Detecting Memory Leaks" in *Programming with the Microsoft Class Library Reference*.

Note Declarations of objects of type **CMemoryState** and calls to member functions should be bracketed by **#if defined(_DEBUG)/#endif** directives. This causes memory diagnostics to be included only in debugging builds of your program.

Construction

CMemoryState   Constructs a class-like structure that controls memory checkpoints.

Checkpoint   Obtains a snapshot or "checkpoint" of the current memory state.

Operations

Difference   Computes the difference between two objects of type **CMemoryState**.

DumpAllObjectsSince   Dumps a summary of all currently allocated objects since a previous checkpoint.

DumpStatistics   Prints memory allocation statistics for a **CMemoryState** object.

Member Functions

CMemoryState::Checkpoint

void Checkpoint( );

Remarks   Takes a snapshot summary of memory and stores it in this **CMemoryState** object. The **CMemoryState** member functions **Difference** and **DumpAllObjectsSince** use this snapshot data.

Example   See the example for the **CMemoryState** constructor.

CMemoryState::CMemoryState

CMemoryState( );

Remarks   Constructs an empty **CMemoryState** object that must be filled in by the **Checkpoint** or **Difference** member functions.

Example

```
// Includes all CMemoryState functions
CMemoryState msOld, msNew, msDif;
msOld.Checkpoint();
CAge* page1 = new CAge( 21 );
CAge* page2 = new CAge( 22 );
msOld.DumpAllObjectsSince();
msNew.Checkpoint();
msDif.Difference( msOld, msNew );
msDif.DumpStatistics();
```

The results from this program are as follows:

```
Dumping objects ->
{2} a CObject at $190A
{1} a CObject at $18EA
Object dump complete.
0 bytes in 0 Free Blocks
8 bytes in 2 Object Blocks
0 bytes in 0 Non-Object Blocks
Largest number used: 8 bytes
Total allocations: 8 bytes
```

CMemoryState::Difference

BOOL Difference(const CMemoryState& *oldState***,**
   const CMemoryState& *newState* **);**

Parameters   *oldState*   The initial memory state as defined by a **CMemoryState** checkpoint.

    newState   The new memory state as defined by a **CMemoryState** checkpoint.

Remarks   Compares two **CMemoryState** objects, then stores the difference into this **CMemoryState** object. **Checkpoint** must have been called for each of the two memory-state parameters.

Example   See the example for the **CMemoryState** constructor.

CMemoryState::DumpAllObjectsSince

void DumpAllObjectsSince( ) const;

Remarks   Calls the **Dump** function for all objects of a type derived from class **CObject** that were allocated (and are still allocated) since the last **Checkpoint** call for this **CMemoryState** object.

    Calling **DumpAllObjectsSince** with an uninitialized **CMemoryState** object will dump out all objects currently in memory.

Example   See the example for the **CMemoryState** constructor.

CMemoryState::DumpStatistics

void DumpStatistics( ) const;

Remarks   Prints a concise memory statistics report from a **CMemoryState** object that is filled by the **Difference** member function. The report, which is printed on the **afxDump** device, shows the following:

- Number of "object" blocks (blocks of memory allocated using **CObject::operator new**) still allocated on the heap.
- Number of non-object blocks still allocated on the heap.
- The maximum memory used by the program at any one time (in bytes).
- The total memory currently used by the program (in bytes).

A sample report looks like this:

```
0 bytes in 0 Free Blocks
8 bytes in 2 Object Blocks
0 bytes in 0 Non-Object Blocks
Largest number used: 8 bytes
Total allocations: 8 bytes
```

- The first line describes the number of blocks whose deallocation was delayed if **afxMemDF** was set to **delayFreeMemDF**. For a description of **afxMemDF**, see "Macros and Globals."
- The second line describes how many object blocks still remain allocated on the heap.
- The third line describes how many nonobject blocks (arrays or structures allocated with new) were allocated on the heap and not deallocated.
- The fourth line gives the maximum memory used by your program at any one time.
- The last line lists the total amount of memory used by your program.

Example   See the example for the **CMemoryState** constructor.

class CMenu : public CObject

The **CMenu** class is an encapsulation of the Windows **HMENU**. It provides member functions for creating, tracking, updating, and destroying a menu.

Create a **CMenu** object on the stack frame as a local, then call **CMenu**'s member functions to manipulate the new menu as needed. Next, call **CWnd::SetMenu** to set the menu to a window, followed immediately by a call to the **Detach** member function. The **CWnd::SetMenu** member function sets the window's menu to the new menu, causes the window to be redrawn to reflect the menu change, and also passes ownership of the menu to the window. The call to **Detach** detaches the **HMENU** from the **CMenu** object, so that when the local **CMenu** variable passes out of scope, the **CMenu** object destructor does not attempt to destroy a menu it no longer owns. The menu itself is automatically destroyed when the window is destroyed.

You can use the **LoadMenuIndirect** member function to create a menu from a template in memory, but a menu created from a resource by a call to **LoadMenu** is more easily maintained, and the menu resource itself can be created and modified by the menu editor.

#include <afxwin.h>

See Also   **CObject**

Data Members
m_hMenu	Specifies the handle to the Windows menu attached to the **CMenu** object.

Construction
CMenu	Constructs a **CMenu** object.

Initialization
Attach	Attaches a Windows menu handle to a **CMenu** object.
Detach	Detaches a Windows menu handle from a **CMenu** object and returns the handle.
FromHandle	Returns a pointer to a **CMenu** object given a Windows menu handle.

GetSafeHmenu	Returns the **m_hMenu** wrapped by this **CMenu** object.
DeleteTempMap	Deletes any temporary **CMenu** objects created by the **FromHandle** member function.
CreateMenu	Creates an empty menu and attaches it to a **CMenu** object.
CreatePopupMenu	Creates an empty pop-up menu and attaches it to a **CMenu** object.
LoadMenu	Loads a menu resource from the executable file and attaches it to a **CMenu** object.
LoadMenuIndirect	Loads a menu from a menu template in memory and attaches it to a **CMenu** object.
DestroyMenu	Destroys the menu attached to a **CMenu** object and frees any memory that the menu occupied.

Menu Operations

| **DeleteMenu** | Deletes a specified item from the menu. If the menu item has an associated pop-up menu, destroys the handle to the pop-up menu and frees the memory used by it. |
| **TrackPopupMenu** | Displays a floating pop-up menu at the specified location and tracks the selection of items on the pop-up menu. |

Menu Item Operations

AppendMenu	Appends a new item to the end of this menu.
CheckMenuItem	Places check marks next to or removes check marks from menu items in the pop-up menu.
EnableMenuItem	Enables, disables, or dims (grays) a menu item.
GetMenuItemCount	Determines the number of items in a pop-up or top-level menu.
GetMenuItemID	Obtains the menu-item identifier for a menu item located at the specified position.
GetMenuState	Returns the status of the specified menu item or the number of items in a pop-up menu.
GetMenuString	Retrieves the label of the specified menu item.
GetSubMenu	Retrieves a pointer to a pop-up menu.

InsertMenu	Inserts a new menu item at the specified position, moving other items down the menu.
ModifyMenu	Changes an existing menu item at the specified position.
RemoveMenu	Deletes a menu item with an associated pop-up menu from the specified menu.
SetMenuItemBitmaps	Associates the specified check-mark bitmaps with a menu item.

Overridables

DrawItem	Called by the framework when a visual aspect of an owner-drawn menu changes.
MeasureItem	Called by the framework to determine menu dimensions when an owner-drawn menu is created.

Member Functions

CMenu::AppendMenu

BOOL AppendMenu(UINT *nFlags***, UINT** *nIDNewItem* **= 0, LPCTSTR** *lpszNewItem* **= NULL);**

BOOL AppendMenu(UINT *nFlags***, UINT** *nIDNewItem***, const CBitmap*** *pBmp* **);**

Return Value   Nonzero if the function is successful; otherwise 0.

Parameters   *nFlags*   Specifies information about the state of the new menu item when it is added to the menu. It consists of one or more of the values listed in the Remarks section below.

nIDNewItem   Specifies either the command ID of the new menu item or, if *nFlags* is set to **MF_POPUP**, the menu handle (**HMENU**) of a pop-up menu. The *nIDNewItem* parameter is ignored (not needed) if *nFlags* is set to **MF_SEPARATOR**.

lpszNewItem   Specifies the content of the new menu item. The *nFlags* parameter is used to interpret *lpszNewItem* in the following way:

nFlags	Interpretation of lpszNewItem
MF_OWNERDRAW	Contains an application-supplied 32-bit value that the application can use to maintain additional data associated with the menu item. This 32-bit value is available to the application when it processes **WM_MEASUREITEM** and **WM_DRAWITEM** messages. The value is stored in the **itemData** member of the structure supplied with those messages.
MF_STRING	Contains a pointer to a null-terminated string. This is the default interpretation.
MF_SEPARATOR	The *lpszNewItem* parameter is ignored (not needed).

pBmp   Points to a **CBitmap** object that will be used as the menu item.

Remarks   Appends a new item to the end of a menu. The application can specify the state of the menu item by setting values in *nFlags*. When *nIDNewItem* specifies a pop-up menu, it becomes part of the menu to which it is appended. If that menu is destroyed, the appended menu will also be destroyed. An appended menu should be detached from a **CMenu** object to avoid conflict. Note that **MF_STRING** and **MF_OWNERDRAW** are not valid for the bitmap version of **AppendMenu**.

The following list describes the flags that may be set in *nFlags*:

- **MF_CHECKED**   Acts as a toggle with **MF_UNCHECKED** to place the default check mark next to the item. When the application supplies check-mark bitmaps (see the **SetMenuItemBitmaps** member function), the "check mark on" bitmap is displayed.
- **MF_UNCHECKED**   Acts as a toggle with **MF_CHECKED** to remove a check mark next to the item. When the application supplies check-mark bitmaps (see the **SetMenuItemBitmaps** member function), the "check mark off" bitmap is displayed.
- **MF_DISABLED**   Disables the menu item so that it cannot be selected but does not dim it.
- **MF_ENABLED**   Enables the menu item so that it can be selected and restores it from its dimmed state.
- **MF_GRAYED**   Disables the menu item so that it cannot be selected and dims it.
- **MF_MENUBARBREAK**   Places the item on a new line in static menus or in a new column in pop-up menus. The new pop-up menu column will be separated from the old column by a vertical dividing line.
- **MF_MENUBREAK**   Places the item on a new line in static menus or in a new column in pop-up menus. No dividing line is placed between the columns.

- **MF_OWNERDRAW**   Specifies that the item is an owner-draw item. When the menu is displayed for the first time, the window that owns the menu receives a **WM_MEASUREITEM** message, which retrieves the height and width of the menu item. The **WM_DRAWITEM** message is the one sent whenever the owner must update the visual appearance of the menu item. This option is not valid for a top-level menu item.

- **MF_POPUP**   Specifies that the menu item has a pop-up menu associated with it. The ID parameter specifies a handle to a pop-up menu that is to be associated with the item. This is used for adding either a top-level pop-up menu or a hierarchical pop-up menu to a pop-up menu item.

- **MF_SEPARATOR**   Draws a horizontal dividing line. Can only be used in a pop-up menu. This line cannot be dimmed, disabled, or highlighted. Other parameters are ignored.

- **MF_STRING**   Specifies that the menu item is a character string.

Each of the following groups lists flags that are mutually exclusive and cannot be used together:

- **MF_DISABLED**, **MF_ENABLED**, and **MF_GRAYED**
- **MF_STRING**, **MF_OWNERDRAW**, **MF_SEPARATOR**, and the bitmap version
- **MF_MENUBARBREAK** and **MF_MENUBREAK**
- **MF_CHECKED** and **MF_UNCHECKED**

Whenever a menu that resides in a window is changed (whether or not the window is displayed), the application should call **CWnd::DrawMenuBar**.

See Also   **CWnd::DrawMenuBar**, **CMenu::InsertMenu**, **CMenu::RemoveMenu**, **CMenu::SetMenuItemBitmaps**, **CMenu::Detach**, **::AppendMenu**

CMenu::Attach

BOOL Attach(HMENU *hMenu* **);**

Return Value   Nonzero if the operation was successful; otherwise 0.

Parameters   *hMenu*   Specifies a handle to a Windows menu.

Remarks   Attaches an existing Windows menu to a **CMenu** object. This function should not be called if a menu is already attached to the **CMenu** object. The menu handle is stored in the **m_hMenu** data member.

See Also   **CMenu::Detach**, **CMenu::CMenu**

CMenu::CheckMenuItem

UINT CheckMenuItem(UINT *nIDCheckItem*, **UINT** *nCheck* **);**

Return Value   The previous state of the item: **MF_CHECKED** or **MF_UNCHECKED**, or –1 if the menu item did not exist.

Parameters   *nIDCheckItem*   Specifies the menu item to be checked, as determined by *nCheck*.

nCheck   Specifies how to check the menu item and how to determine the item's position in the menu. The *nCheck* parameter can be a combination of **MF_CHECKED** or **MF_UNCHECKED** with **MF_BYPOSITION** or **MF_BYCOMMAND** flags. These flags can be combined by using the bitwise OR operator. They have the following meanings:

- **MF_BYCOMMAND**   Specifies that the parameter gives the command ID of the existing menu item. This is the default.

- **MF_BYPOSITION**   Specifies that the parameter gives the position of the existing menu item. The first item is at position 0.

- **MF_CHECKED**   Acts as a toggle with **MF_UNCHECKED** to place the default check mark next to the item.

- **MF_UNCHECKED**   Acts as a toggle with **MF_CHECKED** to remove a check mark next to the item.

Remarks   Adds check marks to or removes check marks from menu items in the pop-up menu. The *nIDCheckItem* parameter specifies the item to be modified. The *nIDCheckItem* parameter may identify a pop-up menu item as well as a menu item. No special steps are required to check a pop-up menu item. Top-level menu items cannot be checked. A pop-up menu item must be checked by position since it does not have a menu-item identifier associated with it.

See Also   **CMenu::GetMenuState**, **::CheckMenuItem**

CMenu::CMenu

CMenu( );

Remarks   The menu is not created until you call one of the create or load member functions of **CMenu**, as listed in "See Also."

See Also   **CMenu::CreateMenu**, **CMenu::CreatePopupMenu**, **CMenu::LoadMenu**, **CMenu::LoadMenuIndirect**, **CMenu::Attach**

CMenu::CreateMenu

BOOL CreateMenu( );

Return Value   Nonzero if the menu was created successfully; otherwise 0.

Remarks   Creates a menu and attaches it to the **CMenu** object. The menu is initially empty. Menu items can be added by using the **AppendMenu** or **InsertMenu** member function. If the menu is assigned to a window, it is automatically destroyed when the window is destroyed.

Before exiting, an application must free system resources associated with a menu if the menu is not assigned to a window. An application frees a menu by calling the **DestroyMenu** member function.

See Also   **CMenu::CMenu**, **CMenu::DestroyMenu**, **CMenu::InsertMenu**, **CWnd::SetMenu**, **::CreateMenu**, **CMenu::AppendMenu**

CMenu::CreatePopupMenu

BOOL CreatePopupMenu( );

Return Value   Nonzero if the pop-up menu was successfully created; otherwise 0.

Remarks   Creates a pop-up menu and attaches it to the **CMenu** object. The menu is initially empty. Menu items can be added by using the **AppendMenu** or **InsertMenu** member function. The application can add the pop-up menu to an existing menu or pop-up menu. The **TrackPopupMenu** member function may be used to display this menu as a floating pop-up menu and to track selections on the pop-up menu. If the menu is assigned to a window, it is automatically destroyed when the window is destroyed. If the menu is added to an existing menu, it is automatically destroyed when that menu is destroyed.

Before exiting, an application must free system resources associated with a pop-up menu if the menu is not assigned to a window. An application frees a menu by calling the **DestroyMenu** member function.

See Also   **CMenu::CreateMenu**, **CMenu::InsertMenu**, **CWnd::SetMenu**, **CMenu::TrackPopupMenu**, **::CreatePopupMenu**, **CMenu::AppendMenu**

CMenu::DeleteMenu

BOOL DeleteMenu(UINT *nPosition*, UINT *nFlags*);

Return Value   Nonzero if the function is successful; otherwise 0.

Parameters   *nPosition*   Specifies the menu item that is to be deleted, as determined by *nFlags*.

nFlags   Is used to interpret *nPosition* in the following way:

nFlags	Interpretation of nPosition
MF_BYCOMMAND	Specifies that the parameter gives the command ID of the existing menu item. This is the default if neither **MF_BYCOMMAND** nor **MF_BYPOSITION** is set.
MF_BYPOSITION	Specifies that the parameter gives the position of the existing menu item. The first item is at position 0.

Remarks   Deletes an item from the menu. If the menu item has an associated pop-up menu, **DeleteMenu** destroys the handle to the pop-up menu and frees the memory used by the pop-up menu. Whenever a menu that resides in a window is changed (whether or not the window is displayed), the application must call **CWnd::DrawMenuBar**.

See Also   **CWnd::DrawMenuBar**, **::DeleteMenu**

CMenu::DeleteTempMap

static void PASCAL DeleteTempMap( );

Remarks   Called automatically by the **CWinApp** idle-time handler, **DeleteTempMap** deletes any temporary **CMenu** objects created by the **FromHandle** member function. **DeleteTempMap** detaches the Windows menu object attached to a temporary **CMenu** object before deleting the **CMenu** object.

CMenu::DestroyMenu

BOOL DestroyMenu( );

Return Value   Nonzero if the menu is destroyed; otherwise 0.

Remarks   Destroys the menu and any Windows resources that were used. The menu is detached from the **CMenu** object before it is destroyed. The Windows **DestroyMenu** function is automatically called in the **CMenu** destructor.

See Also   **::DestroyMenu**

CMenu::Detach

HMENU Detach( );

Return Value   The handle, of type **HMENU**, to a Windows menu, if successful; otherwise **NULL**.

Remarks   Detaches a Windows menu from a **CMenu** object and returns the handle. The **m_hMenu** data member is set to **NULL**.

See Also   **CMenu::Attach**

CMenu::DrawItem

virtual void DrawItem(LPDRAWITEMSTRUCT *lpDrawItemStruct* **);**

Parameters   *lpDrawItemStruct*   A pointer to a **DRAWITEMSTRUCT** structure that contains information about the type of drawing required.

Remarks   Called by the framework when a visual aspect of an owner-drawn menu changes. The *itemAction* member of the **DRAWITEMSTRUCT** structure defines the drawing action that is to be performed. Override this member function to implement drawing for an owner-draw **CMenu** object. The application should restore all graphics device interface (GDI) objects selected for the display context supplied in *lpDrawItemStruct* before the termination of this member function.

See **CWnd::OnDrawItem** on page 1058 for a description of the **DRAWITEMSTRUCT** structure.

CMenu::EnableMenuItem

UINT EnableMenuItem(UINT *nIDEnableItem*, **UINT** *nEnable* **);**

Return Value   Previous state (**MF_DISABLED**, **MF_ENABLED**, or **MF_GRAYED**) or –1 if not valid.

Parameters   *nIDEnableItem*   Specifies the menu item to be enabled, as determined by *nEnable*. This parameter can specify pop-up menu items as well as standard menu items.

nEnable   Specifies the action to take. It can be a combination of **MF_DISABLED**, **MF_ENABLED**, or **MF_GRAYED**, with **MF_BYCOMMAND** or **MF_BYPOSITION**. These values can be combined by using the bitwise OR operator. These values have the following meanings:

- **MF_BYCOMMAND**   Specifies that the parameter gives the command ID of the existing menu item. This is the default.
- **MF_BYPOSITION**   Specifies that the parameter gives the position of the existing menu item. The first item is at position 0.
- **MF_DISABLED**   Disables the menu item so that it cannot be selected but does not dim it.
- **MF_ENABLED**   Enables the menu item so that it can be selected and restores it from its dimmed state.
- **MF_GRAYED**   Disables the menu item so that it cannot be selected and dims it.

Remarks   Enables, disables, or dims a menu item. The **CreateMenu**, **InsertMenu**, **ModifyMenu**, and **LoadMenuIndirect** member functions can also set the state (enabled, disabled, or dimmed) of a menu item.

Using the **MF_BYPOSITION** value requires an application to use the correct **CMenu**. If the **CMenu** of the menu bar is used, a top-level menu item (an item in the menu bar) is affected. To set the state of an item in a pop-up or nested pop-up menu by position, an application must specify the **CMenu** of the pop-up menu. When an application specifies the **MF_BYCOMMAND** flag, Windows checks all pop-up menu items that are subordinate to the **CMenu**; therefore, unless duplicate menu items are present, using the **CMenu** of the menu bar is sufficient.

See Also   **CMenu::GetMenuState**, **::EnableMenuItem**

CMenu::FromHandle

static CMenu* PASCAL FromHandle(HMENU *hMenu*);

Return Value   A pointer to a **CMenu** that may be temporary or permanent.

Parameters   *hMenu*   A Windows handle to a menu.

Remarks   Returns a pointer to a **CMenu** object given a Windows handle to a menu. If a **CMenu** object is not already attached to the Windows menu object, a temporary **CMenu** object is created and attached. This temporary **CMenu** object is only valid until the next time the application has idle time in its event loop, at which time all temporary objects are deleted.

CMenu::GetMenuItemCount

UINT GetMenuItemCount( ) const;

Return Value   The number of items in the menu if the function is successful; otherwise −1.

Remarks   Determines the number of items in a pop-up or top-level menu.

See Also   **CWnd::GetMenu**, **CMenu::GetMenuItemID**, **CMenu::GetSubMenu**, **::GetMenuItemCount**

CMenu::GetMenuItemID

UINT GetMenuItemID(int *nPos*) const;

Return Value   The item ID for the specified item in a pop-up menu if the function is successful. If the specified item is a pop-up menu (as opposed to an item within the pop-up menu), the return value is −1. If *nPos* corresponds to a **SEPARATOR** menu item, the return value is 0.

Parameters   *nPos*   Specifies the position (zero-based) of the menu item whose ID is being retrieved.

Remarks   Obtains the menu-item identifier for a menu item located at the position defined by *nPos*.

See Also   **CWnd::GetMenu**, **CMenu::GetMenuItemCount**, **CMenu::GetSubMenu**, **::GetMenuItemID**

CMenu::GetMenuState

UINT GetMenuState(UINT *nID*, **UINT** *nFlags* **) const;**

Return Value   The value –1 if the specified item does not exist. If *nId* identifies a pop-up menu, the high-order byte contains the number of items in the pop-up menu and the low-order byte contains the menu flags associated with the pop-up menu. Otherwise the return value is a mask (Boolean OR) of the values from the following list (this mask describes the status of the menu item that *nId* identifies):

- **MF_CHECKED**   Acts as a toggle with **MF_UNCHECKED** to place the default check mark next to the item. When the application supplies check-mark bitmaps (see the **SetMenuItemBitmaps** member function), the "check mark on" bitmap is displayed.

- **MF_DISABLED**   Disables the menu item so that it cannot be selected but does not dim it.

- **MF_ENABLED**   Enables the menu item so that it can be selected and restores it from its dimmed state. Note that the value of this constant is 0; an application should not test against 0 for failure when using this value.

- **MF_GRAYED**   Disables the menu item so that it cannot be selected and dims it.

- **MF_MENUBARBREAK**   Places the item on a new line in static menus or in a new column in pop-up menus. The new pop-up menu column will be separated from the old column by a vertical dividing line.

- **MF_MENUBREAK**   Places the item on a new line in static menus or in a new column in pop-up menus. No dividing line is placed between the columns.

- **MF_SEPARATOR**   Draws a horizontal dividing line. Can only be used in a pop-up menu. This line cannot be dimmed, disabled, or highlighted. Other parameters are ignored.

- **MF_UNCHECKED**   Acts as a toggle with **MF_CHECKED** to remove a check mark next to the item. When the application supplies check-mark bitmaps (see the **SetMenuItemBitmaps** member function), the "check mark off" bitmap is displayed. Note that the value of this constant is 0; an application should not test against 0 for failure when using this value.

Parameters	*nID* Specifies the menu item ID, as determined by *nFlags*.

nFlags   Specifies the nature of *nID*. It can be one of the following values:

- **MF_BYCOMMAND**   Specifies that the parameter gives the command ID of the existing menu item. This is the default.
- **MF_BYPOSITION**   Specifies that the parameter gives the position of the existing menu item. The first item is at position 0.

Remarks   Returns the status of the specified menu item or the number of items in a pop-up menu.

See Also   **::GetMenuState, CMenu::CheckMenuItem, CMenu::EnableMenuItem**

CMenu::GetMenuString

int GetMenuString(UINT *nIDItem***, LPTSTR** *lpString***, int** *nMaxCount***, UINT** *nFlags* **) const;**

Return Value   Specifies the actual number of bytes copied to the buffer, not including the null terminator.

Parameters   *nIDItem*   Specifies the integer identifier of the menu item or the offset of the menu item in the menu, depending on the value of *nFlags*.

lpString   Points to the buffer that is to receive the label.

nMaxCount   Specifies the maximum length (in bytes) of the label to be copied. If the label is longer than the maximum specified in *nMaxCount*, the extra characters are truncated.

nFlags   Specifies the interpretation of the *nIDItem* parameter. It can be one of the following values:

nFlags	Interpretation of nIDItem
MF_BYCOMMAND	Specifies that the parameter gives the command ID of the existing menu item. This is the default if neither **MF_BYCOMMAND** nor **MF_BYPOSITION** is set.
MF_BYPOSITION	Specifies that the parameter gives the position of the existing menu item. The first item is at position 0.

Remarks   Copies the label of the specified menu item to the specified buffer. The *nMaxCount* parameter should be one larger than the number of characters in the label to accommodate the null character that terminates a string.

See Also   **CWnd::GetMenu, CMenu::GetMenuItemID, ::GetMenuString**

CMenu::GetSafeHmenu

HMENU GetSafeHmenu( ) const;

Remarks   Returns the **HMENU** wrapped by this **CMenu** object, or a **NULL CMenu** pointer.

CMenu::GetSubMenu

CMenu* GetSubMenu(int *nPos* **) const;**

Return Value   A pointer to a **CMenu** object whose **m_hMenu** member contains a handle to the pop-up menu if a pop-up menu exists at the given position; otherwise **NULL**. If a **CMenu** object does not exist, then a temporary one is created. The **CMenu** pointer returned should not be stored.

Parameters   *nPos*   Specifies the position of the pop-up menu contained in the menu. Position values start at 0 for the first menu item. The pop-up menu's identifier cannot be used in this function.

Remarks   Retrieves the **CMenu** object of a pop-up menu.

See Also   **::GetSubMenu**

CMenu::InsertMenu

BOOL InsertMenu(UINT *nPosition*, **UINT** *nFlags*, **UINT** *nIDNewItem* = 0,
LPCTSTR *lpszNewItem* = **NULL**);

BOOL InsertMenu(UINT *nPosition*, **UINT** *nFlags*, **UINT** *nIDNewItem*,
const CBitmap* *pBmp*);

Return Value   Nonzero if the function is successful; otherwise 0.

Parameters   *nPosition*   Specifies the menu item before which the new menu item is to be inserted. The *nFlags* parameter can be used to interpret *nPosition* in the following ways:

nFlags	Interpretation of nPosition
MF_BYCOMMAND	Specifies that the parameter gives the command ID of the existing menu item. This is the default if neither **MF_BYCOMMAND** nor **MF_BYPOSITION** is set.
MF_BYPOSITION	Specifies that the parameter gives the position of the existing menu item. The first item is at position 0. If *nPosition* is –1, the new menu item is appended to the end of the menu.

nFlags   Specifies how *nPosition* is interpreted and specifies information about the state of the new menu item when it is added to the menu. For a list of the flags that may be set, see the **AppendMenu** member function. To specify more than one value, use the bitwise OR operator to combine them with the **MF_BYCOMMAND** or **MF_BYPOSITION** flag.

nIDNewItem   Specifies either the command ID of the new menu item or, if *nFlags* is set to **MF_POPUP**, the menu handle (**HMENU**) of the pop-up menu. The *nIDNewItem* parameter is ignored (not needed) if *nFlags* is set to **MF_SEPARATOR**.

lpszNewItem   Specifies the content of the new menu item. *nFlags* can be used to interpret *lpszNewItem* in the following ways:

nFlags	Interpretation of lpszNewItem
MF_OWNERDRAW	Contains an application-supplied 32-bit value that the application can use to maintain additional data associated with the menu item. This 32-bit value is available to the application in the **itemData** member of the structure supplied by the **WM_MEASUREITEM** and **WM_DRAWITEM** messages. These messages are sent when the menu item is initially displayed or is changed.
MF_STRING	Contains a long pointer to a null-terminated string. This is the default interpretation.
MF_SEPARATOR	The *lpszNewItem* parameter is ignored (not needed).

pBmp   Points to a **CBitmap** object that will be used as the menu item.

Remarks   Inserts a new menu item at the position specified by *nPosition* and moves other items down the menu. The application can specify the state of the menu item by setting values in *nFlags*. Whenever a menu that resides in a window is changed (whether or not the window is displayed), the application should call **CWnd::DrawMenuBar**. When *nIDNewItem* specifies a pop-up menu, it becomes part of the menu in which it is inserted. If that menu is destroyed, the inserted menu will also be destroyed. An inserted menu should be detached from a **CMenu** object to avoid conflict.

If the active multiple document interface (MDI) child window is maximized and an application inserts a pop-up menu into the MDI application's menu by calling this function and specifying the **MF_BYPOSITION** flag, the menu is inserted one position farther left than expected. This happens because the Control menu of the active MDI child window is inserted into the first position of the MDI frame window's menu bar. To position the menu properly, the application must add 1 to the position value that would otherwise be used. An application can use the **WM_MDIGETACTIVE** message to determine whether the currently active child window is maximized.

See Also   CMenu::AppendMenu, CWnd::DrawMenuBar, CMenu::SetMenuItemBitmaps, CMenu::Detach, ::InsertMenu

CMenu::LoadMenu

BOOL LoadMenu(LPCTSTR *lpszResourceName* **);**

BOOL LoadMenu(UINT *nIDResource* **);**

Return Value   Nonzero if the menu resource was loaded successfully; otherwise 0.

Parameters   *lpszResourceName*   Points to a null-terminated string that contains the name of the menu resource to load.

nIDResource   Specifies the menu ID of the menu resource to load.

Remarks   Loads a menu resource from the application's executable file and attaches it to the **CMenu** object. Before exiting, an application must free system resources associated with a menu if the menu is not assigned to a window. An application frees a menu by calling the **DestroyMenu** member function.

See Also   CMenu::AppendMenu, CMenu::DestroyMenu, CMenu::LoadMenuIndirect, ::LoadMenu

CMenu::LoadMenuIndirect

BOOL LoadMenuIndirect(const void* *lpMenuTemplate* **);**

Return Value   Nonzero if the menu resource was loaded successfully; otherwise 0.

Parameters   *lpMenuTemplate*   Points to a menu template (which is a single **MENUITEMTEMPLATEHEADER** structure and a collection of one or more **MENUITEMTEMPLATE** structures).

The **MENUITEMTEMPLATEHEADER** structure has the following generic form:

```
typedef struct {
    UINT    versionNumber;
    UINT    offset;
} MENUITEMTEMPLATEHEADER;
```

The **MENUITEMTEMPLATE** structure has the following generic form:

```
typedef struct {
    UINT mtOption;
    UINT mtID;
    char mtString[1];
} MENUITEMTEMPLATE;
```

For more information on the above two structures, see the Windows Software Development Kit (SDK).

Remarks   Loads a resource from a menu template in memory and attaches it to the **CMenu** object. A menu template is a header followed by a collection of one or more **MENUITEMTEMPLATE** structures, each of which may contain one or more menu items and pop-up menus. The version number should be 0. The **mtOption** flags should include **MF_END** for the last item in a pop-up list and for the last item in the main list. See the **AppendMenu** member function for other flags. The **mtId** member must be omitted from the **MENUITEMTEMPLATE** structure when **MF_POPUP** is specified in **mtOption**. The space allocated for the **MENUITEMTEMPLATE** structure must be large enough for **mtString** to contain the name of the menu item as a null-terminated string.

Before exiting, an application must free system resources associated with a menu if the menu is not assigned to a window. An application frees a menu by calling the **DestroyMenu** member function.

See Also   **CMenu::DestroyMenu**, **CMenu::LoadMenu**, **::LoadMenuIndirect**, **CMenu::AppendMenu**

CMenu::MeasureItem

virtual void MeasureItem(LPMEASUREITEMSTRUCT
    lpMeasureItemStruct **);**

Parameters   *lpMeasureItemStruct*   A pointer to a **MEASUREITEMSTRUCT** structure.

Remarks   Called by the framework when a menu with the owner-draw style is created. By default, this member function does nothing. Override this member function and fill in the **MEASUREITEMSTRUCT** structure to inform Windows of the menu's dimensions.

See **CWnd::OnMeasureItem** on page 1073 for a description of the **MEASUREITEMSTRUCT** structure.

CMenu::ModifyMenu

BOOL ModifyMenu(UINT *nPosition,* **UINT** *nFlags,* **UINT** *nIDNewItem* **= 0,**
LPCTSTR *lpszNewItem* **= NULL);**

BOOL ModifyMenu(UINT *nPosition,* **UINT** *nFlags,* **UINT** *nIDNewItem,* **const**
CBitmap* *pBmp* **);**

Return Value   Nonzero if the function is successful; otherwise 0.

Parameters   *nPosition*   Specifies the menu item to be changed. The *nFlags* parameter can be
used to interpret *nPosition* in the following ways:

nFlags	Interpretation of nPosition
MF_BYCOMMAND	Specifies that the parameter gives the command ID of the existing menu item. This is the default if neither **MF_BYCOMMAND** nor **MF_BYPOSITION** is set.
MF_BYPOSITION	Specifies that the parameter gives the position of the existing menu item. The first item is at position 0.

nFlags   Specifies how *nPosition* is interpreted and gives information about the
changes to be made to the menu item. For a list of flags that may be set, see the
AppendMenu member function.

nIDNewItem   Specifies either the command ID of the modified menu item or, if
nFlags is set to **MF_POPUP**, the menu handle (**HMENU**) of a pop-up menu.
The *nIDNewItem* parameter is ignored (not needed) if *nFlags* is set to
MF_SEPARATOR.

lpszNewItem   Specifies the content of the new menu item. The *nFlags* parameter
can be used to interpret *lpszNewItem* in the following ways:

nFlags	Interpretation of lpszNewItem
MF_OWNERDRAW	Contains an application-supplied 32-bit value that the application can use to maintain additional data associated with the menu item. This 32-bit value is available to the application when it processes **MF_MEASUREITEM** and **MF_DRAWITEM**.
MF_STRING	Contains a long pointer to a null-terminated string or to a **CString**.
MF_SEPARATOR	The *lpszNewItem* parameter is ignored (not needed).

pBmp   Points to a **CBitmap** object that will be used as the menu item.

Remarks	Changes an existing menu item at the position specified by *nPosition*. The application specifies the new state of the menu item by setting values in *nFlags*. If this function replaces a pop-up menu associated with the menu item, it destroys the old pop-up menu and frees the memory used by the pop-up menu. When *nIDNewItem* specifies a pop-up menu, it becomes part of the menu in which it is inserted. If that menu is destroyed, the inserted menu will also be destroyed. An inserted menu should be detached from a **CMenu** object to avoid conflict.
	Whenever a menu that resides in a window is changed (whether or not the window is displayed), the application should call **CWnd::DrawMenuBar**. To change the attributes of existing menu items, it is much faster to use the **CheckMenuItem** and **EnableMenuItem** member functions.
See Also	**CMenu::AppendMenu, CMenu::InsertMenu, CMenu::CheckMenuItem, CWnd::DrawMenuBar, CMenu::EnableMenuItem, CMenu::SetMenuItemBitmaps, CMenu::Detach, ::ModifyMenu**

CMenu::RemoveMenu

BOOL RemoveMenu(UINT *nPosition*, **UINT** *nFlags* **);**

Return Value	Nonzero if the function is successful; otherwise 0.
Parameters	*nPosition* Specifies the menu item to be removed. The *nFlags* parameter can be used to interpret *nPosition* in the following ways:

nFlags	Interpretation of nPosition
MF_BYCOMMAND	Specifies that the parameter gives the command ID of the existing menu item. This is the default if neither **MF_BYCOMMAND** nor **MF_BYPOSITION** is set.
MF_BYPOSITION	Specifies that the parameter gives the position of the existing menu item. The first item is at position 0.

nFlags   Specifies how *nPosition* is interpreted.

Remarks	Deletes a menu item with an associated pop-up menu from the menu. It does not destroy the handle for a pop-up menu, so the menu can be reused. Before calling this function, the application may call the **GetSubMenu** member function to retrieve the pop-up **CMenu** object for reuse. Whenever a menu that resides in a window is changed (whether or not the window is displayed), the application must call **CWnd::DrawMenuBar**.
See Also	**CWnd::DrawMenuBar, CMenu::GetSubMenu, ::RemoveMenu**

CMenu::SetMenuItemBitmaps

BOOL SetMenuItemBitmaps(UINT *nPosition*, **UINT** *nFlags*,
const CBitmap* *pBmpUnchecked*, **const CBitmap*** *pBmpChecked* **);**

Return Value   Nonzero if the function is successful; otherwise 0.

Parameters   *nPosition*   Specifies the menu item to be changed. The *nFlags* parameter can be used to interpret *nPosition* in the following ways:

nFlags	Interpretation of nPosition
MF_BYCOMMAND	Specifies that the parameter gives the command ID of the existing menu item. This is the default if neither **MF_BYCOMMAND** nor **MF_BYPOSITION** is set.
MF_BYPOSITION	Specifies that the parameter gives the position of the existing menu item. The first item is at position 0.

nFlags   Specifies how *nPosition* is interpreted.

pBmpUnchecked   Specifies the bitmap to use for menu items that are not checked.

pBmpChecked   Specifies the bitmap to use for menu items that are checked.

Remarks   Associates the specified bitmaps with a menu item. Whether the menu item is checked or unchecked, Windows displays the appropriate bitmap next to the menu item. If either *pBmpUnchecked* or *pBmpChecked* is **NULL**, then Windows displays nothing next to the menu item for the corresponding attribute. If both parameters are **NULL**, Windows uses the default check mark when the item is checked and removes the check mark when the item is unchecked. When the menu is destroyed, these bitmaps are not destroyed; the application must destroy them.

The Windows **GetMenuCheckMarkDimensions** function retrieves the dimensions of the default check mark used for menu items. The application uses these values to determine the appropriate size for the bitmaps supplied with this function. Get the size, create your bitmaps, then set them.

See Also   **::GetMenuCheckMarkDimensions**, **::SetMenuItemBitmaps**

CMenu::TrackPopupMenu

BOOL TrackPopupMenu(UINT *nFlags*, **int** *x*, **int** *y*, **CWnd*** *pWnd*,
LPCRECT *lpRect* **= 0);**

Return Value   Nonzero if the function is successful; otherwise 0.

Parameters   *nFlags*   Specifies a screen-position flag and a mouse-button flag. The screen-position flag can be one of the following:

- **TPM_CENTERALIGN**   Centers the pop-up menu horizontally relative to the coordinate specified by *x*.
- **TPM_LEFTALIGN**   Positions the pop-up menu so that its left side is aligned with the coordinate specified by *x*.
- **TPM_RIGHTALIGN**   Positions the pop-up menu so that its right side is aligned with the coordinate specified by *x*.

The mouse-button flag can be either of the following:

- **TPM_LEFTBUTTON**   Causes the pop-up menu to track the left mouse button.
- **TPM_RIGHTBUTTON**   Causes the pop-up menu to track the right mouse button.

x   Specifies the horizontal position in screen coordinates of the pop-up menu. Depending on the value of the *nFlags* parameter, the menu can be left-aligned, right-aligned, or centered relative to this position.

y   Specifies the vertical position in screen coordinates of the top of the menu on the screen.

pWnd   Identifies the window that owns the pop-up menu. This window receives all **WM_COMMAND** messages from the menu. In Windows versions 3.1 and later, the window does not receive **WM_COMMAND** messages until **TrackPopupMenu** returns. In Windows 3.0, the window receives **WM_COMMAND** messages before **TrackPopupMenu** returns.

lpRect   Points to a **RECT** structure or **CRect** object that contains the screen coordinates of a rectangle within which the user can click without dismissing the pop-up menu. If this parameter is **NULL**, the pop-up menu is dismissed if the user clicks outside the pop-up menu. This must be **NULL** for Windows 3.0.

For Windows 3.1 and later, you can use the following constants:

- **TPM_CENTERALIGN**
- **TPM_LEFTALIGN**
- **TPM_RIGHTALIGN**
- **TPM_RIGHTBUTTON**

Remarks   Displays a floating pop-up menu at the specified location and tracks the selection of items on the pop-up menu. A floating pop-up menu can appear anywhere on the screen.

See Also   **CMenu::CreatePopupMenu, CMenu::GetSubMenu, ::TrackPopupMenu**

Data Members

CMenu::m_hMenu

Remarks   Specifies the **HMENU** handle of the Windows menu attached to the **CMenu** object.

class CMetaFileDC : public CDC

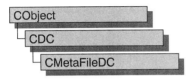

A Windows metafile contains a sequence of graphics device interface (GDI) commands that you can replay to create a desired image or text.

To implement a Windows metafile, first create a **CMetaFileDC** object. Invoke the **CMetaFileDC** constructor, then call the **Create** member function, which creates a Windows metafile device context and attaches it to the **CMetaFileDC** object.

Next send the **CMetaFileDC** object the sequence of **CDC** GDI commands that you intend for it to replay. Only those GDI commands that create output, such as **MoveTo** and **LineTo**, may be used.

After you have sent the desired commands to the metafile, call the **Close** member function, which closes the metafile device contexts and returns a metafile handle. Then dispose of the **CMetaFileDC** object.

CDC::PlayMetaFile can then use the metafile handle to play the metafile repeatedly. The metafile can also be manipulated by Windows functions such as **CopyMetaFile**, which copies a metafile to disk.

When the metafile is no longer needed, delete it from memory with the **DeleteMetaFile**Windows function.

You may also implement the **CMetaFileDC** object so that it can handle both output calls and attribute GDI calls such as **GetTextExtent**. Such a metafile is more flexible and can more easily reuse general GDI code, which often consists of a mix of output and attribute calls. The **CMetaFileDC** class inherits two device contexts, **m_hDC** and **m_hAttribDC**, from **CDC**. The **m_hDC** device context handles all **CDC** GDI output calls and the **m_hAttribDC** device context handles all **CDC** GDI attribute calls. Normally, these two device contexts refer to the same device. In the case of **CMetaFileDC**, the attribute DC is set to **NULL** by default. Create a second device context that points to the screen, a printer, or device other than a metafile, then call the **SetAttribDC** member function to associate the new device context with **m_hAttribDC**. GDI calls for information will now be directed to the new **m_hAttribDC**. Output GDI calls will go to **m_hDC**, which represents the metafile.

#include <afxext.h>

See Also	CDC

Construction

CMetaFileDC	Constructs a **CMetaFileDC** object.

Initialization

Create	Creates the Windows metafile device context and attaches it to the **CMetaFileDC** object.
CreateEnhanced	Creates a metafile device context for an enhanced-format metafile.

Operations

Close	Closes the device context and creates a metafile handle.
CloseEnhanced	Closes an enhanced-metafile device context and creates an enhanced-metafile handle.

Member Functions

CMetaFileDC::Close

HMETAFILE Close( );

Return Value   A valid **HMETAFILE** if the function is successful; otherwise **NULL**.

Remarks   Closes the metafile device context and creates a Windows metafile handle that can be used to play the metafile by using the **CDC::PlayMetaFile** member function. The Windows metafile handle can also be used to manipulate the metafile with Windows functions such as **CopyMetaFile**.

Delete the metafile after use by calling the Windows **DeleteMetaFile** function.

See Also   CDC::PlayMetaFile, ::CloseMetaFile, ::GetMetaFileBits, ::CopyMetaFile, ::DeleteMetaFile

CMetaFileDC::CloseEnhanced

HENHMETAFILE CloseEnhanced( );

Return Value   A handle of an enhanced metafile, if successful; otherwise **NULL**.

Remarks   Closes an enhanced-metafile device context and returns a handle that identifies an enhanced-format metafile. An application can use the enhanced-metafile handle returned by this function to perform the following tasks:

- Display a picture stored in an enhanced metafile
- Create copies of the enhanced metafile
- Enumerate, edit, or copy individual records in the enhanced metafile
- Retrieve an optional description of the metafile contents from the enhanced-metafile header
- Retrieve a copy of the enhanced-metafile header
- Retrieve a binary copy of the enhanced metafile
- Enumerate the colors in the optional palette
- Convert an enhanced-format metafile into a Windows-format metafile

When the application no longer needs the enhanced metafile handle, it should release the handle by calling the **::DeleteEnhMetaFile** function.

See Also   CDC::PlayMetaFile, CMetaFileDC::CreateEnhanced, ::DeleteEnhMetaFile

CMetaFileDC::CMetaFileDC

CMetaFileDC( );

Remarks   Construct a **CMetaFileDC** object in two steps. First, call **CMetaFileDC**, then call **Create**, which creates the Windows metafile device context and attaches it to the **CMetaFileDC** object.

See Also   CMetaFileDC::Create

CMetaFileDC::Create

BOOL Create(LPCTSTR *lpszFilename* **= NULL);**

Return Value   Nonzero if the function is successful; otherwise 0.

Parameters   *lpszFilename*   Points to a null-terminated character string. Specifies the filename of the metafile to create. If *lpszFilename* is **NULL**, a new in-memory metafile is created.

Remarks   Construct a **CMetaFileDC** object in two steps. First, call the constructor **CMetaFileDC**, then call **Create**, which creates the Windows metafile device context and attaches it to the **CMetaFileDC** object.

See Also   CMetaFileDC::CMetaFileDC, CDC::SetAttribDC, ::CreateMetaFile

CMetaFileDC::CreateEnhanced

> **BOOL CreateEnhanced(CDC*** *pDCRef***, LPCTSTR** *lpszFileName***,**
> **LPCRECT** *lpBounds***, LPCTSTR** *lpszDescription* **);**

Return Value

A handle of the device context for the enhanced metafile, if successful; otherwise **NULL**.

Parameters

pDCRef   Identifies a reference device for the enhanced metafile.

lpszFileName   Points to a null-terminated character string. Specifies the filename for the enhanced metafile to be created. If this parameter is **NULL**, the enhanced metafile is memory based and its contents lost when the object is destroyed or when the **::DeleteEnhMetaFile** function is called.

lpBounds   Points to a **RECT** data structure or a **CRect** object that specifies the dimensions in **HIMETRIC** units (in .01-milimeter increments) of the picture to be stored in the enhanced metafile.

lpszDescription   Points to a zero-terminated string that specifies the name of the application that created the picture, as well as the picture's title.

Remarks

Creates a device context for an enhanced-format metafile. This DC can be used to store a device-independent picture.

Windows uses the reference device identified by the *pDCRef* parameter to record the resolution and units of the device on which a picture originally appeared. If the *pDCRef* parameter is **NULL**, it uses the current display device for reference.

The left and top members of the **RECT** data structure pointed to by the *lpBounds* parameter must be smaller than the right and bottom members, respectively. Points along the edges of the rectangle are included in the picture. If *lpBounds* is **NULL**, the graphics device interface (GDI) computes the dimensions of the smallest rectangle that can enclose the picture drawn by the application. The *lpBounds* parameter should be supplied where possible.

The string pointed to by the *lpszDescription* parameter must contain a null character between the application name and the picture name and must terminate with two null characters —for example, "XYZ Graphics Editor\0Bald Eagle\0\0," where \0 represents the null character. If *lpszDescription* is **NULL**, there is no corresponding entry in the enhanced-metafile header.

Applications use the DC created by this function to store a graphics picture in an enhanced metafile. The handle identifying this DC can be passed to any GDI function.

After an application stores a picture in an enhanced metafile, it can display the picture on any output device by calling the **CDC::PlayMetaFile** function. When displaying the picture, Windows uses the rectangle pointed to by the *lpBounds* parameter and the resolution data from the reference device to position and scale the picture. The device context returned by this function contains the same default attributes associated with any new DC.

Applications must use the **::GetWinMetaFileBits** function to convert an enhanced metafile to the older Windows metafile format.

The filename for the enhanced metafile should use the .EMF extension.

See Also   **CMetaFileDC::CloseEnhanced, CDC::PlayMetaFile, ::CloseEnhMetaFile, ::DeleteEnhMetaFile, ::GetEnhMetaFileDescription, ::GetEnhMetaFileHeader, ::GetWinMetaFileBits, ::PlayEnhMetaFile**

class CMiniFrameWnd : public CFrameWnd

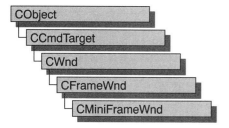

A **CMiniFrameWnd** object represents a half-height frame window typically seen around floating toolbars. These mini-frame windows behave like normal frame windows, except that they do not have minimize/maximize buttons or menus and you only have to single-click on the system menu to dismiss them.

To use a **CMiniFrameWnd** object, first define the object. Then call the **Create** member function to display the mini-frame window.

For more information on how to use **CMiniFrameWnd** objects, see the article "Toolbars: Docking and Floating" in *Programming with the Microsoft Foundation Class Library*.

See Also   **CFrameWnd**

Construction

CMiniFrameWnd	Constructs a **CMiniFrameWnd** object.
Create	Creates a **CMiniFrameWnd** object after construction.

Member Functions

CMiniFrameWnd::CMiniFrameWnd

CMiniFrameWnd( );

Remarks   Constructs a **CMiniFrameWnd** object, but does not create the window. To create the window, call **CMiniFrameWnd::Create**.

See Also   **CFrameWnd**

CMiniFrameWnd::Create

BOOL Create(LPCTSTR *lpClassName*, **LPCTSTR** *lpWindowName*, **DWORD**
dwStyle, **const RECT&** *rect*, **CWnd*** *pParentWnd* = **NULL**, **UINT** *nID* = **0**);

Return Value   Nonzero if successful; otherwise 0.

Parameters   *lpClassName*   Points to a null-terminated character string that names the Windows
class. The class name can be any name registered with the global
AfxRegisterWndClass function. If **NULL**, the window class will be registered
for you by the framework.

lpWindowName   Points to a null-terminated character string that contains the
window name.

dwStyle   Specifies the window style attributes. These may include standard
window styles and one or more of the following special styles:

- **MFS_MOVEFRAME**   Allows the mini-frame window to be moved by
  clicking on any edge of the window, not just the caption.
- **MFS_4THICKFRAME**   Disables resizing of the mini-frame window.
- **MFS_SYNCACTIVE**   Synchronizes the activation of the mini-frame
  window to the activation of its parent window.
- **MFS_THICKFRAME**   Allows the mini-frame window to be sized as
  small as its non-client area.

See **CWnd::Create** for a description of possible window style values. The
typical combination used for mini-frame windows is
WS_POPUP|WS_CAPTION|WS_SYSMENU.

rect   A **RECT** structure specifying the desired dimensions of the window.

pParentWnd   Points to the parent window. Use **NULL** for top-level windows.

nID   If the mini-frame window is created as a child window, this is the identifier
of the child control; otherwise 0.

Remarks   Creates the Windows mini-frame window and attaches it to the **CMiniFrameWnd**
object. **Create** initializes the window's class name and window name and registers
default values for its style and parent.

See Also   **CFrameWnd::Create**, **CWnd::Create**, **CWnd::CreateEx**, **CFrameWnd**

class CMultiDocTemplate : public CDocTemplate

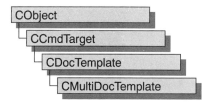

The **CMultiDocTemplate** class defines a document template that implements the multiple document interface (MDI). An MDI application uses the main frame window as a workspace in which the user can open zero or more document frame windows, each of which displays a document. For a more detailed description of the MDI, see *The Windows Interface: An Application Design Guide*.

A document template defines the relationships among three types of classes:

- A document class, which you derive from **CDocument**.

- A view class, which displays data from the document class listed above. You can derive this class from **CView**, **CScrollView**, **CFormView**, or **CEditView**. (You can also use **CEditView** directly.)

- A frame window class, which contains the view. For an MDI document template, you can derive this class from **CMDIChildWnd**, or, if you don't need to customize the behavior of the document frame windows, you can use **CMDIChildWnd** directly without deriving your own class.

An MDI application can support more than one type of document, and documents of different types can be open at the same time. Your application has one document template for each document type that it supports. For example, if your MDI application supports both spreadsheets and text documents, the application has two **CMultiDocTemplate** objects.

The application uses the document template(s) when the user creates a new document. If the application supports more than one type of document, then the framework gets the names of the supported document types from the document templates and displays them in a list in the File New dialog box. Once the user has selected a document type, the application creates a document object, a frame window object, and a view object and attaches them to each other.

You do not need to call any member functions of **CMultiDocTemplate** except the constructor. The framework handles **CMultiDocTemplate** objects internally.

include# **<afxwin.h>**

See Also   **CDocTemplate**, **CDocument**, **CMDIChildWnd**, **CSingleDocTemplate**, **CView**, **CWinApp**

Construction

CMultiDocTemplate   Constructs a **CMultiDocTemplate** object.

Member Functions

CMultiDocTemplate::CMultiDocTemplate

CMultiDocTemplate(UINT *nIDResource*, **CRuntimeClass*** *pDocClass*, **CRuntimeClass*** *pFrameClass*, **CRuntimeClass*** *pViewClass* **);**

Parameters   *nIDResource*   Specifies the ID of the resources used with the document type. This may include menu, icon, accelerator table, and string resources.

The string resource consists of up to seven substrings separated by the '\n' character (the '\n' character is needed as a place holder if a substring is not included; however, trailing '\n' characters are not necessary); these substrings describe the document type. For information on the substrings, see **CDocTemplate::GetDocString**. This string resource is found in the application's resource file. For example:

```
// MYCALC.RC
STRINGTABLE PRELOAD DISCARDABLE
BEGIN
    IDR_SHEETTYPE "\nSheet\nWorksheet\nWorksheets (*.myc)\n.myc\n
MyCalcSheet\nMyCalc Worksheet"
END
```

Note that the string begins with a '\n' character; this is because the first substring is not used for MDI applications and so is not included. You can edit this string using the string editor; the entire string appears as a single entry in the String Editor, not as seven separate entries.

For more information about these resource types, see the *Visual C++ User's Guide*.

pDocClass   Points to the **CRuntimeClass** object of the document class. This class is a **CDocument**-derived class you define to represent your documents.

pFrameClass   Points to the **CRuntimeClass** object of the frame-window class. This class can be a **CMDIChildWnd**-derived class, or it can be **CMDIChildWnd** itself if you want default behavior for your document frame windows.

pViewClass   Points to the **CRuntimeClass** object of the view class. This class is a **CView**-derived class you define to display your documents.

Remarks   Constructs a **CMultiDocTemplate** object. Dynamically allocate one **CMultiDocTemplate** object for each document type that your application supports and pass each one to **CWinApp::AddDocTemplate** from the InitInstance member function of your application class.

See Also   **CDocTemplate::GetDocString**, **CWinApp::AddDocTemplate**, **CWinApp::InitInstance**, **CRuntimeClass**

Example
```
BOOL CMyApp::InitInstance()
{
        // ...
        // Establish all of the document types
        // supported by the application

        AddDocTemplate( new CMultiDocTemplate( IDR_SHEETTYPE,
                            RUNTIME_CLASS( CSheetDoc ),
                            RUNTIME_CLASS( CMDIChildWnd ),
                            RUNTIME_CLASS( CSheetView ) ) );

        AddDocTemplate( new CMultiDocTemplate( IDR_NOTETYPE,
                            RUNTIME_CLASS( CNoteDoc ),
                            RUNTIME_CLASS( CMDIChildWnd ),
                            RUNTIME_CLASS( CNoteView ) ) );
        // ...
}
```

class CNotSupportedException : public CException

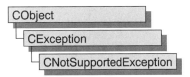

A **CNotSupportedException** object represents an exception that is the result of a request for an unsupported feature. No further qualification is necessary or possible.

#include <afx.h>

Construction
CNotSupportedException   Constructs a **CNotSupportedException** object.

Member Functions

CNotSupportedException::CNotSupportedException

CNotSupportedException( );

Remarks   Constructs a **CNotSupportedException** object. Do not use this constructor directly, but rather call the global function **AfxThrowNotSupportedException**. For more information about exception processing, see the article "Exceptions" in *Programming with the Microsoft Foundation Class Library*.

See Also   **AfxThrowNotSupportedException**

class CObArray : public CObject

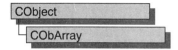

The **CObArray** class supports arrays of **CObject** pointers. These object arrays are similar to C arrays, but they can dynamically shrink and grow as necessary. Array indexes always start at position 0. You can decide whether to fix the upper bound or allow the array to expand when you add elements past the current bound. Memory is allocated contiguously to the upper bound, even if some elements are null.

The elements of a **CObArray** object must fit in one 64K segment together with approximately 100 allocation overhead bytes. If **CObject** pointers are 16-bit near pointers (as they are in the small and medium memory models), then an array size limit is about 32,000 elements; but because there is only one data segment, the objects themselves will probably exhaust memory before the array does.

As with a C array, the access time for a **CObArray** indexed element is constant and is independent of the array size. **CObArray** incorporates the **IMPLEMENT_SERIAL** macro to support serialization and dumping of its elements. If an array of **CObject** pointers is stored to an archive, either with the overloaded insertion operator or with the **Serialize** member function, each **CObject** element is, in turn, serialized along with its array index. If you need a dump of individual **CObject** elements in an array, you must set the depth of the **CDumpContext** object to 1 or greater. When a **CObArray** object is deleted, or when its elements are removed, only the **CObject** pointers are removed, not the objects they reference.

Note Before using an array, use **SetSize** to establish its size and allocate memory for it. If you do not use **SetSize**, adding elements to your array causes it to be frequently reallocated and copied. Frequent reallocation and copying are inefficient and can fragment memory.

Array class derivation is similar to list derivation. For details on the derivation of a special-purpose list class, see the article "Collections" in *Programming with the Microsoft Foundation Class Library*.

Note You must use the **IMPLEMENT_SERIAL** macro in the implementation of your derived class if you intend to serialize the array.

#include <afxcoll.h>

See Also   CStringArray, CPtrArray, CByteArray, CWordArray, CDWordArray

Construction
CObArray	Constructs an empty array for **CObject** pointers.

Bounds
GetSize	Gets the number of elements in this array.
GetUpperBound	Returns the largest valid index.
SetSize	Sets the number of elements to be contained in this array.

Operations
FreeExtra	Frees all unused memory above the current upper bound.
RemoveAll	Removes all the elements from this array.

Element Access
GetAt	Returns the value at a given index.
SetAt	Sets the value for a given index; array not allowed to grow.
ElementAt	Returns a temporary reference to the element pointer within the array.

Growing the Array
SetAtGrow	Sets the value for a given index; grows the array if necessary.
Add	Adds an element to the end of the array; grows the array if necessary.

Insertion/Removal
InsertAt	Inserts an element (or all the elements in another array) at a specified index.
RemoveAt	Removes an element at a specific index.

Operators
operator []	Sets or gets the element at the specified index.

Member Functions

CObArray::Add

int Add(CObject* *newElement*)
    throw(CMemoryException);

Return Value   The index of the added element.

Parameters   *newElement*   The **CObject** pointer to be added to this array.

Remarks   Adds a new element to the end of an array, growing the array by 1. If **SetSize** has been used with an *nGrowBy* value greater than 1, then extra memory may be allocated. However, the upper bound will increase by only 1.

See Also   **CObArray::SetAt**, **CObArray::SetAtGrow**, **CObArray::InsertAt**, **CObArray::operator [ ]**

Example

```
CObArray array;

array.Add( new CAge( 21 ) ); // Element 0
array.Add( new CAge( 40 ) ); // Element 1
#ifdef _DEBUG
    afxDump.SetDepth( 1 );
    afxDump << "Add example: " << &array << "\n";
#endif
```

The results from this program are as follows:

```
Add example: A CObArray with 2 elements
    [0] = a CAge at $442A 21
    [1] = a CAge at $4468 40
```

CObArray::CObArray

CObArray( );

Remarks   Constructs an empty **CObject** pointer array. The array grows one element at a time.

See Also   **CObList::CObList**

Example   See the **CObList** constructor for a listing of the CAge class used in all collection examples.

CObArray::ElementAt

CObject*& ElementAt(int *nIndex*);

Return Value   A reference to a **CObject** pointer.

Parameters   *nIndex*   An integer index that is greater than or equal to 0 and less than or equal to the value returned by **GetUpperBound**.

Remarks   Returns a temporary reference to the element pointer within the array. It is used to implement the left-side assignment operator for arrays. Note that this is an advanced function that should be used only to implement special array operators.

See Also   **CObArray::operator [ ]**

CObArray::FreeExtra

void FreeExtra( );

Remarks   Frees any extra memory that was allocated while the array was grown. This function has no effect on the size or upper bound of the array.

CObArray::GetAt

CObject* GetAt(int *nIndex*) const;

Return Value   The **CObject** pointer element currently at this index; **NULL** if no element is stored at the index.

Parameters   *nIndex*   An integer index that is greater than or equal to 0 and less than or equal to the value returned by **GetUpperBound**.

Remarks   Returns the array element at the specified index.

See Also   **CObArray::SetAt, CObArray::operator [ ]**

Example
```
CObArray array;

array.Add( new CAge( 21 ) ); // Element 0
array.Add( new CAge( 40 ) ); // Element 1
ASSERT( *(CAge*) array.GetAt( 0 ) == CAge( 21 ) );
```

CObArray::GetSize

int GetSize( ) const;

Remarks   Returns the size of the array. Since indexes are zero-based, the size is 1 greater than the largest index.

See Also   **CObArray::GetUpperBound, CObArray::SetSize**

CObArray::GetUpperBound

int GetUpperBound( ) const;

Remarks   Returns the current upper bound of this array. Because array indexes are zero-based, this function returns a value 1 less than **GetSize**. The condition **GetUpperBound( )** = −1 indicates that the array contains no elements.

See Also   **CObArray::GetSize, CObArray::SetSize**

Example
```
CObArray array;

array.Add( new CAge( 21 ) ); // Element 0
array.Add( new CAge( 40 ) ); // Element 1
ASSERT( array.GetUpperBound() == 1 ); // Largest index
```

CObArray::InsertAt

void InsertAt(int *nIndex*, **CObject*** *newElement*, **int** *nCount* = **1**)
   throw(CMemoryException);

void InsertAt(int *nStartIndex*, **CObArray*** *pNewArray*)
   throw(CMemoryException);

Parameters   *nIndex*   An integer index that may be greater than the value returned by
   GetUpperBound.

newElement   The **CObject** pointer to be placed in this array. A *newElement* of
   value **NULL** is allowed.

nCount   The number of times this element should be inserted (defaults to 1).

nStartIndex   An integer index that may be greater than the value returned by
   GetUpperBound.

pNewArray   Another array that contains elements to be added to this array.

Remarks   The first version of **InsertAt** inserts one element (or multiple copies of an element)
at a specified index in an array. In the process, it shifts up (by incrementing the
index) the existing element at this index, and it shifts up all the elements above it.
The second version inserts all the elements from another **CObArray** collection,
starting at the *nStartIndex* position. The **SetAt** function, in contrast, replaces one
specified array element and does not shift any elements.

See Also   **CObArray::SetAt**, **CObArray::RemoveAt**

Example
```
CObArray array;

array.Add( new CAge( 21 ) ); // Element 0
array.Add( new CAge( 40 ) ); // Element 1 (will become 2).
array.InsertAt( 1, new CAge( 30 ) );  // New element 1
#ifdef _DEBUG
    afxDump.SetDepth( 1 );
    afxDump << "InsertAt example: " << &array << "\n";
#endif
```

The results from this program are as follows:

```
InsertAt example: A CObArray with 3 elements
    [0] = a CAge at $45C8 21
    [1] = a CAge at $4646 30
    [2] = a CAge at $4606 40
```

CObArray::RemoveAll

void RemoveAll( );

Remarks

Removes all the pointers from this array but does not actually delete the **CObject** objects. If the array is already empty, the function still works. The **RemoveAll** function frees all memory used for pointer storage.

Example

```
CObArray array;
CAge* pa1;
CAge* pa2;

array.Add( pa1 = new CAge( 21 ) ); // Element 0
array.Add( pa2 = new CAge( 40 ) ); // Element 1
ASSERT( array.GetSize() == 2 );
array.RemoveAll(); // Pointers removed but objects not deleted.
ASSERT( array.GetSize() == 0 );
delete pa1;
delete pa2;   // Cleans up memory.
```

CObArray::RemoveAt

void RemoveAt(int *nIndex*, int *nCount* = 1);

Parameters

nIndex   An integer index that is greater than or equal to 0 and less than or equal to the value returned by **GetUpperBound**.

nCount   The number of elements to remove.

Remarks

Removes one or more elements starting at a specified index in an array. In the process, it shifts down all the elements above the removed element(s). It decrements the upper bound of the array but does not free memory. If you try to remove more elements than are contained in the array above the removal point, then the Debug version of the library asserts. The **RemoveAt** function removes the **CObject** pointer from the array, but it does not delete the object itself.

See Also

CObArray::SetAt, CObArray::SetAtGrow, CObArray::InsertAt

Example
```
CObArray array;
CObject* pa;

array.Add( new CAge( 21 ) ); // Element 0
array.Add( new CAge( 40 ) ); // Element 1
if( ( pa = array.GetAt( 0 ) ) != NULL )
{
    array.RemoveAt( 0 );  // Element 1 moves to 0.
    delete pa; // Delete the original element at 0.
}
#ifdef _DEBUG
    afxDump.SetDepth( 1 );
    afxDump << "RemoveAt example: " << &array << "\n";
#endif
```

The results from this program are as follows:

```
RemoveAt example: A CObArray with 1 elements
    [0] = a CAge at $4606 40
```

CObArray::SetAt

void SetAt(int *nIndex,* **CObject*** *newElement* **);**

Parameters   *nIndex*   An integer index that is greater than or equal to 0 and less than or equal to the value returned by **GetUpperBound**.

newElement   The object pointer to be inserted in this array. A **NULL** value is allowed.

Remarks   Sets the array element at the specified index. **SetAt** will not cause the array to grow. Use **SetAtGrow** if you want the array to grow automatically.

You must ensure that your index value represents a valid position in the array. If it is out of bounds, then the Debug version of the library asserts.

See Also   **CObArray::GetAt, CObArray::SetAtGrow, CObArray::ElementAt, CObArray::operator []**

Example

```
CObArray array;
CObject* pa;

array.Add( new CAge( 21 ) ); // Element 0
array.Add( new CAge( 40 ) ); // Element 1
if( ( pa = array.GetAt( 0 ) ) != NULL )
{
    array.SetAt( 0, new CAge( 30 ) );  // Replace element 0.
    delete pa; // Delete the original element at 0.
}
#ifdef _DEBUG
    afxDump.SetDepth( 1 );
    afxDump << "SetAt example: " << &array << "\n";
#endif
```

The results from this program are as follows:

```
SetAt example: A CObArray with 2 elements
    [0] = a CAge at $47E0 30
    [1] = a CAge at $47A0 40
```

CObArray::SetAtGrow

void SetAtGrow(int *nIndex,* **CObject*** *newElement* **)**
    throw(CMemoryException);

Parameters   *nIndex*   An integer index that is greater than or equal to 0.

    newElement   The object pointer to be added to this array. A **NULL** value is
    allowed.

Remarks   Sets the array element at the specified index. The array grows automatically if
necessary (that is, the upper bound is adjusted to accommodate the new element).

See Also   **CObArray::GetAt, CObArray::SetAt, CObArray::ElementAt,
CObArray::operator [ ]**

Example

```
CObArray array;

array.Add( new CAge( 21 ) ); // Element 0
array.Add( new CAge( 40 ) ); // Element 1
array.SetAtGrow( 3, new CAge( 65 ) ); // Element 2 deliberately
                                      // skipped.
#ifdef _DEBUG
    afxDump.SetDepth( 1 );
    afxDump << "SetAtGrow example: " << &array << "\n";
#endif
```

The results from this program are as follows:

```
SetAtGrow example: A CObArray with 4 elements
    [0] = a CAge at $47C0 21
    [1] = a CAge at $4800 40
    [2] = NULL
    [3] = a CAge at $4840 65
```

CObArray::SetSize

void SetSize(int *nNewSize,* **int** *nGrowBy* **= –1)**
   throw(CMemoryException);

Parameters

nNewSize   The new array size (number of elements). Must be greater than or equal to 0.

nGrowBy   The minimum number of element slots to allocate if a size increase is necessary.

Remarks

Establishes the size of an empty or existing array; allocates memory if necessary. If the new size is smaller than the old size, then the array is truncated and all unused memory is released. For efficiency, call **SetSize** to set the size of the array before using it. This prevents the need to reallocate and copy the array each time an item is added.

The *nGrowBy* parameter affects internal memory allocation while the array is growing. Its use never affects the array size as reported by **GetSize** and **GetUpperBound**.

Operators

CObArray::operator [ ]

CObject*& operator [ ](int *nIndex* **);**

CObject* operator [ ](int *nIndex* **) const;**

Remarks

These subscript operators are a convenient substitute for the **SetAt** and **GetAt** functions. The first operator, called for arrays that are not **const**, may be used on either the right (r-value) or the left (l-value) of an assignment statement. The second, called for **const** arrays, may be used only on the right. The Debug version of the library asserts if the subscript (either on the left or right side of an assignment statement) is out of bounds.

See Also

CObArray::GetAt, **CObArray::SetAt**

Example

```
CObArray array;
CAge* pa;

array.Add( new CAge( 21 ) ); // Element 0
array.Add( new CAge( 40 ) ); // Element 1
pa = (CAge*)array[0]; // Get element 0
ASSERT( *pa == CAge( 21 ) ); // Get element 0
array[0] = new CAge( 30 ); // Replace element 0
delete pa;
ASSERT( *(CAge*) array[0] == CAge( 30 ) ); // Get new element 0
```

class CObject

CObject is the principal base class for the Microsoft Foundation Class Library. It serves as the root not only for library classes such as **CFile** and **CObList**, but also for the classes that you write. **CObject** provides basic services, including

- Serialization support
- Run-time class information
- Object diagnostic output
- Compatibility with collection classes

Note that **CObject** does not support multiple inheritance. Your derived classes can have only one **CObject** base class, and that **CObject** must be leftmost in the hierarchy. It is permissible, however, to have structures and non-**CObject**-derived classes in right-hand multiple-inheritance branches.

You will realize major benefits from **CObject** derivation if you use some of the optional macros in your class implementation and declarations. The first-level macros, **DECLARE_DYNAMIC** and **IMPLEMENT_DYNAMIC**, permit run-time access to the class name and its position in the hierarchy. This, in turn, allows meaningful diagnostic dumping. The second-level macros, **DECLARE_SERIAL** and **IMPLEMENT_SERIAL**, include all the functionality of the first-level macros, and they enable an object to be "serialized" to and from an "archive."

For important information about deriving Microsoft Foundation classes and Visual C++ classes in general, see the article "CObject Class" in *Programming with the Microsoft Foundation Class Library*.

#include <afx.h>

Construction

CObject	Default constructor.
CObject	Copy constructor.
operator new	Special **new** operator.
operator delete	Special **delete** operator.
operator =	Assignment operator.

Diagnostics

AssertValid	Validates this object's integrity.
Dump	Produces a diagnostic dump of this object.

Serialization

IsSerializable   Tests to see whether this object can be serialized.

Serialize   Loads or stores an object from/to an archive.

Miscellaneous

GetRuntimeClass   Returns the **CRuntimeClass** structure corresponding to this object's class.

IsKindOf   Tests this object's relationship to a given class.

Member Functions

CObject::AssertValid

virtual void AssertValid( ) const;

Remarks   **AssertValid** performs a validity check on this object by checking its internal state. In the Debug version of the library, **AssertValid** may assert and thus terminate the program with a message that lists the line number and filename where the assertion failed. When you write your own class, you should override the **AssertValid** function to provide diagnostic services for yourself and other users of your class. The overridden **AssertValid** usually calls the **AssertValid** function of its base class before checking data members unique to the derived class.

Because **AssertValid** is a **const** function, you are not permitted to change the object state during the test. Your own derived class **AssertValid** functions should not throw exceptions but rather should assert whether they detect invalid object data. The definition of "validity" depends on the object's class. As a rule, the function should perform a "shallow check." That is, if an object contains pointers to other objects, it should check to see whether the pointers are not null, but it should not perform validity testing on the objects referred to by the pointers.

Example   See **CObList::CObList** for a listing of the CAge class used in all **CObject** examples.

```
void CAge::AssertValid() const
{
    CObject::AssertValid();
    ASSERT( m_years > 0 );
    ASSERT( m_years < 105 );
}
```

CObject::CObject

Protected→
CObject( );
  END Protected

Private →
CObject(constCObject& *objectSrc* **);**
  END Private

Parameters   *objectSrc*   A reference to another **CObject**

Remarks   These functions are the standard **CObject** constructors. The default version is automatically called by the constructor of your derived class. If your class is serializable (it incorporates the **IMPLEMENT_SERIAL** macro), then you must have a default constructor (a constructor with no arguments) in your class declaration. If you do not need a default constructor, declare a private or protected "empty" constructor. For more information, see the article "CObject Class" in *Programming with the Microsoft Foundation Class Library*. The standard Visual C++ default class copy constructor does a member-by-member copy. The presence of the private **CObject** copy constructor guarantees a compiler error message if the copy constructor of your class is needed but not available. You must therefore provide a copy constructor if your class requires this capability.

CObject::Dump

virtual void Dump(CDumpContext& *dc* **) const;**

Parameters   *dc*   The diagnostic dump context for dumping, usually **afxDump**.

Remarks   Dumps the contents of your object to a **CDumpContext** object. When you write your own class, you should override the **Dump** function to provide diagnostic services for yourself and other users of your class. The overridden **Dump** usually calls the **Dump** function of its base class before printing data members unique to the derived class. **CObject::Dump** prints the class name if your class uses the **IMPLEMENT_DYNAMIC** or **IMPLEMENT_SERIAL** macro.

Note Your **Dump** function should not print a newline character at the end of its output.

Dump calls make sense only in the Debug version of the Microsoft Foundation Class Library. You should bracket calls, function declarations, and function implementations with **#ifdef _DEBUG/#endif** statements for conditional compilation. Since **Dump** is a **const** function, you are not permitted to change the object state during the dump. The CDumpContext insertion (**<<**) operator calls **Dump** when a **CObject** pointer is inserted. **Dump** permits only "acyclic" dumping of objects. You can dump a list of objects, for example, but if one of the objects is the list itself, you will eventually overflow the stack.

Example

```
void CAge::Dump( CDumpContext &dc ) const
{
CObject::Dump( dc );
dc << "Age = " << m_years;
}
```

CObject::GetRuntimeClass

virtual CRuntimeClass* GetRuntimeClass( ) const;

Return Value   A pointer to the **CRuntimeClass** structure corresponding to this object's class; never **NULL**.

Remarks   There is one **CRuntimeClass** structure for each **CObject**-derived class. The structure members are as follows:

- **const char* m_pszClassName**   A null-terminated string containing the ASCII class name.
- **int m_nObjectSize**   The actual size of the object. If the object has data members that point to allocated memory, the size of that memory is not included.
- **WORD m_wSchema**   The schema number (–1 for nonserializable classes). See the **IMPLEMENT_SERIAL** macro for a description of schema number.
- **void (*m_pfnConstruct)(void* p)**   A pointer to the default constructor of your class (valid only if the class is serializable).
- **CRuntimeClass* m_pBaseClass**   A pointer to the **CRuntimeClass** structure that corresponds to the base class.

This function requires use of the **IMPLEMENT_DYNAMIC** or **IMPLEMENT_SERIAL** macros in the class implementation. You will get incorrect results otherwise.

See Also   **CObject::IsKindOf, RUNTIME_CLASS Macro**

Example

```
CAge a(21);
CRuntimeClass* prt = a.GetRuntimeClass();
ASSERT( strcmp( prt->m_pszClassName, "CAge" )  == 0 );
```

CObject::IsKindOf

BOOL IsKindOf(const CRuntimeClass* *pClass*) const;

Return Value   Nonzero if the object corresponds to the class; otherwise 0.

Parameters	*pClass* A pointer to a **CRuntimeClass** structure associated with your **CObject**-derived class.
Remarks	Tests *pClass* to see if (1) it is an object of the specified class or (2) it is an object of a class derived from the specified class. This function works only for classes declared with the **DECLARE_DYNAMIC** or **DECLARE_SERIAL** macros. Do not use this function extensively because it defeats the Visual C++ polymorphism feature. Use virtual functions instead.
See Also	**CObject::GetRuntimeClass, RUNTIME_CLASS Macro**
| **Example** | ```
CAge a(21); // Must use IMPLEMENT_DYNAMIC or IMPLEMENT_SERIAL
ASSERT( a.IsKindOf( RUNTIME_CLASS( CAge ) ) );
ASSERT( a.IsKindOf( RUNTIME_CLASS( CObject ) ) );
``` |

CObject::IsSerializable

BOOL IsSerializable( ) const;

Return Value	Nonzero if this object can be serialized; otherwise 0.
Remarks	Tests whether this object is eligible for serialization. For a class to be serializable, its declaration must contain the **DECLARE_SERIAL** macro, and the implementation must contain the **IMPLEMENT_SERIAL** macro.

Note Do not override this function.

See Also	**CObject::Serialize**
| **Example** | ```
CAge a(21);
ASSERT( a.IsSerializable() );
``` |

CObject::Serialize

virtual void Serialize(CArchive& *ar* **)**
    throw(CMemoryException, CArchiveException, CFileException);

Parameters	*ar* A **CArchive** object to serialize to or from.
Remarks	Reads or writes this object from or to an archive. You must override **Serialize** for each class that you intend to serialize. The overridden **Serialize** must first call the **Serialize** function of its base class. You must also use the **DECLARE_SERIAL** macro in your class declaration, and you must use the **IMPLEMENT_SERIAL** macro in the implementation.
	Use **CArchive::IsLoading** or **CArchive::IsStoring** to determine whether the archive is loading or storing. **Serialize** is called by **CArchive::ReadObject** and **CArchive::WriteObject**. These functions are associated with the **CArchive**

insertion operator (**<<**) and extraction operator (**>>**). For serialization examples, see the article "Serialization: CObject Persistence" in *Programming with the Microsoft Foundation Class Library*.

Example

```
void CAge::Serialize( CArchive& ar )
 {
CObject::Serialize( ar );
    if( ar.IsStoring() )
    ar << m_years;
    else
    ar >> m_years;
 }
```

Operators

CObject::operator =

Private →
void operator =(const CObject& *src* **);**
END Private

Remarks

The standard Visual C++ default class assignment behavior is a member-by-member copy. The presence of this private assignment operator guarantees a compiler error message if you assign without the overridden operator. You must therefore provide an assignment operator in your derived class if you intend to assign objects of your derived class.

CObject::operator delete

void operator delete(void* *p* **);**

Remarks

For the Release version of the library, operator **delete** simply frees the memory allocated by operator **new**. In the Debug version, operator **delete** participates in an allocation-monitoring scheme designed to detect memory leaks. If you override operators **new** and **delete**, you forfeit the diagnostic capability.

See Also

CObject::operator new

CObject::operator new

void* operator new(size_t *nSize* **)**
    throw(CMemoryException);

void* operator new(size_t *nSize***, LPCSTR** *lpszFileName***, int** *nLine* **)**
    throw(CMemoryException);

Remarks   For the Release version of the library, operator **new** performs an optimal memory allocation in a manner similar to **malloc**. In the Debug version, operator **new** participates in an allocation-monitoring scheme designed to detect memory leaks. If you use the code line

```
#define new DEBUG_NEW
```

before any of your implementations in a .CPP file, then the second version of **new** will be used, storing the filename and line number in the allocated block for later reporting. You do not have to worry about supplying the extra parameters; a macro takes care of that for you. Even if you do not use **DEBUG_NEW** in Debug mode, you still get leak detection, but without the source-file line-number reporting described above.

Note   If you override this operator, you must also override **delete**. Do not use the standard library **_new_handler** function.

See Also   **CObject::operator delete**

class CObList : public CObject

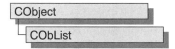

The **CObList** class supports ordered lists of nonunique **CObject** pointers accessible sequentially or by pointer value. **CObList** lists behave like doubly-linked lists. A variable of type **POSITION** is a key for the list. You can use a **POSITION** variable both as an iterator to traverse a list sequentially and as a bookmark to hold a place. A position is not the same as an index, however.

Element insertion is very fast at the list head, at the tail, and at a known **POSITION**. A sequential search is necessary to look up an element by value or index. This search can be slow if the list is long.

CObList incorporates the **IMPLEMENT_SERIAL** macro to support serialization and dumping of its elements. If a list of **CObject** pointers is stored to an archive, either with an overloaded insertion operator or with the **Serialize** member function, each **CObject** element is serialized in turn.

If you need a dump of individual **CObject** elements in the list, you must set the depth of the dump context to 1 or greater. When a **CObList** object is deleted, or when its elements are removed, only the **CObject** pointers are removed, not the objects they reference.

You can derive your own classes from **CObList**. Your new list class, designed to hold pointers to objects derived from **CObject**, adds new data members and new member functions. Note that the resulting list is not strictly type safe, because it allows insertion of any **CObject** pointer.

Note You must use the **IMPLEMENT_SERIAL** macro in the implementation of your derived class if you intend to serialize the list.

#include <afxcoll.h>

See Also   **CStringList, CPtrList**

Construction
CObList   Constructs an empty list for **CObject** pointers.

Head/Tail Access

GetHead	Returns the head element of the list (cannot be empty).
GetTail	Returns the tail element of the list (cannot be empty).

Operations

RemoveHead	Removes the element from the head of the list.
RemoveTail	Removes the element from the tail of the list.
AddHead	Adds an element (or all the elements in another list) to the head of the list (makes a new head).
AddTail	Adds an element (or all the elements in another list) to the tail of the list (makes a new tail).
RemoveAll	Removes all the elements from this list.

Iteration

GetHeadPosition	Returns the position of the head element of the list.
GetTailPosition	Returns the position of the tail element of the list.
GetNext	Gets the next element for iterating.
GetPrev	Gets the previous element for iterating.

Retrieval/Modification

GetAt	Gets the element at a given position.
SetAt	Sets the element at a given position.
RemoveAt	Removes an element from this list, specified by position.

Insertion

InsertBefore	Inserts a new element before a given position.
InsertAfter	Inserts a new element after a given position.

Searching

Find	Gets the position of an element specified by pointer value.
FindIndex	Gets the position of an element specified by a zero-based index.

Status

GetCount	Returns the number of elements in this list.
IsEmpty	Tests for the empty list condition (no elements).

Member Functions

CObList::AddHead

POSITION AddHead(CObject* *newElement* **)**
   throw(CMemoryException);

void AddHead(CObList* *pNewList* **)**
   throw(CMemoryException);

Return Value

The first version returns the **POSITION** value of the newly inserted element.

Parameters

newElement   The **CObject** pointer to be added to this list.

pNewList   A pointer to another **CObList** list. The elements in *pNewList* will be added to this list.

Remarks

Adds a new element or list of elements to the head of this list. The list may be empty before the operation.

See Also

CObList::GetHead, CObList::RemoveHead

Example

```
    CObList list;
    list.AddHead( new CAge( 21 ) ); // 21 is now at head.
    list.AddHead( new CAge( 40 ) ); // 40 replaces 21 at head.
#ifdef _DEBUG
    afxDump.SetDepth( 1 );
    afxDump << "AddHead example: " << &list << "\n";
#endif
```

The results from this program are as follows:

```
AddHead example: A CObList with 2 elements
    a CAge at $44A8 40
    a CAge at $442A 21
```

CObList::AddTail

POSITION AddTail(CObject* *newElement* **)**
   throw(CMemoryException);

void AddTail(CObList* *pNewList* **)**
   throw(CMemoryException);

Return Value

The first version returns the **POSITION** value of the newly inserted element.

Parameters   *newElement*   The **CObject** pointer to be added to this list.

pNewList   A pointer to another **CObList** list. The elements in *pNewList* will be added to this list.

Remarks   Adds a new element or list of elements to the tail of this list. The list may be empty before the operation.

See Also   **CObList::GetTail**, **CObList::RemoveTail**

Example
```
      CObList list;
      list.AddTail( new CAge( 21 ) );
      list.AddTail( new CAge( 40 ) ); // List now contains (21, 40).
#ifdef _DEBUG
      afxDump.SetDepth( 1 );
      afxDump << "AddTail example: " << &list << "\n";
#endif
```

The results from this program are as follows:

```
AddTail example: A CObList with 2 elements
     a CAge at $444A 21
     a CAge at $4526 40
```

CObList::CObList

CObList(int *nBlockSize* **= 10);**

Parameters   *nBlockSize*   The memory-allocation granularity for extending the list.

Remarks   Constructs an empty **CObject** pointer list. As the list grows, memory is allocated in units of *nBlockSize* entries. If a memory allocation fails, a **CMemoryException** is thrown.

Example   Below is a listing of the **CObject**-derived class CAge used in all the collection examples:

```
// Simple CObject-derived class for CObList examples
class CAge : public CObject
{
    DECLARE_SERIAL( CAge )
private:
    int m_years;
public:
    CAge() { m_years = 0; }
    CAge( int age ) { m_years = age; }
    CAge( const CAge& a ) { m_years = a.m_years; } // Copy constructor
    void Serialize( CArchive& ar);
    void AssertValid() const;
    const CAge& operator=( const CAge& a )
    {
        m_years = a.m_years; return *this;
    }
    BOOL operator==(CAge a)
    {
        return m_years == a.m_years;
    }
#ifdef _DEBUG
    void Dump( CDumpContext& dc ) const
    {
        CObject::Dump( dc );
        dc << m_years;
    }
#endif
};
```

Below is an example of **CObList** constructor usage:

```
CObList list( 20 );  // List on the stack with blocksize = 20.

CObList* plist = new CObList; // List on the heap with default
                             // blocksize.
```

CObList::Find

POSITION Find(CObject* *searchValue*, **POSITION** *startAfter* = **NULL)**
const;

Return Value   A **POSITION** value that can be used for iteration or object pointer retrieval; **NULL** if the object is not found.

Parameters   *searchValue*   The object pointer to be found in this list.

startAfter   The start position for the search.

Remarks   Searches the list sequentially to find the first **CObject** pointer matching the specified **CObject** pointer. Note that the pointer values are compared, not the contents of the objects.

See Also   **CObList::GetNext, CObList::GetPrev**

Example
```
CObList list;
CAge* pa1;
CAge* pa2;
POSITION pos;
list.AddHead( pa1 = new CAge( 21 ) );
list.AddHead( pa2 = new CAge( 40 ) );    // List now contains (40, 21).
if( ( pos = list.Find( pa1 ) ) != NULL ) // Hunt for pa1
{                                         // starting at head by default.
    ASSERT( *(CAge*) list.GetAt( pos ) == CAge( 21 ) );
}
```

CObList::FindIndex

POSITION FindIndex(int *nIndex*) const;

Return Value   A **POSITION** value that can be used for iteration or object pointer retrieval; **NULL** if *nIndex* is negative or too large.

Parameters   *nIndex*   The zero-based index of the list element to be found.

Remarks   Uses the value of *nIndex* as an index into the list. It starts a sequential scan from the head of the list, stopping on the *n*th element.

See Also   **CObList::Find, CObList::GetNext, CObList::GetPrev**

Example
```
CObList list;
POSITION pos;

list.AddHead( new CAge( 21 ) );
list.AddHead( new CAge( 40 ) ); // List now contains (40, 21).
if( ( pos = list.FindIndex( 0 )) != NULL )
{
    ASSERT( *(CAge*) list.GetAt( pos ) == CAge( 40 ) );
}
```

CObList::GetAt

CObject*& GetAt(POSITION *position*);

CObject* GetAt(POSITION *position*) const;

Return Value   See the return value description for **GetHead**.

Parameters   *position*   A **POSITION** value returned by a previous **GetHeadPosition** or **Find** member function call.

Remarks   A variable of type **POSITION** is a key for the list. It is not the same as an index, and you cannot operate on a **POSITION** value yourself. **GetAt** retrieves the **CObject** pointer associated with a given position. You must ensure that your **POSITION** value represents a valid position in the list. If it is invalid, then the Debug version of the Microsoft Foundation Class Library asserts.

See Also   **CObList::Find, CObList::SetAt, CObList::GetNext, CObList::GetPrev, CObList::GetHead**

Example   See the example for **FindIndex**.

CObList::GetCount

int GetCount( ) const;

Return Value   An integer value containing the element count.

Remarks   Gets the number of elements in this list.

See Also   **CObList::IsEmpty**

Example
```
CObList list;

list.AddHead( new CAge( 21 ) );
list.AddHead( new CAge( 40 ) ); // List now contains (40, 21).
ASSERT( list.GetCount() == 2 );
```

CObList::GetHead

CObject*& GetHead( );

CObject* GetHead( ) const;

Return Value   If the list is accessed through a pointer to a **const CObList**, then **GetHead** returns a **CObject** pointer. This allows the function to be used only on the right side of an assignment statement and thus protects the list from modification. If the list is accessed directly or through a pointer to a **CObList**, then **GetHead** returns a reference to a **CObject** pointer. This allows the function to be used on either side of an assignment statement and thus allows the list entries to be modified.

Remarks   Gets the **CObject** pointer that represents the head element of this list. You must ensure that the list is not empty before calling **GetHead**. If the list is empty, then the Debug version of the Microsoft Foundation Class Library asserts. Use **IsEmpty** to verify that the list contains elements.

See Also   **CObList::GetTail**, **CObList::GetTailPosition**, **CObList::AddHead**, **CObList::RemoveHead**

Example   The following example illustrates the use of **GetHead** on the left side of an assignment statement.

```
const CObList* cplist;

CObList* plist = new CObList;
CAge* page1 = new CAge( 21 );
CAge* page2 = new CAge( 30 );
CAge* page3 = new CAge( 40 );
plist->AddHead( page1 );
plist->AddHead( page2 );  // List now contains (30, 21).
// The following statement REPLACES the head element.
plist->GetHead() = page3; // List now contains (40, 21).
ASSERT( *(CAge*) plist->GetHead() == CAge( 40 ) );
cplist = plist;  // cplist is a pointer to a const list.
// cplist->GetHead() = page3; // Does not compile!
ASSERT( *(CAge*) plist->GetHead() == CAge( 40 ) ); // OK

delete page1;
delete page2;
delete page3;
delete plist; // Cleans up memory.
```

CObList::GetHeadPosition

POSITION GetHeadPosition( ) const;

Return Value   A **POSITION** value that can be used for iteration or object pointer retrieval; **NULL** if the list is empty.

Remarks   Gets the position of the head element of this list.

See Also   **CObList::GetTailPosition**

Example
```
CObList list;
POSITION pos;

list.AddHead( new CAge( 21 ) );
list.AddHead( new CAge( 40 ) ); // List now contains (40, 21).
if( ( pos = list.GetHeadPosition() ) != NULL )
{
    ASSERT( *(CAge*) list.GetAt( pos ) == CAge( 40 ) );
}
```

CObList::GetNext

CObject*& GetNext(POSITION& *rPosition* **);**

CObject* GetNext(POSITION& *rPosition* **) const;**

Return Value   See the return value description for **GetHead**.

Parameters   *rPosition*   A reference to a **POSITION** value returned by a previous **GetNext**,
GetHeadPosition, or other member function call.

Remarks   Gets the list element identified by *rPosition*, then sets *rPosition* to the **POSITION**
value of the next entry in the list. You can use **GetNext** in a forward iteration loop
if you establish the initial position with a call to **GetHeadPosition** or **Find**.

You must ensure that your **POSITION** value represents a valid position in the list.
If it is invalid, then the Debug version of the Microsoft Foundation Class Library
asserts.

If the retrieved element is the last in the list, then the new value of *rPosition* is set
to **NULL**. It is possible to remove an element during an iteration. See the example
for **RemoveAt**.

See Also   **CObList::Find, CObList::GetHeadPosition, CObList::GetTailPosition,
CObList::GetPrev, CObList::GetHead**

Example
```
CObList list;
POSITION pos;
list.AddHead( new CAge( 21 ) );
list.AddHead( new CAge( 40 ) ); // List now contains (40, 21).
// Iterate through the list in head-to-tail order.
#ifdef _DEBUG
    for( pos = list.GetHeadPosition(); pos != NULL; )
    {
    afxDump << list.GetNext( pos ) << "\n";
    }
#endif
```

The results from this program are as follows:

```
a CAge at $479C 40
a CAge at $46C0 21
```

CObList::GetPrev

CObject*& GetPrev(POSITION& *rPosition* **);**

CObject* GetPrev(POSITION& *rPosition* **) const;**

Return Value   See the return value description for **GetHead**.

Parameters   *rPosition*   A reference to a **POSITION** value returned by a previous **GetPrev** or other member function call.

Remarks   Gets the list element identified by *rPosition*, then sets *rPosition* to the **POSITION** value of the previous entry in the list. You can use **GetPrev** in a reverse iteration loop if you establish the initial position with a call to **GetTailPosition** or **Find**.

You must ensure that your **POSITION** value represents a valid position in the list. If it is invalid, then the Debug version of the Microsoft Foundation Class Library asserts. If the retrieved element is the first in the list, then the new value of *rPosition* is set to **NULL**.

See Also   **CObList::Find, CObList::GetTailPosition, CObList::GetHeadPosition, CObList::GetNext, CObList::GetHead**

Example
```
         CObList list;
         POSITION pos;

         list.AddHead( new CAge(21) );
         list.AddHead( new CAge(40) ); // List now contains (40, 21).
         // Iterate through the list in tail-to-head order.
         for( pos = list.GetTailPosition(); pos != NULL; )
         {
#ifdef _DEBUG
            afxDump << list.GetPrev( pos ) << "\n";
#endif
         }
```

The results from this program are as follows:

```
a CAge at $421C 21
a CAge at $421C 40
```

CObList::GetTail

CObject*& GetTail( );

CObject* GetTail( ) const;

Return Value   See the return value description for **GetHead**.

Remarks   Gets the **CObject** pointer that represents the tail element of this list. You must ensure that the list is not empty before calling **GetTail**. If the list is empty, then the Debug version of the Microsoft Foundation Class Library asserts. Use **IsEmpty** to verify that the list contains elements.

See Also	**CObList::AddTail**, **CObList::AddHead**, **CObList::RemoveHead**, **CObList::GetHead**
| Example | ```
CObList list;

list.AddHead( new CAge( 21 ) );
list.AddHead( new CAge( 40 ) ); // List now contains (40, 21).
ASSERT( *(CAge*) list.GetTail() == CAge( 21 ) );
``` |

CObList::GetTailPosition

POSITION GetTailPosition( ) const;

Return Value	A **POSITION** value that can be used for iteration or object pointer retrieval; **NULL** if the list is empty.
Remarks	Gets the position of the tail element of this list; **NULL** if the list is empty.
See Also	**CObList::GetHeadPosition**, **CObList::GetTail**
| Example | ```
CObList list;
POSITION pos;

list.AddHead( new CAge( 21 ) );
list.AddHead( new CAge( 40 ) ); // List now contains (40, 21).
if( ( pos = list.GetTailPosition() ) != NULL )
{
    ASSERT( *(CAge*) list.GetAt( pos ) == CAge( 21 ) );
}
``` |

CObList::InsertAfter

POSITION InsertAfter(POSITION *position***, CObject*** *newElement* **)**
throw (CMemoryException);

Parameters	*position* A **POSITION** value returned by a previous **GetNext**, **GetPrev**, or **Find** member function call.
	newElement The object pointer to be added to this list.
Remarks	Adds an element to this list after the element at the specified position
See Also	**CObList::Find**, **CObList::InsertBefore**

Example
```
CObList list;
POSITION pos1, pos2;
list.AddHead( new CAge( 21 ) );
list.AddHead( new CAge( 40 ) ); // List now contains (40, 21).
if( ( pos1 = list.GetHeadPosition() ) != NULL )
{
    pos2 = list.InsertAfter( pos1, new CAge( 65 ) );
}
#ifdef _DEBUG
    afxDump.SetDepth( 1 );
    afxDump << "InsertAfter example: " << &list << "\n";
#endif
```

The results from this program are as follows:

```
InsertAfter example: A CObList with 3 elements
    a CAge at $4A44 40
    a CAge at $4A64 65
    a CAge at $4968 21
```

CObList::InsertBefore

POSITION InsertBefore(POSITION *position*, **CObject*** *newElement* **)**
throw (CMemoryException);

Return Value
A **POSITION** value that can be used for iteration or object pointer retrieval;
NULL if the list is empty.

Parameters
position   A **POSITION** value returned by a previous **GetNext**, **GetPrev**, or **Find**
member function call.

newElement   The object pointer to be added to this list.

Remarks
Adds an element to this list before the element at the specified position.

See Also
CObList::Find, CObList::InsertAfter

Example
```
CObList list;
POSITION pos1, pos2;
list.AddHead( new CAge( 21 ) );
list.AddHead( new CAge( 40 ) ); // List now contains (40, 21).
if( ( pos1 = list.GetTailPosition() ) != NULL )
{
    pos2 = list.InsertBefore( pos1, new CAge( 65 ) );
}
#ifdef _DEBUG
    afxDump.SetDepth( 1 );
    afxDump << "InsertBefore example: " << &list << "\n";
#endif
```

The results from this program are as follows:

```
InsertBefore example: A CObList with 3 elements
    a CAge at $4AE2 40
    a CAge at $4B02 65
    a CAge at $49E6 21
```

CObList::IsEmpty

BOOL IsEmpty( ) const;

Return Value   Nonzero if this list is empty; otherwise 0.

Remarks   Indicates whether this list contains no elements.

See Also   **CObList::GetCount**

Example   See the example for **RemoveAll**.

CObList::RemoveAll

void RemoveAll( );

Remarks   Removes all the elements from this list and frees the associated **CObList** memory. No error is generated if the list is already empty. When you remove elements from a **CObList**, you remove the object pointers from the list. It is your responsibility to delete the objects themselves.

Example
```
CObList list;
CAge* pa1;
CAge* pa2;
ASSERT( list.IsEmpty()); // Yes it is.
list.AddHead( pa1 = new CAge( 21 ) );
list.AddHead( pa2 = new CAge( 40 ) ); // List now contains (40, 21).
ASSERT( !list.IsEmpty()); // No it isn't.
list.RemoveAll(); // CAge's aren't destroyed.
ASSERT( list.IsEmpty()); // Yes it is.
delete pa1;     // Now delete the CAge objects.
delete pa2;
```

CObList::RemoveAt

void RemoveAt(POSITION *position* **);**

Parameters   *position*   The position of the element to be removed from the list.

Remarks   Removes the specified element from this list. When you remove an element from a **CObList**, you remove the object pointer from the list. It is your responsibility to delete the objects themselves. You must ensure that your **POSITION** value represents a valid position in the list. If it is invalid, then the Debug version of the Microsoft Foundation Class Library asserts.

Example   Be careful when removing an element during a list iteration. The following example shows a removal technique that guarantees a valid **POSITION** value for **GetNext**:

```
CObList list;
POSITION pos1, pos2;
CObject* pa;

list.AddHead( new CAge( 21 ) );
list.AddHead( new CAge( 40 ) );
list.AddHead( new CAge( 65 ) ); // List now contains (65 40, 21).
for( pos1 = list.GetHeadPosition(); ( pos2 = pos1 ) != NULL; )
{
    if( *(CAge*) list.GetNext( pos1 ) == CAge( 40 ) )
    {
        pa = list.GetAt( pos2 ); // Save the old pointer for
                                 //deletion.
        list.RemoveAt( pos2 );
        delete pa; // Deletion avoids memory leak.
    }
}
#ifdef _DEBUG
    afxDump.SetDepth( 1 );
    afxDump << "RemoveAt example: " << &list << "\n";
#endif
```

The results from this program are as follows:

```
RemoveAt example: A CObList with 2 elements
    a CAge at $4C1E 65
    a CAge at $4B22 21
```

CObList::RemoveHead

CObject* RemoveHead( );

Return Value   The **CObject** pointer previously at the head of the list.

Remarks   Removes the element from the head of the list and returns a pointer to it. You must ensure that the list is not empty before calling **RemoveHead**. If the list is empty, then the Debug version of the Microsoft Foundation Class Library asserts. Use **IsEmpty** to verify that the list contains elements.

See Also   **CObList::GetHead, CObList::AddHead**

Example
```
CObList list;
CAge* pa1;
CAge* pa2;

list.AddHead( pa1 = new CAge( 21 ) );
list.AddHead( pa2 = new CAge( 40 ) ); // List now contains (40, 21).
ASSERT( *(CAge*) list.RemoveHead() == CAge( 40 ) );  // Old head
ASSERT( *(CAge*) list.GetHead() == CAge( 21 ) );  // New head
delete pa1;
delete pa2;
```

CObList::RemoveTail

CObject* RemoveTail( );

Return Value   A pointer to the object that was at the tail of the list.

Remarks   Removes the element from the tail of the list and returns a pointer to it. You must ensure that the list is not empty before calling **RemoveTail**. If the list is empty, then the Debug version of the Microsoft Foundation Class Library asserts. Use **IsEmpty** to verify that the list contains elements.

See Also   **CObList::GetTail**, **CObList::AddTail**

Example
```
CObList list;
CAge* pa1;
CAge* pa2;

list.AddHead( pa1 = new CAge( 21 ) );
list.AddHead( pa2 = new CAge( 40 ) ); // List now contains (40, 21).
ASSERT( *(CAge*) list.RemoveTail() == CAge( 21 ) );  // Old tail
ASSERT( *(CAge*) list.GetTail() == CAge( 40 ) );  // New tail
delete pa1;
delete pa2; // Clean up memory.
```

CObList::SetAt

void SetAt(POSITION *pos*, CObject* *newElement*);

Parameters   *pos*   The **POSITION** of the element to be set.

newElement   The **CObject** pointer to be written to the list.

Remarks   A variable of type **POSITION** is a key for the list. It is not the same as an index, and you cannot operate on a **POSITION** value yourself. **SetAt** writes the **CObject** pointer to the specified position in the list. You must ensure that your **POSITION** value represents a valid position in the list. If it is invalid, then the Debug version of the Microsoft Foundation Class Library asserts.

See Also   **CObList::Find, CObList::GetAt, CObList::GetNext, CObList::GetPrev**

Example
```
CObList list;
CObject* pa;
POSITION pos;

list.AddHead( new CAge( 21 ) );
list.AddHead( new CAge( 40 ) ); // List now contains (40, 21).
if( ( pos = list.GetTailPosition()) != NULL )
{
    pa = list.GetAt( pos ); // Save the old pointer for
                            //deletion.
    list.SetAt( pos, new CAge( 65 ) );  // Replace the tail
                                        //element.
    delete pa;  // Deletion avoids memory leak.
}
#ifdef _DEBUG
    afxDump.SetDepth( 1 );
    afxDump << "SetAt example: " << &list << "\n";
#endif
```

The results from this program are as follows:

```
SetAt example: A CObList with 2 elements
    a CAge at $4D98 40
    a CAge at $4DB8 65
```

class COleBusyDialog : public COleDialog

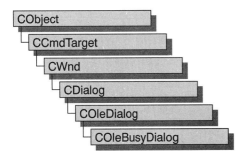

The **COleBusyDialog** class is used for the OLE Server Not Responding or Server Busy dialog boxes. Create an object of class **COleBusyDialog** when you want to call these dialog boxes. After a **COleBusyDialog** object has been constructed, you can use the **m_bz** structure to initialize the values or states of controls in the dialog box. The **m_bz** structure is of type **OLEUIBUSY**.

For more information on OLE 2–specific dialog boxes, see the article "Dialog Boxes in OLE" in *Programming with the Microsoft Foundation Class Library*.

#include <afxodlgs.h>

See Also   **COleDialog**

In the *OLE 2 Programmer's Reference, Volume 1*: **OLEUIBUSY**

Data Members

m_bz	Structure of type **OLEUIBUSY** that controls the behavior of the dialog box.

Construction

COleBusyDialog	Constructs a **COleBusyDialog** object.

Operations

DoModal	Displays the OLE 2 Server Busy dialog box.
GetSelectionType	Determines the choice made in the dialog box.

Member Functions

COleBusyDialog::COleBusyDialog

COleBusyDialog(HTASK *htaskBusy*, **BOOL** *bNotResponding* = **FALSE**, **DWORD** *dwFlags* = **0**, **CWnd*** *pParentWnd* = **NULL**);

Parameters   *htaskBusy*   Handle to the server task that is busy.

bNotResponding   If TRUE, call the Not Responding dialog box instead of the Server Busy dialog box. The wording in the Not Responding dialog box is slightly different than the wording in the Server Busy dialog box, and the Cancel button is disabled.

dwFlags   Creation flag. Can contain zero or more of the following values combined with the bitwise-or operator:

- **BZ_DISABLECANCELBUTTON**   Disable the Cancel button when calling the dialog box.
- **BZ_DISABLESWITCHTOBUTTON**   Disable the Switch To button when calling the dialog box.
- **BZ_DISABLERETRYBUTTON**   Disable the Retry button when calling the dialog box.

pParentWnd   Points to the parent or owner window object (of type **CWnd**) to which the dialog object belongs. If it is **NULL**, the parent window of the dialog object is set to the main application window.

Remarks   This function only constructs a **COleBusyDialog** object. To display the dialog box, call **DoModal**.

See Also   **COleBusyDialog::DoModal**

COleBusyDialog::DoModal

virtual int DoModal( ) const;

Return Value   **IDOK** if the dialog box was successfully displayed, **IDCANCEL** if the user canceled the dialog box, or **IDABORT** if an error occurred. If **IDABORT** is returned, call the **COleDialog::GetLastError** member function to get more information about the type of error that occurred. For a listing of possible errors, see "OleUIBusy" in the *User Interface Dialog* help file.

Remarks   Call this function to display the OLE Server Busy or Server Not Responding dialog box.

If you want to initialize the various dialog box controls by setting members of the **m_bz** structure, you should do this before calling **DoModal**, but after the dialog object is constructed.

If **DoModal** returns **IDOK**, you can call other member functions to retrieve the settings or information that was input by the user into the dialog box.

See Also   **COleDialog::GetLastError, CDialog::DoModal**

COleBusyDialog::GetSelectionType

UINT GetSelectionType( );

Return Value   Type of selection made:

- **COleBusyDialog::switchTo**   Switch To button was pressed.
- **COleBusyDialog::retry**   Retry button was pressed.
- **COleBusyDialog::callUnblocked**   Call to activate the server is now unblocked.

Remarks   Call this function to get the selection type chosen by the user in the Server Busy dialog box.

See Also   **COleBusyDialog::DoModal**

Data Members

COleBusyDialog::m_bz

Remarks   Structure of type **OLEUIBUSY** used to control the behavior of the Server Busy dialog box. Members of this structure can be modified directly or through membe functions.

See Also   **COleBusyDialog::COleBusyDialog**

In the *OLE 2 Programmer's Reference, Volume 1*: **OLEUIBUSY**

class COleChangeIconDialog : public COleDialog

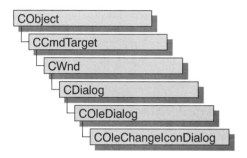

The **COleChangeIconDialog** class is used for the OLE Change Icon dialog box. Create an object of class **COleChangeIconDialog** when you want to call this dialog box. After a **COleChangeIconDialog** object has been constructed, you can use the **m_ci** structure to initialize the values or states of controls in the dialog box. The **m_ci** structure is of type **OLEUICHANGEICON**.

For more information about OLE 2–specific dialog boxes, see the article "Dialog Boxes in OLE" in *Programming with the Microsoft Foundation Class Library*.

#include <afxodlgs.h>

See Also   **COleDialog**

In the *OLE 2 Programmer's Reference, Volume 1*: **OLEUICHANGEICON**

Data Members
m_ci	A structure that controls the behavior of the dialog box.

Construction
COleChangeIconDialog	Constructs a **COleChangeIconDialog** object.

Operations and Attributes
DoChangeIcon	Performs the change specified in the dialog box.
DoModal	Displays the OLE 2 Change Icon dialog box.
GetIconicMetafile	Gets a handle to the metafile associated with the iconic form of this item.

Member Functions

COleChangeIconDialog::COleChangeIconDialog

> **COleChangeIconDialog** (**COleClientItem*** *pItem*, **DWORD** *dwFlags* = **CIF_SELECTCURRENT**, **CWnd*** *pParentWnd* = **NULL**);

Parameters   *pItem*   Points to the item to be converted.

dwFlags   Creation flag, which contains any number of the following values combined using the bitwise-or operator:

- **CIF_SHOWHELP**   Specifies that the Help button will be displayed when the dialog box is called.

- **CIF_SELECTCURRENT**   Specifies that the Current radio button will be selected initially when the dialog box is called. This is the default.

- **CIF_SELECTDEFAULT**   Specifies that the Default radio button will be selected initially when the dialog box is called.

- **CIF_SELECTFROMFILE**   Specifies that the From File radio button will be selected initially when the dialog box is called.

- **CIF_USEICONEXE**   Specifies that the icon should be extracted from the executable specified in the **szIconExe** field of **m_ci** instead of retrieved from the type. This is useful for embedding or linking to non-OLE files.

pParentWnd   Points to the parent or owner window object (of type **CWnd**) to which the dialog object belongs. If it is **NULL**, the parent window of the dialog box will be set to the main application window.

Remarks   This function constructs only a **COleChangeIconDialog** object. To display the dialog box, call the **DoModal** function.

See Also   **COleClientItem, COleChangeIconDialog::DoModal**

In the *OLE 2 Programmer's Reference, Volume 1*: **OLEUICHANGEICON**

COleChangeIconDialog::DoChangeIcon

> **BOOL DoChangeIcon**(**COleClientItem*** *pItem*);

Return Value   Nonzero if change is successful; otherwise 0.

Parameters   *pItem*   Points to the item whose icon is changing.

Remarks   Call this function to change the icon representing the item to the one selected in the dialog box after **DoModal** returns **IDOK**.

See Also   **COleChangeIconDialog::DoModal**

COleChangeIconDialog::DoModal

virtual int DoModal( );

Return Value   **IDOK** if the dialog box was successfully displayed, **IDCANCEL** if the user canceled the dialog box, or **IDABORT** if an error occurred. If **IDABORT** is returned, call the **COleDialog::GetLastError** member function to get more information about the type of error that occurred. For a listing of possible errors, see "OleUIChangeIcon" in the *User Interface Dialog* help file.

Remarks   Call this function to display the OLE Change Icon dialog box.

If you want to initialize the various dialog box controls by setting members of the **m_ci** structure, you should do this before calling **DoModal**, but after the dialog object is constructed.

If **DoModal** returns **IDOK**, you can call other member functions to retrieve the settings or information that was input by the user into the dialog box.

See Also   **COleDialog::GetLastError**, **CDialog::DoModal**

In the *OLE 2 Programmer's Reference, Volume 1*: **OLEUICHANGEICON**

COleChangeIconDialog::GetIconicMetafile

HGLOBAL GetIconicMetafile( ) const;

Return Value   The handle to the metafile containing the iconic aspect of the new icon, if the dialog box was dismissed by choosing OK; otherwise, the icon as it was before the dialog was displayed.

Remarks   Call this function to get a handle to the metafile that contains the iconic aspect of the selected item.

See Also   **COleChangeIconDialog::DoModal**,
COleChangeIconDialog::COleChangeIconDialog

Data Members

COleChangeIconDialog::m_ci

Remarks   Structure of type **OLEUICHANGEICON** used to control the behavior of the Change Icon dialog box. Members of this structure can be modified either directly or through member functions.

See Also   **COleChangeIconDialog::COleChangeIconDialog**

In the *OLE 2 Programmer's Reference, Volume 1*: **OLEUICHANGEICON**

class COleClientItem : public CDocItem

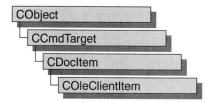

CObject
CCmdTarget
CDocItem
COleClientItem

The **COleClientItem** class defines the container interface to OLE items. An OLE item represents data, created and maintained by a server application, which can be "seamlessly" incorporated into a document so that it appears to the user to be a single document. The result is a "compound document" made up of the OLE item and a containing document.

An OLE item can be either embedded or linked. If it is embedded, its data is stored as part of the compound document. If it is linked, its data is stored as part of a separate file created by the server application, and only a link to that file is stored in the compound document. All OLE items contain information specifying the server application that should be called to edit them.

COleClientItem defines several overridable functions that are called in response to requests from the server application; these overridables usually act as notifications. This allows the server application to inform the container of changes the user makes when editing the OLE item, or to retrieve information needed during editing.

COleClientItem can be used with either the **COleDocument**, **COleLinkingDoc**, or **COleServerDoc** classes. To use **COleClientItem**, derive a class from it and implement the **OnChange** member function, which defines how the container responds to changes made to the item. To support in-place activation, override the **OnGetItemPosition** member function. This function provides information about the displayed position of the OLE item.

For more information about using the container interface, see "Containers: Implementing a Container" and "Activation: Container Issues" in *Programming with the Microsoft Foundation Class Library*.

Note The OLE documentation refers to embedded and linked items as "objects" and refers to types of items as "classes." This reference uses the term "item" to distinguish the OLE entity from the corresponding C++ object and the term "type" to distinguish the OLE category from the C++ class.

#include <afxole.h>

See Also	**COleDocument**, **COleLinkingDoc**, **COleServerItem**

Construction
COleClientItem	Constructs a **COleClientItem** object.

Creation
CreateFromClipboard	Creates an embedded item from the Clipboard.
CreateFromData	Creates an embedded item from a data object.
CanCreateFromData	Indicates whether a container application can create an embedded object.
CreateFromFile	Creates an embedded item from a file.
CreateStaticFromClipboard	Creates a static item from the Clipboard.
CreateStaticFromData	Creates a static item from a data object.
CreateLinkFromClipboard	Creates a linked item from the Clipboard.
CreateLinkFromData	Creates a linked item from a data object.
CanCreateLinkFromData	Indicates whether a container application can create a linked object.
CreateLinkFromFile	Creates a linked item from a file.
CreateNewItem	Creates a new embedded item by launching the server application.
CreateCloneFrom	Creates a duplicate of an existing item.

Status
GetLastStatus	Returns the status of the last OLE operation.
GetType	Returns the type (embedded, linked, or static) of the OLE item.
GetExtent	Returns the bounds of the OLE item's rectangle.
GetClassID	Gets the present item's class ID.
GetUserType	Gets a string describing the item's type.
GetIconicMetafile	Gets the metafile used for drawing the item's icon.
SetIconicMetafile	Caches the metafile used for drawing the item's icon.
GetDrawAspect	Gets the item's current view for rendering.
SetDrawAspect	Sets the item's current view for rendering.
GetItemState	Gets the item's current state.

GetActiveView	Gets the view on which the item is activated in place.
IsModified	Returns **TRUE** if the item has been modified since it was last saved.
IsRunning	Returns **TRUE** if the item's server application is running.
IsInPlaceActive	Returns **TRUE** if the item is in-place active.
IsOpen	Returns **TRUE** if the item is currently open in the server application.

Data Access

GetDocument	Returns the **COleDocument** object that contains the present item.
AttachDataObject	Accesses the data in the OLE object.

Object Conversion

ConvertTo	Converts the item to another type.
ActivateAs	Activates the item as another type.
Reload	Reloads the item after a call to **ActivateAs**.

Clipboard Operations

CanPaste	Indicates whether the Clipboard contains an embeddable or static OLE item.
CanPasteLink	Indicates whether the Clipboard contains a linkable OLE item.
DoDragDrop	Performs a drag-and-drop operation.
CopyToClipboard	Copies the OLE item to the Clipboard.
GetClipboardData	Gets the data that would be placed on the Clipboard by calling the **CopyToClipboard** member function.

General Operations

Close	Closes a link to a server but does not destroy the OLE item.
Release	Releases the connection to an OLE linked item and closes it if it was open. Does not destroy the client item.

Delete	Deletes or closes the OLE item if it was a linked item.
Draw	Draws the OLE item.
Run	Runs the application associated with the item.
SetPrintDevice	Sets the print-target device for this client item.

Activation

Activate	Opens the OLE item for an operation and then executes the specified verb.
DoVerb	Executes the specified verb.
Deactivate	Deactivates the item.
DeactivateUI	Restores the container application's user interface to its original state.
ReactivateAndUndo	Reactivates the item and undoes the last in-place editing operation.
SetItemRects	Sets the item's bounding rectangle.
GetInPlaceWindow	Returns a pointer to the item's in-place editing window.

Embedded Object Operations

SetHostNames	Sets the names the server displays when editing the OLE item.
SetExtent	Sets the bounding rectangle of the OLE item.

Linked Object Operations and Status

GetLinkUpdateOptions	Returns the update mode for a linked item (advanced feature).
SetLinkUpdateOptions	Sets the update mode for a linked item (advanced feature).
UpdateLink	Updates the presentation cache of an item.
IsLinkUpToDate	Returns **TRUE** if a linked item is up to date with its source document.

Overridables

OnChange	Called when the server changes the OLE item. Implementation required.
OnGetClipboardData	Called by the framework to get the data to be copied to the Clipboard.

OnInsertMenus	Called by the framework to create a composite menu.
OnSetMenu	Called by the framework to install and remove a composite menu.
OnRemoveMenus	Called by the framework to remove the container's menus from a composite menu.
OnUpdateFrameTitle	Called by the framework to update the frame window's title bar.
OnShowControlBars	Called by the framework to show and hide control bars.
OnGetItemPosition	Called by the framework to get the item's position relative to the view.
OnScrollBy	Called by the framework to scroll the item into view.
OnDeactivateUI	Called by the framework when the server has removed its in-place user interface.
OnDiscardUndoState	Called by the framework to discard the item's undo state information.
OnDeactivateAndUndo	Called by the framework to undo after activation.
OnShowItem	Called by the framework to display the OLE item.
OnGetClipRect	Called by the framework to get the item's clipping-rectangle coordinates.
CanActivate	Called by the framework to determine whether in-place activation is allowed.
OnActivate	Called by the framework to notify the item that it is activated.
OnActivateUI	Called by the framework to notify the item that it is activated and should show its user interface.
OnGetWindowContext	Called by the framework when an item is activated in place.
OnDeactivate	Called by the framework when an item is deactivated.
OnChangeItemPosition	Called by the framework when an item's position changes.

Member Functions

COleClientItem::Activate

void Activate(LONG *nVerb*, **CVIEW*** *pView*, **LPMSG** *lpMsg* **= NULL);**

Parameters   *nVerb*   Specifies the verb to execute. It can be one of the following:

Value	Meaning	Symbol
0	Primary verb	**OLEIVERB_PRIMARY**
1	Secondary verb	(None)
−1	Display item for editing	**OLEIVERB_SHOW**
−2	Edit item in separate window	**OLEIVERB_OPEN**
−3	Hide item	**OLEIVERB_HIDE**

The −1 value is typically an alias for another verb. If open editing is not supported, −2 has the same effect as −1. For additional values, see **IOleObject::DoVerb** in the *OLE 2 Programmer's Reference, Volume 1*.

pView   Pointer to the container view window that contains the OLE item; this is used by the server application for in-place activation. This parameter should be **NULL** if the container does not support in-place activation.

lpMsg   Pointer to the message that caused the item to be activated.

Remarks   Call this function to execute the specified verb instead of **DoVerb** so that you can do your own processing when an exception is thrown.

If the server application was written using the Microsoft Foundation Class Library, this function causes the **OnDoVerb** member function of the corresponding **COleServerItem** object to be executed.

If the primary verb is Edit and zero is specified in the *nVerb* parameter, the server application is launched to allow the OLE item to be edited. If the container application supports in-place activation, editing can be done in place. If the container does not support in-place activation (or if the Open verb is specified), the server is launched in a separate window and editing can be done there. Typically, when the user of the container application double-clicks the OLE item, the value for the primary verb in the *nVerb* parameter determines which action the user can take. However, if the server supports only one action, it takes that action, no matter which value is specified in the *nVerb* parameter.

See Also   **COleClientItem::DoVerb**, **COleServerItem::OnDoVerb**

In the *OLE 2 Programmer's Reference, Volume 1*: **IOleObject::DoVerb**

COleClientItem::ActivateAs

BOOL ActivateAs(LPCTSTR *lpszUserType*, **REFCLSID** *clsidOld*,
REFCLSID *clsidNew* **);**

Return Value   Nonzero if successful; otherwise 0.

Parameters   *lpszUserType*   Pointer to a string representing the target user type, such as "Word Document."

clsidOld   A reference to the item's current class ID. The class ID should represent the type of the actual object, as stored, unless it is a link. In that case, it should be the CLSID of the item to which the link refers. The **COleConvertDialog** automatically provides the correct class ID for the item.

clsidNew   A reference to the target class ID.

Remarks   Uses OLE's object conversion facilities to activate the item as though it were an item of the type specified by *clsidNew*. This is called automatically by **COleConvertDialog::DoConvert.** It is not usually called directly.

See Also   **COleConvertDialog, COleClientItem::ConvertTo, COleClientItem::Reload**

COleClientItem::AttachDataObject

void AttachDataObject(COleDataObject& *rDataObject* **) const;**

Parameters   *rDataObject*   Reference to a **COleDataObject** object that will be initialized to allow access to the data in the OLE item.

Remarks   Call this function to initialize a **COleDataObject** for accessing the data in the OLE item.

See Also   **COleDataObject**

COleClientItem::CanActivate

virtual BOOL CanActivate( );

Return Value   Nonzero if in-place activation is allowed; otherwise 0.

Remarks   Called by the framework when the user requests in-place activation of the OLE item; this function's return value determines whether in-place activation is allowed. The default implementation allows in-place activation if the container has a valid window. Override this function to implement special logic for accepting or refusing the activation request. For example, an activation request can be refused if the OLE item is too small or not currently visible.

See Also   In the *OLE 2 Programmer's Reference, Volume 1*:
IOleInPlaceSite::CanInPlaceActivate

COleClientItem::CanCreateFromData

static BOOL PASCAL CanCreateFromData(const COleDataObject*
pDataObject **);**

Return Value   Nonzero if the container can create an embedded object from the **COleDataObject** object.

Parameters   *pDataObject*   Pointer to the **COleDataObject** object from which the OLE item is to be created.

Remarks   Checks whether a container application can create an embedded object from the given **COleDataObject** object. The **COleDataObject** class is used in data transfers for retrieving data in various formats from the Clipboard, through drag and drop, or from an embedded OLE item.

Containers can use this function to decide to enable or disable their Edit Paste and Edit Paste Special commands.

See Also   **COleDataObject**

In *Programming with the Microsoft Foundation Class Library*: "Data Objects and Data Sources"

COleClientItem::CanCreateLinkFromData

static BOOL PASCAL CanCreateLinkFromData(const COleDataObject*
pDataObject **);**

Return Value   Nonzero if the container can create a linked object from the **COleDataObject** object.

Parameters   *pDataObject*   Pointer to the **COleDataObject** object from which the OLE item is to be created.

Remarks   Checks whether a container application can create a linked object from the given **COleDataObject** object. The **COleDataObject** class is used in data transfers for retrieving data in various formats from the Clipboard, through drag and drop, or from an embedded OLE item.

Containers can use this function to decide to enable or disable their Edit Paste Special and Edit Paste Link commands.

See Also   COleDataObject

In *Programming with the Microsoft Foundation Class Library*: "Data Objects and Data Sources"

COleClientItem::CanPaste

static BOOL PASCAL CanPaste( );

Return Value   Nonzero if an embedded OLE item can be pasted from the Clipboard; otherwise 0.

Remarks   Call this function to see whether an embedded OLE item can be pasted from the Clipboard.

See Also   COleClientItem::CanPasteLink, COleClientItem::CreateFromClipboard, COleClientItem::CreateStaticFromClipboard, COleDocument

In the *OLE 2 Programmer's Reference, Volume 1*: **::OleGetClipboard**, **::OleQueryCreateFromData**

COleClientItem::CanPasteLink

static BOOL PASCAL CanPasteLink( );

Return Value   Nonzero if a linked OLE item can be pasted from the Clipboard; otherwise 0.

Remarks   Call this function to see whether a linked OLE item can be pasted from the Clipboard.

See Also   COleClientItem::CanPaste, COleClientItem::CreateLinkFromClipboard

In the *OLE 2 Programmer's Reference, Volume 1*: **::OleGetClipboard**, **::OleQueryCreateLinkFromData**

COleClientItem::Close

void Close(OLECLOSE *dwCloseOption* = OLECLOSE_SAVEIFDIRTY);

Parameters   *dwCloseOption*   Flag specifying under what circumstances the OLE item is saved when it returns to the loaded state. It can have one of the following values:

- **OLECLOSE_SAVEIFDIRTY**   Save the OLE item.
- **OLECLOSE_NOSAVE**   Do not save the OLE item.
- **OLECLOSE_PROMPTSAVE**   Prompt the user on whether to save the OLE item.

Remarks   Call this function to change the state of an OLE item from the running state to the loaded state, that is, loaded with its handler in memory but with the server not running. This function has no effect when the OLE item is not running.

See Also   **COleClientItem::UpdateLink**

In the *OLE 2 Programmer's Reference, Volume 1*: **IOleObject::Close**

COleClientItem::COleClientItem

COleClientItem(COleDocument* *pContainerDoc* **= NULL);**

Parameters   *pContainerDoc*   Pointer to the container document that will contain this item. This can be any **COleDocument** derivative.

Remarks   Constructs a **COleClientItem** object and adds it to the container document's collection of document items, which constructs only the C++ object and does not perform any OLE initialization. If you pass a **NULL** pointer, no addition is made to the container document. You must explicitly call **COleDocument::AddItem**.

You must call one of the following creation member functions before you use the OLE item: **CreateFromClipboard**, **CreateFromData**, **CreateFromFile**, **CreateStaticFromClipboard**, **CreateStaticFromData**, **CreateLinkFromClipboard**, **CreateLinkFromData**, **CreateLinkFromFile**, **CreateNewItem**, or **CreateCloneFrom**.

See Also   **COleDocument, COleDocument::AddItem**

COleClientItem::ConvertTo

BOOL ConvertTo(REFCLSID *clsidNew* **);**

Return Value   Nonzero if successful; otherwise 0.

Parameters   *clsidNew*   The class ID of the target type.

Remarks   Call this member function to convert the item to the type specified by *clsidNew*. This is called automatically by **ConvertDialog**. It is not necessary to call it directly.

See Also   **COleClientItem::ActivateAs, COleConvertDialog**

COleClientItem::CopyToClipboard

void CopyToClipboard(BOOL *bIncludeLink* **= FALSE);**

Parameters   *bIncludeLink*   **TRUE** if link information should be copied to the Clipboard, allowing a linked item to bc pasted; otherwise **FALSE**.

Remarks	Call this function to copy the OLE item to the Clipboard. Typically, you call this function when writing message handlers for the Copy or Cut commands from the Edit menu. You must implement item selection in your container application if you want to implement the Copy or Cut commands.
See Also	In the *OLE 2 Programmer's Reference, Volume 1*: **::OleSetClipboard**

COleClientItem::CreateCloneFrom

BOOL CreateCloneFrom(const COleClientItem* *pSrcItem* **);**

Return Value	Nonzero if successful; otherwise 0.
Parameters	*pSrcItem* Pointer to the OLE item to be duplicated.
Remarks	Call this function to create a copy of the specified OLE item. The copy is identical to the source item. You can use this function to support undo operations.
See Also	**COleClientItem::CreateNewItem**

COleClientItem::CreateFromClipboard

BOOL CreateFromClipboard(OLERENDER *render* **= OLERENDER_DRAW, CLIPFORMAT** *cfFormat* **= 0, LPFORMATETC** *lpFormatEtc* **= NULL);**

Return Value	Nonzero if successful; otherwise 0.
Parameters	*render* Flag specifying how the server will render the OLE item. For the possible values, see **COleClientItem::CreateNewItem**.
	cfFormat Specifies the Clipboard data format to be cached when creating the OLE item.
	lpFormatEtc Pointer to a **FORMATETC** structure used if *render* is **OLERENDER_FORMAT** or **OLERENDER_DRAW**. Provide a value for this parameter only if you want to specify additional format information beyond the Clipboard format specified by *cfFormat*. If you omit this parameter, default values are used for the other fields in the **FORMATETC** structure.
Remarks	Call this function to create an embedded item from the contents of the Clipboard. You typically call this function from the message handler for the Paste command on the Edit menu. (The Paste command is enabled by the framework if the **CanPaste** member function returns nonzero.)
See Also	**COleDataObject::AttachClipboard**, **COleClientItem::CreateFromData**, **COleClientItem::CanPaste**

COleClientItem::CreateFromData

> **BOOL CreateFromData(COleDataObject*** *pDataObject*, **OLERENDER**
> *render* **= OLERENDER_DRAW, CLIPFORMAT** *cfFormat* **= 0,**
> **LPFORMATETC** *lpFormatEtc* **= NULL);**

Return Value   Nonzero if successful; otherwise 0.

Parameters   *pDataObject*   Pointer to the **COleDataObject** object from which the OLE item is
to be created.

render   Flag specifying how the server will render the OLE item. For the possible
values, see **COleClientItem::CreateNewItem**.

cfFormat   Specifies the Clipboard data format to be cached when creating the
OLE item.

lpFormatEtc   Pointer to a **FORMATETC** structure used if *render* is
OLERENDER_FORMAT or **OLERENDER_DRAW**. Provide a value for
this parameter only if you want to specify additional format information beyond
the Clipboard format specified by *cfFormat*. If you omit this parameter, default
values are used for the other fields in the **FORMATETC** structure.

Remarks   Call this function to create an embedded item from a **COleDataObject** object.
Data transfer operations, such as pasting from the Clipboard or drag-and-drop
operations, provide **COleDataObject** objects containing the information offered by
a server application. It is usually used in your override of **CView:OnDrop**.

See Also   **COleDataObject::AttachClipboard,**
COleClientItem::CreateFromClipboard, COleDataObject

In the *OLE 2 Programmer's Reference, Volume 1*: **::OleCreateFromData**

COleClientItem::CreateFromFile

> **BOOL CreateFromFile(LPCTSTR** *lpszFileName*, **REFCLSID** *clsid* **=**
> **CLSID_NULL, OLERENDER** *render* **= OLERENDER_DRAW,**
> **CLIPFORMAT** *cfFormat* **= 0, LPFORMATETC** *lpFormatEtc* **= NULL);**

Return Value   Nonzero if successful; otherwise 0.

Parameters   *lpszFileName*   Pointer to the name of the file from which the OLE item is to be
created.

clsid   Reserved for future use.

render   Flag specifying how the server will render the OLE item. For the possible values, see **COleClientItem::CreateNewItem**.

cfFormat   Specifies the Clipboard data format to be cached when creating the OLE item.

lpFormatEtc   Pointer to a **FORMATETC** structure used if *render* is **OLERENDER_FORMAT** or **OLERENDER_DRAW**. Provide a value for this parameter only if you want to specify additional format information beyond the Clipboard format specified by *cfFormat*. If you omit this parameter, default values are used for the other fields in the **FORMATETC** structure.

Remarks   Call this function to create an embedded OLE item from a file. The framework calls this function from **COleInsertObject::CreateItem** if the user chooses OK from the Insert Object dialog box when the Create from File button is selected.

See Also   **COleInsertDialog::CreateItem**

In the *OLE 2 Programmer's Reference, Volume 1*: **::OleCreateFromFile**

COleClientItem::CreateLinkFromClipboard

BOOL CreateLinkFromClipboard(OLERENDER *render* = **OLERENDER_DRAW, CLIPFORMAT** *cfFormat* = **0, LPFORMATETC** *lpFormatEtc* = **NULL**);

Return Value   Nonzero if successful; otherwise 0.

Parameters   *render*   Flag specifying how the server will render the OLE item. For the possible values, see **COleClientItem::CreateNewItem**.

cfFormat   Specifies the Clipboard data format to be cached when creating the OLE item.

lpFormatEtc   Pointer to a **FORMATETC** structure used if *render* is **OLERENDER_FORMAT** or **OLERENDER_DRAW**. Provide a value for this parameter only if you want to specify additional format information beyond the Clipboard format specified by *cfFormat*. If you omit this parameter, default values are used for the other fields in the **FORMATETC** structure.

Remarks   Call this function to create a linked item from the contents of the Clipboard. You typically call this function from the message handler for the Paste Link command on the Edit menu. (The Paste Link command is enabled in the default implementation of **COleDocument** if the Clipboard contains an OLE item that can be linked to.)

See Also   **COleClientItem::CanPasteLink, COleClientItem::CreateLinkFromData, COleDataObject::AttachClipboard**

COleClientItem::CreateLinkFromData

BOOL CreateLinkFromData(COleDataObject* *pDataObject*,
OLERENDER *render* = **OLERENDER_DRAW, CLIPFORMAT** *cfFormat*
= **0, LPFORMATETC** *lpFormatEtc* = **NULL);**

Return Value   Nonzero if successful; otherwise 0.

Parameters   *pDataObject*   Pointer to the **COleDataObject** object from which the OLE item is to be created.

render   Flag specifying how the server will render the OLE item. For the possible values, see **COleClientItem::CreateNewItem**.

cfFormat   Specifies the Clipboard data format to be cached when creating the OLE item.

lpFormatEtc   Pointer to a **FORMATETC** structure used if *render* is **OLERENDER_FORMAT** or **OLERENDER_DRAW**. Provide a value for this parameter only if you want to specify additional format information beyond the Clipboard format specified by *cfFormat*. If you omit this parameter, default values are used for the other fields in the **FORMATETC** structure.

Remarks   Call this function to create a linked item from a **COleDataObject** object. Call this during a drop operation when the user indicates a link should be created. It can also be used to handle the Edit Paste command. It is called by the framework in **COleClientItem::CreateLinkFromClipboard** and in **COlePasteSpecialDialog::CreateItem** when the Link radio button has been selected.

See Also   **COleDataObject::AttachClipboard, COleDataObject, COleClientItem::CreateLinkFromClipboard**

In the *OLE 2 Programmer's Reference, Volume 1*: **::OleCreateLinkFromData**

COleClientItem::CreateLinkFromFile

BOOL CreateLinkFromFile(LPCTSTR *lpszFileName*, **OLERENDER** *render*
= **OLERENDER_DRAW, CLIPFORMAT** *cfFormat* = **0,**
LPFORMATETC *lpFormatEtc* = **NULL);**

Return Value   Nonzero if successful; otherwise 0.

Parameters   *lpszFileName*   Pointer to the name of the file from which the OLE item is to be created.

render   Flag specifying how the server will render the OLE item. For the possible values, see **COleClientItem::CreateNewItem**.

cfFormat   Specifies the Clipboard data format to be cached when creating the OLE item.

lpFormatEtc   Pointer to a **FORMATETC** structure used if *render* is **OLERENDER_FORMAT** or **OLERENDER_DRAW**. Provide a value for this parameter only if you want to specify additional format information beyond the Clipboard format specified by *cfFormat*. If you omit this parameter, default values are used for the other fields in the **FORMATETC** structure.

Remarks   Call this function to create a linked OLE item from a file. The framework calls this function if the user chooses OK from the Insert Object dialog box when the Create from File button is selected and the Link check box is checked. It is called from **COleInsertDialog::CreateItem**.

See Also   **COleInsertDialog::CreateItem**

In the *OLE 2 Programmer's Reference, Volume 1*: **::OleCreateLinkFromFile**

COleClientItem::CreateNewItem

BOOL CreateNewItem(REFCLSID *clsid*, **OLERENDER** *render* = **OLERENDER_DRAW, CLIPFORMAT** *cfFormat* = **0, LPFORMATETC** *lpFormatEtc* = **NULL**);

Return Value   Nonzero if successful; otherwise 0.

Parameters   *clsid*   ID that uniquely identifies the type of OLE item to create.

render   Flag specifying how the server will render the OLE item. For values in addition to **OLERENDER_DRAW**, see the OLE 2 documentation.

cfFormat   Specifies the Clipboard data format to be cached when creating the OLE item.

lpFormatEtc   Pointer to a **FORMATETC** structure used if *render* is **OLERENDER_FORMAT** or **OLERENDER_DRAW**. Provide a value for this parameter only if you want to specify additional format information beyond the Clipboard format specified by *cfFormat*. If you omit this parameter, default values are used for the other fields in the **FORMATETC** structure.

Remarks   Call this function to create an embedded item; this function launches the server application that allows the user to create the OLE item. The framework calls this function if the user chooses OK from the Insert Object dialog box when the Create New button is selected.

See Also   **COleInsertDialog::CreateItem**

In the *OLE 2 Programmer's Reference, Volume 1*: **::OleCreate**

COleClientItem::CreateStaticFromClipboard

BOOL CreateStaticFromClipboard(OLERENDER *render* **= OLERENDER_DRAW, CLIPFORMAT** *cfFormat* **= 0, LPFORMATETC** *lpFormatEtc* **= NULL);**

Return Value   Nonzero if successful; otherwise 0.

Parameters   *render*   Flag specifying how the server will render the OLE item. For the possible values, see **COleClientItem::CreateNewItem**.

cfFormat   Specifies the Clipboard data format to be cached when creating the OLE item.

lpFormatEtc   Pointer to a **FORMATETC** structure used if *render* is **OLERENDER_FORMAT** or **OLERENDER_DRAW**. Provide a value for this parameter only if you want to specify additional format information beyond the Clipboard format specified by *cfFormat*. If you omit this parameter, default values are used for the other fields in the **FORMATETC** structure.

Remarks   Call this function to create a static item from the contents of the Clipboard. A static item contains the presentation data but not the native data; consequently it cannot be edited. You typically call this function if the **CreateFromClipboard** member function fails.

See Also   **COleDataObject::AttachClipboard, COleClientItem::CanPaste, COleClientItem::CreateStaticFromData**

COleClientItem::CreateStaticFromData

BOOL CreateStaticFromData(COleDataObject* *pDataObject*, **OLERENDER** *render* **= OLERENDER_DRAW, CLIPFORMAT** *cfFormat* **= 0, LPFORMATETC** *lpFormatEtc* **= NULL);**

Return Value   Nonzero if successful; otherwise 0.

Parameters   *pDataObject*   Pointer to the **COleDataObject** object from which the OLE item is to be created.

render   Flag specifying how the server will render the OLE item. For the possible values, see **COleClientItem::CreateNewItem**.

cfFormat   Specifies the Clipboard data format to be cached when creating the OLE item.

lpFormatEtc   Pointer to a **FORMATETC** structure used if *render* is **OLERENDER_FORMAT** or **OLERENDER_DRAW**. Provide a value for this parameter only if you want to specify additional format information beyond the Clipboard format specified by *cfFormat*. If you omit this parameter, default values are used for the other fields in the **FORMATETC** structure.

Remarks   Call this function to create a static item from a **COleDataObject** object. A static item contains the presentation data but not the native data; consequently, it cannot be edited. This is essentially the same as **CreateStaticFromClipboard** except that a static item can be created from an arbitrary **COleDataObject**, not just from the Clipboard.

Used in **COlePasteSpecialDialog::CreateItem** when Static is selected.

See Also   **COleDataObject::AttachClipboard**, **COleDataObject**

In the *OLE 2 Programmer's Reference, Volume 1*: **::OleCreateStaticFromData**

COleClientItem::Deactivate

void Deactivate( );

Remarks   Call this function to deactivate the OLE item and free any associated resources. You typically deactivate an in-place active OLE item when the user clicks the mouse on the client area outside the bounds of the item. Note that deactivating the OLE item will discard its undo state, making it impossible to call the **ReactivateAndUndo** member function.

If your application supports undo, do not call **Deactivate**; instead, call **DeactivateUI**.

See Also   **COleClientItem::ReactivateAndUndo**, **COleClientItem::DeactivateUI**

In the *OLE 2 Programmer's Reference, Volume 1*:
IOleInPlaceObject::DeactivateInPlace

COleClientItem::DeactivateUI

void DeactivateUI( );

Remarks

Call this function when the user deactivates an item that was activated in place. This function restores the container application's user interface to its original state, hiding any menus and other controls that were created for in-place activation.

This function does not flush the undo state information for the item. That information is retained so that **ReactivateAndUndo** can later be used to execute an undo command in the server application, in case the container's undo command is chosen immediately after deactivating the item.

See Also

COleClientItem::ReactivateAndUndo, **COleClientItem::DeactivateUI**

In the *OLE 2 Programmer's Reference, Volume 1*:
IOleInPlaceObject::DeactivateInPlace

COleClientItem::Delete

void Delete(BOOL *bAutoDelete* **= TRUE);**

Parameters

bAutoDelete   Specifies whether the item is to be removed from the document.

Remarks

Call this function to delete the OLE item from the container document. This function calls the **Release** member function, which in turn deletes the C++ object for the item, permanently removing the OLE item from the document. If the OLE item is embedded, the native data for the item is deleted. It always closes a running server; therefore, if the item is an open link, this function closes it.

See Also

COleClientItem::Release

COleClientItem::DoDragDrop

DROPEFFECT DoDragDrop(LPCRECT *lpItemRect***, CPoint** *ptOffset***,**
    BOOL *bIncludeLink* **= FALSE,**
    DWORD *dwEffects* **= DROPEFFECT_COPY | DROPEFFECT_MOVE,**
    LPCRECT *lpRectStartDrag* **= NULL);**

Return Value

A **DROPEFFECT** value. If it is **DROPEFFECT_MOVE**, the original data should be removed.

Parameters

lpItemRect   The item's rectangle on screen in client coordinates (pixels).

ptOffset   The offset from *lpItemRect* where the mouse position was at the time of the drag.

bIncludeLink   Set this to **TRUE** if the link data should be copied to the Clipboard. Set it to **FALSE** if your server application does not support links.

dwEffects   Determines the effects that the drag source will allow in the drag operation.

lpRectStartDrag   Pointer to the rectangle that defines where the drag actually starts. It does not start until the mouse cursor leaves the rectangle. If **NULL**, a default rectangle is used so that the drag starts when the mouse cursor moves one pixel.

Remarks   Call the **DoDragDrop** member function to perform a drag-and-drop operation.

See Also   **COleDataSource::DoDragDrop**, **COleClientItem::CopyToClipboard**

COleClientItem::DoVerb

virtual BOOL DoVerb(LONG *nVerb*, **CView*** *pView*, **LPMSG** *lpMsg* = **NULL**);

Return Value   Nonzero if the verb was successfully executed; otherwise 0.

Parameters   *nVerb*   Specifies the verb to execute. It can include one of the following:

Value	Meaning	Symbol
0	Primary verb	**OLEIVERB_PRIMARY**
1	Secondary verb	(None)
−1	Display item for editing	**OLEIVERB_SHOW**
−2	Edit item in separate window	**OLEIVERB_OPEN**
−3	Hide item	**OLEIVERB_HIDE**

The -1 value is typically an alias for another verb. If open editing is not supported, -2 has the same effect as -1. For additional values, see **IOleObject::DoVerb** in the *OLE 2 Programmer's Reference, Volume 1*.

pView   Pointer to the view window; this is used by the server for in-place activation. This parameter should be **NULL** if the container application does not allow in-place activation.

lpMsg   Pointer to the message that caused the item to be activated.

Remarks   Call **DoVerb** to execute the specified verb. This function calls the **Activate** member function to execute the verb. It also catches exceptions and displays a message box to the user if one is thrown.

If the primary verb is Edit and zero is specified in the *nVerb* parameter, the server application is launched to allow the OLE item to be edited. If the container application supports in-place activation, editing can be done in place. If the container does not support in-place activation (or if the Open verb is specified), the server is launched in a separate window and editing can be done there. Typically, when the user of the container application double-clicks the OLE item, the value for the primary verb in the *nVerb* parameter determines which action the user can take. However, if the server supports only one action, it takes that action, no matter which value is specified in the *nVerb* parameter.

See Also   **COleClientItem::Activate**

COleClientItem::Draw

BOOL Draw(CDC* *pDC*, **LPCRECT** *lpBounds*, **DVASPECT** *nDrawAspect* = **(DVASPECT)-1);**

Return Value   Nonzero if successful; otherwise 0.

Parameters   *pDC*   Pointer to a **CDC** object used for drawing the OLE item.

lpBounds   Pointer to a **CRect** object or **RECT** structure that defines the bounding rectangle in which to draw the OLE item (in logical units determined by the device context).

nDrawAspect   Specifies the aspect of the OLE item, that is, how it should be displayed. If *nDrawAspect* is -1, the last aspect set by using **SetDrawAspect** is used. For more information about possible values for this flag, see the OLE 2 documentation.

Remarks   Call this function to draw the OLE item into the specified bounding rectangle using the specified device context. The function may use the metafile representation of the OLE item created by the **OnDraw** member function of **COleServerItem**.

Typically you use **Draw** for screen display, passing the screen device context as *pDC*. In this case, you need to specify only the first two parameters.

The *lpBounds* parameter identifies the rectangle in the target device context (relative to its current mapping mode). Rendering may involve scaling the picture and can be used by container applications to impose a view that scales between the displayed view and the final printed image.

See Also   **COleClientItem::SetExtent**, **COleServerItem::OnDraw**

In the *OLE 2 Programmer's Reference, Volume 1*: **IViewObject::Draw**

COleClientItem::GetActiveView

CView* GetActiveView( ) const;

Return Value   A pointer to the view; otherwise **NULL** if the item is not in-place activated.

Remarks   Returns the view on which the item is in-place activated.

See Also   **COleClientItem::IsInPlaceActive, COleClientItem::GetDocument,**

COleClientItem::GetClassID

void GetClassID(CLSID* *pClassID*) const;

Parameters   *pClassID*   Pointer to a structure of type **CLSID** to retrieve the class ID. For information on the **CLSID** structure, see the OLE 2 documentation.

Remarks   Returns the class ID of the item into the memory pointed to by *pClassID*. The class ID is a 128-bit number that uniquely identifies the application that edits the item.

See Also   In the *OLE 2 Programmer's Reference, Volume 1*: **Persist::GetClassID**

COleClientItem::GetClipboardData

void GetClipboardData(COleDataSource* *pDataSource*, BOOL *bIncludeLink* = FALSE, LPPOINT *lpOffset* = NULL, LPSIZE *lpSize* = NULL);

Parameters   *pDataSource*   Pointer to a **COleDataSource** object that will receive the data contained in the OLE item.

bIncludeLink   **TRUE** if link data should be included; otherwise **FALSE**.

lpOffset   The offset of the mouse cursor from the origin of the object in pixels.

lpSize   The size of the object in pixels.

Remarks   Call this function to get a **COleDataSource** object containing all the data that would be placed on the Clipboard by a call to the **CopyToClipboard** member function.

Override **GetClipboardData** only if you want to offer data formats in addition to those offered by **CopyToClipboard**. Place those formats in the **COleDataSource** object before or after calling **CopyToClipboard**, and then pass the **COleDataSource** object to the **COleDataSource::SetClipboard** function. For example, if you want the OLE item's position in its container document to accompany it on the Clipboard, you would define your own format for passing that information and place it in the **COleDataSource** before calling **CopyToClipboard**.

See Also   **COleDataSource, COleClientItem::CopyToClipboard, COleDataSource::SetClipboard**

COleClientItem::GetDocument

COleDocument* GetDocument( ) const;

Return Value   A pointer to the document that contains the OLE item. **NULL** if the item is not part of a document.

Remarks   Call this function to get a pointer to the document that contains the OLE item. This pointer allows access to the document object that you passed as an argument to the **COleClientItem** constructor.

See Also   **COleClientItem::COleClientItem, COleDocument, COleLinkingDoc**

COleClientItem::GetDrawAspect

DVASPECT GetDrawAspect( ) const;

Return Value   A value from the **DVASPECT** enumeration, whose values are listed in the reference for **COleClientItem::SetDrawAspect**.

Remarks   Call the **GetDrawAspect** member function to determine the current "aspect," or view, of the item. The aspect specifies how the item is to be rendered.

See Also   **COleClientItem::SetDrawAspect, COleClientItem::Draw**

COleClientItem::GetExtent

BOOL GetExtent(LPSIZE *lpSize,* **DVASPECT** *nDrawAspect =* **(DVASPECT)-1);**

Return Value   Nonzero if successful; 0 if the OLE item is blank.

Parameters   *lpSize*   Pointer to a **SIZE** structure or a **CSize** object that will receive the size information.

nDrawAspect   Specifies the aspect of the OLE item whose bounds are to be retrieved. For possible values, see **COleClientItem::Draw**.

Remarks   Call this function to retrieve the OLE item's size. If the server application was written using the Microsoft Foundation Class Library, this function causes the **OnGetExtent** member function of the corresponding **COleServerItem** object to be called. Note that the retrieved size may differ from the size last set by the **SetExtent** member function; the size specified by **SetExtent** is treated as a suggestion. The dimensions are in **MM_HIMETRIC** units.

See Also   **COleClientItem::SetExtent, COleServerItem::OnGetExtent**

In the *OLE 2 Programmer's Reference, Volume 1*: **IOleObject::GetExtent**

COleClientItem::GetIconicMetafile

HGLOBAL GetIconicMetafile( );

Return Value   A handle to the metafile if successful; otherwise **NULL**.

Remarks   Retrieves the metafile used for drawing the item's icon. If there is no current icon, a default icon is returned. This is called automatically by the MFC/OLE dialogs and is usually not called directly.

This function also calls **SetIconicMetafile** to cache the metafile for later use.

See Also   **COleClientItem::SetIconicMetafile**

COleClientItem::GetInPlaceWindow

CWnd* GetInPlaceWindow( );

Return Value   A pointer to the item's in-place editing window; **NULL** if the item is not active or if its server is unavailable.

Remarks   Call the **GetInPlaceWindow** member function to get a pointer to the window in which the item has been opened for in-place editing. This function should be called only for items that are in-place active.

See Also   **COleClientItem::Activate**, **COleClientItem::Deactivate**, **COleClientItem::SetItemRects**

COleClientItem::GetItemState

UINT GetItemState( ) const;

Return Value   A **COleClientItem::ItemState** enumerated value, which can be one of the following: **emptyState**, **loadedState**, **openState**, **activeState**, **activeUIState**. For information about these states, see the article "Containers: Client-Item States" in *Programming with the Microsoft Foundation Class Library*.

Remarks   Call this function to get the OLE item's current state. To be notified when the OLE item's state changes, use the **OnChange** member function.

See Also   **COleClientItem::OnChange**

In *Programming with the Microsoft Foundation Class Library*: "Containers: Client-Item States"

COleClientItem::GetLastStatus

SCODE GetLastStatus( ) const;

Return Value
An **SCODE** value. For a list of status codes that can be returned, see the *OLE 2 Programmer's Reference, Volume 1*.

Remarks
Returns the status code of the last OLE operation. For member functions that return a **BOOL** value of **FALSE**, or other member functions that return **NULL**, **GetLastStatus** returns more detailed failure information. Be aware that most OLE member functions throw exceptions for more serious errors.

COleClientItem::GetLinkUpdateOptions

OLEUPDATE GetLinkUpdateOptions( );

Return Value
One of the following values:

- **OLEUPDATE_ALWAYS**   Update the linked item whenever possible. This option supports the Automatic link-update radio button in the Links dialog box.
- **OLEUPDATE_ONCALL**   Update the linked item only on request from the container application (when the **UpdateLink** member function is called). This option supports the Manual link-update radio button in the Links dialog box.

Remarks
Call this function to get the current value of the link-update option for the OLE item. This is an advanced operation.

This function is called automatically by the **COleLinks** dialog class.

See Also
COleClientItem::SetLinkUpdateOptions, COleLinksDialog

In the *OLE 2 Programmer's Reference, Volume 1*:
IOleLink::GetUpdateOptions

COleClientItem::GetType

OLE_OBJTYPE GetType( ) const;

Return Value
An unsigned integer with one of the following values:

- **OT_LINK**   The OLE item is a link.
- **OT_EMBEDDED**   The OLE item is embedded.
- **OT_STATIC**   The OLE item is static, that is, it contains only presentation data, not native data, and thus cannot be edited.

Remarks   Call this function to determine whether the OLE item is embedded or linked, or static.

See Also   **COleClientItem::GetUserType**

COleClientItem::GetUserType

void GetUserType(USERCLASSTYPE *nUserClassType***, CString&** *rString* **);**

Parameters   *nUserClassType*   A value indicating the desired variant of the string describing the OLE item's type. This can have one of the following values:

- **USERCLASSTYPE_FULL**   The full type name displayed to the user.
- **USERCLASSTYPE_SHORT**   A short name (15 characters maximum) for use in pop-up menus and the Edit Links dialog box.
- **USERCLASSTYPE_APPNAME**   Name of the application servicing the class.

rString   A reference to a **CString** object to which the string describing the OLE item's type is to be returned.

Remarks   Call this function to get the user-visible string describing the OLE item's type, such as "Word document." This is often the entry in the system registration database.

If the full type name is requested but not available, the short name is used instead. If no entry for the type of OLE item is found in the registration database, or if there are no user types registered for the type of OLE item, then the user type currently stored in the OLE item is used. If that user type name is an empty string, "Unknown Object" is used.

See Also   **COleClientItem::GetType**

In the *OLE 2 Programmer's Reference, Volume 1*: **IOleObject::GetUserType**

COleClientItem::IsInPlaceActive

BOOL IsInPlaceActive( ) const;

Return Value   Nonzero if the OLE item is in-place active; otherwise 0.

Remarks   Call this function to see whether the OLE item is in-place active. It is common to execute different logic depending on whether the item is being edited in place. The function checks whether the current item state is equal to either the **activeState** or the **activeUIState**.

See Also   **COleClientItem::GetItemState**

COleClientItem::IsLinkUpToDate

BOOL IsLinkUpToDate( ) const;

Return Value   Nonzero if the OLE item is up to date; otherwise 0.

Remarks   Call this function to see whether the OLE item is up to date. A linked item can be out of date if its source document has been updated. An embedded item that contains links within it can similarly become out of date. The function does a recursive check of the OLE item. Note that determining whether an OLE item is out of date can be as expensive as actually performing an update.

This is called automatically by the **COleLinksDialog** implementation.

See Also   In the *OLE 2 Programmer's Reference, Volume 1*: **OleObject::IsUpToDate**

COleClientItem::IsModified

BOOL IsModified( ) const;

Return Value   Nonzero if the OLE item is dirty; otherwise 0.

Remarks   Call this function to see whether the OLE item is dirty (modified since it was last saved).

See Also   In the *OLE 2 Programmer's Reference, Volume 1*: **IPersistStorage::IsDirty**

COleClientItem::IsOpen

BOOL IsOpen( ) const;

Return Value   Nonzero if the OLE item is open; otherwise 0.

Remarks   Call this function to see whether the OLE item is open; that is, opened in an instance of the server application running in a separate window. It is used to determine when to draw the object with a hatching pattern. An open object should have a hatch pattern drawn on top of the object. You can use a **CRectTracker** object to accomplish this.

See Also   **COleClientItem::GetItemState**, **CRectTracker**

COleClientItem::IsRunning

BOOL IsRunning( ) const;

Return Value   Nonzero if the OLE item is running; otherwise 0.

Remarks   Call this function to see whether the OLE item is running; that is, whether the item is loaded and running in the server application.

See Also   In the *OLE 2 Programmer's Reference, Volume 1*: **::OleIsRunning**

COleClientItem::OnActivate

virtual void OnActivate( );

Remarks   Called by the framework to notify the item that it has just been activated in place. Note that this function is called to indicate that the server is running, not to indicate that its user interface has been installed in the container application. At this point, the object does not have an active user interface (is not **uiActive**). It has not installed its menus or toolbar. The **OnActivateUI** member function is called when that happens.

The default implementation calls the **OnChange** member function with **OLE_CHANGEDSTATE** as a parameter. Override this function to perform custom processing when an item becomes in-place active.

See Also   **COleClientItem::OnDeactivate**, **COleClientItem::OnDeactivateUI**, **COleClientItem::OnActivateUI**, **COleClientItem::CanActivate**

COleClientItem::OnActivateUI

virtual void OnActivateUI( );

Remarks   The framework calls **OnActivateUI** when the object has entered the active UI state. The object has now installed its tool bar and menus.

The default implementation remembers the server's **HWND** for later **GetServerWindow** calls.

See Also   **COleClientItem::OnDeactivate**, **COleClientItem::OnDeactivateUI**, **COleClientItem::OnActivate**, **COleClientItem::CanActivate**

COleClientItem::OnChange

Protected→
virtual void OnChange(OLE_NOTIFICATION *nCode*,
        DWORD *dwParam* **);**
END Protected

Parameters   *nCode*   The reason the server changed this item. It can have one of the following values:

- **OLE_CHANGED**   The OLE item's appearance has changed.
- **OLE_SAVED**   The OLE item has been saved.

- **OLE_CLOSED**   The OLE item has been closed.
- **OLE_CHANGED_STATE**   The OLE item has changed from one state to another.

dwParam   If *nCode* is **OLE_SAVED** or **OLE_CLOSED**, this parameter is not used. If *nCode* is **OLE_CHANGED**, this parameter specifies the aspect of the OLE item that has changed. For possible values, see the *dwParam* parameter of **COleClientItem::Draw**. If *nCode* is **OLE_CHANGED_STATE**, this parameter is a **COleClientItem::ItemState** enumerated value and describes the state being entered. It can have one of the following values: **emptyState**, **loadedState**, **openState**, **activeState**, or **activeUIState**.

Remarks   Called by the framework when the user modifies, saves, or closes the OLE item. (If the server application is written using the Microsoft Foundation Class Library, this function is called in response to the **Notify** member functions of **COleServerDoc** or **COleServerItem**.) The default implementation marks the container document as modified if *nCode* is **OLE_CHANGED** or **OLE_SAVED**.

For **OLE_CHANGED_STATE**, the current state returned from **GetItemState** will still be the old state, meaning the state that was current prior to this state change.

Override this function to respond to changes in the OLE item's state. Typically you update the item's appearance by invalidating the area in which the item is displayed. Call the base class implementation at the beginning of your override.

See Also   **COleClientItem::GetItemState**, **COleServerItem::NotifyChanged**, **COleServerDoc::NotifyChanged**, **COleServerDoc::NotifyClosed**, **COleServerDoc::NotifySaved**

COleClientItem::OnChangeItemPosition

virtual BOOL OnChangeItemPosition(const CRect& *rectPos* **);**

Return Value   Nonzero if the item's position is successfully changed; otherwise 0.

Parameters   *rectPos*   Indicates the item's position relative to the container application's client area.

Remarks   Called by the framework to notify the container that the OLE item's extent has changed during in-place activation. The default implementation determines the new visible rectangle of the OLE item and calls **SetItemRects** with the new values. The default implementation calculates the visible rectangle for the item and passes that information to the server.

Override this function to apply special rules to the resize/move operation. If the application is written in MFC, this call results because the server called **COleServerDoc::RequestPositionChange**.

See Also   **COleServerDoc::RequestPositionChange**

COleClientItem::OnDeactivate

virtual void OnDeactivate( );

Remarks   Called by the framework when the OLE item transitions from the in-place active state (**ActiveState**) to the loaded state, meaning that it is deactivated after an in-place activation. Note that this function is called to indicate that the OLE item is closed, not that its user interface has been removed from the container application. When that happens, the **OnDeactivateUI** member function is called.

The default implementation calls the **OnChange** member function with **OLE_CHANGEDSTATE** as a parameter. Override this function to perform custom processing when an in-place active item is deactivated. For example, if you support the undo command in your container application, you can override this function to discard the undo state, indicating that the last operation performed on the OLE item cannot be undone once the item is deactivated.

See Also   **COleClientItem::OnGetWindowContext**, **COleClientItem::OnDeactivateUI**, **COleClientItem::OnActivateUI**, **COleClientItem::OnActivate**, **COleClientItem::CanActivate**, **CDocTemplate::SetContainerInfo**

COleClientItem::OnDeactivateAndUndo

Protected→
virtual void OnDeactivateAndUndo( );
    END Protected

Remarks   Called by the framework when the user invokes the undo command after activating the OLE item in place. The default implementation calls **DeactivateUI** to deactivate the server's user interface. Override this function if you are implementing the undo command in your container application. In your override, call the base class version of the function and then undo the last command executed in your application.

See Also   **COleClientItem::DeactivateUI**

In the *OLE 2 Programmer's Reference, Volume 1:*
IOleInPlaceSite::DeactivateAndUndo

COleClientItem::OnDeactivateUI

Protected→
virtual void OnDeactivateUI(BOOL *bUndoable* **);**
END Protected

Parameters   *bUndoable*   Specifies whether the editing changes are undoable.

Remarks   Called when the user deactivates an item that was activated in place. This function restores the container application's user interface to its original state, hiding any menus and other controls that were created for in-place activation.

If *bUndoable* is **FALSE**, the container should disable the undo command, in effect discarding the undo state of the container, because it indicates that the last operation performed by the server is not undoable.

See Also   **COleClientItem::OnActivateUI**, **COleClientItem::OnDeactivateAndUndo**, **COleClientItem::OnDeactivate**

COleClientItem::OnDiscardUndoState

virtual void OnDiscardUndoState( );

Remarks   Called by the framework when the user performs an action that discards the undo state while editing the OLE item. The default implementation does nothing. Override this function if you are implementing the undo command in your container application. In your override, discard the container application's undo state.

If the server was written with the Microsoft Foundation Class Library, the server can cause this function to be called by calling **COleServerDoc::DiscardUndoState**.

See Also   **COleServerDoc::DiscardUndoState**

In the *OLE 2 Programmer's Reference, Volume 1*:
IOleInPlaceSite::DiscardUndoState

COleClientItem::OnGetClipboardData

virtual COleDataSource* OnGetClipboardData(BOOL *bIncludeLink*,
   LPPOINT *lpOffset*, **LPSIZE** *lpSize* **);**

Return Value   A pointer to a **COleDataSource** object containing the Clipboard data.

Parameters   *bIncludeLink*   Set this to **TRUE** if link data should be copied to the Clipboard. Set this to **FALSE** if your server application does not support links.

lpOffset   Pointer to the offset of the mouse cursor from the origin of the object in pixels.

lpSize   Pointer to the size of the object in pixels.

Remarks   Called by the framework to get a **COleDataSource** object containing all the data that would be placed on the Clipboard by a call to either the **CopyToClipboard** or the **DoDragDrop** member function. The default implementation of this function calls **GetClipboardData**.

See Also   **COleDataSource**, **COleClientItem::CopyToClipboard**, **COleClientItem::GetClipboardData**, **COleDataSource::SetClipboard**

COleClientItem::OnGetClipRect

virtual void OnGetClipRect(CRect& *rClipRect* **);**

Parameters   *rClipRect*   Pointer to an object of class **CRect** that will hold the clipping-rectangle coordinates of the item.

Remarks   The framework calls the **OnGetClipRect** member function to get the clipping-rectangle coordinates of the item that is being edited in place. Coordinates are in pixels relative to the container application window's client area.

The default implementation simply returns the client rectangle of the view on which the item is in-place active.

See Also   **COleClientItem::OnActivate**

COleClientItem::OnGetItemPosition

Protected→
virtual void OnGetItemPosition(CRect& *rPosition* **);**
END Protected

Parameters   *rPosition*   Reference to the **CRect** object that will contain the item's position coordinates.

Remarks   The framework calls the **OnGetItemPosition** member function to get the coordinates of the item that is being edited in place. Coordinates are in pixels relative to the container application window's client area.

The default implementation of this function does nothing. Applications that support in-place editing require its implementation.

See Also   **COleClientItem::OnActivate**, **COleClientItem::OnActivateUI**

COleClientItem::OnGetWindowContext

virtual BOOL OnGetWindowContext(CFrameWnd** *ppMainFrame*,
  CFrameWnd** *ppDocFrame*, **LPOLEINPLACEFRAMEINFO**
  lpFrameInfo);

Return Value

Nonzero if successful; otherwise 0.

Parameters

ppMainFrame   Pointer to a pointer to the main frame window.

ppDocFrame   Pointer to a pointer to the document frame window.

lpFrameInfo   Pointer to an **LPOLEINPLACEFRAMEINFO** structure that will
  receive frame window information.

Remarks

Called by the framework when an item is activated in place. This function is used to
retrieve information about the OLE item's parent window.

If the container is an MDI application, the default implementation returns a pointer
to the **CMDIFrameWnd** object in *ppMainFrame* and a pointer to the active
CMDIChildWnd object in *ppDocFrame*. If the container is an SDI application,
the default implementation returns a pointer to the **CFrameWnd** object in
ppMainFrame and returns **NULL** in *ppDocFrame*. The default implementation
also fills in the members of *lpFrameInfo*.

Override this function only if the default implementation does not suit your
application; for example, if your application has a user-interface paradigm that
differs from SDI or MDI. This is an advanced overridable.

See Also

In the *OLE 2 Programmer's Reference, Volume 1*:
IOleInPlaceSite::GetWindowContext

COleClientItem::OnInsertMenus

virtual void OnInsertMenus(CMenu* *pMenuShared*,
  LPOLEMENUGROUPWIDTHS *lpMenuWidths*);

Parameters

pMenuShared   Points to an empty menu.

lpMenuWidths   Points to an array of six **LONG** values indicating how many
  menus are in each of the following menu groups: File, Edit, Container, Object,
  Window, Help. The container application is responsible for the File, Container,
  and Window menu groups, corresponding to elements 0, 2, and 4 of this array.

Remarks

Called by the framework during in-place activation to insert the container
application's menus into an empty menu. This menu is then passed to the server,
which inserts its own menus, creating a composite menu. This function can be
called repeatedly to build several composite menus.

The default implementation inserts into *pMenuShared* the in-place container menus; that is, the File, Container, and Window menu groups. **CDocTemplate::SetContainerInfo** is used to set this menu resource. The default implementation also assigns the appropriate values to elements 0, 2, and 4 in *lpMenuWidths*, depending on the menu resource. Override this function if the default implementation is not appropriate for your application; for example, if your application does not use document templates for associating resources with document types. If you override this function, you should also override **OnSetMenu** and **OnRemoveMenus**. This is an advanced overridable.

See Also   **COleClientItem::OnRemoveMenus, COleClientItem::OnSetMenu**

In the *OLE 2 Programmer's Reference, Volume 1*:
IOleInPlaceFrame::InsertMenus

COleClientItem::OnRemoveMenus

virtual void OnRemoveMenus(CMenu* *pMenuShared* **);**

Parameters   *pMenuShared*   Points to the composite menu constructed by calls to the **OnInsertMenus** member function.

Remarks   Called by the framework to remove the container's menus from the specified composite menu when in-place activation ends.

The default implementation removes from *pMenuShared* the in-place container menus, that is, the File, Container, and Window menu groups. Override this function if the default implementation is not appropriate for your application; for example, if your application does not use document templates for associating resources with document types. If you override this function, you should probably override **OnInsertMenus** and **OnSetMenu** as well. This is an advanced overridable.

The submenus on *pMenuShared* may be shared by more than one composite menu if the server has repeatedly called **OnInsertMenus**. Therefore you should not delete any submenus in your override of **OnRemoveMenus**; you should only detach them.

See Also   **COleClientItem::OnInsertMenus, COleClientItem::OnSetMenu**

In the *OLE 2 Programmer's Reference, Volume 1:*
IOleInPlaceFrame::RemoveMenus

COIeClientItem::OnScrollBy

Protected→

virtual BOOL OnScrollBy(CSize *sizeExtent* **);**

END Protected

Return Value   Nonzero if the item was scrolled; 0 if the item could not be scrolled.

Parameters   *sizeExtent*   Specifies the distances, in pixels, to scroll in the x and y directions.

Remarks   Called by the framework to scroll the OLE item in response to requests from the server. For example, if the OLE item is partially visible and the user moves outside the visible region while performing in-place editing, this function is called to keep the cursor visible. The default implementation does nothing. Override this function to scroll the item by the specified amount. Note that as a result of scrolling, the visible portion of the OLE item can change. Call **SetItemRects** to update the item's visible rectangle.

See Also   **COIeClientItem::SetItemRects**

In the *OLE 2 Programmer's Reference, Volume 1*: **IOleInPlaceSite::OnScroll**

COIeClientItem::OnSetMenu

virtual void OnSetMenu(CMenu* *pMenuShared*, **HOLEMENU** *holemenu*, **HWND** *hwndActiveObject* **);**

Parameters   *pMenuShared*   Pointer to the composite menu constructed by calls to the **OnInsertMenus** member function and the **::InsertMenu** function.

holemenu   Handle to the menu descriptor returned by the **::OleCreateMenuDescriptor** function, or **NULL** if the dispatching code is to be removed.

hwndActiveObject   Handle to the editing window for the OLE item. This is the window that will receive editing commands from OLE.

Remarks   Called by the framework two times when in-place activation begins and ends; the first time to install the composite menu and the second time (with *holemenu* equal to **NULL**) to remove it. The default implementation installs or removes the composite menu and then calls the **::OleSetMenuDescriptor** function to install or remove the dispatching code. Override this function if the default implementation is not appropriate for your application. If you override this function, you should probably override **OnInsertMenus** and **OnRemoveMenus** as well. This is an advanced overridable.

See Also   COleClientItem::OnInsertMenus, COleClientItem::OnRemoveMenus

In the *OLE 2 Programmer's Reference, Volume 1:* ::OleCreateMenuDescriptor, ::OleSetMenuDescriptor, IOleInPlaceFrame::SetMenu

COleClientItem::OnShowControlBars

virtual BOOL OnShowControlBars(CFrameWnd* *pFrameWnd*, BOOL *bShow*);

Return Value   Nonzero if the function call causes a change in the control bars' state; 0 if the call causes no change, or if *pFrameWnd* does not point to the container's frame window.

Parameters   *pFrameWnd*   Pointer to the container application's frame window. This can be either a main frame window or an MDI child window.

bShow   Specifies whether control bars are to be shown or hidden.

Remarks   Called by the framework to show and hide the container application's control bars. This function returns 0 if the control bars are already in the state specified by *bShow*. This would occur, for example, if the control bars are hidden and *bShow* is **FALSE**.

The default implementation removes the toolbar from the top-level frame window.

See Also   COleClientItem::OnInsertMenus, COleClientItem::OnSetMenu, COleClientItem::OnRemoveMenus, COleClientItem::OnUpdateFrameTitle

COleClientItem::OnShowItem

virtual void OnShowItem( );

Remarks   Called by the framework to display the OLE item, making it totally visible during editing. It is used when your container application supports links to embedded items (that is, if you have derived your document class from **COleLinkingDoc**). This function is called during in-place activation or when the OLE item is a link source and the user wants to edit it. The default implementation activates the first view on the container document. Override this function to scroll the document so that the OLE item is visible.

See Also   COleLinkingDoc

COleClientItem::OnUpdateFrameTitle

virtual void OnUpdateFrameTitle( );

Remarks   Called by the framework during in-place activation to update the frame window's title bar. The general form of the frame window title is "*server app - item* in *docname*" (for example, "Microsoft Excel - spreadsheet in REPORT.DOC"). The default implementation synthesizes a string and sets it to be the frame window title. Override this function if you want a different frame title for your application. This is an advanced overridable.

COleClientItem::ReactivateAndUndo

BOOL ReactivateAndUndo( );

Return Value   Nonzero if successful; otherwise 0.

Remarks   Call this function to reactivate the OLE item and undo the last operation performed by the user during in-place editing. If your container application supports the undo command, call this function if the user chooses the undo command immediately after deactivating the OLE item.

If the server application is written with the Microsoft Foundation Class Libraries, this function causes the server to call **COleServerDoc::OnReactivateAndUndo**.

See Also   **COleServerDoc::OnReactivateAndUndo**,
COleClientItem::OnDeactivateAndUndo

In the *OLE 2 Programmer's Reference, Volume 1:*
IOleInPlaceObject::ReactivateAndUndo

COleClientItem::Release

virtual void Release(OLECLOSE *dwCloseOption* =
    OLECLOSE_NOSAVE);

Parameters   *dwCloseOption*   Flag specifying under what circumstances the OLE item is saved when it returns to the loaded state. For a list of possible values, see **COleClientItem::Close**.

Remarks   Call this function to clean up resources used by the OLE item. **Release** is called by the **COleClientItem** destructor.

See Also   **COleClientItem::Close, COleClientItem::Delete**

In the *OLE 2 Programmer's Reference, Volume 1*: **IUnknown::Release**,
IStorage::Release

COleClientItem::Reload

BOOL Reload( );

Return Value   Nonzero if successful; otherwise 0.

Remarks   Closes and reloads the item. Call the **Reload** function after activating the item as an item of another type by a call to **ActivateAs**.

See Also   **COleClientItem::ActivateAs**

COleClientItem::Run

void Run( );

Remarks   Runs the application associated with this item.

Call the **Run** member function to launch the server application before activating the item. This is done automatically by **ActivateAndDoVerb**, so it is usually not necessary to call this function. Call this function if it is necessary to run the server in order to set an item attribute, such as **SetExtent**, before executing **DoVerb**.

See Also   **COleClientItem::IsRunning**

COleClientItem::SetDrawAspect

void SetDrawAspect(DVASPECT *nDrawAspect* **);**

Parameters   *nDrawAspect*   A value from the **DVASPECT** enumeration. This parameter can have one of the following values:

- **DVASPECT_CONTENT**   Item is represented in such a way that it can be displayed as an embedded object inside its container.
- **DVASPECT_THUMBNAIL**   Item is rendered in a "thumbnail" representation so that it can be displayed in a browsing tool.
- **DVASPECT_ICON**   Item is represented by an icon.
- **DVASPECT_DOCPRINT**   Item is represented as if it were printed using the Print command from the File menu.

Remarks   Call the **SetDrawAspect** member function to set the "aspect," or view, of the item. The aspect specifies how the item is to be rendered by **COleClientItem::Draw** when the default value for that function's *nDrawAspect* argument is used.

This function is called automatically by the Change Icon (and other dialogs that call the Change Icon dialog directly) to enable the iconic display aspect when requested by the user.

See Also   **COleClientItem::GetDrawAspect, COleClientItem::Draw**

COleClientItem::SetExtent

> void SetExtent(const CSize& *size*, DVASPECT *nDrawAspect* = DVASPECT_CONTENT);

Parameters   *size*   A **CSize** object that contains the size information.

nDrawAspect   Specifies the aspect of the OLE item whose bounds are to be set. For possible values, see **COleClientItem::Draw**.

Remarks   Call this function to specify how much space is available to the OLE item. If the server application was written using the Microsoft Foundation Class Library, this causes the **OnSetExtent** member function of the corresponding **COleServerItem** object to be called. The OLE item can then adjust its display accordingly. The dimensions must be in **MM_HIMETRIC** units. Call this function when the user resizes the OLE item or if you support some form of layout negotiation.

See Also   **COleClientItem::GetExtent, COleServerItem::OnSetExtent**

In the *OLE 2 Programmer's Reference, Volume 1*: **IOleObject::SetExtent**

COleClientItem::SetHostNames

> void SetHostNames(LPCTSTR *lpszHost*, LPCTSTR *lpszHostObj*);

Parameters   *lpszHost*   Pointer to the user-visible name of the container application.

lpszHostObj   Pointer to an identifying string of the container that contains the OLE item.

Remarks   Call this function to specify the name of the container application and the container's name for an embedded OLE item. If the server application was written using the Microsoft Foundation Class Library, this function calls the **OnSetHostNames** member function of the **COleServerDoc** document that contains the OLE item. This information is used in window titles when the OLE item is being edited. Each time a container document is loaded, the framework calls this function for all the OLE items in the document. **SetHostNames** is applicable only to embedded items. It is not necessary to call this function each time an embedded OLE item is activated for editing.

This is also called automatically with the application name and document name when an object is loaded or when a file is saved under a different name. Accordingly, it is not usually necessary to call this function directly.

See Also   **COleServerDoc::OnSetHostNames**

In the *OLE 2 Programmer's Reference, Volume 1*: **IOleObject::SetHostNames**

COleClientItem::SetIconicMetafile

BOOL SetIconicMetafile(HGLOBAL *hMetaPict* **);**

Return Value   Nonzero if successful; otherwise 0.

Parameters   *hMetaPict*   A handle to the metafile used for drawing the item's icon.

Remarks   Caches the metafile used for drawing the item's icon. Use **GetIconicMetafile** to retrieve the metafile.

The *hMetaPict* parameter is copied into the item; therefore, *hMetaPict* must be freed by the caller.

See Also   **COleClientItem::GetIconicMetafile**

COleClientItem::SetItemRects

BOOL SetItemRects(LPCRECT *lpPosRect* **= NULL, LPCRECT** *lpClipRect* **= NULL);**

Parameters   *lprcPosRect*   Pointer to the rectangle containing the bounds of the OLE item relative to its parent window, in client coordinates.

lprcClipRect   Pointer to the rectangle containing the bounds of the visible portion of the OLE item relative to its parent window, in client coordinates.

Remarks   Call this function to set the bounding rectangle or the visible rectangle of the OLE item. This function is called by the default implementation of the **OnChangeItemPosition** member function. You should call this function whenever the position or visible portion of the OLE item changes. Usually this means that you call it from your view's **OnSize** and **OnScrollBy** member functions.

See Also   **COleClientItem::OnChangeItemPosition, COleClientItem::OnGetItemPosition**

In the *OLE 2 Programmer's Reference, Volume 1*: **IOleInPlaceObject::SetObjectRects**

COleClientItem::SetLinkUpdateOptions

void SetLinkUpdateOptions(OLEUPDATE *dwUpdateOpt* **);**

Parameters   *dwUpdateOpt*   The value of the link-update option for this item. This value must be one of the following:

- **OLEUPDATE_ALWAYS**   Update the linked item whenever possible. This option supports the Automatic link-update radio button in the Links dialog box.

- **OLEUPDATE_ONCALL** Update the linked item only on request from the container application (when the **UpdateLink** member function is called). This option supports the Manual link-update radio button in the Links dialog box.

Remarks   Call this function to set the link-update option for the presentation of the specified linked item. Typically, you should not change the update options chosen by the user in the Links dialog box.

See Also   **COleClientItem::GetLinkUpdateOptions**, **COleLinksDialog**

In the *OLE 2 Programmer's Reference, Volume 1*: **IOleLink::SetUpdateOptions**

COleClientItem::SetPrintDevice

BOOL SetPrintDevice(const DVTARGETDEVICE* *ptd*);

BOOL SetPrintDevice(const PRINTDLG* *ppd*);

Return Value   Nonzero if the function was successful; otherwise 0.

Parameters   *ptd*   Pointer to a **DVTARGETDEVICE** data structure, which contains information about the new print-target device. Can be **NULL**.

ppd   Pointer to a **PRINTDLG** data structure, which contains information about the new print-target device. Can be **NULL**.

Remarks   Call this function to change the print-target device for this item. This function updates the print-target device for the item but does not rcfrcsh the presentation cache. To update the presentation cache for an item, call **COleClientItem::UpdateLink**.

The arguments to this function contain information that the OLE system uses to identify the target device. The **PRINTDLG** structure contains information that Windows uses to initialize the common Print dialog box. After the user closes the dialog box, Windows returns information about the user's selections in this structure. The **m_pd** member of a **CPrintDialog** object is a **PRINTDLG** structur For more information about this structure, see the *Windows 3.1 Software Development Kit* (SDK) documentation.

See Also   **COleClientItem::UpdateLink**, **CPrintDialog**

In the *OLE 2 Programmer's Reference, Volume 1*: **DVTARGETDEVICE**

In the *Windows 3.1 Software Development Kit* documentation: **PRINTDLG**

COleClientItem::UpdateLink

BOOL UpdateLink( );

Return Value   Nonzero on success; otherwise 0.

Remarks   Call this function to update the presentation data of the OLE item immediately. For linked items, the function finds the link source to obtain a new presentation for the OLE item. This process may involve running one or more server applications, which could be time-consuming. For embedded items, the function operates recursively, checking whether the embedded item contains links that might be out of date and updating them. The user can also manually update individual links using the Links dialog box.

See Also   **COleLinksDialog**

In the *OLE 2 Programmer's Reference, Volume 1*: **IOleLink::Update**

class COleConvertDialog : public COleDialog

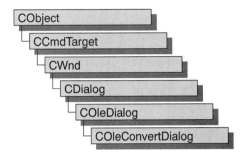

The **COleConvertDialog** class is used for the OLE Convert dialog box. Create an object of class **COleConvertDialog** when you want to call this dialog box. After a **COleConvertDialog** object has been constructed, you can use the **m_cv** structure to initialize the values or states of controls in the dialog box. The **m_cv** structure is of type **OLEUICONVERT**.

For more information about OLE 2–specific dialog boxes, see the article "Dialog Boxes in OLE" in *Programming with the Microsoft Foundation Class Library*.

#include <afxodlgs.h>

See Also   **COleDialog**

In the *OLE 2 Programmer's Reference, Volume 1*: **OLEUICONVERT**

Data Members

m_cv	A structure that controls the behavior of the dialog box.

Construction

COleConvertDialog	Constructs a **COleConvertDialog** object.

Operations and Attributes

DoConvert	Performs the conversion specified in the dialog box.
DoModal	Displays the OLE 2 Change Item dialog box.
GetClassID	Gets the **CLSID** associated with the chosen item.
GetDrawAspect	Specifies whether to draw item as an icon.

| GetIconicMetafile | Gets a handle to the metafile associated with the iconic form of this item. |
| GetSelectionType | Gets the type of selection chosen. |

Member Functions

COleConvertDialog::COleConvertDialog

COleConvertDialog (**COleClientItem*** *pItem*, **DWORD** *dwFlags* = **CF_SELECTCONVERTTO**, **CLSID FAR*** *pClassID* = **NULL**, **CWnd*** *pParentWnd* = **NULL**);

Parameters

pItem   Points to the item to be converted or activated.

dwFlags   Creation flag, which contains any number of the following values combined using the bitwise-or operator:

- **CF_SHOWHELPBUTTON**   Specifies that the Help button will be displayed when the dialog box is called.
- **CF_SETCONVERTDEFAULT**   Specifies that the class whose **CLSID** is specified by the **clsidConvertDefault** member of the **m_cv** structure will be used as the default selection in the class list box when the Convert To radio button is selected.
- **CF_SETACTIVATEDEFAULT**   Specifies that the class whose **CLSID** is specified by the **clsidActivateDefault** member of the **m_cv** structure will be used as the default selection in the class list box when the Activate As radio button is selected.
- **CF_SELECTCONVERTTO**   Specifies that the Convert To radio button will be selected initially when the dialog box is called. This is the default.
- **CF_SELECTACTIVATEAS**   Specifies that the Activate As radio button will be selected initially when the dialog box is called.

pClassID   Points to the **CLSID** of the item to be converted or activated. If **NULL**, the **CLSID** associated with *pItem* will be used.

pParentWnd   Points to the parent or owner window object (of type **CWnd**) to which the dialog object belongs. If it is **NULL**, the parent window of the dialog box is set to the main application window.

Remarks

Constructs only a **COleConvertDialog** object. To display the dialog box, call the **DoModal** function.

See Also   COleConvertDialog::DoModal

In the *OLE 2 Programmer's Reference, Volume 1*: **CLSID, OLEUICONVERT**

COleConvertDialog::DoConvert

BOOL DoConvert(COleClientItem* *pItem* **);**

Return Value   Nonzero if successful; otherwise 0.

Parameters   *pItem*   Points to the item to be converted or activated. Cannot be NULL.

Remarks   Call this function, after returning successfully from **DoModal,** either to convert or to activate an object of type **COleClientItem**. The item is converted or activated according to the information selected by the user in the Convert dialog box.

See Also   **COleClientItem, COleConvertDialog::DoModal,
COleConvertDialog::GetSelectionType, COleClientItem::ConvertTo,
COleClientItem::ActivateAs**

COleConvertDialog::DoModal

virtual int DoModal( );

Return Value   **IDOK** if the dialog box was successfully displayed, **IDCANCEL** if the user canceled the dialog box, or **IDABORT** if an error occurred. If **IDABORT** is returned, call the **COleDialog::GetLastError** member function to get more information about the type of error that occurred. For a listing of possible errors, see "OleUIConvert" in the *User Interface Dialog* help file.

Remarks   Call this function to display the OLE Convert dialog box.

If you want to initialize the various dialog box controls by setting members of the **m_cv** structure, you should do this before calling **DoModal**, but after the dialog object is constructed.

If **DoModal** returns **IDOK**, you can call other member functions to retrieve the settings or information that was input by the user into the dialog box.

See Also   **COleDialog::GetLastError**, **CDialog::DoModal**

COleConvertDialog::GetClassID

const CLSID& GetClassID( ) const;

Return Value   The **CLSID** associated with the item that was selected in the Convert dialog box.

Remarks   Call this function to get the **CLSID** associated with the item the user selected in the Convert dialog box. Call this function only after **DoModal** returns **IDOK**.

See Also   **COleConvertDialog::DoModal**

In the *OLE 2 Programmer's Reference, Volume 1*: **CLSID**

COleConvertDialog::GetDrawAspect

DVASPECT GetDrawAspect( ) const;

Return Value   The method needed to render the object.

- **DVASPECT_CONTENT**   Returned if the Display As Icon check box was not checked.
- **DVASPECT_ICON**   Returned if the Display As Icon check box was checked.

Remarks   Call this function to determine whether the user chose to display the selected item as an icon. Call this function only after **DoModal** returns **IDOK**.

See Also   **COleConvertDialog::DoModal, COleConvertDialog::COleConvertDialog**

In the *OLE 2 Programmer's Reference, Volume 1*: **DVASPECT**

COleConvertDialog::GetIconicMetafile

HGLOBAL GetIconPicture( ) const;

Return Value   The handle to the metafile containing the iconic aspect of the selected item, if the Display As Icon check box was checked when the dialog was dismissed by choosing **OK**; otherwise **NULL**.

Remarks   Call this function to get a handle to the metafile that contains the iconic aspect of the selected item.

See Also   **COleConvertDialog::DoModal, COleConvertDialog::COleConvertDialog, COleConvertDialog::GetDrawAspect**

COleConvertDialog::GetSelectionType

UINT GetSelectionType( ) const;

Return Value   Type of selection made:

- **COleConvertDialog::noConversion**   Returned if either the dialog box was canceled or the user selected no conversion. If **DoModal** returned **IDOK**, it is possible that the user selected a different icon than the one previously selected.
- **COleConvertDialog::convertItem**   Returned if the Convert To radio button was checked, the user selected a different item to convert to, and **DoModal** returned **IDOK**.

- **COleConvertDialog::activateAs**   Returned if the Activate As radio button was checked, the user selected a different item to activate, and **DoModal** returned **IDOK**.

Remarks   Call this function to determine the type of conversion selected in the Convert dialog box.

See Also   **COleConvertDialog::DoModal**, **COleConvertDialog::COleConvertDialog**

Data Members

COleConvertDialog::m_cv

Remarks   Structure of type **OLEUICONVERT** used to control the behavior of the Convert dialog box. Members of this structure can be modified either directly or through member functions.

See Also   **COleConvertDialog::COleConvertDialog**

In the *OLE 2 Programmer's Reference, Volume 1*: **OLEUICONVERT**

class COleDataObject

The **COleDataObject** class is used in data transfers for retrieving data in various formats from the Clipboard, through drag and drop, or from an embedded OLE item. These kinds of data transfers include a source and a destination. The data source is implemented as an object of the **COleDataSource** class. Whenever a destination application has data dropped in it or is asked to perform a paste operation from the Clipboard, an object of the **COleDataObject** class must be created.

This class enables you to determine whether the data exists in a specified format. You can also enumerate the available data formats or check whether a given format is available and then retrieve the data in the preferred format. Object retrieval can be accomplished in several different ways, including the use of a **CFile**, an **HGLOBAL**, or an **STGMEDIUM** structure. For more information about the **STGMEDIUM** structure, see the *OLE 2 Programmer's Reference, Volume 1.*

For more information about using data objects in your application, see the article "Data Objects and Data Sources" in *Programming with the Microsoft Foundation Class Library.*

#include <afxole.h>

See Also   **COleDataSource, COleClientItem, COleServerItem, COleDataSource::DoDragDrop, CView::OnDrop**

Construction

COleDataObject	Constructs a **COleDataObject** object.

Operations

Attach	Attaches the specified OLE data object to the **COleDataObject**.
AttachClipboard	Attaches the data object that is on the Clipboard.
BeginEnumFormats	Prepares for one or more subsequent **GetNextFormat** calls.
Detach	Detaches the associated **IDataObject** object.
GetData	Copies data from the attached OLE data object in a specified format.
GetFileData	Copies data from the attached OLE data object into a **CFile** pointer in the specified format.

GetGlobalData	Copies data from the attached OLE data object into an **HGLOBAL** in the specified format.
GetNextFormat	Returns the next data format available.
IsDataAvailable	Checks whether data is available in a specified format.
Release	Detaches and releases the associated **IDataObject** object.

Member Functions

COleDataObject::Attach

void **Attach(LPDATAOBJECT** *lpDataObject*, **BOOL** *bAutoRelease* = **TRUE**);

Parameters   *lpDataObject*   Points to an OLE data object.

bAutoRelease   **TRUE** if the OLE data object should be released when the **COleDataObject** object is destroyed; otherwise **FALSE**.

Remarks   Call this function to associate the **COleDataObject** object with an OLE data object.

See Also   **COleDataObject::AttachClipboard, COleDataObject::Detach, COleDataObject::Release**

In the *OLE 2 Programmer's Reference, Volume 1*: **IDataObject**

COleDataObject::AttachClipboard

BOOL AttachClipboard( );

Return Value   Nonzero if successful; otherwise 0.

Remarks   Call this function to attach the data object that is currently on the Clipboard to the **COleDataObject** object.

See Also   **COleDataObject::Attach, COleDataObject::Detach, COleDataObject::Release**

COleDataObject::BeginEnumFormats

void **BeginEnumFormats( );**

Remarks   Call this function to prepare for one or more subsequent **GetNextFormat** calls for retrieving data from the item.

After a call to **BeginEnumFormats**, the position of the first format supported by the **GetData**, **GetFileData**, and **GetGlobalData** functions is stored. Successive calls to **GetNextFormat** will enumerate the list of available formats in the data object.

See Also   COleDataObject::GetNextFormat

In the *OLE 2 Programmer's Reference, Volume 1*:
IDataObject::EnumFormatEtc

COleDataObject::COleDataObject

COleDataObject( );

Remarks   Constructs a **COleDataObject** object. A call to **Attach** must be made before calling other **COleDataObject** functions.

See Also   COleDataObject::Attach, COleDataObject::Release

COleDataObject::Detach

LPDATAOBJECT Detach( );

Return Value   A pointer to the OLE data object that was detached.

Remarks   Call this function to detach the **COleDataObject** object from its associated OLE data object without releasing the data object.

See Also   COleDataObject::Attach, COleDataObject::Release

COleDataObject::GetData

BOOL GetData(CLIPFORMAT *cfFormat*, **LPSTGMEDIUM** *lpStgMedium*, **LPFORMATETC** *lpFormatEtc* = **NULL**);

Return Value   Nonzero if successful; otherwise 0.

Parameters   *cfFormat*   The format in which data is to be returned. This parameter can be one of the predefined Clipboard formats or the value returned by the native Windows **RegisterClipboardFormat** function.

lpStgMedium   Points to a **STGMEDIUM** structure that will receive data.

lpFormatEtc   Points to a **FORMATETC** structure describing the format in which data is to be returned. Provide a value for this parameter if you want to specify additional format information beyond the Clipboard format specified by *cfFormat*. If it is **NULL**, the default values are used for the other fields in the **FORMATETC** structure.

Remarks   Call this function to retrieve data from the item in the specified format.

See Also   **COleDataObject::GetFileData**, **COleDataObject::GetGlobalData**

In the *OLE 2 Programmer's Reference, Volume 1*: **IDataObject::GetData**

COleDataObject::GetFileData

CFile* GetFileData(CLIPFORMAT *cfFormat*, **LPFORMATETC**
lpFormatEtc = **NULL**);

Return Value   Pointer to the new **CFile** or **CFile**-derived object containing the data if successful;
otherwise **NULL**.

Parameters   *cfFormat*   The format in which data is to be returned. This parameter can be one
of the predefined Clipboard formats or the value returned by the native
Windows **RegisterClipboardFormat** function.

lpFormatEtc   Points to a **FORMATETC** structure describing the format in which
data is to be returned. Provide a value for this parameter if you want to specify
additional format information beyond the Clipboard format specified by
cfFormat. If it is **NULL**, the default values are used for the other fields in the
FORMATETC structure.

Remarks   Call this function to create a **CFile** or **CFile**-derived object and to retrieve data in
the specified format into a **CFile** pointer. Depending on the medium the data is
stored in, the actual type pointed to by the return value may be **CFile**,
CSharedFile, or **COleStreamFile**.

See Also   **COleDataObject::GetData**, **COleDataObject::GetGlobalData**,
::RegisterClipboardFormat

COleDataObject::GetGlobalData

HGLOBAL GetGlobalData(CLIPFORMAT *cfFormat*, **LPFORMATETC**
lpFormatEtc = **NULL**);

Return Value   The handle of the global memory block containing the data if successful; otherwise
NULL.

Parameters   *cfFormat*   The format in which data is to be returned. This parameter can be one
of the predefined Clipboard formats or the value returned by the native
Windows **RegisterClipboardFormat** function.

lpFormatEtc   Points to a **FORMATETC** structure describing the format in which
data is to be returned. Provide a value for this parameter if you want to specify
additional format information beyond the Clipboard format specified by

cfFormat. If it is **NULL**, the default values are used for the other fields in the **FORMATETC** structure.

Remarks   Call this function to allocate a global memory block and to retrieve data in the specified format into an **HGLOBAL**.

See Also   **COleDataObject::GetData**, **COleDataObject::GetFileData**

COleDataObject::GetNextFormat

BOOL GetNextFormat(LPFORMATETC *lpFormatEtc* **);**

Return Value   Nonzero if another format is available; otherwise 0.

Parameters   *lpFormatEtc*   Points to the **FORMATETC** structure that receives the format information when the function call returns.

Remarks   Call this function repeatedly to obtain all the formats available for retrieving data from the item.

After a call to **BeginEnumFormats**, the position of the first format supported by the **GetData**, **GetFileData**, and **GetGlobalData** functions is stored. Successive calls to **GetNextFormat** will enumerate the list of available formats in the data object. When a desired format is retrieved, call **GetData**, **GetFileData**, or **GetGlobalData** to actually get the data.

See Also   **COleDataObject::BeginEnumFormats**, **COleDataObject::GetData**, **COleDataObject::GetFileData**, **COleDataObject::GetGlobalData**

In the *OLE 2 Programmer's Reference, Volume 1*: **IEnumFORMATETC::Next**

COleDataObject::IsDataAvailable

BOOL IsDataAvailable(CLIPFORMAT *cfFormat*, **LPFORMATETC** *lpFormatEtc* = **NULL**);

Return Value   Nonzero if data is available in the specified format; otherwise 0.

Parameters   *cfFormat*   The Clipboard data format to be used in the structure pointed to by *lpFormatEtc*.

lpFormatEtc   Points to a **FORMATETC** structure describing the format desired. Provide a value for this parameter only if you want to specify additional format information beyond the Clipboard format specified by *cfFormat*. If it is **NULL**, the default values are used for the other fields in the **FORMATETC** structure.

Remarks   Call this function to determine if a particular format is available for retrieving data from the OLE item. This function is useful before calling **GetData**, **GetFileData**, or **GetGlobalData**. It is an alternative to enumerating formats.

See Also   **COleDataObject::BeginEnumFormats**, **COleDataObject::GetData**,
COleDataObject::GetFileData, **COleDataObject::GetGlobalData**,
COleDataObject::GetNextFormat

In the *OLE 2 Programmer's Reference, Volume 1*: **IDataObject::QueryGetData**

COleDataObject::Release

void Release( );

Remarks   Call this function to release ownership of the **IDataObject** object that was
previously associated with the **COleDataObject** object by using **Attach** or one of
the constructors. If the *bAutoRelease* parameter of **Attach** is **FALSE**, the
IDataObject object will not be released. In this case, the caller is responsible for
releasing the **IDataObject** by calling its **Release** method.

See Also   **COleDataObject::Attach**, **COleDataObject::COleDataObject**,
COleDataObject::Detach

class COleDataSource : public CCmdTarget

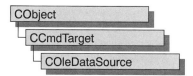

The **COleDataSource** class acts as a cache into which an OLE application places the data that it will offer during data transfer operations, such as Clipboard or drag-and-drop operations.

After an OLE data object has been created using either the **COleClientItem**, **ColeServerItem**, or one derived from one of these classes, the user either chooses Copy or Cut from the Edit menu or begins a drag-and-drop operation. The application calls an appropriate function from the object that has been created, which then calls **OnGetClipboardData**. As a result, that function creates an object of the **COleDataSource** class.

Whenever you want to prepare data for a transfer, you should create an object of this class and fill it with your data using the most appropriate method for your data. The way it is inserted into a data source is directly affected by whether the data is supplied immediately (immediate rendering) or on demand (delayed rendering). For every Clipboard format in which you are providing data by passing the Clipboard format to be used (and an optional **FORMATETC** structure), call **COleDataSource::DelayRenderData**.

For more information about data sources and data transfer, please see the article "Data Objects and Data Sources" in *Programming with the Microsoft Foundation Class Library*.

#include <afxole.h>

See Also **COleClientItem**, **COleDataObject**, **COleServerItem**

In *Programming with the Microsoft Foundation Class Library*: "Clipboard"

Construction
COleDataSource	Constructs a **COleDataSource** object.

Operations
CacheData	Offers data in a specified format using a **STGMEDIUM** structure.
CacheGlobalData	Offers data in a specified format using an **HGLOBAL**.

DelayRenderData	Offers data in a specified format using delayed rendering.
DelayRenderFileData	Offers data in a specified format in a **CFile** pointer.
DelaySetData	Called for every format that is supported in **OnSetData**.
DoDragDrop	Performs Drag and Drop operations with a data source.
Empty	Empties the **COleDataSource** object of data.
FlushClipboard	Renders all data to the clipboard.
GetClipboardOwner	Verifies that the data placed on the clipboard is still there.
OnRenderData	Retrieves data as part of delayed rendering.
OnRenderFileData	Retrieves data into a **CFile** as part of delayed rendering.
OnRenderGlobalData	Retrieves data into an **HGLOBAL** as part of delayed rendering.
OnSetData	Called to replace the data in the **COleDataSource** object.
SetClipboard	Places a **COleDataSource** object on the clipboard.

Member Functions

COleDataSource::CacheData

void CacheData(CLIPFORMAT *cfFormat*, **LPSTGMEDIUM** *lpStgMedium*, **LPFORMATETC** *lpFormatEtc* = **NULL**);

Parameters   *cfFormat*   The Clipboard format in which the data is to be offered.

lpStgMedium   Points to a **STGMEDIUM** structure containing the data in the format specified.

lpFormatEtc   Points to a **FORMATETC** structure describing the format in which the data is to be offered. Provide a value for this parameter if you want to specify additional format information beyond the Clipboard format specified by *cfFormat*. If it is **NULL**, default values are used for the other fields in the **FORMATETC** structure.

Remarks   Call this function to specify a format in which data is offered during data transfer operations. You must supply the data, because this function provides it by using immediate rendering. The data is cached until needed.

Supply the data using a **STGMEDIUM** structure. You can also use the **CacheGlobalData** member function if the amount of data you are supplying is small enough to be transferred efficiently using an **HGLOBAL**.

After the call to **CacheData** the *ptd* member of *lpFormatEtc* and the contents of *lpStgMedium* are owned by the data object, not by the caller.

For more information about the **STGMEDIUM** or **FORMATETC** structures, see the *OLE 2 Programmer's Reference, Volume 1.*

To use delayed rendering, call the **DelayRenderData** or **DelayRenderFileData** member functions.

See Also   COleDataSource::CacheGlobalData, COleDataSource::DelayRenderData, COleDataSource::DelayRenderFileData

COleDataSource::CacheGlobalData

void CacheGlobalData(CLIPFORMAT *cfFormat*, **HGLOBAL** *hGlobal*, **LPFORMATETC** *lpFormatEtc* **= NULL);**

Parameters   *cfFormat*   The Clipboard format in which the data is to be offered.

hGlobal   Handle to the global memory block containing the data in the format specified.

lpFormatEtc   Points to a **FORMATETC** structure describing the format in which the data is to be offered. Provide a value for this parameter if you want to specify additional format information beyond the Clipboard format specified by *cfFormat*. If it is **NULL**, default values are used for the other fields in the **FORMATETC** structure.

Remarks   Call this function to specify a format in which data is offered during data transfer operations. This function provides the data using immediate rendering, so you must supply the data when calling the function; the data is cached until needed. Use the **CacheData** member function if you are supplying a large amount of data or if you require a structured storage medium.

To use delayed rendering, call the **DelayRenderData** or **DelayRenderFileData** member functions.

See Also   COleDataSource::CacheData, COleDataSource::DelayRenderData, COleDataSource::DelayRenderFileData

COleDataSource::COleDataSource

COleDataSource( );

Remarks   Constructs a **COleDataSource** object.

COleDataSource::DelayRenderData

void DelayRenderData(CLIPFORMAT *cfFormat***, LPFORMATETC**
lpFormatEtc **= NULL**);

Parameters   *cfFormat*   The Clipboard format in which the data is to be offered.

lpFormatEtc   Points to a **FORMATETC** structure describing the format in which
the data is to be offered. Provide a value for this parameter if you want to
specify additional format information beyond the Clipboard format specified by
cfFormat. If it is **NULL**, default values are used for the other fields in the
FORMATETC structure.

Remarks   Call this function to specify a format in which data is offered during data transfer
operations. This function provides the data using delayed rendering, so the data is
not supplied immediately. The **OnRenderData** or **OnRenderGlobalData** member
functions are called to request the data.

Use this function if you are not going to supply your data through a **CFile** object. If
you are going to supply the data through a **CFile** object, call the
DelayRenderFileData member function.

To use immediate rendering, call the **CacheData** or **CacheGlobalData** member
functions.

See Also   **COleDataSource::CacheData, COleDataSource::CacheGlobalData,
COleDataSource::DelayRenderFileData, COleDataSource::OnRenderData,
COleDataSource::OnRenderGlobalData**

COleDataSource::DelayRenderFileData

void DelayRenderFileData(CLIPFORMAT *cfFormat***, LPFORMATETC**
lpFormatEtc **= NULL**);

Parameters   *cfFormat*   The Clipboard format in which the data is to be offered.

lpFormatEtc   Points to a **FORMATETC** structure describing the format in which
the data is to be offered. Provide a value for this parameter if you want to
specify additional format information beyond the Clipboard format specified by
cfFormat. If it is **NULL**, default values are used for the other fields in the
FORMATETC structure.

Remarks   Call this function to specify a format in which data is offered during data transfer
operations. This function provides the data using delayed rendering, so the data is
not supplied immediately. The **OnRenderFileData** member function is called to
request the data.

Use this function if you are going to use a **CFile** object to supply the data. If you are not going to use a **CFile** object, call the **DelayRenderData** member function.

To use immediate rendering, call the **CacheData** or **CacheGlobalData** member functions.

See Also   **COleDataSource::CacheData, COleDataSource::CacheGlobalData, COleDataSource::DelayRenderData, COleDataSource::OnRenderFileData**

COleDataSource::DelaySetData

void DelaySetData(CLIPFORMAT *cfFormat*, **LPFORMATETC** *lpFormatEtc* **= NULL) const;**

Parameters   *cfFormat*   The Clipboard format in which the data is to be placed.

lpFormatEtc   Points to a **FORMATETC** structure describing the format in which the data is to be replaced. Provide a value for this parameter if you want to specify additional format information beyond the Clipboard format specified by *cfFormat*. If it is **NULL**, default values are used for the other fields in the **FORMATETC** structure.

Remarks   Call this function to support changing the contents of the data source. **OnSetData** will be called by the framework when this happens. This is only used when the framework returns the data source from **COleServerItem::GetDataSource**. If **DelaySetData** is not called, your **OnSetData** function will never be called. **DelaySetData** should be called for each clipboard or **FORMATETC** format you support.

See Also   **COleServerItem::GetDataSource, COleDataSource::OnSetData**

COleDataSource::DoDragDrop

DROPEFFECT DoDragDrop(DWORD *dwEffects* **= DROPEFFECT_COPY|DROPEFFECT_MOVE|DROPEFFECT_LINK, LPCRECT** *lpRectStartDrag* **= NULL, COleDropSource*** *pDropSource* **= NULL);**

Return Value   Drop effect generated by the drag-and-drop operation; otherwise **DROPEFFECT_NONE** if the operation never begins because the user released the mouse button before leaving the supplied rectangle.

Parameters   *dwEffects*   Drag and drop operations that are allowed on this data source. Can be one or more of the following:

- **DROPEFFECT_COPY**   A copy operation could be performed.
- **DROPEFFECT_MOVE**   A move operation could be performed.

- **DROPEFFECT_LINK**   A link from the dropped data to the original data could be established.

- **DROPEFFECT_SCROLL**   Indicates that a drag scroll operation could occur.

lpRectStartDrag   Points to a rectangle that determines when the drag-and-drop operation actually starts. If **NULL**, an empty rectangle will be used.

pDropSource   Points to a drop source. If **NULL** then a default implementation of **COleDropSource** will be used.

Remarks   Call this function to begin a drag-and-drop operation for this data source. Call this function when the user starts to drag selected data, typically when a **WM_LBUTTONDOWN** message is received. For more information, see the article "Drag and Drop; Implementing a Drop Source" in *Programming with the Microsoft Foundation Class Library*.

See Also   **COleDropSource::OnBeginDrag**, **COleDropSource**

COleDataSource::Empty

void Empty( );

Remarks   Call this function to empty the **COleDataSource** object of data. Both cached and delay render formats are emptied so they can be reused.

See Also   In the *OLE 2 Programmer's Reference, Volume 1*: **::ReleaseStgMedium**

COleDataSource::FlushClipboard

static void FlushClipboard( );

Remarks   Removes data from the clipboard that was placed there by a previous call to **SetClipboard**. This function also causes any data still on the Clipboard to be immediately rendered. Call this function when it is necessary to delete the data object last placed on the clipboard from memory. Calling this function ensures that OLE will not require the original data source to perform clipboard rendering.

See Also   **COleDataSource::GetClipboardOwner**, **COleDataSource::SetClipboard**

COleDataSource::GetClipboardOwner

static COleDataSource* GetClipboardOwner( );

Return Value   Returns the data source currently on the Clipboard, **NULL** if there is nothing on the Clipboard or if the Clipboard is not owned by the calling application.

Remarks   Determines whether the data on the Clipboard has changed since **SetClipboard** was last called and, if so, identifies the current owner.

See Also   COleDataSource::FlushClipboard, COleDataSource::SetClipboard

COleDataSource::OnRenderData

virtual BOOL OnRenderData(LPFORMATETC *lpFormatEtc*,
    LPSTGMEDIUM *lpStgMedium*);

Return Value   Nonzero if successful; otherwise 0.

Parameters   *lpFormatEtc*   Points to the **FORMATETC** structure specifying the format in which information is requested.

              lpStgMedium   Points to a **STGMEDIUM** structure in which the data is to be returned.

Remarks   Called by the framework to retrieve data in the specified format. The specified format is one previously placed in the **COleDataSource** object using the **DelayRenderData** or **DelayRenderFileData** member functions for delayed rendering. The default implementation of this function will call **OnRenderFileData** or **OnRenderGlobalData** if the supplied storage medium is either a file or memory, respectively. If neither of these formats are supplied, then the default implementation will return 0 and do nothing.

If *lpStgMedium->tymed* is **TYMED_NULL**, the **STGMEDIUM** should allocated and filled as specified by *lpFormatEtc->tymed*. If it is not **TYMED_NULL**, the **STGMEDIUM** should be filled in place with the data.

Override this function to supply your data in the requested format and medium. Depending on your data, you may want to override one of the other versions of this function instead. If your data is small and fixed in size, override **OnRenderGlobalData**. If your data is in a file, or is of variable size, override **OnRenderFileData**. This is an advanced overridable.

See Also   COleDataSource::DelayRenderData,
COleDataSource::DelayRenderFileData,
COleDataSource::OnRenderFileData,
COleDataSource::OnRenderGlobalData, COleDataSource::OnSetData

In the *OLE 2 Programmer's Reference, Volume 1*: **IDataObject::GetData**

COleDataSource::OnRenderFileData

virtual BOOL OnRenderFileData(LPFORMATETC *lpFormatEtc***, CFile*** *pFile* **);**

Return Value   Nonzero if successful; otherwise 0.

Parameters   *lpFormatEtc*   Points to the **FORMATETC** structure specifying the format in which information is requested.

pFile   Points to a **CFile** object in which the data is to be rendered.

Remarks   Called by the framework to retrieve data in the specified format when the specified storage medium is a file. The specified format is one previously placed in the **COleDataSource** object using the **DelayRenderData** member function for delayed rendering. The default implementation of this function simply returns **FALSE**.

This is an advanced overridable. Override this function to supply your data in the requested format and medium. Depending on your data, you might want to override one of the other versions of this function instead. If you want to handle multiple storage media, override **OnRenderData**. If your data is in a file, or is of variable size, override **OnRenderFileData**.

See Also   **COleDataSource::DelayRenderData, COleDataSource::DelayRenderFileData, COleDataSource::OnRenderData, COleDataSource::OnRenderGlobalData, COleDataSource::OnSetData**

In the *OLE 2 Programmer's Reference, Volume 1*: **IDataObject::GetData**

COleDataSource::OnRenderGlobalData

virtual BOOL OnRenderGlobalData(LPFORMATETC *lpFormatEtc***, HGLOBAL*** *phGlobal* **);**

Return Value   Nonzero if successful; otherwise 0.

Parameters   *lpFormatEtc*   Points to the **FORMATETC** structure specifying the format in which information is requested.

phGlobal   Points to a handle to global memory in which the data is to be returned. If one has not yet been allocated, this parameter can be **NULL**.

Remarks   Called by the framework to retrieve data in the specified format when the specified storage medium is global memory. The specified format is one previously placed in the **COleDataSource** object using the **DelayRenderData** member function for delayed rendering. The default implementation of this function simply returns **FALSE**.

If *phGlobal* is **NULL**, then a new **HGLOBAL** should be allocated and returned in *phGlobal*. Otherwise, the **HGLOBAL** specified by *phGlobal* should be filled with the data. The amount of data placed in the **HGLOBAL** must not exceed the current size of the memory block. Also, the block cannot be reallocated to a larger size.

This is an advanced overridable. Override this function to supply your data in the requested format and medium. Depending on your data, you may want to override one of the other versions of this function instead. If you want to handle multiple storage media, override **OnRenderData**. If your data is in a file, or is of variable size, override **OnRenderFileData**.

See Also   **COleDataSource::DelayRenderData**,
COleDataSource::DelayRenderFileData, **COleDataSource::OnRenderData**,
COleDataSource::OnRenderFileData, **COleDataSource::OnSetData**

In the *OLE 2 Programmer's Reference, Volume 1*: **IDataObject::GetData**

COleDataSource::OnSetData

virtual BOOL OnSetData(LPFORMATETC *lpFormatEtc*, **LPSTGMEDIUM** *lpStgMedium*, **BOOL** *bRelease* **);**

Return Value   Nonzero if successful; otherwise 0.

Parameters   *lpFormatEtc*   Points to the **FORMATETC** structure specifying the format in which data is being replaced.

lpStgMedium   Points to the **STGMEDIUM** structure containing the data that will replace the current contents of the **COleDataSource** object.

bRelease   Indicates who has ownership of the storage medium after completing the function call. The caller decides who is responsible for releasing the resources allocated on behalf of the storage medium. The caller does this by setting *bRelease*. If *bRelease* is nonzero, the data source takes ownership, freeing the medium when it has finished using it. When *bRelease* is 0, the caller retains ownership and the data source can use the storage medium only for the duration of the call.

Remarks   Called by the framework to set or replace the data in the **COleDataSource** object in the specified format. The data source does not take ownership of the data until it has successfully obtained it. That is, it does not take ownership if **OnSetData** returns 0. If the data source takes ownership, it frees the storage medium by calling the **::ReleaseStgMedium** function.

The default implementation does nothing. Override this function to replace the data in the specified format. This is an advanced overridable.

See Also   **COleDataSource::DelaySetData**, **COleDataSource::OnRenderData**,
COleDataSource::OnRenderFileData,
COleDataSource::OnRenderGlobalData, **COleServerItem::OnSetData**

In the *OLE 2 Programmer's Reference, Volume 1*: **IDataObject::GetData**,
::ReleaseStgMedium

COleDataSource::SetClipboard

void SetClipboard( );

Remarks   Puts the data contained in the **COleDataSource** object on the Clipboard after
calling one of the following functions: **CacheData**, **CacheGlobalData**,
DelayRenderData, or **DelayRenderFileData**.

See Also   **COleDataSource::GetClipboardOwner**, **COleDataSource::FlushClipboard**

class COleDialog : public CDialog

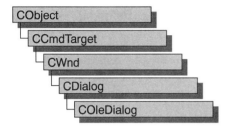

CObject
CCmdTarget
CWnd
CDialog
COleDialog

The **COleDialog** class provides functionality common to dialog boxes for OLE. The Microsoft Foundation Class Library provides several classes derived from **COleDialog**. These are **COleInsertDialog**, **COleConvertDialog**, **COleChangeIconDialog**, **COleLinksDialog**, **COleBusyDialog**, **COleUpdateDialog**, and **COlePasteSpecialDialog**.

For more information about OLE 2–specific dialog boxes, see the article "Dialog Boxes in OLE" in *Programming with the Microsoft Foundation Class Library*.

#include <afxodlgs.h>

See Also   **COleBusyDialog, COleChangeIconDialog, COleConvertDialog, COleInsertDialog, COleLinksDialog, COlePasteSpecialDialog, COleUpdateDialog**

Operations

GetLastError   Gets the error code returned by the dialog box.

Member Functions

COleDialog::GetLastError

UINT GetLastError( ) const;

Return Value   The error codes returned by **GetLastError** depend on the specific dialog box displayed.

Remarks   Calls the **GetLastError** member function to get additional error information when **DoModal** returns **IDABORT**.

See Also   **COleBusyDialog::DoModal, COleChangeIconDialog::DoModal, COleConvertDialog::DoModal, COleInsertDialog::DoModal, COleLinksDialog::DoModal, COlePasteSpecialDialog::DoModal, COleUpdateDialog::DoModal**

class COleDispatchDriver

The **COleDispatchDriver** class implements the client side of OLE automation. OLE dispatch interfaces provide access to an object's methods and properties. Member functions of **COleDispatchDriver** attach, detach, create, and release a dispatch connection of type **IDispatch**. Other member functions use variable argument lists to simplify calling **IDispatch::Invoke**. For more information about **IDispatch::Invoke**, see the *OLE 2 Programmer's Reference, Volume 1*.

This class can be used directly, but it is generally used only by classes created by ClassWizard. When you create new C++ classes by importing a type library, ClassWizard derives the new classes from **COleDispatchDriver**.

#include <afxdisp.h>

See Also   **CCmdTarget**

In *Programming with the Microsoft Foundation Class Library*: "AppWizard: OLE Support," "Automation Clients," "Automation Servers," "ClassWizard: OLE Automation Support"

In the *OLE 2 Programmer's Reference, Volume 1*: **IDispatch**

Construction

COleDispatchDriver	Constructs a **COleDispatchDriver** object.

Operations

CreateDispatch	Creates an **IDispatch** connection and attaches it to the **COleDispatch** object.
AttachDispatch	Attaches an **IDispatch** connection to the **COleDispatchDriver** object.
DetachDispatch	Detaches an **IDispatch** connection, without releasing it.
ReleaseDispatch	Releases an **IDispatch** connection.
InvokeHelper	Helper for calling automation methods.
SetProperty	Sets an automation property.
GetProperty	Gets an automation property.

Member Functions

COleDispatchDriver::AttachDispatch

void AttachDispatch(LPDISPATCH *lpDispatch*, BOOL *bAutoRelease* = TRUE);

Parameters   *lpDispatch*   Pointer to an OLE **IDispatch** object to be attached to the **COleDispatchDriver** object.

bAutoRelease   Specifies whether the dispatch is to be released when this object goes out of scope.

Remarks   Call the **AttachDispatch** member function to attach an **IDispatch** pointer to the **COleDispatchDriver** object. This function releases any **IDispatch** pointer that is already attached to the **COleDispatchDriver** object.

See Also   **COleDispatchDriver::DetachDispatch**, **COleDispatchDriver::ReleaseDispatch**, **COleDispatchDriver::CreateDispatch**

COleDispatchDriver::COleDispatchDriver

COleDispatchDriver( );

Remarks   Constructs a **COleDispatchDriver** object. Before using this object, you should connect an **IDispatch** to it using either **OleDispatchDriver::CreateDispatch** or **OleDispatchDriver::AttachDispatch**.

See Also   **COleDispatchDriver::AttachDispatch**, **COleDispatchDriver::CreateDispatch**

COleDispatchDriver::CreateDispatch

BOOL CreateDispatch(REFCLSID *clsid*, COleException* *pError* = NULL);

BOOL CreateDispatch(LPCTSTR *lpszProgID*, COleException* *pError* = NULL);

Return Value   Nonzero on success; otherwise 0.

Parameters   *clsid*   Class ID of the **IDispatch** connection object to be created.

pError   Pointer to an OLE exception object, which will hold the status code resulting from the creation.

lpszProgID   Pointer to a verbal identifier, such as "Excel.Document.5", of the application for which the dispatch object is to be created.

Remarks   Creates an **IDispatch** object and attaches it to the **COleDispatchDriver** object.

This function throws an exception if *pError* is **NULL**.

See Also   **COleDispatchDriver::DetachDispatch, COleDispatchDriver::ReleaseDispatch, COleDispatchDriver::AttachDispatch, COleException**

COleDispatchDriver::DetachDispatch

LPDISPATCH DetachDispatch( );

Return Value   A pointer to the previously attached OLE **IDispatch** object. For more information about the **LPDISPATCH** type, see the *OLE 2 Programmer's Reference, Volume 1*.

Remarks   Detaches the current **IDispatch** connection from this object. The **IDispatch** is not released.

See Also   **COleDispatchDriver::ReleaseDispatch, COleDispatchDriver::CreateDispatch, COleDispatchDriver::AttachDispatch**

In the *OLE 2 Programmer's Reference*
Volume 1: **LPDISPATCH**

COleDispatchDriver::GetProperty

void GetProperty(DISPID *dwDispID*, **VARTYPE** *vtProp*, **void*** *pvProp* **) const;**

Parameters   *dwDispID*   Identifies the property to be retrieved. This value is usually supplied by ClassWizard.

vtProp   Specifies the property to be retrieved. For possible values, see the "Remarks" for **COleDispatchDriver::InvokeHelper**.

pvProp   Address of the variable that will receive the property value. It must match the type specified by *vtProp*.

Remarks   Gets the object property specified by *vtProp*.

See Also   **COleDispatchDriver::InvokeHelper, COleDispatchDriver::SetProperty**

COleDispatchDriver::InvokeHelper

void InvokeHelper(DISPID *dwDispID*, **WORD** *wFlags*, **VARTYPE** *vtRet*,
void* *pvRet*, **const BYTE FAR*** *pbParamInfo*, **...**);

Parameters   *dwDispID*   Identifies the method or property to be invoked. This value is usually
supplied by ClassWizard.

wFlags   Flags describing the context of the call to **IDispatch::Invoke**. For
possible values, see the *OLE 2 Programmer's Reference, Volume 1*.

vtRet   Specifies the type of the return value. For possible values, see the Remarks
section below.

pvRet   Address of the variable that will receive the property value or return value.
It must match the type specified by *vtRet*.

pbParamInfo   Pointer to a null-terminated string of bytes specifying the types of
the parameters following *pbParamInfo*.

...   Variable list of parameters, of types specified in *pbParamInfo*.

Remarks   Calls the object method or property specified by *dwDispID*, in the context specified
by *wFlags*. The *pbParamInfo* parameter specifies the types of the parameters
passed to the method or property. The variable list of arguments is represented by **...**
in the syntax declaration.

Possible values for the *vtRet* argument are taken from the **VARENUM**
enumeration. Possible values are as follows:

Symbol	Return Type
VT_EMPTY	**void**
VT_I2	**short**
VT_I4	**long**
VT_R4	**float**
VT_R8	**double**
VT_CY	**CY**
VT_DATE	**DATE**
VT_BSTR	**BSTR**
VT_DISPATCH	**LPDISPATCH**
VT_ERROR	**SCODE**
VT_BOOL	**BOOL**
VT_VARIANT	**VARIANT**
VT_UNKNOWN	**LPUNKNOWN**

The *pbParamInfo* argument is a space-separated list of **VTS_**. One or more of these values, separated by spaces (not commas), specifies the function's parameter list. Possible values are as follows:

Symbol	Parameter Type
VTS_I2	**short**
VTS_I4	**long**
VTS_R4	**float**
VTS_R8	**double**
VTS_CY	**const CY***
VTS_DATE	**DATE**
VTS_BSTR	**const char***
VTS_DISPATCH	**LPDISPATCH**
VTS_SCODE	**SCODE**
VTS_BOOL	**BOOL**
VTS_VARIANT	**const VARIANT***
VTS_UNKNOWN	**LPUNKNOWN**
VTS_PI2	**short***
VTS_PI4	**long***
VTS_PR4	**float***
VTS_PR8	**double***
VTS_PCY	**CY***
VTS_PDATE	**DATE***
VTS_PBSTR	**BSTR***
VTS_PDISPATCH	**LPDISPATCH***
VTS_PSCODE	**SCODE***
VTS_PBOOL	**BOOL***
VTS_PVARIANT	**VARIANT***
VTS_PUNKNOWN	**LPUNKNOWN***

See Also   In the *OLE 2 Programmer's Reference, Volume 1:* **IDispatch**

COleDispatchDriver::ReleaseDispatch

void ReleaseDispatch( );

Remarks   Releases the **IDispatch** connection.

See Also   **COleDispatchDriver::DetachDispatch,**
COleDispatchDriver::CreateDispatch, COleDispatchDriver::AttachDispatch

COleDispatchDriver::SetProperty

void SetProperty(DISPID *dwDispID*, **VARTYPE** *vtProp*, **...**);

Parameters

dwDispID   Identifies the property to be set. This value is usually supplied by ClassWizard.

vtProp   Specifies the type of the property to be set. For possible values, see the Remarks for **COleDispatchDriver::InvokeHelper**.

...   A single parameter of the type specified by *vtProp*.

Remarks   Sets the OLE object property specified by *dwDispID*.

See Also   **COleDispatchDriver::InvokeHelper**, **COleDispatchDriver::GetProperty**

class COleDispatchException : public CException

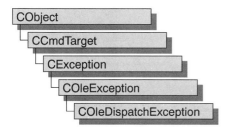

The **COleDispatchException** class handles exceptions specific to the OLE **IDispatch** interface, which is a key part of OLE automation. Like the other exception classes derived from the **CException** base class, **COleDispatchException** is intended to be used with the **THROW**, **THROW_LAST**, **TRY**, **CATCH**, **AND_CATCH**, and **END_CATCH** macros. For more information on exceptions, see the article "Exceptions" in *Programming with the Microsoft Foundation Class Library*.

#include <afxdisp.h>

See Also   **COleDispatchDriver**, **COleException**

Data Members

m_wCode	**IDispatch**-specific error code.
m_strDescription	Verbal error description.
m_dwHelpContext	Help context for error.
m_strHelpFile	Help file to use with **m_dwHelpContext**.
m_strSource	Application that generated the exception.

Data Members

COleDispatchException::m_dwHelpContext

DWORD m_dwHelpContext;

Remarks   Identifies a help context in your application's help (.HLP) file. This member is set by the function **AfxThrowOleDispatchException** when an exception is thrown.

See Also   **COleDispatchException::m_strDescription,
COleDispatchException::m_wCode**

COleDispatchException::m_strDescription

CString m_strDescription;

Remarks   Contains a verbal error description, such as "Disk full." This member is set by the function **AfxThrowOleDispatchException** when an exception is thrown.

See Also   **COleDispatchException::m_dwHelpContext,
COleDispatchException::m_wCode, AfxThrowOleDispatchException**

COleDispatchException::m_strHelpFile

CString m_strHelpFile;

Remarks   The framework fills in this string with the name of the application's help file.

See Also   **AfxThrowOleDispatchException**

COleDispatchException::m_strSource

CString m_strSource;

Remarks   The framework fills in this string with the name of the application that generated the exception.

See Also   **AfxThrowOleDispatchException**

COleDispatchException::m_wCode

WORD m_wCode;

Remarks Contains an error code specific to your application. This member is set by the function **AfxThrowOleDispatchException** when an exception is thrown.

See Also **COleDispatchException::m_strDescription**,
COleDispatchException::m_dwHelpContext,
AfxThrowOleDispatchException

class COleDocument : public CDocument

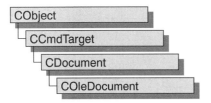

COleDocument is the base class for OLE documents that support visual editing. COleDocument is derived from CDocument, which allows your OLE applications to use the document/view architecture provided by the Microsoft Foundation Class Library.

COleDocument treats a document as a collection of CDocItem objects. Both container and server applications require such an architecture because their documents must be able to contain OLE items. The COleServerItem and COleClientItem classes, both derived from CDocItem, manage the interactions between applications and OLE items.

If you are writing a simple container application, derive your document class from COleDocument. If you are writing a container application that supports linking to the embedded items contained by its documents, derive your document class from COleLinkingDoc. If you are writing a server application or combination container/server, derive your document class from COleServerDoc. COleLinkingDoc and COleServerDoc are derived from COleDocument, so these classes inherit all the services available in COleDocument and CDocument.

To use COleDocument, derive a class from it and add functionality to manage the application's non-OLE data as well as embedded or linked items. If you define CDocItem-derived classes to store the application's native data, you can use the default implementation defined by COleDocument to store both your OLE and non-OLE data. You can also design your own data structures for storing your non-OLE data separately from the OLE items. For more information, see the article "Containers: Compound Files" in *Programming with the Microsoft Foundation Class Library*.

#include <afxole.h>

See Also   COleLinkingDoc, COleServerDoc, COleClientItem, COleServerItem, CDocItem

Construction

COleDocument   Constructs a COleDocument object.

Operations

HasBlankItems	Checks for blank items in the document.
EnableCompoundFile	Causes documents to be stored using the OLE Structured Storage file format.
GetInPlaceActiveItem	Returns the OLE item that is currently in-place active.
GetNextClientItem	Gets the next client item for iterating.
GetNextServerItem	Gets the next server item for iterating.
UpdateModifiedFlag	Marks the document as modified if any of the contained OLE items have been modified.
ApplyPrintDevice	Sets the print-target device for all client items in the document.
AddItem	Adds an item to the list of items maintained by the document.
GetNextItem	Gets the next document item for iterating.
GetStartPosition	Gets the initial position to begin iteration.
RemoveItem	Removes an item from the list of items maintained by the document.

Overridables

GetPrimarySelectedItem	Returns the primary selected OLE item in the document.
OnShowViews	Called when the document becomes visible or invisible.

Member Functions

COleDocument::AddItem

virtual void AddItem(CDocItem* *pItem*);

Parameters   *pItem*   Pointer to the document item being added.

Remarks   Call this function to add an item to the document. You do not need to call this function explicitly when it is called by the **COleClientItem** or **COleServerItem** constructor that accepts a pointer to a document.

See Also   **CDocItem, COleDocument::RemoveItem, COleServerItem::COleServerItem, COleClientItem::COleClientItem**

COleDocument::ApplyPrintDevice

BOOL ApplyPrintDevice(const DVTARGETDEVICE FAR* *ptd* **);**

BOOL ApplyPrintDevice(const PRINTDLG* *ppd* **);**

Return Value   Nonzero if the function was successful; otherwise 0.

Parameters   *ptd*   Pointer to a **DVTARGETDEVICE** data structure, which contains information about the new print-target device. Can be **NULL**.

ppd   Pointer to a **PRINTDLG** data structure, which contains information about the new print-target device. Can be **NULL**.

Remarks   Call this function to change the print-target device for all embedded **COleClientItem** items in your application's container document. This function updates the print-target device for all items but does not refresh the presentation cache for those items. To update the presentation cache for an item, call **COleClientItem::UpdateLink**.

The arguments to this function contain information that OLE uses to identify the target device. The **PRINTDLG** structure contains information that Windows uses to initialize the common Print dialog box. After the user closes the dialog box, Windows returns information about the user's selections in this structure. The **m_pd** member of a **CPrintDialog** object is a **PRINTDLG** structure. For more information about this structure, see the *Windows 3.1 Software Development Kit (SDK)* documentation.

See Also   **CPrintDialog**

In the *OLE 2 Programmer's Reference, Volume 1*: **DVTARGETDEVICE**

COleDocument::COleDocument

COleDocument( );

Remarks   Constructs a **COleDocument** object.

COleDocument::EnableCompoundFile

void EnableCompoundFile(BOOL *bEnable* = **TRUE);**

Parameters   *bEnable*   Specifies whether compound file support is enabled or disabled.

Remarks   Call this function if you want to store the document using the compound-document structured file format. You typically call this function from the constructor of your **COleDocument**-derived class. For more information about compound documents, see the article "Containers: Compound Files" in *Programming with the Microsoft Foundation Class Library*.

If you do not call this member function, documents will be stored in a nonstructured ("flat") file format.

After compound file support is enabled or disabled for a document, the setting should not be changed during the document's lifetime.

See Also   **COleClientItem**

In *Programming with the Microsoft Foundation Class Library*: "Containers: Compound Files"

COleDocument::GetInPlaceActiveItem

COleClientItem* GetInPlaceActiveItem(CWnd* *pWnd* **);**

Return Value   A pointer to the single, in-place active OLE item; **NULL** if there is no OLE item currently in the "in-place active" state.

Parameters   *pWnd*   Pointer to the window that displays the container document.

Remarks   Call this function to get the OLE item that is currently activated in place in the frame window containing the view identified by *pWnd*.

See Also   **COleClientItem**

COleDocument::GetNextClientItem

COleClientItem* GetNextClientItem(POSITION& *pos* **) const;**

Return Value   A pointer to the next client item in the document, or **NULL** if there are no more client items.

Parameters   *pos*   A reference to a **POSITION** value set by a previous call to **GetNextClientItem**; the initial value is returned by the **GetStartPosition** member function.

Remarks   Call this function repeatedly to access each of the client items in your document. After each call, the value of *pos* is set for the next item in the document, which might or might not be a client item.

See Also   **COleClientItem**, **COleDocument::GetStartPosition**

Example

```
// pDoc points to a COleDocument object
POSITION pos = pDoc->GetStartPosition();
COleClientItem *pItem;
while ( ( pItem = pDoc->GetNextClientItem( pos ) ) != NULL )
{
    // Use pItem
}
```

COleDocument::GetNextItem

virtual CDocItem* GetNextItem(POSITION& *pos* **) const;**

Return Value   A pointer to the document item at the specified position.

Parameters   *pos*   A reference to a **POSITION** value set by a previous call to **GetNextItem**; the initial value is returned by the **GetStartPosition** member function.

Remarks   Call this function repeatedly to access each of the items in your document. After each call, the value of *pos* is set to the **POSITION** value of the next item in the document. If the retrieved element is the last element in the document, the new value of *pos* is **NULL**.

See Also   **COleDocument::GetStartPosition**

Example

```
// pDoc points to a COleDocument object
POSITION pos = pDoc->GetStartPosition();
CDocItem *pItem;
while( pos != NULL )
{
    pItem = pDoc->GetNextItem( pos );
    // Use pItem
}
```

COleDocument::GetNextServerItem

COleServerItem* GetNextServerItem(POSITION& *pos* **) const;**

Return Value   A pointer to the next server item in the document, or **NULL** if there are no more server items.

Parameters   *pos*   A reference to a **POSITION** value set by a previous call to **GetNextServerItem**; the initial value is returned by the **GetStartPosition** member function.

Remarks   Call this function repeatedly to access each of the server items in your document. After each call, the value of *pos* is set for the next item in the document, which might or might not be a server item.

See Also   **COleServerItem, COleDocument::GetStartPosition**

Example
```
// pDoc points to a COleDocument object
POSITION pos = pDoc->GetStartPosition();
COleServerItem *pItem;
while ( ( pItem = pDoc->GetNextServerItem( pos ) ) != NULL )
{
    // Use pItem
}
```

COleDocument::GetPrimarySelectedItem

virtual COleClientItem* GetPrimarySelectedItem(CView* *pView*);

Return Value   A pointer to the single, selected OLE item; **NULL** if no OLE items are selected or if more than one is selected.

Parameters   *pView*   Pointer to the active view object displaying the document.

Remarks   Called by the framework to retrieve the currently selected OLE item in the specified view. The default implementation searches the list of contained OLE items for a single selected item and returns a pointer to it. If there is no item selected, or if there is more than one item selected, the function returns **NULL**. You must override the **CView::IsSelected** member function in your view class for this function to work. Override this function if you have your own method of storing contained OLE items.

See Also   **CView::IsSelected**

COleDocument::GetStartPosition

virtual POSITION GetStartPosition( ) const;

Return Value   A **POSITION** value that can be used to begin iterating through the document's items; **NULL** if the document has no items.

Remarks   Call this function to get the position of the first item in the document. Pass the value returned to **GetNextItem**, **GetNextClientItem**, or **GetNextServerItem**.

See Also   **COleDocument::GetNextItem, COleDocument::GetNextClientItem, COleDocument::GetNextServerItem**

COleDocument::HasBlankItems

BOOL HasBlankItems( ) const;

Return Value   Nonzero if the document contains any blank items; otherwise 0.

Remarks   Call this function to determine whether the document contains any blank items. A blank item is one whose rectangle is empty.

See Also   **CDocItem::IsBlank**

COleDocument::OnShowViews

virtual void OnShowViews(BOOL *bVisible* **);**

Parameters   *bVisible*   Indicates whether the document has become visible or invisible.

Remarks   The framework calls this function after the document's visibility state changes.

The default version of this function does nothing. Override it if your application must perform any special processing when the document's visibility changes.

COleDocument::UpdateModifiedFlag

void UpdateModifiedFlag( );

Remarks   Call this function to mark the document as modified if any of the contained OLE items have been modified. This allows the framework to prompt the user to save the document before closing, even if the native data in the document has not been modified.

See Also   **CDocument::SetModifiedFlag**, **COleClientItem::IsModified**

COleDocument::RemoveItem

virtual void RemoveItem(CDocItem* *pItem* **);**

Parameters   *pItem*   Pointer to the document item to be removed.

Remarks   Call this function to remove an item from the document. You typically do not need to call this function explicitly; it is called by the destructors for **COleClientItem** and **COleServerItem**.

See Also   **COleServerItem, COleClientItem, COleDocument::AddItem CDocItem**

class COleDropSource : public CCmdTarget

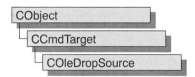

A **COleDropSource** object allows data to be dragged to a drop target. The **COleDropSource** object is responsible for determining when a drag operation begins, providing feedback during the drag operation, and determining when the drag operation ends.

To use a **COleDropSource** object, just call the constructor. This simplifies the process of determining what events, such as a mouse click, begin a drag operation and the selection of an appropriate **DoDragDrop** function. You might also want to modify the default behavior of the overridable functions listed below. These member functions will be called at the appropriate times by the framework.

For more information on drag-and-drop operations using OLE, see the article "Drag and Drop" in *Programming with the Microsoft Foundation Class Library*.

#include <afxole.h>

See Also   **COleDropTarget**

In the *OLE 2 Programmer's Reference, Volume 1*: **IDropSource**

Construction
COleDropSource	Constructs a **COleDropSource** object.

Overridables
GiveFeedback	Changes the cursor during a drag-and-drop operation.
OnBeginDrag	Handles mouse capture during a drag-and-drop operation.
QueryContinueDrag	Checks to see whether dragging should continue.

Member Functions

COleDropSource::COleDropSource

COleDropSource( );

Remarks   Constructs a **COleDropSource** object.

See Also   **COleDropTarget**

COleDropSource::GiveFeedback

virtual SCODE GiveFeedback(DROPEFFECT *dropEffect* **);**

Return Value   Returns **DRAGDROP_S_USEDEFAULTCURSORS** if dragging is in progress, **NOERROR** if it is not.

Parameters   *dropEffect*   The effect you would like to display to the user, usually indicating what would happen if a drop occurred at this point with the selected data. Typically, this is the value returned by the most recent call to **CView::OnDragEnter** or **CView::OnDragOver**. It can be one or more of the following:

- **DROPEFFECT_NONE**   A drop would not be allowed.
- **DROPEFFECT_COPY**   A copy operation would be performed.
- **DROPEFFECT_MOVE**   A move operation would be performed.
- **DROPEFFECT_LINK**   A link from the dropped data to the original data would be established.
- **DROPEFFECT_SCROLL**   A drag scroll operation is about to occur or is occurring in the target.

Remarks   Called by the framework after calling **IDropTarget::DragOver** or **DragEnter**. Override this function to provide feedback to the user about what would happen if a drop occurred at this point. The default implementation uses the OLE 2 default cursors.

See Also   **CView::OnDragEnter**, **CView::OnDragOver**

In the *OLE 2 Programmer's Reference, Volume 1*: **IDropSource::GiveFeedback**

COleDropSource::OnBeginDrag

virtual BOOL OnBeginDrag(CWnd* *pWnd* **);**

Return Value   Nonzero if dragging is allowed, otherwise 0.

Parameters   *pWnd*   Points to the window that contains the selected data.

Remarks   Called by the framework when an event occurs that could begin a drag operation, such as pressing the left mouse button. Override this function if you want to modify the way the dragging process is started. The default implementation captures the mouse and stays in drag mode until the user clicks the left or right mouse button or hits ESC, at which time it releases the mouse.

See Also   **COleDropSource::GiveFeedback**

COleDropSource::QueryContinueDrag

virtual SCODE QueryContinueDrag(BOOL *bEscapePressed,* **DWORD** *dwKeyState*);

Return Value   **DRAGDROP_S_CANCEL** if the ESC key or right button is pressed, or left button is raised before dragging starts. **DRAGDROP_S_DROP** if a drop operation should occur. Otherwise **S_OK**.

Parameters   *bEscapePressed*   States whether the ESC key has been pressed since the last call to **COleDropSource::QueryContinueDrag**.

   dwKeyState   Contains the state of the modifier keys on the keyboard. This is a combination of any number of the following: **MK_CONTROL, MK_SHIFT, MK_ALT, MK_LBUTTON, MK_MBUTTON,** and **MK_RBUTTON**.

Remarks   After dragging has begun, this function is called repeatedly by the framework until the drag operation is either canceled or completed. Override this function if you want to change the point at which dragging is canceled or a drop occurs.

   The default implementation initiates the drop or cancels the drag as follows. It cancels a drag operation when the ESC key or the right mouse button is pressed. It initiates a drop operation when the left mouse button is raised after dragging has started. Otherwise, it returns **S_OK** and performs no further operations.

   Because this function is called frequently, it should be optimized as much as possible.

See Also   **COleDropSource::OnBeginDrag, COleDropTarget::OnDrop**

class COleDropTarget : public CCmdTarget

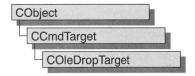

A **COleDropTarget** object provides the communication mechanism between a window and the OLE 2 libraries. Creating an object of this class allows a window to accept data through the OLE 2 drag-and-drop mechanism.

To get a window to accept drop commands, you should first create an object of the **COleDropTarget** class, and then call the **Register** function with a pointer to the desired **CWnd** object as the only parameter.

For more information on drag-and-drop operations using OLE, see the article "Drag and Drop" in *Programming with the Microsoft Foundation Class Library*.

#include <afxole.h>

See Also   **COleDropSource**

Construction
COleDropTarget   Constructs a **COleDropTarget** object.

Operations

Register	Registers the window as a valid drop target.
Revoke	Causes the window to cease being a valid drop target.

Overridables

OnDragEnter	Called when the cursor first enters the window.
OnDragLeave	Called when the cursor is dragged out of the window.
OnDragOver	Called repeatedly when the cursor is dragged over the window.
OnDragScroll	Called to determine whether the cursor is dragged into the scroll region of the window.
OnDrop	Called when data is dropped into the window.

Member Functions

COleDropTarget::COleDropTarget

COleDropTarget( );

Remarks   Constructs an object of class **COleDropTarget**. Call **Register** to associate this object with a window.

See Also   **COleDropSource**

COleDropTarget::OnDragEnter

virtual DROPEFFECT OnDragEnter(CWnd* *pWnd*, **COleDataObject***
pDataObject, **DWORD** *dwKeyState*, **CPoint** *point* **);**

Return Value   The effect that would result if a drop were attempted at the location specified by *point*. It can be one or more of the following:

- **DROPEFFECT_NONE**   A drop would not be allowed.
- **DROPEFFECT_COPY**   A copy operation would be performed.
- **DROPEFFECT_MOVE**   A move operation would be performed.

- **DROPEFFECT_LINK**   A link from the dropped data to the original data would be established.
- **DROPEFFECT_SCROLL**   A drag scroll operation is about to occur or is occurring in the target.

Parameters   *pWnd*   Points to the window the cursor is entering.

pDataObject   Points to the data object containing the data that may be dropped.

dwKeyState   Contains the state of the modifier keys on the keyboard. This is a combination of any number of the following: **MK_CONTROL, MK_SHIFT, MK_ALT, MK_LBUTTON, MK_MBUTTON**, and **MK_RBUTTON**.

point   Contains the current location of the cursor in client coordinates.

Remarks   Called by the framework when the cursor is first dragged into the window. Override this function to allow drop operations to occur in the window. The default implementation calls **CView::OnDragEnter**, which simply returns **DROPEFFECT_NONE** by default.

See Also   **COleDropTarget::OnDragOver, COleDropTarget::OnDragLeave, COleDropTarget::OnDrop**

COleDropTarget::OnDragLeave

virtual void OnDragLeave(CWnd* *pWnd* **);**

Parameters   *pWnd*   Points to the window the cursor is leaving.

Remarks   Called by the framework when the cursor leaves the window while a dragging operation is in effect. Override this function if you want special behavior when the drag operation leaves the specified window. The default implementation of this function calls **CView::OnDragLeave,** which returns **DROPEFFECT_NONE**.

See Also   **COleDropTarget::OnDragEnter, COleDropTarget::OnDragOver, COleDropTarget::OnDrop**

In the *OLE 2 Programmer's Reference, Volume 1*: **IDropTarget::DragLeave**

COleDropTarget::OnDragOver

virtual DROPEFFECT OnDragOver(CWnd* *pWnd*, **COleDataObject*** *pDataObject*, **DWORD** *dwKeyState*, **CPoint** *point* **);**

Return Value   The effect that would result if a drop were attempted at the location specified by *point*. It can be one or more of the following:

- **DROPEFFECT_NONE**   A drop would not be allowed.
- **DROPEFFECT_COPY**   A copy operation would be performed.

- **DROPEFFECT_MOVE**   A move operation would be performed.
- **DROPEFFECT_LINK**   A link from the dropped data to the original data would be established.
- **DROPEFFECT_SCROLL**   Indicates that a drag scroll operation is about to occur or is occurring in the target.

Parameters

pWnd   Points to the window that the cursor is over.

pDataObject   Points to the data object that contains the data to be dropped.

dwKeyState   Contains the state of the modifier keys on the keyboard. This is a combination of any number of the following: **MK_CONTROL**, **MK_SHIFT**, **MK_ALT**, **MK_LBUTTON**, **MK_MBUTTON**, and **MK_RBUTTON**.

point   Contains the current location of the cursor in client coordinates.

Remarks

Called by the framework when the cursor is dragged over the window. This function should be overridden to allow drop operations to occur in the window. The default implementation of this function calls **CView::OnDragOver**, which returns **DROPEFFECT_NONE** by default. Because this function is called frequently during a drag-and-drop operation, it should be optimized as much as possible.

See Also

COIeDropTarget::OnDragEnter, **COIeDropTarget::OnDragLeave**, **COIeDropTarget::OnDrop**

COIeDropTarget::OnDragScroll

virtual BOOL OnDragScroll(CWnd* *pWnd*, **DWORD** *dwKeyState*, **CPoint** *point* **);**

Return Value

Nonzero if the window supports scrolling and it is appropriate to do so; otherwise 0.

Parameters

pWnd   Points to the window the cursor is currently over.

dwKeyState   Contains the state of the modifier keys on the keyboard. This is a combination of any number of the following: **MK_CONTROL**, **MK_SHIFT**, **MK_ALT**, **MK_LBUTTON**, **MK_MBUTTON**, and **MK_RBUTTON**.

point   Contains the location of the cursor, in pixels, relative to the screen.

Remarks

Called by the framework before calling **OnDragEnter** or **OnDragOver** to determine whether *point* is in the scrolling region. Override this function when you want to provide special behavior for this event. The default implementation automatically scrolls windows when the cursor is dragged into the default scroll region inside the border of each window.

See Also

COIeDropTarget::OnDragEnter, **COIeDropTarget::OnDragOver**

COleDropTarget::OnDrop

virtual BOOL OnDrop(CWnd* *pWnd,* **COleDataObject*** *pDataObject,*
DROPEFFECT *dropEffect,* **CPoint** *point*);

Return Value   Nonzero if the drop is successful; otherwise 0.

Parameters   *pWnd*   Points to the window the cursor is currently over.

pDataObject   Points to the data object that contains the data to be dropped.

dropEffect   The effect that the user chose for the drop operation. It can be one or more of the following:

- **DROPEFFECT_NONE**   A drop would not be allowed.
- **DROPEFFECT_COPY**   A copy operation would be performed.
- **DROPEFFECT_MOVE**   A move operation would be performed.
- **DROPEFFECT_LINK**   A link from the dropped data to the original data would be established.
- **DROPEFFECT_SCROLL**   A drag scroll operation is about to occur or is occurring in the target.

point   Contains the location of the cursor, in pixels, relative to the screen.

Remarks   Called by the framework when a drop operation is to occur. This function should be overridden to handle data being dropped into the specified window. The default implementation calls **CView::OnDrop**, which simply returns **FALSE** by default.

See Also   **COleDropTarget::OnDragOver**, **COleDropTarget::OnDragEnter**

In the *OLE 2 Programmer's Reference, Volume 1*: **IDropTarget::Drop**

COleDropTarget::Register

BOOL Register(CWnd* *pWnd*);

Return Value   Nonzero if registration is successful; otherwise 0.

Parameters   *pWnd*   Points to the window that is to be registered as a drop target.

Remarks   Call this function to register your window with the OLE 2 DLLs as a valid drop target. This function must be called for drop operations to be accepted.

See Also   **COleDropTarget::Revoke**

In the *OLE 2 Programmer's Reference, Volume 1*: **::RegisterDragDrop**, **::RevokeDragDrop**

COleDropTarget::Revoke

virtual void Revoke( );

Remarks   Call this function before destroying any window that has been registered as a drop target through a call to **COleDropTarget::Register** to remove it from the list of drop targets. This function is called automatically from the **OnDestroy** handler for the window that was registered, so it is usually not necessary to call this function explicitly.

See Also   **COleDropTarget::Register**

In the *OLE 2 Programmer's Reference, Volume 1*: **::RevokeDragDrop**, **::RegisterDragDrop**

class COleException : public CException

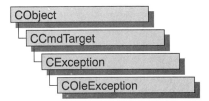

A **COleException** object represents an exception condition related to an OLE operation. The **COleException** class includes a public data member that holds the status code indicating the reason for the exception.

You will seldom need to create a **COleException** object directly; instead, you should call **AfxThrowOleException.**

#include <afxole.h>

See Also   **AfxThrowOleException**

Data Members
m_sc   Contains the status code that indicates the reason for the exception.

Operations
Process   Translates a caught exception into an OLE return code.

Construction
COleException   Constructs a **COleException** object.

Member Functions

COleException::COleException

COleException( );

Remarks   Constructs a **COleException** object. Do not use this constructor directly; instead, call the global function **AfxThrowOleException**.

See Also   **AfxThrowOleException**

COleException::Process

static SCODE PASCAL Process(const CException* *pAnyException***);**

Return Value   An OLE status code.

Parameters   *pAnyException*   Pointer to a caught exception.

Remarks   Call the **Process** member function to translate a caught exception into an OLE status code.

See Also   **CException**

In the *OLE 2 Programmer's Reference, Volume 1*: **SCODE**

Data Members

COleException::m_sc

SCODE m_sc;

Remarks   This data member holds the OLE 2 status code that indicates the reason for the exception. This variable's value is set by the constructor.

See Also   **COleException::COleException**

In the *OLE 2 Programmer's Reference, Volume 1*: **SCODE**

class COleInsertDialog : public COleDialog

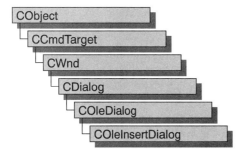

The **COleInsertDialog** class is used for the OLE Insert Object dialog box. Create an object of class **COleInsertDialog** when you want to call this dialog box. After a **COleInsertDialog** object has been constructed, you can use the **m_io** structure to initialize the values or states of controls in the dialog box. The **m_io** structure is of type **OLEUIINSERTOBJECT**.

For more information regarding OLE 2–specific dialog boxes, see the article "Dialog Boxes in OLE" in *Programming with the Microsoft Foundation Class Library*.

#include <afxodlgs.h>

See Also   **COleDialog**

In the *OLE 2 Programmer's Reference, Volume 1*: **OLEUIINSERTOBJECT**

Data Members
m_io	A structure of type **OLEUIINSERTOBJECT** that controls the behavior of the dialog box.

Construction
COleInsertDialog	Constructs a **COleInsertDialog** object.

Operations and Attributes
CreateItem	Creates the item selected in the dialog box.
DoModal	Displays the OLE 2 Insert Object dialog box.
GetClassID	Gets the **CLSID** associated with the chosen item.
GetDrawAspect	Tells whether to draw the item as an icon.

GetIconicMetafile	Gets a handle to the metafile associated with the iconic form of this item.
GetPathName	Gets the full path to the file chosen in the dialog box.
GetSelectionType	Gets the type of object selected.

Member Functions

COleInsertDialog::COleInsertDialog

COleInsertDialog (DWORD *dwFlags* **= IOF_SELECTCREATENEW,
CWnd*** *pParentWnd* **= NULL);**

Parameters   *dwFlags*   Creation flag that contains any number of the following values to be combined using the bitwise OR operator:

- **IOF_SHOWHELP**   Specifies that the Help button will be displayed when the dialog box is called.

- **IOF_SELECTCREATENEW**   Specifies that the Create New radio button will be selected initially when the dialog box is called. This is the default and cannot be used with **IOF_SELECTCREATEFROMFILE**.

- **IOF_SELECTCREATEFROMFILE**   Specifies that the Create From File radio button will be selected initially when the dialog box is called. Cannot be used with **IOF_SELECTCREATENEW**.

- **IOF_CHECKLINK**   Specifies that the Link check box will be checked initially when the dialog box is called.

- **IOF_CHECKDISPLAYASICON**   Specifies that the Display As Icon check box will be checked initially, the current icon will be displayed, and the Change Icon button will be enabled when the dialog box is called.

- **IOF_DISABLELINK**   Specifies that the Link check box will be disabled when the dialog box is called.

- **IOF_VERIFYSERVERSEXIST**   Specifies that the dialog box should validate the classes it adds to the list box by ensuring that the servers specified in the registration database exist before the dialog box is displayed. Setting this flag can significantly impair performance.

pParentWnd   Points to the parent or owner window object (of type **CWnd**) to which the dialog object belongs. If it is **NULL**, the parent window of the dialog object is set to the main application window.

Remarks   This function constructs only a **COIeInsertDialog** object. To display the dialog box, call the **DoModal** function.

See Also   **COIeInsertDialog::DoModal**

COIeInsertDialog::CreateItem

BOOL CreateItem(COIeClientItem* *pItem*);

Return Value   Nonzero if item was created; otherwise 0.

Parameters   *pItem*   Points to the item to be created.

Remarks   Call this function to create an object of type **COIeClientItem** only if **DoModal** returns **IDOK**. You must allocate the **COIeClientItem** object before you can call this function.

See Also   **COIeClientItem::CreateLinkFromFile, COIeClientItem::CreateFromFile, COIeClientItem::CreateNewItem, COIeClientItem::SetDrawAspect, COIeInsertDialog::GetSelectionType, COIeInsertDialog::DoModal**

COIeInsertDialog::DoModal

virtual int DoModal( );

Return Value   **IDOK** if the dialog box was successfully displayed, **IDCANCEL** if the user canceled the dialog box, or **IDABORT** if an error occurred. If **IDABORT** is returned, call the **COIeDialog::GetLastError** member function to get more information about the type of error that occurred. For a listing of possible errors, see "OleUIInsertObject" in the *User Interface Dialog* help file.

Remarks   Call this function to display the OLE Insert Object dialog box.

If you want to initialize the various dialog box controls by setting members of the **m_io** structure, you should do this before calling **DoModal**, but after the dialog object is constructed.

If **DoModal** returns **IDOK**, you can call other member functions to retrieve the settings or information input into the dialog box by the user.

See Also   **COIeDialog::GetLastError, CDialog::DoModal**

COIeInsertDialog::GetClassID

const CLSID& GetClassID( ) const;

Return Value   Returns the **CLSID** associated with the selected item.

Remarks	Call this function to get the **CLSID** associated with the selected item only if **DoModal** returns **IDOK** and the selection type is **COleInsertDialog::createNewItem**.
See Also	**COleInsertDialog::DoModal**

In the *OLE 2 Programmer's Reference, Volume 1*: **CLSID**

COleInsertDialog::GetDrawAspect

DVASPECT GetDrawAspect( ) const;

Return Value	The method needed to render the object.

- **DVASPECT_CONTENT**   Returned if the Display As Icon check box was not checked.
- **DVASPECT_ICON**   Returned if the Display As Icon check box was checked.

Remarks	Call this function to determine if the user chose to display the selected item as an icon. Call this function only after **DoModal** returns **IDOK**.
See Also	**COleInsertDialog::DoModal, COleInsertDialog::COleInsertDialog**

In the *OLE 2 Programmer's Reference, Volume 1*: **DVASPECT**

COleInsertDialog::GetIconicMetafile

HGLOBAL GetIconicMetafile( ) const;

Return Value	The handle to the metafile containing the iconic aspect of the selected item, if the Display As Icon check box was checked when the dialog was dismissed by choosing **OK**; otherwise **NULL**.
Remarks	Call this function to get a handle to the metafile that contains the iconic aspect of the selected item.
See Also	**COleInsertDialog::DoModal, COleInsertDialog::GetDrawAspect**

COleInsertDialog::GetPathName

CString GetPathName( ) const;

Return Value	The full path to the file selected in the dialog box. If the selection type is **createNewItem**, this function returns **NULL** in release mode or causes an assertion in debug mode.
Remarks	Call this function to get the full path of the selected file only if **DoModal** returns **IDOK** and the selection type is not **COleInsertDialog::createNewItem**.

See Also   **COleInsertDialog::GetSelectionType, COleInsertDialog::DoModal**

COleInsertDialog::GetSelectionType

UINT GetSelectionType( ) const;

Return Value   Type of selection made:

- **COleInsertDialog::createNewItem**   The Create New radio button was selected.

- **COleInsertDialog::insertFromFile**   The Create From File radio button was selected and the Link check box was not checked.

- **COleInsertDialog::linkToFile**   The Create From File radio button was selected and the Link check box was checked.

Remarks   Call this function to get the selection type chosen when the Insert Object dialog box was dismissed by choosing OK.

See Also   **COleInsertDialog::DoModal, COleInsertDialog::COleInsertDialog**

Data Members

COleInsertDialog::m_io

Remarks   Structure of type **OLEUIINSERTOBJECT** used to control the behavior of the Insert Object dialog box. Members of this structure can be modified either directly or through member functions.

See Also   **COleInsertDialog::COleInsertDialog**

In the *OLE 2 Programmer's Reference, Volume 1*: **OLEUIINSERTOBJECT**

class COIeIPFrameWnd : public CFrameWnd

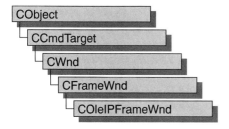

Use the **COIeIPFrameWnd** class as the base for your application's in-place editing window. This class creates and positions control bars within the container application's document window. It also handles notifications generated by an embedded **COIeResizeBar** object when the user resizes the in-place editing window.

#include <afxole.h>

See Also   **COIeResizeBar**, **CFrameWnd**

Construction

COIeIPFrameWnd	Constructs a **COIeIPFrameWnd** object.

Overridables

OnCreateControlBars	Called by the framework when an item is activated for in-place editing.
RepositionFrame	Called by the framework to reposition the in-place editing window.

Member Functions

COIeIPFrameWnd::COIeIPFrameWnd

COIeIPFrameWnd( );

Remarks   Constructs a **COIeIPFrameWnd** object and initializes its in-place state information, which is stored in a structure of type **OLEINPLACEFRAMEINFO**.

See Also   **COIeServerDoc::ActivateInPlace**

In the *OLE 2 Programmer's Reference, Volume 1*:
OLEINPLACEFRAMEINFO

COIeIPFrameWnd::OnCreateControlBars

virtual BOOL OnCreateControlBars(CWnd* *pWndFrame*,
CWnd* *pWndDoc* **);**

Return Value   Nonzero on success; otherwise, 0.

Parameters   *pWndFrame*   Pointer to the container application's frame window.

pWndDoc   Pointer to the container's document-level window. May be **NULL** if the container is an SDI application.

Remarks   The framework calls the **OnCreateControlBars** function when an item is activated for in-place editing.

The default implementation does nothing. Override this function to perform any special processing required when control bars are created.

See Also   **COleServerDoc::ActivateInPlace**

COIeIPFrameWnd::RepositionFrame

virtual void RepositionFrame(LPCRECT *lpPosRect*, **LPCRECT** *lpClipRect* **);**

Parameters   *lpPosRect*   Pointer to a **RECT** structure or a **CRect** object containing the in-place frame window's current position coordinates, in pixels, relative to the client area.

lpClipRect   Pointer to a **RECT** structure or a **CRect** objcct containing the in-place frame window's current clipping-rectangle coordinates, in pixels, relative to the client area.

Remarks   The framework calls the **RepositionFrame** member function to lay out control bars and reposition the in-place editing window so all of it is visible.

Layout of control bars in the container window differs from that performed by a non-OLE frame window. The non-OLE frame window calculates the positions of control bars and other objects from a given frame-window size, as in a call to **CFrameWnd::RecalcLayout**. The client area is what remains after space for control bars and other objects is subtracted. A **COleIPFrameWnd** window, on the other hand, positions toolbars in accordance with a given client area. In other words, **CFrameWnd::RecalcLayout** works "from the outside in," whereas **COleIPFrameWnd::RepositionFrame** works "from the inside out."

See Also   **CFrameWnd::RecalcLayout**

class COleLinkingDoc : public COleDocument

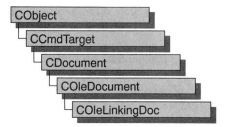

The **COleLinkingDoc** class is the base class for OLE container documents that support linking to the embedded items they contain. A container application that supports linking to embedded items is called a "link container." The Oclient sample application is an example of a link container.

When a linked item's source is an embedded item in another document, that containing document must be loaded in order for the embedded item to be edited. For this reason, a link container must be able to be launched by another container application when the user wants to edit the source of a linked item. Your application must also use the **COleTemplateServer** class so that it can create documents when launched programmatically.

To make your container a link container, derive your document class from **COleLinkingDoc** instead of **COleDocument**. As with any other OLE container, you must design your class for storing the application's native data as well as embedded or linked items. Also, you must design data structures for storing your native data. If you define a **CDocItem**-derived class for your application's native data, you can use the interface defined by **COleDocument** to store your native data as well as your OLE data.

To allow your application to be launched programmatically by another container, declare a **COleTemplateServer** object as a member of your application's **CWinApp**-derived class:

```
class COleClientApp : public CWinApp
{
// ...
protected:
    COleTemplateServer m_server;
// ...
};
```

In the **InitInstance** member function of your **CWinApp**-derived class, create a document template and specify your **COleLinkingDoc**-derived class as the document class:

```
// CMainDoc is derived from COleLinkingDoc
CMultiDocTemplate* pDocTemplate = new CMultiDocTemplate(IDR_OCLIENTTYPE,
        RUNTIME_CLASS(CMainDoc),
        RUNTIME_CLASS(CSplitFrame),
        RUNTIME_CLASS(CMainView));
pDocTemplate->SetContainerInfo(IDR_OCLIENTTYPE_CNTR_IP);
AddDocTemplate(pDocTemplate);
```

Connect your **COleTemplateServer** object to your document templates by calling the object's **ConnectTemplate** member function, and register all class objects with the OLE system by calling **COleTemplateServer::RegisterAll**:

```
m_server.ConnectTemplate(clsid, pDocTemplate, FALSE);
COleTemplateServer::RegisterAll();
```

For a sample **CWinApp**-derived class definition and **InitInstance** function, see OCLIENT.H and OCLIENT.CPP in \MSVC20\MFC\SAMPLES\OCLIENT.

#include <afxole.h>

See Also   **COleDocument**, **COleTemplateServer**, **CDocTemplate**

In *Programming with the Microsoft Foundation Class Library*: "Containers: Advanced Issues"

Construction

COleLinkingDoc	Constructs a **COleLinkingDoc** object.

Operations

Register	Registers the document with the OLE system DLLs.
Revoke	Revokes the document's registration.

Overridables

OnFindEmbeddedItem	Finds the specified embedded item.
OnGetLinkedItem	Finds the specified linked item.

Member Functions

COleLinkingDoc::COleLinkingDoc

COleLinkingDoc( );

Remarks   Constructs a **COleLinkingDoc** object without beginning communications with the OLE system DLLs. You must call the **Register** member function to inform OLE that the document is open.

See Also   **COleLinkingDoc::Register**

COleLinkingDoc::OnFindEmbeddedItem

virtual COleClientItem* OnFindEmbeddedItem(LPCTSTR *lpszItemName* **);**

Parameters   *lpszItemName*   Pointer to the name of the embedded OLE item requested.

Remarks   Called by the framework to determine whether the document contains an embedded OLE item with the specified name. The default implementation searches the list of embedded items for an item with the specified name (the name comparison is case sensitive). Override this function if you have your own method of storing or naming embedded OLE items.

See Also   **COleClientItem**, **COleLinkingDoc::OnGetLinkedItem**

COleLinkingDoc::OnGetLinkedItem

virtual COleServerItem* OnGetLinkedItem(LPCTSTR *lpszItemName* **);**

Return Value   A pointer to the specified item; **NULL** if the item is not found.

Parameters   *lpszItemName*   Pointer to the name of the linked OLE item requested.

Remarks   Called by the framework to check whether the document contains a linked server item with the specified name. The default **COleLinkingDoc** implementation always returns **NULL**. This function is overriden in the derived class **COleServerDoc** to search the list of OLE server items for a linked item with the specified name (the name comparison is case sensitive). Override this function if you have implemented your own method of storing or retrieving linked server items.

See Also   **COleServerItem::GetItemName**, **COleServerItem::SetItemName**, **COleLinkingDoc::OnFindEmbeddedItem**

COleLinkingDoc::Register

BOOL Register(COleObjectFactory* *pFactory*, **LPCTSTR** *lpszPathName* **);**

Return Value   Nonzero if the document is successfully registered; otherwise 0.

Parameters   *pFactory*   Pointer to an OLE factory object (can be **NULL**).

lpszPathName   Pointer to the fully qualified path of the container document.

Remarks   Informs the OLE system DLLs that the document is open. Call this function when creating or opening a named file to register the document with the OLE system DLLs. There is no need to call this function if the document represents an embedded item.

If you are using **COleTemplateServer** in your application, **Register** is called for you by **COleLinkingDoc**'s implementation of **OnNewDocument**, **OnOpenDocument**, and **OnSaveDocument**.

See Also   **COleTemplateServer**, **COleObjectFactory**

CDocument::OnNewDocument
CDocument::OnOpenDocument

COleLinkingDoc::Revoke

void Revoke( );

Remarks   Informs the OLE system DLLs that the document is no longer open. Call this function to revoke the document's registration with the OLE system DLLs.

You should call this function when closing a named file, but you usually do not need to call it directly. **Revoke** is called for you by **COleLinkingDoc**'s implementation of **OnCloseDocument**, **OnNewDocument**, **OnOpenDocument**, and **OnSaveDocument**.

See Also   **COleTemplateServer, CDocument::OnCloseDocument,**
CDocument::OnNewDocument, CDocument::OnOpenDocument,
CDocument::OnSaveDocument

class COleLinksDialog : public COleDialog

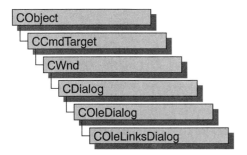

The **COleLinksDialog** object is used for the OLE Edit Links dialog box. Create an object of class **COleLinksDialog** when you want to call this dialog box. After a **COleLinksDialog** object has been constructed, you can use the **m_el** structure to initialize the values or states of controls in the dialog box. The **m_el** structure is of type **OLEUIEDITLINKS**.

For more information regarding OLE 2–specific dialog boxes, see the article "Dialog Boxes in OLE" in *Programming with the Microsoft Foundation Class Library*.

#include <afxodlgs.h>

See Also   **COleDialog**

In the *OLE 2 Programmer's Reference, Volume 1*: **OLEUIEDITLINKS**

Data Members
m_el	A structure of type **OLEUIEDITLINKS** that controls the behavior of the dialog box.

Construction
COleLinksDialog	Constructs a **COleLinksDialog** object.

Operations and Attributes
DoModal	Displays the OLE 2 Edit Links dialog box.

Member Functions

COleLinksDialog::COleLinksDialog

COleLinksDialog (COleDocument* *pDoc***, CView*** *pView***, DWORD** *dwFlags*
= 0, CWnd* *pParentWnd* **= NULL);**

Parameters   *pDoc*   Points to the OLE client document that contains the links to be edited.

pView   Points to the current view on *pDoc*.

dwFlags   Creation flag, which contains either 0 or **ELF_SHOWHELP** to specify
whether the Help button will be displayed when the dialog box is displayed.

pParentWnd   Points to the parent or owner window object (of type **CWnd**) to
which the dialog object belongs. If it is **NULL**, the parent window of the dialog
box is set to the main application window.

Remarks   This function constructs only a **COleLinksDialog** object. To display the dialog
box, call the **DoModal** function.

See Also   **COleDocument**, **COleLinksDialog::DoModal**, **CView**, **CWnd**

COleLinksDialog::DoModal

virtual int DoModal( );

Return Value   **IDOK** if the dialog box was successfully displayed, **IDCANCEL** if the user
canceled the dialog box, or **IDABORT** if an error occurred. If **IDABORT** is
returned, call the **COleDialog::GetLastError** member function to get more
information about the type of error that occurred. For a listing of possible errors,
see "OleUIEditLinks" in the *User Interface Dialog* help file.

Remarks   Call this function to display the OLE Edit Links dialog box.

If you want to initialize the various dialog box controls by setting members of the
m_el structure, you should do it before calling **DoModal**, but after the dialog object
is constructed.

If **DoModal** returns **IDOK**, you can call other member functions to retrieve the
settings or information input by the user into the dialog box.

See Also   **COleDialog::GetLastError**, **CDialog::DoModal**

Data Members

COleLinksDialog::m_el

Remarks

Structure of type **OLEUIEDITLINKS** used to control the behavior of the Edit Links dialog. Members of this structure can be modified either directly or through member functions.

See Also

COleLinksDialog::COleLinksDialog

In the *OLE 2 Programmer's Reference, Volume 1*: **OLEUIEDITLINKS**

class COleMessageFilter : public CCmdTarget

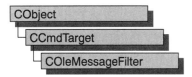

The **COleMessageFilter** class manages the concurrency required by the interaction of OLE applications.

The **COleMessageFilter** class is useful in visual editing server and container applications, as well as OLE automation applications. For server applications that are being called, this class can be used to make the application "busy" so that incoming calls from other container applications are either canceled or retried later. This class can also be used to determine the action to be taken by a calling application when the called application is busy.

Common usage is for a server application to call **BeginBusyState** and **EndBusyState** when it would be dangerous for a document or other OLE accessible object to be destroyed. These calls are made in **CWinApp::OnIdle** during user-interface updates.

By default, a **COleMessageFilter** object is allocated when the application is initialized. It can be retrieved with **AfxOleGetMessageFilter**.

This is an advanced class: you seldom need to work with it directly.

#include <afxole.h>

See Also   **AfxOleGetMessageFilter**, **CCmdTarget**

Construction
COleMessageFilter	Constructs a **COleMessageFilter** object.

Operations
Register	Registers the message filter with the OLE system DLLs.
Revoke	Revokes the message filter's registration with the OLE system DLLs.
BeginBusyState	Puts the application in the busy state.
EndBusyState	Terminates the application's busy state.

SetBusyReply	Determines the busy application's reply to an OLE call.
SetRetryReply	Determines the calling application's reply to a busy application.
SetMessagePendingDelay	Determines how long the application waits for a response to an OLE call.
EnableBusyDialog	Enables and disables the dialog box that appears when a called application is busy.
EnableNotRespondingDialog	Enables and disables the dialog box that appears when a called application is not responding.

Overridables

OnMessagePending	Called by the framework to process messages while an OLE call is in progress.

Member Functions

COleMessageFilter::BeginBusyState

virtual void BeginBusyState( );

Remarks Call this function to begin a busy state. It works in conjunction with **EndBusyState** to control the application's busy state. The function **SetBusyReply** determines the application's reply to calling applications when it is busy.

The **BeginBusyState** and **EndBusyState** calls increment and decrement, respectively, a counter that determines whether the application is busy. For example, two calls to **BeginBusyState** and one call to **EndBusyState** still result in a busy state. To cancel a busy state it is necessary to call **EndBusyState** the same number of times **BeginBusyState** has been called.

By default, the framework enters the busy state during idle processing, which is performed by **CWinApp::OnIdle**. While the application is handling **ON_COMMANDUPDATEUI** notifications, incoming calls are handled later, after idle processing is complete.

See Also COleMessageFilter::EndBusyState, COleMessageFilter::SetBusyReply

COleMessageFilter::COleMessageFilter

COleMessageFilter( );

Remarks Creates a **COleMessageFilter** object.

See Also COleMessageFilter::Register, COleMessageFilter::Revoke

COleMessageFilter::EnableBusyDialog

void **EnableBusyDialog**(BOOL *bEnableBusy* = **TRUE**);

Parameters   *bEnableBusy*   Specifies whether the "busy" dialog is enabled or disabled.

Remarks   Enables and disables the busy dialog, which is displayed when the message-pending delay expires (see **SetRetryReply**) during an OLE call.

See Also   **COleMessageFilter::EnableNotRespondingDialog**, **COleMessageFilter::BeginBusyState**, **COleMessageFilter::SetBusyReply**, **COleMessageFilter::SetRetryReply**, **COleBusyDialog**

COleMessageFilter::EnableNotRespondingDialog

void **EnableNotRespondingDialog**(BOOL *bEnableNotResponding* = **TRUE**);

Parameters   *bEnableNotResponding*   Specifies whether the "not responding" dialog is enabled or disabled.

Remarks   Enables and disables the "not responding" dialog, which is displayed if a keyboard or mouse message is pending during an OLE call and the call has timed out.

See Also   **COleMessageFilter::EnableBusyDialog**, **COleMessageFilter::BeginBusyState**, **COleMessageFilter::SetBusyReply**, **COleBusyDialog**

COleMessageFilter::EndBusyState

virtual void **EndBusyState**( );

Remarks   Call this function to end a busy state. It works in conjunction with **BeginBusyState** to control the application's busy state. The function **SetBusyReply** determines the application's reply to calling applications when it is busy.

The **BeginBusyState** and **EndBusyState** calls increment and decrement, respectively, a counter that determines whether the application is busy. For example, two calls to **BeginBusyState** and one call to **EndBusyState** still result in a busy state. To cancel a busy state it is necessary to call **EndBusyState** the same number of times **BeginBusyState** has been called.

By default, the framework enters the busy state during idle processing, which is performed by **CWinApp::OnIdle**. While the application is handling ON_UPDATE_COMMAND_UI notifications, incoming calls are handled after idle processing is complete.

See Also   **COleMessageFilter::BeginBusyState**, **COleMessageFilter::SetBusyReply**

COleMessageFilter::OnMessagePending

virtual BOOL OnMessagePending(const MSG* *pMsg* **);**

Return Value Nonzero on success; otherwise 0.

Parameters *pMsg* Pointer to the pending message.

Remarks Called by the framework to process messages while an OLE call is in progress.

When a calling application is waiting for a call to be completed, the framework calls **OnMessagePending** with a pointer to the pending message. By default, the framework dispatches **WM_PAINT** messages, so that window updates can occur during a call that is taking a long time.

You must register your message filter by means of a call to **COleMessageFilter::Register** before it can become active.

See Also **COleMessageFilter::Register, AfxOleInit, CWinApp::InitInstance**

COleMessageFilter::Register

BOOL Register( );

Return Value Nonzero on success; otherwise 0.

Remarks Registers the message filter with the OLE system DLLs. A message filter has no effect unless it is registered with the system DLLs. Usually your application's initialization code registers the application's message filter. Any other message filter registered by your application should be revoked before the program terminates by a call to **Revoke**.

The framework's default message filter is automatically registered during initialization and revoked at termination.

See Also **COleMessageFilter::Revoke**

COleMessageFilter::Revoke

void Revoke( );

Remarks Revokes a previous registration performed by a call to **Register**. A message filter should be revoked before the program terminates.

The default message filter, which is created and registered automatically by the framework, is also automatically revoked.

See Also **COleMessageFilter::Register**

COleMessageFilter::SetBusyReply

void SetBusyReply(SERVERCALL *nBusyReply* **);**

Parameters   *nBusyReply*   A value from the **SERVERCALL** enumeration, which is defined in COMPOBJ.H. It can have any one of the following values:

- **SERVERCALL_ISHANDLED**   The application can accept calls but may fail in processing a particular call.
- **SERVERCALL_REJECTED**   The application probably will never be able to process a call.
- **SERVERCALL_RETRYLATER**   The application is temporarily in a state in which it cannot process a call.

Remarks   This function sets the application's "busy reply." The **BeginBusyState** and **EndBusyState** functions control the application's busy state.

When an application has been made busy with a call to **BeginBusyState**, it responds to calls from the OLE system DLLs with a value determined by the last setting of **SetBusyReply**. The calling application uses this busy reply to determine what action to take.

By default, the busy reply is **SERVERCALL_RETRYLATER**. This reply causes the calling application to retry the call as soon as possible.

See Also   **COleMessageFilter::BeginBusyState**, **COleMessageFilter::EndBusyState**

COleMessageFilter::SetMessagePendingDelay

void SetMessagePendingDelay(DWORD *nTimeout* **= 5000);**

Parameters   *nTimeout*   Number of milliseconds for the message-pending delay.

Remarks   Determines how long the calling application waits for a response from the called application before taking further action.

This function works in concert with **SetRetryReply**.

See Also   **COleMessageFilter::SetRetryReply**

COleMessageFilter::SetRetryReply

void SetRetryReply(DWORD *nRetryReply* **= 0);**

Parameters   *nRetryReply*   Number of milliseconds between retries.

Remarks   Determines the calling application's action when it receives a busy response from a called application.

When a called application indicates that it is busy, the calling application may decide to wait until the server is no longer busy, to retry right away, or to retry after a specified interval. It may also decide to cancel the call altogether.

The caller's response is controlled by the functions **SetRetryReply** and **SetMessagePendingDelay**. **SetRetryReply** determines how long the calling application should wait between retries for a given call. **SetMessagePendingDelay** determines how long the calling application waits for a response from the server before taking further action.

Usually the defaults are acceptable and do not need to be changed. The framework retries the call every *nRetryReply* milliseconds until the call goes through or the message-pending delay has expired. A value of 0 for *nRetryReply* specifies an immediate retry, and −1 specifies cancellation of the call.

When the message-pending delay has expired, the OLE "busy dialog box" (see **COleBusyDialog**) is displayed so that the user can choose to cancel or retry the call. Call **EnableBusyDialog** to enable or disable this dialog.

When a keyboard or mouse message is pending during a call and the call has timed out (exceeded the message-pending delay), the "not responding" dialog box is displayed. Call **EnableNotRespondingDialog** to enable or disable this dialog box. Usually this state of affairs indicates that something has gone wrong and the user is getting impatient.

When the dialogs are disabled, the current "retry reply" is always used for calls to busy applications. (See **SetRetryReply**.)

See Also   **COleBusyDialog**, **COleMessageFilter::SetRetryReply**, **COleMessageFilter::SetMessagePendingDelay**

class COleObjectFactory : public CObject

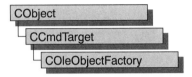

The **COleObjectFactory** class implements the OLE class factory, which creates OLE objects such as servers, automation objects, and documents.

The **COleObjectFactory** class also manages the registration of objects. It has member functions for updating the OLE system register, as well as the run-time registration that informs OLE that objects are running and ready to receive messages.

For more information about object creation, see the article "Data Objects and Data Sources: Creation and Destruction." For more about registration, see the article "Registration." Both are in *Programming with the Microsoft Foundation Class Library*.

#include <afxdisp.h>

See Also   **COleTemplateServer**

Construction

COleObjectFactory	Constructs a **COleObjectFactory** object.

Operations

Register	Registers this object factory with the OLE system DLLs.
RegisterAll	Registers all of the application's object factories with OLE system DLLs.
Revoke	Revokes this object factory's registration with the OLE system DLLs.
RevokeAll	Revokes an application's object factories' registrations with the OLE system DLLs.
UpdateRegistry	Registers this object factory with the OLE system registry.
UpdateRegistryAll	Registers all of the application's object factories with the OLE system registry.

Attributes

IsRegistered	Indicates whether the object factory is registered with the OLE system DLLs.
GetClassID	Returns the OLE class ID of the objects this factory creates.

Overridables

OnCreateInstance	Called by the framework to create a new object of this factory's type.

Member Functions

COleObjectFactory::COleObjectFactory

COleObjectFactory(REFCLSID *clsid***, CRuntimeClass*** *pRuntimeClass***,**
BOOL *bMultiInstance***, LPCTSTR** *lpszProgID* **);**

Parameters   *clsid*   Reference to the OLE class ID this object factory represents.

pRuntimeClass   Pointer to the run-time class of the C++ objects this factory can create.

bMultiInstance   Indicates whether a single instance of the application can support multiple instantiations. If **TRUE**, multiple instances of the application are launched for each request to create an object.

lpszProgID   Pointer to a string containing a verbal program identifier, such as "Microsoft Excel."

Remarks   Constructs a **COleObjectFactory** object, initializes it as an unregistered object factory, and adds it to the list of factories. To use the object, however, you must register it.

See Also   **RUNTIME_CLASS**

In the *OLE 2 Programmer's Reference. Volume 1*: **REFCLSID**

COleObjectFactory::GetClassID

REFCLSID GetClassID( ) const;

Return Value   Reference to the OLE class ID this factory represents.

Remarks   Returns a reference to the OLE class ID this factory represents.

See Also   In the *OLE 2 Programmer's Reference, Volume 1*: **REFCLSID**

COleObjectFactory::IsRegistered

BOOL IsRegistered( ) const;

Return Value   Nonzero if the factory is registered; otherwise 0.

Remarks   Returns a nonzero value if the factory is registered with the OLE system DLLs.

See Also   **COleObjectFactory::Register**, **COleObjectFactory::Revoke**

COleObjectFactory::OnCreateObject

virtual CCmdTarget* OnCreateObject( );

Return Value   A pointer to the created object. It can throw a memory exception if it fails.

Remarks   Called by the framework to create a new object. Override this function to create the object from something other than the **CRuntimeClass** passed to the constructor.

COleObjectFactory::Register

BOOL Register( );

Return Value   Nonzero if the factory is successfully registered; otherwise 0.

Remarks   Registers this object factory with the OLE system DLLs. This function is usually called by **CWinApp::InitInstance** when the application is launched.

See Also   **COleObjectFactory::Revoke**, **COleObjectFactory::RegisterAll**, **CWinApp::InitInstance**

COleObjectFactory::RegisterAll

static BOOL PASCAL RegisterAll( );

Return Value   Nonzero if the factories are successfully registered; otherwise 0.

Remarks   Registers all of the application's object factories with the OLE system DLLs. This function is usually called by **CWinApp::InitInstance** when the application is launched.

See Also   **COleObjectFactory::Revoke**, **COleObjectFactory::Register**, **CWinApp::InitInstance**

COleObjectFactory::Revoke

void Revoke( );

Remarks   Revokes this object factory's registration with the OLE system DLLs. The framework calls this function automatically before the application terminates. If necessary, call it from an override of **CWinApp::ExitInstance**.

See Also   **COleObjectFactory::RevokeAll, COleObjectFactory::Register, CWinApp::ExitInstance**

COleObjectFactory::RevokeAll

static void PASCAL RevokeAll( );

Remarks   Revokes all of the application's object factories' registrations with the OLE system DLLs. The framework calls this function automatically before the application terminates. If necessary, call it from an override of **CWinApp::ExitInstance**.

See Also   **COleObjectFactory::Revoke, COleObjectFactory::RegisterAll, CWinApp::ExitInstance**

COleObjectFactory::UpdateRegistry

void UpdateRegistry(LPCTSTR *lpszProgID* **= NULL);**

Parameters   *lpszProgID*   Pointer to a string containing the human-readable program identifier, such as "Excel.Document.5".

Remarks   Registers this object factory with the OLE system registry. This function is usually called by **CWinApp::InitInstance** when the application is launched.

See Also   **COleObjectFactory::Revoke, COleObjectFactory::Register, COleObjectFactory::UpdateRegistryAll, CWinApp::InitInstance**

COleObjectFactory::UpdateRegistryAll

static void PASCAL UpdateRegistry( );

Remarks   Registers all of the application's object factories with the OLE system registry. This function is usually called by **CWinApp::InitInstance** when the application is launched.

See Also   **COleObjectFactory::Revoke, COleObjectFactory::Register, COleObjectFactory::UpdateRegistry, CWinApp::InitInstance**

class COlePasteSpecialDialog : public COleDialog

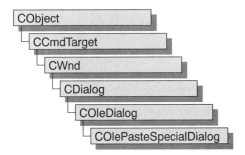

The **COlePasteSpecialDialog** class is used for the OLE Paste Special dialog box. Create an object of class **COlePasteSpecialDialog** when you want to call this dialog box. After a **COlePasteSpecialDialog** object has been constructed, you can use the **m_ps** structure to initialize the values or states of controls in the dialog box. The **m_ps** structure is of type **OLEUIPASTESPECIAL**.

For more information regarding OLE 2-specific dialog boxes, see the article "Dialog Boxes in OLE" in *Programming with the Microsoft Foundation Class Library*.

#include <afxodlgs.h>

See Also   **COleDialog**

In the *OLE 2 Programmer's Reference, Volume 1*: **OLEUIPASTESPECIAL**

Data Members

m_ps	A structure of type **OLEUIPASTESPECIAL** that controls the function of the dialog box.

Construction

COlePasteSpecialDialog	Constructs a **COlePasteSpecialDialog** object.

Operations and Attributes

AddFormat	Adds custom formats to the list of formats your application can paste.
AddStandardFormats	Adds **CF_BITMAP**, **CF_DIB**, **CF_METAFILEPICT**, and optionally **CF_LINKSOURCE** to the list of formats your application can paste.
CreateItem	Creates the item in the container document using the specified format.
DoModal	Displays the OLE 2 Paste Special dialog box.
GetDrawAspect	Tells whether to draw item as an icon or not.
GetIconicMetafile	Gets a handle to the metafile associated with the iconic form of this item.
GetPasteIndex	Gets the index of available paste options that was chosen by the user.
GetSelectionType	Gets the type of selection chosen.

Member Functions

COlePasteSpecialDialog::AddFormat

void AddFormat(const FORMATETC& *fmt*, **LPTSTR** *lpstrFormat*, **LPTSTR** *lpstrResult*, **DWORD** *flags* **);**

void AddFormat(UINT *cf*, **DWORD** *tymed*, **UINT** *nFormatID*, **BOOL** *bEnableIcon*, **BOOL** *bLink* **);**

Parameters

fmt   Reference to the data type to add.

lpstrFormat   String that describes the format to the user.

lpstrResult   String that describes the result if this format is chosen in the dialog box.

flags   The different linking and embedding options available for this format. This flag is a bitwise combination of one or more of the different values in the **OLEUIPASTEFLAG** enumerated type.

cf   The clipboard format to add.

tymed   The types of media available in this format. This is a bitwise combination of one or more of the values in the **TYMED** enumerated type.

nFormatID   The ID of the string that identifies this format. The format of this string is two separate strings separated by a '\n' character. The first string is the same that would be passed in the *lpstrFormat* parameter, and the second is the same as the *lpstrResult* parameter.

bEnableIcon   Flag that determines whether the Display As Icon check box is activated when this format is chosen in the list box.

bLink   Flag that determines whether the Paste Link radio button is activated when this format is chosen in the list box.

Remarks   Call this function to add new formats to the list of formats your application can support in a Paste Special operation. This function can be called to add either standard formats such as **CF_TEXT** or **CF_TIFF** or custom formats that your application has registered with the OLE system. For more information about pasting data objects into your application, see the article "Data Objects and Data Sources: Manipulation" in *Programming with the Microsoft Foundation Class Library*.

See Also   In the *OLE 2 Programmer's Reference, Volume 1*: **OLEUIPASTEFLAG**, **TYMED**, **FORMATETC**

COlePasteSpecialDialog::AddStandardFormats

void COlePasteSpecialDialog(BOOL *bEnableLink* **= TRUE);**

Parameters   *bEnableLink*   Flag that determines whether to add **CF_LINKSOURCE** to the list of formats your application can paste.

Remarks   Call this function to add the following Clipboard formats to the list of formats your application can support in a Paste Special operation:

- **CF_BITMAP**
- **CF_DIB**
- **CF_METAFILEPICT**
- (optionally) **CF_LINKSOURCE**

See Also   **COlePasteSpecialDialog::AddFormat**

COlePasteSpecialDialog::COlePasteSpecialDialog

COlePasteSpecialDialog(DWORD *dwFlags* **= PSF_SELECTPASTE, COleDataObject*** *pDataObject* **= NULL, CWnd*** *pParentWnd* **= NULL);**

Parameters   *dwFlags*   Creation flag, contains any number of the following flags combined using the bitwise OR operator:

- **PSF_SHOWHELP**   Specifies that the Help button will be displayed when the dialog box is called.

- **PSF_SELECTPASTE**   Specifies that the Paste radio button will be checked initially when the dialog box is called. Cannot be used in combination with **PSF_SELECTPASTELINK**. This is the default.

- **PSF_SELECTPASTELINK**   Specifies that the Paste Link radio button will be checked initially when the dialog box is called. Cannot be used in combination with **PSF_SELECTPASTE**.

- **PSF_CHECKDISPLAYASICON**   Specifies that the Display As Icon check box will be checked initially when the dialog box is called.

pDataObject   Points to the **COleDataObject** that is on the Clipboard.

pParentWnd   Points to the parent or owner window object (of type **CWnd**) to which the dialog object belongs. If it is **NULL**, the parent window of the dialog box is set to the main application window.

Remarks   This function only constructs a **COlePasteSpecialDialog** object. To display the dialog box, call the **DoModal** function.

See Also   **COleDataObject**, **COlePasteSpecialDialog::DoModal**

In the *OLE 2 Programmer's Reference, Volume 1*: **OLEUIPASTEFLAG**

COlePasteSpecialDialog::CreateItem

BOOL CreateItem(COleClientItem* *pNewItem* **);**

Return Value   Nonzero if the item was created successfully; otherwise 0.

Parameters   *pNewItem*   Points to a **COleClientItem** instance. Cannot be **NULL**.

Remarks   Call this function to create the new item that was chosen in the Paste Special dialog box. This function should only be called after **DoModal** returns **IDOK**.

See Also   **COleClientItem**, **COlePasteSpecialDialog::DoModal**, **COlePasteSpecialDialog::GetSelectionType**

COlePasteSpecialDialog::DoModal

virtual int DoModal( );

Return Value   **IDOK** if the dialog box was successfully displayed, **IDCANCEL** if the user canceled the dialog box, or **IDABORT** if an error occurred. If **IDABORT** is returned, call the **COleDialog::GetLastError** member function to get more information about the type of error that occurred. For a listing of possible errors, see "OleUIPasteSpecial" in the *User Interface Dialog* help file.

Remarks   Call this function to display the OLE Paste Special dialog box.

If you want to initialize the various dialog box controls by setting members of the **m_ps** structure, you should do this before calling **DoModal**, but after the dialog object is constructed.

If **DoModal** returns **IDOK**, you can call other member functions to retrieve the settings or information input by the user into the dialog box.

See Also   **COleDataObject, COleDialog::GetLastError, CDialog::DoModal**

COlePasteSpecialDialog::GetDrawAspect

DVASPECT GetDrawAspect( ) const;

Return Value   The method needed to render the object.

- **DVASPECT_CONTENT**   Returned if the Display As Icon check box was not checked when the dialog was dismissed.
- **DVASPECT_ICON**   Returned if the Display As Icon check box was checked when the dialog was dismissed.

Remarks   Call this function to determine if the user chose to display the selected item as an icon. Only call this function after **DoModal** returns **IDOK**.

See Also   **COlePasteSpecialDialog::DoModal, DVASPECT**

COlePasteSpecialDialog::GetIconicMetafile

HGLOBAL GetIconicMetafile( ) const;

Return Value   The handle to the metafile containing the iconic aspect of the selected item, if the Display As Icon check box was selected when the dialog was dismissed by choosing OK; otherwise **NULL**.

Remarks   Gets the metafile associated with the item selected by the user.

See Also   **COlePasteSpecialDialog::GetDrawAspect**

COlePasteSpecialDialog::GetPasteIndex

int GetPasteIndex( ) const;

Return Value   The index into the array of **OLEUIPASTEENTRY** structures that was selected by the user. The format that corresponds to the selected index should be used when performing the paste operation.

Remarks   Gets the index value associated with the entry the user selected.

See Also   **OLEUIPASTEENTRY**

COlePasteSpecialDialog::GetSelectionType

UINT GetSelectionType( ) const;

Return Value   Returns type of selection made:

- **COlePasteSpecialDialog::pasteLink**   The Paste Link radio button was
  checked and the chosen format was not a metafile.

- **COlePasteSpecialDialog::pasteNormal**   The Paste radio button was checked
  and the chosen format was not a metafile.

- **COlePasteSpecialDialog::pasteOther**   The selected format is not a standard
  OLE format.

- **COlePasteSpecialDialog::pasteStatic**   The chosen format was a metafile.

Remarks   Call this function to determine the type of selection the user made.

See Also   **COlePasteSpecialDialog::DoModal**

Data Members

COlePasteSpecialDialog::m_ps

Remarks   Structure of type **OLEUIPASTESPECIAL** used to control the behavior of the
                    Paste Special dialog. Members of this structure can be modified directly or through
                    member functions.

See Also   **COlePasteSpecialDialog::COlePasteSpecialDialog**

                    In the *OLE 2 Programmer's Reference, Volume 1*: **OLEUIPASTESPECIAL**

class COleResizeBar : public CControlBar

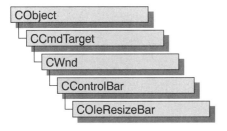

An object of the class **COleResizeBar** is a type of control bar that supports resizing of in-place OLE items. **COleResizeBar** objects appear as a **CRectTracker** with a hatched border and outer resize handles.

COleResizeBar objects are usually embedded members of frame-window objects derived from the **COleIPFrameWnd** class.

#include <afxole.h>

See Also   **CRectTracker**, **COleIPFrameWnd**, **COleServerDoc**

Construction

COleResizeBar	Constructs a **COleResizeBar** object.
Create	Creates and initializes a Windows child window and associates it to the **COleResizeBar** object.

Member Functions

COleResizeBar::Create

BOOL Create(CWnd* *pParentWnd***, DWORD** *dwStyle* **= WS_CHILD |**
    WS_VISIBLE, UINT *nID* **= AFX_IDW_RESIZE_BAR);**

Return Value   Nonzero if the resize bar was created; otherwise 0.

Parameters   *pParentWnd*   Pointer to the parent window of the resize bar.

    dwStyle   Specifies the window style attributes. For a list of window styles, see the section "Window Styles" on page 1253.

    nID   The resize bar's child window ID.

Remarks	Creates a child window and associates it with the **COleResizeBar** object.
See Also	**CWnd::Create**, **CControlBar**

COleResizeBar::COleResizeBar

COleResizeBar( );

Remarks	Constructs a **COleResizeBar** object. Call **Create** to create the resize bar object.
See Also	**COleResizeBar::Create**

class COleServerDoc : public COleLinkingDoc

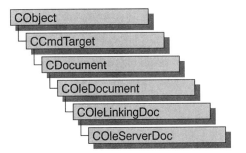

COleServerDoc is the base class for OLE server documents. A server document can contain COleServerItem objects, which represent the server interface to embedded or linked items. When a server application is launched by a container to edit an embedded item, the item is loaded as its own server document; the COleServerDoc object contains just one COleServerItem object, consisting of the entire document. When a server application is launched by a container to edit a linked item, an existing document is loaded from disk; a portion of the document's contents is highlighted to indicate the linked item.

COleServerDoc objects can also contain items of the COleClientItem class. This allows you to create container-server applications. The framework provides functions to properly store the COleClientItem items while servicing the COleServerItem objects.

If your server application does not support links, a server document will always contain only one server item, which represents the entire embedded object as a document. If your server application does support links, it must create a server item each time a selection is copied to the Clipboard.

To use COleServerDoc, derive a class from it and implement the OnGetEmbeddedItem member function, which allows your server to support embedded items. Derive a class from COleServerItem to implement the items in your documents, and return objects of that class from OnGetEmbeddedItem.

To support linked items, COleServerDoc provides the OnGetLinkedItem member function. You can use the default implementation or override it if you have your own way of managing document items.

You need one COleServerDoc-derived class for each type of server document your application supports. For example, if your server application supports worksheets and charts, you need two COleServerDoc-derived classes.

#include <afxole.h>

See Also   COIeDocument, COIeLinkingDoc, COIeTemplateServer, COIeServerItem

Construction

COIeServerDoc   Constructs a **COIeServerDoc** object.

Attributes

IsEmbedded   Indicates whether the document is embedded in a
                                 container document or running stand-alone.

IsInPlaceActive   Returns TRUE if the item is currently activated in place.

GetEmbeddedItem   Returns a pointer to an item representing the entire
                                 document.

GetItemPosition   Returns the current position rectangle, relative to the
                                 container application's client area, for in-place editing.

GetItemClipRect   Returns the current clipping rectangle for in-place
                                 editing.

GetZoomFactor   Returns the zoom factor in pixels.

Operations

NotifyChanged   Notifies containers that the user has changed the
                                 document.

NotifyRename   Notifies containers that the user has renamed the
                                 document.

NotifySaved   Notifies containers that the user has saved the
                                 document.

NotifyClosed   Notifies containers that the user has closed the
                                 document.

SaveEmbedding   Tells the container application to save the document.

ActivateInPlace   Activates the document for in-place editing.

DeactivateAndUndo   Deactivates the server's user interface.

DiscardUndoState   Discards undo-state information.

RequestPositionChange   Changes the position of the in-place editing frame.

ScrollContainerBy   Scrolls the container document.

UpdateAllItems   Notifies containers that the user has changed the
                                 document.

Overridables

OnUpdateDocument	Called by the framework when a server document that is an embedded item is saved, updating the container's copy of the item.
OnGetEmbeddedItem	Called to get a **COleServerItem** that represents the entire document; used to get an embedded item. Implementation required.
OnClose	Called by the framework when a container requests to close the document.
OnSetHostNames	Called by the framework when a container sets the window title for an embedded object.
OnShowDocument	Called by the framework to show or hide the document.
OnDeactivate	Called by the framework when the user deactivates an item that was activated in place.
OnDeactivateUI	Called by the framework to destroy controls and other user-interface elements created for in-place activation.
OnSetItemRects	Called by the framework to position the in-place editing frame window within the container application's window.
OnReactivateAndUndo	Called by the framework to undo changes made during in-place editing.
OnFrameWindowActivate	Called by the framework when the container's frame window is activated or deactivated.
OnDocWindowActivate	Called by the framework when the container's document frame window is activated or deactivated.
OnShowControlBars	Called by the framework to show or hide control bars for in-place editing.
OnResizeBorder	Called by the framework when the container application's frame window or document window is resized.
CreateInPlaceFrame	Called by the framework to create a frame window for in-place editing.
DestroyInPlaceFrame	Called by the framework to destroy a frame window for in-place editing.

Member Functions

COleServerDoc::ActivateInPlace

BOOL ActivateInPlace( );

Return Value   Nonzero if successful; otherwise 0, which indicates that the item is fully open.

Remarks   Activates the item for in-place editing.

This function performs all operations necessary for in-place activation. It creates an in-place frame window, activates it and sizes it to the item, sets up shared menus and other controls, scrolls the item into view, and sets the focus to the in-place frame window.

This function is called by the default implementation of **COleServerItem::OnShow**. Call this function if your application supports another verb for in-place activation (such as Play).

See Also   **COleServerItem::OnShow**

COleServerDoc::COleServerDoc

COleServerDoc( );

Remarks   Constructs a **COleServerDoc** object without connecting with the OLE system DLLs. You must call **COleLinkingDoc::Register** to open communications with OLE. If you are using **COleTemplateServer** in your application, **COleLinkingDoc::Register** is called for you by **COleLinkingDoc**'s implementation of **OnNewDocument**, **OnOpenDocument**, and **OnSaveDocument**.

See Also   **COleLinkingDoc::Register**

COleServerDoc::DeactivateAndUndo

BOOL DeactivateAndUndo( );

Return Value   Nonzero on success; otherwise 0.

Remarks   Call this function if your application supports Undo and the user chooses Undo after activating an item but before editing it. If the container application is written using the Microsoft Foundation Class Library, calling this function causes **COleClientItem::OnDeactivateAndUndo** to be called, which deactivates the server's user interface.

See Also   **COleClientItem::OnDeactivateAndUndo**

COleServerDoc::CreateInPlaceFrame

Protected→
virtual COleIPFrameWnd* CreateInPlaceFrame(CWnd* *pParentWnd*);
END Protected

Return Value   A pointer to the in-place frame window, or **NULL** if unsuccessful.

Parameters   *pParentWnd*   Pointer to the container application's parent window.

Remarks   The framework calls this function to create a frame window for in-place editing. The default implementation uses information specified in the document template to create the frame. The view used is the first view created for the document. This view is temporarily detached from the original frame and attached to the newly created frame.

This is an advanced overridable.

See Also   **COleServerDoc::DestroyInPlaceFrame**

COleServerDoc::DestroyInPlaceFrame

Protected→
virtual void DestroyInPlaceFrame(COleIPFrameWnd* *pFrame*);
END Protected

Parameters   *pFrame*   Pointer to the in-place frame window to be destroyed.

Remarks   The framework calls this function to destroy an in-place frame window and return the server application's document window to its state before in-place activation.

This is an advanced overridable.

See Also   **COleServerDoc::CreateInPlaceFrame**

COleServerDoc::DiscardUndoState

BOOL DiscardUndoState( );

Return Value   Nonzero on success; otherwise 0.

Remarks   If the user performs an editing operation that cannot be undone, call this function to force the container application to discard its undo-state information.

This function is provided so that servers that support Undo can free resources that would otherwise be consumed by undo-state information that cannot be used.

See Also   **COleServerDoc::OnReactivateAndUndo**

COleServerDoc::GetEmbeddedItem

COleServerItem* GetEmbeddedItem( );

Return Value   A pointer to an item representing the entire document; **NULL** if the operation failed.

Remarks   Call this function to get a pointer to an item representing the entire document. It calls **COleServerDoc::OnGetEmbeddedItem**, a virtual function with no default implementation.

See Also   **COleServerDoc::OnGetEmbeddedItem**

COleServerDoc::GetItemClipRect

void GetItemClipRect(LPRECT *lpClipRect* **) const;**

Parameters   *lpClipRect*   Pointer to a **RECT** structure or a **CRect** object to receive the clipping-rectangle coordinates of the item.

Remarks   Call the **GetItemClipRect** member function to get the clipping-rectangle coordinates of the item that is being edited in place. Coordinates are in pixels relative to the container application window's client area.

Drawing should not occur outside the clipping rectangle. Usually, drawing is automatically restricted. Use this function to determine whether the user has scrolled outside the visible portion of the document; if so, scroll the container document as needed by means of a call to **ScrollContainerBy**.

See Also   **COleServerDoc::GetItemPosition, COleServerDoc::ScrollContainerBy**

COleServerDoc::GetItemPosition

void GetItemPosition(LPRECT *lpPosRect* **) const;**

Parameters   *lpPosRect*   Pointer to a **RECT** structure or a **CRect** object to receive the coordinates of the item.

Remarks   Call the **GetItemPosition** member function to get the coordinates of the item being edited in place. Coordinates are in pixels relative to the container application window's client area.

The item's position can be compared with the current clipping rectangle to determine the extent to which the item is visible (or not visible) on the screen.

See Also   **COleServerDoc::GetItemClipRect**

COleServerDoc::GetZoomFactor

BOOL GetZoomFactor(LPSIZE *lpSizeNum* **= NULL, LPSIZE** *lpSizeDenom* **= NULL, LPCRECT** *lpPosRect* **= NULL) const;**

Return Value

Nonzero if the item is activated for in-place editing and its zoom factor is other than 100% (1:1); otherwise 0.

Parameters

lpSizeNum   Pointer to an object of class **CSize** that will hold the zoom factor's numerator. Can be **NULL**.

lpSizeDenom   Pointer to an object of class **CSize** that will hold the zoom factor's denominator. Can be **NULL**.

lpPosRect   Pointer to an object of class **CRect** that describes the item's new position. If this argument is **NULL**, the function uses the item's current position.

Remarks

The **GetZoomFactor** member function determines the "zoom factor" of an item that has been activated for in-place editing. The zoom factor, in pixels, is the proportion of the item's size to its current extent. If the container application has not set the item's extent, its natural extent (as determined by **COleServerItem::OnGetExtent**) is used.

The function sets its first two arguments to the numerator and denominator of the item's "zoom factor." If the item is not being edited in place, the function sets these arguments to a default value of 100% (or 1:1) and returns zero. For further information, see Technical Note 40, "OLE In-Place Resizing and Zooming."

See Also

COleServerDoc::GetItemPosition, **COleServerDoc::GetItemClipRect**, **COleServerDoc::OnSetItemRects**

COleServerDoc::IsEmbedded

BOOL IsEmbedded( ) const;

Return Value

Nonzero if the **OleServerDoc** object is a document that represents an object embedded in a container; otherwise 0.

Remarks

Call the **IsEmbedded** member function to determine whether the document represents an object embedded in a container. A document loaded from a file is not embedded although it may be manipulated by a container application as a link. A document which is an embedding in a container document is considered to be embedded.

COleServerDoc::IsInPlaceActive

BOOL IsInPlaceActive( ) const;

Return Value   Nonzero if the **OleServerDoc** object is active in place; otherwise 0.

Remarks   Call the **IsInPlaceActive** member function to determine whether the item is currently in the in-place active state.

See Also   **COleClientItem::OnActivate**, **COleServerDoc::OnReactivateAndUndo**, **COleServerDoc::ActivateInPlace**

COleServerDoc::NotifyChanged

void NotifyChanged( );

Remarks   Call this function to notify all linked items connected to the document that the document has changed. Typically, you call this function after the user changes some global attribute such as the dimensions of the server document. If an OLE item is linked to the document with an automatic link, the item is updated to reflect the changes. In container applications written with the Microsoft Foundation Class Library, the **OnChange** member function of **COleClientItem** is called.

Note   This function is included for compatibility with OLE 1. New applications should use **UpdateAllItems**.

See Also   **COleServerDoc::NotifyClosed**, **COleServerDoc::NotifySaved**, **COleClientItem::OnChange**

COleServerDoc::NotifyClosed

void NotifyClosed( );

Remarks   Call this function to notify the container(s) that the document has been closed. When the user chooses the Close command from the File menu, **NotifyClosed** is called by **COleServerDoc**'s implementation of the **OnCloseDocument** member function. In container applications written with the Microsoft Foundation Class Library, the **OnChange** member function of **COleClientItem** is called.

See Also   **COleServerDoc::NotifyChanged**, **COleServerDoc::NotifySaved**, **COleClientItem::OnChange**, **CDocument::OnCloseDocument**

COleServerDoc::NotifyRename

void NotifyRename(LPCTSTR *lpszNewName* **);**

Parameters   *lpszNewName*   Pointer to a string specifying the new name of the server
              document; this is typically a fully qualified path.

Remarks   Call this function after the user renames the server document. When the user
              chooses the Save As command from the File menu, **NotifyRename** is called by
              COleServerDoc's implementation of the **OnSaveDocument** member function.
              This function notifies the OLE system DLLs, which in turn notify the containers. In
              container applications written with the Microsoft Foundation Class Library, the
              OnRenamed member function of **COleClientItem** is called.

See Also   **COleServerDoc::NotifySaved, CDocument::OnSaveDocument**

COleServerDoc::NotifySaved

void NotifySaved( );

Remarks   Call this function after the user saves the server document. When the user chooses
              the Save command from the File menu, **NotifySaved** is called for you by
              COleServerDoc's implementation of **OnSaveDocument**. This function notifies
              the OLE system DLLs, which in turn notify the containers. In container applications
              written with the Microsoft Foundation Class Library, the **OnChange** member
              function of **COleClientItem** is called.

See Also   **COleServerDoc::NotifyChanged, COleServerDoc::NotifyClosed,**
              COleClientItem::OnChange, ::OleSavedServerDoc,
              CDocument::OnSaveDocument

COleServerDoc::OnClose

Protected→
virtual void OnClose(OLECLOSE *dwCloseOption* **);**
END Protected

Parameters   *dwCloseOption*   A value from the enumeration **OLECLOSE**. This parameter can
              have one of the following values:

- **OLECLOSE_SAVEIFDIRTY**   The file is saved if it has been modified.
- **OLECLOSE_NOSAVE**   The file is closed without being saved.
- **OLECLOSE_PROMPTSAVE**   If the file has been modified, the user is
  prompted about saving it.

Remarks   Called by the framework when a container requests that the server document be closed. The default implementation calls **CDocument::OnCloseDocument**. For more information and additional values for **OLECLOSE**, see the *OLE 2 Programmer's Reference, Volume 1.*

See Also   **COleException, CDocument::OnCloseDocument**

In the *OLE 2 Programmer's Reference, Volume 1*: **OLECLOSE**

COleServerDoc::OnDeactivate

Protected→
virtual void OnDeactivate( );
    END Protected

Remarks   Called by the framework when the user deactivates an embedded or linked item that is currently in-place active. This function restores the container application's user interface to its original state and destroys any menus and other controls that were created for in-place activation.

The undo state information should be unconditionally released at this point.

See Also   **COleServerDoc::ActivateInPlace, COleServerDoc::OnDeactivateUI, COleServerDoc::DestroyInPlaceFrame**

In *Programming with the Microsoft Foundation Class Library*: "Activation"

COleServerDoc::OnDeactivateUI

Protected→
virtual void OnDeactivateUI(BOOL *bUndoable* **);**
    END Protected

Parameters   *bUndoable*   Specifies whether the editing changes can be undone.

Remarks   Called when the user deactivates an item that was activated in place. This function restores the container application's user interface to its original state, hiding any menus and other controls that were created for in-place activation.

The framework always sets *bUndoable* to **FALSE**. If the server supports undo and there is an operation that can be undone, call the base-class implementation with *bUndoable* set to **TRUE**.

See Also   **COleServerDoc::OnDeactivate**

COleServerDoc::OnDocWindowActivate

Protected→
virtual void OnDocWindowActivate(BOOL *bActivate* **);**
END Protected

Parameters   *bActivate*   Specifies whether the document window is to be activated or deactivated.

Remarks   The framework calls this function to activate or deactivate a document window for in-place editing. The default implementation removes or adds the frame-level user interface elements as appropriate. Override this function if you want to perform additional actions when the document containing your item is activated or deactivated.

See Also   **COleServerDoc::ActivateInPlace, COleServerDoc::OnReactivateAndUndo, COleServerDoc::OnShowControlBars, COleServerDoc::OnDeactivateUI, COleServerDoc::OnFrameWindowActivate, COleIPFrameWnd**

In *Programming with the Microsoft Foundation Class Library*: "Activation"

COleServerDoc::OnFrameWindowActivate

Protected→
virtual void OnFrameWindowActivate(BOOL *bActivate* **);**
END Protected

Parameters   *bActivate*   Specifies whether the frame window is to be activated or deactivated.

Remarks   The framework calls this function when the container application's frame window is activated or deactivated.

The default implementation cancels any help modes the frame window might be in. Override this function if you want to perform special processing when the frame window is activated or deactivated.

See Also   **COleServerDoc::OnDocWindowActivate**

In *Programming with the Microsoft Foundation Class Library*: "Activation"

COleServerDoc::OnGetEmbeddedItem

Protected→
virtual COleServerItem* OnGetEmbeddedItem( ) = 0;
END Protected

Return Value   A pointer to an item representing the entire document; **NULL** if the operation failed.

Remarks   Called by the framework when a container application calls the server application to create or edit an embedded item. There is no default implementation. You must override this function to return an item that represents the entire document. This return value should be an object of a **COleServerItem**-derived class.

See Also   **COleLinkingDoc::OnGetLinkedItem**, **COleServerItem**

COleServerDoc::OnReactivateAndUndo

Protected→
virtual BOOL OnReactivateAndUndo( );
END Protected

Return Value   Nonzero if successful; otherwise 0.

Remarks   The framework calls this function when the user chooses to undo changes made to an item that has been activated in place, changed, and subsequently deactivated. The default implementation does nothing except return **FALSE** to indicate failure.

Override this function if your application supports undo. Usually you would perform the undo operation, then activate the item by calling **ActivateInPlace**. If the container application is written with the Microsoft Foundation Class Library, calling **COleClientItem::ReactivateAndUndo** causes this function to be called.

See Also   **COleServerDoc::ActivateInPlace**, **COleServerDoc::IsInPlaceActive**, **COleClientItem::ReactivateAndUndo**

COleServerDoc::OnResizeBorder

Protected→
virtual void OnResizeBorder(LPCRECT *lpRectBorder*,
    LPOLEINPLACEUIWINDOW *lpUIWindow*, **BOOL** *bFrame* **);**
END Protected

Parameters   *lpRectBorder*   Pointer to a **RECT** structure or a **CRect** object that specifies the coordinates of the border.

lpUIWindow   Pointer to an object of class **IOleInPlaceUIWindow** that owns the current in-place editing session.

bFrame   **TRUE** if *lpUIWindow* points to the container application's top-level frame window, or **FALSE** if *lpUIWindow* points to the container application's document-level frame window.

Remarks	The framework calls this function when the container application's frame windows change size. This function resizes and adjusts toolbars and other user-interface elements in accordance with the new window size.

This is an advanced overridable.

See Also	**COleServerDoc::OnShowControlBars**

In the *OLE 2 Programmer's Reference*
Volume 1: **IOleInPlaceUIWindow**

COleServerDoc::OnSetHostNames

Protected→
virtual void OnSetHostNames(LPCTSTR *lpszHost*, **LPCTSTR** *lpszHostObj* **);**
END Protected

Parameters   *lpszHost*   Pointer to a string that specifies the name of the container application.

lpszHostObj   Pointer to a string that specifies the container's name for the document.

Remarks   Called by the framework when the container sets or changes the host names for this document. The default implementation changes the document title for all views referring to this document.

Override this function if your application sets the titles through a different mechanism.

See Also   **COleClientItem::SetHostNames**

COleServerDoc::OnSetItemRects

Protected→
virtual void OnSetItemRects(LPCRECT *lpPosRect*,
    LPCRECT *lpClipRect* **);**
END Protected

Parameters   *lpPosRect*   Pointer to a **RECT** structure or a **CRect** object that specifies the in-place frame window's position relative to the container application's client area.

lpClipRect   Pointer to a **RECT** structure or a **CRect** object that specifies the in-place frame window's clipping rectangle relative to the container application's client area.

Remarks	The framework calls this function to position the in-place editing frame window within the container application's frame window. Override this function to update the view's zoom factor, if necessary.

The framework calls this function to position the in-place editing frame window within the container application's frame window. Override this function to update the view's zoom factor, if necessary.

This function is usually called in response to a **RequestPositionChange** call, although it can be called at any time by the container to request a position change for the in-place item.

See Also   **COleServerDoc::RequestPositionChange**,
COleIPFrameWnd::RepositionFrame, **COleClientItem::SetItemRects**,
COleServerDoc::GetZoomFactor

COleServerDoc::OnShowControlBars

Protected→
virtual void OnShowControlBars(CFrameWnd **pFrameWnd***, BOOL**
bShow **)**;
END Protected

Parameters   *pFrameWnd*   Pointer to the frame window whose control bars should be hidden or shown.

bShow   Determines whether control bars are shown or hidden.

Remarks   The framework calls this function to show or hide the server application's control bars associated with the frame window identified by *pFrameWnd*. The default implementation enumerates all control bars owned by that frame window and hides or shows them.

See Also   **COleServerDoc::ActivateInPlace**, **COleServerDoc::OnReactivateAndUndo**,
COleServerDoc::OnFrameWindowActivate,
COleServerDoc::IsInPlaceActive

COleServerDoc::OnShowDocument

Protected→
virtual void OnShowDocument(BOOL *bShow* **)**;
END Protected

Parameters   *bShow*   Specifies whether the user interface to the document is to be shown or hidden.

Remarks   The framework calls the **OnShowDocument** function when the server document must be hidden or shown. If *bShow* is **TRUE**, the default implementation activates the server application, if necessary, and causes the container application to scroll its window so that the item is visible. If *bShow* is **FALSE**, the default implementation deactivates the item through a call to **OnDeactivate**, then destroys or hides all frame windows that have been created for the document, except the first one. If no visible documents remain, the default implementation hides the server application.

See Also   **COleServerDoc::ActivateInPlace**, **COleServerItem::OnDoVerb**,
COleServerDoc::IsInPlaceActive, **COleServerDoc::OnDeactivateUI**

COleServerDoc::OnUpdateDocument

virtual BOOL OnUpdateDocument( );

Return Value   Nonzero if the document was successfully updated; otherwise 0.

Remarks   Called by the framework when saving a document that is an embedded item in a compound document. The default implementation calls the **COleServerDoc::NotifySaved** and **COleServerDoc::SaveEmbedding** member functions and then marks the document as clean. Override this function if you want to perform special processing when updating an embedded item.

See Also   **COleServerDoc::NotifySaved**, **COleServerDoc::SaveEmbedding**,
CDocument::OnSaveDocument

COleServerDoc::RequestPositionChange

void RequestPositionChange(LPCRECT *lpPosRect* **);**

Parameters   *lpPosRect*   Pointer to a **RECT** structure or a **CRect** object containing the item's new position.

Remarks   Call this member function to have the container application change the item's position. This function is usually called (in conjunction with **UpdateAllItems**) when the data in an in-place active item has changed. Following this call, the container might or might not perform the change by calling **OnSetItemRects**. The resulting position might be different from the one requested.

See Also   **COleServerDoc::ScrollContainerBy**

COleServerDoc::SaveEmbedding

void SaveEmbedding( );

Remarks   Call this function to tell the container application to save the embedded object. This function is called automatically from **OnUpdateDocument**. Note that this function causes the item to be updated on disk, so it is usually called only as a result of a specific user action.

See Also   **COleServerDoc::NotifyClosed**

COleServerDoc::ScrollContainerBy

BOOL ScrollContainerBy(CSize *sizeScroll* **);**

Return Value   Nonzero if successful; otherwise 0.

Parameters   *sizeScroll*   Indicates how far the container document is to scroll.

Remarks   Call the **ScrollContainerBy** member function to scroll the container document by the amount, in pixels, indicated by *sizeScroll*. Positive values indicate scrolling down and to the right; negative values indicate scrolling up and to the left.

See Also   **COleClientItem::OnScrollBy**

COleServerDoc::UpdateAllItems

void UpdateAllItems(COleServerItem* *pSender*, **LPARAM** *lHint* = 0L, **CObject*** *pHint* = **NULL, DVASPECT** *nDrawAspect* = **DVASPECT_CONTENT);**

Parameters   *pSender*   Pointer to the item that modified the document, or **NULL** if all items are to be updated.

lHint   Contains information about the modification.

pHint   Pointer to an object storing information about the modification.

nDrawAspect   Determines how the item is to be drawn. This is a value from the **DVASPECT** enumeration. This parameter can have one of the following values:

- **DVASPECT_CONTENT**   Item is represented in such a way that it can be displayed as an embedded object inside its container.
- **DVASPECT_THUMBNAIL**   Item is rendered in a "thumbnail" representation so that it can be displayed in a browsing tool.
- **DVASPECT_ICON**   Item is represented by an icon.
- **DVASPECT_DOCPRINT**   Item is represented as if it were printed using the Print command from the File menu.

Remarks   Call this function to notify all linked items connected to the document that the document has changed. You typically call this function after the user changes the server document. If an OLE item is linked to the document with an automatic link, the item is updated to reflect the changes. In container applications written with the Microsoft Foundation Class Library, the **OnChange** member function of **COleClientItem** is called.

This function calls the **OnUpdate** member function for each of the document's items except the sending item, passing *pHint*, *lHint*, and *nDrawAspect*. Use these parameters to pass information to the items about the modifications made to the document. You can encode information using *lHint* or you can define a **CObject**-derived class to store information about the modifications and pass an object of that class using *pHint*. Override the **OnUpdate** member function in your **COleServerItem**-derived class to optimize the updating of each item depending on whether its presentation has changed.

See Also   **COleServerDoc::NotifyChanged, COleServerItem::OnUpdate, COleServerDoc::NotifySaved, COleClientItem::OnChange**

class COleServerItem : public CDocItem

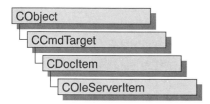

The **COleServerItem** class provides the server interface to OLE items. A linked item can represent some or all of a server document. An embedded item always represents an entire server document.

The **COleServerItem** class defines several overridable member functions that are called by the OLE system dynamic-link libraries (DLLs), usually in response to requests from the container application. These member functions allow the container application to manipulate the item indirectly in various ways, such as by displaying it, executing its verbs, or retrieving its data in various formats.

To use **COleServerItem**, derive a class from it and implement the **OnDraw** and **Serialize** member functions. The **OnDraw** function provides the metafile representation of an item, allowing it to be displayed when a container application opens a compound document. The **Serialize** function of **CObject** provides the native representation of an item, allowing an embedded item to be transferred between the server and container applications. **OnGetExtent** provides the natural size of the item to the container, enabling the container to size the item.

For more information about servers and related topics, see the article "Creating a Container/Server Application" in *Programming with the Microsoft Foundation Class Library*.

#include <afxole.h>

See Also   **COleClientItem**, **COleServerItem**, **COleServerDoc**, **COleTemplateServer**, **CObject::Serialize**

Status

GetDocument	Returns the server document that contains the item.
GetItemName	Returns the name of the item. Used for linked items only.
SetItemName	Sets the name of the item. Used for linked items only.
IsConnected	Indicates whether the item is currently attached to an active container.
IsLinkedItem	Indicates whether the item represents a linked OLE item.

Operations

CopyToClipboard	Copies the item to the Clipboard.
NotifyChanged	Updates all containers with automatic link update.
DoDragDrop	Performs a drag-and-drop operation.
GetClipboardData	Gets the data source for use in data transfer (drag and drop or Clipboard).
GetEmbedSourceData	Gets the **CF_EMBEDSOURCE** data for an OLE item.
AddOtherClipboardData	Places presentation and conversion formats in a **COleDataSource** object.
GetLinkSourceData	Gets the **CF_LINKSOURCE** data for an OLE item.
GetObjectDescriptorData	Gets the **CF_OBJECTDESCRIPTOR** data for an OLE item.

Construction

COleServerItem	Constructs a **COleServerItem** object.
GetDataSource	Gets the object used to store conversion formats.

Overridables

OnDraw	Called when the container requests to draw the item; implementation required.
OnDrawEx	Called for specialized item drawing.
OnUpdate	Called when some portion of the document the item belongs in is changed.
OnInitFromData	Called by the framework to initialize an OLE item using the contents of the data transfer object specified.
OnGetExtent	Called by the framework to retrieve the size of the OLE item.
OnSetExtent	Called by the framework to set the size of the OLE item.
OnGetClipboardData	Called by the framework to get the data that would be copied to the clipboard.
OnSetColorScheme	Called to set the item's color scheme.
OnSetData	Called to set the item's data.
OnDoVerb	Called to execute a verb.
OnQueryUpdateItems	Called to determine whether any linked items require updating.
OnRenderData	Retrieves data as part of delayed rendering.
OnRenderFileData	Retrieves data into a **CFile** object as part of delayed rendering.

OnRenderGlobalData	Retrieves data into an **HGLOBAL** as part of delayed rendering.
OnUpdateItems	Called to update the presentation cache of all items in the server document.
OnOpen	Called by the framework to display the OLE item in its own top-level window.
OnShow	Called when the container requests to show the item.
OnHide	Called by the framework to hide the OLE item.

Data Members

| m_sizeExtent | Informs the server about how much of the OLE item is visible. |

Member Functions

COleServerItem::AddOtherClipboardData

void AddOtherClipboardData(COleDataSource* *pDataSource* **);**

Parameters   *pDataSource*   Pointer to the **COleDataSource** object in which the data should be placed.

Remarks   Call this function to place the presentation and conversion formats for the OLE item in the specified **COleDataSource** object. You must have implemented the **OnDraw** member function to provide the presentation format (a metafile picture) for the item. To support other conversion formats, register them using the **COleDataSource** object returned by **GetDataSource** and override the **OnRenderData** member function to provide data in the formats you want to support.

See Also   **COleDataSource, COleServerItem::GetDataSource, COleServerItem::GetEmbedSourceData, COleServerItem::OnDraw**

COleServerItem::COleServerItem

Protected→
COleServerItem(COleServerDoc* *pServerDoc*, **BOOL** *bAutoDelete* **);**
END Protected

Parameters   *pServerDoc*   Pointer to the document that contains the item.

bAutoDelete   Flag indicating whether the object can be deleted when a link to it is released. Set this to **FALSE** if the **COleServerItem** object is an integral part of your document's data which you must delete. Set this to **TRUE** if the object is a secondary structure used to identify a range in your document's data that can be deleted by the framework.

Remarks   Constructs a **COleServerItem** object and adds it to the server document's collection of document items.

See Also   **COleDocument::AddItem**

COleServerItem::CopyToClipboard

void **CopyToClipboard**(**BOOL** *bIncludeLink* = **FALSE**);

Parameters   *bIncludeLink*   Set this to **TRUE** if link data should be copied to the Clipboard. Set this to **FALSE** if your server application does not support links.

Remarks   Call this function to copy the OLE item to the Clipboard. The function uses the **OnGetClipboardData** member function to create a **COleDataSource** object containing the OLE item's data in the formats supported. The function then places the **COleDataSource** object on the Clipboard by using the **COleDataSource::SetClipboard** function. The **COleDataSource** object includes the item's native data and its representation in **CF_METAFILEPICT** format, as well as data in any conversion formats you choose to support. You must have implemented **Serialize** and **OnDraw** for this member function to work.

See Also   **COleDataSource::SetClipboard, COleDataSource, COleServerItem::AddOtherClipboardData, COleServerItem::GetClipboardData, COleServerItem::OnDraw, CObject::Serialize**

COleServerItem::DoDragDrop

DROPEFFECT DoDragDrop(**LPCRECT** *lpItemRect*, **CPoint** *ptOffset*, **BOOL** *bIncludeLink* = **FALSE**, **DWORD** *dwEffects* = **DROPEFFECT_COPY** | **DROPEFFECT_MOVE**, **LPCRECT** *lpRectStartDrag* = **NULL**);

Return Value   A value from the **DROPEFFECT** enumeration. If it is **DROPEFFECT_MOVE**, the original data should be removed.

Parameters   *lpItemRect*   The item's rectangle on screen, in pixels, relative to the client area.

ptOffset   The offset from *lpItemRect* where the mouse position was at the time of the drag.

bIncludeLink   Set this to **TRUE** if link data should be copied to the Clipboard. Set it to **FALSE** if your application does not support links.

dwEffects   Determines the effects that the drag source will allow in the drag operation (a combination of Copy, Move, and Link).

lpRectStartDrag   Pointer to the rectangle that defines where the drag actually starts. It does not start until the mouse cursor leaves the rectangle. If **NULL**, a default drag rectangle is used so that the drag does not start until the cursor moves by at least one pixel.

Remarks   Call the **DoDragDrop** member function to perform a drag-and-drop operation.

See Also   **COleDataSource::DoDragDrop**, **COleServerItem::CopyToClipboard**

COleServerItem::GetClipboardData

void GetClipboardData(COleDataSource* *pDataSource*,
   BOOL *bIncludeLink* = **FALSE, LPPOINT** *lpOffset* = **NULL,**
   LPSIZE *lpSize* = **NULL);**

Parameters   *pDataSource*   Pointer to the **COleDataSource** object that will receive the OLE item's data in all supported formats.

bIncludeLink   **TRUE** if link data should be copied to the Clipboard. **FALSE** if your server application does not support links.

lpOffset   The offset, in pixels, of the mouse cursor from the origin of the object.

lpSize   The size of the object in pixels.

Remarks   Call this function to fill the specified **COleDataSource** object with all the data that would be copied to the Clipboard if you called **CopyToClipboard** (the same data would also be transferred if you called **DoDragDrop**). This function calls the **GetEmbedSourceData** member function to get the native data for the OLE item and calls the **AddOtherClipboardData** member function to get the presentation format and any supported conversion formats. If *bIncludeLink* is **TRUE**, the function also calls **GetLinkSourceData** to get the link data for the item.

Override this function if you want to put formats in a **COleDataSource** object before or after those formats supplied by **CopyToClipboard**.

See Also   **COleDataSource, COleServerItem::AddOtherClipboardData,**
   COleServerItem::CopyToClipboard, COleServerItem::DoDragDrop,
   COleServerItem::GetEmbedSourceData,
   COleServerItem::GetLinkSourceData

COleServerItem::GetDataSource

COleDataSource* GetDataSource( );

Remarks   Call this function to get the **COleDataSource** object used to store the conversion formats that the server application supports. If you want your server application to offer data in a variety of formats during data transfer operations, register those formats with the **COleDataSource** object returned by this function. For example, if you want to supply a **CF_TEXT** representation of the OLE item for Clipboard or drag-and-drop operations, you would register the format with the **COleDataSource** object this function returns, and then override the **OnRenderxxxData** member function to provide the data.

See Also   **COleDataSource, COleDataSource::DelayRenderData, COleServerItem::CopyToClipboard, COleServerItem::DoDragDrop**

COleServerItem::GetDocument

COleServerDoc* GetDocument( ) const;

Return Value   A pointer to the document that contains the item; **NULL** if the item is not part of a document.

Remarks   Call this function to get a pointer to the document that contains the item. This allows access to the server document that you passed as an argument to the **COleServerItem** constructor.

See Also   **COleServerItem::COleServerItem, COleServerDoc**

COleServerItem::GetEmbedSourceData

void GetEmbedSourceData(LPSTGMEDIUM *lpStgMedium* **);**

Parameters   *lpStgMedium*   Pointer to the **STGMEDIUM** structure that will receive the **CF_EMBEDSOURCE** data for the OLE item.

Remarks   Call this function to get the **CF_EMBEDSOURCE** data for an OLE item. This format includes the item's native data. You must have implemented the **Serialize** member function for this function to work properly.

The result can then be added to a data source by using **COleDataSource::CacheData**. This function is called automatically by **OnGetClipboard**.

See Also   **COleServerItem::GetLinkSourceData, COleServerItem::GetObjectDescriptorData, COleDataSource::CacheData, CObject::Serialize**

COleServerItem::GetItemName

const CString& GetItemName( ) const;

Return Value   The name of the item.

Remarks   Call this function to get the name of the item. You typically call this function only for linked items.

See Also   **COleServerItem::SetItemName**, **COleLinkingDoc::OnGetLinkedItem**

COleServerItem::GetLinkSourceData

BOOL GetLinkSourceData(LPSTGMEDIUM *lpStgMedium* **);**

Return Value   Nonzero if successful; otherwise 0.

Parameters   *lpStgMedium*   Pointer to the **STGMEDIUM** structure that will receive the **CF_LINKSOURCE** data for the OLE item.

Remarks   Call this function to get the **CF_LINKSOURCE** data for an OLE item. This format includes the CLSID describing the type of the OLE item and the information needed to locate the document containing the OLE item.

The result can then be added to a data source with **COleDataSource::CacheData**. This function is called automatically by **OnGetClipboard**.

See Also   **COleServerItem::GetEmbedSourceData**,
COleServerItem::GetObjectDescriptorData

COleServerItem::GetObjectDescriptorData

void GetObjectDescriptorData(LPPOINT* *lpOffset*, **LPSIZE*** *lpSize*,
LPSTGMEDIUM *lpStgMedium* **);**

Parameters   *lpOffset*   Offset of the mouse click from the upper-left corner of the OLE item. Can be **NULL**.

lpSize   Size of the OLE item. Can be **NULL**.

lpStgMedium   Pointer to the **STGMEDIUM** structure that will receive the **CF_OBJECTDESCRIPTOR** data for the OLE item.

Remarks   Call this function to get the **CF_OBJECTDESCRIPTOR** data for an OLE item. The information is copied into the **STGMEDIUM** structure pointed to by *lpStgMedium*. This format includes the information needed for the Paste Special dialog.

See Also   COleServerItem::AddOtherClipboardData,
COleServerItem::GetEmbedSourceData,
COleServerItem::GetLinkSourceData

In the *OLE 2 Programmer's Reference, Volume 1*: **STGMEDIUM**

COleServerItem::IsConnected

BOOL IsConnected( ) const;

Return Value   Nonzero if the item is connected; otherwise 0.

Remarks   Call this function to see if the OLE item is connected. An OLE item is considered connected if one or more containers have references to the item. An item is connected if its reference count is greater than 0 or if it is an embedded item.

See Also   **COleServerItem::IsLinkedItem, COleLinkingDoc::OnGetLinkedItem**

COleServerItem::IsLinkedItem

BOOL IsLinkedItem( ) const;

Return Value   Nonzero if the item is a linked item; otherwise 0.

Remarks   Call this function to see if the OLE item is a linked item. An item is linked if the item is valid and is not returned in the document's list of embedded items. A linked item might or might not be connected to a container.

It is common to use the same class for both linked and embedded items. **IsLinkedItem** allows you to make linked items behave differently than embedded items although many times the code is common.

See Also   **COleServerItem::IsConnected, COleLinkingDoc::OnGetLinkedItem**

COleServerItem::NotifyChanged

void NotifyChanged(DVASPECT *nDrawAspect* **= DVASPECT_CONTENT);**

Parameters   *nDrawAspect*   A value from the **DVASPECT** enumeration that indicates which aspect of the OLE item has changed. For possible values, see **COleServerItem::OnUpdate**.

Remarks   Call this function after the linked item has been changed. If a container item is linked to the document with an automatic link, the item is updated to reflect the changes. In container applications written using the Microsoft Foundation Class Library, the **OnChange** member function of **COleClientItem** is called in response.

See Also   **COleClientItem::OnChange, COleServerItem::OnUpdate,
COleServerDoc::NotifyChanged**

COleServerItem::OnDoVerb

virtual void OnDoVerb(LONG *iVerb* **);**

Parameters
iVerb Specifies the verb to execute. It can be any one of the following:

Value	Meaning	Symbol
0	Primary verb	**OLEIVERB_PRIMARY**
1	Secondary verb	(None)
−1	Display item for editing	**OLEIVERB_SHOW**
−2	Edit item in separate window	**OLEIVERB_OPEN**
−3	Hide item	**OLEIVERB_HIDE**

The −1 value is typically an alias for another verb. If open editing is not supported, −2 has the same effect as −1. For additional values, see **IOleObject::DoVerb** in the *OLE 2 Programmer's Reference, Volume 1*.

Remarks
Called by the framework to execute the specified verb. If the container application was written with the Microsoft Foundation Class Library, this function is called when the **COleClientItem::Activate** member function of the corresponding **COleClientItem** object is called. The default implementation calls the **OnShow** member function if the primary verb or **OLEIVERB_SHOW** is specified, **OnOpen** if the secondary verb or **OLEIVERB_OPEN** is specified, and **OnHide** if **OLEIVERB_HIDE** is specified. The default implementation calls **OnShow** if *iVerb* is not one of the verbs listed above.

Override this function if your primary verb does not show the item. For example, if the item is a sound recording and its primary verb is Play, you would not have to display the server application to play the item.

See Also
COleClientItem::Activate, COleServerItem::OnShow, COleServerItem::OnOpen, COleServerItem::OnHide

In the *OLE 2 Programmer's Reference, Volume 1*: **IOleObject::DoVerb**

COleServerItem::OnDraw

virtual BOOL OnDraw(CDC* *pDC*, **CSize&** *rSize* **) = 0;**

Return Value
Nonzero if the item was successfully drawn; otherwise 0.

Parameters
pDC A pointer to the **CDC** object on which to draw the item. The display context is automatically connected to the attribute display context so you can call attribute functions, although doing so would make the metafile device-specific.

rSize Size, in **HIMETRIC** units, in which to draw the metafile.

Remarks	Called by the framework to render the OLE item into a metafile. The metafile representation of the OLE item is used to display the item in the container application. If the container application was written with the Microsoft Foundation Class Library, the metafile is used by the **Draw** member function of the corresponding **COleClientItem** object. There is no default implementation. You must override this function to draw the item into the device context specified.
See Also	**COleClientItem::Draw**

COleServerItem::OnDrawEx

virtual BOOL OnDrawEx(CDC* *pDC*, **DVASPECT** *nDrawAspect*, **CSize&** *rSize* **);**

Return Value	Nonzero if the item was successfully drawn; otherwise 0.
Parameters	*pDC* A pointer to the **CDC** object on which to draw the item. The DC is automatically connected to the attribute DC so you can call attribute functions, although doing so would make the metafile device-specific.
	nDrawAspect A value from the **DVASPECT** enumeration. For possible values, see **COleServerItem::OnUpdate**.
	rSize Size of the item in **HIMETRIC** units.
Remarks	Called by the framework for all drawing. The default implementation calls **OnDraw** when **DVASPECT** is equal to **DVASPECT_CONTENT**; otherwise it fails.
	Override this function to provide presentation data for aspects other than **DVASPECT_CONTENT**, such as **DVASPECT_ICON** or **DVASPECT_THUMBNAIL**.
See Also	**COleServerItem::OnDraw**
	In the *OLE 2 Programmer's Reference* *Volume 1*: **DVASPECT**

COleServerItem::OnGetClipboardData

virtual COleDataSource* OnGetClipboardData(BOOL *bIncludeLink*, **LPPOINT** *lpOffset*, **LPSIZE** *lpSize* **);**

Return Value	A pointer to a **COleDataSource** object containing the Clipboard data.
Parameters	*bIncludeLink* Set this to **TRUE** if link data should be copied to the Clipboard. Set this to **FALSE** if your server application does not support links.

lpOffset   The offset of the mouse cursor from the origin of the object in pixels.

lpSize   The size of the object in pixels.

Remarks   Called by the framework to get a **COleDataSource** object containing all the data that would be placed on the Clipboard by a call to the **CopyToClipboard** member function. The default implementation of this function calls **GetClipboardData**.

See Also   **COleDataSource**, **COleDataSource::SetClipboard**, **COleServerItem::CopyToClipboard**, **COleServerItem::GetClipboardData**

COleServerItem::OnGetExtent

virtual BOOL OnGetExtent(DVASPECT *nDrawAspect*, **CSize&** *rSize* **);**

Return Value   Nonzero if successful; otherwise 0.

Parameters   *nDrawAspect*   Specifies the aspect of the OLE item whose bounds are to be retrieved. For possible values, see **COleClientItem::Draw**.

rSize   Reference to a **CSize** object that will receive the size of the OLE item.

Remarks   Called by the framework to retrieve the size, in **HIMETRIC** units, of the OLE item.

If the container application was written with the Microsoft Foundation Class Library, this function is called when the **GetExtent** member function of the corresponding **COleClientItem** object is called. The default implementation does nothing. You must implement it yourself. Override this function if you want to perform special processing when handling a request for the size of the OLE item.

See Also   **COleClientItem::Draw**, **COleClientItem::GetExtent**

COleServerItem::OnHide

Protected→
virtual void OnHide( );
    END Protected

Remarks   Called by the framework to hide the OLE item. The default calls **OnShowDocument(FALSE)**. The function also notifies the container that the OLE item has been hidden. Override this function if you want to perform special processing when hiding an OLE item.

See Also   **COleServerItem::OnOpen**, **COleServerItem::OnShow**, **COleServerDoc::OnShowDocument**

COleServerItem::OnInitFromData

virtual BOOL OnInitFromData(COleDataObject* *pDataObject*, **BOOL**
bCreation **);**

Return Value   Nonzero if successful; otherwise 0.

Parameters   *pDataObject*   Pointer to an OLE data object containing data in various formats for
initializing the OLE item.

bCreation   **TRUE** if the function is called to initialize an OLE item being newly
created by a container application. **FALSE** if the function is called to replace
the contents of an already existing OLE item.

Remarks   Called by the framework to initialize an OLE item using the contents of
pDataObject. If *bCreation* is **TRUE**, this function is called if a container
implements Insert New Object based on the current selection. The data selected is
used when creating the new OLE item. For example, when selecting a range of cells
in a spreadsheet program and then using the Insert New Object to create a chart
based on the values in the selected range. The default implementation does nothing.
Override this function to choose an acceptable format from those offered by
pDataObject and initialize the OLE item based on the data provided. This is an
advanced overridable.

See Also   In the *OLE 2 Programmer's Reference, Volume 1:* **IOleObject::InitFromData**

COleServerItem::OnOpen

Protected→
virtual void OnOpen( );
END Protected

Remarks   Called by the framework to display the OLE item in a separate instance of the
server application, rather than in place.

The default implementation activates the first frame window displaying the
document that contains the OLE item; if the application is a mini-server, the default
implementation shows the main window. The function also notifies the container
that the OLE item has been opened.

Override this function if you want to perform special processing when opening an
OLE item. This is especially common with linked items where you want to set the
selection to the link when it is opened.

See Also   **COleServerItem::OnShow**

In the *OLE 2 Programmer's Reference, Volume 1*:
IOleClientSite::OnShowWindow

COleServerItem::OnQueryUpdateItems

virtual BOOL OnQueryUpdateItems( );

Return Value   Nonzero if the document has items needing updates; 0 if all items are up to date.

Remarks   Called by the framework to determine whether any linked items in the current server document are out of date. An item is out of date if its source document has been changed but the linked item has not been updated to reflect the changes in the document.

See Also   **COleServerItem::OnUpdate**, **COleServerItem::OnUpdateItems**

COleServerItem::OnRenderData

virtual BOOL OnRenderData(LPFORMATETC *lpFormatEtc***,**
LPSTGMEDIUM *lpStgMedium* **);**

Return Value   Nonzero if successful; otherwise 0.

Parameters   *lpFormatEtc*   Points to the **FORMATETC** structure specifying the format in which information is requested.

lpStgMedium   Points to a **STGMEDIUM** structure in which the data is to be returned.

Remarks   Called by the framework to retrieve data in the specified format. The specified format is one previously placed in the **COleDataSource** object using the **DelayRenderData** or **DelayRenderFileData** member functions for delayed rendering. The default implementation of this function calls **OnRenderFileData** or **OnRenderGlobalData**, respectively, if the supplied storage medium is either a file or memory. If neither of these formats is supplied, the default implementation returns 0 and does nothing.

If *lpStgMedium->tymed* is **TYMED_NULL**, the **STGMEDIUM** should allocated and filled as specified by *lpFormatEtc->tymed*. If not **TYMED_NULL**, the **STGMEDIUM** should be filled in place with the data.

Override this function to provide your data in the requested format and medium. Depending on your data, you may want to override one of the other versions of this function instead. If your data is small and fixed in size, override **OnRenderGlobalData**. If your data is in a file, or is of variable size, override **OnRenderFileData**. This is an advanced overridable.

See Also   **COleServerItem::OnRenderFileData**

In the *OLE 2 Programmer's Reference, Volume 1*: **IDataObject::GetData**

COleServerItem::OnRenderFileData

virtual BOOL OnRenderFileData(LPFORMATETC *lpFormatEtc*, **CFile*** *pFile* **);**

Return Value   Nonzero if successful; otherwise 0.

Parameters   *lpFormatEtc*   Points to the **FORMATETC** structure specifying the format in which information is requested.

     pFile   Points to a **CFile** object in which the data is to be rendered.

Remarks   Called by the framework to retrieve data in the specified format when the storage medium is a file. The specified format is one previously placed in the **COleDataSource** object using the **DelayRenderData** member function for delayed rendering. The default implementation of this function simply returns **FALSE**.

     This is an advanced overridable. Override this function to provide your data in the requested format and medium. Depending on your data, you might want to override one of the other versions of this function instead. If you want to handle multiple storage mediums, override **OnRenderData**. If your data is in a file, or is of variable size, override **OnRenderFileData**.

See Also   **COleServerItem::OnRenderData**

     In the *OLE 2 Programmer's Reference, Volume 1*: **IDataObject::GetData**

COleServerItem::OnRenderGlobalData

virtual BOOL OnRenderGlobalData(LPFORMATETC *lpFormatEtc*, **HGLOBAL*** *phGlobal* **);**

Return Value   Nonzero if successful; otherwise 0.

Parameters   *lpFormatEtc*   Points to the **FORMATETC** structure specifying the format in which information is requested.

     phGlobal   Points to a handle to global memory in which the data is to be returned. If no memory has been allocated, this parameter can be **NULL**.

Remarks   Called by the framework to retrieve data in the specified format when the specified storage medium is global memory. The specified format is one previously placed in the **COleDataSource** object using the **DelayRenderData** member function for delayed rendering. The default implementation of this function simply returns **FALSE**.

If *phGlobal* is **NULL**, then a new **HGLOBAL** should be allocated and returned in *phGlobal*. Otherwise, the **HGLOBAL** specified by *phGlobal* should be filled with the data. The amount of data placed in the **HGLOBAL** must not exceed the current size of the memory block. Also, the block cannot be reallocated to a larger size.

This is an advanced overridable. Override this function to provide your data in the requested format and medium. Depending on your data, you may want to override one of the other versions of this function instead. If you want to handle multiple storage mediums, override **OnRenderData**. If your data is in a file, or is of variable size, override **OnRenderFileData**.

See Also　　COleServerItem::OnRenderData

In the *OLE 2 Programmer's Reference, Volume 1*: **IDataObject::GetData**

COleServerItem::OnSetColorScheme

Protected→
virtual BOOL OnSetColorScheme(const LOGPALETTE FAR* *lpLogPalette*);
END Protected

Return Value　　Nonzero if the color palette is used; otherwise 0.

Parameters　　*lpLogPalette*　　Pointer to a Windows **LOGPALETTE** structure.

Remarks　　Called by the framework to specify a color palette to be used when editing the OLE item. If the container application was written using the Microsoft Foundation Class Library, this function is called when the **IOleObject::SetColorScheme** function of the corresponding **COleClientItem** object is called. The default implementation returns **FALSE**. Override this function if you want to use the recommended palette. The server application is not required to use the suggested palette.

See Also　　In the *OLE 2 Programmer's Reference, Volume 1:* **OleObject::SetColorScheme**

COleServerItem::OnSetData

virtual BOOL OnSetData(LPFORMATETC *pFormatEtc*, **LPSTGMEDIUM** *pStgMedium*, **BOOL** *bRelease*);

Return Value　　Nonzero if successful; otherwise 0.

Parameters　　*pFormatEtc*　　Pointer to a **FORMATETC** structure specifying the format of the data.

pStgMedium   Pointer to a **STGMEDIUM** structure in which the data resides.

bRelease   Indicates who has ownership of the storage medium after completing the function call. The caller decides who is responsible for releasing the resources allocated on behalf of the storage medium. The caller does this by setting *bRelease*. If *bRelease* is nonzero, the server item takes ownership, freeing the medium when it has finished using it. When *bRelease* is 0, the caller retains ownership and the server item can use the storage medium only for the duration of the call.

Remarks   Called by the framework to replace the OLE item's data with the specified data. The server item does not take ownership of the data until it has successfully obtained it. That is, it does not take ownership if it returns 0. If the data source takes ownership, it frees the storage medium by calling the **::ReleaseStgMedium** function.

The default implementation does nothing. Override this function to replace the OLE item's data with the specified data. This is an advanced overridable.

For more information about the **FORMATETC** and **::ReleaseStgMedium**, see the *OLE 2 Programmer's Reference, Volume 1.*

See Also   **COleDataSource::OnSetData**

COleServerItem::OnSetExtent

virtual BOOL OnSetExtent(DVASPECT n*DrawAspect,* **const CSize&** *size* **);**

Return Value   Nonzero if successful; otherwise 0.

Parameters   *nDrawAspect*   Specifies the aspect of the OLE item whose bounds are being specified. For possible values, see **COleClientItem::Draw**.

size   A **CSize** structure specifying the new size of the OLE item.

Remarks   Called by the framework to tell the OLE item how much space is available to it in the container document. If the container application was written with the Microsoft Foundation Class Library, this function is called when the **SetExtent** member function of the corresponding **COleClientItem** object is called. The default implementation sets the **m_sizeExtent** member to the specified size if *nDrawAspect* is **DVASPECT_CONTENT**; otherwise it returns 0. Override this function to perform special processing when you change the size of the item.

See Also   **COleClientItem::SetExtent**, **COleServerItem::OnGetExtent**

COleServerItem::OnShow

Protected→
virtual void OnShow( );
    END Protected

Remarks   Called by the framework to instruct the server application to display the OLE item in place. This function is typically called when the user of the container application creates an item or executes a verb, such as Edit, that requires the item to be shown. The default implementation attempts in-place activation. If this fails, the function calls the **OnOpen** member function to display the OLE item in a separate window.

Override this function if you want to perform special processing when an OLE item is shown.

See Also   **COleServerItem::OnOpen, COleClientItem::Activate**

COleServerItem::OnUpdate

virtual void COleServerItem::OnUpdate(COleServerItem* *pSender*,
LPARAM *lHint*, **CObject*** *pHint*, **DVASPECT** *nDrawAspect* **);**

Parameters   *pSender*   Pointer to the item that modified the document. Can be **NULL**.

lHint   Contains information about the modification.

pHint   Pointer to an object storing information about the modification.

nDrawAspect   A value from the **DVASPECT** enumeration. This parameter can have any one of the following values:

- **DVASPECT_CONTENT**   Item is represented in such a way that it can be displayed as an embedded object inside its container.
- **DVASPECT_THUMBNAIL**   Item is rendered in a "thumbnail" representation so that it can be displayed in a browsing tool.
- **DVASPECT_ICON**   Item is represented by an icon.
- **DVASPECT_DOCPRINT**   Item is represented as if it were printed using the Print command from the File menu.

Remarks   Called by the framework when an item has been modified. The default implementation calls **COleServerItem::NotifyChanged**, regardless of the hint or sender.

See Also   **COleServerItem::NotifyChanged**

COleServerItem::OnUpdateItems

virtual void OnUpdateItems( );

Remarks   Called by the framework to update all items in the server document. The default implementation calls **UpdateLink** for all **COleClientItem** objects in the document.

See Also   **COleServerItem::OnUpdate**, **COleServerItem::OnQueryUpdateItems**

COleServerItem::SetItemName

void SetItemName(LPCTSTR *lpszItemName* **);**

Parameters   *lpszItemName*   Pointer to the new name of the item.

Remarks   Call this function when you create a linked item to set its name. The name must be unique within the document. When a server application is called to edit a linked item, the application uses this name to find the item. You do not need to call this function for embedded items.

See Also   **COleServerItem::GetItemName**, **COleLinkingDoc::OnGetLinkedItem**

Data Members

COleServerItem::m_sizeExtent

CSize m_sizeExtent;

Remarks   This member tells the server how much of the object is visible in the container document. The default implementation of **OnSetExtent** sets this member.

See Also   **COleServerItem::OnSetExtent**

class COleStreamFile : public CFile

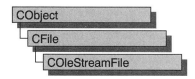

A **COleStreamFile** object represents a stream of data (**IStream**) in a compound file as part of OLE 2 Structured Storage. An **IStorage** object must exist before the stream can be opened or created unless it is a memory stream.

COleStreamFile objects are manipulated exactly like **CFile** objects.

For more information about manipulating streams and storages, see the article "Containers: Compound Files" in *Programming with the Microsoft Foundation Class Library*.

#include <afxole.h>

See Also   **CFile**

In the *OLE 2 Programmer's Reference, Volume 1*: **IStream**, **IStorage**

Construction
COleStreamFile	Constructs a **COleStreamFile** object.

Attributes and Operations
Attach	Associates a stream with the object.
CreateMemoryStream	Creates a stream from global memory and associates it with the object.
CreateStream	Creates a stream and associates it with the object.
Detach	Disassociates the stream from the object.
OpenStream	Safely opens a stream and associates it with the object.

Member Functions

COleStreamFile::Attach

void Attach(LPSTREAM *lpStream* **);**

Parameters   *lpStream*   Points to the OLE stream to be associated with the object. Cannot be **NULL**.

Remarks   Associates the supplied OLE stream with the **COleStreamFile** object. The object must not already be associated with an OLE stream.

See Also   **COleStreamFile::Detach**

In the *OLE 2 Programmer's Reference, Volume 1*: **LPStream**

COleStreamFile::COleStreamFile

COleStreamFile(LPSTREAM *lpStream* **= NULL);**

Parameters   *lpStream*   Pointer to the OLE stream to be associated with the object.

Remarks   Creates a **COleStreamFile** object. If *lpStream* is **NULL**, the object is not associated with an OLE stream, otherwise, the object is associated with the supplied OLE stream.

See Also   **COleStreamFile::Attach**, **CFile**

In the *OLE 2 Programmer's Reference, Volume 1*: **LPSTREAM**

COleStreamFile::CreateMemoryStream

BOOL CreateMemoryStream(CFileException* *pError* **= NULL);**

Return Value   Nonzero if the stream is created successfully; otherwise 0.

Parameters   *pError*   Points to a **CFileException** object or **NULL** that indicates the completion status of the create operation. Supply this parameter if you want to monitor possible exceptions generated by attempting to create the stream.

Remarks   Safely creates a new stream out of global, shared memory where a failure is a normal, expected condition. The memory is allocated by the OLE subsystem.

See Also   **COleStreamFile::OpenStream**, **COleStreamFile::CreateStream**, **CFileException**

In the *OLE 2 Programmer's Reference, Volume 1*: **::CreateStreamOnHGlobal**

COleStreamFile::CreateStream

BOOL CreateStream(LPSTORAGE *lpStorage,* **LPCTSTR** *lpszName,*
DWORD *nOpenFlags* = **modeReadWrite|shareExclusive|modeCreate,**
CFileException* *pError* = **NULL);**

Return Value   Nonzero if the stream is created successfully; otherwise 0.

Parameters   *lpStorage*   Points to the OLE storage object that contains the stream to be created. Cannot be **NULL.**

lpszStreamName   Name of the stream to be created. Cannot be **NULL.**

nOpenFlags   Access mode to use when opening the stream. Exclusive, read/write, and create modes are used by default. For a complete list of the available modes, see **CFile::CFile.**

pError   Points to a **CFileException** object or **NULL.** Supply this parameter if you want to monitor possible exceptions generated by attempting to create the stream.

Remarks   Safely creates a new stream in the supplied storage object where a failure is a normal, expected condition. A file exception will be thrown if the open fails and *pError* is not **NULL.**

See Also   **COleStreamFile::OpenStream, COleStreamFile::CreateMemoryStream, CFileException**

In the *OLE 2 Programmer's Reference, Volume 1*: **IStorage::CreateStream**

COleStreamFile::Detach

LPSTREAM Detach( );

Return Value   A pointer to the stream that was associated with the object.

Remarks   Disassociates the stream from the object without closing the stream. The stream must be closed in some other fashion before the program terminates.

See Also   **COleStreamFile::Attach**

In the *OLE 2 Programmer's Reference, Volume 1*: **LPSTREAM**

COleStreamFile::OpenStream

BOOL OpenStream(LPSTORAGE *lpStorage***, LPCTSTR** *lpszName***,
DWORD** *nOpenFlags* **= modeReadWrite|shareExclusive,
CFileException*** *pError* **= NULL);**

Return Value   Nonzero if the stream is opened successfully; otherwise 0.

Parameters   *lpStorage*   Points to the OLE storage object that contains the stream to be opened.
Cannot be **NULL**.

lpszName   Name of the stream to be opened. Cannot be **NULL**.

nOpenFlags   Access mode to use when opening the stream. Exclusive and
read/write modes are used by default. For the complete list of the available
modes, see **CFile::CFile**.

pError   Points to a **CFileException** object or **NULL**. Supply this parameter if
you want to monitor possible exceptions generated by attempting to open the
stream.

Remarks   Opens an existing stream. A file exception will be thrown if the open fails and
pError is not **NULL**.

See Also   **COleStreamFile::CreateStream**, **COleStreamFile::CreateMemoryStream**,
CFileException

In the *OLE 2 Programmer's Reference, Volume 1*: **IStorage::OpenStream**

class COleTemplateServer : public COleObjectFactory

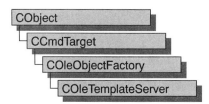

The **COleTemplateServer** class is used for OLE visual editing servers, automation servers, and link containers (applications that support links to embeddings). This class is derived from the class **COleObjectFactory**; usually, you can use **COleTemplateServer** directly rather than deriving your own class. **COleTemplateServer** uses a **CDocTemplate** object to manage the server documents. Use **COleTemplateServer** when implementing a full server, that is, a server that can be run as a standalone application. Full servers are typically multiple document interface (MDI) applications, although single document interface (SDI) applications are supported. One **COleTemplateServer** object is needed for each type of server document an application supports; that is, if your server application supports both worksheets and charts, you must have two **COleTemplateServer** objects.

COleTemplateServer overrides the **OnCreateInstance** member function defined by **COleObjectFactory**. This member function is called by the framework to create a C++ object of the proper type.

#include <afxdisp.h>

See Also   **COleObjectFactory**, **COleServerDoc**, **COleServerItem**, **CDocTemplate**

Construction

COleTemplateServer	Constructs a **COleTemplateServer** object.

Operations

ConnectTemplate	Connects a document template to the underlying **COleObjectFactory** object.
UpdateRegistry	Registers the document type with the OLE system registry.

Member Functions

COleTemplateServer::COleTemplateServer

COleTemplateServer( );

Remarks   Constructs a **COleTemplateServer** object.

COleTemplateServer::ConnectTemplate

void ConnectTemplate(REFCLSID *clsid***, CDocTemplate*** *pDocTemplate***,**
BOOL *bMultiInstance* **);**

Parameters   *clsid*   Reference to the OLE class ID that the template requests.

pDocTemplate   Pointer to the document template.

bMultiInstance   Indicates whether a single instance of the application can support
multiple instantiations. If **TRUE**, multiple instances of the application are
launched for each request to create an object.

Remarks   Connects the document template pointed to by *pDocTemplate* to the underlying
COleObjectFactory object.

See Also   **CDocTemplate**

In the *OLE 2 Programmer's Reference, Volume 1*: **REFCLSID**

COleTemplateServer::UpdateRegistry

void UpdateRegistry(OLE_APPTYPE *nAppType* **=**
OAT_INPLACE_SERVER, LPCSTR* *rglpszRegister* **= NULL, LPCSTR**
FAR* *rglpszOverwrite* **= NULL);**

Parameters   *nAppType*   A value from the **OLE_APPTYPE** enumeration, which is defined in
AFXDISP.H. It can have any one of the following values:

- **OAT_INPLACE_SERVER**   Server has full server user-interface.
- **OAT_SERVER**   Server supports only embedding.
- **OAT_CONTAINER**   Container supports links to embeddings.
- **OAT_DISPATCH_OBJECT**   **IDispatch**-capable object.

rglpszRegister   A list of entries that is written into the registry only if no entries
exist.

rglpszOverwrite   A list of entries that is written into the registry regardless of whether any preceding entries exist.

Remarks

Loads file-type information from the document-template string and places that information in the OLE system registry.

The registration information is loaded by means of a call to **CDocTemplate::GetDocString**. The substrings retrieved are those identified by the indexes **regFileTypeId**, **regFileTypeName**, and **fileNewName**, as described in the **GetDocString** reference pages.

This function fails, and the file information is not entered in the registry, if the **regFileTypeId** substring is empty or if the call to **GetDocString** fails for any other reason.

The information in the arguments *rglpszRegister* and *rglpszOverwrite* is written to the registry through a call to **AfxOleRegisterServerClass**. The default information, which is registered when the two arguments are **NULL**, is suitable for most applications. For information on the structure of the information in these arguments, see **AfxOleRegisterServerClass**.

See Also

CDocTemplate::GetDocString

class COleUpdateDialog : public COleLinksDialog

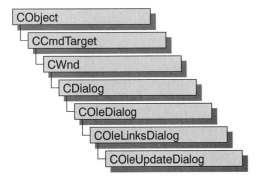

The **COleUpdateDialog** class is used for a special case of the OLE Edit Links dialog box, which should be used when you need to update only existing linked or embedded objects in a document.

For more information regarding OLE 2–specific dialog boxes, see the article "Dialog Boxes in OLE" in *Programming with the Microsoft Foundation Class Library*.

#include <afxodlgs.h>

See Also   **COleLinksDialog**

Construction
COleUpdateDialog	Constructs a **COleUpdateDialog** object.

Operations
DoModal	Displays the Edit Links dialog box in an update mode.

Member Functions

COleUpdateDialog::COleUpdateDialog

COleUpdateDialog(COleDocument* *pDoc*, BOOL *bUpdateLinks* = TRUE, BOOL *bUpdateEmbeddings* = FALSE, CWnd* *pParentWnd* = NULL);

Parameters   *pDoc*   Points to the document containing the links that may need updating.

bUpdateLinks   Flag that determines whether linked objects are to be updated.

bUpdateEmbeddings   Flag that determines whether embedded objects are to be updated.

pParentWnd   Points to the parent or owner window object (of type **CWnd**) to which the dialog object belongs. If it is **NULL**, the parent window of the dialog box will be set to the main application window.

Remarks   This function constructs only a **COleUpdateDialog** object. To display the dialog box, call **DoModal**. This class should be used instead of **COleLinksDialog** when you want to update only existing linked or embedded items.

See Also   **COleDialog**, **COleLinksDialog**, **COleDocument**, **CWnd**, **CDialog**

COleUpdateDialog::DoModal

virtual int DoModal( );

Return Value   **IDOK** if the dialog box returned successfully, **IDCANCEL** if none of the linked or embedded items in the current document need updating, or **IDABORT** if an error occurred. If **IDABORT** is returned, call the **COleDialog::GetLastError** member function to get more information about the type of error that occurred. For a listing of possible errors, see "OleUIEditLinks" in the *User Interface Dialog* help file.

Remarks   Call this function to display the Edit Links dialog box in update mode. All links and/or embeddings are updated unless the user selects the Cancel button.

See Also   **COleDialog::GetLastError**, **COleLinksDialog::DoModal**

class CPaintDC : public CDC

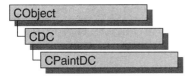

The **CPaintDC** class is a device-context class derived from **CDC**. It performs a **CWnd::BeginPaint** at construction time and **CWnd::EndPaint** at destruction time. A **CPaintDC** object can only be used when responding to a **WM_PAINT** message, usually in your **OnPaint** message-handler member function.

#include <afxwin.h>

See Also   CDC

Data Members
m_ps	Contains the **PAINTSTRUCT** used to paint the client area.
m_hWnd	The **HWND** to which this **CPaintDC** object is attached.

Construction
CPaintDC	Constructs a **CPaintDC** connected to the specified **CWnd**.

Member Functions

CPaintDC::CPaintDC

CPaintDC(CWnd* *pWnd*)
   throw(CResourceException);

Parameters   *pWnd*   Points to the **CWnd** object to which the **CPaintDC** object belongs.

Remarks   Constructs a **CPaintDC** object, prepares the application window for painting, and stores the **PAINTSTRUCT** structure in the **m_ps** member variable. An exception (of type **CResourceException**) is thrown if the Windows **GetDC** call fails. A device context may not be available if Windows has already allocated all of its available device contexts. Your application competes for the five common display contexts available at any given time under Windows.

Data Members

CPaintDC::m_hWnd

Remarks
The **HWND** to which this **CPaintDC** object is attached. **m_hWnd** is a protected variable of type **HWND**.

CPaintDC::m_ps

Remarks
m_ps is a public member variable of type **PAINTSTRUCT**. It is the **PAINTSTRUCT** that is passed to and filled out by **CWnd::BeginPaint**. The **PAINTSTRUCT** contains information that the application uses to paint the client area of the window associated with a **CPaintDC** object. Note that you can access the device-context handle through the **PAINTSTRUCT**. However, you can access the handle more directly through the **m_hDC** member variable that **CPaintDC** inherits from **CDC**.

class CPalette : public CGdiObject

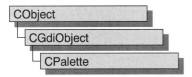

The **CPalette** class encapsulates a Windows color palette. A palette provides an interface between an application and a color output device (such as a display device). The interface allows the application to take full advantage of the color capabilities of the output device without severely interfering with the colors displayed by other applications. Windows uses the application's logical palette (a list of needed colors) and the system palette (which defines available colors) to determine the colors used.

A **CPalette** object provides member functions for manipulating the palette referred to by the object. Construct a **CPalette** object and use its member functions to create the actual palette, a graphics device interface (GDI) object, and to manipulate its entries and other properties.

#include <afxwin.h>

Construction

CPalette	Constructs a **CPalette** object with no attached Windows palette. You must initialize the **CPalette** object with one of the other member functions before it can be used.

Initialization

CreatePalette	Initializes a **CPalette** object by creating a Windows color palette and attaching the palette to the **CPalette** object.
CreateHalftonePalette	Creates a halftone palette for the device context.

Operations

FromHandle	Returns a pointer to a **CPalette** object when given a handle to a Windows palette object. If a **CPalette** object is not already attached to the Windows palette, a temporary **CPalette** object is created and attached.
GetPaletteEntries	Retrieves a range of palette entries in a logical palette.

SetPaletteEntries	Sets RGB color values and flags in a range of entries in a logical palette.
AnimatePalette	Replaces entries in the logical palette identified by the **CPalette** object. The application does not have to update its client area because Windows maps the new entries into the system palette immediately.
GetNearestPaletteIndex	Returns the index of the entry in the logical palette that most closely matches a color value.
ResizePalette	Changes the size of the logical palette specified by the **CPalette** object to the specified number of entries.

Member Functions

CPalette::AnimatePalette

void AnimatePalette(UINT *nStartIndex*, **UINT** *nNumEntries*, **LPPALETTEENTRY** *lpPaletteColors* **);**

Parameters *nStartIndex* Specifies the first entry in the palette to be animated.

nNumEntries Specifies the number of entries in the palette to be animated.

lpPaletteColors Points to the first member of an array of **PALETTEENTRY** structures to replace the palette entries identified by *nStartIndex* and *nNumEntries*.

Remarks Replaces entries in the logical palette attached to the **CPalette** object. When an application calls **AnimatePalette**, it does not have to update its client area because Windows maps the new entries into the system palette immediately. The **AnimatePalette** function will only change entries with the **PC_RESERVED** flag set in the corresponding **palPaletteEntry** member of the **LOGPALETTE** structure that is attached to the **CPalette** object.

See Also **CPalette::CreatePalette, ::AnimatePalette**

CPalette::CPalette

CPalette( );

Remarks Constructs a **CPalette** object. The object has no attached palette until you call **CreatePalette** to attach one.

See Also **CPalette::CreatePalette**

CPalette::CreateHalftonePalette

BOOL CreateHalftonePalette(CDC* *pDC* **);**

Return Value   Nonzero if the function is successful; otherwise 0.

Parameters   *pDC*   Identifies the device context.

Remarks   Creates a halftone palette for the device context. An application should create a halftone palette when the stretching mode of a device context is set to **HALFTONE**. The logical halftone palette returned by the **CreateHalftonePalette** member function should then be selected and realized into the device context before the **CDC::StretchBlt** or **::StretchDIBits** function is called.

See Also   **CDC::RealizePalette**, **CDC::SelectPalette**, **CDC::SetStretchBltMode**, **::CreateHalftonePalette**

CPalette::CreatePalette

BOOL CreatePalette(LPLOGPALETTE *lpLogPalette* **);**

Return Value   Nonzero if successful; otherwise 0.

Parameters   *lpLogPalette*   Points to a **LOGPALETTE** structure that contains information about the colors in the logical palette.

The **LOGPALETTE** structure has the following form:

```
typedef struct tagLOGPALETTE {
    WORD         palVersion;
    WORD         palNumEntries;
    PALETTEENTRY palPalEntry[1];
} LOGPALETTE;
```

Remarks   Initializes a **CPalette** object by creating a Windows logical color palette and attaching it to the **CPalette** object.

See Also   **::CreatePalette**

CPalette::FromHandle

static CPalette* PASCAL FromHandle(HPALETTE *hPalette* **);**

Return Value   A pointer to a **CPalette** object if successful; otherwise **NULL**.

Parameters   *hPalette*   A handle to a Windows GDI color palette.

Remarks   Returns a pointer to a **CPalette** object when given a handle to a Windows palette object. If a **CPalette** object is not already attached to the Windows palette, a temporary **CPalette** object is created and attached. This temporary **CPalette** object is valid only until the next time the application has idle time in its event loop, at which time all temporary graphic objects are deleted. In other words, the temporary object is valid only during the processing of one window message.

CPalette::GetNearestPaletteIndex

UINT GetNearestPaletteIndex(COLORREF *crColor* **) const;**

Return Value   The index of an entry in a logical palette. The entry contains the color that most nearly matches the specified color.

Parameters   *crColor*   Specifies the color to be matched.

Remarks   Returns the index of the entry in the logical palette that most closely matches the specified color value.

See Also   **::GetNearestPaletteIndex**

CPalette::GetPaletteEntries

UINT GetPaletteEntries(UINT *nStartIndex*, **UINT** *nNumEntries*,
      LPPALETTEENTRY *lpPaletteColors* **) const;**

Return Value   The number of entries retrieved from the logical palette; 0 if the function failed.

Parameters   *nStartIndex*   Specifies the first entry in the logical palette to be retrieved.

nNumEntries   Specifies the number of entries in the logical palette to be retrieved.

lpPaletteColors   Points to an array of **PALETTEENTRY** data structures to receive the palette entries. The array must contain at least as many data structures as specified by *nNumEntries*.

Remarks   Retrieves a range of palette entries in a logical palette.

See Also   **::GetPaletteEntries**

CPalette::ResizePalette

BOOL ResizePalette(UINT *nNumEntries* **);**

Return Value   Nonzero if the palette was successfully resized; otherwise 0.

Parameters   *nNumEntries*   Specifies the number of entries in the palette after it has been resized.

Remarks   Changes the size of the logical palette attached to the **CPalette** object to the number of entries specified by *nNumEntries*. If an application calls **ResizePalette** to reduce the size of the palette, the entries remaining in the resized palette are unchanged. If the application calls **ResizePalette** to enlarge the palette, the additional palette entries are set to black (the red, green, and blue values are all 0), and the flags for all additional entries are set to 0.

See Also   **::ResizePalette**

CPalette::SetPaletteEntries

UINT SetPaletteEntries(UINT *nStartIndex***, UINT** *nNumEntries***,**
   LPPALETTEENTRY *lpPaletteColors* **);**

Return Value   The number of entries set in the logical palette; 0 if the function failed.

Parameters   *nStartIndex*   Specifies the first entry in the logical palette to be set.

nNumEntries   Specifies the number of entries in the logical palette to be set.

lpPaletteColors   Points to an array of **PALETTEENTRY** data structures to receive the palette entries. The array must contain at least as many data structures as specified by *nNumEntries*.

Remarks   Sets RGB color values and flags in a range of entries in a logical palette.

If the logical palette is selected into a device context when the application calls **SetPaletteEntries**, the changes will not take effect until the application calls **CDC::RealizePalette**.

See Also   **CDC::RealizePalette**, **::SetPaletteEntries**

class CPen : public CGdiObject

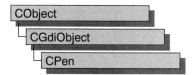

The **CPen** class encapsulates a Windows graphics device interface (GDI) pen.

#include <afxwin.h>

Construction

CPen	Constructs a **CPen** object.

Initialization

CreatePen	Creates a logical cosmetic or geometric pen with the specified style, width, and brush attributes.
CreatePenIndirect	Initializes a pen with the style, width, and color given in a **LOGPEN** structure.

Operations

FromHandle	Returns a pointer to a **CPen** object when given a Windows **HPEN**.

Member Functions

CPen::CPen

CPen( );

CPen(int *nPenStyle*, **int** *nWidth*, **COLORREF** *crColor*)
    throw(CResourceException);

CPen(int *nPenStyle*, **int** *nWidth*, **const LOGBRUSH*** *pLogBrush*, **int**
    nStyleCount = **0, const DWORD*** *lpStyle* = **NULL**)
    throw(CResourceException);

Parameters   *nPenStyle*   Specifies the pen style. This parameter in the first version of the constructor can be one of the following values:

- **PS_SOLID**   Creates a solid pen.
- **PS_DASH**   Creates a dashed pen. Valid only when the pen width is 1.
- **PS_DOT**   Creates a dotted pen. Valid only when the pen width is 1.
- **PS_DASHDOT**   Creates a pen with alternating dashes and dots. Valid only when the pen width is 1.
- **PS_DASHDOTDOT**   Creates a pen with alternating dashes and double dots. Valid only when the pen width is 1.
- **PS_NULL**   Creates a null pen.
- **PS_INSIDEFRAME**   Creates a pen that draws a line inside the frame of closed shapes produced by the Windows GDI output functions that specify a bounding rectangle (for example, the **Ellipse**, **Rectangle**, **RoundRect**, **Pie**, and **Chord** member functions). When this style is used with Windows GDI output functions that do not specify a bounding rectangle (for example, the **LineTo** member function), the drawing area of the pen is not limited by a frame.

The second version of the **CPen** constructor specifies a combination of type, style, end cap, and join attributes. The values from each category should be combined by using the bitwise OR operator (|). The pen type can be one of the following values:

- **PS_GEOMETRIC**   Creates a geometric pen.
- **PS_COSMETIC**   Creates a cosmetic pen.

The second version of the **CPen** constructor adds the following pen styles for *nPenStyle*:

- **PS_ALTERNATE**   Creates a pen that sets every other pixel. (This style is applicable only for cosmetic pens.)
- **PS_USERSTYLE**   Creates a pen that uses a styling array supplied by the user.

The end cap can be one of the following values:

- **PS_ENDCAP_ROUND**   End caps are round.
- **PS_ENDCAP_SQUARE**   End caps are square.
- **PS_ENDCAP_FLAT**   End caps are flat.

The join can be one of the following values:

- **PS_JOIN_BEVEL**   Joins are beveled.
- **PS_JOIN_MITER**   Joins are mitered when they are within the current limit set by the **::SetMiterLimit** function. If the join exceeds this limit, it is beveled.
- **PS_JOIN_ROUND**   Joins are round.

nWidth   Specifies the width of the pen.

- For the first version of the constructor, if this value is 0, the width in device units is always 1 pixel, regardless of the mapping mode.
- For the second version of the constructor, if *nPenStyle* is **PS_GEOMETRIC**, the width is given in logical units. If *nPenStyle* is **PS_COSMETIC**, the width must be set to 1.

crColor   Contains an RGB color for the pen.

pLogBrush   Points to a **LOGBRUSH** structure. If *nPenStyle* is **PS_COSMETIC**, the *lbColor* member of the **LOGBRUSH** structure specifies the color of the pen and the *lbStyle* member of the **LOGBRUSH** structure must be set to **BS_SOLID**. If *nPenStyle* is **PS_GEOMETRIC**, all members must be used to specify the brush attributes of the pen.

nStyleCount   Specifies the length, in doubleword units, of the *lpStyle* array. This value must be zero if *nPenStyle* is not **PS_USERSTYLE**.

lpStyle   Points to an array of doubleword values. The first value specifies the length of the first dash in a user-defined style, the second value specifies the length of the first space, and so on. This pointer must be **NULL** if *nPenStyle* is not **PS_USERSTYLE**.

Remarks   If you use the constructor with no arguments, you must initialize the resulting **CPen** object with the **CreatePen**, **CreatePenIndirect**, or **CreateStockObject** member functions. If you use the constructor that takes arguments, then no further initialization is necessary. The constructor with arguments can throw an exception if errors are encountered, while the constructor with no arguments will always succeed.

See Also   **CPen::CreatePen**, **CPen::CreatePenIndirect**, **CGdiObject::CreateStockObject**

CPen::CreatePen

BOOL CreatePen(int *nPenStyle,* **int** *nWidth,* **COLORREF** *crColor* **);**

BOOL ExtCreatePen(int *nPenStyle,* **int** *nWidth,* **const LOGBRUSH*** *pLogBrush,* **int** *nStyleCount* **= 0, const DWORD*** *lpStyle* **= NULL);**

Return Value

Nonzero, or the handle of a logical pen, if successful; otherwise 0.

Parameters

nPenStyle   Specifies the style for the pen. For a list of possible values, see the *nPenStyle* parameter in the **CPen** constructor.

nWidth   Specifies the width of the pen.

- For the first version of **CreatePen**, if this value is 0, the width in device units is always 1 pixel, regardless of the mapping mode.

- For the second version of **CreatePen**, if *nPenStyle* is **PS_GEOMETRIC**, the width is given in logical units. If *nPenStyle* is **PS_COSMETIC**, the width must be set to 1.

crColor   Contains an RGB color for the pen.

pLogBrush   Points to a **LOGBRUSH** structure. If *nPenStyle* is **PS_COSMETIC**, the **lbColor** member of the **LOGBRUSH** structure specifies the color of the pen and the **lbStyle** member of the **LOGBRUSH** structure must be set to **BS_SOLID**. If *nPenStyle* is **PS_GEOMETRIC**, all members must be used to specify the brush attributes of the pen.

nStyleCount   Specifies the length, in doubleword units, of the *lpStyle* array. This value must be zero if *nPenStyle* is not **PS_USERSTYLE**.

lpStyle   Points to an array of doubleword values. The first value specifies the length of the first dash in a user-defined style, the second value specifies the length of the first space, and so on. This pointer must be **NULL** if *nPenStyle* is not **PS_USERSTYLE**.

Remarks

The first version of **CreatePen** initializes a pen with the specified style, width, and color. The pen can be subsequently selected as the current pen for any device context. Pens that have a width greater than 1 pixel should always have either the **PS_NULL, PS_SOLID,** or **PS_INSIDEFRAME** style. If a pen has the **PS_INSIDEFRAME** style and a color that does not match a color in the logical color table, the pen is drawn with a dithered color. The **PS_SOLID** pen style cannot be used to create a pen with a dithered color. The style **PS_INSIDEFRAME** is identical to **PS_SOLID** if the pen width is less than or equal to 1.

The second version of **CreatePen** initializes a logical cosmetic or geometric pen that has the specified style, width, and brush attributes. The width of a cosmetic pen is always 1; the width of a geometric pen is always specified in world units. After an application creates a logical pen, it can select that pen into a device context by calling the SelectObject function. After a pen is selected into a device context, it can be used to draw lines and curves.

- If *nPenStyle* is **PS_COSMETIC** and **PS_USERSTYLE**, the entries in the *lpStyle* array specify lengths of dashes and spaces in style units. A style unit is defined by the device in which the pen is used to draw a line.

- If *nPenStyle* is **PS_GEOMETRIC** and **PS_USERSTYLE**, the entries in the *lpStyle* array specify lengths of dashes and spaces in logical units.

- If *nPenStyle* is **PS_ALTERNATE**, the style unit is ignored and every other pixel is set.

When an application no longer requires a given pen, it should call the **CGdiObject::DeleteObject** member function to delete the pen from the device context.

See Also   CPen::CreatePenIndirect, CPen::CPen

CPen::CreatePenIndirect

BOOL CreatePenIndirect(LPLOGPEN *lpLogPen*);

Return Value   Nonzero if the function is successful; otherwise 0.

Parameters   *lpLogPen*   Points to the Windows **LOGPEN** structure that contains information about the pen.

Remarks   Initializes a pen that has the style, width, and color given in the structure pointed to by *lpLogPen*. Pens that have width greater than 1 pixel should always have either the **PS_NULL, PS_SOLID,** or **PS_INSIDEFRAME** style. If a pen has the **PS_INSIDEFRAME** style and a color that does not match a color in the logical color table, the pen is drawn with a dithered color. The **PS_INSIDEFRAME** style is identical to **PS_SOLID** if the pen width is less than or equal to 1.

See Also   CPen::CreatePen, CPen::CPen

CPen::FromHandle

static CPen* PASCAL FromHandle(HPEN *hPen*);

Return Value   A pointer to a **CPen** object if successful; otherwise **NULL**.

Parameters   *hPen*   HPEN handle to Windows GDI pen.

Remarks   Returns a pointer to a **CPen** object given a handle to a Windows GDI pen object. If a **CPen** object is not attached to the handle, a temporary **CPen** object is created and attached. This temporary **CPen** object is valid only until the next time the application has idle time in its event loop, at which time all temporary graphic objects are deleted. In other words, the temporary object is only valid during the processing of one window message.

class CPoint : public tagPOINT

The **CPoint** class is similar to the Windows **POINT** structure and also includes member functions to manipulate **CPoint** and **POINT** structures. A **CPoint** object can be used wherever a **POINT** structure is used. The operators of this class that interact with a "size" accept either **CSize** objects or **SIZE** structures, since the two are interchangeable.

#include <afxwin.h>

See Also   **CRect**, **CSize**

Construction
CPoint   Constructs a **CPoint**.

Operations
Offset   Adds separate values to the **x** and **y** members of the **CPoint**.

operator ==   Checks for equality between two points.

operator !=   Checks for inequality between two points.

operator +=   Offsets a **CPoint** by a size.

operator –=   Subtracts a size from the **CPoint**.

Operators Returning CPoint Values
operator +   Returns a **CPoint** offset by a size.

operator –   Returns a **CPoint** offset by a negative size.

Operators Returning CSize Values
operator –   Returns the size difference between two points.

Member Functions

CPoint::CPoint

CPoint( );

CPoint(int *initX*, **int** *initY* **)**;

CPoint(POINT *initPt* **)**;

CPoint(SIZE *initSize* **)**;

CPoint(DWORD *dwPoint* **)**;

Parameters   *initX*   Sets the **x** member for the **CPoint**.

initY   Sets the **y** member for the **CPoint**.

initPt   Windows **POINT** structure or **CPoint** used to initialize **CPoint**.

initSize   Sets the **x** and **y** members equal to the corresponding values in **cx** and **cy** values in *initSize*.

dwPoint   Sets the low-order word to the **x** member and the high-order word to the **y** member.

Remarks   Constructs a **CPoint** object. If no arguments are given, **x** and **y** members are not initialized.

CPoint::Offset

void Offset(int *xOffset*, **int** *yOffset* **)**;

void Offset(POINT *point* **)**;

void Offset(SIZE *size* **)**;

Return Value   A **CPoint** offset by a **POINT**, **CPoint**, **CSize**, or **SIZE**.

Parameters   *xOffset*   Specifies the amount to offset the **x** member of the **CPoint**.

yOffset   Specifies the amount to offset the **y** member of the **CPoint**.

point   Specifies the amount (**POINT** or **CPoint**) to offset the **CPoint**.

size   Specifies the amount (**SIZE** or **CSize**) to offset the **CPoint**.

Remarks   Adds separate values to the **x** and **y** members of the **CPoint**.

Operators

CPoint::operator ==

BOOL operator ==(POINT *point* **) const;**

Return Value   Nonzero if the points are equal; otherwise 0.

Parameters   *point*   Contains a **POINT** structure or **CPoint** object.

Remarks   Checks for equality between two points.

CPoint::operator !=

BOOL operator !=(POINT *point* **) const;**

Return Value   Nonzero if the points are not equal; otherwise 0.

Parameters   *point*   Contains a **POINT** structure or **CPoint** object.

Remarks   Checks for inequality between two points.

CPoint::operator +=

void operator +=(SIZE *size* **);**

Parameters   *size*   Contains a **SIZE** structure or **CSize** object.

Remarks   Offsets a **CPoint** by a size.

CPoint::operator –=

void operator –=(SIZE *size* **);**

Parameters   *size*   Contains a **SIZE** structure or **CSize** object.

Remarks   Subtracts a size from the **CPoint**.

CPoint::operator +

CPoint operator +(SIZE *size* **) const;**

Return Value   A **CPoint** that is offset by a size.

Parameters   *size*   Contains a **SIZE** structure or **CSize** object.

CPoint::operator –

CSize operator –(POINT *point* **) const;**

CPoint operator –(SIZE *size* **) const;**

CPoint operator –( ) const;

Return Value   A **CSize** that is the difference between two points, or returns a **CPoint** that is offset by a negative size.

Parameters   *point*   Contains a **POINT** structure or **CPoint** object.

size   Contains a **SIZE** structure or **CSize** object.

class CPrintDialog : public CDialog

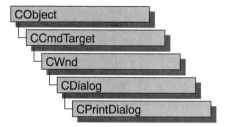

The **CPrintDialog** class encapsulates the services provided by the Windows common dialog box for printing. Common print dialog boxes provide an easy way to implement Print and Print Setup dialog boxes in a manner consistent with Windows standards.

If you wish, you can rely on the framework to handle many aspects of the printing process for your application. In this case, the framework automatically displays the Windows common dialog box for printing. You can also have the framework handle printing for your application but override the common Print dialog box with your own print dialog box. For more information on using the framework to handle printing tasks, see the article "Printing" in *Programming with the Microsoft Foundation Class Library*.

If you want your application to handle printing without the framework's involvement, you can use the **CPrintDialog** class "as is" with the constructor provided, or you can derive your own dialog class from **CPrintDialog** and write a constructor to suit your needs. In either case, these dialog boxes will behave like standard MFC dialog boxes because they are derived from class **CDialog**.

To use a **CPrintDialog** object, first create the object using the **CPrintDialog** constructor. Once the dialog box has been constructed, you can set or modify any values in the **m_pd** structure to initialize the values of the dialog box's controls. The **m_pd** structure is of type **PRINTDLG**. For more information on this structure, see the Windows Software Development Kit (SDK) documentation.

If you do not supply your own handles in **m_pd** for the **hDevMode** and **hDevNames** members, be sure to call the Windows function **GlobalFree** for these handles when you are done with the dialog box. When using the framework's Print Setup implementation provided by **CWinApp::OnFilePrintSetup**, you do not have to free these handles. The handles are maintained by **CWinApp** and are freed in **CWinApp**'s destructor. It is only necessary to free these handles when using **CPrintDialog** standalone.

After initializing the dialog box controls, call the **DoModal** member function to display the dialog box and allow the user to select print options. **DoModal** returns whether the user selected the OK (**IDOK**) or Cancel (**IDCANCEL**) button.

If **DoModal** returns **IDOK**, you can use one of **CPrintDialog**'s member functions to retrieve the information input by the user.

The **CPrintDialog::GetDefaults** member function is useful for retrieving the current printer defaults without displaying a dialog box. This member function requires no user interaction.

You can use the Windows **CommDlgExtendedError** function to determine whether an error occurred during initialization of the dialog box and to learn more about the error. For more information on this function, see the Windows SDK documentation.

CPrintDialog relies on the COMMDLG.DLL file that ships with Windows versions 3.1 and later. For details about redistributing COMMDLG.DLL to Windows version 3.0 users, see the *Getting Started* manual for the Windows SDK.

To customize the dialog box, derive a class from **CPrintDialog**, provide a custom dialog template, and add a message map to process the notification messages from the extended controls. Any unprocessed messages should be passed on to the base class. Customizing the hook function is not required.

To process the same message differently depending on whether the dialog box is Print or Print Setup, you must derive a class for each dialog box. You must also override the Windows **AttachOnSetup** function, which handles the creation of a new dialog box when the Print Setup button is selected within a Print dialog box.

#include <afxdlgs.h>

Data Members

m_pd	A structure used to customize a **CPrintDialog** object.

Construction

CPrintDialog	Constructs a **CPrintDialog** object.

Operations

CreatePrinterDC	Creates a printer device context without displaying the Print dialog box.
DoModal	Displays the dialog box and allows the user to make a selection.
GetCopies	Retrieves the number of copies requested.
GetDefaults	Retrieves device defaults without displaying a dialog box.
GetDeviceName	Retrieves the name of the currently selected printer device.

GetDevMode	Retrieves the **DEVMODE** structure.
GetDriverName	Retrieves the name of the currently selected printer driver.
GetFromPage	Retrieves the starting page of the print range.
GetToPage	Retrieves the ending page of the print range.
GetPortName	Retrieves the name of the currently selected printer port.
GetPrinterDC	Retrieves a handle to the printer device context.
PrintAll	Determines whether to print all pages of the document.
PrintCollate	Determines whether collated copies are requested.
PrintRange	Determines whether to print only a specified range of pages.
PrintSelection	Determines whether to print only the currently selected items.

Member Functions

CPrintDialog::CPrintDialog

CPrintDialog(BOOL *bPrintSetupOnly*, **DWORD** *dwFlags* **= PD_ALLPAGES | PD_USEDEVMODECOPIES | PD_NOPAGENUMS | PD_HIDEPRINTTOFILE | PD_NOSELECTION, CWnd*** *pParentWnd* **= NULL);**

Parameters *bPrintSetupOnly*   Specifies whether the standard Windows Print dialog box or Print Setup dialog box is displayed. Set this parameter to **TRUE** to display the standard Windows Print Setup dialog box. Set it to **FALSE** to display the Windows Print dialog box. If *bPrintSetupOnly* is **FALSE**, a Print Setup option button is still displayed in the Print dialog box.

dwFlags   One or more flags you can use to customize the settings of the dialog box, combined using the bitwise OR operator. For example, the **PD_ALLPAGES** flag sets the default print range to all pages of the document. See the **PRINTDLG** structure in the Windows SDK for more information on these flags.

pParentWnd   A pointer to the dialog box's parent or owner window.

Remarks   Constructs either a Windows Print or Print Setup dialog object. This member function only constructs the object. Use the **DoModal** member function to display the dialog box.

See Also   **CPrintDialog::DoModal, ::PrintDlg, PRINTDLG**

CPrintDialog::CreatePrinterDC

HDC CreatePrinterDC( );

Return Value Handle to the newly created printer device context.

Class **CPrintDialog**

Remarks Creates a printer device context (DC) from the **DEVMODE** and **DEVNAMES** structures. This DC is assumed to be the current printer DC, and any other previously obtained printer DCs must be deleted by the user. This function can be called, and the resulting DC used, without ever displaying the Print dialog box.

See Also **CPrintDialog::GetDevMode**

CPrintDialog::DoModal

virtual int DoModal( );

Return Value **IDOK** or **IDCANCEL** if the function is successful; otherwise 0. **IDOK** and **IDCANCEL** are constants that indicate whether the user selected the OK or Cancel button.

If **IDCANCEL** is returned, you can call the Windows **CommDlgExtendedError** function to determine whether an error occurred.

Remarks Call this function to display the Windows common print dialog box and allow the user to select various printing options such as the number of copies, page range, and whether copies should be collated.

If you want to initialize the various print dialog options by setting members of the **m_pd** structure, you should do this before calling **DoModal**, but after the dialog object is constructed.

After calling **DoModal**, you can call other member functions to retrieve the settings or information input by the user into the dialog box.

See Also **CPrintDialog::CPrintDialog**, **CDialog::DoModal**

CPrintDialog::GetCopies

int GetCopies( ) const;

Return Value The number of copies requested.

Remarks Call this function after calling **DoModal** to retrieve the number of copies requested.

See Also **CPrintDialog::PrintCollate**

CPrintDialog::GetDefaults

BOOL GetDefaults( );

Return Value   Nonzero if the function was successful; otherwise 0.

Remarks   Call this function to retrieve the device defaults of the default printer without displaying a dialog box. The retrieved values are placed in the **m_pd** structure.

See Also   **CPrintDialog::m_pd**

CPrintDialog::GetDeviceName

CString GetDeviceName( ) const;

Return Value   The name of the currently selected printer.

Remarks   Call this function after calling **DoModal** to retrieve the name of the currently selected printer.

See Also   **CPrintDialog::GetDriverName, CPrintDialog::GetDevMode, CPrintDialog::GetPortName**

CPrintDialog::GetDevMode

LPDEVMODE GetDevMode( ) const;

Return Value   The **DEVMODE** data structure, which contains information about the device initialization and environment of a print driver. You must free the memory taken by this structure with the Windows **GlobalFree** function. See **PRINTDLG** in the Windows SDK reference for more information about using **GlobalFree**.

Remarks   Call this function after calling **DoModal** to retrieve information about the printing device.

See Also   **CDC::GetDeviceCaps**

CPrintDialog::GetDriverName

CString GetDriverName( ) const;

Return Value   The name of the currently selected printer device driver.

Remarks   Call this function after calling **DoModal** to retrieve the name of the currently selected printer device driver.

See Also   **CPrintDialog::GetDeviceName, CPrintDialog::GetDevMode, CPrintDialog::GetPortName**

CPrintDialog::GetFromPage

int GetFromPage( ) const;

Return Value   The starting page number in the range of pages to be printed.

Remarks   Call this function after calling **DoModal** to retrieve the starting page number in the range of pages to be printed.

See Also   **CPrintDialog::GetToPage, CPrintDialog::PrintRange**

CPrintDialog::GetPortName

CString GetPortName( ) const;

Return Value   The name of the currently selected printer port.

Remarks   Call this function after calling **DoModal** to retrieve the name of the currently selected printer port.

See Also   **CPrintDialog::GetDriverName, CPrintDialog::GetDeviceName**

CPrintDialog::GetPrinterDC

HDC GetPrinterDC( ) const;

Return Value   A handle to the printer device context if successful; otherwise **NULL**.

Remarks   If the *bPrintSetupOnly* parameter of the **CPrintDialog** constructor was **FALSE** (indicating that the Print dialog box is displayed), then **GetPrinterDC** returns a handle to the printer device context. You must call the Windows **DeleteDC** function to delete the device context when you are done using it.

CPrintDialog::GetToPage

int GetToPage( ) const;

Return Value   The ending page number in the range of pages to be printed.

Remarks   Call this function after calling **DoModal** to retrieve the ending page number in the range of pages to be printed.

See Also   **CPrintDialog::GetFromPage, CPrintDialog::PrintRange**

CPrintDialog::PrintAll

BOOL PrintAll( ) const;

Return Value   Nonzero if all pages in the document are to be printed; otherwise 0.

Remarks   Call this function after calling **DoModal** to determine whether to print all pages in the document.

See Also   **CPrintDialog::PrintRange, CPrintDialog::PrintSelection**

CPrintDialog::PrintCollate

BOOL PrintCollate( ) const;

Return Value   Nonzero if the user selects the collate check box in the dialog box; otherwise 0.

Remarks   Call this function after calling **DoModal** to determine whether the printer should collate all printed copies of the document.

See Also   **CPrintDialog::GetCopies**

CPrintDialog::PrintRange

BOOL PrintRange( ) const;

Return Value   Nonzero if only a range of pages in the document are to be printed; otherwise 0.

Remarks   Call this function after calling **DoModal** to determine whether to print only a range of pages in the document.

See Also   **CPrintDialog::PrintAll, CPrintDialog::PrintSelection,
CPrintDialog::GetFromPage, CPrintDialog::GetToPage**

CPrintDialog::PrintSelection

BOOL PrintSelection( ) const;

Return Value   Nonzero if only the selected items are to be printed; otherwise 0.

Remarks   Call this function after calling **DoModal** to determine whether to print only the currently selected items.

See Also   **CPrintDialog::PrintRange, CPrintDialog::PrintAll**

Data Members

CPrintDialog::m_pd

PRINTDLG& m_pd;

Remarks   A structure whose members store the characteristics of the dialog object. After
constructing a **CPrintDialog** object, you can use **m_pd** to set various aspects of the
dialog box before calling the **DoModal** member function. For more information on
the **m_pd** structure, see **PRINTDLG** in the Windows SDK documentation.

If you modify the **m_pd** data member directly, you will override any default
behavior.

structure CPrintInfo

CPrintInfo stores information about a print or print-preview job. The framework creates an object of **CPrintInfo** each time the Print or Print Preview command is chosen and destroys it when the command is completed.

CPrintInfo contains information about both the print job as a whole, such as the range of pages to be printed, and the current status of the print job, such as the page currently being printed. Some information is stored in an associated **CPrintDialog** object; this object contains the values entered by the user in the Print dialog box.

A **CPrintInfo** object is passed between the framework and your view class during the printing process and is used to exchange information between the two. For example, the framework informs the view class which page of the document to print by assigning a value to the **m_nCurPage** member of **CPrintInfo**; the view class retrieves the value and performs the actual printing of the specified page.

Another example is the case in which the length of the document is not known until it is printed. In this situation, the view class tests for the end of the document each time a page is printed. When the end is reached, the view class sets the **m_bContinuePrinting** member of **CPrintInfo** to **FALSE**; this informs the framework to stop the print loop.

CPrintInfo is used by the member functions of **CView** listed under "See Also." For more information about the printing architecture provided by the Microsoft Foundation Class Library, see Chapter 3 and the article "Printing" in *Programming with the Microsoft Foundation Class Library*.

#include <afxext.h>

See Also   **CView::OnBeginPrinting**, **CView::OnEndPrinting**,
CView::OnEndPrintPreview, **CView::OnPrepareDC**,
CView::OnPreparePrinting, **CView::OnPrint**

Data Members

m_pPD	Contains a pointer to **CPrintDialog** object used for the Print dialog box.
m_bPreview	Contains a flag indicating whether the document is being previewed.
m_bContinuePrinting	Contains a flag indicating whether the framework should continue the print loop.
m_nCurPage	Identifies the number of the page currently being printed.
m_nNumPreviewPages	Identifies the number of pages displayed in the preview window; either 1 or 2.

m_lpUserData	Contains a pointer to a user-created structure.
m_rectDraw	Specifies a rectangle defining the current usable page area.
m_strPageDesc	Contains a format string for page-number display.

Attributes

SetMinPage	Sets the number of the first page of the document.
SetMaxPage	Sets the number of the last page of the document.
GetMinPage	Returns the number of the first page of the document.
GetMaxPage	Returns the number of the last page of the document.
GetFromPage	Returns the number of the first page being printed.
GetToPage	Returns the number of the last page being printed.

Member Functions

CPrintInfo::GetFromPage

UINT GetFromPage( );

Remarks   Call this function to retrieve the number of the first page to be printed. This is the value specified by the user in the Print dialog box, and it is stored in the **CPrintDialog** object referenced by the **m_pPD** member. If the user has not specified a value, the default is the first page of the document.

See Also   **CPrintInfo::m_nCurPage**, **CPrintInfo::m_pPD**, **CPrintInfo::GetToPage**

CPrintInfo::GetMaxPage

UINT GetMaxPage( );

Remarks   Call this function to retrieve the number of the last page of the document. This value is stored in the **CPrintDialog** object referenced by the **m_pPD** member.

See Also   **CPrintInfo::m_nCurPage**, **CPrintInfo::m_pPD**, **CPrintInfo::GetMinPage**, **CPrintInfo::SetMaxPage**, **CPrintInfo::SetMinPage**

CPrintInfo::GetMinPage

UINT GetMinPage( );

Remarks   Call this function to retrieve the number of the first page of the document. This value is stored in the **CPrintDialog** object referenced by the **m_pPD** member.

See Also   **CPrintInfo::m_nCurPage**, **CPrintInfo::m_pPD**, **CPrintInfo::GetMaxPage**, **CPrintInfo::SetMaxPage**, **CPrintInfo::SetMinPage**

CPrintInfo::GetToPage

UINT GetToPage( );

Remarks   Call this function to retrieve the number of the last page to be printed. This is the value specified by the user in the Print dialog box, and it is stored in the **CPrintDialog** object referenced by the **m_pPD** member. If the user has not specified a value, the default is the last page of the document.

See Also   **CPrintInfo::m_nCurPage**, **CPrintInfo::m_pPD**, **CPrintInfo::GetFromPage**

CPrintInfo::SetMaxPage

void SetMaxPage(UINT *nMaxPage* **);**

Parameters   *nMaxPage*   Number of the last page of the document.

Remarks   Call this function to specify the number of the last page of the document. This value is stored in the **CPrintDialog** object referenced by the **m_pPD** member. If the length of the document is known before it is printed, call this function from your override of **CView::OnPreparePrinting**. If the length of the document depends on a setting specified by the user in the Print dialog box, call this function from your override of **CView::OnBeginPrinting**. If the length of the document is not known until it is printed, use the **m_bContinuePrinting** member to control the print loop.

See Also   **CPrintInfo::m_bContinuePrinting**, **CPrintInfo::m_nCurPage**, **CPrintInfo::m_pPD**, **CPrintInfo::GetMinPage**, **CPrintInfo::GetToPage**, **CPrintInfo::SetMinPage**, **CView::OnBeginPrinting**, **CView::OnPreparePrinting**

CPrintInfo::SetMinPage

void SetMinPage(UINT *nMinPage* **);**

Parameters   *nMinPage*   Number of the first page of the document.

Remarks   Call this function to specify the number of the first page of the document. Page numbers normally start at 1. This value is stored in the **CPrintDialog** object referenced by the **m_pPD** member.

See Also   **CPrintInfo::m_nCurPage**, **CPrintInfo::m_pPD**, **CPrintInfo::GetMaxPage**, **CPrintInfo::GetMinPage**, **CPrintInfo::SetMaxPage**

Data Members

CPrintInfo::m_bContinuePrinting

Remarks   Contains a flag indicating whether the framework should continue the print loop. If you are doing print-time pagination, you can set this member to **FALSE** in your override of **CView::OnPrepareDC** once the end of the document has been reached. You do not have to modify this variable if you have specified the length of the document at the beginning of the print job using the **SetMaxPage** member function. The **m_bContinuePrinting** member is a public variable of type **BOOL**.

See Also   **CPrintInfo::SetMaxPage**, **CView::OnPrepareDC**

CPrintInfo::m_bPreview

Remarks   Contains a flag indicating whether the document is being previewed. This is set by the framework depending on which command the user executed. The Print dialog box is not displayed for a print-preview job. The **m_bPreview** member is a public variable of type **BOOL**.

See Also   **CView::DoPreparePrinting**, **CView::OnPreparePrinting**

CPrintInfo::m_lpUserData

Remarks   Contains a pointer to a user-created structure. You can use this to store printing-specific data that you do not want to store in your view class. The **m_lpUserData** member is a public variable of type **LPVOID**.

CPrintInfo::m_nCurPage

Remarks   Contains the number of the current page. The framework calls **CView::OnPrepareDC** and **CView::OnPrint** once for each page of the document, specifying a different value for this member each time; its values range from the value returned by **GetFromPage** to that returned by **GetToPage**. Use this member in your overrides of **CView::OnPrepareDC** and **CView::OnPrint** to print the specified page of the document.

When preview mode is first invoked, the framework reads the value of this member to determine which page of the document should be previewed initially. You can set the value of this member in your override of **CView::OnPreparePrinting** to maintain the user's current position in the document when entering preview mode. The **m_nCurPage** member is a public variable of type **UINT**.

See Also   **CPrintInfo::GetFromPage**, **CPrintInfo::GetToPage**, **CView::OnPrepareDC**, **CView::OnPreparePrinting**, **CView::OnPrint**

CPrintInfo::m_nNumPreviewPages

Remarks   Contains the number of pages displayed in preview mode; it can be either 1 or 2. The **m_nNumPreviewPages** member is a public variable of type **UINT**.

See Also   **CPrintInfo::m_strPageDesc**

CPrintInfo::m_pPD

Remarks   Contains a pointer to the **CPrintDialog** object used to display the Print dialog box for the print job. The **m_pPD** member is a public variable declared as a pointer to **CPrintDialog**.

See Also   **CPrintDialog**

CPrintInfo::m_rectDraw

Remarks   Specifies the usable drawing area of the page in logical coordinates. You may want to refer to this in your override of **CView::OnPrint**. You can use this member to keep track of what area remains usable after you print headers, footers, etc. The **m_rectDraw** member is a public variable of type **CRect**.

See Also   **CView::OnPrint**

CPrintInfo::m_strPageDesc

Remarks   Contains a format string used to display the page numbers during print preview; this string consists of two substrings, one for single-page display and one for double-page display, each terminated by a '\n' character. The framework uses "Page %u\nPages %u-%u\n" as the default value. If you want a different format for the page numbers, specify a format string in your override of **CView::OnPreparePrinting**. The **m_strPageDesc** member is a public variable of type **CString**.

See Also   **CView::OnPreparePrinting**

class CPropertyPage : public CDialog

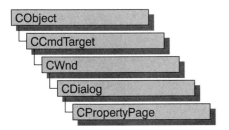

CObject
CCmdTarget
CWnd
CDialog
CPropertyPage

Objects of class **CPropertyPage** represent individual pages of a property sheet, otherwise known as a tab dialog box. As with standard dialog boxes, you derive a class from **CPropertyPage** for each page in your property sheet. To use **CPropertyPage**-derived objects, first create a **CPropertySheet** object, and then create an object for each page that goes in the property sheet. Call **CPropertySheet::AddPage** for each page in the sheet, and then display the property sheet by calling **CPropertySheet::DoModal** for a modal property sheet, or **CPropertySheet::Create** for a modeless property sheet.

For more information on using **CPropertyPage** objects, see the article "Property Sheets" in *Programming with the Microsoft Foundation Class Library*.

#include <afxdlgs.h>

See Also   **CPropertySheet, CDialog**

Construction
CPropertyPage   Constructs a **CPropertyPage** object.

Operations
CancelToClose   Changes the Cancel button to read Close after an unrecoverable change in the page of a modal property sheet.

SetModified   Call to activate or deactivate the Apply Now button.

Overridables

OnCancel	Called by the framework when the Cancel button is clicked.
OnKillActive	Called by the framework when the current page is no longer the active page. Perform data validation here.
OnOK	Called by the framework when the OK, Apply Now, or Close button is clicked.
OnSetActive	Called by the framework when the page is made the active page.

Member Functions

CPropertyPage::CancelToClose

void CancelToClose( );

Remarks   Call this function after an unrecoverable change has been made to the data in a page of a modal property sheet. This function will change the text of the Cancel button to read Close. This alerts the user that he has made a permanent change and cannot cancel the modifications he has made.

The **CancelToClose** member function does nothing in a modeless property sheet, because a modeless property sheet does not have a Cancel button by default.

See Also   **CPropertyPage::OnKillActive**, **CPropertyPage::SetModified**

CPropertyPage::CPropertyPage

CPropertyPage(UINT *nIDTemplate*, **UINT** *nIDCaption* = **0**);

CPropertyPage(LPCTSTR *lpszTemplateName*, **UINT** *nIDCaption* = **0**);

Parameters   *nIDTemplate*   ID of the template used for this page.

nIDCaption   ID of the name to be placed in the tab for this page. If 0, the name will be taken from the dialog template for this page.

lpszTemplateName   Points to a string containing the name of the template for this page. Cannot be **NULL**.

Remarks   Constructs a **CPropertyPage** object. The object is displayed after all of the following conditions are met:

- The page has been added to a property sheet using **CPropertySheet::AddPage**.
- The property sheet's **DoModal** or **Create** function has been called.
- The user has selected (tabbed to) this page.

See Also   **CPropertySheet::DoModal**, **CPropertySheet::AddPage**

CPropertyPage::OnCancel

virtual void OnCancel( );

Remarks   Called by the framework when the Cancel button is selected.

Override this function to perform Cancel button actions. The default negates any changes that have been made.

See Also   **CDialog::OnCancel**, **CPropertyPage::OnOK**

CPropertyPage::OnKillActive

virtual BOOL OnKillActive( );

Return Value   Nonzero if data was updated successfully, otherwise 0.

Remarks   Called by the framework when the page is no longer the active page. Override this function to perform special data validation tasks.

The default implementation of this function copies settings from the controls in the property page to the member variables of the property page. If the data was not updated successfully due to a dialog data validation (DDV) error, the page retains focus.

After this function returns successfully, the framework will call the page's **OnOK** function.

See Also   **CWnd::UpdateData**, **CPropertyPage::OnOK**, **CPropertyPage::OnSetActive**

CPropertyPage::OnOK

virtual void OnOK( );

Remarks   Called by the framework when the user chooses either the OK or Apply Now button, immediately after the framework calls **OnKillActive**. Override this function to implement additional behavior specific to the currently active page when user dismisses the entire property sheet.

The default implementation marks the page as "clean" to reflect that the data was updated in the **OnKillActive** function.

See Also   CDialog::OnOK, CPropertyPage::OnKillActive

CPropertyPage::OnSetActive

virtual BOOL OnSetActive( );

Return Value   Nonzero if the page was successfully set active; otherwise 0.

Remarks   Called by the framework when the page is chosen by the user and becomes the active page. Override this function to perform tasks when a page is activated. Your override of this function should call the default version before any other processing is done.

The default implementation creates the window for the page, if not previously created, and makes it the active page.

See Also   CPropertyPage::OnKillActive

CPropertyPage::SetModified

void SetModified(BOOL *bChanged* **= TRUE);**

Parameters   *bChanged*   **TRUE** to indicate that the property page settings have been modified since the last time they were applied; **FALSE** to indicate that the property page settings have been applied, or should be ignored.

Remarks   Call this function to enable or disable the Apply Now button, based on whether the settings in the property page should be applied to the appropriate external object.

The framework keeps track of which pages are "dirty," that is, property pages for which you have called **SetModified(TRUE)**. The Apply Now button will always be enabled if you call **SetModified(TRUE)** for one of the pages. The Apply Now button will be disabled when you call **SetModified(FALSE)** for one of the pages, but only if none of the other pages is "dirty."

See Also   CPropertyPage::CancelToClose

class CPropertySheet : public CWnd

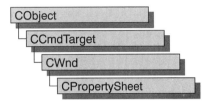

Objects of class **CPropertySheet** represent property sheets, otherwise known as tab dialog boxes. A property sheet consists of a **CPropertySheet** object and one or more **CPropertyPage** objects. A property sheet is displayed by the framework as a window with a set of tab indices, with which the user selects the current page, and an area for the currently selected page.

Even though **CPropertySheet** is not derived from **CDialog**, managing a **CPropertySheet** object is similar to managing a **CDialog** object. For example, creation of a property sheet requires two-part construction: call the constructor, and then call **DoModal** for a modal property sheet or **Create** for a modeless property sheet.

Exchanging data between a **CPropertySheet** object and some external object is similar to exchanging data with a **CDialog** object. The important difference is that the settings of a property sheet are normally member variables of the **CPropertyPage** objects rather than of the **CPropertySheet** object itself.

For more information on how to use **CPropertySheet** objects, see the article **#include <afxdlgs.h>**

See Also   **CPropertyPage, CWnd**

Construction

CPropertySheet	Constructs a **CPropertySheet** object.

Attributes

GetPageCount	Retrieves the number of pages in the property sheet.
GetPage	Retrieves a pointer to the specified page.

Operations

DoModal	Displays a modal property sheet.
Create	Displays a modeless property sheet.

AddPage	Adds a page to the property sheet.
RemovePage	Removes a page from the property sheet.
EndDialog	Terminates the property sheet.

Member Functions

CPropertySheet::AddPage

void AddPage(CPropertyPage **pPage* **);**

Parameters *pPage*   Points to the page to be added to the property sheet. Cannot be **NULL**.

Remarks This function adds the supplied page as the rightmost page in the property sheet. Add pages to the property sheet in the left-to-right order you want them to appear.

AddPage adds the **CPropertyPage** object to the **CPropertySheet** object's list of pages but does not actually create the window for the page. The framework postpones creation of the window for the page until the user selects that page.

It is not necessary to wait until creation of the property sheet window to call **AddPage**. Typically, you will call **AddPage** before calling **DoModal** or **Create**.

If you call **AddPage** after displaying the property page, the tab row will reflect the newly added page.

See Also **CPropertySheet::RemovePage**

CPropertySheet::CPropertySheet

CPropertySheet(UINT *nIDCaption*, **CWnd** **pParentWnd* = **NULL, UINT** *iSelectPage* = **0);**

CPropertySheet(LPCTSTR *pszCaption*, **CWnd** **pParentWnd* = **NULL, UINT** *iSelectPage* = **0);**

Parameters *nIDCaption*   ID of the caption to be used for the property sheet.

pParentWnd   Points to the parent window of the property sheet. If **NULL**, the parent window will be the main window of the application.

iSelectPage   The index of the page that will initially be on top. Default is the first page added to the sheet.

pszCaption   Points to a string containing the caption to be used for the property sheet. Cannot be **NULL**.

Remarks   Constructs a **CPropertySheet** object. To display the property sheet, call **DoModal** or **Create**. The string contained in the first parameter will be placed in the caption bar for the property sheet.

See Also   **CPropertySheet::DoModal**, **CPropertySheet::Create**, **CPropertyPage**

CPropertySheet::Create

BOOL Create(CWnd* *pParentWnd* = NULL, DWORD *dwStyle* =
    WS_SYSMENU | WS_POPUP | WS_CAPTION | DS_MODALFRAME |
    WS_VISIBLE, DWORD *dwExStyle* = WS_EX_DLGMODALFRAME);

Return Value   Nonzero if the property sheet is created successfully; otherwise 0.

Parameters   *pParentWnd*   Points to parent window. If **NULL**, parent is the desktop.

dwStyle   Window styles for property sheet. For a complete list of available styles, see Window Styles on page 1253.

dwExStyle   Extended window styles for property sheet. For a complete list of available styles, see Extended Window Styles on page 1254.

Remarks   Call this function to display a modeless property sheet. The call to **Create** can be inside the constructor, or you can call it after the constructor is invoked.

The **Create** member function returns immediately after creating the property sheet. To destroy the property sheet, call **DestroyWindow**.

Modeless property sheets displayed with a call to **Create** do not have OK, Cancel, Apply Now, and Help buttons as modal property sheets do. Desired buttons must be created by the user.

To display a modal property sheet, call **DoModal** instead.

See Also   **CDialog::Create**, **CPropertySheet::DoModal**

CPropertySheet::DoModal

int DoModal( );

Return Value   **IDOK** or **IDCANCEL** if the function was successful; otherwise 0.

Remarks   Call this function to display a modal property sheet. The return value corresponds to the ID of the control that closed the property sheet. After this function returns, the windows corresponding to the property sheet and all the pages will have been destroyed. The objects themselves will still exist. Typically, you will retrieve data from the **CPropertyPage** objects after **DoModal** returns **IDOK**.

To display a modeless property sheet, call **Create** instead.

See Also   **CDialog::DoModal**, **CPropertySheet::Create**

CPropertySheet::EndDialog

void EndDialog(int *nEndID* **);**

Parameters   *nEndID*   Identifier to be used as return value of the property sheet.

Remarks   Terminates the property sheet. This is called by the framework when the OK, Cancel or Close button is pressed. Call this function if an event occurs that should close the property sheet.

See Also   **CPropertyPage::OnOK**, **CPropertyPage::OnCancel**, **CWnd::DestroyWindow**

CPropertySheet::GetPage

CPropertyPage* GetPage(int *nPage* **) const;**

Return Value   Pointer to the page corresponding to the *nPage* parameter.

Parameters   *nPage*   Index of the desired page, starting at 0. Must be between 0 and one less than the number of pages in the property sheet, inclusive.

Remarks   This function retrieves a pointer to the specified page in this property sheet.

See Also   **CPropertySheet::GetPageCount**, **CPropertySheet::AddPage**, **CPropertySheet::RemovePage**

CPropertySheet::GetPageCount

int GetPageCount( );

Return Value   The number of pages in the property sheet.

Remarks   Call this function to determine the number of pages currently in the property sheet.

See Also   **CPropertySheet::GetPage**, **CPropertySheet::AddPage**, **CPropertySheet::RemovePage**

CPropertySheet::RemovePage

void RemovePage(CPropertyPage *pPage **);**

void RemovePage(int *nPage* **);**

Parameters   *pPage*   Points to the page to be removed from the property sheet. Cannot be **NULL**.

nPage   Index of the page to be removed. Must be between 0 and one less than the number of pages in the property sheet, inclusive.

Remarks   Removes a page from the property sheet and destroys the associated window. The **CPropertyPage** object itself is not destroyed until the owner of the **CPropertySheet** window is closed.

See Also   **CPropertySheet::AddPage**

class CPtrArray : public CObject

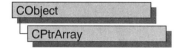

The **CPtrArray** class supports arrays of void pointers.

The member functions of **CPtrArray** are similar to the member functions of class **CObArray**. Because of this similarity, you can use the **CObArray** reference documentation for member function specifics. Wherever you see a **CObject** pointer as a function parameter or return value, substitute a pointer to **void**.

```
CObject* CObArray::GetAt( int <nIndex> ) const;
```

for example, translates to

```
void* CPtrArray::GetAt( int <nIndex> ) const;
```

Note Before using an array, use **SetSize** to establish its size and allocate memory for it. If you do not use **SetSize**, adding elements to your array causes it to be frequently reallocated and copied. Frequent reallocation and copying are inefficient and can fragment memory.

Pointer arrays cannot be serialized. When a pointer array is deleted, or when its elements are removed, only the pointers are removed, not the entities they reference.

#include <afxcoll.h>

Construction
CPtrArray   Constructs an empty array for void pointers.

Bounds
GetSize   Gets number of elements in this array.

GetUpperBound   Returns the largest valid index.

SetSize   Sets the number of elements to be contained in this array.

Operations
FreeExtra   Frees all unused memory above the current upper bound.

RemoveAll   Removes all the elements from this array.

Element Access

GetAt	Returns the value at a given index.
SetAt	Sets the value for a given index; array is not allowed to grow.
ElementAt	Returns a temporary reference to the element pointer within the array.

Growing the Array

SetAtGrow	Sets the value for a given index; grows the array if necessary.
Add	Adds an element to the end of the array; grows the array if necessary.

Insertion/Removal

InsertAt	Inserts an element (or all the elements in another array) at a specified index.
RemoveAt	Removes an element at a specific index.

Operators

operator []	Sets or gets the element at the specified index.

class CPtrList : public CObject

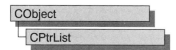

The **CPtrList** class supports lists of void pointers. The member functions of **CPtrList** are similar to the member functions of class **CObList**. Because of this similarity, you can use the **CObList** reference documentation for member function specifics. Wherever you see a **CObject** pointer as a function parameter or return value, substitute a pointer to **void**.

```
CObject*& CObList::GetHead() const;
```

for example, translates to

```
void*& CPtrList::GetHead() const;
```

CPtrList incorporates the **IMPLEMENT_DYNAMIC** macro to support run-time type access and dumping to a **CDumpContext** object. If you need a dump of individual pointer list elements, you must set the depth of the dump context to 1 or greater. Pointer lists cannot be serialized. When a **CPtrList** object is deleted, or when its elements are removed, only the pointers are removed, not the entities they reference.

#include <afxcoll.h>

Construction

CPtrList	Constructs an empty list for void pointers.

Head/Tail Access

GetHead	Returns the head element of the list (cannot be empty).
GetTail	Returns the tail element of the list (cannot be empty).

Operations

RemoveHead	Removes the element from the head of the list.
RemoveTail	Removes the element from the tail of the list.
AddHead	Adds an element (or all the elements in another list) to the head of the list (makes a new head).
AddTail	Adds an element (or all the elements in another list) to the tail of the list (makes a new tail).
RemoveAll	Removes all the elements from this list.

Iteration

GetHeadPosition	Returns the position of the head element of the list.
GetTailPosition	Returns the position of the tail element of the list.
GetNext	Gets the next element for iterating.
GetPrev	Gets the previous element for iterating.

Retrieval/Modification

GetAt	Gets the element at a given position.
SetAt	Sets the element at a given position.
RemoveAt	Removes an element from this list, specified by position.

Insertion

InsertBefore	Inserts a new element before a given position.
InsertAfter	Inserts a new element after a given position.

Searching

Find	Gets the position of an element specified by pointer value.
FindIndex	Gets the position of an element specified by a zero-based index.

Status

GetCount	Returns the number of elements in this list.
IsEmpty	Tests for the empty list condition (no elements).

class CRecordset : public CObject

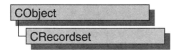

A **CRecordset** object represents a set of records selected from a data source. Known as "recordsets," **CRecordset** objects are available in two forms: dynasets and snapshots. A dynaset is a dynamic recordset that stays synchronized with updates by other users. A snapshot is a static recordset that reflects the state of the database at the time of the snapshot. Each form represents a set of records fixed at the time the recordset is opened, but when you scroll to a record in a dynaset, it reflects changes subsequently made to the record, either by other users or by other recordsets in your application. To work with either kind of recordset, you must derive an application-specific recordset class from **CRecordset**. Recordsets select records from a data source, and you can then

- Scroll through the records.
- Update the records and specify a locking mode.
- Filter the recordset to constrain which records it selects from those available on the data source.
- Sort the recordset.
- Parameterize the recordset to customize its selection with information not known until run time.

To use your class, open a database and construct a recordset object, passing the constructor a pointer to your **CDatabase** object. Then call the recordset's **Open** member function, specifying whether the object is a dynaset or a snapshot. Calling **Open** selects data from the data source and retrieves the first record. Use the object's member functions and data members to scroll through the records and operate on them. The operations available depend on whether the object is a dynaset or a snapshot, and whether it is updatable or read-only—this depends on the capability of the Open Database Connectivity (ODBC) data source. To refresh records that may have been changed or added since the **Open** call, call the object's **Requery** member function. Call the object's **Close** member function and destroy the object when you finish with it.

CRecordset uses record field exchange (RFX) to support reading and updating of record fields through type-safe C++ members of your **CRecordset**-derived class.

For more information about recordsets in general and record field exchange, see the encyclopedia articles "Recordset" and "Record Field Exchange." For a focus on dynasets and snapshots, see the articles "Dynaset" and "Snapshot." All articles are in *Programming with the Microsoft Foundation Class Library*.

#include <afxdb.h>

See Also   **CDatabase**, **CRecordView**

Data Members

m_hstmt	Contains the ODBC statement handle for the recordset. Type **HSTMT**.
m_nFields	Contains the number of field data members in the recordset. Type **UINT**.
m_nParams	Contains the number of parameter data members in the recordset. Type **UINT**.
m_pDatabase	Contains a pointer to the **CDatabase** object through which the recordset is connected to a data source.
m_strFilter	Contains a **CString** that specifies a Structured Query Language (SQL) **WHERE** clause. Used as a filter to select only those records that meet certain criteria.
m_strSort	Contains a **CString** that specifies an SQL **ORDER BY** clause. Used to control how the records are sorted.

Construction

CRecordset	Constructs a **CRecordset** object. Your derived class must provide a constructor that calls this one.
Open	Opens the recordset by retrieving the table or performing the query that the recordset represents.
Close	Closes the recordset and the ODBC **HSTMT** associated with it.

Recordset Attributes

CanAppend	Returns nonzero if new records can be added to the recordset via the **AddNew** member function.
CanRestart	Returns nonzero if **Requery** can be called to run the recordset's query again.
CanScroll	Returns nonzero if you can scroll through the records.
CanTransact	Returns nonzero if the data source supports transactions.
CanUpdate	Returns nonzero if the recordset can be updated (you can add, update, or delete records).
GetRecordCount	Returns the number of records in the recordset.

GetStatus	Gets the status of the recordset: the index of the current record and whether a final count of the records has been obtained.
GetTableName	Gets the name of the table on which the recordset is based.
GetSQL	Gets the SQL string used to select records for the recordset.
IsOpen	Returns nonzero if **Open** has been called previously.
IsBOF	Returns nonzero if the recordset has been positioned before the first record. There is no current record.
IsEOF	Returns nonzero if the recordset has been positioned after the last record. There is no current record.
IsDeleted	Returns nonzero if the recordset is positioned on a deleted record.

Recordset Update Operations

AddNew	Prepares for adding a new record. Call **Update** to complete the addition.
Delete	Deletes the current record from the recordset. You must explicitly scroll to another record after the deletion.
Edit	Prepares for changes to the current record. Call **Update** to complete the edit.
Update	Completes an **AddNew** or **Edit** operation by saving the new or edited data on the data source.

Recordset Navigation Operations

Move	Positions the recordset to a specified number of records from the current record in either direction.
MoveFirst	Positions the current record on the first record in the recordset. Test for **IsBOF** first.
MoveLast	Positions the current record on the last record in the recordset. Test for **IsEOF** first.
MoveNext	Positions the current record on the next record in the recordset. Test for **IsEOF** first.
MovePrev	Positions the current record on the previous record in the recordset. Test for **IsBOF** first.

Other Recordset Operations

Cancel	Cancels an asynchronous operation.
IsFieldDirty	Returns nonzero if the specified field in the current record has been changed.
IsFieldNull	Returns nonzero if the specified field in the current record is Null (has no value).
IsFieldNullable	Returns nonzero if the specified field in the current record can be set to Null (having no value).
Requery	Runs the recordset's query again to refresh the selected records.
SetFieldDirty	Marks the specified field in the current record as changed.
SetFieldNull	Sets the value of the specified field in the current record to Null (having no value).
SetLockingMode	Sets the locking mode to "optimistic" locking (the default) or "pessimistic" locking. Determines how records are locked for updates.

Recordset Overridables

DoFieldExchange	Called to exchange data (in both directions) between the field data members of the recordset and the corresponding record on the data source. Implements record field exchange (RFX).
GetDefaultConnect	Called to get the default connect string.
GetDefaultSQL	Called to get the default SQL string to execute.
OnSetOptions	Called to set options for the specified ODBC statement.
OnWaitForDataSource	Called to yield processing time to other applications for asynchronous operations.

Member Functions

CRecordset::AddNew

> **virtual void AddNew( );**
> **throw(CDBException, CFileException);**

Remarks   Call this member function to prepare for adding a new record to the table. You must call the **Requery** member function to see the newly added record. The record's fields are initially Null. (In database terminology, Null means "having no value" and is not the same as **NULL** in C++.) To complete the operation, you must call the **Update** member function. **Update** saves your changes to the data source.

AddNew prepares a new, empty record using the recordset's field data members. After you call **AddNew**, set the values you want in the recordset's field data members. (You do not have to call the **Edit** member function for this purpose; use **Edit** only for existing records.) When you subsequently call **Update**, changed values in the field data members are saved on the data source.

Caution If you scroll to a new record before you call **Update**, the new record is lost, and no warning is given.

If the data source supports transactions, you can make your **AddNew** call part of a transaction. For more information about transactions, see class **CDatabase**. Note that you should call **CDatabase::BeginTrans** before calling **AddNew**.

Important For dynasets, new records are added to the recordset as the last record. Added records are not added to snapshots—you must call **Requery** to refresh the recordset.

It is illegal to call **AddNew** for a recordset whose **Open** member function has not been called. A **CDBException** is thrown if you call **AddNew** for a recordset that cannot be appended to. You can determine whether the recordset is updatable by calling **CanAppend**.

See Also   **CRecordset::Update, CRecordset::Requery, CDatabase::BeginTrans, CRecordset::SetFieldDirty, CRecordset::SetFieldNull, CRecordset::IsFieldNull, CRecordset::IsFieldNullable, CDBException**

In *Programming with the Microsoft Foundation Class Library*: "Recordset: How Recordsets Update Records," "Recordset: Adding, Updating, and Deleting Records," "Transaction"

Example   See the article "Transaction: Performing a Transaction in a Recordset" in *Programming with the Microsoft Foundation Class Library*.

CRecordset::CanAppend

BOOL CanAppend( ) const;

Return Value   Nonzero if the recordset allows adding new records; otherwise 0. **CanAppend** will return 0 if you opened the recordset as read-only.

Remarks   Call this member function to determine whether the previously opened recordset allows you to add new records by calling the **AddNew** member function.

See Also   **CRecordset::AddNew**, **CRecordset::Requery**

CRecordset::Cancel

void Cancel( );

Remarks   Call this member function to request that the data source cancel an asynchronous operation in progress. The **OnWaitForDataSource** member function will continue to call the ODBC function until it no longer returns **SQL_STILL_EXECUTING**.

See Also   **CDatabase::SetSynchronousMode**, **CDatabase::InWaitForDataSource**, **CRecordset::OnWaitForDataSource**

CRecordset::CanRestart

BOOL CanRestart( ) const;

Return Value   Nonzero if requery is allowed; otherwise 0.

Remarks   Call this member function to determine whether the recordset allows restarting its query (to refresh its records) by calling the **Requery** member function.

See Also   **CRecordset::Requery**

CRecordset::CanScroll

BOOL CanScroll( ) const;

Return Value   Nonzero if the recordset allows scrolling; otherwise 0.

Remarks   Call this member function to determine whether the recordset allows scrolling.

See Also   In *Programming with the Microsoft Foundation Class Library*: "Recordset: Scrolling"

CRecordset::CanTransact

BOOL CanTransact( ) const;

Return Value   Nonzero if the recordset allows transactions; otherwise 0.

Remarks   Call this member function to determine whether the recordset allows transactions.

See Also   **CDatabase::BeginTrans**, **CDatabase::CommitTrans**, **CDatabase::Rollback**

In *Programming with the Microsoft Foundation Class Library*: "Transaction"

CRecordset::CanUpdate

BOOL CanUpdate( ) const;

Return Value   Nonzero if the recordset can be updated; otherwise 0.

Remarks   Call this member function to determine whether the recordset can be updated. A recordset might be read-only if the underlying data source is read-only or if you specified **CRecordset::readOnly** for *dwOptions* when you opened the recordset.

See Also   **CRecordset::Open, CRecordset::Edit**

CRecordset::Close

virtual void Close( );

Remarks   Call this member function to close the recordset. The ODBC **HSTMT** and all memory the framework allocated for the recordset are deallocated. Usually after calling **Close**, you delete the C++ recordset object if it was allocated with **new**.

You can call **Open** again after calling **Close**. This lets you reuse the recordset object. The alternative is to call **Requery**.

See Also   **CRecordset::CRecordset, CRecordset::Open, CRecordset::Requery**

Example
```
CCustSet rsCustSet( NULL ); // Construct a snapshot object
if( !rsCustSet.Open( ) )
    return FALSE;
// Use the snapshot ...
// Close the snapshot
rsCustSet.Close( );
// Destructor is called when the function exits
```

CRecordset::CRecordset

CRecordset(CDatabase* *pDatabase* **= NULL);**

Parameters   *pDatabase*   Contains a pointer to a **CDatabase** object or the value **NULL**. If not **NULL** and the **CDatabase** object's **Open** member function has not been called to connect it to the data source, the recordset attempts to open it for you during its own **Open** call. If you pass **NULL**, a **CDatabase** object is constructed and connected for you using the data source information you specified when you derived your recordset class with ClassWizard.

Remarks   Constructs a **CRecordset** object. Your recordset objects must be objects of an application-specific class derived from **CRecordset**. Use ClassWizard to derive your recordset classes.

> **Note** Your derived class *must* supply its own constructor. In the constructor of your derived class, call the constructor **CRecordset::CRecordset**, passing the appropriate parameters along to it.

Pass **NULL** to your recordset constructor to have a **CDatabase** object constructed and connected for you automatically. This is a useful shorthand that does not require you to construct and connect a **CDatabase** object prior to constructing your recordset.

See Also   **CRecordset::Open**, **CRecordset::Close**

Example   See the article "Recordset: Declaring a Class for a Table" in *Programming with the Microsoft Foundation Class Library*.

CRecordset::Delete

    virtual void Delete( );
        throw(CDBException);

Remarks   Call this member function to delete the current record. After a successful deletion, the recordset's field data members are set to a Null value, and you must explicitly call one of the **Move** functions in order to move off the deleted record. Once you move off the deleted record, it is not possible to return to it. If the data source supports transactions, you can make the **Delete** call part of a transaction. For more information, see the article "Transaction" in *Programming with the Microsoft Foundation Class Library*.

> **Caution** The recordset must be updatable and there must be a valid record current in the recordset when you call **Delete**; otherwise, an error occurs. For example, if you delete a record but do not scroll to a new record before you call **Delete** again, **Delete** throws a **CDBException**.

Unlike **AddNew** and **Edit**, a call to **Delete** is not followed by a call to **Update**. If a **Delete** call fails, the field data members are left unchanged.

See Also   **CDatabase::BeginTrans**, **CDatabase::CommitTrans**, **CDatabase::Rollback**, **CDBException**

Example   This example shows a recordset created on the frame of a function. The example assumes the existence of m_dbCust, a member variable of type **CDatabase** already connected to the data source.

```
// Create a derived CRecordset object
CCustSet rsCustSet( &m_dbCust );
rsCustSet.Open( );

if( rsCustSet.IsEOF( ) || !rsCustSet.CanUpdate( ) ||
            !rsCustSet.CanTransact( ) )
    return;
if( !m_dbCust.BeginTrans( ) )
{
    // Do something to handle a failure
}
else
{
    // Perhaps scroll to a new record...
    // Delete the current record
    rsCustSet.Delete( );
    // ...

    // Finished commands for this transaction
    if( <the user confirms the transaction> )
        m_dbCust.CommitTrans( );
    else // User changed mind
        m_dbCust.Rollback( );
}
// ...
```

CRecordset::DoFieldExchange

virtual void DoFieldExchange(CFieldExchange* *pFX* **) = 0;**
 throw(CDBException);

Parameters

pFX   Contains a pointer to a **CFieldExchange** object. The framework will already
have set up this object to specify a context for the field exchange operation.

Remarks

The framework calls this member function to automatically exchange data between
the field data members of your recordset object and the corresponding columns of
the current record on the data source. It also binds your parameter data members, if
any, to parameter placeholders in the SQL statement string for the recordset's
selection. The exchange of field data, called record field exchange (RFX), works in
both directions: from the recordset object's field data members to the fields of the
record on the data source, and from the record on the data source to the recordset
object.

The only action you must normally take to implement **DoFieldExchange** for your
derived recordset class is to create the class with ClassWizard and specify the
names and data types of the field data members. You might also add code to what
ClassWizard writes to specify parameter data members or to deal with any columns
you bind dynamically. For more information, see the article "Recordset:

Dynamically Binding Data Columns" in *Programming with the Microsoft Foundation Class Library*.

When you declare your derived recordset class with ClassWizard, the wizard writes an override of **DoFieldExchange** for you, which resembles the following example:

```
void CCustSet::DoFieldExchange(CFieldExchange* pFX)
{
    //{{AFX_FIELD_MAP(CCustSet)
    pFX->SetFieldType(CFieldExchange::outputColumn);
    RFX_Text(pFX, "Name", m_strName);
    RFX_Int(pFX, "Age", m_wAge);
    //}}AFX_FIELD_MAP
}
```

For further examples and details about **DoFieldExchange**, see the article "Record Field Exchange: How RFX Works." For general information about RFX, see the article "Record Field Exchange." Both articles are in *Programming with the Microsoft Foundation Class Library*.

See Also   **CFieldExchange, CRecordset::m_nFields, CRecordset::m_nParams**

CRecordset::Edit

virtual void Edit( );
    throw(CDBException, CMemoryException, CFileException);

Remarks   Call this member function to allow changes to the current record. After you call **Edit**, you can change the field data members by directly resetting their values. The operation is completed when you subsequently call the **Update** member function to save your changes on the data source.

Edit saves the values of the recordset's data members. If you call **Edit**, make changes, then call **Edit** again, the record's values are restored to what they were before the first **Edit** call.

In some cases, you may want to update a column by making it Null (containing no data). To do so, call **SetFieldNull** with a parameter of **TRUE** to mark the field Null; this also causes the column to be updated. If you want a field to be written to the data source even though its value has not changed, call **SetFieldDirty** with a parameter of **TRUE**. This works even if the field had the value Null.

If the data source supports transactions, you can make the **Edit** call part of a transaction. Note that you should call **CDatabase::BeginTrans** before calling **Edit** and after the recordset has been opened. Also note that calling **CDatabase::CommitTrans** is not a substitute for calling **Update** to complete the **Edit** operation. For more information about transactions, see class **CDatabase**.

Depending on the current locking mode, the record being updated may be locked by **Edit** until you call **Update** or scroll to another record, or it may be locked only during the **Edit** call. You can change the locking mode with **SetLockingMode**.

The previous value of the current record is restored if you scroll to a new record before calling **Update**. A **CDBException** is thrown if you call **Edit** for a recordset that cannot be updated or if there is no current record.

See Also   **CRecordset::Update**, **CRecordset::AddNew**, **CRecordset::Delete**, **CRecordset::SetFieldDirty**, **CRecordset::SetFieldNull**, **CRecordset::CanUpdate**, **CRecordset::CanTransact**, **CRecordset::SetLockingMode**

In *Programming with the Microsoft Foundation Class Library*: "Transaction," "Recordset: Locking Records"

Example

```
// To edit a record,
// First set up the edit buffer
rsCustSet.Edit( );
// Then edit field data members for the record
rsCustSet.m_dwCustID = 2795;
rsCustSet.m_strCustomer = "Jones Mfg";
// Finally, complete the operation
if( !rsCustSet.Update( ) )
    // Handle the failure to update
```

CRecordset::GetDefaultConnect

virtual CString GetDefaultConnect( );

Return Value   A pointer to a string that contains the default connect string.

Remarks   The framework calls this member function to get the default connect string for the data source on which the recordset is based. ClassWizard implements this function for you by identifying the same data source you use in ClassWizard to get information about tables and columns. You will probably find it convenient to rely on this default connection while developing your application. But the default connection may not be appropriate for users of your application. If that is the case, you should reimplement this function, discarding ClassWizard's version. For more information about connect strings, see the article "Data Source" in *Programming with the Microsoft Foundation Class Library*.

CRecordset::GetDefaultSQL

virtual CString GetDefaultSQL( ) = 0;

Return Value   A pointer to a string that contains the default SQL statement.

Remarks   The framework calls this member function to get the default SQL statement on which the recordset is based. This might be a table name or an SQL **SELECT** statement.

You indirectly define the default SQL statement by declaring your recordset class with ClassWizard. Your derived **CRecordset** class must override **GetDefaultSQL**, but ClassWizard performs this task for you.

If you need the SQL statement string for your own use, call **GetSQL**, which returns the SQL statement used to select the recordset's records when it was opened. You can edit the default SQL string in your class's override of **GetDefaultSQL**. For example, you could specify a call to a predefined query using a **CALL** statement. For more information, see the article "Recordset: Declaring a Class for a Table" in *Programming with the Microsoft Foundation Class Library*.

Caution The table name will be empty if the framework could not identify a table name, if multiple table names were supplied, or if a **CALL** statement could not be interpreted.

See Also   CRecordset::GetSQL

CRecordset::GetRecordCount

long GetRecordCount( ) const;

Return Value   The number of records in the recordset; 0 if the recordset contains no records; or −1 if the record count cannot be determined.

Remarks   Call this member function to determine the size of the recordset.

Caution The record count is maintained as a "high water mark"—the highest-numbered record yet seen as the user moves through the records. The total number of records is only known after the user has moved beyond the last record. For performance reasons, the count is not updated when you call **MoveLast**. To count the records yourself, call **MoveNext** repeatedly until **IsEOF** returns nonzero. Adding a record via **CRecordView:AddNew** increases the count; deleting a record via **CRecordView::Delete** decreases the count. Adding or deleting records by directly calling **CRecordset::AddNew** and **Delete** will not change the record count, and should therefore be avoided if you are working with a record view.

See Also   **CRecordset::MoveLast, CRecordset::MoveNext, CRecordset::IsEOF, CRecordset::GetStatus**

CRecordset::GetStatus

void GetStatus(CRecordsetStatus& *rStatus* **) const;**

Parameters   *rStatus*   A reference to a **CRecordsetStatus** object. The **CRecordsetStatus** structure has the following form:

```
struct CRecordsetStatus
{
    long m_lCurrentRecord;
    BOOL m_bRecordCountFinal;
};
```

The two members of **CRecordsetStatus** have the following meanings:

- **m_lCurrentRecord**   Contains the zero-based index of the current record in the recordset, if known. If the index cannot be determined, this member contains **AFX_CURRENT_RECORD_UNDEFINED** (−2). If **IsBOF** is **TRUE** (empty recordset or attempt to scroll before first record) then **m_lCurrentRecord** is set to **AFX_CURRENT_RECORD_BOF** (−1). If on the first record, then it is set to 0, second record 1, and so on.

- **m_bRecordCountFinal**   Nonzero if the total number of records in the recordset has been determined. Generally this must be accomplished by starting at the beginning of the recordset and calling **MoveNext** until **IsEOF** returns nonzero. If this member is zero, the record count as returned by **GetRecordCount**, if not −1, is only a "high water mark" count of the records.

Remarks   Call this member function to determine the index of the current record in the recordset and/or whether the last record has been seen. **CRecordset** attempts to track the index, but under some circumstances this may not be possible. See **GetRecordCount** for an explanation.

See Also   **CRecordset::GetRecordCount**

CRecordset::GetSQL

const CString& GetSQL( ) const;

Return Value   A **const** reference to a **CString** that contains the SQL statement.

Remarks   Call this member function to get the SQL statement that was used to select the recordset's records when it was opened. This will generally be an SQL **SELECT** statement. The string returned by **GetSQL** is read-only.

The string returned by **GetSQL** is typically different from any string you may have passed to the recordset in the *lpszSQL* parameter to the **Open** member function. This is because the recordset constructs a full SQL statement based on what you passed to **Open**, what you specified with ClassWizard, what you may have specified in the **m_strFilter** and **m_strSort** data members, and any parameters you may have specified. For details about how the recordset constructs this SQL statement, see the article "Recordset: How Recordsets Select Records" in *Programming with the Microsoft Foundation Class Library*.

Important Call this member function only after calling **Open**.

See Also   **CRecordset::GetDefaultSQL**, **CRecordset::Open**, **CRecordset::m_strFilter**, **CRecordset::m_strSort**

CRecordset::GetTableName

const CString& GetTableName( ) const;

Return Value   A **const** reference to a **CString** that contains the table name, if the recordset is based on a table; otherwise, an empty string.

Remarks   Call this member function to get the name of the SQL table on which the recordset's query is based. **GetTableName** is only valid if the recordset is based on a table, not a join of multiple tables or a predefined query (stored procedure). The name is read-only.

Important Call this member function only after calling **Open**.

CRecordset::IsBOF

BOOL IsBOF( ) const;

Return Value   Nonzero if the recordset contains no records or if you have scrolled backward before the first record; otherwise 0.

Remarks   Call this member function before you scroll from record to record to learn whether you have gone before the first record of the recordset. You can also use **IsBOF** along with **IsEOF** to determine whether the recordset contains any records or is empty. Immediately after you call **Open**, if the recordset contains no records, **IsBOF** returns nonzero.When you open a recordset that has at least one record, the first record is the current record and **IsBOF** returns 0.

If the first record is the current record and you call **MovePrev**, **IsBOF** will subsequently return nonzero. If **IsBOF** returns nonzero and you call **MovePrev**, an error occurs. If **IsBOF** returns nonzero, the current record is undefined, and any action that requires a current record will result in an error.

See Also   **CRecordset::IsEOF**, **CRecordset::MoveFirst**, **CRecordset::MovePrev**

Example This example uses **IsBOF** and **IsEOF** to detect the limits of a recordset as the code scrolls through the recordset in both directions.

```
// Open a recordset; first record is current
CCustSet rsCustSet( NULL );
rsCustSet.Open( );
if( rsCustSet.IsBOF( ) )
    return;                        // The recordset is empty
while ( !rsCustSet.IsEOF( ) )     // Scroll to the end of the recordset
    rsCustSet.MoveNext( );
// Past last record, so no record is current
rsCustSet.MoveLast( );            // Move to the last record
while( !rsCustSet.IsBOF( ) )      // Scroll to beginning of the recordset
    rsCustSet.MovePrev( );
// Past first record, so no record is current
rsCustSet.MoveFirst( );           // First record is current again
```

CRecordset::IsDeleted

BOOL IsDeleted( ) const;

Return Value Nonzero if the recordset is positioned on a deleted record; otherwise 0.

Remarks Call this member function to determine whether the current record has been deleted. If it has, you must scroll to another record before you can perform any other recordset operations. **IsDeleted** returns nonzero only if *you* deleted a record and did not scroll off that record.

See Also **CRecordset::IsBOF, CRecordset::IsEOF, CRecordset::Delete**

CRecordset::IsEOF

BOOL IsEOF( ) const;

Return Value Nonzero if the recordset contains no records or if you have scrolled beyond the last record; otherwise 0.

Remarks Call this member function as you scroll from record to record to learn whether you have gone beyond the last record of the recordset. You can also use **IsEOF** to determine whether the recordset contains any records or is empty. Immediately after you call **Open**, if the recordset contains no records, **IsEOF** returns nonzero. When you open a recordset that has at least one record, the first record is the current record and **IsEOF** returns 0.

If the last record is the current record when you call **MoveNext**, **IsEOF** will subsequently return nonzero. If **IsEOF** returns nonzero and you call **MoveNext**, an error occurs. If **IsEOF** returns nonzero, the current record is undefined, and any action that requires a current record will result in an error.

See Also   **CRecordset::IsBOF**, **CRecordset::MoveLast**, **CRecordset::MoveNext**

Example   See the example for **IsBOF**.

CRecordset::IsFieldDirty

BOOL IsFieldDirty(void* *pv* **);**
   throw(CMemoryException);

Return Value   Nonzero if the specified field data member is flagged as dirty; otherwise 0.

Parameters   *pv*   A pointer to the field data member whose status you want to check, or **NULL** to determine if any of the fields are dirty.

Remarks   Call this member function to determine whether the specified field data member of a dynaset has been flagged as "dirty" (changed). The data in all dirty field data members will be transferred to the record on the data source when the current record is updated by a call to the **Update** member function of **CRecordset** (following a call to **Edit** or **AddNew**). With this knowledge, you can take further steps, such as unflagging the field data member to mark the column so it will not be written to the data source. For more information on the dirty flag, see the article "Recordset: How Recordsets Select Records" in *Programming with the Microsoft Foundation Class Library*.

Using **NULL** for the first argument of the function will apply the function only to **outputColumns**, not **params**. For instance, the call

```
SetFieldNull( NULL );
```

will set only **outputColumns** to **NULL**. **Params** will be unaffected.

To work on **params**, you must supply the actual address of the individual **param** you want to work on, such as:

```
SetFieldNull( &m_strParam );
```

This means you cannot set all **params NULL**, as you can with **outputColumns**.

IsFieldDirty is implemented through **DoFieldExchange**.

See Also   **CRecordset::SetFieldDirty**, **CRecordset::IsFieldNull**

CRecordset::IsFieldNull

BOOL IsFieldNull(void* *pv* **);**
   throw(CMemoryException);

Return Value   Nonzero if the specified field data member is flagged as Null; otherwise 0.

Parameters   *pv*   A pointer to the field data member whose status you want to check, or **NULL** to determine if any of the fields are Null.

Remarks   Call this member function to determine whether the specified field data member of a dynaset has been flagged as Null. (In database terminology, Null means "having no value" and is not the same as **NULL** in C++.) If a field data member is flagged as Null, it is interpreted as a column of the current record for which there is no value.

Using **NULL** for the first argument of the function will apply the function only to **outputColumns**, not **params**. For instance, the call

```
SetFieldNull( NULL );
```

will set only **outputColumns** to **NULL**. **Params** will be unaffected.

To work on **params**, you must supply the actual address of the individual **param** you want to work on, such as:

```
SetFieldNull( &m_strParam );
```

This means you cannot set all **params NULL**, as you can with **outputColumns**.

IsFieldNull is implemented through **DoFieldExchange**.

See Also   **CRecordset::SetFieldNull, CRecordset::IsFieldDirty**

CRecordset::IsFieldNullable

BOOL IsFieldNullable(void* *pv* **);**
  throw(CDBException)

Parameters   *pv*   A pointer to the field data member whose status you want to check, or **NULL** to determine if any of the fields can be set to a Null value.

Remarks   Call this member function to to determine whether the specified field data member is "nullable" (can be set to a Null value; C++ **NULL** is not the same as Null, which, in database terminology, means "having no value").

A field that cannot be Null must have a value. If you attempt to set a such a field to Null when adding or updating a record, the data source rejects the addition or update, and **Update** will throw an exception. The exception occurs when you call **Update**, not when you call **SetFieldNull**.

Using **NULL** for the first argument of the function will apply the function only to **outputColumns**, not **params**. For instance, the call

```
SetFieldNull( NULL );
```

will set only **outputColumns** to **NULL**. **Params** will be unaffected.

To work on **params**, you must supply the actual address of the individual **param** you want to work on, such as:

```
SetFieldNull( &m_strParam );
```

This means you cannot set all **params NULL**, as you can with **outputColumns**.

IsFieldNullable is implemented through **DoFieldExchange**.

See Also   **CRecordset::IsFieldNull**, **CRecordset::SetFieldNull**

CRecordset::IsOpen

BOOL IsOpen( ) const;

Return Value   Nonzero if the recordset object's **Open** or **Requery** member function has previously been called and the recordset has not been closed; otherwise 0.

Remarks   Call this member function to determine if the recordset is already open.

CRecordset::Move

virtual void Move(long *lRows* **);**
    throw(CDBException, CFileException, CMemoryException);

Parameters   *lRows*   The number of rows to move forward or backward. Positive values move forward, toward the end of the recordset. Negative values move backward, toward the beginning.

Remarks   Call this member function to position the recordset *lRows* records from the current record. You can move forward or backward. Move(1) is equivalent to **MoveNext**, and Move(-1) is equivalent to **MovePrev**. For more information, see the article "Recordset: Scrolling" in *Programming with the Microsoft Foundation Class Library*.

Call **Move** with the parameter **AFX_MOVE_REFRESH** to refresh the current record by restoring the value it had before an **AddNew** or **Edit** call. This call also ends any current **AddNew** or **Edit** mode if you were in one. This call does not refresh data in a snapshot, since a snapshot is, by definition a static copy of the data, but you can use it to end an **AddNew** or **Edit** mode.

Caution Calling any of the **Move** functions throws an exception if the recordset has no records. Call both **IsBOF** and **IsEOF** before any move operation to determine whether the recordset has any records.

If you have scrolled past the beginning or end of the recordset (**IsBOF** or **IsEOF** returns nonzero), a call to **Move** results in an error. **Move** throws a **CDBException**.

If you call any of the **Move** functions while the current record is being updated or added, the updates are lost without warning.

See Also   CRecordset::MoveNext, CRecordset::MovePrev, CRecordset::MoveFirst, CRecordset::MoveLast, CRecordset::IsBOF, CRecordset::IsEOF

Example   This example uses **Move** to move from the first record of a newly opened recordset to the sixth.

```
rsCust.MoveFirst( );
rsCust.Move( 5 );
```

CRecordset::MoveFirst

void MoveFirst( );
    throw(CDBException, CMemoryException, CFileException);

Remarks   Call this member function to make the first record in the recordset (if any) the current record.

You do not have to call **MoveFirst** immediately after you open the recordset. At that time, the first record (if any) is automatically the current record.

Caution Calling any of the **Move** functions throws an exception if the recordset has no records. Call both **IsBOF** and **IsEOF** before any move operation to determine whether the recordset has any records.

If you call any of the **Move** functions while the current record is being updated or added, the updates are lost without warning.

See Also   CRecordset::MoveLast, CRecordset::MoveNext, CRecordset::MovePrev, CRecordset::IsBOF

Example   See the example for **IsBOF**.

CRecordset::MoveLast

> **void MoveLast( );**
>   **throw(CDBException, CMemoryException, CFileException);**

Remarks   Call this member function to make the last record (if any) in the recordset the current record.

> **Caution** Calling any of the **Move** functions throws an exception if the recordset has no records. Call both **IsBOF** and **IsEOF** before any move operation to determine whether the recordset has any records.

See Also   **CRecordset::MoveFirst, CRecordset::MoveNext, CRecordset::MovePrev, CRecordset::IsEOF**

Example   See the example for **IsBOF**.

CRecordset::MoveNext

> **void MoveNext( );**
>   **throw(CDBException, CMemoryException, CFileException);**

Remarks   Call this member function to make the next record in the recordset the current record.

It is recommended that you call **IsEOF** before you attempt to move to the next record. If you call **MoveNext** when the last record is current, **IsEOF** will subsequently return nonzero, and calling **MoveNext** again results in an error. A call to **MoveNext** will throw a **CDBException** if **IsEOF** returns nonzero, indicating that you have already scrolled past the last record, or that no records were selected by the recordset.

> **Caution** Calling any of the **Move** functions throws an exception if the recordset has no records. Call both **IsBOF** and **IsEOF** before any move operation to determine whether the recordset has any records.

See Also   **CRecordset::MovePrev, CRecordset::MoveFirst, CRecordset::MoveLast, CRecordset::IsEOF**

Example   See the example for **IsBOF**.

CRecordset::MovePrev

void MovePrev( );
   throw(CDBException, CMemoryException, CFileException);

Remarks

Call this member function to make the previous record in the recordset the current record.

It is recommended that you call **IsBOF** before you attempt to move to the previous record. If you call **MovePrev** when the first record is current, **IsBOF** will subsequently return nonzero, and calling **MovePrev** again results in an error. A call to **MovePrev** will throw a **CDBException** if **IsBOF** returns nonzero, indicating either that you have already scrolled before the first record or that no records were selected by the recordset.

Caution Calling any of the **Move** functions throws an exception if the recordset has no records. Call both **IsBOF** and **IsEOF** before any move operation to determine whether the recordset has any records.

See Also

CRecordset::MoveNext, CRecordset::MoveFirst, CRecordset::MoveLast, CRecordset::IsBOF

Example

See the example for **IsBOF**.

CRecordset::OnSetOptions

virtual void OnSetOptions(HSTMT *hstmt* **);**

Parameters

hstmt   The **HSTMT** of the ODBC statement whose options are to be set.

Remarks

The framework calls this member function to set initial options for the recordset. **OnSetOptions** determines the data source's support for scrollable cursors and for cursor concurrency and sets the recordset's options accordingly.

Override **OnSetOptions** to set additional options specific to the driver or the data source. For example, if your data source supports opening for exclusive access, you might override **OnSetOptions** to take advantage of that ability.

For more information about cursors, see the article "ODBC" in *Programming with the Microsoft Foundation Class Library.*

See Also

CDatabase::OnSetOptions

CRecordset::OnWaitForDataSource

virtual void OnWaitForDataSource(BOOL *bStillExecuting* **);**

Parameters

bStillExecuting Nonzero if the data source is still executing an asynchronous operation begun previously, or 0 if the data source has finished execution.

Remarks

The framework calls this member function to yield processing time to other applications.

Override **OnWaitForDataSource** if you want to give the user a chance to cancel a long operation for this recordset. You must check whether the user wants to abort; if so, call the **Cancel** member function. The framework will eventually break out of the **OnWaitForDataSource** loop. The default implementation calls the **OnWaitForDataSource** member function of class **CDatabase**. (See **CDatabase::OnWaitForDataSource** for details.) Override the **CDatabase** version if you need to customize the handling of all recordsets associated with a **CDatabase** object, but in general override this version instead.

See Also

CDatabase::OnWaitForDataSource, CRecordset::Cancel

CRecordset::Open

virtual BOOL Open(UINT *nOpenType* **= snapshot, LPCSTR** *lpszSql* **= NULL, DWORD** *dwOptions* **= none);**
throw(CDBException, CMemoryException, CFileException);

Return Value

Nonzero if the **CRecordset** object was successfully opened; otherwise 0 if **CDatabase::Open** (if called) returns 0.

Parameters

nOpenType One of the following values from the **enum OpenType**:

- **CRecordset::dynaset** A dynamic recordset with bi-directional scrolling.
- **CRecordset::snapshot** A static recordset with bi-directional scrolling.
- **CRecordset::forwardOnly** A read-only recordset with only forward scrolling.

Caution If the requested type is not supported, the framework throws an exception.

lpszSql A string pointer containing one of the following:

- A **NULL** pointer.
- The name of a table.
- An SQL **SELECT** statement (optionally with an SQL **WHERE** or **ORDER BY** clause).

- A **CALL** statement specifying the name of a predefined query (stored procedure).

For more information about this string, see the table and the discussion of ClassWizard's role under "Remarks."

Note The order of the columns in your result set must match the order of the RFX function calls in your `DoFieldExchange` function override.

---

dwOptions   One of the mutually exclusive values listed below. The default value is **none**. Possible values are as follows:

- **CRecordset::none**   No options set. By default, the recordset can be updated with **Edit** or **Delete** and allows appending new records with **AddNew**. Updatability depends on the data source as well as on the option you specify.
- **CRecordset::appendOnly**   Do not allow **Edit** or **Delete** on the recordset. Allow **AddNew** only.
- **CRecordset::readOnly**   Open the recordset as read-only.

Remarks   You must call this member function to run the query defined by the recordset. Before calling **Open**, you must construct the recordset object.

This recordset's connection to the data source depends on how you construct the recordset before calling **Open**. If you pass a **CDatabase** object to the recordset constructor that has not been connected to the data source, this member function uses **GetDefaultConnect** to attempt to open the database object. If you pass **NULL** to the recordset constructor, the constructor constructs a **CDatabase** object for you, and **Open** attempts to connect the database object. For details on closing the recordset and the connection under these varying circumstances, see **Close**.

Note Access to a data source through a recordset is always shared. You cannot use a recordset to open a data source with exclusive access.

When you call **Open**, a query, usually an SQL **SELECT** statement, selects records based on criteria shown in the following table.

Value of the lpszSQL Parameter	Records Selected Are Determined By	Example
NULL	The string returned by **GetDefaultSQL**.	
SQL table name	All columns of the table-list in **DoFieldExchange**.	`"Customer"`
Predefined query (stored procedure) name.	The columns the query is defined to return.	`"{call OverDueAccts}"`
SELECT column-list **FROM** table-list	The specified columns from the specified table(s).	`"SELECT CustId, CustName FROM Customer"`

The usual procedure is to pass **NULL** to **Open**; in that case, **Open** calls **GetDefaultSQL**, whose value is generated by ClassWizard. This value gives the table name you specified in ClassWizard. You can instead specify other information in the *lpszSQL* parameter.

Whatever you pass, **Open** constructs a final SQL string for the query (the string may have SQL **WHERE** and **ORDER BY** clauses appended to the *lpszSQL* string you passed) and then executes the query. You can examine the constructed string by calling **GetSQL** after calling **Open**. For additional details about how the recordset constructs an SQL statement and selects records, see the article "Recordset: How Recordsets Select Records" in *Programming with the Microsoft Foundation Class Library*.

The field data members of your recordset class are bound to the columns of the data selected. If any records are returned, the first record becomes the current record.

If you want to set options for the recordset, such as a filter or sort, specify these after you construct the recordset object but before you call **Open**. If you want to refresh the records in the recordset after the recordset is already open, call **Requery**.

For more information, including additional examples, see the articles "Recordset: How Recordsets Select Records" and "Recordset: Creating and Closing Recordsets" in *Programming with the Microsoft Foundation Class Library*.

See Also   **CRecordset::CRecordset, CRecordset::Close, CRecordset::GetDefaultSQL, CRecordset::GetSQL, CRecordset::m_strFilter, CRecordset::m_strSort, CRecordset::Requery**

In *Programming with the Microsoft Foundation Class Library*: "Recordset"

Example

The first example shows how to use *dwOptions* to open a read-only recordset based on the recordset class's default SQL statement. The second example gives several different forms of the **Open** call.

```
void CMyDocument::MyCustomerFunction( )
{
    // Construct the recordset object
    CCustSet dsCustSet( NULL );
    // Initialize the recordset
    dsCustSet.Open( CRecordset::snapshot, NULL, CRecordset::readOnly );
    // ...
}

// Pass a complete SELECT statement
dsCustSet.Open( CRecordset::snapshot, "Select L_Name from Customer" );
// Pass just a table name
dsCustSet.Open( CRecordset::snapshot, "Customer" );
// Accept all defaults
dsCustSet.Open( );
}
```

CRecordset::Requery

virtual BOOL Requery( );
    throw(CDBException, CMemoryException, CFileException);

Return Value

Nonzero if the recordset was successfully rebuilt; otherwise 0.

Remarks

Call this member function to rebuild (refresh) a recordset. If any records are returned, the first record becomes the current record.

In order for the recordset to reflect the additions and deletions that you or other users are making to the data source, you must rebuild the recordset by calling **Requery**. If the recordset is a dynaset, it automatically reflects updates that you or other users make to its existing records (but not additions). If the recordset is a snapshot, you must call **Requery** to reflect edits by other users as well as additions and deletions.

For either a dynaset or a snapshot, call **Requery** any time you want to rebuild the recordset using a new filter or sort, or new parameter values. Set the new filter or sort property by assigning new values to **m_strFilter** and **m_strSort** before calling **Requery**. Set new parameters by assigning new values to parameter data members before calling **Requery**. If the filter and sort strings are unchanged, you can reuse the query, which improves performance.

If the attempt to rebuild the recordset fails, the recordset is closed. Before you call **Requery**, you can determine whether the recordset can be requeried by calling the **CanRestart** member function. **CanRestart** does not guarantee that **Requery** will succeed.

Caution Call **Requery** only after you have called **Open**.

See Also   **CRecordset::CanRestart, CRecordset::m_strFilter, CRecordset::m_strSort**

Example   This example rebuilds a recordset to apply a different sort order.

```
CCustSet rsCustSet( NULL ); // Open the recordset
rsCustSet.Open( );
// Use the recordset ...
// Set the sort order and Requery the recordset
rsCustSet.m_strSort = "District, Last_Name";
if( !rsCustSet.CanRestart( ) )
    return;                    // Unable to requery
if( !rsCustSet.Requery( ) )
    // Requery failed, so take action
```

CRecordset::SetFieldDirty

void SetFieldDirty(void* *pv*, **BOOL** *bDirty* **= TRUE**);

Parameters   *pv*   Contains the address of a field data member in the recordset or **NULL**. If
NULL, all field data members in the recordset are flagged. (C++ **NULL** is not
the same as Null in database terminology, which means "having no value.")

bDirty   **TRUE** if the field data member is to be flagged as "dirty" (changed).
Otherwise **FALSE** if the field data member is to be flagged as "clean"
(unchanged).

Remarks   Call this member function to flag a field data member of the recordset as changed or
as unchanged. Marking fields as unchanged ensures the field is not updated and
results in less SQL traffic.

The framework marks changed field data members to ensure they will be written to
the record on the data source by the record field exchange (RFX) mechanism.
Changing the value of a field generally sets the field dirty automatically, so you will
seldom need to call **SetFieldDirty** yourself, but you might sometimes want to
ensure that columns will be explicitly updated or inserted regardless of what value
is in the field data member.

Important Call this member function only after you have called **Edit** or **AddNew**.

Using **NULL** for the first argument of the function will apply the function only to **outputColumns**, not **params**. For instance, the call

```
SetFieldNull( NULL );
```

will set only **outputColumns** to **NULL**. **Params** will be unaffected.

To work on **params**, you must supply the actual address of the individual **param** you want to work on, such as:

```
SetFieldNull( &m_strParam );
```

This means you cannot set all **params NULL**, as you can with **outputColumns**.

SetFieldDirty is implemented through **DoFieldExchange**.

See Also   **CRecordset::IsFieldDirty**, **CRecordset::SetFieldNull**, **CRecordset::Edit**, **CRecordset::Update**

CRecordset::SetFieldNull

void SetFieldNull(void* *pv*, **BOOL** *bNull* = **TRUE**);

Parameters   *pv*   Contains the address of a field data member in the recordset or **NULL**. If **NULL**, all field data members in the recordset are flagged. (C++ **NULL** is not the same as Null in database terminology, which means "having no value.")

bNull   Nonzero if the field data member is to be flagged as having no value (Null). Otherwise 0 if the field data member is to be flagged as non-Null.

Remarks   Call this member function to flag a field data member of the recordset as Null (specifically having no value) or as non-Null. When you add a new record to a recordset, all field data members are initially set to a Null value and flagged as "dirty" (changed). When you retrieve a record from a data source, its columns either already have values or are Null.

For example, if you specifically wish to designate a field of the current record as not having a value, call **SetFieldNull** with *bNull* set to **TRUE** to flag it as Null. If a field was previously marked Null and you now want to give it a value, simply set its new value. You do not have to remove the Null flag with **SetFieldNull**. To determine whether the field is allowed to be Null, call **IsFieldNullable**.

Important   Call this member function only after you have called **Edit** or **AddNew**.

Using **NULL** for the first argument of the function will apply the function only to **outputColumns**, not **params**. For instance, the call

```
SetFieldNull( NULL );
```

will set only **outputColumns** to **NULL**. **Params** will be unaffected.

To work on **params**, you must supply the actual address of the individual **param** you want to work on, such as:

```
SetFieldNull( &m_strParam );
```

This means you cannot set all **params NULL**, as you can with **outputColumns**.

SetFieldNull is implemented through **DoFieldExchange**.

See Also   **CRecordset::IsFieldNull, CRecordset::SetFieldDirty, CRecordset::Edit, CRecordset::Update, CRecordset::IsFieldNullable**

CRecordset::SetLockingMode

void SetLockingMode(UINT *nMode* **);**

Parameters   *nMode*   Contains one of the following values from the **enum LockMode**:

- **optimistic**   Optimistic locking locks the record being updated only during the call to **Update**.
- **pessimistic**   Pessimistic locking locks the record as soon as **Edit** is called and keeps it locked until the **Update** call completes or you move to a new record.

Remarks   Call this member function if you need to specify which of two record-locking strategies the recordset is using for updates. By default, the locking mode of a recordset is **optimistic**. You can change that to a more cautious **pessimistic** locking strategy. Call **SetLockingMode** after you construct and open the recordset object but before you call **Edit**.

See Also   **CRecordset::Edit, CRecordset::Update**

CRecordset::Update

virtual BOOL Update( );
throw(CDBException);

Return Value   Nonzero if one record was successfully updated; otherwise 0 if no columns have changed. If no records were updated, or if more than one record was updated, an exception is thrown. An exception is also thrown for any other failure on the data source.

Remarks
Call this member function after a call to the **AddNew** or **Edit** member function. This call is required to complete the **AddNew** or **Edit** operation.

Both **AddNew** and **Edit** prepare an edit buffer in which the added or edited data is placed for saving to the data source. **Update** saves the data. Only those fields marked or detected as changed are updated.

If the data source supports transactions, you can make the **Update** call (and its corresponding **AddNew** or **Edit** call) part of a transaction. For more information about transactions, see the article "Transaction" in *Programming with the Microsoft Foundation Class Library*.

> **Caution** If you call **Update** without first calling either **AddNew** or **Edit**, **Update** throws a **CDBException**. If you call **AddNew** or **Edit**, you must call **Update** before you call **MoveNext** or close either the recordset or the data source connection. Otherwise, your changes are lost without notification.

For details on handling **Update** failures, see the article "Recordset: How Recordsets Update Records" in *Programming with the Microsoft Foundation Class Library*.

See Also
CRecordset::Edit, CRecordset::AddNew, CRecordset::SetFieldDirty, CDBException

Example
See the example for **CRecordset::AddNew**.

Data Members

CRecordset::m_hstmt

Remarks
Contains a handle to the ODBC statement data structure, of type **HSTMT**, associated with the recordset. Each query to an ODBC data source is associated with an **HSTMT**.

> **Caution** Do not use **m_hstmt** before **Open** has been called.

Normally you do not need to access the **HSTMT** directly, but you might need it for direct execution of SQL statements. The **ExecuteSQL** member function of class **CDatabase** provides an example of using **m_hstmt**.

See Also
CDatabase::ExecuteSQL

CRecordset::m_nFields

Remarks
Contains the number of field data members in the recordset class—the number of columns selected by the recordset from the data source. The constructor for the recordset class must initialize **m_nFields** with the correct number. ClassWizard writes this initialization for you when you use it to declare your recordset class. You can also write it manually.

The framework uses this number to manage interaction between the field data members and the corresponding columns of the current record on the data source.

Important This number must correspond to the number of "output columns" registered in **DoFieldExchange** after a call to **SetFieldType** with the parameter **CFieldExchange::outputColumn**.

You can bind columns dynamically, as explained in the article "Recordset: Dynamically Binding Data Columns." If you do so, you must increase the count in **m_nFields** to reflect the number of RFX function calls in your **DoFieldExchange** member function for the dynamically bound columns.

See Also
CRecordset::m_nParams

In *Programming with the Microsoft Foundation Class Library*: "Recordset: Dynamically Binding Data Columns"

Example
See the article "Record Field Exchange: Using RFX" in Programming with the Microsoft Foundation Class Library

CRecordset::m_nParams

Remarks
Contains the number of parameter data members in the recordset class—the number of parameters passed with the recordset's query. If your recordset class has any parameter data members, the constructor for the class must initialize **m_nParams** with the correct number. The value of **m_nParams** defaults to 0. If you add parameter data members—which you must do manually—you must also manually add an initialization in the class constructor to reflect the number of parameters (which must be at least as large as the number of '?' placeholders in your **m_strFilter** or **m_strSort** string).

The framework uses this number when it parameterizes the recordset's query.

Important This number must correspond to the number of "params" registered in **DoFieldExchange** after a call to **SetFieldType** with the parameter **CFieldExchange::param**.

See Also
CRecordset::m_nFields

Example See the articles "Recordset: Parameterizing a Recordset" and "Record Field Exchange: Using RFX." in *Programming with the Microsoft Foundation Class Library*.

CRecordset::m_pDatabase

Remarks Contains a pointer to the **CDatabase** object through which the recordset is connected to a data source. This variable is set in two ways. Typically, you pass a pointer to an already connected **CDatabase** object when you construct the recordset object. If you pass **NULL** instead, **CRecordset** creates a **CDatabase** object for you and connects it. In either case, **CRecordset** stores the pointer in this variable.

Normally you will not directly need to use the pointer stored in **m_pDatabase**. If you write your own extensions to **CRecordset**, however, you might need to use the pointer. For example, you might need the pointer if you throw your own **CDBException**s. Or you might need it if you need to do something using the same **CDatabase** object, such as running transactions, setting timeouts, or calling the **ExecuteSQL** member function of class **CDatabase** to execute SQL statements directly.

CRecordset::m_strFilter

Remarks After you construct the recordset object, but before you call its **Open** member function, use this data member to store a **CString** containing an SQL **WHERE** clause. The recordset uses this string to constrain—or filter—the records it selects during the **Open** or **Requery** call. This is useful for selecting a subset of records, such as "all salespersons based in California" ("state = CA"). The ODBC SQL syntax for a **WHERE** clause is

```
WHERE search-condition
```

Note that you do not include the **WHERE** keyword in your string. The framework supplies it.

You can also parameterize your filter string by placing '?' placeholders in it, declaring a parameter data member in your class for each placeholder, and passing parameters to the recordset at run time. This lets you construct the filter at run time.

For more information about SQL **WHERE** clauses, see the article "SQL." For more information about selecting and filtering records, see the article "Recordset: Filtering Records."

See Also **CRecordset::m_strSort**, **CRecordset::Requery**

In *Programming with the Microsoft Foundation Class Library*: "Recordset: Parameterizing a Recordset," "SQL," "Recordset: Filtering Records."

Example
```
CCustSet rsCustSet( NULL );              // Construct a snapshot object
rsCustSet.m_strFilter = "state = 'CA'";  // Set its filter
// Run the filtered query
rsCustSet.Open( CRecordset::snapshot, "Customers" );
```

CRecordset::m_strSort

Remarks

After you construct the recordset object, but before you call its **Open** member function, use this data member to store a **CString** containing an SQL **ORDER BY** clause. The recordset uses this string to sort the records it selects during the **Open** or **Requery** call. You can use this feature to sort a recordset on one or more columns. The ODBC SQL syntax for an **ORDER BY** clause is

```
ORDER BY sort-specification [, sort-specification]...
```

where a sort-specification is an integer or a column name. You can also specify ascending or descending order (the order is ascending by default) by appending "ASC" or "DESC" to the column list in the sort string. The selected records are sorted first by the first column listed, then by the second, and so on. For example, you might order a "Customers" recordset by last name, then first name. The number of columns you can list depends on the data source. For more information, see the ODBC SDK *Programmer's Reference*.

Note that you do not include the **ORDER BY** keyword in your string. The framework supplies it.

See Also

CRecordset::m_strFilter, **CRecordset::Requery**

In *Programming with the Microsoft Foundation Class Library*: "SQL," "Recordset: Sorting Records."

Example
```
CCustSet rsCustSet( NULL );              // Construct a snapshot object
rsCustSet.m_strSort = "District, Last_Name"; // Set its sort string
rsCustSet.Open( CRecordset::snapshot, "Customers" );    // Run the
sorted query
```

class CRecordView : public CFormView

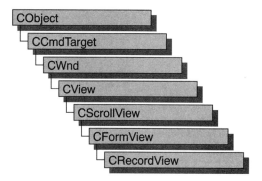

A **CRecordView** object is a view that displays database records in controls. The view is a form view directly connected to a **CRecordset** object. The view is created from a dialog template resource and displays the fields of the **CRecordset** object in the dialog template's controls. The **CRecordView** object uses dialog data exchange (DDX) and record field exchange (RFX) to automate the movement of data between the controls on the form and the fields of the recordset. **CRecordView** also supplies a default implementation for moving to the first, next, previous, or last record and an interface for updating the record currently on view.

The most common way to create your record view is with AppWizard. AppWizard creates both the record view class and its associated recordset class as part of your skeleton starter application. If you don't create the record view class with AppWizard, you can create it later with ClassWizard. If you simply need a single form, the AppWizard approach is easier. ClassWizard lets you decide to use a record view later in the development process. Using ClassWizard to create a record view and a recordset separately and then connect them is the most flexible approach because it gives you more control in naming the recordset class and its .H/.CPP files. This approach also lets you have multiple record views on the same recordset class.

To make it easy for end-users to move from record to record in the record view, AppWizard creates menu (and optionally toolbar) resources for moving to the first, next, previous, or last record. If you create a record view class with ClassWizard, you need to create these resources yourself with the menu and bitmap editors. For more information about these resources, see the articles "AppWizard: Database Support" and "ClassWizard: Creating a Database Form."

For information about the default implementation for moving from record to record, see **IsOnFirstRecord** and **IsOnLastRecord** and the article "Record Views: Using a Record View."

CRecordView keeps track of the user's position in the recordset so that the record view can update the user interface. When the user moves to either end of the recordset, the record view disables user interface objects—such as menu items or toolbar buttons—for moving further in the same direction.

For more information about declaring and using your record view and recordset classes, see the article "Designing and Creating a Record View." For more information about how record views work and how to use them, see the articles "Forms" and "Record Views: Using a Record View. All the articles mentioned above are in *Programming with the Microsoft Foundation Class Library*.

#include <afxdb.h>

See Also   **CRecordset**, **CFormView**

In *Programming with the Microsoft Foundation Class Library*: "AppWizard," "ClassWizard"

Construction

CRecordView	Constructs a CRecordView object.

Attributes

OnGetRecordset	Returns a pointer to an object of a class derived from CRecordset. ClassWizard overrides this function for you and creates the recordset if necessary.
IsOnFirstRecord	Returns nonzero if the current record is the first record in the associated recordset.
IsOnLastRecord	Returns nonzero if the current record is the last record in the associated recordset.

Operations

OnMove	If the current record has changed, updates it on the data source, then moves to the specified record (next, previous, first, or last).

Member Functions

CRecordView::CRecordView

CRecordView(LPCSTR *lpszTemplateName* **);**

CRecordView(UINT *nIDTemplate* **);**

Parameters   *lpszTemplateName*   Contains a null-terminated string that is the name of a dialog template resource.

nIDTemplate   Contains the ID number of a dialog template resource.

Remarks   When you create an object of a type derived from **CRecordView**, call either form of the constructor to initialize the view object and identify the dialog resource on which the view is based. You can either identify the resource by name (pass a string as the argument to the constructor) or by its ID (pass an unsigned integer as the argument). Using a resource ID is recommended.

Note Your derived class *must* supply its own constructor. In the constructor of your derived class, call the constructor **CRecordView::CRecordView** with the resource name or ID as an argument, as shown in the example below.

CRecordView::OnInitialUpdate calls **UpdateData**, which calls **DoDataExchange**. This initial call to **DoDataExchange** connects **CRecordView** controls (indirectly) to **CRecordset** field data members created by ClassWizard. These data members cannot be used until after you call the base class **CFormView::OnInitialUpdate** member function.

Note If you use ClassWizard, the wizard defines an **enum** value `CRecordView::IDD` and specifies it in the member initialization list for the constructor where you see `IDD_MYFORM` in the example. The example shows how you can specify the dialog template resource ID if you write the code yourself without the wizard.

See Also   **CRecordset::DoFieldExchange**, **CView::OnInitialUpdate**, **CWnd::UpdateData**

Example
```
CMyRecordView::CMyRecordView()
    : CRecordView( IDD_MYFORM )
{
    //{{AFX_DATA_INIT( CMyRecordView )
        // NOTE: the ClassWizard will add member initialization here
    //}}AFX_DATA_INIT
    // Other construction code, such as data initialization
}
```

CRecordView::IsOnFirstRecord

BOOL IsOnFirstRecord( );

Return Value   Nonzero if the current record is the first record in the recordset; otherwise 0.

Remarks   Call this member function to determine whether the current record is the first record in the recordset object associated with this record view. This function is useful for writing your own implementations of the default command update handlers written by ClassWizard.

If the user moves to the first record, the framework disables any user interface objects you have for moving to the first or the previous record.

See Also   **CRecordView::OnMove, CRecordView::IsOnLastRecord, CRecordset::IsBOF, CRecordset::GetRecordCount**

CRecordView::IsOnLastRecord

BOOL IsOnLastRecord( );

Return Value   Nonzero if the current record is the last record in the recordset; otherwise 0.

Remarks   Call this member function to determine whether the current record is the last record in the recordset object associated with this record view. This function is useful for writing your own implementations of the default command update handlers that ClassWizard writes to support a user interface for moving from record to record.

Caution The result of this function is reliable except that the view cannot detect the end of the recordset until the user has moved past it. The user must move beyond the last record before the record view can tell that it must disable any user interface objects for moving to the next or last record. If the user moves past the last record and then moves back to the last record (or before it), the record view can track the user's position in the recordset and disable user interface objects correctly. **IsOnLastRecord** is also unreliable after a call to the implementation function **OnRecordLast**, which handles the **ID_RECORD_LAST** command, or **CRecordset::MoveLast**.

See Also   **CRecordView::OnMove, CRecordView::IsOnFirstRecord, CRecordset::IsEOF, CRecordset::GetRecordCount**

CRecordView::OnGetRecordset

virtual CRecordset* OnGetRecordset( ) = 0;

Return Value   A pointer to a **CRecordset**-derived object if the object was successfully created; otherwise a **NULL** pointer.

Remarks   Returns a pointer to the **CRecordset**-derived object associated with the record view. You must override this member function to construct or obtain a recordset object and return a pointer to it. If you declare your record view class with ClassWizard, the wizard writes a default override for you. ClassWizard's default implementation returns the recordset pointer stored in the record view if one exists. If not, it constructs a recordset object of the type you specified with ClassWizard and calls its **Open** member function to open the table or run the query, and then returns a pointer to the object.

For more information and examples, see the article "Record Views: Using a Record View" in *Programming with the Microsoft Foundation Class Library*.

See Also   **CRecordset, CRecordset::Open**

CRecordView::OnMove

virtual BOOL OnMove(UINT *nIDMoveCommand*);
  throw(CDBException);

Return Value   Nonzero if the move was successful; otherwise 0 if the move request was denied.

Parameters   *nIDMoveCommand*   One of the following standard command ID values:

- **ID_RECORD_FIRST**   Move to the first record in the recordset.
- **ID_RECORD_LAST**   Move to the last record in the recordset.
- **ID_RECORD_NEXT**   Move to the next record in the recordset.
- **ID_RECORD_PREV**   Move to the previous record in the recordset.

Remarks   Call this member function to move to a different record in the recordset and display its fields in the controls of the record view. The default implementation calls the appropriate Move member function of the **CRecordset** object associated with the record view.

By default, **OnMove** updates the current record on the data source if the user has changed it in the record view.

AppWizard creates a menu resource with First Record, Last Record, Next Record, and Previous Record menu items. If you select the Initial Toolbar option, AppWizard also creates a toolbar with buttons corresponding to these commands.

If you move past the last record in the recordset, the record view continues to display the last record. If you move backward past the first record, the record view continues to display the first record.

Caution   Calling **OnMove** throws an exception if the recordset has no records. Call the appropriate user interface update handler function—**OnUpdateRecordFirst**, **OnUpdateRecordLast**, **OnUpdateRecordNext**, or **OnUpdateRecordPrev**—before the corresponding move operation to determine whether the recordset has any records. For information about the update handlers, see the article "AppWizard: Database Support" in *Programming with the Microsoft Foundation Class Library*.

See Also   **CRecordset::Move**

class CRect : public tagRECT

The **CRect** class is similar to a Windows **RECT** structure and also includes member functions to manipulate **CRect** objects and Windows **RECT** structures. A **CRect** object can be passed as a function parameter wherever an **LPRECT** or **RECT** structure can be passed.

A **CRect** contains member variables that define the top-left and bottom-right points of a rectangle. The width or height of the rectangle defined by **CRect** must not exceed 32,767 units.

When specifying a **CRect**, you must be careful to construct it so that the top-left point is above and to the left of the bottom-right point in the Windows coordinate system; otherwise, the **CRect** will not be recognized by some functions, such as **IntersectRect**, **UnionRect**, and **PtInRect**. For example, a top left of (10,10) and bottom right of (20,20) defines a valid rectangle; a top left of (20,20) and bottom right of (10,10), an empty rectangle.

Use caution when manipulating a **CRect** with the **CDC::DPtoLP** and **CDC::LPtoDP** member functions. If the mapping mode of a display context is such that the y-extent is negative, as in **MM_LOENGLISH**, then **CDC::DPtoLP** will transform the **CRect** so that its top is greater than the bottom. Functions such as **Height** and **Size** will then return negative values for the height of the transformed **CRect**.

When using overloaded **CRect** operators, the first operator must be a **CRect**; the second can be either a **RECT** structure or a **CRect** object.

#include <afxwin.h>

See Also   **CPoint**, **CSize**

Construction
CRect   Constructs a **CRect** object.

Operations
Width	Calculates the width of **CRect**.
Height	Calculates the height of **CRect**.
Size	Calculates the size of **CRect**.
TopLeft	Returns a reference to the top-left point of **CRect**.
BottomRight	Returns a reference to the bottom-right point of **CRect**.
IsRectEmpty	Determines whether **CRect** is empty. **CRect** is empty if the width and/or height are 0.

IsRectNull	Determines whether the **top**, **bottom**, **left**, and **right** member variables are all equal to 0.
PtInRect	Determines whether the specified point lies within **CRect**.
SetRect	Sets the dimensions of **CRect**.
SetRectEmpty	Sets **CRect** to an empty rectangle (all coordinates equal to 0).
CopyRect	Copies the dimensions of a source rectangle to **CRect**.
EqualRect	Determines whether **CRect** is equal to the given rectangle.
InflateRect	Increases or decreases the width and height of **CRect**.
NormalizeRect	Standardizes the height and width of **CRect**.
OffsetRect	Moves **CRect** by the specified offsets.
SubtractRect	Subtracts one rectangle from another.
IntersectRect	Sets **CRect** equal to the intersection of two rectangles.
UnionRect	Sets **CRect** equal to the union of two rectangles.

Operators

operator LPCRECT	Converts a **CRect** to an **LPCRECT**.
operator LPRECT	Converts a **CRect** to an **LPRECT**.
operator =	Copies the dimensions of a rectangle to **CRect**.
operator ==	Determines whether **CRect** is equal to a rectangle.
operator !=	Determines whether **CRect** is not equal to a rectangle.
operator +=	Adds the specified offsets to **CRect**.
operator -=	Subtracts the specified offsets from **CRect**.
operator &=	Sets **CRect** equal to the intersection of **CRect** and a rectangle.
operator |=	Sets **CRect** equal to the union of **CRect** and a rectangle.
operator +	Adds the given offsets to **CRect** and returns the resulting **CRect**.
operator -	Subtracts the given offsets from **CRect** and returns the resulting **CRect**.
operator &	Creates the intersection of **CRect** and a rectangle and returns the resulting **CRect**.
operator |	Creates the union of **CRect** and a rectangle and returns the resulting **CRect**.

Member Functions

CRect::BottomRight

CPoint& BottomRight( );

Return Value   **CPOINT&**, a reference to a **CPoint** object.

Remarks   Returns a reference to the bottom-right point of **CRect**.

CRect::CopyRect

void CopyRect(LPCRECT *lpSrcRect* **);**

Parameters   *lpSrcRect*   Points to the **RECT** structure or **CRect** object whose dimensions are to be copied.

Remarks   Copies the *lpSrcRect* rectangle to the **CRect** object.

See Also   **::CRect**, **CRect::operator =**

CRect::CRect

CRect( );

CRect(int *l*, **int** *t*, **int** *r*, **int** *b* **);**

CRect(const RECT& *srcRect* **);**

CRect(LPCRECT *lpSrcRect* **);**

CRect(POINT *point*, **SIZE** *size* **);**

Parameters   *l*   Specifies the left position of the **CRect**.

t   Specifies the top of the **CRect**.

r   Specifies the right position of the **CRect**.

b   Specifies the bottom of the **CRect**.

srcRect   Refers to the **RECT** structure with the coordinates for the **CRect** object.

lpSrcRect   Points to the **RECT** structure with the coordinates for the **CRect** object.

point   Specifies the origin point for the rectangle to be constructed. Corresponds to the top-left corner.

size   Specifies the displacement from the top-left corner to the bottom-right corner of the rectangle to be constructed.

Remarks   Constructs a **CRect** object. The **CRect(const RECT&)** and **CRect(LPCRECT)** constructors perform a **CopyRect**. The other constructors initialize the member variables of the object directly.

See Also   **CRect::SetRect**, **CRect::CopyRect**, **CRect::operator =**

CRect::EqualRect

BOOL EqualRect(LPCRECT *lpRect* **) const;**

Return Value   Nonzero if the two rectangles have the same top, left, bottom, and right values; otherwise 0.

Parameters   *lpRect*   Points to a **RECT** structure or **CRect** object that contains the upper-left and lower-right corner coordinates of a rectangle.

See Also   In the Win32 *Programmer's Reference*: **::EqualRect**

CRect::Height

int Height( ) const;

Return Value   The height of **CRect**.

Remarks   Calculates the height of **CRect** by subtracting the top value from the bottom value. The resulting value may be negative.

CRect::InflateRect

void InflateRect(int *x*, **int** *y* **);**

void InflateRect(SIZE *size* **);**

Parameters   *x*   Specifies the amount to increase or decrease the width of **CRect**. It must be negative to decrease the width.

y   Specifies the amount to increase or decrease the height of **CRect**. It must be negative to decrease the height.

size   Contains a **SIZE** or **CSize** that specifies the amounts to add to the **CRect**'s height and width.

Remarks   The parameters of **InflateRect** are signed values; positive values inflate the **CRect** and negative values deflate it. When inflated, the width of **CRect** is increased by two times *x* and its height is increased by two times *y*.

See Also   In the Win32 *Programmer's Reference*: **::InflateRect**

CRect::IntersectRect

BOOL IntersectRect(LPCRECT *lpRect1*, **LPCRECT** *lpRect2* **);**

Return Value   Nonzero if the intersection is not empty; 0 if the intersection is empty.

Parameters   *lpRect1*   Points to a **RECT** structure or **CRect** object that contains a source rectangle.

lpRect2   Points to a **RECT** structure or **CRect** object that contains a source rectangle.

Remarks   Makes a **CRect** equal to the intersection of two existing rectangles. The intersection is the largest rectangle contained in both existing rectangles.

Note   The value of the left coordinate must be less than the right and the top less than the bottom for both *lpRect1* and *lpRect2*.

See Also   **CRect::operator &=**, **CRect::operator &**

In the Win32 *Programmer's Reference*: **::IntersectRect**

CRect::IsRectEmpty

BOOL IsRectEmpty( ) const;

Return Value   Nonzero if **CRect** is empty; 0 if **CRect** is not empty.

Remarks   Determines whether **CRect** is empty. A rectangle is empty if the width and/or height are 0 or negative. Differs from **IsRectNull**, which determines whether the rectangle is **NULL**.

See Also   **CRect::IsRectNull**

In the Win32 *Programmer's Reference*: **::IsRectEmpty**

CRect::IsRectNull

BOOL IsRectNull( ) const;

Return Value   Nonzero if the **CRect** object's top, left, bottom, and right values are all equal to 0; otherwise 0.

Remarks   Determines whether the top, left, bottom, and right values of the **CRect** are all equal to 0. Differs from **IsRectEmpty**, which determines whether the rectangle is empty.

See Also   **CRect::IsRectEmpty**

CRect::NormalizeRect

void NormalizeRect( );

Remarks   Normalizes the **CRect** object so that both the height and width are positive. The function does a comparison of the top and bottom values, swapping them if the bottom is greater than the top. The same action is performed on the left and right values. This function is useful when dealing with different mapping modes and inverted rectangles.

Note Some functions, such as **IntersectRect** and **UnionRect**, recognize only normalized **CRect** objects.

See Also   **CRect::IntersectRect**, **CRect::UnionRect**

CRect::OffsetRect

void **OffsetRect**(int *x*, int *y*);

void **OffsetRect**(**POINT** *point*);

void **OffsetRect**(**SIZE** *size*);

Parameters   *x*   Specifies the amount to move left or right. It must be negative to move left.

y   Specifies the amount to move up or down. It must be negative to move up.

point   Contains a **POINT** or **CPoint** specifying both dimensions by which to move.

size   Contains a **SIZE** or **CSize** specifying both dimensions by which to move.

Remarks   Moves **CRect** by the specified offsets. Moves **CRect** *x* units along the x-axis and *y* units along the y-axis. The *x* and *y* parameters are signed values, so **CRect** can be moved left or right and up or down.

CRect::PtInRect

BOOL **PtInRect**(**POINT** *point*) const;

Return Value   Nonzero if the point lies within **CRect**; otherwise 0.

Parameters   *point*   Contains a **POINT** structure or **CPoint** object.

Remarks   Determines whether the specified point lies within **CRect**. A point is within **CRect** if it lies on the left or top side or is within all four sides. A point on the right or bottom side is outside **CRect**.

Note   The value of the left coordinate of **CRect** must be less than the right and the top less than the bottom.

See Also   In the Win32 *Programmer's Reference*: **::PtInRect**

CRect::SetRect

void SetRect(int *x1***, int** *y1***, int** *x2***, int** *y2* **);**

Parameters   *x1*   Specifies the x-coordinate of the upper-left corner.

y1   Specifies the y-coordinate of the upper-left corner.

x2   Specifies the x-coordinate of the lower-right corner.

y2   Specifies the y-coordinate of the lower-right corner.

Remarks   Sets the dimensions of **CRect** to the specified coordinates.

See Also   **CRect::CRect, CRect::SetRectEmpty**

In the Win32 *Programmer's Reference*: **::SetRect**

CRect::SetRectEmpty

void SetRectEmpty( );

Remarks   Creates a **NULL** rectangle (all coordinates equal to 0).

See Also   In the Win32 *Programmer's Reference*: **::SetRectEmpty**

CRect::Size

CSize Size( ) const;

Return Value   The **CRect** width and height encapsulated as the **cx** and **cy** member variables of a **CSize** object.

CRect::SubtractRect

BOOL SubtractRect(LPCRECT *lpRectSrc1*, **LPCRECT** *lpRectSrc2* **);**

Return Value   Nonzero if the function is successful; otherwise 0.

Parameters   *lpRectSrc1*   Points to the **RECT** structure from which a rectangle is to be subtracted.

    lpRectSrc2   Points to the **RECT** structure that is to be subtracted from the rectangle pointed to by the *lpRectSrc1* parameter.

Remarks   Makes the dimensions of a **CRect** object equal to the subtraction of *lpRectSrc2* from *lpRectSrc1*. The rectangle specified by *lpRectSrc2* is subtracted from the rectangle specified by *lpRectSrc1* only when the rectangles intersect completely in either the x- or y-direction. For example, if *lpRectSrc1* were (10,10, 100,100) and *lpRectSrc2* were (50,50, 150,150), the rectangle pointed to by *lpRectSrc1* would contain the same coordinates as the original *lpRectSrc1* when the function returned. If *lpRectSrc1* were (10,10, 100,100) and *lpRectSrc2* were (50,10, 150,150), however, the rectangle pointed to by *lpRectSrc1* would contain the coordinates (10,10, 50,100) when the function returned.

See Also   **CRect::IntersectRect**

    In the Win32 *Programmer's Reference*: **::UnionRect**, **::SubtractRect**

CRect::TopLeft

CPoint& TopLeft( );

Return Value   A reference to the top-left point of **CRect**.

CRect::UnionRect

BOOL UnionRect(LPCRECT *lpRect1*, **LPCRECT** *lpRect2* **);**

Return Value   Nonzero if the union is not empty; 0 if the union is empty.

Parameters   *lpRect1*   Points to a **RECT** or **CRect** that contains a source rectangle.

    lpRect2   Points to a **RECT** or **CRect** that contains a source rectangle.

Remarks   Makes the dimensions of **CRect** equal to the union of the two source rectangles. The union is the smallest rectangle that contains both source rectangles. Windows ignores the dimensions of an empty rectangle; that is, a rectangle that has no height or has no width.

Note	The value of the left coordinate must be less than the right and the top less than the bottom for both *lpRect1* and *lpRect2*.

See Also   **CRect::operator |=**, **CRect::operator |**

In the Win32 *Programmer's Reference*: **::UnionRect**

CRect::Width

int Width( ) const;

Return Value   The width of **CRect**.

Remarks   Calculates the width of **CRect** by subtracting the left value from the right value. The width may be negative.

Operators

CRect::operator LPCRECT

operator LPCRECT( ) const;

Remarks   Converts a **CRect** to an **LPCRECT** with no need for the address-of (**&**) operator.

CRect::operator LPRECT

operator LPRECT( );

Remarks   Converts a **CRect** defined as a constant to an **LPRECT** with no need for the address-of (**&**) operator.

CRect::operator =

void operator =(const RECT& *srcRect* **);**

Parameters   *srcRect*   Refers to a source rectangle. May be a **RECT** or **CRect**.

Remarks   Copies the dimensions of *srcRect* to **CRect**.

See Also   **CRect::SetRect**

In the Win32 *Programmer's Reference*: **::CopyRect**

CRect::operator ==

BOOL operator ==(const RECT& *rect* **) const;**

Return Value If the values of these coordinates are equal, returns nonzero; otherwise 0.

Parameters *rect* Refers to a source rectangle. May be a **RECT** or **CRect**.

Remarks Determines whether *rect* is equal to **CRect** by comparing the coordinates of their upper-left and lower-right corners.

See Also In the Win32 *Programmer's Reference*: **::EqualRect**

CRect::operator !=

BOOL operator !=(const RECT& *rect* **) const;**

Return Value Nonzero if not equal; otherwise 0.

Parameters *rect* Refers to a source rectangle. May be a **RECT** or **CRect**.

Remarks Determines whether *rect* is not equal to **CRect** by comparing the coordinates of their upper-left and lower-right corners.

See Also **CRect::operator ==**

CRect::operator +=

void operator +=(POINT *point* **);**

Parameters *point* Contains a **POINT** or **CPoint**.

Remarks Moves **CRect** by the specified offsets. The *point* parameter's *x* and *y* parameters are added to **CRect**.

See Also **CRect::OffsetRect**

CRect::operator –=

void operator –=(POINT *point* **);**

Parameters *point* Contains a **POINT** or **CPoint**.

Remarks Moves **CRect** by the specified offsets. The *point* parameter's *x* and *y* parameters are subtracted from **CRect**.

See Also **CRect::OffsetRect**

CRect::operator &=

void operator &=(const RECT& *rect* **);**

Parameters   *rect*   Contains a **RECT** or **CRect**.

Remarks   Sets **CRect** equal to the intersection of **CRect** and *rect*. The intersection is the largest rectangle contained in both rectangles.

Note The value of the left coordinate must be less than the right and the top less than the bottom for both **CRect** and *rect*.

See Also   **CRect::IntersectRect**

CRect::operator |=

void operator |=(const RECT& *rect* **);**

Parameters   *rect*   Contains a **CRect** or **RECT**.

Remarks   Sets **CRect** equal to the union of **CRect** and *rect*. The union is the smallest rectangle that contains both source rectangles. Windows ignores the dimensions of an empty rectangle; that is, a rectangle that has no height or has no width.

Note The value of the left coordinate must be less than the right and the top less than the bottom for both **CRect** and *rect*.

See Also   **CRect::UnionRect**

CRect::operator +

CRect operator +(POINT *point* **) const;**

Return Value   The **CRect** resulting from the offset by *point*.

Parameters   *point*   Contains a **POINT** or **CPoint**.

Remarks   Returns a new **CRect** that is equal to **CRect** displaced by *point*. The *point* parameter's *x* and *y* parameters are added to **CRect**'s position.

See Also   **CRect::OffsetRect**

CRect::operator –

CRect operator –(POINT *point* **) const;**

Return Value   The **CRect** resulting from the offset by *point*.

Parameters   *point*   Contains a **POINT** or **CPoint**.

Remarks   A new **CRect** that is equal to **CRect** displaced by *–point*. The *point* parameter's *x* and *y* parameters are subtracted from **CRect**'s dimensions.

See Also   **CRect::OffsetRect**

CRect::operator &

CRect operator &(const RECT& *rect2* **) const;**

Return Value   A **CRect** that is the intersection of **CRect** and *rect2*. The intersection is the largest rectangle contained in both rectangles.

Note The value of the left coordinate must be less than the right and the top less than the bottom for both **CRect** and *rect2*.

Parameters   *rect2*   Contains a **RECT** or **CRect**.

See Also   **CRect::IntersectRect**

CRect::operator |

CRect operator |(const RECT& *rect2* **) const;**

Return Value   A **CRect** that is the union of **CRect** and *rect2*. A union is the smallest rectangle that contains both source rectangles. Windows ignores the dimensions of an empty rectangle; that is, a rectangle that has no height or has no width.

Note The value of the left coordinate must be less than the right and the top less than the bottom for both **CRect** and *rect2*.

Parameters   *rect2*   Contains a **RECT** or **CRect**.

See Also   **CRect::UnionRect**

class CRectTracker

The **CRectTracker** class allows an in-place item to be displayed, moved, and resized in different fashions. Borders can be solid or dotted lines. You can place eight resize handles on either the outside or the inside border of the item. The item can be given a hatched border or overlaid with a hatched pattern to indicate different states of the in-place item. Finally, a **CRectTracker** allows you to change the orientation of an item during resizing. Although the **CRectTracker** class is designed to allow the user to interact with OLE items by using a graphical interface, its use is not restricted to OLE-enabled applications. It can be used anywhere such a user interface is required.

To use **CRectTracker**, construct a **CRectTracker** object and specify which display states are initialized. You can then use this interface to give the user visual feedback on the current status of the OLE item associated with the **CRectTracker** object.

#include <afxext.h>

See Also   **COleResizeBar**, **CRect**

In *Programming with the Microsoft Foundation Class Library*: "Trackers"

Data Members

m_nHandleSize	Determines size of handles.
m_rect	Current position (in pixels) of the rectangle.
m_sizeMin	Determines minimum rectangle width and height.
m_nStyle	Current style(s) of the tracker.

Construction

CRectTracker	Constructs a **CRectTracker** object.

Operations

Draw	Renders the rectangle.
GetTrueRect	Returns width and height of rectangle including resize handles.
HitTest	Returns the current position of the cursor related to the **CRectTracker** object.
NormalizeHit	Normalizes a hit-test code.

SetCursor	Sets the cursor, depending on its position over the rectangle.
Track	Allows the user to manipulate the rectangle.
TrackRubberBand	Allows the user to "rubber-band" the selection.

Overridables

AdjustRect	Called when the rectangle is resized.
DrawTrackerRect	Called when drawing the border of a **CRectTracker** object.
OnChangedRect	Called when the rectangle has been resized or moved.

Member Functions

CRectTracker::AdjustRect

virtual void AdjustRect(int *nHandle***, LPRECT** *lpRect* **);**

Parameters   *nHandle*   Index of handle used.

lpRect   Pointer to the current size of the rectangle.

Remarks   Called by the framework when the tracking rectangle is resized by using a resize handle. Default behavior of this function allows the rectangle's orientation to change only when **Track** and **TrackRubberBand** are called with inverting allowed.

Override this function to control the adjustment of the tracking rectangle during a dragging operation. One method is to adjust the coordinates specified by *lpRect* before returning.

Special features that are not directly supported by **CRectTracker**, such as snap-to-grid or keep-aspect-ratio, can be implemented by overriding this function.

See Also   **CRectTracker::Track, CRectTracker::TrackRubberBand, CRectTracker::OnChangedRect**

CRectTracker::CRectTracker

CRectTracker( );

CRectTracker(LPCRECT *lpSrcRect***, UINT** *nStyle* **);**

Parameters   *lpSrcRect*   The coordinates of the rectangle object.

nStyle   Specifies the style of the **CRectTracker** object. The following styles are supported:

- **CRectTracker::solidLine**   Use a solid line for the rectangle border.
- **CRectTracker::dottedLine**   Use a dotted line for the rectangle border.
- **CRectTracker::hatchedBorder**   Use a hatched pattern for the rectangle border.
- **CRectTracker::resizeInside**   Resize handles located inside the rectangle.
- **CRectTracker::resizeOutside**   Resize handles located outside the rectangle.
- **CRectTracker::hatchInside**   Hatched pattern covers the entire rectangle.

Remarks   Creates and initializes a **CRectTracker** object.

The default constructor initializes the **CRectTracker** object with the values from *lpSrcRect* and initializes other sizes to system defaults. If the object is created with no parameters, the **m_rect** and **m_nStyle** data members are uninitialized.

See Also   **CRect::CRect**

CRectTracker::Draw

void Draw(CDC* *pDC* **) const;**

Parameters   *pDC*   Pointer to the device context on which to draw.

Remarks   Call this function to draw the rectangle's outer lines and inner region. The style of the tracker determines how the drawing is done. See the constructor for **CRectTracker** for more information on the styles available.

See Also   **CRectTracker::DrawTrackerRect**, **CRectTracker::CRectTracker**, **CRect::NormalizeRect**

CRectTracker::DrawTrackerRect

virtual void DrawTrackerRect(LPCRECT *lpRect*, **CWnd*** *pWndClipTo*, **CDC*** *pDC*, **CWnd*** *pWnd* **);**

Parameters   *lpRect*   Pointer to the **RECT** that contains the rectangle to draw.

pWndClipTo   Pointer to the window to use in clipping the rectangle.

pDC   Pointer to the device context on which to draw.

pWnd   Pointer to the window on which the drawing will occur.

Remarks   Called by the framework whenever the position of the tracker has changed while inside the **Track** or **TrackRubberBand** member function. The default implementation makes a call to **CDC::DrawFocusRect**, which draws a dotted rectangle.

Override this function to provide different feedback during the tracking operation.

See Also   **CRectTracker::Track**, **CRectTracker::TrackRubberBand**, **CDC::DrawFocusRect**

CRectTracker::GetTrueRect

void GetTrueRect(LPRECT *lpTrueRect* **) const;**

Parameters   *lpTrueRect*   Pointer to the **RECT** structure that will contain the device coordinates of the **CRectTracker** object.

Remarks   Call this function to retrieve the coordinates of the rectangle. The dimensions of the rectangle include the height and width of any resize handles located on the outer border. Upon returning, **lpTrueRect* is always a normalized rectangle in device coordinates.

See Also   **CRect::NormalizeRect**

CRectTracker::HitTest

int HitTest(CPoint *point* **) const;**

Return Value   The value returned is based on the enumerated type **CRectTracker::TrackerHit** and can have one of the following values:

- **CRectTracker::hitNothing**   −1
- **CRectTracker::hitTopLeft**   0
- **CRectTracker::hitTopRight**   1
- **CRectTracker::hitBottomRight**   2
- **CRectTracker:hitBottomLeft**   3
- **CRectTracker:hitTop**   4
- **CRectTracker:hitRight**   5
- **CRectTracker:hitBottom**   6
- **CRectTracker:hitLeft**   7
- **CRectTracker:hitMiddle**   8

Parameters   *point*   The point, in device coordinates, to test.

Remarks	Call this function to find out whether the user has grabbed a resize handle.
See Also	**CRectTracker::NormalizeHit**, **CRectTracker::SetCursor**

CRectTracker::NormalizeHit

int NormalizeHit(int *nHandle* **) const;**

Return Value	The index of the normalized handle.
Parameters	*nHandle* Handle selected by the user.
Remarks	Call this function to convert a potentially inverted handle.
	When **CRectTracker::Track** or **CRectTracker::TrackRubberBand** are called with inverting allowed, it is possible for the rectangle to be inverted on the x-axis, the y-axis, or both. When this happens, **HitTest** will return handles that are also inverted with respect to the rectangle. This is inappropriate for drawing cursor feedback because the feedback depends on the screen position of the rectangle, not the portion of the rectangle data structure that will be modified.
See Also	**CRectTracker::HitTest**, **CRectTracker::Track**, **CRectTracker::TrackRubberBand**

CRectTracker::OnChangedRect

virtual void OnChangedRect(const CRect& *rectOld* **);**

Parameters	*rectOld* Contains the old device coordinates of the **CRectTracker** object.
Remarks	Called by the framework whenever the tracker rectangle has changed during a call to **Track**. At the time this function is called, all feedback drawn with **DrawTrackerRect** has been removed. The default implementation of this function does nothing.
	Override this function when you want to perform any actions after the rectangle has been resized.
See Also	**CRectTracker::AdjustRect**, **CRectTracker::Track**, **CRectTracker::TrackRubberBand**

CRectTracker::SetCursor

BOOL SetCursor(CWnd* *pWnd***, UINT** *nHitTest* **) const;**

Return Value	Nonzero if the previous hit was over the tracker rectangle; otherwise 0.
Parameters	*pWnd* Points to the window that currently contains the cursor.

nHitTest   Results of the previous hit test, from the **WM_SETCURSOR** message.

Remarks   Call this function to change the cursor shape while it is over the **CRectTracker** object's region.

Call this function from inside the function of your window that handles the **WM_SETCURSOR** message (typically **OnSetCursor**).

See Also   **CRectTracker::NormalizeHit**, **CRectTracker::HitTest**, **CWinApp::LoadCursor**, **CWnd::OnSetCursor**

CRectTracker::Track

BOOL Track(CWnd* *pWnd*, **CPoint** *point*, **BOOL** *bAllowInvert* = **FALSE**, **CWnd*** *pWndClipTo* = **NULL**);

Return Value   If the ESC key is pressed, the tracking process is halted, the rectangle stored in the tracker is not altered, and 0 is returned. If the change is committed, by moving the mouse and releasing the left mouse button, the new position and/or size is recorded in the tracker's rectangle and nonzero is returned.

Parameters   *pWnd*   The window object that contains the rectangle.

point   Device coordinates of the current mouse position relative to the client area.

bAllowInvert   If **TRUE**, the rectangle can be inverted along the x-axis or y-axis; otherwise **FALSE**.

pWndClipTo   The window that drawing operations will be clipped to. If **NULL**, *pWnd* is used as the clipping rectangle.

Remarks   Call this function to display the user interface for resizing the rectangle. This is usually called from inside the function of your application that handles the **WM_LBUTTONDOWN** message (typically **OnLButtonDown**).

This function will capture the mouse until the user releases the left mouse button, hits the ESC key, or hits the right mouse button. As the user moves the mouse cursor, the feedback is updated by calling **DrawTrackerRect** and **OnChangeRect**.

If *bAllowInvert* is **TRUE**, the tracking rectangle can be inverted on either the x-axis or y-axis.

See Also   **CRectTracker::DrawTrackerRect**, **CRectTracker::OnChangedRect**, **CRectTracker::CRectTracker**, **CRectTracker::TrackRubberBand**

CRectTracker::TrackRubberBand

BOOL TrackRubberBand(CWnd* *pWnd***, CPoint** *point***, BOOL** *bAllowInvert*
= TRUE);

Return Value   Nonzero if the mouse has moved and the rectangle is not empty; otherwise 0.

Parameters   *pWnd*   The window object that contains the rectangle.

point   Device coordinates of the current mouse position relative to the client area.

bAllowInvert   If **TRUE,** the rectangle can be inverted along the x-axis or y-axis; otherwise **FALSE.**

Remarks   Call this function to do rubber-band selection. It is usually called from inside the function of your application that handles the **WM_LBUTTONDOWN** message (typically **OnLButtonDown**).

This function will capture the mouse until the user releases the left mouse button, hits the ESC key, or hits the right mouse button. As the user moves the mouse cursor, the feedback is updated by calling **DrawTrackerRect** and **OnChangeRect**.

Tracking is performed with a rubber-band-type selection from the lower-right handle. If inverting is allowed, the rectangle can be sized by dragging either up and to the left or down and to the right.

See Also   **CRectTracker::DrawTrackerRect**, **CRectTracker::OnChangedRect**, **CRectTracker::CRectTracker**

Data Members

CRectTracker::m_nHandleSize

Remarks   The size, in pixels, of the **CRectTracker** resize handles. Initialized with the default system value.

CRectTracker::m_rect

Remarks   The current position of the rectangle in client coordinates (pixels).

See Also   **CRectTracker::CRectTracker, CRectTracker::Track,**
CRectTracker::TrackRubberBand

CRectTracker::m_sizeMin

Remarks   The minimum size of the rectangle. Both default values, **cx** and **cy**, are calculated from the default system value for the border width. This data member is used only by the **AdjustRect** member function.

See Also   **CRectTracker::Track**, **CRectTracker::TrackRubberBand**

CRectTracker::m_nStyle

Remarks   Current style of the rectangle. See **CRectTracker::CRectTracker** for a list of possible styles.

See Also   **CRectTracker::CRectTracker**, **CRectTracker::Draw**

class CResourceException : public CException

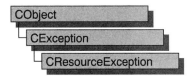

A **CResourceException** object is generated when Windows cannot find or allocate a requested resource. No further qualification is necessary or possible.

#include <afxwin.h>

Construction

CResourceException   Constructs a **CResourceException** object.

Member Functions

CResourceException::CResourceException

CResourceException( );

Remarks   Constructs a **CResourceException** object.

Do not use this constructor directly, but rather call the global function **AfxThrowResourceException**. For more information about exceptions, see the article "Exceptions" in *Programming with the Microsoft Foundation Class Library*.

See Also   **AfxThrowResourceException**

class CRgn : public CGdiObject

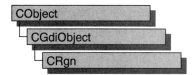

The **CRgn** class encapsulates a Windows graphics device interface (GDI) region. A region is an elliptical or polygonal area within a window. To use regions, you use the member functions of class **CRgn** with the clipping functions defined as members of class **CDC**. The member functions of **CRgn** create, alter, and retrieve information about the region object for which they are called.

#include <afxwin.h>

Construction

CRgn	Constructs a **CRgn** object.

Initialization

CreateRectRgn	Initializes a **CRgn** object with a rectangular region.
CreateRectRgnIndirect	Initializes a **CRgn** object with a rectangular region defined by a **RECT** structure.
CreateEllipticRgn	Initializes a **CRgn** object with an elliptical region.
CreateEllipticRgnIndirect	Initializes a **CRgn** object with an elliptical region defined by a **RECT** structure.
CreatePolygonRgn	Initializes a **CRgn** object with a polygonal region. The system closes the polygon automatically, if necessary, by drawing a line from the last vertex to the first.
CreatePolyPolygonRgn	Initializes a **CRgn** object with a region consisting of a series of closed polygons. The polygons may be disjoint or they may overlap.
CreateRoundRectRgn	Initializes a **CRgn** object with a rectangular region with rounded corners.
CombineRgn	Sets a **CRgn** object so that it is equivalent to the union of two specified **CRgn** objects.
CopyRgn	Sets a **CRgn** object so that it is a copy of a specified **CRgn** object.

CreateFromPath	Creates a region from the path that is selected into the given device context.
CreateFromData	Creates a region from the given region and transformation data.

Operations

EqualRgn	Checks two **CRgn** objects to determine whether they are equivalent.
FromHandle	Returns a pointer to a **CRgn** object when given a handle to a Windows region.
GetRegionData	Fills the specified buffer with data describing the given region.
GetRgnBox	Retrieves the coordinates of the bounding rectangle of a **CRgn** object.
OffsetRgn	Moves a **CRgn** object by the specified offsets.
PtInRegion	Determines whether a specified point is in the region.
RectInRegion	Determines whether any part of a specified rectangle is within the boundaries of the region.
SetRectRgn	Sets the **CRgn** object to the specified rectangular region.

Member Functions

CRgn::CombineRgn

int CombineRgn(CRgn* *pRgn1*, CRgn* *pRgn2*, int *nCombineMode*);

Return Value   Specifies the type of the resulting region. It can be one of the following values:

- **COMPLEXREGION**   New region has overlapping borders.
- **ERROR**   No new region created.
- **NULLREGION**   New region is empty.
- **SIMPLEREGION**   New region has no overlapping borders.

Parameters   *pRgn1*   Identifies an existing region.

pRgn2   Identifies an existing region.

nCombineMode   Specifies the operation to be performed when combining the two source regions. It can be any one of the following values:

- **RGN_AND**   Uses overlapping areas of both regions (intersection).
- **RGN_COPY**   Creates a copy of region 1 (identified by *pRgn1*).
- **RGN_DIFF**   Creates a region consisting of the areas of region 1 (identified by *pRgn1*) that are not part of region 2 (identified by *pRgn2*).
- **RGN_OR**   Combines both regions in their entirety (union).
- **RGN_XOR**   Combines both regions but removes overlapping areas.

Remarks   Creates a new GDI region by combining two existing regions. The regions are combined as specified by *nCombineMode*. The two specified regions are combined, and the resulting region handle is stored in the **CRgn** object. Thus, whatever region is stored in the **CRgn** object is replaced by the combined region. The size of a region is limited to 32,767 by 32,767 logical units or 64K of memory, whichever is smaller. Use **CopyRgn** to simply copy one region into another region.

See Also   **CRgn::CopyRgn**, **::CombineRgn**

CRgn::CopyRgn

int CopyRgn(CRgn* *pRgnSrc* **);**

Return Value   Specifies the type of the resulting region. It can be one of the following values:

- **COMPLEXREGION**   New region has overlapping borders.
- **ERROR**   No new region created.
- **NULLREGION**   New region is empty.
- **SIMPLEREGION**   New region has no overlapping borders.

Parameters   *pRgnSrc*   Identifies an existing region.

Remarks   Copies the region defined by *pRgnSrc* into the **CRgn** object. The new region replaces the region formerly stored in the **CRgn** object. This function is a special case of the **CombineRgn** member function.

See Also   **CRgn::CombineRgn**, **::CombineRgn**

CRgn::CreateEllipticRgn

BOOL CreateEllipticRgn(int *x1*, **int** *y1*, **int** *x2*, **int** *y2* **);**

Return Value   Nonzero if the operation succeeded; otherwise 0.

Parameters   *x1*   Specifies the logical x-coordinate of the upper-left corner of the bounding rectangle of the ellipse.

	y1 Specifies the logical y-coordinate of the upper-left corner of the bounding rectangle of the ellipse.
	x2 Specifies the logical x-coordinate of the lower-right corner of the bounding rectangle of the ellipse.
	y2 Specifies the logical y-coordinate of the lower-right corner of the bounding rectangle of the ellipse.
Remarks	Creates an elliptical region. The region is defined by the bounding rectangle specified by *x1*, *y1*, *x2*, and *y2*. The region is stored in the **CRgn** object. The size of a region is limited to 32,767 by 32,767 logical units or 64K of memory, whichever is smaller. When it has finished using a region created with the **CreateEllipticRgn** function, an application should select the region out of the device context and use the **DeleteObject** function to remove it.
See Also	**CRgn::CreateEllipticRgnIndirect**, **::CreateEllipticRgn**

CRgn::CreateEllipticRgnIndirect

BOOL CreateEllipticRgnIndirect(LPCRECT *lpRect* **);**

Return Value	Nonzero if the operation succeeded; otherwise 0.
Parameters	*lpRect* Points to a **RECT** structure or a **CRect** object that contains the logical coordinates of the upper-left and lower-right corners of the bounding rectangle of the ellipse.
Remarks	Creates an elliptical region. The region is defined by the structure or object pointed to by *lpRect* and is stored in the **CRgn** object. The size of a region is limited to 32,767 by 32,767 logical units or 64K of memory, whichever is smaller. When it has finished using a region created with the **CreateEllipticRgnIndirect** function, an application should select the region out of the device context and use the **DeleteObject** function to remove it.
See Also	**CRgn::CreateEllipticRgn**, **::CreateEllipticRgnIndirect**

CRgn::CreateFromData

BOOL CreateFromData(const XFORM* *lpXForm***, int** *nCount***, const RGNDATA*** *pRgnData* **);**

Return Value	Nonzero if the function is successful; otherwise 0.
Parameters	*lpXForm* Points to an **XFORM** data structure that defines the transformation to be performed on the region. If this pointer is **NULL**, the identity transformation is used.

nCount   Specifies the number of bytes pointed to by *pRgnData*.

pRgnData   Points to a **RGNDATA** data structure that contains the region data.

Remarks   Creates a region from the given region and transformation data. An application can retrieve data for a region by calling the **CRgn::GetRegionData** function.

See Also   **CRgn::GetRegionData**, **::ExtCreateRegion**

CRgn::CreateFromPath

BOOL CreateFromPath(CDC* *pDC*);

Return Value   Nonzero if the function is successful; otherwise 0.

Parameters   *pDC*   Identifies a device context that contains a closed path.

Remarks   Creates a region from the path that is selected into the given device context. The device context identified by the *pDC* parameter must contain a closed path. After **CreateFromPath** converts a path into a region, Windows discards the closed path from the device context.

See Also   **CDC::BeginPath**, **CDC::EndPath**, **CDC::SetPolyFillMode**

CRgn::CreatePolygonRgn

BOOL CreatePolygonRgn(LPPOINT *lpPoints*, int *nCount*, int *nMode*);

Return Value   Nonzero if the operation succeeded; otherwise 0.

Parameters   *lpPoints*   Points to an array of **POINT** structures or an array of **CPoint** objects. Each structure specifies the x-coordinate and y-coordinate of one vertex of the polygon. The **POINT** structure has the following form:

```
typedef struct tagPOINT {
    int x;
    int y;
} POINT;
```

nCount   Specifies the number of **POINT** structures or **CPoint** objects in the array pointed to by *lpPoints*.

nMode   Specifies the filling mode for the region. This parameter may be either **ALTERNATE** or **WINDING**.

Remarks   Creates a polygonal region. The system closes the polygon automatically, if necessary, by drawing a line from the last vertex to the first. The resulting region is stored in the **CRgn** object. The size of a region is limited to 32,767, by 32,767, logical units or 64K of memory, whichever is smaller.

When the polygon-filling mode is **ALTERNATE**, the system fills the area between odd-numbered and even-numbered polygon sides on each scan line. That is, the system fills the area between the first and second side, between the third and fourth side, and so on. When the polygon-filling mode is **WINDING**, the system uses the direction in which a figure was drawn to determine whether to fill an area. Each line segment in a polygon is drawn in either a clockwise or a counterclockwise direction. Whenever an imaginary line drawn from an enclosed area to the outside of a figure passes through a clockwise line segment, a count is incremented. When the line passes through a counterclockwise line segment, the count is decremented. The area is filled if the count is nonzero when the line reaches the outside of the figure.

When an application has finished using a region created with the **CreatePolygonRgn** function, it should select the region out of the device context and use the **DeleteObject** function to remove it.

See Also   **CRgn::CreatePolyPolygonRgn**, **::CreatePolygonRgn**

CRgn::CreatePolyPolygonRgn

BOOL **CreatePolyPolygonRgn**(LPPOINT *lpPoints*, LPINT *lpPolyCounts*, int *nCount*, int *nPolyFillMode*);

Return Value   Nonzero if the operation succeeded; otherwise 0.

Parameters   *lpPoints*   Points to an array of **POINT** structures or an array of **CPoint** objects that defines the vertices of the polygons. Each polygon must be explicitly closed because the system does not close them automatically. The polygons are specified consecutively. The **POINT** structure has the following form:

```
typedef struct tagPOINT {
    int x;
    int y;
} POINT;
```

lpPolyCounts   Points to an array of integers. The first integer specifies the number of vertices in the first polygon in the *lpPoints* array, the second integer specifies the number of vertices in the second polygon, and so on.

nCount   Specifies the total number of integers in the *lpPolyCounts* array.

nPolyFillMode   Specifies the polygon-filling mode. This value may be either **ALTERNATE** or **WINDING**.

Remarks   Creates a region consisting of a series of closed polygons. The resulting region is stored in the **CRgn** object. The polygons may be disjoint or they may overlap. The size of a region is limited to 32,767, by 32,767 logical units or 64K of memory, whichever is smaller.

When the polygon-filling mode is **ALTERNATE**, the system fills the area between odd-numbered and even-numbered polygon sides on each scan line. That is, the system fills the area between the first and second side, between the third and fourth side, and so on. When the polygon-filling mode is **WINDING**, the system uses the direction in which a figure was drawn to determine whether to fill an area. Each line segment in a polygon is drawn in either a clockwise or a counterclockwise direction. Whenever an imaginary line drawn from an enclosed area to the outside of a figure passes through a clockwise line segment, a count is incremented. When the line passes through a counterclockwise line segment, the count is decremented. The area is filled if the count is nonzero when the line reaches the outside of the figure.

When an application has finished using a region created with the **CreatePolyPolygonRgn** function, it should select the region out of the device context and use the **DeleteObject** function to remove it.

See Also   **CRgn::CreatePolygonRgn, CDC::SetPolyFillMode, ::CreatePolyPolygonRgn**

CRgn::CreateRectRgn

BOOL CreateRectRgn(int *x1*, **int** *y1*, **int** *x2*, **int** *y2* **);**

Return Value   Nonzero if the operation succeeded; otherwise 0.

Parameters   *x1*   Specifies the logical x-coordinate of the uppeoperationsr-left corner of the region.

    y1   Specifies the logical y-coordinate of the upper-left corner of the region.

    x2   Specifies the logical x-coordinate of the lower-right corner of the region.

    y2   Specifies the logical y-coordinate of the lower-right corner of the region.

Remarks   Creates a rectangular region that is stored in the **CRgn** object. The size of a region is limited to 32,767 by 32,767 logical units or 64K of memory, whichever is smaller. When it has finished using a region created by **CreateRectRgn**, an application should use the **DeleteObject** function to remove the region.

See Also   **CRgn::CreateRectRgnIndirect, CRgn::CreateRoundRectRgn, ::CreateRectRgn**

CRgn::CreateRectRgnIndirect

BOOL CreateRectRgnIndirect(LPCRECT *lpRect* **);**

Return Value   Nonzero if the operation succeeded; otherwise 0.

Parameters   *lpRect*   Points to a **RECT** structure or **CRect** object that contains the logical coordinates of the upper-left and lower-right corners of the region. The **RECT** structure has the following form:

```
typedef struct tagRECT {
    int left;
    int top;
    int right;
    int bottom;
} RECT;
```

Remarks   Creates a rectangular region that is stored in the **CRgn** object. The size of a region is limited to 32,767 by 32,767 logical units or 64K of memory, whichever is smaller. When it has finished using a region created by **CreateRectRgnIndirect**, an application should use the **DeleteObject** function to remove the region.

See Also   **CRgn::CreateRectRgn, CRgn::CreateRoundRectRgn, ::CreateRectRgnIndirect**

CRgn::CreateRoundRectRgn

BOOL CreateRoundRectRgn(int *x1*, **int** *y1*, **int** *x2*, **int** *y2*, **int** *x3*, **int** *y3* **);**

Return Value   Nonzero if the operation succeeded; otherwise 0.

Parameters   *x1*   Specifies the logical x-coordinate of the upper-left corner of the region.

y1   Specifies the logical y-coordinate of the upper-left corner of the region.

x2   Specifies the logical x-coordinate of the lower-right corner of the region.

y2   Specifies the logical y-coordinate of the lower-right corner of the region.

x3   Specifies the width of the ellipse used to create the rounded corners.

y3   Specifies the height of the ellipse used to create the rounded corners.

Remarks   Creates a rectangular region with rounded corners that is stored in the **CRgn** object. The size of a region is limited to 32,767 by 32,767 logical units or 64K of memory, whichever is smaller. When an application has finished using a region created with the **CreateRoundRectRgn** function, it should select the region out of the device context and use the **DeleteObject** function to remove it.

See Also   **CRgn::CreateRectRgn, CRgn::CreateRectRgnIndirect, ::CreateRoundRectRgn**

CRgn::CRgn

CRgn( );

Remarks   Constructs a **CRgn** object. The **m_hObject** data member does not contain a valid Windows GDI region until the object is initialized with one or more of the other **CRgn** member functions.

CRgn::EqualRgn

BOOL EqualRgn(CRgn* *pRgn* **) const;**

Return Value   Nonzero if the two regions are equivalent; otherwise 0.

Parameters   *pRgn*   Identifies a region.

Remarks   Determines whether the given region is equivalent to the region stored in the **CRgn** object.

See Also   **::EqualRgn**

CRgn::FromHandle

static CRgn* PASCAL FromHandle(HRGN *hRgn* **);**

Return Value   A pointer to a **CRgn** object. If the function was not successful, the return value is **NULL**.

Parameters   *hRgn*   Specifies a handle to a Windows region.

Remarks   Returns a pointer to a **CRgn** object when given a handle to a Windows region. If a **CRgn** object is not already attached to the handle, a temporary **CRgn** object is created and attached. This temporary **CRgn** object is valid only until the next time the application has idle time in its event loop, at which time all temporary graphic objects are deleted. Another way of saying this is that the temporary object is only valid during the processing of one window message.

CRgn::GetRegionData

BOOL GetRegionData(LPRGNDATA *lpRgnData*, **int** *nCount* **) const;**

Return Value   Nonzero if the function is successful; otherwise 0.

Parameters   *lpRgnData*   Points to a **RGNDATA** data structure that receives the information. If this parameter is **NULL**, the return value contains the number of bytes needed for the region data.

nCount   Specifies the size, in bytes, of the *lpRgnData* buffer.

Remarks   Fills the specified buffer with data describing the region. This data includes the dimensions of the rectangles that make up the region. This function is used in conjunction with the **CRgn::CreateFromData** function.

See Also   **CRgn::CreateFromData**

CRgn::GetRgnBox

                   int GetRgnBox(LPRECT *lpRect* **) const;**

Return Value   Specifies the region's type. It can be any of the following values:

- **COMPLEXREGION**   Region has overlapping borders.
- **NULLREGION**   Region is empty.
- **ERROR**   **CRgn** object does not specify a valid region.
- **SIMPLEREGION**   Region has no overlapping borders.

Parameters   *lpRect*   Points to a **RECT** structure or **CRect** object to receive the coordinates of the bounding rectangle. The **RECT** structure has the following form:

```
typedef struct tagRECT {
    int left;
    int top;
    int right;
    int bottom;
} RECT;
```

Remarks   Retrieves the coordinates of the bounding rectangle of the **CRgn** object.

See Also   **::GetRgnBox**

CRgn::OffsetRgn

                   int OffsetRgn(int *x***, int** *y* **);**

                   int OffsetRgn(POINT *point* **);**

Return Value   The new region's type. It can be any one of the following values:

- **COMPLEXREGION**   Region has overlapping borders.
- **ERROR**   Region handle is not valid.
- **NULLREGION**   Region is empty.
- **SIMPLEREGION**   Region has no overlapping borders.

Parameters   *x*   Specifies the number of units to move left or right.

                   y   Specifies the number of units to move up or down.

point   The x-coordinate of *point* specifies the number of units to move left or right. The y-coordinate of *point* specifies the number of units to move up or down. The *point* parameter may be either a **POINT** structure or a **CPoint** object.

Remarks

Moves the region stored in the **CRgn** object by the specified offsets. The function moves the region x units along the x-axis and y units along the y-axis. The coordinate values of a region must be less than or equal to 32,767 and greater than or equal to –32,768. The x and y parameters must be carefully chosen to prevent invalid region coordinates.

See Also

::**OffsetRgn**

CRgn::PtInRegion

BOOL PtInRegion(int *x*, **int** *y*) **const;**

BOOL PtInRegion(POINT *point*) **const;**

Return Value

Nonzero if the point is in the region; otherwise 0.

Parameters

x   Specifies the logical x-coordinate of the point to test.

y   Specifies the logical y-coordinate of the point to test.

point   The x- and y-coordinates of *point* specify the x- and y-coordinates of the point to test the value of. The *point* parameter can either be a **POINT** structure or a **CPoint** object.

Remarks

Checks whether the point given by x and y is in the region stored in the **CRgn** object.

See Also

::**PtInRegion**

CRgn::RectInRegion

BOOL RectInRegion(LPCRECT *lpRect*) **const;**

Return Value

Nonzero if any part of the specified rectangle lies within the boundaries of the region; otherwise 0.

Parameters

lpRect   Points to a **RECT** structure or **CRect** object. The **RECT** structure has the following form:

```
typedef struct tagRECT {
    int left;
    int top;
    int right;
    int bottom;
} RECT;
```

Remarks   Determines whether any part of the rectangle specified by *lpRect* is within the boundaries of the region stored in the **CRgn** object.

See Also   **::RectInRegion**

CRgn::SetRectRgn

void SetRectRgn(int *x1*, **int** *y1*, **int** *x2*, **int** *y2* **);**

void SetRectRgn(LPCRECT *lpRect* **);**

Parameters   *x1*   Specifies the x-coordinate of the upper-left corner of the rectangular region.

           y1   Specifies the y-coordinate of the upper-left corner of the rectangular region.

           x2   Specifies the x-coordinate of the lower-right corner of the rectangular region.

           y2   Specifies the y-coordinate of the lower-right corner of the rectangular region.

           lpRect   Specifies the rectangular region. Can be either a pointer to a **RECT** structure or a **CRect** object.

Remarks   Creates a rectangular region. Unlike **CreateRectRgn**, however, it does not allocate any additional memory from the local Windows application heap. Instead, it uses the space allocated for the region stored in the **CRgn** object. This means that the **CRgn** object must already have been initialized with a valid Windows region before calling **SetRectRgn**. The points given by *x1*, *y1*, *x2*, and *y2* specify the minimum size of the allocated space. Use this function instead of the **CreateRectRgn** member function to avoid calls to the local memory manager.

See Also   **CRgn::CreateRectRgn**, **::SetRectRgn**

structure CRuntimeClass

Each class derived from **CObject** is associated with a **CRuntimeClass** structure that you can use to obtain information about an object or its base class at run time. The ability to determine the class of an object at run time is useful when extra type checking of function arguments is needed, or when you must write special-purpose code based on the class of an object. Run-time class information is not supported directly by the C++ language.

The structure has the following members:

LPCSTR m_lpszClassName
A null-terminated string containing the ASCII class name.

int m_nObjectSize
The size of the object, in bytes. If the object has data members that point to allocated memory, the size of that memory is not included.

WORD m_wSchema
The schema number (−1 for nonserializable classes). See the **IMPLEMENT_SERIAL** macro for a description of the schema number.

void (*m_pfnConstruct)(void* p)
A pointer to the default constructor of your class (valid only if the class supports dynamic creation).

CRuntimeClass* m_pBaseClass
A pointer to the **CRuntimeClass** structure that corresponds to the base class.

CObject* CreateObject( );
Classes derived from **CObject** can support dynamic creation, which is the ability to create an object of a specified class at run time. Document, view, and frame classes, for example, should support dynamic creation. The **CreateObject** member function can be used to implement this function and create objects for these classes during run time. For more information on dynamic creation and the **CreateObject** member, see the article "CObject Class" in *Programming with the Microsoft Foundation Class Library*.

Note To use the **CRuntimeClass** structure, you must include the **IMPLEMENT_DYNAMIC, IMPLEMENT_DYNCREATE** or **IMPLEMENT_SERIAL** macro in the implementation of the class for which you want to retrieve run-time object information.

See Also   **CObject::GetRuntimeClass, CObject::IsKindOf, RUNTIME_CLASS, IMPLEMENT_DYNAMIC, IMPLEMENT_DYNCREATE, IMPLEMENT_SERIAL**

class CScrollBar : public CWnd

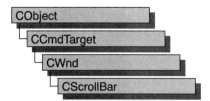

The **CScrollBar** class provides the functionality of a Windows scroll-bar control. You create a scroll-bar control in two steps. First, call the constructor **CScrollBar** to construct the **CScrollBar** object, then call the **Create** member function to create the Windows scroll-bar control and attach it to the **CScrollBar** object.

If you create a **CScrollBar** object within a dialog box (through a dialog resource), the **CScrollBar** is automatically destroyed when the user closes the dialog box. If you create a **CScrollBar** object within a window, you may also need to destroy it.

If you create the **CScrollBar** object on the stack, it is destroyed automatically. If you create the **CScrollBar** object on the heap by using the **new** function, you must call **delete** on the object to destroy it when the user terminates the Windows scroll bar. If you allocate any memory in the **CScrollBar** object, override the **CScrollBar** destructor to dispose of the allocations.

#include <afxwin.h>

See Also   **CWnd, CButton, CComboBox, CEdit, CListBox, CStatic, CDialog**

Construction
CScrollBar	Constructs a **CScrollBar** object.

Initialization
Create	Creates the Windows scroll bar and attaches it to the **CScrollBar** object.

Operations
GetScrollPos	Retrieves the current position of a scroll box.
SetScrollPos	Sets the current position of a scroll box.
GetScrollRange	Retrieves the current minimum and maximum scroll-bar positions for the given scroll bar.

SetScrollRange	Sets minimum and maximum position values for the given scroll bar.
ShowScrollBar	Shows or hides a scroll bar.
EnableScrollBar	Enables or disables one or both arrows of a scroll bar.

Member Functions

CScrollBar::Create

BOOL Create(DWORD *dwStyle*, **const RECT&** *rect*, **CWnd*** *pParentWnd*, **UINT** *nID* **);**

Return Value Nonzero if successful; otherwise 0.

Parameters *dwStyle* Specifies the scroll bar's style. Apply any combination of scroll-bar styles to the scroll bar. For a list of scroll-bar styles, see the section "Scroll-Bar Styles" on page 1251.

rect Specifies the scroll bar's size and position. Can be either a **RECT** structure or a **CRect** object.

pParentWnd Specifies the scroll bar's parent window, usually a **CDialog** object. It must not be **NULL**.

nID The scroll bar's control ID.

Remarks You construct a **CScrollBar** object in two steps. First call the constructor, which constructs the **CScrollBar** object; then call **Create**, which creates and initializes the associated Windows scroll bar and attaches it to the **CScrollBar** object.

Apply the following window styles to a scroll bar: For a list of window styles, see the section "Window Styles" on page 1253.

- **WS_CHILD** Always
- **WS_VISIBLE** Usually
- **WS_DISABLED** Rarely
- **WS_GROUP** To group controls

See Also **CScrollBar::CScrollBar**

CScrollBar::CScrollBar

CScrollBar( );

Remarks   Constructs a **CScrollBar** object. After constructing the object, call the **Create** member function to create and initialize the Windows scroll bar.

See Also   **CScrollBar::Create**

CScrollBar::EnableScrollBar

BOOL EnableScrollBar(UINT *nArrowFlags* **= ESB_ENABLE_BOTH);**

Return Value   Nonzero if the arrows are enabled or disabled as specified; otherwise 0, which indicates that the arrows are already in the requested state or that an error occurred.

Parameters   *nArrowFlags*   Specifies whether the scroll arrows are enabled or disabled and which arrows are enabled or disabled. This parameter can be one of the following values:

- **ESB_ENABLE_BOTH**   Enables both arrows of a scroll bar.
- **ESB_DISABLE_LTUP**   Disables the left arrow of a horizontal scroll bar or the up arrow of a vertical scroll bar.
- **ESB_DISABLE_RTDN**   Disables the right arrow of a horizontal scroll bar or the down arrow of a vertical scroll bar.
- **ESB_DISABLE_BOTH**   Disables both arrows of a scroll bar.

Remarks   Enables or disables one or both arrows of a scroll bar.

See Also   **CWnd::EnableScrollBar**, **::EnableScrollBar**

CScrollBar::GetScrollPos

int GetScrollPos( ) const;

Return Value   Specifies the current position of the scroll box if successful; otherwise 0.

Remarks   Retrieves the current position of a scroll box. The current position is a relative value that depends on the current scrolling range. For example, if the scrolling range is 100 to 200 and the scroll box is in the middle of the bar, the current position is 150.

See Also   **CScrollBar::SetScrollPos, CScrollBar::GetScrollRange,** **CScrollBar::SetScrollRange, ::GetScrollPos**

CScrollBar::GetScrollRange

void GetScrollRange(LPINT *lpMinPos*, **LPINT** *lpMaxPos* **) const;**

Parameters *lpMinPos*   Points to the integer variable that is to receive the minimum position.

lpMaxPos   Points to the integer variable that is to receive the maximum position.

Remarks Copies the current minimum and maximum scroll-bar positions for the given scroll bar to the locations specified by *lpMinPos* and *lpMaxPos*. The default range for a scroll-bar control is empty (both values are 0).

See Also **::GetScrollRange**, **CScrollBar::SetScrollRange**, **CScrollBar::GetScrollPos**, **CScrollBar::SetScrollPos**

CScrollBar::SetScrollPos

int SetScrollPos(int *nPos*, **BOOL** *bRedraw* **= TRUE);**

Return Value Specifies the previous position of the scroll box if successful; otherwise 0.

Parameters *nPos*   Specifies the new position for the scroll box. It must be within the scrolling range.

bRedraw   Specifies whether the scroll bar should be redrawn to reflect the new position. If *bRedraw* is **TRUE**, the scroll bar is redrawn. If it is **FALSE**, it is not redrawn. The scroll bar is redrawn by default.

Remarks Sets the current position of a scroll box to that specified by *nPos* and, if specified, redraws the scroll bar to reflect the new position. Set *bRedraw* to **FALSE** whenever the scroll bar will be redrawn by a subsequent call to another function to avoid having the scroll bar redrawn twice within a short interval.

See Also **CScrollBar::GetScrollPos**, **CScrollBar::GetScrollRange**, **CScrollBar::SetScrollRange**, **::SetScrollPos**

CScrollBar::SetScrollRange

void SetScrollRange(int *nMinPos*, **int** *nMaxPos*, **BOOL** *bRedraw* **= TRUE);**

Parameters *nMinPos*   Specifies the minimum scrolling position.

nMaxPos   Specifies the maximum scrolling position.

bRedraw   Specifies whether the scroll bar should be redrawn to reflect the change. If *bRedraw* is **TRUE**, the scroll bar is redrawn; if **FALSE**, it is not redrawn. It is redrawn by default.

Remarks   Sets minimum and maximum position values for the given scroll bar. Set *nMinPos* and *nMaxPos* to 0 to hide standard scroll bars. Do not call this function to hide a scroll bar while processing a scroll-bar notification message. If a call to **SetScrollRange** immediately follows a call to the **SetScrollPos** member function, set *bRedraw* in **SetScrollPos** to 0 to prevent the scroll bar from being redrawn twice.

The difference between the values specified by *nMinPos* and *nMaxPos* must not be greater than 32,767. The default range for a scroll-bar control is empty (both *nMinPos* and *nMaxPos* are 0).

See Also   **CScrollBar::GetScrollPos**, **CScrollBar::SetScrollPos**, **CScrollBar::GetScrollRange**, **::SetScrollRange**

CScrollBar::ShowScrollBar

void ShowScrollBar(BOOL *bShow* **= TRUE);**

Parameters   *bShow*   Specifies whether the scroll bar is shown or hidden. If this parameter is **TRUE**, the scroll bar is shown; otherwise it is hidden.

Remarks   Shows or hides a scroll bar. An application should not call this function to hide a scroll bar while processing a scroll-bar notification message.

See Also   **CScrollBar::GetScrollPos**, **CScrollBar::GetScrollRange**, **CWnd::ScrollWindow**, **CScrollBar::SetScrollPos**, **CScrollBar::SetScrollRange**

class CScrollView : public CView

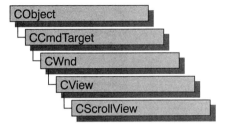

The **CScrollView** class is a **CView** with scrolling capabilities.

You can handle scrolling yourself in any class derived from **CView** by overriding the message-mapped **OnHScroll** and **OnVScroll** member functions. But **CScrollView** adds the following features to its **CView** capabilities:

- It manages window and viewport sizes and mapping modes.
- It scrolls automatically in response to scroll-bar messages.

To take advantage of automatic scrolling, derive your view class from **CScrollView** instead of from **CView**. When the view is first created, if you want to calculate the size of the scrollable view based on the size of the document, call the **SetScrollSizes** member function from your override of either **CView::OnInitialUpdate** or **CView::OnUpdate**. (You must write your own code to query the size of the document. For an example, see Chapter 13 in *Introducing Visual C++*.)

The call to the **SetScrollSizes** member function sets the view's mapping mode, the total dimensions of the scroll view, and the amounts to scroll horizontally and vertically. All sizes are in logical units. The logical size of the view is usually calculated from data stored in the document, but in some cases you may want to specify a fixed size. For examples of both approaches, see **CScrollView::SetScrollSizes**.

You specify the amounts to scroll horizontally and vertically in logical units. By default, if the user clicks a scroll bar shaft outside of the scroll box, **CScrollView** scrolls a "page." If the user clicks a scroll arrow at either end of a scroll bar, **CScrollView** scrolls a "line." By default, a page is 1/10 of the total size of the view; a line is 1/10 of the page size. Override these default values by passing custom sizes in the **SetScrollSizes** member function. For example, you might set the horizontal size to some fraction of the width of the total size and the vertical size to the height of a line in the current font.

Instead of scrolling, **CScrollView** can automatically scale the view to the current window size. In this mode, the view has no scroll bars and the logical view is stretched or shrunk to exactly fit the window's client area. To use this scale-to-fit capability, call **CScrollView::SetScaleToFitSize**. (Call either **SetScaleToFitSize** or **SetScrollSizes**, but not both.)

Before the OnDraw member function of your derived view class is called, **CScrollView** automatically adjusts the viewport origin for the **CPaintDC** device-context object that it passes to OnDraw.

To adjust the viewport origin for the scrolling window, **CScrollView** overrides **CView::OnPrepareDC**. This adjustment is automatic for the **CPaintDC** device context that **CScrollView** passes to OnDraw, but you must call **CScrollView::OnPrepareDC** yourself for any other device contexts you use, such as a **CClientDC**. You can override **CScrollView::OnPrepareDC** to set the pen, background color, and other drawing attributes, but call the base class to do scaling.

Scroll bars may appear in three places relative to a view, as shown in the following cases:

- Standard window-style scroll bars can be set for the view using the **WS_HSCROLL** and **WS_VSCROLL** styles. For more information on window styles, see the section "Window Styles" on page 1253.

- Scroll-bar controls can also be added to the frame containing the view, in which case the framework forwards **WM_HSCROLL** and **WM_VSCROLL** messages from the frame window to the currently active view.

- The framework also forwards scroll messages from a **CSplitterWnd** splitter control to the currently active splitter pane (a view). When placed in a **CSplitterWnd** with shared scroll bars, a **CScrollView** object will use the shared ones rather than creating its own.

#include <afxwin.h>

See Also   CView, CSplitterWnd

Operations

FillOutsideRect	Fills the area of a view outside the scrolling area.
GetDeviceScrollPosition	Gets the current scroll position in device units.
GetDeviceScrollSizes	Gets the current mapping mode, the total size, and the line and page sizes of the scrollable view. Sizes are in device units.
GetScrollPosition	Gets the current scroll position in logical units.
GetTotalSize	Gets the total size of the scroll view in logical units.
ResizeParentToFit	Causes the size of the view to dictate the size of its frame.
ScrollToPosition	Scrolls the view to a given point, specified in logical units.
SetScaleToFitSize	Puts the scroll view into scale-to-fit mode.
SetScrollSizes	Sets the scroll view's mapping mode, total size, and horizontal and vertical scroll amounts.

Construction

CScrollView	Constructs a **CScrollView** object.

Member Functions

CScrollView::CScrollView

Protected→
CScrollView( );
END Protected

Remarks   Constructs a **CScrollView** object. You must call either **SetScrollSizes** or **SetScaleToFitSize** before the scroll view is usable.

See Also   **CScrollView::SetScrollSizes**, **CScrollView::SetScaleToFitSize**

CScrollView::FillOutsideRect

void FillOutsideRect(CDC* *pDC***, CBrush*** *pBrush* **)**;

Parameters   *pDC*   Device context in which the filling is to be done.

pBrush   Brush with which the area is to be filled.

Remarks   Call **FillOutsideRect** to fill the area of the view that appears outside of the scrolling area. Use **FillOutsideRect** in your scroll view's **OnEraseBkgnd** handler function to prevent excessive background repainting.

See Also   **CWnd::OnEraseBkgnd**

Example
```
BOOL CScaleView::OnEraseBkgnd( CDC* pDC )
{
    CBrush br( GetSysColor( COLOR_WINDOW ) );
    FillOutsideRect( pDC, &br );
    return TRUE;                    // Erased
}
```

CScrollView::GetDeviceScrollPosition

CPoint GetDeviceScrollPosition( ) const;

Remarks   Call **GetDeviceScrollPosition** when you need the current horizontal and vertical positions of the scroll boxes in the scroll bars. This coordinate pair corresponds to the location in the document to which the upper-left corner of the view has been scrolled. This is useful for offsetting mouse-device positions to scroll-view device positions.

GetDeviceScrollPosition returns values in device units. If you want logical units, use **GetScrollPosition** instead.

See Also   **CScrollView::GetScrollPosition**

CScrollView::GetDeviceScrollSizes

void GetDeviceScrollSizes(int& *nMapMode*, **SIZE&** *sizeTotal*,
  SIZE& *sizePage*, **SIZE&** *sizeLine* **) const;**

Parameters *nMapMode*   Returns the current mapping mode for this view. For a list of possible values, see **SetScrollSizes**.

sizeTotal   Returns the current total size of the scroll view in device units.

sizePage   Returns the current horizontal and vertical amounts to scroll in each direction in response to a mouse click in a scroll-bar shaft. The **cx** member contains the horizontal amount. The **cy** member contains the vertical amount.

sizeLine   Returns the current horizontal and vertical amounts to scroll in each direction in response to a mouse click in a scroll arrow. The **cx** member contains the horizontal amount. The **cy** member contains the vertical amount.

Remarks **GetDeviceScrollSizes** gets the current mapping mode, the total size, and the line and page sizes of the scrollable view. Sizes are in device units. This member function is rarely called.

See Also **CScrollView::SetScrollSizes, CScrollView::GetTotalSize**

CScrollView::GetScrollPosition

CPoint GetScrollPosition( ) const;

Remarks Call **GetScrollPosition** when you need the current horizontal and vertical positions of the scroll boxes in the scroll bars. This coordinate pair corresponds to the location in the document to which the upper-left corner of the view has been scrolled.

GetScrollPosition returns values in logical units. If you want device units, use **GetDeviceScrollPosition** instead.

See Also **CScrollView::GetDeviceScrollPosition**

CScrollView::GetTotalSize

CSize GetTotalSize( ) const;

Return Value The total size of the scroll view in logical units. The horizontal size is in the **cx** member of the **CSize** return value. The vertical size is in the **cy** member.

Remarks Call **GetTotalSize** to retrieve the current horizontal and vertical sizes of the scroll view.

See Also **CScrollView::GetDeviceScrollSizes, CScrollView::SetScrollSizes**

CScrollView::ResizeParentToFit

void ResizeParentToFit(BOOL *bShrinkOnly* **= TRUE);**

Parameters *bShrinkOnly* The kind of resizing to perform. The default value, **TRUE**, shrinks the frame window if appropriate. Scroll bars will still appear for large views or small frame windows. A value of **FALSE** causes the view always to resize the frame window exactly. This can be somewhat dangerous since the frame window could get too big to fit inside the multiple document interface (MDI) frame window or the screen.

Remarks Call **ResizeParentToFit** to let the size of your view dictate the size of its frame window. This is recommended only for views in MDI child frame windows. Use **ResizeParentToFit** in the **OnInitialUpdate** handler function of your derived **CScrollView** class. For an example of this member function, see **CScrollView::SetScrollSizes**.

ResizeParentToFit assumes that the size of the view window has been set. If the view window size has not been set when **ResizeParentToFit** is called, you will get an assertion. To ensure that this does not happen, make the following call before calling **ResizeParentToFit**:

```
GetParentFrame()->RecalcLayout();
```

See Also   **CView::OnInitialUpdate**, **CScrollView::SetScrollSizes**

CScrollView::ScrollToPosition

void ScrollToPosition(POINT *pt* **);**

Parameters   *pt*   The point to scroll to, in logical units. The **cx** member must be a positive value (greater than or equal to 0, up to the total size of the view). The same is true for the **cy** member when the mapping mode is **MM_TEXT**. The **cy** member is negative in mapping modes other than **MM_TEXT**.

Remarks   Call **ScrollToPosition** to scroll to a given point in the view. The view will be scrolled so that this point is at the upper-left corner of the window. This member function must not be called if the view is scaled to fit.

See Also   **CScrollView::GetDeviceScrollPosition**, **CScrollView::SetScaleToFitSize**, **CScrollView::SetScrollSizes**

CScrollView::SetScaleToFitSize

void SetScaleToFitSize(SIZE *sizeTotal* **);**

Parameters   *sizeTotal*   The horizontal and vertical sizes to which the view is to be scaled. The scroll view's size is measured in logical units. The horizontal size is contained in the **cx** member. The vertical size is contained in the **cy** member. Both **cx** and **cy** must be greater than or equal to 0.

Remarks   Call **SetScaleToFitSize** when you want to scale the viewport size to the current window size automatically. With scroll bars, only a portion of the logical view may be visible at any time. But with the scale-to-fit capability, the view has no scroll bars and the logical view is stretched or shrunk to exactly fit the window's client area. When the window is resized, the view draws its data at a new scale based on the size of the window.

You'll typically place the call to **SetScaleToFitSize** in your override of the view's **OnInitialUpdate** member function. If you do not want automatic scaling, call the **SetScrollSizes** member function instead.

SetScaleToFitSize can be used to implement a "Zoom to Fit" operation. Use **SetScrollSizes** to reinitialize scrolling.

SetScaleToFitSize assumes that the size of the view window has been set. If the view window size has not been set when **SetScaleToFitSize** is called, you will get an assertion. To ensure that this does not happen, make the following call before calling **SetScaleToFitSize**:

```
GetParentFrame()->RecalcLayout();
```

See Also   **CScrollView::SetScrollSizes**, **CView::OnInitialUpdate**

CScrollView::SetScrollSizes

void SetScrollSizes(int *nMapMode***, SIZE** *sizeTotal***, const SIZE&** *sizePage* **= sizeDefault, const SIZE&** *sizeLine* **= sizeDefault);**

Parameters   *nMapMode*   The mapping mode to set for this view. Possible values include:

Mapping Mode	Logical Unit	Positive y-axis Extends...
MM_TEXT	1 pixel	Downward
MM_HIMETRIC	0.01 mm	Upward
MM_TWIPS	1/1440 in	Upward
MM_HIENGLISH	0.001 in	Upward
MM_LOMETRIC	0.1 mm	Upward
MM_LOENGLISH	0.01 in	Upward

All of these modes are defined by Windows. Two standard mapping modes, **MM_ISOTROPIC** and **MM_ANISOTROPIC**, are not used for **CScrollView**. The class library provides the **SetScaleToFitSize** member function for scaling the view to window size. Column three in the table above describes the coordinate orientation.

sizeTotal   The total size of the scroll view. The **cx** member contains the horizontal extent. The **cy** member contains the vertical extent. Sizes are in logical units. Both **cx** and **cy** must be greater than or equal to 0.

sizePage   The horizontal and vertical amounts to scroll in each direction in response to a mouse click in a scroll-bar shaft. The **cx** member contains the horizontal amount. The **cy** member contains the vertical amount.

sizeLine   The horizontal and vertical amounts to scroll in each direction in response to a mouse click in a scroll arrow. The **cx** member contains the horizontal amount. The **cy** member contains the vertical amount.

Remarks   Call **SetScrollSizes** when the view is about to be updated. Call it in your override of the **OnUpdate** member function to adjust scrolling characteristics when, for example, the document is initially displayed or when it changes size.

You will typically obtain size information from the view's associated document by calling a document member function, perhaps called `GetMyDocSize`, that you supply with your derived document class. The following code shows this approach:

```
SetScrollSizes( nMapMode, GetDocument( )->GetMyDocSize( ) );
```

Alternatively, you might sometimes need to set a fixed size, as in the following code:

```
SetScrollSizes( nMapMode, CSize(100, 100) );
```

You must set the mapping mode to any of the Windows mapping modes except **MM_ISOTROPIC** or **MM_ANISOTROPIC**. If you want to use an unconstrained mapping mode, call the **SetScaleToFitSize** member function instead of **SetScrollSizes**.

See Also   **CScrollView::SetScaleToFitSize**, **CScrollView::GetDeviceScrollSizes**, **CScrollView::GetTotalSize**

Example
```
void CScaleView::OnUpdate( )
{
    // ...
    // Implement a GetDocSize( ) member function in
    // your document class; it returns a CSize.
    SetScrollSizes( MM_LOENGLISH, GetDocument( )->GetDocSize( ) );
    ResizeParentToFit( );   // Default bShrinkOnly argument
    // ...
}
```

class CSingleDocTemplate : public CDocTemplate

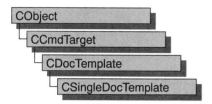

The **CSingleDocTemplate** class defines a document template that implements the single document interface (SDI). An SDI application uses the main frame window to display a document; only one document can be open at a time. For a more detailed description of the SDI, see *The Windows Interface: An Application Design Guide*.

A document template defines the relationship between three types of classes:

- A document class, which you derive from **CDocument**.
- A view class, which displays data from the document class listed above. You can derive this class from **CView**, **CScrollView**, **CFormView**, or **CEditView**. (You can also use **CEditView** directly.)
- A frame window class, which contains the view. For an SDI document template, you can derive this class from **CFrameWnd**; if you do not need to customize the behavior of the main frame window, you can use **CFrameWnd** directly without deriving your own class.

An SDI application typically supports one type of document, so it has only one **CSingleDocTemplate** object. Only one document can be open at a time.

You don't need to call any member functions of **CSingleDocTemplate** except the constructor. The framework handles **CSingleDocTemplate** objects internally.

See Also   **CDocTemplate**, **CDocument**, **CFrameWnd**, **CMultiDocTemplate**, **CView**, **CWinApp**

Construction

CSingleDocTemplate   Constructs a **CSingleDocTemplate** object.

Member Functions

CSingleDocTemplate::CSingleDocTemplate

> **CSingleDocTemplate(UINT** *nIDResource*, **CRuntimeClass*** *pDocClass*,
> **CRuntimeClass*** *pFrameClass*, **CRuntimeClass*** *pViewClass* **);**

Parameters   *nIDResource*   Specifies the ID of the resources used with the document type. This
may include menu, icon, accelerator table, and string resources.

The string resource consists of up to seven substrings separated by the '\n'
character (the '\n' character is needed as a placeholder if a substring is not
included; however, trailing '\n' characters are not necessary); these substrings
describe the document type. For information about the substrings, see
CDocTemplate::GetDocString. This string resource is found in the
application's resource file. For example:

```
// MYCALC.RC
STRINGTABLE PRELOAD DISCARDABLE
BEGIN
    IDR_MAINFRAME "MyCalc Windows Application\nSheet\nWorksheet\n
Worksheets (*.myc)\n.myc\nMyCalcSheet\n MyCalc Worksheet"
END
```

You can edit this string using the string editor; the entire string appears as a
single entry in the String Editor, not as seven separate entries.

For more information about these resource types, see the *Visual C++ User's
Guide*.

pDocClass   Points to the **CRuntimeClass** object of the document class. This class
is a **CDocument**-derived class you define to represent your documents.

pFrameClass   Points to the **CRuntimeClass** object of the frame window class.
This class can be a **CFrameWnd**-derived class, or it can be **CFrameWnd**
itself if you want default behavior for your main frame window.

pViewClass   Points to the **CRuntimeClass** object of the view class. This class is a
CView-derived class you define to display your documents.

Remarks   Constructs a **CSingleDocTemplate** object. Dynamically allocate a
CSingleDocTemplate object and pass it to **CWinApp::AddDocTemplate** from
the `InitInstance` member function of your application class.

See Also   **CDocTemplate::GetDocString**, **CWinApp::AddDocTemplate**,
CWinApp::InitInstance, **CRuntimeClass**

In the Win32 *Programmer's Reference*: **RUNTIME_CLASS**

Example
```
BOOL CMyApp::InitInstance()
{
        // ...
        // Establish the document type
        // supported by the application

        AddDocTemplate( new CSingleDocTemplate( IDR_MAINFRAME,
                               RUNTIME_CLASS( CSheetDoc ),
                               RUNTIME_CLASS( CFrameWnd ),
                               RUNTIME_CLASS( CSheetView ) ) );

        // ...
}
```

class CSize : public tagSIZE

The **CSize** class is similar to the Windows **SIZE** structure, which implements a relative coordinate or position. Because **CSize** derives from **tagSIZE**, **CSize** objects may be used as **SIZE** structures. The operators of this class that interact with a "size" accept either **CSize** objects or **SIZE** structures.

The **cx** and **cy** members of **SIZE** (and **CSize**) are public. In addition, **CSize** implements member functions to manipulate the **SIZE** structure.

#include <afxwin.h>

See Also   **CRect, CPoint**

Construction
CSize   Constructs a **CSize** object.

Operators
operator ==   Checks for equality between **CSize** and a size.
operator !=   Checks for inequality between **CSize** and a size.
operator +=   Adds a size to **CSize**.
operator –=   Subtracts a size from **CSize**.

Operators Returning CSize Values
operator +   Adds two sizes.
operator –   Subtracts two sizes.

Member Functions

CSize::CSize

CSize( );

CSize(int *initCX***, int** *initCY* **);**

CSize(SIZE *initSize* **);**

CSize(POINT *initPt* **);**

CSize(DWORD *dwSize* **);**

Parameters

initCX   Sets the **cx** member for the **CSize**.

initCY   Sets the **cy** member for the **CSize**.

initSize   **SIZE** structure or **CSize** object used to initialize **CSize**.

initPt   **POINT** structure or **CPoint** object used to initialize **CSize**.

dwSize   **DWORD** used to initialize **CSize**. The low-order word is the **cx** member and the high-order word is the **cy** member.

Remarks   Constructs a **CSize** object. If no arguments are given, **cx** and **cy** members are not initialized.

Operators

CSize::operator ==

BOOL operator ==(SIZE *size* **) const;**

Return Value   Nonzero if the sizes are equal; otherwise 0.

Remarks   Checks for equality between two sizes.

CSize::operator !=

BOOL operator !=(SIZE *size* **) const;**

Return Value   Nonzero if the sizes are not equal; otherwise 0.

Remarks   Checks for inequality between two sizes.

CSize::operator +=

void operator +=(SIZE *size* **);**

Remarks   Adds a size to a **CSize**.

CSize::operator -=

void operator -=(SIZE *size* **);**

Remarks   Subtracts a size from a **CSize**.

CSize::operator +

CSize operator +(SIZE *size*) const;

Return Value   A **CSize** that is the sum of two sizes.

CSize::operator –

CSize operator –(SIZE *size*) const;

CSize operator –( ) const;

Return Value   A **CSize** that is the difference between two sizes.

class CSplitterWnd : public CWnd

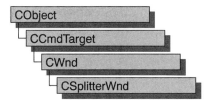

CObject
CCmdTarget
CWnd
CSplitterWnd

The **CSplitterWnd** class provides the functionality of a splitter window, which is a window that contains multiple panes. A pane is usually an application-specific object derived from **CView**, but it can be any **CWnd** object that has the appropriate child window ID.

A **CSplitterWnd** object is usually embedded in a parent **CFrameWnd** or **CMDIChildWnd** object. Create a **CSplitterWnd** object using the following steps:

1. Embed a **CSplitterWnd** member variable in the parent frame.
2. Override the parent frame's **OnCreateClient** member function.
3. From within the overridden **OnCreateClient**, call the **Create** or **CreateStatic** member function of **CSplitterWnd**.

Call the **Create** member function to create a dynamic splitter window. A dynamic splitter window typically is used to create and scroll a number of individual panes, or views, of the same document. The framework automatically creates an initial pane for the splitter; then the framework creates, resizes, and disposes of additional panes as the user operates the splitter window's controls.

When you call **Create**, you specify a minimum row height and column width that determine when the panes are too small to be fully displayed. After you call **Create**, you can adjust these minimums by calling the **SetColumnInfo** and **SetRowInfo** member functions.

Also use the **SetColumnInfo** and **SetRowInfo** member functions to set an "ideal" width for a column and "ideal" height for a row. When the framework displays a splitter window, it first displays the parent frame, then the splitter window. The framework then lays out the panes in columns and rows according to their ideal dimensions, working from the upper-left to the lower-right corner of the splitter window's client area.

All panes in a dynamic splitter window must be of the same class. Familiar applications that support dynamic splitter windows include Microsoft Word and Microsoft Excel.

Use the **CreateStatic** member function to create a static splitter window. The user can change only the size of the panes in a static splitter window, not their number or order.

You must specifically create all the static splitter's panes when you create the static splitter. Make sure you create all the panes before the parent frame's **OnCreateClient** member function returns, or the framework will not display the window correctly.

The **CreateStatic** member function automatically initializes a static splitter with a minimum row height and column width of 0. After you call **Create**, adjust these minimums by calling the **SetColumnInfo** and **SetRowInfo** member functions. Also use **SetColumnInfo** and **SetRowInfo** after you call **CreateStatic** to indicate desired ideal pane dimensions.

The individual panes of a static splitter often belong to different classes. For examples of static splitter windows, see the graphics editor and the Windows File Manager.

A splitter window supports special scroll bars (apart from the scroll bars that panes may have). These scroll bars are children of the **CSplitterWnd** object and are shared with the panes.

You create these special scroll bars when you create the splitter window. For example, a **CSplitterWnd** that has one row, two columns, and the **WS_VSCROLL** style will display a vertical scroll bar that is shared by the two panes. When the user moves the scroll bar, **WM_VSCROLL** messages are sent to both panes. When the panes set the scroll-bar position, the shared scroll bar is set.

For further information on splitter windows, see Technical Note 29 under MFC in Books Online. For more information on how to create dynamic splitter windows, see the Scribble sample application in Chapter 13 of *Introducing Visual C++*, and the VIEWEX sample under MFC in Books Online.

#include <afxext.h>

See Also   CWnd

Construction

CSplitterWnd	Call to construct a **CSplitterWnd** object.
Create	Call to create a dynamic splitter window and attach it to the **CSplitterWnd** object.
CreateStatic	Call to create a static splitter window and attach it to the **CSplitterWnd** object.
CreateView	Call to create a pane in a splitter window.

Operations

GetRowCount	Returns the current pane row count.
GetColumnCount	Returns the current pane column count.
GetRowInfo	Returns information on the specified row.
SetRowInfo	Call to set the specified row information.
GetColumnInfo	Returns information on the specified column.
SetColumnInfo	Call to set the specified column information.
GetPane	Returns the pane at the specified row and column.
IsChildPane	Call to determine whether the window is currently a child pane of this splitter window.
IdFromRowCol	Returns the child window ID of the pane at the specified row and column.
RecalcLayout	Call to redisplay the splitter window after adjusting row or column size.
GetScrollStyle	Returns the shared scroll-bar style.
SetScrollStyle	Specifies the new scroll-bar style for the splitter window's shared scroll-bar support.

Member Functions

CSplitterWnd::Create

BOOL Create(CWnd* *pParentWnd*, **int** *nMaxRows*, **int** *nMaxCols*, **SIZE** *sizeMin*, **CCreateContext*** *pContext*, **DWORD** *dwStyle* = **WS_CHILD | WS_VISIBLE |WS_HSCROLL | WS_VSCROLL | SPLS_DYNAMIC_SPLIT, UINT** *nID* = **AFX_IDW_PANE_FIRST**);

Return Value   Nonzero if successful; otherwise 0.

Parameters   *pParentWnd*   The parent frame window of the splitter window.

nMaxRows   The maximum number of rows in the splitter window. This value must not exceed 2.

nMaxCols   The maximum number of columns in the splitter window. This value must not exceed 2.

sizeMin   Specifies the minimum size at which a pane may be displayed.

pContext   A pointer to a **CCreateContext** structure. In most cases, this can be the *pContext* passed to the parent frame window.

dwStyle   Specifies the window style.

nID   The child window ID of the window. The ID can be **AFX_IDW_PANE_FIRST** unless the splitter window is nested inside another splitter window.

Remarks   To create a dynamic splitter window, call the **Create** member function.

You can embed a **CSplitterWnd** in a parent **CFrameWnd** or **CMDIChildWnd** object by taking the following steps:

1. Embed a **CSplitterWnd** member variable in the parent frame.
2. Override the parent frame's **OnCreateClient** member function.
3. Call the **Create** member function from within the overridden **OnCreateClient**.

When you create a splitter window from within a parent frame, pass the parent frame's *pContext* parameter to the splitter window. Otherwise, this parameter can be **NULL**.

The initial minimum row height and column width of a dynamic splitter window are set by the *sizeMin* parameter. These minimums, which determine whether a pane is too small to be shown in its entirety, can be changed with the **SetRowInfo** and **SetColumnInfo** member functions.

For more on dynamic splitter windows, see Chapter 3, "Working with Frame Windows, Documents, and Views," in *Programming with the Microsoft Foundation Class Library*, Technical Note 29, and the **CSplitterWnd** class overview.

See Also   **CSplitterWnd::CreateStatic**, **CFrameWnd::OnCreateClient**, **CSplitterWnd::SetRowInfo**, **CSplitterWnd::SetColumnInfo**, **CSplitterWnd::CreateView**

CSplitterWnd::CreateStatic

BOOL CreateStatic(CWnd* *pParentWnd*, **int** *nRows*, **int** *nCols*, **DWORD** *dwStyle* **= WS_CHILD | WS_VISIBLE, UINT** *nID* **= AFX_IDW_PANE_FIRST);**

Return Value   Nonzero if successful; otherwise 0.

Parameters   *pParentWnd*   The parent frame window of the splitter window.

nRows   The number of rows. This value must not exceed 16.

nCols   The number of columns. This value must not exceed 16.

dwStyle   Specifies the window style.

nID   The child window ID of the window. The ID can be **AFX_IDW_PANE_FIRST** unless the splitter window is nested inside another splitter window.

Remarks

To create a static splitter window, call the **CreateStatic** member function.

A **CSplitterWnd** is usually embedded in a parent **CFrameWnd** or **CMDIChildWnd** object by taking the following steps:

1. Embed a **CSplitterWnd** member variable in the parent frame.
2. Override the parent frame's **OnCreateClient** member function.
3. Call the **CreateStatic** member function from within the overridden **OnCreateClient**.

A static splitter window contains a fixed number of panes, often from different classes.

When you create a static splitter window, you must at the same time create all its panes. The **CreateView** member function is usually used for this purpose, but you can create other nonview classes as well.

The initial minimum row height and column width for a static splitter window is 0. These minimums, which determine when a pane is too small to be shown in its entirety, can be changed with the **SetRowInfo** and **SetColumnInfo** member functions.

To add scroll bars to a static splitter window, add the **WS_HSCROLL** and **WS_VSCROLL** styles to *dwStyle*.

See Chapter 3, "Working with Frame Windows, Documents and Views" in *Programming with the Microsoft Foundation Class Library*, Technical Note 29, and the **CSplitterWnd** class overview for more on static splitter windows.

See Also

CSplitterWnd::Create, **CFrameWnd::OnCreateClient**, **CSplitterWnd::SetRowInfo**, **CSplitterWnd::SetColumnInfo**, **CSplitterWnd::CreateView**

CSplitterWnd::CreateView

virtual BOOL CreateView(int *row*, **int** *col*, **CRuntimeClass*** *pViewClass*, **SIZE** *sizeInit*, **CCreateContext*** *pContext* **);**

Return Value

Nonzero if successful; otherwise 0.

Parameters

row   Specifies the splitter window row in which to place the new view.

col   Specifies the splitter window column in which to place the new view.

pViewClass   Specifies the **CRuntimeClass** of the new view.

sizeInit   Specifies the initial size of the new view.

pContext   A pointer to a creation context used to create the view (usually the *pContext* passed into the parent frame's overridden **OnCreateClient** member function in which the splitter window is being created).

Remarks   Call this member function to create the panes for a static splitter window. All panes of a static splitter window must be created before the framework displays the splitter.

The framework also calls this member function to create new panes when the user of a dynamic splitter window splits a pane, row, or column.

See Also   **CSplitterWnd::Create**

CSplitterWnd::CSplitterWnd

CSplitterWnd( );

Remarks   Construct a **CSplitterWnd** object in two steps. First call the constructor, which creates the **CSplitterWnd** object, then call the **Create** member function, which creates the splitter window and attaches it to the **CSplitterWnd** object.

See Also   **CSplitterWnd::Create**

CSplitterWnd::GetColumnCount

int GetColumnCount( );

Return Value   Returns the current number of columns in the splitter. For a static splitter this will also be the maximum number of columns.

See Also   **CSplitterWnd::GetRowCount**

CSplitterWnd::GetColumnInfo

void GetColumnInfo(int *col*, int& *cxCur*, int& *cxMin*);

Parameters   *col*   Specifies a column.

cxCur   A reference to an **int** to be set to the current width of the column.

cxMin   A reference to an **int** to be set to the current minimum width of the column.

Remarks   Call this member function to obtain information about the specified column.

See Also   **CSplitterWnd::SetColumnInfo, CSplitterWnd::GetRowInfo**

CSplitterWnd::GetPane

CWnd* GetPane(int *row*, **int** *col* **);**

Return Value   Returns the pane at the specified row and column. The returned pane is usually a
CView-derived class.

Parameters   *row*   Specifies a row.

col   Specifies a column.

See Also   **CSplitterWnd::IdFromRowCol, CSplitterWnd::IsChildPane**

CSplitterWnd::GetRowCount

int GetRowCount( );

Return Value   Returns the current number of rows in the splitter window. For a static splitter
window, this will also be the maximum number of rows.

See Also   **CSplitterWnd::GetColumnCount**

CSplitterWnd::GetRowInfo

void GetRowInfo(int *row*, **int&** *cyCur*, **int&** *cyMin* **);**

Return Value   The *cyCur* parameter is filled with the current height of the specified row, and
cyMin is filled with the minimum height of the row.

Parameters   *row*   Specifies a row.

cyCur   Reference to **int** to be set to the current height of the row in pixels.

cyMin   Reference to **int** to be set to the current minimum height of the row in
    pixels.

Remarks   Call this member function to obtain information about the specified row.

See Also   **CSplitterWnd::SetRowInfo, CSplitterWnd::GetColumnInfo**

CSplitterWnd::GetScrollStyle

DWORD GetScrollStyle( ) const;

Return Value   One or more of the following windows style flags, if successful:

- **WS_HSCROLL**   If the splitter currently manages shared horizontal scroll
  bars.
- **WS_VSCROLL**   If the splitter currently manages shared vertical scroll bars.

If zero, the splitter window does not currently manage any shared scroll bars.

Remarks   Returns the shared scroll-bar style for the splitter window.

See Also   **CSplitterWnd::SetScrollStyle**

CSplitterWnd::IdFromRowCol

int IdFromRowCol(int *row*, **int** *col* **);**

Return Value   The child window ID for the pane.

Parameters   *row*   Specifies the splitter window row.

col   Specifies the splitter window column.

Remarks   Call this member function to obtain the child window ID for the pane at the specified row and column. This member function is used for creating nonviews as panes and may be called before the pane exists.

See Also   **CSplitterWnd::GetPane**, **CSplitterWnd::IsChildPane**

CSplitterWnd::IsChildPane

BOOL IsChildPane(CWnd* *pWnd*, **int&** *row*, **int&** *col* **);**

Return Value   If nonzero, *pWnd* is currently a child pane of this splitter window, and *row* and *col* are filled in with the position of the pane in the splitter window. If *pWnd* is not a child pane of this splitter window, 0 is returned.

Parameters   *pWnd*   A pointer to a **CWnd** object to be tested.

row   Reference to an **int** in which to store row number.

col   Reference to an **int** in which to store a column number.

Remarks   Call this member function to determine whether *pWnd* is currently a child pane of this splitter window.

See Also   **CSplitterWnd::GetPane**

CSplitterWnd::RecalcLayout

void RecalcLayout( );

Remarks   Call this member function to correctly redisplay the splitter window after you have adjusted row and column sizes with the **SetRowInfo** and **SetColumnInfo** member functions. If you change row and column sizes as part of the creation process before the splitter window is visible, it is not necessary to call this member function.

The framework calls this member function whenever the user resizes the splitter window or moves a split.

See Also   **CSplitterWnd::SetRowInfo**, **CSplitterWnd::SetColumnInfo**

CSplitterWnd::SetColumnInfo

void SetColumnInfo(int *col*, **int** *cxIdeal*, **int** *cxMin* **);**

Parameters   *col*   Specifies a splitter window column.

cxIdeal   Specifies an ideal width for the splitter window column in pixels.

cxMin   Specifies a minimum width for the splitter window column in pixels.

Remarks   Call this member function to set a new minimum width and ideal width for a column. The column minimum value determines when the column will be too small to be fully displayed.

When the framework displays the splitter window, it lays out the panes in columns and rows according to their ideal dimensions, working from the upper-left to the lower-right corner of the splitter window's client area.

See Also   **CSplitterWnd::GetRowInfo**, **CSplitterWnd::RecalcLayout**

CSplitterWnd::SetRowInfo

void SetRowInfo(int *row*, **int** *cyIdeal*, **int** *cyMin* **);**

Parameters   *row*   Specifies a splitter window row.

cyIdeal   Specifies an ideal height for the splitter window row in pixels.

cyMin   Specifies a minimum height for the splitter window row in pixels.

Remarks   Call this member function to set a new minimum height and ideal height for a row. The row minimum value determines when the row will be too small to be fully displayed.

When the framework displays the splitter window, it lays out the panes in columns and rows according to their ideal dimensions, working from the upper-left to the lower-right corner of the splitter window's client area.

See Also   **CSplitterWnd::GetRowInfo**, **CSplitterWnd::SetColumnInfo**,
CSplitterWnd::RecalcLayout

CSplitterWnd::SetScrollStyle

void SetScrollStyle(DWORD *dwStyle* **);**

Return Value   The new scroll bar style if successful; otherwise 0.

Parameters   *dwStyle*   The new scroll style for the splitter window's shared scroll-bar support, which can be one of the following values:

- **WS_HSCROLL**   Create/show horizontal shared scroll bars.
- **WS_VSCROLL**   Create/show vertical shared scroll bars.

Remarks   Specifies the new scroll style for the splitter window's shared scroll-bar support. Once a scroll bar is created it will not be destroyed even if **SetScrollStyle** is called without that style; instead those scroll bars are hidden. This allows the scroll bars to retain their state even though they are hidden. After calling **SetScrollStyle** it is necessary to call **CSplitterWnd::RecalcLayout** for all the changes to take effect.

See Also   **CSplitterWnd::GetScrollStyle**

class CStatic : public CWnd

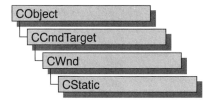

The **CStatic** class provides the functionality of a Windows static control. A static control is a simple text field, box, or rectangle that can be used to label, box, or separate other controls. A static control takes no input and provides no output.

Create a static control in two steps. First, call the constructor **CStatic** to construct the **CStatic** object, then call the **Create** member function to create the static control and attach it to the **CStatic** object.

If you create a **CStatic** object within a dialog box (through a dialog resource), the **CStatic** object is automatically destroyed when the user closes the dialog box. If you create a **CStatic** object within a window, you may also need to destroy it. A **CStatic** object created on the stack within a window is automatically destroyed. If you create the **CStatic** object on the heap by using the **new** function, you must call **delete** on the object to destroy it when the user terminates the Windows static control.

#include <afxwin.h>

See Also   **CWnd**, **CButton**, **CComboBox**, **CEdit**, **CListBox**, **CScrollBar**, **CDialog**

Construction
CStatic   Constructs a **CStatic** object.

Initialization
Create   Creates the Windows static control and attaches it to the **CStatic** object.

Operations
SetIcon   Associates an icon with an icon resource.

GetIcon   Retrieves the handle of the icon associated with an icon resource.

Member Functions

CStatic::Create

> **BOOL Create(LPCTSTR** *lpszText***, DWORD** *dwStyle***, const RECT&** *rect***,**
> **CWnd*** *pParentWnd***, UINT** *nID* **= 0xffff);**

Return Value   Nonzero if successful; otherwise 0.

Parameters   *lpszText*   Specifies the text to place in the control. If **NULL**, no text will be visible.

dwStyle   Specifies the static control's window style. Apply any combination of static control styles to the control. For a list of static styles, see the section "Static Styles" on page 1252.

rect   Specifies the position and size of the static control. It can be either a **RECT** structure or a **CRect** object.

pParentWnd   Specifies the **CStatic** parent window, usually a **CDialog** object. It must not be **NULL**.

nID   Specifies the static control's control ID.

Remarks   Construct a **CStatic** object in two steps. First call the constructor **CStatic**, then call **Create**, which creates the Windows static control and attaches it to the **CStatic** object. Apply the following window styles to a static control:

- **WS_CHILD**   Always
- **WS_VISIBLE**   Usually
- **WS_DISABLED**   Rarely

See Also   **CStatic::CStatic**

CStatic::CStatic

> **CStatic( );**

Remarks   Constructs a **CStatic** object.

See Also   **CStatic::Create**

CStatic::GetIcon

HICON GetIcon( ) const;

Return Value   Returns the handle of the icon associated with an icon resource. This function should be called only for **CStatic** objects that represent icons created with the **SS_ICON** style.

See Also   **STM_GETICON, CStatic::SetIcon**

CStatic::SetIcon

HICON SetIcon(HICON *hIcon* **);**

Return Value   The handle of the icon that was previously associated with the icon resource; 0 if an error occurred.

Parameters   *hIcon*   Identifies the icon to associate with an icon resource.

Remarks   Associates an icon with an icon resource. This is a **CStatic** object created with the **SS_ICON** style.

See Also   **STM_SETICON, ::LoadIcon, CStatic::GetIcon**

class CStatusBar : public CControlBar

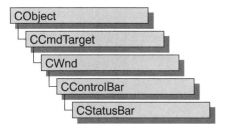

A **CStatusBar** object is a control bar with a row of text output panes, or "indicators." The output panes commonly are used as message lines and as status indicators. Examples include the menu help-message lines that briefly explain the selected menu command and the indicators that show the status of the SCROLL LOCK, NUM LOCK, and other keys.

The framework stores indicator information in an array with the leftmost indicator at position 0. When you create a status bar, you use an array of string IDs that the framework associates with the corresponding indicators. You can then use either a string ID or an index to access an indicator.

By default, the first indicator is "elastic": it takes up the status-bar length not used by the other indicator panes, so that the other panes are right-aligned.

To create a status bar, follow these steps:

1. Construct the **CStatusBar** object.
2. Call the **Create** function to create the status-bar window and attach it to the **CStatusBar** object.
3. Call **SetIndicators** to associate a string ID with each indicator.

There are three ways to update the text in a status-bar pane:

1. Call **SetWindowText** to update the text in pane 0 only.
2. Call **SetText** in the status bar's **ON_UPDATE_COMMAND_UI** handler.
3. Call **SetPaneText** to update the text for any pane.

#include <afxext.h>

See Also   **CControlBar, CWnd::SetWindowText, CStatusBar::SetIndicators**

Construction

CStatusBar	Constructs a **CStatusBar** object.
Create	Creates the Windows status bar, attaches it to the **CStatusBar** object, and sets the initial font and bar height.
SetIndicators	Sets indicator IDs.

Attributes

CommandToIndex	Gets index for a given indicator ID.
GetItemID	Gets indicator ID for a given index.
GetItemRect	Gets display rectangle for a given index.
GetPaneText	Gets indicator text for a given index.
SetPaneText	Sets indicator text for a given index.
GetPaneInfo	Gets indicator ID, style, and width for a given index.
SetPaneInfo	Sets indicator ID, style, and width for a given index.

Member Functions

CStatusBar::CommandToIndex

int CommandToIndex(UINT *nIDFind* **) const;**

Return Value   The index of the indicator if successful; –1 if not successful.

Parameters   *nIDFind*   String ID of the indicator whose index is to be retrieved.

Remarks   Gets the indicator index for a given ID. The index of the first indicator is 0.

See Also   **CStatusBar::GetItemID**

CStatusBar::Create

BOOL Create(CWnd* *pParentWnd***, DWORD** *dwStyle* **= WS_CHILD | WS_VISIBLE | CBRS_BOTTOM, UINT** *nID* **= AFX_IDW_STATUS_BAR);**

Return Value   Nonzero if successful; otherwise 0.

Parameters   *pParentWnd*   Pointer to the **CWnd** object whose Windows window is the parent of the status bar.

dwStyle   The status-bar style. In addition to the standard Windows styles, these styles are supported. For a list of window styles, see the section "Window Styles" on page 1253.

- **CBRS_TOP**   Control bar is at top of frame window.
- **CBRS_BOTTOM**   Control bar is at bottom of frame window.
- **CBRS_NOALIGN**   Control bar is not repositioned when the parent is resized.

nID   The toolbar's child-window ID.

Remarks   Creates a status bar (a child window) and associates it with the **CStatusBar** object. Also sets the initial font and sets the status bar's height to a default value.

See Also   **CStatusBar::SetIndicators**

CStatusBar::CStatusBar

CStatusBar( );

Remarks   Constructs a **CStatusBar** object, creates a default status-bar font if necessary, and sets the font characteristics to default values.

See Also   **CStatusBar::Create**

CStatusBar::GetItemID

UINT GetItemID(int *nIndex* **) const;**

Return Value The ID of the indicator specified by *nIndex*.

Parameters   *nIndex*   Index of the indicator whose ID is to be retrieved.

Remarks   Returns the ID of the indicator specified by *nIndex*.

See Also   **CStatusBar::CommandToIndex**

CStatusBar::GetItemRect

void GetItemRect(int *nIndex***, LPRECT** *lpRect* **) const;**

Parameters   *nIndex*   Index of the indicator whose rectangle coordinates are to be retrieved.

lpRect   Points to a **RECT** structure or a **CRect** object that will receive the coordinates of the indicator specified by *nIndex*.

Remarks   Copies the coordinates of the indicator specified by *nIndex* into the structure pointed to by *lpRect*. Coordinates are in pixels relative to the upper left corner of the status bar.

See Also   **CStatusBar::CommandToIndex, CStatusBar::GetPaneInfo**

CStatusBar::GetPaneInfo

void GetPaneInfo(int *nIndex***, UINT&** *nID***, UINT&** *nStyle***, int&** *cxWidth* **)**
const;

Parameters *nIndex*   Index of the pane whose information is to be retrieved.

nID   Reference to a **UINT** that is set to the ID of the pane.

nStyle   Reference to a **UINT** that is set to the style of the pane.

cxWidth   Reference to an integer that is set to the width of the pane.

Remarks Sets *nID*, *nStyle*, and *cxWidth* to the ID, style, and width of the indicator pane at
the location specified by *nIndex*.

See Also **CStatusBar::SetPaneInfo, CStatusBar::GetItemID,**
CStatusBar::GetItemRect

CStatusBar::GetPaneText

void GetPaneText(int *nIndex***, CString&** *s* **) const;**

Parameters *nIndex*   Index of the pane whose text is to be retrieved.

s   Reference to a **CString** object to which the pane's text is copied.

Remarks Copies the pane's text to the **CString** object.

See Also **CStatusBar::SetPaneText**

CStatusBar::SetIndicators

BOOL SetIndicators(const UINT* *lpIDArray***, int** *nIDCount* **);**

Return Value Nonzero if successful; otherwise 0.

Parameters *lpIDArray*   Pointer to an array of IDs.

nIDCount   Number of elements in the array pointed to by *lpIDArray*.

Remarks Sets each indicator's ID to the value specified by the corresponding element of the
array *lpIDArray*, loads the string resource specified by each ID, and sets the
indicator's text to the string.

See Also **CStatusBar::CStatusBar, CStatusBar::Create, CStatusBar::SetPaneInfo,**
CStatusBar::SetPaneText

CStatusBar::SetPaneInfo

void SetPaneInfo(int *nIndex,* **UINT** *nID,* **UINT** *nStyle,* **int** *cxWidth* **);**

Parameters   *nIndex*   Index of the indicator pane whose style is to be set.

nID   New ID for the indicator pane.

nStyle   New style for the indicator pane.

cxWidth   New width for the indicator pane.

Remarks   Sets the specified indicator pane to a new ID, style, and width.

The following indicator styles are supported:

- **SBPS_NOBORDERS**   No 3-D border around the pane.
- **SBPS_POPOUT**   Reverse border so that text "pops out."
- **SBPS_DISABLED**   Do not draw text.
- **SBPS_STRETCH**   Stretch pane to fill unused space. Only one pane per status bar can have this style.
- **SBPS_NORMAL**   No stretch, borders, or pop-out.

See Also   **CStatusBar::GetPaneInfo**

CStatusBar::SetPaneText

BOOL SetPaneText(int *nIndex,* **LPCTSTR** *lpszNewText,*
    BOOL *bUpdate* **= TRUE);**

Return Value   Nonzero if successful; otherwise 0.

Parameters   *nIndex*   Index of the pane whose text is to be set.

lpszNewText   Pointer to the new pane text.

bUpdate   If TRUE, the pane is invalidated after the text is set.

Remarks   Sets the pane text to the string pointed to by *lpszNewText*.

See Also   **CStatusBar::GetPaneText**

class CStdioFile : public CFile

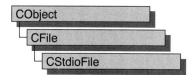

A **CStdioFile** object represents a C run-time stream file as opened by the **fopen** function. Stream files are buffered and can be opened in either text mode (the default) or binary mode. Text mode provides special processing for carriage return–linefeed pairs. When you write a newline character (0x0A) to a text-mode **CStdioFile** object, the byte pair (0x0A, 0x0D) is sent to the file. When you read, the byte pair (0x0A, 0x0D) is translated to a single 0x0A byte.

The **CFile** functions **Duplicate**, **LockRange**, and **UnlockRange** are not implemented for **CStdioFile**. If you call these functions on a **CStdioFile**, you will get a **CNotSupportedException**.

#include <afx.h>

Data Members
m_pStream   Contains a pointer to an open file.

Construction
CStdioFile   Constructs a **CStdioFile** object from a path or file pointer.

Text Read/Write
ReadString   Reads a single line of text.
WriteString   Writes a single line of text.

Member Functions

CStdioFile::CStdioFile

CStdioFile( );

CStdioFile(FILE* *pOpenStream* **);**

CStdioFile(LPCTSTR *lpszFileName*, **UINT** *nOpenFlags* **)**
   throw(CFileException);

Parameters   *pOpenStream*   Specifies the file pointer returned by a call to the C run-time function **fopen**.

lpszFileName   Specifies a string that is the path to the desired file. The path can be relative or absolute.

nOpenFlags   Sharing and access mode. Specifies the action to take when the file is opened. You can combine options by using the bitwise OR (|) operator. One access permission and a text-binary specifier are required; the **create** and **noInherit** modes are optional. See **CFile::CFile** for a list of mode options. The share flags do not apply.

Remarks   The default version of the constructor works in conjunction with the **CFile::Open** member function to test errors. The one-parameter version constructs a **CStdioFile** object from a pointer to a file that is already open. Allowed pointer values include the predefined input/output file pointers **stdin**, **stdout**, or **stderr**. The two-parameter version constructs a **CStdioFile** object and opens the corresponding operating-system file with the given path. **CFileException** is thrown if the file cannot be opened or created.

Example
```
char* pFileName = "test.dat";
CStdioFile f1;
if( !f1.Open( pFileName,
        CFile::modeCreate | CFile::modeWrite | CFile::typeText ) ) {
    #ifdef _DEBUG
        afxDump << "Unable to open file" << "\n";
    #endif
    exit( 1 );
}
CStdioFile f2( stdout );
TRY
{
    CStdioFile f3( pFileName,
        CFile::modeCreate | CFile::modeWrite | CFile::typeText );
}
CATCH( CFileException, e )
{
    #ifdef _DEBUG
        afxDump << "File could not be opened " << e->m_cause << "\n";
    #endif
}
END_CATCH
```

CStdioFile::ReadString

virtual LPTSTR ReadString(LPTSTR *lpsz*, **UINT** *nMax* **)**
  throw(CFileException);

Return Value   A pointer to the buffer containing the text data; **NULL** if end-of-file was reached.

Parameters   *lpsz*   Specifies a pointer to a user-supplied buffer that will receive a null-
          terminated text string.

   nMax   Specifies the maximum number of characters to read. Should be one less
          than the size of the *lpsz* buffer.

Remarks   Reads text data into a buffer, up to a limit of *nMax*–1 characters, from the file
       associated with the **CStdioFile** object. Reading is stopped by a carriage
       return–linefeed pair. If, in that case, fewer than *nMax*–1 characters have been read,
       a newline character is stored in the buffer. A null character ('\0') is appended in
       either case. **CFile::Read** is also available for text-mode input, but it does not
       terminate on a carriage return–linefeed pair.

Example
```
extern CStdioFile f;
char buf[100];

f.ReadString( buf, 100 );
```

CStdioFile::WriteString

virtual void WriteString(LPCTSTR *lpsz* **)**
  throw(CFileException);

Parameters   *lpsz*   Specifies a pointer to a buffer containing a null-terminated text string.

Remarks   Writes data from a buffer to the file associated with the **CStdioFile** object. The
       terminating null character ('\0') is not written to the file. Any newline character in
       lpsz is written to the file as a carriage return–linefeed pair. **WriteString** throws an
       exception in response to several conditions, including the disk-full condition.

       This is a text-oriented write function available only to **CStdioFile** and its
       descendents. **CFile::Write** is also available, but rather than terminating on a null
       character, it writes the requested number of bytes to the file.

Example
```
extern CStdioFile f;
char buf[] = "test string";

f.WriteString( buf );
```

Data Members

CStdioFile::m_pStream

Remarks

The **m_pStream** data member is the pointer to an open file as returned by the C run-time function **fopen**. It is **NULL** if the file has never been opened or has been closed.

class CString

A **CString** object consists of a variable-length sequence of characters. **CString** provides functions and operators using a syntax similar to that of BASIC. Concatenation and comparison operators, together with simplified memory management, make **CString** objects easier to use than ordinary character arrays.

CString is based on the **TCHAR** data type. If the symbol **_UNICODE** is defined for your program, **TCHAR** is defined as type **wchar_t**, a 16-bit character type; otherwise, it is defined as **char**, the normal 8-bit character type. Under Unicode, then, **CString** objects are composed of 16-bit characters. Without Unicode, they are composed of 8-bit **char**s.

CString objects also have the following characteristics:

- **CString** objects can grow as a result of concatenation operations.
- **CString** objects follow "value semantics." Think of a **CString** as an actual string, not as a pointer to a string.
- You can freely substitute **CStrings** for **const char*** and **LPCTSTR** function arguments.
- A conversion operator gives direct access to the string's characters as a read-only array of characters (a C-style string).

Tip Where possible, allocate **CString** objects on the frame rather than on the heap. This saves memory and simplifies parameter passing.

For more information, see the "Strings" article in *Programming with the Microsoft Foundation Class Library*.

#include <afx.h>

See Also In *Programming with the Microsoft Foundation Class Library*: "Strings: Basic CString Operations," "Strings: CString Semantics," "Strings: CString Operations Relating to C-Style Strings," "Strings: CString Exception Cleanup," "Strings: CString Argument Passing," "Strings: Unicode and Multibyte Character Set (MBCS) Support"

Construction

CString   Constructs **CString** objects in various ways.

The String as an Array

GetLength	Returns the number of characters in a **CString** object.
IsEmpty	Tests whether a **CString** object contains no characters.
Empty	Forces a string to have 0 length.
GetAt	Returns the character at a given position.
operator [ ]	Returns the character at a given position—operator substitution for **GetAt**.
SetAt	Sets a character at a given position.
operator LPCTSTR ( )	Directly accesses characters stored in a **CString** object as a C-style string.

Assignment/Concatenation

operator =	Assigns a new value to a **CString** object.
operator +	Concatenates two strings and returns a new string.
operator +=	Concatenates a new string to the end of an existing string.

Comparison

operator == <, etc.	Comparison operators (case sensitive).
Compare	Compares two strings (case sensitive).
CompareNoCase	Compares two strings (case insensitive).
Collate	Obsolete. See **Compare**.

Extraction

Mid	Extracts the middle part of a string (like the BASIC MID$ function).
Left	Extracts the left part of a string (like the BASIC LEFT$ function).
Right	Extracts the right part of a string (like the BASIC RIGHT$ function).
SpanIncluding	Extracts a substring that contains only the characters in a set.
SpanExcluding	Extracts a substring that contains only the characters not in a set.

Other Conversions

MakeUpper	Converts all the characters in this string to uppercase characters.
MakeLower	Converts all the characters in this string to lowercase characters.
MakeReverse	Reverses the characters in this string.
Format	Format the string as **sprintf** does.

Searching

Find	Finds a character or substring inside a larger string.
ReverseFind	Finds a character inside a larger string; starts from the end.
FindOneOf	Finds the first matching character from a set.

Archive/Dump

operator <<	Inserts a **CString** object to an archive or dump context.
operator >>	Extracts a **CString** object from an archive.

Buffer Access

GetBuffer	Returns a pointer to the characters in the **CString**.
GetBufferSetLength	Returns a pointer to the characters in the **CString**, truncating to the specified length.
ReleaseBuffer	Releases control of the buffer returned by **GetBuffer**.
FreeExtra	Removes any overhead of this string object by freeing any extra memory previously allocated to the string.

Windows-Specific

AllocSysString	Allocates a **BSTR** from **CString** data.
SetSysString	Sets an existing **BSTR** object with data from a **CString** object.
LoadString	Loads an existing **CString** object from a Windows resource.
AnsiToOem	Makes an in-place conversion from the ANSI character set to the OEM character set.
OemToAnsi	Makes an in-place conversion from the OEM character set to the ANSI character set.

Member Functions

CString::AllocSysString

BSTR AllocSysString ( );
   throw(CMemoryException)

Return Value   Points to the newly allocated string.

Remarks   Allocates a new OLE Automation–compatible string of the type **BSTR** and copies the contents of the **CString** object into it, including the terminating null character. A **CMemoryException** is thrown if insufficient memory exists. This function is normally used to return strings for OLE Automation.

Use **::SysFreeString** in the rare case that you need to deallocate the returned string.

See Also   **::SysAllocString**, **::SysFreeString**

CString::AnsiToOem

void AnsiToOem( );

Remarks   Converts all the characters in this **CString** object from the ANSI character set to the OEM character set. See the ANSI table in the *Programmer's Reference* in the Windows Software Development Kit (SDK). The function is not available if **_UNICODE** is defined.

See Also   **CString::OemToAnsi**

CString::Collate

int Collate(LPCTSTR *lpsz* **) const;**

Return Value   0 if the strings are identical, −1 if this **CString** object is less than *lpsz*, or 1 if this **CString** object is greater than *lpsz*.

Parameters   *lpsz*   The other string used for comparison.

Remarks   This member function is obsolete. Use **Compare** instead.

See Also   **CString::Compare, CString::CompareNoCase**

Example
```
CString s1( "abc" );
CString s2( "abd" );
ASSERT( s1.Collate( s2 ) == -1 );
```

CString::Compare

int Compare(LPCTSTR *lpsz* **) const;**

Return Value   The function returns 0 if the strings are identical, −1 if this **CString** object is less than *lpsz*, or 1 if this **CString** object is greater than *lpsz*.

Parameters   *lpsz*   The other string used for comparison.

Remarks   Compares this **CString** object with another string using the function **lstrcmp**. The current locale is used to get the correct language-specific sort ordering.

See Also   **CString::CompareNoCase, ::lstrcmp**

Example
```
CString s1( "abc" );
CString s2( "abd" );
ASSERT( s1.Compare( s2 ) == -1 ); // Compare with another CString.
ASSERT( s1.Compare( "abe" ) == -1 ); // Compare with LPTSTR string.
```

CString::CompareNoCase

int CompareNoCase(LPCTSTR *lpsz* **) const;**

Remarks   Compares this **CString** object with another string using the function **lstrcmpi**.

The current locale is used to get the correct language-specific sort ordering.

See Also   **CString::Compare, CString::Collate**

Example
```
CString s1( "abc" );
CString s2( "ABD" );
ASSERT( s1.CompareNoCase( s2 ) == -1 ); // Compare with a CString.
ASSERT( s1.Compare( "ABE" ) == -1 ); // Compare with LPTSTR string.
```

CString::CString

CString( );

CString(const CString& *stringSrc* **)**
  throw(CMemoryException);

CString(TCHAR *ch*, **int** *nRepeat* **= 1)**
  throw(CMemoryException);

CString(LPCTSTR *lpch*, **int** *nLength* **)**
  throw(CMemoryException);

CString(const unsigned char* *psz* **)**
  throw(CMemoryException);

CString(LPCWSTR *lpsz* **)**
  throw(CMemoryException);

CString(LPCSTR *lpsz* **)**
  throw(CMemoryException);

Return Value   The function returns 0 if the strings are identical (ignoring case), –1 if this **CString** object is less than *lpsz* (ignoring case), or 1 if this **CString** object is greater than *lpsz* (ignoring case).

Parameters   *stringSrc*   An existing **CString** object to be copied into this **CString** object.

lpsz   A null-terminated string to be copied into this **CString** object.

ch   A single character to be repeated *nRepeat* times.

nRepeat   The repeat count for *ch*.

lpch   A pointer to an array of characters of length *nLength*, not null-terminated.

nLength   A count of the number of characters in *pch*.

Remarks   Each of these constructors initializes a new **CString** object with the specified data.

Because the constructors copy the input data into new allocated storage, you should be aware that memory exceptions may result. Note that some of these constructors act as conversion functions. This allows you to substitute, for example, an **LPTSTR** where a **CString** object is expected.

Several forms of the constructor have special purposes:

CString(LPCSTR *lpsz* **)**
  Constructs a Unicode **CString** from an ANSI string.

CString(LPCWSTR *lpsz* **)**
Constructs a **CString** from a Unicode string.

CString(const unsigned char* *psz* **)**
Allows you to construct a **CString** from a pointer to **unsigned char**.

See Also　**CString::operator =**

In *Programming with the Microsoft Foundation Class Library*: "Strings: CString Exception Cleanup"

Example
```
CString s1;                       // Empty string
CString s2( "cat" );              // From a C string literal
CString s3 = s2;                  // Copy constructor
CString s4( s2 + " " + s3 );      // From a string expression

CString s5( 'x' );                // s5 = "x"
CString s6( 'x', 6 );             // s6 = "xxxxxx"

CString city = "Philadelphia";    // NOT the assignment operator
```

CString::Empty

void Empty( );

Remarks　Makes this **CString** object an empty string and frees memory as appropriate.

See Also　**CString::IsEmpty**

In *Programming with the Microsoft Foundation Class Library*: "Strings: CString Exception Cleanup"

Example
```
CString s( "abc" );
s.Empty();
ASSERT( s.GetLength( ) == 0 );
```

CString::Find

int Find(TCHAR *ch* **) const;**

int Find(LPCTSTR *lpszSub* **) const;**

Return Value　The zero-based index of the first character in this **CString** object that matches the requested substring or characters; –1 if the substring or character is not found.

Parameters　*ch*　A single character to search for.

lpszSub　A substring to search for.

Remarks   Searches this string for the first match of a substring. The function is overloaded to accept both single characters (similar to the run-time function **strchr**) and strings (similar to **strstr**).

See Also   **CString::ReverseFind, CString::FindOneOf**

Example
```
CString s( "abcdef" );
ASSERT( s.Find( 'c' ) == 2 );
ASSERT( s.Find( "de" ) == 3 );
```

CString::FindOneOf

int FindOneOf(LPCTSTR *lpszCharSet* **) const;**

Return Value   The zero-based index of the first character in this string that is also in *lpszCharSet*; −1 if there is no match.

Parameters   *lpszCharSet*   String containing characters for matching.

Remarks   Searches this string for the first character that matches any character contained in *lpszCharSet*.

See Also   **CString::Find**

Example
```
CString s( "abcdef" );
ASSERT( s.FindOneOf( "xd" ) == 3 ); // 'd' is first match
```

CString::Format

void Format(LPCTSTR *lpszFormat*, **...);**

Parameters   *lpszFormat*   A format-control string.

Remarks   Call this member function to write formatted data to a **CString** in the same way that **sprintf** formats data into a C-style character array. This function formats and stores a series of characters and values in the **CString**. Each argument (if any) is converted and output according to the corresponding format specification in *lpszFormat*. The format consists of ordinary characters and has the same form and function as the format argument for the **printf** function. (For a description of the format and arguments, see **printf**.) A null character is appended to the end of the characters written.

See Also   **sprintf, printf**

CString::FreeExtra

void FreeExtra( );

Remarks   Call this member function to free any extra memory previously allocated by the string but no longer needed. This should reduce the memory overhead consumed by the string object. The function reallocates the buffer to the exact length returned by **CString::GetLength**.

CString::GetAt

TCHAR GetAt(int *nIndex* **) const;**

Return Value   A **TCHAR** containing the character at the specified position in the string.

Parameters   *nIndex*   Zero-based index of the character in the **CString** object. The *nIndex* parameter must be greater than or equal to 0 and less than the value returned by **GetLength**. The Debug version of the Microsoft Foundation Class Library validates the bounds of *nIndex*; the Release version does not.

Remarks   You can think of a **CString** object as an array of characters. The **GetAt** member function returns a single character specified by an index number. The overloaded subscript (**[ ]**) operator is a convenient alias for **GetAt**.

See Also   **CString::SetAt**, **CString::GetLength**, **CString::operator [ ]**

Example
```
CString s( "abcdef" );
ASSERT( s.GetAt(2) == 'c' );
```

CString::GetBuffer

LPTSTR GetBuffer(int *nMinBufLength* **)**
    throw(CMemoryException);

Return Value   An **LPTSTR** pointer to the object's (null-terminated) character buffer.

Parameters   *nMinBufLength*   The minimum size of the character buffer in characters. You do not need to allow space for a null terminator.

Remarks   Returns a pointer to the internal character buffer for the **CString** object. The returned **LPTSTR** is not **const** and thus allows direct modification of **CString** contents.

If you use the pointer returned by **GetBuffer** to change the string contents, you must call **ReleaseBuffer** before using any other **CString** member functions.

The address returned by **GetBuffer** may not be valid after the call to **ReleaseBuffer** since additional **CString** operations may cause the **CString** buffer to be reallocated. The buffer will not be reassigned if you do not change the length of the **CString**.

The buffer memory will be freed automatically when the **CString** object is destroyed.

Note that if you keep track of the string length yourself, you should not append the terminating null character. You must, however, specify the final string length when you release the buffer with **ReleaseBuffer**. If you do append a terminating null character, you should pass –1 for the length and **ReleaseBuffer** will perform a **strlen** on the buffer to determine its length.

See Also   **CString::GetBufferSetLength**, **CString::ReleaseBuffer**

Example
```
CString s( "abcd" );
#ifdef _DEBUG
afxDump << "CString s " << s << "\n";
#endif
LPTSTR p = s.GetBuffer( 10 );
strcpy( p, "Hello" );    // directly access CString buffer
s.ReleaseBuffer( );
#ifdef _DEBUG
afxDump << "CString s " << s << "\n";
#endif
```

CString::GetBufferSetLength

LPTSTR GetBufferSetLength(int *nNewLength* **)**
   throw(CMemoryException);

Return Value   An **LPTSTR** pointer to the object's (null-terminated) character buffer.

Parameters   *nNewLength*   The exact size of the **CString** character buffer in characters.

Remarks   Returns a pointer to the internal character buffer for the **CString** object, truncating or growing its length if necessary to exactly match the length specified in *nNewLength*. The returned **LPTSTR** pointer is not **const** and thus allows direct modification of **CString** contents.

If you use the pointer returned by **GetBuffer** to change the string contents, you must call **ReleaseBuffer** before using any other **CString** member functions.

The address returned by **GetBufferSetLength** may not be valid after the call to **ReleaseBuffer** since additional **CString** operations may cause the **CString** buffer to be reallocated. The buffer will not be reassigned if you do not change the length of the **CString**.

The buffer memory will be freed automatically when the **CString** object is destroyed.

Note that if you keep track of the string length yourself, you should not append the terminating null character. You must, however, specify the final string length when you release the buffer with **ReleaseBuffer**. If you do append a terminating null character, you should pass –1 for the length and **ReleaseBuffer** will perform a **strlen** on the buffer to determine its length.

See Also   **CString::GetBuffer**, **CString::ReleaseBuffer**

CString::GetLength

int GetLength( ) const;

Remarks   Returns a count of the characters in this **CString** object. The count does not include a null terminator.

See Also   **CString::IsEmpty**

Example
```
CString s( "abcdef" );
ASSERT( s.GetLength() == 6 );
```

CString::IsEmpty

BOOL IsEmpty( ) const;

Return Value   Nonzero if the **CString** object has 0 length; otherwise 0.

Remarks   Tests a **CString** object for the empty condition.

See Also   **CString::GetLength**

Example
```
CString s;
ASSERT( s.IsEmpty() );
```

CString::Left

CString Left(int *nCount* **) const**
    throw(CMemoryException);

Return Value   A **CString** object containing a copy of the specified range of characters. Note that the returned **CString** object may be empty.

Parameters   *nCount*   The number of characters to extract from this **CString** object.

Remarks   Extracts the first (that is, leftmost) *nCount* characters from this **CString** object and returns a copy of the extracted substring. If *nCount* exceeds the string length, then the entire string is extracted. **Left** is similar to the BASIC LEFT$ function (except that indexes are zero-based).

See Also   **CString::Mid**, **CString::Right**

Example

```
CString s( _T("abcdef") );
ASSERT( s.Left(3) == _T("abc") );
```

CString::LoadString

BOOL LoadString(UINT *nID* **)**
   throw(CMemoryException);

Return Value   Nonzero if resource load was successful; otherwise 0.

Parameters   *nID*   A Windows string resource ID.

Remarks   Reads a Windows string resource, identified by *nID*, into an existing **CString** object. The maximum string size is 255 characters.

Example

```
#define IDS_FILENOTFOUND 1
CString s;
s.LoadString( IDS_FILENOTFOUND );
```

CString::MakeLower

void MakeLower( );

Remarks   Converts this **CString** object to a lowercase string.

See Also   **CString::MakeUpper**

Example

```
CString s( "ABC" );
s.MakeLower();
ASSERT( s == "abc" );
```

CString::MakeReverse

void MakeReverse( );

Remarks   Reverses the order of the characters in this **CString** object.

Example

```
CString s( "abc" );
s.MakeReverse();
ASSERT( s == "cba" );
```

CString::MakeUpper

void MakeUpper( );

Remarks   Converts this **CString** object to an uppercase string.

See Also   **CString::MakeLower**

| **Example** | ```
CString s( "abc" );
s.MakeUpper();
ASSERT( s == "ABC" );
``` |

CString::Mid

CString Mid(int *nFirst*) const
    throw(CMemoryException);

CString Mid(int *nFirst*, int *nCount*) const
    throw(CMemoryException);

Return Value   A **CString** object that contains a copy of the specified range of characters. Note that the returned **CString** object may be empty.

Parameters   *nFirst*   The zero-based index of the first character in this **CString** object that is to be included in the extracted substring.

              nCount   The number of characters to extract from this **CString** object. If this parameter is not supplied, then the remainder of the string is extracted.

Remarks   Extracts a substring of length *nCount* characters from this **CString** object, starting at position *nFirst* (zero-based). The function returns a copy of the extracted substring. **Mid** is similar to the BASIC MID$ function (except that indexes are zero-based).

See Also   **CString::Left, CString::Right**

Example
```
CString s( _T("abcdef") );
ASSERT( s.Mid( 2, 3 ) == _T("cde") );
```

CString::OemToAnsi

void OemToAnsi( );

Remarks   Converts all the characters in this **CString** object from the OEM character set to the ANSI character set. See the ANSI table in the *Programmer's Reference* in the Windows SDK.

    This function is not available if **_UNICODE** is defined.

See Also   **CString::AnsiToOem**
```

CString::ReleaseBuffer

void ReleaseBuffer(int *nNewLength* **= –1);**

Parameters   *nNewLength*   The new length of the string in characters, not counting a null terminator. If the string is null-terminated, the –1 default value sets the **CString** size to the current length of the string.

Remarks   Use **ReleaseBuffer** to end use of a buffer allocated by **GetBuffer**. If you know that the string in the buffer is null-terminated, you can omit the *nNewLength* argument. If your string is not null-terminated, then use *nNewLength* to specify its length. The address returned by **GetBuffer** is invalid after the call to **ReleaseBuffer** or any other **CString** operation.

See Also   **CString::GetBuffer**

Example
```
CString s;
s = "abc";
LPTSTR p = s.GetBuffer( 1024 );
strcpy(p, "abc");    // use the buffer directly
ASSERT( s.GetLength() == 3 ); // String length = 3
s.ReleaseBuffer();  // Surplus memory released, p is now invalid.
ASSERT( s.GetLength() == 3 ); // Length still 3
```

CString::ReverseFind

int ReverseFind(TCHAR *ch* **) const;**

Return Value   The index of the last character in this **CString** object that matches the requested character; –1 if the character is not found.

Parameters   *ch*   The character to search for.

Remarks   Searches this **CString** object for the last match of a substring. The function is similar to the run-time function **strrchr**.

See Also   **CString::Find, CString::FindOneOf**

Example
```
CString s( "abcabc" );
ASSERT( s.ReverseFind( 'b' ) == 4 );
```

CString::Right

CString Right(int *nCount* **) const**
    throw(CMemoryException);

Return Value   A **CString** object that contains a copy of the specified range of characters. Note that the returned **CString** object may be empty.

Parameters	*nCount* The number of characters to extract from this **CString** object.
Remarks	Extracts the last (that is, rightmost) *nCount* characters from this **CString** object and returns a copy of the extracted substring. If *nCount* exceeds the string length, then the entire string is extracted. **Right** is similar to the BASIC RIGHT$ function (except that indexes are zero-based).
See Also	**CString::Mid, CString::Left**
Example	``` CString s(_T("abcdef")); ASSERT(s.Right(3) == _T("def")); ```

CString::SetAt

void SetAt(int *nIndex*, TCHAR *ch*);

Parameters	*nIndex* Zero-based index of the character in the **CString** object. The *nIndex* parameter must be greater than or equal to 0 and less than the value returned by **GetLength**. The Debug version of the Microsoft Foundation Class Library will validate the bounds of *nIndex*; the Release version will not.
	ch The character to insert. Must not be '\0'.
Remarks	You can think of a **CString** object as an array of characters. The **SetAt** member function overwrites a single character specified by an index number. **SetAt** will not enlarge the string if the index exceeds the bounds of the existing string.
See Also	**CString::GetAt, CString::operator [ ]**

CString::SetSysString

BSTR SetSysString(BSTR* *pbstr*);

Return Value	The new string.
Parameters	*pbstr* A pointer to a character string.
Remarks	Reallocates the **BSTR** pointed to by *pbstr* and copies the contents of the **CString** object into it, including the **NULL** character. The value of the **BSTR** referenced by *pbstr* may change. Throws a **CMemoryException** if insufficient memory exists.
	This function is normally used to change the value of strings passed by reference for OLE Automation.
See Also	**::SysReallocStringLen, ::SysFreeString**

CString::SpanExcluding

CString SpanExcluding(LPCTSTR *lpszCharSet* **) const**
  throw(CMemoryException);

Return Value   A substring that contains all characters in the string beginning with the first character in the string that is <u>not</u> in *lpszCharSet*; or an empty string if the first character in the string is <u>not</u> in *lpszCharSet*.

Parameters   *lpszCharSet*   A string interpreted as a set of characters.

Remarks   Searches the string for the first occurrence of any character not found in the specified set *lpszCharSet*. Extracts all characters in the string from the character found by the search to the end of the string. If the first character of the string is included in the specified set, then **SpanExcluding** returns an empty string.

See Also   **CString::SpanIncluding**

CString::SpanIncluding

CString SpanIncluding(LPCTSTR *lpszCharSet* **) const**
  throw(CMemoryException);

Return Value   A substring that contains all characters in the string beginning with the first character in the string that is in *lpszCharSet*; or an empty string if the first character in the string is in *lpszCharSet*.

Parameters   *lpszCharSet*   A string interpreted as a set of characters.

Remarks   Searches the string for the first occurrence of any character not found in the specified set *lpszCharSet*. Extracts all characters in the string from the character found by the search to the end of the string. If the first character of the string is <u>not</u> in the character set, then **SpanIncluding** returns an empty string.

See Also   **CString::SpanExcluding**

Operators

CString::operator =

const CString& operator =(const CString& *stringSrc* **)**
  throw(CMemoryException);

const CString& operator =(TCHAR *ch* **)**
  throw(CMemoryException);

const CString& operator =(const unsigned char* *psz* **)**
  throw(CMemoryException);

const CString& operator =(LPCWSTR *lpsz* **)**
  throw(CMemoryException);

const CString& operator =(LPCSTR *lpsz* **)**
  throw(CMemoryException);

Remarks   The **CString** assignment (=) operator reinitializes an existing **CString** object with new data. If the destination string (that is, the left side) is already large enough to store the new data, no new memory allocation is performed. You should be aware that memory exceptions may occur whenever you use the assignment operator because new storage is often allocated to hold the resulting **CString** object.

See Also   **CString::CString**

Example

```
CString s1, s2;              // Empty CString objects

s1 = "cat";                  // s1 = "cat"
s2 = s1;                     // s1 and s2 each = "cat"
s1 = "the " + s1;            // Or expressions
s1 = 'x';                    // Or just individual characters
```

CString::operator LPCTSTR ( )

operator LPCTSTR ( ) const;

Return Value   A character pointer to the string's data.

Remarks   This useful casting operator provides an efficient method to access the null-terminated C string contained in a **CString** object. No characters are copied; only a pointer is returned. Be careful with this operator. If you change a **CString** object after you have obtained the character pointer, you may cause a reallocation of memory that invalidates the pointer.

CString::operator <<, >>

friend CArchive& operator <<(CArchive& *ar*, **const CString&** *string* **)**
  throw(CArchiveException);

friend CArchive& operator >>(CArchive& *ar*, **CString&** *string* **)**
  throw(CArchiveException);

friend CDumpContext& operator <<(CDumpContext& *dc*,
  const CString& *string* **);**

Remarks

The **CString** insertion (**<<**) operator supports diagnostic dumping and storing to an archive. The extraction (**>>**) operator supports loading from an archive.

The **CDumpContext** operators are valid only in the Debug version of the Microsoft Foundation Class Library.

Example

```
// Operator <<, >> example
    extern CArchive ar;
    CString s( "abc" );
#ifdef _DEBUG
    afxDump << s;  // Prints the value (abc)
    afxDump << &s;  // Prints the address
#endif

    if( ar.IsLoading() )
        ar >> s;
    else
        ar << s;
```

CString::operator +

friend CString operator +(const CString& *string1*, **const CString&** *string2* **)**
  throw(CMemoryException);

friend CString operator +(const CString& *string*, **TCHAR** *ch* **)**
  throw(CMemoryException);

friend CString operator +(TCHAR *ch*, **const CString&** *string* **)**
  throw(CMemoryException);

friend CString operator +(const CString& *string*, **LPCTSTR** *lpsz* **)**
  throw(CMemoryException);

friend CString operator +(LPCTSTR *lpsz*, **const CString&** *string* **)**
  throw(CMemoryException);

Return Value

A **CString** object that is the temporary result of the concatenation. This return value makes it possible to combine several concatenations in the same expression.

Parameters	*string*, *string1*, *string2* **CString** objects to concatenate.

ch   A character to concatenate to a string or to concatenate a string to.

lpsz   A pointer to a null-terminated character string.

Remarks   The + concatenation operator joins two strings and returns a **CString** object. One of the two argument strings must be a **CString** object. The other can be a character pointer or a character. You should be aware that memory exceptions may occur whenever you use the concatenation operator since new storage may be allocated to hold temporary data.

See Also   **CString::operator +=**

Example
```
CString s1( "abc" );
    CString s2( "def" );
    ASSERT( (s1 + s2 ) == "abcdef" );
    CString s3;
    s3 = CString( "abc" ) + "def" ; // Correct
// s3 = "abc" + "def"; // Wrong! One argument must be a CString.
```

CString::operator +=

const CString& operator +=(const CString& *string* **)**
   throw(CMemoryException);

const CString& operator +=(TCHAR *ch* **)**
   throw(CMemoryException);

const CString& operator +=(LPCTSTR *lpsz* **)**
   throw(CMemoryException);

Parameters   *string*   A **CString** to concatenate to this string.

ch   A character to concatenate to this string.

lpsz   A pointer to a null-terminated string to concatenate to this string.

Remarks   The += concatenation operator joins characters to the end of this string. The operator accepts another **CString** object, a character pointer, or a single character. You should be aware that memory exceptions may occur whenever you use this concatenation operator because new storage may be allocated for characters added to this **CString** object.

See Also   **CString::operator +**

Example
```
CString s( "abc" );
ASSERT( ( s += "def" ) == "abcdef" );
```

CString Comparison Operators

BOOL operator ==(const CString& *s1*, **const CString&** *s2*);

BOOL operator ==(const CString& *s1*, **LPCTSTR** *s2*);

BOOL operator ==(LPCTSTR *s1*, **const CString&** *s2*);

BOOL operator !=(const CString& *s1*, **const CString&** *s2*);

BOOL operator !=(const CString& *s1*, **LPCTSTR** *s2*);

BOOL operator !=(LPCTSTR *s1*, **const CString&** *s2*);

BOOL operator <(const CString& *s1*, **const CString&** *s2*);

BOOL operator <(const CString& *s1*, **LPCTSTR** *s2*);

BOOL operator <(LPCTSTR *s1*, **const CString&** *s2*);

BOOL operator >(const CString& *s1*, **const CString&** *s2*);

BOOL operator >(const CString& *s1*, **LPCTSTR** *s2*);

BOOL operator >(LPCTSTR *s1*, **const CString&** *s2*);

BOOL operator <=(const CString& *s1*, **const CString&** *s2*);

BOOL operator <=(const CString& *s1*, **LPCTSTR** *s2*);

BOOL operator <=(LPCTSTR *s1*, **const CString&** *s2*);

BOOL operator >=(const CString& *s1*, **const CString&** *s2*);

BOOL operator >=(const CString& *s1*, **LPCTSTR** *s2*);

BOOL operator >=(LPCTSTR *s1*, **const CString&** *s2*);

Return Value Nonzero if the strings meet the comparison condition; otherwise 0.

Parameters *s1*, *s2* **CString** objects to compare.

Remarks These comparison operators compare two strings. The operators are a convenient substitute for the case-sensitive **Compare** member function.

Example
```
CString s1( "abc" );
CString s2( "abd" );
ASSERT( s1 < s2 ); // Operator is overloaded for both.
ASSERT( "ABC" < s1 ); // CString and char*
ASSERT( s2 > "abe" );
```

CString::operator [ ]

TCHAR operator [ ](int *nIndex*) const;

Parameters   *nIndex*   Zero-based index of a character in the string.

Remarks   You can think of a **CString** object as an array of characters. The overloaded subscript ([ ]) operator returns a single character specified by the zero-based index in *nIndex*. This operator is a convenient substitute for the **GetAt** member function.

Important   You can use the subscript ([ ]) operator to get the value of a character in a **CString**, but you cannot use it to change the value of a character in a **CString**.

See Also   **CString::GetAt, CString::SetAt**

Example
```
CString s( "abc" );
ASSERT( s[1] == 'b' );
```

Note   The **CString** "Application Notes" have been moved to *Programming with the Microsoft Foundation Class Library*. See the articles "Strings: Exception Cleanup" and "Strings: CString Argument Passing."

---

class CStringArray : public CObject

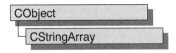

The **CStringArray** class supports arrays of **CString** objects. The member functions of **CStringArray** are similar to the member functions of class **CObArray**. Because of this similarity, you can use the **CObArray** reference documentation for member function specifics. Wherever you see a **CObject** pointer as a return value, substitute a **CString** (not a **CString** pointer). Wherever you see a **CObject** pointer as a function parameter, substitute a **LPCTSTR**.

```
CObject* CObArray::GetAt( int <nIndex> ) const;
```

for example, translates to

```
CString CStringArray::GetAt( int <nIndex> ) const;
```

and

```
void SetAt( int <nIndex>, CObject* <newElement> )
```

translates to

```
void SetAt( int <nIndex>, LPCTSTR <newElement> )
```

Note Before using an array, use **SetSize** to establish its size and allocate memory for it. If you do not use **SetSize**, adding elements to your array causes it to be frequently reallocated and copied. Frequent reallocation and copying are inefficient and can fragment memory.

If you need a dump of individual string elements in the array, you must set the depth of the dump context to 1 or greater. When a **CString** array is deleted, or when its elements are removed, string memory is freed as appropriate.

#include <afxcoll.h>

Construction

CStringArray   Constructs an empty array for **CString** objects.

Bounds

GetSize	Gets number of elements in this array.
GetUpperBound	Returns the largest valid index.
SetSize	Sets the number of elements to be contained in this array.

Operations

FreeExtra	Frees all unused memory above the current upper bound.
RemoveAll	Removes all the elements from this array.

Element Access

GetAt	Returns the value at a given index.
SetAt	Sets the value for a given index; array not allowed to grow.
ElementAt	Returns a temporary reference to the element pointer within the array.

Growing the Array

SetAtGrow	Sets the value for a given index; grows the array if necessary.
Add	Adds an element to the end of the array; grows the array if necessary.

Insertion/Removal

InsertAt	Inserts an element (or all the elements in another array) at a specified index.
RemoveAt	Removes an element at a specific index.

Operators

operator []	Sets or gets the element at the specified index.

class CStringList : public CObject

The **CStringList** class supports lists of **CString** objects. All comparisons are done by value, meaning that the characters in the string are compared instead of the addresses of the strings. The member functions of **CStringList** are similar to the member functions of class **CObList**. Because of this similarity, you can use the **CObArray** reference documentation for member function specifics. Wherever you see a **CObject** pointer as a return value, substitute a **CString** (not a **CString** pointer). Wherever you see a **CObject** pointer as a function parameter, substitute an **LPCTSTR**.

```
CObject*& CObList::GetHead() const;
```

for example, translates to

```
CString& CStringList::GetHead() const;
```

and

```
POSITION AddHead( CObject* <newElement> );
```

translates to

```
POSITION AddHead( LPCTSTR <newElement> );
```

CStringList incorporates the **IMPLEMENT_SERIAL** macro to support serialization and dumping of its elements. If a list of **CString** objects is stored to an archive, either with an overloaded insertion operator or with the **Serialize** member function, each **CString** element is serialized in turn.

If you need a dump of individual **CString** elements, you must set the depth of the dump context to 1 or greater. When a **CStringList** object is deleted, or when its elements are removed, the **CString** objects are deleted as appropriate.

#include <afxcoll.h>

Construction

CStringList   Constructs an empty list for **CString** objects.

Head/Tail Access

GetHead	Returns the head element of the list (cannot be empty).
GetTail	Returns the tail element of the list (cannot be empty).

Operations

RemoveHead	Removes the element from the head of the list.
RemoveTail	Removes the element from the tail of the list.
AddHead	Adds an element (or all the elements in another list) to the head of the list (makes a new head).
AddTail	Adds an element (or all the elements in another list) to the tail of the list (makes a new tail).
RemoveAll	Removes all the elements from this list.

Iteration

GetHeadPosition	Returns the position of the head element of the list.
GetTailPosition	Returns the position of the tail element of the list.
GetNext	Gets the next element for iterating.
GetPrev	Gets the previous element for iterating.

Retrieval/Modification

GetAt	Gets the element at a given position.
SetAt	Sets the element at a given position.
RemoveAt	Removes an element from this list as specified by position.

Insertion

InsertBefore	Inserts a new element before a given position.
InsertAfter	Inserts a new element after a given position.

Searching

Find	Gets the position of an element specified by string value.
FindIndex	Gets the position of an element specified by a zero-based index.

Status

GetCount	Returns the number of elements in this list.
IsEmpty	Tests for the empty list condition (no elements).

class CTime

A **CTime** object represents an absolute time and date. The **CTime** class incorporates the ANSI **time_t** data type and its associated run-time functions, including the ability to convert to and from a Gregorian date and 24-hour time. **CTime** values are based on universal coordinated time (UCT), which is equivalent to Greenwich mean time (GMT). The local time zone is controlled by the **TZ** environment variable. See the *Run-Time Library Reference* for more information on the **time_t** data type and the run-time functions that are used by **CTime**. Note that **CTime** uses the **strftime** function, which is not supported for Windows dynamic-link libraries (DLL). Therefore, **CTime** cannot be used in Windows DLLs. A companion class, **CTimeSpan**, represents a time interval—the difference between two **CTime** objects.

The **CTime** and **CTimeSpan** classes are not designed for derivation. Because there are no virtual functions, the size of **CTime** and **CTimeSpan** objects is exactly 4 bytes. Most member functions are inline.

#include <afx.h>

See Also   Run-time functions: **asctime**, **_ftime**, **gmtime**, **localtime**, **strftime**, **time**

Construction

CTime	Constructs **CTime** objects in various ways.
GetCurrentTime	Creates a **CTime** object that represents the current time (static member function).

Extraction

GetTime	Returns a **time_t** that corresponds to this **CTime** object.
GetYear	Returns the year that this **CTime** object represents.
GetMonth	Returns the month that this **CTime** object represents (1 through 12).
GetDay	Returns the day that this **CTime** object represents (1 through 31).
GetHour	Returns the hour that this **CTime** object represents (0 through 23).
GetMinute	Returns the minute that this **CTime** object represents (0 through 59).

GetSecond	Returns the second that this **CTime** object represents (0 through 59).
GetDayOfWeek	Returns the day of the week (1 for Sunday, 2 for Monday, and so forth).

Conversion

GetGmtTm	Breaks down a **CTime** object into components—based on UCT.
GetLocalTm	Breaks down a **CTime** object into components—based on the local time zone.
Format	Converts a **CTime** object into a formatted string—based on the local time zone.
FormatGmt	Converts a **CTime** object into a formatted string—based on UCT.

Operators

operator =	Assigns new time values.
operator + –	Add and subtract **CTimeSpan** and **CTime** objects.
operator + =, – =	Add and subtract a **CTimeSpan** object to and from this **CTime** object.
operator ==, < , etc.	Compare two absolute times.

Archive/Dump

operator <<	Outputs a **CTime** object to **CArchive** or **CDumpContext**.
operator >>	Inputs a **CTime** object from **CArchive**.

Member Functions

CTime::CTime

CTime( );

CTime(const CTime& *timeSrc* **);**

CTime(time_t *time* **);**

CTime(int *nYear*, **int** *nMonth*, **int** *nDay*, **int** *nHour*, **int** *nMin*, **int** *nSec* **);**

CTime(WORD *wDosDate*, **WORD** *wDosTime* **);**

CTime(const SYSTEMTIME& *sysTime* **);**

CTime(const FILETIME& *fileTime* **);**

Parameters   *timeSrc*   Indicates a **CTime** object that already exists.

time   Indicates a time value.

nYear, *nMonth*, *nDay*, *nHour*, *nMin*, *nSec*   Indicate year, month, day, hour, minute, and second.

wDosDate, *wDosTime*   Indicate the date and time in the form obtained through the MS-DOS function **_dos_getftime**.

sysTime   Indicates the date and time retrieved from Windows NT. The *fileTime* parameter is a reference to a Windows NT **FILETIME** structure, which represents time as a 64-bit value, a more convenient format for internal storage than a **SYSTEMTIME** structure and the format used by Windows NT to represent the time of file creation.

fileTime   Indicates a file time stamp in Windows NT.

Remarks   All these constructors create a new **CTime** object initialized with the specified absolute time, based on the current time zone. Each constructor is described below:

- **CTime( );**   Constructs a **CTime** object with a 0 (illegal) value. Note that 0 is an invalid time. This constructor allows you to define **CTime** object arrays. You should initialize such arrays with valid times prior to use.

- **CTime(const CTime&);**   Constructs a **CTime** object from another **CTime** value.

- **CTime(time_t);**   Constructs a **CTime** object from a **time_t** type.

- **CTime(int, int,** etc.**);**   Constructs a **CTime** object from local time components with each component constrained to the following ranges:

Component	Range
nYear	1970–2038
nMonth	1–12
nDay	1–31
nHour	0–23
nMin	0–59
nSec	0–59

This constructor makes the appropriate conversion to UCT. The Debug version of the Microsoft Foundation Class Library asserts if one or more of the time-day components is out of range. It is your responsibility to validate the arguments prior to calling.

- **CTime(WORD, WORD);**   Constructs a **CTime** object from a date and time in the form obtained through the MS-DOS function **_dos_get ftime**.

- **CTime(const SYSTEMTIME&);**   Constructs a **CTime** object from a Windows NT **SYSTEMTIME** structure.

- **CTime(const FILETIME&);**   Constructs a **CTime** object from a Windows NT **FILETIME** structure. You most likely will not use **CTime FILETIME** initialization directly. If you use a **CFile** object to manipulate a file, **CFile::GetStatus** retrieves the file time stamp for you via a **CTime** object initialized with a **FILETIME** structure.

Example

```
time_t osBinaryTime; // C run-time time (defined in <time.h>)
time( &osBinaryTime ) ; // Get the current time from the
                        // operating system.
CTime time1; // Empty CTime. (0 is illegal time value.)
CTime time2 = time1; // Copy constructor.
CTime time3( osBinaryTime );  // CTime from C run-time time
CTime time4( 1999, 3, 19, 22, 15, 0 ); // 10:15PM March 19, 1999
```

CTime::Format

CString Format(const char* *pFormat* **);**

Return Value   A **CString** that contains the formatted time.

Parameters   *pFormat*   Specifies a formatting string similar to the **printf** formatting string. See the run-time function **strftime** for details.

Remarks   Generates a formatted string that corresponds to this **CTime** object. The time value is converted to local time.

See Also   **CTime::FormatGmt**

Example
```
CTime t( 1999, 3, 19, 22, 15, 0 ); // 10:15PM March 19, 1999
CString s = t.Format( "%A, %B %d, %Y" );
ASSERT( s == "Friday, March 19, 1999" );
```

CTime::FormatGmt

CString FormatGmt(const char* *pFormat* **);**

Return Value   A **CString** that contains the formatted time.

Parameters   *pFormat*   Specifies a formatting string similar to the **printf** formatting string. See the run-time function **strftime** for details.

Remarks   Generates a formatted string that corresponds to this **CTime** object. The time value is not converted and thus reflects UCT.

See Also   **CTime::Format**

CTime::GetCurrentTime

static CTime PASCAL GetCurrentTime( );

Remarks   Returns a **CTime** object that represents the current time.

Example
```
CTime t = CTime::GetCurrentTime();
```

CTime::GetDay

int GetDay( ) const;

Remarks   Returns the day of the month, based on local time, in the range 1 through 31. This function calls **GetLocalTm**, which uses an internal, statically allocated buffer. The data in this buffer is overwritten as a result of calls to other **CTime** member functions.

See Also   **CTime::GetDayOfWeek**

Example
```
CTime t( 1999, 3, 19, 22, 15, 0 ); // 10:15PM March 19, 1999
ASSERT( t.GetDay() == 19 );
ASSERT( t.GetMonth() == 3 );
ASSERT( t.GetYear() == 1999 );
```

CTime::GetDayOfWeek

int GetDayOfWeek( ) const;

Remarks   Returns the day of the week based on local time; 1 = Sunday, 2 = Monday, ..., 7 = Saturday. This function calls **GetLocalTm**, which uses an internal, statically allocated buffer. The data in this buffer is overwritten as a result of calls to other **CTime** member functions.

CTime::GetGmtTm

struct tm* GetGmtTm(struct tm* *ptm* **= NULL) const;**

Return Value

A pointer to a filled-in **struct tm** as defined in the include file TIME.H. The members and the values they store are as follows:

- **tm_sec**   Seconds
- **tm_min**   Minutes
- **tm_hour**   Hours (0–23)
- **tm_mday**   Day of month (1–31)
- **tm_mon**   Month (0–11; January = 0)
- **tm_year**   Year (actual year minus 1900)
- **tm_wday**   Day of week (1–7; Sunday = 1)
- **tm_yday**   Day of year (0–365; January 1 = 0)
- **tm_isdst**   Always 0

Note   The year in **struct tm** is in the range 70 to 138; the year in the **CTime** interface is in the range 1970 to 2038 (inclusive).

Parameters

ptm   Points to a buffer that will receive the time data. If this pointer is **NULL**, an internal, statically allocated buffer is used. The data in this default buffer is overwritten as a result of calls to other **CTime** member functions.

This function calls **GetLocalTm**, which uses an internal, statically allocated buffer. The data in this buffer is overwritten as a result of calls to other **CTime** member functions.

Remarks

Gets a **struct tm** that contains a decomposition of the time contained in this **CTime** object. **GetGmtTm** returns UCT.

Example

See the example for **GetLocalTm**.

CTime::GetHour

int GetHour( ) const;

Remarks

Returns the hour, based on local time, in the range 0 through 23. This function calls **GetLocalTm**, which uses an internal, statically allocated buffer. The data in this buffer is overwritten as a result of calls to other **CTime** member functions.

Example

```
CTime t( 1999, 3, 19, 22, 15, 0 ); // 10:15PM March 19, 1999
ASSERT( t.GetSecond() == 0 );
ASSERT( t.GetMinute() == 15 );
ASSERT( t.GetHour() == 22 );
```

CTime::GetLocalTm

struct tm* GetLocalTm(struct tm* *ptm* **= NULL) const;**

Return Value

A pointer to a filled-in **struct tm** as defined in the include file TIME.H. See **GetGmtTm** for the structure layout.

Parameters

ptm   Points to a buffer that will receive the time data. If this pointer is **NULL**, an internal, statically allocated buffer is used. The data in this default buffer is overwritten as a result of calls to other **CTime** member functions.

Remarks

Gets a **struct tm** containing a decomposition of the time contained in this **CTime** object. **GetLocalTm** returns local time.

Example

```
CTime t( 1999, 3, 19, 22, 15, 0 ); // 10:15PM March 19, 1999
struct tm* osTime;  // A pointer to a structure containing time
                    // elements.
osTime = t.GetLocalTm( NULL );
ASSERT( osTime->tm_mon == 2 ); // Note zero-based month!
```

CTime::GetMinute

int GetMinute( ) const;

Remarks

Returns the minute, based on local time, in the range 0 through 59. This function calls **GetLocalTm**, which uses an internal, statically allocated buffer. The data in this buffer is overwritten as a result of calls to other **CTime** member functions.

CTime::GetMonth

int GetMonth( ) const;

Remarks

Returns the month, based on local time, in the range 1 through 12 (1 = January). This function calls **GetLocalTm**, which uses an internal, statically allocated buffer. The data in this buffer is overwritten as a result of calls to other **CTime** member functions.

Example

See the example for **GetDay**.

CTime::GetSecond

int GetSecond( ) const;

Remarks   Returns the second, based on local time, in the range 0 through 59. This function calls **GetLocalTm**, which uses an internal, statically allocated buffer. The data in this buffer is overwritten as a result of calls to other **CTime** member functions.

CTime::GetTime

time_t GetTime( ) const;

Remarks   Returns a **time_t** value for the given **CTime** object.

See Also   **CTime::CTime**

Example
```
CTime t( 1999, 3, 19, 22, 15, 0 ); // 10:15PM March 19, 1999
time_t osBinaryTime = t.GetTime(); // time_t defined in <time.h>
printf( "time_t = %ld\n", osBinaryTime );
```

CTime::GetYear

int GetYear( ) const;

Remarks   Returns the year, based on local time, in the range 1970 to 2038. This function calls **GetLocalTm**, which uses an internal, statically allocated buffer. The data in this buffer is overwritten as a result of calls to other **CTime** member functions.

Example   See the example for **GetDay**.

Operators

CTime::operator =

const CTime& operator =(const CTime& *timeSrc*);

const CTime& operator =(time_t *t*);

Remarks   These overloaded assignment operators copy the source time into this **CTime** object. The internal time storage in a **CTime** object is independent of time zone. Time-zone conversion is not necessary during assignment.

See Also   **CTime::CTime**

Example
```
time_t osBinaryTime;  // C run-time time (defined in <time.h>)
CTime t1 = osBinaryTime; // Assignment from time_t
CTime t2 = t1; // Assignment from CTime
```

CTime::operator +, –

CTime operator +(CTimeSpan *timeSpan* **) const;**

CTime operator –(CTimeSpan *timeSpan* **) const;**

CTimeSpan operator –(CTime *time* **) const;**

Remarks   **CTime** objects represent absolute time. **CTimeSpan** objects represent relative time. The first two operators allow you to add and subtract **CTimeSpan** objects to and from **CTime** objects. The third allows you to subtract one **CTime** object from another to yield a **CTimeSpan** object.

Example
```
CTime t1( 1999, 3, 19, 22, 15, 0 ); // 10:15PM March 19, 1999
CTime t2( 1999, 3, 20, 22, 15, 0 ); // 10:15PM March 20, 1999
CTimeSpan ts = t2 - t1;  // Subtract 2 CTimes
ASSERT( ts.GetTotalSeconds() == 86400L );
ASSERT( ( t1 + ts ) == t2 );  // Add a CTimeSpan to a CTime.
ASSERT( ( t2 - ts ) == t1 );  // Subtract a CTimeSpan from a CTime.
```

CTime::operator +=, –=

const CTime& operator +=(CTimeSpan *timeSpan* **);**

const CTime& operator –=(CTimeSpan *timeSpan* **);**

Remarks   These operators allow you to add and subtract a **CTimeSpan** object to and from this **CTime** object.

Example
```
CTime t( 1999, 3, 19, 22, 15, 0 ); // 10:15PM March 19, 1999
t += CTimeSpan( 0, 1, 0, 0 ); // 1 hour exactly
ASSERT( t.GetHour() == 23 );
```

CTime Comparison Operators

BOOL operator ==(CTime *time* **) const;**

BOOL operator !=(CTime *time* **) const;**

BOOL operator <(CTime *time* **) const;**

BOOL operator >(CTime *time* **) const;**

BOOL operator <=(CTime *time* **) const;**

BOOL operator >=(CTime *time* **) const;**

Remarks   These operators compare two absolute times and return nonzero if the condition is true; otherwise 0.

Example
```
CTime t1 = CTime::GetCurrentTime();
CTime t2 = t1 + CTimeSpan( 0, 1, 0, 0 );     // 1 hour later
ASSERT( t1 != t2 );
ASSERT( t1 < t2 );
ASSERT( t1 <= t2 );
```

CTime::operators <<, >>

friend CDumpContext& operator <<(CDumpContext& *dc*, **CTime** *time* **);**

friend CArchive& operator <<(CArchive& *ar*, **CTime** *time* **);**

friend CArchive& operator >>(CArchive& *ar*, **CTime&** *rtime* **);**

Remarks   The **CTime** insertion (**<<**) operator supports diagnostic dumping and storing to an archive. The extraction (**>>**) operator supports loading from an archive.

When you send a **CTime** object to the dump context, the local time is displayed in readable date-time format.

See Also   **CArchive**, **CDumpContext**

Example
```
CTime t( 1999, 3, 19, 22, 15, 0 ); // 10:15PM March 19, 1999
afxDump << t << "\n"; // Prints 'CTime("Fri Mar 19 22:15:00 1999")'.

extern CArchive ar;
if( ar.IsLoading() )
  ar >> t;
else
  ar << t;
```

class CTimeSpan

A **CTimeSpan** object represents a relative time span. The **CTimeSpan** class incorporates the ANSI **time_t** data type and its associated run-time functions. These functions convert seconds to various combinations of days, hours, minutes, and seconds. A **CTimeSpan** object keeps time in seconds. Because the **CTimeSpan** object is stored as a signed number in 4 bytes, the maximum allowed span is approximately ± 68 years.

A companion class, **CTime**, represents an absolute time. A **CTimeSpan** is the difference between two **CTime** values. The **CTime** and **CTimeSpan** classes are not designed for derivation. Because there are no virtual functions, the size of both **CTime** and **CTimeSpan** objects is exactly 4 bytes. Most member functions are inline.

#include <afx.h>

See Also   Run-time functions: **asctime**, **_ftime**, **gmtime**, **localtime**, **strftime**, **time**

Construction

CTimeSpan	Constructs **CTimeSpan** objects in various ways.

Extraction

GetDays	Returns the number of complete days in this **CTimeSpan**.
GetHours	Returns the number of hours in the current day (–23 through 23).
GetTotalHours	Returns the total number of complete hours in this **CTimeSpan**.
GetMinutes	Returns the number of minutes in the current hour (–59 through 59).
GetTotalMinutes	Returns the total number of complete minutes in this **CTimeSpan**.
GetSeconds	Returns the number of seconds in the current minute (–59 through 59).
GetTotalSeconds	Returns the total number of complete seconds in this **CTimeSpan**.

Conversion

Format	Converts a **CTimeSpan** into a formatted string.

Operators

operator =	Assigns new time-span values.
operator + –	Add and subtract **CTimeSpan** objects.
operator += –=	Add and subtract a **CTimeSpan** object to and from this **CTimeSpan**.
operator == < etc.	Compare two relative time values.

Archive/Dump

| operator << | Outputs a **CTimeSpan** object to **CArchive** or **CDumpContext**. |
| operator >> | Inputs a **CTimeSpan** object from **CArchive**. |

Member Functions

CTimeSpan::CTimeSpan

CTimeSpan( );

CTimeSpan(const CTimeSpan& *timeSpanSrc* **);**

CTimeSpan(time_t *time* **);**

CTimeSpan(LONG *lDays*, **int** *nHours*, **int** *nMins*, **int** *nSecs* **);**

Parameters   *timeSpanSrc*   A **CTimeSpan** object that already exists.

time   A **time_t** time value.

lDays, *nHours*, *nMins*, *nSecs*   Days, hours, minutes, and seconds, respectively.

Remarks   All these constructors create a new **CTimeSpan** object initialized with the specified relative time. Each constructor is described below:

- **CTimeSpan( );**   Constructs an uninitialized **CTimeSpan** object.
- **CTimeSpan(const CTimeSpan&);**   Constructs a **CTimeSpan** object from another **CTimeSpan** value.
- **CTimeSpan(time_t);**   Constructs a **CTimeSpan** object from a **time_t** type. This value should be the difference between two absolute **time_t** values.
- **CTimeSpan(LONG, int, int, int);**   Constructs a **CTimeSpan** object from components with each component constrained to the following ranges:

Component	Range
lDays	0–25,000 (approximately)
nHours	0–23
nMins	0–59
nSecs	0–59

Note that the Debug version of the Microsoft Foundation Class Library asserts if one or more of the time-day components is out of range. It is your responsibility to validate the arguments prior to calling.

Example
```
CTimeSpan ts1;  // Uninitialized time value
CTimeSpan ts2a( ts1 ); // Copy constructor
CTimeSpan ts2b = ts1; // Copy constructor again
CTimeSpan ts3( 100 ); // 100 seconds
CTimeSpan ts4( 0, 1, 5, 12 );    // 1 hour, 5 minutes, and 12 seconds
```

CTimeSpan::Format

CString Format(const char* *pFormat* **);**

Return Value   A **CString** object that contains the formatted time.

Parameters   *pFormat*   A formatting string similar to the **printf** formatting string. Formatting codes, preceded by a percent (**%**) sign, are replaced by the corresponding **CTimeSpan** component. Other characters in the formatting string are copied unchanged to the returned string. The value and meaning of the formatting codes for **Format** are listed below:

- **%D**   Total days in this **CTimeSpan**
- **%H**   Hours in the current day
- **%M**   Minutes in the current hour
- **%S**   Seconds in the current minute
- **%%**   Percent sign

Remarks   Generates a formatted string that corresponds to this **CTimeSpan**. The Debug version of the library checks the formatting codes and asserts if the code is not in the table above.

Example
```
CTimeSpan ts( 3, 1, 5, 12 ); // 3 days, 1 hour, 5 min, and 12 sec
CString s = ts.Format( "Total days: %D, hours: %H, mins: %M, secs: %S"
    );
ASSERT( s == "Total days: 3, hours: 01, mins: 05, secs: 12" );
```

CTimeSpan::GetDays

LONG GetDays( ) const;

Remarks   Returns the number of complete days. This value may be negative if the time span is negative.

Example
```
CTimeSpan ts( 3, 1, 5, 12 ); // 3 days, 1 hour, 5 min, and 12 sec
ASSERT( ts.GetDays() == 3 );
```

CTimeSpan::GetHours

int GetHours( ) const;

Remarks   Returns the number of hours in the current day. The range is −23 through 23.

Example
```
CTimeSpan ts( 3, 1, 5, 12 ); // 3 days, 1 hour, 5 min, and 12 sec
ASSERT( ts.GetHours() == 1 );
ASSERT( ts.GetMinutes() == 5 );
ASSERT( ts.GetSeconds() == 12 );
```

CTimeSpan::GetMinutes

int GetMinutes( ) const;

Remarks   Returns the number of minutes in the current hour. The range is −59 through 59.

Example   See the example for **GetHours**.

CTimeSpan::GetSeconds

int GetSeconds( ) const;

Remarks   Returns the number of seconds in the current minute. The range is −59 through 59.

Example   See the example for **GetHours**.

CTimeSpan::GetTotalHours

LONG GetTotalHours( ) const;

Remarks   Returns the total number of complete hours in this **CTimeSpan**.

Example
```
CTimeSpan ts( 3, 1, 5, 12 ); // 3 days, 1 hour, 5 min, and 12 sec
ASSERT( ts.GetTotalHours() == 73 );
ASSERT( ts.GetTotalMinutes() == 4385 );
ASSERT( ts.GetTotalSeconds() == 263112 );
```

CTimeSpan::GetTotalMinutes

LONG GetTotalMinutes( ) const;

Remarks   Returns the total number of complete minutes in this **CTimeSpan**.

Example   See the example for **GetTotalHours**.

CTimeSpan::GetTotalSeconds

LONG GetTotalSeconds( ) const;

Remarks   Returns the total number of complete seconds in this **CTimeSpan**.

Example   See the example for **GetTotalHours**.

Operators

CTimeSpan::operator =

const CTimeSpan& operator =(const CTimeSpan& *timeSpanSrc* **);**

Remarks   The overloaded assignment operator copies the source **CTimeSpan** *timeSpanSrc*
object into this **CTimeSpan** object.

See Also   **CTimeSpan::CTimeSpan**

Example
```
CTimeSpan ts1;
CTimeSpan ts2( 3, 1, 5, 12 ); // 3 days, 1 hour, 5 min, and 12 sec
ts1 = ts2;
ASSERT( ts1 == ts2 );
```

CTimeSpan::operator +, –

CTimeSpan operator +(CTimeSpan *timeSpan* **) const;**

CTimeSpan operator –(CTimeSpan *timeSpan* **) const;**

Remarks   These two operators allow you to add and subtract **CTimeSpan** objects to and from
each other.

Example
```
CTimeSpan ts1( 3, 1, 5, 12 ); // 3 days, 1 hour, 5 min, and 12 sec
CTimeSpan ts2( 100 ); // 100 seconds
CTimeSpan ts3 = ts1 + ts2;
ASSERT( ts3.GetSeconds() == 52 ); // 6 mins, 52 secs
```

CTimeSpan::operator +=, −=

const CTimeSpan& operator +=(CTimeSpan *timeSpan* **);**

const CTimeSpan& operator −=(CTimeSpan *timeSpan* **);**

Remarks   These operators allow you to add and subtract a **CTimeSpan** object to and from this **CTimeSpan**.

Example
```
CTimeSpan ts1( 10 ); // 10 seconds
CTimeSpan ts2( 100 ); // 100 seconds
ts2 -= ts1;
ASSERT( ts2.GetTotalSeconds() == 90 );
```

CTimeSpan Comparison Operators

BOOL operator ==(CTimeSpan *timeSpan* **) const;**

BOOL operator !=(CTimeSpan *timeSpan* **) const;**

BOOL operator <(CTimeSpan *timeSpan* **) const;**

BOOL operator >(CTimeSpan *timeSpan* **) const;**

BOOL operator <=(CTimeSpan *timeSpan* **) const;**

BOOL operator >=(CTimeSpan *timeSpan* **) const;**

Remarks   These operators compare two relative time values. They return nonzero if the condition is true; otherwise 0.

Example
```
CTimeSpan ts1( 100 );
CTimeSpan ts2( 110 );
ASSERT( ( ts1 != ts2 ) && ( ts1 < ts2 ) && ( ts1 <= ts2 ) );
```

CTimeSpan::operators <<, >>

friend CDumpContext& operator <<(CDumpContext& *dc,* **CTimeSpan** *timeSpan* **);**

friend CArchive& operator <<(CArchive& *ar,* **CTimeSpan** *timeSpan* **);**

friend CArchive& operator >>(CArchive& *ar,* **CTimeSpan&** *timeSpan* **);**

Remarks   The **CTimeSpan** insertion (**<<**) operator supports diagnostic dumping and storing to an archive. The extraction (**>>**) operator supports loading from an archive.

When you send a **CTimeSpan** object to the dump context, the value is displayed in an alphanumeric format that shows days, hours, minutes, and seconds.

Example

```
CTimeSpan ts( 3, 1, 5, 12 ); // 3 days, 1 hour, 5 min, and 12 sec
#ifdef _DEBUG
afxDump << ts << "\n";
#endif
// Prints 'CTimeSpan(3 days, 1 hours, 5 minutes and 12 seconds)'

extern CArchive ar;
if( ar.IsLoading( ))
  ar >> ts;
else
  ar << ts;
```

class CToolBar : public CControlBar

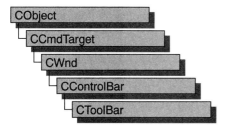

Objects of the class **CToolBar** are control bars that have a row of bitmapped buttons and optional separators. The buttons can act like pushbuttons, check-box buttons, or radio buttons. **CToolBar** objects are usually embedded members of frame-window objects derived from the class **CFrameWnd** or **CMDIFrameWnd**.

To create a toolbar from within a frame-window object, follow these steps:

1. Construct the **CToolBar** object.
2. Call the **Create** function to create the Windows toolbar and attach it to the **CToolBar** object.
3. Call **LoadBitmap** to load the bitmap that contains the toolbar button images.
4. Call **SetButtons** to set the button style and associate each button with an image in the bitmap.

All the button images in the toolbar are taken from one bitmap, which must contain one image for each button. All images must be the same size; the default is 16 pixels wide and 15 pixels high. Images must be side by side in the bitmap.

The **SetButtons** function takes a pointer to an array of control IDs and an integer that specifies the number of elements in the array. The function sets each button's ID to the value of the corresponding element of the array and assigns each button an image index, which specifies the position of the button's image in the bitmap. If an array element has the value **ID_SEPARATOR**, no image index is assigned.

The order of the images in the bitmap is typically the order in which they are drawn on the screen, but you can use the **SetButtonInfo** function to change the relationship between image order and drawing order.

All buttons in a toolbar are the same size. The default is 24 × 22 pixels, in accordance with *The Windows Interface: An Application Design Guide*. Any additional space between the image and button dimensions is used to form a border around the image.

Each button has one image. The various button states and styles (pressed, up, down, disabled, disabled down, and indeterminate) are generated from that one image. Although bitmaps can be any color, you can achieve the best results with images in black and shades of gray.

Toolbar buttons imitate pushbuttons by default. However, toolbar buttons can also imitate check-box buttons or radio buttons. Check-box buttons have three states: checked, cleared, and indeterminate. Radio buttons have only two states: checked and cleared.

To create a check-box button, assign it the style **TBBS_CHECKBOX** or use a **CCmdUI** object's **SetCheck** member function in an **ON_UPDATE_COMMAND_UI** handler. Calling **SetCheck** turns a pushbutton into a check-box button. Pass **SetCheck** an argument of 0 for unchecked, 1 for checked, or 2 for indeterminate.

To create a radio button, call a **CCmdUI** object's **SetRadio** member function from an **ON_UPDATE_COMMAND_UI** handler. Pass **SetRadio** an argument of 0 for unchecked or nonzero for checked. In order to provide a radio group's mutually exclusive behavior, you must have **ON_UPDATE_COMMAND_UI** handlers for all of the buttons in the group.

See Also   **CControlBar**, **CToolBar::Create**, **CToolBar::LoadBitmap**, **CToolBar::SetButtons**, **CCmdUI::SetCheck**, **CCmdUI::SetRadio**

Construction

CToolBar	Constructs a **CToolBar** object.
Create	Creates the Windows toolbar and attaches it to the **CToolBar** object.
SetSizes	Sets the sizes of buttons and their bitmaps.
SetHeight	Sets the height of the toolbar.
LoadBitmap	Loads the bitmap containing bitmap-button images.
SetButtons	Sets button styles and an index of button images within the bitmap.

Attributes

CommandToIndex	Returns the index of a button with the given command ID.
GetItemID	Returns the command ID of a button or separator at the given index.
GetItemRect	Gets the display rectangle for the item at the given index.
GetButtonInfo	Gets a button's ID, style, and image number.
SetButtonInfo	Sets a button's ID, style, and image number.

Member Functions

CToolBar::CommandToIndex

int CommandToIndex(UINT *nIDFind* **);**

Return Value   The index of the button, or –1 if no button has the given command ID.

Parameters   *nIDFind*   Command ID of a toolbar button.

Remarks   Returns the index of the first toolbar button, starting at position 0, whose command ID matches *nIDFind*.

See Also   **CToolBar::GetItemId**

CToolBar::Create

BOOL Create(CWnd* *pParentWnd***, DWORD** *dwStyle* **= WS_CHILD | WS_VISIBLE | CBRS_TOP, UINT** *nID* **= AFX_IDW_TOOLBAR);**

Return Value   Nonzero if successful; otherwise 0.

Parameters   *pParentWnd*   Pointer to the window that is the toolbar's parent.

                dwStyle   The toolbar style. Additional toolbar styles supported are:

- **CBRS_TOP**   Control bar is at top of the frame window.
- **CBRS_BOTTOM**   Control bar is at bottom of the frame window.
- **CBRS_NOALIGN**   Control bar is not repositioned when the parent is resized.
- **CBRS_TOOLTIPS**   Control bar displays tool tips.

                nID   The toolbar's child-window ID.

Remarks   Creates a Windows toolbar (a child window) and associates it with the **CToolBar** object. Also sets the toolbar height to a default value.

See Also   **CToolBar::CToolBar, CToolBar::LoadBitmap, CToolBar::SetButtons**

CToolBar::CToolBar

CToolBar( );

Remarks   Constructs a **CToolBar** object and sets the default sizes.

Call **Create** to create the toolbar window.

See Also   **CToolBar::Create**

CToolBar::GetButtonInfo

void **GetButtonInfo**(int *nIndex*, UINT& *nID*, UINT& *nStyle*, int& *iImage*) **const;**

Parameters   *nIndex*   Index of the toolbar button or separator whose information is to be retrieved.

nID   Reference to a **UINT** that is set to the command ID of the button.

nStyle   Reference to a **UINT** that is set to the style of the button.

iImage   Reference to an integer that is set to the index of the button's image within the bitmap.

Remarks   Gets the control ID, style, and image index of the toolbar button or separator at the location specified by *nIndex*. Those values are assigned to the variables referenced by *nID*, *nStyle*, and *iImage*. The image index is the position of the image within the bitmap that contains images for all the toolbar buttons. The first image is at position 0.

If *nIndex* specifies a separator, *iImage* is set to the separator width in pixels.

See Also   **CToolBar::SetButtonInfo, CToolBar::GetItemID**

CToolBar::GetItemID

UINT **GetItemID**(int *nIndex*) **const;**

Return Value   The command ID of the button or separator specified by *nIndex*.

Parameters   *nIndex*   Index of the item (B1) whose ID is to be retrieved.

Remarks   Returns the command ID of the button or separator specified by *nIndex*. Separators return **ID_SEPARATOR**.

See Also   **CToolBar::CommandToIndex, CControlBar::GetCount**

CToolBar::GetItemRect

void **GetItemRect**(int *nIndex*, LPRECT *lpRect*);

Parameters   *nIndex*   Index of the item (button or separator) whose rectangle coordinates are to be retrieved.

lpRect   Address of the **RECT** structure that will contain the item's coordinates.

Remarks   Fills the **RECT** structure whose address is contained in *lpRect* with the coordinates of the button or separator specified by *nIndex*. Coordinates are in pixels relative to the upper-left corner of the toolbar.

Use **GetItemRect** to get the coordinates of a separator you want to replace with a combo box or other control.

See Also   **CToolBar::CommandToIndex**

CToolBar::LoadBitmap

BOOL LoadBitmap(LPCTSTR *lpszResourceName* **);**

BOOL LoadBitmap(UINT *nIDResource* **);**

Return Value   Nonzero if successful; otherwise 0.

Parameters   *lpszResourceName*   Pointer to the resource name of the bitmap to be loaded.

nIDResource   Resource ID of the bitmap to be loaded.

Remarks   Loads the bitmap specified by *lpszResourceName* or *nIDResource*. The bitmap should contain one image for each toolbar button. If the images are not of the standard size (16 pixels wide and 15 pixels high), call **SetSizes** to set the button sizes and their images.

See Also   **CToolBar::Create**, **CToolBar::SetButtons**, **CToolBar::SetSizes**

CToolBar::SetButtonInfo

void SetButtonInfo(int *nIndex*, **UINT** *nID*, **UINT** *nStyle*, **int** *iImage* **);**

Parameters   *nIndex*   Index of the button or separator whose information is to be set.

nID   The value to which the button's command ID is set.

nStyle   The new button style. The following button styles are supported:

- **TBBS_BUTTON**   Standard pushbutton (default)
- **TBBS_SEPARATOR**   Separator
- **TBBS_CHECKBOX**   Auto check-box button

iImage   New index for the button's image within the bitmap.

Remarks   Sets the button's command ID, style, and image number. For separators, which have the style **TBBS_SEPARATOR**, this function sets the separator's width in pixels to the value stored in *iImage*.

For information on bitmap images and buttons, see **CToolBar** and **CToolBar::LoadBitmap**.

See Also   **CToolBar::GetButtonInfo**, **CToolBar::LoadBitmap**

CToolBar::SetButtons

BOOL SetButtons(const UINT* *lpIDArray*, **int** *nIDCount* **);**

Return Value   Nonzero if successful; otherwise 0.

Parameters   *lpIDArray*   Pointer to an array of command IDs.

nIDCount   Number of elements in the array pointed to by *lpIDArray*.

Remarks   Sets each toolbar button's command ID to the value specified by the corresponding element of the array *lpIDArray*. If an element of the array has the value **ID_SEPARATOR**, a separator is created in the corresponding position of the toolbar. This function also sets each button's style to **TBBS_BUTTON** and each separator's style to **TBBS_SEPARATOR**, and assigns an image index to each button. The image index specifies the position of the button's image within the bitmap.

You do not need to account for separators in the bitmap because this function does not assign image indexes for separators. If your toolbar has buttons at positions 0, 1, and 3 and a separator at position 2, the images at positions 0, 1, and 2 in your bitmap are assigned to the buttons at positions 0, 1, and 3, respectively.

If *lpIDArray* is **NULL**, this function allocates space for the number of items specified by *nIDCount*. Use **SetButtonInfo** to set each item's attributes.

See Also   **CToolBar::Create**, **CToolBar::SetButtonInfo**

CToolBar::SetHeight

void SetHeight(int *cyHeight* **);**

Parameters   *cyHeight*   The height in pixels of the toolbar.

Remarks   Sets the toolbar's height to the value, in pixels, specified in *cyHeight*.

After calling **SetSizes**, use this function to override the standard toolbar height. If the height is too small, the buttons will be clipped at the bottom.

If this function is not called, the framework uses the size of the button to determine the toolbar height.

See Also   **CToolBar::SetSizes**, **CToolBar::SetButtonInfo**, **CToolBar::SetButtons**

CToolBar::SetSizes

void SetSizes(SIZE *sizeButton***, SIZE** *sizeImage* **);**

Parameters   *sizeButton*   The size in pixels of each button.

sizeImage   The size in pixels of each image.

Remarks   Sets the toolbar's buttons to the size, in pixels, specified in *sizeButton*. The *sizeImage* parameter must contain the size, in pixels, of the images in the toolbar's bitmap. The dimensions in *sizeButton* must be sufficient to hold the image plus 3 pixels on each side for the button outline. This function also sets the toolbar height to fit the buttons.

Call this function only for toolbars that do not follow *The Windows Interface: An Application Design Guide* recommendations for button and image sizes.

See Also   **CToolBar::LoadBitmap**, **CToolBar::SetButtonInfo**, **CToolBar::SetButtons**, **CToolBar::SetHeight**

class CTypedPtrArray : public BASE_CLASS

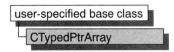

user-specified base class

CTypedPtrArray

template< class *BASE_CLASS*, class *TYPE* >
    class CTypedPtrArray : public BASE_CLASS

Parameters

BASE_CLASS   Base class of the typed pointer array class; must be an array class (**CObArray** or **CPtrArray**).

TYPE   Type of the elements stored in the base-class array.

Remarks

The **CTypedPtrArray** class provides a type-safe "wrapper" for objects of class **CPtrArray** or **CObArray**. When you use **CTypedPtrArray** rather than **CPtrArray** or **CObArray**, the C++ type-checking facility helps eliminate errors caused by mismatched pointer types.

In addition, the **CTypedPtrArray** wrapper performs much of the casting that would be required if you used **CObArray** or **CPtrArray**.

Because all **CTypedPtrArray** functions are in-line, use of this template does not significantly affect the size or speed of your code.

#include <afxtempl.h>

See Also

CPtrArray, **CObArray**

Element Access

GetAt	Returns the value at a given index.
ElementAt	Returns a temporary reference to the element pointer within the array.

Operators

operator[]	Sets or gets the element at the specified index.

Member Functions

CTypedPtrArray::ElementAt

TYPE& **ElementAt**(int *nIndex*);

Return Value   A temporary reference to the element at the location specified by *nIndex*. This element is of the type specified by the template parameter *TYPE*.

Parameters   *TYPE*   Template parameter specifying the type of elements stored in this array.

nIndex   An integer index that is greater than or equal to 0 and less than or equal to the value returned by *BASE_CLASS*::**GetUpperBound**.

Remarks   This inline function calls *BASE_CLASS*::**ElementAt**.

See Also   **CObArray::ElementAt, CObArray::GetUpperBound**

CTypedPtrArray::GetAt

TYPE **GetAt**(int *nIndex*) **const**;

Parameters   *TYPE*   Template parameter specifying the type of elements stored in the array.

nIndex   An integer index that is greater than or equal to 0 and less than or equal to the value returned by *BASE_CLASS*::**GetUpperBound**.

Remarks   This inline function calls *BASE_CLASS*::**GetAt**.

Return Value   A copy of the element at the location specified by *nIndex*. This element is of the type specified by the template parameter *TYPE*.

See Also   **CObArray::GetAt, CObArray::GetUpperBound**

Operators

CTypedPtrArray::operator [ ]

TYPE& **operator[]**(int *nIndex*);

TYPE **operator[]**(int *nIndex*) **const**;

Parameters   *TYPE*   Template parameter specifying the type of elements stored in the array.

nIndex   An integer index that is greater than or equal to 0 and less than or equal to the value returned by *BASE_CLASS*::**GetUpperBound**.

Remarks   These inline operators call *BASE_CLASS*::**operator [ ]**.

The first operator, called for arrays that are not **const**, may be used on either the right (r-value) or the left (l-value) of an assignment statement. The second, invoked for **const** arrays, may be used only on the right.

The Debug version of the library asserts if the subscript (either on the left or right side of an assignment statement) is out of bounds.

See Also   **CObArray::operator [ ]**

class CTypedPtrList : public BASE_CLASS

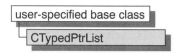

user-specified base class

CTypedPtrList

template< class *BASE_CLASS***, class** *TYPE* **>**
    class CTypedPtrList : public *BASE_CLASS*

Parameters   *BASE_CLASS*   Base class of the typed pointer list class; must be a pointer list class (**CObList** or **CPtrList**).

TYPE   Type of the elements stored in the base-class list.

Remarks   The **CTypedPtrList** class provides a type-safe "wrapper" for objects of class **CPtrList**. When you use **CTypedPtrList** rather than **CObList** or **CPtrList**, the C++ type-checking facility helps eliminate errors caused by mismatched pointer types.

In addition, the **CTypedPtrList** wrapper performs much of the casting that would be required if you used **CObList** or **CPtrList**.

Because all **CTypedPtrList** functions are inline, use of this template does not significantly affect the size or speed of your code.

Lists derived from **CObList** can be serialized, but those derived from **CPtrList** cannot.

When a **CTypedPtrList** object is deleted, or when its elements are removed, only the pointers are removed, not the entities they reference.

#include <afxtempl.h>

See Also   **CPtrList, CObList**

Head/Tail Access

GetHead	Returns the head element of the list (cannot be empty).
GetTail	Returns the tail element of the list (cannot be empty).

Operations

RemoveHead	Removes the element from the head of the list.
RemoveTaill	Removes the element from the tail of the list.

Iteration

GetNext	Gets the next element for iterating.
GetPrev	Gets the previous element for iterating.

Retrieval/Modification

GetAt	Gets the element at a given position.

Member Functions

CTypedPtrList::GetAt

TYPE& **GetAt(POSITION** *position* **)**;

TYPE **GetAt(POSITION** *position* **) const;**

Return Value

If the list is accessed through a pointer to a **const CTypedPtrList**, then **GetAt** returns a pointer of the type specified by the template parameter *TYPE*. This allows the function to be used only on the right side of an assignment statement and thus protects the list from modification.

If the list is accessed directly or through a pointer to a **CTypedPtrList**, then **GetAt** returns a reference to a pointer of the type specified by the template parameter *TYPE*. This allows the function to be used on either side of an assignment statement and thus allows the list entries to be modified.

Parameters

TYPE   Template parameter specifying the type of elements stored in the list.

position   A **POSITION** value returned by a previous **GetHeadPosition** or **Find** member function call.

Remarks

A variable of type **POSITION** is a key for the list. It is not the same as an index, and you cannot operate on a **POSITION** value yourself. **GetAt** retrieves the **CObject** pointer associated with a given position.

You must ensure that your **POSITION** value represents a valid position in the list. If it is invalid, then the Debug version of the Microsoft Foundation Class Library asserts.

This inline function calls *BASE_CLASS*::**GetAt**.

See Also   **CObList::GetAt**

CTypedPtrList::GetHead

TYPE& GetHead( );

TYPE **GetHead( ) const;**

Return Value   If the list is accessed through a pointer to a **const CTypedPtrList**, then **GetHead** returns a pointer of the type specified by the template parameter *TYPE*. This allows the function to be used only on the right side of an assignment statement and thus protects the list from modification.

If the list is accessed directly or through a pointer to a **CTypedPtrList**, then **GetHead** returns a reference to a pointer of the type specified by the template parameter *TYPE*. This allows the function to be used on either side of an assignment statement and thus allows the list entries to be modified.

Parameters   *TYPE*   Template parameter specifying the type of elements stored in the list.

Remarks   Gets the pointer that represents the head element of this list.

You must ensure that the list is not empty before calling **GetHead**. If the list is empty, then the Debug version of the Microsoft Foundation Class Library asserts. Use **IsEmpty** to verify that the list contains elements.

See Also   **CPtrList::IsEmpty**

CTypedPtrList::GetNext

TYPE& GetNext(**POSITION&** *rPosition*);

TYPE **GetNext(POSITION&** *rPosition*) const;

Return Value   If the list is accessed through a pointer to a **const CTypedPtrList**, then **GetNext** returns a pointer of the type specified by the template parameter *TYPE*. This allows the function to be used only on the right side of an assignment statement and thus protects the list from modification.

If the list is accessed directly or through a pointer to a **CTypedPtrList**, then **GetNext** returns a reference to a pointer of the type specified by the template parameter *TYPE*. This allows the function to be used on either side of an assignment statement and thus allows the list entries to be modified.

Parameters   *TYPE*   Template parameter specifying the type of elements contained in this list.

rPosition   A reference to a **POSITION** value returned by a previous **GetNext**, **GetHeadPosition**, or other member function call.

Remarks   Gets the list element identified by *rPosition*, then sets *rPosition* to the **POSITION** value of the next entry in the list. You can use **GetNext** in a forward iteration loop if you establish the initial position with a call to **GetHeadPosition** or **CPtrList::Find**.

You must ensure that your **POSITION** value represents a valid position in the list. If it is invalid, then the Debug version of the Microsoft Foundation Class Library asserts.

If the retrieved element is the last in the list, then the new value of *rPosition* is set to **NULL**.

It is possible to remove an element during an iteration. See the example for **CObList::RemoveAt**.

See Also   **CObList::Find**, **CObList::GetHeadPosition**, **CObList::GetTailPosition**, **CTypedPtrList::GetPrev**, **CTypedPtrList::GetHead**

CTypedPtrList::GetPrev

TYPE& **GetPrev(POSITION&** *rPosition*);

TYPE **GetPrev(POSITION&** *rPosition*) **const;**

Return Value   If the list is accessed through a pointer to a **const CTypedPtrList**, then **GetPrev** returns a pointer of the type specified by the template parameter *TYPE*. This allows the function to be used only on the right side of an assignment statement and thus protects the list from modification.

If the list is accessed directly or through a pointer to a **CTypedPtrList**, then **GetPrev** returns a reference to a pointer of the type specified by the template parameter *TYPE*. This allows the function to be used on either side of an assignment statement and thus allows the list entries to be modified.

Parameters   *TYPE*   Template parameter specifying the type of elements contained in this list.

rPosition   A reference to a **POSITION** value returned by a previous **GetPrev** or other member function call.

Remarks   Gets the list element identified by *rPosition*, then sets *rPosition* to the **POSITION** value of the previous entry in the list. You can use **GetPrev** in a reverse iteration loop if you establish the initial position with a call to **GetTailPosition** or **Find**.

You must ensure that your **POSITION** value represents a valid position in the list. If it is invalid, then the Debug version of the Microsoft Foundation Class Library asserts.

If the retrieved element is the first in the list, then the new value of *rPosition* is set to **NULL**.

See Also   **CPtrList::Find**, **CPtrList::GetTailPosition**, **CPtrList::GetHeadPosition**, **CTypedPtrList::GetNext**, **CTypedPtrList::GetHead**

CTypedPtrList::GetTail

TYPE& **GetTail( );**

TYPE **GetTail( ) const;**

Return Value   If the list is accessed through a pointer to a **const CTypedPtrList**, then **GetTail** returns a pointer of the type specified by the template parameter *TYPE*. This allows the function to be used only on the right side of an assignment statement and thus protects the list from modification.

If the list is accessed directly or through a pointer to a **CTypedPtrList**, then **GetTail** returns a reference to a pointer of the type specified by the template parameter *TYPE*. This allows the function to be used on either side of an assignment statement and thus allows the list entries to be modified.

Parameters   *TYPE*   Template parameter specifying the type of elements stored in the list.

Remarks   Gets the pointer that represents the head element of this list.

You must ensure that the list is not empty before calling **GetTail**. If the list is empty, then the Debug version of the Microsoft Foundation Class Library asserts. Use **IsEmpty** to verify that the list contains elements.

See Also   **CPtrList::IsEmpty**, **CPtrList::Find**, **CPtrList::GetTailPosition**, **CPtrList::GetHeadPosition**, **CTypedPtrList::GetNext**, **CTypedPtrList::GetHead**

CTypedPtrList::RemoveHead

TYPE **RemoveHead( );**

Return Value   The pointer previously at the head of the list. This pointer is of the type specified by the template parameter *TYPE*.

Parameters   *TYPE*   Template parameter specifying the type of elements stored in the list.

Remarks   Removes the element from the head of the list and returns it.

You must ensure that the list is not empty before calling **RemoveHead**. If the list is empty, then the Debug version of the Microsoft Foundation Class Library asserts. Use **IsEmpty** to verify that the list contains elements.

See Also   **CTypedPtrList::RemoveTail**, **CPtrList::IsEmpty**, **CPtrList::GetHead**, **CPtrList::AddHead**

CTypedPtrList::RemoveTail

TYPE **RemoveTail( );**

Return Value   The pointer previously at the tail of the list. This pointer is of the type specified by the template parameter *TYPE*.

Parameters   *TYPE*   Template parameter specifying the type of elements stored in the list.

Remarks   Removes the element from the tail of the list and returns it.

You must ensure that the list is not empty before calling **RemoveTail**. If the list is empty, then the Debug version of the Microsoft Foundation Class Library asserts. Use **IsEmpty** to verify that the list contains elements.

See Also   **CTypedPtrList::RemoveTail**, **CPtrList::IsEmpty**, **CPtrList::GetTail**, **CPtrList::AddTail**

class CTypedPtrMap : public BASE_CLASS

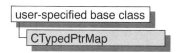

user-specified base class
CTypedPtrMap

> **template< class** *BASE_CLASS*, **class** *KEY*, **class** *VALUE* **>**
> **class CTypedPtrMap : public BASE_CLASS**

Parameters
> *BASE_CLASS*   Base class of the typed pointer map class; must be a pointer map class (**CMapPtrToPtr**, **CMapPtrToWord**, **CMapWordToPtr**, or **CMapStringToPtr**).
>
> *KEY*   Class of the object used as the key to the map.
>
> *VALUE*   Class of the object stored in the map.

Remarks
> The **CTypedPtrMap** class provides a type-safe "wrapper" for objects of the pointer-map classes **CMapPtrToPtr**, **CMapPtrToWord**, **CMapWordToPtr**, and **CMapStringToPtr**. When you use **CTypedPtrMap**, the C++ type-checking facility helps eliminate errors caused by mismatched pointer types.
>
> Because all **CTypedPtrMap** functions are in-line, use of this template does not significantly affect the size or speed of your code.
>
> **#include <afxtempl.h>**

See Also
> **CMapPtrToPtr**, **CMapPtrToWord**, **CMapWordToPtr**, **CMapStringToPtr**

Element Access
Lookup	Returns a *KEY* based on a *VALUE*.
GetNextAssoc	Gets the next element for iterating.

Operators
operator[]	Inserts an element into the map.

Member Functions

CTypedPtrMap::GetNextAssoc

> void GetNextAssoc(POSITION& *rPosition*, *KEY*& *rKey*, *VALUE*& *rValue*)
> const;

Parameters   *rPosition*   Specifies a reference to a **POSITION** value returned by a previous **GetNextAssoc** or *BASE_CLASS*::**GetStartPosition** call.

KEY   Template parameter specifying the type of the map's keys.

rKey   Specifies the returned key of the retrieved element.

VALUE   Template parameter specifying the type of the map's values.

rValue   Specifies the returned value of the retrieved element.

Remarks   Retrieves the map element at *rNextPosition*, then updates *rNextPosition* to refer to the next element in the map. This function is most useful for iterating through all the elements in the map. Note that the position sequence is not necessarily the same as the key value sequence.

If the retrieved element is the last in the map, then the new value of *rNextPosition* is set to **NULL**.

This inline functon calls *BASE_CLASS*::**GetNextAssoc**.

See Also   **CMapStringToOb::GetNextAssoc, CMapStringToOb::GetStartPosition**

CTypedPtrMap::Lookup

> BOOL Lookup(*BASE_CLASS*::**BASE_ARG_KEY** *key*, *VALUE*& *rValue*)
> const;

Return Value   Nonzero if the element was found; otherwise 0.

Parameters   *BASE_CLASS*   Template parameter specifying the base class of this map's class.

key   The key of the element to be looked up.

VALUE   Template parameter specifying the type of values stored in this map.

rValue   Specifies the returned value of the retrieved element.

Remarks	**Lookup** uses a hashing algorithm to quickly find the map element with a key that matches exactly.

This inline functon calls *BASE_CLASS*::**Lookup**. |
| **See Also** | **CMapStringToOb::Lookup** |

Operators

CTypedPtrMap::operator [ ]

VALUE& **operator [ ]**(*BASE_CLASS*::**BASE_ARG_KEY** *key*);

Parameters	*VALUE* Template parameter specifying the type of values stored in this map.

BASE_CLASS   Template parameter specifying the base class of this map's class.

key   The key of the element to be looked created in the map. |
| **Remarks** | This operator can be used only on the left side of an assignment statement (an l-value). If there is no map element with the specified key, then a new element is created.There is no "right side" (r-value) equivalent to this operator because there is a possibility that a key may not be found in the map. Use the **Lookup** member function for element retrieval. |
| **See Also** | **CTypedPtrMap::Lookup** |

class CUIntArray : public CObject

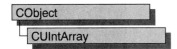

The **CUIntArray** class supports arrays of unsigned integers. An unsigned integer, or **UINT**, differs from words and doublewords in that the physical size of a **UINT** can change depending on the target operating environment. Under Windows version 3.1, a **UINT** is the same size as a **WORD**. Under Windows NT, a **UINT** is the same size as a doubleword. The member functions of **CUIntArray** are similar to the member functions of class **CObArray**. Because of this similarity, you can use the **CObArray** reference documentation for member function specifics. Wherever you see a **CObject** pointer as a function parameter or return value, substitute a **UINT**.

```
CObject* CObArray::GetAt( int <nIndex> ) const;
```

for example, translates to

```
UINT CUIntArray::GetAt( int <nIndex> ) const;
```

CUIntArray incorporates the **IMPLEMENT_DYNAMIC** macro to support runtime type access and dumping to a **CDumpContext** object. If you need a dump of individual unsigned integer elements, you must set the depth of the dump context to 1 or greater. Unsigned integer arrays may not be serialized.

Note   Before using an array, use **SetSize** to establish its size and allocate memory for it. If you do not use **SetSize**, adding elements to your array causes it to be frequently reallocated and copied. Frequent reallocation and copying are inefficient and can fragment memory.

#include <afxcoll.h>

Construction
CUIntArray	Constructs an empty array for unsigned integers.

Bounds
GetSize	Gets the number of elements in this array.
GetUpperBound	Returns the largest valid index.
SetSize	Sets the number of elements to be contained in this array.

Operations

FreeExtra   Frees all unused memory above the current upper bound.

RemoveAll   Removes all the elements from this array.

Element Access

GetAt   Returns the value at a given index.

SetAt   Sets the value for a given index; the array is not allowed to grow.

ElementAt   Returns a temporary reference to the element pointer within the array.

Growing the Array

SetAtGrow   Sets the value for a given index; grows the array if necessary.

Add   Adds an element to the end of the array; grows the array if necessary.

Insertion/Removal

InsertAt   Inserts an element (or all the elements in another array) at a specified index.

RemoveAt   Removes an element at a specific index.

Operators

operator [ ]   Sets or gets the element at the specified index.

class CUserException : public CException

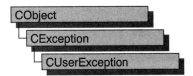

A **CUserException** is thrown to stop an end-user operation. Use **CUserException** when you want to use the throw/catch exception mechanism for application-specific exceptions. "User" in the class name can be interpreted as "my user did something exceptional that I need to handle."

A **CUserException** is usually thrown after calling the global function **AfxMessageBox** to notify the user that an operation has failed. When you write an exception handler, handle the exception specially since the user usually has already been notified of the failure. The framework throws this exception in some cases. To throw a **CUserException** yourself, alert the user and then call the global function **AfxThrowUserException**.

In the example below, a function containing operations that may fail alerts the user and throws a **CUserException**. The calling function catches the exception and handles it specially:

```
void DoSomeOperation( )
{
    // Processing
    // If something goes wrong...
    AfxMessageBox( "The x operation failed" );
    AfxThrowUserException( );
}

BOOL TrySomething( )
{
    TRY
    {
        // Could throw a CUserException or other exception.
        DoSomeOperation( );
    }
    CATCH( CUserException, e )
    {
        return FALSE;    // User already notified.
    }
```

```
AND_CATCH( CException, e )
{
    // For other exception types, notify user here.
    AfxMessageBox( "Some operation failed" );
    return FALSE;
}
END_CATCH
return TRUE;   // No exception thrown.
}
```

#include <afxwin.h>

See Also   **CException, AfxMessageBox, AfxThrowUserException**

class CView : public CWnd

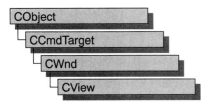

The **CView** class provides the basic functionality for user-defined view classes. A view is attached to a document and acts as an intermediary between the document and the user: the view renders an image of the document on the screen or printer and interprets user input as operations upon the document.

A view is a child of a frame window. More than one view can share a frame window, as in the case of a splitter window. The relationship between a view class, a frame window class, and a document class is established by a **CDocTemplate** object. When the user opens a new window or splits an existing one, the framework constructs a new view and attaches it to the document.

A view can be attached to only one document, but a document can have multiple views attached to it at once—for example, if the document is displayed in a splitter window or in multiple child windows in a multiple document interface (MDI) application. Your application can support different types of views for a given document type; for example, a word-processing program might provide both a complete text view of a document and an outline view that shows only the section headings. These different types of views can be placed in separate frame windows or in separate panes of a single frame window if you use a splitter window.

A view may be responsible for handling several different types of input, such as keyboard input, mouse input or input via drag-and-drop, as well as commands from menus, toolbars, or scroll bars. A view receives commands forwarded by its frame window. If the view does not handle a given command, it forwards the command to its associated document. Like all command targets, a view handles messages via a message map.

The view is responsible for displaying and modifying the document's data but not for storing it. The document provides the view with the necessary details about its data. You can let the view access the document's data members directly, or you can provide member functions in the document class for the view class to call.

When a document's data changes, the view responsible for the changes typically calls the **CDocument::UpdateAllViews** function for the document, which notifies all the other views by calling the **OnUpdate** member function for each. The default implementation of **OnUpdate** invalidates the view's entire client area. You can override it to invalidate only those regions of the client area that map to the modified portions of the document.

To use **CView**, derive a class from it and implement the **OnDraw** member function to perform screen display. You can also use **OnDraw** to perform printing and print preview. The framework handles the print loop for printing and previewing your document.

A view handles scroll-bar messages in its **OnHScroll** and **OnVScroll** member functions. You can implement scroll-bar message handling in these functions, or you can use the derived class **CScrollView** to handle scrolling for you.

Besides **CScrollView**, the Microsoft Foundation Class Library provides two other classes derived from **CView**:

- **CFormView**, a scrollable view that contains dialog-box controls and is based on a dialog template resource.

- **CEditView**, a view that provides a simple multiline text editor. You can use a **CEditView** object as a control in a dialog box as well as a view on a document.

The **CView** class also has a derived class named **CPreviewView**, which is used by the framework to perform print previewing. This class provides support for the features unique to the print-preview window, such as a toolbar, single- or double-page preview, and zooming, that is, enlarging the previewed image. You don't need to call or override any of **CPreviewView**'s member functions unless you want to implement your own interface for print preview (for example, if you want to support editing in print preview mode). See Technical Note 30 under MFC in Books Online for more details on customizing print preview.

#include <afxwin.h>

See Also

CWnd, **CFrameWnd**, **CSplitterWnd**, **CDC**, **CDocTemplate**, **CDocument**, **CFormView**, **CEditView**, **CScrollView**

Operations

DoPreparePrinting	Displays Print dialog box and creates printer device context; call when overriding the **OnPreparePrinting** member function.
GetDocument	Returns the document associated with the view.

OLE 2 Overridables

OnDragEnter	Called when an item is first dragged into the drag-and-drop region of a view.
OnDragLeave	Called when a dragged item leaves the drag-and-drop region of a view.
OnDragOver	Called when an item is dragged over the drag-and-drop region of a view.
OnDrop	Called when an item has been dropped into the drag-and-drop region of a view.
OnInitialUpdate	Called after a view is first attached to a document.
OnScrollBy	Called when a view containing active in-place OLE items is scrolled.
OnScroll	Called when OLE items are dragged beyond the borders of the view.

Overridables

IsSelected	Tests whether a document item is selected. Required for OLE support.
OnActivateView	Called when a view is activated.
OnBeginPrinting	Called when a print job begins; override to allocate graphics device interface (GDI) resources.
OnDraw	Called to render an image of the document for screen display, printing, or print preview. Implementation required.
OnEndPrinting	Called when a print job ends; override to deallocate GDI resources.
OnEndPrintPreview	Called when preview mode is exited.
OnPrepareDC	Called before the **OnDraw** member function is called for screen display or the **OnPrint** member function is called for printing or print preview.
OnPreparePrinting	Called before a document is printed or previewed; override to initialize Print dialog box.
OnPrint	Called to print or preview a page of the document.
OnUpdate	Called to notify a view that its document has been modified.

Constructors

CView	Constructs a **CView** object.

Member Functions

CView::CView

Protected→
CView( );
END Protected

Remarks   Constructs a **CView** object. The framework calls the constructor when a new frame window is created or a window is split. Override the **OnInitialUpdate** member function to initialize the view after the document is attached.

See Also   **CView::OnInitialUpdate**

CView::DoPreparePrinting

BOOL DoPreparePrinting(CPrintInfo* *pInfo* **);**

Return Value   Nonzero if printing or print preview can begin; 0 if the operation has been canceled.

Parameters   *pInfo*   Points to a **CPrintInfo** structure that describes the current print job.

Remarks   Call this function from your override of **OnPreparePrinting** to invoke the Print dialog box and create a printer device context.

This function's behavior depends on whether it is being called for printing or print preview (specified by the **m_bPreview** member of the *pInfo* parameter). If a file is being printed, this function invokes the Print dialog box, using the values in the **CPrintInfo** structure that *pInfo* points to; after the user has closed the dialog box, the function creates a printer device context based on settings the user specified in the dialog box and returns this device context through the *pInfo* parameter. This device context is used to print the document.

If a file is being previewed, this function creates a printer device context using the current printer settings; this device context is used for simulating the printer during preview.

See Also   **CPrintInfo, CView::OnPreparePrinting**

CView::GetDocument

CDocument* GetDocument( ) const;

Return Value   A pointer to the **CDocument** object associated with the view. **NULL** if the view is not attached to a document.

Remarks	Call this function to get a pointer to the view's document. This allows you to call the document's member functions.
See Also	**CDocument**

CView::IsSelected

virtual BOOL IsSelected(const CObject* *pDocItem* **) const;**

Return Value	Nonzero if the specified document item is selected; otherwise 0.
Parameters	*pDocItem* Points to the document item being tested.
Remarks	Called by the framework to check whether the specified document item is selected. The default implementation of this function returns **FALSE**. Override this function if you are implementing selection using **CDocItem** objects. You must override this function if your view contains OLE items.
See Also	**CDocItem**, **COleClientItem**

CView::OnActivateView

Protected→
virtual void OnActivateView(BOOL *bActivate*, **CView*** *pActivateView*,
  CView* *pDeactiveView* **);**
END Protected

Parameters	*bActivate* Indicates whether the view is being activated or deactivated.
	pActivateView Points to the view object that is being activated.
	pDeactiveView Points to the view object that is being deactivated.
Remarks	Called by the framework when a view is activated or deactivated. The default implementation of this function sets the focus to the view being activated. Override this function if you want to perform special processing when a view is activated or deactivated. For example, if you want to provide special visual cues that distinguish the active view from the inactive views, you would examine the *bActivate* parameter and update the view's appearance accordingly.
	The *pActivateView* and *pDeactiveView* parameters point to the same view if the application's main frame window is activated with no change in the active view— for example, if the focus is being transferred from another application to this one, rather than from one view to another within the application. This allows a view to re-realize its palette, if needed.
See Also	**CWnd::OnActivate**

CView::OnBeginPrinting

Protected→

virtual void OnBeginPrinting(CDC* *pDC,* **CPrintInfo*** *pInfo* **);**

END Protected

Parameters *pDC* Points to the printer device context.

pInfo Points to a **CPrintInfo** structure that describes the current print job.

Remarks Called by the framework at the beginning of a print or print preview job, after **OnPreparePrinting** has been called. The default implementation of this function does nothing. Override this function to allocate any GDI resources, such as pens or fonts, needed specifically for printing. Select the GDI objects into the device context from within the **OnPrint** member function for each page that uses them. If you are using the same view object to perform both screen display and printing, use separate variables for the GDI resources needed for each display; this allows you to update the screen during printing.

You can also use this function to perform initializations that depend on properties of the printer device context. For example, the number of pages needed to print the document may depend on settings that the user specified from the Print dialog box (such as page length). In such a situation, you cannot specify the document length in the **OnPreparePrinting** member function, where you would normally do so; you must wait until the printer device context has been created based on the dialog box settings. **OnBeginPrinting** is the first overridable function that gives you access to the **CDC** object representing the printer device context, so you can set the document length from this function. Note that if the document length is not specified by this time, a scroll bar is not displayed during print preview.

See Also **CView::OnEndPrinting, CView::OnPreparePrinting, CView::OnPrint**

CView::OnDragEnter

virtual DROPEFFECT OnDragEnter(COleDataObject* *pDataObject,*
    DWORD *dwKeyState,* **CPoint** *point* **);**

Return Value A value from the **DROPEFFECT** enumerated type, which indicates the type of drop that would occur if the user dropped the object at this position. The type of drop usually depends on the current key state indicated by *dwKeyState*. A standard mapping of keystates to **DROPEFFECT** values is:

- **DROPEFFECT_LINK** for **MK_CONTROL | MK_SHIFT**   Creates a linkage between the object and its server.

- **DROPEFFECT_COPY** for **MK_CONTROL**   Creates a copy of the dropped object.

- **DROPEFFECT_MOVE** for **MK_ALT**   Creates a copy of the dropped object and delete the original object.

For more information see the OCLIENT sample found under MFC in Books Online.

Parameters   *pDataObject*   Points to the **COleDataObject** being dragged into the drop area of the view.

dwKeyState   The state of the SHIFT, ALT, and CTRL keys at the time the object is dragged into the drop area of the view.

point   The current mouse position relative to the client area of the view .

Remarks   Called by the framework when the mouse first enters the non-scrolling region of the drop target window. Default implementation is to do nothing and return **DROPEFFECT_NONE**.

Override this function to prepare for future calls to the **OnDragOver** member function. Any data required from the data object should be retrieved at this time for later use in the **OnDragOver** member function. The view should also be updated at this time to give the user visual feedback. For more information, see the article "Drag and Drop: Implementing a Drop Target" in *Programming with the Microsoft Foundation Class Library*.

See Also   **CView::OnDragOver**, **CView::OnDrop**, **CView::OnDragLeave**, **COleDropTarget**

CView::OnDragLeave

virtual void OnDragLeave( );

Remarks   Called by the framework during a drag operation when the mouse is moved out of the valid drop area for that window.

Override this function if the current view needs to clean up any actions taken during **OnDragEnter** or **OnDragOver** calls, such as removing any visual user feedback while the object was dragged and dropped.

See Also   **CView::OnDragEnter**, **CView::OnScroll**, **COleDropTarget**

CView::OnDragOver

virtual DROPEFFECT OnDragOver(COleDataObject* *pDataObject***,**
    DWORD *dwKeyState***, CPoint** *point* **);**

Return Value   A value from the **DROPEFFECT** enumerated type, which indicates the type of drop that would occur if the user dropped the object at this position. The type of drop often depends on the current key state as indicated by *dwKeyState*. A standard mapping of keystates to **DROPEFFECT** values is as follows:

- **DROPEFFECT_LINK** for **MK_CONTROL | MK_SHIFT**   Creates a linkage between the object and its server.
- **DROPEFFECT_COPY** for **MK_CONTROL**   Creates a copy of the dropped object.
- **DROPEFFECT_MOVE** for **MK_ALT**   Creates a copy of the dropped object and delete the original object.

For more information see the OCLIENT sample found under MFC in Books Online.

Parameters   *pDataObject*   Points to the **COleDataObject** being dragged over the drop target.

dwKeyState   The state of the SHIFT, ALT, and CTRL keys at the time the object is dragged over the drop area of the view.

point   The current mouse position relative to the view client area.

Remarks   Called by the framework during a drag operation when the mouse is moved over the drop target window. The default implementation is to do nothing and return **DROPEFFECT_NONE**.

Override this function to give the user visual feedback during the drag operation. Since this function is called continuously, any code contained within it should be optimized as much as possible. For more information, see the article "Drag and Drop: Implementing a Drop Target" in *Programming with the Microsoft Foundation Class Library*.

See Also   **CView::OnDragEnter**, **CView::OnDrop**, **CView::OnDragLeave**, **COleDropTarget**

CView::OnDraw

Protected→
virtual void OnDraw(CDC* *pDC* **) = 0;**
END Protected

Parameters   *pDC*   Points to the device context to be used for rendering an image of the document.

Remarks   Called by the framework to render an image of the document. The framework calls this function to perform screen display, printing, and print preview, and it passes a different device context in each case. There is no default implementation.

You must override this function to display your view of the document. You can make graphic device interface (GDI) calls using the **CDC** object pointed to by the *pDC* parameter. You can select GDI resources, such as pens or fonts, into the device context before drawing and then deselect them afterwards. Often your drawing code can be device-independent; that is, it doesn't require information about what type of device is displaying the image.

To optimize drawing, call the **RectVisible** member function of the device context to find out whether a given rectangle will be drawn. If you need to distinguish between normal screen display and printing, call the **IsPrinting** member function of the device context.

See Also   **CDC::IsPrinting, CDC::RectVisible, CView::OnPrint, CWnd::OnCreate, CWnd::OnDestroy, CWnd::PostNcDestroy**

CView::OnDrop

virtual BOOL OnDrop(COleDataObject* *pDataObject*, **DROPEFFECT** *dropEffect*, **CPoint** *point* **);**

Return Value   Nonzero if the drop was successful; otherwise 0.

Parameters   *pDataObject*   Points to the **COleDataObject** that is dropped into the drop target.

dropEffect   The drop effect that the user has requested.

- **DROPEFFECT_COPY**   Creates a copy of the data object being dropped.
- **DROPEFFECT_MOVE**   Moves the data object to the current mouse location.
- **DROPEFFECT_LINK**   Creates a link between a data object and its server.

point   The current mouse position relative to the view client area.

Remarks   Called by the framework when the user releases a data object over a valid drop target. The default implementation is to do nothing and return **DROPEFFECT_NONE**.

Override this function to implement the effect of an OLE drop into the client area of the view. The data object can be examined via *pDataObject* for "clipboard" data and data dropped at the specified point.

See Also   **CView::OnDragEnter, CView::OnDragOver, CView::OnDragLeave, COleDropTarget**

CView::OnEndPrinting

Protected→
virtual void OnEndPrinting(CDC* *pDC*, **CPrintInfo*** *pInfo* **);**
END Protected

Parameters   *pDC*   Points to the printer device context.

pInfo   Points to a **CPrintInfo** structure that describes the current print job.

Remarks   Called by the framework after a document has been printed or previewed. The default implementation of this function does nothing. Override this function to free any GDI resources you allocated in the **OnBeginPrinting** member function.

See Also   **CView::OnBeginPrinting**

CView::OnEndPrintPreview

Protected→
virtual void OnEndPrintPreview(CDC* *pDC***, CPrintInfo*** *pInfo***, POINT**
    *point***, CPreviewView*** *pView* **);**
END Protected

Parameters   *pDC*   Points to the printer device context.

pInfo   Points to a **CPrintInfo** structure that describes the current print job.

point   Specifies the point on the page that was last displayed in preview mode.

pView   Points to the view object used for previewing.

Remarks   Called by the framework when the user exits print preview mode. The default implementation of this function calls the **OnEndPrinting** member function and restores the main frame window to the state it was in before print preview began. Override this function to perform special processing when preview mode is terminated. For example, if you want to maintain the user's position in the document when switching from preview mode to normal display mode, you can scroll to the position described by the *point* parameter and the **m_nCurPage** member of the **CPrintInfo** structure that the *pInfo* parameter points to.

Always call the base class version of **OnEndPrintPreview** from your override, typically at the end of the function.

See Also   **CPrintInfo, CView::OnEndPrinting**

CView::OnInitialUpdate

virtual void OnInitialUpdate( );

Remarks   Called by the framework after the view is first attached to the document, but before the view is initially displayed. The default implementation of this function calls the **OnUpdate** member function with no hint information (that is, using the default values of 0 for the *lHint* parameter and **NULL** for the *pHint* parameter). Override this function to perform any one-time initialization that requires information about the document. For example, if your application has fixed-sized documents, you can use this function to initialize a view's scrolling limits based on the document size. If your application supports variable-sized documents, use **OnUpdate** to update the scrolling limits every time the document changes.

See Also   **CView::OnUpdate**

CView::OnPrepareDC

Protected→
virtual void OnPrepareDC(CDC* *pDC*, **CPrintInfo*** *pInfo* = NULL **);**
END Protected

Parameters   *pDC*   Points to the device context to be used for rendering an image of the document.

pInfo   Points to a **CPrintInfo** structure that describes the current print job if **OnPrepareDC** is being called for printing or print preview; the **m_nCurPage** member specifies the page about to be printed. This parameter is **NULL** if **OnPrepareDC** is being called for screen display.

Remarks   Called by the framework before the **OnDraw** member function is called for screen display and before the **OnPrint** member function is called for each page during printing or print preview. The default implementation of this function does nothing if the function is called for screen display. However, this function is overridden in derived classes, such as **CScrollView**, to adjust attributes of the device context; consequently, you should always call the base class implementation at the beginning of your override.

If the function is called for printing, the default implementation examines the page information stored in the *pInfo* parameter. If the length of the document has not been specified, **OnPrepareDC** assumes the document to be one page long and stops the print loop after one page has been printed. The function stops the print loop by setting the **m_bContinuePrinting** member of the structure to **FALSE**.

Override **OnPrepareDC** for any of the following reasons:

- To adjust attributes of the device context as needed for the specified page. For example, if you need to set the mapping mode or other characteristics of the device context, do so in this function.

- To perform print-time pagination. Normally you specify the length of the document when printing begins, using the **OnPreparePrinting** member function. However, if you don't know in advance how long the document is (for example, when printing an undetermined number of records from a database), override **OnPrepareDC** to test for the end of the document while it is being printed. When there is no more of the document to be printed, set the **m_bContinuePrinting** member of the **CPrintInfo** structure to **FALSE**.

- To send escape codes to the printer on a page-by-page basis. To send escape codes from **OnPrepareDC**, call the **Escape** member function of the *pDC* parameter.

Call the base class version of **OnPrepareDC** at the beginning of your override.

See Also   CDC::Escape, CPrintInfo, CView::OnBeginPrinting, CView::OnDraw, CView::OnPreparePrinting, CView::OnPrint

CView::OnPreparePrinting

Protected→
virtual BOOL OnPreparePrinting(CPrintInfo* *pInfo* **);**
END Protected

Return Value   Nonzero to begin printing; 0 if the print job has been canceled.

Parameters   *pInfo*   Points to a **CPrintInfo** structure that describes the current print job.

Remarks   Called by the framework before a document is printed or previewed. The default implementation does nothing.

You must override this function to enable printing and print preview. Call the **DoPreparePrinting** member function, passing it the *pInfo* parameter, and then return its return value; **DoPreparePrinting** displays the Print dialog box and creates a printer device context. If you want to initialize the Print dialog box with values other than the defaults, assign values to the members of *pInfo*. For example, if you know the length of the document, pass the value to the **SetMaxPages** member function of *pInfo* before calling **DoPreparePrinting**. This value is displayed in the To: box in the Range portion of the Print dialog box.

DoPreparePrinting does not display the Print dialog box for a preview job. If you want to bypass the Print dialog box for a print job, check that the **m_bPreview** member of *pInfo* is **FALSE** and then set it to **TRUE** before passing it to **DoPreparePrinting**; reset it to **FALSE** afterwards.

If you need to perform initializations that require access to the **CDC** object representing the printer device context (for example, if you need to know the page size before specifying the length of the document), override the **OnBeginPrinting** member function.

If you want to set the value of the **m_nNumPreviewPages** or **m_strPageDesc** members of the *pInfo* parameter, do so after calling **DoPreparePrinting**. The **DoPreparePrinting** member function sets **m_nNumPreviewPages** to the value found in the application's .INI file and sets **m_strPageDesc** to its default value.

See Also   CPrintInfo, CView::DoPreparePrinting, CView::OnBeginPrinting, CView::OnPrepareDC, CView::OnPrint

Example   The following is an override of **OnPreparePrinting** provided by AppWizard if you select the printing option when you create a set of starter files. This override is sufficient unless you want to initialize the Print dialog box.

```
void CMyView::OnPreparePrinting( CPrintInfo *pInfo )
{
    return DoPreparePrinting( pInfo );
}
```

CView::OnPrint

Protected→
virtual void OnPrint(CDC* *pDC*, **CPrintInfo*** *pInfo* **);**
END Protected

Parameters   *pDC*   Points to the printer device context.

pInfo   Points to a **CPrintInfo** structure that describes the current print job.

Remarks   Called by the framework to print or preview a page of the document. For each page being printed, the framework calls this function immediately after calling the **OnPrepareDC** member function. The page being printed is specified by the **m_nCurPage** member of the **CPrintInfo** structure that *pInfo* points to. The default implementation calls the **OnDraw** member function and passes it the printer device context.

Override this function for any of the following reasons:

- To allow printing of multipage documents. Render only the portion of the document that corresponds to the page currently being printed. If you're using **OnDraw** to perform the rendering, you can adjust the viewport origin so that only the appropriate portion of the document is printed.

- To make the printed image look different from the screen image (that is, if your application is not WYSIWYG). Instead of passing the printer device context to **OnDraw**, use the device context to render an image using attributes not shown on the screen.

  If you need GDI resources for printing that you don't use for screen display, select them into the device context before drawing and deselect them afterwards. These GDI resources should be allocated in **OnBeginPrinting** and released in **OnEndPrinting**.

- To implement headers or footers. You can still use **OnDraw** to do the rendering by restricting the area that it can print on.

Note that the **m_rectDraw** member of the *pInfo* parameter describes the printable area of the page in logical units.

Do not call **OnPrepareDC** in your override of **OnPrint**; the framework calls **OnPrepareDC** automatically before calling **OnPrint**.

See Also   **CView::OnBeginPrinting**, **CView::OnEndPrinting**, **CView::OnPrepareDC**, **CView::OnDraw**

Example   The following is a skeleton for an overridden **OnPrint** function:

```
void CMyView::OnPrint( CDC *pDC, CPrintInfo *pInfo )
{
    // Print headers and/or footers, if desired.
    // Find portion of document corresponding to pInfo->m_nCurPage.
    OnDraw( pDC );
}
```

CView::OnScroll

virtual BOOL CView::OnScroll(UINT *nScrollCode***, UINT** *nPos***, BOOL** *bDoScroll* **= TRUE);**

Return Value   If *bDoScroll* is **TRUE** and the view was actually scrolled, then return nonzero; otherwise 0. If *bDoScroll* is **FALSE**, then return the value that you would have returned if *bDoScroll* were **TRUE**, even though you don't actually do the scrolling.

Parameters   *nScrollCode*   A scroll-bar code that indicates the user's scrolling request. This parameter is composed of two parts: a low-order byte, which determines the type of scrolling occurring horizontally, and a high-order byte, which determines the type of scrolling occurring vertically:

- **SB_BOTTOM**   Scrolls to bottom.
- **SB_LINEDOWN**   Scrolls one line down.
- **SB_LINEUP**   Scrolls one line up.
- **SB_PAGEDOWN**   Scrolls one page down.
- **SB_PAGEUP**   Scrolls one page up.
- **SB_THUMBTRACK**   Dragsscroll box to specified position. The current position is specified in *nPos*.
- **SB_TOP**   Scrolls to top.

nPos   Contains the current scroll-box position if the scroll-bar code is **SB_THUMBTRACK**; otherwise it is not used. Depending on the initial scroll range, *nPos* may be negative and should be cast to an **int** if necessary.

bDoScroll   Determines whether you should actually do the specified scrolling action. If **TRUE,** then scrolling should take place; if **FALSE,** then scrolling should not occur.

Remarks   Called by the framework to determine whether scrolling is possible.

In one case this function is called by the framework with *bDoScroll* set to **TRUE** when the view receives a scrollbar message.In this case, you should actually scroll the view. In the other case this function is called with *bDoScroll* set to **FALSE** when an OLE item is initially dragged into the auto-scrolling region of a drop target before scrolling actually takes place. In this case, you should not actually scroll the view.

See Also   **CView::OnScrollBy, COleClientItem**

CView::OnScrollBy

BOOL CView::OnScrollBy(CSize *sizeScroll***, BOOL** *bDoScroll* **= TRUE);**

Return Value   Nonzero if the view was able to be scrolled; otherwise 0.

Parameters   *sizeScroll*   Number of pixels scrolled horizontally and vertically.

bDoScroll   Determines whether scrolling of the view occurs. If **TRUE,** then scrolling takes place; if **FALSE**, then scrolling does not occur.

Remarks   Called by the framework when the user views an area beyond the present view of the document, either by dragging an OLE item against the view's current borders or by manipulating the vertical or horizontal scrollbars. The default implementation does nothing. In derived classes the function checks to see whether the view is scrollable in the direction the user requested and then updates the new region if necessary. This function is automatically called by **CScrollView::OnHScroll** and **CScrollView::OnVScroll**to perform the actual scrolling request.

CView::OnUpdate

Protected→
virtual void OnUpdate(CView* *pSender***, LPARAM** *lHint***, CObject*** *pHint* **);**
END Protected

Parameters   *pSender*   Points to the view that modified the document, or **NULL** if all views are to be updated.

lHint   Contains information about the modifications.

pHint   Points to an object storing information about the modifications.

Remarks   Called by the framework after the view's document has been modified; this function is called by **CDocument::UpdateAllViews** and allows the view to update its display to reflect those modifications. It is also called by the default implementation of **OnInitialUpdate**. The default implementation invalidates the entire client area, marking it for painting when the next **WM_PAINT** message is received. Override this function if you want to update only those regions that map to the modified portions of the document. To do this you must pass information about the modifications using the hint parameters.

To use *lHint*, define special hint values, typically a bitmask or an enumerated type, and have the document pass one of these values. To use *pHint*, derive a hint class from **CObject** and have the document pass a pointer to a hint object; when overriding **OnUpdate**, use the **CObject::IsKindOf** member function to determine the run-time type of the hint object.

Typically you should not perform any drawing directly from **OnUpdate**. Instead, determine the rectangle describing, in device coordinates, the area that requires updating; pass this rectangle to **CWnd::InvalidateRect**. This causes painting to occur the next time a **WM_PAINT** message is received.

If *lHint* is 0 and *pHint* is **NULL**, the document has sent a generic update notification. If a view receives a generic update notification, or if it cannot decode the hints, it should invalidate its entire client area.

See Also   **CDocument::UpdateAllViews**, **CView::OnInitialUpdate**, **CWnd::Invalidate**, **CWnd::InvalidateRect**

class CWinApp : public CWinThread

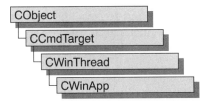

The **CWinApp** class is the base class from which you derive a Windows application object. An application object provides member functions for initializing your application (and each instance of it) and for running the application.

Each application that uses the Microsoft Foundation classes can only contain one object derived from **CWinApp**. This object is constructed when other C++ global objects are constructed and is already available when Windows calls the **WinMain** function, which is supplied by the Microsoft Foundation Class Library. Declare your derived **CWinApp** object at the global level.

When you derive an application class from **CWinApp**, override the **InitInstance** member function to create your application's main window object. In addition to the **CWinApp** member functions, the Microsoft Foundation Class Library provides the following global functions to access your **CWinApp** object and other global information:

- **AfxGetApp**   Obtains a pointer to the **CWinApp** object.

- **AfxGetInstanceHandle**   Obtains a handle to the current application instance.

- **AfxGetResourceHandle**   Obtains a handle to the application's resources.

- **AfxGetAppName**   Obtains a pointer to a string containing the application's name. Alternately, if you have a pointer to the **CWinApp** object, use **m_pszExeName** to get the application's name.

For more information about these global functions, see "Macros and Globals" in this manual.

See Chapter 1, "Using the Classes to Write Applications for Windows," in *Programming with the Microsoft Foundation Class Library* for more on the **CWinApp** class, including an overview of the following:

- **CWinApp**-derived code written by AppWizard.

- **CWinApp**'s role in the execution sequence of your application.

- **CWinApp**'s default member function implementations.

- **CWinApp**'s key overridables.

#include \<afxwin.h\>

Data Members

m_pszAppName	Specifies the name of the application.
m_hInstance	Identifies the current instance of the application.
m_hPrevInstance	Identifies the previous instance of the application.
m_lpCmdLine	Points to a null-terminated string that specifies the command line for the application.
m_nCmdShow	Specifies how the window is to be shown initially.
m_bHelpMode	Indicates if the user is in Help context mode (typically invoked with SHIFT+F1).
m_pActiveWnd	Pointer to the main window of the container application when an OLE server is in-place active.
m_pszExeName	The module name of the application.
m_pszHelpFilePath	The path to the application's Help file.
m_pszProfileName	The application's .INI filename.
m_pszRegistryKey	Used to determine the full registry key for storing application profile settings.

Construction

CWinApp	Constructs a **CWinApp** object.

Operations

LoadCursor	Loads a cursor resource.
LoadStandardCursor	Loads a Windows predefined cursor that the **IDC_** constants specify in WINDOWS.H.
LoadOEMCursor	Loads a Windows OEM predefined cursor that the **OCR_** constants specify in WINDOWS.H.
LoadIcon	Loads an icon resource.
LoadStandardIcon	Loads a Windows predefined icon that the **IDI_** constants specify in WINDOWS.H.
LoadOEMIcon	Loads a Windows OEM predefined icon that the **OIC_** constants specify in WINDOWS.H.
RunAutomated	Tests the application's command line for the /**Automation** option.

RunEmbedded	Tests the application's command line for the **/Embedding** option.
GetProfileInt	Retrieves an integer from an entry in the application's .INI file.
WriteProfileInt	Writes an integer to an entry in the application's .INI file.
GetProfileString	Retrieves a string from an entry in the application's .INI file.
WriteProfileString	Writes a string to an entry in the application's .INI file.
AddDocTemplate	Adds a document template to the application's list of available document templates.
OpenDocumentFile	Called by the framework to open a document from a file.
AddToRecentFileList	Adds a filename to the most recently used (MRU) file list.
GetPrinterDeviceDefaults	Retrieves the printer device defaults.

Overridables

InitApplication	Override to perform any application-level initialization.
InitInstance	Override to perform Windows instance initialization, such as creating your window objects.
Run	Runs the default message loop. Override to customize the message loop.
OnIdle	Override to perform application-specific idle-time processing.
ExitInstance	Override to clean up when your application terminates.
PreTranslateMessage	Filters messages before they are dispatched to the Windows functions **TranslateMessage** and **DispatchMessage**.
SaveAllModified	Prompts the user to save all modified documents.
DoMessageBox	Implements **AfxMessageBox** for the application.
ProcessMessageFilter	Intercepts certain messages before they reach the application.

ProcessWndProcException	Intercepts all unhandled exceptions thrown by the application's message and command handlers.
DoWaitCursor	Turns the wait cursor on and off.
OnDDECommand	Called by the framework in response to a dynamic data exchange (DDE) execute command.
WinHelp	Calls the **WinHelp** Windows function.

Initialization

LoadStdProfileSettings	Loads standard .INI file settings and enables the MRU file list feature.
SetDialogBkColor	Sets the default background color for dialog boxes and message boxes.
SetRegistryKey	Causes application settings to be stored in the registry instead of .INI files.
EnableShellOpen	Allows the user to open data files from the Windows File Manager.
RegisterShellFileTypes	Registers all the application's document types with the Windows File Manager.
Enable3dControls	Enables controls with three-dimensional appearance.

Command Handlers

OnFileNew	Implements the **ID_FILE_NEW** command.
OnFileOpen	Implements the **ID_FILE_OPEN** command.
OnFilePrintSetup	Implements the **ID_FILE_PRINT_SETUP** command.
OnContextHelp	Handles SHIFT+F1 Help within the application.
OnHelp	Handles F1 Help within the application (using the current context).
OnHelpIndex	Handles the **ID_HELP_INDEX** command and provides a default Help topic.
OnHelpUsing	Handles the **ID_HELP_USING** command.

Member Functions

CWinApp::AddDocTemplate

void AddDocTemplate(CDocTemplate* *pTemplate* **);**

Parameters   *pTemplate*   A pointer to the **CDocTemplate** to be added.

Remarks   Call this member function to add a document template to the list of available document templates that the application maintains. You should add all document templates to an application before you call **RegisterShellFileTypes**.

See Also   **CWinApp::RegisterShellFileTypes**, **CMultiDocTemplate**, **CSingleDocTemplate**

Example
```
BOOL CMyApp::InitInstance()
{
    // ...
    // The following code is produced by AppWizard when you
    // choose the MDI (multiple document interface) option.
    CMultiDocTemplate* pDocTemplate;
    pDocTemplate = new CMultiDocTemplate(
        IDR_MYTYPE,
        RUNTIME_CLASS(CMyDoc),
        RUNTIME_CLASS(CMDIChildWnd),          // standard MDI child frame
        RUNTIME_CLASS(CMyView));
    AddDocTemplate(pDocTemplate);
    // ...
}
```

CWinApp::AddToRecentFileList

virtual void AddToRecentFileList(LPCTSTR *lpszPathName* **);**

Parameters   *lpszPathName*   The path of the file.

Remarks   Call this member function to add *lpszPathName* to the MRU file list. You should call the **LoadStdProfileSettings** member function to load the current MRU file list before you use this member function.

The framework calls this member function when it opens a file or executes the Save As command to save a file with a new name.

See Also   **CWinApp::LoadStdProfileSettings**

Example
```
// This adds the pathname c:\temp\test.doc to the top of
// the most recently used (MRU) list in the File menu.
AfxGetApp()->AddToRecentFileList("c:\\temp\\test.doc");
```

CWinApp::CWinApp

CWinApp(LPCTSTR *lpszAppName* **= NULL);**

Parameters   *lpszAppName*   A null-terminated string that contains the application name that Windows uses. If this argument is not supplied or is **NULL**, **CWinApp** uses the resource string **AFX_IDS_APP_TITLE** or the filename of the executable file.

Remarks   Constructs a **CWinApp** object and passes *lpszAppName* to be stored as the application name. You should construct one global object of your **CWinApp**-derived class. You can have only one **CWinApp** object in your application. The constructor stores a pointer to the **CWinApp** object so that **WinMain** can call the object's member functions to initialize and run the application.

CWinApp::DoMessageBox

virtual int DoMessageBox(LPCTSTR *lpszPrompt*, **UINT** *nType*, **UINT** *nIDPrompt* **);**

Return Value   Returns the same values as **AfxMessageBox**.

Parameters   *lpszPrompt*   Address of text in the message box.

nType   The message box style.

nIDPrompt   An index to a Help context string.

Remarks   The framework calls this member function to implement a message box for the global function **AfxMessageBox**. Do not call this member function to open a message box; use **AfxMessageBox** instead.

Override this member function to customize your application-wide processing of **AfxMessageBox** calls.

See Also   **AfxMessageBox, ::MessageBox**

CWinApp::DoWaitCursor

virtual void DoWaitCursor(int *nCode* **);**

Parameters   *nCode*   If this parameter is 0, the original cursor is restored. If 1, a wait cursor appears. If −1, the wait cursor ends.

Remarks   Called by the framework to implement **CCmdTarget::BeginWaitCursor**, **CCmdTarget::EndWaitCursor**, and **CCmdTarget::RestoreWaitCursor**. Implements an hourglass cursor. **DoWaitCursor** maintains a reference count. When positive, the hourglass cursor is displayed.

If your code changes the cursor, call `DoWaitCursor(0)` to restore the cursor to the state the framework is maintaining.

Override this member function to change the wait cursor or to do additional processing while the wait cursor is displayed.

See Also   **CCmdTarget::BeginWaitCursor**, **CCmdTarget::EndWaitCursor**, **CCmdTarget::RestoreWaitCursor**

Example
```
// This illustrates the normal usage of DoWaitCursor.
AfxGetApp()->DoWaitCursor(1);

// do some lengthy processing

AfxGetApp()->DoWaitCursor(-1);
```

CWinApp::Enable3dControls

BOOL Enable3dControls( );

Return Value   Nonzero if the CTL3D32.DLL is loaded successfully; otherwise 0.

Remarks   Call this function from your override of the **InitInstance** member function to enable dialog boxes and windows whose controls have a three-dimensional appearance. **Enable3dControls** loads the CTL3D32.DLL and registers the application with the DLL. If you call **Enable3dControls**, you do not need to call the **SetDialogBkColor** member function.

MFC automatically provides 3D control effects for the following classes of windows:

- **CDialog**
- **CDialogBar**
- **CFormView**
- **CPropertyPage**
- **CPropertySheet**
- **CControlBar**
- **CToolBar**

If the controls for which you want a 3D effect are in a window of any of these types, all you need is the enabling call to **Enable3dControls**. If you want to give a 3D effect to controls in windows based on other classes, you must call the CTL3D32 API functions directly.

See Also   **CWinApp::InitInstance**, **CWinApp::SetDialogBkColor**

CWinApp::EnableShellOpen

Protected→
void EnableShellOpen( );
END Protected

Remarks

Call this function, typically from your **InitInstance** override, to enable your application's users to open data files when they double-click the files from within the Windows File Manager. Call the **RegisterShellFileTypes** member function in conjunction with this function, or provide a .REG file with your application for manual registration of document types.

See Also

CWinApp::OnDDECommand, **CWinApp::RegisterShellFileTypes**

Example

```
BOOL CMyApp::InitInstance()
{
    // ...

    CMultiDocTemplate* pDocTemplate;
    pDocTemplate = new CMultiDocTemplate(
        IDR_MYTYPE,
        RUNTIME_CLASS(CMyDoc),
        RUNTIME_CLASS(CMDIChildWnd),        // standard MDI child frame
        RUNTIME_CLASS(CMyView));
    AddDocTemplate(pDocTemplate);


    // Create main MDI Frame window.
    CMainFrame* pMainFrame = new CMainFrame;
    if (!pMainFrame->LoadFrame(IDR_MAINFRAME))
        return FALSE;
    // Save the pointer to the main frame window.  This is the
    // only way the framework will have knowledge of what the
    // main frame window is.
    m_pMainWnd = pMainFrame;

    // enable file manager drag/drop and DDE Execute open
    EnableShellOpen();
    RegisterShellFileTypes();
    // ...

    // Show the main window using the nCmdShow parameter
    // passed to the application when it was first launched.
    pMainFrame->ShowWindow(m_nCmdShow);
    pMainFrame->UpdateWindow();

    // ...
}
```

CWinApp::ExitInstance

virtual int ExitInstance( );

Return Value   The application's exit code; 0 indicates no errors, and values greater than 0 indicate an error. This value is used as the return value from **WinMain**.

Remarks   Called by the framework from within the **Run** member function to exit this instance of the application. Do not call this member function from anywhere but within the **Run** member function.

The default implementation of this function writes framework options to the application's .INI file. Override this function to clean up when your application terminates.

See Also   **CWinApp::Run**, **CWinApp::InitInstance**

CWinApp::GetPrinterDeviceDefaults

BOOL GetPrinterDeviceDefaults(PRINTDLG* *pPrintDlg* **);**

Return Value   Nonzero if successful; otherwise 0.

Parameters   *pPrintDlg*   A pointer to a **PRINTDLG** structure.

Remarks   Call this member function to prepare a printer device context for printing. Retrieves the current printer defaults from the Windows .INI file as necessary, or uses the last printer configuration set by the user in Print Setup.

See Also   **CPrintDialog**

In the *Programmer's Reference*: **PRINTDLG**

CWinApp::GetProfileInt

UINT GetProfileInt(LPCTSTR *lpszSection*, **LPCTSTR** *lpszEntry*,
int *nDefault* **);**

Return Value   The integer value of the string that follows the specified entry if the function is successful. The return value is the value of the *nDefault* parameter if the function does not find the entry. The return value is 0 if the value that corresponds to the specified entry is not an integer.

This member function supports hexadecimal notation for the value in the .INI file. When you retrieve a signed integer, you should cast the value into an **int**.

Parameters   *lpszSection*   Points to a null-terminated string that specifies the section containing the entry.

lpszEntry   Points to a null-terminated string that contains the entry whose value is to be retrieved.

nDefault   Specifies the default value to return if the framework cannot find the entry. This value can be an unsigned value in the range 0 through 65,535 or a signed value in the range –32,768 through 32,767.

Remarks   Call this member function to retrieve the value of an integer from an entry within a specified section of the application's .INI file.

This member function is not case sensitive, so the strings in the *lpszSection* and *lpszEntry* parameters may differ in case.

See Also   **CWinApp::GetProfileString**, **CWinApp::WriteProfileInt** , **::GetPrivateProfileInt**

CWinApp::GetProfileString

CString GetProfileString(LPCTSTR *lpszSection*, **LPCTSTR** *lpszEntry*, **LPCTSTR** *lpszDefault* = **NULL**);

Return Value   The return value is the string from the application's .INI file or *lpszDefault* if the string cannot be found. The maximum string length supported by the framework is **_MAX_PATH**. If *lpszDefault* is **NULL**, the return value is an empty string.

Parameters   *lpszSection*   Points to a null-terminated string that specifies the section containing the entry.

lpszEntry   Points to a null-terminated string that contains the entry whose string is to be retrieved. This value must not be **NULL**.

lpszDefault   Points to the default string value for the given entry if the entry cannot be found in the initialization file.

Remarks   Call this member function to retrieve the string associated with an entry within the specified section in the application's .INI file.

See Also   **CWinApp::GetProfileInt, CWinApp::WriteProfileString**, **::GetPrivateProfileString**

Example

```
CString strSection       = "My Section";
CString strStringItem    = "My String Item";
CString strIntItem       = "My Int Item";

CWinApp* pApp = AfxGetApp();

pApp->WriteProfileString(strSection, strStringItem, "test");

CString strValue;
strValue = pApp->GetProfileString(strSection, strStringItem);
ASSERT(strValue == "test");

pApp->WriteProfileInt(strSection, strIntItem, 1234);
int nValue;
nValue = pApp->GetProfileInt(strSection, strIntItem, 0);
ASSERT(nValue == 1234);
```

CWinApp::InitApplication

virtual BOOL InitApplication( );

Return Value   Nonzero if initialization is successful; otherwise 0.

Remarks   Windows allows several copies of the same program to run at the same time. There are two types of application initialization:

1. One-time application initialization that is done the first time the program runs.
2. Instance initialization that runs each time a copy of the program runs, including the first time.

This function is called by the version of **WinMain** that the framework provides. Override **InitApplication** to implement one-time initialization such as Windows class registration. Override **InitInstance** to implement per-instance initialization.

See Also   **CWinApp::InitInstance**

Example
```
// If you need to register your own Windows window class (rare),
// then do it in an override of CWinApp::InitApplication.
BOOL CMyApp::InitApplication()
{
    m_strMyWndClass = AfxRegisterWndClass(
        CS_HREDRAW | CS_VREDRAW,
        LoadCursor(IDC_MYCURSOR),
        0,
        LoadIcon(IDI_MYWINDOWICON));

    return TRUE;
}
```

CWinApp::InitInstance

virtual BOOL InitInstance( );

Return Value   Nonzero if initialization is successful; otherwise 0.

Remarks   Windows allows several copies of the same program to run at the same time. Application initialization is conceptually divided into two sections: one-time application initialization that is done the first time the program runs, and instance initialization that runs each time a copy of the program runs, including the first time. The framework's implementation of **WinMain** calls this function.

Override **InitInstance** to initialize each new instance of your application running under Windows. Typically, you override **InitInstance** to construct your main window object and set the **CWinThread::m_pMainWnd** data member to point to that window. For more information on overriding this member function, see Chapter 1, "Using the Classes to Write Applications for Windows." in *Programming with the Microsoft Foundation Class Library*.

See Also   **CWinApp::InitApplication**

Example
```
// AppWizard implements the InitInstance overridable function
// according to options you select.  For example, the single document
// interface (SDI) option was chosen for the AppWizard code created
// below. You can add other per-instance initializations to the code
// created by AppWizard.

BOOL CMyApp::InitInstance()
{
    // Standard initialization
    // If you are not using these features and wish to reduce the size
    //  of your final executable, you should remove from the following
    //  the specific initialization routines you do not need.

    SetDialogBkColor();        // Set dialog background color to gray
    LoadStdProfileSettings();  // Load standard INI file options
(including MRU)

    // Register the application's document templates.  Document templates
    //  serve as the connection between documents, frame windows and
views.

    CSingleDocTemplate* pDocTemplate;
    pDocTemplate = new CSingleDocTemplate(
        IDR_MAINFRAME,
        RUNTIME_CLASS(CMyDoc),
        RUNTIME_CLASS(CMainFrame),     // main SDI frame window
        RUNTIME_CLASS(CMyView));
    AddDocTemplate(pDocTemplate);
```

```
                    // create a new (empty) document
                    OnFileNew();

                    if (m_lpCmdLine[0] != '\0')
                    {
                        // TODO: add command line processing here
                    }

                    return TRUE;
                }
```

CWinApp::LoadCursor

HCURSOR LoadCursor(LPCTSTR *lpszResourceName* **) const;**

HCURSOR LoadCursor(UINT *nIDResource* **) const;**

Return Value   A handle to a cursor. If unsuccessful, returns **NULL**.

Parameters   *lpszResourceName*   Points to a null-terminated string that contains the name of the cursor resource. You can use a **CString** for this argument.

nIDResource   ID number of the cursor resource.

Remarks   Loads the cursor resource named by *lpszResourceName* or specified by *nIDResource* from the current executable file. **LoadCursor** loads the cursor into memory only if it has not been previously loaded; otherwise, it retrieves a handle of the existing resource. Use the **LoadStandardCursor** or **LoadOEMCursor** member function to access the predefined Windows cursors.

See Also   **CWinApp::LoadStandardCursor**, **CWinApp::LoadOEMCursor**, **::LoadCursor**

Example
```
HCURSOR hCursor;
// Load a cursor resource that was originally created using
// the Graphics Editor and assigned the i.d. IDC_MYCURSOR.
hCursor = AfxGetApp()->LoadCursor(IDC_MYCURSOR);
```

CWinApp::LoadIcon

HICON LoadIcon(LPCTSTR *lpszResourceName* **) const;**

HICON LoadIcon(UINT *nIDResource* **) const;**

Return Value   A handle to an icon. If unsuccessful, returns **NULL**.

Parameters	*lpszResourceName* Points to a null-terminated string that contains the name of the icon resource. You can also use a **CString** for this argument. *nIDResource* ID number of the icon resource.
Remarks	Loads the icon resource named by *lpszResourceName* or specified by *nIDResource* from the executable file. **LoadIcon** loads the icon only if it has not been previously loaded; otherwise, it retrieves a handle of the existing resource. You can use the **LoadStandardIcon** or **LoadOEMIcon** member function to access the predefined Windows icons.
See Also	**CWinApp::LoadStandardIcon, CWinApp::LoadOEMIcon, ::LoadIcon**

CWinApp::LoadOEMCursor

HCURSOR LoadOEMCursor(UINT *nIDCursor*) const;

Return Value	A handle to a cursor. If unsuccessful, returns **NULL**.
Parameters	*nIDCursor* An **OCR_** manifest constant identifier that specifies a predefined Windows cursor. You must have **#define OEMRESOURCE** before **#include <afxwin.h>** to gain access to the **OCR_** constants in WINDOWS.H.
Remarks	Loads the Windows predefined cursor resource specified by *nIDCursor*. Use the **LoadOEMCursor** or **LoadStandardCursor** member function to access the predefined Windows cursors.
See Also	**CWinApp::LoadCursor, CWinApp::LoadStandardCursor, ::LoadCursor**
Example	```\n// In the stdafx.h file, add #define OEMRESOURCE to\n// include the windows.h definitions of OCR_ values.\n#define OEMRESOURCE\n#include <afxwin.h> // MFC core and standard components\n#include <afxext.h> // MFC extensions (including VB)\n\n HCURSOR hCursor;\n // Load the predefined WIndows "size all" cursor.\n hCursor = AfxGetApp()->LoadOEMCursor(OCR_SIZEALL);\n```

CWinApp::LoadOEMIcon

HICON LoadOEMIcon(UINT *nIDIcon*) const;

Return Value	A handle to an icon. If unsuccessful, returns **NULL**.
Parameters	*nIDIcon* An **OIC_** manifest constant identifier that specifies a predefined Windows icon. You must have **#define OEMRESOURCE** before **#include afxwin.h** to access the **OIC_** constants in WINDOWS.H.

Remarks   Loads the Windows predefined icon resource specified by *nIDIcon*. Use the
LoadOEMIcon or **LoadStandardIcon** member function to access the predefined
Windows icons.

See Also   **CWinApp::LoadStandardIcon**, **CWinApp::LoadIcon**, **::LoadIcon**

CWinApp::LoadStandardCursor

HCURSOR LoadStandardCursor(LPCTSTR *lpszCursorName* **) const;**

Return Value   A handle to a cursor. If unsuccessful, returns **NULL**.

Parameters   *lpszCursorName*   An **IDC_** manifest constant identifier that specifies a predefined
Windows cursor. These identifiers are defined in WINDOWS.H. The following list
shows the possible predefined values and meanings for *lpszCursorName*:

- **IDC_ARROW**   Standard arrow cursor
- **IDC_IBEAM**   Standard text-insertion cursor
- **IDC_WAIT**   Hourglass cursor used when Windows performs a time-consuming task
- **IDC_CROSS**   Cross-hair cursor for selection
- **IDC_UPARROW**   Arrow that points straight up
- **IDC_SIZE**   Cursor to use to resize a window
- **IDC_ICON**   Cursor to use to drag a file
- **IDC_SIZENWSE**   Two-headed arrow with ends at upper left and lower right
- **IDC_SIZENESW**   Two-headed arrow with ends at upper right and lower left
- **IDC_SIZEWE**   Horizontal two-headed arrow
- **IDC_SIZENS**   Vertical two-headed arrow

Remarks   Loads the Windows predefined cursor resource that *lpszCursorName* specifies. Use
the **LoadStandardCursor** or **LoadOEMCursor** member function to access the
predefined Windows cursors.

See Also   **CWinApp::LoadOEMCursor**, **CWinApp::LoadCursor**, **::LoadCursor**

Example
```
HCURSOR hCursor;
// Load the predefined Windows "up arrow" cursor.
hCursor = AfxGetApp()->LoadStandardCursor(IDC_UPARROW);
```

CWinApp::LoadStandardIcon

HICON LoadStandardIcon(LPCTSTR *lpszIconName* **) const;**

Return Value   A handle to an icon. If unsuccessful, returns **NULL**.

Parameters   *lpszIconName*   A manifest constant identifier that specifies a predefined Windows icon. These identifiers are defined in WINDOWS.H. The following list shows the possible predefined values and meanings for *lpszIconName*:

- **IDI_APPLICATION**   Default application icon
- **IDI_HAND**   Hand-shaped icon used in serious warning messages
- **IDI_QUESTION**   Question-mark shape used in prompting messages
- **IDI_EXCLAMATION**   Exclamation point shape used in warning messages
- **IDI_ASTERISK**   Asterisk shape used in informative messages

Remarks   Loads the Windows predefined icon resource that *lpszIconName* specifies. Use the **LoadStandardIcon** or **LoadOEMIcon** member function to access the predefined Windows icons.

See Also   **CWinApp::LoadOEMIcon, CWinApp::LoadIcon, ::LoadIcon**

CWinApp::LoadStdProfileSettings

Protected→
void LoadStdProfileSettings(UINT *nMaxMRU* **= _AFX_MRU_COUNT);**
END Protected

Parameters   *nMaxMRU*   The number of recently used files to track.

Remarks   Call this member function from within the **InitInstance** member function to enable and load the list of most recently used (MRU) files and last preview state. If *nMaxMRU* is 0, no MRU list will be maintained.

See Also   **CWinApp::OnFileOpen, CWinApp::AddToRecentFileList**

CWinApp::OnContextHelp

Protected→
afx_msg void OnContextHelp( );
END Protected

Remarks   You must add an

```
ON_COMMAND( ID_CONTEXT_HELP, OnContextHelp )
```

statement to your **CWinApp** class message map and also add an accelerator table entry, typically SHIFT+F1, to enable this member function.

OnContextHelp puts the application into Help mode. The cursor changes to an arrow and a question mark, and the user can then move the mouse pointer and press the left mouse button to select a dialog box, window, menu, or command button. This member function retrieves the Help context of the object under the cursor and calls the Windows function **WinHelp** with that Help context.

See Also   **CWinApp::OnHelp**, **CWinApp::WinHelp**

CWinApp::OnDDECommand

virtual BOOL OnDDECommand(LPTSTR *lpszCommand* **);**

Return Value   Nonzero if the command is handled; otherwise 0.

Parameters   *lpszCommand*   Points to a DDE command string received by the application.

Remarks   Called by the framework when the main frame window receives a DDE execute message. The default implementation checks whether the command is a request to open a document and, if so, opens the specified document. The Windows File Manager usually sends such DDE command strings when the user double-clicks a data file. Override this function to handle other DDE execute commands, such as the command to print.

See Also   **CWinApp::EnableShellOpen**

Example
```
BOOL CMyApp::OnDDECommand(LPTSTR lpszCommand)
{
    if (CWinApp::OnDDECommand(lpszCommand))
        return TRUE;

    // Handle any DDE commands recognized by your application
    // and return TRUE.  See implementation of CWinApp::OnDDEComand
    // for example of parsing the DDE command string.

    // Return FALSE for any DDE commands you do not handle.
    return FALSE;
}
```

CWinApp::OnFileNew

Protected→
afx_msg void OnFileNew( );
END Protected

Remarks

You must add an

```
ON_COMMAND( ID_FILE_NEW, OnFileNew )
```

statement to your **CWinApp** class message map to enable this member function.

If enabled, this function handles execution of the File New command.

See Technical Note 22 under MFC in Books Online for information on default behavior and guidance on how to override this member function.

See Also   **CWinApp::OnFileOpen**

Example

```
// The following message map, produced by AppWizard, binds the
// File New, Open, and Print Setup menu commands to default
// framework implementations of these commands.
BEGIN_MESSAGE_MAP(CMyApp, CWinApp)
    //{{AFX_MSG_MAP(CMyApp)
    ON_COMMAND(ID_APP_ABOUT, OnAppAbout)
        // NOTE - the ClassWizard will add and remove mapping macros here.
        //    DO NOT EDIT what you see in these blocks of generated code!
    //}}AFX_MSG_MAP
    // Standard file based document commands
    ON_COMMAND(ID_FILE_NEW, CWinApp::OnFileNew)
    ON_COMMAND(ID_FILE_OPEN, CWinApp::OnFileOpen)
    // Standard print setup command
    ON_COMMAND(ID_FILE_PRINT_SETUP, CWinApp::OnFilePrintSetup)
END_MESSAGE_MAP()

// The following message map illustrates how to rebind the
// File New, Open and Print Setup menu commands to handlers that
// you implement in your CWinApp-derived class.  You can use
// ClassWizard to bind the commands, as illustrated below, since
// the message map entries are bracketed by //{{AFX_MSG_MAP
// and //}}AFX_MSG_MAP.  Note, you can name the handler
// CMyApp::OnFileNew instead of CMyApp::OnMyFileNew, and likewise
// for the other handlers, if desired.
BEGIN_MESSAGE_MAP(CMyApp, CWinApp)
    //{{AFX_MSG_MAP(CMyApp)
    ON_COMMAND(ID_APP_ABOUT, OnAppAbout)
    ON_COMMAND(ID_FILE_NEW, OnMyFileNew)
    ON_COMMAND(ID_FILE_OPEN, OnMyFileOpen)
    ON_COMMAND(ID_FILE_PRINT_SETUP, OnMyFilePrintSetup)
    //}}AFX_MSG_MAP
END_MESSAGE_MAP()
```

CWinApp::OnFileOpen

Protected→
afx_msg void OnFileOpen( );
END Protected

Remarks

You must add an

```
ON_COMMAND( ID_FILE_OPEN, OnFileOpen )
```

statement to your **CWinApp** class message map to enable this member function.

If enabled, this function handles execution of the File Open command.

For information on default behavior and guidance on how to override this member function, see Technical Note 22 under MFC in Books Online.

See Also   **CWinApp::OnFileNew**

Example

```
// The following message map, produced by AppWizard, binds the
// File New, Open, and Print Setup menu commands to default
// framework implementations of these commands.
BEGIN_MESSAGE_MAP(CMyApp, CWinApp)
   //{{AFX_MSG_MAP(CMyApp)
   ON_COMMAND(ID_APP_ABOUT, OnAppAbout)
      // NOTE - the ClassWizard will add and remove mapping macros here.
      //    DO NOT EDIT what you see in these blocks of generated code!
   //}}AFX_MSG_MAP
   // Standard file based document commands
   ON_COMMAND(ID_FILE_NEW, CWinApp::OnFileNew)
   ON_COMMAND(ID_FILE_OPEN, CWinApp::OnFileOpen)
   // Standard print setup command
   ON_COMMAND(ID_FILE_PRINT_SETUP, CWinApp::OnFilePrintSetup)
END_MESSAGE_MAP()

// The following message map illustrates how to rebind the
// File New, Open and Print Setup menu commands to handlers that
// you implement in your CWinApp-derived class.  You can use
// ClassWizard to bind the commands, as illustrated below, since
// the message map entries are bracketed by //{{AFX_MSG_MAP
// and //}}AFX_MSG_MAP.  Note, you can name the handler
// CMyApp::OnFileNew instead of CMyApp::OnMyFileNew, and likewise
// for the other handlers, if desired.
BEGIN_MESSAGE_MAP(CMyApp, CWinApp)
   //{{AFX_MSG_MAP(CMyApp)
   ON_COMMAND(ID_APP_ABOUT, OnAppAbout)
   ON_COMMAND(ID_FILE_NEW, OnMyFileNew)
   ON_COMMAND(ID_FILE_OPEN, OnMyFileOpen)
   ON_COMMAND(ID_FILE_PRINT_SETUP, OnMyFilePrintSetup)
   //}}AFX_MSG_MAP
END_MESSAGE_MAP()
```

CWinApp::OnFilePrintSetup

Protected→

afx_msg void OnFilePrintSetup( );

END Protected

Remarks

You must add an

```
ON_COMMAND( ID_FILE_PRINT_SETUP, OnFilePrintSetup )
```

statement to your **CWinApp** class message map to enable this member function.

If enabled, this function handles execution of the File Print command.

For information on default behavior and guidance on how to override this member function, see Technical Note 22 under MFC in Books Online.¤

See Also

CWinApp::OnFileNew

Example

```
// The following message map, produced by AppWizard, binds the
// File New, Open, and Print Setup menu commands to default
// framework implementations of these commands.
BEGIN_MESSAGE_MAP(CMyApp, CWinApp)
   //{{AFX_MSG_MAP(CMyApp)
   ON_COMMAND(ID_APP_ABOUT, OnAppAbout)
      // NOTE - the ClassWizard will add and remove mapping macros here.
      //     DO NOT EDIT what you see in these blocks of generated code!
   //}}AFX_MSG_MAP
   // Standard file based document commands
   ON_COMMAND(ID_FILE_NEW, CWinApp::OnFileNew)
   ON_COMMAND(ID_FILE_OPEN, CWinApp::OnFileOpen)
   // Standard print setup command
   ON_COMMAND(ID_FILE_PRINT_SETUP, CWinApp::OnFilePrintSetup)
END_MESSAGE_MAP()

// The following message map illustrates how to rebind the
// File New, Open and Print Setup menu commands to handlers that
// you implement in your CWinApp-derived class.  You can use
// ClassWizard to bind the commands, as illustrated below, since
// the message map entries are bracketed by //{{AFX_MSG_MAP
// and //}}AFX_MSG_MAP.  Note, you can name the handler
// CMyApp::OnFileNew instead of CMyApp::OnMyFileNew, and likewise
// for the other handlers, if desired.
```

```
BEGIN_MESSAGE_MAP(CMyApp, CWinApp)
  //{{AFX_MSG_MAP(CMyApp)
  ON_COMMAND(ID_APP_ABOUT, OnAppAbout)
  ON_COMMAND(ID_FILE_NEW, OnMyFileNew)
  ON_COMMAND(ID_FILE_OPEN, OnMyFileOpen)
  ON_COMMAND(ID_FILE_PRINT_SETUP, OnMyFilePrintSetup)
  //}}AFX_MSG_MAP
END_MESSAGE_MAP()
```

CWinApp::OnHelp

Protected→
afx_msg void OnHelp( );
END Protected

Remarks   You must add an

```
ON_COMMAND( ID_ON_HELP, OnHelp )
```

statement to your **CWinApp** class message map to enable this member function. Usually you will also add an accelerator-key entry for the F1 key. Enabling the F1 key is only a convention, not a requirement.

If enabled, called by the framework when the user presses the F1 key.

The default implementation of this message-handler function determines the Help context that corresponds to the current window, dialog box, or menu item and then calls WINHELP.EXE. If no context is currently available, the function uses the default context.

Override this member function to set the Help context to something other than the window, dialog box, menu item, or toolbar button that currently has the focus. Call **WinHelp** with the desired Help context ID.

See Also   **CWinApp::OnContextHelp, CWinApp::OnHelpUsing, CWinApp::OnHelpIndex, CWinApp::WinHelp**

CWinApp::OnHelpIndex

Protected→
afx_msg void OnHelpIndex( );
END Protected

Remarks   You must add an

```
ON_COMMAND( ID_HELP_INDEX, OnHelpIndex )
```

statement to your **CWinApp** class message map to enable this member function.

If enabled, the framework calls this message-handler function when the user of your application selects the Help Index command to invoke **WinHelp** with the standard **HELP_INDEX** topic.

See Also   **CWinApp::OnHelp, CWinApp::OnHelpUsing, CWinApp::WinHelp**

CWinApp::OnHelpUsing

Protected→
afx_msg void OnHelpUsing( );
END Protected

Remarks   You must add an

```
ON_COMMAND( ID_HELP_USING, OnHelpUsing )
```

statement to your **CWinApp** class message map to enable this member function.

The framework calls this message-handler function when the user of your application selects the Help Using command to invoke the **WinHelp** application with the standard **HELP_HELPONHELP** topic.

See Also   **CWinApp::OnHelp, CWinApp::OnHelpIndex, CWinApp::WinHelp**

CWinApp::OnIdle

virtual BOOL OnIdle(LONG *lCount*);

Return Value   Nonzero to receive more idle processing time; 0 if no more idle time is needed.

Parameters   *lCount*   A counter incremented each time **OnIdle** is called when the application's message queue is empty. This count is reset to 0 each time a new message is processed. You can use the *lCount* parameter to determine the relative length of time the application has been idle without processing a message.

Remarks   Override this member function to perform idle-time processing. **OnIdle** is called in the default message loop when the application's message queue is empty. Use your override to call your own background idle-handler tasks.

OnIdle should return 0 to indicate that no idle processing time is required. The *lCount* parameter is incremented each time **OnIdle** is called when the message queue is empty and resets to 0 each time a new message is processed. You can call your different idle routines based on this count.

The following summarizes idle loop processing:

1. If the message loop in the Microsoft Foundation Class Library checks the message queue and finds no pending messages, it calls `OnIdle` for the application object and supplies 0 as the *lCount* argument.

2. `OnIdle` performs some processing and returns a nonzero value to indicate it should be called again to do further processing.

3. The message loop checks the message queue again. If no messages are pending, it calls `OnIdle` again, incrementing the *lCount* argument.

4. Eventually, `OnIdle` finishes processing all its idle tasks and returns 0. This tells the message loop to stop calling `OnIdle` until the next message is received from the message queue, at which point the idle cycle restarts with the argument set to 0.

Do not perform lengthy tasks during **OnIdle** because your application cannot process user input until **OnIdle** returns.

Note The default implementation of **OnIdle** updates command user-interface objects such as menu items and toolbar buttons, and it performs internal data structure cleanup. Therefore, if you override **OnIdle**, you must call **CWinApp::OnIdle** with the *lCount* in your overridden version. First call all base-class idle processing (that is, until the base class **OnIdle** returns 0). If you need to perform work before the base-class processing completes, review the base-class implementation to select the proper *lCount* during which to do your work.

Example

The following two examples show how to use **OnIdle**. The first example processes two idle tasks using the *lCount* argument to prioritize the tasks. The first task is high priority, and you should do it whenever possible. The second task is less important and should be done only when there is a long pause in user input. Note the call to the base-class version of **OnIdle**. The second example manages a group of idle tasks with different priorities.

First Example

```
BOOL CMyApp::OnIdle(LONG lCount)
{
    BOOL bMore = CWinApp::OnIdle(lCount);

    if (lCount == 0)
    {
    TRACE("App idle for short period of time\n");
    bMore = TRUE;
    }
    else if (lCount == 10)
    {
    TRACE("App idle for longer amount of time\n");
        bMore = TRUE;
    }
    else if (lCount == 100)
    {
        TRACE("App idle for even longer amount of time\n");
        bMore = TRUE;
    }
    else if (lCount == 1000)
    {
        TRACE("App idle for quite a long period of time\n");
     // bMore is not set to TRUE, no longer need idle
     // IMPORTANT: bMore is not set to FALSE since CWinApp::OnIdle may
     // have more idle tasks to complete.
    }

    return bMore;
     // return TRUE as long as there is any more idle tasks
}
```

Second Example

```
// In this example, four idle loop tasks are given various
// opportunities to run:
// Task1 is always given a chance to run during idle time, provided
//   that no message has queued up while the framework was processing
//   its own idle loop tasks (at lCount levels 0 and 1).
// Task2 is given a chance to run only if Task1 has already run,
//   provided that no message has queued up while Task1 was running.
// Task3 and Task4 are given a chance to run only if both Task1 and
//   Task2 have already run, and no message has queued up in the mean
//   time.  If Task3 gets its chance to run, then Task4 always gets
//   a chance to run immediately after Task3.
```

```
BOOL CMyApp::OnIdle(LONG lCount)
{
   // In this example, as in most applications, you should let the
   // base class CWinApp::OnIdle complete its processing before you
   // attempt any additional idle loop processing.
   if (CWinApp::OnIdle(lCount))
      return TRUE;

   // The base class CWinApp::OnIdle reserves the lCount values 0
   // and 1 for the framework's own idle processing.  If you wish to
   // share idle processing time at a peer level with the framework,
   // then replace the above if-statement with a straight call to
   // CWinApp::OnIdle; and then add a case statement for lCount value
   // 0 and/or 1. Study the base class implementation first to
   // understand how your idle loop tasks will compete with the
   // framework's idle loop processing.

   switch (lCount)
   {
      case 2:
         Task1();
         return TRUE; // next time give Task2 a chance
      case 3:
         Task2();
         return TRUE; // next time give Task3 and Task4 a chance
      case 4:
         Task3();
         Task4();
         return FALSE; // cycle through the idle loop tasks again
   }
   return FALSE;
}
```

CWinApp::OpenDocumentFile

virtual CDocument* OpenDocumentFile(LPCTSTR *lpszFileName* **);**

Return Value   A pointer to a **CDocument** if successful; otherwise **NULL**.

Parameters   *lpszFileName*   The name of the file to be opened.

Remarks   The framework calls this member function to open the named **CDocument** file for
                     the application. If a document with that name is already open, the first frame
                     window that contains that document will be activated. If an application supports
                     multiple document templates, the framework uses file extension to find the
                     appropriate document template to attempt to load the document. If successful, the
                     document template then creates a frame window and view for the document.

Example

```
BOOL CMyApp::InitInstance()
{
  // ...
  if (m_lpCmdLine[0] == '\0')
  {
    // Create a new (empty) document.
    OnFileNew();
  }
  else
  {
    // Open a file passed as the first command line parameter.
    OpenDocumentFile(m_lpCmdLine);
  }
  // ...
}
```

CWinApp::PreTranslateMessage

virtual BOOL PreTranslateMessage(MSG* *pMsg*);

Return Value   Nonzero if the message was fully processed in **PreTranslateMessage** and should not be processed further. Zero if the message should be processed in the normal way.

Parameters   *pMsg*   A pointer to an **MSG** structure that contains the message to process.

Remarks   Override this function to filter window messages before they are dispatched to the Windows functions **TranslateMessage** and **DispatchMessage**. The default implementation performs accelerator-key translation, so you must call the **CWinApp::PreTranslateMessage** member function in your overridden version.

See Also   **::DispatchMessage**, **::TranslateMessage**

CWinApp::ProcessMessageFilter

virtual BOOL ProcessMessageFilter(int *code*, LPMSG *lpMsg*);

Return Value   Nonzero if the message is processed; otherwise 0.

Parameters   *code*   Specifies a hook code. This member function uses the code to determine how to process *lpMsg*.

lpMsg   A pointer to a Windows **MSG** structure.

Remarks   The framework's hook function calls this member function to filter and respond to certain Windows messages. A hook function processes events before they are sent to the application's normal message processing.

If you override this advanced feature, be sure to call the base-class version to maintain the framework's hook processing.

See Also   **MessageProc**, **WH_MSGFILTER**

CWinApp::ProcessWndProcException

virtual LRESULT ProcessWndProcException(CException* *e*,
const MSG* *pMsg* **);**

Return Value   The value that should be returned to Windows. Normally this is 0L for windows messages, 1L (**TRUE**) for command messages.

Parameters   *e*   A pointer to an uncaught exception.

pMsg   An **MSG** structure that contains information about the windows message that caused the framework to throw an exception.

Remarks   The framework calls this member function whenever the handler does not catch an exception thrown in one of your application's message or command handlers.

Do not call this member function directly.

The default implementation of this member function creates a message box. If the uncaught exception originates with a menu, toolbar, or accelerator command failure, the message box displays a "Command failed" message; otherwise, it displays an "Internal application error" message.

Override this member function to provide global handling of your exceptions. Only call the base functionality if you wish the message box to be displayed.

See Also   **CWnd::WindowProc**, **CException**

CWinApp::RegisterShellFileTypes

Protected→
void RegisterShellFileTypes( );
END Protected

Remarks   Call this function to register all of your application's document types with the Windows File Manager. This allows the user to open a data file created by your application by double-clicking it from within File Manager. Call this member function after you call **AddDocTemplate** for each of the document templates in your application. Also call the **EnableShellOpen** member function when you call this member function.

This function iterates through the list of **CDocTemplate** objects that the application maintains and, for each document template, adds entries to the registration database that Windows maintains for file associations. File Manager uses these entries to open a data file when the user double-clicks it. This eliminates the need to ship a .REG file with your application.

If the registration database already associates a given filename extension with another file type, no new association is created. See the **CDocTemplate** class for the format of strings necessary to register this information.

See Also   **CDocTemplate**, **CWinApp::EnableShellOpen**, **CWinApp::AddDocTemplate**

CWinApp::Run

virtual int Run( );

Return Value   An **int** value that is returned by **WinMain**.

Remarks   Provides a default message loop. **Run** acquires and dispatches Windows messages until the application receives a **WM_QUIT** message. If the application's message queue currently contains no messages, **Run** calls **OnIdle** to perform idle-time processing. Incoming messages go to the **PreTranslateMessage** member function for special processing and then to the Windows function **TranslateMessage** for standard keyboard translation; finally, the **DispatchMessage** Windows function is called. **Run** is rarely overridden, but you can override it to provide special behavior.

See Also   **CWinApp::PreTranslateMessage**, **WM_QUIT**, **::DispatchMessage**, **::TranslateMessage**

CWinApp::RunAutomated

BOOL RunAutomated( );

Return Value   Nonzero if the option was found; otherwise 0.

Remarks   Call this function to determine whether the "/**Automation**" or "**-Automation**" option is present, which indicates whether the server application was launched by a client application. If present, the option is removed from the command line. For more information on OLE Automation, see the article "Servers: Implementing a Server" in *Programming with the Microsoft Foundation Class Library*.

See Also   **CWinApp::RunEmbedded**

CWinApp::RunEmbedded

BOOL RunEmbedded( );

Return Value   Nonzero if the option was found; otherwise 0.

Remarks   Call this function to determine whether the "/**Embedding**" or "**-Embedding**" option is present, which indicates whether the server application was launched by a client application. If present, the option is removed from the command line. For more information on embedding, see the article "Containers: Implementing a Container" in *Programming with the Microsoft Foundation Class Library*.

See Also   **CWinApp::RunAutomated**

CWinApp::SaveAllModified

virtual BOOL SaveAllModified( );

Return Value   Nonzero if safe to terminate the application; 0 if not safe to terminate the application.

Remarks   Called by the framework to save all documents when the application's main frame window is to be closed, or through a **WM_QUERYENDSESSION** message.

The default implementation of this member function calls the **SaveModified** member function in turn for all modified documents within the application.

CWinApp::SetDialogBkColor

Protected→
void SetDialogBkColor(COLORREF *clrCtlBk* **= RGB(192, 192, 192),**
COLORREF *clrCtlText* **= RGB(0, 0, 0));**
END Protected

Parameters   *clrCtlBk*   The dialog background color for the application.

clrCtlText   The dialog control color for the application.

Remarks   Call this member function from within the **InitInstance** member function to set the default background and text color for dialog boxes and message boxes within your application.

Example
```
BOOL CMyApp::InitInstance()
{
   // Standard initialization

   SetDialogBkColor();      // Set dialog background color to gray
   LoadStdProfileSettings(); // Load standard INI file options
(including MRU)

   // ...
}
```

CWinApp::SetRegistryKey

void SetRegistryKey(LPCTSTR *lpszRegistryKey*);

void SetRegistryKey(UINT *nIDRegistryKey*);

Parameters   *lpszRegistryKey*   Pointer to a string containing the name of the key.

nIDRegistryKey   ID/index of a key in the registry.

Remarks   Causes application settings to be stored in the registry instead of INI files. This function sets *m_pszRegistryKey*, which is then used by the **GetProfileXXX** and **WriteProfileXXX** member functions of **CWinApp**. If this function has been called, the list of most recently-used (MRU) files is also stored in the registry. The registry key is usually the name of a company. It is stored in a key of the following form: HKEY_CURRENT_USER\Software\<company name>\<application name>\<section name>\<value name>.

See Also   **CWinApp::InitInstance, CWinApp::InitApplication, CWinApp::GetProfileString, CWinApp::WriteProfileString**

CWinApp::WinHelp

virtual void WinHelp(DWORD *dwData*, UINT *nCmd* = HELP_CONTEXT);

Parameters   *dwData*   Specifies additional data. The value used depends on the value of the *nCmd* parameter.

nCmd   Specifies the type of help requested. For a list of possible values and how they affect the *dwData* parameter, see the **WinHelp** Windows function.

Remarks   Call this member function to invoke the WinHelp application. The framework also calls this function to invoke the WinHelp application.

The framework will automatically close the WinHelp application when your application terminates.

See Also   **CWinApp::OnContextHelp, CWinApp::OnHelpUsing, CWinApp::OnHelp, CWinApp::OnHelpIndex, ::WinHelp**

Example

```
// Header File: HELPIDS.H
//
// This example header file is #include'd twice:
// (1) It is #include'd by the .CPP file that passes the DWORD
//     context i.d. to CWinApp::WinHelp.
// (2) It is #include'd in the [MAP] section of the .HPJ file,
//     to associate the help context string "HID_MYTOPIC" with
//     the help context numeric i.d., 101.
// The help context string "HID_MYTOPIC" is what identifies the
// help topic in the help .RTF source file, in the "#" footnote:
//     # HID_MYTOPIC
//
// Note, it is not necessary to manage help context id's this way
// for help topics associated with command id's and user interface
// id's defined in your RESOURCE.H file; you should use the MAKEHM
// tool, or the MAKEHELP.BAT file produced by AppWizard's Context
// Help option, to produce a help map (.HM) file for these id's.
// It is necessary to manage help context id's as illustrated here
// only for help topics not associated with command id's or user
// interface id's.

#define HID_MYTOPIC 101

    // Show the custom help topic that has the context string
    // "HID_MYTOPIC" in the help .RTF file, and which is mapped
    // to the DWORD i.d. HID_MYTOPIC in the above HELPIDS.H file.
    AfxGetApp()->WinHelp(HID_MYTOPIC);

// The following is one line of code in the help map (.HM)
// file produced by the MAKEHM tool, which in turn is called
// by the MAKEHELP.BAT file produced by the AppWizard Context
// Help option.  The MAKEHM tool reads the following #define
// in the application's RESOURCE.H file:
//    #define ID_MYCOMMAND 0x08004
// and adds a help id offset value of 0x10000 to create the
// help context DWORD value 0x18004.  See MFC Tech Note 28
// for more information on help id offset values.

HID_MYCOMMAND                        0x18004

    // Rarely will you need to directly call WinHelp yourself
    // with the help context i.d. for a command or user interface
    // object. The framework will call WinHelp automatically when
    // the user, for example, hits F1 when the focus is on a
    // My Command menu item. However, if you do want to directly
    // call WinHelp for the help topic associated with the command,
    // here is how you would do it:

    AfxGetApp()->WinHelp(0x10000 + ID_MYCOMMAND);
```

CWinApp::WriteProfileInt

BOOL WriteProfileInt(LPCTSTR *lpszSection*, **LPCTSTR** *lpszEntry*, **int** *nValue* **);**

Return Value   Nonzero if successful; otherwise 0.

Parameters   *lpszSection*   Points to a null-terminated string that specifies the section containing the entry. If the section does not exist, it is created. The name of the section is case independent; the string may be any combination of uppercase and lowercase letters.

lpszEntry   Points to a null-terminated string that contains the entry into which the value is to be written. If the entry does not exist in the specified section, it is created.

nValue   Contains the value to be written.

Remarks   Call this member function to write the specified value into the specified section of the application's .INI file.

See Also   **CWinApp::GetProfileInt, CWinApp::WriteProfileString**

Example
```
CString strSection      = "My Section";
CString strStringItem   = "My String Item";
CString strIntItem      = "My Int Item";

CWinApp* pApp = AfxGetApp();

pApp->WriteProfileString(strSection, strStringItem, "test");

CString strValue;
strValue = pApp->GetProfileString(strSection, strStringItem);
ASSERT(strValue == "test");

pApp->WriteProfileInt(strSection, strIntItem, 1234);
int nValue;
nValue = pApp->GetProfileInt(strSection, strIntItem, 0);
ASSERT(nValue == 1234);
```

CWinApp::WriteProfileString

BOOL WriteProfileString(LPCTSTR *lpszSection*, **LPCTSTR** *lpszEntry*, **LPCTSTR** *lpszValue* **);**

Return Value   Nonzero if successful; otherwise 0.

Parameters   *lpszSection*   Points to a null-terminated string that specifies the section containing the entry. If the section does not exist, it is created. The name of the section is case independent; the string may be any combination of uppercase and lowercase letters.

lpszEntry   Points to a null-terminated string that contains the entry into which the value is to be written. If the entry does not exist in the specified section, it is created.

lpszValue   Points to the string to be written. If this parameter is **NULL**, the entry specified by the *lpszEntry* parameter is deleted.

Remarks   Call this member function to write the specified string into the specified section of the application's .INI file.

See Also   **CWinApp::GetProfileString, CWinApp::WriteProfileInt**, PrivateProfileString

Example
```
CString strSection      = "My Section";
CString strStringItem   = "My String Item";
CString strIntItem      = "My Int Item";

CWinApp* pApp = AfxGetApp();

pApp->WriteProfileString(strSection, strStringItem, "test");

CString strValue;
strValue = pApp->GetProfileString(strSection, strStringItem);
ASSERT(strValue == "test");

pApp->WriteProfileInt(strSection, strIntItem, 1234);
int nValue;
nValue = pApp->GetProfileInt(strSection, strIntItem, 0);
ASSERT(nValue == 1234);
```

Data Members

CWinApp::m_bHelpMode

Remarks   **TRUE** if the application is in Help context mode (conventionally invoked with SHIFT+F1); otherwise **FALSE**. In Help context mode, the cursor becomes a question mark and the user can move it about the screen. Examine this flag if you want to implement special handling when in the Help mode. **m_bHelpMode** is a public variable of type **BOOL**.

CWinApp::m_hInstance

Remarks   Corresponds to the *hInstance* parameter passed by Windows to **WinMain**. The **m_hInstance** data member is a handle to the current instance of the application running under Windows. This is returned by the global function **AfxGetInstanceHandle**. **m_hInstance** is a public variable of type **HINSTANCE**.

Example
```
// Typically you do not need to pass the application's hInstance
// to Windows APIs directly because there are equivalent MFC
// member functions that pass the hInstance for you.  The following
// example is not typical:

HCURSOR hCursor;
hCursor = ::LoadCursor(AfxGetApp()->m_hInstance,
   MAKEINTRESOURCE(IDC_MYCURSOR));

// A more direct way to get the application's hInstance is to
// call AfxGetInstanceHandle:
hCursor = ::LoadCursor(AfxGetInstanceHandle(),
   MAKEINTRESOURCE(IDC_MYCURSOR));

// If you need the hInstance to load a resource, it is better
// to call AfxGetResourceHandle instead of AfxGetInstanceHandle:
hCursor = ::LoadCursor(AfxGetResourceHandle(),
   MAKEINTRESOURCE(IDC_MYCURSOR));

// A better way to load the cursor resource is to call
// CWinApp::LoadCursor
hCursor = AfxGetApp()->LoadCursor(IDC_MYCURSOR);
```

CWinApp::m_hPrevInstance

Remarks   Corresponds to the *hPrevInstance* parameter passed by Windows to **WinMain**.

Identifies the previous instance of the application. The **m_hPrevInstance** data member has the value **NULL** if this is the first instance of the application that is running. **m_hPrevInstance** is a public variable of type **HINSTANCE**.

CWinApp::m_lpCmdLine

Remarks   Corresponds to the *lpCmdLine* parameter passed by Windows to **WinMain**. Points to a null-terminated string that specifies the command line for the application. Use **m_lpCmdLine** to access any command-line arguments the user entered when the application was started. **m_lpCmdLine** is a public variable of type **LPSTR**.

Example
```
BOOL CMyApp::InitInstance()
{
   // ...
   if (m_lpCmdLine[0] == '\0')
   {
      // Create a new (empty) document.
      OnFileNew();
   }
   else
   {
```

```
                    // Open a file passed as the first command line parameter.
                    OpenDocumentFile(m_lpCmdLine);
            }
            // ...
    }
```

CWinApp::m_nCmdShow

Remarks

Corresponds to the *nCmdShow* parameter passed by Windows to **WinMain**. You should pass **m_nCmdShow** as an argument when you call **ShowWindow** for your application's main window. **m_nCmdShow** is a public variable of type **int**.

Example

```
BOOL CMyApp::InitInstance()
{
    // ...

    // Create main MDI Frame window.
    CMainFrame* pMainFrame = new CMainFrame;
    if (!pMainFrame->LoadFrame(IDR_MAINFRAME))
        return FALSE;
    // Save the pointer to the main frame window.  This is the
    // only way the framework will have knowledge of what the
    // main frame window is.
    m_pMainWnd = pMainFrame;
    // Show the   main window using the nCmdShow parameter
    // passed to the application when it was first launched.
    pMainFrame->ShowWindow(m_nCmdShow);
    pMainFrame->UpdateWindow();
    // ...
}
```

CWinApp::m_pActiveWnd

Remarks

Use this data member to store a pointer to the main window of the OLE container application that has your OLE server application in-place activated. If this data member is **NULL**, the application is not in-place active.

The framework sets this member variable when the frame window is in-place activated by an OLE container application.

See Also   **AfxGetMainWnd, CWinThread::m_pMainWnd**

CWinApp::m_pszAppName

Remarks

Specifies the name of the application. The application name can come from the parameter passed to the **CWinApp** constructor, or, if not specified, to the resource string with the ID of **AFX_IDS_APP_TITLE**. If the application name is not found in the resource, it comes from the program's .EXE filename. Returned by the global function **AfxGetAppName**. **m_pszAppName** is a public variable of type **const char***.

Example

```
CWnd* pWnd;
// Set pWnd to some CWnd object whose window has already
// been created.

// The following call to CWnd::MessageBox uses the application
// title as the message box caption.
pWnd->MessageBox("Some message", AfxGetApp()->m_pszAppName);

// A more direct way to get the application title is to
// call AfxGetAppName:
pWnd->MessageBox("Some message", AfxGetAppName());

// An easier way to display a message box using the application
// title as the message box caption is to call AfxMessageBox:
AfxMessageBox("Some message");
```

CWinApp::m_pszExeName

Remarks   Contains the name of the application's executable file without an extension. Unlike **m_pszAppName**, this name cannot contain blanks. **m_pszExeName** is a public variable of type **const char***.

CWinApp::m_pszHelpFilePath

Remarks   Contains the path to the application's Help file. The framework expects a single Help file, which must have the same name as the application but with a .HLP extension. **m_pszHelpFilePath** is a public variable of type **const char***.

CWinApp::m_pszProfileName

Remarks   Contains the name of the application's .INI file. **m_pszProfileName** is a public variable of type **const char***.

See Also   **CWinApp::GetProfileString**, **CWinApp::GetProfileInt**, **CWinApp::WriteProfileInt**, **CWinApp::WriteProfileString**

CWinApp::m_pszRegistryKey

LPCTSTR *m_pszRegistryKey*;

Remarks   Used to determine the full registry key for storing application profile settings. Normally, this data member is treated as read-only.

See Also   **CWinApp::SetRegistryKey**

class CWindowDC : public CDC

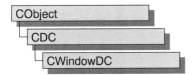

The **CWindowDC** class is derived from **CDC**. It calls the Windows functions **GetWindowDC** at construction time and **ReleaseDC** at destruction time. This means that a **CWindowDC** object accesses the entire screen area of a **CWnd** (both client and nonclient areas).

#include <afxwin.h>

See Also   **CDC**

Construction
CWindowDC   Constructs a **CWindowDC** object.

Data Members
m_hWnd   The **HWND** to which this **CWindowDC** is attached.

Member Functions

CWindowDC::CWindowDC

CWindowDC(CWnd* *pWnd* **)**
    throw(CResourceException);

Parameters   *pWnd*   The window whose client area the device-context object will access.

Remarks   Constructs a **CWindowDC** object that accesses the entire screen area (both client and nonclient) of the **CWnd** object pointed to by *pWnd*. The constructor calls the Windows function **GetDC**. An exception (of type **CResourceException**) is thrown if the Windows **GetDC** call fails. A device context may not be available if Windows has already allocated all of its available device contexts. Your application competes for the five common display contexts available at any given time under Windows.

See Also   **CDC, CClientDC, CWnd**

Data Members

CWindowDC::m_hWnd

Remarks   The **HWND** of the **CWnd** pointer is used to construct the **CWindowDC** object. **m_hWnd** is a protected variable of type **HWND**.

class CWinThread : public CCmdTarget

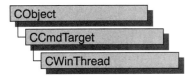

A **CWinThread** object represents a thread of execution within an application. The main thread of execution is usually provided by an object derived from **CWinApp**; **CWinApp** is derived from **CWinThread**. Additional **CWinThread** objects allow multiple threads within a given application.

There are two general types of threads that **CWinThread** supports: worker threads and user-interface threads. Worker threads have no message pump: for example, a thread that performs background calculations in a spreadsheet application. User-interface threads have a message pump and process messages received from the system. **CWinApp** and classes derived from it are examples of user-interface threads. Other user-interface threads can also be derived directly from **CWinThread**.

Objects of class **CWinThread** typically exist for the duration of the thread. If you wish to modify this behavior, set **m_bAutoDelete** to **FALSE**.

The **CWinThread** class is necessary to make your code and MFC fully thread-safe. Thread-local data used by the framework to maintain thread-specific information is managed by **CWinThread** objects. Because of this dependence on **CWinThread** to handle thread-local data, any thread that uses MFC must be created by MFC. For example, a thread created by the run-time function **_beginthreadex** cannot use any MFC APIs.

To create a thread, call **AfxBeginThread**. There are two forms, depending on whether you want a worker or user-interface thread. If you want a user-interface thread, pass to **AfxBeginThread** a pointer to the **CRuntimeClass** of your **CWinThread**-derived class. If you want to create a worker thread, pass to **AfxBeginThread** a pointer to the controlling function and the parameter to the controlling function. For both worker threads and user-interface threads, you can specify optional parameters that modify priority, stack size, creation flags, and security attributes. **AfxBeginThread** will return a pointer to your new **CWinThread** object.

Instead of calling **AfxBeginThread**, you can construct a **CWinThread**-derived object and then call **CreateThread**. This two-stage construction method is useful if you want to reuse the **CWinThread** object between successive creation and terminations of thread executions.

For more information, see the article "Multithreading: Creating User-Interface Threads" or "Multithreading: Creating Worker Threads" in *Programming with the Microsoft Foundation Class Library* for more information.

See Also   **CWinApp**, **CCmdTarget**

In *Programming with the Microsoft Foundation Class Library:* Multithreading

Data Members

m_bAutoDelete	Specifies whether to destroy the object at thread termination.
m_hThread	Handle to the current thread.
m_nThreadID	ID of the current thread.
m_pMainWnd	Holds a pointer to the application's main window.

Construction

CWinThread	Constructs a **CWinThread** object.
CreateThread	Starts execution of a **CWinThread** object.

Operations

GetMainWnd	Retrieves a pointer to the main window for the thread.
GetThreadPriority	Gets the priority of the current thread.
ResumeThread	Decrements a thread's suspend count.
SetThreadPriority	Sets the priority of the current thread.
SuspendThread	Increments a thread's suspend count.

Overridables

ExitInstance	Override to clean up when your thread terminates.
InitInstance	Override to perform thread instance initialization.
OnIdle	Override to perform thread-specific idle-time processing.
PreTranslateMessage	Filters messages before they are dispatched to the Windows functions **TranslateMessage** and **DispatchMessage**.

ProcessWndProcException	Intercepts all unhandled exceptions thrown by the thread's message and command handlers.
Run	Controlling function for threads with a message pump. Override to customize the default message loop.

Member Functions

CWinThread::CreateThread

BOOL CreateThread(DWORD *dwCreateFlags* **= 0, UINT** *nStackSize* **= 0, LPSECURITY_ATTRIBUTES** *lpSecurityAttrs* **= NULL);**

Return Value   Nonzero if the thread is created successfully; otherwise 0.

Parameters   *dwCreateFlags*   Specifies an additional flag that controls the creation of the thread. This flag can contain one of two values:

- **CREATE_SUSPENDED**   Start the thread with a suspend count of one. The thread will not execute until **ResumeThread** is called.
- **0**   Start the thread immediately after creation.

nStackSize   Specifies the size in bytes of the stack for the new thread. If **0**, the stack size defaults to the same size as that of the process's primary thread.

lpSecurityAttrs   Points to a **SECURITY_ATTRIBUTES** structure that specifies the security attributes for the thread.

Remarks   Creates a thread to execute within the address space of the calling process. Use **AfxBeginThread** to create a thread object and execute it in one step. Use **CreateThread** if you want to reuse the thread object between successive creation and termination of thread executions.

See Also   **AfxBeginThread, CWinThread::CWinThread, ::CreateThread**

CWinThread::CWinThread

CWinThread( );

Remarks   Constructs a **CWinThread** object. To begin the thread's execution, call the **CreateThread** member function. You will usually create threads by calling **AfxBeginThread**, which will call this constructor and **CreateThread**.

See Also   **CWinThread::CreateThread**

CWinThread::ExitInstance

virtual int ExitInstance( );

Return Value
The thread's exit code; 0 indicates no errors, and values greater than 0 indicate an error. This value can be retrieved by calling **::GetExitCodeThread**.

Remarks
Called by the framework from within a rarely overridden **Run** member function to exit this instance of the thread, or if a call to **InitInstance** fails.

Do not call this member function from anywhere but within the **Run** member function. This member function is used only in user-interface threads.

The default implementation of this function deletes the **CWinThread** object if **m_bAutoDelete** is **TRUE**. Override this function if you wish to perform additional clean-up when your thread terminates. Your implementation of **ExitInstance** should call the base class's version after your code is executed.

See Also
CWinApp::ExitInstance

CWinThread::GetMainWnd

virtual CWnd * GetMainWnd( );

Return Value
This function returns a pointer to one of two types of windows. If your thread is part of an OLE server and has an object that is in-place active inside an active container, this function returns the **CWinApp::m_pActiveWnd** data member of your application object.

If there is no object that is in-place active within a container or your application is not an OLE server, this function returns the **m_pMainWnd** data member of your thread object.

Remarks
If your application is an OLE server, call this function to retrieve a pointer to the active main window of the application instead of directly referring to the **m_pMainWnd** member of the application object. For user-interface threads, this is equivalent to directly referring to the **m_pActiveWnd** member of your application object.

If your application is not an OLE server, then calling this function is equivalent to directly referring to the **m_pMainWnd** member of your application object.

Override this function to modify the default behavior.

See Also
AfxGetMainWnd

CWinThread::GetThreadPriority

int GetThreadPriority( );

Return Value   The current thread priority level within its priority class. The value returned will be one of the following, listed from highest priority to lowest:

- **THREAD_PRIORITY_TIME_CRITICAL**
- **THREAD_PRIORITY_HIGHEST**
- **THREAD_PRIORITY_ABOVE_NORMAL**
- **THREAD_PRIORITY_NORMAL**
- **THREAD_PRIORITY_BELOW_NORMAL**
- **THREAD_PRIORITY_LOWEST**
- **THREAD_PRIORITY_IDLE**

For more information on these priorities, see **::SetThreadPriority** in the Win32 *Programmer's Reference, Volume 4.*

Remarks   Gets the current thread priority level of this thread.

See Also   **CWinThread::SetThreadPriority**, **::GetThreadPriority**

CWinThread::InitInstance

virtual BOOL InitInstance( );

Return Value   Nonzero if initialization is successful; otherwise 0.

Remarks   **InitInstance** must be overridden to initialize each new instance of a user-interface thread. Typically, you override **InitInstance** to perform tasks that must be completed when a thread is first created.

This member function is used only in user-interface threads. Perform initialization of worker threads in the controlling function passed to **AfxBeginThread**.

See Also   **CWinApp::InitInstance**

CWinThread::OnIdle

virtual BOOL OnIdle(LONG *lCount*);

Return Value   Nonzero to receive more idle processing time; 0 if no more idle processing time is needed.

Parameters	*lCount* A counter incremented each time **OnIdle** is called when the thread's message queue is empty. This count is reset to 0 each time a new message is processed. You can use the *lCount* parameter to determine the relative length of time the thread has been idle without processing a message.
Remarks	Override this member function to perform idle-time processing. **OnIdle** is called in the default message loop when the thread's message queue is empty. Use your override to call your own background idle-handler tasks.

OnIdle should return 0 to indicate that no additional idle processing time is required. The *lCount* parameter is incremented each time **OnIdle** is called when the message queue is empty and is reset to 0 each time a new message is processed. You can call your different idle routines based on this count.

The default implementation of this member function frees temporary objects and unused dynamic link libraries from memory.

This member function is used only in user-interface threads.

Because the application cannot process messages until **OnIdle** returns, do not perform lengthy tasks in this function.

See Also	**CWinApp::OnIdle**

CWinThread::PreTranslateMessage

virtual BOOL PreTranslateMessage(MSG **pMsg**);

Return Value	Nonzero if the message was fully processed in **PreTranslateMessage** and should not be processed further. Zero if the message should be processed in the normal way.
Parameters	*pMsg* Points to a **MSG** structure containing the message to process.
Remarks	Override this function to filter window messages before they are dispatched to the Windows functions **::TranslateMessage** and **::DispatchMessage**.

This member function is used only in user-interface threads.

See Also	**CWinApp::PreTranslateMessage**

CWinThread::ProcessWndProcException

virtual LRESULT ProcessWndProcException(CException **e**, const MSG**
        ****pMsg**);

Return Value	–1 if a **WM_CREATE** exception is generated; otherwise 0.

Parameters   *e*   Points to an unhandled exception.

pMsg   Points to an **MSG**structure containing information about the windows message that caused the framework to throw an exception.

Remarks   The framework calls this member function whenever the handler does not catch an exception thrown in one of your thread's message or command handlers.

Do not call this member function directly.

The default implementation of this member function handles only exceptions generated from the following messages:

Command	Action
WM_CREATE	Fail.
WM_PAINT	Validate the affected window, thus preventing another **WM_PAINT** message from being generated.

Override this member function to provide global handling of your exceptions. Call the base functionality only if you wish to display the default behavior.

This member function is used only in threads that have a message pump.

See Also   **CWinApp::ProcessWndProcException**

CWinThread::ResumeThread

DWORD ResumeThread( );

Return Value   The thread's previous suspend count if successful; 0xFFFFFFFF otherwise. If the return value is zero, the current thread was not suspended. If the return value is one, the thread was suspended, but is now restarted. Any return value greater than one means the thread remains suspended.

Remarks   Called to resume execution of a thread that was suspended by the **SuspendThread** member function, or a thread created with the **CREATE_SUSPENDED** flag. The suspend count of the current thread is reduced by one. If the suspend count is reduced to zero, the thread resumes execution; otherwise the thread remains suspended.

See Also   **CWinThread::SuspendThread**, **::ResumeThread**

CWinThread::Run

virtual int Run( );

Return Value   An **int** value that is returned by the thread. This value can be retrieved by calling **::GetExitCodeThread**.

Remarks	Provides a default message loop for user-interface threads. **Run** acquires and dispatches Windows messages until the application receives a **WM_QUIT** message. If the thread's message queue currently contains no messages, **Run** calls **OnIdle** to perform idle-time processing. Incoming messages go to the **PreTranslateMessage** member function for special processing and then to the Windows function **::TranslateMessage** for standard keyboard translation. Finally, the **::DispatchMessage** Windows function is called.
	Run is rarely overridden, but you can override it to implement special behavior.
	This member function is used only in user-interface threads.
See Also	**CWinApp::Run**

CWinThread::SetThreadPriority

BOOL SetThreadPriority(int *nPriority* **);**

Return Value	Nonzero if function was successful; otherwise 0.
Parameters	*nPriority* Specifies the new thread priority level within its priority class. This parameter must be one of the following values, listed from highest priority to lowest:

- **THREAD_PRIORITY_TIME_CRITICAL**
- **THREAD_PRIORITY_HIGHEST**
- **THREAD_PRIORITY_ABOVE_NORMAL**
- **THREAD_PRIORITY_NORMAL**
- **THREAD_PRIORITY_BELOW_NORMAL**
- **THREAD_PRIORITY_LOWEST**
- **THREAD_PRIORITY_IDLE**

For more information on these priorities, see **::SetThreadPriority** in the Win32 *Programmer's Reference, Volume 4*.

Remarks	This function sets the priority level of the current thread within its priority class. It can only be called after **CreateThread** successfully returns.
See Also	**CWinThread::GetThreadPriority**, **::SetThreadPriority**

CWinThread::SuspendThread

DWORD SuspendThread( );

Return Value	The thread's previous suspend count if successful; 0xFFFFFFFF otherwise.

Remarks   Increments the current thread's suspend count. If any thread has a suspend count above zero, that thread does not execute. The thread can be resumed by calling the **ResumeThread** member function.

See Also   **CWinThread::ResumeThread**, **::SuspendThread**

CWinThread::m_bAutoDelete

Remarks   Specifies whether the **CWinThread** object should be automatically deleted at thread termination. The **m_bAutoDelete** data member is a public variable of type **BOOL**.

CWinThread::m_hThread

Remarks   Handle to the thread attached to this **CWinThread**. The **m_hThread** data member is a public variable of type **HANDLE**. It is only valid if underlying thread currently exists.

CWinThread::m_nThreadID

Remarks   ID of the thread attached to this **CWinThread**. The **m_nThreadID** data member is a public variable of type **DWORD**. It is only valid if underlying thread currently exists.

CWinThread::m_pMainWnd

Remarks   Use this data member to store a pointer to your thread's main window object. The Microsoft Foundation Class Library will automatically terminate your thread when the window referred to by **m_pMainWnd** is closed. If this thread is the primary thread for an application, the application will also be terminated. If this data member is **NULL**, the main window for the application's **CWinApp** object will be inherited. **m_pMainWnd** is a public variable of type **CWnd***.

Typically, you set this member variable when you override **InitInstance**. In a worker thread, the value of this data member is inherited from its parent thread.

See Also   **CWinThread::InitInstance**

class CWnd : public CCmdTarget

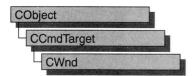

The **CWnd** class provides the base functionality of all window classes in the Microsoft Foundation Class Library. A **CWnd** object is distinct from a Windows window, but the two are tightly linked. A **CWnd** object is created or destroyed by the **CWnd** constructor and destructor. The Windows window, on the other hand, is a data structure internal to Windows that is created by a **Create** member function and destroyed by the **CWnd** virtual destructor. The **DestroyWindow** function destroys the Windows window without destroying the object. The **CWnd** class and the message-map mechanism hide the **WndProc** function. Incoming Windows notification messages are automatically routed through the message map to the proper **On***Message* **CWnd** member functions. You override an **On***Message* member function to handle a member's particular message in your derived classes.

The **CWnd** class also lets you create a Windows child window for your application. Derive a class from **CWnd**, then add member variables to the derived class to store data specific to your application. Implement message-handler member functions and a message map in the derived class to specify what happens when messages are directed to the window.

You create a child window in two steps. First, call the constructor **CWnd** to construct the **CWnd** object, then call the **Create** member function to create the child window and attach it to the **CWnd** object. When the user terminates your child window, destroy the **CWnd** object, or call the **DestroyWindow** member function to remove the window and destroy its data structures.

Within the Microsoft Foundation Class Library, further classes are derived from **CWnd** to provide specific window types. Many of these classes, including **CFrameWnd**, **CMDIFrameWnd**, **CMDIChildWnd**, **CView**, and **CDialog**, are designed for further derivation. The control classes derived from **CWnd**, such as **CButton**, can be used directly or can be used for further derivation of classes.

#include <afxwin.h>

See Also   **CDialog, CFrameWnd, CView**

Data Members
m_hWnd   Indicates the **HWND** attached to this **CWnd**.

Construction/Destruction

CWnd	Constructs a **CWnd** object.
DestroyWindow	Destroys the attached Windows window.

Initialization

Create	Creates and initializes the child window associated with the **CWnd** object.
PreCreateWindow	Called before the creation of the Windows window attached to this **CWnd** object.
CalcWindowRect	Called to calculate the window rectangle from the client rectangle.
GetStyle	Returns the current window style.
GetExStyle	Returns the window's extended style.
Attach	Attaches a Windows handle to a **CWnd** object.
Detach	Detaches a Windows handle from a **CWnd** object and returns the handle.
SubclassWindow	Attaches a window to a **CWnd** object and makes it route messages through the **CWnd**'s message map.
FromHandle	Returns a pointer to a **CWnd** object when given a handle to a window. If a **CWnd** object is not attached to the handle, a temporary **CWnd** object is created and attached.
FromHandlePermanent	Returns a pointer to a **CWnd** object when given a handle to a window. If a **CWnd** object is not attached to the handle, **NULL** is returned.
DeleteTempMap	Called automatically by the **CWinApp** idle-time handler and deletes any temporary **CWnd** objects created by **FromHandle**.
GetSafeHwnd	Returns **m_hWnd**, or **NULL** if the **this** pointer is **NULL**.
CreateEx	Creates a Windows overlapped, pop-up, or child window and attaches it to a **CWnd** object.

Window State Functions

IsWindowEnabled	Determines whether the window is enabled for mouse and keyboard input.
EnableWindow	Enables or disables mouse and keyboard input.
GetActiveWindow	Retrieves the active window.

SetActiveWindow	Activates the window.
GetCapture	Retrieves the **CWnd** that has the mouse capture.
SetCapture	Causes all subsequent mouse input to be sent to the **CWnd**.
GetFocus	Retrieves the **CWnd** that currently has the input focus.
SetFocus	Claims the input focus.
GetDesktopWindow	Retrieves the Windows desktop window.
GetForegroundWindow	Returns a pointer to the foreground window (the top-level window with which the user is currently working).
SetForegroundWindow	Puts the thread that created the window into the foreground and activates the window.

Window Size and Position

GetWindowPlacement	Retrieves the show state and the normal (restored), minimized, and maximized positions of a window.
SetWindowPlacement	Sets the show state and the normal (restored), minimized, and maximized positions for a window.
IsIconic	Determines whether **CWnd** is minimized (iconic).
IsZoomed	Determines whether **CWnd** is maximized.
MoveWindow	Changes the position and/or dimensions of **CWnd**.
SetWindowPos	Changes the size, position, and ordering of child, pop-up, and top-level windows.
ArrangeIconicWindows	Arranges all the minimized (iconic) child windows.
BringWindowToTop	Brings **CWnd** to the top of a stack of overlapping windows.
GetWindowRect	Gets the screen coordinates of **CWnd**.
GetClientRect	Gets the dimensions of the **CWnd** client area.

Window Access Functions

ChildWindowFromPoint	Determines which, if any, of the child windows contains the specified point.
FindWindow	Returns the handle of the window, which is identified by its window name and window class.
GetNextWindow	Returns the next (or previous) window in the window manager's list.
GetOwner	Retrieves a pointer to the owner of a **CWnd**.
SetOwner	Changes the owner of a **CWnd**.
GetTopWindow	Returns the first child window that belongs to the **CWnd**.
GetWindow	Returns the window with the specified relationship to this window.
GetLastActivePopup	Determines which pop-up window owned by **CWnd** was most recently active.
IsChild	Indicates whether **CWnd** is a child window or other direct descendant of the specified window.
GetParent	Retrieves the parent window of **CWnd** (if any).
SetParent	Changes the parent window.
WindowFromPoint	Identifies the window that contains the given point.
GetDlgItem	Retrieves the control with the specified ID from the specified dialog box.
GetDlgCtrlID	If the **CWnd** is a child window, calling this function returns its ID value.
SetDlgCtrlID	Sets the window or control ID for the window (which can be any child window, not only a control in a dialog box).
GetDescendantWindow	Searches all descendant windows and returns the window with the specified ID.
GetParentFrame	Returns the **CWnd** object's parent frame window.
SendMessageToDescendants	Sends a message to all descendant windows of the window.
UpdateDialogControls	Call to update the state of dialog buttons and other controls.
UpdateData	Initializes or retrieves data from a dialog box.
CenterWindow	Centers a window relative to its parent.

Update/Painting Functions

BeginPaint	Prepares **CWnd** for painting.
EndPaint	Marks the end of painting.
LockWindowUpdate	Disables or reenables drawing in the given window.
GetDC	Retrieves a display context for the client area.
GetDCEx	Retrieves a display context for the client area, and enables clipping while drawing.
RedrawWindow	Updates the specified rectangle or region in the client area.
GetWindowDC	Retrieves the display context for the whole window, including the caption bar, menus, and scroll bars.
ReleaseDC	Releases client and window device contexts, freeing them for use by other applications.
UpdateWindow	Updates the client area.
SetRedraw	Allows changes in **CWnd** to be redrawn or prevents changes from being redrawn.
GetUpdateRect	Retrieves the coordinates of the smallest rectangle that completely encloses the **CWnd** update region.
GetUpdateRgn	Retrieves the **CWnd** update region.
Invalidate	Invalidates the entire client area.
InvalidateRect	Invalidates the client area within the given rectangle by adding that rectangle to the current update region.
InvalidateRgn	Invalidates the client area within the given region by adding that region to the current update region.
ValidateRect	Validates the client area within the given rectangle by removing the rectangle from the current update region.
ValidateRgn	Validates the client area within the given region by removing the region from the current update region.
ShowWindow	Shows or hides the window.
IsWindowVisible	Determines whether the window is visible.
ShowOwnedPopups	Shows or hides all pop-up windows owned by the window.

EnableScrollBar	Enables or disables one or both arrows of a scroll bar.

Coordinate Mapping Functions

MapWindowPoints	Converts (maps) a set of points from the coordinate space of the **CWnd** to the coordinate space of another window.
ClientToScreen	Converts the client coordinates of a given point or rectangle on the display to screen coordinates.
ScreenToClient	Converts the screen coordinates of a given point or rectangle on the display to client coordinates.

Window Text Functions

SetWindowText	Sets the window text or caption title (if it has one) to the specified text.
GetWindowText	Returns the window text or caption title (if it has one).
GetWindowTextLength	Returns the length of the window's text or caption title.
SetFont	Sets the current font.
GetFont	Retrieves the current font.

Scrolling Functions

GetScrollPos	Retrieves the current position of a scroll box.
GetScrollRange	Copies the current minimum and maximum scroll-bar positions for the given scroll bar.
ScrollWindow	Scrolls the contents of the client area.
ScrollWindowEx	Scrolls the contents of the client area. Similar to **ScrollWindow**, with additional features.
SetScrollPos	Sets the current position of a scroll box and, if specified, redraws the scroll bar to reflect the new position.
SetScrollRange	Sets minimum and maximum position values for the given scroll bar.
ShowScrollBar	Displays or hides a scroll bar.
EnableScrollBarCtrl	Enables or disables a sibling scroll-bar control.
GetScrollBarCtrl	Returns a sibling scroll-bar control.
RepositionBars	Repositions control bars in the client area.

Drag-Drop Functions

DragAcceptFiles   Indicates the window will accept dragged files.

Caret Functions

CreateCaret   Creates a new shape for the system caret and gets ownership of the caret.

CreateSolidCaret   Creates a solid block for the system caret and gets ownership of the caret.

CreateGrayCaret   Creates a gray block for the system caret and gets ownership of the caret.

GetCaretPos   Retrieves the client coordinates of the caret's current position.

SetCaretPos   Moves the caret to a specified position.

HideCaret   Hides the caret by removing it from the display screen.

ShowCaret   Shows the caret on the display at the caret's current position. Once shown, the caret begins flashing automatically.

Dialog-Box Item Functions

CheckDlgButton   Places a check mark next to or removes a check mark from a button control.

CheckRadioButton   Checks the specified radio button and removes the check mark from all other radio buttons in the specified group of buttons.

GetCheckedRadioButton   Returns the ID of the currently checked radio button in a group of buttons.

DlgDirList   Fills a list box with a file or directory listing.

DlgDirListComboBox   Fills the list box of a combo box with a file or directory listing.

DlgDirSelect   Retrieves the current selection from a list box.

DlgDirSelectComboBox   Retrieves the current selection from the list box of a combo box.

GetDlgItemInt   Translates the text of a control in the given dialog box to an integer value.

GetDlgItemText   Retrieves the caption or text associated with a control.

GetNextDlgGroupItem   Searches for the next (or previous) control within a group of controls.

GetNextDlgTabItem	Retrieves the first control with the **WS_TABSTOP** style that follows (or precedes) the specified control.
IsDlgButtonChecked	Determines whether a button control is checked.
SendDlgItemMessage	Sends a message to the specified control.
SetDlgItemInt	Sets the text of a control to the string that represents an integer value.
SetDlgItemText	Sets the caption or text of a control in the specified dialog box.
SubclassDlgItem	Attaches a Windows control to a **CWnd** object and makes it route messages through the **CWnd**'s message map.

Menu Functions

GetMenu	Retrieves a pointer to the specified menu.
SetMenu	Sets the menu to the specified menu.
DrawMenuBar	Redraws the menu bar.
GetSystemMenu	Allows the application to access the Control menu for copying and modification.
HiliteMenuItem	Highlights or removes the highlighting from a top-level (menu-bar) menu item.

Timer Functions

SetTimer	Installs a system timer that sends a **WM_TIMER** message when triggered.
KillTimer	Kills a system timer.

Alert Functions

FlashWindow	Flashes the window once.
MessageBox	Creates and displays a window that contains an application-supplied message and caption.

Window Message Functions

PreTranslateMessage	Used by **CWinApp** to filter window messages before they are dispatched to the **TranslateMessage** and **DispatchMessage** Windows functions.
SendMessage	Sends a message to the **CWnd** object and does not return until it has processed the message.

| PostMessage | Places a message in the application queue, then returns without waiting for the window to process the message. |
| SendNotifyMessage | Sends the specified message to the window and returns as soon as possible, depending on whether the calling thread created the window. |

Clipboard Functions

ChangeClipboardChain	Removes **CWnd** from the chain of Clipboard viewers.
SetClipboardViewer	Adds **CWnd** to the chain of windows that are notified whenever the contents of the Clipboard are changed.
OpenClipboard	Opens the Clipboard. Other applications will not be able to modify the Clipboard until the Windows **CloseClipboard** function is called.
GetClipboardOwner	Retrieves a pointer to the current owner of the Clipboard.
GetOpenClipboardWindow	Retrieves a pointer to the window that currently has the Clipboard open.
GetClipboardViewer	Retrieves a pointer to the first window in the chain of Clipboard viewers.

Operations

| GetCurrentMessage | Returns a pointer to the message this window is currently processing. Should only be called when in an **On***Message* message-handler member function. |
| Default | Calls the default window procedure, which provides default processing for any window messages that an application does not process. |

Overridables

GetSuperWndProcAddr	Accesses the default **WndProc** of a subclassed window.
WindowProc	Provides a window procedure for a **CWnd**. The default dispatches messages through the message map.
DefWindowProc	Calls the default window procedure, which provides default processing for any window messages that an application does not process.

PostNcDestroy	This virtual function is called by the default **OnNcDestroy** function after the window has been destroyed.
OnChildNotify	Called by a parent window to give a notifying control a chance to respond to a control notification.
DoDataExchange	For dialog data exchange and validation. Called by **UpdateData**.

Initialization Message Handlers

OnInitMenu	Called when a menu is about to become active.
OnInitMenuPopup	Called when a pop-up menu is about to become active.

System Message Handlers

OnSysChar	Called when a keystroke translates to a system character.
OnSysCommand	Called when the user selects a command from the Control menu, or when the user selects the Maximize or Minimize button.
OnSysDeadChar	Called when a keystroke translates to a system dead character (such as accent characters).
OnSysKeyDown	Called when the user holds down the ALT key and then presses another key.
OnSysKeyUp	Called when the user releases a key that was pressed while the ALT key was held down.
OnCompacting	Called when Windows detects that system memory is low.
OnDevModeChange	Called for all top-level windows when the user changes device-mode settings.
OnFontChange	Called when the pool of font resources changes.
OnPaletteIsChanging	Informs other applications when an application is going to realize its logical palette.
OnPaletteChanged	Called to allow windows that use a color palette to realize their logical palettes and update their client areas.
OnSysColorChange	Called for all top-level windows when a change is made in the system color setting.

OnWindowPosChanging	Called when the size, position, or Z-order is about to change as a result of a call to **SetWindowPos** or another window-management function.
OnWindowPosChanged	Called when the size, position, or Z-order has changed as a result of a call to **SetWindowPos** or another window-management function.
OnDropFiles	Called when the user releases the left mouse button over a window that has registered itself as the recipient of dropped files.
OnSpoolerStatus	Called from Print Manager whenever a job is added to or removed from the Print Manager queue.
OnTimeChange	Called for all top-level windows after the system time changes.
OnWinIniChange	Called for all top-level windows after the Windows initialization file, WIN.INI, is changed.

General Message Handlers

OnCommand	Called when the user selects a command.
OnActivate	Called when **CWnd** is being activated or deactivated.
OnActivateApp	Called when the application is about to be activated or deactivated.
OnCancelMode	Called to allow **CWnd** to cancel any internal modes, such as mouse capture.
OnChildActivate	Called for multiple document interface (MDI) child windows whenever the size or position of **CWnd** changes or **CWnd** is activated.
OnClose	Called as a signal that **CWnd** should be closed.
OnCreate	Called as a part of window creation.
OnCtlColor	Called if **CWnd** is the parent of a control when the control is about to be drawn.
OnDestroy	Called when **CWnd** is being destroyed.
OnEnable	Called when **CWnd** is enabled or disabled.
OnEndSession	Called when the session is ending.
OnEnterIdle	Called to inform an application's main window procedure that a modal dialog box or a menu is entering an idle state.

OnEraseBkgnd	Called when the window background needs erasing.
OnGetMinMaxInfo	Called whenever Windows needs to know the maximized position or dimensions, or the minimum or maximum tracking size.
OnIconEraseBkgnd	Called when **CWnd** is minimized (iconic) and the background of the icon must be filled before painting the icon.
OnKillFocus	Called immediately before **CWnd** loses the input focus.
OnMenuChar	Called when the user presses a menu mnemonic character that doesn't match any of the predefined mnemonics in the current menu.
OnMenuSelect	Called when the user selects a menu item.
OnMove	Called after the position of the **CWnd** has been changed.
OnPaint	Called to repaint a portion of the window.
OnParentNotify	Called when a child window is created or destroyed, or when the user clicks a mouse button while the cursor is over the child window.
OnQueryDragIcon	Called when a minimized (iconic) **CWnd** is about to be dragged by the user.
OnQueryEndSession	Called when the user chooses to end the Windows session.
OnQueryNewPalette	Informs **CWnd** that it is about to receive the input focus.
OnQueryOpen	Called when **CWnd** is an icon and the user requests that the icon be opened.
OnSetFocus	Called after **CWnd** gains the input focus.
OnShowWindow	Called when **CWnd** is to be hidden or shown.
OnSize	Called after the size of **CWnd** has changed.

Control Message Handlers

OnCharToItem	Called by a child list box with the **LBS_WANTKEYBOARDINPUT** style in response to a **WM_CHAR** message.
OnCompareItem	Called to determine the relative position of a new item in a child sorted owner-draw combo box or list box.

OnDeleteItem	Called when an owner-draw child list box or combo box is destroyed or when items are removed from the control.
OnDrawItem	Called when a visual aspect of an owner-draw child button control, combo-box control, list-box control, or menu needs to be drawn.
OnGetDlgCode	Called for a control so the control can process arrow-key and TAB-key input itself.
OnMeasureItem	Called for an owner-draw child combo box, list box, or menu item when the control is created. **CWnd** informs Windows of the dimensions of the control.
OnVKeyToItem	Called by a list box owned by **CWnd** in response to a **WM_KEYDOWN** message.

Input Message Handlers

OnChar	Called when a keystroke translates to a nonsystem character.
OnDeadChar	Called when a keystroke translates to a nonsystem dead character (such as accent characters).
OnHScroll	Called when the user clicks the horizontal scroll bar of **CWnd**.
OnKeyDown	Called when a nonsystem key is pressed.
OnKeyUp	Called when a nonsystem key is released.
OnLButtonDblClk	Called when the user double-clicks the left mouse button.
OnLButtonDown	Called when the user presses the left mouse button.
OnLButtonUp	Called when the user releases the left mouse button.
OnMButtonDblClk	Called when the user double-clicks the middle mouse button.
OnMButtonDown	Called when the user presses the middle mouse button.
OnMButtonUp	Called when the user releases the middle mouse button.
OnMouseActivate	Called when the cursor is in an inactive window and the user presses a mouse button.
OnMouseMove	Called when the mouse cursor moves.

OnRButtonDblClk	Called when the user double-clicks the right mouse button.
OnRButtonDown	Called when the user presses the right mouse button.
OnRButtonUp	Called when the user releases the right mouse button.
OnSetCursor	Called if mouse input is not captured and the mouse causes cursor movement within a window.
OnTimer	Called after each interval specified in **SetTimer**.
OnVScroll	Called when the user clicks the window's vertical scroll bar.

Nonclient-Area Message Handlers

OnNcActivate	Called when the nonclient area needs to be changed to indicate an active or inactive state.
OnNcCalcSize	Called when the size and position of the client area need to be calculated.
OnNcCreate	Called prior to **OnCreate** when the nonclient area is being created.
OnNcDestroy	Called when the nonclient area is being destroyed.
OnNcHitTest	Called by Windows every time the mouse is moved if **CWnd** contains the cursor or has captured mouse input with **SetCapture**.
OnNcLButtonDblClk	Called when the user double-clicks the left mouse button while the cursor is within a nonclient area of **CWnd**.
OnNcLButtonDown	Called when the user presses the left mouse button while the cursor is within a nonclient area of **CWnd**.
OnNcLButtonUp	Called when the user releases the left mouse button while the cursor is within a nonclient area of **CWnd**.
OnNcMButtonDblClk	Called when the user double-clicks the middle mouse button while the cursor is within a nonclient area of **CWnd**.

OnNcMButtonDown	Called when the user presses the middle mouse button while the cursor is within a nonclient area of **CWnd**.
OnNcMButtonUp	Called when the user releases the middle mouse button while the cursor is within a nonclient area of **CWnd**.
OnNcMouseMove	Called when the cursor is moved within a nonclient area of **CWnd**.
OnNcPaint	Called when the nonclient area needs painting.
OnNcRButtonDblClk	Called when the user double-clicks the right mouse button while the cursor is within a nonclient area of **CWnd**.
OnNcRButtonDown	Called when the user presses the right mouse button while the cursor is within a nonclient area of **CWnd**.
OnNcRButtonUp	Called when the user releases the right mouse button while the cursor is within a nonclient area of **CWnd**.

MDI Message Handlers

OnMDIActivate	Called when an MDI child window is activated or deactivated.

Clipboard Message Handlers

OnAskCbFormatName	Called by a Clipboard viewer application when a Clipboard owner will display the Clipboard contents.
OnChangeCbChain	Notifies that a specified window is being removed from the chain.
OnDestroyClipboard	Called when the Clipboard is emptied through a call to the Windows **EmptyClipboard** function.
OnDrawClipboard	Called when the contents of the change.
OnHScrollClipboard	Called when a Clipboard owner should scroll the Clipboard image, invalidate the appropriate section, and update the scroll-bar values.
OnPaintClipboard	Called when the client area of the Clipboard viewer needs repainting.
OnRenderAllFormats	Called when the owner application is being destroyed and needs to render all its formats.

OnRenderFormat	Called for the Clipboard owner when a particular format with delayed rendering needs to be rendered.
OnSizeClipboard	Called when the size of the client area of the Clipboard-viewer window has changed.
OnVScrollClipboard	Called when the owner should scroll the Clipboard image, invalidate the appropriate section, and update the scroll-bar values.

Menu Loop Notification

OnEnterMenuLoop	Called when a menu modal loop has been entered.
OnExitMenuLoop	Called when a menu modal loop has been exited.

Member Functions

CWnd::ArrangeIconicWindows

UINT ArrangeIconicWindows( );

Return Value   The height of one row of icons if the function is successful; otherwise 0.

Remarks   Arranges all the minimized (iconic) child windows. This member function also arranges icons on the desktop window, which covers the entire screen. The **GetDesktopWindow** member function retrieves a pointer to the desktop window object. To arrange iconic MDI child windows in an MDI client window, call **CMDIFrameWnd::MDIIconArrange**.

See Also   **CWnd::GetDesktopWindow, CMDIFrameWnd::MDIIconArrange, ::ArrangeIconicWindows**

CWnd::Attach

BOOL Attach(HWND *hWndNew* **);**

Return Value   Nonzero if successful; otherwise 0.

Parameters   *hWndNew*   Specifies a handle to a Windows window.

Remarks   Attaches a Windows window to a **CWnd** object.

See Also   **CWnd::Detach, CWnd::m_hWnd, CWnd::SubclassWindow**

CWnd::BeginPaint

CDC* BeginPaint(LPPAINTSTRUCT *lpPaint* **);**

Return Value
Identifies the device context for **CWnd**. The pointer may be temporary and should not be stored beyond the scope of **EndPaint**.

Parameters
lpPaint   Points to the **PAINTSTRUCT** structure that is to receive painting information.

Remarks
Prepares **CWnd** for painting and fills a **PAINTSTRUCT** data structure with information about the painting. The paint structure contains a **RECT** data structure that has the smallest rectangle that completely encloses the update region and a flag that specifies whether the background has been erased. The update region is set by the **Invalidate**, **InvalidateRect**, or **InvalidateRgn** member functions and by the system after it sizes, moves, creates, scrolls, or performs any other operation that affects the client area. If the update region is marked for erasing, **BeginPaint** sends an **WM_ONERASEBKGND** message.

Do not call the **BeginPaint** member function except in response to a **WM_PAINT** message. Each call to the **BeginPaint** member function must have a matching call to the **EndPaint** member function. If the caret is in the area to be painted, the **BeginPaint** member function automatically hides the caret to prevent it from being erased.

See Also
CWnd::EndPaint, CWnd::Invalidate, CWnd::InvalidateRgn, ::BeginPaint, CPaintDC

CWnd::BringWindowToTop

void BringWindowToTop( );

Remarks
Brings **CWnd** to the top of a stack of overlapping windows. In addition, **BringWindowToTop** activates pop-up, top-level, and MDI child windows. The **BringWindowToTop** member function should be used to uncover any window that is partially or completely obscured by any overlapping windows. Calling this function is similar to calling the **SetWindowPos** function to change a window's position in the Z order. The **BringWindowToTop** function does not change the window style to make it a top-level window of the desktop.

See Also
::BringWindowToTop

CWnd::CalcWindowRect

virtual void CalcWindowRect(LPRECT *lpClientRect*, **UINT** *nAdjustType* = **adjustBorder);**

Parameters	*lpClientRect* Points to a **RECT** structure or **CRect** object that contains the resultant value of the window rectangle.
	nAdjustType An enumerated type used for in-place editing. It can have the following values: **CWnd::adjustBorder** = 0, which means that scrollbar sizes are ignored in calculation; and **CWnd::adjustOutside** = 1, which means that they are added into the final measurements of the rectangle.
Remarks	Call this member function to compute the required size of the window rectangle based on the desired client-rectangle size. The resulting window rectangle (contained in *lpClientRect*) can then be passed to the **Create** member function to create a window whose client area is the desired size.
	Called by the framework to size windows prior to creation.
	A client rectangle is the smallest rectangle that completely encloses a client area. A window rectangle is the smallest rectangle that completely encloses the window.
See Also	**::AdjustWindowRect**

CWnd::CenterWindow

void CenterWindow(CWnd* *pAlternateOwner* **= NULL);**

Parameters	*pAlternateOwner* Pointer to an alternate window relative to which it will be centered (other than the parent window).
Remarks	Centers a window relative to its parent. Usually called from **CDialog::OnInitDialog** to center dialogs relative to the main window of the application. By default, the function centers child windows relative to their parent window, and popup windows relative to their owner. If the popup window is not owned, it is centered relative to the screen. To center a window relative to a specific window which is not the owner or parent, the *pAlternateOwner* parameter may be set to a valid window. To force centering relative to the screen, pass the value returned by **CWnd::GetDesktopWindow** as *pAlternateOwner*.
See Also	**CWnd::GetDesktopWindow**, **CDialog::OnInitDialog**

CWnd::ChangeClipboardChain

BOOL ChangeClipboardChain(HWND *hWndNext* **);**

Return Value	Nonzero if successful; otherwise 0.
Parameters	*hWndNext* Identifies the window that follows **CWnd** in the Clipboard-viewer chain.

Remarks   Removes **CWnd** from the chain of Clipboard viewers and makes the window specified by *hWndNext* the descendant of the **CWnd** ancestor in the chain.

See Also   **CWnd::SetClipboardViewer**, **::ChangeClipboardChain**

CWnd::CheckDlgButton

void CheckDlgButton(int *nIDButton***, UINT** *nCheck* **);**

Parameters   *nIDButton*   Specifies the button to be modified.

nCheck   Specifies the action to take. If *nCheck* is nonzero, the **CheckDlgButton** member function places a check mark next to the button; if 0, the check mark is removed. For three-state buttons, if *nCheck* is 2, the button state is indeterminate.

Remarks   Selects (places a check mark next to) or clears (removes a check mark from) a button, or it changes the state of a three-state button. The **CheckDlgButton** function sends a **BM_SETCHECK** message to the specified button.

See Also   **CWnd::IsDlgButtonChecked**, **CButton::SetCheck**, **::CheckDlgButton**

CWnd::CheckRadioButton

void CheckRadioButton(int *nIDFirstButton***, int** *nIDLastButton***,**
       int *nIDCheckButton* **);**

Parameters   *nIDFirstButton*   Specifies the integer identifier of the first radio button in the group.

nIDLastButton   Specifies the integer identifier of the last radio button in the group.

nIDCheckButton   Specifies the integer identifier of the radio button to be checked.

Remarks   Selects (adds a check mark to) a given radio button in a group and clears (removes a check mark from) all other radio buttons in the group. The **CheckRadioButton** function sends a **BM_SETCHECK** message to the specified radio button.

See Also   **CWnd::GetCheckedRadioButton**, **CButton::SetCheck**, **::CheckRadioButton**

CWnd::ChildWindowFromPoint

CWnd* ChildWindowFromPoint(POINT *point* **) const;**

Return Value   Identifies the child window that contains the point. It is **NULL** if the given point lies outside of the client area. If the point is within the client area but is not contained within any child window, **CWnd** is returned.

This member function will return a hidden or disabled child window that contains the specified point. More than one window may contain the given point. However, this function returns only the **CWnd*** of the first window encountered that contains the point. The **CWnd*** that is returned may be temporary and should not be stored for later use.

Parameters   *point*   Specifies the client coordinates of the point to be tested.

Remarks   Determines which, if any, of the child windows belonging to **CWnd** contains the specified point.

See Also   **CWnd::WindowFromPoint, ::ChildWindowFromPoint**

CWnd::ClientToScreen

void ClientToScreen(LPPOINT *lpPoint* **) const;**

void ClientToScreen(LPRECT *lpRect* **) const;**

Parameters   *lpPoint*   Points to a **POINT** structure or **CPoint** object that contains the client coordinates to be converted.

lpRect   Points to a **RECT** structure or **CRect** object that contains the client coordinates to be converted.

Remarks   Converts the client coordinates of a given point or rectangle on the display to screen coordinates. The **ClientToScreen** member function uses the client coordinates in the **POINT** or **RECT** structure or the **CPoint** or **CRect** object pointed to by *lpPoint* or *lpRect* to compute new screen coordinates; it then replaces the coordinates in the structure with the new coordinates. The new screen coordinates are relative to the upper-left corner of the system display. The **ClientToScreen** member function assumes that the given point or rectangle is in client coordinates.

See Also   **CWnd::ScreenToClient, ::ClientToScreen**

CWnd::Create

virtual BOOL Create(LPCTSTR *lpszClassName*, **LPCTSTR** *lpszWindowName*, **DWORD** *dwStyle*, **const RECT&** *rect*, **CWnd*** *pParentWnd*, **UINT** *nID*, **CCreateContext*** *pContext* = **NULL);**

Return Value   Nonzero if successful; otherwise 0.

Parameters   *lpszClassName*   Points to a null-terminated character string that names the Windows class (a **WNDCLASS** structure). The class name can be any name registered with the global **AfxRegisterWndClass** function or any of the predefined control-class names. If **NULL**, uses the default **CWnd** attributes.

lpszWindowName   Points to a null-terminated character string that contains the window name.

dwStyle   Specifies the window style attributes. For a list of window styles, see the section "Window Styles" on page 1253. **WS_POPUP** cannot be used. If you wish to create a popup window, use **CWnd::CreateEx** instead.

rect   The size and position of the window, in client coordinates of *pParentWnd*.

pParentWnd   The parent window.

nID   The ID of the child window.

pContext   The create context of the window.

Remarks   Creates a Windows child window and attaches it to the **CWnd** object. You construct a child window in two steps. First, call the constructor, which constructs the **CWnd** object. Then call **Create**, which creates the Windows child window and attaches it to **CWnd**. **Create** initializes the window's class name and window name and registers values for its style, parent, and ID.

See Also   **CWnd::CWnd, CWnd::CreateEx**

CWnd::CreateCaret

void CreateCaret(CBitmap* *pBitmap* **);**

Parameters   *pBitmap*   Identifies the bitmap that defines the caret shape.

Remarks   Creates a new shape for the system caret and claims ownership of the caret. The bitmap must have previously been created by the **CBitmap::CreateBitmap** member function, the **CreateDIBitmap** Windows function, or the **CBitmap::LoadBitmap** member function. **CreateCaret** automatically destroys the previous caret shape, if any, regardless of which window owns the caret. Once created, the caret is initially hidden. To show the caret, the **ShowCaret** member function must be called.

The system caret is a shared resource. **CWnd** should create a caret only when it has the input focus or is active. It should destroy the caret before it loses the input focus or becomes inactive.

See Also   **CBitmap::CreateBitmap, ::CreateDIBitmap, ::DestroyCaret, CBitmap::LoadBitmap, CWnd::ShowCaret, ::CreateCaret**

CWnd::CreateEx

BOOL CreateEx(DWORD *dwExStyle***, LPCTSTR** *lpszClassName***, LPCTSTR** *lpszWindowName***, DWORD** *dwStyle***, int** *x***, int** *y***, int** *nWidth***, int** *nHeight***, HWND** *hwndParent***, HMENU** *nIDorHMenu***, LPVOID** *lpParam* **= NULL);**

Return Value   Nonzero if successful; otherwise 0.

Parameters   *dwExStyle*   Specifies the extended style of the **CWnd** being created. Apply any of the extended window styles to the window. For a list of window styles, see the section "Window Styles" on page 1253.

lpszClassName   Points to a null-terminated character string that names the Windows class (a **WNDCLASS** structure). The class name can be any name registered with the global **AfxRegisterWndClass** function or any of the predefined control-class names. It must not be **NULL**.

lpszWindowName   Points to a null-terminated character string that contains the window name.

dwStyle   Specifies the window style attributes. See **CWnd::Create** for a description of the possible values.

x   Specifies the initial x-position of the **CWnd** window.

y   Specifies the initial top position of the **CWnd** window.

nWidth   Specifies the width (in device units) of the **CWnd** window.

nHeight   Specifies the height (in device units) of the **CWnd** window.

hwndParent   Identifies the parent or owner window of the **CWnd** window being created. Use **NULL** for top-level windows.

nIDorHMenu   Identifies a menu or a child-window identifier. The meaning depends on the style of the window.

lpParam   Points to the data referenced by the **lpCreateParams** field of the **CREATESTRUCT** structure.

Remarks   Creates an overlapped, pop-up, or child window with the extended style specified in *dwExStyle*. The **CreateEx** parameters specify the **WNDCLASS**, window title, window style, and (optionally) initial position and size of the window. **CreateEx** also specifies the window's parent (if any) and ID. When **CreateEx** executes, Windows sends the **WM_GETMINMAXINFO**, **WM_NCCREATE**, **WM_NCCALCSIZE**, and **WM_CREATE** messages to the window.

To extend the default message handling, derive a class from **CWnd**, add a message map to the new class, and provide member functions for the above messages. Override **OnCreate**, for example, to perform needed initialization for a new class. Override further **On***Message* message handlers to add further functionality to your derived class.

If the **WS_VISIBLE** style is given, Windows sends the window all the messages required to activate and show the window. If the window style specifies a title bar, the window title pointed to by the *lpszWindowName* parameter is displayed in the title bar. The *dwStyle* parameter can be any combination of window styles.

See Also   **::CreateWindowEx**

CWnd::CreateGrayCaret

void CreateGrayCaret(int *nWidth***, int** *nHeight* **);**

Parameters   *nWidth*   Specifies the width of the caret (in logical units). If this parameter is 0, the width is set to the system-defined window-border width.

nHeight   Specifies the height of the caret (in logical units). If this parameter is 0, the height is set to the system-defined window-border height.

Remarks   Creates a gray rectangle for the system caret and claims ownership of the caret. The caret shape can be a line or a block. The parameters *nWidth* and *nHeight* specify the caret's width and height (in logical units); the exact width and height (in pixels) depend on the mapping mode. The system's window-border width or height can be retrieved by the **GetSystemMetrics** Windows function with the **SM_CXBORDER** and **SM_CYBORDER** indexes. Using the window-border width or height ensures that the caret will be visible on a high-resolution display.

The **CreateGrayCaret** member function automatically destroys the previous caret shape, if any, regardless of which window owns the caret. Once created, the caret is initially hidden. To show the caret, the **ShowCaret** member function must be called. The system caret is a shared resource. **CWnd** should create a caret only when it has the input focus or is active. It should destroy the caret before it loses the input focus or becomes inactive.

See Also   **::DestroyCaret, ::GetSystemMetrics, CWnd::ShowCaret, ::CreateCaret**

CWnd::CreateSolidCaret

void CreateSolidCaret(int *nWidth***, int** *nHeight* **);**

Parameters   *nWidth*   Specifies the width of the caret (in logical units). If this parameter is 0, the width is set to the system-defined window-border width.

nHeight   Specifies the height of the caret (in logical units). If this parameter is 0, the height is set to the system-defined window-border height.

Remarks   Creates a solid rectangle for the system caret and claims ownership of the caret. The caret shape can be a line or block. The parameters *nWidth* and *nHeight* specify the caret's width and height (in logical units); the exact width and height (in pixels) depend on the mapping mode. The system's window-border width or height can be retrieved by the **GetSystemMetrics** Windows function with the **SM_CXBORDER** and **SM_CYBORDER** indexes. Using the window-border width or height ensures that the caret will be visible on a high-resolution display.

The **CreateSolidCaret** member function automatically destroys the previous caret shape, if any, regardless of which window owns the caret. Once created, the caret is initially hidden. To show the caret, the **ShowCaret** member function must be called. The system caret is a shared resource. **CWnd** should create a caret only when it has the input focus or is active. It should destroy the caret before it loses the input focus or becomes inactive.

See Also   **::DestroyCaret, ::GetSystemMetrics, CWnd::ShowCaret, ::CreateCaret**

CWnd::CWnd

CWnd( );

Remarks   Constructs a **CWnd** object. The Windows window is not created and attached until the **CreateEx** or **Create** member function is called.

See Also   **CWnd::CreateEx, CWnd::Create**

CWnd::Default

Protected→
LRESULT Default( );
END Protected

Return Value   Depends on the message sent.

Remarks   Calls the default window procedure. The default window procedure provides default processing for any window message that an application does not process. This member function ensures that every message is processed.

See Also   **CWnd::DefWindowProc, ::DefWindowProc**

CWnd::DefWindowProc

Protected→
virtual LRESULT DefWindowProc(UINT *message***, WPARAM** *wParam***,**
    LPARAM *lParam* **);**
END Protected

Return Value   Depends on the message sent.

Parameters   *message*   Specifies the Windows message to be processed.

                     wParam   Specifies additional message-dependent information.

                     lParam   Specifies additional message-dependent information.

Remarks   Calls the default window procedure, which provides default processing for any window message that an application does not process. This member function ensures that every message is processed. It should be called with the same parameters as those received by the window procedure.

See Also   **CWnd::Default**, **::DefWindowProc**

CWnd::DeleteTempMap

static void PASCAL DeleteTempMap( );

Remarks   Called automatically by the idle time handler of the **CWinApp** object. Deletes any temporary **CWnd** objects created by the **FromHandle** member function.

See Also   **CWnd::FromHandle**

CWnd::DestroyWindow

virtual BOOL DestroyWindow( );

Return Value   Nonzero if the window is destroyed; otherwise 0.

Remarks   Destroys the Windows window attached to the **CWnd** object. The **DestroyWindow** member function sends appropriate messages to the window to deactivate it and remove the input focus. It also destroys the window's menu, flushes the application queue, destroys outstanding timers, removes Clipboard ownership, and breaks the Clipboard-viewer chain if **CWnd** is at the top of the viewer chain. It sends **WM_DESTROY** and **WM_NCDESTROY** messages to the window. It does not destroy the **CWnd** object.

If the window is the parent of any windows, these child windows are automatically destroyed when the parent window is destroyed. The **DestroyWindow** member function destroys child windows first and then the window itself. The

DestroyWindow member function also destroys modeless dialog boxes created by **CDialog::Create**.

If the **CWnd** being destroyed is a child window and does not have the **WS_EX_NOPARENTNOTIFY** style set, then the **WM_PARENTNOTIFY** message is sent to the parent.

See Also   **CWnd::OnDestroy**, **CWnd::Detach**, **::DestroyWindow**

CWnd::Detach

HWND Detach( );

Return Value   A **HWND** to the Windows object.

Remarks   Detaches a Windows handle from a **CWnd** object and returns the handle.

See Also   **CWnd::Attach**

CWnd::DlgDirList

int DlgDirList(LPTSTR *lpPathSpec***, int** *nIDListBox***, int** *nIDStaticPath***, UINT** *nFileType* **);**

Return Value   Nonzero if the function is successful; otherwise 0.

Parameters   *lpPathSpec*   Points to a null-terminated string that contains the path or filename. **DlgDirList** modifies this string, which should be long enough to contain the modifications. For more information, see the following "Remarks" section.

nIDListBox   Specifies the identifier of a list box. If *nIDListBox* is 0, **DlgDirList** assumes that no list box exists and does not attempt to fill one.

nIDStaticPath   Specifies the identifier of the static-text control used to display the current drive and directory. If *nIDStaticPath* is 0, **DlgDirList** assumes that no such text control is present.

nFileType   Specifies the attributes of the files to be displayed. It can be any combination of the following values:

- **DDL_READWRITE**   Read-write data files with no additional attributes.
- **DDL_READONLY**   Read-only files.
- **DDL_HIDDEN**   Hidden files.
- **DDL_SYSTEM**   System files.
- **DDL_DIRECTORY**   Directories.
- **DDL_ARCHIVE**   Archives.

- **DDL_POSTMSGS**   **LB_DIR** flag. If the **LB_DIR** flag is set, Windows places the messages generated by **DlgDirList** in the application's queue; otherwise, they are sent directly to the dialog-box procedure.

- **DDL_DRIVES**   Drives. If the **DDL_DRIVES** flag is set, the **DDL_EXCLUSIVE** flag is set automatically. Therefore, to create a directory listing that includes drives and files, you must call **DlgDirList** twice: once with the **DDL_DRIVES** flag set and once with the flags for the rest of the list.

- **DDL_EXCLUSIVE**   Exclusive bit. If the exclusive bit is set, only files of the specified type are listed; otherwise normal files and files of the specified type are listed.

Remarks

Fills a list box with a file or directory listing. **DlgDirList** sends **LB_RESETCONTENT** and **LB_DIR** messages to the list box. It fills the list box specified by *nIDListBox* with the names of all files that match the path given by *lpPathSpec*. The *lpPathSpec* parameter has the following form:

[[*drive*:]] [[[[\u]]*directory*[[\i*directory*]]...\u]] [[*filename*]]

In this example, *drive* is a drive letter, *directory* is a valid directory name, and *filename* is a valid filename that must contain at least one wildcard. The wildcards are a question mark (**?**), which means match any character, and an asterisk (*****), meaning match any number of characters.

If you specify a 0-length string for *lpPathSpec*, or if you specify only a directory name but do not include any file specification, the string will be changed to "*.*". I *lpPathSpec* includes a drive and/or directory name, the current drive and directory are changed to the designated drive and directory before the list box is filled. The text control identified by *nIDStaticPath* is also updated with the new drive and/or directory name. After the list box is filled, *lpPathSpec* is updated by removing the drive and/or directory portion of the path.

See Also

CWnd::DlgDirListComboBox, **::DlgDirList**

CWnd::DlgDirListComboBox

int **DlgDirListComboBox**(LPTSTR *lpPathSpec*, int *nIDComboBox*, int *nIDStaticPath*, UINT *nFileType*);

Return Value

Specifies the outcome of the function. It is nonzero if a listing was made, even an empty listing. A 0 return value implies that the input string did not contain a valid search path.

Parameters

lpPathSpec   Points to a null-terminated string that contains the path or filename. **DlgDirListComboBox** modifies this string, which should be long enough to contain the modifications. For more information, see the following "Remarks" section.

nIDComboBox   Specifies the identifier of a combo box in a dialog box. If *nIDComboBox* is 0, **DlgDirListComboBox** assumes that no combo box exists and does not attempt to fill one.

nIDStaticPath   Specifies the identifier of the static-text control used to display the current drive and directory. If *nIDStaticPath* is 0, **DlgDirListComboBox** assumes that no such text control is present.

nFileType   Specifies DOS file attributes of the files to be displayed. It can be any combination of the following values:

- **DDL_READWRITE**   Read-write data files with no additional attributes.
- **DDL_READONLY**   Read-only files.
- **DDL_HIDDEN**   Hidden files.
- **DDL_SYSTEM**   System files.
- **DDL_DIRECTORY**   Directories.
- **DDL_ARCHIVE**   Archives.
- **DDL_POSTMSGS**   **CB_DIR** flag. If the **CB_DIR** flag is set, Windows places the messages generated by **DlgDirListComboBox** in the application's queue; otherwise, they are sent directly to the dialog-box procedure.
- **DDL_DRIVES**   Drives. If the **DDL_DRIVES** flag is set, the **DDL_EXCLUSIVE** flag is set automatically. Therefore, to create a directory listing that includes drives and files, you must call **DlgDirListComboBox** twice: once with the **DDL_DRIVES** flag set and once with the flags for the rest of the list.
- **DDL_EXCLUSIVE**   Exclusive bit. If the exclusive bit is set, only files of the specified type are listed; otherwise normal files and files of the specified type are listed.

Remarks   Fills the list box of a combo box with a file or directory listing. **DlgDirListComboBox** sends **CB_RESETCONTENT** and **CB_DIR** messages to the combo box. It fills the list box of the combo box specified by *nIDComboBox* with the names of all files that match the path given by *lpPathSpec*. The *lpPathSpec* parameter has the following form:

[[*drive*:]] [[[[\u]]*directory*[[\i*directory*]]...\u]] [[*filename*]]

In this example, *drive* is a drive letter, *directory* is a valid directory name, and *filename* is a valid filename that must contain at least one wildcard. The wildcards are a question mark (**?**), which means match any character, and an asterisk (*****), which means match any number of characters.

If you specify a zero-length string for *lpPathSpec*, or if you specify only a directory name but do not include any file specification, the string will be changed to "*.*". If *lpPathSpec* includes a drive and/or directory name, the current drive and directory are changed to the designated drive and directory before the list box is filled. The text control identified by *nIDStaticPath* is also updated with the new drive and/or directory name. After the combo-box list box is filled, *lpPathSpec* is updated by removing the drive and/or directory portion of the path.

See Also   **CWnd::DlgDirList**, **CWnd::DlgDirSelect**, **::DlgDirListComboBox**

CWnd::DlgDirSelect

BOOL DlgDirSelect(LPTSTR *lpString*, **int** *nIDListBox* **);**

Return Value   Nonzero if successful; otherwise 0.

Parameters   *lpString*   Points to a buffer that is to receive the current selection in the list box.

nIDListBox   Specifies the integer ID of a list box in the dialog box.

Remarks   Retrieves the current selection from a list box. It assumes that the list box has been filled by the **DlgDirList** member function and that the selection is a drive letter, a file, or a directory name. The **DlgDirSelect** member function copies the selection to the buffer given by *lpString*. If there is no selection, *lpString* does not change.

DlgDirSelect sends **LB_GETCURSEL** and **LB_GETTEXT** messages to the list box.

It does not allow more than one filename to be returned from a list box. The list box must not be a multiple-selection list box.

See Also   **CWnd::DlgDirList**, **CWnd::DlgDirListComboBox**, **CWnd::DlgDirSelectComboBox**, **::DlgDirSelect**

CWnd::DlgDirSelectComboBox

BOOL DlgDirSelectComboBox(LPTSTR *lpString*, **int** *nIDComboBox* **);**

Return Value   Nonzero if successful; otherwise 0.

Parameters   *lpString*   Points to a buffer that is to receive the selected path.

nIDComboBox   Specifies the integer ID of the combo box in the dialog box.

Remarks   Retrieves the current selection from the list box of a combo box. It assumes that the list box has been filled by the **DlgDirListComboBox** member function and that the selection is a drive letter, a file, or a directory name. The **DlgDirSelectComboBox**

member function copies the selection to the specified buffer. If there is no selection, the contents of the buffer are not changed.

DlgDirSelectComboBox sends **CB_GETCURSEL** and **CB_GETLBTEXT** messages to the combo box. It does not allow more than one filename to be returned from a combo box.

See Also   **CWnd::DlgDirListComboBox**, **::DlgDirSelectComboBox**

CWnd::DoDataExchange

Protected→
virtual void DoDataExchange(CDataExchange* *pDX* **);**
     END Protected

Parameters   *pDX*   A pointer to a **CDataExchange** object.

Remarks   Called by the framework to exchange and validate dialog data.

Never call this function directly. It is called by the **UpdateData** member function. Call **UpdateData** to initialize a dialog box's controls or retrieve data from a dialog box. When you derive an application-specific dialog class from **CDialog**, you need to override this member function if you wish to utilize the framework's automatic data exchange and validation. ClassWizard will write an overridden version of this member function for you containing the desired "data map" of dialog data exchange (DDX) and validation (DDV) global function calls.

To automatically generate an overridden version of this member function, first create a dialog resource with the dialog editor, then derive an application-specific dialog class. Then call ClassWizard and use it to associate variables, data, and validation ranges with various controls in the new dialog box. ClassWizard then writes the overridden **DoDataExchange**, which contains a data map. The following is an example DDX/DDV code block generated by ClassWizard:

```
void CPenWidthsDlg::DoDataExchange(CDataExchange* pDX)
{
    CDialog::DoDataExchange(pDX);
    //{{AFX_DATA_MAP(CPenWidthsDlg)

        DDX_Text(pDX, IDC_THIN_PEN_WIDTH, m_nThinWidth);

        DDV_MinMaxInt(pDX, m_nThinWidth, 1, 20);

        DDX_Text(pDX, IDC_THICK_PEN_WIDTH, m_nThickWidth);

        DDV_MinMaxInt(pDX, m_nThickWidth, 1, 20);
    //}}AFX_DATA_MAP
}
```

ClassWizard will maintain the code within the \\{{ and \\}} delimiters. You should not modify this code.

The **DoDataExchange** overridden member function must precede the macro statements in your source file.

For more information on dialog data exchange and validation, see Displaying and Manipulating Data in a Form in *Programming with the Microsoft Foundation Class Library*, or see Chapter 12 of the *Visual C++ User's Guide*. For a description of the DDX_ and DDV_ macros generated by ClassWizard, see Technical Note 26.

See Also   **CWnd::UpdateData**

CWnd::DragAcceptFiles

void DragAcceptFiles(BOOL *bAccept* **= TRUE);**

Parameters   *bAccept*   Flag that indicates whether dragged files are accepted.

Remarks   Call this member function from within the main window in your application's **CWinApp::InitInstance** function to indicate that your main window and all child windows accept dropped files from the Windows File Manager.

To discontinue receiving dragged files, call the member function with *bAccept* equal to **FALSE**.

See Also   **::DragAcceptFiles**, **WM_DROPFILES**

CWnd::DrawMenuBar

void DrawMenuBar( );

Remarks   Redraws the menu bar. If a menu bar is changed after Windows has created the window, call this function to draw the changed menu bar.

See Also   **::DrawMenuBar**

CWnd::EnableScrollBar

BOOL EnableScrollBar(int *nSBFlags*, **UINT** *nArrowFlags* **= ESB_ENABLE_BOTH);**

Return Value   Nonzero if the arrows are enabled or disabled as specified. Otherwise it is 0, which indicates that the arrows are already in the requested state or that an error occurred.

Parameters   *nSBFlags*   Specifies the scroll-bar type. Can have one of the following values:

- **SB_BOTH**   Enables or disables the arrows of the horizontal and vertical scroll bars associated with the window.
- **SB_HORZ**   Enables or disables the arrows of the horizontal scroll bar associated with the window.
- **SB_VERT**   Enables or disables the arrows of the vertical scroll bar associated with the window.

nArrowFlags   Specifies whether the scroll-bar arrows are enabled or disabled and which arrows are enabled or disabled. Can have one of the following values:

- **ESB_ENABLE_BOTH**   Enables both arrows of a scroll bar (default).
- **ESB_DISABLE_LTUP**   Disables the left arrow of a horizontal scroll bar or the up arrow of a vertical scroll bar.
- **ESB_DISABLE_RTDN**   Disables the right arrow of a horizontal scroll bar or the down arrow of a vertical scroll bar.
- **ESB_DISABLE_BOTH**   Disables both arrows of a scroll bar.

Remarks   Enables or disables one or both arrows of a scroll bar.

See Also   **CWnd::ShowScrollBar**, **CScrollBar::EnableScrollBar**

CWnd::EnableScrollBarCtrl

void EnableScrollBarCtrl(int *nBar*, **BOOL** *bEnable* = **TRUE);**

Parameters   *nBar*   The scroll-bar identifier.

bEnable   Specifies whether the scroll bar is to be enabled or disabled.

Remarks   Call this member function to enable or disable the scroll bar for this window. If the window has a sibling scroll-bar control, that scroll bar is used; otherwise the window's own scroll bar is used.

See Also   **CWnd::GetScrollBarCtrl**

CWnd::EnableWindow

BOOL EnableWindow(BOOL *bEnable* = **TRUE);**

Return Value Indicates the state before the **EnableWindow** member function was called. The return value is nonzero if the window was previously disabled. The return value is 0 if the window was previously enabled or an error occurred.

Parameters

bEnable   Specifies whether the given window is to be enabled or disabled. If this parameter is **TRUE**, the window will be enabled. If this parameter is **FALSE**, the window will be disabled.

Remarks

Enables or disables mouse and keyboard input. When input is disabled, input such as mouse clicks and keystrokes is ignored. When input is enabled, the window processes all input. If the enabled state is changing, the **WM_ENABLE** message is sent before this function returns. If disabled, all child windows are implicitly disabled, although they are not sent **WM_ENABLE** messages.

A window must be enabled before it can be activated. For example, if an application is displaying a modeless dialog box and has disabled its main window, the main window must be enabled before the dialog box is destroyed. Otherwise, another window will get the input focus and be activated. If a child window is disabled, it is ignored when Windows tries to determine which window should get mouse messages. By default, a window is enabled when it is created. An application can specify the **WS_DISABLED** style in the **Create** or **CreateEx** member function to create a window that is initially disabled. After a window has been created, an application can also use the **EnableWindow** member function to enable or disable the window. An application can use this function to enable or disable a control in a dialog box. A disabled control cannot receive the input focus, nor can a user access it.

See Also

::EnableWindow, **CWnd::OnEnable**

CWnd::EndPaint

void EndPaint(LPPAINTSTRUCT *lpPaint* **);**

Parameters

lpPaint   Points to a **PAINTSTRUCT** structure that contains the painting information retrieved by the **BeginPaint** member function.

Remarks

Marks the end of painting in the given window. The **EndPaint** member function is required for each call to the **BeginPaint** member function, but only after painting is complete. If the caret was hidden by the **BeginPaint** member function, **EndPaint** restores the caret to the screen.

See Also

CWnd::BeginPaint, **::EndPaint**, **CPaintDC**

CWnd::FindWindow

static CWnd* PASCAL FindWindow(LPCTSTR *lpszClassName*,
    LPCTSTR *lpszWindowName* **);**

Return Value

Identifies the window that has the specified class name and window name. It is **NULL** if no such window is found. The **CWnd*** may be temporary and should not be stored for later use.

Parameters   *lpszClassName*   Points to a null-terminated string that specifies the window's class name (a **WNDCLASS** structure). If *lpClassName* is **NULL**, all class names match.

lpszWindowName   Points to a null-terminated string that specifies the window name (the window's title). If *lpWindowName* is **NULL**, all window names match.

Remarks   Returns the top-level **CWnd** whose window class is given by *lpszClassName* and whose window name, or title, is given by *lpszWindowName*. This function does not search child windows.

See Also   **::FindWindow**

CWnd::FlashWindow

BOOL FlashWindow(BOOL *bInvert* **);**

Return Value   Nonzero if the window was active before the call to the **FlashWindow** member function; otherwise 0.

Parameters   *bInvert*   Specifies whether the **CWnd** is to be flashed or returned to its original state. The **CWnd** is flashed from one state to the other if *bInvert* is **TRUE**. If *bInvert* is **FALSE**, the window is returned to its original state (either active or inactive).

Remarks   Flashes the given window once. For successive flashing, create a system timer and repeatedly call **FlashWindow**. Flashing the **CWnd** means changing the appearance of its title bar as if the **CWnd** were changing from inactive to active status, or vice versa. (An inactive title bar changes to an active title bar; an active title bar changes to an inactive title bar.) Typically, a window is flashed to inform the user that it requires attention but that it does not currently have the input focus.

The *bInvert* parameter should be **FALSE** only when the window is getting the input focus and will no longer be flashing; it should be **TRUE** on successive calls while waiting to get the input focus. This function always returns nonzero for minimized windows. If the window is minimized, **FlashWindow** will simply flash the window's icon; *bInvert* is ignored for minimized windows.

See Also   **::FlashWindow**

CWnd::FromHandle

static CWnd* PASCAL FromHandle(HWND *hWnd* **);**

Return Value   Returns a pointer to a **CWnd** object when given a handle to a window. If a **CWnd** object is not attached to the handle, a temporary **CWnd** object is created and attached. The pointer may be temporary and should not be stored for later use.

Parameters	*hWnd* An **HWND** of a Windows window.
See Also	**CWnd::DeleteTempMap**

CWnd::FromHandlePermanent

static CWnd* PASCAL FromHandlePermanent(HWND *hWnd* **);**

Return Value	A pointer to a **CWnd** object.
Parameters	*hWnd* An **HWND** of a Windows window.
Remarks	Returns a pointer to a **CWnd** object when given a handle to a window. If a **CWnd** object is not attached to the handle, **NULL** is returned.
	This function, unlike **FromHandle**, does not create temporary objects.
See Also	**CWnd::FromHandle**

CWnd::GetActiveWindow

static CWnd* PASCAL GetActiveWindow( );

Return Value	The active window or **NULL** if no window was active at the time of the call. The pointer may be temporary and should not be stored for later use.
Remarks	Retrieves a pointer to the active window. The active window is either the window that has the current input focus or the window explicitly made active by the **SetActiveWindow** member function.
See Also	**CWnd::SetActiveWindow**, **::GetActiveWindow**

CWnd::GetCapture

static CWnd* PASCAL GetCapture( );

Return Value	Identifies the window that has the mouse capture. It is **NULL** if no window has the mouse capture. The return value may be temporary and should not be stored for later use.
Remarks	Retrieves the window that has the mouse capture. Only one window has the mouse capture at any given time. A window receives the mouse capture when the **SetCapture** member function is called. This window receives mouse input whether or not the cursor is within its borders.
See Also	**CWnd::SetCapture**, **::GetCapture**

CWnd::GetCaretPos

static CPoint PASCAL GetCaretPos( );

Return Value   **CPoint** object containing the coordinates of the caret's position.

Remarks   Retrieves the client coordinates of the caret's current position and returns them as a **CPoint**. The caret position is given in the client coordinates of the **CWnd** window.

See Also   **::GetCaretPos**

CWnd::GetCheckedRadioButton

int GetCheckedRadioButton(int *nIDFirstButton*, **int** *nIDLastButton* **);**

Return Value   ID of the checked radio button, or 0 if none is selected.

Parameters   *nIDFirstButton*   Specifies the integer identifier of the first radio button in the group.

                nIDLastButton   Specifies the integer identifier of the last radio button in the group.

Remarks   Retrieves the ID of the currently checked radio button in the specified group.

See Also   **CWnd::CheckRadioButton**

CWnd::GetClientRect

void GetClientRect(LPRECT *lpRect* **) const;**

Parameters   *lpRect*   Points to a **RECT** structure or a **CRect** object to receive the client coordinates. The **left** and **top** members will be 0. The **right** and **bottom** members will contain the width and height of the window.

Remarks   Copies the client coordinates of the **CWnd** client area into the structure pointed to by *lpRect*. The client coordinates specify the upper-left and lower-right corners of the client area. Since client coordinates are relative to the upper-left corners of the **CWnd** client area, the coordinates of the upper-left corner are (0,0).

See Also   **CWnd::GetWindowRect, ::GetClientRect**

CWnd::GetClipboardOwner

static CWnd* PASCAL GetClipboardOwner( );

Return Value   Identifies the window that owns the Clipboard if the function is successful. Otherwise, it is **NULL**. The returned pointer may be temporary and should not be stored for later use.

Remarks   Retrieves the current owner of the Clipboard. The Clipboard can still contain data even if it is not currently owned.

See Also   **CWnd::GetClipboardViewer**, **::GetClipboardOwner**

CWnd::GetClipboardViewer

static CWnd* PASCAL GetClipboardViewer( );

Return Value   Identifies the window currently responsible for displaying the Clipboard if successful; otherwise **NULL** (for example, if there is no viewer). The returned pointer may be temporary and should not be stored for later use.

Remarks   Retrieves the first window in the Clipboard-viewer chain.

See Also   **CWnd::GetClipboardOwner**, **::GetClipboardViewer**

CWnd::GetCurrentMessage

Protected→
static const MSG* PASCAL GetCurrentMessage( );
END Protected

Return Value   Returns a pointer to the message the window is currently processing. Should only be called when in an **On***Message* handler.

CWnd::GetDC

CDC* GetDC( );

Return Value   Identifies the device context for the **CWnd** client area if successful; otherwise, the return value is **NULL**. The pointer may be temporary and should not be stored for later use.

Remarks   Retrieves a pointer to a common, class, or private device context for the client area depending on the class style specified for the **CWnd**. For common device contexts, **GetDC** assigns default attributes to the context each time it is retrieved. For class and private contexts, **GetDC** leaves the previously assigned attributes unchanged. The device context can be used in subsequent graphics device interface (GDI) functions to draw in the client area.

Unless the device context belongs to a window class, the **ReleaseDC** member function must be called to release the context after painting. Since only five common device contexts are available at any given time, failure to release a device context can prevent other applications from accessing a device context. A device context belonging to the **CWnd** class is returned by the **GetDC** member function if **CS_CLASSDC**, **CS_OWNDC**, or **CS_PARENTDC** was specified as a style in the **WNDCLASS** structure when the class was registered.

See Also   **CWnd::ReleaseDC, ::GetDC, CClientDC**

CWnd::GetDCEx

CDC* GetDCEx(CRgn* *prgnClip***, DWORD** *flags* **);**

Return Value   The device context for the specified window if the function is successful; otherwise **NULL**.

Parameters   *prgnClip*   Identifies a clipping region that may be combined with the visible region of the client window.

flags   Can have one of the following preset values:

- **DCX_CACHE**   Returns a device context from the cache rather than the **OWNDC** or **CLASSDC** window. Overrides **CS_OWNDC** and **CS_CLASSDC**.

- **DCX_CLIPCHILDREN**   Excludes the visible regions of all child windows below the **CWnd** window.

- **DCX_CLIPSIBLINGS**   Excludes the visible regions of all sibling windows above the **CWnd** window.

- **DCX_EXCLUDERGN**   Excludes the clipping region identified by *prgnClip* from the visible region of the returned device context.

- **DCX_INTERSECTRGN**   Intersects the clipping region identified by *prgnClip* within the visible region of the returned device context.

- **DCX_LOCKWINDOWUPDATE**   Allows drawing even if there is a **LockWindowUpdate** call in effect that would otherwise exclude this window. This value is used for drawing during tracking.

- **DCX_PARENTCLIP**   Uses the visible region of the parent window and ignores the parent window's **WS_CLIPCHILDREN** and **WS_PARENTDC** style bits. This value sets the device context's origin to the upper-left corner of the **CWnd** window.

- **DCX_WINDOW**   Returns a device context that corresponds to the window rectangle rather than the client rectangle.

Remarks   Retrieves the handle of a device context for the **CWnd** window. The device context can be used in subsequent GDI functions to draw in the client area. This function, which is an extension to the **GetDC** function, gives an application more control over how and whether a device context for a window is clipped. Unless the device context belongs to a window class, the **ReleaseDC** function must be called to release the context after drawing. Since only five common device contexts are available at any given time, failure to release a device context can prevent other applications from gaining access to a device context.

In order to obtain a cached device context, an application must specify **DCX_CACHE** If **DCX_CACHE** is not specified and the window is neither **CS_OWNDC** nor **CS_CLASSDC**, this function returns **NULL**. A device context with special characteristics is returned by the **GetDCEx** function if the **CS_CLASSDC, CS_OWNDC,** or **CS_PARENTDC** style was specified in the **WNDCLASS** structure when the class was registered. For more information about these characteristics, see the description of the **WNDCLASS** structure in the *Windows Programmer's Reference, Volume 3.*

See Also   **CWnd::BeginPaint, CWnd::GetDC, CWnd::GetWindowDC, CWnd::ReleaseDC, ::GetDCEx**

CWnd::GetDescendantWindow

CWnd* GetDescendantWindow(int *nID,* **BOOL** *bOnlyPerm* **= FALSE) const;**

Return Value   A pointer to a **CWnd** object, or **NULL** if no child window is found.

Parameters   *nID*   Specifies the identifier of the control or child window to be retrieved.

bOnlyPerm   Specifies whether the window to be returned can be temporary. If **TRUE**, the function can return a temporary window; if **FALSE,** only a permanent window can be returned. For more information on temporary windows see Technical Note 3 under MFC in Books Online.

Remarks   Call this member function to find the descendant window specified by the given ID. This member function searches the entire tree of child windows, not only the windows that are immediate children.

See Also   **CWnd::GetParentFrame, CWnd::IsChild, CWnd::GetDlgItem**

CWnd::GetDesktopWindow

static CWnd* PASCAL GetDesktopWindow( );

Return Value   Identifies the Windows desktop window. This pointer may be temporary and should not be stored for later use.

Remarks   Returns the Windows desktop window. The desktop window covers the entire screen and is the area on top of which all icons and other windows are painted.

See Also   **::GetDesktopWindow**

CWnd::GetDlgCtrlID

int GetDlgCtrlID( ) const;

Return Value   The numeric identifier of the **CWnd** child window if the function is successful; otherwise 0.

Remarks   Returns the window or control ID value for any child window, not only that of a control in a dialog box. Since top-level windows do not have an ID value, the return value of this function is invalid if the **CWnd** is a top-level window.

See Also   **::GetDlgCtrlID**

CWnd::GetDlgItem

CWnd* GetDlgItem(int *nID* **) const;**

Return Value   A pointer to the given control or child window. If no control with the integer ID given by the *nID* parameter exists, the value is **NULL**. The returned pointer may be temporary and should not be stored for later use.

Parameters   *nID*   Specifies the identifier of the control or child window to be retrieved.

Remarks   Retrieves a pointer to the specified control or child window in a dialog box or other window. The pointer returned is usually cast to the type of control identified by *nID*.

See Also   **CWnd::Create, CWnd::GetWindow, CWnd::GetDescendantWindow, CWnd::GetWindow, ::GetDlgItem**

CWnd::GetDlgItemInt

UINT GetDlgItemInt(int *nID***, BOOL*** *lpTrans* **= NULL, BOOL** *bSigned* **= TRUE) const;**

Return Value   Specifies the translated value of the dialog-box item text. Since 0 is a valid return value, *lpTrans* must be used to detect errors. If a signed return value is desired, cast it as an **int** type. The function returns 0 if the translated number is greater than 32,767 (for signed numbers) or 65,535 (for unsigned).

When errors occur, such as encountering nonnumeric characters and exceeding the above maximum, **GetDlgItemInt** copies 0 to the location pointed to by *lpTrans*. If there are no errors, *lpTrans* receives a nonzero value. If *lpTrans* is **NULL**, **GetDlgItemInt** does not warn about errors.

Parameters   *nID*   Specifies the integer identifier of the dialog-box control to be translated.

lpTrans   Points to the Boolean variable that is to receive the translated flag.

bSigned   Specifies whether the value to be retrieved is signed.

Remarks   Retrieves the text of the control identified by *nID*. It translates the text of the specified control in the given dialog box into an integer value by stripping any extra spaces at the beginning of the text and converting decimal digits. It stops the translation when it reaches the end of the text or encounters any nonnumeric character.

If *bSigned* is **TRUE**, **GetDlgItemInt** checks for a minus sign (–) at the beginning of the text and translates the text into a signed number. Otherwise, it creates an unsigned value. It sends a **WM_GETTEXT** message to the control.

See Also   **CWnd::GetDlgItemText**, **::GetDlgItemInt**

CWnd::GetDlgItemText

int GetDlgItemText(int *nID*, **LPTSTR** *lpStr*, **int** *nMaxCount* **) const;**

Return Value   Specifies the actual number of bytes copied to the buffer, not including the terminating null character. The value is 0 if no text is copied.

Parameters   *nID*   Specifies the integer identifier of the control whose title is to be retrieved.

lpStr   Points to the buffer to receive the control's title or text.

nMaxCount   Specifies the maximum length (in bytes) of the string to be copied to *lpStr*. If the string is longer than *nMaxCount*, it is truncated.

Remarks   Retrieves the title or text associated with a control in a dialog box. The **GetDlgItemText** member function copies the text to the location pointed to by *lpStr* and returns a count of the number of bytes it copies.

See Also   **CWnd::GetDlgItem**, **CWnd::GetDlgItemInt**, **::GetDlgItemText**, **WM_GETTEXT**

CWnd::GetExStyle

DWORD GetExStyle( ) const;

Return Value   The window's extended style.

See Also   **CWnd::GetStyle**, **::GetExStyle**, **::GetWindowLong**

CWnd::GetFocus

static CWnd* PASCAL GetFocus( );

Return Value   A pointer to the window that has the current focus, or **NULL** if there is no focus window. The pointer may be temporary and should not be stored for later use.

Remarks   Retrieves a pointer to the **CWnd** that currently has the input focus.

See Also   **CWnd::GetActiveWindow, CWnd::GetCapture, CWnd::SetFocus,**
::GetFocus

CWnd::GetFont

CFont* GetFont( ) const;

Return Value   A pointer to the current font. The pointer may be temporary and should not be
stored for later use.

Remarks   Gets the current font for this window.

See Also   **CWnd::SetFont, WM_GETFONT, CFont**

CWnd::GetForegroundWindow

static CWnd* PASCAL GetForegroundWindow( )

Return Value   A pointer to the foreground window. This may be a temporary **CWnd** object.

Remarks   Returns a pointer to the foreground window (the window with which the user is
currently working). The foreground window applies only to top-level windows
(frame windows or dialogs).

See Also   **CWnd::SetForegroundWindow**

CWnd::GetLastActivePopup

CWnd* GetLastActivePopup( ) const;

Return Value   Identifies the most recently active pop-up window. The return value will be the
window itself if any of the following conditions are met:

- The window itself was most recently active.
- The window does not own any pop-up windows.
- The window is not a top-level window or is owned by another window.

The pointer may be temporary and should not be stored for later use.

Remarks   Determines which pop-up window owned by **CWnd** was most recently active.

See Also   **::GetLastActivePopup**

CWnd::GetMenu

CMenu* GetMenu( ) const;

Return Value   Identifies the menu. The value is **NULL** if **CWnd** has no menu. The return value is undefined if **CWnd** is a child window. The returned pointer may be temporary and should not be stored for later use.

Remarks   Retrieves a pointer to the menu for this window. This function should not be used for child windows because they do not have a menu.

See Also   **::GetMenu**

CWnd::GetNextDlgGroupItem

CWnd* GetNextDlgGroupItem(CWnd* *pWndCtl*, **BOOL** *bPrevious* = **FALSE**) const;

Return Value   Pointer to the previous (or next) control in the group if the member function is successful. The returned pointer may be temporary and should not be stored for later use.

Parameters   *pWndCtl*   Identifies the control to be used as the starting point for the search.

bPrevious   Specifies how the function is to search the group of controls in the dialog box. If **TRUE**, the function searches for the previous control in the group; if **FALSE**, it searches for the next control in the group.

Remarks   Searches for the previous (or next) control within a group of controls in a dialog box. A group of controls begins with a control that was created with the **WS_GROUP** style and ends with the last control that was not created with the **WS_GROUP** style. For more information on windows styles, see the section "Windows Styles" on page 1253. By default, the **GetNextDlgGroupItem** member function returns a pointer to the next control in the group. If *pWndCtl* identifies the first control in the group and *bPrevious* is **TRUE**, **GetNextDlgGroupItem** returns a pointer to the last control in the group.

See Also   **CWnd::GetNextDlgTabItem, ::GetNextDlgGroupItem**

CWnd::GetNextDlgTabItem

CWnd* GetNextDlgTabItem(CWnd* *pWndCtl*, **BOOL** *bPrevious* = **FALSE**) const;

Return Value   Pointer to the previous (or next) control that has the **WS_TABSTOP** style, if the member function is successful. The returned pointer may be temporary and should not be stored for later use.

Parameters   *pWndCtl*   Identifies the control to be used as the starting point for the search.

bPrevious   Specifies how the function is to search the dialog box. If **TRUE**, the function searches for the previous control in the dialog box; if **FALSE**, it searches for the next control.

Remarks   Retrieves a pointer to the first control that was created with the **WS_TABSTOP** style and that precedes (or follows) the specified control.

See Also   **CWnd::GetNextDlgGroupItem**, **::GetNextDlgTabItem**

CWnd::GetNextWindow

CWnd* GetNextWindow(UINT *nFlag* **= GW_HWNDNEXT) const;**

Return Value   Identifies the next (or the previous) window in the window manager's list if the member function is successful. The returned pointer may be temporary and should not be stored for later use.

Parameters   *nFlag*   Specifies whether the function returns a pointer to the next window or the previous window. It can be either **GW_HWNDNEXT**, which returns the window that follows the **CWnd** object on the window manager's list, or **GW_HWNDPREV**, which returns the previous window on the window manager's list.

Remarks   Searches for the next (or previous) window in the window manager's list. The window manager's list contains entries for all top-level windows, their associated child windows, and the child windows of any child windows. If **CWnd** is a top-level window, the function searches for the next (or previous) top-level window; if **CWnd** is a child window, the function searches for the next (or previous) child window.

See Also   **::GetNextWindow**

CWnd::GetOpenClipboardWindow

static CWnd* PASCAL GetOpenClipboardWindow( );

Return Value   The handle of the window that currently has the Clipboard open if the function is successful; otherwise **NULL**.

Remarks   Retrieves the handle of the window that currently has the Clipboard open.

See Also   **CWnd::GetClipboardOwner**, **CWnd::GetClipboardViewer**, **CWnd::OpenClipboard**, **::GetOpenClipboardWindow**

CWnd::GetOwner

CWnd* GetOwner( ) const;

Return Value   A pointer to a **CWnd** object.

Remarks   Retrieves a pointer to the owner of the window. If the window has no owner, then a pointer to the parent window object is returned by default. Note that the relationship between the owner and the owned differs from the parent-child aspect in several important aspects. For example, a window with a parent is confined to its parent window's client area. Owned windows can be drawn at any location on the desktop.

See Also   **CWnd::GetParent**, **CWnd::SetOwner**, **CWnd::IsChild**, **CToolbar**

CWnd::GetParent

CWnd* GetParent( ) const;

Return Value   Identifies the parent window if the member function is successful. Otherwise, the value is **NULL**, which indicates an error or no parent window. The returned pointer may be temporary and should not be stored for later use.

Remarks   Retrieves the parent window (if any).

See Also   **::GetParent**

CWnd::GetParentFrame

CFrameWnd* GetParentFrame( ) const;

Return Value   A pointer to a frame window if successful; otherwise **NULL**.

Remarks   Call this member function to retrieve the parent frame window. The member function searches up the parent chain until a **CFrameWnd** (or derived class) object is found.

See Also   **CWnd::GetDescendantWindow**, **CWnd::GetParent**, **CFrameWnd::GetActiveView**

CWnd::GetSafeHwnd

HWND GetSafeHwnd( ) const;

Return Value   Returns the window handle for a window. Returns **NULL** if the **CWnd** is not attached to a window or if it is used with a **NULL CWnd** pointer.

CWnd::GetScrollBarCtrl

virtual CScrollBar* GetScrollBarCtrl(int *nBar*) const;

Return Value   A sibling scroll-bar control, or **NULL** if none.

Parameters	*nBar* Specifies the type of scroll bar. The parameter can take one of the following values:

- **SB_HORZ** Retrieves the position of the horizontal scroll bar.
- **SB_VERT** Retrieves the position of the vertical scroll bar.

Remarks   Call this member function to obtain a pointer to the specified sibling scroll bar or splitter window. This member function does not operate on scroll bars created when the **WS_HSCROLL** or **WS_VSCROLL** bits are set during the creation of a window. The **CWnd** implementation of this function simply returns **NULL**. Derived classes, such as **CView**, implement the described functionality.

See Also   **CWnd::EnableScrollBarCtrl**

CWnd::GetScrollPos

int GetScrollPos(int *nBar* **) const;**

Return Value   Specifies the current position of the scroll box in the scroll bar if successful; otherwise 0.

Parameters   *nBar* Specifies the scroll bar to examine. The parameter can take one of the following values:

- **SB_HORZ** Retrieves the position of the horizontal scroll bar.
- **SB_VERT** Retrieves the position of the vertical scroll bar.

Remarks   Retrieves the current position of the scroll box of a scroll bar. The current position is a relative value that depends on the current scrolling range. For example, if the scrolling range is 50 to 100 and the scroll box is in the middle of the bar, the current position is 75.

See Also   **::GetScrollPos, CScrollBar::GetScrollPos**

CWnd::GetScrollRange

void GetScrollRange(int *nBar*, **LPINT** *lpMinPos*, **LPINT** *lpMaxPos* **) const;**

Parameters   *nBar* Specifies the scroll bar to examine. The parameter can take one of the following values:

- **SB_HORZ** Retrieves the position of the horizontal scroll bar.
- **SB_VERT** Retrieves the position of the vertical scroll bar.

lpMinPos Points to the integer variable that is to receive the minimum position.

lpMaxPos Points to the integer variable that is to receive the maximum position.

Remarks   Copies the current minimum and maximum scroll-bar positions for the given scroll bar to the locations specified by *lpMinPos* and *lpMaxPos*. If **CWnd** does not have a scrollbar, then the **GetScrollRange** member function copies 0 to *lpMinPos* and *lpMaxPos*. The default range for a standard scroll bar is 0 to 100. The default range for a scroll-bar control is empty (both values are 0).

See Also   **::GetScrollRange**

CWnd::GetStyle

DWORD GetStyle( ) const;

Return Value   The window's style.

See Also   **::GetWindowLong**, **CWnd::CreateEx**

CWnd::GetSuperWndProcAddr

Protected→
virtual WNDPROC* GetSuperWndProcAddr( );
END Protected

Return Value   The address in which to store the default **WndProc** for this class.

Remarks   This function is obsolete. You will not need to override this function because the default implementation in **CWnd** now stores this pointer in all **CWnd** objects.

CWnd::GetSystemMenu

CMenu* GetSystemMenu(BOOL *bRevert*) const;

Return Value   Identifies a copy of the Control menu if *bRevert* is **FALSE**. If *bRevert* is **TRUE**, the return value is undefined. The returned pointer may be temporary and should not be stored for later use.

Parameters   *bRevert*   Specifies the action to be taken. If *bRevert* is **FALSE**, **GetSystemMenu** returns a handle to a copy of the Control menu currently in use. This copy is initially identical to the Control menu but can be modified. If *bRevert* is **TRUE**, **GetSystemMenu** resets the Control menu back to the default state. The previous, possibly modified, Control menu, if any, is destroyed. The return value is undefined in this case.

Remarks   Allows the application to access the Control menu for copying and modification. Any window that does not use **GetSystemMenu** to make its own copy of the Control menu receives the standard Control menu. The pointer returned by the **GetSystemMenu** member function can be used with the **CMenu::AppendMenu**, **CMenu::InsertMenu**, or **CMenu::ModifyMenu** functions to change the Control menu.

The Control menu initially contains items identified with various ID values such as **SC_CLOSE**, **SC_MOVE**, and **SC_SIZE**. Items on the Control menu generate **WM_SYSCOMMAND** messages. All predefined Control-menu items have ID numbers greater than 0xF000. If an application adds items to the Control menu, it should use ID numbers less than F000.

Windows may automatically dim items on the standard Control menu. **CWnd** can carry out its own checking or dimming by responding to the **WM_INITMENU** messages, which are sent before any menu is displayed.

See Also   **CMenu::AppendMenu**, **CMenu::InsertMenu**, **CMenu::ModifyMenu**, **::GetSystemMenu**

CWnd::GetTopWindow

CWnd* GetTopWindow( ) const;

Return Value   Identifies the top-level child window in a **CWnd** linked list of child windows. If no child windows exist, the value is **NULL**. The returned pointer may be temporary and should not be stored for later use.

Remarks   Searches for the top-level child window that belongs to **CWnd**. If **CWnd** has no children, this function returns **NULL**.

See Also   **::GetTopWindow**

CWnd::GetUpdateRect

BOOL GetUpdateRect(LPRECT *lpRect*, **BOOL** *bErase* = **FALSE**);

Return Value   Specifies the status of the update region. The value is nonzero if the update region is not empty; otherwise 0. If the *lpRect* parameter is set to **NULL**, the return value is nonzero if an update region exists; otherwise 0.

Parameters   *lpRect*   Points to a **CRect** object or **RECT** structure that is to receive the client coordinates of the update that encloses the update region.

Set this parameter to **NULL** to determine whether an update region exists within the **CWnd**. If *lpRect* is **NULL**, the **GetUpdateRect** member function returns nonzero if an update region exists and 0 if one does not. This provides a way to determine whether a **WM_PAINT** message resulted from an invalid area. Do not set this parameter to **NULL** in Windows version 3.0 and earlier.

bErase   Specifies whether the background in the update region is to be erased.

Remarks   Retrieves the coordinates of the smallest rectangle that completely encloses the update region. If **CWnd** was created with the **CS_OWNDC** style and the mapping mode is not **MM_TEXT**, the **GetUpdateRect** member function gives the rectangle in logical coordinates. Otherwise, **GetUpdateRect** gives the rectangle in client coordinates. If there is no update region, **GetUpdateRect** sets the rectangle to be empty (sets all coordinates to 0).

The *bErase* parameter specifies whether **GetUpdateRect** should erase the background of the update region. If *bErase* is **TRUE** and the update region is not empty, the background is erased. To erase the background, **GetUpdateRect** sends the **WM_ERASEBKGND** message. The update rectangle retrieved by the **BeginPaint** member function is identical to that retrieved by the **GetUpdateRect** member function. The **BeginPaint** member function automatically validates the update region, so any call to **GetUpdateRect** made immediately after a call to **BeginPaint** retrieves an empty update region.

See Also   **CWnd::BeginPaint, ::GetUpdateRect, CWnd::OnPaint,
CWnd::RedrawWindow**

CWnd::GetUpdateRgn

int GetUpdateRgn(CRgn* *pRgn,* **BOOL** *bErase* **= FALSE);**

Return Value   Specifies a short-integer flag that indicates the type of resulting region. The value can take any one of the following:

- **SIMPLEREGION**   The region has no overlapping borders.
- **COMPLEXREGION**   The region has overlapping borders.
- **NULLREGION**   The region is empty.
- **ERROR**   No region was created.

Parameters   *pRgn*   Identifies the update region.

bErase   Specifies whether the background will be erased and nonclient areas of child windows will be drawn. If the value is **FALSE,** no drawing is done.

Remarks   Retrieves the update region into a region identified by *pRgn*. The coordinates of this region are relative to the upper-left corner (client coordinates). The **BeginPaint** member function automatically validates the update region, so any call to **GetUpdateRgn** made immediately after a call to **BeginPaint** retrieves an empty update region.

See Also   **CWnd::BeginPaint, ::GetUpdateRgn**

CWnd::GetWindow

CWnd* GetWindow(UINT *nCmd*) const;

Return Value

Returns a pointer to the window requested, or **NULL** if none. The returned pointer may be temporary and should not be stored for later use.

Parameters

nCmd   Specifies the relationship between **CWnd** and the returned window. It can take one of the following values:

- **GW_CHILD**   Identifies the **CWnd** first child window.
- **GW_HWNDFIRST**   If **CWnd** is a child window, returns the first sibling window. Otherwise, it returns the first top-level window in the list.
- **GW_HWNDLAST**   If **CWnd** is a child window, returns the last sibling window. Otherwise, it returns the last top-level window in the list.
- **GW_HWNDNEXT**   Returns the next window on the window manager's list.
- **GW_HWNDPREV**   Returns the previous window on the window manager's list.
- **GW_OWNER**   Identifies the **CWnd** owner.

See Also

CWnd::GetParent, **CWnd::GetNextWindow**, **::GetWindow**

CWnd::GetWindowDC

CDC* GetWindowDC( );

Return Value

Identifies the display context for the given window if the function is successful; otherwise **NULL**. The returned pointer may be temporary and should not be stored for later use. **ReleaseDC** should be called once for each successful call to **GetWindowDC**.

Remarks

Retrieves the display context for the entire window, including caption bar, menus, and scroll bars. A window display context permits painting anywhere in **CWnd**, since the origin of the context is the upper-left corner of **CWnd** instead of the client area. Default attributes are assigned to the display context each time it retrieves the context. Previous attributes are lost. **GetWindowDC** is intended to be used for special painting effects within the **CWnd** nonclient area. Painting in nonclient areas of any window is not recommended.

The **GetSystemMetrics** Windows function can be used to retrieve the dimensions of various parts of the nonclient area, such as the caption bar, menu, and scroll bars. After painting is complete, the **ReleaseDC** member function must be called to release the display context. Failure to release the display context will seriously affect painting requested by applications due to limitations on the number of device contexts that can be open at the same time.

See Also   ::GetSystemMetrics, CWnd::ReleaseDC, ::GetWindowDC, CWnd::GetDC, CWindowDC

CWnd::GetWindowPlacement

BOOL GetWindowPlacement(WINDOWPLACEMENT* *lpwndpl* **) const;**

Return Value   Nonzero if the function is successful; otherwise 0.

Parameters   *lpwndpl*   Points to the **WINDOWPLACEMENT** structure that receives the show state and position information.

Remarks   Retrieves the show state and the normal (restored), minimized, and maximized positions of a window. The **flags** member of the **WINDOWPLACEMENT** structure retrieved by this function is always 0. If **CWnd** is maximized, the **showCmd** member of **WINDOWPLACEMENT** is **SW_SHOWMAXIMIZED**. If the window is minimized, it is **SW_SHOWMINIMIZED.** It is **SW_SHOWNORMAL** otherwise.

See Also   CWnd::SetWindowPlacement, ::GetWindowPlacement

CWnd::GetWindowRect

void GetWindowRect(LPRECT *lpRect* **) const;**

Parameters   *lpRect*   Points to a **CRect** object or a **RECT** structure that will receive the screen coordinates of the upper-left and lower-right corners.

Remarks   Copies the dimensions of the bounding rectangle of the **CWnd** object to the structure pointed to by *lpRect*. The dimensions are given in screen coordinates relative to the upper-left corner of the display screen. The dimensions of the caption, border, and scroll bars, if present, are included.

See Also   CWnd::GetClientRect, CWnd::MoveWindow, CWnd::SetWindowPos, ::GetWindowRect

CWnd::GetWindowText

int GetWindowText(LPTSTR *lpszStringBuf***, int** *nMaxCount* **) const;**

void GetWindowText(CString& *rString* **) const;**

Return Value   Specifies the length, in bytes, of the copied string, not including the terminating null character. It is 0 if **CWnd** has no caption or if the caption is empty.

Parameters   *lpszStringBuf*   Points to the buffer that is to receive the copied string of the window's title.

nMaxCount   Specifies the maximum number of characters to be copied to the buffer. If the string is longer than the number of characters specified in *nMaxCount*, it is truncated.

rString   A **CString** object that is to receive the copied string of the window's title.

Remarks   Copies the **CWnd** caption title (if it has one) into the buffer pointed to by *lpszStringBuf* or into the destination string *rString*. If the **CWnd** object is a control, the **GetWindowText** member function copies the text within the control instead of copying the caption. This member function causes the **WM_GETTEXT** message to be sent to the **CWnd** object.

See Also   **CWnd::SetWindowText**, **WM_GETTEXT**, **CWnd::GetWindowTextLength**

CWnd::GetWindowTextLength

int GetWindowTextLength( ) const;

Return Value   Specifies the text length, not including any null-termination character. The value is 0 if no such text exists.

Remarks   Returns the length of the **CWnd** object caption title. If **CWnd** is a control, the **GetWindowTextLength** member function returns the length of the text within the control instead of the caption. This member function causes the **WM_GETTEXTLENGTH** message to be sent to the **CWnd** object.

See Also   **::GetWindowTextLength**, **WM_GETTEXTLENGTH**, **CWnd::GetWindowText**

CWnd::HideCaret

void HideCaret( );

Remarks   Hides the caret by removing it from the display screen. Although the caret is no longer visible, it can be displayed again by using the **ShowCaret** member function. Hiding the caret does not destroy its current shape. Hiding is cumulative. If **HideCaret** has been called five times in a row, the **ShowCaret** member function must be called five times before the caret will be shown.

See Also   **CWnd::ShowCaret**, **::HideCaret**

CWnd::HiliteMenuItem

BOOL HiliteMenuItem(CMenu* *pMenu***, UINT** *nIDHiliteItem***,**
    UINT *nHilite* **);**

Return Value   Specifies whether the menu item was highlighted. Nonzero if the item was highlighted; otherwise 0.

Parameters   *pMenu*   Identifies the top-level menu that contains the item to be highlighted.

nIDHiliteItem   Specifies the menu item to be highlighted, depending on the value of the *nHilite* parameter.

nHilite   Specifies whether the menu item is highlighted or the highlight is removed. It can be a combination of **MF_HILITE** or **MF_UNHILITE** with **MF_BYCOMMAND** or **MF_BYPOSITION**. The values can be combined using the bitwise OR operator. These values have the following meanings:

- **MF_BYCOMMAND**   Interprets *nIDHiliteItem* as the menu-item ID (the default interpretation).
- **MF_BYPOSITION**   Interprets *nIDHiliteItem* as the zero-based offset of the menu item.
- **MF_HILITE**   Highlights the item. If this value is not given, the highlight is removed from the item.
- **MF_UNHILITE**   Removes the highlight from the item.

Remarks   Highlights or removes the highlight from a top-level (menu-bar) menu item. The **MF_HILITE** and **MF_UNHILITE** flags can be used only with this member function; they cannot be used with the **ModifyMenu** member function.

See Also   **CMenu::ModifyMenu, ::HiliteMenuItem**

CWnd::Invalidate

void Invalidate(BOOL *bErase* **= TRUE);**

Parameters   *bErase*   Specifies whether the background within the update region is to be erased.

Remarks   Invalidates the entire client area of **CWnd**. The client area is marked for painting when the next **WM_PAINT** message occurs. The region can also be validated before a **WM_PAINT** message occurs by the **ValidateRect** or **ValidateRgn** member function.

The *bErase* parameter specifies whether the background within the update area is to be erased when the update region is processed. If *bErase* is **TRUE**, the background is erased when the **BeginPaint** member function is called; if *bErase* is **FALSE**, the background remains unchanged. If *bErase* is **TRUE** for any part of the update region, the background in the entire region, not just in the given part, is erased. Windows sends a **WM_PAINT** message whenever the **CWnd** update region is not empty and there are no other messages in the application queue for that window.

See Also   **CWnd::BeginPaint, CWnd::ValidateRect, CWnd::ValidateRgn, ::InvalidateRect**

CWnd::InvalidateRect

void InvalidateRect(LPCRECT *lpRect*, **BOOL** *bErase* = **TRUE**);

Parameters   *lpRect*   Points to a **CRect** object or a **RECT** structure that contains the rectangle (in client coordinates) to be added to the update region. If *lpRect* is **NULL**, the entire client area is added to the region.

   bErase   Specifies whether the background within the update region is to be erased.

Remarks   Invalidates the client area within the given rectangle by adding that rectangle to the **CWnd** update region. The invalidated rectangle, along with all other areas in the update region, is marked for painting when the next **WM_PAINT** message is sent. The invalidated areas accumulate in the update region until the region is processed when the next **WM_PAINT** call occurs, or until the region is validated by the **ValidateRect** or **ValidateRgn** member function.

   The *bErase* parameter specifies whether the background within the update area is to be erased when the update region is processed. If *bErase* is **TRUE**, the background is erased when the **BeginPaint** member function is called; if *bErase* is **FALSE**, the background remains unchanged. If *bErase* is **TRUE** for any part of the update region, the background in the entire region is erased, not just in the given part. Windows sends a **WM_PAINT** message whenever the **CWnd** update region is not empty and there are no other messages in the application queue for that window.

See Also   **CWnd::BeginPaint**, **CWnd::ValidateRect**, **CWnd::ValidateRgn**, **::InvalidateRect**

CWnd::InvalidateRgn

void InvalidateRgn(CRgn* *pRgn*, **BOOL** *bErase* = **TRUE**);

Parameters   *pRgn*   Identifies the region to be added to the update region. The region is assumed to have client coordinates. If this parameter is **NULL**, the entire client area is added to the update region.

   bErase   Specifies whether the background within the update region is to be erased.

Remarks   Invalidates the client area within the given region by adding it to the current update region of **CWnd**. The invalidated region, along with all other areas in the update region, is marked for painting when the **WM_PAINT** message is next sent. The invalidated areas accumulate in the update region until the region is processed when a **WM_PAINT** message is next sent, or until the region is validated by the **ValidateRect** or **ValidateRgn** member function.

   The *bErase* parameter specifies whether the background within the update area is to be erased when the update region is processed. If *bErase* is **TRUE**, the background is erased when the **BeginPaint** member function is called; if *bErase* is **FALSE**, the background remains unchanged. If *bErase* is **TRUE** for any part of the update region, the background in the entire region, not just in the given part, is erased. Windows sends a **WM_PAINT** message whenever the **CWnd** update region is not empty and there are no other messages in the application queue for that window. The given region must have been previously created by one of the region functions.

See Also   **CWnd::BeginPaint, CWnd::ValidateRect, CWnd::ValidateRgn,** **::InvalidateRgn**

CWnd::IsChild

BOOL IsChild(const CWnd* *pWnd* **) const;**

Return Value   Specifies the outcome of the function. The value is nonzero if the window identified by *pWnd* is a child window of **CWnd**; otherwise 0.

Parameters   *pWnd*   Identifies the window to be tested.

Remarks   Indicates whether the window specified by *pWnd* is a child window or other direct descendant of **CWnd**. A child window is the direct descendant of **CWnd** if the **CWnd** object is in the chain of parent windows that leads from the original pop-up window to the child window.

See Also   **::IsChild**

CWnd::IsDlgButtonChecked

UINT IsDlgButtonChecked(int *nIDButton* **) const;**

Return Value   Nonzero if the given control is checked, and 0 if it is not checked. Only radio buttons and check boxes can be checked. For three-state buttons, the return value can be 2 if the button is indeterminate. This member function returns 0 for a pushbutton.

Parameters   *nIDButton*   Specifies the integer identifier of the button control.

Remarks   Determines whether a button control has a check mark next to it. If the button is a three-state control, the member function determines whether it is dimmed, checked, or neither.

See Also   **::IsDlgButtonChecked, CButton::GetCheck**

CWnd::IsIconic

BOOL IsIconic( ) const;

Return Value   Nonzero if **CWnd** is minimized; otherwise 0.

Remarks	Specifies whether **CWnd** is minimized (iconic).
See Also	**::IsIconic**

CWnd::IsWindowEnabled

BOOL IsWindowEnabled( ) const;

Return Value	Nonzero if **CWnd** is enabled; otherwise 0.
Remarks	Specifies whether **CWnd** is enabled for mouse and keyboard input.
See Also	**::IsWindowEnabled**

CWnd::IsWindowVisible

BOOL IsWindowVisible( ) const;

Return Value	Nonzero if **CWnd** is visible (has the **WS_VISIBLE** style bit set, and parent window is visible). Because the return value reflects the state of the **WS_VISIBLE** style bit, the return value may be nonzero even though **CWnd** is totally obscured by other windows.
Remarks	Determines the visibility state of the given window. A window possesses a visibility state indicated by the **WS_VISIBLE** style bit. When this style bit is set with a call to the **ShowWindow** member function, the window is displayed and subsequent drawing to the window is displayed as long as the window has the style bit set. Any drawing to a window that has the **WS_VISIBLE** style will not be displayed if the window is covered by other windows or is clipped by its parent window.
See Also	**CWnd::ShowWindow, ::IsWindowVisible**

CWnd::IsZoomed

BOOL IsZoomed( ) const;

Return Value	Nonzero if **CWnd** is maximized; otherwise 0.
Remarks	Determines whether **CWnd** has been maximized.
See Also	**::IsZoomed**

CWnd::KillTimer

BOOL KillTimer(int *nIDEvent*);

Return Value	Specifies the outcome of the function. The value is nonzero if the event was killed. It is 0 if the **KillTimer** member function could not find the specified timer event.

Parameters   *nIDEvent*   The value of the timer event passed to **SetTimer**.

Remarks   Kills the timer event identified by *nIDEvent* from the earlier call to **SetTimer**. Any pending **WM_TIMER** messages associated with the timer are removed from the message queue.

See Also   **CWnd::SetTimer, ::KillTimer**

CWnd::LockWindowUpdate

BOOL LockWindowUpdate( );

Return Value   Nonzero if the function is successful. It is 0 if a failure occurs or if the **LockWindowUpdate** function has been used to lock another window.

Remarks   Disables or reenables drawing in the given window. A locked window cannot be moved. Only one window can be locked at a time. To unlock a window locked with **LockWindowUpdate**, call **CWnd::UnlockWindowUpdate**.

If an application with a locked window (or any locked child windows) calls the **GetDC**, **GetDCEx**, or **BeginPaint** Windows function, the called function returns a device context whose visible region is empty. This will occur until the application unlocks the window by calling the **LockWindowUpdate** member function.

While window updates are locked, the system keeps track of the bounding rectangle of any drawing operations to device contexts associated with a locked window. When drawing is reenabled, this bounding rectangle is invalidated in the locked window and its child windows to force an eventual **WM_PAINT** message to update the screen. If no drawing has occurred while the window updates were locked, no area is invalidated.

The **LockWindowUpdate** member function does not make the given window invisible and does not clear the **WS_VISIBLE** style bit. For more information about window styles, see the section "Window Styles" on page 1253.

See Also   **CWnd::GetDCEx, ::LockWindowUpdate**

CWnd::MapWindowPoints

void MapWindowPoints(CWnd* *pwndTo***, LPRECT** *lpRect* **) const;**

void MapWindowPoints(CWnd* *pwndTo***, LPPOINT** *lpPoint***, UINT** *nCount* **) const;**

Parameters   *pwndTo*   Identifies the window to which points are converted. If this parameter is **NULL**, the points are converted to screen coordinates.

lpRect   Specifies the rectangle whose points are to be converted.

The first version of this function is available only for Windows 3.1 and later.

lpPoint   A pointer to an array of **POINT** structures that contain the set of points to be converted.

nCount   Specifies the number of **POINT** structures in the array pointed to by *lpPoint*.

Remarks   Converts (maps) a set of points from the coordinate space of the **CWnd** to the coordinate space of another window.

See Also   **CWnd::ClientToScreen**, **CWnd::ScreenToClient**, **::MapWindowPoints**

CWnd::MessageBox

int MessageBox(LPCTSTR *lpszText*, **LPCTSTR** *lpszCaption* **= NULL, UINT** *nType* **= MB_OK);**

Return Value   Specifies the outcome of the function. It is 0 if there is not enough memory to create the message box.

Parameters   *lpszText*   Points to a **CString** object or null-terminated string containing the message to be displayed.

lpszCaption   Points to a **CString** object or null-terminated string to be used for the message-box caption. If *lpszCaption* is **NULL**, the default caption "Error" is used.

nType   Specifies the contents and behavior of the message box.

Remarks   Creates and displays a window that contains an application-supplied message and caption, plus a combination of the predefined icons and pushbuttons described in the Message-Box Styles list. For a list of message-box styles, see the section "Message-Box Styles" on page 1250. Use the global function **AfxMessageBox** instead of this member function to implement a message box in your application.

See Also   **::MessageBox**, **AfxMessageBox**

CWnd::MoveWindow

void MoveWindow(int *x*, **int** *y*, **int** *nWidth*, **int** *nHeight*, **BOOL** *bRepaint* **= TRUE);**

void MoveWindow(LPCRECT *lpRect*, **BOOL** *bRepaint* **= TRUE);**

Parameters   *x*   Specifies the new position of the left side of the **CWnd**.

y   Specifies the new position of the top of the **CWnd**.

nWidth   Specifies the new width of the **CWnd**.

nHeight   Specifies the new height of the **CWnd**.

bRepaint   Specifies whether **CWnd** is to be repainted. If **TRUE**, **CWnd** receives a **WM_PAINT** message in its **OnPaint** message handler as usual. If this parameter is **FALSE**, no repainting of any kind occurs. This applies to the client area, to the nonclient area (including the title and scroll bars), and to any part of the parent window uncovered as a result of **Cwnd**'s move. When this parameter is **FALSE**, the application must explicitly invalidate or redraw any parts of **CWnd** and parent window that must be redrawn.

lpRect   The **CRect** object or **RECT** structure that specifies the new size and position.

Remarks   Changes the position and dimensions. For a top-level **CWnd** object, the *x* and *y* parameters are relative to the upper-left corner of the screen. For a child **CWnd** object, they are relative to the upper-left corner of the parent window's client area. The **MoveWindow** function sends the **WM_GETMINMAXINFO** message. Handling this message gives **CWnd** the opportunity to modify the default values for the largest and smallest possible windows. If the parameters to the **MoveWindow** member function exceed these values, the values can be replaced by the minimum or maximum values in the **WM_GETMINMAXINFO** handler.

See Also   **CWnd::SetWindowPos, WM_GETMINMAXINFO, ::MoveWindow**

CWnd::OnActivate

Parameters   *nState*   Specifies whether the **CWnd** is being activated or deactivated. It can be one of the following values:

- **WA_INACTIVE**   The window is being deactivated.
- **WA_ACTIVE**   The window is being activated through some method other than a mouse click (for example, by use of the keyboard interface to select the window).
- **WA_CLICKACTIVE**   The window is being activated by a mouse click.

pWndOther   Pointer to the **CWnd** being activated or deactivated. The pointer can be **NULL**, and it may be temporary.

bMinimized   Specifies the minimized state of the **CWnd** being activated or deactivated. A value of **TRUE** indicates the window is minimized.

If **TRUE**, the **CWnd** is being activated; otherwise deactivated.

Remarks   Called when a **CWnd** object is being activated or deactivated. First, the main window being deactivated has **OnActivate** called, and then the main window being activated has **OnActivate** called.

If the **CWnd** object is activated with a mouse click, it will also receive an **OnMouseActivate** member function call.

See Also   **WM_MOUSEACTIVATE, WM_NCACTIVATE, WM_ACTIVATE**

CWnd::OnActivateApp

Protected→
afx_msg void OnActivateApp(BOOL *bActive*, **HTASK** *hTask*);
END Protected

Parameters   *bActive*   Specifies whether the **CWnd** is being activated or deactivated. **TRUE** means the **CWnd** is being activated. **FALSE** means the **CWnd** is being deactivated.

hTask   Specifies a task handle. If *bActive* is **TRUE**, the handle identifies the task that owns the **CWnd** being deactivated. If *bActive* is **FALSE**, the handle identifies the task that owns the **CWnd** being activated.

Remarks   Called for all top-level windows of the task being activated and for all top-level windows of the task being deactivated.

See Also   **WM_ACTIVATEAPP**

CWnd::OnAskCbFormatName

Protected→
afx_msg void OnAskCbFormatName(UINT *nMaxCount*, **LPTSTR** *lpszString*);
END Protected

Parameters   *nMaxCount*   Specifies the maximum number of bytes to copy.

lpszString   Points to the buffer where the copy of the format name is to be stored.

Remarks   Called when the Clipboard contains a data handle for the **CF_OWNERDISPLAY** format (that is, when the Clipboard owner will display the Clipboard contents). The Clipboard owner should provide a name for its format. Override this member function and copy the name of the **CF_OWNERDISPLAY** format into the specified buffer, not exceeding the maximum number of bytes specified.

See Also   **WM_ASKCBFORMATNAME**

CWnd::OnCancelMode

Protected→
afx_msg void OnCancelMode( );
ÉND Protected

Remarks   Called to inform **CWnd** to cancel any internal mode. If the **CWnd** object has the focus, its **OnCancelMode** member function is called when a dialog box or message box is displayed. This gives the **CWnd** the opportunity to cancel modes such as mouse capture. The default implementation responds by calling the **ReleaseCapture** Windows function. Override this member function in your derived class to handle other modes.

See Also   **CWnd::Default**, **::ReleaseCapture**, **WM_CANCELMODE**

CWnd::OnChangeCbChain

Protected→
afx_msg void OnChangeCbChain(HWND *hWndRemove*, **HWND** *hWndAfter* **);**
END Protected

Parameters   *hWndRemove*   Specifies the window handle that is being removed from the Clipboard-viewer chain.

hWndAfter   Specifies the window handle that follows the window being removed from the Clipboard-viewer chain.

Remarks   Called for each window in the Clipboard-viewer chain to notify it that a window is being removed from the chain. Each **CWnd** object that receives an **OnChangeCbChain** call should use the **SendMessage** Windows function to send the **WM_CHANGECBCHAIN** message to the next window in the Clipboard-viewer chain (the handle returned by **SetClipboardViewer**). If *hWndRemove* is the next window in the chain, the window specified by *hWndAfter* becomes the next window, and Clipboard messages are passed on to it.

See Also   **CWnd::ChangeClipboardChain**, **::SendMessage**

CWnd::OnChar

Protected→
afx_msg void OnChar(UINT *nChar*, **UINT** *nRepCnt*, **UINT** *nFlags* **);**
END Protected

Parameters   *nChar*   Contains the virtual-key code value of the key.

nRepCnt   Contains the repeat count, the number of times the keystroke is repeated when user holds down the key.

nFlags   Contains the scan code, key-transition code, previous key state, and context code, as shown in the following list:

Value	Description of nFlags
0–7	Scan code (OEM-dependent value).
8	Extended key, such as a function key or a key on the numeric keypad (1 if it is an extended key; otherwise 0).
11–12	Used internally by Windows.
13	Context code (1 if the ALT key is held down while the key is pressed; otherwise 0).
14	Previous key state (1 if the key is down before the call; 0 if the key is up).
15	Transition state (1 if the key is being released; 0 if the key is being pressed).

Remarks   Called when a keystroke translates to a nonsystem character. This function is called before the **OnKeyUp** member function and after the **OnKeyDown** member function are called. **OnChar** contains the value of the keyboard key being pressed or released. Because there is not necessarily a one-to-one correspondence between keys pressed and **OnChar** calls generated, the information in *nFlags* is generally not useful to applications. The information in *nFlags* applies only to the most recent call to the **OnKeyUp** member function or the **OnKeyDown** member function that precedes the call to **OnChar**.

For IBM Enhanced 101- and 102-key keyboards, enhanced keys are the right ALT and the right CTRL keys on the main section of the keyboard; the INS, DEL, HOME, END, PAGE UP, PAGE DOWN, and arrow keys in the clusters to the left of the numeric keypad; and the slash (/) and ENTER keys in the numeric keypad. Some other keyboards may support the extended-key bit in *nFlags*.

See Also   **WM_CHAR**, **WM_KEYDOWN**, **WM_KEYUP**

CWnd::OnCharToItem

Protected→
afx_msg int OnCharToItem(UINT *nChar*, **CListBox*** *pListBox,*
    UINT *nIndex* **);**
END Protected

Return Value   Specifies the action that the application performed in response to the call. A return value of –2 indicates that the application handled all aspects of selecting the item and wants no further action by the list box. A return value of –1 indicates that the list box should perform the default action in response to the keystroke. A return value of 0 or greater specifies the zero-based index of an item in the list box and indicates that the list box should perform the default action for the keystroke on the given item.

Parameters	*nChar* Specifies the value of the key pressed by the user.

pListBox   Specifies a pointer to the list box. It may be temporary.

nIndex   Specifies the current caret position.

Remarks   Called when a list box with the **LBS_WANTKEYBOARDINPUT** style sends its owner a **WM_CHARTOITEM** message in response to a **WM_CHAR** message. For a description of list-box styles, see the section "List-Box Styles" on page 1249.

See Also   **WM_CHAR**, **WM_CHARTOITEM**

CWnd::OnChildActivate

Protected→
afx_msg void OnChildActivate( );
     END Protected

Remarks   If the **CWnd** object is a multiple document interface (MDI) child window, **OnChildActivate** is called when the user clicks the window's title bar or when the window is activated, moved, or sized.

See Also   **CWnd::SetWindowPos**, **WM_CHILDACTIVATE**

CWnd::OnChildNotify

Protected→
virtual BOOL OnChildNotify(UINT *message***, WPARAM** *wParam***, LPARAM** *lParam***, LRESULT*** *pLResult* **);**
     END Protected

Return Value   Nonzero if this window handles the message sent to its parent; otherwise 0.

Parameters   *message*   A Windows message number sent to a parent window.

wParam   The **wparam** associated with the message.

lParam   The **lparam** associated with the message.

pLResult   A pointer to a value to be returned from the parent's window procedure. This pointer will be **NULL** if no return value is expected.

Remarks   Called by this window's parent window when it receives a notification message that applies to this window.

Never call this member function directly.

The default implementation of this member function returns 0, which means that the parent should handle the message. Override this member function to extend the manner in which a control responds to notification messages.

CWnd::OnClose

Protected→
afx_msg void OnClose( );
END Protected

Remarks   Called as a signal that the **CWnd** or an application is to terminate. The default implementation calls **DestroyWindow**.

See Also   **CWnd::DestroyWindow, WM_CLOSE**

CWnd::OnCommand

Protected→
virtual BOOL OnCommand(WPARAM *wParam*, **LPARAM** *lParam*);
END Protected

Return Value   An application returns nonzero if it processes this message; otherwise 0.

Parameters   *wParam*   Identifies the command ID of the menu item or control.

lParam   The low-order word of *lParam* identifies the control that sends the message if the message is from a control. Otherwise, the low-order word is 0. The high-order word of *lParam* specifies the notification message if the message is from a control. If the message is from an accelerator, the high-order word is 1. If the message is from a menu, the high-order word is 0.

Remarks   Called when the user selects an item from a menu, when a child control sends a notification message, or when an accelerator keystroke is translated. **OnCommand** processes the message map for control notification and **ON_COMMAND** entries, and calls the appropriate member function. Override this member function in your derived class to handle the **WM_COMMAND** message. An override will not process the message map unless the base class **OnCommand** is called.

See Also   **WM_COMMAND CCmdTarget::OnCmdMsg**

CWnd::OnCompacting

Protected→
afx_msg void OnCompacting(UINT *nCpuTime*);
END Protected

Parameters   *nCpuTime*   Specifies the ratio of CPU time currently spent by Windows compacting memory to CPU time spent performing other operations. For example, 8000h represents 50 percent of CPU time spent compacting memory.

Remarks   Called for all top-level windows when Windows detects that more than 12.5 percent of system time over a 30- to 60-second interval is being spent compacting memory.

This indicates that system memory is low. When a **CWnd** object receives this call, it should free as much memory as possible, taking into account the current level of activity of the application and the total number of applications running in Windows. The application can call the Windows function to determine how many applications are running.

See Also   **WM_COMPACTING**

CWnd::OnCompareItem

Protected→
afx_msg int OnCompareItem(int *nIDCtl***, LPCOMPAREITEMSTRUCT**
lpCompareItemStruct)
END Protected

Return Value   Indicates the relative position of the two items. It may be any of the following values:

Value	Meaning
–1	Item 1 sorts before item 2.
0	Item 1 and item 2 sort the same.
1	Item 1 sorts after item 2.

Parameters   *nIDCtl*   The identifier of the control that sent the **WM_COMPAREITEM** message.

lpCompareItemStruct   Contains a long pointer to a **COMPAREITEMSTRUCT** data structure that contains the identifiers and application-supplied data for two items in the combo or list box.

Remarks   Specifies the relative position of a new item in a child sorted owner-draw combo or list box. If a combo or list box is created with the **CBS_SORT** or **LBS_SORT** style, Windows sends the combo-box or list-box owner a **WM_COMPAREITEM** message whenever the application adds a new item.

Two items in the combo or list box are reformed in a **COMPAREITEMSTRUCT** structure pointed to by *lpCompareItemStruct*. **OnCompareItem** should return a value that indicates which of the items should appear before the other. Typically, Windows makes this call several times until it determines the exact position for the new item.

If the **hwndItem** member of the **COMPAREITEMSTRUCT** structure belongs to a **CListBox** or **CComboBox** object, then the **CompareItem** virtual function of the appropriate class is called. Override **CComboBox::CompareItem** or

CListBox::CompareItem in your derived CListBox or CComboBox class to do the item comparison.

See Also   COMPAREITEMSTRUCT, WM_COMPAREITEM, CListBox::CompareItem, CComboBox::CompareItem

CWnd::OnCreate

Protected→

afx_msg int OnCreate(LPCREATESTRUCT *lpCreateStruct* **);**

END Protected

Return Value   OnCreate must return 0 to continue the creation of the CWnd object. If the application returns –1, the window will be destroyed.

Parameters   *lpCreateStruct*   Points to a CREATESTRUCT structure that contains information about the CWnd object being created.

Remarks   Called when an application requests that the Windows window be created by calling the Create or CreateEx member function. The CWnd object receives this call after the window is created but before it becomes visible. OnCreate is called before the Create or CreateEx member function returns. Override this member function to perform any needed initialization of a derived class. The CREATESTRUCT structure contains copies of the parameters used to create the window.

See Also   CWnd::CreateEx, CWnd::OnNcCreate, WM_CREATE, CWnd::Default, CWnd::FromHandle

CWnd::OnCtlColor

Protected→

afx_msg HBRUSH OnCtlColor(CDC* *pDC*, **CWnd*** *pWnd*, **UINT** *nCtlColor* **);**

END Protected

Return Value   OnCtlColor must return a handle to the brush that is to be used for painting the control background.

Parameters   *pDC*   Contains a pointer to the display context for the child window. May be temporary.

pWnd   Contains a pointer to the control asking for the color. May be temporary.

nCtlColor   Contains one of the following values, specifying the type of control:

- **CTLCOLOR_BTN**   Button control
- **CTLCOLOR_DLG**   Dialog box
- **CTLCOLOR_EDIT**   Edit control
- **CTLCOLOR_LISTBOX**   List-box control
- **CTLCOLOR_MSGBOX**   Message box
- **CTLCOLOR_SCROLLBAR**   Scroll-bar control
- **CTLCOLOR_STATIC**   Static control

Remarks   Called when a child control is about to be drawn. Most controls send this message to their parent (usually a dialog box) to prepare the *pDC* for drawing the control using the correct colors.

To change the text color, call the **SetTextColor** member function with the desired red, green, and blue (RGB) values. To change the background color of a single-line edit control, set the brush handle in both the **CTLCOLOR_EDIT** and **CTLCOLOR_MSGBOX** message codes, and call the **CDC::SetBkColor** function in response to the **CTLCOLOR_EDIT** code.

OnCtlColor will not be called for the list box of a drop-down combo box because the drop-down list box is actually a child of the combo box and not a child of the window. To change the color of the drop-down list box, create a **CComboBox** with an override of **OnCtlColor** that checks for **CTLCOLOR_LISTBOX** in the *nCtlColor* parameter. In this handler, the **SetBkColor** member function must be used to set the background color for the text.

See Also   **CDC::SetBkColor**

CWnd::OnDeadChar

Protected→
afx_msg void OnDeadChar(UINT *nChar*, **UINT** *nRepCnt*, **UINT** *nFlags* **);**
END Protected

Parameters   *nChar*   Specifies the dead-key character value.

nRepCnt   Specifies the repeat count.

nFlags   Specifies the scan code, key-transition code, previous key state, and context code, as shown in the following list:

Value	Description
0–7	Scan code (OEM-dependent value). Low byte of high-order word.
8	Extended key, such as a function key or a key on the numeric keypad (1 if it is an extended key; otherwise 0).
9–10	Not used.
11–12	Used internally by Windows.
13	Context code (1 if the ALT key is held down while the key is pressed; otherwise 0).
14	Previous key state (1 if the key is down before the call, 0 if the key is up).
15	Transition state (1 if the key is being released, 0 if the key is being pressed).

Remarks
Called when the **OnKeyUp** member function and the **OnKeyDown** member functions are called. This member function can be used to specify the character value of a dead key. A dead key is a key, such as the umlaut (double-dot) character, that is combined with other characters to form a composite character. For example, the umlaut-O character consists of the dead key, umlaut, and the O key.

An application typically uses **OnDeadChar** to give the user feedback about each key pressed. For example, an application can display the accent in the current character position without moving the caret. Since there is not necessarily a one-to-one correspondence between keys pressed and **OnDeadChar** calls, the information in *nFlags* is generally not useful to applications. The information in *nFlags* applies only to the most recent call to the **OnKeyUp** member function or the **OnKeyDown** member function that precedes the **OnDeadChar** call.

For IBM Enhanced 101- and 102-key keyboards, enhanced keys are the right ALT and the right CTRL keys on the main section of the keyboard; the INS, DEL, HOME, END, PAGE UP, PAGE DOWN, and arrow keys in the clusters to the left of the numeric keypad; and the slash (/) and ENTER keys in the numeric keypad. Some other keyboards may support the extended-key bit in *nFlags*.

See Also   **WM_DEADCHAR**

CWnd::OnDeleteItem

Protected→
afx_msg void OnDeleteItem(int *nIDCtl*, **LPDELETEITEMSTRUCT**
   lpDeleteItemStruct);
END Protected

Parameters
nIDCtl   The identifier of the control that sent the **WM_DELETEITEM** message.

lpDeleteItemStruct   Specifies a long pointer to a **DELETEITEMSTRUCT** data structure that contains information about the deleted list box item.

Remarks   Called to inform the owner of an owner-draw list box or combo box that the list box or combo box is destroyed or that items have been removed by **CComboBox::DeleteString**, **CListBox::DeleteString**, **CComboBox::ResetContent**, or **CListBox::ResetContent**.

If the **hwndItem** member of the DELETEITEMSTRUCT structure belongs to a combo box or list box, then the **DeleteItem** virtual function of the appropriate class is called. Override the **DeleteItem** member function of the appropriate control's class to delete item-specific data.

See Also   **CComboBox::DeleteString**, **CListBox::DeleteString**, **CComboBox::ResetContent**, **CListBox::ResetContent**, **WM_DELETEITEM**, **CListBox::DeleteItem**, **CComboBox::DeleteItem**

CWnd::OnDestroy

Protected→
afx_msg void OnDestroy( );
    END Protected

Remarks   Called to inform the **CWnd** object that it is being destroyed. **OnDestroy** is called after the **CWnd** object is removed from the screen. **OnDestroy** is called first for the **CWnd** being destroyed, then for the child windows of **CWnd** as they are destroyed. It can be assumed that all child windows still exist while **OnDestroy** runs. If the **CWnd** object being destroyed is part of the Clipboard-viewer chain (set by calling the **SetClipboardViewer** member function), the **CWnd** must remove itself from the Clipboard-viewer chain by calling the **ChangeClipboardChain** member function before returning from the **OnDestroy** function.

See Also   **CWnd::ChangeClipboardChain**, **CWnd::DestroyWindow**, **CWnd::SetClipboardViewer**

CWnd::OnDestroyClipboard

Protected→
afx_msg void OnDestroyClipboard( );
    END Protected

Remarks   Called for the Clipboard owner when the Clipboard is emptied through a call to the **EmptyClipboard** Windows function.

See Also   **::EmptyClipboard**, **WM_DESTROYCLIPBOARD**

CWnd::OnDevModeChange

Protected→

afx_msg void OnDevModeChange(LPTSTR *lpDeviceName* **);**

END Protected

Parameters   *lpDeviceName*   Points to the device name specified in the Windows initialization file, WIN.INI.

Remarks   Called for all top-level **CWnd** objects when the user changes device-mode settings. Applications that handle the **WM_DEVMODECHANGE** message may reinitialize their device-mode settings. Applications that use the Windows **ExtDeviceMode** function to save and restore device settings typically do not process this function. This function is not called when the user changes the default printer from Control Panel. In this case, the **OnWinIniChange** function is called.

See Also   **WM_DEVMODECHANGE**

CWnd::OnDrawClipboard

Protected→

afx_msg void OnDrawClipboard( );

END Protected

Remarks   Called for each window in the Clipboard-viewer chain when the contents of the Clipboard change. Only applications that have joined the Clipboard-viewer chain by calling the **SetClipboardViewer** member function need to respond to this call. Each window that receives an **OnDrawClipboard** call should call the **SendMessage** Windows function to pass a **WM_DRAWCLIPBOARD** message on to the next window in the Clipboard-viewer chain. The handle of the next window is returned by the **SetClipboardViewer** member function; it may be modified in response to an **OnChangeCbChain** member function call.

See Also   **::SendMessage, CWnd::SetClipboardViewer, WM_CHANGECBCHAIN, WM_DRAWCLIPBOARD**

CWnd::OnDrawItem

Protected→

afx_msg void OnDrawItem(int *nIDCtl,* **LPDRAWITEMSTRUCT** *lpDrawItemStruct* **);**

END Protected

Parameters   *nIDCtl*   Contains the identifier of the control that sent the **WM_DRAWITEM** message. If a menu sent the message, *nIDCtl* contains 0.

lpDrawItemStruct   Specifies a long pointer to a **DRAWITEMSTRUCT** data structure that contains information about the item to be drawn and the type of drawing required.

Remarks   Called for the owner of an owner-draw button control, combo-box control, list-box control, or menu when a visual aspect of the control or menu has changed. The **itemAction** member of the **DRAWITEMSTRUCT** structure defines the drawing operation that is to be performed. The data in this member allows the owner of the control to determine what drawing action is required. Before returning from processing this message, an application should ensure that the device context identified by the **hDC** member of the **DRAWITEMSTRUCT** structure is restored to the default state.

If the **hwndItem** member belongs to a **CButton**, **CMenu**, **CListBox** or **CComboBox** object, then the **DrawItem** virtual function of the appropriate class is called. Override the **DrawItem** member function of the appropriate control's class to draw the item.

See Also   DRAWITEMSTRUCT, WM_DRAWITEM, CButton::DrawItem, CMenu::DrawItem, CListBox::DrawItem, CComboBox::DrawItem

CWnd::OnDropFiles

Protected→
afx_msg void OnDropFiles(HDROP *hDropInfo* **);**
END Protected

Parameters   *hDropInfo*   A pointer to an internal data structure that describes the dropped files. This handle is used by the **DragFinish**, **DragQueryFile**, and **DragQueryPoint** Windows functions to retrieve information about the dropped files.

Remarks   Called when the user releases the left mouse button over a window that has registered itself as the recipient of dropped files. Typically, a derived class will be designed to support dropped files and it will register itself during window construction.

See Also   CWnd::DragAcceptFiles, WM_DROPFILES, ::DragAcceptFiles, ::DragFinish, ::DragQueryFile, ::DragQueryPoint

CWnd::OnEnable

Protected→
afx_msg void OnEnable(BOOL *bEnable* **);**
END Protected

Parameters   *bEnable*   Specifies whether the **CWnd** object has been enabled or disabled. This parameter is **TRUE** if the **CWnd** has been enabled; it is **FALSE** if the **CWnd** has been disabled.

Remarks   Called when an application changes the enabled state of the **CWnd** object. **OnEnable** is called before the **EnableWindow** member function returns, but after the window enabled state (**WS_DISABLED** style bit) has changed.

See Also   **CWnd::EnableWindow**, **WM_ENABLE**

CWnd::OnEndSession

Protected→
afx_msg void OnEndSession(BOOL *bEnding* **);**
END Protected

Parameters   *bEnding*   Specifies whether or not the session is being ended. It is **TRUE** if the session is being ended; otherwise **FALSE**.

Remarks   Called after the **CWnd** object has returned a nonzero value from a **OnQueryEndSession** member function call. The **OnEndSession** call informs the **CWnd** object whether the session is actually ending. If *bEnding* is **TRUE**, Windows can terminate any time after all applications have returned from processing this call. Consequently, have an application perform all tasks required for termination within **OnEndSession**. You do not need to call the **DestroyWindow** member function or **PostQuitMessage** Windows function when the session is ending.

See Also   **CWnd::DestroyWindow**, **CWnd::OnQueryEndSession**, **::ExitWindows**, **::PostQuitMessage**, **WM_QUERYENDSESSION**, **CWnd::Default**, **WM_ENDSESSION**

CWnd::OnEnterIdle

Protected→
afx_msg void OnEnterIdle(UINT *nWhy*, **CWnd*** *pWho* **);**
END Protected

Parameters   *nWhy*   Specifies whether the message is the result of a dialog box or a menu being displayed. This parameter can be one of the following values:

- **MSGF_DIALOGBOX**   The system is idle because a dialog box is being displayed.
- **MSGF_MENU**   The system is idle because a menu is being displayed.

pWho   Specifies a pointer to the dialog box (if *nWhy* is **MSGF_DIALOGBOX**), or the window that contains the displayed menu (if *nWhy* is **MSGF_MENU**). This pointer may be temporary and should not be stored for later use.

Remarks   A call to **OnEnterIdle** informs an application's main window procedure that a modal dialog box or a menu is entering an idle state. A modal dialog box or menu enters an idle state when no messages are waiting in its queue after it has processed one or more previous messages.

See Also   **WM_ENTERIDLE**

CWnd::OnEnterMenuLoop

Protected→
afx_msg void OnEnterMenuLoop(BOOL *bIsTrackPopupMenu* **);**
END Protected

Parameters   *bIsTrackPopupMenu*   Specifies whether the menu involved is a popup menu. Has a nonzero value if the function is successful; otherwise 0.

Remarks   Called when a menu modal loop has been entered.

See Also   **CWnd::OnExitMenuLoop, WM_ENTERMENULOOP**

CWnd::OnEraseBkgnd

Protected→
afx_msg BOOL OnEraseBkgnd(CDC* *pDC* **);**
END Protected

Return Value   Nonzero if it erases the background; otherwise 0.

Parameters   *pDC*   Specifies the device-context object.

Remarks   Called when the **CWnd** object background needs erasing (for example, when resized). It is called to prepare an invalidated region for painting.

The default implementation erases the background using the window class background brush specified by the **hbrBackground** member of the window class structure. If the **hbrBackground** member is **NULL**, your overridden version of **OnEraseBkgnd** should erase the background color. Your version should also align the origin of the intended brush with the **CWnd** coordinates by first calling **UnrealizeObject** for the brush, and then selecting the brush.

An overridden **OnEraseBkgnd** should return nonzero in response to **WM_ERASEBKGND** if it processes the message and erases the background; this indicates that no further erasing is required. If it returns 0, the window will remain marked as needing to be erased. (Typically, this means that the **fErase** member of the **PAINTSTRUCT** structure will be **TRUE**.) Windows assumes the background is computed with the **MM_TEXT** mapping mode. If the device context is using any other mapping mode, the area erased may not be within the visible part of the client area.

See Also   **WM_ICONERASEBKGND**, **CGdiObject::UnrealizeObject**, **WM_ERASEBKGND**

CWnd::OnExitMenuLoop

Protected→
afx_msg void **OnExitMenuLoop**(BOOL *bIsTrackPopupMenu*);
END Protected

Parameters   *bIsTrackPopupMenu*   Specifies whether the menu involved is a popup menu. Has a nonzero value if the function is successful; otherwise 0.

Remarks   Called when a menu modal loop has been exited.

See Also   **CWnd::OnEnterMenuLoop**; **WM_EXITMENULOOP**

CWnd::OnFontChange

Protected→
afx_msg void **OnFontChange**( );
END Protected

Remarks   All top-level windows in the system receive an **OnFontChange** call after the application changes the pool of font resources. An application that adds or removes fonts from the system (for example, through the **AddFontResource** or **RemoveFontResource** Windows function) should send the **WM_FONTCHANGE** message to all top-level windows.

To send this message, use the **SendMessage** Windows function with the *hWnd* parameter set to 0xFFFF.

See Also   **::AddFontResource**, **::RemoveFontResource**, **::SendMessage**, **WM_FONTCHANGE**

CWnd::OnGetDlgCode

Protected→
afx_msg UINT **OnGetDlgCode**( );
END Protected

Return Value   One or more of the following values, indicating which type of input the application processes:

- **DLGC_BUTTON**   Button (generic).
- **DLGC_DEFPUSHBUTTON**   Default pushbutton.
- **DLGC_HASSETSEL**   **EM_SETSEL** messages.
- **DLGC_UNDEFPUSHBUTTON**   No default pushbutton processing. (An application can use this flag with **DLGC_BUTTON** to indicate that it processes button input but relies on the system for default pushbutton processing.)
- **DLGC_RADIOBUTTON**   Radio button.
- **DLGC_STATIC**   Static control.
- **DLGC_WANTALLKEYS**   All keyboard input.
- **DLGC_WANTARROWS**   Arrow keys.
- **DLGC_WANTCHARS**   **WM_CHAR** messages.
- **DLGC_WANTMESSAGE**   All keyboard input. The application passes this message on to the control.
- **DLGC_WANTTAB**   TAB key.

Remarks   Normally, Windows handles all arrow-key and TAB-key input to a **CWnd** control. By overriding **OnGetDlgCode**, a **CWnd** control can choose a particular type of input to process itself. The default **OnGetDlgCode** functions for the predefined control classes return a code appropriate for each class.

See Also   **WM_GETDLGCODE**

CWnd::OnGetMinMaxInfo

Protected→
afx_msg void OnGetMinMaxInfo(MINMAXINFO FAR* *lpMMI* **);**
END Protected

Parameters   *lpMMI*   Points to a **MINMAXINFO** structure that contains information about a window's maximized size and position and its minimum and maximum tracking size. For more about this structure, see the **MINMAXINFO** structure on page 1237.

Remarks   Called whenever Windows needs to know the maximized position or dimensions, or the minimum or maximum tracking size. The maximized size is the size of the window when its borders are fully extended. The maximum tracking size of the window is the largest window size that can be achieved by using the borders to size the window. The minimum tracking size of the window is the smallest window size that can be achieved by using the borders to size the window. Windows fills in an array of points specifying default values for the various positions and dimensions. The application may change these values in **OnGetMinMaxInfo**.

See Also   **WM_GETMINMAXINFO**

CWnd::OnHScroll

Protected→

afx_msg void OnHScroll(UINT *nSBCode*, **UINT** *nPos*, **CScrollBar***
pScrollBar);

END Protected

Parameters   *nSBCode*   Specifies a scroll-bar code that indicates the user's scrolling request.
This parameter can be one of the following:

- **SB_LEFT**   Scroll to far left.
- **SB_ENDSCROLL**   End scroll.
- **SB_LINELEFT**   Scroll left.
- **SB_LINERIGHT**   Scroll right.
- **SB_PAGELEFT**   Scroll one page left.
- **SB_PAGERIGHT**   Scroll one page right.
- **SB_RIGHT**   Scroll to far right.
- **SB_THUMBPOSITION**   Scroll to absolute position. The current position
  is specified by the *nPos* parameter.
- **SB_THUMBTRACK**   Drag scroll box to specified position. The current
  position is specified by the *nPos* parameter.

nPos   Specifies the scroll-box position if the scroll-bar code is
SB_THUMBPOSITION or **SB_THUMBTRACK**; otherwise, not used.
Depending on the initial scroll range, *nPos* may be negative and should be cast
to an **int** if necessary.

pScrollBar   If the scroll message came from a scroll-bar control, contains a
pointer to the control. If the user clicked a window's scroll bar, this parameter is
NULL. The pointer may be temporary and should not be stored for later use.

Remarks   Called when the user clicks a window's horizontal scroll bar. The
SB_THUMBTRACK scroll-bar code typically is used by applications that give
some feedback while the scroll box is being dragged. If an application scrolls the
contents controlled by the scroll bar, it must also reset the position of the scroll box
with the **SetScrollPos** member function.

See Also   **CWnd::SetScrollPos, WM_VSCROLL, WM_HSCROLL**

CWnd::OnHScrollClipboard

Protected→

afx_msg void OnHScrollClipboard(CWnd* *pClipAppWnd*, **UINT** *nSBCode*,
UINT *nPos* **);**

END Protected

Parameters   *pClipAppWnd*   Specifies a pointer to a Clipboard-viewer window. The pointer
may be temporary and should not be stored for later use.

nSBCode   Specifies one of the following scroll-bar codes in the low-order word:

- **SB_BOTTOM**   Scroll to lower right.
- **SB_ENDSCROLL**   End scroll.
- **SB_LINEDOWN**   Scroll one line down.
- **SB_LINEUP**   Scroll one line up.
- **SB_PAGEDOWN**   Scroll one page down.
- **SB_PAGEUP**   Scroll one page up.
- **SB_THUMBPOSITION**   Scroll to the absolute position. The current
position is provided in *nPos*.
- **SB_TOP**   Scroll to upper left.

nPos   Contains the scroll-box position if the scroll-bar code is
SB_THUMBPOSITION; otherwise not used.

Remarks   The Clipboard owner's **OnHScrollClipboard** member function is called by the
Clipboard viewer when the Clipboard data has the **CF_OWNERDISPLAY** format
and there is an event in the Clipboard viewer's horizontal scroll bar. The owner
should scroll the Clipboard image, invalidate the appropriate section, and update the
scroll-bar values.

See Also   **CWnd::OnVScrollClipboard, WM_HSCROLLCLIPBOARD**

CWnd::OnIconEraseBkgnd

Protected→

afx_msg void OnIconEraseBkgnd(CDC* *pDC* **);**

END Protected

Parameters   *pDC*   Specifies the device-context object of the icon. May be temporary and
should not be stored for later use.

Remarks   Called for a minimized (iconic) **CWnd** object when the background of the icon
must be filled before painting the icon. **CWnd** receives this call only if a class icon
is defined for the window default implementation; otherwise **OnEraseBkgnd** is

called. The **DefWindowProc** member function fills the icon background with the background brush of the parent window.

See Also **CWnd::OnEraseBkgnd**, **WM_ICONERASEBKGND**

CWnd::OnInitMenu

Protected→
afx_msg void OnInitMenu(CMenu* *pMenu* **);**
    END Protected

Parameters *pMenu* Specifies the menu to be initialized. May be temporary and should not be stored for later use.

Remarks Called when a menu is about to become active. The call occurs when the user clicks an item on the menu bar or presses a menu key. Override this member function to modify the menu before it is displayed. **OnInitMenu** is only called when a menu is first accessed; **OnInitMenu** is called only once for each access. This means, for example, that moving the mouse across several menu items while holding down the button does not generate new calls. This call does not provide information about menu items.

See Also **CWnd::OnInitMenuPopup**, **WM_INITMENU**

CWnd::OnInitMenuPopup

Protected→
afx_msg void OnInitMenuPopup(CMenu* *pPopupMenu*, **UINT** *nIndex*,
    BOOL *bSysMenu* **);**
    END Protected

Parameters *pPopupMenu* Specifies the menu object of the pop-up menu. May be temporary and should not be stored for later use.

nIndex Specifies the index of the pop-up menu in the main menu.

bSysMenu **TRUE** if the pop-up menu is the Control menu; otherwise **FALSE**.

Remarks Called when a pop-up menu is about to become active. This allows an application to modify the pop-up menu before it is displayed without changing the entire menu.

See Also **CWnd::OnInitMenu**, **WM_INITMENUPOPUP**

CWnd::OnKeyDown

Protected→
afx_msg void OnKeyDown(UINT *nChar*, **UINT** *nRepCnt*, **UINT** *nFlags* **);**
END Protected

Parameters

nChar   Specifies the virtual-key code of the given key.

nRepCnt   Repeat count (the number of times the keystroke is repeated as a result of the user holding down the key).

nFlags   Specifies the scan code, key-transition code, previous key state, and context code, as shown in the following list:

Value	Description
0–7	Scan code (OEM-dependent value).
8	Extended key, such as a function key or a key on the numeric keypad (1 if it is an extended key).
9–10	Not used.
11–12	Used internally by Windows.
13	Context code (1 if the ALT key is held down while the key is pressed; otherwise 0).
14	Previous key state (1 if the key is down before the call, 0 if the key is up).
15	Transition state (1 if the key is being released, 0 if the key is being pressed).

For a **WM_KEYDOWN** message, the key-transition bit (bit 15) is 0 and the context-code bit (bit 13) is 0.

Remarks

Called when a nonsystem key is pressed. A nonsystem key is a keyboard key that is pressed when the ALT key is not pressed or a keyboard key that is pressed when **CWnd** has the input focus. Because of auto-repeat, more than one **OnKeyDown** call may occur before an **OnKeyUp** member function call is made. The bit that indicates the previous key state can be used to determine whether the **OnKeyDown** call is the first down transition or a repeated down transition.

For IBM Enhanced 101- and 102-key keyboards, enhanced keys are the right ALT and the right CTRL keys on the main section of the keyboard; the INS, DEL, HOME, END, PAGE UP, PAGE DOWN, and arrow keys in the clusters to the left of the numeric keypad; and the slash (/) and ENTER keys in the numeric keypad. Some other keyboards may support the extended-key bit in *nFlags*.

See Also

WM_CHAR, **WM_KEYUP**, **WM_KEYDOWN**

CWnd::OnKeyUp

Protected→

afx_msg void OnKeyUp(UINT *nChar*, **UINT** *nRepCnt*, **UINT** *nFlags* **);**

END Protected

Parameters

nChar   Specifies the virtual-key code of the given key.

nRepCnt   Repeat count (the number of times the keystroke is repeated as a result of the user holding down the key).

nFlags   Specifies the scan code, key-transition code, previous key state, and context code, as shown in the following list:

Value	Description
0–7	Scan code (OEM-dependent value). Low byte of high-order word.
8	Extended key, such as a function key or a key on the numeric keypad (1 if it is an extended key; otherwise 0).
9–10	Not used.
11–12	Used internally by Windows.
13	Context code (1 if the ALT key is held down while the key is pressed; otherwise 0).
14	Previous key state (1 if the key is down before the call, 0 if the key is up).
15	Transition state (1 if the key is being released, 0 if the key is being pressed).

For a **WM_KEYUP** message, the key-transition bit (bit 15) is 1 and the context-code bit (bit 13) is 0.

Remarks

Called when a nonsystem key is released. A nonsystem key is a keyboard key that is pressed when the ALT key is not pressed or a keyboard key that is pressed when the **CWnd** has the input focus.

For IBM Enhanced 101- and 102-key keyboards, enhanced keys are the right ALT and the right CTRL keys on the main section of the keyboard; the INS, DEL, HOME, END, PAGE UP, PAGE DOWN, and arrow keys in the clusters to the left of the numeric keypad; and the slash (/) and ENTER keys in the numeric keypad. Some other keyboards may support the extended-key bit in *nFlags*.

See Also

WM_CHAR, WM_KEYUP, CWnd::Default, WM_KEYDOWN

CWnd::OnKillFocus

Protected→

afx_msg void OnKillFocus(CWnd* *pNewWnd* **);**

END Protected

Parameters

pNewWnd   Specifies a pointer to the window that receives the input focus (may be **NULL** or may be temporary).

Remarks

Called immediately before losing the input focus. If the **CWnd** object is displaying a caret, the caret should be destroyed at this point.

See Also

CWnd::SetFocus, **WM_KILLFOCUS**

CWnd::OnLButtonDblClk

Protected→

afx_msg void OnLButtonDblClk(UINT *nFlags*, **CPoint** *point* **);**

END Protected

Parameters

nFlags   Indicates whether various virtual keys are down. This parameter can be any combination of the following values:

- **MK_CONTROL**   Set if the CTRL key is down.
- **MK_LBUTTON**   Set if the left mouse button is down.
- **MK_MBUTTON**   Set if the middle mouse button is down.
- **MK_RBUTTON**   Set if the right mouse button is down.
- **MK_SHIFT**   Set if the SHIFT key is down.

point   Specifies the x- and y-coordinate of the cursor. These coordinates are always relative to the upper-left corner of the window.

Remarks

Called when the user double-clicks the left mouse button. Only windows that have the **CS_DBLCLKS WNDCLASS** style will receive **OnLButtonDblClk** calls. This is the default for Microsoft Foundation class windows. Windows calls **OnLButtonDblClk** when the user presses, releases, and then presses the left mouse button again within the system's double-click time limit. Double-clicking the left mouse button actually generates four events: **WM_LBUTTONDOWN**, **WM_LBUTTONUP** messages, the **WM_LBUTTONDBLCLK** call, and another **WM_LBUTTONUP** message when the button is released.

See Also

CWnd::OnLButtonDown, **CWnd::OnLButtonUp**, **WM_LBUTTONDBLCLK**

CWnd::OnLButtonDown

afx_msg void OnLButtonDown(UINT *nFlags*, **CPoint** *point* **);**

Parameters   *nFlags*   Indicates whether various virtual keys are down. This parameter can be any combination of the following values:

- **MK_CONTROL**   Set if the CTRL key is down.
- **MK_LBUTTON**   Set if the left mouse button is down.
- **MK_MBUTTON**   Sct if thc middlc mousc button is down.
- **MK_RBUTTON**   Set if the right mouse button is down.
- **MK_SHIFT**   Set if the SHIFT key is down.

point   Specifies the x- and y-coordinate of the cursor. These coordinates are always relative to the upper-left corner of the window.

Remarks   Called when the user presses the left mouse button.

See Also   **CWnd::OnLButtonDblClk, CWnd::OnLButtonUp, WM_LBUTTONDOWN**

CWnd::OnLButtonUp

afx_msg void OnLButtonUp(UINT *nFlags*, **CPoint** *point* **);**

Parameters   *nFlags*   Indicates whether various virtual keys are down. This parameter can be any combination of the following values:

- **MK_CONTROL**   Set if the CTRL key is down.
- **MK_MBUTTON**   Set if the middle mouse button is down.
- **MK_RBUTTON**   Set if the right mouse button is down.
- **MK_SHIFT**   Set if the SHIFT key is down.

point   Specifies the x- and y-coordinate of the cursor. These coordinates are always relative to the upper-left corner of the window.

Remarks   Called when the user releases the left mouse button.

See Also   **CWnd::OnLButtonDblClk, CWnd::OnLButtonDown, WM_LBUTTONUP**

CWnd::OnMButtonDblClk

Protected→

afx_msg void OnMButtonDblClk(UINT *nFlags*, **CPoint** *point* **);**

END Protected

Parameters
    nFlags   Indicates whether various virtual keys are down. This parameter can be any combination of the following values:

- **MK_CONTROL** Set if the CTRL key is down.
- **MK_LBUTTON** Set if the left mouse button is down.
- **MK_MBUTTON** Set if the middle mouse button is down.
- **MK_RBUTTON** Set if the right mouse button is down.
- **MK_SHIFT** Set if the SHIFT key is down.

    point   Specifies the x- and y-coordinate of the cursor. These coordinates are always relative to the upper-left corner of the window.

Remarks
    Called when the user double-clicks the middle mouse button. Only windows that have the **CS_DBLCLKS WNDCLASS** style will receive **OnMButtonDblClk** calls. This is the default for all Microsoft Foundation class windows. Windows generates an **OnMButtonDblClk** call when the user presses, releases, and then presses the middle mouse button again within the system's double-click time limit. Double-clicking the middle mouse button actually generates four events: **WM_MBUTTONDOWN** and **WM_MBUTTONUP** messages, the **WM_MBUTTONDBLCLK** call, and another **WM_MBUTTONUP** message.

See Also
    CWnd::OnMButtonDown, **CWnd::OnMButtonUp**, **WM_MBUTTONDBLCLK**

CWnd::OnMButtonDown

Protected→

afx_msg void OnMButtonDown(UINT *nFlags*, **CPoint** *point* **);**

END Protected

Parameters
    nFlags   Indicates whether various virtual keys are down. This parameter can be any combination of the following values:

- **MK_CONTROL** Set if the CTRL key is down.
- **MK_LBUTTON** Set if the left mouse button is down.
- **MK_MBUTTON** Set if the middle mouse button is down.
- **MK_RBUTTON** Set if the right mouse button is down.
- **MK_SHIFT** Set if the SHIFT key is down.

point   Specifies the x- and y-coordinate of the cursor. These coordinates are always relative to the upper-left corner of the window.

Remarks   Called when the user presses the middle mouse button.

See Also   **CWnd::OnMButtonDblClk**, **CWnd::OnMButtonUp**, **WM_MBUTTONDOWN**

CWnd::OnMButtonUp

Protected→
afx_msg void OnMButtonUp(UINT *nFlags***, CPoint** *point* **);**
END Protected

Parameters   *nFlags*   Indicates whether various virtual keys are down. This parameter can be any combination of the following values:

- **MK_CONTROL**   Set if the CTRL key is down.
- **MK_LBUTTON**   Set if the left mouse button is down.
- **MK_RBUTTON**   Set if the right mouse button is down.
- **MK_SHIFT**   Set if the SHIFT key is down.

point   Specifies the x- and y-coordinate of the cursor. These coordinates are always relative to the upper-left corner of the window.

Remarks   Called when the user releases the middle mouse button.

See Also   **CWnd::OnMButtonDblClk**, **CWnd::OnMButtonDown**, **WM_MBUTTONUP**

CWnd::OnMDIActivate

Protected→
afx_msg void OnMDIActivate(BOOL *bActivate***, CWnd*** *pActivateWnd***,
CWnd*** *pDeactivateWnd* **);**
END Protected

Parameters   *bActivate*   **TRUE** if the child is being activated and **FALSE** if it is being deactivated.

pActivateWnd   Contains a pointer to the MDI child window to be activated. When received by an MDI child window, *pActivateWnd* contains a pointer to the child window being activated. This pointer may be temporary and should not be stored for later use.

pDeactivateWnd   Contains a pointer to the MDI child window being deactivated. This pointer may be temporary and should not be stored for later use.

Remarks   Called for the child window being deactivated and the child window being activated. An MDI child window is activated independently of the MDI frame window. When the frame becomes active, the child window that was last activated with a **OnMDIActivate** call receives an **WM_NCACTIVATE** message to draw an active window frame and caption bar, but it does not receive another **OnMDIActivate** call.

See Also   **CMDIFrameWnd::MDIActivate**, **WM_MDIACTIVATE**

CWnd::OnMeasureItem

Protected→
afx_msg void OnMeasureItem(int *nIDCtl,* **LPMEASUREITEMSTRUCT**
   lpMeasureItemStruct **);**
END Protected

Parameters   *nIDCtl*   The ID of the control.

lpMeasureItemStruct   Points to a **MEASUREITEMSTRUCT** data structure that contains the dimensions of the owner-draw control.

Remarks   Called by the framework for the owner of an owner-draw button, combo box, list box, or menu item when the control is created.

Override this member function and fill in the **MEASUREITEMSTRUCT** data structure pointed to by *lpMeasureItemStruct* and return; this informs Windows of the dimensions of the control and allows Windows to process user interaction with the control correctly.

If a list box or combo box is created with the **LBS_OWNERDRAWVARIABLE** or **CBS_OWNERDRAWVARIABLE** style, the framework calls this function for the owner for each item in the control; otherwise this function is called once. Windows initiates the call to **OnMeasureItem** for the owner of combo boxes and list boxes created with the **OWNERDRAWFIXED** style before sending the **WM_INITDIALOG** message. As a result, when the owner receives this call, Windows has not yet determined the height and width of the font used in the control; function calls and calculations that require these values should occur in the main function of the application or library.

If the item being measured is a **CMenu**, **CListBox** or **CComboBox** object, then the **MeasureItem** virtual function of the appropriate class is called. Override the **MeasureItem** member function of the appropriate control's class to calculate and set the size of each item.

See Also   **CMenu::MeasureItem, CListBox::MeasureItem, CComboBox::MeasureItem, WM_MEASUREITEM**

CWnd::OnMenuChar

Protected→
afx_msg LRESULT OnMenuChar(UINT *nChar*, **UINT** *nFlags*,
  CMenu* *pMenu* **);**
END Protected

Return Value   The high-order word of the return value should contain one of the following command codes:

Value	Description
0	Tells Windows to discard the character that the user pressed and creates a short beep on the system speaker.
1	Tells Windows to close the current menu.
2	Informs Windows that the low-order word of the return value contains the item number for a specific item. This item is selected by Windows.

The low-order word is ignored if the high-order word contains 0 or 1. Applications should process this message when accelerator (shortcut) keys are used to select bitmaps placed in a menu.

Parameters   *nChar*   Specifies the ASCII character that the user pressed.

nFlags   Contains the **MF_POPUP** flag if the menu is a pop-up menu. It contains the **MF_SYSMENU** flag if the menu is a Control menu.

pMenu   Contains a pointer to the selected **CMenu**. The pointer may be temporary and should not be stored.

Remarks   Called when the user presses a menu mnemonic character that doesn't match any of the predefined mnemonics in the current menu. It is sent to the **CWnd** that owns the menu. **OnMenuChar** is also called when the user presses ALT and any other key, even if the key does not correspond to a mnemonic character. In this case, *pMenu* points to the menu owned by the **CWnd**, and *nFlags* is 0.

See Also   **WM_MENUCHAR**

CWnd::OnMenuSelect

Protected→
afx_msg void OnMenuSelect(UINT *nItemID*, **UINT** *nFl* **HMENU** *hSysMenu* **);**
END Protected

Parameters   *nItemID*   Identifies the item selected. If the selected item is a menu item, *nItemID* contains the menu-item ID. If the selected item contains a pop-up menu, *nItemID* contains the pop-up menu handle.

nFlags   Contains a combination of the following menu flags:

- **MF_BITMAP**   Item is a bitmap.
- **MF_CHECKED**   Item is checked.
- **MF_DISABLED**   Item is disabled.
- **MF_GRAYED**   Item is dimmed.
- **MF_MOUSESELECT**   Item was selected with a mouse.
- **MF_OWNERDRAW**   Item is an owner-draw item.
- **MF_POPUP**   Item contains a pop-up menu.
- **MF_SEPARATOR**   Item is a menu-item separator.
- **MF_SYSMENU**   Item is contained in the Control menu.

hSysMenu   If *nFlags* contains **MF_SYSMENU**, identifies the menu associated with the message; otherwise unused.

Remarks   If the **CWnd** object is associated with a menu, **OnMenuSelect** is called when the user selects a menu item. If *nFlags* contains 0xFFFF and *hSysMenu* contains 0, Windows has closed the menu because the user pressed the ESC key or clicked outside the menu.

See Also   **WM_MENUSELECT**

CWnd::OnMouseActivate

Protected→
afx_msg int OnMouseActivate(CWnd* *pDesktopWnd,* **UINT** *nHitTest,* **UINT** message **);**
END Protected

Return Value   Specifies whether to activate the **CWnd** and whether to discard the mouse event. It must be one of the following values:

- **MA_ACTIVATE**   Activate **CWnd** object.
- **MA_NOACTIVATE**   Do not activate **CWnd** object.
- **MA_ACTIVATEANDEAT**   Activate **CWnd** object and discard the mouse event.
- **MA_NOACTIVATEANDEAT**   Do not activate **CWnd** object and discard the mouse event.

Parameters   *pDesktopWnd*   Specifies a pointer to the top-level parent window of the window being activated. The pointer may be temporary and should not be stored.

nHitTest   Specifies the hit-test area code. A hit test is a test that determines the location of the cursor.

message   Specifies the mouse message number.

Remarks   Called when the cursor is in an inactive window and the user presses a mouse button. The default implementation passes this message to the parent window before any processing occurs. If the parent window returns **TRUE**, processing is halted.

For a description of the individual hit-test area codes, see the **OnNcHitTest** member function.

See Also   **CWnd::OnNcHitTest, WM_MOUSEACTIVATE**

CWnd::OnMouseMove

Protected→
afx_msg void OnMouseMove(UINT *nFlags***, CPoint** *point* **);**
END Protected

Parameters   *nFlags*   Indicates whether various virtual keys are down. This parameter can be any combination of the following values:

- **MK_CONTROL**   Set if the CTRL key is down.
- **MK_LBUTTON**   Set if the left mouse button is down.
- **MK_MBUTTON**   Set if the middle mouse button is down.
- **MK_RBUTTON**   Set if the right mouse button is down.
- **MK_SHIFT**   Set if the SHIFT key is down.

point   Specifies the x- and y-coordinate of the cursor. These coordinates are always relative to the upper-left corner of the window.

Remarks   Called when the mouse cursor moves. If the mouse is not captured, the **WM_MOUSEMOVE** message is received by the **CWnd** object beneath the mouse cursor; otherwise, the message goes to the window that has captured the mouse.

See Also   **CWnd::SetCapture, CWnd::OnNCHitTest, WM_MOUSEMOVE**

CWnd::OnMove

Protected→
afx_msg void OnMove(int *x***, int** *y* **);**
END Protected

Parameters	*x*	Specifies the new x-coordinate location of the upper-left corner of the client area. This new location is given in screen coordinates for overlapped and pop-up windows, and parent-client coordinates for child windows.

y   Specifies the new y-coordinate location of the upper-left corner of the client area. This new location is given in screen coordinates for overlapped and pop-up windows, and parent-client coordinates for child windows.

Remarks   Called after the **CWnd** object has been moved.

See Also   **WM_MOVE**

CWnd::OnNcActivate

Protected→
afx_msg BOOL OnNcActivate(BOOL *bActive* **);**
END Protected

Return Value   Nonzero if Windows should proceed with default processing; 0 to prevent the caption bar or icon from being deactivated.

Parameters   *bActive*   Specifies when a caption bar or icon needs to be changed to indicate an active or inactive state. The *bActive* parameter is **TRUE** if an active caption or icon is to be drawn. It is **FALSE** for an inactive caption or icon.

Remarks   Called when the nonclient area needs to be changed to indicate an active or inactive state. The default implementation draws the title bar and title-bar text in their active colors if *bActive* is **TRUE** and in their inactive colors if *bActive* is **FALSE**.

See Also   **CWnd::Default**, **WM_NCACTIVATE**

CWnd::OnNcCalcSize

Protected→
afx_msg void OnNcCalcSize(BOOL *bCalcValidRects*,
    NCCALCSIZE_PARAMS* *lpncsp* **);**
END Protected

Parameters   *bCalcValidRects*   Specifies whether the application should specify which part of the client area contains valid information. Windows will copy the valid information to the specified area within the new client area. If this parameter is **TRUE**, the application should specify which part of the client area is valid.

lpncsp   Points to a **NCCALCSIZE_PARAMS** data structure that contains information an application can use to calculate the new size and position of the **CWnd** rectangle (including client area, borders, caption, scroll bars, and so on).

Remarks   Called when the size and position of the client area needs to be calculated. By processing this message, an application can control the contents of the window's client area when the size or position of the window changes.

Regardless of the value of *bCalcValidRects*, the first rectangle in the array specified by the **rgrc** structure member of the NCCALCSIZE_PARAMS structure contains the coordinates of the window. For a child window, the coordinates are relative to the parent window's client area. For top-level windows, the coordinates are screen coordinates. An application should modify the **rgrc[0]** rectangle to reflect the size and position of the client area. The **rgrc[1]** and **rgrc[2]** rectangles are valid only if *bCalcValidRects* is **TRUE**. In this case, the **rgrc[1]** rectangle contains the coordinates of the window before it was moved or resized. The **rgrc[2]** rectangle contains the coordinates of the window's client area before the window was moved. All coordinates are relative to the parent window or screen.

The default implementation calculates the size of the client area based on the window characteristics (presence of scroll bars, menu, and so on), and places the result in *lpncsp*.

See Also   **WM_NCCALCSIZE, CWnd::MoveWindow, CWnd::SetWindowPos**

CWnd::OnNcCreate

Protected→
afx_msg BOOL OnNcCreate(LPCREATESTRUCT *lpCreateStruct* **);**
      END Protected

Return Value   Nonzero if the nonclient area is created. It is 0 if an error occurs; the **Create** function will return **failure** in this case.

Parameters   *lpCreateStruct*   Points to the **CREATESTRUCT** data structure for **CWnd**.

Remarks   Called prior to the **WM_CREATE** message when the **CWnd** object is first created.

See Also   **CWnd::CreateEx, WM_NCCREATE**

CWnd::OnNcDestroy

Protected→
afx_msg void OnNcDestroy( );
      END Protected

Remarks   Called by the framework when the nonclient area is being destroyed, and is the last member function called when the Windows window is destroyed. The default implementation performs some cleanup, then calls the virtual member function **PostNcDestroy**. Override **PostNcDestroy** if you want to perform your own cleanup, such as a **delete this** operation. If you override **OnNcDestroy**, you must call **OnNcDestroy** in your base class to ensure that any memory internally allocated for the window is freed.

See Also   **CWnd::DestroyWindow**, **CWnd::OnNcCreate**, **WM_NCDESTROY**, **CWnd::Default**, **CWnd::PostNcDestroy**

CWnd::OnNcHitTest

Protected→
afx_msg UINT OnNcHitTest(CPoint *point* **);**
END Protected

Return Value   One of the mouse hit-test enumerated values listed below.

Parameters   *point*   Contains the x- and y-coordinates of the cursor. These coordinates are always screen coordinates.

Remarks   Called for the **CWnd** object that contains the cursor (or the **CWnd** object that used the **SetCapture** member function to capture the mouse input) every time the mouse is moved.

See Also   **CWnd::GetCapture**, **WM_NCHITTEST**

**Mouse
Enumerated
Values**

- **HTBORDER**   In the border of a window that does not have a sizing border.
- **HTBOTTOM**   In the lower horizontal border of the window.
- **HTBOTTOMLEFT**   In the lower-left corner of the window border.
- **HTBOTTOMRIGHT**   In the lower-right corner of the window border.
- **HTCAPTION**   In a title-bar area.
- **HTCLIENT**   In a client area.
- **HTERROR**   On the screen background or on a dividing line between windows (same as **HTNOWHERE** except that the **DefWndProc** Windows function produces a system beep to indicate an error).
- **HTGROWBOX**   In a size box.
- **HTHSCROLL**   In the horizontal scroll bar.
- **HTLEFT**   In the left border of the window.
- **HTMAXBUTTON**   In a Maximize button.
- **HTMENU**   In a menu area.
- **HTMINBUTTON**   In a Minimize button.
- **HTNOWHERE**   On the screen background or on a dividing line between windows.
- **HTREDUCE**   In a Minimize button.
- **HTRIGHT**   In the right border of the window.

- **HTSIZE**   In a size box (same as **HTGROWBOX**).
- **HTSYSMENU**   In a Control menu or in a Close button in a child window.
- **HTTOP**   In the upper horizontal border of the window.
- **HTTOPLEFT**   In the upper-left corner of the window border.
- **HTTOPRIGHT**   In the upper-right corner of the window border.
- **HTTRANSPARENT**   In a window currently covered by another window.
- **HTVSCROLL**   In the vertical scroll bar.
- **HTZOOM**   In a Maximize button.

CWnd::OnNcLButtonDblClk

Protected→
afx_msg void OnNcLButtonDblClk(UINT *nHitTest*, **CPoint** *point* **);**
END Protected

Parameters   *nHitTest*   Specifies the hit-test code. A hit test is a test that determines the location of the cursor.

point   Specifies a **CPoint** object that contains the x and y screen coordinates of the cursor position. These coordinates are always relative to the upper-left corner of the screen.

Remarks   Called when the user double-clicks the left mouse button while the cursor is within a nonclient area of **CWnd**. If appropriate, the **WM_SYSCOMMAND** message is sent.

See Also   **WM_NCLBUTTONDBLCLK, CWnd::OnNcHitTest**

CWnd::OnNcLButtonDown

Protected→
afx_msg void OnNcLButtonDown(UINT *nHitTest*, **CPoint** *point* **);**
END Protected

Parameters   *nHitTest*   Specifies the hit-test code. A hit test is a test that determines the location of the cursor.

point   Specifies a **CPoint** object that contains the x and y screen coordinates of the cursor position. These coordinates are always relative to the upper-left corner of the screen.

Remarks   Called when the user presses the left mouse button while the cursor is within a nonclient area of the **CWnd** object. If appropriate, the **WM_SYSCOMMAND** is sent.

See Also CWnd::OnNcHitTest, CWnd::OnNcLButtonDblClk,
CWnd::OnNcLButtonUp, CWnd::OnSysCommand,
WM_NCLBUTTONDOWN, CWnd::Default

CWnd::OnNcLButtonUp

Protected→
afx_msg void OnNcLButtonUp(UINT *nHitTest*, **CPoint** *point* **);**
END Protected

Parameters *nHitTest* Specifies the hit-test code. A hit test is a test that determines the location of the cursor.

point Specifies a **CPoint** object that contains the x and y screen coordinates of the cursor position. These coordinates are always relative to the upper-left corner of the screen.

Remarks Called when the user releases the left mouse button while the cursor is within a nonclient area. If appropriate, **WM_SYSCOMMAND** is sent.

See Also CWnd::OnNcHitTest, CWnd::OnNcLButtonDown,
CWnd::OnSysCommand, WM_NCLBUTTONUP

CWnd::OnNcMButtonDblClk

Protected→
afx_msg void OnNcMButtonDblClk(UINT *nHitTest*, **CPoint** *point* **);**
END Protected

Parameters *nHitTest* Specifies the hit-test code. A hit test is a test that determines the location of the cursor.

point Specifies a **CPoint** object that contains the x and y screen coordinates of the cursor position. These coordinates are always relative to the upper-left corner of the screen.

Remarks Called when the user double-clicks the middle mouse button while the cursor is within a nonclient area.

See Also CWnd::OnNcHitTest, CWnd::OnNcMButtonDown,
CWnd::OnNcMButtonUp, WM_NCMBUTTONDBLCLK

CWnd::OnNcMButtonDown

Protected→
afx_msg void OnNcMButtonDown(UINT *nHitTest***, CPoint** *point* **);**
END Protected

Parameters   *nHitTest*   Specifies the hit-test code. A hit test is a test that determines the location of the cursor.

point   Specifies a **CPoint** object that contains the x and y screen coordinates of the cursor position. These coordinates are always relative to the upper-left corner of the screen.

Remarks   Called when the user presses the middle mouse button while the cursor is within a nonclient area.

See Also   **CWnd::OnNcHitTest, CWnd::OnNcMButtonDblClk, CWnd::OnNcMButtonUp, WM_NCMBUTTONDOWN**

CWnd::OnNcMButtonUp

Protected→
afx_msg void OnNcMButtonUp(UINT *nHitTest***, CPoint** *point* **);**
END Protected

Parameters   *nHitTest*   Specifies the hit-test code. A hit test is a test that determines the location of the cursor.

point   Specifies a **CPoint** object that contains the x and y screen coordinates of the cursor position. These coordinates are always relative to the upper-left corner of the screen.

Remarks   Called when the user releases the middle mouse button while the cursor is within a nonclient area.

See Also   **CWnd::OnNcHitTest, CWnd::OnNcMButtonDblClk, CWnd::OnNcMButtonDown, WM_NCMBUTTONUP**

CWnd::OnNcMouseMove

Protected→
afx_msg void OnNcMouseMove(UINT *nHitTest***, CPoint** *point* **);**
END Protected

Parameters   *nHitTest*   Specifies the hit-test code. A hit test is a test that determines the location of the cursor.

point   Specifies a **CPoint** object that contains the x and y screen coordinates of the cursor position. These coordinates are always relative to the upper-left corner of the screen.

Remarks   Called when the cursor is moved within a nonclient area. If appropriate, the **WM_SYSCOMMAND** message is sent.

See Also   **CWnd::OnNcHitTest**, **CWnd::OnSysCommand**, **WM_NCMOUSEMOVE**

CWnd::OnNcPaint

Protected→
afx_msg void OnNcPaint( );
END Protected

Remarks   Called when the nonclient area needs to be painted. The default implementation paints the window frame. An application can override this call and paint its own custom window frame. The clipping region is always rectangular, even if the shape of the frame is altered.

See Also   **WM_NCPAINT**

CWnd::OnNcRButtonDblClk

Protected→
afx_msg void OnNcRButtonDblClk(UINT *nHitTest*, CPoint *point*);
END Protected

Parameters   *nHitTest*   Specifies the hit-test code. A hit test is a test that determines the location of the cursor.

point   Specifies a **CPoint** object that contains the x and y screen coordinates of the cursor position. These coordinates are always relative to the upper-left corner of the screen.

Remarks   Called when the user double-clicks the right mouse button while the cursor is within a nonclient area of **CWnd**.

See Also   **CWnd::OnNcHitTest**, **CWnd::OnNcRButtonDown**, **CWnd::OnNcRButtonUp**, **WM_NCRBUTTONDBLCLK**

CWnd::OnNcRButtonDown

Protected→
afx_msg void OnNcRButtonDown(UINT *nHitTest***, CPoint** *point* **);**
END Protected

Parameters   *nHitTest*   Specifies the hit-test code. A hit test is a test that determines the location of the cursor.

point   Specifies a **CPoint** object that contains the x and y screen coordinates of the cursor position. These coordinates are always relative to the upper-left corner of the screen.

Remarks   Called when the user presses the right mouse button while the cursor is within a nonclient area.

See Also   **CWnd::OnNcHitTest, CWnd::OnNcRButtonDblClk, CWnd::OnNcRButtonUp,**

CWnd::OnNcRButtonUp

Protected→
afx_msg void OnNcRButtonUp(UINT *nHitTest***, CPoint** *point* **);**
END Protected

Parameters   *nHitTest*   Specifies the hit-test code. A hit test is a test that determines the location of the cursor.

point   Specifies a **CPoint** object that contains the x and y screen coordinates of the cursor position. These coordinates are always relative to the upper-left corner of the screen.

Remarks   Called when the user releases the right mouse button while the cursor is within a nonclient area.

See Also   **CWnd::OnNcHitTest, CWnd::OnNcRButtonDblClk, CWnd::OnNcRButtonDown, WM_NCRBUTTONUP**

CWnd::OnPaint

Protected→
afx_msg void OnPaint( );
END Protected

Remarks   Called when Windows or an application makes a request to repaint a portion of an application's window. The **WM_PAINT** message is sent when the **UpdateWindow** or **RedrawWindow** member function is called.

A window may receive internal paint messages as a result of calling the **RedrawWindow** member function with the **RDW_INTERNALPAINT** flag set. In this case, the window may not have an update region. An application should call the **GetUpdateRect** member function to determine whether the window has an update region. If **GetUpdateRect** returns 0, the application should not call the **BeginPaint** and **EndPaint** member functions.

It is an application's responsibility to check for any necessary internal repainting or updating by looking at its internal data structures for each **WM_PAINT** message because a **WM_PAINT** message may have been caused by both an invalid area and a call to the **RedrawWindow** member function with the **RDW_INTERNALPAINT** flag set. An internal **WM_PAINT** message is sent only once by Windows. After an internal **WM_PAINT** message is sent to a window by the **UpdateWindow** member function, no further **WM_PAINT** messages will be sent or posted until the window is invalidated or until the **RedrawWindow** member function is called again with the **RDW_INTERNALPAINT** flag set.

See Also   **CWnd::BeginPaint**, **CWnd::EndPaint**, **CWnd::RedrawWindow**, **CPaintDC**

CWnd::OnPaintClipboard

Protected→
afx_msg void OnPaintClipboard(CWnd* *pClipAppWnd*,
    HGLOBAL *hPaintStruct* **);**
END Protected

Parameters   *pClipAppWnd*   Specifies a pointer to the Clipboard-application window. The pointer may be temporary and should not be stored for later use.

hPaintStruct   Identifies a **PAINTSTRUCT** data structure that defines what part of the client area to paint.

Remarks   A Clipboard owner's **OnPaintClipboard** member function is called by a Clipboard viewer when the Clipboard owner has placed data on the Clipboard in the **CF_OWNERDISPLAY** format and the Clipboard viewer's client area needs repainting. To determine whether the entire client area or just a portion of it needs repainting, the Clipboard owner must compare the dimensions of the drawing area given in the **rcpaint** member of the **PAINTSTRUCT** structure to the dimensions given in the most recent **OnSizeClipboard** member function call.

OnPaintClipboard should use the **GlobalLock** Windows function to lock the memory that contains the **PAINTSTRUCT** data structure and unlock that memory with the **GlobalUnlock** Windows function before it exits.

See Also   **::GlobalLock ::GlobalUnlock CWnd::OnSizeClipboard**,
WM_PAINTCLIPBOARD

CWnd::OnPaletteChanged

Protected→
afx_msg void OnPaletteChanged(CWnd* *pFocusWnd* **);**
END Protected

Parameters   *pFocusWnd*   Specifies a pointer to the window that caused the system palette to change. The pointer may be temporary and should not be stored.

Remarks   Called for all top-level windows after the window with input focus has realized its logical palette thereby changing the system palette. This call allows a window without the input focus that uses a color palette to realize its logical palettes and update its client area. The **OnPaletteChanged** member function is called for all top-level and overlapped windows, including the one that changed the system palette and caused the **WM_PALETTECHANGED** message to be sent. If any child window uses a color palette, this message must be passed on to it. To avoid an infinite loop, the window shouldn't realize its palette unless it determines that *pFocusWnd* does not contain a pointer to itself.

See Also   **::RealizePalette, WM_PALETTECHANGED, CWnd::OnPaletteIsChanging, CWnd::OnQueryNewPalette**

CWnd::OnPaletteIsChanging

Protected→
afx_msg void OnPaletteIsChanging(CWnd* *pRealizeWnd* **);**
END Protected

Parameters   *pRealizeWnd*   Specifies the window that is about to realize its logical palette.

Remarks   Informs applications that an application is going to realize its logical palette.

See Also   **CWnd::OnPaletteChanged, CWnd::OnQueryNewPalette, ::OnPaletteIsChanging**

CWnd::OnParentNotify

Protected→
afx_msg void OnParentNotify(UINT *message***, LPARAM** *lParam* **);**
END Protected

Parameters   *message*   Specifies the event for which the parent is being notified. It can be any of these values:

- **WM_CREATE**   The child window is being created.
- **WM_DESTROY**   The child window is being destroyed.

- **WM_LBUTTONDOWN** The user has placed the mouse cursor over the child window and clicked the left mouse button.
- **WM_MBUTTONDOWN** The user has placed the mouse cursor over the child window and clicked the middle mouse button.
- **WM_RBUTTONDOWN** The user has placed the mouse cursor over the child window and clicked the right mouse button.

lParam If *message* is **WM_CREATE** or **WM_DESTROY** specifies the window handle of the child window in the low-order word and the identifier of the child window in the high-order word; otherwise *lParam* contains the x and y coordinates of the cursor. The x coordinate is in the low-order word and the y coordinate is in the high-order word.

Remarks

A parent's **OnParentNotify** member function is called when its child window is created or destroyed, or when the user clicks a mouse button while the cursor is over the child window. When the child window is being created, the system calls **OnParentNotify** just before the **Create** member function that creates the window returns. When the child window is being destroyed, the system calls **OnParentNotify** before any processing takes place to destroy the window. **OnParentNotify** is called for all ancestor windows of the child window, including the top-level window.

All child windows except those that have the **WS_EX_NOPARENTNOTIFY** style send this message to their parent windows. By default, child windows in a dialog box have the **WS_EX_NOPARENTNOTIFY** style unless the child window was created without this style by calling the **CreateEx** member function. For more information on extended window styles, see the section "Extended Window Styles" on page 1254.

See Also

CWnd::OnCreate, **CWnd::OnDestroy**, **CWnd::OnLButtonDown**, **CWnd::OnMButtonDown**, **CWnd::OnRButtonDown**, **WM_PARENTNOTIFY**

CWnd::OnQueryDragIcon

Protected→
afx_msg HCURSOR OnQueryDragIcon( );
END Protected

Return Value

A doubleword value that contains a cursor or icon handle in the low-order word. The cursor or icon must be compatible with the display driver's resolution. If the application returns **NULL**, the system displays the default cursor. The default return value is **NULL**.

Remarks   Called by a minimized (iconic) window that does not have an icon defined for its class. The system makes this call to obtain the cursor to display while the user drags the minimized window. If an application returns the handle of an icon or cursor, the system converts it to black-and-white. If an application returns a handle, the handle must identify a monochrome cursor or icon compatible with the display driver's resolution. The application can call the **CWinApp::LoadCursor** or **CWinApp::LoadIcon** member functions to load a cursor or icon from the resources in its executable file and to obtain this handle.

See Also   **CWinApp::LoadCursor**, **CWinApp::LoadIcon**, **WM_QUERYDRAGICON**

CWnd::OnQueryEndSession

Protected→
afx_msg BOOL OnQueryEndSession( );
    END Protected

Return Value   Nonzero if an application can be conveniently shut down; otherwise 0.

Remarks   Called when the user chooses to end the Windows session or when an application calls the **ExitWindows** Windows function. If any application returns 0, the Windows session is not ended. Windows stops calling **OnQueryEndSession** as soon as one application returns 0 and sends the **WM_ENDSESSION** message with a parameter value of **FALSE** for any application that has already returned nonzero.

See Also   **::ExitWindows**, **CWnd::OnEndSession**, **WM_QUERYENDSESSION**

CWnd::OnQueryNewPalette

Protected→
afx_msg BOOL OnQueryNewPalette( );
    END Protected

Return Value   Nonzero if the **CWnd** realizes its logical palette; otherwise 0.

Remarks   Called when the **CWnd** object is about to receive the input focus, giving the **CWnd** an opportunity to realize its logical palette when it receives the focus.

See Also   **CWnd::Default**, **CWnd::OnPaletteChanged**, **WM_QUERYNEWPALETTE**

CWnd::OnQueryOpen

Protected→
afx_msg BOOL OnQueryOpen( );
    END Protected

Return Value   Nonzero if the icon can be opened, or 0 to prevent the icon from being opened.

Remarks   Called when the **CWnd** object is minimized and the user requests that the **CWnd** be restored to its preminimized size and position. While in **OnQueryOpen**, **CWnd** should not perform any action that would cause an activation or focus change (for example, creating a dialog box).

See Also   **WM_QUERYOPEN**

CWnd::OnRButtonDblClk

Protected→
afx_msg void OnRButtonDblCik(UINT *nFlags*, **CPoint** *point*);
END Protected

Parameters   *nFlags*   Indicates whether various virtual keys are down. This parameter can be any combination of the following values:

- **MK_CONTROL**   Set if CTRL key is down.
- **MK_LBUTTON**   Set if left mouse button is down.
- **MK_MBUTTON**   Set if middle mouse button is down.
- **MK_RBUTTON**   Set if right mouse button is down.
- **MK_SHIFT**   Set if SHIFT key is down.

point   Specifies the x and y coordinates of the cursor. These coordinates are always relative to the upper-left corner of the window.

Remarks   Called when the user double-clicks the right mouse button. Only windows that have the **CS_DBLCLKS WNDCLASS** style can receive **OnRButtonDblClk** calls. This is the default for windows within the Microsoft Foundation Class Library. Windows calls **OnRButtonDblClk** when the user presses, releases, and then again presses the right mouse button within the system's double-click time limit. Double-clicking the right mouse button actually generates four events: **WM_RBUTTONDOWN** and **WM_RBUTTONUP** messages, the **OnRButtonDblClk** call, and another **WM_RBUTTONUP** message when the button is released.

See Also   **CWnd::OnRButtonDown**, **CWnd::OnRButtonUp**, **WM_RBUTTONDBLCLK**

CWnd::OnRButtonDown

Protected→
afx_msg void OnRButtonDown(UINT *nFlags*, **CPoint** *point*);
END Protected

Parameters   *nFlags*   Indicates whether various virtual keys are down. This parameter can be any combination of the following values:

- **MK_CONTROL**   Set if CONTROL key is down.
- **MK_LBUTTON**   Set if left mouse button is down.
- **MK_MBUTTON**   Set if middle mouse button is down.
- **MK_RBUTTON**   Set if right mouse button is down.
- **MK_SHIFT**   Set if SHIFT key is down.

point   Specifies the x and y coordinates of the cursor. These coordinates are always relative to the upper-left corner of the window.

Remarks   Called when the user presses the right mouse button.

See Also   **CWnd::OnRButtonDblClk, CWnd::OnRButtonUp, WM_RBUTTONDOWN**

CWnd::OnRButtonUp

Protected→
afx_msg void OnRButtonUp(UINT *nFlags***, CPoint** *point* **);**
END Protected

Parameters   *nFlags*   Indicates whether various virtual keys are down. This parameter can be any combination of the following values:

- **MK_CONTROL**   Set if CTRL key is down.
- **MK_LBUTTON**   Set if left mouse button is down.
- **MK_MBUTTON**   Set if middle mouse button is down.
- **MK_SHIFT**   Set if SHIFT key is down.

point   Specifies the x and y coordinates of the cursor. These coordinates are always relative to the upper-left corner of the window.

Remarks   Called when the user releases the right mouse button.

See Also   **CWnd::OnRButtonDblClk, CWnd::OnRButtonDown, WM_RBUTTONUP**

CWnd::OnRenderAllFormats

Protected→
afx_msg void OnRenderAllFormats( );
END Protected

Remarks   The Clipboard owner's **OnRenderAllFormats** member function is called when the owner application is being destroyed. The Clipboard owner should render the data in all the formats it is capable of generating and pass a data handle for each format to the Clipboard by calling the **SetClipboardData** Windows function. This ensures that the Clipboard contains valid data even though the application that rendered the data is destroyed. The application should call the **OpenClipboard** member function before calling the **SetClipboardData** Windows function and call the **CloseClipboard** Windows function afterward.

See Also   **::CloseClipboard**, **CWnd::OpenClipboard**, **::SetClipboardData**, **CWnd::OnRenderFormat**, **WM_RENDERALLFORMATS**

CWnd::OnRenderFormat

Protected→
afx_msg void OnRenderFormat(UINT *nFormat* **);**
END Protected

Parameters   *nFormat*   Specifies the Clipboard format.

Remarks   The Clipboard owner's **OnRenderFormat** member function is called when a particular format with delayed rendering needs to be rendered. The receiver should render the data in that format and pass it to the Clipboard by calling the **SetClipboardData** Windows function. Do not call the **OpenClipboard** member function or the **CloseClipboard** Windows function from within **OnRenderFormat**.

See Also   **::CloseClipboard**, **CWnd::OpenClipboard**, **::SetClipboardData**, **WM_RENDERFORMAT**

CWnd::OnSetCursor

Protected→
afx_msg BOOL OnSetCursor(CWnd* *pWnd***, UINT** *nHitTest***,**
     UINT *message* **);**
END Protected

Return Value   Nonzero to halt further processing, or 0 to continue.

Parameters   *pWnd*   Specifies a pointer to the window that contains the cursor. The pointer may be temporary and should not be stored for later use.

nHitTest   Specifies the hit-test area code. The hit test determines the cursor's location.

message   Specifies the mouse message number.

Remarks   Called if mouse input is not captured and the mouse causes cursor movement within the **CWnd** object. The default implementation calls the parent window's **OnSetCursor** before processing. If the parent window returns **TRUE**, further processing is halted. Calling the parent window gives the parent window control over the cursor's setting in a child window. The default implementation sets the cursor to an arrow if it is not in the client area or to the registered-class cursor if it is.

If *nHitTest* is **HTERROR** and *message* is a mouse button-down message, the **MessageBeep** member function is called. The *message* parameter is 0 when **CWnd** enters menu mode.

See Also   **CWnd::OnNcHitTest**, **WM_SETCURSOR**

CWnd::OnSetFocus

Protected→
afx_msg void OnSetFocus(CWnd* *pOldWnd* **);**
END Protected

Parameters   *pOldWnd*   Contains the **CWnd** object that loses the input focus (may be **NULL**). The pointer may be temporary and should not be stored for later use.

Remarks   Called after gaining the input focus. To display a caret, **CWnd** should call the appropriate caret functions at this point.

See Also   **WM_SETFOCUS**

CWnd::OnShowWindow

Protected→
afx_msg void OnShowWindow(BOOL *bShow*, **UINT** *nStatus* **);**
END Protected

Parameters   *bShow*   Specifies whether a window is being shown. It is **TRUE** if the window is being shown; it is **FALSE** if the window is being hidden.

nStatus   Specifies the status of the window being shown. It is 0 if the message is sent because of a **ShowWindow** member function call; otherwise *nStatus* is one of the following:

- **SW_PARENTCLOSING**   Parent window is closing (being made iconic) or a pop-up window is being hidden.
- **SW_PARENTOPENING**   Parent window is opening (being displayed) or a pop-up window is being shown.

Remarks   Called when the **CWnd** object is about to be hidden or shown. A window is hidden or shown when the **ShowWindow** member function is called, when an overlapped window is maximized or restored, or when an overlapped or pop-up window is closed (made iconic) or opened (displayed on the screen). When an overlapped window is closed, all pop-up windows associated with that window are hidden.

See Also   **WM_SHOWWINDOW**

CWnd::OnSize

Protected→
afx_msg void OnSize(UINT *nType*, **int** *cx*, **int** *cy* **);**
END Protected

Parameters   *nType*   Specifies the type of resizing requested. This parameter can be one of the following values:

- **SIZE_MAXIMIZED**   Window has been maximized.
- **SIZE_MINIMIZED**   Window has been minimized.
- **SIZE_RESTORED**   Window has been resized, but neither **SIZE_MINIMIZED** nor **SIZE_MAXIMIZED** applies.
- **SIZE_MAXHIDE**   Message is sent to all pop-up windows when some other window is maximized.
- **SIZE_MAXSHOW**   Message is sent to all pop-up windows when some other window has been restored to its former size.

cx   Specifies the new width of the client area.

cy   Specifies the new height of the client area.

Remarks   Called after the window's size has changed. If the **SetScrollPos** or **MoveWindow** member function is called for a child window from **OnSize**, the *bRedraw* parameter of **SetScrollPos** or **MoveWindow** should be nonzero to cause the **CWnd** to be repainted.

See Also   **CWnd::MoveWindow**, **CWnd::SetScrollPos**, **WM_SIZE**

CWnd::OnSizeClipboard

Protected→
afx_msg void OnSizeClipboard(CWnd* *pClipAppWnd*, **HGLOBAL** *hRect* **);**
END Protected

Parameters   *pClipAppWnd*   Identifies the Clipboard-application window. The pointer may be temporary and should not be stored.

hRect   Identifies a global memory object. The memory object contains a **RECT** data structure that specifies the area for the Clipboard owner to paint.

Remarks   The Clipboard owner's **OnSizeClipboard** member function is called by the Clipboard viewer when the Clipboard contains data with the **CF_OWNERDISPLAY** attribute and the size of the client area of the Clipboard-viewer window has changed. The **OnSizeClipboard** member function is called with a null rectangle (0,0,0,0) as the new size when the Clipboard application is about to be destroyed or minimized. This permits the Clipboard owner to free its display resources. Within **OnSizeClipboard**, an application must use the **GlobalLock** Windows function to lock the memory that contains the **RECT** data structure. Have the application unlock that memory with the **GlobalUnlock** Windows function before it yields or returns control.

See Also   **::GlobalLock**, **::GlobalUnlock**, **::SetClipboardData**, **CWnd::SetClipboardViewer**, **WM_SIZECLIPBOARD**

CWnd::OnSpoolerStatus

Protected→
afx_msg void OnSpoolerStatus(UINT *nStatus***, UINT** *nJobs* **);**
    END Protected

Parameters   *nStatus*   Specifies the **SP_JOBSTATUS** flag.

nJobs   Specifies the number of jobs remaining in the Print Manager queue.

Remarks   Called from Print Manager whenever a job is added to or removed from the Print Manager queue. This call is for informational purposes only.

See Also   **WM_SPOOLERSTATUS**

CWnd::OnSysChar

Protected→
afx_msg void OnSysChar(UINT *nChar***, UINT** *nRepCnt***, UINT** *nFlags* **);**
    END Protected

Parameters   *nChar*   Specifies the ASCII-character key code of a Control-menu key.

nRepCnt   Specifies the repeat count (the number of times the keystroke is repeated as a result of the user holding down the key).

nFlags   The *nFlags* parameter can have these values:

Value	Meaning
0–7	Scan code (OEM-dependent value). Low byte of high-order word.
8	Extended key, such as a function key or a key on the numeric keypad (1 if it is an extended key; otherwise 0).
9–10	Not used.
11–12	Used internally by Windows.
13	Context code (1 if the ALT key is held down while the key is pressed; otherwise 0).
14	Previous key state (1 if the key is down before the message is sent, 0 if the key is up).
15	Transition state (1 if the key is being released, 0 if the key is being pressed).

Remarks   Called if **CWnd** has the input focus and the **WM_SYSKEYUP** and **WM_SYSKEYDOWN** messages are translated. It specifies the virtual-key code of the Control-menu key. When the context code is 0, **WM_SYSCHAR** can pass the **WM_SYSCHAR** message to the **TranslateAccelerator** Windows function, which will handle it as though it were a normal key message instead of a Control-menu key message. This allows accelerator keys to be used with the active window even if the active window does not have the input focus.

For IBM Enhanced 101- and 102-key keyboards, enhanced keys are the right ALT and the right CTRL keys on the main section of the keyboard; the INS, DEL, HOME, END, PAGE UP, PAGE DOWN, and arrow keys in the clusters to the left of the numeric keypad; and the slash (/) and ENTER keys in the numeric keypad. Some other keyboards may support the extended-key bit in *nFlags*.

See Also   **::TranslateAccelerator**, **WM_SYSKEYDOWN**, **WM_SYSKEYUP**, **WM_SYSCHAR**

CWnd::OnSysColorChange

Protected→
afx_msg void OnSysColorChange( );
END Protected

Remarks   Called for all top-level windows when a change is made in the system color setting. Windows calls **OnSysColorChange** for any window that is affected by a system color change. Applications that have brushes that use the existing system colors should delete those brushes and re-create them with the new system colors.

See Also   **::SetSysColors**, **WM_SYSCOLORCHANGE**

CWnd::OnSysCommand

Protected→
afx_msg void OnSysCommand(UINT *nID,* **LPARAM** *lParam* **);**
END Protected

Parameters
nID   Specifies the type of system command requested. This parameter can be any one of the following values:

- **SC_CLOSE**   Close the **CWnd** object.
- **SC_HOTKEY**   Activate the **CWnd** object associated with the application-specified hot key. The low-order word of *lParam* identifies the **HWND** of the window to activate.
- **SC_HSCROLL**   Scroll horizontally.
- **SC_KEYMENU**   Retrieve a menu through a keystroke.
- **SC_MAXIMIZE** (or **SC_ZOOM**)   Maximize the **CWnd** object.
- **SC_MINIMIZE** (or **SC_ICON**)   Minimize the **CWnd** object.
- **SC_MOUSEMENU**   Retrieve a menu through a mouse click.
- **SC_MOVE**   Move the **CWnd** object.
- **SC_NEXTWINDOW**   Move to the next window.
- **SC_PREVWINDOW**   Move to the previous window.
- **SC_RESTORE**   Restore window to normal position and size.
- **SC_SCREENSAVE**   Executes the screen-saver application specified in the [boot] section of the SYSTEM.INI file.
- **SC_SIZE**   Size the **CWnd** object.
- **SC_TASKLIST**   Execute or activate the Windows Task Manager application.
- **SC_VSCROLL**   Scroll vertically.

lParam   If a Control-menu command is chosen with the mouse contains the cursor coordinates. The low-order word contains the x coordinate, and the high-order word contains the y coordinate. Otherwise this parameter is not used.

- **SC_HOTKEY**   Activate the window associated with the application-specified hot key. The low-order word of *lParam* identifies the window to activate.
- **SC_SCREENSAVE**   Execute the screen-save application specified in the Desktop section of Control Panel.

Remarks
Called when the user selects a command from the Control menu, or when the user selects the Maximize or the Minimize button. By default, **OnSysCommand** carries out the Control-menu request for the predefined actions specified in the preceding

table. In **WM_SYSCOMMAND** messages, the four low-order bits of the *nID* parameter are used internally by Windows. When an application tests the value of *nID*, it must combine the value 0xFFF0 with the *nID* value by using the bitwise-AND operator to obtain the correct result.

The menu items in a Control menu can be modified with the **GetSystemMenu**, **AppendMenu**, **InsertMenu**, and **ModifyMenu** member functions. Applications that modify the Control menu must process **WM_SYSCOMMAND** messages, and any **WM_SYSCOMMAND** messages not handled by the application must be passed on to **OnSysCommand**. Any command values added by an application must be processed by the application and cannot be passed to **OnSysCommand**.

An application can carry out any system command at any time by passing a **WM_SYSCOMMAND** message to **OnSysCommand**. Accelerator (shortcut) keystrokes that are defined to select items from the Control menu are translated into **OnSysCommand** calls; all other accelerator keystrokes are translated into **WM_COMMAND** messages.

See Also   **WM_SYSCOMMAND**

CWnd::OnSysDeadChar

Protected→
afx_msg void OnSysDeadChar(UINT *nChar*, **UINT** *nRepCnt*, **UINT** *nFlags* **);**
END Protected

Parameters   *nChar*   Specifies the dead-key character value.

nRepCnt   Specifies the repeat count.

nFlags   Specifies the scan code, key-transition code, previous key state, and context code, as shown in the following list:

Value	Meaning
0–7	Scan code (OEM-dependent value). Low byte of high-order word.
8	Extended key, such as a function key or a key on the numeric keypad (1 if it is an extended key; otherwise 0).
9–10	Not used.
11–12	Used internally by Windows.
13	Context code (1 if the ALT key is held down while the key is pressed; otherwise 0).
14	Previous key state (1 if the key is down before the call, 0 if the key is up).
15	Transition state (1 if the key is being released, 0 if the key is being pressed).

Remarks   Called if the **CWnd** object has the input focus when the **OnSysKeyUp** or **OnSysKeyDown** member function is called. It specifies the character value of a dead key.

See Also   **CWnd::OnSysKeyDown**, **CWnd::OnSysKeyUp**, **WM_SYSDEADCHAR**, **CWnd::OnDeadChar**

CWnd::OnSysKeyDown

Protected→
afx_msg void OnSysKeyDown(UINT *nChar*, **UINT** *nRepCnt*, **UINT** *nFlags* **);**
END Protected

Parameters   *nChar*   Specifies the virtual-key code of the key being pressed.

nRepCnt   Specifies the repeat count.

nFlags   Specifies the scan code, key-transition code, previous key state, and context code, as shown in the following list:

Value	Meaning
0–7	Scan code (OEM-dependent value). Low byte of high-order word.
8	Extended key, such as a function key or a key on the numeric keypad (1 if it is an extended key; otherwise 0).
9–10	Not used.
11–12	Used internally by Windows.
13	Context code (1 if the ALT key is held down while the key is pressed, 0 otherwise).
14	Previous key state (1 if the key is down before the message is sent, 0 if the key is up).
15	Transition state (1 if the key is being released, 0 if the key is being pressed).

For **OnSysKeyDown** calls, the key-transition bit (bit 15) is 0. The context-code bit (bit 13) is 1 if the ALT key is down while the key is pressed; it is 0 if the message is sent to the active window because no window has the input focus.

Remarks   If the **CWnd** object has the input focus, the **OnSysKeyDown** member function is called when the user holds down the ALT key and then presses another key. If no window currently has the input focus, the active window's **OnSysKeyDown** member function is called. The **CWnd** object that receives the message can distinguish between these two contexts by checking the context code in *nFlags*. When the context code is 0, the **WM_SYSKEYDOWN** message received by **OnSysKeyDown** can be passed to the **TranslateAccelerator** Windows function, which will handle it as though it were a normal key message instead of a system-key message. This allows accelerator keys to be used with the active window even if the active window does not have the input focus.

Because of auto-repeat, more than one **OnSysKeyDown** call may occur before the **WM_SYSKEYUP** message is received. The previous key state (bit 14) can be used to determine whether the **OnSysKeyDown** call indicates the first down transition or a repeated down transition.

For IBM Enhanced 101- and 102-key keyboards, enhanced keys are the right ALT and the right CTRL keys on the main section of the keyboard; the INS, DEL, HOME, END, PAGE UP, PAGE DOWN, and arrow keys in the clusters to the left of the numeric keypad; and the slash (/) and ENTER keys in the numeric keypad. Some other keyboards may support the extended-key bit in *nFlags*.

See Also   ::**TranslateAccelerator**, **WM_SYSKEYUP**, **WM_SYSKEYDOWN**

CWnd::OnSysKeyUp

Protected→
afx_msg void OnSysKeyUp(UINT *nChar*, **UINT** *nRepCnt*, **UINT** *nFlags* **);**
END Protected

Parameters   *nChar*   Specifies the virtual-key code of the key being pressed.

nRepCnt   Specifies the repeat count.

nFlags   Specifies the scan code, key-transition code, previous key state, and context code, as shown in the following list:

Value	Meaning
0–7	Scan code (OEM-dependent value). Low byte of high-order word.
8	Extended key, such as a function key or a key on the numeric keypad (1 if it is an extended key; otherwise 0).
9–10	Not used.
11–12	Used internally by Windows.
13	Context code (1 if the ALT key is held down while the key is pressed, 0 otherwise).
14	Previous key state (1 if the key is down before the message is sent, 0 if the key is up).
15	Transition state (1 if the key is being released, 0 if the key is being pressed).

For **OnSysKeyUp** calls, the key-transition bit (bit 15) is 1. The context-code bit (bit 13) is 1 if the ALT key is down while the key is pressed; it is 0 if the message is sent to the active window because no window has the input focus.

Remarks   If the **CWnd** object has the focus, the **OnSysKeyUp** member function is called when the user releases a key that was pressed while the ALT key was held down. If no window currently has the input focus, the active window's **OnSysKeyUp** member function is called. The **CWnd** object that receives the call can distinguish between these two contexts by checking the context code in *nFlags*. When the context code is 0, the **WM_SYSKEYUP** message received by **OnSysKeyUp** can be passed to the **TranslateAccelerator** Windows function, which will handle it as though it were a normal key message instead of a system-key message. This allows accelerator (shortcut) keys to be used with the active window even if the active window does not have the input focus.

For IBM Enhanced 101- and 102-key keyboards, enhanced keys are the right ALT and the right CTRL keys on the main section of the keyboard; the INS, DEL, HOME, END, PAGE UP, PAGE DOWN, and arrow keys in the clusters to the left of the numeric keypad; and the slash (/) and ENTER keys in the numeric keypad. Some other keyboards may support the extended-key bit in *nFlags*.

For non-U.S. Enhanced 102-key keyboards, the right ALT key is handled as the CTRL+ALT key combination. The following shows the sequence of messages and calls that result when the user presses and releases this key:

Sequence	Function Accessed	Message Passed
1.	**WM_KEYDOWN**	**VK_CONTROL**
2.	**WM_KEYDOWN**	**VK_MENU**
3.	**WM_KEYUP**	**VK_CONTROL**
4.	**WM_SYSKEYUP**	**VK_MENU**

See Also   ::**TranslateAccelerator**, **WM_SYSKEYDOWN**, **WM_SYSKEYUP**

CWnd::OnTimeChange

Protected→
afx_msg void OnTimeChange( );
END Protected

Remarks   Called after the system time is changed. Have any application that changes the system time send this message to all top-level windows. To send the **WM_TIMECHANGE** message to all top-level windows, an application can use the **SendMessage** Windows function with its *hwnd* parameter set to **HWND_BROADCAST**.

See Also   ::**SendMessage**, **WM_TIMECHANGE**

CWnd::OnTimer

Protected→
afx_msg void OnTimer(UINT *nIDEvent* **);**
    END Protected

Parameters   *nIDEvent*   Specifies the identifier of the timer.

Remarks   Called after each interval specified in the **SetTimer** member function used to install a timer. The **DispatchMessage** Windows function sends a **WM_TIMER** message when no other messages are in the application's message queue.

See Also   **CWnd::SetTimer**, **WM_TIMER**

CWnd::OnVKeyToItem

protafx_msg int OnVKeyToItem(UINT *nKey*, **CListBox*** *pListBox*, **UINT** *nIndex* **);**
    END Protected

Return Value   Specifies the action that the application performed in response to the message. A return value of –2 indicates that the application handled all aspects of selecting the item and requires no further action by the list box. A return value of –1 indicates that the list box should perform the default action in response to the keystroke. A return value of 0 or greater specifies the zero-based index of an item in the list box and indicates that the list box should perform the default action for the keystroke on the given item.

Parameters   *nKey*   Specifies the virtual-key code of the key that the user pressed.

     pListBox   Specifies a pointer to the list box. The pointer may be temporary and should not be stored for later use.

     nIndex   Specifies the current caret position.

Remarks   If the **CWnd** object owns a list box with the **LBS_WANTKEYBOARDINPUT** style, the list box will send the **WM_VKEYTOITEM** message in response to a **WM_KEYDOWN** message. This member function is called only for list boxes that have the **LBS_HASSTRINGS** style. For more information on list-box styles, see the section "List-Box Styles" on page 1249.

See Also   **WM_KEYDOWN**, **WM_VKEYTOITEM**

CWnd::OnVScroll

Protected→
afx_msg void OnVScroll(UINT *nSBCode*, **UINT** *nPos*, **CScrollBar***
pScrollBar **);**
END Protected

Parameters

nSBCode   Specifies a scroll-bar code that indicates the user's scrolling request. This parameter can be one of the following:

- **SB_BOTTOM**   Scroll to bottom.
- **SB_ENDSCROLL**   End scroll.
- **SB_LINEDOWN**   Scroll one line down.
- **SB_LINEUP**   Scroll one line up.
- **SB_PAGEDOWN**   Scroll one page down.
- **SB_PAGEUP**   Scroll one page up.
- **SB_THUMBPOSITION**   Scroll to the absolute position. The current position is provided in *nPos*.
- **SB_THUMBTRACK**   Drag scroll box to specified position. The current position is provided in *nPos*.
- **SB_TOP**   Scroll to top.

nPos   Contains the current scroll-box position if the scroll-bar code is **SB_THUMBPOSITION** or **SB_THUMBTRACK**; otherwise not used. Depending on the initial scroll range, *nPos* may be negative and should be cast to an **int** if necessary.

pScrollBar   If the scroll message came from a scroll-bar control, contains a pointer to the control. If the user clicked a window's scroll bar, this parameter is **NULL**. The pointer may be temporary and should not be stored for later use.

Remarks

Called when the user clicks the window's vertical scroll bar. **OnVScroll** typically is used by applications that give some feedback while the scroll box is being dragged. If **OnVScroll** scrolls the contents of the **CWnd** object, it must also reset the position of the scroll box with the **SetScrollPos** member function.

See Also

CWnd::SetScrollPos, CWnd::OnHScroll, WM_VSCROLL

CWnd::OnVScrollClipboard

Protected→
afx_msg void OnVScrollClipboard(CWnd* *pClipAppWnd***, UINT** *nSBCode***, UINT** *nPos* **);**
END Protected

Parameters

pClipAppWnd   Specifies a pointer to a Clipboard-viewer window. The pointer may be temporary and should not be stored for later use.

nSBCode   Specifies one of the following scroll-bar values:

- **SB_BOTTOM**   Scroll to bottom.
- **SB_ENDSCROLL**   End scroll.
- **SB_LINEDOWN**   Scroll one line down.
- **SB_LINEUP**   Scroll one line up.
- **SB_PAGEDOWN**   Scroll one page down.
- **SB_PAGEUP**   Scroll one page up.
- **SB_THUMBPOSITION**   Scroll to the absolute position. The current position is provided in *nPos*.
- **SB_TOP**   Scroll to top.

nPos   Contains the scroll-box position if the scroll-bar code is **SB_THUMBPOSITION**; otherwise *nPos* is not used.

Remarks

The Clipboard owner's **OnVScrollClipboard** member function is called by the Clipboard viewer when the Clipboard data has the **CF_OWNERDISPLAY** format and there is an event in the Clipboard viewer's vertical scroll bar. The owner should scroll the Clipboard image, invalidate the appropriate section, and update the scroll-bar values.

See Also

CWnd::Invalidate, CWnd::OnHScrollClipboard, CWnd::InvalidateRect, WM_VSCROLLCLIPBOARD, CWnd::Default

CWnd::OnWindowPosChanged

Protected→
afx_msg void OnWindowPosChanged(WINDOWPOS* *lpwndpos* **);**
END Protected

Parameters

lpwndpos   Points to a **WINDOWPOS** data structure that contains information about the window's new size and position.

Remarks

Called when the size, position, or Z-order has changed as a result of a call to the **SetWindowPos** member function or another window-management function. The default implementation sends the **WM_SIZE** and **WM_MOVE** messages to the window. These messages are not sent if an application handles the **OnWindowPosChanged** call without calling its base class. It is more efficient to perform any move or size change processing during the call to **OnWindowPosChanged** without calling its base class.

See Also   **WM_WINDOWPOSCHANGED**

CWnd::OnWindowPosChanging

Protected→
afx_msg void OnWindowPosChanging(WINDOWPOS* *lpwndpos* **);**
END Protected

Parameters   *lpwndpos*   Points to a **WINDOWPOS** data structure that contains information about the window's new size and position.

Remarks   Called when the size, position, or Z-order is about to change as a result of a call to the **SetWindowPos** member function or another window-management function. An application can prevent changes to the window by setting or clearing the appropriate bits in the **flags** member of the **WINDOWPOS** structure. For a window with the **WS_OVERLAPPED** or **WS_THICKFRAME** style, the default implementation sends a **WM_GETMINMAXINFO** message to the window. This is done to validate the new size and position of the window and to enforce the **CS_BYTEALIGNCLIENT** and **CS_BYTEALIGN** client styles. An application can override this functionality by not calling its base class.

See Also   **CWnd::OnWindowPosChanged**, **WM_WINDOWPOSCHANGING**

CWnd::OnWinIniChange

Protected→
afx_msg void OnWinIniChange(LPCTSTR *lpszSection* **);**
END Protected

Parameters   *lpszSection*   Points to a string that specifies the name of the section that has changed. (The string does not include the square brackets that enclose the section name.)

Remarks   Called after a change has been made to the Windows initialization file, WIN.INI. The **SystemParametersInfo** Windows function calls **OnWinIniChange** after an application uses the function to change a setting in the WIN.INI file. To send the **WM_WININICHANGE** message to all top-level windows, an application can use the **SendMessage** Windows function with its *hwnd* parameter set to **HWND_BROADCAST**.

If an application changes many different sections in WIN.INI at the same time, the application should send one **WM_WININICHANGE** message with *lpszSection* set to **NULL**. Otherwise, an application should send **WM_WININICHANGE** each time it makes a change to WIN.INI.

If an application receives an **OnWinIniChange** call with *lpszSection* set to **NULL**, the application should check all sections in WIN.INI that affect the application.

See Also   **::SendMessage**, **::SystemParametersInfo**, **WM_WININICHANGE**

CWnd::OpenClipboard

BOOL OpenClipboard( );

Return Value   Nonzero if the Clipboard is opened via **CWnd**, or 0 if another application or window has the Clipboard open.

Remarks   Opens the Clipboard. Other applications will not be able to modify the Clipboard until the **CloseClipboard** Windows function is called. The current **CWnd** object will not become the owner of the Clipboard until the **EmptyClipboard** Windows function is called.

See Also   **::CloseClipboard**, **::EmptyClipboard**, **::OpenClipboard**

CWnd::PostMessage

BOOL PostMessage(UINT *message*, **WPARAM** *wParam* **= 0,**
LPARAM *lParam* **= 0);**

Return Value   Nonzero if the message is posted; otherwise 0.

Parameters   *message*   Specifies the message to be posted.

wParam   Specifies additional message information. The content of this parameter depends on the message being posted.

lParam   Specifies additional message information. The content of this parameter depends on the message being posted.

Remarks   Places a message in the window's message queue and then returns without waiting for the corresponding window to process the message. Messages in a message queue are retrieved by calls to the **GetMessage** or **PeekMessage** Windows function. The Windows **PostMessage** function can be used to access another application.

See Also   **::GetMessage**, **::PeekMessage**, **::PostMessage**, **::PostAppMessage**,
CWnd::SendMessage

CWnd::PostNcDestroy

Protected→

virtual void PostNcDestroy( );

END Protected

Remarks   Called by the default **OnNcDestroy** member function after the window has been destroyed. Derived classes can use this function for custom cleanup such as the deletion of the **this** pointer.

See Also   **CWnd::OnNcDestroy**

CWnd::PreCreateWindow

virtual BOOL PreCreateWindow(CREATESTRUCT& *cs* **);**

Return Value   Nonzero if the window creation should continue; 0 to indicate creation failure.

Parameters   *cs*   A **CREATESTRUCT** structure.

Remarks   Called by the framework before the creation of the Windows window attached to this **CWnd** object.

Never call this function directly.

The default implementation of this function checks for a NULL window class name and substitutes an appropriate default.

Override this member function to modify the **CREATESTRUCT** structure before the window is created. If you override this member function, you should examine the source code to determine whether or not you need to invoke the base class implementation.

See Also   **CWnd::Create, CREATESTRUCT**

CWnd::PreTranslateMessage

virtual BOOL PreTranslateMessage(MSG* *pMsg* **);**

Return Value   Nonzero if the message was translated and should not be dispatched; 0 if the message was not translated and should be dispatched.

Parameters   *pMsg*   Points to a **MSG** structure that contains the message to process.

Remarks   Used by class **CWinApp** to translate window messages before they are dispatched to the **TranslateMessage** and **DispatchMessage** Windows functions.

See Also   **::TranslateMessage, ::IsDialogMessage, CWinApp::PreTranslateMessage**

CWnd::RedrawWindow

BOOL RedrawWindow(LPCRECT *lpRectUpdate* = **NULL,**
CRgn* *prgnUpdate* = **NULL, UINT** *flags* = **RDW_INVALIDATE |**
RDW_UPDATENOW | RDW_ERASE);

Parameters

lpRectUpdate   Points to a **RECT** structure containing the coordinates of the
update rectangle. This parameter is ignored if *prgnUpdate* contains a valid
region handle.

prgnUpdate   Identifies the update region. If both *prgnUpdate* and *lpRectUpdate*
are **NULL**, the entire client area is added to the update region.

flags   The following flags are used to invalidate the window:

- **RDW_ERASE**   Causes the window to receive a **WM_ERASEBKGND**
  message when the window is repainted. The **RDW_INVALIDATE** flag
  must also be specified; otherwise **RDW_ERASE** has no effect.

- **RDW_FRAME**   Causes any part of the nonclient area of the window that
  intersects the update region to receive a **WM_NCPAINT** message. The
  RDW_INVALIDATE flag must also be specified; otherwise
  RDW_FRAME has no effect.

- **RDW_INTERNALPAINT**   Causes a **WM_PAINT** message to be posted
  to the window regardless of whether the window contains an invalid region.

- **RDW_INVALIDATE**   Invalidate *lpRectUpdate* or *prgnUpdate* (only one
  may be not **NULL**). If both are **NULL**, the entire window is invalidated.

The following flags are used to validate the window:

- **RDW_NOERASE**   Suppresses any pending **WM_ERASEBKGND**
  messages.

- **RDW_NOFRAME**   Suppresses any pending **WM_NCPAINT** messages.
  This flag must be used with **RDW_VALIDATE** and is typically used with
  RDW_NOCHILDREN. This option should be used with care, as it could
  prevent parts of a window from painting properly.

- **RDW_NOINTERNALPAINT**   Suppresses any pending internal
  WM_PAINT messages. This flag does not affect **WM_PAINT** messages
  resulting from invalid areas.

- **RDW_VALIDATE**   Validates *lpRectUpdate* or *prgnUpdate* (only one
  may be not **NULL**). If both are **NULL**, the entire window is validated. This
  flag does not affect internal **WM_PAINT** messages.

The following flags control when repainting occurs. Painting is not performed by
the **RedrawWindow** function unless one of these bits is specified.

- **RDW_ERASENOW**   Causes the affected windows (as specified by the **RDW_ALLCHILDREN** and **RDW_NOCHILDREN** flags) to receive **WM_NCPAINT** and **WM_ERASEBKGND** messages, if necessary, before the function returns. **WM_PAINT** messages are deferred.

- **RDW_UPDATENOW**   Causes the affected windows (as specified by the **RDW_ALLCHILDREN** and **RDW_NOCHILDREN** flags) to receive **WM_NCPAINT**, **WM_ERASEBKGND**, and **WM_PAINT** messages, if necessary, before the function returns.

By default, the windows affected by the **RedrawWindow** function depend on whether the specified window has the **WS_CLIPCHILDREN** style. The child windows of **WS_CLIPCHILDREN** windows are not affected. However, those windows that are not **WS_CLIPCHILDREN** windows are recursively validated or invalidated until a **WS_CLIPCHILDREN** window is encountered. The following flags control which windows are affected by the **RedrawWindow** function:

- **RDW_ALLCHILDREN**   Includes child windows, if any, in the repainting operation.

- **RDW_NOCHILDREN**   Excludes child windows, if any, from the repainting operation.

Remarks   Updates the specified rectangle or region in the given window's client area.

When the **RedrawWindow** member function is used to invalidate part of the desktop window, that window does not receive a **WM_PAINT** message. To repaint the desktop, an application should use **CWnd::ValidateRgn**, **CWnd::InvalidateRgn**, **CWnd::UpdateWindow**, or **::RedrawWindow**

CWnd::ReleaseDC

int ReleaseDC(CDC* *pDC*);

Return Value   Nonzero if successful; otherwise 0.

Parameters   *pDC*   Identifies the device context to be released.

Remarks   Releases a device context, freeing it for use by other applications. The effect of the **ReleaseDC** member function depends on the device-context type. The application must call the **ReleaseDC** member function for each call to the **GetWindowDC** member function and for each call to the **GetDC** member function.

See Also   **CWnd::GetDC, CWnd::GetWindowDC, ::ReleaseDC**

CWnd::RepositionBars

void RepositionBars(UINT *nIDFirst*, **UINT** *nIDLast*, **UINT** *nIDLeftOver*,
UINT *nFlag* = **CWnd::reposDefault, LPRECT** *lpRectParam* = **NULL**,
LPCRECT *lpRectClient* = **NULL**);

Parameters   *nIDFirst*   The ID of the first in a range of control bars to reposition and resize.

nIDLast   The ID of the last in a range of control bars to reposition and resize.

nIDLeftOver   Specifies ID of pane that fills the rest of the client area.

nFlag   Can have one of the following values:

- **CWnd::reposDefault**   Performs the layout of the control bars. *lpRectParam* is not used and can be **NULL**.
- **CWnd::reposQuery**   The layout of the control bars is not done; instead *lpRectParam* is initialized with the size of the client area, as if the layout had actually been done.
- **CWnd::reposExtra**   Adds the values of *lpRectParam* to the client area of *nIDLast* and also performs the layout.

lpRectParam   Points to a **RECT** structure; the usage of which depends on the value of *nFlag*.

lpRectClient   Points to a **RECT** structure containing the available client area. If **NULL**, the window's client area will be used.

Remarks   Called to reposition and resize control bars in the client area of a window. The *nIDFirst* and *nIDLast* parameters define a range of control-bar IDs to be repositioned in the client area. The *nIDLeftOver* parameter specifies the ID of the child window (normally the view) which is repositioned and resized to fill the rest of the client area not filled by control bars.

See Also   **CFrameWnd::RecalcLayout**

CWnd::ScreenToClient

void ScreenToClient(LPPOINT *lpPoint*) **const;**

void ScreenToClient(LPRECT *lpRect*) **const;**

Parameters   *lpPoint*   Points to a **CPoint** object or **POINT** structure that contains the screen coordinates to be converted.

lpRect   Points to a **CRect** object or **RECT** structure that contains the screen coordinates to be converted.

Remarks   Converts the screen coordinates of a given point or rectangle on the display to client coordinates.

The **ScreenToClient** member function replaces the screen coordinates given in *lpPoint* or *lpRect* with client coordinates. The new coordinates are relative to the upper-left corner of the **CWnd** client area.

See Also   **CWnd::ClientToScreen**, **::ScreenToClient**

CWnd::ScrollWindow

void ScrollWindow(int *xAmount*, **int** *yAmount*, **LPCRECT** *lpRect* = **NULL**, **LPCRECT** *lpClipRect* = **NULL**);**

Parameters   *xAmount*   Specifies the amount, in device units, of horizontal scrolling. This parameter must be a negative value to scroll to the left.

yAmount   Specifies the amount, in device units, of vertical scrolling. This parameter must be a negative value to scroll up.

lpRect   Points to a **CRect** object or **RECT** structure that specifies the portion of the client area to be scrolled. If *lpRect* is **NULL**, the entire client area is scrolled. The caret is repositioned if the cursor rectangle intersects the scroll rectangle.

lpClipRect   Points to a **CRect** object or **RECT** structure that specifies the clipping rectangle to scroll. Only bits inside this rectangle are scrolled. Bits outside this rectangle are not affected even if they are in the *lpRect* rectangle. If *lpClipRect* is **NULL**, no clipping is performed on the scroll rectangle.

Remarks   Scrolls the contents of the client area of the current **CWnd** object. If the caret is in the **CWnd** being scrolled, **ScrollWindow** automatically hides the caret to prevent it from being erased and then restores the caret after the scroll is finished. The caret position is adjusted accordingly.

The area uncovered by the **ScrollWindow** member function is not repainted but is combined into the current **CWnd** object's update region. The application will eventually receive a **WM_PAINT** message notifying it that the region needs repainting. To repaint the uncovered area at the same time the scrolling is done, call the **UpdateWindow** member function immediately after calling **ScrollWindow**.

If *lpRect* is **NULL**, the positions of any child windows in the window are offset by the amount specified by *xAmount* and *yAmount*, and any invalid (unpainted) areas in the **CWnd** are also offset. **ScrollWindow** is faster when *lpRect* is **NULL**. If *lpRect* is not **NULL**, the positions of child windows are not changed, and invalid areas in **CWnd** are not offset. To prevent updating problems when *lpRect* is not

NULL, call the **UpdateWindow** member function to repaint **CWnd** before calling **ScrollWindow**.

See Also   **CWnd::UpdateWindow**, **::ScrollWindow**

CWnd::ScrollWindowEx

int ScrollWindowEx(int *dx*, **int** *dy*, **LPCRECT** *lpRectScroll*, **LPCRECT** *lpRectClip*, **CRgn*** *prgnUpdate*, **LPRECT** *lpRectUpdate*, **UINT** *flags*);

Return Value   The return value is **SIMPLEREGION** (rectangular invalidated region), **COMPLEXREGION** (nonrectangular invalidated region; overlapping rectangles), or **NULLREGION** (no invalidated region), if the function is successful; otherwise the return value is **ERROR**.

Parameters   *dx*   Specifies the amount, in device units, of horizontal scrolling. This parameter must have a negative value to scroll to the left.

dy   Specifies the amount, in device units, of vertical scrolling. This parameter must have a negative value to scroll up.

lpRectScroll   Points to a **RECT** structure that specifies the portion of the client area to be scrolled. If this parameter is **NULL**, the entire client area is scrolled.

lpRectClip   Points to a **RECT** structure that specifies the clipping rectangle to scroll. This structure takes precedence over the rectangle pointed to by *lpRectScroll*. Only bits inside this rectangle are scrolled. Bits outside this rectangle are not affected even if they are in the *lpRectScroll* rectangle. If this parameter is **NULL**, no clipping is performed on the scroll rectangle.

prgnUpdate   Identifies the region that is modified to hold the region invalidated by scrolling. This parameter may be **NULL**.

lpRectUpdate   Points to a **RECT** structure that will receive the boundaries of the rectangle invalidated by scrolling. This parameter may be **NULL**.

flags   Can have one of the following values:

- **SW_ERASE**   When specified with **SW_INVALIDATE**, erases the newly invalidated region by sending a **WM_ERASEBKGND** message to the window.

- **SW_INVALIDATE**   Invalidates the region identified by *prgnUpdate* after scrolling.

- **SW_SCROLLCHILDREN**   Scrolls all child windows that intersect the rectangle pointed to by *lpRectScroll* by the number of pixels specified in *dx* and *dy*. Windows sends a **WM_MOVE** message to all child windows that intersect *lpRectScroll*, even if they do not move. The caret is repositioned when a child window is scrolled and the cursor rectangle intersects the scroll rectangle.

Remarks

Scrolls the contents of a window's client area. This function is similar to the **ScrollWindow** function, with some additional features. If **SW_INVALIDATE** and **SW_ERASE** are not specified, the **ScrollWindowEx** member function does not invalidate the area that is scrolled away from. If either of these flags is set, **ScrollWindowEx** invalidates this area. The area is not updated until the application calls the **UpdateWindow** member function, calls the **RedrawWindow** member function (specifying **RDW_UPDATENOW** or **RDW_ERASENOW**), or retrieves the **WM_PAINT** message from the application queue.

If the window has the **WS_CLIPCHILDREN** style, the returned areas specified by *prgnUpdate* and *lpRectUpdate* represent the total area of the scrolled window that must be updated, including any areas in child windows that need updating. If the **SW_SCROLLCHILDREN** flag is specified, Windows will not properly update the screen if part of a child window is scrolled. The part of the scrolled child window that lies outside the source rectangle will not be erased and will not be redrawn properly in its new destination. Use the **DeferWindowPos** Windows function to move child windows that do not lie completely within the *lpRectScroll* rectangle. The cursor is repositioned if the **SW_SCROLLCHILDREN** flag is set and the caret rectangle intersects the scroll rectangle.

All input and output coordinates (for *lpRectScroll*, *lpRectClip*, *lpRectUpdate*, and *prgnUpdate*) are assumed to be in client coordinates, regardless of whether the window has the **CS_OWNDC** or **CS_CLASSDC** class style. Use the **LPtoDP** and **DPtoLP** Windows functions to convert to and from logical coordinates, if necessary.

See Also

CWnd::RedrawWindow, **CDC::ScrollDC**, **CWnd::ScrollWindow**, **CWnd::UpdateWindow**, **::DeferWindowPos**, **::ScrollWindowEx**

CWnd::SendDlgItemMessage

LRESULT SendDlgItemMessage(int *nID*, **UINT** *message*,
    WPARAM *wParam* **= 0, LPARAM** *lParam* **= 0);**

Return Value

Specifies the value returned by the control's window procedure, or 0 if the control was not found.

Parameters

nID   Specifies the identifier of the dialog control that will receive the message.

message   Specifies the message to be sent.

wParam   Specifies additional message-dependent information.

lParam   Specifies additional message-dependent information.

Remarks   Sends a message to a control. The **SendDlgItemMessage** member function does not return until the message has been processed. Using **SendDlgItemMessage** is identical to obtaining a **CWnd*** to the given control and calling the **SendMessage** member function.

See Also   **CWnd::SendMessage**, **::SendDlgItemMessage**

CWnd::SendMessage

LRESULT SendMessage(UINT *message***, WPARAM** *wParam* **= 0,**
    LPARAM *lParam* **= 0);**

Return Value   The result of the message processing; its value depends on the message sent.

Parameters   *message*   Specifies the message to be sent.

    wParam   Specifies additional message-dependent information.

    lParam   Specifies additional message-dependent information.

Remarks   Sends the specified message to this window. The **SendMessage** member function calls the window procedure directly and does not return until that window procedure has processed the message. This is in contrast to the **PostMessage** member function, which places the message into the window's message queue and returns immediately.

See Also   **::InSendMessage**, **CWnd::PostMessage**, **CWnd::SendDlgItemMessage**, **::SendMessage**

CWnd::SendMessageToDescendants

void SendMessageToDescendants(UINT *message* **WPARAM** *wParam* **= 0,**
    LPARAM *lParam* **= 0, BOOL** *bDeep* **= TRUE, BOOL** *bOnlyPerm* **= FALSE);**

Parameters   *message*   Specifies the message to be sent.

    wParam   Specifies additional message-dependent information.

    lParam   Specifies additional message-dependent information.

    bDeep   Specifies the level to which to search. If **TRUE**, recursively search all children; if **FALSE**, search only immediate children.

    bOnlyPerm   Specifies whether the message will be received by temporary windows. If **TRUE**, temporary windows can receive the message; if **FALSE**, only permanent windows receive the message. For more information on temporary windows see Technical Note 3 found under MFC in Books Online.

Remarks	Call this member function to send the specified Windows message to all descendant windows.

If *bDeep* is **FALSE**, the message is sent to just to the immediate children of the window; otherwise the message is sent to all descendant windows.

If *bDeep* and *bOnlyPerm* are **TRUE**, the search continues below temporary windows. In this case only permanent windows encountered during the search receive the message. If *bDeep* is **FALSE**, the message is sent only to the immediate children of the window.

See Also	**CWnd::SendMessage**, **CWnd::FromHandlePermanent**, **CWnd::FromHandle**

CWnd::SendNotifyMessage

BOOL SendNotifyMessage(UINT *message***, WPARAM** *wParam***, LPARAM** *lParam* **);**

Return Value	Nonzero if the function is successful; otherwise 0.
Parameters	*message* Specifies the message to be sent.
	wParam Specifies additional message-dependent information.
	lParam Specifies additional message-dependent information.
Remarks	Sends the specified message to the window. If the window was created by the calling thread, **SendNotifyMessage** calls the window procedure for the window and does not return until the window procedure has processed the message. If the window was created by a different thread, **SendNotifyMessage** passes the message to the window procedure and returns immediately; it does not wait for the window procedure to finish processing the message.
See Also	**CWnd::SendMessage**, **::SendNotifyMessage**

CWnd::SetActiveWindow

CWnd* SetActiveWindow( );

Return Value	The window that was previously active. The returned pointer may be temporary and should not be stored for later use.
Remarks	Makes **CWnd** the active window. The **SetActiveWindow** member function should be used with care since it allows an application to arbitrarily take over the active window and input focus. Normally, Windows takes care of all activation.
See Also	**::SetActiveWindow**, **CWnd::GetActiveWindow**

CWnd::SetCapture

CWnd* SetCapture( );

Return Value A pointer to the window object that previously received all mouse input. It is **NULL** if there is no such window. The returned pointer may be temporary and should not be stored for later use.

Remarks Causes all subsequent mouse input to be sent to the current **CWnd** object regardless of the position of the cursor. When **CWnd** no longer requires all mouse input, the application should call the **ReleaseCapture** function so that other windows can receive mouse input.

See Also **::ReleaseCapture**, **::SetCapture**, **CWnd::GetCapture**

CWnd::SetCaretPos

static void PASCAL SetCaretPos(POINT *point* **);**

Parameters *point* Specifies the new x and y coordinates (in client coordinates) of the caret.

Remarks Sets the position of the caret. The **SetCaretPos** member function moves the caret only if it is owned by a window in the current task. **SetCaretPos** moves the caret whether or not the caret is hidden. The caret is a shared resource. A window should not move the caret if it does not own the caret.

See Also **CWnd::GetCaretPos**, **::SetCaretPos**

CWnd::SetClipboardViewer

HWND SetClipboardViewer( );

Return Value A handle to the next window in the Clipboard-viewer chain if successful. Applications should save this handle (it can be stored as a member variable) and use it when responding to Clipboard-viewer chain messages.

Remarks Adds this window to the chain of windows that are notified (by means of the **WM_DRAWCLIPBOARD** message) whenever the content of the Clipboard is changed. A window that is part of the Clipboard-viewer chain must respond to **WM_DRAWCLIPBOARD, WM_CHANGECBCHAIN**, and **WM_DESTROY** messages and pass the message to the next window in the chain. This member function sends a **WM_DRAWCLIPBOARD** message to the window. Since the handle to the next window in the Clipboard-viewer chain has not yet been returned, the application should not pass on the

WM_DRAWCLIPBOARD message that it receives during the call to **SetClipboardViewer**. To remove itself from the Clipboard-viewer chain, an application must call the **ChangeClipboardChain** member function.

See Also   **CWnd::ChangeClipboardChain**, **::SetClipboardViewer**

CWnd::SetDlgCtrlID

int SetDlgCtrlID(int *nID* **);**

Return Value   The previous identifier of the window, if successful; otherwise 0.

Parameters   *nID*   The new value to set for the control's identifier.

Remarks   Sets the window ID or control ID for the window to a new value. The window can be any child window, not only a control in a dialog box. The window cannot be a top-level window.

See Also   **CWnd::GetDlgCtrlID**, **CWnd::Create**, **CWnd::CreateEx**, **CWnd::GetDlgItem**

CWnd::SetDlgItemInt

void SetDlgItemInt(int *nID***, UINT** *nValue***, BOOL** *bSigned* = **TRUE);**

Parameters   *nID*   Specifies the integer ID of the control to be changed.

nValue   Specifies the integer value used to generate the item text.

bSigned   Specifies whether the integer value is signed or unsigned. If this parameter is **TRUE**, *nValue* is signed. If this parameter is **TRUE** and *nValue* is less than 0, a minus sign is placed before the first digit in the string. If this parameter is **FALSE**, *nValue* is unsigned.

Remarks   Sets the text of a given control in a dialog box to the string representation of a specified integer value. **SetDlgItemInt** sends a **WM_SETTEXT** message to the given control.

See Also   **CWnd::GetDlgItemInt**, **::SetDlgItemInt**, **WM_SETTEXT**

CWnd::SetDlgItemText

void SetDlgItemText(int *nID***, LPCTSTR** *lpszString* **);**

Parameters   *nID*   Identifies the control whose text is to be set.

lpszString   Points to a **CString** object or null-terminated string that contains the text to be copied to the control.

Remarks	Sets the caption or text of a control owned by a window or dialog box. **SetDlgItemText** sends a **WM_SETTEXT** message to the given control.
See Also	**::SetDlgItemText**, **WM_SETTEXT**, **CWnd::GetDlgItemText**

CWnd::SetForegroundWindow

BOOL SetForegroundWindow( );

Return Value	Nonzero if the function is successful; otherwise 0.
Remarks	Puts the thread that created the window into the foreground and activates the window. Keyboard input is directed to the window, and various visual cues are changed for the user. The foreground window is the window with which the user is currently working. The foreground window applies only to top-level windows (frame windows or dialogs).
See Also	**CWnd::GetForegroundWindow**

CWnd::SetFocus

CWnd* SetFocus( );

Return Value	A pointer to the window object that previously had the input focus. It is **NULL** if there is no such window. The returned pointer may be temporary and should not be stored.
Remarks	Claims the input focus. The input focus directs all subsequent keyboard input to this window. Any window that previously had the input focus loses it. The **SetFocus** member function sends a **WM_KILLFOCUS** message to the window that loses the input focus and a **WM_SETFOCUS** message to the window that receives the input focus. It also activates either the window or its parent. If the current window is active but does not have the focus (that is, no window has the focus), any key pressed will produce the messages **WM_SYSCHAR**, **WM_SYSKEYDOWN**, or **WM_SYSKEYUP**.
See Also	**::SetFocus**, **CWnd::GetFocus**

CWnd::SetFont

void SetFont(CFont* *pFont*, **BOOL** *bRedraw* = **TRUE**);

Parameters	*pFont* Specifies the new font.
	bRedraw If **TRUE**, redraw the **CWnd** object.

Remarks   Sets the window's current font to the specified font. If *bRedraw* is **TRUE**, the window will also be redrawn.

See Also   **CWnd::GetFont**, **WM_SETFONT**

CWnd::SetMenu

BOOL SetMenu(CMenu* *pMenu* **);**

Return Value Nonzero if the menu is changed; otherwise 0.

Parameters   *pMenu*   Identifies the new menu. If this parameter is **NULL**, the current menu is removed.

Remarks   Sets the current menu to the specified menu. Causes the window to be redrawn to reflect the menu change. **SetMenu** will not destroy a previous menu. An application should call the **CMenu::DestroyMenu** member function to accomplish this task.

See Also   **CMenu::DestroyMenu**, **CMenu::LoadMenu**, **::SetMenu**, **CWnd::GetMenu**

CWnd::SetOwner

void SetOwner(CWnd* *pOwnerWnd* **);**

Parameters   *pOwnerWnd*   Identifies the new owner of the window object. If this parameter is **NULL**, the window object has no owner.

Remarks   Sets the current window's owner to the specified window object. This owner can then receive command messages from the current window object. By default, the parent of the current window is its owner.

It is often useful to establish connections between window objects that are unrelated to the window hierarchy. For example, **CToolBar** sends notifications to its owner instead of to its parent. This allows the toolbar to become the child of one window (such as an OLE container application window) while sending notifications to another window (such as the in-place frame window). Furthermore, when a server window is deactivated or activated during in-place editing, any window owned by the frame window is hidden or shown. This ownership is explicitly set with a call to **SetOwner**.

See Also   **CWnd::GetOwner**, **CToolBar**, **::SetWindowWord**

CWnd::SetParent

CWnd* SetParent(CWnd* *pWndNewParent* **);**

Return Value A pointer to the previous parent window object if successful. The returned pointer may be temporary and should not be stored for later use.

Parameters   *pWndNewParent*   Identifies the new parent window.

Remarks   Changes the parent window of a child window. If the child window is visible, Windows performs the appropriate redrawing and repainting.

See Also   **::SetParent**, **CWnd::GetParent**

CWnd::SetRedraw

void SetRedraw(BOOL *bRedraw* **= TRUE);**

Parameters   *bRedraw*   Specifies the state of the redraw flag. If this parameter is **TRUE**, the redraw flag is set; if **FALSE**, the flag is cleared.

Remarks   An application calls **SetRedraw** to allow changes to be redrawn or to prevent changes from being redrawn. This member function sets or clears the redraw flag. While the redraw flag is cleared, the contents will not be updated after each change and will not be repainted until the redraw flag is set. For example, an application that needs to add several items to a list box can clear the redraw flag, add the items, and then set the redraw flag. Finally, the application can call the **Invalidate** or **InvalidateRect** member function to cause the list box to be repainted.

See Also   **WM_SETREDRAW**

CWnd::SetScrollPos

int SetScrollPos(int *nBar*, **int** *nPos*, **BOOL** *bRedraw* **= TRUE);**

Return Value   The previous position of the scroll box.

Parameters   *nBar*   Specifies the scroll bar to be set. This parameter can be either of the following:

- **SB_HORZ**   Sets the position of the scroll box in the horizontal scroll bar of the window.
- **SB_VERT**   Sets the position of the scroll box in the vertical scroll bar of the window.

nPos   Specifies the new position of the scroll box. It must be within the scrolling range.

bRedraw   Specifies whether the scroll bar should be repainted to reflect the new scroll-box position. If this parameter is **TRUE**, the scroll bar is repainted; if **FALSE**, the scroll bar is not repainted.

Remarks   Sets the current position of a scroll box and, if requested, redraws the scroll bar to reflect the new position of the scroll box. Setting *bRedraw* to **FALSE** is useful whenever the scroll bar will be redrawn by a subsequent call to another function.

See Also   **::SetScrollPos**, **CWnd::GetScrollPos**, **CScrollBar::SetScrollPos**

CWnd::SetScrollRange

void SetScrollRange(int *nBar*, int *nMinPos*, int *nMaxPos*,
      BOOL *bRedraw* = **TRUE**);

Parameters   *nBar*   Specifies the scroll bar to be set. This parameter can be either of the following values:

- **SB_HORZ**   Sets the range of the horizontal scroll bar of the window.
- **SB_VERT**   Sets the range of the vertical scroll bar of the window.

nMinPos   Specifies the minimum scrolling position.

nMaxPos   Specifies the maximum scrolling position.

bRedraw   Specifies whether the scroll bar should be redrawn to reflect the change. If *bRedraw* is **TRUE**, the scroll bar is redrawn; if **FALSE**, the scroll bar is not redrawn.

Remarks   Sets minimum and maximum position values for the given scroll bar. It can also be used to hide or show standard scroll bars. An application should not call this function to hide a scroll bar while processing a scroll-bar notification message. If the call to **SetScrollRange** immediately follows a call to the **SetScrollPos** member function, the *bRedraw* parameter in the **SetScrollPos** member function should be 0 to prevent the scroll bar from being drawn twice. The default range for a standard scroll bar is 0 through 100. The default range for a scroll bar control is empty (both the *nMinPos* and *nMaxPos* values are 0). The difference between the values specified by *nMinPos* and *nMaxPos* must not be greater than **INT_MAX**.

See Also   **CWnd::SetScrollPos**, **::SetScrollRange**, **CWnd::GetScrollRange**

CWnd::SetTimer

UINT SetTimer(UINT *nIDEvent*, UINT *nElapse*, void
      (CALLBACK EXPORT* *lpfnTimer*)(HWND, UINT, UINT, DWORD));

Return Value   The timer identifier of the new timer if the function is successful. An application passes this value to the **KillTimer** member function to kill the timer. Nonzero if successful; otherwise 0.

Parameters   *nIDEvent*   Specifies a nonzero timer identifier.

nElapse   Specifies the time-out value, in milliseconds.

lpfnTimer   Specifies the address of the application-supplied `TimerProc` callback function that processes the **WM_TIMER** messages. If this parameter is **NULL**, the **WM_TIMER** messages are placed in the application's message queue and handled by the **CWnd** object.

Remarks   Installs a system timer. A time-out value is specified, and every time a time-out occurs, the system posts a **WM_TIMER** message to the installing application's message queue or passes the message to an application-defined **TimerProc** callback function. The *lpfnTimer* callback function need not be named `TimerProc`, but it must be defined as follows and return 0.

```
void CALLBACK EXPORT TimerProc(
    HWND hWnd,       //handle of CWnd that called SetTimer
    UINT nMsg,       //WM_TIMER
    UINT nIDEvent    //timer identification
    DWORD dwTime//system time
);
```

Timers are a limited global resource; therefore it is important that an application check the value returned by the **SetTimer** member function to verify that a timer is actually available.

See Also   **WM_TIMER**, **CWnd::KillTimer**, **::SetTimer**, **CWnd::FromHandle**

CWnd::SetWindowPlacement

BOOL SetWindowPlacement(const WINDOWPLACEMENT* *lpwndpl* **);**

Return Value   Nonzero if the function is successful; otherwise 0.

Parameters   *lpwndpl*   Points to a **WINDOWPLACEMENT** structure that specifies the new show state and positions.

Remarks   Sets the show state and the normal (restored), minimized, and maximized positions for a window.

See Also   **CWnd::GetWindowPlacement**, **::SetWindowPlacement**

CWnd::SetWindowPos

BOOL SetWindowPos(const CWnd* *pWndInsertAfter***, int** *x***, int** *y***, int** *cx***, int** *cy***, UINT** *nFlags* **);**

Return Value   Nonzero if the function is successful; otherwise 0.

Parameters   *pWndInsertAfter*   Identifies the **CWnd** object that will precede this **CWnd** object in the Z-order. This parameter can be a pointer to a **CWnd** or one of the following values:

- **wndBottom**   Places the window at the bottom of the Z-order. If this **CWnd** is a topmost window, the window loses its topmost status; the system places the window at the bottom of all other windows.

- **wndTop**   Places the window at the top of the Z-order.

- **wndTopMost**   Places the window above all nontopmost windows. The window maintains its topmost position even when it is deactivated.

- **wndNoTopMost**   Repositions the window to the top of all nontopmost windows (that is, behind all topmost windows). This flag has no effect if the window is already a nontopmost window.

See the "Remarks" section for this function below for rules about how this parameter is used.

x   Specifies the new position of the left side of the window.

y   Specifies the new position of the top of the window.

cx   Specifies the new width of the window.

cy   Specifies the new height of the window.

nFlags   Specifies sizing and positioning options. This parameter can be a combination of the following:

- **SWP_DRAWFRAME**   Draws a frame (defined when the window was created) around the window.

- **SWP_HIDEWINDOW**   Hides the window.

- **SWP_NOACTIVATE**   Does not activate the window. If this flag is not set, the window is activated and moved to the top of either the topmost or the nontopmost group (depending on the setting of the *pWndInsertAfter* parameter).

- **SWP_NOMOVE**   Retains current position (ignores the *x* and *y* parameters).

- **SWP_NOREDRAW**   Does not redraw changes. If this flag is set, no repainting of any kind occurs. This applies to the client area, the nonclient area (including the title and scroll bars), and any part of the parent window uncovered as a result of the moved window. When this flag is set, the application must explicitly invalidate or redraw any parts of the window and parent window that must be redrawn.

- **SWP_NOSIZE**   Retains current size (ignores the *cx* and *cy* parameters).
- **SWP_NOZORDER**   Retains current ordering (ignores *pWndInsertAfter*).
- **SWP_SHOWWINDOW**   Displays the window.

Remarks   Call this member function to change the size, position, and Z-order of child, pop-up, and top-level windows.

Windows are ordered on the screen according to their Z-order; the window at the top of the Z-order appears on top of all other windows in the order.

All coordinates for child windows are client coordinates (relative to the upper-left corner of the parent window's client area).

A window can be moved to the top of the Z-order either by setting the *pWndInsertAfter* parameter to **&wndTopMost** and ensuring that the **SWP_NOZORDER** flag is not set or by setting a window's Z-order so that it is above any existing topmost windows. When a nontopmost window is made topmost, its owned windows are also made topmost. Its owners are not changed. A topmost window is no longer topmost if it is repositioned to the bottom (**&wndBottom**) of the Z-order or after any nontopmost window. When a topmost window is made nontopmost, all of its owners and its owned windows are also made nontopmost windows.

If neither **SWP_NOACTIVATE** nor **SWP_NOZORDER** is specified (that is, when the application requests that a window be simultaneously activated and placed in the specified Z-order), the value specified in *pWndInsertAfter* is used only in the following circumstances:

- Neither **&wndTopMost** nor **&wndNoTopMost** is specified in the *pWndInsertAfter* parameter.
- This window is not the active window.

An application cannot activate an inactive window without also bringing it to the top of the Z-order. Applications can change the Z-order of an activated window without restrictions.

A nontopmost window may own a topmost window, but not vice versa. Any window (for example, a dialog box) owned by a topmost window is itself made a topmost window to ensure that all owned windows stay above their owner.

With Windows versions 3.1 and later, windows can be moved to the top of the Z-order and locked there by setting their **WS_EX_TOPMOST** styles. Such a topmost window maintains its topmost position even when deactivated. For example, selecting the WinHelp Always On Top command makes the Help window topmost, and it then remains visible when you return to your application.

To create a topmost window, call **SetWindowPos** with the *pWndInsertAfter* parameter equal to **&wndTopMost**, or set the **WS_EX_TOPMOST** style when you create the window.

If the Z-order contains any windows with the **WS_EX_TOPMOST** style, a window moved with the **&wndTopMost** value is placed at the top of all nontopmost windows, but below any topmost windows. When an application activates an inactive window without the **WS_EX_TOPMOST** bit, the window is moved above all nontopmost windows but below any topmost windows.

If **SetWindowPos** is called when the *pWndInsertAfter* parameter is **&wndBottom** and **CWnd** is a topmost window, the window loses its topmost status (**WS_EX_TOPMOST** is cleared), and the system places the window at the bottom of the Z-order.

See Also   **::DeferWindowPos, ::SetWindowPos**

CWnd::SetWindowText

void SetWindowText(LPCTSTR *lpszString* **);**

Parameters   *lpszString*   Points to a **CString** object or null-terminated string to be used as the new title or control text.

Remarks   Sets the window's title to the specified text. If the window is a control, the text within the control is set. This function causes a **WM_SETTEXT** message to be sent to this window.

See Also   **CWnd::GetWindowText, ::SetWindowText**

CWnd::ShowCaret

void ShowCaret( );

Remarks   Shows the caret on the screen at the caret's current position. Once shown, the caret begins flashing automatically. The **ShowCaret** member function shows the caret only if it has a current shape and has not been hidden two or more times consecutively. If the caret is not owned by this window, the caret is not shown.

Hiding the caret is cumulative. If the **HideCaret** member function has been called five times consecutively, **ShowCaret** must be called five times to show the caret. The caret is a shared resource. The window should show the caret only when it has the input focus or is active.

See Also   **CWnd::HideCaret, ::ShowCaret**

CWnd::ShowOwnedPopups

void ShowOwnedPopups(BOOL *bShow* **= TRUE);**

Parameters   *bShow*   Specifies whether pop-up windows are to be shown or hidden. If this parameter is **TRUE**, all hidden pop-up windows are shown. If this parameter is **FALSE**, all visible pop-up windows are hidden.

Remarks   Shows or hides all pop-up windows owned by this window.

See Also   **::ShowOwnedPopups**

CWnd::ShowScrollBar

void ShowScrollBar(UINT *nBar***, BOOL** *bShow* **= TRUE);**

Parameters   *nBar*   Specifies whether the scroll bar is a control or part of a window's nonclient area. If it is part of the nonclient area, *nBar* also indicates whether the scroll bar is positioned horizontally, vertically, or both. It must be one of the following:

- **SB_BOTH**   Specifies the horizontal and vertical scroll bars of the window.
- **SB_HORZ**   Specifies that the window is a horizontal scroll bar.
- **SB_VERT**   Specifies that the window is a vertical scroll bar.

bShow   Specifies whether Windows shows or hides the scroll bar. If this parameter is **TRUE**, the scroll bar is shown; otherwise the scroll bar is hidden.

Remarks   Shows or hides a scroll bar. An application should not call **ShowScrollBar** to hide a scroll bar while processing a scroll-bar notification message.

See Also   **::ShowScrollBar**, **CScrollBar::ShowScrollBar**

CWnd::ShowWindow

BOOL ShowWindow(int *nCmdShow* **);**

Return Value   Nonzero if the window was previously visible; 0 if the **CWnd** was previously hidden.

Parameters   *nCmdShow*   Specifies how the **CWnd** is to be shown. It must be one of the following values:

- **SW_HIDE**   Hides this window and passes activation to another window.
- **SW_MINIMIZE**   Minimizes the window and activates the top-level window in the system's list.

- **SW_RESTORE**   Activates and displays the window. If the window is minimized or maximized, Windows restores it to its original size and position.
- **SW_SHOW**   Activates the window and displays it in its current size and position.
- **SW_SHOWMAXIMIZED**   Activates the window and displays it as a maximized window.
- **SW_SHOWMINIMIZED**   Activates the window and displays it as an icon.
- **SW_SHOWMINNOACTIVE**   Displays the window as an icon. The window that is currently active remains active.
- **SW_SHOWNA**   Displays the window in its current state. The window that is currently active remains active.
- **SW_SHOWNOACTIVATE**   Displays the window in its most recent size and position. The window that is currently active remains active.
- **SW_SHOWNORMAL**   Activates and displays the window. If the window is minimized or maximized, Windows restores it to its original size and position.

Remarks   Sets the visibility state of the window. **ShowWindow** must be called only once per application for the main window with **CWinApp::m_nCmdShow**. Subsequent calls to **ShowWindow** must use one of the values listed above instead of the one specified by **m_nCmdShow**.

See Also   **::ShowWindow**, **CWnd::OnShowWindow**, **CWnd::ShowOwnedPopups**,

CWnd::SubclassDlgItem

BOOL SubclassDlgItem(UINT *nID*, **CWnd*** *pParent* **);**

Return Value   Nonzero if the function is successful; otherwise 0.

Parameters   *nID*   The control's ID.

pParent   The control's parent (usually a dialog box).

Remarks   Call this member function to "dynamically subclass" a control created from a dialog template and attach it to this **CWnd** object. When a control is dynamically subclassed, windows messages will route through the **CWnd**'s message map and call message handlers in the **CWnd**'s class first. Messages that are passed to the base class will be passed to the default message handler in the control.

This member function attaches the Windows control to a **CWnd** object and replaces the control's **WndProc** and **AfxWndProc** functions. The function stores the old **WndProc** in the location returned by the **GetSuperWndProcAddr** member function. You must override the **GetSuperWndProcAddr** member function for every unique window class to provide a place to store the old **WndProc**.

See Also   CWnd::GetSuperWndProcAddr, CWnd::DefWindowProc, CWnd::SubclassWindow, CWnd::Attach

CWnd::SubclassWindow

BOOL SubclassWindow(HWND *hWnd*);

Return Value   Nonzero if the function is successful; otherwise 0.

Parameters   *hWnd*   A handle to the window.

Remarks   Call this member function to "dynamically subclass" a window and attach it to this **CWnd** object. When a window is dynamically subclassed, windows messages will route through the **CWnd**'s message map and call message handlers in the **CWnd**'s class first. Messages that are passed to the base class will be passed to the default message handler in the window.

This member function attaches the Windows control to a **CWnd** object and replaces the window's **WndProc** and **AfxWndProc** functions. The function stores the old **WndProc** in the location returned by the **GetSuperWndProcAddr** member function. You must override the **GetSuperWndProcAddr** member function for every unique window class to provide a place to store the old **WndProc**.

See Also   CWnd::GetSuperWndProcAddr, CWnd::DefWindowProc, CWnd::SubclassDlgItem, CWnd::Attach

CWnd::UpdateData

BOOL **UpdateData**(BOOL *bSaveAndValidate* = TRUE);

Return Value   Nonzero if the operation is successful; otherwise 0. If *bSaveAndValidate* is **TRUE**, then a return value of nonzero means that the data is successfully validated.

Parameters   *bSaveAndValidate*   Flag that indicates whether dialog box is being initialized (**FALSE**) or data is being retrieved (**TRUE**).

Remarks   Call this member function to initialize data in a dialog box, or to retrieve and validate dialog data.

The framework automatically calls **UpdateData** with *bSaveAndValidate* set to **FALSE** when a modal dialog box is created in the default implementation of **CDialog::OnInitDialog**. The call occurs before the dialog box is visible. The default implementation of **CDialog::OnOK** calls this member function with *bSaveAndValidate* set to **TRUE** to retrieve the data, and if successful, will close the dialog box. (If the Cancel button is clicked in the dialog box, the dialog box is closed without the data being retrieved.)

See Also   **CWnd::DoDataExchange**

CWnd::UpdateDialogControls

void UpdateDialogControls(CCmdTarget* *pTarget*, **BOOL** *bDisableIfNoHndler* **);**

Parameters   *pTarget*   Points to the main frame window of the application, and used for routing update messages.

bDisableIfNoHndler   Flag that indicates whether a control that has no update handler should be automatically displayed as disabled.

Remarks   Call this member function to update the state of dialog buttons and other controls in a dialog box or window that uses the **ON_UPDATE_COMMAND_UI** callback mechanism.

If a child control does not have a handler and *bDisableIfNoHndler* is **TRUE**, then the child control will be disabled.

The framework calls this member function for controls in dialog bars or toolbars as part of the application's idle processing.

See Also   **CFrameWnd::m_bAutoMenuEnable**

CWnd::UpdateWindow

void UpdateWindow( );

Remarks   Updates the client area by sending a **WM_PAINT** message if the update region is not empty. The **UpdateWindow** member function sends a **WM_PAINT** message directly, bypassing the application queue. If the update region is empty, **WM_PAINT** is not sent.

See Also   **::UpdateWindow**, **CWnd::RedrawWindow**

CWnd::ValidateRect

void ValidateRect(LPCRECT *lpRect* **);**

Parameters   *lpRect*   Points to a **CRect** object or **RECT** structure that contains client coordinates of the rectangle to be removed from the update region. If *lpRect* is **NULL**, the entire window is validated.

Remarks   Validates the client area within the given rectangle by removing the rectangle from the update region of the window. The **BeginPaint** member function automatically validates the entire client area. Neither the **ValidateRect** nor **ValidateRgn** member function should be called if a portion of the update region needs to be validated before **WM_PAINT** is next generated. Windows continues to generate **WM_PAINT** messages until the current update region is validated.

See Also   **CWnd::BeginPaint**, **::ValidateRect**, **CWnd::ValidateRgn**

CWnd::ValidateRgn

void ValidateRgn(CRgn* *pRgn* **);**

Parameters   *pRgn*   Identifies a region that defines the area to be removed from the update region. If this parameter is **NULL**, the entire client area is removed.

Remarks   Validates the client area within the given region by removing the region from the current update region of the window. The given region must have been created previously by a region function. The region coordinates are assumed to be client coordinates. The **BeginPaint** member function automatically validates the entire client area. Neither the **ValidateRect** nor the **ValidateRgn** member function should be called if a portion of the update region must be validated before the next **WM_PAINT** message is generated.

See Also   **::ValidateRgn**, **CWnd::ValidateRect**

CWnd::WindowFromPoint

static CWnd* PASCAL WindowFromPoint(POINT *point* **);**

Return Value   A pointer to the window object in which the point lies. It is **NULL** if no window exists at the given point. The returned pointer may be temporary and should not be stored for later use.

Parameters   *point*   Specifies a **CPoint** object or **POINT** data structure that defines the point to be checked.

Remarks   Retrieves the window that contains the specified point; *point* must specify the screen coordinates of a point on the screen. **WindowFromPoint** does not retrieve a hidden, disabled, or transparent window, even if the point is within the window. An application should use the **ChildWindowFromPoint** member function for a nonrestrictive search.

See Also   **::WindowFromPoint**, **CWnd::ChildWindowFromPoint**

CWnd::WindowProc

Protected→

virtual LRESULT WindowProc(UINT *message***, WPARAM** *wParam***,**
LPARAM *lParam* **);**

END Protected

Return Value   The return value depends on the message.

Parameters   *message*   Specifies the Windows message to be processed.

wParam   Provides additional information used in processing the message. The parameter value depends on the message.

lParam   Provides additional information used in processing the message. The parameter value depends on the message.

Remarks   Provides a Windows procedure (**WindowProc**) for a **CWnd** object. It dispatches messages through the window's message map.

Data Members

CWnd::m_hWnd

Remarks   The handle of the Windows window attached to this **CWnd**. The **m_hWnd** data member is a public variable of type **HWND**.

See Also   **CWnd::Attach**, **CWnd::Detach**, **CWnd::FromHandle**

class CWordArray : public CObject

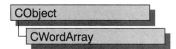

The **CWordArray** class supports arrays of 16-bit words. The member functions of **CWordArray** are similar to the member functions of class **CObArray**. Because of this similarity, you can use the **CObArray** reference documentation for member function specifics. Wherever you see a **CObject** pointer as a function parameter or return value, substitute a **WORD**.

```
CObject* CObArray::GetAt( int <nIndex> ) const;
```

for example, translates to

```
WORD CWordArray::GetAt( int <nIndex> ) const;
```

Note   Before using an array, use **SetSize** to establish its size and allocate memory for it. If you do not use **SetSize**, adding elements to your array causes it to be frequently reallocated and copied. Frequent reallocation and copying are inefficient and can fragment memory.

If you need a dump of individual elements in the array, you must set the depth of the dump context to 1 or greater.

#include <afxcoll.h>

Construction
CWordArray   Constructs an empty array for words.

Bounds
GetSize   Gets number of elements in this array.

GetUpperBound   Returns the largest valid index.

SetSize   Sets the number of elements to be contained in this array.

Operations
FreeExtra   Frees all unused memory above the current upper bound.

RemoveAll   Removes all the elements from this array.

Element Access

GetAt   Returns the value at a given index.

SetAt   Sets the value for a given index; array is not allowed to grow.

ElementAt   Returns a temporary reference to the element pointer within the array.

Growing the Array

SetAtGrow   Sets the value for a given index; grows the array if necessary.

Add   Adds an element to the end of the array; grows the array if necessary.

Insertion/Removal

InsertAt   Inserts an element (or all the elements in another array) at a specified index.

RemoveAt   Removes an element at a specific index.

Operators

operator [ ]   Sets or gets the element at the specified index.

Macros and Globals

The Microsoft Foundation Class Library can be divided into two major sections: 1) the MFC classes and 2) macros and globals. If a function or variable is not a member of a class, it is a global function or variable.

The MFC macros and globals offer functionality in the following categories:

- Data types
- Run-time object-model services
- Diagnostic services
- Exception processing
- **CString** formatting and message-box display
- Message maps
- ClassWizard comment delimiters
- Application information and management
- Standard commands and window IDs
- OLE support in the following categories:
  - OLE initialization
  - Application control
  - Dispatch maps
- Database support in the following categories:
  - Record Field Exchange (RFX) functions
  - Dialog Data Exchange (DDX) functions for class **CRecordView**
  - Macros to aid in calling Open Database Connectivity (ODBC) application programming interface (API) functions directly

The first part of this section briefly discusses each of the above categories and lists each global and macro in the category, along with a brief description of what it does. Following this is a complete alphabetical listing of all the global functions, global variables, and macros in the MFC classes.

The main supporting reference for the "Macros and Globals" section is *Programming with the Microsoft Foundation Class Library*. This is usually the first place you should look to find more information on macros and globals. When necessary, the appropriate article in *Programming with the Microsoft Foundation Class Library* is mentioned with the function or macro description.

Note Most global functions start with the prefix "Afx"—the RFX functions and DDX functions are an exception to this convention. All global variables start with the prefix "afx". Macros do not start with any particular prefix, but they are written all in uppercase.

Data Types

This section lists the data types most commonly used in the Microsoft Foundation Class Library. Most of these data types are exactly the same as those in the Windows Software Development Kit (SDK) version 3.1, while others are unique to MFC.

Commonly used Windows SDK and MFC data types are as follows:

- **BOOL** A boolean value.
- **BSTR** A 32-bit character pointer.
- **BYTE** An 8-bit unsigned integer.
- **COLORREF** A 32-bit value used as a color value.
- **DWORD** A 32-bit unsigned integer or the address of a segment and its associated offset.
- **LONG** A 32-bit signed integer.
- **LPARAM** A 32-bit value passed as a parameter to a window procedure or callback function.
- **LPCSTR** A 32-bit pointer to a constant character string.
- **LPSTR** A 32-bit pointer to a character string.
- **LPCTSTR** A 32-bit pointer to a constant character string that is portable for Unicode and DBCS.
- **LPTSTR** A 32-bit pointer to a character string that is portable for Unicode and DBCS.
- **LPVOID** A 32-bit pointer to an unspecified type.
- **LRESULT** A 32-bit value returned from a window procedure or callback function.
- **UINT** A 16-bit unsigned integer on Windows versions 3.0 and 3.1; a 32-bit unsigned integer on Win32.

- **WNDPROC** A 32-bit pointer to a window procedure.
- **WORD** A 16-bit unsigned integer.
- **WPARAM** A value passed as a parameter to a window procedure or callback function; 16 bits on Windows versions 3.0 and 3.1; 32 bits on Win32.

Data types unique to the Microsoft Foundation Class Library include the following:

- **POSITION** A value used to denote the position of an element in a collection; used by MFC collection classes.
- **LPCRECT** A 32-bit pointer to a constant (nonmodifiable) **RECT** structure.

For a list of the less common data types, see the Windows SDK reference.

Run-Time Object Model Services

The classes **CObject** and **CRuntimeClass** encapsulate several object services, including access to run-time class information, serialization, and dynamic object creation. All classes derived from **CObject** inherit this functionality.

Access to run-time class information enables you to determine information about an object's class at run time. The ability to determine the class of an object at run time is useful when you need extra type-checking of function arguments and when you must write special-purpose code based on the class of an object. Run-time class information is not supported directly by the C++ language.

Serialization is the process of writing or reading an object's contents to or from a file. You can use serialization to store an object's contents even after the application exits. The object can then be read from the file when the application is restarted. Such data objects are said to be "persistent."

Dynamic object creation enables you to create an object of a specified class at run time. For example, document, view, and frame objects must support dynamic creation because the framework needs to create them dynamically.

The following table lists the MFC macros that support run-time class information, serialization, and dynamic creation. For more information on these run-time object services and serialization, see *Programming with the Microsoft Foundation Class Library*.

Run-Time Object Model Services

DECLARE_DYNAMIC	Enables access to run-time class information (must be used in the class declaration).
DECLARE_DYNCREATE	Enables dynamic creation and access to run-time class information (must be used in the class declaration).
DECLARE_SERIAL	Enables serialization and access to run-time class information (must be used in the class declaration).
IMPLEMENT_DYNAMIC	Enables access to run-time class information (must be used in the class implementation).
IMPLEMENT_DYNCREATE	Enables dynamic creation and access to run-time information (must be used in the class implementation).
IMPLEMENT_SERIAL	Permits serialization and access to run-time class information (must be used in the class implementation).
RUNTIME_CLASS	Returns the **CRuntimeClass** structure that corresponds to the named class.

OLE frequently requires the dynamic creation of objects at run time. For example, an OLE server application must be able to create OLE items dynamically in response to a request from a client. Similarly, an automation server must be able to create items in response to requests from automation clients.

The Microsoft Foundation Class Library provides two macros specific to OLE.

DECLARE_OLECREATE	Enables objects to be created through OLE automation.
IMPLEMENT_OLECREATE	Enables objects to be created by the OLE system.

Diagnostic Services

The Microsoft Foundation Class Library supplies many diagnostic services that make debugging your programs easier. These diagnostic services include macros and global functions that allow you to track your program's memory allocations, dump the contents of objects during run time, and print debugging messages during run time. The macros and global functions for diagnostic services are grouped into the following categories:

- General diagnostic macros
- General diagnostic functions and variables
- Object diagnostic functions

These macros and functions are available for all classes derived from **CObject** in the Debug and Release versions of MFC. However, all except **DEBUG_NEW** and **VERIFY** do nothing in the Release version.

In the Debug library, all allocated memory blocks are bracketed with a series of "guard bytes." If these bytes are disturbed by an errant memory write, then the diagnostic routines can report a problem. If you include the line

```
#define new DEBUG_NEW
```

in your implementation file, all calls to **new** will store the filename and line number where the memory allocation took place. The function **CMemoryState::DumpAllObjectsSince** will display this extra information, allowing you to identify memory leaks. Refer also to the class **CDumpContext** for additional information on diagnostic output.

For a general discussion of diagnostic facilities and the use of some of the key memory diagnostic functions, see *Programming with the Microsoft Foundation Class Library.*

General Diagnostic Macros

ASSERT	Prints a message and then aborts the program if the specified expression evaluates to **FALSE** in the Debug version of the library.
ASSERT_VALID	Tests the internal validity of an object by calling its **AssertValid** member function; typically overridden from **CObject**.
DEBUG_NEW	Supplies a filename and line number for all object allocations in Debug mode to help find memory leaks.

TRACE	Provides **printf**-like capability in the Debug version of the library.
TRACE0	Similar to **TRACE** but takes a format string with no arguments.
TRACE1	Similar to **TRACE** but takes a format string with a single argument.
TRACE2	Similar to **TRACE** but takes a format string with two arguments.
TRACE3	Similar to **TRACE** but takes a format string with three arguments.
VERIFY	Similar to **ASSERT** but evaluates the expression in the Release version of the library as well as in the Debug version.

General Diagnostic Functions and Variables

afxDump	Global variable that sends **CDumpContext** information to the debugger output window or to the debug terminal.
afxMemDF	Global variable that controls the behavior of the debugging memory allocator.
afxTraceEnabled	Global variable used to enable or disable output from the **TRACE** macro.
afxTraceFlags	Global variable used to turn on the built-in reporting features of MFC.
AfxCheckMemory	Checks the integrity of all currently allocated memory.
AfxDump	If called while in the debugger, dumps the state of an object while debugging.
AfxEnableMemoryTracking	Turns memory tracking on and off.
AfxIsMemoryBlock	Verifies that a memory block has been properly allocated.
AfxIsValidAddress	Verifies that a memory address range is within the program's bounds.
AfxIsValidString	Determines whether a pointer to a string is valid.
AfxSetAllocHook	Enables the calling of a function on each memory allocation.

Object Diagnostic Functions

AfxDoForAllClasses	Performs a specified function on all **CObject**-derived classes that support run-time type checking.
AfxDoForAllObjects	Performs a specified function on all **CObject**-derived objects that were allocated with **new**.

Exception Processing

When a program executes, a number of abnormal conditions and errors called "exceptions" can occur. These may include running out of memory, resource allocation errors, and failure to find files.

The Microsoft Foundation Class Library uses an exception-handling scheme that is modeled closely after the one proposed by the ANSI standards committee for C++. An exception handler must be set up before calling a function that may encounter an abnormal situation. If the function encounters an abnormal condition, it throws an exception and control is passed to the exception handler.

Several macros included with the Microsoft Foundation Class Library will set up exception handlers. A number of other global functions help to throw specialized exceptions and terminate programs, if necessary. These macros and global functions fall into the following categories:

- Exception macros, which structure your exception handler
- Exception-throwing functions, which generate exceptions of specific types
- Termination functions, which cause program termination

For examples and more details, see the article "Exceptions" in *Programming with the Microsoft Foundation Class Library*.

See Also   **CException**

Exception Macros

TRY	Designates a block of code for exception processing.
CATCH	Designates a block of code for catching an exception from the preceding **TRY** block.
AND_CATCH	Designates a block of code for catching additional exception types from the preceding **TRY** block.

END_CATCH	Ends the last **CATCH** or **AND_CATCH** code block.
THROW	Throws a specified exception.
THROW_LAST	Throws the currently handled exception to the next outer handler.

Exception-Throwing Functions

AfxThrowArchiveException	Throws an archive exception.
AfxThrowFileException	Throws a file exception.
AfxThrowMemoryException	Throws a memory exception.
AfxThrowNotSupportedException	Throws a not-supported exception.
AfxThrowResourceException	Throws a Windows resource-not-found exception.
AfxThrowUserException	Throws an exception in a user-initiated program action.

MFC provides two exception-throwing functions specifically for OLE exceptions:

| **AfxThrowOleDispatchException** | Throws an exception within an OLE automation function. |
| **AfxThrowOleException** | Throws an OLE exception. |

To support database exceptions, the database classes provide a new exception class, **CDBException**, and one global function to support the exception type:

| **AfxThrowDBException** | Throws a **CDBException** from your own code when an exceptional condition occurs during database processing. |

Termination Functions

| **AfxAbort** | Called to terminate an application when a fatal error occurs. |

CString Formatting and Message-Box Display

A number of functions are provided to format and parse **CString** objects. You can use these functions whenever you have to manipulate **CString** objects, but they are particularly useful for formatting strings that will appear in message-box text.

This group of functions also includes a global routine for displaying a message box.

See Also   **CString**

CString Functions

AfxFormatString1　　Substitutes a given string for the format characters "%1" in a string contained in the string table.

AfxFormatString2　　Substitutes two strings for the format characters "%1" and "%2" in a string contained in the string table.

AfxMessageBox　　Displays a message box.

Message Maps

Since Windows is a message-oriented operating system, a large portion of programming for the Windows environment involves message handling. Each time an event such as a keystroke or mouse click occurs, a message is sent to the application, which must then handle the event.

The Microsoft Foundation Class Library offers a programming model optimized for message-based programming. In this model, "message maps" are used to designate which functions will handle various messages for a particular class. Message maps contain one or more macros that specify which messages will be handled by which functions. For example, a message map containing an **ON_COMMAND** macro might look something like this:

```
BEGIN_MESSAGE_MAP( CMyDoc, CDocument )
    //{{AFX_MSG_MAP( CMyDoc )
    ON_COMMAND( ID_MYCMD, OnMyCommand )
    // ... More entries to handle additional commands
    //}}AFX_MSG_MAP
END_MESSAGE_MAP( )
```

The **ON_COMMAND** macro is used to handle command messages generated by menus, buttons, and accelerator keys. Macros are available to map the following:

Windows Messages
- Control notifications
- User-defined messages

Command Messages
- Registered user-defined messages
- User-interface update messages

Ranges of Messages

- Commands
- Update handler messages
- Control notifications

Although message-map macros are important, you generally won't have to use them directly. This is because ClassWizard automatically creates message-map entries in your source files when you use it to associate message-handling functions with messages. Any time you want to edit or add a message-map entry, you can use ClassWizard.

Note ClassWizard does not support message map ranges. You must write these message map entries yourself.

However, message maps are important part of the Microsoft Foundation Class Library. You should understand what they do, and documentation is provided for them.

To support message maps, MFC supplies the following macros:

Message-Map Declaration and Demarcation

DECLARE_MESSAGE_MAP	Declares that a message map will be used in a class to map messages to functions (must be used in the class declaration).
BEGIN_MESSAGE_MAP	Begins the definition of a message map (must be used in the class implementation).
END_MESSAGE_MAP	Ends the definition of a message map (must be used in the class implementation).

Message-Mapping Macros

ON_COMMAND	Indicates which function will handle a specified command message.
ON_CONTROL	Indicates which function will handle a specified control-notification message.
ON_MESSAGE	Indicates which function will handle a user-defined message.

ON_REGISTERED_MESSAGE	Indicates which function will handle a registered user-defined message.
ON_UPDATE_COMMAND_UI	Indicates which function will handle a specified user-interface update command message.

Message-Map Range Macros

ON_COMMAND_RANGE	Indicates which function will handle the range of command IDs specified in the first two parameters to the macro.
ON_UPDATE_COMMAND_UI_RANGE	Indicates which update handler will handle the range of command IDs specified in the first two parameters to the macro.
ON_CONTROL_RANGE	Indicates which function will handle notifications from the range of control IDs specified in the second and third parameters to the macro. The first parameter is a control-notification message, such as **BN_CLICKED**.

For more information on message maps, the message-map declaration and demarcation macros, and the message-mapping macros, see Chapter 2 in *Programming with the Microsoft Foundation Class Library*. For more information about message map ranges, see the article "Message Map: Ranges of Messages" in Part 2 of *Programming with the Microsoft Foundation Class Library*. For more information on how to use ClassWizard, see the *Visual C++ User's Guide*.

Application Information and Management

When you write an application, you create a single **CWinApp**-derived object. At times, you may wish to get information about this object from outside the **CWinApp**-derived object.

See Also   **CWinApp**

The Microsoft Foundation Class Library provides the following global functions to help you accomplish these tasks:

Application Information and Management

AfxGetApp	Returns a pointer to the application's single **CWinApp** object.
AfxGetAppName	Returns a string containing the application's name.
AfxGetInstanceHandle	Returns an **HINSTANCE** representing this instance of the application.
AfxGetMainWnd	Returns a pointer to the current "main" window of a non-OLE application, or the in-place frame window of a server application.
AfxGetResourceHandle	Returns an **HINSTANCE** to the source of the application's default resources. Use this to access the application's resources directly.
AfxRegisterWndClass	Registers a Windows window class to supplement those registered automatically by MFC.
AfxSetResourceHandle	Sets the **HINSTANCE** handle where the default resources of the application are loaded.
AfxRegisterClass	Registers a window class in a DLL that uses MFC.
AfxBeginThread	Creates a new thread.
AfxEndThread	Terminates the current thread.
AfxGetThread	Retrieves a pointer to the current **CWinThread** object.

Standard Command and Window IDs

The Microsoft Foundation Class Library defines a number of standard command and window IDs in AFXRES.H. These IDs are most commonly used within the resource editors and ClassWizard to map messages to your handler functions. All standard commands have an **ID_** prefix. For example, when you use the menu editor, you normally bind the File Open menu item to the standard **ID_FILE_OPEN** command ID.

For most standard commands, application code does not need to refer to the command ID, because the framework itself handles the commands through message-maps in its primary framework classes (**CWinThread**, **CWinApp**, **CView**, **CDocument**, and so forth).

In addition to standard command IDs, a number of other standard IDs are defined which have a prefix of **AFX_ID**. These IDs include standard window IDs (prefix **AFX_IDW_**), string IDs (prefix **AFX_IDS_**), and several other types.

IDs that begin with the **AFX_ID** prefix are rarely used by programmers, but you might need to refer to these IDs when overriding framework functions which also refer to the **AFX_ID**s.

IDs are not individually documented in this reference. You can find more information on them in Technical Notes 20, 21, and 22, which can be found under MFC in Books Online.

Note The header file AFXRES.H is indirectly included in AFXWIN.H. You must explicitly include the statement

```
#include afxres.h
```
in your application's resource script (.RC) file.

OLE Initialization

Before an application can use OLE system services, it must initialize the OLE system DLLs and verify that the DLLs are the correct version. The **AfxOleInit** function initializes the OLE system DLLs.

OLE Initialization

AfxOleInit	Initializes the OLE libraries.

Application Control

OLE requires substantial control over applications and their objects. The OLE system DLLs must be able to launch and release applications automatically, coordinate their production and modification of objects, and so on. The functions in this section meet those requirements. In addition to being called by the OLE system DLLs, these functions must sometimes be called by applications as well.

Application Control

AfxOleCanExitApp	Indicates whether the application can terminate.
AfxOleGetMessageFilter	Retrieves the application's current message filter.
AfxOleGetUserCtrl	Retrieves the current user-control flag.
AfxOleSetUserCtrl	Sets or clears the user-control flag.
AfxOleLockApp	Increments the framework's global count of the number of active objects in an application.
AfxOleUnlockApp	Decrements the framework's count of the number of active objects in an application.
AfxOleRegisterServerClass	Registers a server in the OLE system registry.
AfxOleSetEditMenu	Implements the user interface for the *typename* Object command.

Dispatch Maps

OLE Automation provides ways to call methods and to access properties across applications. The mechanism supplied by the Microsoft Foundation Class Library for dispatching these requests is the "dispatch map," which designates the internal and external names of object functions and properties, as well as the data types of the properties themselves and of function arguments.

Dispatch Maps

DECLARE_DISPATCH_MAP	Declares that a dispatch map will be used to expose a class's methods and properties (must be used in the class declaration).
BEGIN_DISPATCH_MAP	Starts the definition of a dispatch map.
END_DISPATCH_MAP	Ends the definition of a dispatch map.
DISP_FUNCTION	Used in a dispatch map to define an OLE automation function.

DISP_PROPERTY	Defines an OLE automation property.
DISP_PROPERTY_EX	Defines an OLE automation property and names the "get" and "set" functions.
DISP_DEFVALUE	Makes an existing property the default value of an object.

Record Field Exchange Functions

This section lists the Record Field Exchange (RFX) functions used to automate transfer of data between a recordset object and its data source and to perform other operations on the data. For each field data member in your recordset class, ClassWizard writes an RFX function in the overriding **DoFieldExchange** member function of the recordset class—specifically within the "data map" portion of the function. Depending on the context, these functions can move data, either from data source to recordset or from recordset to data source, each time the framework calls **DoFieldExchange**. Each RFX function transfers a specific data type.

An RFX function call specifies the name of the recordset data member it represents. There are two types of data members for which you make RFX calls: field data members and parameter data members. ClassWizard does not support parameter data members, so you must write your own RFX function calls for them. (For more information about parameters, see the article "Recordset: Parameterizing a Recordset" in *Programming with the Microsoft Foundation Class Library*.)

You must precede each group of RFX calls for a particular type of data member with a call to **CFieldExchange::SetFieldType**.

For more information about how these functions are used, see the article "Record Field Exchange: How RFX Works." For columns of data that you bind dynamically, you can also call the RFX functions yourself, rather than using ClassWizard, as explained in the article "Recordset: Dynamically Binding Data Columns." Both articles are found in *Programming with the Microsoft Foundation Class Library*. Additionally, you can write your own custom RFX routines, as explained in Technical Note 43. For an example of RFX functions as they appear in a **DoFieldExchange** function, see **RFX_Text**.

RFX Functions

RFX_Text	Transfers string data.
RFX_Bool	Transfers Boolean data.
RFX_Byte	Transfers a single byte of data.
RFX_Int	Transfers integer data.
RFX_Long	Transfers long integer data.
RFX_Single	Transfers float data.

RFX_Double	Transfers double-precision float data.
RFX_Date	Transfers time and date data.
RFX_Binary	Transfers arrays of bytes.
RFX_LongBinary	Transfers binary-large-object (BLOB) data via an object of the **CLongBinary** class.

Dialog Data Exchange Functions for CRecordView

This section lists the DDX_Field functions used to exchange data between a recordset and a **CRecordView** form.

Important DDX_Field functions are like DDX functions in that they exchange data with controls in a form. But unlike DDX, they exchange data with the fields of the view's associated recordset object rather than with fields of the record view itself. For more information, see class **CRecordView** and the article "ClassWizard: Mapping Form Controls to Recordset Fields" in *Programming with the Microsoft Foundation Class Library*.

DDX Functions

DDX_FieldText	Overloaded versions are available for transferring **int**, **UINT**, **long**, **DWORD**, **CString**, **float**, and **double** data between a recordset field data member and an edit box in a **CRecordView**.
DDX_FieldRadio	Transfers integer data between a recordset field data member and a group of radio buttons in a **CRecordView**.
DDX_FieldLBString	Manages the transfer of **CString** data between a list-box control and the field data members of a recordset. When moving data from the recordset to the control, this function selects the item in the list box that begins with the characters in the specified string.
DDX_FieldLBStringExact	Manages the transfer of **CString** data between a list-box control and the field data members of a recordset. When moving data from the recordset to the control, this function selects the first item that exactly matches the specified string.

DDX_FieldCBString	Transfers **CString** data between a recordset field data member and the edit control of a combo box in a **CRecordView**. When moving data from the recordset to the control, this function selects the item in the combo box that begins with the characters in the specified string.
DDX_FieldCBStringExact	Transfers **CString** data between a recordset field data member and the edit control of a combo box in a **CRecordView**. When moving data from the recordset to the control, this function selects the item in the combo box that exactly matches the specified string.

Database Macros

This section lists the macros you can use in your database applications. When you find it necessary to call Open Database Connectivity (ODBC) API functions directly, using the macros gives asynchronous operations an opportunity to yield time to other processes. These macros assume you that have declared a variable, `nRetCode`, of type **RETCODE**, and that it is in current scope.

Database Macros

AFX_SQL_ASYNC	Use this macro to call ODBC API functions that may return **SQL_STILL_EXECUTING**.
AFX_SQL_SYNC	Use this macro to call ODBC API functions that will not return **SQL_STILL_EXECUTING**.

Collection Class Helpers

The collection classes **CMap**, **CList**, and **CArray** use templated global helper functions for such purposes as constructing, destroying, and serializing elements. As part of your implementation of classes based on **CMap**, **CList**, and **CArray**, you must override these functions as necessary with versions tailored to the type of data stored in your map, list, or array. For information on overriding **ConstructElements**, **DestructElements**, and **SerializeElements**, see the article "Collections: How to Make a Type-Safe Collection" in *Programming with the Microsoft Foundation Class Library*.

See Also   **CMap**, **CList**, **CArray**

The Microsoft Foundation Class Library provides the following global functions to help you customize your collection classes:

Collection Class Helpers

CompareElements	Indicates whether elements are the same.
ConstructElements	Performs any action necessary when an element is constructed.
DestructElements	Performs any action necessary when an element is destroyed.
DumpElements	Provides stream-oriented diagnostic output.
HashKey	Calculates a hash key.
SerializeElements	Stores or retrieves elements to or from an archive.

Macros, Global Functions and Global Variables

AfxAbort

void AfxAbort( );

Remarks   The default termination function supplied by MFC. **AfxAbort** is called internally by MFC member functions when there is a fatal error, such as an uncaught exception that cannot be handled. You can call **AfxAbort** in the rare case when you encounter a catastrophic error from which you cannot recover.

AfxBeginThread

CWinThread* AfxBeginThread(AFX_THREADPROC *pfnThreadProc*, **LPVOID** *pParam*, **int** *nPriority* = **THREAD_PRIORITY_NORMAL, UINT** *nStackSize* = **0, DWORD** *dwCreateFlags* = **0, LPSECURITY_ATTRIBUTES** *lpSecurityAttrs* = **NULL);**

CWinThread* AfxBeginThread(CRuntimeClass* *pThreadClass*, **int** *nPriority* = **THREAD_PRIORITY_NORMAL, UINT** *nStackSize* = **0, DWORD** *dwCreateFlags* = **0, LPSECURITY_ATTRIBUTES** *lpSecurityAttrs* = **NULL);**

Return Value   Pointer to the newly created thread object.

Parameters   *pfnThreadProc*   Points to the controlling function for the worker thread. Cannot be **NULL**. This function must be declared as follows:

```
UINT MyControllingFunction( LPVOID pParam );
```

pThreadClass   The **RUNTIME_CLASS** of an object derived from **CWinThread**.

pParam   Parameter to be passed to the controlling function as shown in the parameter to the function declaration in *pfnThreadProc*.

nPriority   The desired priority of the thread. If 0, the same priority as the creating thread will be used. For a full list and description of the available priorities, see **::SetThreadPriority** in the *Win32 Programmer's Reference, Volume 4.*

nStackSize   Specifies the size in bytes of the stack for the new thread. If 0, the stack size defaults to the same size stack as the creating thread.

dwCreateFlags   Specifies an additional flag that controls the creation of the thread. This flag can contain one of two values:

- **CREATE_SUSPENDED**   Start the thread with a suspend count of one. The thread will not execute until **ResumeThread** is called.

- **0**   Start the thread immediately after creation.

lpSecurityAttrs   Points to a **SECURITY_ATTRIBUTES** structure that specifies the security attributes for the thread. If **NULL**, the same security attributes as the creating thread will be used.

Remarks

Call this function to create a new thread. The first form of **AfxBeginThread** creates a worker thread. The second form creates a user-interface thread.

AfxBeginThread creates a new **CWinThread** object, calls its **CreateThread** function to start executing the thread, and returns a pointer to the thread. Checks are made throughout the procedure to make sure all objects are deallocated properly should any part of the creation fail. To end the thread, call **AfxEndThread** from within the thread, or return from the controlling function of the worker thread.

See Also

AfxGetThread

In *Programming with the Microsoft Foundation Class Library*: "Multithreading: Creating Worker Threads," "Multithreading: Creating User-Interface Threads"

AfxCheckMemory

BOOL AfxCheckMemory( );

Remarks

This function validates the free memory pool and prints error messages as required. If the function detects no memory corruption, it prints nothing.

All memory blocks currently allocated on the heap are checked, including those allocated by **new** but not those allocated by direct calls to underlying memory allocators, such as the **malloc** function or the **GlobalAlloc** Windows function. If any block is found to be corrupted, a message is printed to the debugger output.

If you include the line

```
#define new DEBUG_NEW
```

in a program module, then subsequent calls to **AfxCheckMemory** show the filename and line number where the memory was allocated.

> **Note** If your module contains one or more implementations of serializable classes, then you must put the #define line after the last **IMPLEMENT_SERIAL** macro call.

Return Value

Nonzero if no memory errors; otherwise 0.

Example

```
CAge* pcage = new CAge( 21 ); // CAge is derived from CObject.
Age* page = new Age( 22 );      // Age is NOT derived from CObject.
*(((char*) pcage) - 1) = 99;  // Corrupt preceding guard byte
*(((char*) page) - 1) = 99;   // Corrupt preceding guard byte
AfxCheckMemory();
```

The results from the program are as follows:

```
memory check error at $0067495F = $63, should be $FD
DAMAGE: before Non-Object block at $00674960
Non-Object allocated at file test02.cxx(48)
Non-Object located at $00674960 is 2 bytes long
memory check error at $00674905 = $63, should be $FD
DAMAGE: before Object block at $00674906
Object allocated at file test02.cxx(47)
Object located at $00674906 is 6 bytes long
```

> **Note** This function works only in the Debug version of MFC.

AfxDoForAllClasses

void AfxDoForAllClasses(void (*_pfn_)(const CRuntimeClass* _pClass_**, void*** _pContext_**), void*** _pContext_ **);**

Parameters

pfn   Points to an iteration function to be called for each class. The function arguments are a pointer to a **CRuntimeClass** object and a void pointer to extra data that the caller supplies to the function.

pContext   Points to optional data that the caller can supply to the iteration function. This pointer can be **NULL**.

Remarks

Calls the specified iteration function for all **CObject**-derived classes in the application's memory space that support run-time type checking using the macros **DECLARE_DYNAMIC**, **DECLARE_DYNCREATE**, or **DECLARE_SERIAL**. The pointer that is passed to **AfxDoForAllClasses** in _pContext_ is passed to the specified iteration function each time it is called.

Note   This function works only in the Debug version of MFC.

AfxDoForAllObjects

void AfxDoForAllObjects(void (*_pfn_)(CObject* _pObject_**, void*** _pContext_**), void*** _pContext_ **);**

Parameters

pfn   Points to an iteration function to execute for each object. The function arguments are a pointer to a **CObject** and a void pointer to extra data that the caller supplies to the function.

pContext   Points to optional data that the caller can supply to the iteration function. This pointer can be **NULL**.

Remarks

Executes the specified iteration function for all objects derived from **CObject** that have been allocated with **new**. Stack, global, or embedded objects are not enumerated. The pointer passed to **AfxDoForAllObjects** in _pContext_ is passed to the specified iteration function each time it is called.

Note   This function works only in the Debug version of MFC.

afxDump

CDumpContext afxDump;

Remarks

Use this variable to provide basic object-dumping capability in your application. **afxDump** is a predefined **CDumpContext** object that allows you to send

CDumpContext information to the debugger output window or to a debug terminal. Typically, you supply **afxDump** as a parameter to **CObject::Dump**.

Under Windows, **afxDump** output is sent to the debugger.

In Windows NT, **afxDump** output is sent to the Output-Debug window of Visual C++ when you debug your application. In Console applications, **afxDump** output is sent to **stderr**.

This variable is defined only in the Debug version of MFC. For more information on **afxDump**, see the article "Diagnostics: Debugging Features" in *Programming with the Microsoft Foundation Class Library*. Technical Notes 7 and 12 also contain additional information.

Note   This function works only in the Debug version of MFC.

See Also   **CObject::Dump**

Example
```
CPerson myPerson = new CPerson;
// set some fields of the CPerson object...
//..
// now dump the contents
#ifdef _DEBUG
afxDump << "Dumping myPerson:\n";
myPerson->Dump( afxDump );
afxDump << "\n";
#endif
```

AfxDump

void AfxDump(const CObject* *pOb* **);**

Parameters   *pOb*   A pointer to an object of a class derived from **CObject**.

Remarks   Call this function while in the debugger to dump the state of an object while debugging. **AfxDump** calls an object's **Dump** member function and sends the information to the location specified by the **afxDump** variable. **AfxDump** is available only in the Debug version of MFC.

Your program code should not call **AfxDump**, but should instead call the **Dump** member function of the appropriate object.

For example, the following command prints the state of the current object when you enter it at the > prompt in the CodeView command window:

```
? AfxDump(this)
```

See Also   **CObject::Dump, afxDump**

AfxEnableMemoryTracking

BOOL AfxEnableMemoryTracking(BOOL *bTrack* **);**

Parameters *bTrack*   Setting this value to **TRUE** turns on memory tracking; **FALSE** turns it off.

Return Value The previous setting of the tracking-enable flag.

Remarks Diagnostic memory tracking is normally enabled in the Debug version of MFC. Use this function to disable tracking on sections of your code that you know are allocating blocks correctly.

For more information on **AfxEnableMemoryTracking**, see the article "Diagnostics" in *Programming with the Microsoft Foundation Class Library*.

Note This function works only in the Debug version of MFC.

AfxEndThread

void AfxEndThread(UINT *nExitCode* **);**

Parameters *nExitCode*   Specifies the exit code of the thread.

Remarks Call this function to terminate the currently executing thread. Must be called from within the thread to be terminated.

See Also **AfxBeginThread**

In *Programming with the Microsoft Foundation Class Library*: "Multithreading: Terminating Threads"

AfxFormatString1

void AfxFormatString1(CString& *rString*, **UINT** *nIDS*, **LPCTSTR** *lpsz1* **);**

Parameters *rString*   A reference to a **CString** object that will contain the resultant string after the substitution is performed.

nIDS   The resource ID of the template string on which the substitution will be performed.

lpsz1   A string that will replace the format characters "%1" in the template string.

Remarks Loads the specified string resource and substitutes the characters "%1" for the string pointed to by *lpsz1*. The newly formed string is stored in *rString*. For example, if the string in the string table is "File %1 not found", and *lpsz1* is equal to "C:\MYFILE.TXT", then *rString* will contain the string "File C:\MYFILE.TXT not found". This function is useful for formatting strings sent to message boxes and other windows.

If the format characters "%1" appear in the string more than once, multiple substitutions will be made.

See Also   **AfxFormatString2**

AfxFormatString2

void **AfxFormatString2**(**CString&** *rString*, **UINT** *nIDS*, **LPCTSTR** *lpsz1*, **LPCTSTR** *lpsz2*);

Parameters   *rString*   A reference to the **CString** that will contain the resultant string after the substitution is performed.

nIDS   The string table ID of the template string on which the substitution will be performed.

lpsz1   A string that will replace the format characters "%1" in the template string.

lpsz2   A string that will replace the format characters "%2" in the template string.

Remarks   Loads the specified string resource and substitutes the characters "%1" and "%2" for the strings pointed to by *lpsz1* and *lpsz2*. The newly formed string is stored in *rString*. For example, if the string in the string table is "File %1 not found in directory %2", *lpsz1* points to "MYFILE.TXT", and *lpsz2* points to "C:\MYDIR", then rString will contain the string "File MYFILE.TXT not found in directory C:\MYDIR".

If the format characters "%1" or "%2" appear in the string more than once, multiple substitutions will be made. They do not have to be in numerical order.

See Also   **AfxFormatString1**

AfxGetApp

CWinApp* AfxGetApp( );

Return Value   A pointer to the single **CWinApp** object for the application.

Remarks   The pointer returned by this function can be used to access application information such as the main message-dispatch code or the topmost window.

AfxGetAppName

LPCTSTR AfxGetAppName( );

Return Value   A null-terminated string containing the application's name.

Remarks   The string returned by this function can be used for diagnostic messages or as a root for temporary string names.

AfxGetInstanceHandle

HINSTANCE AfxGetInstanceHandle( );

Return Value   An **HINSTANCE** to the current instance of the application. If called from within a DLL linked with the USRDLL version of MFC, an **HINSTANCE** to the DLL is returned.

Remarks   This function allows you to retrieve the instance handle of the current application. **AfxGetInstanceHandle** always returns the **HINSTANCE** of your executable (.EXE) unless it is called from within a DLL linked with the USRDLL version of MFC. In this case, it returns an **HINSTANCE** to the DLL.

See Also   **AfxGetResourceHandle, AfxSetResourceHandle**

AfxGetMainWnd

CWnd* AfxGetMainWnd( );

Return Value   If the server has an object that is in-place active inside a container, and this container is active, this function returns a pointer to the frame window object that contains the in-place active document.

If there is no object that is in-place active within a container, or your application is not an OLE server, this function simply returns the **m_pMainWnd** of your application object.

Remarks   If your application is an OLE server, call this function to retrieve a pointer to the active main window of the application instead of directly referring to the **m_pMainWnd** member of the application object.

If your application is not an OLE server, then calling this function is equivalent to directly referring to the **m_pMainWnd** member of your application object.

See Also   **CWinThread::m_pMainWnd**

AfxGetResourceHandle

HINSTANCE AfxGetResourceHandle( );

Return Value   An **HINSTANCE** handle where the default resources of the application are loaded.

Remarks   Use the **HINSTANCE** handle returned by this function to access the application's resources directly, for example, in calls to the Windows function **FindResource**.

See Also   **AfxGetInstanceHandle, AfxSetResourceHandle**

AfxGetThread

CWinThread* AfxGetThread( );

Return Value   Pointer to the currently executing thread.

Remarks   Call this function to get a pointer to the **CWinThread** object representing the currently executing thread. Must be called from within the desired thread.

See Also   **AfxBeginThread**

AfxIsMemoryBlock

BOOL AfxIsMemoryBlock(const void* *p*, **UINT** *nBytes*, **LONG*** *plRequestNumber* = **NULL**);

Parameters   *p*   Points to the block of memory to be tested.

nBytes   Contains the length of the memory block in bytes.

plRequestNumber   Points to a **long** integer that will be filled in with the memory block's allocation sequence number. The variable pointed to by *plRequestNumber* will only be filled in if **AfxIsMemoryBlock** returns nonzero.

Return Value   Nonzero if the memory block is currently allocated and the length is correct; otherwise 0.

Remarks   Tests a memory address to make sure it represents a currently active memory block that was allocated by the diagnostic version of **new**. It also checks the specified size against the original allocated size. If the function returns nonzero, the allocation sequence number is returned in *plRequestNumber*. This number represents the order in which the block was allocated relative to all other **new** allocations.

See Also   **AfxIsValidAddress**

Example
```
CAge* pcage = new CAge( 21 ); // CAge is derived from CObject.
ASSERT( AfxIsMemoryBlock( pcage, sizeof( CAge ) ) )
```

AfxIsValidAddress

BOOL AfxIsValidAddress(const void* *lp*,
UINT *nBytes*, **BOOL** *bReadWrite* = **TRUE**);

Parameters   *lp*   Points to the memory address to be tested.

nBytes   Contains the number of bytes of memory to be tested.

bReadWrite   Specifies whether the memory is both for reading and writing (**TRUE**) or just reading (**FALSE**).

Return Value	Nonzero if the specified memory block is contained entirely within the program's memory space; otherwise 0.
Remarks	Tests any memory address to ensure that it is contained entirely within the program's memory space. The address is not restricted to blocks allocated by **new**.
See Also	**AfxIsMemoryBlock**, **AfxIsValidString**

AfxIsValidString

BOOL AfxIsValidString(LPCSTR *lpsz*, **int** *nLength* = –1 **);**

Parameters	*lpsz* The pointer to test.
	nLength Specifies the length of the string to be tested, in bytes. A value of –1 indicates that the string will be null-terminated.
Return Value	Nonzero if the specified pointer points to a string of the specified size; otherwise 0.
Remarks	Use this function to determine whether a pointer to a string is valid.
See Also	**AfxIsMemoryBlock**, **AfxIsValidAddress**

afxMemDF

int afxMemDF;

Remarks	This variable is accessible from a debugger or your program and allows you to tune allocation diagnostics. It can have the following values as specified by the enumeration **afxMemDF**:

- **allocMemDF**   Turns on debugging allocator (default setting in Debug library).
- **delayFreeMemDF**   Delays freeing memory. While your program frees a memory block, the allocator does not return that memory to the underlying operating system. This will place maximum memory stress on your program.
- **checkAlwaysMemDF**   Calls **AfxCheckMemory** every time memory is allocated or freed. This will significantly slow memory allocations and deallocations.

Example	`afxMemDF = allocMemDF	checkAlwaysMemDF;`

AfxMessageBox

int AfxMessageBox(LPCTSTR *lpszText*, **UINT** *nType* = **MB_OK, UINT** *nIDHelp* = **0);**

int AFXAPI AfxMessageBox(UINT *nIDPrompt*, **UINT** *nType* = **MB_OK, UINT** *nIDHelp* = **(UINT) –1);**

Parameters   *lpszText*   Points to a **CString** object or null-terminated string containing the message to be displayed in the message box.

nType   The style of the message box. Apply any of the message-box styles to the box. For a list of message-box styles, see the section "Message-Box Styles" on page 1250.

nIDHelp   The Help-context ID for the message; 0 indicates no Help context.

nIDPrompt   A unique ID used to reference a string in the string table.

Return Value   Zero if there is not enough memory to display the message box; otherwise one of the following values is returned:

- **IDABORT**   The Abort button was selected.
- **IDCANCEL**   The Cancel button was selected.
- **IDIGNORE**   The Ignore button was selected.
- **IDNO**   The No button was selected.
- **IDOK**   The OK button was selected.
- **IDRETRY**   The Retry button was selected.
- **IDYES**   The Yes button was selected.

If a message box has a Cancel button, the **IDCANCEL** value will be returned if either the ESC key is pressed or the Cancel button is selected. If the message box has no Cancel button, pressing the ESC key has no effect.

The functions **AfxFormatString1** and **AfxFormatString2** can be useful in formatting text that appears in a message box.

Remarks   Displays a message box on the screen. The first form of this overloaded function displays a text string pointed to by *lpszText* in the message box and uses *nIDHelp* to describe a Help context. The Help context is used to jump to an associated Help topic when the user presses the Help key (typically F1).

The second form of the function uses the string resource with the ID *nIDPrompt* to display a message in the message box. The associated Help page is found through the value of *nIDHelp*. If *nIDHelp* is not specified, the string resource ID, *nIDPrompt*, is used for the Help context. For more information about defining Help contexts, see the article "Help" in *Programming with the Microsoft Foundation Class Library* and Technical Note 28.

See Also   **CWnd::MessageBox**

AfxOleCanExitApp

BOOL AFXAPI AfxOleCanExitApp( );

#include <afxdisp.h>

Return Value   Nonzero if the application can exit; otherwise 0.

Remarks   Indicates whether the application can terminate. An application should not terminate if there are outstanding references to its objects. The global functions **AfxOleLockApp** and **AfxOleUnlockApp** increment and decrement, respectively, a counter of references to the application's objects. The application should not terminate when this counter is nonzero. If the counter is nonzero, the application's main window is hidden (not destroyed) when the user chooses Close from the system menu or Exit from the File menu.

See Also   **AfxOleLockApp**, **AfxOleUnlockApp**

AfxOleGetMessageFilter

COleMessageFilter* AFXAPI AfxOleGetMessageFilter( );

#include <afxwin.h>

Return Value   A pointer to the current message filter.

Remarks   Retrieves the application's current message filter. Call this function to access the current **COleMessageFilter**-derived object, just as you would call **AfxGetApp** to access the current application object.

See Also   **COleMessageFilter**, **AfxGetApp**

Example
```
COleMessageFilter* pFilter = AfxOleGetMessageFilter();
ASSERT_VALID(pFilter);
pFilter->BeginBusyState();
// do things requiring a busy state
pFilter->EndBusyState();
```

AfxOleGetUserCtrl

BOOL AFXAPI AfxOleGetUserCtrl( );

#include <afxdisp.h>

Return Value   Nonzero if the user is in control of the application; otherwise 0.

Remarks   Retrieves the current user-control flag. The user is "in control" of the application when the user has explicitly opened or created a new document. The user is also in control if the application was not launched by the OLE system DLLs — in other words, if the user launched the application with the system shell.

See Also   **AfxOleSetUserCtrl**

AfxOleInit

BOOL AFXAPI AfxOleInit( );

#include <afxdisp.h>

Return Value   Nonzero if successful; 0 if initialization fails, possibly because incorrect versions of the OLE system DLLs are installed.

Remarks   Initializes the OLE DLLs.

AfxOleLockApp

void AFXAPI AfxOleLockApp( );

#include <afxdisp.h>

Remarks   Increments the framework's global count of the number of active objects in the application.

The framework keeps a count of the number of objects active in an application. The **AfxOleLockApp** and **AfxOleUnlockApp** functions, respectively, increment and decrement this count.

When the user attempts to close an application that has active objects—an application for which the count of active objects is nonzero—the framework hides the application from the user's view instead of completely shutting it down. The **AfxOleCanExitApp** function indicates whether the application can terminate.

Call **AfxOleLockApp** from any object that exposes OLE interfaces, if it would be undesirable for that object to be destroyed while still being used by a client application. Also call **AfxOleUnlockApp** in the destructor of any object that calls **AfxOleLockApp** in the constructor. By default, **COleDocument** (and derived classes) automatically lock and unlock the application.

See Also   **AfxOleUnlockApp**, **AfxOleCanExitApp**, **COleDocument**

AfxOleRegisterServerClass

BOOL AFXAPI AfxOleRegisterServerClass(REFCLSID *clsid*, LPCTSTR
lpszClassName, LPCTSTR *lpszShortTypeName*, LPCTSTR *lpszLongTypeName*,
OLE_APPTYPE *nAppType* = OAT_SERVER, LPCTSTR* *rglpszRegister* =
NULL, LPCTSTR* *rglpszOverwrite* =
NULL);

#include <afxdisp.h>

Return Value   Nonzero if the server class is successfully registered; otherwise 0.

Parameters   *clsid*   Reference to the server's OLE class ID.

lpszClassName   Pointer to a string containing the class name of the server's
objects.

lpszShortTypeName   Pointer to a string containing the short name of the server's
object type, such as "Chart."

lpszLongTypeName   Pointer to a string containing the long name of the server's
object type, such as "Microsoft Excel 4.0 Chart."

nAppType   A value, taken from the **OLE_APPTYPE** enumeration, specifying the
type of OLE application. Possible values are the following:

- **OAT_INPLACE_SERVER**   Server has full server user-interface.
- **OAT_SERVER**   Server supports only embedding.
- **OAT_CONTAINER**   Container supports links to embeddings.
- **OAT_DISPATCH_OBJECT**   **IDispatch**-capable object.

rglpszRegister   Array of pointers to strings representing the keys and values to be
added to the OLE system registry if no existing values for the keys are found.

rglpszOverwrite   Array of pointers to strings representing the keys and values to
be added to the OLE system registry if the registry contains existing values for the
given keys.

Remarks   This function allows you to register your server in the OLE system registry. Most
applications can use **COleTemplateServer::Register** to register the application's
document types. If your application's system-registry format does not fit the typical
pattern, you can use **AfxOleRegisterServerClass** for more control.

The registry consists of a set of keys and values. The *rglpszRegister* and
rglpszOverwrite arguments are arrays of pointers to strings, each consisting of a
key and a value separated by a **NULL** character (' \0 '). Each of these strings can

have replaceable parameters whose places are marked by the character sequences %1 through %5.

The symbols are filled in as follows:

Symbol	Value
%1	Class ID, formatted as a string
%2	Class name
%3	Path to executable file
%4	Short type name
%5	Long type name

See Also   **COleTemplateServer::UpdateRegistry**

AfxOleSetEditMenu

void AFXAPI AfxOleSetEditMenu(COleClientItem* *pClient***, CMenu*** *pMenu***, UINT** *iMenuItem***, UINT** *nIDVerbMin***, UINT** *nIDVerbMax* **= 0, UINT** *nIDConvert* **= 0);**

#include <afxole.h>

Parameters   *pClient*   A pointer to the client OLE item.

pMenu   A pointer to the menu object to be updated.

iMenuItem   The index of the menu item to be updated.

nIDVerbMin   The command ID that corresponds to the primary verb.

nIDVerbMax   The command ID that corresponds to the last verb.

nIDConvert   ID for the Convert menu item.

Remarks   Implements the user interface for the *typename* Object command. If the server recognizes only a primary verb, the menu item becomes "verb *typename* Object" and the *nIDVerbMin* command is sent when the user chooses the command. If the server recognizes several verbs, then the menu item becomes "*typename* Object" and a submenu listing all the verbs appears when the user chooses the command. When the user chooses a verb from the submenu, *nIDVerbMin* is sent if the first verb is chosen, *nIDVerbMin* + 1 is sent if the second verb is chosen, and so forth. The default **COleDocument** implementation automatically handles this feature.

You must have the following statement in your client's application resource script (.RC) file:

```
#include <afxolecl.rc>
```

To add this include file to your .RC file, choose the Set Include item on the Visual C++ File menu and add #include <afxolecl.rc> to the list of compile-time directives.

See Also   **COleDocument**

AfxOleSetUserCtrl

void AFXAPI AfxOleSetUserCtrl(BOOL *bUserCtrl* **);**

#include <afxdisp.h>

Parameters   *bUserCtrl*   Specifies whether the user-control flag is to be set or cleared.

Remarks   Sets or clears the user-control flag, which is explained in the reference for **AfxOleGetUserCtrl**. The framework calls this function when the user creates or loads a document, but not when a document is loaded or created through an indirect action such as loading an embedded object from a container application.

Call this function if other actions in your application should put the user in control of the application.

See Also   **AfxOleGetUserCtrl**

AfxOleUnlockApp

void AFXAPI AfxOleUnlockApp( );

#include <afxdisp.h>

Remarks   Decrements the framework's count of active objects in the application. See **AfxOleLockApp** for further information.

When the number of active objects reaches zero, **AfxOleOnReleaseAllObjects** is called.

See Also   **AfxOleLockApp, CCmdTarget::OnFinalRelease**

AfxRegisterClass

BOOL AFXAPI AfxRegisterClass(WNDCLASS* *lpWndClass* **);**

Parameters   *lpWndClass*   Pointer to a WNDCLASS structure containing information about the window class to be registered.

Return Value   **TRUE** if the class is successfully registered; otherwise **FALSE**.

Remarks   Use this function to register window classes in a DLL that uses MFC. If you use this function, the class is automatically unregistered when the DLL is unloaded.

In non-DLL builds, the **AfxRegisterClass** identifier is defined as a macro that maps to the Windows function **RegisterClass**, since classes registered in an application are automatically unregistered. If you use **AfxRegisterClass** instead of **RegisterClass**, your code can be used without change both in an application and in a DLL.

AfxRegisterWndClass

LPCTSTR AFXAPI AfxRegisterWndClass(UINT *nClassStyle***, HCURSOR** *hCursor* **= 0, HBRUSH** *hbrBackground* **= 0, HICON** *hIcon* **= 0);**

Return Value   A null-terminated string containing the class name. You can pass this class name to the **Create** member function in **CWnd** or other **CWnd**-derived classes to create a window. The name is generated by the Microsoft Foundation Class Library.

> **Note**   The return value is a pointer to a static buffer. To save this string, assign it to a **CString** variable.

Parameters   *nClassStyle*   Specifies the Windows class style or combination of styles for the window class. This parameter can be any valid window style or control style, or a combination of styles created by using the bitwise OR (|) operator. For a list of class styles, see the **WNDCLASS** structure in the Windows SDK documentation.

hCursor   Specifies a handle to the cursor resource to be installed in each window created from the window class.

hbrBackground   Specifies a handle to the brush resource to be installed in each window created from the window class.

hIcon   Specifies a handle to the icon resource to be installed in each window created from the window class.

Remarks   The Microsoft Foundation Class Library automatically registers several standard window classes for you. Call this function if you want to register your own window classes.

See Also   **CWnd::Create**, **CWnd::PreCreateWindow**, **WNDCLASS**

AfxSetAllocHook

AFX_ALLOC_HOOK AfxSetAllocHook(AFX_ALLOC_HOOK *pfnAllocHook* **);**

Parameters   *pfnAllocHook*   Specifies the name of the function to call. See below for the prototype of an allocation function.

Return Value   Nonzero if you want to permit the allocation; otherwise 0.

Remarks   Sets a hook that enables calling of the specified function before each memory block is allocated. The hook function is described below.

Hook Function

The Microsoft Foundation Class Library debug-memory allocator can call a user-defined hook function to allow the user to monitor a memory allocation and to control whether the allocation is permitted. Allocation hook functions are prototyped as follows:

BOOL AllocHook(size_t *nSize,* **BOOL** *bObject,* **LONG** *lRequestNumber* **);**

nSize   The size of the proposed memory allocation.

bObject   **TRUE** if the allocation is for a **CObject**-derived object.

lRequestNumber   The memory allocation's sequence number.

AfxSetResourceHandle

void AfxSetResourceHandle(HINSTANCE *hInstResource* **);**

Parameters   *hInstResource*   The instance or module handle to an .EXE or DLL file from which the application's resources are loaded.

Remarks   Use this function to set the **HINSTANCE** handle that determines where the default resources of the application are loaded.

See Also   **AfxGetInstanceHandle, AfxGetResourceHandle**

AFX_SQL_ASYNC

AFX_SQL_ASYNC(*prs, SQLFunc* **)**

Parameters   *prs*   A pointer to a **CRecordset** object or a **CDatabase** object. You must pass this pointer, but it can be to either type of object—both have the member functions that the macro calls. This parameter enables the macro to decide when to yield processing time while handling an asynchronous function.

SQLFunc   An ODBC API function. For more information about ODBC API functions, see the *Programmer's Reference* for the ODBC Software Development Kit (SDK).

Remarks   The **AFX_SQL_ASYNC** macro repeatedly calls an asynchronous function until it no longer returns **SQL_STILL_EXECUTING**. It also calls **CDatabase::OnWaitForDataSource**, which keeps track of how long the asynchronous process has been running. **OnWaitForDataSource** may decide to yield processing time. Use this macro to call any ODBC API function that may return **SQL_STILL_EXECUTING**. Using the AFX_SQL macros saves you time and code by generating code to check server status before a call to an ODBC API function.

This macro assumes it is called from within the scope of "this" recordset object. Before invoking the macro, you must declare a variable, nRetCode, of type **RETCODE**. You can use **CRecordset::Check** to check the value of nRetCode after the macro call (**Check** is a public implementation function). Asynchronous processing is the default for the database classes. To change the mode, call **CDatabase::SetSynchronousMode**.

As a prerequisite, call **CDatabase::InWaitForDataSource**. If that call returns **TRUE**, you should not call this macro. Once you make the asynchronous ODBC call, **InWaitForDataSource** will return **TRUE** until the asynchronous call completes. See the example below.

See Also   **AFX_SQL_SYNC**

Example   This example uses AFX_SQL_ASYNC to call the ::SQLColumns API function, which returns a list of the columns in the table named by strTableName. Note the declaration of nRetCode and the use of recordset data members to pass parameters to the function. The example also illustrates checking the results of the call with Check, a public implementation member of class CRecordset. The variable prs is a pointer to a CRecordset object, declared elsewhere. if(

```
CDatabase::InWaitForDataSource( ) )
    return;     // Yield control to Windows, try again later
RETCODE nRetCode;
AFX_SQL_ASYNC( prs, ::SQLColumns( prs->m_hstmt,
    (UCHAR *)NULL, SQL_NTS, (UCHAR *)NULL, SQL_NTS,
    (UCHAR *)(const char *)strTableName, SQL_NTS,
    (UCHAR *)NULL, SQL_NTS ) );
if ( !prs->Check( nRetCode ) )
{
    AfxThrowDBException( nRetCode, prs->m_pdb, prs->m_hstmt );
    TRACE( "SQLColumns failed\n" );
}
```

AFX_SQL_SYNC

AFX_SQL_SYNC(*SQLFunc*)

Parameters   *SQLFunc*   An ODBC API function. For more information about these functions, see the *Programmer's Reference* for the Open Database Connectivity Software Development Kit (SDK).

Remarks   The **AFX_SQL_SYNC** macro simply calls the function, but before doing so it asserts whether the application is already waiting for the server. Use this macro to call ODBC API functions that will not return **SQL_STILL_EXECUTING**. Using the AFX_SQL macros saves you time by generating code to check server status before a call to an ODBC API function.

Before calling the macro, you must declare a variable, nRetCode, of type **RETCODE**. You can check the value of nRetCode after the macro call.

Note You should first call **CDatabase::InWaitForDataSource**, even for **AFX_SQL_SYNC**, if it is possible that some other ODBC call in your application is still executing.

See Also **AFX_SQL_ASYNC**

Example
```
HSTMT hstmtUpdate;
RETCODE nRetCode;
AFX_SQL_SYNC( ::SQLAllocStmt( prs->m_pdb->m_hdbc, &hstmtUpdate ) );
if (!Check( nRetCode ) )
{
    AfxThrowDBException( nRetCode, prs->m_pdb, hstmtUpdate );
}
```

AfxThrowArchiveException

void AfxThrowArchiveException(int *cause* **);**

Parameters *cause* Specifies an integer that indicates the reason for the exception. For a list of the possible values, see **CArchiveException::m_cause**.

Remarks Throws an archive exception.

See Also **CArchiveException**, **THROW**

AfxThrowDBException

void AfxThrowDBException(RETCODE *nRetCode***, CDatabase*** *pdb***, HSTMT** *hstmt* **);**

Parameters *nRetCode* A value of type **RETCODE**, defining the type of error that caused the exception to be thrown.

pdb A pointer to the **CDatabase** object that represents the data source connection with which the exception is associated.

hstmt An ODBC **HSTMT** handle that specifies the statement handle with which the exception is associated.

Remarks   Call this function to throw an exception of type **CDBException** from your own code. The framework calls **AfxThrowDBException** when it receives an ODBC **RETCODE** from a call to an ODBC API function and interprets the **RETCODE** as an exceptional condition rather than an expectable error. For example, a data access operation might fail because of a disk read error.

For information about the **RETCODE** values defined by ODBC, see Chapter 8 in the ODBC SDK *Programmer's Reference*. For information about MFC extensions to these codes, see class **CDBException**.

See Also   **CDBException::m_nRetCode**

AfxThrowFileException

void AfxThrowFileException(int *cause***, LONG** *lOsError* **= –1);**

Parameters   *cause*   Specifies an integer that indicates the reason for the exception. For a list of the possible values, see **CFileException::m_cause**.

lOsError   Contains the operating-system error number (if available) that states the reason for the exception. See your operating-system manual for a listing of error codes.

Remarks   Throws a file exception. You are responsible for determining the cause based on the operating-system error code.

See Also   **CFileException::ThrowOsError**, **THROW**

AfxThrowMemoryException

void AfxThrowMemoryException( );

Remarks   Throws a memory exception. Call this function if calls to underlying system memory allocators (such as **malloc** and the **GlobalAlloc** Windows function) fail. You do not need to call it for **new** because **new** will throw a memory exception automatically if the memory allocation fails.

See Also   **CMemoryException**, **THROW**

AfxThrowNotSupportedException

void AfxThrowNotSupportedException( );

Remarks   Throws an exception that is the result of a request for an unsupported feature.

See Also   **CNotSupportedException**, **THROW**

AfxThrowOleDispatchException

void AFXAPI AfxThrowOleDispatchException(WORD *wCode***, LPCSTR** *lpszDescription***, UINT** *nHelpID* **= 0);**

void AFXAPI AfxThrowOleDispatchException(WORD *wCode***, UINT** *nDescriptionID***, UINT** *nHelpID* **= –1);**

#include <afxdisp.h>

Parameters   *wCode*   An error code specific to your application.

lpszDescription   Verbal description of the error.

nDescriptionID   Resource ID for the verbal error description.

nHelpID   A help context for your application's help (.HLP) file.

Remarks   Use this function to throw an exception within an OLE automation function. The information provided to this function can be displayed by the driving application (Visual Basic or another OLE automation client application).

See Also   **COleException**

AfxThrowOleException

void AFXAPI AfxThrowOleException(SCODE *sc* **);**

void AFXAPI AfxThrowOleException(HRESULT *hr* **);**

#include <afxdisp.h>

Parameters   *sc*   An OLE status code that indicates the reason for the exception.

hr   Handle to a result code that indicates the reason for the exception.

Remarks   Creates an object of type **COleException** and throws an exception. The version that takes an **HRESULT** as an argument converts that result code into the corresponding **SCODE**.

See Also   **COleException, THROW**

In the *OLE 2 Programmer's Reference, Volume 1*: **SCODE, HRESULT**

AfxThrowResourceException

void AfxThrowResourceException( );

Remarks   Throws a resource exception. This function is normally called when a Windows resource cannot be loaded.

See Also   **CResourceException**, **THROW**

AfxThrowUserException

void AfxThrowUserException( );

Remarks   Throws an exception to stop an end-user operation. This function is normally called immediately after **AfxMessageBox** has reported an error to the user.

See Also   **CUserException**, **THROW**, **AfxMessageBox**

afxTraceEnabled

BOOL afxTraceEnabled;

Remarks   A global variable used to enable or disable output from the **TRACE** macro.

By default, output from the **TRACE** macro is disabled. Set **afxTraceEnabled** to a nonzero value if you want **TRACE** macros in your program to produce output. Set it to 0 if you don't want **TRACE** macros in your program to produce output.

Usually, the value of **afxTraceEnabled** is set in your AFX.INI file. Alternately, you can set the value of **afxTraceEnabled** with the TRACER.EXE utility. For more information on **afxTraceEnabled**, see Technical Note 7.

See Also   **afxTraceFlags**, **TRACE**

afxTraceFlags

int afxTraceFlags;

Remarks   Used to turn on the built-in reporting features of the Microsoft Foundation Class Library.

This variable can be set under program control or while using the debugger. Each bit of **afxTraceFlags** selects a trace reporting option. You can turn any one of these bits on or off as desired using TRACER.EXE. There is never a need to set these flags manually.

The following is a list of the bit patterns and the resulting trace report option:

- **0x01**   Multiapplication debugging. This will prefix each **TRACE** output with the name of the application and affects both the explicit **TRACE** output of your program as well as the additional report options described below.

- **0x02**   Main message pump. Reports each message received in the main **CWinApp** message-handling mechanism. Lists the window handle, the message name or number, **wParam**, and **lParam**.

The report is made after the Windows **GetMessage** call but before any message translation or dispatch occurs.

Dynamic data exchange (DDE) messages will display additional data that can be used for some debugging scenarios in OLE.

This flag displays only messages that are posted, not those that are sent.

- **0x04**   Main message dispatch. Like option **0x02** above but applies to messages dispatched in **CWnd::WindowProc**, and therefore handles both posted and sent messages that are about to be dispatched.

- **0x08**   **WM_COMMAND** dispatch. A special case used for extended **WM_COMMAND/OnCommand** handling to report progress of the command-routing mechanism.

Also reports which class receives the command (when there is a matching message-map entry), and when classes do not receive a command (when there is no matching message map entry). This report is especially useful to track the flow of command messages in multiple document interface (MDI) applications.

- **0x10**   OLE tracing. Reports significant OLE notifications or requests.

Turn this option on for an OLE client or server to track communication between the OLE DLLs and an OLE application.

For more information, see Technical Note 7.

See Also   **afxTraceEnabled**, **TRACE**

AND_CATCH

AND_CATCH(*exception_class*, *exception_object_pointer_name*)

Parameters   *exception_class*   Specifies the exception type to test for. For a list of standard exception classes, see class **CException**.

exception_object_pointer_name   A name for an exception-object pointer that will be created by the macro. You can use the pointer name to access the exception object within the **AND_CATCH** block. This variable is declared for you.

Remarks   Defines a block of code for catching additional exception types thrown in a preceding **TRY** block. Use the **CATCH** macro to catch one exception type, then the **AND_CATCH** macro to catch each subsequent type.

The exception-processing code can interrogate the exception object, if appropriate, to get more information about the specific cause of the exception. Call the **THROW_LAST** macro within the **AND_CATCH** block to shift processing to the next outer exception frame. **AND_CATCH** marks the end of the preceding **CATCH** or **AND_CATCH** block.

> **Note** The **AND_CATCH** block is defined as a C++ scope (delineated by curly braces). If you declare variables in this scope, remember that they are accessible only within that scope. This also applies to the *exception_object_pointer_name* variable.

See Also **TRY, CATCH, THROW, END_CATCH, THROW_LAST, CException**

ASSERT

ASSERT(*booleanExpression*)

Parameters *booleanExpression* Specifies an expression (including pointer values) that evaluates to nonzero or 0.

Remarks Evaluates its argument. If the result is 0, the macro prints a diagnostic message and aborts the program. If the condition is nonzero, it does nothing.

The diagnostic message has the form

```
assertion failed in file <name> in line <num>
```

where *name* is the name of the source file, and *num* is the line number of the assertion that failed in the source file.

In the Release version of MFC, **ASSERT** does not evaluate the expression and thus will not interrupt the program. If the expression must be evaluated regardless of environment, use the **VERIFY** macro in place of **ASSERT**.

> **Note** This function is available only in the Debug version of MFC.

See Also **VERIFY**

Example
```
CAge* pcage = new CAge( 21 ); // CAge is derived from CObject.
ASSERT( pcage!= NULL )
ASSERT( pcage->IsKindOf( RUNTIME_CLASS( CAge ) ) )
// Terminates program only if pcage is NOT a CAge*.
```

ASSERT_VALID

ASSERT_VALID(*pObject*)

Parameters *pObject* Specifies an object of a class derived from **CObject** that has an overriding version of the **AssertValid** member function.

Remarks Use to test your assumptions about the validity of an object's internal state. **ASSERT_VALID** calls the **AssertValid** member function of the object passed as its argument.

In the Release version of MFC, **ASSERT_VALID** does nothing. In the Debug version, it validates the pointer, checks against **NULL**, and calls the object's own **AssertValid** member functions. If any of these tests fails, this displays an alert message in the same manner as **ASSERT**.

Note This function is available only in the Debug version of MFC.

For more information and examples, see the article "Diagnostics" in *Programming with the Microsoft Foundation Class Library*.

See Also **ASSERT**, **VERIFY**, **CObject**, **CObject::AssertValid**

BASED_CODE

Remarks Under Win32, this macro expands to nothing and is provided for backward compatibility. Under 16-bit MFC, the macro ensures that data will be placed in the code segment rather than in the data segment. The result is less impact on your data segment.

BEGIN_DISPATCH_MAP

BEGIN_DISPATCH_MAP(*theClass*, *baseClass*)

#include <afxdisp.h>

Parameters *theClass*   Specifies the name of the class that owns this dispatch map.

baseClass   Specifies the base class name of *theClass*.

Remarks Use the **BEGIN_DISPATCH_MAP** macro to declare the definition of your dispatch map.

In the implementation (.CPP) file that defines the member functions for your class, start the dispatch map with the **BEGIN_DISPATCH_MAP** macro, add macro entries for each of your dispatch functions and properties, and complete the dispatch map with the **END_DISPATCH_MAP** macro.

See Also **DECLARE_DISPATCH_MAP, END_DISPATCH_MAP, DISP_FUNCTION, DISP_PROPERTY, DISP_PROPERTY_EX, DISP_DEFVALUE**

BEGIN_MESSAGE_MAP

BEGIN_MESSAGE_MAP(*theClass*, *baseClass*)

Parameters *theClass*   Specifies the name of the class whose message map this is.

baseClass   Specifies the name of the base class of *theClass*.

Remarks

Use the **BEGIN_MESSAGE_MAP** macro to begin the definition of your message map.

In the implementation (.CPP) file that defines the member functions for your class, start the message map with the **BEGIN_MESSAGE_MAP** macro, then add macro entries for each of your message-handler functions and complete the message map with the **END_MESSAGE_MAP** macro.

For more information on message maps and the **BEGIN_MESSAGE_MAP** macro, see Chapter 12, "Adding a Dialog Box," in *Introducing Visual C++*.

See Also

DECLARE_MESSAGE_MAP, **END_MESSAGE_MAP**

Example

```
BEGIN_MESSAGE_MAP( CMyWindow, CFrameWnd )
    //{{AFX_MSG_MAP( CMyWindow )
    ON_WM_PAINT()
    ON_COMMAND( IDM_ABOUT, OnAbout )
    //}}AFX_MSG_MAP
END_MESSAGE_MAP( )
```

CATCH

CATCH(*exception_class*, *exception_object_pointer_name*)

Parameters

exception_class   Specifies the exception type to test for. For a list of standard exception classes, see class **CException**.

exception_object_pointer_name   Specifies a name for an exception-object pointer that will be created by the macro. You can use the pointer name to access the exception object within the **CATCH** block. This variable is declared for you.

Remarks

Use this macro to define a block of code that catches the first exception type thrown in the preceding **TRY** block. The exception-processing code can interrogate the exception object, if appropriate, to get more information about the specific cause of the exception. Invoke the **THROW_LAST** macro to shift processing to the next outer exception frame.

If *exception_class* is the class **CException**, then all exception types will be caught. You can use the **CObject::IsKindOf** member function to determine which specific exception was thrown. A better way to catch several kinds of exceptions is to use sequential **AND_CATCH** statements, each with a different exception type.

The exception object pointer is created by the macro. You do not need to declare it yourself.

> **Note** The **CATCH** block is defined as a C++ scope (delineated by curly braces). If you declare variables in this scope, remember that they are accessible only within that scope. This also applies to *exception_object_pointer_name*.

For more information on exceptions and the **CATCH** macro, see the article "Exceptions" in *Programming with the Microsoft Foundation Class Library*.

See Also   **TRY**, **AND_CATCH**, **END_CATCH**, **THROW**, **THROW_LAST**, **CException**

CompareElements

template< class *TYPE***, class** *ARG_TYPE* **>**
BOOL CompareElements(const *TYPE** pElement1*,
const *ARG_TYPE** pElement2* **);**

Parameters   *TYPE*   The type of the first element to be compared.

pElement1   Pointer to the first element to be compared.

ARG_TYPE   The type of the second element to be compared.

pElement2   Pointer to the second element to be compared.

Return Value   Non-zero if the object pointed to by *pElement1* is equal to the object pointed to by *pElement2*; otherwise 0.

Remarks   This function is called directly by **CList::Find** and indirectly by **CMap::Lookup** and **CMap::operator []**. The **CMap** calls use the **CMap** template parameters *KEY* and *ARG_KEY*.

The default implementation returns the result of the comparison of **pElement1* and **pElement2*. Override this function so that it compares the elements in a way that is appropriate for your application.

The C++ language defines the comparison operator (= =)for simple types (**char**, **int**, **float**, etc.) but does not define a comparison operator for classes and structures. If you want to use **CompareElements** or to instantiate one of the collection classes that uses it, you must either define the comparison operator or overload **CompareElements** with a version that returns appropriate values.

See Also   **CList**, **CMap**

ConstructElements

template< class *TYPE* **>**
void ConstructElements(*TYPE** pElements*, **int** *nCount* **);**

Parameters   *TYPE*   Template parameter specifying the type of the elements to be constructed.

pElements   Pointer to the elements.

nCount   Number of elements to be constructed.

Remarks   This function is called when new array, list, and map elements are constructed. The default version initializes all bits of the new elements to zero.

For information on implementing this and other helper functions, see the article "Collections: How to Make a Type-Safe Collection" in *Programming with the Microsoft Foundation Class Library*.

See Also   **CArray, CList, CMap**

DDX_FieldCBString

void DDX_FieldCBString(**CDataExchange*** *pDX*, **int** *nIDC*, **CString&** *value*, **CRecordset*** *pRecordset* **);**

Parameters   *pDX*   A pointer to a **CDataExchange** object. The framework supplies this object to establish the context of the data exchange, including its direction.

nIDC   The ID of a control in the **CRecordView** object.

value   A reference to a field data member in the associated **CRecordset** object.

pRecordset   A pointer to the **CRecordset** object with which data is exchanged.

Remarks   The **DDX_FieldCBString** function manages the transfer of **CString** data between the edit control of a combo box control in a record view and a **CString** field data member of a recordset associated with the record view. When moving data from the recordset to the control, this function sets the current selection in the combo box to the first row that begins with the characters in the string specified in *value*. On a transfer from the recordset to the control, if the recordset field is Null, any selection is removed from the combo box and the edit control of the combo box is set to empty. On a transfer from control to recordset, if the control is empty, the recordset field is set to Null if the field permits.

For more information about DDX, see Chapter 12, "Adding a Dialog Box," of the *Visual C++ User's Guide*. For examples and more information about DDX for **CRecordView** fields, see the article "Record Views" in *Programming with the Microsoft Foundation Class Library*.

See Also   DDX_FieldText, DDX_FieldRadio, DDX_FieldLBString,
DDX_FieldLBStringExact, DDX_FieldCBStringExact

Example   See **DDX_FieldText** for a general DDX_Field example. The example includes a
call to **DDX_FieldCBString**.

DDX_FieldCBStringExact

void DDX_FieldCBStringExact(CDataExchange* *pDX*, int *nIDC*, CString&
value, CRecordset* *pRecordset*);

Parameters   *pDX*   A pointer to a **CDataExchange** object. The framework supplies this object
to establish the context of the data exchange, including its direction.

nIDC   The ID of a control in the **CRecordView** object.

value   A reference to a field data member in the associated **CRecordset** object.

pRecordset   A pointer to the **CRecordset** object with which data is exchanged.

Remarks   The **DDX_FieldCBStringExact** function manages the transfer of **CString** data
between the edit control of a combo box control in a record view and a **CString**
field data member of a recordset associated with the record view. When moving
data from the recordset to the control, this function sets the current selection in the
combo box to the first row that exactly matches the string specified in *value*. On a
transfer from the recordset to the control, if the recordset field is Null, any selection
is removed from the combo box and the edit box of the combo box is set to empty.
On a transfer from control to recordset, if the control is empty, the recordset field is
set to Null.

For more information about DDX, see Chapter 12, "Adding a Dialog Box," of the
Visual C++ User's Guide. For examples and more information about DDX for
CRecordView fields, see the article "Record Views" in *Programming with the
Microsoft Foundation Class Library.*

See Also   DDX_FieldText, DDX_FieldRadio, DDX_FieldLBString,
DDX_FieldLBStringExact, DDX_FieldCBString

Example   See **DDX_FieldText** for a general DDX_Field example. Calls to
DDX_FieldCBStringExact would be similar.

DDX_FieldLBString

void DDX_FieldLBString(CDataExchange* *pDX*, **int** *nIDC*, **CString&** *value*, **CRecordset*** *pRecordset* **);**

Parameters   *pDX*   A pointer to a **CDataExchange** object. The framework supplies this object to establish the context of the data exchange, including its direction.

nIDC   The ID of a control in the **CRecordView** object.

value   A reference to a field data member in the associated **CRecordset** object.

pRecordset   A pointer to the **CRecordset** object with which data is exchanged.

Remarks   The **DDX_FieldLBString** copies the current selection of a list box control in a record view to a **CString** field data member of a recordset associated with the record view. In the reverse direction, this function sets the current selection in the list box to the first row that begins with the characters in the string specified by *value*. On a transfer from the recordset to the control, if the recordset field is Null, any selection is removed from the list box. On a transfer from control to recordset, if the control is empty, the recordset field is set to Null.

For more information about DDX, see Chapter 12, "Adding a Dialog Box," of the *Visual C++ User's Guide.* For examples and more information about DDX for **CRecordView** fields, see the article "Record Views" in *Programming with the Microsoft Foundation Class Library.*

See Also   **DDX_FieldText, DDX_FieldRadio, DDX_FieldLBStringExact, DDX_FieldCBString, DDX_FieldCBStringExact**

Example   See **DDX_FieldText** for a general DDX_Field example. Calls to **DDX_FieldLBString** would be similar.

DDX_FieldLBStringExact

void DDX_FieldLBStringExact(CDataExchange* *pDX*, **int** *nIDC*, **CString&** *value*, **CRecordset*** *pRecordset* **);**

Parameters   *pDX*   A pointer to a **CDataExchange** object. The framework supplies this object to establish the context of the data exchange, including its direction.

nIDC   The ID of a control in the **CRecordView** object.

value   A reference to a field data member in the associated **CRecordset** object.

pRecordset   A pointer to the **CRecordset** object with which data is exchanged.

Remarks   The **DDX_FieldLBStringExact** function copies the current selection of a list box control in a record view to a CString field data member of a recordset associated with the record view. In the reverse direction, this function sets the current selection in the list box to the first row that exactly matches the string specified in *value*. On a transfer from the recordset to the control, if the recordset field is Null, any selection is removed from the list box. On a transfer from control to recordset, if the control is empty, the recordset field is set to Null.

For more information about DDX, see Chapter 12, "Adding a Dialog Box," of the *Visual C++ User's Guide.* For examples and more information about DDX for **CRecordView** fields, see the article "Record Views" in *Programming with the Microsoft Foundation Class Library*.

See Also   **DDX_FieldText, DDX_FieldRadio, DDX_FieldLBString, DDX_FieldCBString, DDX_FieldCBStringExact**

Example   See **DDX_FieldText** for a general DDX_Field example. Calls to **DDX_FieldLBStringExact** would be similar.

DDX_FieldRadio

void **DDX_FieldRadio**(**CDataExchange*** *pDX*, **int** *nIDC*, **int&** *value*, **CRecordset*** *pRecordset*);

Parameters   *pDX*   A pointer to a **CDataExchange** object. The framework supplies this object to establish the context of the data exchange, including its direction.

nIDC   The ID of the first in a group (with style **WS_GROUP**) of adjacent radio button controls in the **CRecordView** object.

value   A reference to a field data member in the associated **CRecordset** object.

pRecordset   A pointer to the **CRecordset** object with which data is exchanged.

Remarks   The **DDX_FieldRadio** function associates a zero-based **int** member variable of a record view's recordset with the currently selected radio button in a group of radio buttons in the record view. When transferring from the recordset field to the view, this function turns on the *nth* radio button (zero-based) and turns off the other buttons. In the reverse direction, this function sets the recordset field to the ordinal number of the radio button that is currently on (checked). On a transfer from the recordset to the control, if the recordset field is Null, no button is selected. On a transfer from control to recordset, if no control is selected, the recordset field is set to Null if the field permits that.

For more information about DDX, see Chapter 12, "Adding a Dialog Box," of the *Visual C++ User's Guide.* For examples and more information about DDX for **CRecordView** fields, see the article "Record Views" in *Programming with the Microsoft Foundation Class Library*.

See Also   **DDX_FieldText, DDX_FieldLBString, DDX_FieldLBStringExact, DDX_FieldCBString, DDX_FieldCBStringExact**

Example   See **DDX_FieldText** for a general DDX_Field example. Calls to
DDX_FieldRadio would be similar.

DDX_FieldText

void DDX_FieldText(CDataExchange* *pDX*, int *nIDC*, int& *value*,
CRecordset* *pRecordset*);

void DDX_FieldText(CDataExchange* *pDX*, int *nIDC*, UINT& *value*,
CRecordset* *pRecordset*);

void DDX_FieldText(CDataExchange* *pDX*, int *nIDC*, long& *value*,
CRecordset* *pRecordset*);

void DDX_FieldText(CDataExchange* *pDX*, int *nIDC*, DWORD& *value*,
CRecordset* *pRecordset*);

void DDX_FieldText(CDataExchange* *pDX*, int *nIDC*, CString& *value*,
CRecordset* *pRecordset*);

void DDX_FieldText(CDataExchange* *pDX*, int *nIDC*, float& *value*);

void DDX_FieldText(CDataExchange* *pDX*, int *nIDC*, double& *value*);

Parameters   *pDX*   A pointer to a **CDataExchange** object. The framework supplies this object
to establish the context of the data exchange, including its direction.

nIDC   The ID of a control in the **CRecordView** object.

value   A reference to a field data member in the associated **CRecordset** object.
The data type of value depends on which of the overloaded versions of
DDX_FieldText you use.

pRecordset   A pointer to the **CRecordset** object with which data is exchanged.
This pointer enables **DDX_FieldText** to detect and set Null values.

Remarks   The **DDX_FieldText** function manages the transfer of **int**, **UINT**, **long**, **DWORD**,
CString, **float**, or **double** data between an edit box control and the field data
members of a recordset. An empty edit box control indicates a Null value. On a
transfer from the recordset to the control, if the recordset field is Null, the edit box
is set to empty. On a transfer from control to recordset, if the control is empty, the
recordset field is set to Null.

For more information about DDX, see Chapter 12, "Adding a Dialog Box," of the
Visual C++ User's Guide. For examples and more information about DDX for
CRecordView fields, see the article "Record Views" in *Programming with the
Microsoft Foundation Class Library.*

See Also   **DDX_FieldRadio, DDX_FieldLBString, DDX_FieldLBStringExact,
DDX_FieldCBString, DDX_FieldCBStringExact**

Example

The following **DoDataExchange** function for a **CRecordView**-derived class contains **DDX_FieldText** function calls for three data types: IDC_COURSELIST is a combo box; the other two controls are edit boxes.

```
void CSectionForm::DoDataExchange( CDataExchange* pDX )
{
    CRecordView::DoDataExchange( pDX );
    //{{AFX_DATA_MAP(CSectionForm)
    DDX_FieldCBString( pDX, IDC_COURSELIST,
                                m_pSet->m_strCourseID, m_pSet);
    DDX_FieldText( pDX, IDC_ROOM, m_pSet->m_nRoomNo, m_pSet );
    DDX_FieldText( pDX, IDC_TUITION, m_pSet->m_dwTuition, m_pSet );
    //}}AFX_DATA_MAP
}
```

DEBUG_NEW

#define new DEBUG_NEW

Remarks

Assists in finding memory leaks. You can use **DEBUG_NEW** everywhere in your program that you would ordinarily use the **new** operator to allocate heap storage.

In Debug mode (when the _**DEBUG** symbol is defined), **DEBUG_NEW** keeps track of the filename and line number for each object that it allocates. Then, when you use the **CMemoryState::DumpAllObjectsSince** member function, each object allocated with **DEBUG_NEW** is shown with the filename and line number where it was allocated.

To use **DEBUG_NEW**, insert the following directive into your source files:

```
#define new DEBUG_NEW
```

Once you insert this directive, the preprocessor will insert **DEBUG_NEW** wherever you use **new**, and MFC does the rest. When you compile a release version of your program, **DEBUG_NEW** resolves to a simple **new** operation, and the filename and line number information is not generated.

Note You must place the **#define** statement after all statements that call the **IMPLEMENT_DYNCREATE** or **IMPLEMENT_SERIAL** macros in your module, or you will get a compile-time error.

For more information on the **DEBUG_NEW** macro, see the article "Diagnostics" in *Programming with the Microsoft Foundation Class Library*.

DECLARE_DISPATCH_MAP

DECLARE_DISPATCH_MAP( )

Remarks   If a **CCmdTarget**-derived class in your program supports OLE Automation, that class must provide a dispatch map to expose its methods and properties. Use the **DECLARE_DISPATCH_MAP** macro at the end of your class declaration. Then, in the .CPP file that defines the member functions for the class, use the **BEGIN_DISPATCH_MAP** macro. Then include macro entries for each of your class's exposed methods and properties (**DISP_FUNCTION**, **DISP_PROPERTY**, etc.). Finally, use the **END_DISPATCH_MAP** macro.

Note If you declare any members after **DECLARE_DISPATCH_MAP**, you must specify a new access type (**public, private**, or **protected**) for them.

AppWizard and ClassWizard assist in creating OLE Automation classes and in maintaining dispatch maps: see "AppWizard: OLE Support," "AppWizard: Creating an OLE Visual Editing Application," and "ClassWizard: OLE Automation Support." For more information on dispatch maps, see "Automation Servers." All these articles are in *Programming with the Microsoft Foundation Class Library*.

See Also   **BEGIN_DISPATCH_MAP, END_DISPATCH_MAP, DISP_FUNCTION, DISP_PROPERTY, DISP_PROPERTY_EX, DISP_DEFVALUE**

Example
```
class CMyDoc : public CDocument
{
    // Member declarations

    DECLARE_DISPATCH_MAP()
};
```

DECLARE_DYNAMIC

DECLARE_DYNAMIC(*class_name*)

Parameters   *class_name*   The actual name of the class (not enclosed in quotation marks).

Remarks   When deriving a class from **CObject**, this macro adds the ability to access run-time information about an object's class.

Add the **DECLARE_DYNAMIC** macro to the header (.H) module for the class, then include that module in all .CPP modules that need access to objects of this class.

If you use the **DECLARE_DYNAMIC** and **IMPLEMENT_DYNAMIC** macros as described, you can then use the **RUNTIME_CLASS** macro and the **CObject::IsKindOf** function to determine the class of your objects at run time.

If **DECLARE_DYNAMIC** is included in the class declaration, then **IMPLEMENT_DYNAMIC** must be included in the class implementation.

For more information on the **DECLARE_DYNAMIC** macro, see the article "CObject Class" in *Programming with the Microsoft Foundation Class Library*.

See Also   **IMPLEMENT_DYNAMIC, DECLARE_DYNCREATE, DECLARE_SERIAL, RUNTIME_CLASS, CObject::IsKindOf**

DECLARE_DYNCREATE

DECLARE_DYNCREATE(*class_name* **)**

Parameters   *class_name*   The actual name of the class (not enclosed in quotation marks).

Remarks   Use the **DECLARE_DYNCREATE** macro to enable objects of **CObject**-derived classes to be created dynamically at run time. The framework uses this ability to create new objects dynamically, for example, when it reads an object from disk during serialization. Document, view, and frame classes should support dynamic creation because the framework needs to create them dynamically.

Add the **DECLARE_DYNCREATE** macro in the .H module for the class, then include that module in all .CPP modules that need access to objects of this class.

If **DECLARE_DYNCREATE** is included in the class declaration, then **IMPLEMENT_DYNCREATE** must be included in the class implementation.

For more information on the **DECLARE_DYNCREATE** macro, see the article "CObject Class" in *Programming with the Microsoft Foundation Class Library*.

See Also   **DECLARE_DYNAMIC, IMPLEMENT_DYNAMIC, IMPLEMENT_DYNCREATE, RUNTIME_CLASS, CObject::IsKindOf**

DECLARE_MESSAGE_MAP

DECLARE_MESSAGE_MAP( )

Remarks   Each **CCmdTarget**-derived class in your program must provide a message map to handle messages. Use the **DECLARE_MESSAGE_MAP** macro at the end of your class declaration. Then, in the .CPP file that defines the member functions for the class, use the **BEGIN_MESSAGE_MAP** macro, macro entries for each of your message-handler functions and the **END_MESSAGE_MAP** macro.

> **Note** If you declare any member after **DECLARE_MESSAGE_MAP**, you must specify a new access type (public, private, protected) for them.

For more information on message maps and the **DECLARE_MESSAGE_MAP** macro, see Chapter 2, "Working with Messages and Commands," in *Programming with the Microsoft Foundation Class Library*.

See Also   **BEGIN_MESSAGE_MAP, END_MESSAGE_MAP**

Example

```
class CMyWnd : public CFrameWnd
{
    // Member declarations

    DECLARE_MESSAGE_MAP( )
};
```

DECLARE_OLECREATE

DECLARE_OLECREATE(*class_name* **)**

#include <afxdisp.h>

Parameters   *class_name*   The actual name of the class (not enclosed in quotation marks).

Remarks   Use the **DECLARE_OLECREATE** macro to enable objects of **CCmdTarget**-derived classes to be created through OLE automation. This macro enables other OLE-enabled applications to create objects of this type.

Add the **DECLARE_OLECREATE** macro in the .H module for the class, then include that module in all .CPP modules that need access to objects of this class.

If **DECLARE_OLECREATE** is included in the class declaration, then **IMPLEMENT_OLECREATE** must be included in the class implementation. A class declaration using **DECLARE_OLECREATE** must also use **DECLARE_DYNCREATE** or **DECLARE_SERIAL**.

See Also   **IMPLEMENT_OLECREATE, DECLARE_DYNCREATE, DECLARE_SERIAL**

DECLARE_SERIAL

DECLARE_SERIAL(*class_name* **)**

Parameters   *class_name*   The actual name of the class (not enclosed in quotation marks).

Remarks   **DECLARE_SERIAL** generates the C++ header code necessary for a **CObject**-derived class that can be serialized. Serialization is the process of writing or reading the contents of an object to and from a file.

Use the **DECLARE_SERIAL** macro in a .H module, then include that module in all .CPP modules that need access to objects of this class.

If **DECLARE_SERIAL** is included in the class declaration, then **IMPLEMENT_SERIAL** must be included in the class implementation. The **DECLARE_SERIAL** macro includes all the functionality of **DECLARE_DYNAMIC** and **DECLARE_DYNCREATE**.

For more information on the **DECLARE_SERIAL** macro, see the article "CObject Class" in *Programming with the Microsoft Foundation Class Library*.

See Also   **DECLARE_DYNAMIC, IMPLEMENT_SERIAL, RUNTIME_CLASS, CObject::IsKindOf**

DestructElements

template< class *TYPE* **>**
void DestructElements(*TYPE* * *pElements*, **int** *nCount* **);**

Parameters   *TYPE*   Template parameter specifying the type of the elements to be destroyed.

pElements   Pointer to the elements.

nCount   Number of elements to be destroyed.

Remarks   The **CArray**, **CList**, and **CMap** class members call this function when elements are destroyed.

The default implementation does nothing. For information on implementing this and other helper functions, see the article "Collections: How to Make a Type-Safe Collection" in *Programming with the Microsoft Foundation Class Library*.

See Also   **CArray, CList, CMap**

DISP_DEFVALUE

DISP_DEFVALUE(*theClass*, *pszName* **)**

#include <afxdisp.h>

Parameters   *theClass*   Name of the class.

pszName   External name of the property that represents the "value" of the object.

Remarks   This macro makes an existing property the default value of an object. Using a default value can make programming your automation object simpler for Visual Basic applications.

The "default value" of your object is the property that is retrieved or set when a reference to an object does not specify a property or member function.

See Also   **DECLARE_DISPATCH_MAP**, **DISP_PROPERTY_EX**, **DISP_FUNCTION**, **BEGIN_DISPATCH_MAP**, **END_DISPATCH_MAP**

DISP_FUNCTION

DISP_FUNCTION(*theClass*, *pszName*, *pfnMember*, *vtRetVal*, *vtsParams*)

#include <afxdisp.h>

Parameters   *theClass*   Name of the class.

pszName   External name of the function.

pfnMember   Name of the member function.

vtRetVal   A value specifying the function's return type.

vtsParams   A space-separated list of one or more constants specifying the function's parameter list.

Remarks   The **DISP_FUNCTION** macro is used in a dispatch map to define an OLE automation function.

The *vtRet* argument is of type **VARTYPE**. Possible values for this argument are taken from the **VARENUM** enumeration. They are as follows:

Symbol	Return Type
VT_EMPTY	**void**
VT_I2	**short**
VT_I4	**long**
VT_R4	**float**
VT_R8	**double**
VT_CY	**CY**
VT_DATE	**DATE**
VT_BSTR	**BSTR**
VT_DISPATCH	**LPDISPATCH**
VT_ERROR	**SCODE**
VT_BOOL	**BOOL**
VT_VARIANT	**VARIANT**
VT_UNKNOWN	**LPUNKNOWN**

The *vtsParams* argument is a space-separated list of values from the **VTS_** constants. One or more of these values separated by spaces (not commas) specifies the function's parameter list. For example,

```
VTS_I2 VTS_PI2
```

specifies a list containing a short integer followed by a pointer to a short integer.

The **VTS_** constants and their meanings are as follows:

Symbol	Parameter Type
VTS_I2	**short**
VTS_I4	**long**
VTS_R4	**float**
VTS_R8	**double**
VTS_CY	**const CY** or **CY***
VTS_DATE	**DATE**
VTS_BSTR	**LPCSTR**
VTS_DISPATCH	**LPDISPATCH**
VTS_SCODE	**SCODE**
VTS_BOOL	**BOOL**
VTS_VARIANT	**const VARIANT*** or **VARIANT&**
VTS_UNKNOWN	**LPUNKNOWN**
VTS_PI2	**short***
VTS_PI4	**long***
VTS_PR4	**float***
VTS_PR8	**double***
VTS_PCY	**CY***
VTS_PDATE	**DATE***
VTS_PBSTR	**BSTR***
VTS_PDISPATCH	**LPDISPATCH***
VTS_PSCODE	**SCODE***
VTS_PBOOL	**BOOL***
VTS_PVARIANT	**VARIANT***
VTS_PUNKNOWN	**LPUNKNOWN***

See Also   **DECLARE_DISPATCH_MAP, DISP_PROPERTY, DISP_PROPERTY_EX, BEGIN_DISPATCH_MAP, END_DISPATCH_MAP**

DISP_PROPERTY

DISP_PROPERTY(*theClass*, *pszName*, *memberName*, *vtPropType*)

#include <afxdisp.h>

Parameters   *theClass*   Name of the class.

pszName   External name of the property.

memberName   Name of the member variable in which the property is stored.

vtPropType   A value specifying the property's type.

Remarks   The **DISP_PROPERTY** macro is used in a dispatch map to define an OLE automation property.

The *vtPropType* argument is of type **VARTYPE**. Possible values for this argument are taken from the **VARENUM** enumeration:

Symbol	Property Type
VT_I2	**short**
VT_I4	**long**
VT_R4	**float**
VT_R8	**double**
VT_CY	**CY**
VT_DATE	**DATE**
VT_BSTR	**CString**
VT_DISPATCH	**LPDISPATCH**
VT_ERROR	**SCODE**
VT_BOOL	**BOOL**
VT_VARIANT	**VARIANT**
VT_UNKNOWN	**LPUNKNOWN**

When an external client changes the property, the value of the member variable specified by *memberName* changes; there is no notification of the change.

See Also   **DECLARE_DISPATCH_MAP, DISP_PROPERTY, DISP_FUNCTION, BEGIN_DISPATCH_MAP, END_DISPATCH_MAP**

DISP_PROPERTY_EX

DISP_PROPERTY_EX(*theClass*, *pszName*, *memberGet*, *memberSet*, *vtPropType*)

#include <afxdisp.h>

Parameters   *theClass*   Name of the class.

pszName   External name of the property.

memberGet   Name of the member function used to get the property.

memberSet   Name of the member function used to set the property.

vtPropType   A value specifying the property's type.

Remarks   The **DISP_PROPERTY_EX** macro is used in a dispatch map to define an OLE automation property and name the functions used to get and set the property's value.

The *memberGet* and *memberSet* functions have signatures determined by the *vtPropType* argument. The *memberGet* function takes no arguments and returns a value of the type specified by *vtPropType*. The *memberSet* function takes an argument of the type specified by *vtPropType* and returns nothing.

The *vtPropType* argument is of type **VARTYPE**. Possible values for this argument are taken from the the **VARENUM** enumeration. For a list of these values, see the Remarks for the *vtRet* parameter in **DISP_FUNCTION**. Note that **VT_EMPTY**, listed in the **DISP_FUNCTION** remarks, is not permitted as a property data type.

See Also   **DECLARE_DISPATCH_MAP**, **DISP_PROPERTY**, **DISP_FUNCTION**, **BEGIN_DISPATCH_MAP**, **END_DISPATCH_MAP**

DumpElements

template< class *TYPE* >
void DumpElements(CDumpContext& *dc*, **const** *TYPE** *pElements*,
int *nCount* **);**

Parameters   *dc*   Dump context for dumping elements.

TYPE   Template parameter specifying the type of the elements.

pElements   Pointer to the elements to be dumped.

nCount   Number of elements to be dumped.

Remarks   Override this function to provide stream-oriented diagnostic output in text form for the elements of your collection. The **CArray::Dump**, **CList::Dump**, and **CMap::Dump** functions call this if the depth of the dump is greater than 0.

The default implementation does nothing. If the elements of your collection are derived from **CObject**, your override will typically iterate through the collection's elements, calling **Dump** for each element in turn.

For information on diagnostics and on the **Dump** function, see the article "Diagnostics: Dumping Object Contents" in *Programming with the Microsoft Foundation Class Library*.

See Also   **CDumpContext::SetDepth**, **CObject::Dump**, **CArray**, **CList**, **CMap**

END_CATCH

END_CATCH

Remarks   Marks the end of the last **CATCH** or **AND_CATCH** block.

For more information on the **END_CATCH** macro, see the article "Exceptions" in *Programming with the Microsoft Foundation Class Library*.

See Also   **TRY**, **CATCH**, **THROW**, **AND_CATCH**, **THROW_LAST**

END_DISPATCH_MAP

END_DISPATCH_MAP( )

#include <afxdisp.h>

Remarks   Use the **END_DISPATCH_MAP** macro to end definition of your dispatch map. It must be used in conjunction with **BEGIN_DISPATCH_MAP**.

See Also   **DECLARE_DISPATCH_MAP**, **BEGIN_DISPATCH_MAP**, **DISP_FUNCTION**, **DISP_PROPERTY**, **DISP_PROPERTY_EX**, **DISP_DEFVALUE**

END_MESSAGE_MAP

END_MESSAGE_MAP( )

Remarks   Use the **END_MESSAGE_MAP** macro to end the definition of your message map.

For more information on message maps and the **END_MESSAGE_MAP** macro, see Chapter 2, "Working with Messages and Commands," in *Programming with the Microsoft Foundation Class Library*.

See Also   **DECLARE_MESSAGE_MAP**, **BEGIN_MESSAGE_MAP**, **Message Map Function Categories**

HashKey

template< class *ARG_KEY* **>**
UINT HashKey(*ARG_KEY key* **);**

Parameters   *ARG_KEY*   Template parameter specifying the data type used to access map keys.

key   The key whose hash value is to be calculated.

Return Value   The key's hash value.

Remarks   Calculates a hash value for the given key.

This function is called directly by **CMap::RemoveKey** and indirectly by **CMap::Lookup** and **CMap::Operator []**.

The default implementation creates a hash value by shifting *key* rightward by four positions. Override this function so that it returns hash values appropriate for your application.

See Also   **CMap**

IMPLEMENT_DYNAMIC

IMPLEMENT_DYNAMIC(*class_name***,** *base_class_name* **)**

Parameters   *class_name*   The actual name of the class (not enclosed in quotation marks).

base_class_name   The name of the base class (not enclosed in quotation marks).

Remarks   Generates the C++ code necessary for a dynamic **CObject**-derived class with run-time access to the class name and position within the hierarchy. Use the **IMPLEMENT_DYNAMIC** macro in a .CPP module, then link the resulting object code only once.

For more information, see the article "CObject Class" in *Programming with the Microsoft Foundation Class Library*.

See Also   **DECLARE_DYNAMIC, RUNTIME_CLASS, CObject::IsKindOf**

IMPLEMENT_DYNCREATE

IMPLEMENT_DYNCREATE(*class_name, base_class_name* **)**

Parameters   *class_name*   The actual name of the class (not enclosed in quotation marks).

base_class_name   The actual name of the base class (not enclosed in quotation marks).

Remarks   Use the **IMPLEMENT_DYNCREATE** macro with the **DECLARE_DYNCREATE** macro to enable objects of **CObject**-derived classes to be created dynamically at run time. The framework uses this ability to create new objects dynamically, for example, when it reads an object from disk during serialization. Add the **IMPLEMENT_DYNCREATE** macro in the class implementation file. For more information, see the article "CObject Class" in *Programming with the Microsoft Foundation Class Library*.

If you use the **DECLARE_DYNCREATE** and **IMPLEMENT_DYNCREATE** macros, you can then use the **RUNTIME_CLASS** macro and the **CObject::IsKindOf** member function to determine the class of your objects at run time.

If **DECLARE_DYNCREATE** is included in the class declaration, then **IMPLEMENT_DYNCREATE** must be included in the class implementation.

See Also   **DECLARE_DYNCREATE**, **RUNTIME_CLASS**, **CObject::IsKindOf**

IMPLEMENT_OLECREATE

IMPLEMENT_OLECREATE(*class_name*, *external_name*, *l*, *w1*, *w2*, *b1*, *b2*, *b3*, *b4*, *b5*, *b6*, *b7*, *b8*)

#include <afxdisp.h>

Parameters   *class_name*   The actual name of the class (not enclosed in quotation marks).

external_name   The object name exposed to other applications (enclosed in quotation marks).

l, *w1*, *w2*, *b1*, *b2*, *b3*, *b4*, *b5*, *b6*, *b7*, *b8*   Components of the class's **CLSID**.

Remarks   This macro must appear in the implementation file for any class that uses **DECLARE_OLECREATE**.

The external name is the identifier exposed to other applications. Client applications use the external name to request an object of this class from an automation server.

The OLE class ID is a unique 128-bit identifier for the object. It consists of one **long**, two **WORD**s, and eight **BYTE**s, as represented by *l*, *w1*, *w2*, and *b1* through *b8* in the syntax description. ClassWizard and AppWizard create unique OLE class IDs for you as required.

See Also   **DECLARE_OLECREATE**

In the *OLE 2 Programmer's Reference, Volume 1:* **CLSID**

IMPLEMENT_SERIAL

IMPLEMENT_SERIAL(*class_name*, *base_class_name*, *wSchema*)

Parameters   *class_name*   The actual name of the class (not enclosed in quotation marks).

base_class_name   The name of the base class (not enclosed in quotation marks).

wSchema   A **UINT** "version number" that will be encoded in the archive to enable a deserializing program to identify and handle data created by earlier program versions. The class schema number must not be –1.

Remarks   Generates the C++ code necessary for a dynamic **CObject**-derived class with run-time access to the class name and position within the hierarchy. Use the **IMPLEMENT_SERIAL** macro in a .CPP module; then link the resulting object code only once.

For more information, see the article "CObject Class" in *Programming with the Microsoft Foundation Class Library*.

See Also   **DECLARE_SERIAL**, **RUNTIME_CLASS**, **CObject::IsKindOf**

ON_COMMAND

ON_COMMAND(*id*, *memberFxn*)

Parameters   *id*   The command ID.

memberFxn   The name of the message-handler function to which the command is mapped.

Remarks   This macro is usually inserted in a message map by ClassWizard or manually. It indicates which function will handle a command message from a command user-interface object such as a menu item or toolbar button.

When a command-target object receives a Windows **WM_COMMAND** message with the specified ID, **ON_COMMAND** will call the member function *memberFxn* to handle the message.

There should be exactly one **ON_COMMAND** macro statement in your message map for every menu or accelerator command that must be mapped to a message-handler function.

For more information and examples, see Chapter 2, "Working with Messages and Commands," in *Programming with the Microsoft Foundation Class Library*.

See Also   **ON_UPDATE_COMMAND_UI**

Example
```
BEGIN_MESSAGE_MAP( CMyDoc, CDocument )
    //{{AFX_MSG_MAP( CMyDoc )
    ON_COMMAND( ID_MYCMD, OnMyCommand )
    // ... More entries to handle additional commands
    //}}AFX_MSG_MAP
END_MESSAGE_MAP( )
```

ON_COMMAND_RANGE

ON_COMMAND_RANGE(*id1*, *id2*, *memberFxn*)

Parameters   *id1*   Command ID at the beginning of a contiguous range of command IDs.

id2   Command ID at the end of a contiguous range of command IDs.

memberFxn   The name of the message-handler function to which the commands are mapped.

Remarks   Use this macro to map a contiguous range of command IDs to a single message handler function. The range of IDs starts with *id1* and ends with *id2*.

ClassWizard does not support message map ranges, so you must place the macro yourself. Be sure to put it outside the message map //{{AFX_MSG_MAP delimiters.

See Also   **ON_UPDATE_COMMAND_UI_RANGE**, **ON_CONTROL_RANGE**

ON_CONTROL

ON_CONTROL(*wNotifyCode*, *id*, *memberFxn*)

Parameters   *wNotifyCode*   The notification code of the control.

id   The command ID.

memberFxn   The name of the message-handler function to which the command is mapped.

Remarks   Indicates which function will handle a custom-control notification message. Control notification messages are those sent from a control to its parent window.

There should be exactly one **ON_CONTROL** macro statement in your message map for every control notification message that must be mapped to a message-handler function.

For more information and examples, see Chapter 2, "Working with Messages and Commands," in *Programming with the Microsoft Foundation Class Library*.

See Also   **ON_MESSAGE**, **ON_REGISTERED_MESSAGE**

ON_CONTROL_RANGE

ON_CONTROL_RANGE(*wNotifyCode*, *id1*, *id2*, *memberFxn* **)**

Parameters   *wNotifyCode*   The notification code to which your handler is responding.

id1   Command ID at the beginning of a contiguous range of control IDs.

id2   Command ID at the end of a contiguous range of control IDs.

memberFxn   The name of the message-handler function to which the controls are mapped.

Remarks   Use this macro to map a contiguous range of control IDs to a single message handler function for a specified Windows notification message, such as **BN_CLICKED**. The range of IDs starts with *id1* and ends with *id2*. The handler is called for the specified notification coming from any of the mapped controls.

ClassWizard does not support message map ranges, so you must place the macro yourself. Be sure to put it outside the message map //{{AFX_MSG_MAP delimiters.

See Also   **ON_UPDATE_COMMAND_UI_RANGE, ON_COMMAND_RANGE**

ON_MESSAGE

ON_MESSAGE(*message*, *memberFxn* **)**

Parameters   *message*   The message ID.

memberFxn   The name of the message-handler function to which the message is mapped.

Remarks   Indicates which function will handle a user-defined message. User-defined messages are usually defined in the range **WM_USER** to 0x7FFF. User-defined messages are any messages that are not standard Windows **WM_MESSAGE** messages. There should be exactly one **ON_MESSAGE** macro statement in your message map for every user-defined message that must be mapped to a message-handler function.

For more information and examples, see Chapter 2, "Working with Messages and Commands," in *Programming with the Microsoft Foundation Class Library*.

See Also   **ON_UPDATE_COMMAND_UI, ON_CONTROL, ON_REGISTERED_MESSAGE, ON_COMMAND**, User-Defined Handlers

Example
```
#define WM_MYMESSAGE (WM_USER + 1)
BEGIN_MESSAGE_MAP( CMyWnd, CMyParentWndClass )
    //{{AFX_MSG_MAP( CMyWnd
    ON_MESSAGE( WM_MYMESSAGE, OnMyMessage )
    // ... Possibly more entries to handle additional messages
    //}}AFX_MSG_MAP
END_MESSAGE_MAP( )
```

ON_REGISTERED_MESSAGE

ON_REGISTERED_MESSAGE(*nMessageVariable***,** *memberFxn* **)**

Parameters
nMessageVariable   The registered window-message ID variable.

memberFxn   The name of the message-handler function to which the message is mapped.

Remarks
The Windows **RegisterWindowMessage** function is used to define a new window message that is guaranteed to be unique throughout the system. This macro indicates which function will handle the registered message.

For more information and examples, see Chapter 2, "Working with Messages and Commands," in *Programming with the Microsoft Foundation Class Library*.

See Also
ON_MESSAGE, **ON_UPDATE_COMMAND_UI**, **ON_CONTROL**, **ON_COMMAND**, **::RegisterWindowMessage**, User-Defined Handlers

Example
```
const UINT   wm_Find = RegisterWindowMessage( FINDMSGSTRING )
BEGIN_MESSAGE_MAP( CMyWnd, CMyParentWndClass )
    //{{AFX_MSG_MAP( CMyWnd )
    ON_REGISTERED_MESSAGE( wm_Find, OnFind )
    // ... Possibly more entries to handle additional messages
    //}}AFX_MSG_MAP
END_MESSAGE_MAP( )
```

ON_UPDATE_COMMAND_UI

ON_UPDATE_COMMAND_UI(*id***,** *memberFxn* **)**

Parameters
id   The message ID.

memberFxn   The name of the message-handler function to which the message is mapped.

Remarks
This macro is usually inserted in a message map by ClassWizard to indicate which function will handle a user-interface update command message.

There should be exactly one **ON_UPDATE_COMMAND_UI** macro statement in your message map for every user-interface update command that must be mapped to a message-handler function.

For more information and examples, see Chapter 2, "Working with Messages and Commands," in *Programming with the Microsoft Foundation Class Library*.

See Also   **ON_MESSAGE, ON_REGISTED_MESSAGE, ON_CONTROL, ON_COMMAND, CCmdUI**

ON_UPDATE_COMMAND_UI_RANGE

ON_UPDATE_COMMAND_UI_RANGE(*id1*, *id2*, *memberFxn* **)**

Parameters   *id1*   Command ID at the beginning of a contiguous range of command IDs.

id2   Command ID at the end of a contiguous range of command IDs.

memberFxn   The name of the update message-handler function to which the commands are mapped.

Remarks   Use this macro to map a contiguous range of command IDs to a single update message handler function. Update message handlers update the state of menu items and toolbar buttons associated with the command. The range of IDs starts with *id1* and ends with *id2*.

ClassWizard does not support message map ranges, so you must place the macro yourself. Be sure to put it outside the message map `//{{AFX_MSG_MAP` delimiters.

See Also   **ON_COMMAND_RANGE, ON_CONTROL_RANGE**

RFX_Binary

void RFX_Binary(CFieldExchange* *pFX*, **const char*** *szName*, **CByteArray&** *value*, **int** *nMaxLength* = 255 **);**

Parameters   *pFX*   A pointer to an object of class **CFieldExchange**. This object contains information to define the context for each call of the function. For more information about the operations a **CFieldExchange** object can specify, see the article "Record Field Exchange: How RFX Works" in *Programming with the Microsoft Foundation Class Library*.

szName   The name of a data column.

value   The value stored in the indicated data member—the value to be transferred. For a transfer from recordset to data source, the value, of type **CByteArray**, is taken from the specified data member. For a transfer from data source to recordset, the value is stored in the specified data member.

nMaxLength   The maximum allowed length of the string or array being transferred. The default value of *nMaxLength* is 255. Legal values are 1 to 32,767. The framework allocates this amount of space for the data. Passing a value smaller than 255 bytes saves allocation space. The value passed constrains the amount of data retrieved from the data source. Longer incoming data values are truncated and a trace message is sent.

Remarks

The **RFX_Binary** function transfers arrays of bytes between the field data members of a **CRecordset** object and the columns of a record on the data source of ODBC type **SQL_BINARY**, **SQL_VARBINARY**, or **SQL_LONGVARBINARY**. Data in the data source of these types is mapped to and from type **CByteArray** in the recordset.

See Also

RFX_Text, **RFX_Bool**, **RFX_Long**, **RFX_Int**, **RFX_Single**, **RFX_Double**, **RFX_Date**, **RFX_Byte**, **RFX_LongBinary**, **CFieldExchange::SetFieldType**

Example

See **RFX_Text**.

RFX_Bool

void RFX_Bool(CFieldExchange* *pFX*, **const char*** *szName*, **BOOL&** *value* **);**

Parameters

pFX   A pointer to an object of class **CFieldExchange**. This object contains information to define the context for each call of the function. For more information about the operations a **CFieldExchange** object can specify, see the article "Record Field Exchange: How RFX Works" in *Programming with the Microsoft Foundation Class Library*.

szName   The name of a data column.

value   The value stored in the indicated data member—the value to be transferred. For a transfer from recordset to data source, the value, of type **BOOL**, is taken from the specified data member. For a transfer from data source to recordset, the value is stored in the specified data member.

Remarks

The **RFX_BOOL** function transfers Boolean data between the field data members of a **CRecordset** object and the columns of a record on the data source of ODBC type **SQL_BIT**.

See Also

RFX_Text, **RFX_Long**, **RFX_Int**, **RFX_Single**, **RFX_Double**, **RFX_Date**, **RFX_Byte**, **RFX_Binary**, **RFX_LongBinary**, **CFieldExchange::SetFieldType**

Example

See **RFX_Text**.

RFX_Byte

void RFX_Byte(CFieldExchange* *pFX*, **const char*** *szName*, **int&** *value* **);**

Parameters
    pFX   A pointer to an object of class **CFieldExchange**. This object contains information to define the context for each call of the function. For more information about the operations a **CFieldExchange** object can specify, see the article "Record Field Exchange: How RFX Works" in *Programming with the Microsoft Foundation Class Library*.

    szName   The name of a data column.

    value   The value stored in the indicated data member—the value to be transferred. For a transfer from recordset to data source, the value, of type **int**, is taken from the specified data member. For a transfer from data source to recordset, the value is stored in the specified data member.

Remarks
    The **RFX_Byte** function transfers single bytes between the field data members of a **CRecordset** object and the columns of a record on the data source of ODBC type **SQL_TINYINT**.

See Also
    RFX_Text, RFX_Bool, RFX_Long, RFX_Int, RFX_Single, RFX_Double, RFX_Date, RFX_Binary, RFX_LongBinary, CFieldExchange::SetFieldType

Example
    See **RFX_Text**.

RFX_Date

void RFX_Date(CFieldExchange* *pFX*, **const char*** *szName*, **CTime&** *value* **);**

void RFX_Date(CFieldExchange* *pFX*, **const char*** *szName*,
TIMESTAMP_STRUCT& *value***);**

Parameters
    pFX   A pointer to an object of class **CFieldExchange**. This object contains information to define the context for each call of the function. For more information about the operations a **CFieldExchange** object can specify, see the article "Record Field Exchange: How RFX Works" in *Programming with the Microsoft Foundation Class Library*.

    szName   The name of a data column.

    value   The value stored in the indicated data member—the value to be transferred. The two versions of the function take different data types for value. The first version of the function takes a reference to a **CTime** object. For a transfer from recordset to data source, this value is taken from the specified data member. For a transfer from data source to recordset, the value is stored in the specified data member. The second version of the function takes a reference to a **TIMESTAMP_STRUCT**. You must set up this structure yourself prior to the call. Neither dialog data exchange (DDX) support nor ClassWizard support is available for this version. In your field map, place your call to the second version of **RFX_Date** outside the ClassWizard comment delimiters.

Remarks   The **RFX_Date** function transfers **CTime** or **TIMESTAMP_STRUCT** data between the field data members of a **CRecordset** object and the columns of a record on the data source of ODBC type **SQL_DATE**, **SQL_TIME**, or **SQL_TIMESTAMP**.

The **CTime** version of the function imposes the overhead of some intermediate processing and has a somewhat limited range. If you find either of these factors too limiting, use the second version of the function. But note its lack of ClassWizard and DDX support and the requirement that you set up the structure yourself.

See Also   **RFX_Text**, **RFX_Bool**, **RFX_Long**, **RFX_Int**, **RFX_Single**, **RFX_Double**, **RFX_Byte**, **RFX_Binary**, **RFX_LongBinary**, **CFieldExchange::SetFieldType**

Example   See **RFX_Text**.

In the ODBC *Programmer's Reference*: "SQL to C: Timestamp" in Appendix D

RFX_Double

void RFX_Double(CFieldExchange* *pFX*, const char* *szName*, double& *value*);

Parameters   *pFX*   A pointer to an object of class **CFieldExchange**. This object contains information to define the context for each call of the function. For more information about the operations a **CFieldExchange** object can specify, see the article "Record Field Exchange: How RFX Works" in *Programming with the Microsoft Foundation Class Library*.

szName   The name of a data column.

value   The value stored in the indicated data member—the value to be transferred. For a transfer from recordset to data source, the value, of type **double**, is taken from the specified data member. For a transfer from data source to recordset, the value is stored in the specified data member.

Remarks   The **RFX_Double** function transfers **double float** data between the field data members of a **CRecordset** object and the columns of a record on the data source of ODBC type **SQL_DOUBLE**.

See Also   **RFX_Text**, **RFX_Bool**, **RFX_Long**, **RFX_Int**, **RFX_Single**, **RFX_Date**, **RFX_Byte**, **RFX_Binary**, **RFX_LongBinary**, **CFieldExchange::SetFieldType**

Example   See **RFX_Text**.

RFX_Int

void RFX_Int(CFieldExchange* *pFX***, const char*** *szName***, int&** *value* **);**

Parameters
pFX   A pointer to an object of class **CFieldExchange**. This object contains information to define the context for each call of the function. For more information about the operations a **CFieldExchange** object can specify, see the article "Record Field Exchange: How RFX Works" in *Programming with the Microsoft Foundation Class Library*.

szName   The name of a data column.

value   The value stored in the indicated data member—the value to be transferred. For a transfer from recordset to data source, the value, of type **int**, is taken from the specified data member. For a transfer from data source to recordset, the value is stored in the specified data member.

Remarks
The **RFX_Int** function transfers integer data between the field data members of a **CRecordset** object and the columns of a record on the data source of ODBC type **SQL_SMALLINT**.

See Also
RFX_Text, RFX_Bool, RFX_Long, RFX_Single, RFX_Double, RFX_Date, RFX_Byte, RFX_Binary, RFX_LongBinary, CFieldExchange::SetFieldType

Example
See **RFX_Text**.

RFX_Long

void RFX_Long(CFieldExchange* *pFX***, const char*** *szName***, LONG&** *value* **);**

Parameters
pFX   A pointer to an object of class **CFieldExchange**. This object contains information to define the context for each call of the function. For more information about the operations a **CFieldExchange** object can specify, see the article "Record Field Exchange: How RFX Works" in *Programming with the Microsoft Foundation Class Library*.

szName   The name of a data column.

value   The value stored in the indicated data member—the value to be transferred. For a transfer from recordset to data source, the value, of type **long**, is taken from the specified data member. For a transfer from data source to recordset, the value is stored in the specified data member.

Remarks
The **RFX_Long** function transfers long integer data between the field data members of a **CRecordset** object and the columns of a record on the data source of ODBC type **SQL_INTEGER**.

See Also
RFX_Text, RFX_Bool, RFX_Int, RFX_Single, RFX_Double, RFX_Date, RFX_Byte, RFX_Binary, RFX_LongBinary, CFieldExchange::SetFieldType

Example   See **RFX_Text**.

RFX_LongBinary

void RFX_LongBinary(CFieldExchange* *pFX*, **const char*** *szName*,
CLongBinary& *value*);

Parameters   *pFX*   A pointer to an object of class **CFieldExchange**. This object contains
information to define the context for each call of the function. For more information
about the operations a **CFieldExchange** object can specify, see the article "Record
Field Exchange: How RFX Works" in *Programming with the Microsoft
Foundation Class Library*.

szName   The name of a data column.

value   The value stored in the indicated data member—the value to be transferred.
For a transfer from recordset to data source, the value, of type **CLongBinary**, is
taken from the specified data member. For a transfer from data source to recordset,
the value is stored in the specified data member.

Remarks   The **RFX_LongBinary** function transfers binary large object (BLOB) data using
class **CLongBinary** between the field data members of a **CRecordset** object and
the columns of a record on the data source of ODBC type
SQL_LONGVARBINARY or **SQL_LONGVARCHAR**.

See Also   **RFX_Text, RFX_Bool, RFX_Long, RFX_Int, RFX_Single, RFX_Double,
RFX_Date, RFX_Byte, RFX_Binary, CFieldExchange::SetFieldType,
CLongBinary**

Example   See **RFX_Text**.

RFX_Single

void RFX_Single(CFieldExchange* *pFX*, **const char*** *szName*, **float&** *value*);

Parameters   *pFX*   A pointer to an object of class **CFieldExchange**. This object contains
information to define the context for each call of the function. For more information
about the operations a **CFieldExchange** object can specify, see the article "Record
Field Exchange: How RFX Works" in *Programming with the Microsoft
Foundation Class Library*.

szName   The name of a data column.

value   The value stored in the indicated data member—the value to be transferred.
For a transfer from recordset to data source, the value, of type **float**, is taken from
the specified data member. For a transfer from data source to recordset, the value is
stored in the specified data member.

Remarks   The **RFX_Single** function transfers floating point data between the field data members of a **CRecordset** object and the columns of a record on the data source of ODBC type **SQL_REAL**.

See Also   **RFX_Text, RFX_Bool, RFX_Long, RFX_Int, RFX_Double, RFX_Date, RFX_Byte, RFX_Binary, RFX_LongBinary, CFieldExchange::SetFieldType**

Example   See **RFX_Text**.

RFX_Text

void RFX_Text(CFieldExchange* *pFX*, **const char*** *szName*, **CString&** *value*, **int** *nMaxLength* **= 255, int** *nColumnType* **= SQL_VARCHAR);**

Parameters   *pFX*   A pointer to an object of class **CFieldExchange**. This object contains information to define the context for each call of the function. For more information about the operations a **CFieldExchange** object can specify, see the article "Record Field Exchange: How RFX Works" in *Programming with the Microsoft Foundation Class Library*.

szName   The name of a data column.

value   The value stored in the indicated data member—the value to be transferred. For a transfer from recordset to data source, the value, of type **CString**, is taken from the specified data member. For a transfer from data source to recordset, the value is stored in the specified data member.

nMaxLength   The maximum allowed length of the string or array being transferred. The default value of *nMaxLength* is 255. Legal values are 1 to 32,767. The framework allocates this amount of space for the data. Passing a value smaller than 255 bytes saves allocation space. The value passed constrains the amount of data retrieved from the data source. Longer incoming data values are truncated and a trace message is sent.

nColumnType   Used mainly for parameters. An integer indicating the data type of the parameter. The type is an ODBC data type of the form **SQL_XXX**.

Remarks   The **RFX_Text** function transfers **CString** data between the field data members of a **CRecordset** object and columns of a record on the data source of ODBC type **SQL_LONGVARCHAR, SQL_CHAR, SQL_VARCHAR, SQL_DECIMAL,** or **SQL_NUMERIC**. Data in the data source of all of these types is mapped to and from **CString** in the recordset.

See Also   **RFX_Bool, RFX_Long, RFX_Int, RFX_Single, RFX_Double, RFX_Date, RFX_Byte, RFX_Binary, RFX_LongBinary, CFieldExchange::SetFieldType**

Example   This example shows several calls to **RFX_Text**. Notice also the two calls to **CFieldExchange::SetFieldType**. ClassWizard normally writes the second call to **SetFieldType** and its associated RFX calls. You must write the first call and its

RFX call. It is recommended that you put any parameter items before the "//{{AFX_FIELD_MAP" comment. You must put parameters outside the comments.

```
void CSections::DoFieldExchange(CFieldExchange* pFX)
{
    pFX->SetFieldType(CFieldExchange::param);
    RFX_Text(pFX, "Name," m_strNameParam);
    //{{AFX_FIELD_MAP(CSections)
    pFX->SetFieldType(CFieldExchange::outputColumn);
    RFX_Text(pFX, "CourseID", m_strCourseID);
    RFX_Text(pFX, "InstructorID", m_strInstructorID);
    RFX_Int(pFX, "RoomNo", m_nRoomNo);
    RFX_Text(pFX, "Schedule", m_strSchedule);
    RFX_Int(pFX, "SectionNo", m_nSectionNo);
    RFX_Single(pFX, "LabFee", m_flLabFee);
    //}}AFX_FIELD_MAP
}
```

RUNTIME_CLASS

RUNTIME_CLASS(*class_name* **)**

Parameters   *class_name*   The actual name of the class (not enclosed in quotation marks).

Remarks   Use this macro to get the run-time class structure from the name of a C++ class.

RUNTIME_CLASS returns a pointer to a **CRuntimeClass** structure for the class specified by *class_name*. Only **CObject**-derived classes declared with **DECLARE_DYNAMIC**, **DECLARE_DYNCREATE**, or **DECLARE_SERIAL** will return pointers to a **CRuntimeClass** structure.

For more information, see the article "CObject Class" in *Programming with the Microsoft Foundation Class Library*.

See Also   **DECLARE_DYNAMIC, DECLARE_DYNCREATE, DECLARE_SERIAL, CObject::GetRuntimeClass, CRuntimeClass**

Example
```
CRuntimeClass* prt = RUNTIME_CLASS( CAge );
ASSERT( lstrcmp( prt->m_lpszClassName, "CAge" )  == 0 );
```

SerializeElements

template< class *TYPE* **>**
void SerializeElements(CArchive& *ar*, *TYPE* * *pElements*, **int** *nCount* **);**

Parameters   *TYPE*   Template parameter specifying the type of the elements.

ar   An archive object to archive to or from.

pElements   Pointer to the elements being archived.

nCount   Number of elements being archived

Remarks   **CArray**, **CList**, and **CMap** call this function to serialize elements. The default implementation does a bit-wise read or write.

For information on implementing this and other helper functions, see the article "Collections: How to Make a Type-Safe Collection" in *Programming with the Microsoft Foundation Class Library*.

See Also   **CArchive**

THIS_FILE

Remarks   This macro expands to the name of the file that is being compiled. The information is used by the **ASSERT** and **VERIFY** macros. AppWizard and ClassWizard place the macro in source code files they create.

See Also   **ASSERT**, **VERIFY**

THROW

THROW(*exception_object_pointer*)

Parameters   *exception_object_pointer*   Points to an exception object derived from **CException**.

Remarks   Throws the specified exception. **THROW** interrupts program execution, passing control to the associated **CATCH** block in your program. If you have not provided the **CATCH** block, then control is passed to a Microsoft Foundation Class Library module that prints an error message and exits.

For more information, see the article "Exceptions" in *Programming with the Microsoft Foundation Class Library*.

See Also   **TRY, CATCH, THROW, THROW_LAST, AND_CATCH, END_CATCH, AfxThrowArchiveException, AfxThrowFileException, AfxThrowMemoryException, AfxThrowNotSupportedException, AfxThrowResourceException, AfxThrowUserException**

THROW_LAST

THROW_LAST( )

Remarks   Throws the exception back to the next outer **CATCH** block.

This macro allows you to throw a locally created exception. If you try to throw an exception that you have just caught, it will normally go out of scope and be deleted.

With **THROW_LAST**, the exception is passed correctly to the next **CATCH** handler.

For more information, see the article "Exceptions" in *Programming with the Microsoft Foundation Class Library*.

See Also   **TRY**, **CATCH**, **THROW**, **AND_CATCH**, **END_CATCH**

TRACE

TRACE(*exp* **)**

Parameters   *exp*   Specifies a variable number of arguments that are used in exactly the same way that a variable number of arguments are used in the run-time function **printf.**

Remarks   Provides similar functionality to the **printf** function by sending a formatted string to a dump device such as a file or debug monitor. Like **printf** for C programs under MS-DOS, the **TRACE** macro is a convenient way to track the value of variables as your program executes. In the Debug environment, the **TRACE** macro output goes to **afxDump**. In the Release environment, it does nothing.

Note   This macro is available only in the Debug version of MFC.

For more information, see the article "Diagnostics" in *Programming with the Microsoft Foundation Class Library*.

See Also   **TRACE0**, **TRACE1**, **TRACE2**, **TRACE3**, **AfxDump**, **afxTraceEnabled**

Example
```
int i = 1;
char sz[] = "one";
TRACE( "Integer = %d, String = %s\n", i, sz );
// Output: 'Integer = 1, String = one'
```

TRACE0

TRACE0(*exp* **)**

Parameters   *exp*   A format string as used in the run-time function **printf**.

Remarks   Similar to **TRACE**, but places the trace string in a code segment rather than DGROUP, thus using less DGROUP space. **TRACE0** is one variant of a group of trace macros that you can use for debug output. This group includes **TRACE0**, **TRACE1**, **TRACE2**, and **TRACE3**. The difference between these macros is the number of parameters taken. **TRACE0** only takes a format string and can be used for simple text messages. **TRACE1** takes a format string plus one argument—a variable to be dumped. Likewise, **TRACE2** and **TRACE3** take two and three parameters after the format string, respectively.

TRACE0 does nothing if you have compiled a release version of your application. As with **TRACE**, it only dumps data to **afxDump** if you have compiled a debug version of your application.

Note This macro is available only in the Debug version of MFC.

Example

```
TRACE0( "Start Dump of MyClass members:" );
```

See Also   **TRACE, TRACE1, TRACE2, TRACE3**

TRACE1

TRACE1(*exp, param1*)

Parameters   *exp*   A format string as used in the run-time function **printf**.

param1   The name of the variable whose value should be dumped.

Remarks   See **TRACE0** for a description of the **TRACE1** macro.

Example
```
int i = 1;
TRACE1( "Integer = %d\n", i );
// Output: 'Integer = 1'
```

TRACE2

TRACE2(*exp, param1, param2*)

Parameters   *exp*   A format string as used in the run-time function **printf**.

param1   The name of the variable whose value should be dumped.

param2   The name of the variable whose value should be dumped.

Remarks   See **TRACE0** for a description of the **TRACE2** macro.

Example

```
int i = 1;
char sz[] = "one";
TRACE2( "Integer = %d, String = %s\n", i, sz );
// Output: 'Integer = 1, String = one'
```

TRACE3

TRACE3(*exp, param1, param2, param3*)

Parameters   *exp*   A format string as used in the run-time function **printf**.

param1   The name of the variable whose value should be dumped.

param2   The name of the variable whose value should be dumped.

param3   The name of the variable whose value should be dumped.

Remarks   See **TRACE0** for a description of the **TRACE3** macro.

TRY

TRY

Remarks   Use this macro to set up a **TRY** block. A **TRY** block identifies a block of code that might throw exceptions. Those exceptions are handled in the following **CATCH** and **AND_CATCH** blocks. Recursion is allowed: exceptions may be passed to an outer **TRY** block, either by ignoring them or by using the **THROW_LAST** macro.

For more information, see the article "Exceptions" in *Programming with the Microsoft Foundation Class Library*.

See Also   **THROW, CATCH, AND_CATCH, END_CATCH**

VERIFY

VERIFY(*booleanExpression*)

Parameters   *booleanExpression*   Specifies an expression (including pointer values) that evaluates to nonzero or 0.

Remarks   In the Debug version of MFC, the **VERIFY** macro evaluates its argument. If the result is 0, the macro prints a diagnostic message and halts the program. If the condition is nonzero, it does nothing.

The diagnostic message has the form

```
assertion failed in file <name> in line <num>
```

where *name* is the name of the source file and *num* is the line number of the assertion that failed in the source file.

In the Release version of MFC, **VERIFY** evaluates the expression but does not print or interrupt the program. For example, if the expression is a function call, the call will be made.

See Also   **ASSERT**

Structures, Styles, and Callback Functions

Structures

A description of structures that are called from various member functions follows. For further information on individual structure usage, refer to the classes and member functions noted in the "See Also" section of each structure.

ABC Structure

The **ABC** structure has the following form:

```
typedef struct _ABC { /* abc */
    int     abcA;
    UINT    abcB;
    int     abcC;
} ABC;
```

The ABC structure contains the width of a character in a TrueType® font.

Members

abcA   Specifies the "A" spacing of the character. The "A" spacing is the distance to add to the current position before drawing the character glyph.

abcB   Specifies the "B" spacing of the character. The "B" spacing is the width of the drawn portion of the character glyph.

abcC   Specifies the "C" spacing of the character. The "C" spacing is the distance to add to the current position to provide white space to the right of the character glyph.

Comments

The total width of a character is the summation of the "A," "B," and "C" spaces. Either the "A" or the "C" space can be negative to indicate underhangs or overhangs.

See Also

CDC::GetCharABCWidths

ABCFLOAT Structure

The **ABCFLOAT** structure has the following form:

```
typedef struct _ABCFLOAT { /* abcf */
    FLOAT    abcfA;
    FLOAT    abcfB;
    FLOAT    abcfC;
} ABCFLOAT;
```

The **ABCFLOAT** structure contains the A, B, and C widths of a font character.

Members   **abcfA**   Specifies the "A" spacing of the character. The "A" spacing is the distance to add to the current position before drawing the character glyph.

abcfB   Specifies the "B" spacing of the character. The "B" spacing is the width of the drawn portion of the character glyph.

abcfC   Specifies the "C" spacing of the character. The "C" spacing is the distance to add to the current position to provide white space to the right of the character glyph.

Comments   The A, B, and C widths are measured along the base line of the font. The character increment (total width) of a character is the sum of the "A," "B," and "C" spaces. Either the "A" or the "C" space can be negative to indicate underhangs or overhangs.

See Also   **CDC::Get CharABCWidths**

BITMAP Structure

A **BITMAP** structure has the following form:

```
typedef struct tagBITMAP {  /* bm */
    int     bmType;
    int     bmWidth;
    int     bmHeight;
    int     bmWidthBytes;
    BYTE    bmPlanes;
    BYTE    bmBitsPixel;
    LPVOID  bmBits;
} BITMAP;
```

The **BITMAP** structure defines the height, width, color format, and bit values of a logical bitmap.

Members   **bmType**   Specifies the bitmap type. For logical bitmaps, this member must be 0.

bmWidth   Specifies the width of the bitmap in pixels. The width must be greater than 0.

bmHeight   Specifies the height of the bitmap in raster lines. The height must be greater than 0.

bmWidthBytes   Specifies the number of bytes in each raster line. This value must be an even number since the graphics device interface (GDI) assumes that the bit values of a bitmap form an array of integer (2-byte) values. In other words, **bmWidthBytes** * 8 must be the next multiple of 16 greater than or equal to the value obtained when the **bmWidth** member is multiplied by the **bmBitsPixel** member.

bmPlanes   Specifies the number of color planes in the bitmap.

bmBitsPixel   Specifies the number of adjacent color bits on each plane needed to define a pixel.

bmBits   Points to the location of the bit values for the bitmap. The **bmBits** member must be a long pointer to an array of 1-byte values.

Comments   The currently used bitmap formats are monochrome and color. The monochrome bitmap uses a 1-bit, 1-plane format. Each scan is a multiple of 16 bits.

Scans are organized as follows for a monochrome bitmap of height *n*:

```
Scan 0
Scan 1
.
.
.
Scan n-2
Scan n-1
```

The pixels on a monochrome device are either black or white. If the corresponding bit in the bitmap is 1, the pixel is turned on (white). If the corresponding bit in the bitmap is 0, the pixel is turned off (black).

All devices support bitmaps that have the **RC_BITBLT** bit set in the **RASTERCAPS** index of the **GetDeviceCaps** member function.

Each device has its own unique color format. In order to transfer a bitmap from one device to another, use the **GetDIBits** and **SetDIBits** Windows functions.

See Also   **CBitmap::CreateBitmapIndirect**

BITMAPINFO Structure

The **BITMAPINFO** structure has the following form:

```
typedef struct tagBITMAPINFO {
    BITMAPINFOHEADER     bmiHeader;
    RGBQUAD              bmiColors[1];
} BITMAPINFO;
```

The **BITMAPINFO** structure defines the dimensions and color information for a Windows device-independent bitmap (DIB).

Members   **bmiHeader**   Specifies a **BITMAPINFOHEADER** structure that contains information about the dimensions and color format of a device-independent bitmap.

bmiColors   Specifies an array of **RGBQUAD** or **DWORD** data types that define the colors in the bitmap.

Comments   A device-independent bitmap consists of two distinct parts: a **BITMAPINFO** structure describing the dimensions and colors of the bitmap, and an array of bytes defining the pixels of the bitmap. The bits in the array are packed together, but each scan line must be padded with zeroes to end on a **LONG** boundary. If height is positive the origin of the bitmap is the lower-left corner. If the height is negative then the origin is the upper-left corner.

The **biBitCount** member of the **BITMAPINFOHEADER** structure determines the number of bits that define each pixel and the maximum number of colors in the bitmap. This member can be one of the following values:

- The bitmap is monochrome, and the **bmiColors** member contains two entries. Each bit in the bitmap array represents a pixel. If the bit is clear, the pixel is displayed with the color of the first entry in the **bmiColors** table; if the bit is set, the pixel has the color of the second entry in the table.

- The bitmap has a maximum of 16 colors, and the **bmiColors** member contains up to 16 entries. Each pixel in the bitmap is represented by a 4-bit index into the color table. For example, if the first byte in the bitmap is 0x1F, the byte represents two pixels. The first pixel contains the color in the second table entry, and the second pixel contains the color in the sixteenth table entry.

- The bitmap has a maximum of 256 colors, and the **bmiColors** member contains up to 256 entries. In this case, each byte in the array represents a single pixel.

- The bitmap has a maximum of 2^{16} colors. The **biCompression** member of the **BITMAPINFOHEADER** must be **BI_BITFIELDS**. The **bmiColors** member contains 3 **DWORD** color masks which specify the red, green, and blue components, respectively, of each pixel. Bits set in the **DWORD** mask must be contiguous and should not overlap the bits of another mask. All the bits in the pixel do not have to be used. Each **WORD** in the array represents a single pixel.

- The bitmap has a maximum of 224 colors, and the **bmiColors** member is **NULL**. Each 3-byte triplet in the bitmap array represents the relative intensities of blue, green, and red, respectively, of a pixel.

- The bitmap has a maximum of 2^{32} colors. The **biCompression** member of the **BITMAPINFOHEADER** must be **BI_BITFIELDS**. The **bmiColors** member contains 3 **DWORD** color masks which specify the red, green, and blue components, respectively, of each pixel. Bits set in the **DWORD** mask must be contiguous and should not overlap the bits of another mask. All the bits in the pixel do not have to be used. Each **DWORD** in the array represents a single pixel.

The **biClrUsed** member of the **BITMAPINFOHEADER** structure specifies the number of color indices in the color table that are actually used by the bitmap. If the **biClrUsed** member is set to zero, the bitmap uses the maximum number of colors corresponding to the value of the **biBitCount** member.

The colors in the **bmiColors** table should appear in order of importance. Alternatively, for functions that use DIBs, the **bmiColors** member can be an array of 16-bit unsigned integers that specify indices into the currently realized logical palette, instead of explicit RGB values. In this case, an application using the bitmap must call the DIB functions (**::CreateDIBitmap**, **::CreateDIBPatternBrush**, and **::CreateDIBSection**) with the **iUsage** parameter set to **DIB_PAL_COLORS**.

If the bitmap is a packed bitmap (that is, a bitmap in which the bitmap array immediately follows the **BITMAPINFO** header and which is referenced by a single pointer), the biClrUsed member must be set to an even number when using the **DIB_PAL_COLORS** mode so the DIB bitmap array starts on a **DWORD** boundary.

Note The **bmiColors** member should not contain palette indices if the bitmap is to be stored in a file or transferred to another application. Unless the application has exclusive use and control of the bitmap, the bitmap color table should contain explicit RGB values.

See Also   **CBrush::CreateDIBPatternBrush**

COLORADJUSTMENT Structure

The **COLORADJUSTMENT** structure has the following format:

```
typedef struct  tagCOLORADJUSTMENT {     /* ca */
    WORD  caSize;
    WORD  caFlags;
    WORD  caIlluminantIndex;
    WORD  caRedGamma;
    WORD  caGreenGamma;
    WORD  caBlueGamma;
    WORD  caReferenceBlack;
    WORD  caReferenceWhite;
    SHORT caContrast;
    SHORT caBrightness;
    SHORT caColorfulness;
    SHORT caRedGreenTint;
} COLORADJUSTMENT;
```

The **COLORADJUSTMENT** structure defines the color adjustment values used by the **::StretchBlt** and **::StretchDIBits** functions when the **::StretchBlt** mode is **HALFTONE**.

Members   **caSize**   Specifies the size of the structure in bytes.

caFlags   Specifies how the output image should be prepared. This member may be set to **NULL** or any combination of the following values:

- **CA_NEGATIVE**   Specifies that the negative of the original image should be displayed.
- **CA_LOG_FILTER**   Specifies that a logarithmic function should be applied to the final density of the output colors. This will increase the color contrast when the luminance is low.

caIlluminantIndex   Specifies the luminance of the light source under which the image object is viewed. This member may be set to one of the following values:

- **ILLUMINANT_EQUAL_ENERGY**
- **ILLUMINANT_A**
- **ILLUMINANT_B**
- **ILLUMINANT_C**
- **ILLUMINANT_D50**
- **ILLUMINANT_D55**
- **ILLUMINANT_D65**
- **ILLUMINANT_D75**
- **ILLUMINANT_F2**
- **ILLUMINANT_TURNGSTEN**
- **ILLUMINANT_DAYLIGHT**
- **ILLUMINANT_FLUORESCENT**
- **ILLUMINANT_NTSC**

caRedGamma   Specifies the n-th power gamma-correction value for the red primary of the source colors. The value must be in the range from 2,500 to 65,000. A value of 10,000 means no gamma-correction.

caGreenGamma   Specifies the n-th power gamma-correction value for the green primary of the source colors. The value must be in the range from 2,500 to 65,000. A value of 10,000 means no gamma-correction.

caBlueGamma   Specifies the n-th power gamma-correction value for the blue primary of the source colors. The value must be in the range from 2,500 to 65,000. A value of 10,000 means no gamma-correction.

caReferenceBlack   Specifies the black reference for the source colors. Any colors that are darker than this are treated as black. The value must be in the range from 0 to 4,000.

caReferenceWhite Specifies the white reference for the source colors. Any colors that are lighter than this are treated as white. The value must be in the range from 6,000 to 10,000.

caContrast Specifies the amount of contrast to be applied to the source object. The value must be in the range from -100 to 100. A value of 0 means no contrast adjustment.

caBrightness Specifies the amount of brightness to be applied to the source object. The value must be in the range from -100 to 100. A value of 0 means no brightness adjustment.

caColorfulness Specifies the amount of colorfulness to be applied to the source object. The value must be in the range from -100 to 100. A value of 0 means no colorfulness adjustment.

caRedGreenTint Specifies the amount of red or green tint adjustment to be applied to the source object. The value must be in the range from -100 to 100. Positive numbers would adjust towards red and negative numbers adjust towards green. A 0 means no tint adjustment.

See Also   **CDC::GetColorAdjustment**

COMPAREITEMSTRUCT Structure

A **COMPAREITEMSTRUCT** data structure has this form:

```
typedef struct tagCOMPAREITEMSTRUCT {
    UINT    CtlType;
    UINT    CtlID;
    HWND    hwndItem;
    UINT    itemID1;
    DWORD   itemData1;
    UINT    itemID2;
    DWORD   itemData2;
} COMPAREITEMSTRUCT;
```

Members   **CtlType   ODT_LISTBOX** (which specifies an owner-draw list box) or **ODT_COMBOBOX** (which specifies an owner-draw combo box).

CtlID   The control ID for the list box or combo box.

hwndItem   The window handle of the control.

itemID1   The index of the first item in the list box or combo box being compared.

itemData1   Application-supplied data for the first item being compared. This value was passed in the call that added the item to the combo or list box.

itemID2   Index of the second item in the list box or combo box being compared.

itemData2   Application-supplied data for the second item being compared. This value was passed in the call that added the item to the combo or list box.

See Also   **CWnd::OnCompareItem**

CREATESTRUCT Structure

A **CREATESTRUCT** structure has the following form:

```
typedef struct tagCREATESTRUCT {
    LPVOID    lpCreateParams;
    HANDLE    hInstance;
    HMENU     hMenu;
    HWND      hwndParent;
    int       cy;
    int       cx;
    int       y;
    int       x;
    LONG      style;
    LPCSTR    lpszName;
    LPCSTR    lpszClass;
    DWORD     dwExStyle;
} CREATESTRUCT;
```

Members   **lpCreateParams**   Points to data to be used to create the window.

hInstance   Identifies the module-instance handle of the module that owns the new window.

hMenu   Identifies the menu to be used by the new window. If a child window, contains the integer ID.

hwndParent   Identifies the window that owns the new window. This member is **NULL** if the new window is a top-level window.

cy   Specifies the height of the new window.

cx   Specifies the width of the new window.

y   Specifies the y-coordinate of the upper-left corner of the new window. Coordinates are relative to the parent window if the new window is a child window; otherwise coordinates are relative to the screen origin.

x   Specifies the x-coordinate of the upper-left corner of the new window. Coordinates are relative to the parent window if the new window is a child window; otherwise coordinates are relative to the screen origin.

style   Specifies the new window's style.

lpszName   Points to a null-terminated string that specifies the new window's name.

lpszClass   Points to a null-terminated string that specifies the new window's Windows class name (a **WNDCLASS** structure).

dwExStyle   Specifies the extended style for the new window.

See Also   **CWnd::OnCreate**

DELETEITEMSTRUCT Structure

A **DELETEITEMSTRUCT** structure has the following form:

```
typedef struct tagDELETEITEMSTRUCT { /* ditms */
    UINT CtlType;
    UINT CtlID;
    UINT itemID;
    HWND hwndItem;
    UINT itemData;
} DELETEITEMSTRUCT;
```

The **DELETEITEMSTRUCT** structure describes a deleted owner-drawn list-box or combo-box item. When an item is removed from the list box or combo box or when the list box or combo box is destroyed, Windows sends the **WM_DELETEITEM** message to the owner for each deleted item. The **lParam** parameter of the message contains a pointer to this structure.

Members   **CtlType**   Specifies ODT_LISTBOX (an owner-drawn list box) or ODT_COMBOBOX (an owner-drawn combo box).

CtlID   Specifies the identifier of the list box or combo box.

itemID   Specifies index of the item in the list box or combo box being removed.

hwndItem   Identifies the control.

itemData   Specifies application-defined data for the item. This value is passed to the control in the lParam parameter of the message that adds the item to the list box or combo box.

See Also   **CWnd::OnDeleteItem**

DEVMODE Structure

The **DEVMODE** structure has the following form:

```
typedef struct _devicemode {    /* dvmd */
    TCHAR  dmDeviceName[32];
    WORD   dmSpecVersion;
    WORD   dmDriverVersion;
    WORD   dmSize;
    WORD   dmDriverExtra;
```

```
    DWORD  dmFields;
    short  dmOrientation;
    short  dmPaperSize;
    short  dmPaperLength;
    short  dmPaperWidth;
    short  dmScale;
    short  dmCopies;
    short  dmDefaultSource;
    short  dmPrintQuality;
    short  dmColor;
    short  dmDuplex;
    short  dmYResolution;
    short  dmTTOption;
    short  dmCollate;
    TCHAR  dmFormName[32];
    WORD   dmUnusedPadding;
    USHORT dmBitsPerPel;
    DWORD  dmPelsWidth;
    DWORD  dmPelsHeight;
    DWORD  dmDisplayFlags;
    DWORD  dmDisplayFrequency;
} DEVMODE;
```

The **DEVMODE** data structure contains information about the device initialization and environment of a printer.

Members   **dmDeviceName**   Specifies the name of the device the driver supports; for example, "PCL/HP LaserJet" in the case of PCL/HP LaserJet®. This string is unique among device drivers.

dmSpecVersion   Specifies the version number of the initialization data specification on which the structure is based.

dmDriverVersion   Specifies the printer driver version number assigned by the printer driver developer.

dmSize   Specifies the size, in bytes, of the **DEVMODE** structure except the dmDriverData (device-specific) member. If an application manipulates only the driver-independent portion of the data, it can use this member to determine the length of the structure without having to account for different versions.

dmDriverExtra   Contains the number of bytes of private driver-data that follow this structure. If a device driver does not use device-specific information, set this member to zero.

dmFields   Specifies which of the remaining members in the **DEVMODE** structure have been initialized. Bit 0 (defined as **DM_ORIENTATION**) corresponds to **dmOrientation**; bit 1 (defined as **DM_PAPERSIZE**) specifies **dmPaperSize**, and so on. A printer driver supports only those members that are appropriate for the printer technology.

dmOrientation   Selects the orientation of the paper. This member can be either **DMORIENT_PORTRAIT** (1) or **DMORIENT_LANDSCAPE** (2).

dmPaperSize   Selects the size of the paper to print on. This member can be set to zero if the length and width of the paper are both set by the **dmPaperLength** and **dmPaperWidth** members. Otherwise, the dmPaperSize member can be set to one of the following predefined values:

- **DMPAPER_LETTER**   Letter, 8 1/2 by 11 inches
- **MPAPER_LEGAL**   Legal, 8 1/2 by 14 inches
- **DMPAPER_A4**   A4 Sheet, 210 by 297 millimeters
- **DMPAPER_CSHEET**   C Sheet, 17 by 22 inches
- **DMPAPER_DSHEET**   D Sheet, 22 by 34 inches
- **DMPAPER_ESHEET**   E Sheet, 34 by 44 inches
- **DMPAPER_LETTERSMALL**   Letter Small, 8 1/2 by 11 inches
- **DMPAPER_TABLOID**   Tabloid, 11 by 17 inches
- **DMPAPER_LEDGER**   Ledger, 17 by 11 inches
- **DMPAPER_STATEMENT**   Statement, 5 1/2 by 8 1/2 inches
- **DMPAPER_EXECUTIVE**   Executive, 7 1/4 by 10 1/2 inches
- **DMPAPER_A3**   A3 sheet, 297 by 420 millimeters
- **DMPAPER_A4SMALL**   A4 small sheet, 210 by 297 millimeters
- **DMPAPER_A5**   A5 sheet, 148 by 210 millimeters
- **DMPAPER_B4**   B4 sheet, 250 by 354 millimeters
- **DMPAPER_B5**   B5 sheet, 182 by 257 millimeter paper
- **DMPAPER_FOLIO**   Folio, 8 1/2 by 13 inch paper
- **DMPAPER_QUARTO**   Quarto, 215 by 275 millimeter paper

- **DMPAPER_10X14**   10 by 14 inch sheet
- **DMPAPER_11X17**   11 by 17 inch sheet
- **DMPAPER_NOTE**   Note, 8 1/2 by 11 inches
- **DMPAPER_ENV_9**   #9 Envelope, 3 7/8 by 8 7/8 inches
- **DMPAPER_ENV_10**   #10 Envelope, 4 1/8 by 9 1/2 inches
- **DMPAPER_ENV_11**   #11 Envelope, 4 1/2 by 10 3/8 inches
- **DMPAPER_ENV_12**   #12 Envelope, 4 3/4 by 11 inches
- **DMPAPER_ENV_14**   #14 Envelope, 5 by 11 1/2 inches
- **DMPAPER_ENV_DL**   DL Envelope, 110 by 220 millimeters
- **DMPAPER_ENV_C5**   C5 Envelope, 162 by 229 millimeters
- **DMPAPER_ENV_C3**   C3 Envelope, 324 by 458 millimeters
- **DMPAPER_ENV_C4**   C4 Envelope, 229 by 324 millimeters
- **DMPAPER_ENV_C6**   C6 Envelope, 114 by 162 millimeters
- **DMPAPER_ENV_C65**   C65 Envelope, 114 by 229 millimeters
- **DMPAPER_ENV_B4**   B4 Envelope, 250 by 353 millimeters
- **DMPAPER_ENV_B5**   B5 Envelope, 176 by 250 millimeters
- **DMPAPER_ENV_B6**   B6 Envelope, 176 by 125 millimeters
- **DMPAPER_ENV_ITALY**   Italy Envelope, 110 by 230 millimeters
- **DMPAPER_ENV_MONARCH**   Monarch Envelope, 3 7/8 by 7 1/2 inches
- **DMPAPER_ENV_PERSONAL**   6 3/4 Envelope, 3 5/8 by 6 1/2 inches
- **DMPAPER_FANFOLD_US**   US Std Fanfold, 14 7/8 by 11 inches
- **DMPAPER_FANFOLD_STD_GERMAN**   German Std Fanfold, 8 1/2 by 12 inches
- **DMPA PER_FANFOLD_LGL_GERMAN**   German Legal Fanfold, 8 1/2 by 13 inches

dmPaperLength   Overrides the length of the paper specified by the **dmPaperSize** member, either for custom paper sizes or for devices such as dot-matrix printers, which can print on a page of arbitrary length. These values, along with all other values in this structure that specify a physical length, are in tenths of a millimeter.

dmPaperWidth   Overrides the width of the paper specified by the **dmPaperSize** member.

dmScale   Specifies the factor by which the printed output is to be scaled. The apparent page size is scaled from the physical page size by a factor of **dmScale**/100. For example, a letter-sized page with a dmScale value of 50 would contain as much data as a page of 17- by 22-inches because the output text and graphics would be half their original height and width.

dmCopies   Selects the number of copies printed if the device supports multiple-page copies.

dmDefaultSource   Reserved; must be zero.

dmPrintQuality   Specifies the printer resolution. There are four predefined device-independent values:

- **DMRES_HIGH**
- **DMRES_MEDIUM**
- **DMRES_LOW**
- **DMRES_DRAFT**

If a positive value is given, it specifies the number of dots per inch (DPI) and is therefore device dependent.

dmColor   Switches between color and monochrome on color printers. Following are the possible values:

- **DMCOLOR_COLOR**
- **DMCOLOR_MONOCHROME**

dmDuplex   Selects duplex or double-sided printing for printers capable of duplex printing. Following are the possible values:

- **DMDUP_SIMPLEX**
- **DMDUP_HORIZONTAL**
- **DMDUP_VERTICAL**

dmYResolution   Specifies the y-resolution, in dots per inch, of the printer. If the printer initializes this member, the dmPrintQuality member specifies the x-resolution, in dots per inch, of the printer.

dmTTOption   Specifies how TrueType® fonts should be printed. This member can be one of the following values:

- **DMTT_BITMAP**   Prints TrueType fonts as graphics. This is the default action for dot-matrix printers.
- **DMTT_DOWNLOAD**   Downloads TrueType fonts as soft fonts. This is the default action for Hewlett-Packard printers that use Printer Control Language (PCL).
- **DMTT_SUBDEV**   Substitute device fonts for TrueType fonts. This is the default action for PostScript® printers.

dmUnusedPadding   Used to align the structure to a **DWORD** boundary. This should not be used or referenced. Its name and usage is reserved, and can change in future releases.

dmCollate   Specifies whether collation should be used when printing multiple copies. This member can be be one of the following values:

- **DMCOLLATE_TRUE**   Collate when printing multiple copies.
- **DMCOLLATE_FALSE**   Do NOT collate when printing multiple copies.

Using **DMCOLLATE_FALSE** provides faster, more efficient output, since the data is sent to a page printer just once, no matter how many copies are required. The printer is told to simply print the page again.

dmFormName   Specifies the name of the form to use; for example, "Letter" or "Legal." A complete set of names can be retrieved through the **::EnumForms** function.

dmBitsPerPel   Specifies in bits per pixel the color resolution of the display device. For example: 4 bits for 16 colors, 8 bits for 256 colors, or 16 bits for 65536 colors.

dmPelsWidth   Specifies the width, in pixels, of the visible device surface.

dmPelsHeight   Specifies the height, in pixels, of the visible device surface.

dmDisplayFlags   Specifies the device's display mode. The following are valid flags:

- **DM_GRAYSCALE**   Specifies that the display is a NON-color device. If this flag is not set, color is assumed.
- **DM_INTERLACED**   Specifies that the display mode is interlaced. If the flag is not set, NON-interlaced is assumed.

dmDisplayFrequency   Specifies the frequency, in hertz (cycles per second), of the display device in a particular mode.

Comments   A device driver's private data will follow the **dmDisplayMode** member. The number of bytes of private data is specified by the **dmDriverExtra** member.

See Also   **CDC::ResetDC, CPrintDialog::GetDevMode**

DEVNAMES Structure

```
typedef struct tagDEVNAMES { /* dvnm */
    WORD wDriverOffset;
    WORD wDeviceOffset;
    WORD wOutputOffset;
```

```
    WORD wDefault;
    /* driver, device, and port-name strings follow wDefault */
} DEVNAMES;
```

The **DEVNAMES** structure contains strings that identify the driver, device, and output-port names for a printer. The **PrintDlg** function uses these strings to initialize members in the system-defined Print dialog box. When the user closes the dialog box, information about the selected printer is returned in this structure.

Members

wDriverOffset   (Input/Output) Specifies the offset to a null-terminated string that contains the filename (without the extension) of the device driver. On input, this string is used to determine the printer to display initially in the dialog box.

wDeviceOffset   (Input/Output) Specifies the offset to the null-terminated string (maximum of 32 bytes including the null) that contains the name of the device. This string must be identical to the **dmDeviceName** member of the **DEVMODE** structure.

wOutputOffset   (Input/Output) Specifies the offset to the null-terminated string that contains the DOS device name for the physical output medium (output port).

wDefault   Specifies whether the strings contained in the **DEVNAMES** structure identify the default printer. This string is used to verify that the default printer has not changed since the last print operation. On input, if the **DN_DEFAULTPRN** flag is set, the other values in the **DEVNAMES** structure are checked against the current default printer. If any of the strings do not match, a warning message is displayed informing the user that the document may need to be reformatted.

On output, the **wDefault** member is changed only if the Print Setup dialog box was displayed and the user chose the OK button. The **DN_DEFAULTPRN** flag is set if the default printer was selected. If a specific printer is selected, the flag is not set. All other bits in this member are reserved for internal use by the Print Dialog box procedure.

See Also   **CPrintDialog::CreatePrinterDC**

DOCINFO Structure

A **DOCINFO** structure has the following form:

```
typedef struct {    /* di */
    int     cbSize;
    LPCSTR  lpszDocName;
    LPCSTR  lpszOutput;
} DOCINFO;
```

The **DOCINFO** structure contains the input and output filenames used by the **StartDoc** function.

Members   **cbSize**   Specifies the size of the structure, in bytes.

lpszDocName   Points to a null-terminated string specifying the name of the document. This string must not be longer than 32 characters, including the null terminating character.

lpszOutput   Points to a null-terminated string specifying the name of an output file. This allows a print job to be redirected to a file. If this value is **NULL**, output goes to the device for the specified device context.

See Also   **CDC::StartDoc**

DRAWITEMSTRUCT Structure

A **DRAWITEMSTRUCT** structure has the following form:

```
typedef struct tagDRAWITEMSTRUCT {
    UINT    CtlType;
    UINT    CtlID;
    UINT    itemID;
    UINT    itemAction;
    UINT    itemState;
    HWND    hwndItem;
    HDC     hDC;
    RECT    rcItem;
    DWORD   itemData;
} DRAWITEMSTRUCT;
```

Members   **CtlType**   The control type. The values for control types are as follows:

- **ODT_BUTTON**   Owner-draw button
- **ODT_COMBOBOX**   Owner-draw combo box
- **ODT_LISTBOX**   Owner-draw list box
- **ODT_MENU**   Owner-draw menu

CtlID   The control ID for a combo box, list box, or button. This member is not used for a menu.

itemID   The menu-item ID for a menu or the index of the item in a list box or combo box. For an empty list box or combo box, this member is a negative value, which allows the application to draw only the focus rectangle at the coordinates specified by the **rcItem** member even though there are no items in the control. The user can thus be shown whether the list box or combo box has the input focus. The setting of the bits in the **itemAction** member determines whether the rectangle is to be drawn as though the list box or combo box has input focus.

itemAction   Defines the drawing action required. This will be one or more of the following bits:

- **ODA_DRAWENTIRE**   This bit is set when the entire control needs to be drawn.

- **ODA_FOCUS**   This bit is set when the control gains or loses input focus. The **itemState** member should be checked to determine whether the control has focus.

- **ODA_SELECT**   This bit is set when only the selection status has changed. The **itemState** member should be checked to determine the new selection state.

itemState   Specifies the visual state of the item after the current drawing action takes place. That is, if a menu item is to be dimmed, the state flag **ODS_GRAYED** will be set. The state flags are as follows:

- **ODS_CHECKED**   This bit is set if the menu item is to be checked. This bit is used only in a menu.

- **ODS_DISABLED**   This bit is set if the item is to be drawn as disabled.

- **ODS_FOCUS**   This bit is set if the item has input focus.

- **ODS_GRAYED**   This bit is set if the item is to be dimmed. This bit is used only in a menu.

- **ODS_SELECTED**   This bit is set if the item's status is selected.

hwndItem   Specifies the window handle of the control for combo boxes, list boxes, and buttons. Specifies the handle of the menu (**HMENU**) that contains the item for menus.

hDC   Identifies a device context. This device context must be used when performing drawing operations on the control.

rcItem   A rectangle in the device context specified by the **hDC** member that defines the boundaries of the control to be drawn. Windows automatically clips anything the owner draws in the device context for combo boxes, list boxes, and buttons, but it does not clip menu items. When drawing menu items, the owner must not draw outside the boundaries of the rectangle defined by the **rcItem** member.

itemData   For a combo box or list box, this member contains the value that was passed to the list box by one of the following:

CComboBox::AddStringCComboBox::InsertStringCListBox::AddStringCListBox::InsertString

For a menu, this member contains the value that was passed to the menu by one of the following:

CMenu::AppendMenu
CMenu::InsertMenu
CMenu::ModifyMenu

See Also   **CWnd::OnDrawItem**

FILETIME Structure

A Windows NT **FILETIME** structure has the following form:

```
typedef struct _FILETIME {
    DWORD dwLowDateTime;    /* low 32 bits  */
    DWORD dwHighDateTime;   /* high 32 bits */
} FILETIME, *PFILETIME, *LPFILETIME;
```

Members   **ateTidwLowDme**   Specifies the low 32 bits of the file time.

dwHighDateTime   Specifies the high 32 bits of the file time.

See Also   **CTime::CTime**

LOGBRUSH Structure

The **LOGBRUSH** structure has the following form:

```
typedef struct tag LOGBRUSH { /* lb */
   UINT      lbStyle;
   COLORREF  lbColor;
   LONG      lbHatch;
} LOGBRUSH;
```

The **LOGBRUSH** structure defines the style, color, and pattern of a physical brush. It is used by the **::CreateBrushIndirect** and **::ExtCreatePen** functions.

Members   **lbStyle**   Specifies the brush style. The **lbStyle** member must be one of the following styles:

- **BS_DIBPATTERN**   A pattern brush defined by a device-independent bitmap (DIB) specification. If **lbStyle** is **BS_DIBPATTERN**, the **lbHatch** member contains a handle to a packed DIB.

- **BS_DIBPATTERNPT**   A pattern brush defined by a device-independent bitmap (DIB) specification. If **lbStyle** is **BS_DIBPATTERNPT**, the **lbHatch** member contains a pointer to a packed DIB.

- **BS_HATCHED**   Hatched brush.

- **BS_HOLLOW**   Hollow brush.

- **BS_NULL**   Same as BS_HOLLOW.

- **BS_PATTERN**   Pattern brush defined by a memory bitmap.

- **BS_SOLID**   Solid brush.

lbColor   Specifies the color in which the brush is to be drawn. If **lbStyle** is the **BS_HOLLOW** or **BS_PATTERN** style, **lbColor** is ignored. If **lbStyle** is **BS_DIBPATTERN** or **BS_DIBPATTERNBT**, the low-order word of **lbColor** specifies whether the **bmiColors** members of the **BITMAPINFO** structure contain explicit red, green, blue (RGB) values or indices into the currently realized logical palette. The **lbColor** member must be one of the following values:

- **DIB_PAL_COLORS**   The color table consists of an array of 16-bit indices into the currently realized logical palette.

- **DIB_RGB_COLORS**   The color table contains literal RGB values.

lbHatch   Specifies a hatch style. The meaning depends on the brush style defined by **lbStyle**. If **lbStyle** is **BS_DIBPATTERN**, the **lbHatch** member contains a handle to a packed DIB. If **lbStyle** is **BS_DIBPATTERNPT**, the **lbHatch** member contains a pointer to a packed DIB. If **lbStyle** is **BS_HATCHED**, the **lbHatch** member specifies the orientation of the lines used to create the hatch. It can be one of the following values:

- **HS_BDIAGONAL**   A 45-degree upward, left-to-right hatch

- **HS_CROSS**   Horizontal and vertical cross-hatch

- **HS_DIAGCROSS**   45-degree crosshatch

- **HS_FDIAGONAL**   A 45-degree downward, left-to-right hatch
- **HS_HORIZONTAL**   Horizontal hatch
- **HS_VERTICAL**   Vertical hatch

If **lbStyle** is **BS_PATTERN**, **lbHatch** is a handle to the bitmap that defines the pattern. If **lbStyle** is **BS_SOLID** or **BS_HOLLOW**, **lbHatch** is ignored.

Comments   Although **lbColor** controls the foreground color of a hatch brush, the **SetBkMode** and **SetBkColor** functions control the background color.

See Also   **CDC::GetCharABCWidths**

LOGFONT Structure

The **LOGFONT** structure has the following form:

```
typedef struct tagLOGFONT { /* lf */
    LONG lfHeight;
    LONG lfWidth;
    LONG lfEscapement;
    LONG lfOrientation;
    LONG lfWeight;
    BYTE lfItalic;
    BYTE lfUnderline;
    BYTE lfStrikeOut;
    BYTE lfCharSet;
    BYTE lfOutPrecision;
    BYTE lfClipPrecision;
    BYTE lfQuality;
    BYTE lfPitchAndFamily;
    CHAR lfFaceName[LF_FACESIZE];
} LOGFONT;
```

The **LOGFONT** structure defines the attributes of a font.

Members   **lfHeight**   Specifies the height, in logical units, of the font. The font height can be specified in one of three ways. If **lfHeight** is greater than zero, it is transformed into device units and matched against the cell height of the available fonts. If it is zero, a reasonable default size is used. If it is less than zero, it is transformed into device units and the absolute value is matched against the character height of the available fonts. For all height comparisons, the font mapper looks for the largest font that does not exceed the requested size; if there is no such font, it looks for the smallest font available. This mapping occurs when the font is actually used for the first time.

lfWidth   Specifies the average width, in logical units, of characters in the font. If **lfWidth** is zero, the aspect ratio of the device is matched against the digitization aspect ratio of the available fonts to find the closest match, determined by the absolute value of the difference.

lfEscapement   Specifies the angle, in tenths of degrees, of each line of text written in the font (relative to the bottom of the page).

lfOrientation   Specifies the angle, in tenths of degrees, of each character's base line (relative to the bottom of the page).

lfWeight   Specifies the weight of the font, in the range 0 through 1000 (for example, 400 is normal and 700 is bold). If lfWeight is zero, a default weight is used.

lfItalic   Specifies an italic font if set to **TRUE**.

lfUnderline   Specifies an underlined font if set to **TRUE**.

lfStrikeOut   Specifies a strikeout font if set to **TRUE**.

lfCharSet   Specifies the character set. The following values are predefined:

- **ANSI_CHARSET**
- **OEM_CHARSET**
- **SYMBOL_CHARSET**
- **UNICODE_CHARSET**

The OEM character set is system dependent.

Fonts with other character sets may exist in the system. If an application uses a font with an unknown character set, it should not attempt to translate or interpret strings that are to be rendered with that font.

lfOutPrecision   Specifies the output precision. The output precision defines how closely the output must match the requested font's height, width, character orientation, escapement, and pitch. It can be one of the following values:

- **OUT_CHARACTER_PRECIS**
- **OUT_DEFAULT_PRECIS**
- **OUT_STRING_PRECIS**
- **OUT_STROKE_PRECIS**

lfClipPrecision   Specifies the clipping precision. The clipping precision defines how to clip characters that are partially outside the clipping region. It can be one of the following values:

- **CLIP_CHARACTER_PRECIS**

- **CLIP_DEFAULT_PRECIS**
- **CLIP_STROKE_PRECIS**

lfQuality   Specifies the output quality. The output quality defines how carefully graphics device interface (GDI) must attempt to match the logical-font attributes to those of an actual physical font. It can be one of the following values:

- **DEFAULT_QUALITY**   Appearance of the font does not matter.
- **DRAFT_QUALITY**   Appearance of the font is less important than when **PROOF_QUALITY** is used. For GDI fonts, scaling is enabled, which means that more font sizes are available, but the quality may be lower. Bold, italic, underline, and strikeout fonts are synthesized if necessary.
- **PROOF_QUALITY**   Character quality of the font is more important than exact matching of the logical-font attributes. For GDI fonts, scaling is disabled and the font closest in size is chosen. Although the chosen font size may not be mapped exactly when **PROOF_QUALITY** is used, the quality of the font is high and there is no distortion of appearance. Bold, italic, underline, and strikeout fonts are synthesized if necessary.

lfPitchAndFamily   Specifies the pitch and family of the font. The two low-order bits specify the pitch of the font and can be one of the following values:

- **DEFAULT_PITCH**
- **FIXED_PITCH**
- **VARIABLE_PITCH**

Bits 4 through 7 of the member specify the font family and can be one of the following values:

- **FF_DECORATIVE**
- **FF_DONTCARE**
- **FF_MODERN**
- **FF_ROMAN**
- **FF_SCRIPT**
- **FF_SWISS**

The proper value can be obtained by using the Boolean OR operator to join one pitch constant with one family constant. Font families describe the look of a font in a general way. They are intended for specifying fonts when the exact typeface desired is not available. The values for font families are as follows:

FF_DECORATIVE   Novelty fonts. Old English is an example.

FF_DONTCARE   Don't care or don't know.

FF_MODERN   Fonts with constant stroke width (fixed-pitch), with or without serifs. Fixed-pitch fonts are usually modern. Pica, Elite, and CourierNew® are examples.

FF_ROMAN   Fonts with variable stroke width (proportionally spaced) and with serifs. MS® Serif is an example.

FF_SCRIPT   Fonts designed to look like handwriting. Script and Cursive are examples.

FF_SWISS   Fonts with variable stroke width (proportionally spaced) and without serifs. MS® Sans Serif is an example.

lfFaceName   Points to a null-terminated string that specifies the typeface name of the font. The length of this string must not exceed 32 characters. The **::EnumFonts** function can be used to enumerate the typeface names of all currently available fonts. If **lfFaceName** is **NULL**, GDI uses a default typeface.

See Also   **CDC::GetCharABCWidths**, **CFontDialog::CFontDialog**, **CGdiObject::GetObject**

LOGPEN Structure

A **LOGPEN** structure has the following form:

```
typedef struct tagLOGPEN {  /* lgpn */
    UINT     lopnStyle;
    POINT    lopnWidth;
    COLORREF lopnColor;
} LOGPEN;
```

The **LOGPEN** structure defines the style, width, and color of a pen, a drawing object used to draw lines and borders. The **CreatePenIndirect** function uses the **LOGPEN** structure.

Members   **lopnStyle**   Specifies the pen type. This member can be one of the following values:

- **PS_SOLID**   Creates a solid pen.
- **PS_DASH**   Creates a dashed pen. (Valid only when the pen width is 1.)
- **PS_DOT**   Creates a dotted pen. (Valid only when the pen width is 1.)

- **PS_DASHDOT**   Creates a pen with alternating dashes and dots. (Valid only when the pen width is 1.)
- **PS_DASHDOTDOT**   Creates a pen with alternating dashes and double dots. (Valid only when the pen width is 1.)
- **PS_NULL**   Creates a null pen.
- **PS_INSIDEFRAME**   Creates a pen that draws a line inside the frame of closed shapes produced by GDI output functions that specify a bounding rectangle (for example, the **Ellipse**, **Rectangle**, **RoundRect**, **Pie**, and **Chord** member functions). When this style is used with GDI output functions that do not specify a bounding rectangle (for example, the **LineTo** member function), the drawing area of the pen is not limited by a frame.

  If a pen has the **PS_INSIDEFRAME** style and a color that does not match a color in the logical color table, the pen is drawn with a dithered color. The **PS_SOLID** pen style cannot be used to create a pen with a dithered color. The **PS_INSIDEFRAME** style is identical to **PS_SOLID** if the pen width is less than or equal to 1.

  When the **PS_INSIDEFRAME** style is used with GDI objects produced by functions other than **Ellipse**, **Rectangle**, and **RoundRect**, the line may not be completely inside the specified frame.

lopnWidth   Specifies the pen width, in logical units. If the **lopnWidth** member is 0, the pen is 1 pixel wide on raster devices regardless of the current mapping mode.

lopnColor   Specifies the pen color.

Comments   The **y** value in the **POINT** structure for the **lopnWidth** member is not used.

See Also   **CPen::CreatePenIndirect**

MEASUREITEMSTRUCT Structure

A **MEASUREITEMSTRUCT** data structure has the following form:

```
typedef struct tagMEASUREITEMSTRUCT {
    UINT    CtlType;
    UINT    CtlID;
    UINT    itemID;
    UINT    itemWidth;
    UINT    itemHeight;
    DWORD   itemData
} MEASUREITEMSTRUCT;
```

Failure to fill out the proper members in the **MEASUREITEMSTRUCT** structure will cause improper operation of the control.

Members   **CtlType**   Contains the control type. The values for control types are as follows:

- **ODT_COMBOBOX**   Owner-draw combo box
- **ODT_LISTBOX**   Owner-draw list box
- **ODT_MENU**   Owner-draw menu

CtlID   Contains the control ID for a combo box, list box, or button. This member is not used for a menu.

itemID   Contains the menu-item ID for a menu or the list-box-item ID for a variable-height combo box or list box. This member is not used for a fixed-height combo box or list box, or for a button.

itemWidth   Specifies the width of a menu item. The owner of the owner-draw menu item must fill this member before it returns from the message.

itemHeight   Specifies the height of an individual item in a list box or a menu. Before it returns from the message, the owner of the owner-draw combo box, list box, or menu item must fill out this member. The maximum height of a list box item is 255.

itemData   For a combo box or list box, this member contains the value that was passed to the list box by one of the following:

CComboBox::AddString

CComboBox::InsertString

CListBox::AddString

CListBox::InsertString

For a menu, this member contains the value that was passed to the menu by one of the following:

CMenu::AppendMenu

CMenu::InsertMenu

CMenu::ModifyMenu

See Also   **CWnd::OnMeasureItem**

MINMAXINFO Structure

A **MINMAXINFO** structure has the following form:

```
typedef struct tagMINMAXINFO {
    POINT ptReserved;
    POINT ptMaxSize;
    POINT ptMaxPosition;
    POINT ptMinTrackSize;
    POINT ptMaxTrackSize;
} MINMAXINFO;
```

Members   **ptReserved**   Reserved for internal use.

ptMaxSize   Specifies the maximized width (point.x) and the maximized height (point.y) of the window.

ptMaxPosition   Specifies the position of the left side of the maximized window (point.x) and the position of the top of the maximized window (point.y).

ptMinTrackSize   Specifies the minimum tracking width (point.x) and the minimum tracking height (point.y) of the window.

ptMaxTrackSize   Specifies the maximum tracking width (point.x) and the maximum tracking height (point.y) of the window.

See Also   **CWnd::OnGetMinMaxInfo**

NCCALCSIZE_PARAMS Structure

An **NCCALCSIZE_PARAMS** structure has the following form:

```
typedef struct tagNCCALCSIZE_PARAMS {
    RECT          rgrc[3];
    PWINDOWPOS    lppos;
} NCCALCSIZE_PARAMS;
```

The **NCCALCSIZE_PARAMS** structure contains information that an application can use while processing the **WM_NCCALCSIZE** message to calculate the size, position, and valid contents of the client area of a window.

Members   **rgrc**   Specifies an array of rectangles. The first contains the new coordinates of a window that has been moved or resized. The second contains the coordinates of the window before it was moved or resized. The third contains the coordinates of the client area of a window before it was moved or resized. If the window is a child window, the coordinates are relative to the client area of the parent window. If the window is a top-level window, the coordinates are relative to the screen.

lppos   Points to a **WINDOWPOS** structure that contains the size and position values specified in the operation that caused the window to be moved or resized.

See Also   **CWnd::OnNcCalcSize**

PAINTSTRUCT Structure

A **PAINTSTRUCT** structure has the following form:

```
typedef struct tagPAINTSTRUCT {
    HDC  hdc;
    BOOL fErase;
    RECT rcPaint;
    BOOL fRestore;
    BOOL fIncUpdate;
    BYTE rgbReserved[16];
} PAINTSTRUCT;
```

The **PAINTSTRUCT** structure contains information that can be used to paint the client area of a window.

Members   **hdc**   Identifies the display context to be used for painting.

fErase   Specifies whether the background needs to be redrawn. It is not 0 if the application should redraw the background. The application is responsible for drawing the background if a Windows window-class is created without a background brush (see the description of the **hbrBackground** member of the **WNDCLASS** structure in the Windows Software Development Kit documentation).

rcPaint   Specifies the upper-left and lower-right corners of the rectangle in which the painting is requested.

fRestore   Reserved member. It is used internally by Windows.

fIncUpdate   Reserved member. It is used internally by Windows.

rgbReserved[16]   Reserved member. A reserved block of memory used internally by Windows.

See Also   **CPaintDC::m_ps**

POINT Structure

A **POINT** data structure has the following form:

```
typedef struct tagPOINT {
   int x;
   int y;
} POINT;
```

The **POINT** structure defines the x- and y-coordinates of a point.

Members   **x**   Specifies the x-coordinate of a point.

y   Specifies the y-coordinate of a point.

See Also   **CPoint**

RECT Structure

A **RECT** data structure has the following form:

```
typedef struct tagRECT {
   int left;
   int top;
   int right;
   int bottom;
} RECT;
```

The **RECT** structure defines the coordinates of the upper-left and lower-right corners of a rectangle.

Members   **left**   Specifies the x-coordinate of the upper-left corner of a rectangle.

top   Specifies the y-coordinate of the upper-left corner of a rectangle.

right   Specifies the x-coordinate of the lower-right corner of a rectangle.

bottom   Specifies the y-coordinate of the lower-right corner of a rectangle.

See Also   **CRect**

RGNDATA Structure

The **RGNDATA** structure has the following form:

```
typedef struct _RGNDATA { /* rgnd */
   RGNDATAHEADER rdh;
   char          Buffer[1];
} RGNDATA;
```

The **RGNDATA** structure contains a header and an array of rectangles that compose a region. These rectangles, sorted top to bottom left to right, do not overlap.

Members   **rdh**   Specifies a **RGNDATAHEADER** structure. The members of this structure specify the type of region (whether it is rectangular or trapezoidal), the number of rectangles that make up the region, the size of the buffer that contains the rectangle structures, and so on.

Buffer   Specifies an arbitrary-size buffer that contains the **RECT** structures that make up the region.

See Also   **CRgn::CreateFromData**, **CRgn::GetRegionData**

SIZE Structure

A **SIZE** structure has the following form:

```
typedef struct tagSIZE {
    int cx;
    int cy;
} SIZE;
```

Members   **cx**   Specifies the x-extent when a function returns.

cy   Specifies the y-extent when a function returns.

The rectangle dimensions stored in this structure may correspond to viewport extents, window extents, text extents, bitmap dimensions, or the aspect-ratio filter for some extended functions.

See Also   **CSize**

SYSTEMTIME Structure

A Windows NT **SYSTEMTIME** structure has the following form:

```
typedef struct _SYSTEMTIME {
    WORD wYear;
    WORD wMonth;
    WORD wDayOfWeek;
    WORD wDay;
    WORD wHour;
    WORD wMinute;
    WORD wSecond;
    WORD wMilliseconds;
} SYSTEMTIME;
```

Members   **wYear**   The current year

wMonth   The current month; January is 1

wDayOfWeek   The current day of the week; Sunday is 0, Monday is 1, etc.

wDay   The current day of the month

wHour   The current hour

wMinute   The current minute

wSecond   The current second

wMilliseconds   The current millisecond

See Also   **CTime::CTime**

TEXTMETRIC Structure

A **TEXTMETRIC** structure has the following form:

```
typedef struct tagTEXTMETRIC {  /* tm */
    int   tmHeight;
    int   tmAscent;
    int   tmDescent;
    int   tmInternalLeading;
    int   tmExternalLeading;
    int   tmAveCharWidth;
    int   tmMaxCharWidth;
    int   tmWeight;
    BYTE  tmItalic;
    BYTE  tmUnderlined;
    BYTE  tmStruckOut;
    BYTE  tmFirstChar;
    BYTE  tmLastChar;
    BYTE  tmDefaultChar;
    BYTE  tmBreakChar;
    BYTE  tmPitchAndFamily;
    BYTE  tmCharSet;
    int   tmOverhang;
    int   tmDigitizedAspectX;
    int   tmDigitizedAspectY;
} TEXTMETRIC;
```

For more complete information about this structure, see **TEXTMETRIC** in the Windows SDK documentation.

See Also   **CDC::GetTextMetrics**, **TEXTMETRIC**

WINDOWPLACEMENT Structure

A **WINDOWPLACEMENT** data structure has the following form:

```
typedef struct tagWINDOWPLACEMENT {     /* wndpl */
    UINT  length;
    UINT  flags;
    UINT  showCmd;
    POINT ptMinPosition;
    POINT ptMaxPosition;
    RECT  rcNormalPosition;
} WINDOWPLACEMENT;
```

The **WINDOWPLACEMENT** structure contains information about the placement of a window on the screen.

Members

length   Specifies the length, in bytes, of the structure.

flags   Specifies flags that control the position of the minimized window and the method by which the window is restored. This member can be one or both of the following flags:

- **WPF_SETMINPOSITION**   Specifies that the x- and y-positions of the minimized window may be specified. This flag must be specified if the coordinates are set in the **ptMinPosition** member.

- **WPF_RESTORETOMAXIMIZED**   Specifies that the restored window will be maximized, regardless of whether it was maximized before it was minimized. This setting is valid only the next time the window is restored. It does not change the default restoration behavior. This flag is valid only when the **SW_SHOWMINIMIZED** value is specified for the **showCmd** member.

showCmd   Specifies the current show state of the window. This member may be one of the following values:

- **SW_HIDE**   Hides the window and passes activation to another window.

- **SW_MINIMIZE**   Minimizes the specified window and activates the top-level window in the system's list.

- **SW_RESTORE**   Activates and displays a window. If the window is minimized or maximized, Windows restores it to its original size and position (same as **SW_SHOWNORMAL**).

- **SW_SHOW**   Activates a window and displays it in its current size and position.

- **SW_SHOWMAXIMIZED**   Activates a window and displays it as a maximized window.

- **SW_SHOWMINIMIZED**   Activates a window and displays it as an icon.

- **SW_SHOWMINNOACTIVE**   Displays a window as an icon. The window that is currently active remains active.
- **SW_SHOWNA**   Displays a window in its current state. The window that is currently active remains active.
- **SW_SHOWNOACTIVATE**   Displays a window in its most recent size and position. The window that is currently active remains active.
- **SW_SHOWNORMAL**   Activates and displays a window. If the window is minimized or maximized, Windows restores it to its original size and position (same as **SW_RESTORE**).

ptMinPosition   Specifies the position of the window's top-left corner when the window is minimized.

ptMaxPosition   Specifies the position of the window's top-left corner when the window is maximized.

rcNormalPosition   Specifies the window's coordinates when the window is in the normal (restored) position.

See Also   **CWnd::SetWindowPlacement**

WINDOWPOS Structure

A **WINDOWPOS** data structure has the following form:

```
typedef struct tagWINDOWPOS { /* wp */
    HWND    hwnd;
    HWND    hwndInsertAfter;
    int     x;
    int     y;
    int     cx;
    int     cy;
    UINT    flags;
} WINDOWPOS;
```

The **WINDOWPOS** structure contains information about the size and position of a window.

Members   **hwnd**   Identifies the window.

hwndInsertAfter   Identifies the window behind which this window is placed.

x   Specifies the position of the left edge of the window.

y   Specifies the position of the right edge of the window.

cx   Specifies the window width.

cy   Specifies the window height.

flags   Specifies window-positioning options. This member can be one of the following values:

- **SWP_DRAWFRAME**   Draws a frame (defined in the class description for the window) around the window. The window receives a **WM_NCCALCSIZE** message.

- **SWP_HIDEWINDOW**   Hides the window.

- **SWP_NOACTIVATE**   Does not activate the window.

- **SWP_NOMOVE**   Retains current position (ignores the **x** and **y** members).

- **SWP_NOOWNERZORDER**   Does not change the owner window's position in the Z order.

- **SWP_NOSIZE**   Retains current size (ignores the **cx** and **cy** members).

- **SWP_NOREDRAW**   Does not redraw changes.

- **SWP_NOREPOSITION**   Same as **SWP_NOOWNERZORDER**.

- **SWP_NOZORDER**   Retains current ordering (ignores the **hwndInsertAfter** member).

- **SWP_SHOWWINDOW**   Displays the window.

See Also   **Cwnd::OnWindowPosChanging**

XFORM Structure

The **XFORM** structure has the following form:

```
typedef struct  tagXFORM {  /* xfrm */
    FLOAT eM11;
    FLOAT eM12;
    FLOAT eM21;
    FLOAT eM22;
    FLOAT eDx;
    FLOAT eDy;
} XFORM;
```

The **XFORM** structure specifies a world-space to page-space transformation.

Members   **eM11**   Specifies the following:

- **Scaling**   Horizontal scaling component
- **Rotation**   Cosine of rotation angle
- **Reflection**   Horizontal component

eM12   Specifies the following:

- **Shear**   Horizontal proportionality constant
- **Rotation**   Sine of the rotation angle

eM21   Specifies the following:

- **Shear**   Vertical proportionality constant
- **Rotation**   Negative sine of the rotation angle

eM22   Specifies the following:

- **Scaling**   Vertical scaling component
- **Rotation**   Cosine of rotation angle
- **Reflection**   Vertical reflection component

eDx   Specifies the horizontal translation component.

eDy   Specifies the vertical translation component.

The following list describes how the members are used for each operation:

Operation	eM11	eM12	eM22	eM21
Rotation	Cosine	Sine	Negative sine	Cosine
Scaling	Horizontal scaling component	Nothing	Nothing	Vertical Scaling Component
Shear	Nothing	Horizontal Proportionality Constant	Vertical Proportionality Constant	Nothing
Reflection	Horizontal Reflection Component	Nothing	Nothing	Vertical Reflection Component

See Also   **CRgn::CreateFromData**

Styles

The styles described in the following topics are, in most cases, specified with the *dwstyle* parameter. For further information, refer to the member functions listed in the See Also sections of each style.

Button Styles

- **BS_AUTOCHECKBOX**   Same as a check box, except that an **X** appears in the check box when the user selects the box; the **X** disappears the next time the user selects the box.

- **BS_AUTORADIOBUTTON**   Same as a radio button, except that when the user selects it, the button automatically highlights itself and removes the selection from any other radio buttons with the same style in the same group.

- **BS_AUTO3STATE**   Same as a three-state check box, except that the box changes its state when the user selects it.

- **BS_CHECKBOX**   Creates a small square that has text displayed to its right (unless this style is combined with the **BS_LEFTTEXT** style).

- **BS_DEFPUSHBUTTON**   Creates a button that has a heavy black border. The user can select this button by pressing the ENTER key. This style enables the user to quickly select the most likely option (the default option).

- **BS_GROUPBOX**   Creates a rectangle in which other buttons can be grouped. Any text associated with this style is displayed in the rectangle's upper-left corner.

- **BS_LEFTTEXT**   When combined with a radio-button or check-box style, the text appears on the left side of the radio button or check box.

- **BS_OWNERDRAW**   Creates an owner-drawn button. The framework calls the **DrawItem** member function when a visual aspect of the button has changed. This style must be set when using the **CBitmapButton** class.

- **BS_PUSHBUTTON**   Creates a pushbutton that posts a **WM_COMMAND** message to the owner window when the user selects the button.

- **BS_RADIOBUTTON**   Creates a small circle that has text displayed to its right (unless this style is combined with the **BS_LEFTTEXT** style). Radio buttons are usually used in groups of related but mutually exclusive choices.

- **BS_3STATE**   Same as a check box, except that the box can be dimmed as well as checked. The dimmed state typically is used to show that a check box has been disabled.

See Also   **CButton::Create**

Combo-Box Styles

- **CBS_AUTOHSCROLL**   Automatically scrolls the text in the edit control to the right when the user types a character at the end of the line. If this style is not set, only text that fits within the rectangular boundary is allowed.
- **CBS_DROPDOWN**   Similar to **CBS_SIMPLE**, except that the list box is not displayed unless the user selects an icon next to the edit control.
- **CBS_DROPDOWNLIST**   Similar to **CBS_DROPDOWN**, except that the edit control is replaced by a static-text item that displays the current selection in the list box.
- **CBS_HASSTRINGS**   An owner-draw combo box contains items consisting of strings. The combo box maintains the memory and pointers for the strings so the application can use the **GetText** member function to retrieve the text for a particular item.
- **CBS_OEMCONVERT**   Text entered in the combo-box edit control is converted from the ANSI character set to the OEM character set and then back to ANSI. This ensures proper character conversion when the application calls the **AnsiToOem** Windows function to convert an ANSI string in the combo box to OEM characters. This style is most useful for combo boxes that contain filenames and applies only to combo boxes created with the **CBS_SIMPLE** or **CBS_DROPDOWN** styles.
- **CBS_OWNERDRAWFIXED**   The owner of the list box is responsible for drawing its contents; the items in the list box are all the same height.
- **CBS_OWNERDRAWVARIABLE**   The owner of the list box is responsible for drawing its contents; the items in the list box are variable in height.
- **CBS_SIMPLE**   The list box is displayed at all times. The current selection in the list box is displayed in the edit control.
- **CBS_SORT**   Automatically sorts strings entered into the list box.
- **CBS_DISABLENOSCROLL**   The list box shows a disabled vertical scroll bar when the list box does not contain enough items to scroll. Without this style, the scroll bar is hidden when the list box does not contain enough items.
- **CBS_NOINTEGRALHEIGHT**   Specifies that the size of the combo box is exactly the size specified by the application when it created the combo box. Normally, Windows sizes a combo box so that the combo box does not display partial items.

See Also   **CComboBox::Create**

Edit Styles

- **ES_AUTOHSCROLL** Automatically scrolls text to the right by 10 characters when the user types a character at the end of the line. When the user presses the ENTER key, the control scrolls all text back to position 0.

- **ES_AUTOVSCROLL** Automatically scrolls text up one page when the user presses ENTER on the last line.

- **ES_CENTER** Centers text in a multiline edit control.

- **ES_LEFT** Aligns text flush left.

- **ES_LOWERCASE** Converts all characters to lowercase as they are typed into the edit control.

- **ES_MULTILINE** Designates a multiple-line edit control. (The default is single line.) If the **ES_AUTOVSCROLL** style is specified, the edit control shows as many lines as possible and scrolls vertically when the user presses the ENTER key. If **ES_AUTOVSCROLL** is not given, the edit control shows as many lines as possible and beeps if ENTER is pressed when no more lines can be displayed. If the **ES_AUTOHSCROLL** style is specified, the multiple-line edit control automatically scrolls horizontally when the caret goes past the right edge of the control. To start a new line, the user must press ENTER. If **ES_AUTOHSCROLL** is not given, the control automatically wraps words to the beginning of the next line when necessary; a new line is also started if ENTER is pressed. The position of the wordwrap is determined by the window size. If the window size changes, the wordwrap position changes and the text is redisplayed. Multiple-line edit controls can have scroll bars. An edit control with scroll bars processes its own scroll-bar messages. Edit controls without scroll bars scroll as described above and process any scroll messages sent by the parent window.

- **ES_NOHIDESEL** Normally, an edit control hides the selection when the control loses the input focus and inverts the selection when the control receives the input focus. Specifying **ES_NOHIDESEL** deletes this default action.

- **ES_OEMCONVERT** Text entered in the edit control is converted from the ANSI character set to the OEM character set and then back to ANSI. This ensures proper character conversion when the application calls the **AnsiToOem** Windows function to convert an ANSI string in the edit control to OEM characters. This style is most useful for edit controls that contain filenames.

- **ES_PASSWORD** Displays all characters as an asterisk (*****) as they are typed into the edit control. An application can use the **SetPasswordChar** member function to change the character that is displayed.

- **ES_RIGHT** Aligns text flush right in a multiline edit control.

- **ES_UPPERCASE** Converts all characters to uppercase as they are typed into the edit control.

- **ES_READONLY**   Prevents the user from entering or editing text in the edit control.
- **ES_WANTRETURN**   Specifies that a carriage return be inserted when the user presses the ENTER key while entering text into a multiple-line edit control in a dialog box. Without this style, pressing the ENTER key has the same effect as pressing the dialog box's default pushbutton. This style has no effect on a single-line edit control.

See Also   **CEdit::Create**

List-Box Styles

- **LBS_EXTENDEDSEL**   The user can select multiple items using the SHIFT key and the mouse or special key combinations.
- **LBS_HASSTRINGS**   Specifies an owner-draw list box that contains items consisting of strings. The list box maintains the memory and pointers for the strings so the application can use the **GetText** member function to retrieve the text for a particular item.
- **LBS_MULTICOLUMN**   Specifies a multicolumn list box that is scrolled horizontally. The **SetColumnWidth** member function sets the width of the columns.
- **LBS_MULTIPLESEL**   String selection is toggled each time the user clicks or double-clicks the string. Any number of strings can be selected.
- **LBS_NOINTEGRALHEIGHT**   The size of the list box is exactly the size specified by the application when it created the list box. Usually, Windows sizes a list box so that the list box does not display partial items.
- **LBS_NOREDRAW**   List-box display is not updated when changes are made. This style can be changed at any time by sending a **WM_SETREDRAW** message.
- **LBS_NOTIFY**   Parent window receives an input message whenever the user clicks or double-clicks a string.
- **LBS_OWNERDRAWFIXED**   The owner of the list box is responsible for drawing its contents; the items in the list box are the same height.
- **LBS_OWNERDRAWVARIABLE**   The owner of the list box is responsible for drawing its contents; the items in the list box are variable in height.
- **LBS_SORT**   Strings in the list box are sorted alphabetically.
- **LBS_STANDARD**   Strings in the list box are sorted alphabetically, and the parent window receives an input message whenever the user clicks or double-clicks a string. The list box contains borders on all sides.
- **LBS_USETABSTOPS**   Allows a list box to recognize and expand tab characters when drawing its strings. The default tab positions are 32 dialog units. (A dialog unit is a horizontal or vertical distance. One horizontal dialog

unit is equal to one-fourth of the current dialog base width unit. The dialog base units are computed based on the height and width of the current system font. The **GetDialogBaseUnits** Windows function returns the current dialog base units in pixels.)

- **LBS_WANTKEYBOARDINPUT**   The owner of the list box receives **WM_VKEYTOITEM** or **WM_CHARTOITEM** messages whenever the user presses a key while the list box has input focus. This allows an application to perform special processing on the keyboard input.

- **LBS_DISABLENOSCROLL**   The list box shows a disabled vertical scroll bar when the list box does not contain enough items to scroll. Without this style, the scroll bar is hidden when the list box does not contain enough items.

See Also   **CListBox::Create**

Message-Box Styles

Message_Box Types

- **MB_ABORTRETRYIGNORE**   The message box contains three pushbuttons: Abort, Retry, and Ignore.

- **MB_OK**   The message box contains one pushbutton: OK.

- **MB_OKCANCEL**   The message box contains two pushbuttons: OK and Cancel.

- **MB_RETRYCANCEL**   The message box contains two pushbuttons: Retry and Cancel.

- **MB_YESNO**   The message box contains two pushbuttons: Yes and No.

- **MB_YESNOCANCEL**   The message box contains three pushbuttons: Yes, No, and Cancel.

Message-Box Modality

- **MB_APPLMODAL**   The user must respond to the message box before continuing work in the current window. However, the user can move to the windows of other applications and work in those windows. The default is **MB_APPLMODAL** if neither **MB_SYSTEMMODAL** nor **MB_TASKMODAL** is specified.

- **MB_SYSTEMMODAL**   All applications are suspended until the user responds to the message box. System-modal message boxes are used to notify the user of serious, potentially damaging errors that require immediate attention and should be used sparingly.

- **MB_TASKMODAL**   Similar to **MB_APPLMODAL**, but not useful within a Microsoft Foundation class application. This flag is reserved for a calling application or library that does not have a window handle available.

Message-Box Icons

- **MB_ICONEXCLAMATION**   An exclamation-point icon appears in the message box.
- **MB_ICONINFORMATION**   An icon consisting of an "i" in a circle appears in the message box.
- **MB_ICONQUESTION**   A question-mark icon appears in the message box.
- **MB_ICONSTOP**   A stop-sign icon appears in the message box.

Message-Box Default Buttons

- **MB_DEFBUTTON1**   The first button is the default. Note that the first button is always the default unless **MB_DEFBUTTON2** or **MB_DEFBUTTON3** is specified.
- **MB_DEFBUTTON2**   The second button is the default.
- **MB_DEFBUTTON3**   The third button is the default.

See Also   **AfxMessageBox**

Scroll-Bar Styles

- **SBS_BOTTOMALIGN**   Used with the **SBS_HORZ** style. The bottom edge of the scroll bar is aligned with the bottom edge of the rectangle specified in the **Create** member function. The scroll bar has the default height for system scroll bars.
- **SBS_HORZ**   Designates a horizontal scroll bar. If neither the **SBS_BOTTOMALIGN** nor **SBS_TOPALIGN** style is specified, the scroll bar has the height, width, and position given in the **Create** member function.
- **SBS_LEFTALIGN**   Used with the **SBS_VERT** style. The left edge of the scroll bar is aligned with the left edge of the rectangle specified in the **Create** member function. The scroll bar has the default width for system scroll bars.
- **SBS_RIGHTALIGN**   Used with the **SBS_VERT** style. The right edge of the scroll bar is aligned with the right edge of the rectangle specified in the **Create** member function. The scroll bar has the default width for system scroll bars.
- **SBS_SIZEBOX**   Designates a size box. If neither the **SBS_SIZEBOXBOTTOMRIGHTALIGN** nor **SBS_SIZEBOXTOPLEFTALIGN** style is specified, the size box has the height, width, and position given in the **Create** member function.
- **SBS_SIZEBOXBOTTOMRIGHTALIGN**   Used with the **SBS_SIZEBOX** style. The lower-right corner of the size box is aligned with the lower-right corner of the rectangle specified in the **Create** member function. The size box has the default size for system size boxes.
- **SBS_SIZEBOXTOPLEFTALIGN**   Used with the **SBS_SIZEBOX** style. The upper-left corner of the size box is aligned with the upper-left corner of the

rectangle specified in the **Create** member function. The size box has the default size for system size boxes.

- **SBS_TOPALIGN**   Used with the **SBS_HORZ** style. The top edge of the scroll bar is aligned with the top edge of the rectangle specified in the **Create** member function. The scroll bar has the default height for system scroll bars.

- **SBS_VERT**   Designates a vertical scroll bar. If neither the **SBS_RIGHTALIGN** nor **SBS_LEFTALIGN** style is specified, the scroll bar has the height, width, and position given in the **Create** member function.

See Also   **CScrollBar::Create**

Static Styles

- **SS_BLACKFRAME**   Specifies a box with a frame drawn with the same color as window frames. The default is black.

- **SS_BLACKRECT**   Specifies a rectangle filled with the color used to draw window frames. The default is black.

- **SS_CENTER**   Designates a simple rectangle and displays the given text centered in the rectangle. The text is formatted before it is displayed. Words that would extend past the end of a line are automatically wrapped to the beginning of the next centered line.

- **SS_GRAYFRAME**   Specifies a box with a frame drawn with the same color as the screen background (desktop). The default is gray.

- **SS_GRAYRECT**   Specifies a rectangle filled with the color used to fill the screen background. The default is gray.

- **SS_ICON**   Designates an icon displayed in the dialog box. The given text is the name of an icon (not a filename) defined elsewhere in the resource file. The *nWidth* and *nHeight* parameters are ignored; the icon automatically sizes itself.

- **SS_LEFT**   Designates a simple rectangle and displays the given text flush-left in the rectangle. The text is formatted before it is displayed. Words that would extend past the end of a line are automatically wrapped to the beginning of the next flush-left line.

- **SS_LEFTNOWORDWRAP**   Designates a simple rectangle and displays the given text flush-left in the rectangle. Tabs are expanded, but words are not wrapped. Text that extends past the end of a line is clipped.

- **SS_NOPREFIX**   Unless this style is specified, Windows will interpret any ampersand (&) characters in the control's text to be accelerator prefix characters. In this case, the ampersand (&) is removed and the next character in the string is underlined. If a static control is to contain text where this feature is not wanted, **SS_NOPREFIX** may be added. This static-control style may be included with any of the defined static controls. You can combine **SS_NOPREFIX** with other styles by using the bitwise OR operator. This is most often used when filenames or other strings that may contain an ampersand (&) need to be displayed in a static control in a dialog box.

- **SS_RIGHT**   Designates a simple rectangle and displays the given text flush-right in the rectangle. The text is formatted before it is displayed. Words that would extend past the end of a line are automatically wrapped to the beginning of the next flush-right line.

- **SS_SIMPLE**   Designates a simple rectangle and displays a single line of text flush-left in the rectangle. The line of text cannot be shortened or altered in any way. (The control's parent window or dialog box must not process the **WM_CTLCOLOR** message.)

- **SS_USERITEM**   Specifies a user-defined item.

- **SS_WHITEFRAME**   Specifies a box with a frame drawn with the same color as the window background. The default is white.

- **SS_WHITERECT**   Specifies a rectangle filled with the color used to fill the window background. The default is white.

See Also   **CStatic::Create**

Window Styles

- **WS_BORDER**   Creates a window that has a border.

- **WS_CAPTION**   Creates a window that has a title bar (implies the **WS_BORDER** style). Cannot be used with the **WS_DLGFRAME** style.

- **WS_CHILD**   Creates a child window. Cannot be used with the **WS_POPUP** style.

- **WS_CLIPCHILDREN**   Excludes the area occupied by child windows when you draw within the parent window. Used when you create the parent window.

- **WS_CLIPSIBLINGS**   Clips child windows relative to each other; that is, when a particular child window receives a paint message, the **WS_CLIPSIBLINGS** style clips all other overlapped child windows out of the region of the child window to be updated. (If **WS_CLIPSIBLINGS** is not given and child windows overlap, when you draw within the client area of a child window, it is possible to draw within the client area of a neighboring child window.) For use with the **WS_CHILD** style only.

- **WS_DISABLED**   Creates a window that is initially disabled.

- **WS_DLGFRAME**   Creates a window with a double border but no title.

- **WS_GROUP**   Specifies the first control of a group of controls in which the user can move from one control to the next with the arrow keys. All controls defined with the **WS_GROUP** style after the first control belong to the same group. The next control with the **WS_GROUP** style ends the style group and starts the next group (that is, one group ends where the next begins).

- **WS_HSCROLL**   Creates a window that has a horizontal scroll bar.
- **WS_MAXIMIZE**   Creates a window of maximum size.
- **WS_MAXIMIZEBOX**   Creates a window that has a Maximize button.
- **WS_MINIMIZE**   Creates a window that is initially minimized. For use with the **WS_OVERLAPPED** style only.
- **WS_MINIMIZEBOX**   Creates a window that has a Minimize button.
- **WS_OVERLAPPED**   Creates an overlapped window. An overlapped window usually has a caption and a border.
- **WS_OVERLAPPEDWINDOW**   Creates an overlapped window with the **WS_OVERLAPPED**, **WS_CAPTION**, **WS_SYSMENU**, **WS_THICKFRAME**, **WS_MINIMIZEBOX**, and **WS_MAXIMIZEBOX** styles.
- **WS_POPUP**   Creates a pop-up window. Cannot be used with the **WS_CHILD** style.
- **WS_POPUPWINDOW**   Creates a pop-up window with the **WS_BORDER**, **WS_POPUP**, and **WS_SYSMENU** styles. The **WS_CAPTION** style must be combined with the **WS_POPUPWINDOW** style to make the Control menu visible.
- **WS_SYSMENU**   Creates a window that has a Control-menu box in its title bar. Used only for windows with title bars.
- **WS_TABSTOP**   Specifies one of any number of controls through which the user can move by using the TAB key. The TAB key moves the user to the next control specified by the **WS_TABSTOP** style.
- **WS_THICKFRAME**   Creates a window with a thick frame that can be used to size the window.
- **WS_VISIBLE**   Creates a window that is initially visible.
- **WS_VSCROLL**   Creates a window that has a vertical scroll bar.

See Also   **CWnd::Create**

Extended Window Styles

- **WS_EX_DLGMODALFRAME**   Designates a window with a double border that may (optionally) be created with a title bar when you specify the **WS_CAPTION** style flag in the *dwStyle* parameter.
- **WS_EX_NOPARENTNOTIFY**   Specifies that a child window created with this style will not send the **WM_PARENTNOTIFY** message to its parent window when the child window is created or destroyed.
- **WS_EX_ACCEPTFILES**   Specifies that a window created with this style accepts drag-and-drop files.

- **WS_EX_TOPMOST**   Specifies that a window created with this style should be placed above all nontopmost windows and stay above them even when the window is deactivated. An application can use the **SetWindowPos** member function to add or remove this attribute.

- **WS_EX_TRANSPARENT**   Specifies that a window created with this style is to be transparent. That is, any windows that are beneath the window are not obscured by the window. A window created with this style receives **WM_PAINT** messages only after all sibling windows beneath it have been updated.

See Also   **CWnd::CreateEx**

Callback Functions

Three callback functions appear in the Microsoft Foundation Class Library. A description of callback functions that are passed to **CDC::EnumObjects**; **CDC::GrayString**, and **CDC::SetAbortProc** follows this topic. For the general usage of the callback functions, see the Remarks section of these member functions. Note that all callback functions must trap MFC exceptions before returning to Windows, since exceptions cannot be thrown across callback boundaries. For more information about exceptions, see the article "Exceptions" in *Programming with the Microsoft Foundation Class Library*."

Callback Function for CDC::EnumObjects

int CALLBACK EXPORT ObjectFunc(**LPSTR** *lpszLogObject*, **LPSTR*** *lpData*);

Parameters   *lpszLogObject*   Points to a **LOGPEN** or **LOGBRUSH** data structure that contains information about the logical attributes of the object.

lpData   Points to the application-supplied data passed to the **EnumObjects** function.

Return Value   The callback function returns an **int**. The value of this return is user-defined. If the callback function returns 0, **EnumObjects** stops enumeration early.

Remarks   The *ObjectFunc* name is a placeholder for the application-supplied function name. The actual name must be exported.

See Also   **CDC::EnumObjects**

Callback Function for CDC::GrayString

BOOL CALLBACK EXPORT *OutputFunc*(**HDC** *hDC*, **LPARAM** *lpData*, **int** *nCount*);

Return Value   The callback function's return value must be **TRUE** to indicate success; otherwise it is **FALSE**.

Parameters   *hDC*   Identifies a memory device context with a bitmap of at least the width and height specified by *nWidth* and *nHeight* to **GrayString**.

lpData   Points to the character string to be drawn.

nCount   Specifies the number of characters to output.

Remarks   *OutputFunc* is a placeholder for the application-supplied callback function name. The callback function (*OutputFunc*) must draw an image relative to the coordinates (0,0) rather than (*x, y*).

See Also   **CDC::GrayString**

Callback Function for CDC::SetAbortProc

BOOL CALLBACK EXPORT AbortFunc(**HDC** *hPr*, **int** *code*);

Return Value   The return value of the abort-handler function is nonzero if the print job is to continue, and 0 if it is canceled.

Parameters   *hPr*   Identifies the device context.

code   Specifies whether an error has occurred. It is 0 if no error has occurred. It is **SP_OUTOFDISK** if the Print Manager is currently out of disk space and more disk space will become available if the application waits. If *code* is **SP_OUTOFDISK**, the application does not have to abort the print job. If it does not, it must yield to the Print Manager by calling the **PeekMessage** or **GetMessage** Windows function.

Remarks   The name AbortFunc is a placeholder for the application-supplied function name. The actual name must be exported as described in the "Remarks" section above.

See Also   **CDC::SetAbortProc**

Index

H

Contributors to *MFC Reference*

Richard Carlson, Index Editor
Mike Eddy, Production
Jocelyn Garner, Writer
Eric Landes, Writer
Steve Murray, Editor/Production
Mark Olson, Art Director
Chuck Sphar, Writer

Tools of the Trade

Inside Visual C++,™ 2nd ed.
David J. Kruglinski

Now updated to cover Visual C++ version 1.5, this book covers
OLE, ODBC enhancements, and Microsoft Foundation Class (MFC)
Library version 2.5. This is the foundation book for Visual C++ developers programming in Windows. Through fast-paced examples, this book takes readers from the
basics through the advanced capabilities of this rich programming environment,
while explaining the methodologies and the tools. The CD-ROM includes all
the source code files necessary to create the sample programs in the book.

768 pages, softcover with one CD-ROM
$39.95 ($53.95 Canada)   ISBN 1-55615-661-8

Inside OLE 2
Kraig Brockschmidt

Here's the inside scoop on how to build powerful object-oriented applications
for Windows. Written by a leading OLE expert, this guide shows experienced
programmers how to take advantage of OLE 2 to develop next-generation
applications that will take Windows to a new level. Brockschmidt explains how
to build OLE 2 applications from scratch as well as how to convert existing
applications. The disks contain 44 source code examples that demonstrate how
to implement objects and how to integrate OLE 2 features in your applications.

1008 pages, softcover with two 1.44-MB 3.5-inch disks
$49.95 ($67.95 Canada)   ISBN 1-55615-618-9

Code Complete
Steve McConnell

"We were impressed.... A pleasure to read, either straight through or as a
reference." **PC Week**

This practical handbook of software construction covers the art and
science of software development, from design to testing. Examples
are provided in C, Pascal, Basic, FORTRAN, and Ada—but the focus is on programming techniques. Topics include up-front planning, applying good design
techniques to construction, using data effectively, reviewing for errors, managing
construction activities, and relating personal character to superior software.

880 pages, softcover $35.00 ($44.95 Canada)   ISBN 1-55615-484-4

Microsoft Press®